TWENTIE
ETHICAL THEORY

Edited by
Steven M. Cahn
Graduate School
of the City University of New York

Joram G. Haber
Bergen Community College

PRENTICE-HALL
Upper Saddle River, New Jersey 07458

Library of Congress Cataloging-in-Publication Data

Twentieth century ethical theory / [edited by] Steven M. Cahn, Joram G. Haber.
p. cm.
ISBN 0-02-318031-5
1. Ethics, Modern—20th century—Sources. 2. Ethics. I. Cahn, Steven M. II. Haber, Joram Graf.
BJ319.T84 1995
170'.9'04—dc20 94-33204
CIP

Acquisitions editor: Ted Bolen
Editorial assistant: Meg McGuane
Editorial/production supervision: Linda Pawelchak
Cover design: Anthony Gemmellaro
Manufacturing buyer: Lynn Pearlman
Cover art: Vasily Kandinsky:
Sketch for "Composition II" 1909–1910.
Oil on canvas. 38 ³⁄₈ x 51 ⁵⁄₈ inches.
Solomon R. Guggenheim Museum, New York
Photograph by David Heald. Copyright The Solomon Guggenheim Foundation, New York.

Printed in the United States of America
10 9 8 7 6 5 4 3 2 1

ISBN 0-02-318031-5

Prentice-Hall International (UK) Limited, London
Prentice-Hall of Australia Pty. Limited, Sydney
Prentice-Hall Canada Inc., Toronto
Prentice-Hall Hispanoamericana, S.A., Mexico
Prentice-Hall of India Private Limited, New Delhi
Prentice-Hall of Japan, Inc., Tokyo
Pearson Education Asia Pte. Ltd., Singapore
Editora Prentice-Hall do Brasil, Ltda., Rio de Janeiro

Contents

PART II 1931–1950

PART III 1951–1970

Preface

This volume is a compilation of the complete texts of many of the most influential or provocative papers in twentieth-century, Anglo-American ethical theory. Selections from some major books of the period have also been included. The readings are presented chronologically in order to clarify and emphasize their historical sequence. Biographical information arranged by topic can be found in the *Encyclopedia of Ethics* (Garland, 1992), edited by Lawrence C. Becker.

We are grateful to James Rachels for providing an introductory overview of the subject, and we thank him and Professor Becker for their suggestions concerning the book's contents. We want to express our appreciation for the support we received from Ted Bolen, philosophy editor at Prentice Hall and from Maggie Barbieri, who initially took an interest in publishing the book. We also wish to acknowledge the help of Ms. Barbieri's editorial assistant, Ami Johnston; our student researchers, Marge Laver and Michelle Roberts; and our proofreaders Yael Dank and Ian Gardiner. We are also grateful for the suggestions made by the following reviewers: Bernard Elevitch, Boston University; Chin Tia Kim, Case Western Reserve University; and Thomas Loughran, University of Portland.

Introduction: Moral Philosophy in the Twentieth Century

James Rachels

"It is a salutary reflection," wrote John Passmore at the beginning of his *A Hundred Years of Philosophy*, "that had I written this book in 1800 I should probably have dismissed Berkeley and Hume in a few lines, in order to concentrate my attention on Dugald Stewart."[1] As the year 2000 approaches, we will no doubt be flooded with reviews of the past century, and they will contain plenty of misperceptions to amuse future generations. Perhaps history will judge the greatest thinker of the age to have been someone whom today we do not deem worthy of attention.

But even if we cannot be sure what will seem important to future generations, at least we know what has seemed important to us. From our present perspective, the story of what has happened during the last hundred years is clear enough. During the twentieth century, moral philosophers in the English-speaking countries have been preoccupied with two broad questions. The first concerns the objectivity of ethics: Is there any sense in which our moral judgments express truths that are independent of our feelings and conventions? And the second is about substantive moral theory: What is the best way to explain and summarize how we ought to live? As we shall see, these questions are not entirely independent of one another. Nevertheless, they provide a convenient way to organize our subject.

[1]John Passmore, *A Hundred Years of Philosophy* (Harmondsworth, Middlesex: Penguin, 1966), 8.

Our story begins in 1903 with the publication of G. E. Moore's *Principia Ethica,* a book that would become a classic as much for its way of framing issues, its style of argument, and its criticisms of familiar views as for its positive doctrines. Moore, who taught at Cambridge University in England, was revered as a gentle, saintly man. But he began his book with the contentious declaration that previous moral philosophy had been based on a mistake. Earlier philosophers, he said, had gone wrong by failing to be clear about what questions they were asking. The central question is "What is goodness?" We must know what goodness is before we can broach other important matters, such as what things are good, how we know they are good, and how we ought to live.

Like Socrates, Moore wanted a definition of goodness, and not just a verbal definition, but an analysis that would lay bare the essence of the thing. He soon concluded, however, that no such definition was possible. Earlier thinkers had suggested that goodness might be the same as pleasure, or evolutionary progress, or conformity to the will of God. But, Moore said, none of these views will do. They all commit a certain mistake, which he dubbed "the naturalistic fallacy." Moore argued, instead, that "good" is the name of a simple, unanalyzable property. "Good" is like "yellow": We can perceive its presence in things, but we cannot define it by breaking it down into simpler notions.

Moore thought it was obvious that goodness is an objective property of things; for him the only real issue was what sort of property it was. He was the first of a distinguished line of British philosophers, known as the intuitionists, who would defend this view throughout the first half of the century—a line that included, most prominently, H. A. Prichard, W. D. Ross, and A. C. Ewing. What united the intuitionists, despite their differences on many points, was the conviction that good and bad are matters of fact entirely independent of what we think or how we feel. They were English gentlemen who did not see how it could be otherwise. The alternative, as they saw it, was subjectivism, the idea that our evaluative judgments are nothing more than reports of our feelings. Subjectivism, in their view, could not possibly be true. They gave argument after argument against it.

To other philosophers, however, Moore's view seemed incredible. How can goodness be a property of things? We cannot see it or touch it. We cannot detect it with any scientific instrument. To say that we "intuit" goodness with some sort of sixth sense seems like so much occult mumbo jumbo. Hume had made the right point about this sort of view two centuries before:

> Take any action allow'd to be vicious: Willful murder, for instance. Examine it in all lights, and see if you can find that matter of fact, or real existence, which you call *vice.* In which-ever way you take it, you find only certain passions, motives, volitions and thoughts. There is no other matter of fact in the case. The vice entirely escapes you, so long as you consider the object. You never can find it, till you turn your reflection into your own breast, and find a sentiment of disapprobation, which arises in you, towards this action.[2]

So Moore's critics did not reject subjectivism. Instead, they embraced it enthusiastically—or, more precisely, they embraced a new, sophisticated version of subjectivism known as emotivism.

Emotivisim was the ethical theory favored by the Vienna Circle, a group of scientifically minded thinkers whose ideas would be enormously influential on the subsequent development of philosophy. The Circle formed in Vienna in the early 1920s; its members included such figures as Rudolf Carnap, Mortiz Schlick, and Kurt Gödel.

[2]David Hume, *A Treatise of Human Nature,* Selby-Bigge edition (Oxford: Oxford University Press, 1888; originally published in 1739), 468–69.

They believed that any meaningful statement about the world must be expressible in the language of science, and they dismissed religion and metaphysics as mere nonsense. Ethical utterances they allowed might serve the purpose of ventilating feelings and recommending actions. A. J. Ayer popularized these ideas in his 1936 book *Language, Truth and Logic,* but it was the American philosopher Charles Stevenson who gave emotivism its definitive formulation in 1944 in his *Ethics and Language.* Emotivism became the principal alternative to Moorean intuitionism, and soon it eclipsed the older view in influence and popularity.

What made emotivism more sophisticated than earlier versions of subjectivism was its analysis of moral language. The key idea exploited by the emotivists was that *not every utterance is meant to be true or false.* An imperative—"Don't do that!"—is neither true nor false. It does not convey information; rather, it gives an instruction about what is to be done. Similarly, a cheer—"Hurrah"—is not a statement of fact, not even the fact that we like something. It is merely a verbal manifestation of an attitude. According to the emotivists, ethical "statements" are like this. They are not used to state facts; they are, really, disguised imperatives or avowals. Thus, when someone says "Lying is wrong," it is as if he or she had said "Don't lie!" or "Lying—yech."

We can now understand, said the emotivists, why ethical disputes go on endlessly, with neither side being able to convert the other. Ethical disagreement is like disagreeing about the choice of a restaurant: People may agree on all the facts about restaurants and yet disagree about where to eat, because some prefer Chinese food while others like Italian. That's the way ethics is. We may agree fully about the facts and yet disagree profoundly in what we like and what we want to see happen.

During the heyday of emotivism, many philosophers believed that the final truth about ethics had at last been found. But by the early 1950s there was a growing consensus, even among those sympathetic to this approach, that it was a deeply flawed theory. The problem was that emotivism could not adequately account for the place of reason in ethics. It is a point of logic that moral judgments, if they are to be acceptable, must be founded on good reasons. If I tell you that such-and-such action is wrong, you are entitled to ask why it is wrong; and if I have no good reply, you may reject my advice as unfounded. This is what separates moral judgments from mere statements of preference.

But what could the emotivists say about the nature of moral reasoning? Remember that in their view, if I tell you that such-and-such action is wrong, I am not trying to alter your beliefs; I am trying to influence your attitudes. Therefore, if you challenge me to explain why it is wrong, I will want to cite whatever considerations will influence your attitudes in the desired way. The business of giving reasons, therefore, turns out to be nothing more than an exercise in psychological manipulation.

This might strike us as a realistic, if somewhat cynical, view. What is wrong with it? The problem is that if this view is correct, then *any* fact that influences attitudes would count as a reason for the attitude produced. Thus, if the thought that Goldberg is Jewish causes someone to distrust him, then "Goldberg is a Jew" would become a reason in support of the judgment that he is a shady character. Could this possibly be right? Stevenson embraced this consequence of his view without flinching: "Any statement," he said, "about any fact which any speaker considers likely to alter attitudes may be adduced as a reason for or against an ethical judgment."[3] But in the end, not many would agree with him. This account of reasons proved to be the Achilles' heel of emotivism.

[3] C. L. Stevenson, *Ethics and Language* (New Haven: Yale University Press, 1944), 114.

Sometimes philosophy advances because new ideas appear that are unlike anything seen before. But genuinely revolutionary conceptions are rare. More commonly, progress is made as old ideas are rethought and combined in new ways, sidestepping difficulties that previously caused trouble. This happened when the emotivists reformulated the basic idea of Humean subjectivism, rescuing it from the objections of the intuitionists. It happened again when emotivism seemed to be finished. In 1952 R. M. Hare of Oxford University published *The Language of Morals,* in which he recast the basic idea of emotivism in a way that permitted a better account of moral reasoning. Hare's "universal prescriptivism," as he called it, became the most widely debated view in moral philosophy for the next twenty years.

The emotivists had been right, Hare argued, in thinking that moral language is prescriptive rather than descriptive. Moral language is typically used to prescribe what is to be done rather than to describe what is the case. But the emotivists erred by overlooking an important logical feature of words such as "right" and "ought." When we use such words to make moral judgments, we implicitly commit ourselves to universal principles. If, for example, we say on a particular occasion that someone ought not to lie, we are committing ourselves to the general principle that lying is wrong. This, in turn, commits us to other judgments on other occasions, when lying is at issue. If we are to be consistent, we may not appeal to a principle at one time that we would not be willing to accept at other times. Hare refers to this logical feature of moral judgment as its "universalizability."

Emotivism had been faulted for implying that "anything goes"—it imposed no rational constraints at all on what could count as a moral reason. The requirement of universalizability, however, imposes severe constraints, because it means that we must apply to ourselves the same principles we use in judging others.

Did universal prescriptivism provide a satisfactory account of moral reasoning? During the 1950s and 1960s many philosophers argued that it was vulnerable to the same kind of objection that had brought down emotivism. What if someone were to insist, for example, that it is wrong to walk around pear trees in the light of the moon? And suppose that person was willing to universalize this, applying the rule to him- or herself and to others equally? Would there be any way, within the limits of universal prescriptivism, to object that this was a silly notion that has nothing to do with morality? The problem was not just that someone might be willing to universalize a bad moral principle. The problem was that *any* sort of "principle" could turn out to be moral. Philippa Foot pressed this sort of objection in some important papers published in the 1950s. If something vital was missing from Stevenson's account, something equally important seemed to be missing from Hare's.

The missing element, in the opinion of many, was the social content of morality. Morality, as John Dewey had insisted, is not just a matter of individuals ventilating their feelings or prescribing what they would like to see happen. It is, rather, a set of social practices that has a purpose—namely, the promotion of the common welfare. In his 1958 book *The Moral Point of View,* Kurt Baier suggested that the moral rules are, by definition, "for the good of everyone alike." Moral reasoning, therefore, is simply a matter of trying to figure out what is best from this perspective. Does it help or harm people to walk around pear trees in the moonlight? If not, then it has nothing to do with morality. Only by viewing morality as essentially social, Baier argued, can we firmly distinguish good moral reasons from other kinds of reasons and from sheer imposters.

During the 1960s the philosophical journals were filled with articles debating issues connected with these theories. What is the relation between moral judgment and emotion? Is there a logical gap between "is" and "ought"? In what sense, if any, are moral judgments universalizable? Is morality necessarily social, or is an ethics of pure self-interest possible? If morality does impose social duties, why should a rational person bother with it? Then, around 1970, a great deal changed. Philosophers began to think about some entirely different questions.

The preceding account might seem strangely bloodless. It summarizes a main line of moral philosophy for the first seventy years of this century, but there is no reference to the century's great tragedies and struggles. The two world wars, the Great Depression, the rise of communism, the holocaust, and the struggles against colonialism and racism are all missing. Is it possible that a philosophical debate about the nature of good and evil could have been carried on in isolation from such matters? Equally conspicuous by their absence are the human sciences. Can moral philosophy proceed in ignorance of what psychology, sociology, politics, and history teach us? Critics viewing the field from the outside were puzzled by philosophy's lack of engagement. Moral philosophy seemed to have drifted away from the human concerns that gave it life, and the educated public began to look elsewhere for enlightenment about right and wrong.

The philosophers whose work we have been considering were unmoved by such criticism. After all, what was the task of philosophy supposed to be? Were philosophers supposed to be amateur scientists or social commentators? The distinctively philosophical task, they contended, was the logical analysis of concepts—or, as many preferred to put it, the analysis of language. In *Language, Truth and Logic,* perhaps the most widely read book of philosophy during this period, Ayer proclaimed that the philosopher is not concerned with the nature of things: "He is concerned only with the way in which we speak about them. In other words, the propositions of philosophy are not factual, but linguistic in character."[4] Not everyone agreed that philosophy should be limited to linguistic analysis. Nevertheless, many insisted that only works of conceptual analysis were "really" philosophical (this was often said with a disdainful sniff), and from the 1930s to the 1960s it was standard practice for philosophers to express their ideas as theses about language.

The conception of philosophy as logical analysis placed limits on what moral philosophers could do. It was not their business to issue instructions about how people should live. "A philosopher is not a parish priest or Universal Aunt or Citizens' Advice Bureau," said P. H. Nowell-Smith in his book *Ethics.*[5] A moral philosopher might tell you that "good" is the name of an unanalyzable property of things, but it is not his business to tell you what things have that property; or, she might tell you that "Chastity is good" means something like "Hurrah for chastity!"; but it is not her business to join in the cheers either for or against sexual abstinence. Philosophers, it was said, are no more moralists than they are scientists or mathematicians.

Meanwhile, despite all this, philosophers were in fact discussing how we ought to live, at least in an abstract and general way. While the debate continued over moral language and the objectivity of ethics, a somewhat less prominent debate was going on about substantive moral theory. It was mainly a debate about utilitarianism.

In the nineteenth century Jeremy Bentham and John Stuart Mill had argued that all moral duties may be derived from one ultimate principle, which they called the principle of utility. This principle required that we do whatever will have the best overall results for everyone who is affected by our actions—in Bentham's memorable phrase, that we should promote "the greatest happiness for the greatest number." Moore aligned

[4]A. J. Ayer, *Language Truth and Logic,* 2nd ed. (New York: Dover Books, 1946; first edition published in 1936), 57.

[5]P. H. Nowell-Smith, *Ethics* (Baltimore: Penguin Books, 1954), 12.

himself with this view when he defined "right" in utilitarian terms: After explaining that "good" was the name of an unanalyzable property, Moore turned to the question "What actions are right?" and his answer was that right actions are the ones that produce the most good.

Utilitarianism seemed to its partisans to be an enlightened ethic that set aside the superstitions and irrationalities of the past. It dismissed as mere "rule worship" the idea that virtue consists in blindly following moral rules, and it grounded morality firmly in the necessities of this world rather than deferring to demands imposed from some supernatural realm. Utilitarianism was a revolutionary ethical outlook that would have enormous influence in law, economics, and philosophy, as well as affecting how ordinary people think.

Soon, however, the theory came under attack. The most influential criticisms were advanced in 1930 by W. D. Ross in his book *The Right and the Good.* Ross pointed out that utilitarianism leads to conclusions about what should be done in particular cases that, on reflection, seem plainly wrong. When you promise someone to do something, for example, you create an obligation that is independent of how much good you might accomplish. Suppose, when the time comes to do it, you realize that breaking your promise would have slightly better consequences than keeping it. The principle of utility would say that you should break the promise. But should you? Doesn't the fact that you promised impose an obligation on you that might outweigh the slight gain in utility? If not, what was the point of promising in the first place? More generally, Ross wrote:

> It [utilitarianism] says, in effect, that the only morally significant relation in which my neighbors stand to me is that of being possible beneficiaries by my action. They do stand in this relation to me, and this relation is morally significant. But they may also stand to me in the relation of promisee to promiser, of creditor to debtor, of wife to husband, of child to parent, of friend to friend, of fellow countryman to fellow countryman, and the like; and each of these relations is the foundation of the *prima facie* duty, which is more or less incumbent on me according to the circumstances of the case.[6]

Ross argued that we have an indefinite number of independent duties that must be balanced against one another when they come into conflict. These include at least the following: (1) duties resting on some previous act of our own, such as the duty to keep our promises and the duty to make restitution for wrongs we have done; (2) the duty of gratitude, to return favors others have done for us; (3) the duty of justice, to distribute goods fairly; (4) the duty of self-improvement, to develop our own talents and abilities; (5) the duty of beneficence, to act so as to benefit others; and (6) the duty of nonmaleficence, not to injure others. The problem with utilitarianism, Ross argued, was that it recognizes only the last two as fundamental duties. But these others are important, too, and they cannot be reduced to (5) and (6).

Many philosophers were persuaded by Ross's criticisms and concluded that utilitarianism could not be right. Others, however, tried to defend the theory. One of the main strategies of defense was to cast the theory in a new form that would not be vulnerable to Ross's objections. A distinction was drawn between act-utilitarianism and rule-utilitarianism. The former is the idea that the principle of utility is to be applied to each individual action, one by one. So, to determine whether you ought to keep a promise you have made, you would ask whether this particular act of promise keeping would lead to the best possible outcome for everyone concerned. This is the method of

[6] W. D. Ross, *The Right and the Good* (Oxford: Oxford University Press, 1930), 19.

classical utilitarianism, and it generated the difficulties that Ross noticed. Rule-utilitarianism, however, suggests a more sophisticated approach. First, the principle of utility is used to select a set of rules that it would be good to follow. We would all be better off, for example, if we were to follow such rules as "Keep your promises," "Tell the truth," "Respect one another's privacy," and so on. Then, to determine whether a particular action is mandatory—such as keeping a particular promise you have made—we refer to this set of rules. The key point is that the principle of utility is not applied directly to particular actions; it is used only to identify the general rules that are to be followed. Rule-utilitarianism, it was said, does not lead to the difficulties Ross noted. Indeed, all of Ross's "*prima facie* duties" could be understood as nothing more than rules that are themselves ultimately validated by appeal to the principle of utility.

As the debate about the best moral theory continued, Ross's theory of *prima facie* duties and utilitarianism were seen as the main alternatives. But both outlooks came under attack from a minority of philosophers who believed that this debate was radically misconceived. Their banner was raised in 1958 by G. E. M. Anscombe when she published an article called "Modern Moral Philosophy" in the British journal *Philosophy*. Anscombe contended that moral philosophers were discussing the wrong subject. They ought not to be discussing moral obligation and right action at all. Those notions, she argued, are tied to a conception of "moral law" that makes no sense apart from a divine lawgiver. Instead, like Aristotle, modern philosophers should scale back their ambitions and turn their attention to the everyday virtues and vices that make us good or bad people. The primary concern of moral philosophy, in other words, should be questions about *character* rather than action. Anscombe called for nothing less than a radical reorientation of the whole subject.

Eventually, "virtue theory" did emerge as a main alternative, and dozens of books and articles were written about moral character and about particular virtues such as courage, honesty, and friendship. But this did not happen right away. Throughout the 1960s philosophical attention remained focused on theories of right action and on issues of conceptual analysis. Virtue theory came into its own only in the 1970s, when the field of moral philosophy changed.

In the early 1970s two things happened that opened the field to an avalanche of new ideas. The first was the advent of the applied ethics movement. Previously the philosophical discussion of how we ought to live had been general and abstract. Now suddenly academic philosophers began to write about such matters as abortion, racial and sexual discrimination, civil disobedience, economic injustice, war, and even the treatment of nonhuman animals. It was a startling about-face for thinkers who, only a few years before, had agreed that "A philosopher is not a parish priest or Universal Aunt or Citizens' Advice Bureau."

The turn toward concrete issues was, in part, a delayed reaction to the failure of emotivism. It wasn't just that emotivism failed; it was the way it failed. Emotivism failed because it could not account for the place of reason in ethics. So in retrospect it seems inevitable that philosophers would turn their attention to the way in which reasons support moral judgments. And what better way to do this than to study the reasons that might be given in support of particular judgments, in particular moral controversies?

The second thing that happened was the publication of John Rawls's *A Theory of Justice* in 1971. Rarely has a single work had such impact. Rawls, a Harvard professor, had published a series of articles outlining his ideas beginning in the 1950s. But it was not until his book was published that those ideas became the leading topic of debate among moral philosophers. Rawls sought to construct a general theory describing how moral judgments—in particular, judgments about the justice of social institutions—might be made and justified. His theory was a variant of the familiar idea of the social contract.

Rawls proposed that the rules of justice be conceived as whatever rules we would accept in special circumstances called "the original position." The original position is an imaginary situation in which we are negotiating with other people about how the basic institutions of our society are to be structured. But the negotiation takes place under special constraint: Everyone is ignorant of his or her own personal qualities and social position. No one knows whether he or she is male or female, black or white, talented or clumsy, smart or stupid, rich or poor. This influences how the negotiations will go. Because we lack this information, we cannot press for social arrangements that will favor ourselves or people like us. Instead we will be motivated to seek an arrangement in which everyone is as well-off as possible, so that we will have a maximum chance of flourishing regardless of who we turn out to be when the "veil of ignorance" is lifted.

What would be the result of negotiating under such a constraint? Rawls argues that we would agree on two general principles: First, that everyone should have the most extensive liberty compatible with a similar liberty for others; and second, that social or economic inequalities should not be permitted unless they work to everyone's advantage and are attached to positions open to everyone. These are the basic principles of justice: Social institutions are acceptable, from the point of view of justice, only if they satisfy them. These institutions would obviously be egalitarian and democratic.

Future historians might find it difficult to understand why Rawls's book seemed, to philosophers working in the field at the time, such a complete break with the past. True, it was a work of substantive moral theory that had nothing to say about the logic of moral language. But substantive theory had been under discussion, off and on, for the whole century, in the debate over utilitarianism. True, Rawls offered an alternative to both utilitarianism and Ross's theory of *prima facie* duties. But his alternative was a kind of theory, contractarianism, that dates back to the seventeenth century. Rawls himself disclaimed any particular originality. So what was all the fuss about?

Several things might be said about this. First, Rawls was too modest in assessing his own originality. In fact he did something that no one else in this century had done when he constructed a unified, systematic moral theory. Although his view incorporated some older ideas, taken as a whole it was strikingly different from anything that had been seen in a long time. Second, Rawls "changed the subject" of the ongoing philosophical debate by focusing on the notions of justice and rights. When it turned out, in his view, that justice requires social institutions that benefit all people equally, the notion of equality was also brought to center stage. Third, the theory he constructed was rich with implications for all sorts of related matters: the development of the theory involved the elaboration of such notions as autonomy, human life-plans, desert, self-respect, and the basic human goods. A wealth of topics was opened up for discussion within a systematic context. Philosophers were happy to jump in and talk about them rather than continue with the hoary questions of conceptual analysis that had occupied them for so long.

Finally, Rawls's work was attractive in the way it cast off the disciplinary blinders that other philosophers had worn. He saw connections between his work in ethics and theoretical work in economics, law, and psychology. Because of the way he appropriated material from those areas, thinkers in those fields, who had found little of interest in previous philosophical writing, began to see important connections between their work and moral theory. So *A Theory of Justice* signaled the reuniting of ethical theory with these other subjects, as well as with social and political philosophy of the traditional kind. It provided, for many philosophers, a new paradigm of how ethics might be done.

In the continuing debate about the best substantive moral theory, the main contenders have now become utilitarianism and contractarianism. In the 1980s significant new contributions were made to the development of both sorts of views, with Derek Parfit's *Reasons and Persons* breaking new ground in utilitarian theory and David Gauthier's *Morals by Agreement* offering a powerful contractarian view different in important ways from the theory propounded by Rawls.

Gauthier's contractarianism is more general than Rawls's theory because it is a view about the nature of morality as a whole, rather than being limited to the justice of social institutions. Gauthier's idea is more in line with the classical view of Thomas Hobbes, which sees morality as essentially a scheme of social cooperation established by rational, self-interested people for their mutual benefit. (Each of us is better off living in a society in which murder, theft, and so on are prohibited, and in which people can be relied upon to tell the truth and keep their promises.) Moral principles, then, are nothing more or less than the rules rational people would agree to accept, for their own benefit, provided that others accept them as well.

One of the striking features of this view is the way that it finesses the traditional question about the objectivity of ethics. Contractarianism provides the resources for an elegant solution to this problem. Morality is a rational enterprise. It really is true—independent of what anyone thinks or how anyone feels—that certain goods cannot be obtained without social cooperation and that, therefore, rational self-interested people will be motivated to agree to cooperate with one another to obtain those goods. It is further true that this cooperation will involve accepting rules that constrain behavior. If this is what moral rules are like, then it is easy to explain their rationality and objectivity without resorting to any strange or mystifying conception of "objective values." In this form of contractarianism the two concerns with which we began—the concerns about moral objectivity and about the best substantive theory—seem to have merged.

I have not tried to determine which of these views is best; my only purpose has been to describe, in the most general way possible, the course moral philosophy has taken since Moore. It is easy to describe history from a distance. Hindsight enables us to select from the mass of detail just the thoughts and events we need to make up a coherent narrative. Although this inevitably involves some distortion, the exercise helps to put ideas in perspective. The closer one comes to the present, however, the messier and more confusing things become. Current debates cover a dizzying array of topics. Many of the positions taken in these debates are associated with the theories we have been describing, but some are connected to other points of view entirely. And meanwhile, some philosophers argue that a systematic moral theory is not even possible.

Some observers might find this situation chaotic and think that in the twenty-four hundred years since Socrates greater progress should have been made. But Derek Parfit's assessment might be more accurate. Secular moral philosophy, as distinct from theological ethics, is not an old subject—it is, on the contrary, a fairly young discipline that has only recently begun to be developed in a rigorous way. The variety of options still being tested may be just a sign of youthful vigor.

Part I

1901–1930

1903

The Subject-Matter of Ethics

G. E. Moore

1. It is very easy to point out some among our every-day judgments, with the truth of which Ethics is undoubtedly concerned. Whenever we say, "So and so is a good man," or "That fellow is a villain"; whenever we ask, "What ought I to do?" or "Is it wrong for me to do like this?"; whenever we hazard such remarks as "Temperance is a virtue and drunkenness a vice"—it is undoubtedly the business of Ethics to discuss such questions and such statements; to argue what is the true answer when we ask what it is right to do, and to give reasons for thinking that our statements about the character of persons or the morality of actions are true or false. In the vast majority of cases, where we make statements involving any of the terms "virtue," "vice," "duty," "right," "ought," "good," "bad," we are making ethical judgments; and if we wish to discuss their truth, we shall be discussing a point of Ethics.

So much as this is not disputed; but it falls very far short of defining the province of Ethics. That province may indeed be defined as the whole truth about that which is at the same time common to all such judgments and peculiar to them. But we have still to ask the question: What is it that is thus common and peculiar? And this is a question to

G. E. Moore, "The Subject-Matter of Ethics" from PRINCIPIA ETHICA (New York: Cambridge). Reprinted with the permission of the publishers.

which very different answers have been given by ethical philosophers of acknowledged reputation and none of them, perhaps, completely satisfactory.

2. If we take such examples as those given above, we shall not be far wrong in saying that they are all of them concerned with the question of "conduct"—with the question, what, in the conduct of us, human beings, is good, and what is bad, what is right, and what is wrong. For when we say that a man is good, we commonly mean that he acts rightly; when we say that drunkenness is a vice, we commonly mean that to get drunk is a wrong or wicked action. And this discussion of human conduct is, in fact, that with which the name "Ethics" is most intimately associated. It is so associated by derivation; and conduct is undoubtedly by far the most commonest and most generally interesting object of ethical judgments.

Accordingly, we find that many ethical philosophers are disposed to accept as an adequate definition of "Ethics" the statement that it deals with the question what is good or bad in human conduct. They hold that its enquiries are properly confined to "conduct" or to "practice"; they hold that the name "practical philosophy" covers all the matter with which it has to do. Now, without discussing the proper meaning of the word (for verbal questions are properly left to the writers of dictionaries and other persons interested in literature; philosophy, as we shall see, has no concern with them), I may say that I intend to use "Ethics" to cover more than this—a usage, for which there is, I think, quite sufficient authority. I am using it to cover an enquiry for which, at all events, there is no other word: the general enquiry into what is good.

Ethics is undoubtedly concerned with the question what good conduct is; but, being concerned with this, it obviously does not start at the beginning, unless it is prepared to tell us what is good as well as what is conduct. For "good conduct" is a complex notion: all conduct is not good; for some is certainly bad and some may be indifferent. And on the other hand, other things, beside conduct, may be good; and if they are so, then, "good" denotes some property, that is common to them and conduct; and if we examine good conduct alone of all good things, then we shall be in danger of mistaking for this property, some property which is not shared by those other things. and thus we shall have made a mistake about Ethics even in this limited sense; for we shall not know what good conduct really is. This is a mistake which many writers have actually made, from limiting their enquiry to conduct. And hence I shall try to avoid it by considering first what is good in general; hoping, that if we can arrive at any certainty about this, it will be much easier to settle the question of good conduct: for we all know pretty well what "conduct" is. This, then, is our first question: What is good? and What is bad? and to the discussion of this question (or these questions) I give the name of Ethics, since that science must, at all events, include it.

3. But this is a question which may have many meanings. If, for example, each of us were to say "I am doing good now" or "I had a good dinner yesterday," these statements would each of them be some sort of answer to our question, although perhaps a false one. So, too, when A asks B what school he ought to send his son to, B's answer will certainly be an ethical judgment. And similarly all distribution of praise or blame to any personage or thing that has existed, now exists, or will exist, does give some answer to the question "What is good?" In all such cases some particular thing is judged to be good or bad: the question "What?" is answered by "This." But this is not the sense in which a scientific Ethics asks the question. Not one, of all the many million answers of this kind, which must be true, can form a part of an ethical system; although that science must contain reasons and principles sufficient for deciding on the truth of all of them. There are far too many persons, things and events in the world, past, present, or to come, for a discussion of their individual merits to be embraced in any science. Ethics, therefore, does not deal at all with facts of this nature, facts that are unique, individual, absolutely particular; facts with which such studies as history, geography, astronomy, are compelled, in part at least, to deal. And, for this reason, it is not the business of the ethical philosopher to give personal advice or exhortation.

4. But there is another meaning which may be given to the question "What is good?" "Books are good" would be an answer to it, though an answer obviously false; for some books are very bad indeed. And ethical judgments of this kind do indeed belong to Ethics; though I shall not deal with many of them. Such is the judgment "Pleasure is good"—a judgment, of which Ethics should discuss the truth, although it is not nearly as important as that other judgment, with which we shall be much occupied presently—"Pleasure *alone* is good." It is judgments of this sort, which are made in such books on Ethics as contain a list of "virtues"—in Aristotle's "Ethics" for example. But it is judgments of precisely the same kind, which form the substance of what is commonly supposed to be a study different from Ethics, and one much less respectable—the study of Casuistry. We may be told that Casuistry differs from Ethics, in that it is much more detailed and particular, Ethics much more general. But it is most important to notice that Casuistry does not deal with anything that is absolutely particular—particular in the only sense in which a perfectly precise line can be drawn between it and what is general. It is not particular in the sense just noticed, the sense in which this book is a particular book, and A's friend's advice particular advice. Casuistry may indeed be *more* particular and Ethics *more* general; but that means that they differ only in degree and not in kind. And this is universally true of "particular" and "general," when used in this common, but inaccurate, sense. So far as Ethics allows itself to give lists of virtues or even to name constituents of the Ideal, it is indistinguishable from Casuistry. Both alike deal with what is general, in the sense in which physics and chemistry deal with what is general. Just as chemistry aims at discovering what are the properties of oxygen, *wherever it occurs,* and not only of this or that particular specimen of oxygen; so Casuistry aims at discovering what actions are good, *whenever they occur.* In this respect Ethics and Casuistry alike are to be classed with such sciences as physics, chemistry and physiology, in their absolute distinction from those of which history and geography are instances. And it is to be noted that, owing to their detailed nature, casuistical investigations are actually nearer to physics and to chemistry than are the investigations usually assigned to Ethics. For just as physics cannot rest content with the discovery that light is propagated by waves of ether, but must go on to discover the particular nature of the ether-waves corresponding to each several color; so Casuistry, not content with the general law that charity is a virtue must attempt to discover the relative merits of every different form of charity. Casuistry forms, therefore, part of the ideal of ethical science: Ethics cannot be complete without it. The defects of Casuistry are not defects of principle; no objection can be taken to its aim and object. It has failed only because it is far too difficult a subject to be treated adequately in our present state of knowledge. The casuist has been unable to distinguish, in the cases which he treats, those elements upon which their value depends. Hence he often thinks two cases to be alike in respect of value, when in reality they are alike only in some other respect. It is to mistakes of this kind that the pernicious influence of such investigations has been due. For Casuistry is the goal of ethical investigation. It cannot be safely attempted at the beginning of our studies, but only at the end.

5. But our question "What is good?" may have still another meaning. We may, in the third place, mean to ask, not what thing or things are good, but how "good" is to be

defined. This is an enquiry which belongs only to Ethics, not to Casuistry; and this is the enquiry which will occupy us first.

It is an enquiry to which most special attention should be directed; since this question, how "good" is to be defined, is the most fundamental question in all Ethics. That which is meant by "good" is, in fact, except its converse "bad," the *only* simple object of thought which is peculiar to Ethics. Its definition is, therefore, the most essential point in the definition of Ethics; and moreover a mistake with regard to it entails a far larger number of erroneous ethical judgments than any other. Unless this first question be fully understood, and its true answer clearly recognized, the rest of Ethics is as good as useless from the point of view of systematic knowledge. True ethical judgments, of the two kinds last dealt with, may indeed be made by those who do not know the answer to this question as well as by those who do; and it goes without saying that the two classes of people may lead equally good lives. But it is extremely unlikely that the *most general* ethical judgments will be equally valid, in the absence of a true answer to this question: I shall presently try to show that the gravest errors have been largely due to beliefs in a false answer. And, in any case, it is impossible that, till the answer to this question be known, any one should know *what is the evidence* for any ethical judgment whatsoever. But the main object of Ethics, as a systematic science, is to give correct *reasons* for thinking that this or that is good; and, unless this question be answered, such reasons cannot be given. Even, therefore, apart from the fact that a false answer leads to false conclusions, the present enquiry is a most necessary and important part of the science of Ethics.

6. What, then, is good? How is good to be defined? Now, it may be thought that this is a verbal question. A definition does indeed often mean the expressing of one word's meaning in other words. But this is not the sort of definition I am asking for. Such a definition can never be of ultimate importance in any study except lexicography. If I wanted that kind of definition I should have to consider in the first place how people generally used the word "good"; but my business is not with its proper usage, as established by custom. I should, indeed, be foolish, if I tried to use it for something which it did not usually denote: if, for instance, I were to announce that, whenever I used the word "good," I must be understood to be thinking of that object which is usually denoted by the word "table." I shall, therefore, use the word in the sense in which I think it is ordinarily used; but at the same time I am not anxious to discuss whether I am right in thinking that it is so used. My business is solely with that object or idea, which I hold, rightly or wrongly, that the word is generally used to stand for. What I want to discover is the nature of that object or idea, and about this I am extremely anxious to arrive at an agreement.

But, if we understand the question in this sense, my answer to it may seem a very disappointing one. If I am asked "What is good?" my answer is that good is good, and that is the end of the matter. Or if I am asked "How is good to be defined?" my answer is that it cannot be defined, and that is all I have to say about it. But disappointing as these answers may appear, they are of the very last importance. To readers who are familiar with philosophic terminology, I can express their importance by saying that they amount to this: That propositions about the good are all of them synthetic and never analytic; and that is plainly no trivial matter. And the same thing may be expressed more popularly, by saying that, if I am right, then nobody can foist upon us such an axiom as that "Pleasure is the only good" or that "The good is the desired" on the pretence that this is "the very meaning of the word."

7. Let us, then, consider this position. My point is that "good" is a simple notion, just as "yellow" is a simple notion; that, just as you cannot, by any manner of means, explain to any one who does not already know it, what yellow is, so you cannot explain what good is. Definitions of the kind that I was asking for, definitions which describe the real nature of the object or notion denoted by a word, and which do not merely tell us what the word is used to mean, are only possible when the object or notion in question is something complex. You can give a definition of a horse, because a horse has many different properties and qualities, all of which you can enumerate. But when you have enumerated them all, when you have reduced a horse to his simplest terms, then you can no longer define those terms. They are simply something which you think of or perceive, and to any one who cannot think of or perceive them, you can never, by any definition, make their nature known. It may perhaps be objected to this that we are able to describe to others, objects which they have never seen or thought of. We can, for instance, make a man understand what a chimaera is, although he has never heard of one or seen one. You can tell him that it is an animal with a lioness's head and body, with a goat's head growing from the middle of its back, and with a snake in place of a tail. But here the object which you are describing is a complex object; it is entirely composed of parts, with which we are all perfectly familiar—a snake, a goat, a lioness; and we know, too, the manner in which those parts are to be put together, because we know what is meant by the middle of a lioness's back, and where her tail is wont to grow. And so it is with all objects, not previously known, which we are able to define: they are all complex; all composed of parts, which may themselves, in the first instance, be capable of similar definition, but which must in the end be reducible to simplest parts, which can no longer be defined. But yellow and good, we say, are not complex: they are notions of that simple kind, out of which definitions are composed and with which the power of further defining ceases.

8. When we say, as Webster says, "The definition of horse is 'A hoofed quadruped of the genus Equus,' " we may, in fact, mean three different things. (1) We may mean merely: "When I say 'horse,' you are to understand that I am talking about a hoofed quadruped of the genus Equus." This might be called the arbitrary verbal definition: and I do not mean that good is indefinable in that sense. (2) We may mean, as Webster ought to mean: "When most English people say 'horse,' they mean a hoofed quadruped of the genus Equus." This may be called the verbal definition proper, and I do not say that good is indefinable in this sense either; for it is certainly possible to discover how people use a word: otherwise, we could never have known that "good" may be translated by "gut" in German and by "bon" in French. But (3) we may, when we define horse, mean something much more important. We may mean that a certain object, which we all of us know, is composed in a certain manner: that it has four legs, a head, a heart, a liver, etc., etc., all of them arranged in definite relations to one another. It is in this sense that I deny good to be definable. I say that it is not composed of any parts, which we can substitute for it in our minds when we are thinking of it. We might think just as clearly and correctly about a horse, if we thought of all its parts and their arrangement instead of thinking of the whole: we could, I say, think how a horse differed from a donkey just as well, just as truly, in this way, as now we do, only not so easily; but there is nothing whatsoever which we could so substitute for good; and that is what I mean, when I say that good is indefinable.

9. But I am afraid I have still not removed the chief difficulty which may prevent acceptance of the proposition that good is indefinable. I do not mean to say that *the* good, that which is good, is thus indefinable; if I did think so, I should not be writing on Ethics, for my main object is to help towards discovering that definition. It is just because I think there will be less risk of error in our search for a definition of "the good," that I am now insisting that *good* is indefinable. I must try to explain the difference between these two.

I suppose it may be granted that "good" is an adjective. Well "the good," "that which is good," must therefore be the substantive to which the adjective "good" will apply: it must be the whole of that to which the adjective will apply, and the adjective must *always* truly apply to it. But if it is that to which the adjective will apply, it must be something different from that adjective itself; and the whole of that something different, whatever it is, will be our definition of *the* good. Now it may be that this something will have other adjectives, beside "good," that will apply to it. It may be full of pleasure, for example; it may be intelligent: and if these two adjectives are really part of its definition, then it will certainly be true, that pleasure and intelligence are good. And many people appear to think that, if we say "Pleasure and intelligence are good," or if we say "Only pleasure and intelligence are good," we are defining "good." Well, I cannot deny that propositions of this nature may sometimes be called definitions; I do not know well enough how the word is generally used to decide upon this point. I only wish it to be understood that that is not what I mean when I say there is no possible definition of good, and that I shall not mean this if I use the word again. I do most fully believe that some true proposition of the form "Intelligence is good and intelligence alone is good" can be found; if none could be found, our definition of *the* good would be impossible. As it is, I believe *the* good to be definable; and yet I still say that good itself is indefinable.

10. "Good," then, if we mean by it that quality which we assert to belong to a thing, when we say that the thing is good, is incapable of any definition, in the most important sense of that word. The most important sense of "definition" is that in which a definition states what are the parts which invariably compose a certain whole; and in this sense "good" has no definition because it is simple and has no parts. It is one of those innumerable objects of thought which are themselves incapable of definition, because they are the ultimate terms by reference to which whatever *is* capable of definition must be defined. That there must be an indefinite number of such terms is obvious, on reflection; since we cannot define anything except by analysis, which, when carried as far as it will go, refers us to something, which is simply different from anything else, and which by that ultimate difference explains the peculiarity of the whole which we are defining: for every whole contains some parts which are common to other wholes also. There is, therefore, no intrinsic difficulty in the contention that "good" denotes a simple and indefinable quality. There are many other instances of such qualities.

Consider yellow, for example. We may try to define it, by describing its physical equivalent; we may state what kind of light-vibrations must stimulate the normal eye, in order that we may perceive it. But a moment's reflection is sufficient to show that those light-vibrations are not themselves what we mean by yellow. *They* are not what we perceive. Indeed we should never have been able to discover their existence, unless we had first been struck by the patent difference of quality between the different colors. The most we can be entitled to say of those vibrations is that they are what corresponds in space to the yellow which we actually perceive.

Yet a mistake of this simple kind has commonly been made about "good." It may be true that all things which are good are *also* something else, just as it is true that all things which are yellow produce a certain kind of vibration in the light. And it is a fact, that Ethics aims at discovering what are those other properties belonging to all things which are good. But far too many philosophers have thought that when they named those other properties they were actually defining good; that these properties, in fact, were simply not "other," but absolutely and entirely the same with goodness. This view I propose to call the "naturalistic fallacy" and of it I shall now endeavor to dispose.

11. Let us consider what it is such philosophers say. And first it is to be noticed that they do not agree among themselves. They not only say that they are right as to what good is, but they endeavor to prove that other people who say that it is something else, are wrong. One, for instance, will affirm that good is pleasure, another, perhaps, that good is that which is desired; and each of these will argue eagerly to prove that the other is wrong. But how is that possible? One of them says that good is nothing but the object of desire, and at the same time tries to prove that it is not pleasure. But from his first assertion, that good just means the object of desire, one of two things must follow as regards his proof:

(1) He may be trying to prove that the object of desire is not pleasure. But, if this be all, where is his Ethics? The position he is maintaining is merely a psychological one. Desire is something which occurs in our minds, and pleasure is something else which so occurs; and our would-be ethical philosopher is merely holding that the latter is not the object of the former. But what has that to do with the question in dispute? His opponent held the ethical position that pleasure was the good, and although he should prove a million times over the psychological proposition that pleasure is not the object of desire, he is no nearer proving his opponent to be wrong. The position is like this. One man says a triangle is a circle: another replies "A triangle is a straight line, and I will prove to you that I am right: *for*" (this is the only argument) "a straight line is not a circle." "That is quite true," the other may reply; "but nevertheless a triangle is a circle, and you have said nothing whatever to prove the contrary. What is proved is that one of us is wrong, for we agree that a triangle cannot be both a straight line and a circle: but which is wrong, there can be no earthly means of proving, since you define triangle as straight line and I define it as circle."—Well, that is one alternative which any naturalistic Ethics has to face; if good is *defined* as something else, it is then impossible either to prove that any other definition is wrong or even to deny such definition.

(2) The other alternative will scarcely be more welcome. It is that the discussion is after all a verbal one. When A says "Good means pleasant" and B says "Good means desired," they may merely wish to assert that most people have used the word for what is pleasant and for what is desired respectively. And this is quite an interesting subject for discussion: only it is not a whit more an ethical discussion than the last was. Nor do I think that any exponent of naturalistic Ethics would be willing to allow that this was all he meant. They are all so anxious to persuade us that what they call the good is what we really ought to do. "Do, pray, act so, because the word 'good' is generally used to denote actions of this nature": such, on this view, would be the substance of their teaching. And in so far as they tell us how we ought to act, their teaching is truly ethical, as they mean it to be. But how perfectly absurd is the reason they would give for it! "You are to do this, because most people use a certain word to denote conduct such as this." "You are to say the thing which is not, because most people call it lying." That is an argument just as good!—My dear sirs, what we want to know from you as ethical teachers, is not how people use a word; it is not even, what kind of actions they approve, which the use of this word "good" may certainly imply: what we want to know is simply what *is* good. We may indeed agree that what most people do think good, is actually so; we shall at all events be glad to know their opinions: but when we say their opinions about what *is* good, we do mean what we say; we do not care whether they call that thing which they mean "horse" or "table" or "chair," "gut" or "bon" or "ἀγαθός"; we want to know what it is that they so call. When they say "Pleasure is good," we cannot believe that they merely mean "Pleasure is pleasure" and nothing more than that.

12. Suppose a man says "I am pleased"; and suppose that is not a lie or a mistake but the truth. Well, if it is true, what does that mean? It means that his mind, a certain definite mind, distinguished by certain definite marks from all others, has at this moment a certain definite feeling called pleasure. "Pleased" *means* nothing but having pleasure, and though we may be more pleased or less pleased, and even, we may admit for the present, have one or another kind of pleasure; yet in so far as it is pleasure we have, whether there be more or less of it, and whether it be of one kind of another, what we have is one definite thing, absolutely indefinable, some one thing that is the same in all the various degrees and in all the various kinds of it that there may be. We may be able to say how it is related to other things: that, for example, it is in the mind, that it causes desire, that we are conscious of it, etc., etc. We can, I say, describe its relations to other things, but define it we can *not*. And if anybody tried to define pleasure for us as being any other natural object; if anybody were to say, for instance, that pleasure *means* the sensation of red, and were to proceed to deduce from that that pleasure is a color, we should be entitled to laugh at him and to distrust his future statements about pleasure. Well, that would be the same fallacy which I have called the naturalistic fallacy. That "pleased" does not mean "having the sensation of red," or anything else whatever, does not prevent us from understanding what it does mean. It is enough for us to know that "pleased" does mean "having the sensation of pleasure," and though pleasure is absolutely indefinable, though pleasure is pleasure and nothing else whatever, yet we feel no difficulty in saying that we are pleased. The reason is, of course, that when I say "I am pleased," I do *not* mean that "I" am the same thing as "having pleasure." And similarly no difficulty need be found in my saying that "pleasure is good" and yet not meaning that "pleasure" is the same thing as "good," that pleasure *means* good, and that good *means* pleasure. If I were to imagine that when I said "I am pleased," I meant that I was exactly the same thing as "pleased," I should not indeed call that a naturalistic fallacy, although it would be the same fallacy as I have called naturalistic with reference to Ethics. The reason of this is obvious enough. When a man confuses two natural objects with one another, defining the one by the other, if for instance, he confuses himself, who is one natural object, with "pleased" or with "pleasure" which are others, then there is no reason to call the fallacy naturalistic. But if he confuses "good," which is not in the same sense a natural object, with any natural object whatever, then there is a reason for calling that a naturalistic fallacy; its being made with regard to "good" marks it as something quite specific, and this specific mistake deserves a name because it is so common. As for the reasons why good is not to be considered a natural object, they may be reserved for discussion in another place. But, for the present, it is sufficient to notice this: Even if it were a natural object, that would not alter the nature of the fallacy nor diminish its importance one whit. All that I have said about it would remain quite equally true: only the name which I have called it would not be so appropriate as I think it is. And I do not care about the name: what I do care about is the fallacy. It does not matter what we call it, provided we recognize it when we meet with it. It is to be met with in almost every book on Ethics; and yet it is not recognized: and that is why it is necessary to multiply illustrations of it, and convenient to give it a name. It is a very simple fallacy indeed. When we say that an orange is yellow, we do not think our statement binds us to hold that "orange" means nothing else than "yellow," or that nothing can be yellow but an orange. Supposing the orange is also sweet! Does that bind us to say that "sweet" is exactly the same thing as "yellow," that "sweet" must be defined as "yellow"? And supposing it be recognized that "yellow" just means "yellow" and nothing else whatever, does that make it any more difficult to hold that oranges are yellow? Most certainly it does not: on the contrary, it would be absolutely meaningless to say that oranges were yellow, unless yellow did in the end mean just "yellow" and nothing else whatever—unless it was absolutely indefinable. We should not get any very clear notion about things which are yellow—we should not get very far with our science, if we were bound to hold that everything which was yellow, *meant* exactly the same thing as yellow. We should find we had to hold that an orange was exactly the same thing as a stool, a piece of paper, a lemon, anything you like. We could prove any number of absurdities; but should we be the nearer to the truth? Why, then, should it be different with "good"? Why, if good is good and indefinable, should I be held to deny that pleasure is good? Is there any difficulty in holding both to be true at once? On the contrary, there is no meaning in saying that pleasure is good, unless good is something different from pleasure. It is absolutely useless, so far as Ethics is concerned, to prove, as Mr. Spencer tries to do, that increase of pleasure coincides with increase of life, unless good *means* something different from either life or pleasure. He might just as well try to prove that an orange is yellow by showing that it always is wrapped up in paper.

13. In fact, if it is not the case that "good" denotes something simple and indefinable, only two alternatives are possible: either it is a complex, a given whole, about the correct analysis of which there may be disagreement; or else it means nothing at all, and there is no such subject as Ethics. In general, however, ethical philosophers have attempted to define good, without recognizing what such an attempt must mean. They actually use arguments which involve one or both of the absurdities considered in § 11. We are, therefore, justified in concluding that the attempt to define good is chiefly due to want of clearness as to the possible nature of definition. There are, in fact, only two serious alternatives to be considered, in order to establish the conclusion that "good" does denote a simple and indefinable notion. It might possibly denote a complex, as "horse" does; or it might have no meaning at all. Neither of these possibilities has, however, been clearly conceived and seriously maintained, as such, by those who presume to define good; and both may be dismissed by a simple appeal to facts.

(1) The hypothesis that disagreement about the meaning of good is disagreement with regard to the correct analysis of a given whole, may be most plainly seen to be incorrect by consideration of the fact that, whatever definition be offered, it may be always asked, with significance, of the complex so defined, whether it is itself good. To take, for instance, one of the more plausible, because one of the more complicated, of such proposed definitions, it may easily be thought, at first sight, that to be good may mean to be that which we desire to desire. Thus if we apply this definition to a particular instance and say "When we think that A is good, we are thinking that A is one of the things which we desire to desire," our proposition may seem quite plausible. But, if we carry the investigation further, and ask ourselves "Is it good to desire to desire A?" it is apparent, on a little reflection, that this question is itself as intelligible, as the original question "Is A good?"—that we are, in fact, now asking for exactly the same information about the desire to desire A, for which we formerly asked with regard to A itself. But it is also apparent that the meaning of this second question cannot be correctly analyzed into "Is the desire to desire A one of the things which we desire to desire?": we have not before our minds anything so complicated as the question "Do we desire to desire to desire to desire A?" Moreover any one can easily convince himself by inspection that the predicate of this proposition—"good"—is positively different from the notion of "desiring to desire" which enters into its subject: "That we should desire to desire A is good" is *not* merely equivalent to "That A should be good is good." It may indeed be true that what we desire to desire is always also good; perhaps, even the converse may be true: but it is very doubtful whether this is the case, and the mere fact that we understand very well what is meant by doubting it, shows clearly that we have two different notions before our minds.

(2) And the same consideration is sufficient to dismiss the hypothesis that "good" has no meaning whatsoever. It is very natural to make the mistake of supposing that what is universally true is of such a nature that its negation would be self-contradictory: the importance which has been assigned to analytic propositions in the history of philosophy shows how easy such a mistake is. And thus it is very easy to conclude that what seems to be a universal ethical principle is in fact an identical proposition; that, if, for example, whatever is called "good" seems to be pleasant, the proposition "Pleasure is the good" does not assert a connection between two different notions, but involves only one, that of pleasure, which is easily recognized as a distinct entity. But whoever will attentively consider with himself what is actually before his mind when he asks the question "Is pleasure (or whatever it may be) after all good?" can easily satisfy himself that he is not merely wondering whether pleasure is pleasant. And if he will try this experiment with each suggested definition in succession, he may become expert enough to recognize that in every case he has before his mind a unique object, with regard to the connection of which with any other object, a distinct question may be asked. Every one does in fact understand the question "Is this good?" When he thinks of it, his state of mind is different from what it would be, were he asked "Is this pleasant, or desired, or approved?" It has a distinct meaning for him, even though he may not recognize in what respect it is distinct. Whenever he thinks of "intrinsic value," or "intrinsic worth," or says that a thing "ought to exist," he has before his mind the unique object—the unique property of things—which I mean by "good." Everybody is constantly aware of this notion, although he may never become aware at all that it is different from other notions of which he is also aware. But, for correct ethical reasoning, it is extremely important that he should become aware of this fact; and, as soon as the nature of the problem is clearly understood, there should be little difficulty in advancing so far in analysis.

14. "Good," then, is indefinable; and yet, so far as I know, there is only one ethical writer, Prof. Henry Sidgwick, who has clearly recognized and stated this fact. We shall see, indeed, how far many of the most reputed ethical systems fall short of drawing the conclusions which follow from such a recognition. At present I will only quote one instance, which will serve to illustrate the meaning and importance of this principle that "good" is indefinable, or, as Prof. Sidgwick says, an "unanalyzable notion." It is an instance to which Prof. Sidgwick himself refers in a note on the passage, in which he argues that "ought" is unanalyzable.[1]

"Bentham," says Sidgwick, "explains that his fundamental principle 'states the greatest happiness of all those whose interest is in question as being the right and proper end of human action' "; and yet "his language in other passages of the same chapter would seem to imply" that he *means* by the word "right" "conducive to the general happiness." Prof. Sidgwick sees that, if you take these two statements together, you get the absurd result that "greatest happiness is the end of human action, which is conducive to the general happiness"; and so absurd does it seem to him to call this result, as Bentham calls it, "the fundamental principle of a moral system," that he suggests that Bentham cannot have meant it. Yet Prof. Sidgwick himself states elsewhere[2] that Psychological Hedonism is "not seldom confounded with Egoistic Hedonism"; and that confusion, as we shall see, rests chiefly on that same fallacy, the naturalistic fallacy, which is implied in Bentham's statements. Prof. Sidgwick admits therefore that this fallacy is sometimes committed, absurd as it is; and I am inclined to think that Bentham may really have been one of those who committed it. Mill, as we shall see, certainly did commit it. In any case, whether Bentham committed it or not, his doctrine, as above quoted, will

[1] *Methods of Ethics*, Bk. I, Chap. iii, § 1 (6th edition).
[2] *Methods of Ethics*, Bk. I, Chap. iv, § 1.

serve as a very good illustration of this fallacy, and of the importance of the contrary proposition that good is indefinable.

Let us consider this doctrine. Bentham seems to imply, so Prof. Sidgwick says, that the word "right" *means* "conducive to general happiness." Now this, by itself, need not necessarily involve the naturalistic fallacy. For the word "right" is very commonly appropriated to actions which lead to the attainment of what is good; which are regarded as *means* to the ideal and not as ends-in-themselves. This use of "right," as denoting what is good as a means, whether or not it be also good as an end, is indeed the use to which I shall confine the word. Had Bentham been using "right" in this sense, it might be perfectly consistent for him to *define* right as "conducive to the general happiness," *provided only* (and notice this proviso) he had already proved, or laid down as an axiom, that general happiness was *the* good, or (what is equivalent to this) that general happiness alone was good. For in that case he would have already defined *the* good as general happiness (a position perfectly consistent, as we have seen, with the contention that "good" is indefinable), and, since right was to be defined as "conducive to *the* good," it would actually *mean* "conducive to general happiness." But this method of escape from the charge of having committed the naturalistic fallacy has been closed by Bentham himself. For his fundamental principle is, we see, that the greatest happiness of all concerned is the *right* and proper *end* of human action. He applies the word "right," therefore, to the end, as such, not only to the means which are conducive to it; and, that being so, right can no longer be defined as "conducive to the general happiness," without involving the fallacy in question. For now it is obvious that the definition of right as conducive to general happiness can be used by him in support of the fundamental principle that general happiness is the right end; instead of being itself derived from that principle. If right, by definition, means conducive to general happiness, then it is obvious that general happiness is the right end. It is not necessary now first to prove or assert that general happiness is the right end, before right is defined as conducive to general happiness—a perfectly valid procedure; but on the contrary the definition of right as conducive to general happiness proves general happiness to be the right end—a perfectly invalid procedure, since in this case the statement that "general happiness is the right end of human action" is not an ethical principle at all, but either, as we have seen, a proposition about the meaning of words, or else a proposition about the *nature* of general happiness, not about its rightness or goodness.

Now, I do not wish the importance I assign to this fallacy to be misunderstood. The discovery of it does not at all refute Bentham's contention that greatest happiness is the proper end of human action, if that be understood as an ethical proposition, as he undoubtedly intended it. That principle may be true all the same; we shall consider whether it is so in succeeding chapters [of *Principia Ethica*]. Bentham might have maintained it, as Prof. Sidgwick does, even if the fallacy had been pointed out to him. What I am maintaining is that the *reasons* which he actually gives for his ethical proposition are fallacious ones so far as they consist in the definition of right. What I suggest is that he did not perceive them to be fallacious; that, if he had done so, he would have been led to seek for other reasons in support of his Utilitarianism; and that, had he sought for other reasons, he *might* have found none which he thought to be sufficient. In that case he would have changed his whole system—a most important consequence. It is undoubtedly also possible that he would have thought other reasons to be sufficient, and in that case his ethical system, in its main results, would still have stood. But, even in this latter case, his use of the fallacy would be a serious objection to him as an ethical philosopher. For it is the business of Ethics, I must insist, not only to obtain true results, but also to find valid reasons for them. The direct object of Ethics is knowledge and not practice; and any one who uses the naturalistic fallacy has certainly not fulfilled this first object, however correct his practical principles may be.

My objections to Naturalism are then, in the first place, that it offers no reason at all, far less any valid reason, for any ethical principle whatever; and in this it already fails to satisfy the requirements of Ethics, as a scientific study. But in the second place I contend that, though it gives a reason for no ethical principle, it is a *cause* of the acceptance of false principles—it deludes the mind into accepting ethical principles, which are false; and in this it is contrary to every aim of Ethics. It is easy to see that if we start with a definition of right conduct as conduct conducive to general happiness; then, knowing that right conduct is universally conduct conducive to the good, we very easily arrive at the result that the good is general happiness. If, on the other hand, we once recognize that we must start our Ethics without a definition, we shall be much more apt to look about us, before we adopt any ethical principle whatever; and the more we look about us, the less likely are we to adopt a false one. It may be replied to this: Yes, but we shall look about us just as much, before we settle on our definition, and are therefore just as likely to be right. But I will try to show that this is not the case. If we start with the conviction that a definition of good can be found, we start with the conviction that good *can mean* nothing else than some one property of things; and our only business will then be to discover what that property is. But if we recognize that, so far as the meaning of good goes, anything whatever may be good, we start with a much more open mind. Moreover, apart from the fact that, when we think we have a definition, we cannot logically defend our ethical principles in any way whatever, we shall also be much less apt to defend them well, even if illogically. For we shall start with the conviction that good must mean so and so, and shall therefore be inclined either to misunderstand our opponent's arguments or to cut them short with the reply, "This is not an open question: the very meaning of the word decides it; no one can think otherwise except through confusion."

15. Our first conclusion as to the subject-matter of Ethics is, then, that there is a simple, indefinable, unanalyzable object of thought by reference to which it must be defined. By what name we call this unique object is a matter of indifference, so long as we clearly recognize what it is and that it does differ from other objects. The words which are commonly taken as the signs of ethical judgments all do refer to it; and they are expressions of ethical judgments solely because they do so refer. But they may refer to it in two different ways, which it is very important to distinguish, if we are to have a complete definition of the range of ethical judgments. Before I proceeded to argue that there was such an indefinable notion involved in ethical notions, I stated (§ 4) that it was necessary for Ethics to enumerate all true universal judgments, asserting that such and such a thing was good, whenever it occurred. But, although all such judgments do refer to that unique notion which I have called "good," they do not all refer to it in the same way. They may either assert that this unique property does always attach to the thing in question, or else they may assert only that the thing in question is *a cause or necessary condition* for the existence of other things to which this unique property does attach. The nature of these two species of universal ethical judgments is extremely different; and a great part of the difficulties, which are met with in ordinary ethical speculation, are due to the failure to distinguish them clearly. Their difference has, indeed, received expression in ordinary language by the contrast between the terms "good as means" and "good in itself," "value as a means" and "intrinsic value." But these terms are apt to be applied correctly only in the more obvious instances; and this seems to be due to the fact that the distinction between the conceptions which they denote has not been made a separate object of investigation. This distinction may be briefly pointed out as follows.

16. Whenever we judge that a thing is "good as a means," we are making a judgment with regard to its causal relations: we judge *both* that it will have a particular kind of effect, *and* that that effect will be good in itself. But to find causal judgments that are universally true is notoriously a matter of extreme difficulty. The late date at which most of the physical sciences become exact, and the comparative fewness of the laws which they have succeeded in establishing even now, are sufficient proofs of this difficulty. With regard, then, to what are the most frequent objects of ethical judgments, namely actions, it is obvious that we cannot be satisfied that any of our universal causal judgments are true, even in the sense in which scientific laws are so. We cannot even discover hypothetical laws of the form "Exactly this action will always, under these conditions, produce exactly that effect." But for a correct ethical judgment with regard to the effects of certain actions we require more than this in two respects. (1) We require to know that a given action will produce a certain effect, *under whatever circumstances it occurs*. But this is certainly impossible. It is certain that in different circumstances the same action may produce effects which are utterly different in all respects upon which the value of the effects depends. Hence we can never be entitled to more than a *generalization*—to a proposition of the form "This result *generally* follows this kind of action"; and even this generalization will only be true, if the circumstances under which the action occurs are generally the same. This is in fact the case, to a great extent, within any one particular age and state of society. But, when we take other ages into account, in many most important cases the normal circumstances of a given kind of action will be so different, that the generalization which is true for one will not be true for another. With regard then to ethical judgments which assert that a certain kind of action is good as a means to a certain kind of effect, none will be *universally* true; and many, though *generally* true at one period, will be generally false at others. But (2) we require to know not only that *one* good effect will be produced, but that, among all subsequent events affected by the action in question, the balance of good will be greater than if any other possible action had been performed. In other words, to judge that an action is generally a means to good is to judge not only that it generally does *some* good, but that it generally does the greatest good of which the circumstances admit. In this respect ethical judgments about that effects of action involve a difficulty and a complication far greater than that involved in the establishment of scientific laws. For the latter we need only consider a single effect; for the former it is essential to consider not only this, but the effects of that effect, and so on as far as our view into the future can reach. It is, indeed, obvious that our view can never reach far enough for us to be certain that any action will produce the best possible effects. We must be content, if the greatest possible balance of good seems to be produced within a limited period. But it is important to notice that the whole series of effects within a period of considerable length is actually taken account of in our common judgments that an action is good as a means; and that hence this additional complication, which makes ethical generalizations so far more difficult to establish than scientific laws, is one which is involved in actual ethical discussions, and is of practical importance. The commonest rules of conduct involve such considerations as the balancing of future bad health against immediate gains; and even if we can never settle with any certainty how we shall secure the greatest possible total of good, we try at least to assure ourselves that probable future evils will not be greater than the immediate good.

17. There are, then, judgments which state that certain kinds of things have good effects; and such judgments, for the reasons just given, have the important characteristics (1) that they are unlikely to be true, if they state that the kind of thing in question *always* has good effects, and (2) that, even if they only state that it *generally* has good

effects, many of them will only be true of certain periods in the world's history. On the other hand there are judgments which state that certain kinds of things are themselves good; and these differ from the last in that, if true at all, they are all of them universally true. It is, therefore, extremely important to distinguish these two kinds of possible judgments. Both may be expressed in the same language: in both cases we commonly say "Such and such a thing is good." But in the one case "good" will mean "good as means," *i.e.* merely that the thing is a means to good—will have good effects: in the other case it will mean "good as end"—we shall be judging that the thing itself has the property which, in the first case, we asserted only to belong to its effects. It is plain that these are very different assertions to make about a thing; it is plain that either or both of them may be made, both truly and falsely, about all manner of things; and it is certain that unless we are clear as to which of the two we mean to assert, we shall have a very poor chance of deciding rightly whether our assertion is true or false. It is precisely this clearness as to the meaning of the question asked which has hitherto been almost entirely lacking in ethical speculation. Ethics has always been predominantly concerned with the investigation of a limited class of actions. With regard to these we may ask *both* how far they are good in themselves *and* how far they have a general tendency to produce good results. And the arguments brought forward in ethical discussion have always been of both classes—both such as would prove the conduct in question to be good in itself and such as would prove it to be good as a means. But that these are the only questions which any ethical discussion can have to settle, and that to settle the one is *not* the same thing as to settle the other—these two fundamental facts have in general escaped the notice of ethical philosophers. Ethical questions are commonly asked in an ambiguous form. It is asked "What is a man's duty under these circumstances?" or "Is it right to act in this way?" or "What ought we to aim at securing?" But all these questions are capable of further analysis; a correct answer to any of them involves both judgments of what is good in itself and causal judgments. This is implied even by those who maintain that we have a direct and immediate judgment of absolute rights and duties. Such a judgment can only mean that the course of action in question is *the* best thing to do; that, by acting so, every good that *can* be secured will have been secured. Now we are not concerned with the question whether such a judgment will ever be true. The question is: What does it imply, if it is true? And the only possible answer is that, whether true or false, it implies both a proposition as to the degree of goodness of the action in question, as compared with other things, and a number of causal propositions. For it cannot be denied that the action will have consequences: and to deny that the consequences matter is to make a judgment of their intrinsic value, as compared with the action itself. In asserting that the action is *the* best thing to do, we assert that it together with its consequences presents a greater sum of intrinsic value than any possible alternative. And this condition may be realized by any of the three cases:—*(a)* If the action itself has greater intrinsic value than any alternative, whereas both its consequences and those of the alternatives are absolutely devoid either of intrinsic merit or intrinsic demerit; or *(b)* if, though its consequences are intrinsically bad, the balance of intrinsic value is greater than would be produced by any alternative; or *(c)* if, its consequences being intrinsically good, the degree of value belonging to them and it conjointly is greater than that of any alternative series. In short, to assert that a certain line of conduct is, at a given time, absolutely right to obligatory, is obviously to assert that more good or less evil will exist in the world, if it be adopted than if anything else be done instead. But this implies a judgment as to the value both of its own consequences and of those of any possible alternative. And that an action will have such and such consequences involves a number of causal judgments.

Similarly, in answering the question "What ought we to aim at securing?" causal judgments are again involved, but in a somewhat different way. We are liable to forget, because it is so obvious, that this question can never be answered correctly except by naming something which *can* be secured. Not everything can be secured; and, even if we judge that nothing which cannot be obtained would be of equal value with that which can, the possibility of the latter, as well as its value, is essential to its being a proper end of action. Accordingly neither our judgments as to what actions we ought to perform, nor even our judgments as to the ends which they ought to produce, are pure judgments of intrinsic value. With regard to the former, an action which is absolutely obligatory *may* have no intrinsic value whatsoever; that it is perfectly virtuous may mean merely that it causes the best possible effects. And with regard to the latter, these best possible results which justify our action can, in any case, have only so much of intrinsic value as the laws of nature allow us to secure; and they in their turn *may* have no intrinsic value whatsoever, but may merely be a means to the attainment (in a still further future) of something that has such value. Whenever, therefore, we ask "What ought we to do?" or "What ought we to try to get?" we are asking questions which involve a correct answer to two others, completely different in kind from one another. We must know *both* what degree of intrinsic value different things have, *and* how these different things may be obtained. But the vast majority of questions which have actually been discussed in Ethics—*all* practical questions, indeed—involve this double knowledge; and they have been discussed without any clear separation of the two distinct questions involved. A great part of the vast disagreements prevalent in Ethics is to be attributed to this failure in analysis. By the use of conceptions which involve both that of intrinsic value and that of causal relation, as if they involved intrinsic value only, two different errors have been rendered almost universal. Either it is assumed that nothing has intrinsic value which is not possible, or else it is assumed that what is necessary must have intrinsic value. Hence the primary and peculiar business of Ethics, the determination what things have intrinsic value and in what degrees, has received no adequate treatment at all. And on the other hand a *thorough* discussion of means has been also largely neglected, owing to an obscure perception of the truth that it is perfectly irrelevant to the question of intrinsic values. But however this may be, and however strongly any particular reader may be convinced that some one of the mutually contradictory systems which hold the field has given a correct answer either to the question what has intrinsic value, or to the question what we ought to do, or to both, it must at least be admitted that the questions what is best in itself and what will bring about the best possible, are utterly distinct; that both belong to the actual subject-matter of Ethics; and that the more clearly distinct questions are distinguished, the better is our chance of answering both correctly.

18. There remains one point which must not be omitted in a complete description of the kind of questions which Ethics has to answer. The main division of those questions is, as I have said, into two; the question what things are good in themselves, and the question to what other things these are related as effects. The first of these, which is the primary ethical question and is presupposed by the other, includes a correct comparison of the various things which have intrinsic value (if there are many such) in respect of the degree of value which they have; and such comparison involves a difficulty of principle which has greatly aided the confusion of intrinsic value with mere "goodness as a means." It has been pointed out that one difference between a judgment which asserts that a thing is good in itself, and a judgment which asserts that it is a means to good, consists in the fact that the first, if true of one instance of the thing in question, is necessarily true of all; whereas a thing which has good effects under some circumstances may have bad ones under others. Now it is certainly true that all judgments of intrinsic value are in this sense universal; but the principle which I have now to enunciate may easily make it appear as if they were not so but resembled the judgment of means in being merely general. There is, as will presently be maintained, a vast number of different things, each of which has intrinsic value; there are also very many which are positively bad; and there is a still larger class of things, which appear to be indifferent. But a thing belonging to any of these three classes may occur as part of a whole, which includes among its other parts other things belonging both to the same and to the other two classes; and these wholes, as such, may also have intrinsic value. The paradox, to which it is necessary to call attention, is that *the value of such a whole bears no regular proportion to the sum of the values of its parts.* It is certain that a good thing may exist in such a relation to another good thing that the value of the whole thus formed is immensely greater than the sum of the values of the two good things. It is certain that a whole formed of a good thing and an indifferent thing may have immensely greater value than that good thing itself possesses. It is certain that two bad things or a bad thing and an indifferent thing may form a whole much worse than the sum of badness of its parts. And it seems as if indifferent things may also be the sole constituents of a whole which has great value, either positive or negative. Whether the addition of a bad thing to a good whole may increase the positive value of the whole, or the addition of a bad thing to a bad may produce a whole having positive value, may seem more doubtful; but it is, at least, possible, and this possibility must be taken into account in our ethical investigations. However we may decide particular questions, the principle is clear. *The value of a whole must not be assumed to be the same as the sum of the values of its parts.*

A single instance will suffice to illustrate the kind of relation in question. It seems to be true that to be conscious of a beautiful object is a thing of great intrinsic value; whereas the same object, if no one be conscious of it, has certainly comparatively little value, and is commonly held to have none at all. But the consciousness of a beautiful object is certainly a whole of some sort in which we can distinguish as parts the object on the one hand and the being conscious on the other. Now this latter factor occurs as part of a different whole, whenever we are conscious of anything; and it would seem that some of these wholes have at all events very little value, and may even be indifferent or positively bad. Yet we cannot always attribute the slightness of their value to any positive demerit in the object which differentiates them from the consciousness of beauty; the object itself may approach as near as possible to absolute neutrality. Since, therefore, mere consciousness does not always confer great value upon the whole of which it forms a part, even though its object may have no great demerit, we cannot attribute the great superiority of the consciousness of a beautiful thing over the beautiful thing itself to the mere addition of the value of consciousness to that of the beautiful thing. Whatever the intrinsic value of consciousness may be, it does not give to the whole of which it forms a part a value proportioned to the sum of its value and that of its object. If this be so, we have here an instance of a whole possessing a different intrinsic value from the sum of that of its parts; and whether it be so or not, what is meant by such a difference is illustrated by this case.

19. There are, then, wholes which possess the property that their value is different from the sum of the values of their parts; and the relations which subsist between such parts and the whole of which they form a part have not hitherto been distinctly recognized or received a separate name. Two points are especially worthy of notice. (1) It is plain that the existence of any such part is a necessary condition for the existence of that good which is constituted by the whole. And exactly the same language will also express the relation between a means and the good thing which is its effect. But yet there is a most important difference between the two cases, constituted by the fact that the part is, whereas the means is not, a part of the good thing for the existence of which its existence is a necessary condition. The necessity by which, if the good in question is to exist, the means to it must exist is merely a natural or causal necessity. If the laws of nature were different, exactly the same good might exist, although what is now a necessary condition of its existence did not exist. The existence of the means has no intrinsic value; and its utter annihilation would leave the value of that which it is now necessary to secure entirely unchanged. But in the case of a part of such a whole as we are now considering, it is otherwise. In this case the good in question cannot conceivably exist, unless the part exist also. The necessity which connects the two is quite independent of natural law. What is asserted to have intrinsic value is the existence of the whole; and the existence of the whole includes the existence of its part. Suppose the part removed, and what remains is *not* what was asserted to have intrinsic value; but if we suppose a means removed, what remains is just what *was* asserted to have intrinsic value. And yet (2) the existence of the part may *itself* have no more intrinsic value than that of the means. It is this fact which constitutes the paradox of the relation which we are discussing. It has just been said that what has intrinsic value is the existence of the whole, and that this includes the existence of the part; and from this it would seem a natural inference that the existence of the part has intrinsic value. But the inference would be as false as if we were to conclude that, because the number of two stones was two, each of the stones was also two. The part of a valuable whole retains exactly the same value when it is, as when it is not, a part of that whole. If it had value under other circumstances, its value is not any greater, when it is part of a far more valuable whole; and if it had no value by itself, it has none still, however great be that of the whole of which it now forms a part. We are not then justified in asserting that one and the same thing is under some circumstances intrinsically good, and under others not so; as we are justified in asserting of a means that it sometimes does and sometimes does not produce good results. And yet we are justified in asserting that it is far more desirable that a certain thing should exist under some circumstances than under others; namely when other things will exist in such relations to it as to form a more valuable whole. *It* will not have more intrinsic value under these circumstances than under others; *it* will not necessarily even be a means to the existence of things having more intrinsic value: but it will, like a means, be a necessary condition for the existence of that which *has* greater intrinsic value, although, unlike a means, it will itself form a part of this more valuable existent.

20. I have said that the peculiar relation between part and whole which I have just been trying to define is one which has received no separate name. It would, however, be useful that it should have one; and there is a name, which might well be appropriated to it, if only it could be divorced from its present unfortunate usage. Philosophers, especially those who profess to have derived great benefit from the writings of Hegel, have latterly made much use of the terms "organic whole," "organic unity," "organic relation." The reason why these terms might well be appropriated to the use suggested is that the peculiar relation of parts to whole, just defined, is one of the properties which distinguishes the wholes to which they are actually applied with the greatest frequency. And the reason why it is desirable that they should be divorced from their present usage is that, as at present used, they have no distinct sense and, on the contrary, both imply and propagate errors of confusion.

To say that a thing is an "organic whole" is generally understood to imply that its parts are related to one another and to itself as means to end; it is also understood to imply that they have a property described in some such phrase as that they have "no meaning of significance apart from the whole"; and finally such a whole is also treated as if it had the property to which I am proposing that the name should be confined. But those who use the term give us, in general, no hint as to how they suppose these three properties to be related to one another. It seems generally to be assumed that they are identical; and always, at least, that they are necessarily connected with one another. That they are not identical I have already tried to show; to suppose them so is to neglect the very distinctions pointed out in the last paragraph; and the usage might well be discontinued merely because it encourages such neglect. But a still more cogent reason for its discontinuance is that, so far from being necessarily connected, the second is a property which can attach to nothing, being a self-contradictory conception; whereas the first, if we insist on its most important sense, applies to many cases, to which we have no reason to think that the third applies also, and the third certainly applies to many to which the first does not apply.

21. These relations between the three properties just distinguished may be illustrated by reference to a whole of the kind from which the name "organic" was derived—a whole which is an organism in the scientific sense—namely the human body.

(1) There exists between many parts of our body (though not between all) a relation which has been familiarized by the fable, attributed to Menenius Agrippa, concerning the belly and its members. We can find in its parts such that the continued existence of the one is a necessary condition of the continued existence of the other; while the continued existence of this latter is also a necessary condition for the continued existence of the former. This amounts to no more than saying that in the body we have instances of two things, both enduring for some time, which have a relation of mutual causal dependence on one another—a relation of "reciprocity." Frequently no more than this is meant by saying that the parts of the body form an "organic unity," or that they are mutually means and ends to one another. And we certainly have here a striking characteristic of living things. But it would be extremely rash to assert that this relation of mutual causal dependence was only exhibited by living things and hence was sufficient to define their peculiarity. And it is obvious that of two things which have this relation of mutual dependence, neither may have intrinsic value, or one may have it and the other lack it. They are not necessarily "ends" to one another in any sense except that in which "end" means "effect." And moreover it is plain that in this sense the whole cannot be an end to any of its parts. We are apt to talk of "the whole" in contrast to one of its parts, when in fact we mean only *the rest* of the parts. But strictly the whole must include all its parts and no part can be a cause of the whole, because it cannot be a cause of itself. It is plain, therefore, that this relation of mutual causal dependence implies nothing with regard to the value of either of the objects which have it; and that, even if both of them happen also to have value, this relation between them is one which cannot hold between part and whole.

But (2) it may also be the case that our body as a whole has a value greater than the sum of values of its parts; and this may be what is meant when it is said that the parts are means to the whole. It is obvious that if we ask the question "Why *should* the parts be such as they are?" a proper answer may be "Because the whole they form has so much value." But it is equally obvious that the relation which we thus assert to exist between part and whole is quite different from that which we assert to exist between part and part when we say "This part exists, because that one could not exist without it." In the latter case we assert the two parts to be causally connected; but, in the former, part and whole cannot be causally connected, and the relation which we assert to exist between them may exist even though the parts are not causally connected either. All of the parts of a picture do not have that relation of mutual causal dependence, which certain parts of the body have, and yet the existence of those which do not have it may be absolutely essential to the value of the whole. The two relations are quite distinct in kind, and we cannot infer the existence of the one from that of the other. It can, therefore, serve no useful purpose to include them both under the same name; and if we are to say that a whole is organic because its parts are (in this sense) "means" to the whole, we must *not* say that it is organic because its parts are causally dependent on one another.

22. But finally (3) the sense which has been most prominent in recent uses of the term "organic whole" is one whereby it asserts the parts of such a whole to have a property which the parts of no whole can possibly have. It is supposed that just as the whole would not be what it is but for the existence of the parts, so the parts would not be what they are but for the existence of the whole; and this is understood to mean not merely that any particular part could not exist unless the others existed too (which is the case where relation (1) exists between the parts), but actually that the part is no distinct object of thought—that the whole, of which it is a part, is in its turn a part of it. That this supposition is self-contradictory a very little reflection should be sufficient to show. We may admit, indeed, that when a particular thing is a part of a whole, it does possess a predicate which it would not otherwise possess—namely that it is a part of that whole. But what cannot be admitted is that this predicate alters the nature or enters into the definition of the thing which has it. When we think of the part *itself,* we mean just *that which* we assert, in this case, to *have* the predicate that it is part of the whole; and the mere assertion that *it* is a part of the whole involves that it should itself be distinct from that which we assert of it. Otherwise we contradict ourselves since we assert that, not *it,* but something else—namely it together with that which we assert of it—has the predicate which we assert of it. In short, it is obvious that no part contains analytically the whole to which it belongs, or any other parts of that whole. The relation of part to whole is *not* the same as that of whole to part; and the very definition of the latter is that it does contain analytically that which is said to be its part. And yet this very self-contradictory doctrine is the chief mark which shows the influence of Hegel upon modern philosophy—an influence which pervades almost the whole of orthodox philosophy. This is what is generally implied by the cry against falsification by abstraction: that a whole is always a part of its part! "If you want to know the truth about a part," we are told, "you must consider *not* that part, but something else—namely the whole: *nothing* is true of the part, but only of the whole." Yet plainly it must be true of the part at least that it is a part of the whole; and it is obvious that when we say it is, we do *not* mean merely that the whole is a part of itself. This doctrine, therefore, that a part can have "no meaning or significance apart from its whole" must be utterly rejected. It implies itself that the statement "This is a part of that whole" has a meaning; and in order that this may have one, both subject and predicate must have a distinct meaning. And it is easy to see how this false doctrine has arisen by confusion with the two relations (1) and (2) which may really be properties of wholes.

(a) The *existence* of a part may be connected by a natural or causal necessity with the existence of the other parts of its whole; and further what is a part of a whole and what has ceased to be such a part, although differing intrinsically from one another, may be called by one and the same name. Thus, to take a typical example, if an arm be cut off from the human body, we still call it an arm. Yet an arm, when it is a part of the body, undoubtedly differs from a dead arm: and hence we may easily be led to say "The arm which is a part of the body would not be what it is, if it were not such a part," and to think that the contradiction thus expressed is in reality a characteristic of things. But, in fact, the dead arm never was a part of the body; it is only *partially* identical with the living arm. Those parts of it which are identical with parts of the living arm are exactly the

same, whether they belong to the body or not; and in them we have an undeniable instance of one and the same thing at one time forming a part, and at another not forming a part of the presumed "organic whole." On the other hand those properties which *are* possessed by the living, and *not* by the dead, arm, do not exist in a changed form in the latter: they simply do not exist there *at all.* By a causal necessity their existence depends on their having that relation to the other parts of the body which we express by saying that they form part of it. Yet, most certainly, *if* they ever did not form part of the body, they *would* be exactly what they are when they do. That they differ intrinsically from the properties of the dead arm and that they form part of the body are propositions not analytically related to one another. There is no contradiction in supposing them to retain such intrinsic differences and yet not to form part of the body.

But *(b)* when we are told that a living arm has no *meaning* or *significance* apart from the body to which it belongs, a different fallacy is also suggested. "To have meaning or significance" is commonly used in the sense of "to have importance"; and this again means "to have value either as a means or as an end." Now it is quite possible that even a living arm, apart from its body, would have no intrinsic value whatever; although the whole of which it is a part has great intrinsic value owing to its presence. Thus we may easily come to say that, *as* a part of the body, it has great value, whereas *by itself* it would have none; and thus that its whole "meaning" lies in its relation to the body. But in fact the value in question obviously does not belong to *it* at all. To have value merely as a part is equivalent to having no value at all, but merely being a part of that which has it. Owing, however, to neglect of this distinction, the assertion that a part has value, *as a part,* which it would not otherwise have, easily leads to the assumption that it is also different, as a part, from what it would otherwise be; for it is, in fact, true that two things which have a different value must also differ in other respects. Hence the assumption that one and the same thing, because it is a part of a more valuable whole at one time than at another, therefore has more intrinsic value at one time than at another, has encouraged the self-contradictory belief that one and the same thing may be two different things, and that only in one of its forms is it truly what it is.

For these reasons, I shall, where it seems convenient, take the liberty to use the term "organic" with a special sense. I shall use it to denote the fact that a whole has an intrinsic value different in amount from the sum of the values of its parts. I shall use it to denote this and only this. The term will not imply any causal relation whatever between the parts of the whole in question. And it will not imply either, that the parts are inconceivable except as parts of that whole, or that, when they form parts of such a whole, they have a value different from that which they would have if they did not. Understood in this special and perfectly definite sense the relation of an organic whole to its parts is one of the most important which Ethics has to recognize. A chief part of that science should be occupied on comparing the relative values of various goods; and the grossest errors will be committed in such comparison if it be assumed that wherever two things form a whole, the value of that whole is merely the sum of the values of those two things. With this question of "organic wholes," then, we complete the enumeration of the kind of problems, with which it is the business of Ethics to deal.

23. In this chapter I have endeavored to enforce the following conclusions. (1) The peculiarity of Ethics is not that it investigates assertions about human conduct, but that it investigates assertions about that property of things which is denoted by the term "good," and the converse property denoted by the term "bad." It must, in order to establish its conclusions, investigate the truth of *all* such assertions, *except* those which assert the relation of this property only to a single existent (1–4). (2) This property, by reference to which the subject-matter of Ethics must be defined, is itself simple and indefinable (5–14). And (3) all assertions about its relation to other things are of two, and only two, kinds: they either assert in what degree things themselves possess this property, or else they assert causal relations between other things and those which possess it (15–17). Finally, (4) in considering the different degrees in which things themselves possess this property, we have to take account of the fact that a whole may possess it in a degree different from that which is obtained by summing the degrees in which its parts possess it (18–22).

1910

The Meaning of Good and Bad

Bertrand Russell

2. THE MEANING OF GOOD AND BAD

4. Good and Bad, in the sense in which the words are here intended (which is, I believe, their usual sense), are ideas which everybody, or almost everybody, possesses. These ideas are apparently among those which form the simplest constituents of our more complex ideas, and are therefore incapable of being analyzed or built up out of other simpler ideas. When people ask "What do you mean by *Good?*" the answer must consist, not in a verbal definition such as could be given if one were asked "What do you mean by *Pentagon?*" but in such a characterization as shall call up the appropriate idea to the mind of the questioner. This characterization may, and probably will, itself contain the idea of *good,* which would be a fault in a definition, but is harmless when

"'The Elements of Ethics' [from which this selection is taken] was written under the influence of Moore's *Principia Ethica.* There are some important points in which, not long after publishing it, I came to disagree with the theory that it advocates. I do not now think that 'good' is undefinable, and I think that whatever objectivity the concept may possess is political rather than logical. I was first led to this view by Santayana's criticisms of my work in his *Winds of Doctrine,* but have since found confirmation in many other directions. I am not, however, quite satisfied with any view of ethics that I have been able to arrive at, and that is why I have abstained from writing again on the subject."

Bertrand Russell, "The Meaning of Good and Bad" from THE ELEMENTS OF ETHICS (London: George Allen & Unwin, 1910). Reprinted with the permission of Routledge.

our purpose is merely to stimulate the imagination to the production of the idea which is intended. It is in this way that children are taught the names of colors: they are shown (say) a red book, and told that that is red; and for fear that they should think *red* means *book,* they are shown also a red flower, a red ball, and so on, and told that these are all red. Thus the idea of redness is conveyed to their minds, although it is quite impossible to analyze redness or to find constituents which compose it.

In the case of *good,* the process is more difficult, both because goodness is not perceived by the senses, like redness, and because there is less agreement as to the things that are good than as to the things that are red. This is perhaps one reason that has led people to think that the notion of *good* could be analyzed into some other notion, such as *pleasure* or *object of desire.* A second reason, probably more potent, is the common confusion that makes people think they cannot understand an idea unless they can define it—forgetting that ideas are defined by other ideas, which must be already understood if the definition is to convey any meaning. When people begin to philosophize, they seem to make a point of forgetting everything familiar and ordinary; otherwise their acquaintance with redness or any other color might show them how an idea can be intelligible where definition, in the sense of analysis, is impossible.

5. To explain what we mean by Good and Bad, we may say that a thing is good when on its own account it ought to exist, and bad when on its own account it ought not to exist. If it seems to be in our power to cause a thing to exist or not to exist, we ought to try to make it exist if it is good, and not exist if it is bad. When a thing is good, it is fitting that we should feel pleasure in its existence; when it is bad, it is fitting that we should feel pain in its existence. But all such characterizations really presuppose the notions of good and bad, and are therefore useful only as means of calling up the right ideas, not as logical definitions.

It might be thought that *good* could be defined as the quality of whatever we ought to try to produce. This would merely put *ought* in the place of *good* as our ultimate undefined notion; but as a matter of fact the good is much wider than what we ought to try to produce. There is no reason to doubt that some of the lost tragedies of Aeschylus were good, but we ought not to try to re-write them, because we should certainly fail. What we ought to do, in fact, is limited by our powers and opportunities, whereas the good is subject to no such limitation. And our knowledge of goods is confined to the things we have experienced or can imagine; but presumably there are many goods of which we human beings have absolutely no knowledge, because they do not come within the very restricted range of our thoughts and feelings. Such goods are still goods, although human conduct can have no reference to them. Thus the notion of good is wider and more fundamental that any notion concerned with conduct; we use the notion of good in explaining what right conduct is, but we do not use the notion of right conduct in explaining what good is.

6. A fairly plausible view is that *good* means the same as *desired,* so that when we say a thing is good we mean that it is desired. Thus anything is good which we either hope to acquire or fear to lose. Yet it is commonly admitted that there are bad desires; and when people speak of bad desires, they seem to mean desires for what is bad. For example, when one man desires another man's pain, it is obvious that what is desired is not good but bad. But the supporter of the view that *good* means *desired* will say that nothing is good or bad in itself, but is good for one person and perhaps bad for another. This must happen, he will say, in every case of a conflict of desires; if I desire your suffering, then your suffering is good for me, though it is bad for you. But the sense of *good* and *bad* which is needed in ethics is not in this way personal; and it is quite essential, in the study of ethics, to realize that there is an impersonal sense. In this sense when a thing is good, it ought to exist on its own account, not on account of its consequences, nor yet of who is going to enjoy it. We cannot maintain that for me a thing ought to exist on its own account, while for you it ought not; that would merely mean that one of us is mistaken, since in fact everything either ought to exist or ought not. Thus the fact that one man's desire may be another man's aversion proves that *good,* in the sense relevant to ethics, does not mean the same as *desired,* since everything is in itself either good or not good, and cannot be at once good for me and bad for you. This could only mean that its effects on me were good, and on you bad; but here good and bad are again impersonal.

7. There is another line of argument, more subtle but more instructive, by which we can refute those who say that *good* means *desired,* or who propose any other idea, such as pleasure, as the actual *meaning* of good. This line of argument will not prove that the things that are good are not the same as the things that are desired; but it will prove that, if this were the case, it could not be proved by appealing to the *meaning* of the word "good." So far, it might be thought that such an argument could only have a purely logical importance. But in fact this is not so. Many ethical theories have been based upon the contention that "good" means so-and-so, and people have accepted consequences of this contention which, if they had relied upon inspection untrammelled by false theory, they would almost certainly have rejected. Whoever believes that "good" means "desired" will try to explain away the cases where it seems as if what is desired is bad; but if he no longer holds this theory, he will be able to allow free play to his unbiased ethical perceptions, and will thus escape errors into which he would otherwise have fallen.

The argument in question is this: If any one affirms that the good is the desired, we consider what he says, and either assent or dissent; but in any case our assent or dissent is decided by considering what the good and the desired really are. When, on the contrary, some one gives a definition of the meaning of a word, our state of mind is quite different. If we are told "a pentagon is a figure which has five sides," we do not consider what we know about pentagons, and then agree or disagree, we accept this as the meaning of the word, and we know that we are getting information, not about pentagons, but merely about the *word* "pentagon." What we are told is the sort of thing that we expect dictionaries to tell us. But when we are told that the good is the desired, we feel at once that we are being told something of philosophical importance, something which has ethical consequences, something which it is quite beyond the scope of a dictionary to tell us. The reason of this is, that we already know what we mean by the good, and what we mean by the desired; and if these two meanings always applied to the same objects, that would not be a verbal definition, but an important truth. The analogue of such a proposition is not the above definition of a pentagon, but rather: "A pentagon (defined as above) is a figure which has five angles." Whenever a proposed definition sets us thinking whether it is true in fact, and not whether that is how the word is used, there is reason to suspect that we are not dealing with a definition, but with a significant proposition, in which the word professedly defined has a meaning already known to us, either as simple or as defined in some other way. By applying this test, we shall easily convince ourselves that all hitherto suggested definitions of the good are significant, not merely verbal, propositions; and that therefore, though they *may* be true in fact, they do not give the meaning of the word "good."

The importance of this result is that so many ethical theories depend upon the denial of it. Some have contended that "good" means "desired," others that "good" means "pleasure," others again that it means "conformity to Nature" or "obedience to the will of God." The mere fact that so many different and incompatible definitions have been proposed is evidence against any of them being really definitions; there have never been two incompatible definitions of the word "pentagon." None of the above are really definitions; they are all to be understood as substantial affirmations concerning the things that are good. All of them are, in my opinion, mistaken in fact as well as in form, but I shall not here undertake to refute them severally.

8. It is important to realize that when we say a thing is good in itself, and not merely as a means, we attribute to the thing a property which it either has or does not have, quite independently of our opinion on the subject, or of our wishes or other people's. Most men are inclined to agree with Hamlet: "There is nothing good or bad but thinking makes it so." It is supposed that ethical preferences are a mere matter of taste, and that if X thinks A is a good thing, and Y thinks it is a bad thing, all we can say is that A is good for X and bad for Y. This view is rendered plausible by the divergence of opinion as to what is good and bad, and by the difficulty of finding arguments to persuade people who differ from us in such a question. But difficulty in discovering the truth does not prove that there is no truth to be discovered. If X says A is good, and Y says A is bad, one of them must be mistaken, though it may be impossible to discover which. If this were not the case, there would be no difference of opinion between them. If, in asserting that A is good, X meant merely to assert that A had a certain relation to himself, say of pleasing his taste in some way; and if Y, in saying that A is not good, meant merely to deny that A had a like relation to himself: then there would be no subject of debate between them. It would be absurd, if X said "I am eating a pigeon pie," for Y to answer "that is false: I am eating nothing." But this is no more absurd than a dispute as to what is good, if, when we say A is good, we mean merely to affirm a relation of A to ourselves. When Christians assert that God is good, they do not mean merely that the contemplation of God arouses certain emotions in them: they may admit that this contemplation rouses no such emotion in the devils who believe and tremble, but the absence of such emotions is one of the things that make devils bad. As a matter of fact, we consider some tastes better than others: we do not hold merely that some tastes are ours and other tastes are other people's. We do not even always consider our own tastes the best: we may prefer bridge to poetry, but think it better to prefer poetry to bridge. And when Christians affirm that a world created by a good God must be a good world, they do not mean that it must be to their taste, for often it is by no means to their taste, but they use its goodness to argue that it *ought* to be to their taste. And they do not mean merely that it is to God's taste: for that would have been equally the case if God had not been good. Thus *good* and *bad* are qualities which belong to objects independently of our opinions, just as much as *round* and *square* do; and when two people differ as to whether a thing is good, only one of them can be right, though it may be very hard to know which is right.

9. One very important consequence of the indefinability of *good* must be emphasized, namely, the fact that knowledge as to what things exist, have existed, or will exist, can throw absolutely no light upon the question as to what things are good. There might, as far as mere logic goes, be some general proposition to the effect "whatever exists, is good," or "whatever exists, is bad," or "what will exist is better (or worse) than what does exist." But no such general proposition can be proved by considering the *meaning* of "good," and no such general proposition can be arrived at empirically from experience, since we do not know the whole of what does exist, nor yet of what has existed or will exist. We cannot therefore arrive at such a general proposition, unless it is itself self-evident, or follows from some self-evident proposition, which must (to warrant the consequence) be of the same general kind. But as a matter of fact, there is, so far as I can discover, no self-evident proposition as to the goodness or badness of all that exists or has existed or will exist. It follows that, from the fact that the existent world is of such and such a nature, nothing can be inferred as to what things are good or bad. . . .

1912

Does Moral Philosophy Rest on a Mistake?

H. A. Prichard

Probably to most students of Moral Philosophy there comes a time when they feel a vague sense of dissatisfaction with the whole subject. And the sense of dissatisfaction tends to grow rather than to diminish. It is not so much that the positions, and still more the arguments, of particular thinkers seem unconvincing, though this is true. It is rather that the aim of the subject becomes increasingly obscure. "What," it is asked, "are we really going to learn by Moral Philosophy?" "What are books on Moral Philosophy really trying to show, and when their aim is clear, why are they so unconvincing and artificial?" And again: "Why is it so difficult to substitute anything better?" Personally, I have been led by growing dissatisfaction of this kind to wonder whether the reason may not be that the subject, at any rate as usually understood, consists in the attempt to answer an improper question. And in this article I shall venture to contend that the existence of the whole subject, as usually understood, rests on a mistake, and on a mistake parallel to that on which rests, as I think, the subject usually called the Theory of Knowledge.

If we reflect on our own mental history or on the history of the subject, we feel no doubt about the nature of the demand which originates the subject. Any one who, stimulated by education, has come to feel the force of the various obligations in life, at some

H. A. Prichard, "Does Moral Philosophy Rest on a Mistake?," *Mind* 21 (1912). Reprinted with the permission of Oxford University Press.

time or other comes to feel the irksomeness of carrying them out, and to recognize the sacrifice of interest involved; and, if thoughtful, he inevitably puts to himself the question: "Is there really a reason why I should act in the ways in which hitherto I have thought I ought to act? May I not have been all the time under an illusion in so thinking? Should not I really be justified in simply trying to have a good time?" Yet, like Glaucon, feeling that somehow he ought after all to act in these ways, he asks for a *proof* that this feeling is justified. In other words, he asks "*Why* should I do these things?," and his and other people's moral philosophizing is an attempt to supply the answer, i.e. to supply by a process of reflection a proof of the truth of what he and they have prior to reflection believed immediately or without proof. This frame of mind seems to present a close parallel to the frame of mind which originates the Theory of Knowledge. Just as the recognition that the doing of our duty often vitally interferes with the satisfaction of our inclinations leads us to wonder whether we really ought to do what we usually call our duty, so the recognition that we and others are liable to mistakes in knowledge generally lead us, as it did Descartes, to wonder whether hitherto we may not have been always mistaken. And just as we try to find a proof, based on the general consideration of action and of human life, that we ought to act in the ways usually called moral, so we, like Descartes, propose by a process of reflection on our thinking to find a test of knowledge, i.e. a principle by applying which we can show that a certain condition of mind was really knowledge, a condition which *ex hypothesi* existed independently of the process of reflection.

Now, how has the moral question been answered? So far as I can see, the answers all fall, and fall from the necessities of the case, into one of two species. *Either* they state that we ought to do so and so, because, as we see when we fully apprehend the facts, doing so will be for our good, i.e. really, as I would rather say, for our advantage, or, better still, for our happiness; *or* they state that we ought to do so and so, because something realized either in or by the action is good. In other words, the reason "why" is stated in terms either of the agent's happiness or of the goodness of something involved in the action.

To see the prevalence of the former species of answer, we have only to consider the history of Moral Philosophy. To take obvious instances, Plato, Hutcheson, Paley, Mill, each in his own way seeks at bottom to convince the individual that he ought to act in so-called moral ways by showing that to do so will really be for his happiness. Plato is perhaps the most significant instance, because of all philosophers he is the one to whom we are least willing to ascribe a mistake on such matters, and a mistake on his part would be evidence of the deep-rootedness of the tendency to make it. To show that Plato really justifies morality by its profitableness, it is only necessary to point out (1) that the very formulation of the thesis to be met, viz. that justice is *ἀλλότριον ἀγαθὸν* [someone else's good] implies that any refutation must consist in showing that justice is *οἰκεῖον ἀγαθὸν* [one's own good], i.e., really, as the context shows, one's own advantage, and (2) that the term *λυσιτελεῖν* [to be profitable] supplies the key not only to the problem but also to its solution.

The tendency to justify acting on moral rules in this way is natural. For if, as often happens, we put to ourselves the question "Why should we do so and so?," we are satisfied by being convinced either that the doing so will lead to something which we want (e.g. that taking certain medicine will heal our disease), or that the doing so itself, as we see when we appreciate its nature, is something that we want or should like, e.g. playing golf. The formulation of the question implies a state of unwillingness or indifference towards the action, and we are brought into a condition of willingness by the answer. And this process seems to be precisely what we desire when we ask, e.g., "Why should we keep our engagements to our own loss?"; for it is just the fact that the keeping of our engagements runs counter to the satisfaction of our desires which produced the question.

The answer is, of course, not an answer, for it fails to convince us that we ought to keep our engagements; even if successful on its own lines, it only makes us *want* to keep them. And Kant was really only pointing out this fact when he distinguished hypothetical and categorical imperatives, even though he obscured the nature of the fact by wrongly describing his so-called "hypothetical imperatives" as imperatives. But if this answer be no answer, what other can be offered? Only, it seems, an answer which bases the obligation to do something on the *goodness* either of something to which the act leads or of the act itself. Suppose, when wondering whether we really ought to act in the ways usually called moral, we are told as a means of resolving our doubt that those acts are right which produce happiness. We at once ask: "Whose happiness?" If we are told "Our own happiness," then, though we shall lose our hesitation to act in these ways, we shall not recover our sense that we ought to do so. But how can this result be avoided? Apparently, only by being told one of two things: *either* that anyone's happiness is a thing good in itself, and that *therefore* we ought to do whatever will produce it, *or* that working for happiness is itself good, and that the intrinsic goodness of such an action is the reason why we ought to do it. The advantage of this appeal to the goodness of something consists in the fact that it avoids reference to desire, and, instead, refers to something impersonal and objective. In this way it seems possible to avoid the resolution of obligation into inclination. But just for this reason it is of the essence of the answer, that to be effective it must neither include nor involve the view that the apprehension of the goodness of anything necessarily arouses the desire for it. Otherwise the answer resolves itself into a form of the former answer by substituting desire or inclination for the sense of obligation, and in this way it loses what seems its special advantage.

Now it seems to me that both forms of this answer break down, though each for a different reason.

Consider the first form. It is what may be called Utilitarianism in the generic sense, in which what is good is not limited to pleasure. It takes its stand upon the distinction between something which is not itself an action, but which can be produced by an action, and the action which will produce it, and contends that if something which is not an action is good, then we *ought* to undertake the action which will, directly or indirectly, originate it.[1]

But this argument, if it is to restore the sense of obligation to act, must presuppose an intermediate link, viz. the further thesis that what is good ought to be.[2] The necessity of this link is obvious. An "ought," if it is to be derived at all, can only be derived from another "ought." Moreover, this link tacitly presupposes another, viz. that the apprehension that something good which is not an action ought to be involves just the feeling of imperativeness or obligation which is to be aroused by the thought of the action which will originate it. Otherwise the argument will not lead us to feel the obligation to produce it by the action. And, surely, both this link and its implication are false.[3] The word "ought" refers to actions and to actions alone. The proper language is never "So and so ought to be," but "I ought to do so and so." Even if we are sometimes moved to say that

[1]Cf. Dr. Rashdall's *Theory of Good and Evil*, I, 138.

[2]Dr. Rashdall, if I understand him rightly, supplies this link (cf. ibid., 135–36).

[3]When we speak of anything, e.g., of some emotion or of some quality of a human being, as good, we never dream in our ordinary consciousness of going on to say that therefore it ought to be.

the world or something in it is not what it ought to be, what we really mean is that God or some human being has not made something what he ought to have made it. And it is merely stating another side of this fact to urge that we can only feel the imperativeness upon us of something which is in our power; for it is actions and actions alone which, directly at least, are in our power.

Perhaps, however, the best way to see the failure of this view is to see its failure to correspond to our actual moral convictions. Suppose we ask ourselves whether our sense that we ought to pay our debts or to tell the truth arises from our recognition that in doing so we should be originating something good, e.g. material comfort in *A* or true belief in *B*, i.e. suppose we ask ourselves whether it is this aspect of the action which leads to our recognition that we ought to do it. We at once and without hesitation answer "No." Again, if we take as our illustration our sense that we ought to act justly as between two parties, we have, if possible, even less hesitation in giving a similar answer; for the balance of resulting good may be, and often is, not on the side of justice.

At best it can only be maintained that there is this element of truth in the Utilitarian view, that unless we recognize that something which an act will originate is good, we should not recognize that we ought to do the action. Unless we thought knowledge a good thing, it may be urged, we should not think that we ought to tell the truth; unless we thought pain a bad thing, we should not think the infliction of it, without special reason, wrong. But this is not to imply that the badness of error is the reason why it is wrong to lie, or the badness of pain the reason why we ought not to inflict it without special cause.[4]

It is, I think, just because this form of the view is so plainly at variance with our moral consciousness that we are driven to adopt the other form of the view, viz. that the act is good in itself and that its intrinsic goodness is the reason why it ought to be done. It is this form which has always made the most serious appeal; for the goodness of the act itself seems more closely related to the obligation to do it than that of its mere consequences or results, and therefore, if obligation is to be based on the goodness of something, it would seem that this goodness should be that of the act itself. Moreover, the view gains plausibility from the fact that moral actions are most conspicuously those to which the term "intrinsically good" is applicable.

Nevertheless this view, though perhaps less superficial, is equally untenable. For it leads to precisely the dilemma which faces everyone who tries to solve the problem raised by Kant's theory of the good will. To see this, we need only consider the nature of the acts to which we apply the term "intrinsically good."

There is, of course, no doubt that we approve and even admire certain actions, and also that we should describe them as good, and as good in themselves. But it is, I think, equally unquestionable that our approval and our use of the term "good" is always in respect of the motive and refers to actions which have been actually done and of which we think we know the motive. Further, the actions of which we approve and which we should describe as intrinsically good are of two and only two kinds. They are either actions in which the agent did what he did because he thought he ought to do it, or actions of which the motive was a desire prompted by some good emotion, such as gratitude, affection, family feeling, or public spirit, the most prominent of such desires in books on Moral Philosophy being that ascribed to what is vaguely called benevolence. For the sake of simplicity I omit the case of actions done partly from some such

[4]It may be noted that if the badness of pain were the reason why we ought not to inflict pain on another, it would equally be a reason why we ought not to inflict pain on ourselves; yet, though we should allow the wanton infliction of pain on ourselves to be foolish, we should not think of describing it as wrong.

desire and partly from a sense of duty; for even if all good actions are done from a combination of these motives, the argument will not be affected. The dilemma is this. If the motive in respect of which we think an action good is the sense of obligation, then so far from the sense that we ought to do it being derived from our apprehension of its goodness, our apprehension of its goodness will presuppose the sense that we ought to do it. In other words, in this case the recognition that the act is good will plainly *presuppose* the recognition that the act is right, whereas the view under consideration is that the recognition of the goodness of the act *gives rise* to the recognition of its rightness. On the other hand, if the motive in respect of which we think an action good is some intrinsically good desire, such as the desire to help a friend, the recognition of the goodness of the act will equally fail to give rise to the sense of obligation to do it. For we cannot feel that we ought to do that the doing of which is *ex hypothesi* prompted solely by the desire to do it.[5]

The fallacy underlying the view is that while to base the rightness of an act upon its intrinsic goodness implies that the goodness in question is that of the motive, in reality the rightness or wrongness of an act has nothing to do with any question of motives at all. For, as any instance will show, the rightness of an action concerns an action not in the fuller sense of the term in which we include the motive in the action, but in the narrower and commoner sense in which we distinguish an action from its motive and mean by an action merely the conscious origination of something, an origination which on different occasions or in different people may be prompted by different motives. The question "Ought I to pay my bills?" really means simply "Ought I to bring about my tradesmen's possession of what by my previous acts I explicitly or implicitly promised them?" There is, and can be, no question of whether I ought to pay my debts from a particular motive. No doubt we know that if we pay our bills we shall pay them with a motive, but in considering whether we ought to pay them we inevitably think of the act in abstraction from the motive. Even if we knew what our motive would be if we did the act, we should not be any nearer an answer to the question.

Moreover, if we eventually pay our bills from fear of the county court, we shall still have done *what* we ought, even though we shall not have done it *as* we ought. The attempt to bring in the motive involves a mistake similar to that involved in supposing that we can will to will. To feel that I ought to pay my bills is to be *moved towards* paying them. But what I can be moved towards must always be an action and not an action in which I am moved in a particular way, i.e. an action from a particular motive; otherwise I should be moved towards being moved, which is impossible. Yet the view under consideration involves this impossibility, for it really resolves the sense that I ought to do so and so, into the sense that I ought to be moved to do it in a particular way.[6]

So far my contentions have been mainly negative, but they form, I think, a useful, if not a necessary, introduction to what I take to be the truth. This I will now endeavor to state, first formulating what, as I think, is the real nature of our apprehension or appreciation of moral obligations, and then applying the result to elucidate the question of the existence of Moral Philosophy.

The sense of obligation to do, or of the rightness of, an action of a particular kind is absolutely underivative or immediate. The rightness of an action consists in its

[5]It is, I think, on this latter horn of the dilemma that Martineau's view falls; cf. *Types of Ethical Theory*, Part II, Book I.

[6]It is of course not denied here that an action done for a particular motive may be *good;* it is only denied that the *rightness* of an action depends on its being done with a particular motive.

being the origination of something of a certain kind *A* in a situation of a certain kind, a situation consisting in a certain relation *B* of the agent to others or to his own nature. To appreciate its rightness two preliminaries may be necessary. We may have to follow out the consequences of the proposed action more fully than we have hitherto done, in order to realize that in the action we should originate *A*. Thus we may not appreciate the wrongness of telling a certain story until we realize that we should thereby be hurting the feelings of one of our audience. Again, we may have to take into account the relation *B* involved in the situation, which we had hitherto failed to notice. For instance, we may not appreciate the obligation to give *X* a present, until we remember that he has done us an act of kindness. But, given that by a process which is, of course, merely a process of general and not of moral thinking we come to recognize that the proposed act is one by which we shall originate *A* in a relation *B*, then we appreciate the obligation immediately or directly, the appreciation being an activity of *moral* thinking. We recognize, for instance, that this performance of a service to *X*, who has done us a service, just in virtue of its being the performance of a service to one who has rendered a service to the would-be agent, ought to be done by us. This apprehension is immediate, in precisely the sense in which a mathematical apprehension is immediate, e.g. the apprehension that this three-sided figure, in virtue of its being three-sided, must have three angles. Both apprehensions are immediate in the sense that in both insight into the nature of the subject leads us to recognize its possession of the predicate; and it is only stating this fact from the other side to say that in both cases the fact apprehended is self-evident.

The plausibility of the view that obligations are not self-evident but need proof lies in the fact that an act which is referred to as an obligation may be incompletely stated, what I have called the preliminaries to appreciating the obligation being incomplete. If, e.g., we refer to the act of repaying *X* by a present merely as giving *X* a present, it appears, and indeed is, necessary to give a reason. In other words, wherever a moral act is regarded in this incomplete way the question "*Why* should I do it?" is perfectly legitimate. This fact suggests, but suggests wrongly, that even if the nature of the act is completely stated, it is still necessary to give a reason, or, in other words, to supply a proof.

The relations involved in obligations of various kinds are, of course, very different. The relation in certain cases is a relation to others due to a past act of theirs or ours. The obligation to repay a benefit involves a relation due to a past act of the benefactor. The obligation to repay a benefit involves a relation due to a past act of ours in which we have either said or implied that we would make a certain return for something which we have asked for and received. On the other hand, the obligation to speak the truth implies no such definite act; it involves a relation consisting in the fact that others are trusting us to speak the truth, a relation the apprehension of which gives rise to the sense that communication of the truth is something owing by us to them. Again, the obligation not to hurt the feelings of another involves no special relation of us to that other, i.e. no relation other than that involved in our both being men, and men in one and the same world. Moreover, it seems that the relation involved in an obligation need not be a relation to another at all. Thus we should admit that there is an obligation to overcome our natural timidity or greediness, and that this involves no relations to others. Still there is a relation involved, viz. a relation to our own disposition. It is simply because we can and because others cannot directly modify our disposition that it is our business to improve it, and that it is not theirs, or, at least, not theirs to the same extent.

The negative side of all this is, of course, that we do not come to appreciate an obligation by an *argument*, i.e. by a process of nonmoral thinking, and that, in particular, we do not do so by an argument of which a premise is the ethical but not moral activity of appreciating the goodness either of the act or of a consequence of the act; i.e. that our sense of the rightness of an act is not a conclusion from our appreciation of the goodness either of it or of anything else.

It will probably be urged that on this view our various obligations form, like Aristotle's categories, an unrelated chaos in which it is impossible to acquiesce. For, according to it, the obligation to repay a benefit, or to pay a debt, or to keep a promise, presupposes a previous act of another; whereas the obligation to speak the truth or not to harm another does not; and, again, the obligation to remove our timidity involves no relations to others at all. Yet, at any rate, an effective *argumentum ad hominem* is at hand in the fact that the various qualities which we recognize as good are equally unrelated; e.g. courage, humility, and interest in knowledge. If, as is plainly the case, ἀγαθά differ ᾗ ἀγαθά [Goods differ *qua* goods], why should not obligations equally differ *qua* their obligatoriness? Moreover, if this were not so there could in the end be only one obligation, which is palpably contrary to fact.[7]

Certain observations will help to make the view clearer.

In the first place, it may seem that the view, being—as it is—avowedly put forward in opposition to the view that what is right is derived from what is good, must itself involve the opposite of this, viz. the Kantian position that what is good is based upon what is right, i.e. that an act, if it be good, is good because it is right. But this is not so. For, on the view put forward, the rightness of a right action lies solely in the origination in which the act consists, whereas the intrinsic goodness of an action lies solely in its motive; and this implies that a morally good action is morally good not simply because it is a right action but because it is a right action done because it is right, i.e. from a sense of obligation. And this implication, it may be remarked incidentally, seems plainly true.

In the second place, the view involves that when, or rather so far as, we act from a sense of obligation, we have no purpose or end. By a "purpose" or "end" we really mean something the existence of which we desire, and desire of the existence of which leads us to act. Usually our purpose is something which the act will originate, as when we turn round in order to look at a picture. But it may be the action itself, i.e. the origination of something, as when we hit a golf ball into a hole or kill someone out of revenge.[8] Now if by a purpose we mean something the existence of which we desire and desire for which leads us to act, then plainly, so far as we act from a sense

[7]Two other objections may be anticipated: (1) that obligations cannot be self-evident, since many actions regarded as obligations by some are not so regarded by others, and (2) that if obligations are self-evident, the problem of how we ought to act in the presence of conflicting obligations is insoluble.

To the first I should reply:

(a) That the appreciation of an obligation is, of course, only possible for a developed moral being, and that different degrees of development are possible.

(b) That the failure to recognize some particular obligation is usually due to the fact that, owing to a lack of thoughtfulness, what I have called the preliminaries to this recognition are incomplete.

(c) That the view put forward is consistent with the admission that, owing to a lack of thoughtfulness, even the best men are blind to many of their obligations, and that in the end our obligations are seen to be coextensive with almost the whole of our life.

To the second objection I should reply that obligation admits of degrees, and that where obligations conflict, the decision of what we ought to do turns not on the question "Which of the alternative courses of action will originate the greater good?" but on the question "Which is the greater obligation?"

[8]It is no objection to urge that an action cannot be its own purpose, since the purpose of something cannot be the thing itself. For, speaking strictly, the purpose is not the *action's* purpose but *our* purpose, and there is no contradiction in holding that our purpose in acting may be the action.

of obligation, we have no purpose, consisting either in the action or in anything which it will produce. This is so obvious that it scarcely seems worth pointing out. But I do so for two reasons. (1) If we fail to scrutinize the meaning of the terms "end" and "purpose," we are apt to assume uncritically that all deliberate action, i.e. action proper, must have a purpose; we then become puzzled both when we look for the purpose of an action done from a sense of obligation, and also when we try to apply to such an action the distinction of means and end, the truth all the time being that since there is no end, there is no means either. (2) The attempt to base the sense of obligation on the recognition of the goodness of something is really an attempt to find a purpose in a moral action in the shape of something good which, as good, we want. And the expectation that the goodness of something underlies an obligation disappears as soon as we cease to look for a purpose.

The thesis, however, that, so far as we act from a sense of obligation, we have no purpose must not be misunderstood. It must not be taken either to mean or to imply that so far as we so act we have no *motive*. No doubt in ordinary speech the words "motive" and "purpose" are usually treated as correlatives, "motive" standing for the desire which induces us to act, and "purpose" standing for the object of this desire. But this is only because, when we are looking for the motive of the action, say, of some crime, we are usually presupposing that the act in question is prompted by a desire and not by the sense of obligation. At bottom, however, we mean by a motive what moves us to act; a sense of obligation does sometimes move us to act; and in our ordinary consciousness we should not hesitate to allow that the action we were considering might have had as its motive a sense of obligation. Desire and the sense of obligation are coordinate forms or species of motive.

In the third place, if the view put forward be right, we must sharply distinguish morality and virtue as independent, though related, species of goodness, neither being an aspect of something of which the other is an aspect, nor again a form or species of the other, nor again something deducible from the other; and we must at the same time allow that it is possible to do the same act either virtuously or morally or in both ways at once. And surely this is true. An act, to be virtuous, must, as Aristotle saw, be done willingly or with pleasure; as such it is just not done from a sense of obligation but from some desire which is intrinsically good, as arising from some intrinsically good emotion. Thus, in an act of generosity the motive is the desire to help another arising from sympathy with that other; in an act which is courageous and no more, i.e. in an act which is not at the same time an act of public spirit or family affection or the like, we prevent ourselves from being dominated by a feeling of terror, desiring to do so from a sense of shame at being terrified. The goodness of such an act is different from the goodness of an act to which we apply the term moral in the strict and narrow sense, viz. an act done from a sense of obligation. Its goodness lies in the intrinsic goodness of the emotion and of the consequent desire under which we act, the goodness of this motive being different from the goodness of the moral motive proper, viz. the sense of duty or obligation. Nevertheless, at any rate in certain cases, an act can be done either virtuously or morally or in both ways at once. It is possible to repay a benefit either from desire to repay it, or from the feeling that we ought to do so, or from both motives combined. A doctor may tend his patients either from a desire arising out of interest in his patients or in the exercise of skill, or from a sense of duty, or from a desire and a sense of duty combined. Further, although we recognize that in each case the act possesses an intrinsic goodness, we regard that action as the best in which both motives are combined; in other words, we regard as the really best man the man in whom virtue and morality are united.

It may be objected that the distinction between the two kinds of motive is untenable, on the ground that the *desire* to repay a benefit, for example, is only the manifestation of that which manifests itself as the *sense of obligation* to repay whenever we think of something in the action which is other than the repayment and which we should not like, such as the loss or pain involved. Yet the distinction can, I think, easily be shown to be tenable. For, in the analogous case of revenge, the desire to return the injury and the sense that we ought not to do so, leading, as they do, in opposite directions, are plainly distinct; and the obviousness of the distinction here seems to remove any difficulty in admitting the existence of a parallel distinction between the desire to return a benefit and the sense that we ought to return it.[9]

Further, the view implies that an obligation can no more be based on or derived from a virtue than a virtue can be derived from an obligation, in which latter case a virtue would consist in carrying out an obligation. And the implication is surely true and important. Take the case of courage. It is untrue to urge that, since courage is a virtue, we ought to act courageously. It is and must be untrue, because, as we see in the end, to feel an obligation to act courageously would involve a contradiction. For, as I have urged before, we can only feel an obligation to *act;* we cannot feel an obligation to *act from a certain desire,* in this case the desire to conquer one's feelings of terror arising from the sense of shame which they arouse. Moreover, if the sense of obligation to act in a particular way leads to an action, the action will be an action done from a sense of obligation, and therefore not, if the above analysis of virtue be right, an act of courage.

The mistake of supposing that there can be an obligation to act courageously seems to arise from two causes. In the first place, there is often an obligation to do that which involves the conquering or controlling of our fear in the doing of it, e.g. the obligation to walk along the side of a precipice to fetch a doctor for a member of our family. Here the acting on the obligation is externally, though only externally, the same as an act of courage proper. In the second place there is an obligation to acquire courage, i.e. to do such things as will enable us afterwards to act courageously, and this may be mistaken for an obligation to act courageously. The same considerations can, of course, be applied, *mutatis mutandis,* to the other virtues.

The fact, if it be a fact, that virtue is no basis for morality will explain what otherwise it is difficult to account for, viz. the extreme sense of dissatisfaction produced by a close reading of Aristotle's *Ethics.* Why is the *Ethics* so disappointing? Not, I think, because it really answers two radically different questions as if they were one: (1) "What is the happy life?" (2) "What is the virtuous life?" It is, rather, because Aristotle does not do what we as moral philosophers want him to do, viz. to convince us that we really ought to do what in our nonreflective consciousness we have hitherto believed we ought to do, or if not, to tell us what, if any, are the other things which we really ought to do, and to prove to us that he is right. Now, if what I have just been contending is true, a systematic account of the virtuous character cannot possibly satisfy this demand. At best it can only make clear to us the details of one of our obligations, viz. the obligation to make ourselves better men; but the achievement of this does not help us to discover what we ought to do in life as a whole, and why; to think that it did would be to

[9]This sharp distinction of virtue and morality as coordinate and independent forms of goodness will explain a fact which otherwise it is difficult to account for. If we turn from books on Moral Philosophy to any vivid account of human life and action such as we find in Shakespeare, nothing strikes us more than the comparative remoteness of the discussions of Moral Philosophy from the facts of actual life. Is not this largely because, while Moral Philosophy has, quite rightly, concentrated its attention on the fact of obligation, in the case of many of those whom we admire most and whose lives are of the greatest interest, the sense of obligation, though it may be an important, is not a dominating factor in their lives?

think that our only business in life was self-improvement. Hence it is not surprising that Aristotle's account of the good man strikes us as almost wholly of academic value, with little relation to our real demand, which is formulated in Plato's words: *οὐ γὰρ περὶ τοῦ ἐπιυχόντος ὁ λόγος, ἀλλὰ περὶ τοῦ ὅντινα τρόπον χρὴ ζῆν* [for no light matter is at stake, nothing less than the rule of human life].

I am not, of course, *criticizing* Aristotle for failing to satisfy this demand, except so far as here and there he leads us to think that he intends to satisfy it. For my main contention is that the demand cannot be satisfied, and cannot be satisfied because it is illegitimate. Thus we are brought to the question: "Is there really such a thing as Moral Philosophy, and, if there is, in what sense?"

We should first consider the parallel case—as it appears to be—of the Theory of Knowledge. As I urged before, at some time or other in the history of all of us, if we are thoughtful, the frequency of our own and of others' mistakes is bound to lead to the reflection that possibly we and others have *always* been mistaken in consequence of some radical defect of our faculties. In consequence, certain things which previously we should have said without hesitation that we *knew,* as e.g. that $4 \times 7 = 28$, become subject to doubt; we become able only to say that we thought we knew these things. We inevitably go on to look for some general procedure by which we can ascertain that a given condition of mind is really one of knowledge. And this involves the search for a criterion of knowledge, i.e. for a principle by applying which we can settle that a given state of mind is really knowledge. The search for this criterion and the application of it, when found, is what is called the Theory of Knowledge. The search implies that instead of its being the fact that the knowledge that A is B is obtained directly by consideration of the nature of A and B, the knowledge that A is B, in the full or complete sense, can only be obtained by first knowing that A is B, and then knowing that we knew it by applying a criterion, such as Descartes's principle that what we clearly and distinctly conceive is true.

Now it is easy to show that the doubt whether A is B, based on this speculative or general ground, could, if genuine, never be set at rest. For if, in order really to know that A is B, we must first know that we knew it, then really, to know that we knew it, we must first know that we knew that we knew it. But—what is more important—it is also easy to show that this doubt is not a genuine doubt but rests on a confusion the exposure of which removes the doubt. For when we *say* we doubt whether our previous condition was one of knowledge, what we *mean,* if we mean anything at all, is that we doubt whether our previous *belief* was *true,* a belief which we should express as the *thinking* that A is B. For in order to doubt whether our previous condition was one of knowledge, we have to think of it not as knowledge but as only belief, and our only question can be "Was this belief true?" But as soon as we see that we are thinking of our previous condition as only one of belief, we see that what we are now doubting is not what we first *said* we were doubting, viz. whether a previous condition of knowledge was really knowledge. Hence, to remove the doubt, it is only necessary to appreciate the real nature of our consciousness in apprehending, e.g. that $7 \times 4 = 28$, and thereby see that it was no mere condition of believing but a condition of knowing, and then to notice that in our subsequent doubt what we are really doubting is not whether this consciousness was really knowledge, but whether a consciousness of another kind, viz. a belief that $7 \times 4 = 28$, was true. We thereby see that though a doubt based on speculative grounds is possible, it is not a doubt concerning what we believed the doubt concerned, and that a doubt concerning this latter is impossible.

Two results follow. In the first place, if, as is usually the case, we mean by the "Theory of Knowledge" the knowledge which supplies the answer to the question "Is what we have hitherto thought knowledge really knowledge?," there is and can be no such thing, and the supposition that there can is simply due to a confusion. There can be no answer to an illegitimate question, except that the question is illegitimate. Nevertheless the question is one which we continue to put until we realize the inevitable immediacy of knowledge. And it is positive knowledge that knowledge is immediate and neither can be, nor needs to be, improved or vindicated by the further knowledge that it was knowledge. This positive knowledge sets at rest the inevitable doubt, and, so far as by the "Theory of Knowledge" is meant this knowledge, then even though this knowledge be the knowledge that there is no Theory of Knowledge in the former sense, to that extent the Theory of Knowledge exists.

In the second place, suppose we come genuinely to doubt whether, e.g., $7 \times 4 = 28$ owing to a genuine doubt whether we were right in believing yesterday that $7 \times 4 = 28$, a doubt which can in fact only arise if we have lost our hold of, i.e. no longer remember, the real nature of our consciousness of yesterday, and so think of it as consisting in believing. Plainly, the only remedy is to do the sum again. Or, to put the matter generally, if we do come to doubt whether it is true that A is B, as we once thought, the remedy lies not in any process of reflection but in such a reconsideration of the nature of A and B as leads to the knowledge that A is B.

With these considerations in mind, consider the parallel which, as it seems to me, is presented—though with certain differences—by Moral Philosophy. The sense that we ought to do certain things arises in our unreflective consciousness, being an activity of moral thinking occasioned by the various situations in which we find ourselves. At this stage our attitude to these obligations is one of unquestioning confidence. But inevitably the appreciation of the degree to which the execution of these obligations is contrary to our interest raises the doubt whether after all these obligations are really obligatory, i.e. whether our sense that we ought not to do certain things is not illusion. We then want to have it *proved* to us that we ought to do so, i.e. to be convinced of this by a process which, as an argument, is different in kind from our original and unreflective appreciation of it. This demand is, as I have argued, illegitimate.

Hence, in the first place, if, as is almost universally the case, by Moral Philosophy is meant the knowledge which would satisfy this demand, there is no such knowledge, and all attempts to attain it are doomed to failure because they rest on a mistake, the mistake of supposing the possibility of proving what can only be apprehended directly by an act of moral thinking. Nevertheless the demand, though illegitimate, is inevitable until we have carried the process of reflection far enough to realize the self-evidence of our obligations, i.e. the immediacy of our apprehension of them. This realization of their self-evidence is positive knowledge, and so far, and so far only, as the term Moral Philosophy is confined to this knowledge and to the knowledge of the parallel immediacy of the apprehension of the goodness of the various virtues and of good dispositions generally, is there such a thing as Moral Philosophy. But since this knowledge may allay doubts which often affect the whole conduct of life, it is, though not extensive, important, and even vitally important.

In the second place, suppose we come genuinely to doubt whether we ought, for example, to pay our debts, owing to a genuine doubt whether our previous conviction that we ought to do so is true, a doubt which can, in fact, only arise if we fail to remember the real nature of what we now call our past conviction. The only remedy lies in actually getting into a situation which occasions the obligation, or—if our imagination be strong enough—in imagining ourselves in that situation, and then letting our moral capacities of thinking do their work. Or, to put the matter generally, if we do doubt whether there is really an obligation to originate A in a situation B, the remedy lies not in any process of general thinking, but in getting face to face with a particular instance of the situation B, and then directly appreciating the obligation to originate A in that situation.

1913
Hypostatic Ethics
George Santayana

If Mr. Russell, in his essay on "The Elements of Ethics," had wished to propitiate the unregenerate naturalist, before trying to convert him, he could not have chosen a more skillful procedure; for he begins by telling us that "what is called good conduct is conduct which is a means to other things which are good on their own account; and hence . . . the study of what is good or bad on its own account must be included in ethics." Two consequences are involved in this: first, that ethics is concerned with the economy of all values, and not with "moral" goods only, or with duty; and second, that values may and do inhere in a great variety of things and relations, all of which it is the part of wisdom to respect, and if possible to establish. In this matter, according to our author, the general philosopher is prone to one error and the professed moralist to another. "The philosopher, bent on the construction of a system, is inclined to simplify the facts unduly . . . and to twist them into a form in which they can all be deduced from one or two general principles. The moralist, on the other hand, being primarily concerned with conduct, tends to become absorbed in means, to value the actions men ought to perform more than the ends which such actions serve. . . . Hence most of what they value in this world would have to be omitted by many moralists from any imagined heaven, because there such things as self-denial and effort and courage and pity could find no place. . . .

George Santayana, "Hypostatic Ethics" from WINDS OF DOCTRINE (London: J. M. Dent & Sons, 1913). Reprinted with the permission of the publishers.

Kant has the bad eminence of combining both errors in the highest possible degree, since he holds that there is nothing good except the virtuous will—a view which simplifies the good as much as any philosopher could wish, and mistakes means for ends as completely as any moralist could enjoin."

Those of us who are what Mr. Russell would call ethical sceptics will be delighted at this way of clearing the ground; it opens before us the prospect of a moral philosophy that should estimate the various values of things known and of things imaginable, showing what combinations of goods are possible in any one rational system, and (if fancy could stretch so far) what different rational systems would be possible in places and times remote enough from one another not to come into physical conflict. Such ethics, since it would express in reflection the dumb but actual interests of men, might have both influence and authority over them; two things which an alien and dogmatic ethics necessarily lacks. The joy of the ethical sceptic in Mr. Russell is destined, however, to be short-lived. Before proceeding to the expression of concrete ideals, he thinks it necessary to ask a preliminary and quite abstract question, to which his essay is chiefly devoted; namely, what is the right definition of the predicate "good," which we hope to apply in the sequel to such a variety of things? And he answers at once: The predicate "good" is indefinable. This answer he shows to be unavoidable, and so evidently unavoidable that we might perhaps have been absolved from asking the question; for, as he says, the so-called definitions of "good"—that it is pleasure, the desired, and so forth—are not definitions of the predicate "good," but designations of the things to which this predicate is applied by different persons. Pleasure, and its rivals, are not synonyms for the abstract quality "good," but names for classes of concrete facts that are supposed to possess that quality. From this correct, if somewhat trifling, observation, however, Mr. Russell, like Mr. Moore before him, evokes a portentous dogma. Not being able to define good, he hypostasizes it. "Good and bad," he says, "are qualities which belong to objects independently of our opinions, just as much as round and square do; and when two people differ as to whether a thing is good, only one of them can be right, though it may be very hard to know which is right." "We cannot maintain that for me a thing ought to exist on its own account, while for you it ought not; that would merely mean that one of us is mistaken, since in fact everything either ought to exist, or ought not." Thus we are asked to believe that good attaches to things for no reason or cause, and according to no principles of distribution; that it must be found there by a sort of receptive exploration in each separate case; in other words, that it is an absolute, not a relative thing, a primary and not a secondary quality.

That the quality "good" is indefinable is one assertion, and obvious; but that the presence of this quality is unconditioned is another, and astonishing. My logic, I am well aware, is not very accurate or subtle; and I wish Mr. Russell had not left it to me to discover the connection between these two propositions. Green is an indefinable predicate, and the specific quality of it can be given only in intuition; but it is a quality that things acquire under certain conditions, so much so that the same bit of grass, at the same moment, may have it from one point of view and not from another. Right and left are indefinable; the difference could not be explained without being invoked in the explanation; yet everything that is to the right is not to the right on no condition, but obviously on the condition that some one is looking in a certain direction; and if some one else at the same time is looking in the opposite direction, what is truly to the right will be truly to the left also. If Mr. Russell thinks this is a contradiction, I understand why the universe does not please him. The contradiction would be real, undoubtedly, if we suggested that the *idea* of good was at any time or in any relation the *idea* of evil, or the *intuition* of right that of left, or the *quality* of green that of yellow; these disembodied essences are fixed by the intent that selects them, and in that ideal realm they can never have any relations except the dialectical ones implied in their nature, and these relations they must always retain. But the contradiction disappears when, instead of considering the qualities in themselves, we consider the things of which those qualities are aspects; for the qualities of things are not compacted by implication, but are conjoined irrationally by nature, as she will; and the same thing may be, and is, at once yellow and green, to the left and to the right, good and evil, many and one, large and small; and whatever verbal paradox there may be in this way of speaking (for from the point of view of nature it is natural enough) had been thoroughly explained and talked out by the time of Plato, who complained that people should still raise a difficulty so trite and exploded.[1] Indeed, while square is always square, and round round, a thing that is round may actually be square also, if we allow it to have a little body, and to be a cylinder.

But perhaps what suggests this hypostasis of good is rather the fact that what others find good, or what we ourselves have found good in moods with which we retain no sympathy, is sometimes pronounced by us to be bad; and far from inferring from this diversity of experience that the present good, like the others, corresponds to a particular attitude or interest of ours, and is dependent upon it, Mr. Russell and Mr. Moore infer instead that the presence of the good must be independent of all interests, attitudes, and opinions. They imagine that the truth of a proposition attributing a certain relative quality to an object contradicts the truth of another proposition, attributing to the same object an opposite relative quality. Thus if a man here and another man at the antipodes call opposite directions up, "only one of them can be right, though it may be very hard to know which is right."

To protect the belated innocence of this state of mind, Mr. Russell, so far as I can see, has only one argument, and one analogy. The argument is that "if this were not the case, we could not reason with a man as to what is right." "We do in fact hold that when one man approves of a certain act, while another disapproves, one of them is mistaken, which would not be the case with a mere emotion. If one man likes oysters and another dislikes them, we do not say that either of them is mistaken." In other words, we are to maintain our prejudices, however absurd, lest it should become unnecessary to quarrel about them! Truly the debating society has its idols, no less than the cave and the theater. The analogy that comes to buttress somewhat this singular argument is the analogy between ethical propriety and physical or logical truth. An ethical proposition may be correct or incorrect, in a sense justifying argument, when it touches what is good as a means, that is, when it is not intrinsically ethical, but deals with causes and effects, or

[1]Plato, *Philebus,* 14, D. The dialectical element in this dialogue is evidently the basis of Mr. Russell's, as of Mr. Moore's, ethics; but they have not adopted the other elements in it, I mean the political and the theological. As to the political element, Plato everywhere conceives the good as the eligible in life, and refers it to human nature and to the pursuit of happiness—that happiness which Mr. Russell, in a rash moment, says is but a name which some people prefer to give to pleasure. Thus in the *Philebus* (11, D) the good looked for is declared to be "some state and disposition of the soul which has the property of making all men happy"; and later (66, D) the conclusion is that insight is better than pleasure "as an element in human life." As to the theological element. Plato, in hypostasizing the good, does not hypostasize it as good, but as cause or power, which is, it seems to me, the sole category that justifies hypostasis, and logically involves it; for if things have a ground at all, that ground must exist before them and beyond them. Hence the whole Platonic and Christian scheme, in making the good independent of private will and opinion, by no means makes it independent of the direction of nature in general and of human nature in particular; for all things have been created with an innate predisposition towards the creative good, and are capable of finding happiness in nothing else. Obligation, in this system, remains internal and vital. Plato attributes a single vital direction and a single moral source to the cosmos. This is what determines and narrows the scope of the true good; for the true good is that relevant to nature. Plato would not have been a dogmatic moralist, had he not been a theist.

with matters of fact or necessity. But to speak of the truth of an ultimate good would be a false collocation of terms; an ultimate good is chosen, found, or aimed at; it is not opined. The ultimate intuitions on which ethics rests are not debatable, for they are not opinions we hazard but preferences we feel; and it can be neither correct nor incorrect to feel them. We may assert these preferences fiercely or with sweet reasonableness, and we may be more or less incapable of sympathizing with the different preferences of others; about oysters we may be tolerant, like Mr. Russell, and about character intolerant; but that is already a great advance in enlightenment, since the majority of mankind have regarded as hateful in the highest degree any one who indulged in pork, or beans, or frogs' legs, or who had a weakness for anything called "unnatural"; for it is the things that offend their animal instincts that intense natures have always found to be, intrinsically and *par excellence,* abominations.

I am not sure whether Mr. Russell thinks he has disposed of this view where he discusses the proposition that the good is the desired and refutes it on the ground that "it is commonly admitted that there are bad desires; and when people speak of bad desires, they seem to mean desires for what is bad." Most people undoubtedly call desires bad when they are generically contrary to their own desires, and call objects that disgust them bad, even when other people covet them. This human weakness is not, however, a very high authority for a logician to appeal to, being too like the attitude of the German lady who said that Englishmen called a certain object *bread,* and Frenchmen called it *pain,* but that it really was *Brod.* Scholastic philosophy is inclined to this way of asserting itself; and Mr. Russell, though he candidly admits that there are ultimate differences of opinion about good and evil, would gladly minimize these differences, and thinks he triumphs when he feels that the prejudices of his readers will agree with his own; as if the constitutional unanimity of all human animals, supposing it existed, could tend to show that the good they agreed to recognize was independent of their constitution.

In a somewhat worthier sense, however, we may admit that there are desires for what is bad, since desire and will, in the proper psychological sense of these words, are incidental phases of consciousness, expressing but not constituting those natural relations that make one thing good for another. At the same time the words desire and will are often used, in a mythical or transcendental sense, for those material dispositions and instincts by which vital and moral units are constituted. It is in reference to such constitutional interests that things are "really" good or bad; interests which may not be fairly represented by any incidental conscious desire. No doubt any desire, however capricious, represents some momentary and partial interest, which lends to its objects a certain real and inalienable value; yet when we consider, as we do in human society, the interests of men, whom reflection and settled purposes have raised more or less to the ideal dignity of individuals, then passing fancies and passions may indeed have bad objects, and be bad themselves, in that they thwart the more comprehensive interests of the soul that entertains them. Food and poison are such only relatively, and in view of particular bodies, and the same material thing may be food and poison at once; the child, and even the doctor, may easily mistake one for the other. For the human system whiskey is truly more intoxicating than coffee, and the contrary opinion would be an error; but what a strange way of vindicating this real, though relative, distinction, to insist that whiskey is more intoxicating in itself, without reference to any animal; that it is pervaded, as it were, by an inherent intoxication, and stands dead drunk in its bottle! Yet just in this way Mr. Russell and Mr. Moore conceive things to be dead good and dead bad. It is such a view, rather than the naturalistic one, that renders reasoning and self-criticism impossible in morals; for wrong desires, and false opinions as to value, are conceivable only because a point of reference or criterion is available to prove them such. If no point of reference and no criterion were admitted to be relevant, nothing but physical stress could give to one assertion of value greater force than to another. The shouting moralist no doubt has his place, but not in philosophy.

That good is not an intrinsic or primary quality, but relative and adventitious, is clearly betrayed by Mr. Russell's own way of arguing, whenever he approaches some concrete ethical question. For instance, to show that the good is not pleasure, he can avowedly do nothing but appeal "to ethical judgments with which almost every one would agree." He repeats, in effect, Plato's argument about the life of the oyster, having pleasure with no knowledge. Imagine such mindless pleasure, as intense and prolonged as you please, and would you choose it? Is it your good? Here the British reader, like the blushing Greek youth, is expected to answer instinctively, No! It is an *argumentum ad hominem* (and there can be no other kind of argument in ethics); but the man who gives the required answer does so not because the answer is self-evident, which it is not, but because he is the required sort of man. He is shocked at the idea of resembling an oyster. Yet changeless pleasure, without memory or reflection, without the wearisome intermixture of arbitrary images, is just what the mystic, the voluptuary, and perhaps the oyster find to be good. Ideas, in their origin, are probably signals of alarm; and the distress which they marked in the beginning always clings to them in some measure, and causes many a soul, far more profound than that of the young Protarchus or of the British reader, to long for them to cease altogether. Such a radical hedonism is indeed inhuman; it undermines all conventional ambitions, and is not a possible foundation for political or artistic life. But that is all we can say against it. Our humanity cannot annul the incommensurable sorts of good that may be pursued in the world, though it cannot itself pursue them. The impossibility which people labour under of being satisfied with pure pleasure as a goal is due to their want of imagination, or rather to their being dominated by an imagination which is exclusively human.

The author's estrangement from reality reappears in his treatment of egoism, and most of all in his "Free Man's Religion." Egoism, he thinks, is untenable because "if I am right in thinking that my good is the only good, then every one else is mistaken unless he admits that my good, not his, is the only good." "Most people . . . would admit that it is better two people's desires should be satisfied than only one person's. . . . Then what is good is not good *for me* or *for you,* but is simply good." "It is, indeed, so evident that it is better to secure a greater good for *A* than a lesser good for *B,* that it is hard to find any still more evident principle by which to prove this. And if *A* happens to be some one else, and *B* to be myself, that cannot affect the question, since it is irrelevant to the general question who *A* and *B* may be." To the question, as the logician states it after transforming men into letters, it is certainly irrelevant; but it is not irrelevant to the case as it arises in nature. If two goods are somehow rightly pronounced to be equally good, no circumstance can render one better than the other. And if the locus in which the good is to arise is somehow pronounced to be indifferent, it will certainly be indifferent whether that good arises in me or in you. But how shall these two pronouncements be made? In practice, values cannot be compared save as represented or enacted in the private imagination of somebody: for we could not conceive that an alien good *was* a good (as Mr. Russell cannot conceive that the life of an ecstatic oyster is a good) unless we could sympathize with it in some way in our own persons; and on the warmth which we felt in so representing the alien good would hang our conviction that it was truly valuable, and had worth in comparison with our own good. The voice of reason, bidding us prefer the greater good, no matter who is to enjoy it, is also nothing but the force of sympathy, bringing a remote existence before us vividly *sub specie boni.* Capacity for such sympathy measures the capacity to recognize duty and therefore, in a moral sense, to have it. Doubtless it is conceivable that all wills should become co-operative, and that nature should be ruled magically by an exact and universal sympathy; but this situation must be actually attained in part, before it can be conceived or judged to be an authoritative ideal. The tigers cannot regard it as such, for it would suppress the tragic good called ferocity, which makes, in their eyes, the chief glory of the universe. Therefore the inertia of nature, the ferocity of beasts, the optimism of mystics, and the selfishness of men and nations must all be accepted as conditions for the peculiar goods, essentially incommensurable, which they can generate severally. It is misplaced vehemence to call them intrinsically detestable, because they do not (as they cannot) generate or recognize the goods we prize.

In the real world, persons are not abstract egos, like *A* and *B*, so that to benefit one is clearly as good as to benefit another. Indeed, abstract egos could not be benefited, for they could not be modified at all, even if somehow they could be distinguished. It would be the qualities or objects distributed among them that would carry, wherever they went, each its inalienable cargo of value, like ships sailing from sea to sea. But it is quite vain and artificial to imagine different goods charged with such absolute and comparable weights; and actual egoism is not the thin and refutable thing that Mr. Russell makes of it. What it really holds is that a given man, oneself, and those akin to him, are qualitatively better than other beings; that the things they prize are intrinsically better than the things prized by others; and that therefore there is no injustice in treating these chosen interests as supreme. The injustice, it is felt, would lie rather in not treating things so unequal unequally. This feeling may, in many cases, amuse the impartial observer, or make him indignant; yet it may, in every case, according to Mr. Russell, be absolutely just. The refutation he gives of egoism would not dissuade any fanatic from exterminating all his enemies with a good conscience; it would merely encourage him to assert that what he was ruthlessly establishing was the absolute good. Doubtless such conscientious tyrants would be wretched themselves, and compelled to make sacrifices which would cost them dear; but that would only extend, as it were, the pernicious egoism of that part of their being which they had allowed to usurp a universal empire. The twang of intolerance and of self-mutilation is not absent from the ethics of Mr. Russell and Mr. Moore, even as it stands; and one trembles to think what it may become in the mouths of their disciples. Intolerance itself is a form of egoism, and to condemn egoism intolerantly is to share it.

I cannot help thinking that a consciousness of the relativity of values, if it became prevalent, would tend to render people more truly social than would a belief that things have intrinsic and unchangeable values, no matter what the attitude of any one to them may be. If we said that goods, including the right distribution of goods, are relative to specific natures, moral warfare would continue, but not with poisoned arrows. Our private sense of justice itself would be acknowledged to have but a relative authority, and while we could not have a higher duty than to follow it, we should seek to meet those whose aims were incompatible with it as we meet things physically inconvenient, without insulting them as if they were morally vile or logically contemptible. Real unselfishness consists in sharing the interests of others. Beyond the pale of actual unanimity the only possible unselfishness is chivalry—a recognition of the inward right and justification of our enemies fighting against us. This chivalry has long been practiced in the battle-field without abolishing the causes of war; and it might conceivably be extended to all the conflicts of men with one another, and of the warring elements within each breast. Policy, hypnotization, and even surgery may be practiced without exorcisms or anathemas. When a man has decided on a course of action, it is a vain indulgence in expletives to declare that he is sure that course is absolutely right. His moral dogma expresses its natural origin all the more clearly the more hotly it is proclaimed; and ethical absolutism, being a mental grimace of passion, refutes what it says by what it is. Sweeter and more profound, to my sense, is the philosophy of Homer, whose every line seems to breathe the conviction that what is beautiful or precious has not thereby any right to existence; nothing has such a right; nor is it given us to condemn absolutely any force—god or man—that destroys what is beautiful or precious, for it has doubtless something beautiful or precious of its own to achieve.

The consequences of a hypostasis of the good are no less interesting than its causes. If the good were independent of nature, it might still be conceived as relevant to nature, by being its creator or mover; but Mr. Russell is not a theist after the manner of Socrates; his good is not a power. Nor would representing it to be such long help his case; for an ideal hypostasized into a cause achieves only a mythical independence. The least criticism discloses that it is natural laws, zoological species, and human ideals, that have been projected into the empyrean; and it is no marvel that the good should attract the world where the good, by definition, is whatever the world is aiming at. The hypostasis accomplished by Mr. Russell is more serious, and therefore more paradoxical. If I understand it, it may be expressed as follows: In the realm of eternal essences, before anything exists, there are certain essences that have this remarkable property, that they ought to exist, or at least that, if anything exists, it ought to conform to them. What exists, however, is deaf to this moral emphasis in the eternal; nature exists for no reason; and, indeed, why should she have subordinated her own arbitrariness to a good that is no less arbitrary? This good, however, is somehow good notwithstanding; so that there is an abysmal wrong in its not being obeyed. The world is, in principle, totally depraved; but as the good is not a power, there is no one to redeem the world. The saints are those who, imitating the impotent dogmatism on high, and despising their sinful natural propensities, keep asserting that certain things are in themselves good and others bad, and declaring to be detestable any other saint who dogmatizes differently. In this system the Calvinistic God has lost his creative and punitive functions, but continues to decree groundlessly what is good and what evil, and to love the one and hate the other with an infinite love or hatred. Meanwhile the reprobate need not fear hell in the next world, but the elect are sure to find it here.

What shall we say of this strangely unreal and strangely personal religion? Is it a ghost of Calvinism, returned with none of its old force but with its old aspect of rigidity? Perhaps: but then, in losing its force, in abandoning its myths, and threats, and rhetoric, this religion has lost its deceptive sanctimony and hypocrisy; and in retaining its rigidity it has kept what made it noble and pathetic; for it is a clear dramatic expression of that human spirit—in this case a most pure and heroic spirit—which it strives so hard to dethrone. After all, the hypostasis of the good is only an unfortunate incident in a great accomplishment, which is the discernment of the good. I have dwelt chiefly on this incident, because in academic circles it is the abuses incidental to true philosophy that create controversy and form schools. Artificial systems, even when they prevail, after a while fatigue their adherents, without ever having convinced or refuted their opponents, and they fade out of existence not by being refuted in their turn, but simply by a tacit agreement to ignore their claims: so that the true insight they were based on is too often buried under them. The hypostasis of philosophical terms is an abuse incidental to the forthright, unchecked use of the intellect; it substitutes for things the limits and distinctions that divide them. So physics is corrupted by logic; but the logic that corrupts physics is perhaps correct, and when it is moral dialectic, it is more important than physics itself. Mr. Russell's ethics *is* ethics. When we mortals have once assumed the moral attitude, it is certain that an indefinable value accrues to some things as opposed to others, that these things are many, that combinations of them have values not belonging to their parts, and that these valuable things are far more specific than abstract pleasure, and far more diffused than one's personal life. What a pity if this pure morality, in detaching itself impetuously from the earth, whose bright satellite it might be, should fly into the abyss at a tangent, and leave us as much in the dark as before!

1926

Value as Any Object of Any Interest

R. B. Perry

1. PRELIMINARY FORMULATION AND ARGUMENT

§49. Exposition and Illustration. It is characteristic of living mind to be *for* some things and *against* others. This polarity is not reducible to that between "yes" and "no" in the logical or in the purely cognitive sense, because one can say "yes" with reluctance or be glad to say "no." To be "for" or "against" is to view with favor or disfavor; it is a bias of the subject toward or away from. It implies, as we shall see more clearly in the sequel, a tendency to create or conserve, or an opposite tendency to prevent or destroy. This duality appears in many forms, such as liking and disliking, desire and aversion, will and refusal, or seeking and avoiding. It is to this all-pervasive characteristic of the motor-affective life, this *state, act, attitude or disposition of favor or disfavor,* to which we propose to give the name of "*interest.*"[1]

Parts of the present chapter . . . are reprinted from an article entitled "A Behavioristic View of Purpose," published in the *Jour. of Philos.*, Vol. XVIII, 1921.

[1]The term "interest" has been employed for technical purposes by various psychologists, but by none, I think, in the precise sense in which it is employed here. W. Mitchell, in his *Structure and Growth of Mind,*

This, then, we take to be the original source and constant feature of all value. That which is an object of interest is *eo ipso* invested with value.[2] Any object, whatever it be, acquires value when any interest, whatever it be, is taken in it; just as anything whatsoever becomes a target when anyone whosoever aims at it. In other words, Aristotle was fundamentally mistaken when he said, that as a thing's "apparent good" makes it an object of appetite, so its real good makes it the object of "rational desire."[3] By the same token Spinoza was fundamentally correct when he said that

> "in no case do we strive for, wish for, long for, or desire anything, because we deem it to be good, but on the other hand we deem a thing to be good, because we strive for it, wish for it, long for it, or desire it."[4]

The view may otherwise be formulated in the equation: x is valuable = interest is taken in x. Value is thus a specific relation into which things possessing any ontological status whatsoever, whether real or imaginary, may enter with interested subjects.

This is value *simpliciter,*—value in the elementary, primordial and generic sense. It follows that any variation of interest or of its object will determine a variety of value; that any derivative of interest or its object will determine value in a derived sense; and that any condition of interest or its object will determine a conditional value. In short, interest being constitutive of value in the basic sense, theory of value will take this as its point of departure and center of reference; and will classify and systematize values in terms of the different forms which interests and their objects may be found to assume.

This view has rarely found a perfectly clear and consistent expression. It is, however, essentially conveyed in an early work of Mr. George Santayana:

> "Apart from ourselves, and our human bias, we can see in such a mechanical world no element of value whatever. In removing consciousness, we have removed the possibility of worth. But it is not only in the absence of all consciousness that value would be removed from the world; by a less violent abstraction from the totality of human experience, we might conceive beings of a purely intellectual cast, minds in which the transformations of nature were mirrored without any emotion. . . . No event would be repulsive, no situation terrible. . . . In this case, as completely as if consciousness were absent altogether, all value and excellence would be gone. . . . Values spring from the immediate and inexplicable reaction of vital impulse, and from the irrational part of our nature. . . . The ideal of rationality is itself as arbitrary, as much dependent on the needs of a finite organization, as any other ideal."[5]

A more recent statement, and one more explicitly in accord with the view here proposed, is the following:

1907, defines interest as our "feeling towards" an object, or, as how the object "strikes or affects us" (p. 64); whereas I propose to use the term to embrace desire and disposition as well. G. F. Stout, in his *Groundwork of Psychology,* 1903, uses the term for organized and permanent forms of the emotional life, such as sentiments [pp. 221 ff.]. More commonly "interest" is employed by psychology to mean *attention.*

[2]An object is valuable when *qualified* by an act of interest; relation to interest assuming, in the experience or judgment of value, the role of adjective.

[3]*Metaphysica,* XII, Ch. 7, trans. by W. D. Ross, 1072a.

[4]*Ethics,* Part III, Prop. IX, Note, trans. by R. H. M. Elwes, 1901. It is, of course, possible to desire a thing because it is good, where its goodness consists in its being desired by other subjects, or by some other interest of the same subject. But *in the last analysis* good springs from desire and not desire from good.

[5]*The Sense of Beauty,* 1899, pp. 17–19. Cf. also William James: "*The essence of good is to satisfy demand*" (*Will to Believe,* etc., 1898, p. 201).

"Anything is properly said to have value in case, and only in case, it is the object of the affective motor response which we call being *interested* in, positively or negatively. . . . The being liked, or disliked, of the object is its value. And since the being liked or disliked, is being the object of a motor-affective attitude in a subject, some sort of a subject is always requisite to there being value at all—not necessarily a *judging* subject, but a subject capable of at least motor-affective response. For the cat the cream has value, or better and more simply, the cat values the cream, or the warmth, or having her back scratched, quite regardless of her probable inability to conceive cream or to make judgments concerning warmth."[6] . . .

2. REPLY TO THE CHARGE OF RELATIVISM

§53. **Relativism as an Epithet.** Although no conclusive proof of the present view is possible until it is completely elaborated, it has been supposed that there is a conclusive *disproof* which can be urged without further ado. To attribute value to any object of any interest is at once to expose oneself to the charge of *relativism,* whatever the psychological details, and however successful such a definition may prove for purposes of systematic generalization.

No one can afford to disregard this charge. Relativism is an epithet which implies disparagement, when, as is often the case, it implies nothing more. Even the respectable scientific authority which has pronounced in its favor has not saved the physical theory of relativity from being regarded as somewhat *risqué,*—as evidence of the corruption of the times or of the malicious influence of the Semitic mind. There is no man who would not rather be absolute than relative, even though he has not the faintest conception of the meaning of either term.

This sentiment is peculiarly strong in the field of values, and preeminently in the province of morals. Nothing could be more scandalous than these lines of Sir Richard Burton:

"There is no good, there is no bad, these be the whims of mortal will;
What works me weal that call I good, what harms and hurts I hold as ill.
They change with space, they shift with race, and in the veriest space of time,
Each vice has worn a virtue's crown, all good been banned as sin or crime."[7]

How much nobler and more edifying in tone are such utterances as these of Froude and Carlyle:

"The eternal truths and rights of things exist, fortunately, independent of our thoughts or wishes, fixed as mathematics, inherent in the nature of man and the world. They are no more to be trifled with than gravitation."

"What have men to do with interests? There is a right way and a wrong way. That is all we need think about it."[8]

Yet there can scarcely be more offense in the adjective "relative" than there is in the substantive "relation"; and when we investigate the world in which we live, we discover as a rule that what we took to be an absolute does as a matter of fact both stand in

[6]D. W. Prall, *A Study in the Theory of Value,* Univ. of California Publications in Philosophy, Vol. 3, No. 2, 1921, pp. 215, 227. The present writer is in essential agreement with the whole of this admirable monograph.

[7]Quoted by L. Dickinson, *Meaning of Good,* 1907, p. 5.

[8]J. A. Froude, *Inaugural Lecture at St. Andrews,* 1869, p. 41, Letter of Carlyle to Froude, *Longman's Magazine,* 1892, p. 151.

relations and comprise relations. In any case we shall be influenced only by such *theoretical* difficulties as may be urged against a relativistic theory of value, and not in the least by practical or sentimental objections.

§54. **Epistemological Relativism, or Scepticism.** There is unquestionably one form of relativism which is theoretically objectionable. He who identifies the act of *cognizing* values with that act of the subject which *constitutes* them, or holds that values are both known and created in one and the same act, does imply the impossibility of knowing anything whatsoever about value, and thus belies any statements that he himself may make about it. This objection holds against certain philosophers who have identified value with interest, and it therefore behooves us to discover whether our own view is similarly objectionable.

Professor G. E. Moore distinguishes two forms in which this vicious relativism may be stated. In the first place, "it may be held that whenever any man asserts an action to be right or wrong, what he is asserting is merely that he *himself* has some particular feeling toward the action in question."[9] In this case the act of knowing or judging value, is construed as simply an expression of the judge's own interest. The following famous passage from Hobbes is a case in point:

> "But whatsoever is the object of any man's appetite or desire, that is it which he for his part calleth 'good'; and the object of his hate and aversion, 'evil'; and of his contempt 'vile' and 'inconsiderable.' For these words of good, evil, and contemptible, are ever used with relation to the person that useth them: there being nothing simply and absolutely so; nor any common rule of good and evil, to be taken from the nature of the objects themselves."[10]

The *reductio ad absurdum* of such a view, lies, as Professor Moore points out, in the fact that it would lead to the mutual irrelevance of all judgments in which the value-predicates are employed. If in affirming an act to be right or wrong, good or evil, a judge were always referring to *his own present feeling* about it, then no two judges could ever agree or disagree with one another, nor could the same judge ever reaffirm or correct his own past opinions.[11] In other words, on questions of value there could not be any such thing as judgment or opinion in the ordinary sense of these terms. This is not only contrary to fact, but it is inevitably contradicted by the very man who makes the assertion.

A second statement of this vicious relativism is the assertion "that when we judge an action to be right or wrong what we are asserting is merely that somebody or other thinks it to be right or wrong." Generalized and simplified, this assertion is to the effect that value consists in being thought to be valuable—"There is nothing either good or bad, but thinking makes it so." Now the fundamental difficulty with this view lies in the fact that one would then have nothing to think about. If a thing is valuable by virtue of being believed to be valuable, then when one believes a thing to be valuable, one believes that it is believed to be valuable, or one believes that it is believed to be believed to be valuable, and so on *ad infinitum.*[12] In short, there can be no judgment about value, or about anything else, unless there is some content or object other than the act of judgment itself,—a judged as well as a judging.

It is this error or confusion which vitiates the work of Westermarck and others who, not content with a history of moral opinion, have attempted to *define* moral values

[9]*Ethics,* Home University Library, p. 89.
[10]*Leviathan,* Part I, Ch. VI.
[11]Cf. G. E. Moore, *op. cit.,* pp. 100–103.
[12]Cf. G. E. Moore, *op. cit.,* pp. 122–124.

in *terms* of moral opinion.[13] It is the characteristic and besetting error of all anthropological and sociological theories of value, which aim to be scientific or "positive."[14] What has been judged with unanimity to be good or evil by members of a social group, is a matter of record; and is thus a fact ascertainable by archaeological or historical methods, and with a precision and indubitableness peculiar to these methods. But such methodological preferences do not alter the fact that these judgments, if judgments at all, must have been *about* something; and in theory of value it is this *object,* and not the acts of judgment themselves, which is primarily in question. There are also recorded opinions about the stars, and anthropologists may and do investigate these opinions; but one does not therefore propose to substitute a history of astronomical opinions for astronomy.

Let us now inquire whether the view here proposed is guilty of a vicious or sceptical relativism in either or both of these two senses. In the first place, although defining value as relative to interest, we have not defined value as exclusively relative to the present interest of the judge. Thus if Caesar was ambitious when he waged war upon Pompey, the definition implies that power was in fact good, as being coveted by Caesar. But this fact may have been affirmed by Mark Antony, or afterwards denied by Caesar himself in his own defense. Value, therefore, lends itself to judgment in the ordinary sense,—to judgments which are true or false, and which may agree or disagree.

In the second place, having defined value as constituted by interests, such judgments have a content or object other than themselves. They may refer to the interest of the judge, or to any other interests, past or present, common or unique; but the interest that creates the value is always other than the judgment that cognizes it. Theory of value is not a history of opinion about values, but deals with that to which such opinion refers.

§55. The Argument from "Intrinsic" Value. Professor Moore has further weapons in his arsenal which he believes to be fatal not only to the particular forms of epistemological relativism just rejected, but in general to the view that "by calling a thing 'good' or 'bad' we merely mean that some being or beings have a certain mental attitude towards it"; or that "what we mean by calling a thing 'good' is that it is *desired,* or desired in some particular way."[15] Since we have in effect maintained precisely this view, his objections are relevant and must be met.

He appeals, in the first place, to the fact that we may use the word "good" without consciously meaning "object of interest." Judging by what the speaker has in mind, to say that the object is good is not the same as to say that some one is interested in it.[16] This type of argument would prove altogether too much if it proved anything. No definition has ever been formulated that is perfectly in keeping either with verbal usage or conscious meanings. For words may be mere echoes, and conscious meanings careless and obscure. The absurdity of the argument is especially evident in the case of complex entities, such as the exponents of the present view hold value to be. A complex entity is only summarily denoted in common discourse, and analysis will invariably reveal a structure which is not present to a mind which employs terms in a stereotyped sense. It would, for example, scarcely be urged that circularity is indefinable because one can

[13]E. Westermarck, *Origin and Development of Moral Ideas,* 1906, Vol. I, *passim.* Westermarck's confusion is largely due to the ambiguity of the term "approval," and the absence of any clear notion of judgment.

[14]For a general statement of this position, cf. L. Lévy-Bruhl, *La Morale et la Science des Mœurs,* 1910.

[15]*Op. cit.,* pp. 157, 159.

[16]This argument is applied primarily to the term "right," but is equally applicable to the term "good." Cf. *ibid.,* pp. 111, 163.

judge an object to be circular without judging that all points on its perimeter are equidistant from the center. In the one case as in the other the nature of the predicate is revealed not in customary usage, but when doubt has arisen as to its applicability. Where the circularity of an object is in question one falls to measuring; and when its goodness is in question one falls to considering its relation to interests.

A much more serious objection is based upon the notion of *intrinsic* value. We judge a thing to be intrinsically good "where we judge, concerning a particular state of things that it would be worth while—would be "a good thing"—that that state of things should exist, *even if nothing else were to exist besides,* either at the same time or afterwards."[17] If a thing derives value from its relation to an interest taken in it, it would seem impossible that anything whatsoever should possess value in itself. But in that case value would seem always to be borrowed, and never owned; value would shine by a reflected glory having no original source.

The question turns upon the fact that any predicate may be judged synthetically or analytically. Suppose that "good" were to be regarded as a simple quality like yellow. It would then be possible to judge either synthetically, that the primrose was fair or yellow; or, analytically, that the fair, yellow primrose was fair or yellow. Only the fair, yellow primrose would be fair and yellow "even if nothing were to exist besides." But the logic of the situation is not in the least altered if a relational predicate is substituted for a simple quality; indeed it is quite possible to regard a quality as a monadic (a single term) relation. Tangential, for example, is a relational predicate; since a line is a tangent only by virtue of the peculiar relation of single-point contact with another line or surface. Let R^t represent this peculiar relation, and *A, B,* two lines. One can then judge either synthetically, that $(A)\ R^t\ (B)$; or, analytically, that $(A)\ R^t\ (B)$ is R^t. Similarly, let *S* represent an interested subject, *O* an object, and R^i the peculiar relation of interest, taken and received. We can then judge either synthetically, that $(O)\ R^i\ (S)$; or, analytically that $(O)\ R^i\ (S)$ is R^i. In other words, one can say either that *O* is desired by *S,* or that *O-desired-by-S is a case of the general character "desired."*

The situation is complicated, but not logically altered, by the fact that either *O,* or *O*'s-being-desired-by-S^1, may be desired by S^2, and so stand in a second value-relation of the same type. In other words, as we have already seen, the question of value is peculiarly recurrent.[18] But value is intrinsic when it is independent of such ulterior interests. Similarly, the primrose *as enjoyed* is intrinsically good; the primrose *as sought for the sake of* such ulterior enjoyment, is instrumentally, conditionally, or otherwise extrinsically good. In other words, according to the present view an object unrelated to a subject cannot be good in itself, any more than, in Professor Moore's view,[19] an object can be good in itself without possessing the specific superadded quality "good"; but an *object-desired-for-itself,* that is, any value of the variable function $(O)\ R\ (S)$, can and does possess value in itself.[20]

The special case of the universe as a whole[21] furnishes a further and peculiarly instructive example. It is evident that by definition the universe as a whole cannot stand in

[17] *Ibid.*, p. 162.

[18] Cf. §§ 17 and 56.

[19] As set forth above, § 15.

[20] Even Professor Moore says (*ibid.*, p. 167): "I think it is true that no whole can be intrinsically good, unless it *contains* some feeling toward *something* as a part of itself." According to this view the "something" and the "feeling toward," taken together, are "good": there being three factors involved. In my view "good" *means* the "feeling toward," or more precisely, "the being felt toward."

[21] Cf. G. E. Moore, *ibid.*, p. 58.

relation to any desiring subject outside itself. In what sense, therefore, can it be said to possess value in accord with our definition? In the first place, it might, for certain familiar metaphysical reasons which are not here in question, be conceived as a single all-embracing interest. The total universe would be divided between a universal subject and a universal object, with a relation of will or love (perhaps of self-love) uniting the two. In that case the world in its unity would possess intrinsic value. Or, independently of such metaphysical speculation, the universe may be said to possess value in so far as loved or hated by its own members, taken severally. Or it may be said to *contain* value,[22] in that it embraces interests and their objects. Or it may be said to be an instrument of value, in that it provides the conditions by which interests and their objects may arise and be conserved. There is no cosmic paradox which can be urged against the definition of value in terms of the interest-relation which could not with equal force be urged against any other view of value, including the view that value is an indefinable quality. For if it be urged that the universe so defined as to embrace all interests cannot be synthetically good through any interest taken in it, it can equally well be urged that the universe so defined as to embrace the indefinable quality "good," cannot be good through the super-addition of this quality.

We may safely conclude, therefore, that the definition of value herein proposed provides for intrinsic value in such intelligible senses as are provided for in any other theory of value.

§56. The Charge of Circularity. In criticizing the view that value is a "relational attitude," Professor W. M. Urban argues that it involves "a definition in a circle."

> "The value of an object consists, it is said, in its satisfaction of desire, or more broadly, fulfilment of interest. But it is always possible to raise further questions which show conclusively that the value concept is already presupposed. Is the interest itself worthy of being satisfied? Is the object worthy of being of interest? In other words, the fact of intrinsic value requires us to find the essence of value in something other than this type of relation."[23]

This expresses the most popular objection to the present view. The fact of desire is not accepted as final in most judgments of value. Objects of desire are held to be bad despite their being desired, and desires themselves are held to be bad whether or no they are satisfied. Vicious appetites, vulgar taste, o'erweening ambition, are the most notorious of evils. Indeed the general terms "desire" and "interest" have acquired a specific flavor of moral disrepute. Must we not conclude therefore that value, instead of flowing from interest, is an independent, if not antagonistic, principle by which interests and their objects are judged? Despite the strong appeal which this argument must make to common-sense, we shall find not only that it rests upon a confusion, but that the very facts to which it refers can be understood only by such a definition of value as is here proposed.

Let us consider, first, the relatively simple case in which *all* desire is condemned. The argument as presented by Schopenhauer and by other Occidental and Oriental advocates of the cult of apathy, is based upon the generalization that desire is doomed to defeat. Desire asks what in the very nature of the case it can never obtain. It asks for private advantage or special privilege in a world which is indifferent to such claims; or it

[22]And thus to be better than no universe at all, by the principle of "inclusiveness." Cf. Ch. XXII, Sect. III.

[23]"Value and Existence," *Jour. of Philos.*, Vol. XIII, 1916, pp. 452, 453.

perpetually begets new desires out of its own satisfaction, and is thus in a chronic state of bankruptcy. But why, then, condemn it? Pessimism is founded on a conception of evil, which in turn must be assumed to be the converse of good. There would be no reason for condemning the *futility* of desire as evil unless the *success* of desire were supposed to be good. This implication is more clearly evident in the Stoic cult of resignation. Thus Epictetus exhorts his followers to "demand not that events should happen as you wish; but wish them to happen as they do happen and you will go on well."[24] There would be no meaning in such counsel if "going on well" were not conceived as consisting in some sort of accord between events and what men wish.

Let us now consider those cases which arise not from disaccord between interests and their natural environments, but from disaccord between one interest and another. The same object may be liked or desired by one man, and disliked or avoided by another. Our definition requires us to attribute evil to the object as being disliked, *despite* the fact that it is liked. It may, then, be argued that liking cannot make an object good. Or it may be objected that our definition requires us to affirm that the same object is at one and the same time both evil and good, which is contradictory. But *is* it contradictory? The fact is, on the contrary, that a relational definition, such as that here proposed, is the only means of *avoiding* contradiction. It is not denied that the same object may be both liked and disliked; this is the very premise of the objection. If, then, good is *defined* as being liked, and evil as being disliked, it follows that the same object may *in this sense* be without contradiction both good and evil. A term may always possess relational attributes in opposite senses, provided such relations are sustained toward different terms. The same physical object may be both "to the right of" and "to the left of," both "above" and "below"; the same man may be both friend and enemy, both agent and patient.

A yet more common case is that in which one interest is condemned because of being contrary to another interest. Such condemnation arises from the fact that interests conflict, so that the affirmation of one implies the negation of the other. This occurs in sheer struggle where both interests are upon the same plane. When two appetites require for their satisfaction the exclusive use of the same object, the desired object is *good* in relation to each appetite; while each appetite is *evil* in relation to the other, as tending to prevent its satisfaction.

But the case which has most deeply affected popular habits of thought, and which is mainly responsible for the prejudice against the present theory of value, is the case in which an interest or its object is morally condemned. Interests are deemed "bad," and not merely in the sense of being hostile to other rival interests of the same rank; they are deemed "downright" bad, in a sense in which all judges, including the agent himself, are expected to agree.

The explanation of this case lies, however, in the fact that moral judgments are not concerned with value in the generic sense, but with a specific and complex *aspect* of it. They are concerned with organizations of values, whether in the personal or in the social life. They do not deal with interests *per se*, but with the relation of interests to the comprehensive purposes in which they are incorporated. From the moral point of view value *begins* with the bearing of a "lower" interest upon a "higher" interest. To quote Mr. Santayana,

> "It is in reference to such constitutional interests that things are 'really' good or bad; interests which may not be fairly represented by any incidental conscious desire. No doubt any

[24]*Ench.* VIII, translated in Bakewell's *Source Book in Ancient Philosophy*, 1907, p. 318.

desire, however capricious, represents some momentary and partial interest, which lends to its objects a certain real and inalienable value; yet when we consider, as we do in human society, the interests of men, whom reflection and settled purposes have raised more or less to the ideal dignity of individuals, then passing fancies and passions may indeed have bad objects, and be bad themselves, in that they thwart the more comprehensive interests of the soul that entertains them."[25]

It is in this sense that appetites may be vicious in relation to health, or efficiency; that special inclinations or passions may corrupt character, or hinder a life-purpose; and that personal ambition may imperil the well-being of the nation, or of humanity at large. But while such values may be absolutes for the moral consciousness, it is the avowed purpose of a general theory of value to analyze and relate them. Theory of value takes all value for its province, even values which are too evident or ignoble for the judgments of common-sense. This does not imply any neglect of "higher" values, but only the method of understanding the special case in terms of the generic type. . . .

[25]G. Santayana, *Winds of Doctrine,* 1913, p. 146.

1929

The Construction of Good

John Dewey

We saw at the outset of our discussion that insecurity generates the quest for certainty. Consequences issue from every experience, and they are the source of our interest in what is present. Absence of arts of regulation diverted the search for security into irrelevant modes of practice, into rite and cult; thought was devoted to discovery of omens rather than of signs of what is to occur. Gradually there was differentiation of two realms, one higher, consisting of the powers which determine human destiny in all important affairs. With this religion was concerned. The other consisted of the prosaic matters in which man relied upon his own skill and his matter-of-fact insight. Philosophy inherited the idea of this division. Meanwhile in Greece many of the arts had attained a state of development which raised them above a merely routine state; there were intimations of measure, order and regularity in materials dealt with which give intimations of underlying rationality. Because of the growth of mathematics, there arose also the ideal of a purely rational knowledge, intrinsically solid and worthy and the means by which the intimations of rationality within changing phenomena could be comprehended within science. For the intellectual class the stay and consolation, the

John Dewey, "The Construction of Good" from JOHN DEWEY: The Later Works, 1925–1953, Volume 4: 1929, edited by Jo Ann Boydston (Carbondale, IL: Southern Illinois University Press, 1981). Reprinted with the permission of the publishers.

warrant of certainty, provided by religion was henceforth found in intellectual demonstration of the reality of the objects of an ideal realm.

With the expansion of Christianity, ethico-religious traits came to dominate the purely rational ones. The ultimate authoritative standards for regulation of the dispositions and purposes of the human will were fused with those which satisfied the demands for necessary and universal truth. The authority of ultimate Being was, moreover, represented on earth by the Church; that which in its nature transcended intellect was made known by a revelation of which the Church was the interpreter and guardian. The system endured for centuries. While it endured, it provided an integration of belief and conduct for the western world. Unity of thought and practice extended down to every detail of the management of life; efficacy of its operation did not depend upon thought. It was guaranteed by the most powerful and authoritative of all social institutions.

Its seemingly solid foundation was, however, undermined by the conclusions of modern science. They effected, both in themselves and even more in the new interests and activities they generated, a breach between what man is concerned with here and now and the faith concerning ultimate reality which, in determining his ultimate and eternal destiny, had previously given regulation to his present life. The problem of restoring integration and cooperation between man's beliefs about the world in which he lives and his beliefs about the values and purposes that should direct his conduct is the deepest problem of modern life. It is the problem of any philosophy that is not isolated from that life.

The attention which has been given to the fact that in its experimental procedure science has surrendered the separation between knowing and doing has its source in the fact that there is now provided within a limited, specialized and technical field the possibility and earnest, as far as theory is concerned, of effecting the needed integration in the wider field of collective human experience. Philosophy is called upon to be the theory of the practice, through ideas sufficiently definite to be operative in experimental endeavor, by which the integration may be made secure in actual experience. Its central problem is the relation that exists between the beliefs about the nature of things due to natural science and beliefs about values—using that word to designate whatever is taken to have rightful authority in the direction of conduct. A philosophy which should take up this problem is struck first of all by the fact that beliefs about values are pretty much in the position in which beliefs about nature were before the scientific revolution. There is either a basic distrust of the capacity of experience to develop its own regulative standards, and an appeal to what philosophers call eternal values, in order to ensure regulation of belief and action; or there is acceptance of enjoyments actually experienced irrespective of the method or operation by which they are brought into existence. Complete bifurcation between rationalistic method and an empirical method has its final and most deeply human significance in the ways in which good and bad are thought of and acted for and upon.

As far as technical philosophy reflects this situation, there is division of theories of values into two kinds. On the one hand, goods and evils, in every region of life, as they are concretely experienced, are regarded as characteristic of an inferior order of Being—intrinsically inferior. Just because they are things of human experience, their worth must be estimated by reference to standards and ideals derived from ultimate reality. Their defects and perversion are attributed to the same fact; they are to be corrected and controlled through adoption of methods of conduct derived from loyalty to the requirements of Supreme Being. This philosophic formulation gets actuality and force from the fact that it is a rendering of the beliefs of men in general as far as they have come under the influence of institutional religion. Just as rational conceptions were once superimposed upon observed and temporal phenomena, so eternal values are superimposed upon experienced goods. In one case as in the other, the alternative is supposed to be confusion and lawlessness. Philosophers suppose these eternal values are known by reason; the mass of persons that they are divinely revealed.

Nevertheless, with the expansion of secular interests, temporal values have enormously multiplied; they absorb more and more attention and energy. The sense of transcendent values has become enfeebled; instead of permeating all things in life, it is more and more restricted to special times and acts. The authority of the church to declare and impose divine will and purpose has narrowed. Whatever men say and profess, their tendency in the presence of actual evils is to resort to natural and empirical means to remedy them. But in formal belief, the old doctrine of the inherently disturbed and unworthy character of the goods and standards of ordinary experience persists. This divergence between what men do and what they nominally profess is closely connected with the confusions and conflicts of modern thought.

It is not meant to assert that no attempts have been made to replace the older theory regarding the authority of immutable and transcendent values by conceptions more congruous with the practices of daily life. The contrary is the case. The utilitarian theory, to take one instance, has had great power. The idealistic school is the only one in contemporary philosophies, with the exception of one form of neo-realism, that makes much of the notion of a reality which is all one with ultimate moral and religious values. But this school is also the one most concerned with the conservation of "spiritual" life. Equally significant is the fact that empirical theories retain the notion that thought and judgment are concerned with values that are experienced independently of them. For these theories, emotional satisfactions occupy the same place that sensations hold in traditional empiricism. Values are constituted by liking and enjoyment; to be enjoyed and to be a value are two names for one and the same fact. Since science has extruded values from its objects, these empirical theories do everything possible to emphasize their purely subjective character of value. A psychological theory of desire and liking is supposed to cover the whole ground of the theory of values; in it, immediate feeling is the counterpart of immediate sensation.

I shall not object to this empirical theory as far as it connects the theory of values with concrete experiences of desire and satisfaction. The idea that there is such a connection is the only way known to me by which the pallid remoteness of the rationalistic theory, and the only too glaring presence of the institutional theory of transcendental values can be escaped. The objection is that the theory in question holds down value to objects *antecedently* enjoyed, apart from reference to the method by which they come into existence; it takes enjoyments which are casual because unregulated by intelligent operations to be values in and of themselves. Operational thinking needs to be applied to the judgment of values just as it has now finally been applied in conceptions of physical objects. Experimental empiricism in the field of ideas of good and bad is demanded to meet the conditions of the present situation.

The scientific revolution came about when material of direct and uncontrolled experience was taken as problematic; as supplying material to be transformed by reflective operations into known objects. The contrast between experienced and known objects was found to be a temporal one; namely, one between empirical subject-matters which were had or "given" prior to the acts of experimental variation and redisposition and those which succeeded these acts and issued from them. The notion of an act whether of sense or thought which supplied a valid measure of thought in immediate knowledge was discredited. Consequences of operations became the important thing. The suggestion almost imperatively follows that escape from the defects of transcendental absolutism is not to be had by setting up as values enjoyments that happen anyhow, but in defining value by enjoyments which are the consequences of intelligent action. Without the intervention of thought, enjoyments are not values but problematic goods, becoming values when they re-issue in a changed form from intelligent behavior. The fundamental trouble with the current empirical theory of values is that it merely formulates and justifies the socially prevailing habit of regarding enjoyments as they are actually experienced as values in and of themselves. It completely side-steps the question of regulation of these enjoyments. This issue involves nothing less than the problem of the directed reconstruction of economic, political and religious institutions.

There was seemingly a paradox involved in the notion that if we turned our backs upon the immediately perceived qualities of things, we should be enabled to form valid conceptions of objects, and that these conceptions could be used to bring about a more secure and more significant experience of them. But the method terminated in disclosing the connections or interactions upon which perceived objects, viewed as events, depend. Formal analogy suggests that we regard our direct and original experience of things liked and enjoyed as only *possibilities* of values to be achieved; that enjoyment becomes a value when we discover the relations upon which its presence depends. Such a causal and operational definition gives only a conception of a value, not a value itself. But the utilization of the conception in action results in an object having secure and significant value.

The formal statement may be given concrete content by pointing to the difference between the enjoyed and the enjoyable, the desired and the desirable, the satis*fying* and the satis*factory*. To say that something is enjoyed is to make a statement about a fact, something already in existence; it is not to judge the value of that fact. There is no difference between such a proposition and one which says that something is sweet or sour, red or black. It is just correct or incorrect and that is the end of the matter. But to call an object a value is to assert that it satisfies or fulfills certain conditions. Function and status in meeting conditions is a different matter from bare existence. The fact that something is desired only raises the *question* of its desirability; it does not settle it. Only a child in the degree of his immaturity thinks to settle the question of desirability by reiterated proclamation: "I want it, I want it, I want it." What is objected to in the current empirical theory of values is not connection of them with desire and enjoyment but failure to distinguish between enjoyments of radically different sorts. There are many common expressions in which the difference of the two kinds is clearly recognized. Take for example the difference between the ideas of "satisfying" and "satisfactory." To say that something satisfies is to report something as an isolated finality. To assert that it is satis*factory* is to define it in its connections and interactions. The fact that it pleases or is immediately congenial poses a problem to judgment. How shall the satisfaction be rated? Is it a value or is it not? Is it something to be prized and cherished, *to be* enjoyed? Not stern moralists alone but everyday experience informs us that finding satisfaction in a thing may be a warning, a summons to be on the lookout for consequences. To declare something satis*factory* is to assert that it meets specifiable conditions. It is, in effect, a judgment that the thing "will do." It involves a prediction; it contemplates a future in which the thing will continue to serve; it *will* do. It asserts a consequence the thing will actively institute; it will *do*. That it is satisfying is the content of a proposition of fact; that it is satisfactory is a judgment, an estimate, an appraisal. It denotes an attitude *to be* taken, that of striving to perpetuate and to make secure.

It is worth notice that besides the instances given, there are many other recognitions in ordinary speech of the distinction. The endings "able," "worthy" and "ful" are cases in point. Noted and notable, noteworthy; remarked and remarkable; advised and advisable; wondered at and wonderful; pleasing and beautiful; loved and lovable; blamed and blameable, blameworthy; objected to and objectionable; esteemed and estimable; admired and admirable; shamed and shameful; honored and honorable; approved and approvable, worthy of approbation, etc. The multiplication of words adds nothing to the force of the distinction. But it aids in conveying a sense of the fundamental character of the distinction; of the difference between mere report of an already existent fact and judgment as to the importance and need of bringing a fact into existence; or, if it is already there, of sustaining it in existence. The latter is a genuine practical judgment, and marks the only type of judgment that has to do with the direction of action. Whether or no we reserve the term "value" for the latter, (as seems to me proper) is a minor matter; that the distinction be acknowledged as the key to understanding the relation of values to the direction of conduct is the important thing.

This element of direction by an idea of value applies to science as well as anywhere else. For in every scientific undertaking, there is passed a constant succession of estimates; such as "it is worth treating these facts as data or evidence; it is advisable to try this experiment; to make that observation; to entertain such and such a hypothesis; to perform this calculation," etc.

The word "taste" has perhaps got too completely associated with arbitrary liking to express the nature of judgments of value. But if the word be used in the sense of an appreciation at once cultivated and active, one may say that the formation of taste is the chief matter wherever values enter in, whether intellectual, esthetic or moral. Relatively immediate judgments, which we call tact or to which we give the name of intuition, do not precede reflective inquiry, but are the funded products of much thoughtful experience. Expertness of taste is at once the result and the reward of constant exercise of thinking. Instead of there being no disputing about tastes, they are the one thing worth disputing about, if by "dispute" is signified discussion involving reflective inquiry. Taste, if we use the word in its best sense, is the outcome of experience brought cumulatively to bear on the intelligent appreciation of the real worth of likings and enjoyments. There is nothing in which a person so completely reveals himself as in the things which he judges enjoyable and desirable. Such judgments are the sole alternative to the domination of belief by impulse, chance, blind habit and self-interest. The formation of a cultivated and effectively operative good judgment or taste with respect to what is esthetically admirable, intellectually acceptable and morally approvable is the supreme task set to human beings by the incidents of experience.

Propositions about what is or has been liked are of instrumental value in reaching judgments of value, in as far as the conditions and consequences of the thing liked are thought about. In themselves they make no claims; they put forth no demand upon subsequent attitudes and acts; they profess no authority to direct. If one likes a thing he likes it; that *is* a point about which there can be no dispute:—although it is not so easy to state just *what* is liked as is frequently assumed. A judgment about what is *to be* desired and enjoyed is, on the other hand, a claim on future action; it possesses *de jure* and not merely *de facto* quality. It is a matter of frequent experience that likings and enjoyments are of all kinds, and that many are such as reflective judgments condemn. By way of self-justification and "rationalization," an enjoyment creates a tendency to assert that the thing enjoyed is a value. This assertion of validity adds authority to the fact. It is a decision that the object has a right to exist and hence a claim upon action to further its existence.

The analogy between the status of the theory of values and the theory of ideas about natural objects before the rise of experimental inquiry may be carried further. The sensationalistic theory of the origin and test of thought evoked, by way of reaction, the transcendental theory of *a priori* ideas. For it failed utterly to account for objective connection, order and regularity in objects observed. Similarly, any doctrine that identifies the mere fact of being liked with the value of the object liked so fails to give direction to conduct when direction is needed that it automatically calls forth the assertion that there are values eternally in Being that are the standards of all judgments and the obligatory ends of all action. Without the introduction of operational thinking, we oscillate between a theory that, in order to save the objectivity of judgments of values, isolates them from experience and nature, and a theory that, in order to save their concrete and human significance, reduces them to mere statements about our own feelings.

Not even the most devoted adherents of the notion that enjoyment and value are equivalent facts would venture to assert that because we have once liked a thing we should go on liking it; they are compelled to introduce the idea that *some* tastes are to be cultivated. Logically, there is no ground for introducing the idea of cultivation; liking is liking, and one is as good as another. If enjoyments *are* values, the judgment of value cannot regulate the form which liking takes; it cannot regulate its own conditions. Desire and purpose, and hence action, are left without guidance, although the question of regulation of their formation is the supreme problem of practical life. Values (to sum up) may be connected inherently with liking, and yet not with *every* liking but only with those that judgment has approved, after examination of the relation upon which the object liked depends. A casual liking is one that happens without knowledge of how it occurs nor to what effect. The difference between it and one which is sought because of a judgment that it is worth having and is to be striven for, makes just the difference between enjoyments which are accidental and enjoyments that have value and hence a claim upon our attitude and conduct.

In any case, the alternative rationalistic theory does not afford the guidance for the sake of which eternal and immutable norms are appealed to. The scientist finds no help in determining the probable truth of some proposed theory by comparing it with a standard of absolute truth and immutable being. He has to rely upon definite operations undertaken under definite conditions—upon method. We can hardly imagine an architect getting aid in the construction of a building from an ideal at large, though we can understand his framing an ideal on the basis of knowledge of actual conditions and needs. Nor does the ideal of perfect beauty in antecedent Being give direction to a painter in producing a particular work of art. In morals, absolute perfection does not seem to be more than a generalized hypostatization of the recognition that there is a good to be sought, an obligation to be met—both being concrete matters. Nor is the defect in this respect merely negative. An examination of history would reveal, I am confident, that these general and remote schemes of value actually obtain a content definite enough and near enough to concrete situations as to afford guidance in action only by consecrating some institution or dogma already having social currency. Concreteness is gained, but it is by protecting from inquiry some accepted standard which perhaps is outworn and in need of criticism.

When theories of values do not afford intellectual assistance in framing ideas and beliefs about values that are adequate to direct action, the gap must be filled by other means. If intelligent method is lacking, prejudice, the pressure of immediate circumstance, self-interest and class-interest, traditional customs, institutions of accidental historic origin, are *not* lacking, and they tend to take the place of intelligence. Thus we are led to our main proposition: *Judgments about values are judgments about the conditions and the results of experienced objects; judgments about that which should regulate the formation of our desires, affections and enjoyments.* For whatever decides their formation will determine the main course of our conduct, personal and social.

If it sounds strange to hear that we should frame our judgments as to what has value by considering the connections in existence of what we like and enjoy, the reply is not far to seek. As long as we do not engage in this inquiry enjoyments (values if we choose to apply that term) are casual; they are given by "nature," not constructed by art. Like natural objects in their qualitative existence, they at most only supply material for elaboration in rational discourse. A *feeling* of good or excellence is as far removed from goodness in fact as a feeling that objects are intellectually thus and so is removed from their being actually so. To recognize that the truth of natural objects can be reached only by the greatest care in selecting and arranging directed operations, and then to suppose that values can be truly determined by the mere fact of liking seems to leave us in an incredible position. All the serious perplexities of life come back to the genuine difficulty of forming a judgment as to the values of the situation; they come back to a conflict of goods. Only dogmatism can suppose that serious moral conflict is between something clearly bad and something known to be good, and that uncertainty lies wholly in the will of the one choosing. Most conflicts of importance are conflicts between things which are or have been satisfying, not between good and evil. And to suppose that we can make a hierarchical table of values at large once for all, a kind of catalogue in which they are arranged in an order of ascending or descending worth, is to indulge in a gloss on our inability to frame intelligent judgments in the concrete. Or else it is to dignify customary choice and prejudice by a title of honor.

The alternative to definition, classification and systematization of satisfactions just as they happen to occur is judgment of them by means of the relations under which they occur. If we know the conditions under which the act of liking, of desire and enjoyment, takes place, we are in a position to know what are the consequences of that act. The difference between the desired and the desirable, admired and the admirable, becomes effective at just this point. Consider the difference between the proposition "That thing has been eaten," and the judgment "That thing is edible." The former statement involves no knowledge of any relation except the one stated; while we are able to judge of the edibility of anything only when we have a knowledge of its interactions with other things sufficient to enable us to foresee its probable effects when it is taken into the organism and produces effects there.

To assume that anything can be known in isolation from its connections with other things is to identify knowing with merely having some object before perception or in feeling, and is thus to lose the key to the traits that distinguish an object as known. It is futile, even silly, to suppose that some quality that is directly present constitutes the whole of the thing presenting the quality. It does not do so when the quality is that of being hot or fluid or heavy, and it does not when the quality is that of giving pleasure, or being enjoyed. Such qualities are, once more, effects, ends in the sense of closing termini of processes involving causal connections. They are something to be investigated, challenges to inquiry and judgment. The more connections and interactions we ascertain, the more we *know* the object in question. Thinking is a search for these connections. Heat experienced as a consequence of directed operations has a meaning quite different from the heat that is casually experienced without knowledge of how it came about. The same is true of enjoyments. Enjoyments that issue from conduct directed by insight into relations have a meaning and a validity due to the way in which they are experienced. Such enjoyments are not repented of; they generate no after-taste of bitterness. Even in the midst of direct enjoyment, there is a sense of validity, of authorization, which intensifies the enjoyment. There is solicitude for perpetuation of the *object* having value which is radically different from mere anxiety to perpetuate the *feeling* of enjoyment.

Such statements as we have been making are, therefore, far from implying that there are values apart from things actually enjoyed as good. To find a thing enjoy*able* is, so to say, a *plus* enjoyment. We saw that it was foolish to treat the scientific object as a rival to or substitute for the perceived object, since the former is intermediate between uncertain and settled situations and those experienced under conditions of greater control. In the same way, judgment of the value of an object to be experienced is instrumental to appreciation of it when it is realized. But the notion that every object that happens to satisfy has an equal claim with every other to be a value is like supposing that every object of perception has the same cognitive force as every other. There is no knowledge without perception; but objects perceived are *known* only when they are determined as consequences of connective operations. There is no value except where there is satisfaction, but there have to be certain conditions fulfilled to transform a satisfaction into a value.

The time will come when it will be found passing strange that we of this age should take such pains to control by every means at command the formation of ideas of physical things, even those most remote from human concern, and yet are content with haphazard beliefs about the qualities of objects that regulate our deepest interests; that we are scrupulous as to methods of forming ideas of natural objects, and either dogmatic or else driven by immediate conditions in framing those about values. There is, by implication, if not explicitly, a prevalent notion that values are already well known and that all which is lacking is the will to cultivate them in the order of their worth. In fact the most profound lack is not the will to act upon goods already known but the will to know what they are.

It is not a dream that it is possible to exercise some degree of regulation of the occurrence of enjoyments which are of value. Realization of the possibility is exemplified, for example, in the technologies and arts of industrial life—that is, up to a definite limit. Men desired heat, light, and speed of transit and of communication beyond what nature provides of itself. These things have been attained not by lauding the enjoyment of these things and preaching their desirability, but by study of the conditions of their manifestation. Knowledge of relations having been obtained, ability to produce followed, and enjoyment ensued as a matter of course. It is, however, an old story that enjoyment of these things as goods is no warrant of their bringing only good in their train. As Plato was given to pointing out, the physician knows how to heal and the orator to persuade, but the ulterior knowledge of whether it is better for a man to be healed or to be persuaded to the orator's opinion remains unsettled. Here there appears the split between what are traditionally and conventionally called the values of the baser arts and the higher values of the truly personal and humane arts.

With respect to the former, there is no assumption that they can be had and enjoyed without definite operative knowledge. With respect to them it is also clear that the degree in which we value them is measurable by the pains taken to control the conditions of their occurrence. With respect to the latter, it is assumed that no one who is honest can be in doubt what they are; that by revelation, or conscience, or the instruction of others, or immediate feeling, they are clear beyond question. And instead of action in their behalf being taken to be a measure of the extent to which things *are* values to us, it is assumed that the difficulty is to persuade men to act upon what they already know to be good. Knowledge of conditions and consequences is regarded as wholly indifferent to judging what is of serious value, though it is useful in a prudential way in trying to actualize it. In consequence, the existence of values that are by common consent of a secondary and technical sort are under a fair degree of control, while those denominated supreme and imperative are subject to all the winds of impulse, custom and arbitrary authority.

This distinction between higher and lower types of value is itself something to be looked into. Why should there be a sharp division made between some goods as physical and material and others as ideal and "spiritual"? The question touches the whole dualism of the material and the ideal at its root. To denominate anything "matter" or "material" is not in truth to disparage it. It is, if the designation is correctly applied, a way of indicating that the thing in question is a condition or means of the existence of something else. And disparagement of effective means is practically synonymous with disregard of the things that are termed, in eulogistic fashion, ideal and spiritual. For the latter terms if they have any concrete application at all signify something which is a desirable consummation of conditions, a cherished fulfillment of means. The sharp separation between material and ideal good thus deprives the latter of the underpinning of effective support while it opens the way for treating things which should be employed as means as ends in themselves. For since men cannot after all live without some measure of possession of such matters as health and wealth, the latter things will be viewed as values and ends in isolation unless they are treated as integral constituents of the goods that are deemed supreme and final.

The relations that determine the occurrence of what human beings experience, especially when social connections are taken into account, are indefinitely wider and more complex than those that determine the events termed physical; the latter are the outcome of definite selective operations. This is the reason why we know something about remote objects like the stars better than we know significantly characteristic things about our own bodies and minds. We forget the infinite number of things we do not know about the stars, or rather that what we call a star is itself the product of the elimination, enforced and deliberate, of most of the traits that belong to an actual existence. The amount of knowledge we possess about stars would not seem very great or very important if it were carried over to human beings and exhausted our knowledge of them. It is inevitable that genuine knowledge of man and society should lag far behind physical knowledge.

But this difference is not a ground for making a sharp division between the two, nor does it account for the fact that we make so little use of the experimental method of forming our ideas and beliefs about the concerns of man in his characteristic social relations. For this separation religions and philosophies must admit some responsibility. They have erected a distinction between a narrower scope of relations and a wider and fuller one into a difference of kind, naming one kind material, and the other mental and moral. They have charged themselves gratuitously with the office of diffusing belief in the necessity of the division, and with instilling contempt for the material as something inferior in kind in its intrinsic nature and worth. Formal philosophies undergo evaporation of their technical solid contents; in a thinner and more viable form they find their way into the minds of those who know nothing of their original forms. When these diffuse and, so to say, airy emanations re-crystallize in the popular mind they form a hard deposit of opinion that alters slowly and with great difficulty.

What difference would it actually make in the arts of conduct, personal and social, if the experimental theory were adopted not as a mere theory, but as a part of the working equipment of habitual attitudes on the part of everyone? It would be impossible, even were time given, to answer the question in adequate detail, just as men could not foretell in advance the consequences for knowledge of adopting the experimental method. It is the nature of the method that it has to be tried. But there are generic lines of difference which, within the limits of time at disposal, may be sketched.

Change from forming ideas and judgments of value on the basis of conformity to antecedent objects, to constructing enjoyable objects directed by knowledge of consequences, is a change from looking to the past to looking to the future. I do not for a moment suppose that the experiences of the past, personal and social, are of no importance. For without them we should not be able to frame any ideas whatever of the conditions under which objects are enjoyed nor any estimate of the consequences of esteeming and liking them. But past experiences are significant in giving us intellectual instrumentalities of judging just these points. They are tools, not finalities. Reflection upon what we have liked and have enjoyed is a necessity. But it tells us nothing about the *value* of these things until enjoyments are themselves reflectively controlled, or, until, as they are recalled, we form the best judgment possible about what led us to like this sort of thing and what has issued from the fact that we liked it.

We are not, then, to get away from enjoyments experienced in the past and from recall of them, but from the notion that they are the arbiters of things to be further enjoyed. At present, the arbiter is found in the past, although there are many ways of interpreting what in the past is authoritative. Nominally, the most influential conception doubtless is that of a revelation once had or a perfect life once lived. Reliance upon precedent, upon institutions created in the past, especially in law, upon rules of morals that have come to us through unexamined customs, upon uncriticized tradition, are other forms of dependence. It is not for a moment suggested that we can get away from customs and established institutions. A mere break would doubtless result simply in chaos. But there is no danger of such a break. Mankind is too inertly conservative both by constitution and by education to give the idea of this danger actuality. What there is genuine danger of is that the force of new conditions will produce disruption externally and mechanically: this is an ever present danger. The prospect is increased, not mitigated, by that conservatism which insists upon the adequacy of old standards to meet new conditions. What is needed is intelligent examination of the consequences that are actually effected by inherited institutions and customs, in order that there may be intelligent consideration of the ways in which they are to be intentionally modified in behalf of generation of different consequences.

This is the significant meaning of transfer of experimental method from the technical field of physical experience to the wider field of human life. We trust the method in forming our beliefs about things not directly connected with human life. In effect, we distrust it in moral, political and economic affairs. In the fine arts, there are many signs of a change. In the past, such a change has often been an omen and precursor of changes in other human attitudes. But, generally speaking, the idea of actively adopting experimental method in social affairs, in the matters deemed of most enduring and ultimate worth, strikes most persons as a surrender of all standards and regulative authority. But in principle, experimental method does not signify random and aimless action; it implies direction by ideas and knowledge. The question at issue is a practical one. Are there in existence the ideas and the knowledge that permit experimental method to be effectively used in social interests and affairs?

Where will regulation come from if we surrender familiar and traditionally prized values as our directive standards? Very largely from the findings of the natural sciences. For one of the effects of the separation drawn between knowledge and action is to deprive scientific knowledge of its proper service as a guide of conduct—except once more in those technological fields which have been degraded to an inferior rank. Of course, the complexity of the conditions upon which objects of human and liberal value depend is a great obstacle, and it would be too optimistic to say that we have as yet enough knowledge of the scientific type to enable us to regulate our judgments of value very extensively. But we have more knowledge than we try to put to use, and until we try more systematically we shall not know what are the important gaps in our sciences judged from the point of view of their moral and humane use.

For moralists usually draw a sharp line between the field of the natural sciences and the conduct that is regarded as moral. But a moral that frames its judgments of value on the basis of consequences must depend in a most intimate manner upon the conclusions of science. For the knowledge of the relations between changes which enable us to connect things as antecedents and consequences *is* science. The narrow scope which moralists often give to morals, their isolation of some conduct as virtuous and vicious from other large ranges of conduct, those having to do with health and vigor, business, education, with all the affairs in which desires and affection are implicated, is perpetuated by this habit of exclusion of the subject-matter of natural science from a role in formation of moral standards and ideals. The same attitude operates in the other direction to keep natural science a technical specialty, and it works unconsciously to encourage its use exclusively in regions where it can be turned to personal and class advantage, as in war and trade.

Another great difference to be made by carrying the experimental habit into all matter of practice is that it cuts the roots of what is often called subjectivism, but which is better termed egoism. The subjective attitude is much more widespread than would be inferred from the philosophies which have that label attached. It is as rampant in realistic philosophies as in any others, sometimes even more so, although disguised from those who hold these philosophies under the cover of reverence for and enjoyment of ultimate values. For the implication of placing the standard of thought and knowledge in antecedent existence is that our thought makes no difference in what is significantly real. It then affects only our own attitudc toward it.

This constant throwing of emphasis back upon a change made in ourselves instead of one made in the world in which we live seems to me the essence of what is objectionable in "subjectivism." Its taint hangs about even Platonic realism with its insistent evangelical dwelling upon the change made within the mind by contemplation of the realm of essence, and its depreciation of action as transient and all but sordid—a concession to the necessities of organic existence. All the theories which put conversion "of the eye of the soul" in the place of a conversion of natural and social objects that modifies goods actually experienced, are a retreat and escape from existence—and this retraction into self is, once more, the heart of subjective egoisms. The typical example is perhaps the other-worldliness found in religions whose chief concern is with the salvation of the personal soul. But other-worldliness is found as well in estheticism and in all seclusion within ivory towers.

It is not in the least implied that change in personal attitudes, in the disposition of the "subject," is not of great importance. Such change, on the contrary, is involved in any attempt to modify the conditions of the environment. But there is a radical difference between a change in the self that is cultivated and valued as an end, and one that is a means to alteration, through action, of objective conditions. The Aristotelian-medieval conviction that highest bliss is found in contemplative possession of ultimate Being presents an ideal attractive to some types of mind; it sets forth a refined sort of enjoyment. It is a doctrine congenial to minds that despair of the effort involved in creation of a better world of daily experience. It is, apart from theological attachments, a doctrine sure to recur when social conditions are so troubled as to make actual endeavor seem hopeless. But the subjectivism so externally marked in modern thought as compared with ancient is either a development of the old doctrine under new conditions or is of merely technical import. The medieval version of the doctrine at least had the active support of a great social institution by means of which man could be brought into the state of mind that prepared him for ultimate enjoyment of eternal Being. It had a certain solidity and depth which is lacking in modern theories that would attain the result by merely emotional or speculative procedures, or by any means not demanding a change in objective existence so as to render objects of value more empirically secure.

The nature in detail of the revolution that would be wrought by carrying into the region of values the principle now embodied in scientific practice cannot be told; to attempt it would violate the fundamental idea that we know only after we have acted and in consequences of the outcome of action. But it would surely effect a transfer of attention and energy from the subjective to the objective. Men would think of themselves as agents not as ends; ends would be found in experienced enjoyment of the fruits of a transforming activity. In as far as the subjectivity of modern thought represents a discovery of the part played by personal responses, organic and acquired, in the causal production of the qualities and values of objects, it marks the possibility of a decisive gain. It puts us in possession of some of the conditions that control the occurrence of experienced objects, and thereby it supplies us with an instrument of regulation. There is something querulous in the sweeping denial that things as experienced, as perceived and enjoyed, in any way depend upon interaction with human selves. The error of doctrines that have exploited the part played by personal and subjective reactions in determining what is perceived and enjoyed lies either in exaggerating this factor of constitution into the sole condition—as happens in subjective idealism—or else in treating it as a finality instead of, as with all knowledge, an instrument in direction of further action.

A third significant change that would issue from carrying over experimental method from physics to man concerns the import of standards, principles, rules. With the transfer, these, and all tenets and creeds about good and goods, would be recognized to be hypotheses. Instead of being rigidly fixed, they would be treated as intellectual instruments to be tested and confirmed—and altered—through consequences effected by acting upon them. They would lose all pretence of finality—the ulterior source of dogmatism. It is both astonishing and depressing that so much of the energy of mankind has gone into fighting for (with weapons of the flesh as well as of the spirit) the truth of creeds, religious, moral and political, as distinct from what has gone into effort to try creeds by putting them to the test of acting upon them. The change would do away with the intolerance and fanaticism that attend the notion that beliefs and judgments are capable of inherent truth and authority; inherent in the sense of being independent of what they lead to when used as directive principles. The transformation does not imply merely that men are responsible for acting upon what they profess to believe; that is an old doctrine. It goes much further. Any belief as such is tentative, hypothetical; it is not just to be acted upon, but is to be *framed* with reference to its office as a guide to action. Consequently, it should be the last thing in the world to be picked up casually and then clung to rigidly. When it is apprehended as a tool and only a tool, an instrumentality of direction, the same scrupulous attention will go to its formation as now goes into the making of instruments of precision in technical fields. Men, instead of being proud of accepting and asserting beliefs and "principles" on the ground of loyalty, will be as ashamed of that procedure as they would now be to confess their assent to a scientific theory out of reverence for Newton or Helmholtz or whomever, without regard to evidence.

If one stops to consider the matter, is there not something strange in the fact that men should consider loyalty to "laws," principles, standards, ideals to be an inherent virtue, accounted unto them for righteousness? It is as if they were making up for some secret sense of weakness by rigidity and intensity of insistent attachment. A moral law, like a law in physics, is not something to swear by and stick to at all hazards; it is a formula of the way to respond when specified conditions present themselves. Its soundness and pertinence are tested by what happens when it is acted upon. Its claim or authority rests finally upon the imperativeness of the situation that has to be dealt with, not upon its own intrinsic nature—as any tool achieves dignity in the measure of needs served by it. The idea that adherence to standards external to experienced objects is the only alternative to confusion and lawlessness was once held in science. But knowledge became steadily progressive when it was abandoned, and clues and tests found within concrete acts and objects were employed. The test of consequences is more exacting than that afforded by fixed general rules. In addition, it secures constant development, for when new acts are tried new results are experienced, while the lauded immutability of eternal ideals and norms is in itself a denial of the possibility of development and improvement.

The various modifications that would result from adoption in social and humane subjects of the experimental way of thinking are perhaps summed up in saying that it would place *method and means* upon the level of importance that has, in the past, been imputed exclusively to ends. Means have been regarded as menial, and the useful as the servile. Means have been treated as poor relations to be endured, but not inherently welcome. The very meaning of the word "ideals" is significant of the divorce which has obtained between means and ends. "Ideals" are thought to be remote and inaccessible of attainment; they are too high and fine to be sullied by realization. They serve vaguely to arouse "aspiration," but they do not evoke and direct strivings for embodiment in actual existence. They hover in an indefinite way over the actual scene; they are expiring ghosts of a once significant kingdom of divine reality whose rule penetrated to every detail of life.

It is impossible to form a just estimate of the paralysis of effort that has been produced by indifference to means. Logically, it is truistic that lack of consideration for means signifies that so-called ends are not taken seriously. It is as if one professed devotion to painting pictures conjoined with contempt for canvas, brush and paints; or love of music on condition that no instruments, whether the voice or something external, be used to make sounds. The good workman in the arts is known by his respect for his tools and by his interest in perfecting his technique. The glorification in the arts of ends at the expense of means would be taken to be a sign of complete insincerity or even insanity. Ends separated from means are either sentimental indulgences or if they happen to exist are merely accidental. The ineffectiveness in action of "ideals" is due precisely to the supposition that means and ends are not on exactly the same level with respect to the attention and care they demand.

It is, however, much easier to point out the formal contradiction implied in ideals that are professed without equal regard for the instruments and techniques of their realization, than it is to appreciate the concrete ways in which belief in their separation has found its way into life and borne corrupt and poisonous fruits. The separation marks the form in which the traditional divorce of theory and practice has expressed itself in actual life. It accounts for the relative impotency of arts concerned with enduring human welfare. Sentimental attachment and subjective eulogy take the place of action. For there is no art without tools and instrumental agencies. But it also explains the fact that in actual behavior, energies devoted to matters nominally thought to be inferior, material and sordid, engross attention and interest. After a polite and pious deference has been paid to "ideals," men feel free to devote themselves to matters which are more immediate and pressing.

It is usual to condemn the amount of attention paid by people in general to material ease, comfort, wealth, and success gained by competition, on the ground that they give to mere means the attention that ought to be given to ends, or that they have taken for ends things which in reality are only means. Criticisms of the place which economic interest and action occupy in present life are full of complaints that men allow lower aims to usurp the place that belongs to higher and ideal values. The final source of the trouble is, however, that moral and spiritual "leaders" have propagated the notion that ideal ends may be cultivated in isolation from "material" means, as if means and material were not synonymous. While they condemn men for giving to means the thought and energy that ought to go to ends, the condemnation should go to them. For they have not taught their followers to think of material and economic activities as *really* means. They have been unwilling to frame their conception of the values that should be regulative of human conduct on the basis of the actual conditions and operations by which alone values can be actualized.

Practical needs are imminent; with the mass of mankind they are imperative. Moreover, speaking generally, men are formed to act rather than to theorize. Since the ideal ends are so remotely and accidentally connected with immediate and urgent conditions that need attention, after lip service is given to them, men naturally devote themselves to the latter. If a bird in the hand is worth two in a neighboring bush, an actuality in hand is worth, for the direction of conduct, many ideals that are so remote as to be invisible and inaccessible. Men hoist the banner of the ideal, and then march in the direction that concrete conditions suggest and reward.

Deliberate insincerity and hypocrisy are rare. But the notion that action and sentiment are inherently unified in the constitution of human nature has nothing to justify it. Integration is something to be achieved. Division of attitudes and responses, compartmentalizing of interests, is easily acquired. It goes deep just because the acquisition is unconscious, a matter of habitual adaptation to conditions. Theory separated from concrete doing and making is empty and futile; practice then becomes an immediate seizure of opportunities and enjoyments which conditions afford without the direction which theory—knowledge and ideas—has power to supply. The problem of the relation of theory and practice is not a problem of theory alone; it is that, but it is also the most practical problem of life. For it is the question of how intelligence may inform action, and how action may bear the fruit of increased insight into meaning: a clear view of the values that are worth while and of the means by which they are to be made secure in experienced objects. Construction of ideals in general and their sentimental glorification are easy; the responsibilities both of studious thought and of action are shirked. Persons having the advantage of positions of leisure and who find pleasure in abstract theorizing—a most delightful indulgence to those to whom it appeals—have a large measure of liability for a cultivated diffusion of ideals and aims that are separated from the conditions which are the means of actualization. Then other persons who find themselves in positions of social power and authority readily claim to be the bearers and defenders of ideal ends in church and state. They then use the prestige and authority their representative capacity as guardians of the highest ends confers on them to cover actions taken in behalf of the harshest and narrowest of material ends.

The present state of industrial life seems to give a fair index of the existing separation of means and ends. Isolation of economics from ideal ends, whether of morals or of organized social life, was proclaimed by Aristotle. Certain things, he said, are conditions of a worthy life, personal and social, but are not constituents of it. The economic life of man, concerned with satisfaction of wants, is of this nature. Men have wants and they must be satisfied. But they are only prerequisites of a good life, not intrinsic elements in it. Most philosophers have not been so frank nor perhaps so logical. But upon the whole, economics has been treated as on a lower level than either morals or politics.

Yet the life which men, women and children actually lead, the opportunities open to them, the values they are capable of enjoying, their education, their share in all the things of art and science, are mainly determined by economic conditions. Hence we can hardly expect a moral system which ignores economic conditions to be other than remote and empty.

Industrial life is correspondingly brutalized by failure to equate it as the means by which social and cultural values are realized. That the economic life, thus exiled from the pale of higher values, takes revenge by declaring that it is the only social reality, and by means of the doctrine of materialistic determination of institutions and conduct in all fields, denies to deliberate morals and politics any share of causal regulation, is not surprising.

When economists were told that their subject-matter was merely material, they naturally thought they could be "scientific" only by excluding all reference to distinctively human values. Material wants, efforts to satisfy them, even the scientifically regulated technologies highly developed in industrial activity, are then taken to form a complete and closed field. If any reference to social ends and values is introduced it is by way of an external addition, mainly hortatory. That economic life largely determines the conditions under which mankind has access to concrete values may be recognized or it may not be. In either case, the notion that it is the means to be utilized in order to secure significant values as the common and shared possession of mankind is alien and inoperative. To many persons, the idea that the ends professed by morals are impotent save as they are connected with the working machinery of economic life seems like deflowering the purity of moral values and obligations.

The social and moral effects of the separation of theory and practice have been merely hinted at. They are so manifold and so pervasive that an adequate consideration of them would involve nothing less than a survey of the whole field of morals, economics and politics. It cannot be justly stated that these effects are in fact direct consequences of the quest for certainty by thought and knowledge isolated from action. For, as we have seen, this quest was itself a reflex product of actual conditions. But it may be truly asserted that this quest, undertaken in religion and philosophy, has had results which have reinforced the conditions which originally brought it about. Moreover, search for safety and consolation amid the perils of life by means other than intelligent action, by feeling and thought alone, began when actual means of control were lacking, when arts were undeveloped. It had then a relative historic justification that is now lacking. The primary problem for thinking which lays claim to be philosophic in its breadth and depth is to assist in bringing about a reconstruction of all beliefs rooted in a basic separation of knowledge and action; to develop a system of operative ideas congruous with present knowledge and with present facilities of control over natural events and energies.

We have noted more than once how modern philosophy has been absorbed in the problem of effecting an adjustment between the conclusions of natural science and the beliefs and values that have authority in the direction of life. The genuine and poignant issue does not reside where philosophers for the most part have placed it. It does not consist in accommodation to each other of two realms, one physical and the other ideal and spiritual, nor in the reconciliation of the "categories" of theoretical and practical reason. It is found in that isolation of executive means and ideal interests which has grown up under the influence of the separation of theory and practice. For this, by nature, involves the separation of the material and the spiritual. Its solution, therefore, can be found only in action wherein the phenomena of material and economic life are equated with the purposes that command the loyalties of affection and purpose, and in which ends and ideals are framed in terms of the possibilities of actually experienced situations. But while the solution cannot be found in "thought" alone, it can be furthered by thinking which is operative—which frames and defines ideas in terms of what may be done, and which uses the conclusions of science as instrumentalities. William James was well within the bounds of moderation when he said that looking forward instead of backward, looking to what the world and life might become instead of to what they have been, is an alteration in the "seat of authority."

It was incidentally remarked earlier in our discussion that the serious defect in the current empirical philosophy of values, the one which identifies them with things actually enjoyed irrespective of the conditions upon which they depend, is that it formulates and in so far consecrates the conditions of our present social experience. Throughout these chapters, primary attention has perforce been given to the methods and statements of philosophic theories. But these statements are technical and specialized in formulation only. In origin, content and import they are reflections of some condition or some phase of concrete human experience. Just as the theory of the separation of theory and practice has a practical origin and a momentous practical consequence, so the empirical theory that values are identical with whatever men actually enjoy, no matter how or what, formulates an aspect, and an undesirable one, of the present social situation.

For while our discussion has given more attention to the other type of philosophical doctrine, that which holds that regulative and authoritative standards are found in transcendent eternal values, it has not passed in silence over the fact that actually the greater part of the activities of the greater number of human beings is spent in effort to seize upon and hold onto such enjoyments as the actual scene permits. Their energies and their enjoyments are controlled in fact, but they are controlled by external conditions rather than by intelligent judgment and endeavor. If philosophies have any influence over the thoughts and acts of men, it is a serious matter that the most widely held empirical theory should in effect justify this state of things by identifying values with the objects of any interest as such. As long as the only theories of value placed before us for intellectual assent alternate between sending us to a realm of eternal and fixed values and sending us to enjoyments such as actually obtain, the formulation, even as only a theory, of an experimental empiricism which finds values to be identical with goods that are the fruit of intelligently directed activity has its measure of practical significance.

1929–1930

A Lecture on Ethics

Ludwig Wittgenstein

Before I begin to speak about my subject proper let me make a few introductory remarks. I feel I shall have great difficulties in communicating my thoughts to you and I think some of them may be diminished by mentioning them to you beforehand. The first one, which almost I need not mention, is that English is not my native tongue and my expression therefore often lacks that precision and subtlety which would be desirable if one talks about a difficult subject. All I can do is to ask you to make my task easier by trying to get at my meaning in spite of the faults which I will constantly be committing against the English grammar. The second difficulty I will mention is this, that probably many of you come up to this lecture of mine with slightly wrong expectations. And to set you right in this point I will say a few words about the reason for choosing the subject I have chosen: When your former secretary honored me by asking me to read a paper to your society, my first thought was that I would certainly do it and my second thought was that if I was to have the opportunity to speak to you I should speak about something which I am keen on communicating to you and that I should not misuse this opportunity to give you a lecture about, say, logic. I call this a misuse, for to explain a scientific matter to you it would need a course of lectures and not an hour's paper. Another alternative would have been to give you what's called a popular-scientific lecture, that is a lecture intended to make you believe that you understand a thing which actually you don't understand, and to gratify what I believe to be one of the lowest desires of modern people, namely the superficial curiosity about the latest discoveries of science. I rejected these alternatives and decided to talk to you about a subject which seems to me to be of general importance, hoping that it may help to clear up your thoughts about this subject (even if you should entirely disagree with what I will say about it). My third and last difficulty is one which, in fact, adheres to most lengthy philosophical lectures and it is this, that the hearer is incapable of seeing both the road he is led and the goal which it leads to. That is to say: he either thinks: "I understand all he says, but what on earth is he driving at" or else he thinks "I see what he's driving at, but how on earth is he going to get there." All I can do is again to ask you to be patient and to hope that in the end you may see both the way and where it leads to.

I will now begin. My subject, as you know, is Ethics and I will adopt the explanation of that term which Professor Moore has given in his book *Principia Ethica.* He says: "Ethics is the general enquiry into what is good." Now I am going to use the term Ethics in a slightly wider sense, in a sense in fact which includes what I believe to be the most essential part of what is generally called Aesthetics. And to make you see as clearly as possible what I take to be the subject matter of Ethics I will put before you a number of more or less synonymous expressions each of which could be substituted for the above definition, and by enumerating them I want to produce the same sort of effect which Galton produced when he took a number of photos of different faces on the same photographic plate in order to get the picture of the typical features they all had in common. And as by showing to you such a collective photo I could make you see what is the typical—say—Chinese face; so if you look through the row of synonyms which I will put before you, you will, I hope, be able to see the characteristic features they all have in common and these are the characteristic features of Ethics. Now instead of saying "Ethics is the enquiry into what is good" I could have said Ethics is the enquiry into what is valuable, or, into what is really important, or I could have said Ethics is the enquiry into the meaning of life, or into what makes life worth living, or into the right way of living. I believe if you look at all these phrases you will get a rough idea as to what it is that Ethics is concerned with. Now the first thing that strikes one about all these expressions is that each of them is actually used in two very different senses. I will call them the trivial or relative sense on the one hand and the ethical or absolute sense on the other. If for instance I say that this is a *good* chair this means that the chair serves a certain predetermined purpose and the word good here has only meaning so far as this purpose has been previously fixed upon. In fact the word good in the relative sense simply means coming up to a certain predetermined standard. Thus when we say that this man is a good pianist we mean that he can play pieces of a certain degree of difficulty with a certain degree of dexterity. And similarly if I say that it is *important* for me not to catch cold I mean that catching a cold produces certain describable disturbances in my life and if I say that this is the *right* road I mean that it's the right road relative to a certain goal. Used in this way these expressions don't present any difficult or deep problems. But this is not how Ethics uses them. Supposing that I could play tennis and one of you saw me playing and said "Well, you play pretty badly" and suppose I answered "I know, I'm playing badly but I don't want to play any better," all the other man could say would be "Ah then that's all right." But suppose I had told one of you a preposterous lie and he came up to me and said "You're behaving like a beast" and then I were to say "I know I behave badly, but then I don't want to behave any better," could he then say "Ah, then that's all right"? Certainly not; he would say "Well, you *ought* to want to behave better." Here you have an absolute judgment of value, whereas the first instance was one of a relative judgment. The essence of this difference seems to be obviously this: Every judgment of relative value is a mere statement of facts and can therefore be put in such a form that it loses all the appearance of a judgment of value: Instead of saying "This is the right way to Granchester," I could equally well have said, "This is the right way you have to go if you want to get to Granchester in the shortest time"; "This man is a good runner" simply means that he runs a certain number of miles in a certain number of minutes, etc. Now what I wish to contend is that, although all judgments of relative value can be shown to be mere statements of facts, no statement of fact can ever be, or imply, a judgment of absolute value. Let me explain this: Suppose one of you were an omniscient person and therefore knew all the movements of all the bodies in the world dead or alive and that he also knew all the states of mind of all human beings that ever lived, and suppose this man wrote all he knew in a big book, then this book would contain the whole description of the world; and what I want to say is, that this book would contain nothing that we would call an *ethical* judgment or anything that would logically imply such a judgment. It would of course contain all relative judgments of value and all true scientific propositions and in fact all true propositions that can be made. But all the facts described would, as it were, stand on the same level and in the same way all propositions stand on the same level. There are no propositions which, in any absolute sense, are sublime, important, or trivial. Now perhaps some of you will agree to that and be reminded of Hamlet's words: "Nothing is either good or bad, but thinking makes it so." But this again could lead to a misunderstanding. What Hamlet says seems to imply that good and bad, though not qualities of the world outside us, are attributes to our states of mind. But what I mean is that a state of mind, so far as we mean by that a fact which we can describe, is in no ethical sense good or bad. If for instance in our world-book we read the description of a murder with all its details physical and psychological, the mere description of these facts will contain nothing which we could call an *ethical* proposition. The murder will be on exactly the same level as any other event, for instance the falling of a stone. Certainly the reading of this description might cause us pain or rage or any other emotion, or we might read about the pain or rage caused by this murder in other people when they heard of it, but there will simply be facts, facts, and facts but no Ethics. And now I must say that if I contemplate what Ethics really would have to be if there were such a science, this result seems to me quite obvious. It seems to me obvious that nothing we could ever think or say should be *the* thing. That we cannot write a scientific book, the subject matter of which could be intrinsically sublime and above all other subject matters. I can only describe my feeling by the metaphor, that, if a man could write a book on Ethics which really was a book on Ethics, this book would, with an explosion, destroy all the other books in the world. Our words used as we use them in science, are vessels capable only of containing and conveying meaning and sense, *natural* meaning and sense. Ethics, if it is anything, is supernatural and our words will only express facts; as a teacup will only hold a teacup full of water and if I were to pour out a gallon over it. I said that so far as facts and propositions are concerned there is only relative value and relative good, right, etc. And let me, before I go on, illustrate this by a rather obvious example. The right road is the road which leads to an arbitrarily predetermined end and it is quite clear to us all that there is no sense in talking about the right road apart from such a predetermined goal. Now let us see what we could possibly mean by the expression, "*the* absolutely right road." I think it would be the road which *everybody* on seeing it would, *with logical necessity*, have to go, or be ashamed for not going. And similarly the *absolute good*, if it is a describable state of affairs, would be one which everybody, independent of his tastes and inclinations, would *necessarily* bring about or feel guilty for not bringing about. And I want to say that such a state of affairs is a chimera. No state of affairs has, in itself, what I would like to call the coercive power of an absolute judge. Then what have all of us who, like myself, are still tempted to use such expressions as "absolute good," "absolute value," etc., what have we in mind and what do we try to express? Now whenever I try to make this clear to myself it is natural that I should recall cases in which I would certainly use these expressions and I am then in the situation in which you would be if, for instance, I were to give you a lecture on the psychology of pleasure. What you would do then would be to try and recall some typical situation in which you always felt pleasure. For, bearing this situation in mind, all I should say to you would become concrete and, as it were, controllable. One man would perhaps choose as his stock example the sensation when taking a walk on a fine summer's day. Now in this situation I am, if I want to fix my mind on what I mean by absolute or ethical value. And there, in my case, it always happens that the idea of one particular experience presents itself to me which therefore is, in a sense, my experience *par excellence* and this is the reason why, in talking to you now, I will use this experience as my first and foremost example. (As I have said before, this is an entirely personal matter and others would find other examples more striking.) I will describe this experience in order, if possible, to make you recall the same or similar experiences, so that we may have a common ground for our investigation. I believe the best way of describing it is to say that when I have it *I wonder at the existence of the world.* And I am then inclined to use such phrases as "how extraordinary that anything should exist" or "how extraordinary that the world should exist." I will mention another experience straight away which I also know and which others of you might be acquainted with: it is, what one might call, the experience of feeling *absolutely* safe. I mean the state of mind in which one is inclined to say "I am safe, nothing can injure me whatever happens." Now let me consider these experiences, for, I believe, they exhibit the very characteristics we try to get clear about. And there the first thing I have to say is, that the verbal expression which we give to these experiences is nonsense! If I say "I wonder at the existence of the world" I am misusing language. Let me explain this: It has a perfectly good and clear sense to say that I wonder at something being the case, we all understand what it means to say that I wonder at the size of a dog which is bigger than anyone I have ever seen before or at any thing which, in the common sense of the word, is extraordinary. In every such case I wonder at something being the case which I *could* conceive *not* to be the case. I wonder at the size of this dog because I could conceive of a dog of another, namely the ordinary size, at which I should not wonder. To say "I wonder at such and such being the case" has only sense if I can imagine it not to be the case. In this sense one can wonder at the existence of, say, a house when one sees it and has not visited it for a long time and has imagined that it had been pulled down in the meantime. But it is nonsense to say that I wonder at the existence of the world, because I cannot imagine it not existing. I could of course wonder at the world round me being as it is. If for instance I had this experience while looking into the blue sky, I could wonder at the sky being blue as opposed to the case when it's clouded. But that's not what I mean. I am wondering at the sky being *whatever it is.* One might be tempted to say that what I am wondering at is a tautology, namely at the sky being blue or not blue. But then it's just nonsense to say that one is wondering at a tautology. Now the same applies to the other experience which I have mentioned, the experience of absolute safety. We all know what it means in ordinary life to be safe. I am safe in my room, when I cannot be run over by an omnibus. I am safe if I have had whooping cough and cannot therefore get it again. To be safe essentially means that it is physically impossible that certain things should happen to me and therefore it's nonsense to say that I am safe *whatever* happens. Again this is a misuse of the word "safe" as the other example was of a misuse of the word "existence" or "wondering." Now I want to impress on you that a certain characteristic misuse of our language runs through *all* ethical and religious expressions. All these expressions *seem*, prima facie, to be just *similes*. Thus it seems that when we are using the word *right* in an ethical sense, although, what we mean, is not right in its trivial sense, it's something similar, and when we say "This is a good fellow," although the word good here doesn't mean what it means in the sentence "This is a good football player" there seems to be some similarity. And when we say "This man's life was valuable" we don't mean it in the same sense in which we would speak of some valuable jewelry but there seems to be some sort of analogy. Now all religious terms seem in this sense to be used as similes or allegorically. For when we speak of God and that he sees everything and when we kneel and pray to him all our terms and actions seem to be parts of a great and elaborate allegory which represents him as a human being of great power whose grace we try to win, etc., etc. But this allegory also describes the experience which I have just referred to. For the first of them is, I believe, exactly what people were referring to when they said that God had created the world; and the experience of absolute safety has been described by saying that we feel safe in the hands of God. A third experience of the same kind is that of feeling guilty and again this was described by the phrase that God disapproves of our conduct. Thus in ethical and religious language we seem constantly to be using similes. But a simile must be the simile for *something*. And if I can describe a fact by means of a simile I must also be able to drop the simile and to describe the facts without it. Now in our case as soon as we try to drop the simile and simply to state the facts which stand behind it, we find that there are no such facts. And so, what at first appeared to be a simile now seems to be mere nonsense. Now the three experiences which I have mentioned to you (and I could have added others) seem to those who have experienced them, for instance to me, to have in some sense an intrinsic, absolute value. But when I say they are experiences, surely, they are facts; they have taken place then and there, lasted a certain definite time and consequently are describable. And so from what I have said some minutes ago I must admit it is nonsense to say that they have absolute value. And I will make my point still more acute by saying "It is the paradox that an experience, a fact, should seem to have supernatural value." Now there is a way in which I would be tempted to meet this paradox. Let me first consider, again, our first experience of wondering at the existence of the world and let me describe it in a slightly different way; we all know what in ordinary life would be called a miracle. It obviously is simply an event the like of which we have never yet seen. Now suppose such an event happened. Take the case that one of you suddenly grew a lion's head and began to roar. Certainly that would be as extraordinary a thing as I can imagine. Now whenever we should have recovered from our surprise, what I would suggest would be to fetch a doctor and have the case scientifically investigated and if it were not for hurting him I would have him vivisected. And where would the miracle have got to? For it is clear that when we look at it in this way everything miraculous has disappeared; unless what we mean by this term is merely that a fact has not yet been explained by science which again means that we have hitherto failed to group this fact with others in a scientific system. This shows that it is absurd to say "Science has proved that there are no miracles." The truth is that the scientific way of looking at a fact is not the way to look at it as a miracle. For imagine whatever fact you may, it is not in itself miraculous in the absolute sense of that term. For we see now that we have been using the word "miracle" in a relative and an absolute sense. And I will now describe the experience of wondering at the existence of the world by saying: it is the experience of seeing the world as a miracle. Now I am tempted to say that the right expression in language for the miracle of the existence of the world, though it is not any proposition *in* language, is the existence of language itself. But what then does it mean to be aware of this miracle at some times and not at other times? For all I have said by shifting the expression of the miraculous from an expression *by means of* language to the expression *by the existence* of language, all I have said is again that we cannot express what we want to express and that all we *say* about the absolute miraculous remains nonsense. Now the answer to all this will seem perfectly clear to many of you. You will say: Well, if certain experiences constantly tempt us to attribute a quality to them which we call absolute or ethical value and importance, this simply shows that by these words we *don't* mean nonsense, that after all what we mean by saying that an experience has absolute value *is just a fact like other facts* and that all it comes to is that we have not yet succeeded in finding the correct logical analysis of what we mean by our ethical and religious expressions. Now when this is urged against me I at once see clearly, as it were in a flash of light, not only that no description that I can think of would do to describe what I mean by absolute value, but that I would reject every significant description that anybody could possibly suggest, *ab initio,* on the ground of its significance. That is to say: I see now that these nonsensical expressions were not nonsensical because I had not yet found the correct expressions, but that their nonsensicality was their very essence. For all I wanted to do with them was just *to go beyond* the world and that is to say beyond significant language. My whole tendency and I believe the tendency of all men who ever tried to write or talk Ethics or Religion was to run against the boundaries of language. This running against the walls of our cage is perfectly, absolutely hopeless. Ethics so far as it springs from the desire to say something about the ultimate meaning of life, the absolute good, the absolute valuable, can be no science. What it says does not add to our knowledge in any sense. But it is a document of a tendency in the human mind which I personally cannot help respecting deeply and I would not for my life ridicule it.

1930

What Makes Right Acts Right?

W. D. Ross

The real point at issue between hedonism and utilitarianism on the one hand and their opponents on the other is not whether "right" means "productive of so and so"; for it cannot with any plausibility be maintained that it does. The point at issue is that to which we now pass, viz. whether there is any general character which makes right acts right, and if so, what it is. Among the main historical attempts to state a single characteristic of all right actions which is the foundation of their rightness are those made by egoism and utilitarianism. But I do not propose to discuss these, not because the subject is unimportant, but because it has been dealt with so often and so well already, and because there has come to be so much agreement among moral philosophers that neither of these theories is satisfactory. A much more attractive theory has been put forward by Professor Moore: that what makes actions right is that they are productive of more *good* than could have been produced by any other action open to the agent.[1]

This theory is in fact the culmination of all the attempts to base rightness on productivity of some sort of result. The first form this attempt takes is the attempt to base rightness on conduciveness to the advantage or pleasure of the agent. This theory comes

[1]I take the theory which, as I have tried to show, seems to be put forward in *Ethics* rather than the earlier and less plausible theory put forward in *Principia Ethica*. . . .

W. D. Ross, "What Makes Right Acts Right" from THE RIGHT AND THE GOOD (Oxford: Oxford University Press, 1930). Reprinted with the permission of the publishers.

to grief over the fact, which stares us in the face, that a great part of duty consists in an observance of the rights and a furtherance of the interests of others, whatever the cost to ourselves may be. Plato and others may be right in holding that a regard for the rights of others never in the long run involves a loss of happiness for the agent, that "the just life profits a man." But this, even if true, is irrelevant to the rightness of the act. As soon as a man does an action *because* he thinks he will promote his own interests thereby, he is acting not from a sense of its rightness but from self-interest.

To the egoistic theory hedonistic utilitarianism supplies a much-needed amendment. It points out correctly that the fact that a certain pleasure will be enjoyed by the agent is no reason why he *ought* to bring it into being rather than an equal or greater pleasure to be enjoyed by another, though, human nature being what it is, it makes it not unlikely that he *will* try to bring it into being. But hedonistic utilitarianism in its turn needs a correction. On reflection it seems clear that pleasure is not the only thing in life that we think good in itself, that for instance we think the possession of a good character, or an intelligent understanding of the world, as good or better. A great advance is made by the substitution of "productive of the greatest good" for "productive of the greatest pleasure."

Not only is this theory more attractive than hedonistic utilitarianism, but its logical relation to that theory is such that the latter could not be true unless *it* were true, while it might be true though hedonistic utilitarianism were not. It is in fact one of the logical bases of hedonistic utilitarianism. For the view that what produces the maximum pleasure is right has for its bases the views (1) that what produces the maximum good is right, and (2) that pleasure is the only thing good in itself. If they were not assuming that what produces the maximum *good* is right, the utilitarians' attempt to show that pleasure is the only thing good in itself, which is in fact the point they take most pains to establish, would have been quite irrelevant to their attempt to prove that only what produces the maximum *pleasure* is right. If, therefore, it can be shown that productivity of the maximum good is not what makes all right actions right, we shall *a fortiori* have refuted hedonistic utilitarianism.

When a plain man fulfils a promise because he thinks he ought to do so, it seems clear that he does so with no thought of its total consequences, still less with any opinion that these are likely to be the best possible. He thinks in fact much more of the past than of the future. What makes him think it right to act in a certain way is the fact that he has promised to do so—that and, usually, nothing more. That his act will produce the best possible consequences is not his reason for calling it right. What lends color to the theory we are examining, then, is not the actions (which form probably a great majority of our actions) in which some such reflection as "I have promised" is the only reason we give ourselves for thinking a certain action right, but the exceptional cases in which the consequences of fulfilling a promise (for instance) would be so disastrous to others that we judge it right not to do so. It must of course be admitted that such cases exist. If I have promised to meet a friend at a particular time for some trivial purpose, I should certainly think myself justified in breaking my engagement if by doing so I could prevent a serious accident or bring relief to the victims of one. And the supporters of the view we are examining hold that my thinking so is due to my thinking that I shall bring more good into existence by the one action than by the other. A different account may, however, be given of the matter, an account which will, I believe, show itself to be the true one. It may be said that besides the duty of fulfilling promises I have and recognize a duty of relieving distress,[2] and that when I think it right to do the latter at the cost of

[2]These are not strictly speaking duties, but things that tend to be our duty, or *prima facie* duties. Cf. pp. 19–20 [pp. 89–90 this volume].

not doing the former, it is not because I think I shall produce more good thereby but because I think it the duty which is in the circumstances more of a duty. This account surely corresponds much more closely with what we really think in such a situation. If, so far as I can see, I could bring equal amounts of good into being by fulfilling my promise and by helping some one to whom I had made no promise, I should not hesitate to regard the former as my duty. Yet on the view that what is right is right because it is productive of the most good I should not so regard it.

There are two theories, each in its way simple, that offer a solution of such cases of conscience. One is the view of Kant, that there are certain duties of perfect obligation, such as those of fulfilling promises, of paying debts, of telling the truth, which admit of no exception whatever in favor of duties of imperfect obligation, such as that of relieving distress. The other is the view of, for instance, Professor Moore and Dr. Rashdall, that there is only the duty of producing good, and that all "conflicts of duties" should be resolved by asking "by which action will most good be produced?" But it is more important that our theory fit the facts than that it be simple, and the account we have given above corresponds (it seems to me) better than either of the simpler theories with what we really think, viz. that normally promise-keeping, for example, should come before benevolence, but that when and only when the good to be produced by the benevolent act is very great and the promise comparatively trivial, the act of benevolence becomes our duty.

In fact the theory of "ideal utilitarianism," if I may for brevity refer so to the theory of Professor Moore, seems to simplify unduly our relations to our fellows. It says, in effect, that the only morally significant relation in which my neighbors stand to me is that of being possible beneficiaries by my action.[3] They do stand in this relation to me, and this relation is morally significant. But they may also stand to me in the relation of promisee to promiser, of creditor to debtor, of wife to husband, of child to parent, of friend to friend, of fellow countryman to fellow countryman, and the like; and each of these relations is the foundation of a *prima facie* duty, which is more or less incumbent on me according to the circumstances of the case. When I am in a situation, as perhaps I always am, in which more than one of these *prima facie* duties is incumbent on me, what I have to do is to study the situation as fully as I can until I form the considered opinion (it is never more) that in the circumstances one of them is more incumbent than any other; then I am bound to think that to do this *prima facie* duty is my duty *sans phrase* in the situation.

I suggest "*prima facie* duty" or "conditional duty" as a brief way of referring to the characteristic (quite distinct from that of being a duty proper) which an act has, in virtue of being of a certain kind (e.g. the keeping of a promise), of being an act which would be a duty proper if it were not at the same time of another kind which is morally significant. Whether an act is a duty proper or actual duty depends on *all* the morally significant kinds it is an instance of. The phrase "*prima facie* duty" must be apologized for, since (1) it suggests that what we are speaking of is a certain kind of duty, whereas it is in fact not a duty, but something related in a special way to duty. Strictly speaking, we want not a phrase in which duty is qualified by an adjective, but a separate noun. (2) "*Prima" facie* suggests that one is speaking only of an appearance which a moral situation presents at first sight, and which may turn out to be illusory; whereas what I am speaking of is an objective fact involved in the nature of the situation, or more strictly

[3]Some will think it, apart from other considerations, a sufficient refutation of this view to point out that I also stand in that relation to myself, so that for this view the distinction of oneself from others is morally insignificant.

in an element of its nature, though not, as duty proper does, arising from its *whole* nature. I can, however, think of no term which fully meets the case. "Claim" has been suggested by Professor Prichard. The word "claim" has the advantage of being quite a familiar one in this connection, and it seems to cover much of the ground. It would be quite natural to say, "a person to whom I have made a promise has a claim on me," and also, "a person whose distress I could relieve (at the cost of breaking the promise) has a claim on me." But (1) while "claim" is appropriate from *their* point of view, we want a word to express the corresponding fact from the agent's point of view—the fact of his being subject to claims that can be made against him; and ordinary language provides us with no such correlative to "claim." And (2) (what is more important) "claim" seems inevitably to suggest two persons, one of whom might make a claim on the other; and while this covers the ground of social duty, it is inappropriate in the case of that important part of duty which is the duty of cultivating a certain kind of character in oneself. It would be artificial, I think, and at any rate metaphorical, to say that one's character has a claim on oneself.

There is nothing arbitrary about these *prima facie* duties. Each rests on a definite circumstance which cannot seriously be held to be without moral significance. Of *prima facie* duties I suggest, without claiming completeness or finality for it, the following division.[4]

(1) Some duties rest on previous acts of my own. These duties seem to include two kinds, (*a*) those resting on a promise or what may fairly be called an implicit promise, such as the implicit undertaking not to tell lies which seems to be implied in the act of entering into conversation (at any rate by civilized men), or of writing books that purport to be history and not fiction. These may be called the duties of fidelity. (*b*) Those resting on a previous wrongful act. These may be called the duties of reparation. (2) Some rest on previous acts of other men, i.e., services done by them to me. These may be loosely described as the duties of gratitude.[5] (3) Some rest on the fact or possibility of a distribution of pleasure or happiness (or of the means thereto) which is not in accordance with the merit of the persons concerned; in such cases there arises a duty to upset or prevent such a distribution. These are the duties of justice. (4) Some rest on the mere fact that there are other beings in the world whose condition we can make better in respect of virtue, or of intelligence, or of pleasure. These are the duties of beneficence. (5) Some rest on the fact that we can improve our own condition in respect of virtue or of intelligence. These are the duties of self-improvement. (6) I think that we should distinguish from (4) the duties that may be summed up under the title of "not injuring others." No doubt to injure others is incidentally to fail to do them good; but it seems to me clear that non-maleficence is apprehended as a duty distinct from that of beneficence, and as a duty of a more stringent character. It will be noticed that this alone among the types of duty has been stated in a negative way. An attempt might no doubt be made to state this duty, like the others, in a positive way. It might be said that it is really the duty

[4]I should make it plain at this stage that I am *assuming* the correctness of some of our main convictions as to *prima facie* duties, or, more strictly, am claiming that we *know* them to be true. To me it seems as self-evident as anything could be, that to make a promise, for instance, is to create a moral claim on us in someone else. Many readers will perhaps say that they do *not* know this to be true. If so, I certainly cannot prove it to them; I can only ask them to reflect again, in the hope that they will ultimately agree that they also know it to be true. The main moral convictions of the plain man seem to me to be, not opinions which it is for philosophy to prove or disprove, but knowledge from the start; and in my own case I seem to find little difficulty in distinguishing these essential convictions from other moral convictions which I also have, which are merely fallible opinions based on an imperfect study of the working for good or evil of certain institutions or types of action.

[5]For a needed correction of this statement, cf. pp. 22–3 [p. 91 this volume].

to prevent ourselves from acting either from an inclination to harm others or from an inclination to seek our own pleasure, in doing which we should incidentally harm them. But on reflection it seems clear that the primary duty here is the duty not to harm others, this being a duty whether or not we have an inclination that if followed would lead to our harming them; and that when we have such an inclination the primary duty not to harm others gives rise to a consequential duty to resist the inclination. The recognition of this duty of non-maleficence is the first step on the way to the recognition of the duty of beneficence; and that accounts for the prominence of the commands "thou shalt not kill," "thou shalt not commit adultery," "thou shalt not steal," "thou shalt not bear false witness," in so early a code as the Decalogue. But even when we have come to recognize the duty of beneficence, it appears to me that the duty of non-maleficence is recognized as a distinct one, and as *prima facie* more binding. We should not in general consider it justifiable to kill one person in order to keep another alive, or to steal from one in order to give alms to another.

The essential defect of the "ideal utilitarian" theory is that it ignores, or at least does not do full justice to, the highly personal character of duty. If the only duty is to produce the maximum of good, the question who is to have the good—whether it is myself, or my benefactor, or a person to whom I have made a promise to confer that good on him, or a mere fellow man to whom I stand in no such special relation—should make no difference to my having a duty to produce that good. But we are all in fact sure that it makes a vast difference.

One or two other comments must be made on this provisional list of the divisions of duty. (1) The nomenclature is not strictly correct. For by "fidelity" or "gratitude" we mean, strictly, certain states of motivation; and, as I have urged, it is not our duty to have certain motives, but to do certain acts. By "fidelity," for instance, is meant, strictly, the disposition to fulfil promises and implicit promises *because we have made them.* We have no general word to cover the actual fulfillment of promises and implicit promises *irrespective of motive;* and I use "fidelity," loosely but perhaps conveniently, to fill this gap. So too I use "gratitude" for the returning of services, irrespective of motive. The term "justice" is not so much confined, in ordinary usage, to a certain state of motivation, for we should often talk of a man as acting justly even when we did not think his motive was the wish to do what was just simply for the sake of doing so. Less apology is therefore needed for our use of "justice" in this sense. And I have used the word "beneficence" rather than "benevolence," in order to emphasize the fact that it is our duty to do certain things, and not to do them from certain motives.

(2) If the objection be made, that this catalogue of the main types of duty is an unsystematic one resting on no logical principle, it may be replied, first, that it makes no claim to being ultimate. It is a *prima facie* classification of the duties which reflection on our moral convictions seems actually to reveal. And if these convictions are, as I would claim that they are, of the nature of knowledge, and if I have not misstated them, the list will be a list of authentic conditional duties, correct as far as it goes though not necessarily complete. The list of *goods* put forward by the rival theory is reached by exactly the same method—the only sound one in the circumstances—viz. that of direct reflection on what we really think. Loyalty to the facts is worth more than a symmetrical architectonic or a hastily reached simplicity. If further reflection discovers a perfect logical basis for this or for a better classification, so much the better.

(3) It may, again, be objected that our theory that there are these various and often conflicting types of *prima facie* duty leaves us with no principle upon which to discern what is our actual duty in particular circumstances. But this objection is not one

which the rival theory is in a position to bring forward. For when we have to choose between the production of two heterogeneous goods, say knowledge and pleasure, the "ideal utilitarian" theory can only fall back on an opinion, for which no logical basis can be offered, that one of the goods is the greater; and this is no better than a similar opinion that one of two duties is the more urgent. And again, when we consider the infinite variety of the effects of our actions in the way of pleasure, it must surely be admitted that the claim which *hedonism* sometimes makes, that it offers a readily applicable criterion of right conduct, is quite illusory.

I am unwilling, however, to content myself with an *argumentum ad hominem,* and I would contend that in principle there is no reason to anticipate that every act that is our duty is so for one and the same reason. Why should two sets of circumstances, or one set of circumstances, *not* possess different characteristics, any one of which makes a certain act our *prima facie* duty? When I ask what it is that makes me in certain cases sure that I have a *prima facie* duty to do so and so, I find that it lies in the fact that I have made a promise; when I ask the same question in another case, I find the answer lies in the fact that I have done a wrong. And if on reflection I find (as I think I do) that neither of these reasons is reducible to the other, I must not on any *a priori* ground assume that such a reduction is possible.

An attempt may be made to arrange in a more systematic way the main types of duty which we have indicated. In the first place it seems self-evident that if there are things that are intrinsically good, it is *prima facie* a duty to bring them into existence rather than not to do so, and to bring as much of them into existence as possible. It will be argued in our fifth chapter that there are three main things that are intrinsically good—virtue, knowledge, and, with certain limitations, pleasure. And since a given virtuous disposition, for instance, is equally good whether it is realized in myself or in another, it seems to be my duty to bring it into existence whether in myself or in another. So too with a given piece of knowledge.

The case of pleasure is difficult; for while we clearly recognize a duty to produce pleasure for others, it is by no means so clear that we recognize a duty to produce pleasure for ourselves. This appears to arise from the following facts. The thought of an act as our duty is one that presupposes a certain amount of reflection about the act; and for that reason does not normally arise in connection with acts towards which we are already impelled by another strong impulse. So far, the cause of our not thinking of the promotion of our own pleasure as a duty is analogous to the cause which usually prevents a highly sympathetic person from thinking of the promotion of the pleasure of others as a duty. He is impelled so strongly by direct interest in the well-being of others towards promoting their pleasure that he does not stop to ask whether it is his duty to promote it; and we are all impelled so strongly towards the promotion of our own pleasure that we do not stop to ask whether it is a duty or not. But there is a further reason why even when we stop to think about the matter it does not usually present itself as a duty: viz. that, since the performance of most of our duties involves the giving up of some pleasure that we desire, the doing of duty and the getting of pleasure for ourselves come by a natural association of ideas to be thought of as incompatible things. This association of ideas is in the main salutary in its operation, since it puts a check on what but for it would be much too strong, the tendency to pursue one's own pleasure without thought of other considerations. Yet if pleasure is good, it seems in the long run clear that it is right to get it for ourselves as well as to produce it for others, when this does not involve the failure to discharge some more stringent *prima facie* duty. The question is a very difficult one, but it seems that this conclusion can be denied only on one or other of three grounds: (1)

that pleasure is not *prima facie* good (i.e. good when it is neither the actualization of a bad disposition nor undeserved), (2) that there is no *prima facie* duty to produce as much that is good as we can, or (3) that though there is a *prima facie* duty to produce other things that are good, there is no *prima facie* duty to produce pleasure which will be enjoyed by ourselves. I give reasons later[6] for not accepting the first contention. The second hardly admits of argument but seems to me plainly false. The third seems plausible only if we hold that an act that is pleasant or brings pleasure to ourselves must for that reason not be a duty; and this would lead to paradoxical consequences, such as that if a man enjoys giving pleasure to others or working for their moral improvement, it cannot be his duty to do so. Yet it seems to be a very stubborn fact, that in our ordinary consciousness we are not aware of a duty to get pleasure for ourselves; and by way of partial explanation of this I may add that though, as I think, one's own pleasure is a good and there is a duty to produce it, it is only if we *think* of our own pleasure not as simply our own pleasure, but as an objective good, something that an impartial spectator would approve, that we can think of the getting it as a duty; and we do not habitually think of it in this way.

If these contentions are right, what we have called the duty of beneficence and the duty of self-improvement rest on the same ground. No different principles of duty are involved in the two cases. If we feel a special responsibility for improving our own character rather than that of others, it is not because a special principle is involved, but because we are aware that the one is more under our control than the other. It was on this ground that Kant expressed the practical law of duty in the form "seek to make yourself good and other people happy." He was so persuaded of the internality of virtue that he regarded any attempt by one person to produce virtue in another as bound to produce, at most, only a counterfeit of virtue, the doing of externally right acts not from the true principle of virtuous action but out of regard to another person. It must be admitted that one man cannot compel another to be virtuous; compulsory virtue would just not be virtue. But experience clearly shows that Kant overshoots the mark when he contends that one man cannot do anything to *promote* virtue in another, to bring such influences to bear upon him that his own response to them is more likely to be virtuous than his response to other influences would have been. And our duty to do this is not different in kind from our duty to improve our own characters.

It is equally clear, and clear at an earlier stage of moral development, that if there are things that are bad in themselves we ought, *prima facie,* not to bring them upon others; and on this fact rests the duty of non-maleficence.

The duty of justice is particularly complicated, and the word is used to cover things which are really very different—things such as the payment of debts, the reparation of injuries done by oneself to another, and the bringing about of a distribution of happiness between other people in proportion to merit. I use the word to denote only the last of these three. In the fifth chapter I shall try to show that besides the three (comparatively) simple goods, virtue, knowledge, and pleasure, there is a more complex good, not reducible to these, consisting in the proportionment of happiness to virtue. The bringing of this about is a duty which we owe to all men alike, though it may be reinforced by special responsibilities that we have undertaken to particular men. This, therefore, with beneficence and self-improvement, comes under the general principle that we should produce as much good as possible, though the good here involved is different in kind from any other.

[6]pp. 135–8 [*The Right and the Good*].

But besides this general obligation, there are special obligations. These may arise, in the first place, incidentally, from acts which were not essentially meant to create such an obligation, but which nevertheless create it. From the nature of the case such acts may be of two kinds—the infliction of injuries on others, and the acceptance of benefits from them. It seems clear that these put us under a special obligation to other men, and that only these acts can do so incidentally. From these arise the twin duties of reparation and gratitude.

And finally there are special obligations arising from acts the very intention of which, when they were done, was to put us under such an obligation. The name for such acts is "promises"; the name is wide enough if we are willing to include under it implicit promises, i.e. modes of behavior in which without explicit verbal promise we intentionally create an expectation that we can be counted on to behave in a certain way in the interest of another person.

These seem to be, in principle, all the ways in which *prima facie* duties arise. In actual experience they are compounded together in highly complex ways. Thus, for example, the duty of obeying the laws of one's country arises partly (as Socrates contends in the *Crito*) from the duty of gratitude for the benefits one has received from it; partly from the implicit promise to obey which seems to be involved in permanent residence in a country whose laws we know we are *expected* to obey, and still more clearly involved when we ourselves invoke the protection of its laws (this is the truth underlying the doctrine of the social contract); and partly (if we are fortunate in our country) from the fact that its laws are potent instruments for the general good.

Or again, the sense of a general obligation to bring about (so far as we can) a just apportionment of happiness to merit is often greatly reinforced by the fact that many of the existing injustices are due to a social and economic system which we have, not indeed created, but taken part in and assented to; the duty of justice is then reinforced by the duty of reparation.

It is necessary to say something by way of clearing up the relation between *prima facie* duties and the actual or absolute duty to do one particular act in particular circumstances. If, as almost all moralists except Kant are agreed, and as most plain men think, it is sometimes right to tell a lie or to break a promise, it must be maintained that there is a difference between *prima facie* duty and actual or absolute duty. When we think ourselves justified in breaking, and indeed morally obliged to break, a promise in order to relieve some one's distress, we do not for a moment cease to recognize a *prima facie* duty to keep our promise, and this leads us to feel, not indeed shame or repentance, but certainly compunction, for behaving as we do; we recognize, further, that it is our duty to make up somehow to the promisee for the breaking of the promise. We have to distinguish from the characteristic of being our duty that of tending to be our duty. Any act that we do contains various elements in virtue of which it falls under various categories. In virtue of being the breaking of a promise, for instance, it tends to be wrong; in virtue of being an instance of relieving distress it tends to be right. Tendency to be one's duty may be called a parti-resultant attribute, i.e. one which belongs to an act in virtue of some one component in its nature. *Being* one's duty is a toti-resultant attribute, one which belongs to an act in virtue of its whole nature and of nothing less than this.[7] This distinction between parti-resultant and toti-resultant attributes is one which we shall meet in another context also.[8]

Another instance of the same distinction may be found in the operation of natural laws. *Qua* subject to the force of gravitation towards some other body, each body tends

[7]But cf. the qualification in p. 33, n. 2 [p. 97, n. 10 this volume].

[8]Cf. pp. 122–3 [*The Right and The Good*].

to move in a particular direction with a particular velocity; but its actual movement depends on *all* the forces to which it is subject. It is only by recognizing this distinction that we can preserve the absoluteness of laws of nature, and only by recognizing a corresponding distinction that we can preserve the absoluteness of the general principles of morality. But an important difference between the two cases must be pointed out. When we say that in virtue of gravitation a body tends to move in a certain way, we are referring to a causal influence actually exercised on it by another body or other bodies. When we say that in virtue of being deliberately untrue a certain remark tends to be wrong, we are referring to no causal relation, to no relation that involves succession in time, but to such a relation as connects the various attributes of a mathematical figure. And if the word "tendency" is thought to suggest too much a causal relation, it is better to talk of certain types of act as being *prima facie* right or wrong (or of different persons as having different and possibly conflicting claims upon us), than of their tending to be right or wrong.

Something should be said of the relation between our apprehension of the *prima facie* rightness of certain types of act and our mental attitude towards particular acts. It is proper to use the word "apprehension" in the former case and not in the latter. That an act, *qua* fulfilling a promise, or *qua* effecting a just distribution of good, or *qua* returning services rendered, or *qua* promoting the good of others, or *qua* promoting the virtue or insight of the agent, is *prima facie* right, is self-evident; not in the sense that it is evident from the beginning of our lives, or as soon as we attend to the proposition for the first time, but in the sense that when we have reached sufficient mental maturity and have given sufficient attention to the proposition it is evident without any need of proof, or of evidence beyond itself. It is self-evident just as a mathematical axiom, or the validity of a form of inference, is evident. The moral order expressed in these propositions is just as much part of the fundamental nature of the universe (and, we may add, of any possible universe in which there were moral agents at all) as is the spatial or numerical structure expressed in the axioms of geometry or arithmetic. In our confidence that these propositions are true there is involved the same trust in our reason that is involved in our confidence in mathematics; and we should have no justification for trusting it in the latter sphere and distrusting it in the former. In both cases we are dealing with propositions that cannot be proved, but that just as certainly need no proof.

Some of these general principles of *prima facie* duty may appear to be open to criticism. It may be thought, for example, that the principle of returning good for good is a falling off from the Christian principle, generally and rightly recognized as expressing the highest morality, of returning good for evil. To this it may be replied that I do not suggest that there is a principle commanding us to return good for good and forbidding us to return good for evil, and that I do suggest that there is a positive duty to seek the good of all men. What I maintain is that an act in which good is returned for good is recognized as *specially* binding on us just because it is of that character, and that *ceteris paribus* any one would think it his duty to help his benefactors rather than his enemies, if he could not do both; just as it is generally recognized that *ceteris paribus* we should pay our debts rather than give our money in charity, when we cannot do both. A benefactor is not only a man, calling for our effort on his behalf on that ground, but also our benefactor, calling for our *special* effort on *that* ground.

Our judgments about our actual duty in concrete situations have none of the certainty that attaches to our recognition of the general principles of duty. A statement is certain, i.e. is an expression of knowledge, only in one or other of two cases: when it is either self-evident, or a valid conclusion from self-evident premisses. And our judgments about our particular duties have neither of these characters. (1) They are not self-evident. Where a possible act is seen to have two characteristics, in virtue of one of which it is *prima facie* right, and in virtue of the other *prima facie* wrong, we are (I think) well aware that we are not certain whether we ought or ought not to do it; that whether we do it or not, we are taking a moral risk. We come in the long run, after consideration, to think one duty more pressing than the other, but we do not feel certain that it is so. And though we do not always recognize that a possible act has two such characteristics, and though there *may* be cases in which it has not, we are never certain that any particular possible act has not, and therefore never certain that it is right, nor certain that it is wrong. For, to go no further in the analysis, it is enough to point out that any particular act will in all probability in the course of time contribute to the bringing about of good or of evil for many human beings, and thus have a *prima facie* rightness or wrongness of which we know nothing. (2) Again, our judgments about our particular duties are not logical conclusions from self-evident premisses. The only possible premisses would be the general principles stating their *prima facie* rightness or wrongness *qua* having the different characteristics they do have; and even if we could (as we cannot) apprehend the extent to which an act will tend on the one hand, for example, to bring about advantages for our benefactors, and on the other hand to bring about disadvantages for fellow men who are not our benefactors, there is no principle by which we can draw the conclusion that it is on the whole right or on the whole wrong. In this respect the judgment as to the rightness of a particular act is just like the judgment as to the beauty of a particular natural object or work of art. A poem is, for instance, in respect of certain qualities beautiful and in respect of certain others not beautiful; and our judgment as to the degree of beauty it possesses on the whole is never reached by logical reasoning from the apprehension of its particular beauties or particular defects. Both in this and in the moral case we have more or less probable opinions which are not logically justified conclusions from the general principles that are recognized as self-evident.

There is therefore much truth in the description of the right act as a fortunate act. If we cannot be certain that it is right, it is our good fortune if the act we do is the right act. This consideration does not, however, make the doing of our duty a mere matter of chance. There is a parallel here between the doing of duty and the doing of what will be to our personal advantage. We never *know* what act will in the long run be to our advantage. Yet it is certain that we are more likely in general to secure our advantage if we estimate to the best of our ability the probable tendencies of our actions in this respect, than if we act on caprice. And similarly we are more likely to do our duty if we reflect to the best of our ability on the *prima facie* rightness or wrongness of various possible acts in virtue of the characteristics we perceive them to have, than if we act without reflection. With this greater likelihood we must be content.

Many people would be inclined to say that the right act for me is not that whose general nature I have been describing, viz. that which if I were omniscient I should see to be my duty, but that which on all the evidence available to me I should think to be my duty. But suppose that from the state of partial knowledge in which I think act *A* to be my duty, I could pass to a state of perfect knowledge in which I saw act *B* to be my duty, should I not say "act *B* was the right act for me to do"? I should no doubt add "though I am not to be blamed for doing act *A*." But in adding this, am I not passing from the question "what is right" to the question "what is morally good"? At the same time I am not making the *full* passage from the one notion to the other; for in order that the act should be morally good, or an act I am not to be blamed for doing, it must not merely be the act which it is reasonable for me to think my duty; it must also be done for that reason, or from some other morally good motive. Thus the conception of the right act as the act which it is reasonable for me to think my duty is an unsatisfactory compromise between the true notion of the right act and the notion of the morally good action.

The general principles of duty are obviously not self-evident from the beginning of our lives. How do they come to be so? The answer is, that they come to be self-evident to us just as mathematical axioms do. We find by experience that this couple of matches and that couple make four matches, that this couple of balls on a wire and that couple make four balls: and by reflection on these and similar discoveries we come to see that it is of the nature of two and two to make four. In a precisely similar way, we see the *prima facie* rightness of an act which would be the fulfilment of a particular promise, and of another which would be the fulfilment of another promise, and when we have reached sufficient maturity to think in general terms, we apprehend *prima facie* rightness to belong to the nature of any fulfilment of promise. What comes first in time is the apprehension of the self-evident *prima facie* rightness of an individual act of a particular type. From this we come by reflection to apprehend the self-evident general principle of *prima facie* duty. From this, too, perhaps along with the apprehension of the self-evident *prima facie* rightness of the same act in virtue of its having another characteristic as well, and perhaps in spite of the apprehension of its *prima facie* wrongness in virtue of its having some third characteristic, we come to believe something not self-evident at all, but an object of probable opinion, viz. that this particular act is (not *prima facie* but) actually right.

In this respect there is an important difference between rightness and mathematical properties. A triangle which is isosceles necessarily has two of its angles equal, whatever other characteristics the triangle may have—whatever, for instance, be its area, or the size of its third angle. The equality of the two angles is a parti-resultant attribute.[9] And the same is true of all mathematical attributes. It is true, I may add, of *prima facie* rightness. But no act is ever, in virtue of falling under some general description, necessarily actually right; its rightness depends on its whole nature[10] and not on any element in it. The reason is that no mathematical object (no figure, for instance, or angle) ever has two characteristics that tend to give it opposite resultant characteristics, while moral acts often (as every one knows) and indeed always (as on reflection we must admit) have different characteristics that tend to make them at the same time *prima facie* right and *prima facie* wrong; there is probably no act, for instance, which does good to any one without doing harm to some one else, and *vice versa*.

Supposing it to be agreed, as I think on reflection it must, that no one *means* by "right" just "productive of the best possible consequences," or "optimific," the attributes "right" and "optimific" might stand in either of two kinds of relation to each other. (1) They might be so related that we could apprehend *a priori*, either immediately or deductively, that any act that is optimific is right and any act that is right is optimific, as we can apprehend that any triangle that is equilateral is equiangular and *vice versa*. Professor Moore's view is, I think, that the coextensiveness of "right" and "optimific" is apprehended immediately.[11] He rejects the possibility of any proof of it. Or (2) the two attributes might be such that the question whether they are invariably connected had to be answered by means of an inductive inquiry. Now at first sight it might seem as if the constant connection of the two attributes could be immediately apprehended. It might seem

[9]Cf. pp. 28 [p. 94 this volume], 122–3 [*The Right and the Good*].

[10]To avoid complicating unduly the statement of the general view I am putting forward, I have here rather overstated it. Any act is the origination of a great variety of things many of which make no difference to its rightness or wrongness. But there are always many elements in its nature (i.e. in what it is the origination of) that make a difference to its rightness or wrongness, and no element in its nature can be dismissed without consideration as indifferent.

[11]*Ethics*, p. 181.

absurd to suggest that it could be right for any one to do an act which would produce consequences less good than those which would be produced by some other act in his power. Yet a little thought will convince us that this is not absurd. The type of case in which it is easiest to see that this is so is, perhaps, that in which one has made a promise. In such a case we all think that *prima facie* it is our duty to fulfil the promise irrespective of the precise goodness of the total consequences. And though we do not think it is necessarily our actual or absolute duty to do so, we are far from thinking that any, even the slightest, gain in the value of the total consequences will necessarily justify us in doing something else instead. Suppose, to simplify the case by abstraction, that the fulfilment of a promise to *A* would produce 1,000 units of good[12] for him, but that by doing some other act I could produce 1,001 units of good for *B*, to whom I have made no promise, the other consequences of the two acts being of equal value; should we really think it self-evident that it was our duty to do the second act and not the first? I think not. We should, I fancy, hold that only a much greater disparity of value between the total consequences would justify us in failing to discharge our *prima facie* duty to *A*. After all, a promise is a promise, and is not to be treated so lightly as the theory we are examining would imply. What, exactly, a promise is, is not so easy to determine, but we are surely agreed that it constitutes a serious moral limitation to our freedom of action. To produce the 1,001 units of good for *B* rather than fulfil our promise to *A* would be to take, not perhaps our duty as philanthropists too seriously, but certainly our duty as makers of promises too lightly.

Or consider another phase of the same problem. If I have promised to confer on *A* a particular benefit containing 1,000 units of good, is it self-evident that if by doing some different act I could produce 1,001 units of good for *A* himself (the other consequences of the two acts being supposed equal in value), it would be right for me to do so? Again, I think not. Apart from my general *prima facie* duty to do *A* what good I can, I have another *prima facie* duty to do him the particular service I have promised to do him, and this is not to be set aside in consequence of a disparity of good of the order of 1,001 to 1,000, though a much greater disparity might justify me in so doing.

Or again, suppose that *A* is a very good and *B* a very bad man, should I then, even when I have made no promise, think it self-evidently right to produce 1,001 units of good for *B* rather than 1,000 for *A*? Surely not. I should be sensible of a *prima facie* duty of justice, i.e. of producing a distribution of goods in proportion to merit, which is not outweighed by such a slight disparity in the total goods to be produced.

Such instances—and they might easily be added to—make it clear that there is no self-evident connection between the attributes "right" and "optimific." The theory we are examining has a certain attractiveness when applied to our decision that a particular act is our duty (though I have tried to show that it does not agree with our actual moral judgments even here). But it is not even plausible when applied to our recognition of *prima facie* duty. For if it were self-evident that the right coincides with the optimific, it should be self-evident that what is *prima facie* right is *prima facie* optimific. But whereas we are certain that keeping a promise is *prima facie* right, we are not certain that it is *prima facie* optimific (though we are perhaps certain that it is *prima facie* bonific). Our certainty that it is *prima facie* right depends not on its consequences but on its being the fulfilment of a promise. The theory we are examining involves too much difference between the evident ground of our conviction about *prima facie* duty and the alleged ground of our conviction about actual duty.

[12] I am assuming that good is objectively quantitative (cf. pp. 142–4 [*The Right and the Good*]), but not that we can accurately assign an exact quantitative measure to it. Since it is of a definite amount, we can make the *supposition* that its amount is so-and-so, though we cannot with any confidence *assert* that it is.

The coextensiveness of the right and the optimific is, then, not self-evident. And I can see no way of proving it deductively; nor, so far as I know, has any one tried to do so. There remains the question whether it can be established inductively. Such an inquiry, to be conclusive, would have to be very thorough and extensive. We should have to take a large variety of the acts which we, to the best of our ability, judge to be right. We should have to trace as far as possible their consequences, not only for the persons directly affected but also for those indirectly affected, and to these no limit can be set. To make our inquiry thoroughly conclusive, we should have to do what we cannot do, viz. trace these consequences into an unending future. And even to make it reasonably conclusive, we should have to trace them far into the future. It is clear that the most we could possibly say is that a large variety of typical acts that are judged right appear, so far as we can trace their consequences, to produce more good than any other acts possible to the agents in the circumstances. And such a result falls far short of proving the constant connection of the two attributes. But it is surely clear that no inductive inquiry justifying even this result has ever been carried through. The advocates of utilitarian systems have been so much persuaded either of the identity or of the self-evident connection of the attributes "right" and "optimific" (or "felicific") that they have not attempted even such an inductive inquiry as is possible. And in view of the enormous complexity of the task and the inevitable inconclusiveness of the result, it is worth no one's while to make the attempt. What, after all, would be gained by it? If, as I have tried to show, for an act to be right and to be optimific are not the same thing, and an act's being optimific is not even the ground of its being right, then if we could ask ourselves (though the question is really unmeaning) which we ought to do, right acts because they are right or optimific acts because they are optimific, our answers must be "the former." If they are optimific as well as right, that is interesting but not morally important; if not, we still ought to do them (which is only another way of saying that they *are* the right acts), and the question whether they are optimific has no importance for moral theory.

There is one direction in which a fairly serious attempt has been made to show the connection of the attributes "right" and "optimific." One of the most evident facts of our moral consciousness is the sense which we have of the sanctity of promises, a sense which does not, on the face of it, involve the thought that one will be bringing more good into existence by fulfilling the promise than by breaking it. It is plain, I think, that in our normal thought we consider that the fact that we have made a promise is in itself sufficient to create a duty of keeping it, the sense of duty resting on remembrance of the past promise and not on thoughts of the future consequences of its fulfilment. Utilitarianism tries to show that this is not so, that the sanctity of promises rests on the good consequences of the fulfilment of them and the bad consequences of their non-fulfilment. It does so in this way: it points out that when you break a promise you not only fail to confer a certain advantage on your promisee but you diminish his confidence, and indirectly the confidence of others, in the fulfilment of promises. You thus strike a blow at one of the devices that have been found most useful in the relations between man and man—the device on which, for example, the whole system of commercial credit rests—and you tend to bring about a state of things wherein each man, being entirely unable to rely on the keeping of promises by others, will have to do everything for himself, to the enormous impoverishment of human well-being.

To put the matter otherwise, utilitarians say that when a promise ought to be kept it is because the total good to be produced by keeping it is greater than the total good to be produced by breaking it, the former including as its main element the maintenance and strengthening of general mutual confidence, and the latter being greatly diminished by a weakening of this confidence. They say, in fact, that the case I put some pages back[13] never arises—the case in which by fulfilling a promise I shall bring into being 1,000 units of good for my promisee, and by breaking it 1,001 units of good for some one else, the other effects of the two acts being of equal value. The other effects, they say, never are of equal value. By keeping my promise I am helping to strengthen the system of mutual confidence; by breaking it I am helping to weaken this; so that really the first act produces $1{,}000 + x$ units of good, and the second $1{,}001 - y$ units, and the difference between $+x$ and $-y$ is enough to outweigh the slight superiority in the *immediate* effects of the second act. In answer to this it may be pointed out that there must be *some* amount of good that exceeds the difference between $+x$ and $-y$ (i.e. exceeds $x + y$); say, $x + y + z$. Let us suppose the *immediate* good effects of the second act to be assessed not at 1,001 but at $1{,}000 + x + y + z$. Then its *net* good effects are $1{,}000 + x + z$, i.e. greater than those of the fulfillment of the promise; and the utilitarian is bound to say forthwith that the promise should be broken. Now, we may ask whether that is really the way we think about promises? Do we really think that the production of the slightest balance of good, no matter who will enjoy it, by the breach of a promise frees us from the obligation to keep our promise? We need not doubt that a system by which promises are made and kept is one that has great advantages for the general well-being. But that is not the whole truth. To make a promise is not merely to adapt an ingenious device for promoting the general well-being; it is to put oneself in a new relation to one person in particular, a relation which creates a specifically new *prima facie* duty to him, not reducible to the duty of promoting the general well-being of society. By all means let us try to foresee the net good effects of keeping one's promise and the net good effects of breaking it, but even if we assess the first at $1{,}000 + x$ and the second at $1{,}000 + x + z$, the question still remains whether it is not our duty to fulfil the promise. It may be suspected, too, that the effect of a single keeping or breaking of a promise in strengthening or weakening the fabric of mutual confidence is greatly exaggerated by the theory we are examining. And if we suppose two men dying together alone, do we think that the duty of one to fulfil before he dies a promise he has made to the other would be extinguished by the fact that neither act would have any effect on the general confidence? Any one who holds this may be suspected of not having reflected on what a promise is.

I conclude that the attributes "right" and "optimific" are not identical, and that we do not know either by intuition, by deduction, or by induction that they coincide in their application, still less that the latter is the foundation of the former. It must be added, however, that if we are ever under no special obligation such as that of fidelity to a promisee or of gratitude to a benefactor, we ought to do what will produce most good; and that even when we are under a special obligation the tendency of acts to promote general good is one of the main factors in determining whether they are right.

In what has preceded, a good deal of use has been made of "what we really think" about moral questions; a certain theory has been rejected because it does not agree with what we really think. It might be said that this is in principle wrong; that we should not be content to expound what our present moral consciousness tells us but should aim at a criticism of our existing moral consciousness in the light of theory. Now I do not doubt that the moral consciousness of men has in detail undergone a good deal of modification as regards the things we think right, at the hands of moral theory. But if we are

[13]p. 34 [p. 97 this volume].

told, for instance, that we should give up our view that there is a special obligatoriness attaching to the keeping of promises because it is self-evident that the only duty is to produce as much good as possible, we have to ask ourselves whether we really, when we reflect, *are* convinced that this is self-evident, and whether we really *can* get rid of our view that promise-keeping has a bindingness independent of productiveness of maximum good. In my own experience I find that I cannot, in spite of a very genuine attempt to do so; and I venture to think that most people will find the same, and that just because they cannot lose the sense of special obligation, they cannot accept as self-evident, or even as true, the theory which would require them to do so. In fact it seems, on reflection, self-evident that a promise, simply as such, is something that *prima facie* ought to be kept, and it does *not*, on reflection, seem self-evident that production of maximum good is the only thing that makes an act obligatory. And to ask us to give up at the bidding of a theory our actual apprehension of what is right and what is wrong seems like asking people to repudiate their actual experience of beauty, at the bidding of a theory which says "only that which satisfies such and such conditions can be beautiful." If what I have called our actual apprehension is (as I would maintain that it is) truly an apprehension, i.e. an instance of knowledge, the request is nothing less than absurd.

I would maintain, in fact, that what we are apt to describe as "what we think" about moral questions contains a considerable amount that we do not think but know, and that this forms the standard by reference to which the truth of any moral theory has to be tested, instead of having itself to be tested by reference to any theory. I hope that I have in what precedes indicated what in my view these elements of knowledge are that are involved in our ordinary moral consciousness.

It would be a mistake to found a natural science on "what we really think," i.e. on what reasonably thoughtful and well-educated people think about the subjects of the science before they have studied them scientifically. For such opinions are interpretations, and often misinterpretations, of sense-experience; and the man of science must appeal from these to sense-experience itself, which furnishes his real data. In ethics no such appeal is possible. We have no more direct way of access to the facts about rightness and goodness and about what things are right or good, than by thinking about them; the moral convictions of thoughtful and well-educated people are the data of ethics just as sense-perceptions are the data of a natural science. Just as some of the latter have to be rejected as illusory, so have some of the former; but as the latter are rejected only when they are in conflict with other more accurate sense-perceptions, the former are rejected only when they are in conflict with other convictions which stand better the test of reflection. The existing body of moral convictions of the best people is the cumulative product of the moral reflection of many generations, which has developed an extremely delicate power of appreciation of moral distinctions; and this the theorist cannot afford to treat with anything other than the greatest respect. The verdicts of the moral consciousness of the best people are the foundation on which he must build; though he must first compare them with one another and eliminate any contradictions they may contain.

It is worth while to try to state more definitely the nature of the acts that are right. We may try to state first what (if anything) is the universal nature of *all* acts that are right. It is obvious that any of the acts that we do has countless effects, directly or indirectly, on countless people, and the probability is that any act, however right it be, will have adverse effects (though these may be very trivial) on some innocent people. Similarly, any wrong act will probably have beneficial effects on some deserving people. Every act therefore, viewed in some aspects, will be *prima facie* right, and viewed in others, *prima facie* wrong, and right acts can be distinguished from wrong acts only as being those which, of all those possible for the agent in the circumstances, have the greatest balance of *prima facie* rightness, in those respects in which they are *prima facie* right, over their *prima facie* wrongness, in those respects in which they are *prima facie* wrong—*prima facie* rightness and wrongness being understood in the sense previously explained. For the estimation of the comparative stringency of these *prima facie* obligations no general rules can, so far as I can see, be laid down. We can only say that a great deal of stringency belongs to the duties of "perfect obligation"—the duties of keeping our promises, of repairing wrongs we have done, and of returning the equivalent of services we have received. For the rest, ἐν τῇ αἰσθήσει ἡ κρίσις.[14] This sense of our particular duty in particular circumstances, preceded and informed by the fullest reflection we can bestow on the act in all its bearings, is highly fallible, but it is the only guide we have to our duty.

When we turn to consider the nature of individual right acts, the first point to which attention should be called is that any act may be correctly described in an indefinite, and in principle infinite, number of ways. An act is the production of a change in the state of affairs (if we ignore, for simplicity's sake, the comparatively few cases in which it is the maintenance of an existing state of affairs; cases which, I think, raise no special difficulty). Now the only changes we can *directly* produce are changes in our own bodies or in our own minds. But these are not, as such, what as a rule we think it our duty to produce. Consider some comparatively simple act, such as telling the truth or fulfilling a promise. In the first case what I produce directly is movements of my vocal organs. But what I think it my duty to produce is a true view in some one else's mind about some fact, and between my movement of my vocal organs and this result there intervenes a series of physical events and events in his mind. Again, in the second case, I may have promised, for instance, to return a book to a friend. I may be able, by a series of movements of my legs and hands, to place it in his hands. But what I am just as likely to do, and to think I have done my duty in doing, is to send it by a messenger or to hand it to his servant or to send it by post; and in each of these cases what I *do* directly is worthless in itself and is connected by a series of intermediate links with what I do think it is my duty to bring about, viz. his receiving what I have promised to return to him. This being so, it *seems* as if what I *do* has no obligatoriness in itself and as if one or other of three accounts should be given of the matter, each of which makes rightness not belong to what I do, considered in its own nature.

(1) One of them would be that what is obligatory is not *doing* anything in the natural sense of producing any change in the state of affairs, but *aiming* at something—at, for instance, my friend's reception of the book. But this account will not do. For (*a*) to aim at something is to act from a motive consisting of the wish to bring that thing about. But we have seen[15] that motive never forms part of the content of our duty; if anything is certain about morals, that, I think, is certain. And (*b*) if I have promised to return the book to my friend, I obviously do not fulfil my promise and do my duty merely by aiming at his receiving the book; I must see that he actually receives it. (2) A more plausible account is that which says I must do that which is likely to produce the result. But this account is open to the second of these objections, and probably also to the first. For in the first place, however likely my act may seem, even on careful consideration, and even however likely it may in fact be, to produce the result, if it does not produce it I have not done what I promised to do, i.e. have not done my duty. And secondly, when it

[14]"The decision rests with perception." Arist. *Nic. Eth.* 1109 b 23, 1126 b 4.

[15]pp. 5–6 [*The Right and the Good*].

is said that I ought to do what is likely to produce the result, what is *probably* meant is that I ought to do a certain thing as a result of the wish to produce a certain result, and of the thought that my act is likely to produce it; and this again introduces motive into the content of duty. (3) Much the most plausible of the three accounts is that which says, "I ought to do that which will actually produce a certain result." This escapes objection (*b*). Whether it escapes objection (*a*) or not depends on what exactly is meant. If it is meant that I ought to do a certain thing from the wish to produce a certain result and the thought that it will do so, the account is still open to objection (*a*). But if it is meant simply that I ought to do a certain thing, and that the reason why I ought to do it is that it will produce a certain result, objection (*a*) is avoided. Now this account in its second form is that which utilitarianism gives. It says what is right is certain acts, not certain acts motivated in a certain way; and it says that acts are never right by their own nature but by virtue of the goodness of their actual results. And this account is, I think, clearly nearer the truth than one which makes the rightness of an act depend on the goodness of either the *intended* or the *likely* results.

Nevertheless, this account appears not to be the true one. For it implies that what we consider right or our duty is what we do *directly*. It is this, e.g. the packing up and posting of the book, that derives its moral significance not from its own nature but from its consequences. But this is *not* what we should describe, strictly, as our duty; our duty is to fulfill our promise, i.e. to put the book into our friend's possession. This we consider obligatory in its own nature, just because it is a fulfilment of promise, and not because of *its* consequences. But, it might be replied by the utilitarian, I do not do this; I only do something that leads up to this, and what I do has no moral significance in itself but only because of its consequences. In answer to this, however, we may point out that a cause produces not only its immediate, but also its remote consequences, and the latter no less than the former. I, therefore, not only produce the immediate movements of parts of my body but also my friend's reception of the book, which results from these. Or, if this be objected to on the grounds that I can hardly be said to have produced my friend's reception of the book when I have packed and posted it, owing to the time that has still to elapse before he receives it, and that to say I have produced the result hardly does justice to the part played by the Post Office, we may at least say that I have *secured* my friend's reception of the book. What I do is as truly describable in this way as by saying that it is the packing and posting of a book. (It is equally truly describable in many other ways; e.g. I have provided a few moments' employment for Post Office officials. But this is irrelevant to the argument.) And if we ask ourselves whether it is *qua* the packing and posting of a book, or *qua* the securing of my friend's getting what I have promised to return to him, that my action is right, it is clear that it is in the second capacity that it is right; and in this capacity, the only capacity in which it is right, it is right by its own nature and not because of its consequences.

This account may no doubt be objected to, on the ground that we are ignoring the freedom of will of the other agents—the sorter and the postman, for instance—who are equally responsible for the result. Society, it may be said, is not like a machine, in which event follows event by rigorous necessity. Some one may, for instance, in the exercise of his freedom of will, steal the book on the way. But it is to be observed that I have excluded that case, and any similar case. I am dealing with the case in which I secure my friend's receiving the book; and if he does not receive it I have not secured his receiving it. If on the other hand the book reaches its destination, that alone shows that, the system of things being what it is, the trains by which the book travels and the railway lines along which it travels being such as they are and subject to the laws they are subject to, the postal officials who handle it being such as they are, having the motives they have and being subject to the psychological laws they are subject to, my posting the book was the one further thing which was sufficient to procure my friend's receiving it. If it had not been sufficient, the result would not have followed. The attainment of the result proves the sufficiency of the means. The objection in fact rests on the supposition that there can be unmotived action, i.e. an event without a cause, and may be refuted by reflection on the universality of the law of causation.

It is equally true that non-attainment of the result proves the insufficiency of the means. If the book had been destroyed in a railway accident or stolen by a dishonest postman, that would prove that my immediate act was not sufficient to produce the desired result. We get the curious consequence that however carelessly I pack or dispatch the book, if it comes to hand I have done my duty, and however carefully I have acted, if the book does not come to hand I have not done my duty. Success and failure are the only test, and a sufficient test, of the performance of duty. Of course, I should deserve more praise in the second case than in the first; but that is an entirely different question; we must not mix up the question of right and wrong with that of the morally good and the morally bad. And that our conclusion is not as strange as at first sight it might seem is shown by the fact that if the carelessly dispatched book comes to hand, it is not my duty to send another copy, while if the carefully dispatched book does not come to hand I must send another copy to replace it. In the first case I have not my duty still to do, which shows that I have done it; in the second I have it still to do, which shows that I have not done it.

We have reached the result that my act is right *qua* being an ensuring of one of the particular states of affairs of which it is an ensuring, viz., in the case we have taken, of my friend's receiving the book I have promised to return to him. But this answer requires some correction; for it refers only to the *prima facie* rightness of my act. If to be a fulfilment of promise were a sufficient ground of the rightness of an act, all fulfilments of promises would be right, whereas it seems clear that there are cases in which some other *prima facie* duty overrides the *prima facie* duty of fulfilling a promise. The more correct answer would be that the ground of the actual rightness of the act is that, of all acts possible for the agent in the circumstances, it is that whose *prima facie* rightness in the respects in which it is *prima facie* right most outweighs its *prima facie* wrongness in any respects in which it is *prima facie* wrong. But since its *prima facie* rightness is mainly due to its being a fulfilment of promise, we may call its being so the salient element in the ground of its rightness.

Subject to this qualification, then, it is as being the production (or if we prefer the word, the securing or ensuring) of the reception by my friend of what I have promised him (or in other words as the fulfilment of my promise) that my act is right. It is not right as a packing and posting of a book. The packing and posting of the book is only incidentally right, right only because it is a fulfilment of promise, which is what is directly or essentially right.

Our duty, then, is not to do certain things which will produce certain results. Our acts, at any rate our acts of special obligation, are not right because they will produce certain results—which is the view common to all forms of utilitarianism. To say that is to say that in the case in question what is essentially right is to pack and post a book, whereas what is essentially right is to secure the possession by my friend of what I have promised to return to him. An act is not right because it, being one thing, produces good results different from itself; it is right because it is itself the production of a certain state of affairs. Such production is right in itself, apart from any consequence.

But, it might be said, this analysis applies only to acts of special obligation; the utilitarian account still holds good for the acts in which we are not under a special obligation to any person or set of persons but only under that of augmenting the general good. Now merely to have established that there *are* special obligations to do certain things irrespective of their consequences would be already to have made a considerable breach in the utilitarian walls; for according to utilitarianism there is no such thing, there is only the single obligation to promote the general good. But, further, on reflection it is clear that just as (in the case we have taken) my act is not only the packing and posting of a book but the fulfilling of a promise, and just as it is in the latter capacity and not in the former that it is my duty, so an act whereby I augment the general good is not only, let us say, the writing of a begging letter on behalf of a hospital, but the producing (or ensuring) of whatever good ensues therefrom, and it is in the latter capacity and not in the former that it is right, if it *is* right. That which is right is right not because it is an act, one thing, which will produce another thing, an increase of the general welfare, but because it is itself the producing of an increase in the general welfare. Or, to qualify this in the necessary way, its being the production of an increase in the general welfare is the salient element in the ground of its rightness. Just as before we were led to recognize the *prima facie* rightness of the fulfilment of promises, we are now led to recognize the *prima facie* rightness of promoting the general welfare. In both cases we have to recognize the *intrinsic* rightness of a certain type of act, not depending on its consequences but on its own nature.

Part II

1931–1950

1936

A Critique of Ethics

A. J. Ayer

There is still one objection to be met before we can claim to have justified our view that all synthetic propositions are empirical hypotheses. This objection is based on the common supposition that our speculative knowledge is of two distinct kinds—that which relates to questions of empirical fact, and that which relates to questions of value. It will be said that "statements of value" are genuine synthetic propositions, but that they cannot with any show of justice be represented as hypotheses, which are used to predict the course of our sensations; and, accordingly, that the existence of ethics and æsthetics as branches of speculative knowledge presents an insuperable objection to our radical empiricist thesis.

In face of this objection, it is our business to give an account of "judgments of value" which is both satisfactory in itself and consistent with our general empiricist principles. We shall set ourselves to show that in so far as statements of value are significant, they are ordinary "scientific" statements; and that in so far as they are not scientific, they are not in the literal sense significant, but are simply expressions of emotion which can be neither true nor false. In maintaining this view, we may confine ourselves for the present to the case of ethical statements. What is said about them will be found to apply, *mutatis mutandis*, to the case of æsthetic statements also.

A. J. Ayer, "A Critique of Ethics" from LANGUAGE, TRUTH AND LOGIC (New York: Dover, 1952). Reprinted with the permission of the publishers.

The ordinary system of ethics, as elaborated in the works of ethical philosophers, is very far from being a homogeneous whole. Not only is it apt to contain pieces of metaphysics, and analyses of non-ethical concepts: its actual ethical contents are themselves of very different kinds. We may divide them, indeed, into four main classes. There are, first of all, propositions which express definitions of ethical terms, or judgments about the legitimacy or possibility of certain definitions. Secondly, there are propositions describing the phenomena of moral experience, and their causes. Thirdly, there are exhortations to moral virtue. And, lastly, there are actual ethical judgments. It is unfortunately the case that the distinction between these four classes, plain as it is, is commonly ignored by ethical philosophers; with the result that it is often very difficult to tell from their works what it is that they are seeking to discover or prove.

In fact, it is easy to see that only the first of our four classes, namely that which comprises the propositions relating to the definitions of ethical terms, can be said to constitute ethical philosophy. The propositions which describe the phenomena of moral experience, and their causes, must be assigned to the science of psychology, or sociology. The exhortations to moral virtue are not propositions at all, but ejaculations or commands which are designed to provoke the reader to action of a certain sort. Accordingly, they do not belong to any branch of philosophy or science. As for the expressions of ethical judgments, we have not yet determined how they should be classified. But inasmuch as they are certainly neither definitions nor comments upon definitions, nor quotations, we may say decisively that they do not belong to ethical philosophy. A strictly philosophical treatise on ethics should therefore make no ethical pronouncements. But it should, by giving an analysis of ethical terms, show what is the category to which all such pronouncements belong. And this is what we are now about to do.

A question which is often discussed by ethical philosophers is whether it is possible to find definitions which would reduce all ethical terms to one or two fundamental terms. But this question, though it undeniably belongs to ethical philosophy, is not relevant to our present enquiry. We are not now concerned to discover which term, within the sphere of ethical terms, is to be taken as fundamental; whether, for example, "good" can be defined in terms of "right" or "right" in terms of "good," or both in terms of "value." What we are interested in is the possibility of reducing the whole sphere of ethical terms to non-ethical terms. We are enquiring whether statements of ethical value can be translated into statements of empirical fact.

That they can be so translated is the contention of those ethical philosophers who are commonly called subjectivists, and of those who are known as utilitarians. For the utilitarian defines the rightness of actions, and the goodness of ends, in terms of the pleasure, or happiness, or satisfaction, to which they give rise; the subjectivist, in terms of the feelings of approval which a certain person, or group of people, has towards them. Each of these types of definition makes moral judgments into a sub-class of psychological or sociological judgments; and for this reason they are very attractive to us. For, if either was correct, it would follow that ethical assertions were not generically different from the factual assertions which are ordinarily contrasted with them; and the account which we have already given of empirical hypotheses would apply to them also.

Nevertheless we shall not adopt either a subjectivist or a utilitarian analysis of ethical terms. We reject the subjectivist view that to call an action right, or a thing good, is to say that it is generally approved of, because it is not self-contradictory to assert that some actions which are generally approved of are not right, or that some things which are generally approved of are not good. And we reject the alternative subjectivist view that a man who asserts that a certain action is right, or that a certain thing is good, is saying that he himself approves of it, on the ground that a man who confessed that he sometimes approved of what was bad or wrong would not be contradicting himself. And a similar argument is fatal to utilitarianism. We cannot agree that to call an action right is to say that of all the actions possible in the circumstances it would cause, or be likely to cause, the greatest happiness, or the greatest balance of pleasure over pain, or the greatest balance of satisfied over unsatisfied desire, because we find that it is not self-contradictory to say that it is sometimes wrong to perform the action which would actually or probably cause the greatest happiness, or the greatest balance of pleasure over pain, or of satisfied over unsatisfied desire. And since it is not self-contradictory to say that some pleasant things are not good, or that some bad things are desired, it cannot be the case that the sentence "*x* is good" is equivalent to "*x* is pleasant," or to "*x* is desired." And to every other variant of utilitarianism with which I am acquainted the same objection can be made. And therefore we should, I think, conclude that the validity of ethical judgments is not determined by the felicific tendencies of actions, any more than by the nature of people's feelings; but that it must be regarded as "absolute" or "intrinsic," and not empirically calculable.

If we say this, we are not, of course, denying that it is possible to invent a language in which all ethical symbols are definable in non-ethical terms, or even that it is desirable to invent such a language and adopt it in place of our own; what we are denying is that the suggested reduction of ethical to non-ethical statements is consistent with the conventions of our actual language. That is, we reject utilitarianism and subjectivism, not as proposals to replace our existing ethical notions by new ones, but as analyses of our existing ethical notions. Our contention is simply that, in our language, sentences which contain normative ethical symbols are not equivalent to sentences which express psychological propositions, or indeed empirical propositions of any kind.

It is advisable here to make it plain that it is only normative ethical symbols, and not descriptive ethical symbols, that are held by us to be indefinable in factual terms. There is a danger of confusing these two types of symbols, because they are commonly constituted by signs of the same sensible form. Thus a complex sign of the form "*x* is wrong" may constitute a sentence which expresses a moral judgment concerning a certain type of conduct, or it may constitute a sentence which states that a certain type of conduct is repugnant to the moral sense of a particular society. In the latter case, the symbol "wrong" is a descriptive ethical symbol, and the sentence in which it occurs expresses an ordinary sociological proposition; in the former case, the symbol "wrong" is a normative ethical symbol, and the sentence in which it occurs does not, we maintain, express an empirical proposition at all. It is only with normative ethics that we are at present concerned; so that whenever ethical symbols are used in the course of this argument without qualification, they are always to be interpreted as symbols of the normative type.

In admitting that normative ethical concepts are irreducible to empirical concepts, we seem to be leaving the way clear for the "absolutist" view of ethics—that is, the view that statements of value are not controlled by observation, as ordinary empirical propositions are, but only by a mysterious "intellectual intuition." A feature of this theory, which is seldom recognized by its advocates, is that it makes statements of value unverifiable. For it is notorious that what seems intuitively certain to one person may seem doubtful, or even false, to another. So that unless it is possible to provide some criterion by which one may decide between conflicting intuitions, a mere appeal to intuition is worthless as a test of a proposition's validity. But in the case of moral judgments, no such criterion can be given. Some moralists claim to settle the matter by saying that they "know" that their own moral judgments are correct. But such an assertion is of purely psychological interest, and has not the slightest tendency to prove the validity of any moral judgment. For dissentient moralists may equally well "know" that their ethical views are correct. And, as far as subjective certainty goes, there will be nothing to choose between them. When such differences of opinion arise in connection with an ordinary empirical proposition, one may attempt to resolve them by referring to, or actually carrying out, some relevant empirical test. But with regard to ethical statements, there is, on the "absolutist" or "intuitionist" theory, no relevant empirical test. We are therefore justified in saying that on this theory ethical statements are held to be unverifiable. They are, of course, also held to be genuine synthetic propositions.

Considering the use which we have made of the principle that a synthetic proposition is significant only if it is empirically verifiable, it is clear that the acceptance of an "absolutist" theory of ethics would undermine the whole of our main argument. And as we have already rejected the "naturalistic" theories which are commonly supposed to provide the only alternative to "absolutism" in ethics, we seem to have reached a difficult position. We shall meet the difficulty by showing that the correct treatment of ethical statements is afforded by a third theory, which is wholly compatible with our radical empiricism.

We begin by admitting that the fundamental ethical concepts are unanalyzable, inasmuch as there is no criterion by which one can test the validity of the judgments in which they occur. So far we are in agreement with the absolutists. But, unlike the absolutists, we are able to give an explanation of this fact about ethical concepts. We say that the reason why they are unanalyzable is that they are mere pseudo-concepts. The presence of an ethical symbol in a proposition adds nothing to its factual content. Thus if I say to someone, "You acted wrongly in stealing that money," I am not stating anything more than if I had simply said, "You stole that money." In adding that this action is wrong I am not making any further statement about it. I am simply evincing my moral disapproval of it. It is as if I had said, "You stole that money," in a peculiar tone of horror, or written it with the addition of some special exclamation marks. The tone, or the exclamation marks, adds nothing to the literal meaning of the sentence. It merely serves to show that the expression of it is attended by certain feelings in the speaker.

If now I generalize my previous statement and say, "Stealing money is wrong," I produce a sentence which has no factual meaning—that is, expresses no proposition which can be either true or false. It is as if I had written "Stealing money!!"—where the shape and thickness of the exclamation marks show, by a suitable convention, that a special sort of moral disapproval is the feeling which is being expressed. It is clear that there is nothing said here which can be true or false. Another man may disagree with me about the wrongness of stealing, in the sense that he may not have the same feelings about stealing as I have, and he may quarrel with me on account of my moral sentiments. But he cannot, strictly speaking, contradict me. For in saying that a certain type of action is right or wrong, I am not making any factual statement, not even a statement about my own state of mind. I am merely expressing certain moral sentiments. And the man who is ostensibly contradicting me is merely expressing his moral sentiments. So that there is plainly no sense in asking which of us is in the right. For neither of us is asserting a genuine proposition.

What we have just been saying about the symbol "wrong" applies to all normative ethical symbols. Sometimes they occur in sentences which record ordinary empirical facts besides expressing ethical feeling about those facts: sometimes they occur in sentences which simply express ethical feeling about a certain type of action, or situation, without making any statement of fact. But in every case in which one would commonly be said to be making an ethical judgment, the function of the relevant ethical word is purely "emotive." It is used to express feeling about certain objects, but not to make any assertion about them.

It is worth mentioning that ethical terms do not serve only to express feeling. They are calculated also to arouse feeling, and so to stimulate action. Indeed some of them are used in such a way as to give the sentences in which they occur the effect of commands. Thus the sentence "It is your duty to tell the truth" may be regarded both as the expression of a certain sort of ethical feeling about truthfulness and as the expression of the command "Tell the truth." The sentence "You ought to tell the truth" also involves the command "Tell the truth," but here the tone of the command is less emphatic. In the sentence "It is good to tell the truth" the command has become little more than a suggestion. And thus the "meaning" of the word "good," in its ethical usage, is differentiated from that of the word "duty" or the word "ought." In fact we may define the meaning of the various ethical words in terms both of the different feelings they are ordinarily taken to express, and also the different responses which they are calculated to provoke.

We can now see why it is impossible to find a criterion for determining the validity of ethical judgments. It is not because they have an "absolute" validity which is mysteriously independent of ordinary sense-experience, but because they have no objective validity whatsoever. If a sentence makes no statement at all, there is obviously no sense in asking whether what it says is true or false. And we have seen that sentences which simply express moral judgments do not say anything. They are pure expressions of feeling and as such do not come under the category of truth and falsehood. They are unverifiable for the same reason as a cry of pain or a word of command is unverifiable—because they do not express genuine propositions.

Thus, although our theory of ethics might fairly be said to be radically subjectivist, it differs in a very important respect from the orthodox subjectivist theory. For the orthodox subjectivist does not deny, as we do, that the sentences of a moralizer express genuine propositions. All he denies is that they express propositions of a unique non-empirical character. His own view is that they express propositions about the speaker's feelings. If this were so, ethical judgments clearly would be capable of being true or false. They would be true if the speaker had the relevant feelings, and false if he had not. And this is a matter which is, in principle, empirically verifiable. Furthermore they could be significantly contradicted. For if I say, "Tolerance is a virtue," and someone answers, "You don't approve of it," he would, on the ordinary subjectivist theory, be contradicting me. On our theory, he would not be contradicting me, because, in saying that tolerance was a virtue, I should not be making any statement about my own feelings or about anything else. I should simply be evincing my feelings, which is not at all the same thing as saying that I have them.

The distinction between the expression of feeling and the assertion of feeling is complicated by the fact that the assertion that one has a certain feeling often accompanies the expression of that feeling, and is then, indeed, a factor in the expression of that feeling. Thus I may simultaneously express boredom and say that I am bored, and in that case my utterance of the words, "I am bored," is one of the circumstances which make it true to say that I am expressing or evincing boredom. But I can express boredom without actually saying that I am bored. I can express it by my tone and gestures, while making a statement about something wholly unconnected with it, or by an ejaculation, or without uttering any words at all. So that even if the assertion that one has a certain feeling always involves the expression of that feeling, the expression of a feeling assuredly does not always involve the assertion that one has it. And this is the important point to grasp in considering the distinction between our theory and the ordinary subjectivist theory. For whereas the subjectivist holds that ethical statements actually assert the existence of certain feelings, we hold that ethical statements are expressions and excitants of feeling which do not necessarily involve any assertions.

We have already remarked that the main objection to the ordinary subjectivist theory is that the validity of ethical judgments is not determined by the nature of their author's feelings. And this is an objection which our theory escapes. For it does not imply that the existence of any feelings is a necessary and sufficient condition of the validity of an ethical judgment. It implies, on the contrary, that ethical judgments have no validity.

There is, however, a celebrated argument against subjectivist theories which our theory does not escape. It has been pointed out by Moore that if ethical statements were simply statements about the speaker's feelings, it would be impossible to argue about questions of value.[1] To take a typical example: if a man said that thrift was a virtue, and another replied that it was a vice, they would not, on this theory, be disputing with one another. One would be saying that he approved of thrift, and the other that *he* didn't; and there is no reason why both these statements should not be true. Now Moore held it to be obvious that we do dispute about questions of value, and accordingly concluded that the particular form of subjectivism which he was discussing was false.

It is plain that the conclusion that it is impossible to dispute about questions of value follows from our theory also. For as we hold that such sentences as "Thrift is a virtue" and "Thrift is a vice" do not express propositions at all, we clearly cannot hold that they express incompatible propositions. We must therefore admit that if Moore's argument really refutes the ordinary subjectivist theory, it also refutes ours. But, in fact, we deny that it does refute even the ordinary subjectivist theory. For we hold that one really never does dispute about questions of value.

This may seem, at first sight, to be a very paradoxical assertion. For we certainly do engage in disputes which are ordinarily regarded as disputes about questions of value. But, in all such cases, we find, if we consider the matter closely, that the dispute is not really about a question of value, but about a question of fact. When someone disagrees with us about the moral value of a certain action or type of action, we do admittedly resort to argument in order to win him over to our way of thinking. But we do not attempt to show by our arguments that he has the "wrong" ethical feeling towards a situation whose nature he has correctly apprehended. What we attempt to show is that he is mistaken about the facts of the case. We argue that he has misconceived the agent's motive: or that he has misjudged the effects of the action, or its probable effects in view of the agent's knowledge; or that he has failed to take into account the special circumstances in which the agent was placed. Or else we employ more general arguments about the effects which actions of a certain type tend to produce, or the qualities which are usually manifested in their performance. We do this in the hope that we have only to get our opponent to agree with us about the nature of the empirical facts for him to adopt the same moral attitude towards them as we do. And as the people with whom we argue have generally received the same moral education as ourselves, and live in the same social order, our expectation is usually justified. But if our opponent happens to have undergone a different process of moral "conditioning" from ourselves, so that, even when he acknowledges all the facts, he still disagrees with us about the moral value of the actions under discussion, then we abandon the attempt to convince him by argument. We say that it is impossible to argue with him because he has a distorted or undeveloped moral sense; which signifies merely that he employs a different set of val-

[1]cf. *Philosophical Studies*, "The Nature of Moral Philosophy."

ues from our own. We feel that our own system of values is superior, and therefore speak in such derogatory terms of his. But we cannot bring forward any arguments to show that our system is superior. For our judgment that it is so is itself a judgment of value, and accordingly outside the scope of argument. It is because argument fails us when we come to deal with pure questions of value, as distinct from questions of fact, that we finally resort to mere abuse.

In short, we find that argument is possible on moral questions only if some system of values is presupposed. If our opponent concurs with us in expressing moral disapproval of all actions of a given type *t*, then we may get him to condemn a particular action A, by bringing forward arguments to show that A is of type *t*. For the question whether A does or does not belong to that type is a plain question of fact. Given that a man has certain moral principles, we argue that he must, in order to be consistent, react morally to certain things in a certain way. What we do not and cannot argue about is the validity of these moral principles. We merely praise or condemn them in the light of our own feelings.

If anyone doubts the accuracy of this account of moral disputes, let him try to construct even an imaginary argument on a question of value which does not reduce itself to an argument about a question of logic or about an empirical matter of fact. I am confident that he will not succeed in producing a single example. And if that is the case, he must allow that its involving the impossibility of purely ethical arguments is not, as Moore thought, a ground of objection to our theory, but rather a point in favor of it.

Having upheld our theory against the only criticism which appeared to threaten it, we may now use it to define the nature of all ethical enquiries. We find that ethical philosophy consists simply in saying that ethical concepts are pseudo-concepts and therefore unanalyzable. The further task of describing the different feelings that the different ethical terms are used to express, and the different reactions that they customarily provoke, is a task for the psychologist. There cannot be such a thing as ethical science, if by ethical science one means the elaboration of a "true" system of morals. For we have seen that, as ethical judgments are mere expressions of feeling, there can be no way of determining the validity of any ethical system, and, indeed, no sense in asking whether any such system is true. All that one may legitimately enquire in this connection is, What are the moral habits of a given person or group of people, and what causes them to have precisely those habits and feelings? And this enquiry falls wholly within the scope of the existing social sciences.

It appears, then, that ethics, as a branch of knowledge, is nothing more than a department of psychology and sociology. And in case anyone thinks that we are overlooking the existence of casuistry, we may remark that casuistry is not a science, but is a purely analytical investigation of the structure of a given moral system. In other words, it is an exercise in formal logic.

When one comes to pursue the psychological enquiries which constitute ethical science, one is immediately enabled to account for the Kantian and hedonistic theories of morals. For one finds that one of the chief causes of moral behavior is fear, both conscious and unconscious, of a god's displeasure, and fear of the enmity of society. And this, indeed, is the reason why moral precepts present themselves to some people as "categorical" commands. And one finds, also, that the moral code of a society is partly determined by the beliefs of that society concerning the conditions of its own happiness—or, in other words, that a society tends to encourage or discourage a given type of conduct by the use of moral sanctions according as it appears to promote or detract from the contentment of the society as a whole. And this is the reason why altruism is recommended in most moral codes and egotism condemned. It is from the observation of this connection between morality and happiness that hedonistic or eudæmonistic theories of morals ultimately spring, just as the moral theory of Kant is based on the fact, previously explained, that moral precepts have for some people the force of inexorable commands. As each of these theories ignores the fact which lies at the root of the other, both may be criticized as being one-sided; but this is not the main objection to either of them. Their essential defect is that they treat propositions which refer to the causes and attributes of our ethical feelings as if they were definitions of ethical concepts. And thus they fail to recognize that ethical concepts are pseudo-concepts and consequently indefinable. . . .

1937

The Emotive Meaning of Ethical Terms

C. L. Stevenson

1

Ethical questions first arise in the form "is so and so good?" or "is this alternative better than that?" These questions are difficult partly because we don't quite know what we are seeking. We are asking, "is there a needle in the haystack?" without even knowing just what a needle is. So the first thing to do is to examine the questions themselves. We must try to make them clearer, either by defining the terms in which they are expressed or by any other method that is available.

The present essay is concerned wholly with this preliminary step of making ethical questions clear. In order to help answer the question "is X good?" we must *substitute* for it a question that is free from ambiguity and confusion.

It is obvious that in substituting a clearer question we must not introduce some utterly different kind of question. It won't do (to take an extreme instance of a prevalent fallacy) to substitute for "is X good?" the question "is X pink with yellow trimmings?" and then point out how easy the question really is. This would beg the original question, not help answer it. On the other hand, we must not expect the substituted question to be strictly "identical" with the original one. The original question may embody hypostati-

C. L. Stevenson, "The Emotive Meaning of Ethical Terms," *Mind* 46 (1937). Reprinted with the permission of Oxford University Press.

zation, anthropomorphism, vagueness, and all the other ills to which our ordinary discourse is subject. If our substituted question is to be clearer it must remove these ills. The questions will be identical only in the sense that a child is identical with the man he later becomes. Hence we must not demand that the substitution strike us, on immediate introspection, as making no change in meaning.

Just how, then, must the substituted question be related to the original? Let us assume (inaccurately) that it must result from replacing "good" by some set of terms that define it. The question then resolves itself to this: How must the defined meaning of "good" be related to its original meaning?

I answer that it must be *relevant.* A defined meaning will be called "relevant" to the original meaning under these circumstances: Those who have understood the definition must be able to say all that they then want to say by using the term in the defined way. They must never have occasion to use the term in the old, unclear sense. (If a person did have to go on using the word in the old sense, then to this extent his meaning would not be clarified and the philosophical task would not be completed.) It frequently happens that a word is used so confusedly and ambiguously that we must give it *several* defined meanings, rather than one. In this case only the whole set of defined meanings will be called "relevant," and any one of them will be called "partially relevant." This is not a rigorous treatment of *relevance,* by any means, but it will serve for the present purposes.

Let us now turn to our particular task—that of giving a relevant definition of "good." Let us first examine some of the ways in which others have attempted to do this.

The word "good" has often been defined in terms of *approval,* or similar psychological attitudes. We may take as typical examples: "good" means *desired by me* (Hobbes); and "good" means *approved by most people* (Hume, in effect).[1] It will be convenient to refer to definitions of this sort as "interest theories," following R. B. Perry, although neither "interest" nor "theory" is used in the most usual way.[2]

Are definitions of this sort relevant?

It is idle to deny their *partial relevance.* The most superficial inquiry will reveal that "good" is exceedingly ambiguous. To maintain that "good" is *never* used in Hobbes' sense, and never in Hume's, is only to manifest an insensitivity to the complexities of language. We must recognize, perhaps, not only these senses, but a variety of similar ones, differing both with regard to the kind of interest in question and with regard to the people who are said to have the interest.

But that is a minor matter. The essential question is not whether interest theories are *partially* relevant, but whether they are *wholly* relevant. This is the only point for intelligent dispute. Briefly: Granted that some senses of "good" may relevantly be defined in terms of interest, is there some *other* sense which is *not* relevantly so defined? We must give this question careful attention. For it is quite possible that when philosophers (and many others) have found the question "is X good?" so difficult, they have been grasping for this *other* sense of "good" and not any sense relevantly defined in terms of interest. If we insist on defining "good" in terms of interest, and answer the question when thus interpreted, we may be begging *their* question

[1]The definition ascribed to Hume is oversimplified, but not, I think, in a way that weakens the force of the observations that I am about to make. Perhaps the same should be said of Hobbes.

A more accurate account of Hume's Ethics is given in *Ethics and Language* (New Haven, 1944), pp. 273–76.

[2]In *General Theory of Value* (New York, 1926) Perry used "interest" to refer to any sort of favoring or disfavoring, or any sort of disposition to be for or against something. And he used "theory" where he might, alternatively, have used "proposed definition," or "proposed analysis of a common sense meaning." . . .

entirely. Of course this *other* sense of "good" may not exist, or it may be a complete confusion; but that is what we must discover.

Now many have maintained that interest theories are *far* from being completely relevant. They have argued that such theories neglect the very sense of "good" that is most typical of ethics. And certainly, their arguments are not without plausibility.

Only—what *is* this typical sense of "good"? The answers have been so vague and so beset with difficulties that one can scarcely determine.

There are certain requirements, however, with which the typical sense has been expected to comply—requirements which appeal strongly to our common sense. It will be helpful to summarize these, showing how they exclude the interest theories:

In the first place, we must be able sensibly to *disagree* about whether something is "good." This condition rules out Hobbes' definition. For consider the following argument: "This is good." "That isn't so; it's not good." As translated by Hobbes, this becomes: "I desire this." "That isn't so, for *I* don't." The speakers are not contradicting one another, and think they are only because of an elementary confusion in the use of pronouns. The definition, "good" means *desired by my community,* is also excluded, for how could people from different communities disagree?[3]

In the second place, "goodness" must have, so to speak, a magnetism. A person who recognizes X to be "good" must ipso facto acquire a stronger tendency to act in its favor than he otherwise would have had. This rules out the Humian type of definition. For according to Hume, to recognize that something is "good" is simply to recognize that the majority approve of it. Clearly, a man may see that the majority approve of X without having, himself, a stronger tendency to favor it. This requirement excludes any attempt to define "good" in terms of the interest of people *other* than the speaker.[4]

In the third place, the "goodness" of anything must not be verifiable solely by use of the scientific method. "Ethics must not be psychology." This restriction rules out all of the traditional interest theories without exception. It is so sweeping a restriction that we must examine its plausibility. What are the methodological implications of interest theories which are here rejected?

According to Hobbes' definition a person can prove his ethical judgments with finality by showing that he is not making an introspective error about his desires. According to Hume's definition one may prove ethical judgments (roughly speaking) by taking a vote. *This* use of the empirical method, at any rate, seems highly remote from what we usually accept as proof and reflects on the complete relevance of the definitions that imply it.

But are there not more complicated interest theories that are immune from such methodological implications? No, for the same factors appear; they are only put off for a while. Consider, for example, the definition: "X is good" means *most people would approve of* X *if they knew its nature and consequences.* How, according to this definition, could we prove that a certain X was good? We should first have to find out, empirically, just what X was like and what its consequences would be. To this extent the empirical method as required by the definition seems beyond intelligent objection. But what remains? We should next have to discover whether most people would approve of the sort of thing we had discovered X to be. This could not be determined by popular vote—but only because it would be too difficult to explain to the voters, beforehand, what the nature and consequences of X really were. Apart from this, voting would be a pertinent method. We are again reduced to counting noses as a *perfectly final* appeal.

[3]See G. E. Moore, *Philosophical Studies* (New York, 1922), pp. 332–34.

[4]See G. C. Field, *Moral Theory* (London, 1921) pp. 52, 56–57.

Now we need not scorn voting entirely. A man who rejected interest theories as irrelevant might readily make the following statement: "If I believed that X would be approved by the majority, when they knew all about it, I should be strongly *led* to say that X was good." But he would continue: "*Need* I say that X was good, under the circumstances? Wouldn't my acceptance of the alleged 'final proof' result simply from my being democratic? What about the more aristocratic people? They would simply say that the approval of most people, even when they knew all about the object of their approval, simply had nothing to do with the goodness of anything, and they would probably add a few remarks about the low state of people's interests." It would indeed seem, from these considerations, that the definition we have been considering has presupposed democratic ideals from the start; it has dressed up democratic propaganda in the guise of a definition.

The omnipotence of the empirical method, as implied by interest theories and others, may be shown unacceptable in a somewhat different way. G. E. Moore's familiar objection about the open question is chiefly pertinent in this regard. No matter what set of scientifically knowable properties a thing may have (says Moore, in effect), you will find, on careful introspection, that it is an open question to ask whether anything having these properties is *good.* It is difficult to believe that this recurrent question is a totally confused one, or that it seems open only because of the ambiguity of "good." Rather, we must be using some sense of "good" which is not definable, relevantly, in terms of anything scientifically knowable. That is, the scientific method is not sufficient for ethics.[5]

These, then, are the requirements with which the "typical" sense of "good" is expected to comply: (1) goodness must be a topic for intelligent disagreement; (2) it must be "magnetic"; and (3) it must not be discoverable solely through the scientific method.

2

I can now turn to my proposed analysis of ethical judgments. First let me present my position dogmatically, showing to what extent I vary from tradition.

I believe that the three requirements given above are perfectly sensible, that there is some *one* sense of "good" which satisfies all three requirements, and that no traditional interest theory satisfies them all. But this does not imply that "good" must be explained in terms of a Platonic Idea, or of a categorical imperative, or of a unique, unanalyzable property. On the contrary, the three requirements can be met by a *kind* of interest theory. *But we must give up a presupposition that all the traditional interest theories have made.*

Traditional interest theories hold that ethical statements are *descriptive* of the existing state of interests—that they simply *give information* about interests. (More accurately, ethical judgments are said to describe what the state of interests is, was, or will be, or to indicate what the state of interests *would* be under specified circumstances.) It is this emphasis on description, on information, which leads to their incomplete relevance. Doubtless there is always *some* element of description in ethical judgments, but this is by no means all. Their major use is not to indicate facts but to *create an influence.* Instead of merely describing people's interests they *change* or *intensify* them. They *recommend* an interest in an object, rather than state that the interest already exists.

[5]See G. E. Moore, *Principia Ethica* (Cambridge, 1903), ch. 1. I am simply trying to preserve the spirit of Moore's objection and not the exact form of it.

For instance: When you tell a man that he ought not to steal, your object is not merely to let him know that people disapprove of stealing. You are attempting, rather, to get *him* to disapprove of it. Your ethical judgment has a quasi-imperative force which, operating through suggestion and intensified by your tone of voice, readily permits you to begin to *influence,* to *modify,* his interests. If in the end you do not succeed in getting *him* to disapprove of stealing, you will feel that you have failed to convince him that stealing is wrong. You will continue to feel this, even though he fully acknowledges that you disapprove of it and that almost everyone else does. When you point out to him the consequences of his actions—consequences which you suspect he already disapproves of—these *reasons* which support your ethical judgment are simply a means of facilitating your influence. If you think you can change his interests by making vivid to him how others will disapprove of him, you will do so, otherwise not. So the consideration about other people's interest is just an additional means you may employ in order to move him and is not a part of the ethical judgment itself. Your ethical judgment does not merely describe interests to him, it directs his very interests. The difference between the traditional interest theories and my view is like the difference between describing a desert and irrigating it.

Another example: A munitions maker declares that war is a good thing. If he merely meant that he approved of it, he would not have to insist so strongly nor grow so excited in his argument. People would be quite easily convinced that he approved of it. If he merely meant that most people approved of war, or that most people would approve of it if they knew the consequences, he would have to yield his point if it were proved that his was not so. But he would not do this, nor does consistency require it. He is not *describing* the state of people's approval; he is trying to *change* it by his influence. If he found that few people approved of war, he might insist all the more strongly that it was good, for there would be more changing to be done.

This example illustrates how "good" may be used for what most of us would call bad purposes. Such cases are as pertinent as any others. I am not indicating the *good* way of using "good." I am not influencing people but am describing the way this influence sometimes goes on. If the reader wishes to say that the munitions maker's influence is bad—that is, if the reader wishes to awaken people's disapproval of the man, and to make him disapprove of his own actions—I should at another time be willing to join in this undertaking. But this is not the present concern. I am not using ethical terms but am indicating how they *are* used. The munitions maker, in his use of "good," illustrates the persuasive character of the word just as well as does the unselfish man who, eager to encourage in each of us a desire for the happiness of all, contends that the supreme good is peace.

Thus ethical terms are *instruments* used in the complicated interplay and readjustment of human interests. This can be seen plainly from more general observations. People from widely separated communities have different moral attitudes. Why? To a great extent because they have been subject to different social influences. Now clearly this influence does not operate through sticks and stones alone; words play a great part. People praise one another to encourage certain inclinations and blame one another to discourage others. Those of forceful personalities issue commands which weaker people, for complicated instinctive reasons, find it difficult to disobey, quite apart from fears of consequences. Further influence is brought to bear by writers and orators. Thus social influence is exerted, to an enormous extent, by means that have nothing to do with physical force or material reward. The ethical terms facilitate such influence. Being suited for use in *suggestion,* they are a means by which men's attitudes may be led this way or that. The reason, then, that we find a greater similarity in the moral attitudes of one community than in those of different communities is largely this: ethical judgments propagate themselves. One man says "this is good"; this may influence the approval of another person, who then makes the same ethical judgment, which in turn influences another person, and so on. In the end, by a process of mutual influence, people take up more or less the same attitudes. Between people of widely separated communities, of course, the influence is less strong; hence different communities have different attitudes.

These remarks will serve to give a general idea of my point of view. We must now go into more detail. There are several questions which must be answered: How does an ethical sentence acquire its power of influencing people—why is it suited to suggestion? Again, what has this influence to do with the *meaning* of ethical terms? And finally, do these considerations really lead us to a sense of "good" which meets the requirements mentioned in the preceding section?

Let us deal first with the question about *meaning*. This is far from an easy question, so we must enter into a preliminary inquiry about meaning in general. Although a seeming digression this will prove indispensable.

3

Broadly speaking, there are two different *purposes* which lead us to use language. On the one hand we use words (as in science) to record, clarify, and communicate *beliefs*. On the other hand we use words to give vent to our feelings (interjections), or to create moods (poetry), or to incite people to actions or attitudes (oratory).

The first use of words I shall call "descriptive," the second, "dynamic." Note that the distinction depends solely upon the *purpose* of the *speaker*.

When a person says "hydrogen is the lightest known gas," his purpose *may* be simply to lead the hearer to believe this, or to believe that the speaker believes it. In that case the words are used descriptively. When a person cuts himself and says "damn," his purpose is not ordinarily to record, clarify, or communicate any belief. The word is used dynamically. The two ways of using words, however, are by no means mutually exclusive. This is obvious from the fact that our purposes are often complex. Thus when one says "I want you to close the door," part of his purpose, ordinarily, is to lead the hearer to believe that he has this want. To that extent the words are used descriptively. But the major part of one's purpose is to lead the hearer to *satisfy* the want. To that extent the words are used dynamically.

It very frequently happens that the same sentence may have a dynamic use on one occasion and not on another, and that it may have different dynamic uses on different occasions. For instance: A man says to a visiting neighbor, "I am loaded down with work." His purpose may be to let the neighbor know how life is going with him. This would *not* be a dynamic use of words. He may make the remark, however, in order to drop a hint. This *would* be dynamic usage (as well as descriptive). Again, he may make the remark to arouse the neighbor's sympathy. This would be a *different* dynamic usage from that of hinting.

Or again, when we say to a man, "of course you won't make those mistakes any more," we *may* simply be making a prediction. But we are more likely to be using "suggestion," in order to encourage him and hence *keep* him from making mistakes. The first use would be descriptive, the second, mainly dynamic.

From these examples it will be clear that we can not determine whether words are used dynamically or not merely by reading the dictionary—even assuming that everyone is faithful to dictionary meanings. Indeed, to know whether a person is using a word dynamically we must note his tone of voice, his gestures, the general circumstances under which he is speaking, and so on.

We must now proceed to an important question: What has the dynamic use of words to do with their *meaning?* One thing is clear—we must not define "meaning" in a way that would make meaning vary with dynamic usage. If we did, we should have no use for the term. All that we could say about such "meaning" would be that it is very complicated and subject to constant change. So we must certainly distinguish between the dynamic use of words and their meaning.

It does not follow, however, that we must define "meaning" in some nonpsychological fashion. We must simply restrict the psychological field. Instead of identifying meaning with *all* the psychological causes and effects that attend a word's utterance, we must identify it with those that it has a *tendency* (causal property, dispositional property) to be connected with. The tendency must be of a particular kind, moreover. It must exist for all who speak the language; it must be persistent and must be realizable more or less independently of determinate circumstances attending the word's utterance. There will be further restrictions dealing with the interrelations of word in different contexts. Moreover, we must include, under the psychological responses which the words tend to produce, not only immediately introspectable experiences but *dispositions* to react in a given way with appropriate stimuli. I hope to go into these matters in a subsequent essay.[6] Suffice it now to say that I think "meaning" may be thus defined in a way to include "propositional" meaning as an important kind.

The definition will readily permit a distinction between meaning and dynamic use. For when words are accompanied by dynamic purposes, it does not follow that they *tend* to be accompanied by them in the way mentioned above. E.g. there need be no tendency realizable more or less independently of the determinate circumstances under which the words are uttered.

There will be a kind of meaning, however, in the sense above defined, which has an intimate relation to dynamic usage. I refer to "emotive" meaning (in a sense roughly like that employed by Ogden and Richards).[7] The emotive meaning of a word is a tendency of a word, arising through the history of its usage, to produce (result from) *affec-*

[6]The "subsequent essay" became, instead, Chapter 3 of *Ethics and Language,* which among other points defends those that follow:

(1) When used in a generic sense that emphasizes what C. W. Morris calls the *pragmatic* aspects of language, the term "meaning" designates a tendency of words to express or evoke states of mind in the people who use the words. The tendency is of a special kind, however, and many qualifications are needed (including some that bear on syntax) to specify its nature.

(2) When the states of mind in question are cognitive, the meaning can conveniently be called *descriptive;* and when they are feelings, emotions, or attitudes, the meanings can conveniently be called *emotive.*

(3) The states of mind (in a rough and tentative sense of that term) are normally quite complicated. They are not necessarily images or feelings but may in their turn be further tendencies—tendencies to respond to various stimuli that may subsequently arise. A word may have a constant meaning, accordingly, even though it is accompanied, at various times that it is used, by different images or feelings.

(4) Emotive meaning is sometimes more than a by-product of descriptive meaning. When a term has both sorts of meaning, for example, a change in its descriptive meaning may not be attended by a change in emotive meaning.

(5) When a speaker's use of emotive terms evokes an attitude in a hearer (as it sometimes may not, since it has only a *tendency* to do so), it must not be conceived as merely adding to the hearer's attitude in the way that a spark might add its heat to the atmosphere. For a more appropriate analogy, in many cases, we must think rather of a spark that ignites tinder.

[7]See C. K. Ogden and I. A. Richards, *The Meaning of Meaning* (2nd ed. London, 1927). On p. 125 there is a passage on ethics which is the source of the ideas embodied in this essay.

tive responses in people. It is the immediate aura of feeling which hovers about a word.[8] Such tendencies to produce affective responses cling to words very tenaciously. It would be difficult, for instance, to express merriment by using the interjection "alas." Because of the persistence of such affective tendencies (among other reasons) it becomes feasible to classify them as "meanings."

Just *what* is the relation between emotive meaning and the dynamic use of words? Let us take an example. Suppose that a man tells his hostess, at the end of a party, that he thoroughly enjoyed himself, and suppose that he was in fact bored. If we consider his remark an innocent one, are we likely to remind him, later, that he "lied" to his hostess? Obviously not, or at least, not without a broad smile; for although he told her something that he believed to be false, and with the intent of making her believe that it was true—those being the ordinary earmarks of a lie—the expression, "you lied to her," would be emotively too strong for our purposes. It would seem to be a reproach, even if we intended it not to be a reproach. So it will be evident that such words as "lied" (and many parallel examples could be cited) become suited, on account of their emotive meaning, to a certain kind of dynamic use—so well suited, in fact, that the hearer is likely to be misled when we use them in any other way. The more pronounced a word's emotive meaning is, the less likely people are to use it purely descriptively. Some words are suited to encourage people, some to discourage them, some to quiet them, and so on.

Even in these cases, of course, the dynamic purposes are not to be identified with any sort of meaning; for the emotive meaning accompanies a word much more persistently than do the dynamic purposes. But there is an important contingent relation between emotive meaning and dynamic purpose: the former assists the latter. Hence if we define emotively laden terms in a way that neglects their emotive meaning, we become seriously confused. *We lead people to think that the terms defined are used dynamically less often than they are.*

4

Let us now apply these remarks in defining "good." This word may be used morally or nonmorally. I shall deal with the nonmoral usage almost entirely, but only because it is simpler. The main points of the analysis will apply equally well to either usage.

As a preliminary definition let us take an inaccurate approximation. It may be more misleading than helpful but will do to begin with. Roughly, then, the sentence "X is good" means *we like* X. ("We" includes the hearer or hearers.)

At first glance this definition sounds absurd. If used, we should expect to find the following sort of conversation: A. "This is good." B. "But I *don't* like it. What led you to believe that I did?" The unnaturalness of B's reply, judged by ordinary word usage, would seem to cast doubt on the relevance of my definition.

[8] In *Ethics and Language* the phrase "aura of feeling" was expressly repudiated. If the present essay had been more successful in anticipating the analysis given in that later work, it would have introduced the notion of emotive meaning in some such way as this:

The emotive meaning of a word or phrase is a strong and persistent tendency, built up in the course of linguistic history, to give direct expression (quasi-interjectionally) to certain of the speaker's feelings or emotions or attitudes; and it is also a tendency to evoke (quasi-imperatively) corresponding feelings, emotions, or attitudes in those to whom the speaker's remarks are addressed. It is the emotive meaning of a word, accordingly, that leads us to characterize it as *laudatory* or *derogatory*—that rather generic characterization being of particular importance when we are dealing with terms like "good" and "bad" or "right and wrong." But emotive meanings are of great variety: they may yield terms that express or evoke horror, amazement, sadness, sympathy, and so on.

B's unnaturalness, however, lies simply in this: he is assuming that "we like it" (as would occur implicitly in the use of "good") is being used descriptively. This will not do. When "we like it" is to take the place of "this is good," the former sentence must be used not purely descriptively, but dynamically. More specifically, it must be used to promote a very subtle (and for the nonmoral sense in question, a very easily resisted) kind of *suggestion.* To the extent that "we" refers to the hearer it must have the dynamic use, essential to suggestion, of leading the hearer to *make* true what is said, rather than merely to believe it. And to the extent that "we" refers to the speaker, the sentence must have not only the descriptive use of indicating belief about the speaker's interest, but the quasi-interjectory, dynamic function of giving direct expression to the interest. (This immediate expression of feelings assists in the process of suggestion. It is difficult to disapprove in the face of another's enthusiasm.)

For an example of a case where "we like this" is used in the dynamic way that "this is good" is used, consider the case of a mother who says to her several children, "one thing is certain, *we all like to be neat.*" If she really believed this, she would not bother to say so. But she is not using the words descriptively. She is *encouraging* the children to like neatness. By telling them that they like neatness, she will lead them to *make* her statement true, so to speak. If, instead of saying "we all like to be neat" in this way, she had said "it's a good thing to be neat," the effect would have been approximately the same.

But these remarks are still misleading. Even when "we like it" is used for suggestion, it is not quite like "this is good." The latter is more subtle. With such a sentence as "this is a good book," for example, it would be practically impossible to use instead "we like this book." When the latter is used it must be accompanied by so exaggerated an intonation, to prevent its becoming confused with a descriptive statement, that the force of suggestion becomes stronger and ludicrously more overt than when "good" is used.

The definition is inadequate, further, in that the definiens has been restricted to dynamic usage. Having said that dynamic usage was different from meaning, I should not have to mention it in giving the *meaning* of "good."

It is in connection with this last point that we must return to emotive meaning. The word "good" has a laudatory emotive meaning that fits it for the dynamic use of suggesting favorable interest. But the sentence "we like it" has no such emotive meaning. Hence my definition has neglected emotive meaning entirely. Now to neglect emotive meaning serves to foster serious confusions, as I have previously intimated; so I have sought to make up for the inadequacy of the definition by letting the restriction about dynamic usage take the place of emotive meaning. What I should do, of course, is to find a definiens whose emotive meaning, like that of "good," simply does *lead* to dynamic usage.

Why did I not do this? I answer that it is not possible if the definition is to afford us increased clarity. No two words, in the first place, have quite the same emotive meaning. The most we can hope for is a rough approximation. But if we seek for such an approximation for "good," we shall find nothing more than synonyms, such as "desirable" or "valuable"; and these are profitless because they do not clear up the connection between "good" and favorable interest. If we reject such synonyms, in favor of nonethical terms, we shall be highly misleading. For instance "this is good" has something like the meaning of "I *do* like this; do so as well." But this is certainly not accurate. For the imperative makes an appeal to the conscious efforts of the hearer. Of course he cannot like something just by trying. He must be led to like it through suggestion. Hence an ethical sentence differs from an imperative in that it enables one to make changes in a much more subtle, less fully conscious way. Note that the ethical sentence centers the hearer's attention not on his interests but on the object of interest, and thereby facilitates suggestion. Because of its subtlety, moreover, an ethical sentence readily permits counter-suggestion and leads to the give and take situation that is so characteristic of arguments about values.

Strictly speaking, then, it is impossible to define "good" in terms of favorable interest if emotive meaning is not to be distorted. Yet it is possible to say that "this is good" is *about* the favorable interest of the speaker and the hearer or hearers, and that it has a laudatory emotive meaning which fits the words for use in suggestion. This is a rough description of meaning, not a definition. But it serves the same clarifying function that a definition ordinarily does, and that, after all, is enough.

A word must be added about the moral use of "good." This differs from the above in that it is about a different kind of interest. Instead of being about what the hearer and speaker *like,* it is about a stronger sort of approval. When a person *likes* something, he is pleased when it prospers and disappointed when it does not. When a person *morally approves* of something he experiences a rich feeling of security when it prospers and is indignant or "shocked" when it does not. These are rough and inaccurate examples of the many factors which one would have to mention in distinguishing the two kinds of interest. In the moral usage, as well as in the nonmoral, "good" has an emotive meaning which adapts it to suggestion.

And now, are these considerations of any importance? Why do I stress emotive meanings in this fashion? Does the omission of them really lead people into errors? I think, indeed, that the errors resulting from such omissions are enormous. In order to see this, however, we must return to the restrictions, mentioned in Section I, with which the typical sense of "good" has been expected to comply.

5

The first restriction, it will be remembered, had to do with disagreement. Now there is clearly some sense in which people disagree on ethical points, but we must not rashly assume that all disagreement is modeled after the sort that occurs in the natural sciences. We must distinguish between "disagreement in belief" (typical of the sciences) and "disagreement in interest." Disagreement in belief occurs when A believes *p* and B disbelieves it. Disagreement in interest occurs when A has a favorable interest in X and when B has an unfavorable one in it. (For a full-bodied disagreement, neither party is content with the discrepancy.)

Let me give an example of disagreement in interest. A. "Let's go to a cinema tonight." B. "I don't want to do that. Let's go to the symphony." A continues to insist on the cinema, B on the symphony. This is disagreement in a perfectly conventional sense. They cannot agree on where they want to go, and each is trying to redirect the other's interest. (Note that imperatives are used in the example.)

It is disagreement in *interest* which takes places in ethics. When C says "this is good," and D says "no, it's bad," we have a case of suggestion and counter-suggestion. Each man is trying to redirect the other's interest. There obviously need be no domineering, since each may be willing to give ear to the other's influence; but each is trying to move the other none the less. It is in this sense that they disagree. Those who argue that certain interest theories make no provision for disagreement have been misled, I believe, simply because the traditional theories, in leaving out emotive meaning, give the impression that ethical judgments are used descriptively only; and of course when judgments are used purely descriptively, the only disagreement that can arise is disagreement *in belief.* Such disagreement may be disagreement in belief *about* interests, but this is not the same as disagreement *in* interest. My definition does not provide for disagreement in belief about interests any more than does Hobbes'; but that is no matter, for there is no reason to believe, at least on common sense grounds, that this kind of disagreement exists. There is only disagreement *in* interest. (We shall see in a moment that disagreement in interest does not remove ethics from sober argument—that this kind of disagreement may often be resolved through empirical means.)

The second restriction, about "magnetism," or the connection between goodness and actions, requires only a word. This rules out only those interest theories that do *not* include the interest of the speaker in defining "good." My account does include the speaker's interest, hence is immune.

The third restriction, about the empirical method, may be met in a way that springs naturally from the above account of disagreement. Let us put the question in this way: When two people disagree over an ethical matter, can they completely resolve the disagreement through empirical considerations, assuming that each applies the empirical method exhaustively, consistently, and without error?

I answer that sometimes they can and sometimes they cannot, and that at any rate, even when they can, the relation between empirical knowledge and ethical judgments is quite different from the one that traditional interest theories seem to imply.

This can best be seen from an analogy. Let us return to the example where A and B could not agree on a cinema or a symphony. The example differed from an ethical argument in that imperatives were used, rather than ethical judgments, but was analogous to the extent that each person was endeavoring to modify the other's interest. Now how would these people argue the case, assuming that they were too intelligent just to shout at one another?

Clearly, they would give "reasons" to support their imperatives. A might say, "but you know, Garbo is at the Bijou." His hope is that B, who admires Garbo, will acquire a desire to go to the cinema when he knows what film will be there. B may counter, "but Toscanini is guest conductor tonight, in an all-Beethoven program." And so on. Each supports his imperative ("*let's* do so and so") by reasons which may be empirically established.

To generalize from this: disagreement in interest may be rooted in disagreement in belief. That is to say, people who disagree in interest would often cease to do so if they knew the precise nature and consequences of the object of their interest. To this extent disagreement in interest may be resolved by securing agreement in belief, which in turn may be secured empirically.

This generalization holds for ethics. If A and B, instead of using imperatives, had said, respectively, "it would be *better* to go to the cinema," and "it would be better to go to the symphony," the reasons which they would advance would be roughly the same. They would each give a more thorough account of the object of interest, with the purpose of completing the redirection of interest which was begun by the suggestive force of the ethical sentence. On the whole, of course, the suggestive force of the ethical statement merely exerts enough pressure to start such trains of reasons, since the reasons are much more essential in resolving disagreement in interest than the persuasive effect of the ethical judgment itself.

Thus the empirical method is relevant to ethics simply because our knowledge of the world is a determining factor to our interests. But note that empirical facts are not inductive grounds from which the ethical judgment problematically follows. (This is what traditional interest theories imply.) If someone said "close the door," and added the reason "we'll catch cold," the latter would scarcely be called an inductive ground of the former. Now imperatives are related to the reasons which support them in the same way that ethical judgments are related to reasons.

Is the empirical method *sufficient* for attaining ethical agreement? Clearly not. For empirical knowledge resolves disagreement in interest only to the extent that such disagreement is rooted in disagreement in belief. Not all disagreement in interest is of this sort. For instance: A is of a sympathetic nature and B is not. They are arguing about whether a public dole would be good. Suppose that they discovered all the consequences of the dole. Is it not possible, even so, that A will say that it is good and B that it is bad? The disagreement in interest may arise not from limited factual knowledge but simply from A's sympathy and B's coldness. Or again, suppose in the above argument that A was poor and unemployed and that B was rich. Here again the disagreement might not be due to different factual knowledge. It would be due to the different social positions of the men, together with their predominant self-interest.

When ethical disagreement is not rooted in disagreement in belief, is there *any* method by which it may be settled? If one means by "method" a *rational* method, then there is no method. But in any case there is a "way." Let us consider the above example again, where disagreement was due to A's sympathy and B's coldness. Must they end by saying, "well, it's just a matter of our having different temperaments"? Not necessarily. A, for instance, may try to *change* the temperament of his opponent. He may pour out his enthusiasms in such a moving way—present the sufferings of the poor with such appeal—that he will lead his opponent to see life through different eyes. He may build up by the contagion of his feelings an influence which will modify B's temperament and create in him a sympathy for the poor which did not previously exist. This is often the only way to obtain ethical agreement, if there is any way at all. It is persuasive, not empirical or rational; but that is no reason for neglecting it. There is no reason to scorn it, either, for it is only by such means that our personalities are able to grow, through our contact with others.

The point I wish to stress, however, is simply that the empirical method is instrumental to ethical agreement only to the extent that disagreement in interest is rooted in disagreement in belief. There is little reason to believe that all disagreements is of this sort. Hence the empirical method is not sufficient for ethics. In any case, ethics is not psychology, since psychology does not endeavour to *direct* our interests; it discovers facts about the ways in which interests are or can be directed, but that is quite another matter.

To summarize this section: my analysis of ethical judgments meets the three requirements for the typical sense of "good" that were mentioned in Section I. The traditional interest theories fail to meet these requirements simply because they neglect emotive meaning. This neglect leads them to neglect dynamic usage, and the sort of disagreement that results from such usage, together with the method of resolving the disagreement. I may add that my analysis answers Moore's objection about the open question. Whatever scientifically knowable properties a thing may have, it *is* always open to question whether a thing having these (enumerated) qualities is good. For to ask whether it is good is to ask for *influence*. And whatever I may know about an object, I can still ask, quite pertinently, to be influenced with regard to my interest in it.

6

And now, have I really pointed out the "typical" sense of "good"?

I suppose that many will still say "no," claiming that I have simply failed to set down *enough* requirements that this sense must meet, and that my analysis, like all others given in terms of interest, is a way of begging the issue. They will say: "When we ask 'is X good?' we don't want mere influence, mere advice. We decidedly don't want to be influenced through persuasion, nor are we fully content when the influence is supported by a wide scientific knowledge of X. The answer to our question will, of course, modify our interests. But this is only because a unique sort of truth will be revealed to us—a truth that must be apprehended a priori. We want our interests to be guided by this truth and by nothing else. To substitute for this special truth mere emotive meaning and mere factual truth is to conceal from us the very object of our search."

I can only answer that I do not understand. What is this truth to be *about?* For I recollect no Platonic Idea, nor do I know what to *try* to recollect. I find no indefinable property nor do I know what to look for. And the "self-evident" deliverances of reason, which so many philosophers have mentioned, seem on examination to be deliverances of their respective reasons only (if of anyone's) and not of mine.

I strongly suspect, indeed, that any sense of "good" which is expected both to unite itself in synthetic a priori fashion with other concepts and to influence interests as well, is really a great confusion. I extract from this meaning the power of influence alone, which I find the only intelligible part. If the rest is confusion, however, then it certainly deserves more than the shrug of one's shoulders. What I should like to do is to *account* for the confusion—to examine the psychological needs which have given rise to it and show how these needs may be satisfied in another way. This is *the* problem, if confusion is to be stopped at its source. But it is an enormous problem and my reflections on it, which are at present worked out only roughly, must be reserved until some later time.

I may add that if "X is good" has the meaning that I ascribe to it, then it is not a judgment that professional philosophers and only professional philosophers are qualified to make. To the extent that ethics predicates the ethical terms of anything, rather that explains their meaning, it becomes more than a purely intellectual study. Ethical judgments are social instruments. They are used in a cooperative enterprise that leads to a mutual readjustment of human interests. Philosophers have a part in this; but so too do all men.

1939

The Naturalistic Fallacy

W. K. Frankena

The future historian of "thought and expression" in the twentieth century will no doubt record with some amusement the ingenious trick, which some of the philosophical controversialists of the first quarter of our century had, of labelling their opponents' views "fallacies." He may even list some of these alleged fallacies for a certain sonority which their inventors embodied in their titles: the fallacy of initial predication, the fallacy of simple location, the fallacy of misplaced concreteness, the naturalistic fallacy.

Of these fallacies, real or supposed, perhaps the most famous is the naturalistic fallacy. For the practitioners of a certain kind of ethical theory, which is dominant in England and capably represented in America, and which is variously called objectivism, non-naturalism, or intuitionism, have frequently charged their opponents with committing the naturalistic fallacy. Some of these opponents have strongly repudiated the charge of fallacy, others have at least commented on it in passing, and altogether the notion of a naturalistic fallacy has had a considerable currency in ethical literature. Yet, in spite of its repute, the naturalistic fallacy has never been discussed at any length, and, for this reason, I have elected to make a study of it in this paper. I hope incidentally to clarify certain confusions which have been made in connection with the naturalistic fallacy, but my main interest is to free the controversy between

W. K. Frankena, "The Naturalistic Fallacy," *Mind* 48 (1939). Reprinted with the permission of Oxford University Press.

the intuitionists and their opponents of the notion of a logical or quasi-logical fallacy, and to indicate where the issue really lies.

The prominence of the concept of a naturalistic fallacy in recent moral philosophy is another testimony to the great influence of the Cambridge philosopher, Mr. G. E. Moore, and his book, *Principia Ethica.* Thus Mr. Taylor speaks of the "vulgar mistake" which Mr. Moore has taught us to call "the naturalistic fallacy,"[1] and Mr. G. S. Jury, as if to illustrate how well we have learned this lesson, says, with reference to naturalistic definitions of value, "All such definitions stand charged with Dr. Moore's 'naturalistic fallacy.'"[2] Now, Mr. Moore coined the notion of the naturalistic fallacy in his polemic against naturalistic and metaphysical systems of ethics. "The naturalistic fallacy is a fallacy," he writes, and it "must not be committed." All naturalistic and metaphysical theories of ethics, however, "are *based* on the naturalistic fallacy, in the sense that the commission of this fallacy has been the main cause of their wide acceptance."[3] The best way to dispose of them, then, is to expose this fallacy. Yet it is not entirely clear just what is the status of the naturalistic fallacy in the polemics of the intuitionists against other theories. Sometimes it is used as a weapon, as when Miss Clarke says that if we call a thing good simply because it is liked we are guilty of the naturalistic fallacy.[4] Indeed, it presents this aspect to the reader in many parts of *Principia Ethica* itself. Now, in taking it as a weapon, the intuitionists use the naturalistic fallacy as if it were a logical fallacy on all fours with the fallacy of composition, the revelation of which disposes of naturalistic and metaphysical ethics and leaves intuitionism standing triumphant. That is, it is taken as a fallacy in advance, for use in controversy. But there are signs in *Principia Ethica* which indicate that the naturalistic fallacy has a rather different place in the intuitionist scheme, and should not be used as a weapon at all. In this aspect, the naturalistic fallacy must be proved to be a fallacy. It cannot be used to settle the controversy, but can only be asserted to be a fallacy when the smoke of battle has cleared. Consider the following passages: (*a*) "the naturalistic fallacy consists in the contention that good *means* nothing but some simple or complex notion, that can be defined in terms of natural qualities"; (*b*) "the point that good is indefinable and that to deny this involves a fallacy, is a point capable of strict proof."[5] These passages seem to imply that the fallaciousness of the naturalistic fallacy is just what is at issue in the controversy between the intuitionists and their opponents, and cannot be wielded as a weapon in that controversy. One of the points I wish to make in this paper is that the charge of committing the naturalistic fallacy can be made, if at all, only as a conclusion from the discussion and not as an instrument of deciding it.

The notion of a naturalistic fallacy has been connected with the notion of a bifurcation between the "ought" and the "is," between value and fact, between the normative and the descriptive. Thus Mr. D. C. Williams says that some moralists have thought it appropriate to chastise as the naturalistic fallacy the attempt to derive the Ought from the Is.[6] We may begin, then, by considering this bifurcation, emphasis on which, by Sidgwick, Sorley, and others, came largely as a reaction to the procedures of Mill and Spencer. Hume affirms the bifurcation in his *Treatise:* "I cannot forbear adding to these reasonings an observation, which may, perhaps, be found of some importance. In every

[1] A. E. Taylor, *The Faith of a Moralist,* vol. i, p. 104 n.

[2] *Value and Ethical Objectivity,* p. 58.

[3] *Principia Ethica,* pp. 38, 64.

[4] M. E. Clarke, "Cognition and Affection in the Experience of Value," *Journal of Philosophy* (1938).

[5] *Principia Ethica,* pp. 73, 77. See also p. xix.

[6] "Ethics as Pure Postulate." *Philosophical Review* (1933). See also T. Whittaker. *The Theory of Abstract Ethics,* pp. 19 f.

system of morality which I have hitherto met with, I have always remarked, that the author proceeds for some time in the ordinary way of reasoning, and establishes the being of a God, or makes observations concerning human affairs; when of a sudden I am surprised to find, that instead of the usual copulations of propositions, *is,* and *is not,* I meet with no proposition that is not connected with an *ought,* or an *ought not.* This change is imperceptible; but is, however, of the last consequence. For as this *ought,* or *ought not,* expresses some new relation or affirmation, it is necessary that it should be observed and explained; and at the same time that a reason should be given, for what seems altogether inconceivable, how this new relation can be a deduction from others, which are entirely different from it. But as authors do not commonly use this precaution, I shall presume to recommend it to the readers; and am persuaded, that this small attention would subvert all the vulgar systems of morality, and let us see that the distinction of vice and virtue is not founded merely on the relations of objects, nor is perceived by reason."[7]

Needless to say, the intuitionists *have* found this observation of some importance.[8] They agree with Hume that it subverts all the vulgar systems of morality, though, of course, they deny that it lets us see that the distinction of virtue and vice is not founded on the relations of objects, nor is perceived by reason. In fact, they hold that a small attention to it subverts Hume's own system also, since this gives naturalistic definitions of virtue and vice and of good and evil.[9]

Hume's point is that ethical conclusions cannot be drawn validly from premises which are non-ethical. But when the intuitionists affirm the bifurcation of the "ought" and the "is," they mean more than that ethical propositions cannot be deduced from non-ethical ones. For this difficulty in the vulgar systems of morality could be remedied, as we shall see, by the introduction of definitions of ethical notions in non-ethical terms. They mean, further, that such definitions of ethical notions in non-ethical terms are impossible. "The essential point," says Mr. Laird, "is the irreducibility of values to non-values."[10] But they mean still more. Yellow and pleasantness are, according to Mr. Moore, indefinable in non-ethical terms, but they are natural qualities and belong on the "is" side of the fence. Ethical properties, however, are not, for him, mere indefinable natural qualities, descriptive or expository. They are properties of a different *kind*—non-descriptive or non-natural.[11] The intuitionist bifurcation consists of three statements:—

1. Ethical propositions are not deducible from non-ethical ones.[12]
2. Ethical characteristics are not definable in terms of non-ethical ones.
3. Ethical characteristics are different in kind from non-ethical ones.

Really it consists of but one statement, namely, (3), since (3) entails (2) and (2) entails (1). It does not involve saying that any ethical characteristics are absolutely indefinable. That is another question, although this is not always noticed.

What, now, has the naturalistic fallacy to do with the bifurcation of the "ought" and the "is"? To begin with, the connection is this: many naturalistic and metaphysical moralists proceed as if ethical conclusions can be deduced from premises all of which

[7]Book III, part ii, section i.
[8]See J. Laird, *A Study in Moral Theory,* pp. 16 f.; Whittaker, op. cit., p. 19.
[9]See C. D. Broad, *Five Types of Ethical Theory,* ch. iv.
[10]*A Study in Moral Theory,* p. 94 n.
[11]See *Philosophical Studies,* pp. 259, 273 f.
[12]See J. Laird, op. cit., p. 318. Also pp. 12 ff.

are non-ethical, the classical examples being Mill and Spencer. That is, they violate (1). This procedure has lately been referred to as the "factualist fallacy" by Mr. Wheelwright and as the "valuational fallacy" by Mr. Wood.[13] Mr. Moore sometimes seems to identify it with the naturalistic fallacy, but in the main he holds only that it involves, implies, or rests upon this fallacy.[14] We may now consider the charge that the procedure in question is or involves a fallacy.

It may be noted at once that, even if the deduction of ethical conclusions from non-ethical premises is in no way a fallacy, Mill certainly did commit a fallacy in drawing an analogy between visibility and desirability in his argument for hedonism; and perhaps his committing *this* fallacy, which, as Mr. Broad has said, we all learn about at our mothers' knees, is chiefly responsible for the notion of a naturalistic *fallacy*. But is it a fallacy to deduce ethical conclusions from non-ethical premises? Consider the Epicurean argument for hedonism which Mill so unwisely sought to embellish: pleasure is good, since it is sought by all men. Here an ethical conclusion is being derived from a non-ethical premise. And, indeed, the argument, taken strictly as it stands, *is* fallacious. But it is not fallacious because an *ethical* term occurs in the conclusion which does not occur in the premise. It is fallacious because any argument of the form "A is B, therefore A is C" is invalid, if taken strictly as it stands. For example, it is invalid to argue that Crœsus is rich because he is wealthy. Such arguments are, however, not intended to be taken strictly as they stand. They are enthymemes and contain a suppressed premise. And, when this suppressed premise is made explicit, they are valid and involve no logical fallacy.[15] Thus the Epicurean inference from psychological to ethical hedonism is valid when the suppressed premise is added to the effect that what is sought by all men is good. Then the only question left is whether the premises are true.

It is clear, then, that the naturalistic fallacy is not a logical fallacy, since it may be involved even when the argument is valid. How does the naturalistic fallacy enter such 'mixed ethical arguments'[16] as that of the Epicureans? Whether it does or not depends on the nature of the suppressed premise. This may be either an induction, an intuition, a deduction from a "pure ethical argument," a definition, or a proposition which is true by definition. If it is one of the first three, then the naturalistic fallacy does not enter at all. In fact, the argument does not then involve violating (1), since one of its premises will be ethical. But if the premise to be supplied is a definition or a proposition which is true by definition, as it probably was for the Epicureans, then the argument, while still valid, involves the naturalistic fallacy, and will run as follows:—

a. Pleasure is sought by all men.
b. What is sought by all men is good (by definition).
c. Therefore, pleasure is good.

Now I am not greatly interested in deciding whether the argument as here set up violates (1). If it does not, then no "mixed ethical argument" actually commits any factualist or valuational fallacy, except when it is unfairly taken as complete in its en-

[13] P. E. Wheelwright, *A Critical Introduction to Ethics*, pp. 40–51, 91 f.; L. Wood, "Cognition and Moral Value," *Journal of Philosophy*, (1937), p. 237.

[14] See *Principia Ethica*, pp. 114, 57, 43, 49. Whittaker identifies it with the naturalistic fallacy and regards it as a "logical" fallacy, op. cit., pp. 19 f.

[15] See ibid., pp. 50, 139; Wheelwright, loc. cit.

[16] See C. D. Broad, *The Mind and its Place in Nature*, pp. 488 f.; Laird, loc. cit.

thymematic form. If it does, then a valid argument may involve the deduction of an ethical conclusion from non-ethical premises and the factualist or valuational fallacy is not really a fallacy. The question depends on whether or not (*b*) and (*c*) are to be regarded as ethical propositions. Mr. Moore refuses so to regard them, contending that, by hypothesis, (*b*) is analytic or tautologous, and that (*c*) is psychological, since it really says only that pleasure is sought by all men.[17] But to say that (*b*) is analytic and not ethical and that (*c*) is not ethical but psychological is to prejudge the question whether "good" can be defined; for the Epicureans would contend precisely that if their definition is correct then (*b*) is ethical but analytic and (*c*) ethical though psychological. Thus, unless the question of the definability of goodness is to be begged, (*b*) and (*c*) must be regarded as ethical, in which case our argument does not violate (1). However, suppose, if it be not nonsense, that (*b*) is non-ethical and (*c*) ethical, then the argument will violate (1), but it will still obey all of the canons of logic, and it is only confusing to talk of a "valuational logic" whose basic rule is that an evaluative conclusion cannot be deduced from non-evaluative premises.[18]

For the only way in which either the intuitionists or postulationists like Mr. Wood can cast doubt upon the conclusion of the argument of the Epicureans (or upon the conclusion of any parallel argument) is to attack the premises, in particular (*b*). Now, according to Mr. Moore, it is due to the presence of (*b*) that the argument involves the naturalistic fallacy. (*b*) involves the identification of goodness with "being sought by all men," and to make this or any other such identification is to commit the naturalistic fallacy. The naturalistic fallacy is not the procedure of violating (1). It is the procedure, implied in many mixed ethical arguments and explicitly carried out apart from such arguments by many moralists, of defining such characteristics as goodness or of substituting some other characteristic for them. To quote some passages from *Principia Ethica:*—

(*a*) ". . . far too many philosophers have thought that when they named those other properties [belonging to all things which are good] they were actually defining good; that these properties, in fact, were simply not 'other,' but absolutely and entirely the same with goodness. This view I propose to call the 'naturalistic fallacy'. . . ."[19]

(*b*) "I have thus appropriated the name Naturalism to a particular method of approaching Ethics. . . . This method consists in substituting for 'good' some one property of a natural object or of a collection of natural objects. . . ."[20]

(*c*) ". . . the naturalistic fallacy [is] the fallacy which consists in identifying the simple notion which we mean by 'good' with some other notion."[21]

Thus, to identify "better" and "more evolved," "good" and "desired," etc., is to commit the naturalistic fallacy.[22] But just why is such a procedure fallacious or erroneous? And is it a fallacy only when applied to good? We must now study Section 12 of *Principia Ethica.* Here Mr. Moore makes some interesting statements:—

". . . if anybody tried to define pleasure for us as being any other natural object; if anybody were to say, for instance that pleasure *means* the sensation of red. . . . Well, that would be the same fallacy which I have called the naturalistic fallacy. . . . I should not indeed call that a naturalistic fallacy, although it is the same fallacy as I

[17]See op. cit., pp. 11 f.; 19, 38, 73, 139.
[18]See L. Wood, loc. cit.
[19]p. 10.
[20]p. 40.
[21]p. 58, cf. pp. xiii, 73.
[22]Cf. pp. 49, 53, 108, 139.

have called naturalistic with reference to Ethics. . . . When a man confuses two natural objects with one another, defining the one by the other. . . . then there is no reason to call the fallacy naturalistic. But if he confuses 'good,' which is not . . . a natural object, with any natural object whatever, then there is a reason for calling that a naturalistic fallacy. . . ."[23]

Here Mr. Moore should have added that, when one confuses "good," which is not a metaphysical object or quality, with any metaphysical object or quality, as metaphysical moralists do, according to him, then the fallacy should be called the metaphysical fallacy. Instead he calls it a naturalistic fallacy in this case too, though he recognizes that the case is different since metaphysical properties are non-natural[24]—a procedure which has misled many readers of *Principia Ethica.* For example, it has led Mr. Broad to speak of "theological naturalism."[25]

To resume: "Even if [goodness] were a natural object, that would not alter the nature of the fallacy nor diminish its importance one whit."[26]

From these passages it is clear that the fallaciousness of the procedure which Mr. Moore calls the naturalistic fallacy is not due to the fact that it is applied to good or to an ethical or non-natural characteristic. When Mr. R. B. Perry defines "good" as "being an object of interest" the trouble is not merely that he is defining *good.* Nor is the trouble that he is defining an *ethical* characteristic in terms of *non-ethical* ones. Nor is the trouble that he is regarding a *non-natural* characteristic as a *natural* one. The trouble is more generic than that. For clarity's sake I shall speak of the definist fallacy as the generic fallacy which underlies the naturalistic fallacy. The naturalistic fallacy will then, by the above passages, be a species or form of the definist fallacy, as would the metaphysical fallacy if Mr. Moore had given that a separate name.[27] That is, the naturalistic fallacy, as illustrated by Mr. Perry's procedure, is a fallacy, not because it is naturalistic or confuses a non-natural quality with a natural one, but solely because it involves the definist fallacy. We may, then, confine our attention entirely to an understanding and evaluation of the definist fallacy.

To judge by the passages I have just quoted, the definist fallacy is the process of confusing or identifying two properties, of defining one property by another, or of substituting one property for another. Furthermore, the fallacy is always simply that two properties are being treated as one, and it is irrelevant, if it be the case, that one of them is natural or non-ethical and the other non-natural or ethical. One may commit the definist fallacy without infringing on the bifurcation of the ethical and the non-ethical, as when one identifies pleasantness and redness or rightness and goodness. But even when one infringes on that bifurcation in committing the definist fallacy, as when one identifies goodness and pleasantness or goodness and satisfaction, then the *mistake* is still not that the bifurcation is being infringed on, but only that two properties are being treated as one. Hence, on the present interpretation, the definist *fallacy* does not, in any of its forms, consist in violating (3), and has no essential connection with the bifurcation of the "ought" and the "is."

This formulation of the definist fallacy explains or reflects the motto of *Principia Ethica,* borrowed from Bishop Butler: "Everything is what it is, and not another thing." It follows from this motto that goodness is what it is and not another thing. It follows

[23]p. 13.
[24]See pp. 38–40, 110–112.
[25]*Five Types of Ethical Theory,* p. 259.
[26]p. 14.
[27]As Whittaker has, loc. cit.

that views which try to identify it with something else are making a mistake of an elementary sort. For it *is* a mistake to confuse or identify two properties. If the properties really are two, then they simply are not identical. But do those who define ethical notions in non-ethical terms make this mistake? They will reply to Mr. Moore that they are not identifying two properties; what they are saying is that two words or sets of words stand for or mean one and the same property. Mr. Moore was being, in part, misled by the material mode of speech, as Mr. Carnap calls it, in such sentences as "Goodness is pleasantness," "Knowledge is true belief," etc. When one says instead, "The word 'good' and the word 'pleasant' mean the same thing," etc., it is clear that one is not identifying two things. But Mr. Moore kept himself from seeing this by his disclaimer that he was interested in any statement about the use of words.[28]

The definist fallacy, then, as we have stated it, does not rule out any naturalistic or metaphysical definitions of ethical terms. Goodness is not identifiable with any "other" characteristic (if it is a characteristic at all). But the question is: *which* characteristics are other than goodness, which names stand for characteristics other than goodness? And it is begging the question of the definability of goodness to say out of hand that Mr. Perry, for instance, is identifying goodness with something else. The point is that goodness is what it is, even if it is definable. That is why Mr. Perry can take as the motto of his naturalistic *Moral Economy* another sentence from Bishop Butler: "Things and actions are what they are, and the consequences of them will be what they will be: why then should we desire to be deceived?" The motto of *Principia Ethica* is a tautology, and should be expanded as follows: Everything is what it is, and not another thing, unless it is another thing, and even then it is what it is.

On the other hand, if Mr. Moore's motto (or the definist fallacy) rules out any definitions, for example of "good," then it rules out all definitions of any term whatever. To be effective at all, it must be understood to mean, "Every term means what it means, and not what is meant by any other term." Mr. Moore seems implicitly to understand his motto in this way in Section 13, for he proceeds as if "good" has no meaning, if it has no unique meaning. If the motto be taken in this way, it will follow that "good" is an indefinable term, since no synonyms can be found. But it will also follow that no term is definable. And then the method of analysis is as useless as an English butcher in a world without sheep.

Perhaps we have misinterpreted the definist fallacy. And, indeed, some of the passages which I quoted earlier in this paper seem to imply that the definist fallacy is just the error of defining an indefinable characteristic. On this interpretation, again, the definist fallacy has, in all of its forms, no essential connection with the bifurcation of the ethical and the non-ethical. Again, one may commit the definist fallacy without violating that bifurcation, as when one defines pleasantness in terms of redness or goodness in terms of rightness (granted Mr. Moore's belief that pleasantness and goodness are indefinable). But even when one infringes on that bifurcation and defines goodness in terms of desire, the *mistake* is not that one is infringing on the bifurcation by violating (3), but only that one is defining an indefinable characteristic. This is possible because the proposition that goodness is indefinable is logically independent of the proposition that goodness is non-natural: as is shown by the fact that a characteristic may be indefinable and yet natural, as yellowness is; or non-natural and yet definable, as rightness is (granted Mr. Moore's views about yellowness and rightness).

[28]See op. cit., pp. 6, 8, 12.

Consider the definist fallacy as we have just stated it. It is, of course, an error to define an indefinable quality. But the question, again, is: which qualities are indefinable? It is begging the question in favor of intuitionism to say in advance that the quality goodness is indefinable and that, therefore, all naturalists commit the definist fallacy. One must know that goodness is indefinable before one can argue that the definist fallacy *is* a fallacy. Then, however, the definist fallacy can enter only at the end of the controversy between intuitionism and definism, and cannot be used as a weapon in the controversy.

The definist fallacy may be stated in such a way as to involve the bifurcation between the "ought" and the "is."[29] It would then be committed by anyone who offered a definition of any ethical characteristic in terms of non-ethical ones. The trouble with such a definition, on this interpretation, would be that an *ethical* characteristic is being reduced to a *non-ethical* one, a *non-natural* one to a *natural* one. That is, the definition would be ruled out by the fact that the characteristic being defined is ethical or non-natural and therefore cannot be defined in non-ethical or natural terms. But on this interpretation, too, there is danger of a *petitio* in the intuitionist argumentation. To assume that the ethical characteristic is exclusively ethical is to beg precisely the question which is at issue when the definition is offered. Thus, again, one must know that the characteristic is non-natural and indefinable in natural terms before one can say that the definists are making a mistake.

Mr. Moore, McTaggart, and others formulate the naturalistic fallacy sometimes in a way somewhat different from any of those yet discussed. They say that the definists are confusing a universal synthetic proposition about *the good* with a definition of *goodness*.[30] Mr. Abraham calls this the "fallacy of misconstrued proposition."[31] Here again the difficulty is that, while it is true that it is an error to construe a universal synthetic proposition as a definition, it is a *petitio* for the intuitionists to say that what the definist is taking for a definition is really a universal synthetic proposition.[32]

At last, however, the issue between the intuitionists and the definists (naturalistic or metaphysical) is becoming clearer. The definists are all holding that certain propositions involving ethical terms are analytic, tautologous, or true by definition, e.g., Mr. Perry so regards the statement, "All objects of desire are good." The intuitionists hold that such statements are synthetic. What underlies this difference of opinion is that the intuitionists claim to have at least a dim awareness of a simple unique quality or relation of goodness or rightness which appears in the region which our ethical terms roughly indicate, whereas the definists claim to have no awareness of any such quality or relation in that region, which is different from all other qualities and relations which belong to the same context but are designated by words other than "good" and "right" and their obvious synonyms.[33] The definists are in all honesty claiming to find but one characteristic where the intuitionists claim to find two, as Mr. Perry claims to find only the property of being desired where Mr. Moore claims to find both it and the property of being good. The issue, then, is one of inspection or intuition, and concerns the awareness or discernment of qualities and relations.[34] That is why it cannot be decided by the use of the notion of a fallacy.

If the definists may be taken at their word, then they are not actually confusing two characteristics with each other, nor defining an indefinable characteristic, not con-

[29]See J. Wisdom, *Mind* (1931), p. 213, note 1.

[30]See *Principia Ethica*, pp. 10, 16, 38; *The Nature of Existence*, vol. ii, p. 398.

[31]Leo Abraham, "The Logic of Intuitionism," *International Journal of Ethics*, (1933).

[32]As Mr. Abraham points out, loc. cit.

[33]See R. B. Perry, *General Theory of Value*, p. 30; cf.; *Journal of Philosophy*, (1931), p. 520.

[34]See H. Osborne, *Foundations of the Philosophy of Value*, pp. 15, 19, 70.

fusing definitions and universal synthetic propositions—in short they are not committing the naturalistic or definist fallacy in any of the interpretations given above. Then the only fallacy which they commit—the real naturalistic or definist fallacy—is the failure to descry the qualities and relations which are central to morality. But this is neither a logical fallacy nor a logical confusion. It is not even, properly speaking, an error. It is rather a kind of blindness, analogous to color-blindness. Even this moral blindness can be ascribed to the definists only if they are correct in their claim to have no awareness of any unique ethical characteristics and if the intuitionists are correct in affirming the existence of such characteristics, but certainly to call it a "fallacy," even in a loose sense, is both unamiable and profitless.

On the other hand, of course, if there are no such characteristics in the objects to which we attach ethical predicates, then the intuitionists, if we may take them at their word, are suffering from a corresponding moral hallucination. Definists might then call this the intuitionistic or moralistic fallacy, except that it is no more a "fallacy" than is the blindness just described. Anyway, they do not believe the claim of the intuitionists to be aware of unique ethical characteristics, and consequently do not attribute to them this hallucination. Instead, they simply deny that the intuitionists really do find such unique qualities or relations, and then they try to find some plausible way of accounting for the fact that very respectable and trustworthy people think they find them.[35] Thus they charge the intuitionists with verbalism, hypostatization, and the like. But this half of the story does not concern us now.

What concerns us more is the fact that the intuitionists do not credit the claim of the definists either. They would be much disturbed, if they really thought that their opponents were morally blind, for they do not hold that we must be regenerated by grace before we can have moral insight, and they share the common feeling that morality is something democratic even though not all men are good. Thus they hold that "we are all aware" of certain unique characteristics when we use the terms "good," "right," etc., only due to a lack of analytic clearness of mind, abetted perhaps by a philosophical prejudice, we may not be aware at all that they are different from other characteristics of which we are also aware.[36] Now, I have been arguing that the intuitionists cannot charge the definists with committing any fallacy unless and until they have shown that we are all, the definists included, aware of the disputed unique characteristics. If, however, they were to show this, then, at least at the end of the controversy, they could accuse the definists of the error of confusing two characteristics, or of the error of defining an indefinable one, and these errors might, since the term is somewhat loose in its habits, be called "fallacies," though they are not logical fallacies in the sense in which an invalid argument is. The fallacy of misconstrued proposition depends on the error of confusing two characteristics, and hence could also on our present supposition, be ascribed to the definists, but it is not really a *logical* confusion,[37] since it does not actually involve being confused about the difference between a proposition and a definition.

Only it is difficult to see how the intuitionists can prove that the definists are at least vaguely aware of the requisite unique characteristics.[38] The question must surely be left to the inspection or intuition of the definists themselves, aided by whatever suggestions the intuitionists may have to make. If so, we must credit the verdict of their inspection, espe-

[35]Cf. R. B. Perry, *Journal of Philosophy,* (1931), pp. 520 ff.

[36]*Principia Ethica,* pp. 17, 38, 59, 61.

[37]But see H. Osborne, op. cit., pp. 18 f.

[38]For a brief discussion of their arguments, see ibid., p. 67; L. Abraham, op. cit. I think they are all inconclusive, but cannot show this here.

cially of those among them who have read the writings of the intuitionists reflectively, and, then, as we have seen, the most they can be charged with is moral blindness.

Besides trying to discover just what is meant by the naturalistic fallacy, I have tried to show that the notion that a logical or quasilogical fallacy is committed by the definists only confuses the issue between the intuitionists and the definists (and the issue between the latter and the emotists or postulationists), and misrepresents the way in which the issue is to be settled. No logical fallacy need appear anywhere in the procedure of the definists. Even fallacies in any less accurate sense cannot be implemented to decide the case against the definists; at best they can be ascribed to the definists only after the issue has been decided against them on independent grounds. But the only defect which can be attributed to the definists, *if* the intuitionists are right in affirming the existence of unique indefinable ethical characteristics, is a peculiar moral blindness, which is not a fallacy even in the looser sense. The issue in question must be decided by whatever method we may find satisfactory for determining whether or not a word stands for a characteristic at all, and, if it does, whether or not it stands for a unique characteristic. What method is to be employed is, perhaps, in one form or another, the basic problem of contemporary philosophy, but no generally satisfactory solution of the problem has yet been reached. I shall venture to say only this: it does seem to me that the issue is not to be decided against the intuitionists by the application *ab extra* to ethical judgments of any empirical or ontological meaning dictum.[39]

[39]See *Principia Ethica,* pp. 124 f., 140.

1941

The Nature of Ethical Disagreement

C. L. Stevenson

1

When people disagree about the value of something—one saying that it is good or right and another that it is bad or wrong—by what methods of argument or inquiry can their disagreement be resolved? Can it be resolved by the methods of science, or does it require methods of some other kind, or is it open to no rational solution at all?

The question must be clarified before it can be answered. And the word that is particularly in need of clarification, as we shall see, is the word "disagreement."

Let us begin by noting that "disagreement" has two broad senses: In the first sense it refers to what I shall call "disagreement in belief." This occurs when Mr. A believes *p,* when Mr. B believes *not-p,* or something incompatible with *p,* and when neither is content to let the belief of the other remain unchallenged. Thus doctors may disagree in belief about the causes of an illness; and friends may disagree in belief about the exact date on which they last met.

In the second sense the word refers to what I shall call "disagreement in attitude." This occurs when Mr. A has a favorable attitude to something, when Mr. B has an unfavorable or less favorable attitude to it, and when neither is content to let the other's atti-

C. L. Stevenson, "The Nature of Ethical Disagreement" from FACTS AND VALUES (New Haven, CT: Yale University Press, 1963). Reprinted with the permission of the publishers.

tude remain unchanged. The term "attitude" is here used in much the same sense that R. B. Perry uses "interest"; it designates any psychological disposition of being *for* or *against* something. Hence love and hate are relatively specific kinds of attitudes, as are approval and disapproval, and so on.

This second sense can be illustrated in this way: Two men are planning to have dinner together. One wants to eat at a restaurant that the other doesn't like. Temporarily, then, the men cannot "agree" on where to dine. Their argument may be trivial, and perhaps only half serious; but in any case it represents a disagreement *in attitude*. The men have divergent preferences and each is trying to redirect the preference of the other—though normally, of course, each is willing to revise his own preference in the light of what the other may say.

Further examples are readily found. Mrs. Smith wishes to cultivate only the four hundred; Mr. Smith is loyal to his old poker-playing friends. They accordingly disagree, in attitude, about whom to invite to their party. The progressive mayor wants modern school buildings and large parks; the older citizens are against these "newfangled" ways; so they disagree on civic policy. These cases differ from the one about the restaurant only in that the clash of attitudes is more serious and may lead to more vigorous argument.

The difference between the two senses of "disagreement" is essentially this: the first involves an opposition of beliefs, both of which cannot be true, and the second involves an opposition of attitudes, both of which cannot be satisfied.

Let us apply this distinction to a case that will sharpen it. Mr. A believes that most voters will favor a proposed tax and Mr. B disagrees with him. The disagreement concerns attitudes—those of the voters—but note that A and B are *not* disagreeing in attitude. Their disagreement is *in belief about* attitudes. It is simply a special kind of disagreement in belief, differing from disagreement in belief about head colds only with regard to subject matter. It implies not an opposition of the actual attitudes of the speakers but only of their beliefs about certain attitudes. Disagreement *in* attitude, on the other hand, implies that the very attitudes of the speakers are opposed. A and B may have opposed beliefs about attitudes without having opposed attitudes, just as they may have opposed beliefs about head colds without having opposed head colds. Hence we must not, from the fact that an argument is concerned with attitudes, infer that it necessarily involves disagreement *in* attitude.

2

We may now turn more directly to disagreement about values, with particular reference to normative ethics. When people argue about what is good, do they disagree in belief, or do they disagree in attitude? A long tradition of ethical theorists strongly suggest, whether they always intend to or not, that the disagreement is one *in belief.* Naturalistic theorists, for instance, identify an ethical judgment with some sort of scientific statement, and so make normative ethics a branch of science. Now a scientific argument typically exemplifies disagreement in belief, and if an ethical argument is simply a scientific one, then it too exemplifies disagreement in belief. The usual naturalistic theories of ethics that stress attitudes—such as those of Hume, Westermarck, Perry, Richards, and so many others—stress disagreement in belief no less than the rest. They imply, of course, that disagreement about what is good is disagreement *in belief* about attitudes; but we have seen that that is simply one sort of disagreement in belief, and by no means the same as disagreement *in* attitude. Analyses that stress disagreement *in* attitude are extremely rare.

If ethical arguments, as we encounter them in everyday life, involved disagreement in belief exclusively—whether the beliefs were about attitudes or about something else—then I should have no quarrel with the ordinary sort of naturalistic analysis. Normative judgments could be taken as scientific statements and amenable to the usual scientific proof. But a moment's attention will readily show that disagreement in belief has not the exclusive role that theory has so repeatedly ascribed to it. It must be readily granted that ethical arguments usually involve disagreement in belief; but they *also* involve disagreement in attitude. And the conspicuous role of disagreement in attitude is what we usually take, whether we realize it or not, as the distinguishing feature of ethical arguments. For example:

Suppose that the representative of a union urges that the wage level in a given company ought to be higher—that it is only right that the workers receive more pay. The company representative urges in reply that the workers ought to receive no more than they get. Such an argument clearly represents a disagreement in attitude. The union is *for* higher wages; the company is *against* them, and neither is content to let the other's attitude remain unchanged. *In addition* to this disagreement in attitude, of course, the argument may represent no little disagreement in belief. Perhaps the parties disagree about how much the cost of living has risen and how much the workers are suffering under the present wage scale. Or perhaps they disagree about the company's earnings and the extent to which the company could raise wages and still operate at a profit. Like any typical ethical argument, then, this argument involves both disagreement in attitude and disagreement in belief.

It is easy to see, however, that the disagreement in attitude plays a unifying and predominating role in the argument. This is so in two ways:

In the first place, disagreement in attitude determines what beliefs are *relevant* to the argument. Suppose that the company affirms that the wage scale of fifty years ago was far lower than it is now. The union will immediately urge that this contention, even though true, is irrelevant. And it is irrelevant simply because information about the wage level of fifty years ago, maintained under totally different circumstances, is not likely to affect the present attitudes of either party. To be relevant, any belief that is introduced into the argument must be one that is likely to lead one side or the other to have a different attitude, and so reconcile disagreement in attitude. Attitudes are often functions of beliefs. We often change our attitudes to something when we change our beliefs about it; just as a child ceases to *want* to touch a live coal when he comes to *believe* that it will burn him. Thus in the present argument any beliefs that are at all likely to alter attitudes, such as those about the increasing cost of living or the financial state of the company, will be considered by both sides to be relevant to the argument. Agreement in belief on these matters may lead to agreement in attitude toward the wage scale. But beliefs that are likely to alter the attitudes of neither side will be declared irrelevant. They will have no bearing on the disagreement in attitude, with which both parties are primarily concerned.

In the second place, ethical argument usually terminates when disagreement in attitude terminates, even though a certain amount of disagreement in belief remains. Suppose, for instance, that the company and the union continue to disagree in belief about the increasing cost of living, but that the company, even so, ends by favoring the higher wage scale. The union will then be content to end the argument and will cease to press its point about living costs. It may bring up that point again, in some future argument of the same sort, or in urging the righteousness of its victory to the newspaper columnists; but for the moment the fact that the company has agreed in attitude is sufficient to terminate the argument. On the other hand: suppose that both parties agreed on all beliefs that were introduced into the argument, but even so continued to disagree in attitude. In that case neither party would feel that their dispute had been successfully terminated. They might look for other beliefs that could be introduced into the argument. They might use words to play on each other's emotions. They might agree (in attitude) to submit the case to arbitration, both feeling that a decision, even if strongly adverse to one party or the other, would be preferable to a continued impasse. Or, perhaps, they might abandon hope of settling their dispute by any peaceable means.

In many other cases, of course, men discuss ethical topics without having the strong, uncompromising attitudes that the present example has illustrated. They are often as much concerned with redirecting their own attitudes, in the light of greater knowledge, as with redirecting the attitudes of others. And the attitudes involved are often altruistic rather than selfish. Yet the above example will serve, so long as that is understood, to suggest the nature of ethical disagreement. Both disagreement in attitude and disagreement in belief are involved, but the former predominates in that (1) it determines what sort of disagreement in belief is relevantly disputed in a given ethical argument, and (2) it determines by its continued presence or its resolution whether or not the argument has been settled. We may see further how intimately the two sorts of disagreement are related: since attitudes are often functions of beliefs, an agreement in belief may lead people, as a matter of psychological fact, to agree in attitude.

3

Having discussed disagreement, we may turn to the broad question that was first mentioned, namely: By what methods of argument or inquiry may disagreement about matters of value be resolved?

It will be obvious that to whatever extent an argument involves disagreement in belief, it is open to the usual methods of the sciences. If these methods are the *only* rational methods for supporting beliefs—as I believe to be so, but cannot now take time to discuss—then scientific methods are the only rational methods for resolving the disagreement in *belief* that arguments about values may include.

But if science is granted an undisputed sway in reconciling beliefs, it does not thereby acquire, without qualification, an undisputed sway in reconciling attitudes. We have seen that arguments about values include disagreement in attitude, no less than disagreement in belief, and that in certain ways the disagreement in attitude predominates. By what methods shall the latter sort of disagreement be resolved?

The methods of science are still available for that purpose, but only in an indirect way. Initially, these methods have only to do with establishing agreement in belief. If they serve further to establish agreement in attitude, that will be due simply to the psychological fact that altered beliefs may cause altered attitudes. Hence scientific methods are conclusive in ending arguments about values only to the extent that their success in obtaining agreement in belief will in turn lead to agreement in attitude.

In other words: the extent to which scientific methods can bring about agreement on values depends on the extent to which a commonly accepted body of scientific beliefs would cause us to have a commonly accepted set of attitudes.

How much is the development of science likely to achieve, then, with regard to values? To what extent *would* common beliefs lead to common attitudes? It is, perhaps, a pardonable enthusiasm to *hope* that science will do everything—to hope that in some rosy future, when all men know the consequences of their acts, they will all have common aspirations and live peaceably in complete moral accord. But if we speak not from our enthusiastic hopes but from our present knowledge, the answer must be far less exciting. We usually *do not know,* at the beginning of any argument about values, whether an agreement in belief, scientifically established, will lead to an agreement in attitude or not. It is logically possible, at least, that two men should continue to disagree in attitude even though they had all their beliefs in common, and even though neither had made any logical or inductive error, or omitted any relevant evidence. Differences in temperament, or in early training, or in social status, might make the men retain different attitudes even though both were possessed of the complete scientific truth. Whether this logical possibility is an empirical likelihood I shall not presume to say; but it is unquestionably a possibility that must not be left out of account.

To say that science can always settle arguments about value, we have seen, is to make this assumption: Agreement in attitude will always be consequent upon complete agreement in belief, and science can always bring about the latter. Taken as purely heuristic, this assumption has its usefulness. It leads people to discover the discrepancies in their beliefs and to prolong enlightening argument that *may* lead, as a matter of fact, from commonly accepted beliefs to commonly accepted attitudes. It leads people to reconcile their attitudes in a rational, permanent way, rather than by rhapsody or exhortation. But the assumption is *nothing more,* for present knowledge, than a heuristic maxim. It is wholly without any proper foundation of probability. I conclude, therefore, that scientific methods cannot be guaranteed the definite role in the so-called normative sciences that they may have in the natural sciences. Apart from a heuristic assumption to the contrary, it is possible that the growth of scientific knowledge may leave many disputes about values permanently unsolved. Should these disputes persist, there are nonrational methods for dealing with them, of course, such as impassioned, moving oratory. But the purely intellectual methods of science, and, indeed, *all* methods of reasoning, may be insufficient to settle disputes about values even though they may greatly help to do so.

For the same reasons I conclude that normative ethics is not a branch of any science. It deliberately deals with a type of disagreement that science deliberately avoids. Ethics is not psychology, for instance; for although psychologists may, of course, agree or disagree in belief about attitudes, they need not, as psychologists, be concerned with whether they agree or disagree with one another *in* attitude. Insofar as normative ethics draws from the sciences, in order to change attitudes *via* changing people's beliefs, it *draws* from *all* the sciences; but a moralist's peculiar aim—that of *redirecting* attitudes—is a type of activity, rather than knowledge, and falls within no science. Science may study that activity and may help indirectly to forward it; but is not *identical* with that activity.

4

I can take only a brief space to explain why the ethical terms, such as "good," "wrong," "ought," and so on, are so habitually used to deal with disagreement in attitude. On account of their repeated occurrence in emotional situations they have acquired a strong emotive meaning. This emotive meaning makes them serviceable in initiating changes in a hearer's attitudes. Sheer emotive impact is not likely, under many circumstances, to change attitudes in any permanent way; but it *begins* a process that can then be supported by other means.

There is no occasion for saying that the meaning of ethical terms is *purely* emotive, like that of "alas" or "hurrah." We have seen that ethical *arguments* include many expressions of *belief,* and the rough rules of ordinary language permit us to say that some of these beliefs are expressed by an ethical judgment itself. But the beliefs so expressed are by no means always the same. Ethical terms are notable for their ambiguity, and opponents in an argument may use them in different senses. Sometimes this leads to artificial issues, but it usually does not. So long as one person says "this is good" with emotive praise, and another says "no, it is bad," with emotive condemnation, a disagreement in attitude is manifest. Whether or not the beliefs that these statements express are logically incompatible may not be discovered until later in the argument; but even if they are actually compatible, disagreement in attitude will be preserved by emotive meaning; and this disagreement, so central to ethics, may lead to an argument that is certainly not artificial in its issues so long as it is taken for what it is.

The many theorists who have refused to identify ethical statements with scientific ones have much to be said in their favor. They have seen that ethical judgments mold or alter attitudes, rather than describe them, and they have seen that ethical judgments can be guaranteed no definitive scientific support. But one need not on that account provide ethics with any extramundane, sui generis *subject matter.* The distinguishing features of an ethical judgment can be preserved by a recognition of emotive meaning and disagreement in attitude, rather than by some nonnatural quality—and with far greater intelligibility. If a unique subject matter is *postulated,* as it usually is, to preserve the important distinction between normative ethics and science, it serves no purpose that is not served by the very simple analysis I have here suggested. Unless nonnatural qualities can be defended by positive arguments, rather than as an "only resort" from the acknowledged weakness of ordinary forms of naturalism, they would seem nothing more than the invisible shadows cast by emotive meaning.

1946

A Refutation of Morals

John Mackie

[In this paper I do not pretend to be advancing any particularly new ideas: hardly any of the arguments are original, and indeed most are the stock instruments of all modern discussions of morals. But I think I am justified in offering this re-statement of them, because it is seldom realized how they may be brought together and interrelated, or how radically destructive they are of all common views of morality, when this is done.]

We all have moral feelings: all of us find that there are human actions and states of affairs of which we approve and disapprove, and which we therefore try to encourage and develop or to oppose. (This emotion of approval is different from liking, one difference being that its object is more general. If someone stands me a pint, I like it: if someone stands an enemy of mine a pint, I dislike it: but I should approve of a state of society which provided free beer all round. So if I hear of someone whom I have never met and to whom I am personally indifferent being stood a pint, I should not say that I like it, for I am not directly affected, but I may well approve of it, because it is an instance of the sort of thing I want to see everywhere. A thorough distinction of approval from liking and other relations would require further discussion, but perhaps this will serve to indicate a contrast between classes with which we are all in fact acquainted. I shall suggest later a possible source of these generalized emotions.) But most of us do not merely

John Mackie, "A Refutation of Morals," *Australasian Journal of Philosophy.* Reprinted with the permission of Joan Mackie and *Australasian Journal of Philosophy.*

admit that we have such *feelings,* we think we can also *judge* that actions and states are right and good, just as we judge about other matters of fact, that these judgments are either true or false, and that the qualities with which they deal exist objectively. This view, which almost everyone holds, may be crudely called "believing in morals." A few sceptics, however, think that there are only feelings of approval, no objective moral facts. (Of course the existence of a feeling is an objective fact, but not what is commonly called a moral fact.) One of their main arguments is that moral facts would be "queer," in that unlike other facts they cannot be explained in terms of arrangements of matter, or logical constructions out of sense-data, or whatever the particular theorist takes to be the general form of real things. This argument is not in itself very strong, or even very plausible, for unless we have good *a priori* grounds for whatever is taken as the basic principle of criticism, the criterion of reality, the mere fact that we seem to observe moral qualities and facts would be a reason for modifying that principle. Their other main argument, which is both older and more convincing, though not logically conclusive, is that although at any one time, in a particular social group, there is fairly complete agreement about what is right, in other classes, other countries, and above all in other periods of history and other cultures, the actual moral judgments or feelings are almost completely different, though perhaps there are a few feelings so natural to man that they are found everywhere. Now feelings may well change with changing conditions, but a judgment about objective fact should be everywhere the same: if we have a faculty of moral perception, it must be an extremely faulty one, liable not only to temporary illusions, as sight is, but to great and lasting error. Of course it may be that every society except our own is mistaken, that savages are morally backward because they lack our illuminating experience of the long-term effects of various kinds of action, and so on. But this complacent view (not indeed very popular now) is shaken by the observation that the variations in moral feelings can be explained much more plausibly not as being due to mistakes, but as reflections of social habits. This moral relativity would be less alarming if we could say that the varying judgments were not ultimate, but were applications to different circumstances of a single principle or a small number of principles, which were everywhere recognized—for example, that whatever produces pleasure is good, that whatever society commands is right, or, at the very least, that we should always do what we believe to be right. But these principles are not commonly laid down first, and the particular judgments deduced from them: rather the particular judgments are made by ordinary people, whereas the principles are later invented by philosophers and manipulated in order to explain them. In any case there is just as little agreement about principles as about particular judgments.

We find on further enquiry that most, perhaps all, actual moral judgments are fairly closely correlated with what we may call social demands: any society or social group has regular ways of working, and, in order to maintain these, requires that its members should act in certain ways: the members—from whatever motive, perhaps mainly habit, which has compelled them to adapt their desires to the established customs—obey these requirements themselves and force their fellows to do so, or at least feel obliged to obey and approve of others obeying. They call "right" and "good" whatever accords with these ways of working. Moreover as the science of social history develops, it is more and more strongly suggested that ways of working and institutions have their own laws of growth, and that the desires or moral views of individuals do not so much control the history of society as arise out of it.

Belief in the objectivity of moral qualities is further undermined when we remark that whenever anyone calls an action or activity or state of affairs right or good (unless he is speaking in an ironical tone or puts these words in inverted commas) he himself either has a feeling of approval, or desires that the action should be done or the activity pursued or the state of affairs come into existence. (Only one of these alternatives is necessary, but they are often found together.)

None of these considerations is conclusive, but each has a certain weight: together they move the moral sceptic (who is often of a scientific and inductive turn of mind, and less devoted than some others to the clear light of intuition or the authority of reason) to conclude that in all probability we do not recognize moral facts, but merely have feelings of approval and disapproval, which arise in general from social demands and therefore vary from one society to another. This view I intend to examine and restate, and to advance what I regard as decisive arguments for one of its more important aspects.

The simplest formulation of this view is that when someone says "this act is right" he means merely "I approve of this act." The well-known reply simply leaps into the reader's mind: when one person says that an act is right, another that the same act is wrong, they would not on this theory be disagreeing, whereas in fact they think they are. It will not do to say, with Stevenson,[1] that there is a disagreement in attitude, but not in belief: they think, at any rate, that they disagree in belief. Nor does one mean that "society approves of this act," since we frequently meet people who say "I know society approves of this, but it is wrong all the same." But there is no need for argument: direct introspection shows that when we use the terms "right," "good," and the rest, we never intend merely to state that there are feelings of approval. An improved formulation of the sceptical view is that in saying "this is right," and so on, we are not *stating* any approval, but only *expressing* one, that words like "right" and "wrong," "good" and "bad" are to be compared not with "red" and "square" but with exclamations or ejaculations like "ow!," "boo!," and "hurray!" This is certainly nearer the truth, and avoids the previous difficulties, but is, in another way, just as unplausible. For we do not think that we are merely ejaculating when we talk in moral terms. If we did, and if someone disagreed with us, we should merely disapprove of his approvals, and either try to coax him into a different emotional attitude, or if he proved obstinate, knock him down. In fact we reason with him. These facts, and the logical tangles that we get into when we try to re-state fairly complex moral situations in the "boo-hurray" language, prove that we think, at least, that we are not merely expressing our emotions but are describing objective facts, and therefore that the meaning of moral terms is not parallel with that of ejaculations. Many refutations of the "boo-hurray" theory have been worked out, but they all depend upon and illustrate the fact that we *think* that we are doing things of quite different sorts when we say "right" and when we say "ow!" Now if philosophy could do no more than elucidate the meaning of the terms of common speech, remove confusions and rationalize the thought of ordinary men, there would be nothing more to be said. Moral terms do mean objective qualities, and everyone who uses them does so because he believes in objective moral facts. But if the very terms of common speech may include errors and confusions within themselves, so that they cannot be used at all without falsity, if, we may add, philosophy may be permitted to enquire into these errors by observing a few facts for itself and founding inductive conclusions on them, the moral sceptic need not be so soon disheartened.

But he must modify his view again, and say that in using moral terms we are as it were objectifying our own feelings, thinking them into qualities existing independently of us. For example, we may see a plant, say a fungus, that fills us with disgust, but in-

[1]*Ethics and Language*, Chapter I.

stead of stating that we have this feeling, or merely expressing and relieving it by an exclamation, we may ascribe to the fungus a semi-moral quality of foulness, over and above all the qualities that a physical scientist could find in it. Of course, in objectifying our feelings we are also turning them inside out: our feeling about the fungus is one of being disgusted, while the foulness we ascribe to the fungus means that it is disgusting. The supposed objective quality is not simply the feeling itself transferred to an external object, but is something that would inevitably arouse that feeling. (No one would say, "That fungus is foul, but I feel no disgust at it.") The feeling and the supposed quality are related as a seal or stamp and its impression.

This process of objectification is, I think, well known to psychologists and is not new in philosophy. I believe that it resembles what Hume says we do when we manufacture the idea of necessary connection out of our feeling of being compelled, by the association of ideas, to pass from cause to effect, though here the process of turning inside out does not occur.

There are strong influences which might lead us thus to objectify moral feelings. As I have mentioned, our moral judgments seem to arise from approvals borrowed from society, or from some social group, and these are felt by the individual as external to himself. It is for this reason that they are universal in form, applying equally to himself and to others. They are thus formally capable of being objective laws, in contrast to the "selfish" desires of the individual. This generality or universality, which I mentioned as characteristic of the emotion of approval, is reflected in Rousseau's doctrine that the general will and therefore law must be general in their object, and in Kant's criterion of the possibility of universalization of a moral law. Since we inevitably tend to encourage what we approve of, and to impose it upon others, we want everyone to adopt our approvals, and this will most surely come about if they have only to perceive a genuinely existing objective fact, for what we feel is in general private, what we perceive may be common to all. Suppose that we approve of hard work: then if as well as a feeling of approval in our own minds there were an objective fact like "hard work is good," such that everyone could observe the fact and such that the mere observation would arouse in him a like feeling of approval, and even perhaps stimulate him to work, we should eventually get what we want done: people would work hard. And since what we want does not exist in fact, we naturally construct it in imagination: we objectify our feelings so thoroughly that we completely deceive ourselves. I imagine that this is the reason why our belief in moral objectivity is so firm: we much more readily admit that the foulness of a fungus is an objectification than that the depravity of people who break our windows is. If moral predicates were admitted to be what the moral sceptic says they are, we should never be able to extol a state of affairs as good in any sense which would induce people to bring it about, unless they already wanted it, though we might point out that this state had features which in fact they did desire, though they had not realized this: we should never be able to recommend any course of action, except in such terms as "if you want to be rich, be economical"; nor could we give commands by any moral authority, though we might again advise "if you don't want a bullet through your brains, come quietly"; and we should never be able to lecture anyone on his wickedness—an alarming prospect. The temptations to objectify feelings of approval, and to retain our belief in morals, are clearly strong ones.

This process of objectifying our feelings is, then, neither impossible nor improbable: there is also abundant evidence that it is just what has occurred. It is commonly believed by moralists that good means desirable in a sense such that the mere recognition that a thing is good makes us desire it, and similarly the conclusion of the practical syllogism is both "this is right" and the performance of the action. This is what we should expect if "right" were the objectification of a tendency to compel or command the kind of act so described, and "good" of desire and approval. This is again indicated by the use of the term "value" which is clearly borrowed from spheres like economics where value is created by demand—in fact a quality manufactured in imagination out of the relation of being demanded by someone, the abstraction being the easier because the demand is not essentially that of a single buyer, but of an indeterminate crowd of potential buyers: the analogy with the objectification of moral feelings, aided by their generality, is very plain. Anderson has pointed out (in "The Meaning of Good", published in the Journal for September, 1942) that whenever anyone argues "Y is good, X is a means to Y, therefore X is good" he must be using "good" in an economic sense, as relative to some demand: now this is one of the commonest forms of argument in ordinary moral thought. There is nothing inconsistent in saying that "good" is the objectification of both desire and approval: its meaning is not quite fixed, and approval both is a development from liking and desiring, and attains its end when its object is generally desired. Further evidence is given by the categorical imperative, which looks very much like an abstraction from the commonplace hypothetical imperative, "if you want this, do that," and which may be described as the making objective and so absolute of advice which is properly relative to the condition of the presence of the desire. "Naturalistic" theories of ethics, which seem so absurd to a logician like G. E. Moore, who insists on the objective-quality aspect of moral terms, represent as it were partially successful attempts at objectification. "The good is the desired" and suchlike statements, which recur with remarkable persistence in philosophic history, plainly betray the emotional origin of moral terms. But there is no need to multiply examples: almost every moral term and style of moral thought may be seen to be borrowed from less lofty spheres, and in the course of the transfer objective qualities have appeared where only emotions were previously recognized.

In attempting to give an account of the origin of moral terms in this process of objectification, I do not, of course, claim that it is complete or precise in all respects. It is still open to discussion and correction on empirical grounds. We might go on to consider this process as a psychological process, investigating its causes, its similarities and contrasts with other mental processes, and the steps of which it is made up. We might ask whether "objectification" or some other name is really the most suitable, and also what are the precise motives objectified: we might consider, for example, Westermarck's argument[2] that "ought" normally expresses a conation, is sometimes but not necessarily or essentially imperative, and has its origin in disapproval rather than approval.

My discussion in this paper is intended to open the way for such discussions, not to settle them once and for all. What I am concerned to establish is simply the logical status of moral terms, not the psychological details of their origin; in effect I am asserting only that there are no facts of the form "this is right," that when we use such words the only fact is the existence of some feelings in ourselves or in others or in both, but that in using these terms we are falsely postulating or asserting something of the simple, objective form "this is right."

I am not, of course, disagreeing with the point mentioned several times by Anderson (for example in "The Meaning of Good," p. 120) that "I like this," "I approve of this," "this society approves of this," are all statements of objective fact and would in any particular case be true or false. But they are all of a different form from statements

[2]*The Origin and Development of the Moral Ideas*, Chapter VI.

like "this is right," the latter attributing a predicate to a subject, the former asserting a relation between two or more things. When I say that we objectify, I mean that we believe in the truth of statements of the subject-predicate form.

This re-statement does away with the logical difficulties previously encountered by moral scepticism. Nor are there, I think, any non-logical difficulties in the way of our accepting this view, except the persistence of the belief that moral facts are objective. It might be claimed that this firm belief is based on an intuition, but it has no further arguments to support it, and we have indicated social and psychological causes which would produce such a belief even if it had no foundation. However firm the belief may be, therefore, it is not valid evidence for the existence of moral facts. But the true moralist will not be deterred by lack of evidence: he will perhaps be compelled to admit that moral judgments are evolved, historically, by objectification of feelings. But none the less, he will maintain, when evolved they *are* valid. But now we remind him of their variability, their correlation with social demands. Actual moral judgments, en masse, cannot be valid, since they are mutually contradictory: in fact all the evidence suggests that not only are moral judgments derived from feelings, but there are no objective moral facts: the feelings are *all* that exists. We may now legitimately be influenced by the "queerness" of the alleged moral facts, their striking differences from most of the other objects of knowledge and belief. But we must not be over-emphatic. We have only attained probability. Even when our assumptions and observations are accepted it is still possible that there may be facts of the forms "this act is right," "this activity or state of affairs is good," though our recognition of them is very much confused by desires and approvals. We have seen that a great deal of so-called moral judging is really the objectifying of feelings, but perhaps not all of it is. (This leaves the field open for a positive system of ethics like that upheld by Anderson.) But this concession will give the moralist no pleasure when we add that we can show, by a different line of argument, that that part of morals to which moralists are most devoted, which is absolutely essential to their purpose, is certainly not objectively valid, and is therefore to be explained in terms of objectification. I mean everything connected with the notion of obligation.

The demonstration is merely a re-enactment of the drama in which moral thinkers of opposing schools have shown that both determinism and indeterminism are absolutely required by (and may be deduced from) our common views about obligation. We begin with the principle that "ought implies can." It is obvious that if we meet someone who is clearly not in a fit state to be wandering about the streets and say to him "you ought to go home" we are assuming that it is physically possible for him to go home, if he wants to. This kind of freedom no one will deny. But suppose that we know that he has a strong and inflexible determination not to go home, and in fact are certain that he will not go, can we still say that he ought to go? Not, I think, in the full sense of "ought." We may feel regretfully that it is a pity, that going home is the act that would have produced most good, or something like that, but we no longer say he ought to go. (I have seen it suggested that the phrase "he ought not to have done it" shows that we do not restrict obligation to what is undetermined, since we speak of a present obligation about a past act. But this phrase results merely from the perversity of the English language, and we should be speaking more accurately, as well as translating more literally the learned tongues, if we said "he didn't ought to do it." It is then clear that the alleged obligation existed before the act was performed, when it might still be regarded as undetermined.) In the case described, we should probably change our ground, and say that he ought to want to go, or that, given his present unreasonably obstinate nature, he ought to set himself to change it. (We may, of course, go back in time to a point at which the determination began, saying, for example, that now the man is drunk we cannot expect him to do anything but what he does, but he ought not to have started drinking. But we cannot go back indefinitely; we must fix on a moment at which the man might have acted in either of two opposite ways, and if the way in which he acted was determined by his character and circumstances, we must say that he ought not to have this character, or rather, since this is at present an inescapable fact, that he ought to set about reforming himself.) That is to say, if we assume that motives and circumstances fully determine action, we shift the obligation from the external act to its motives. In doing this, we assume that motives themselves are not determined, for clearly we cannot both say "it is right that the man should have such motives" and realize that it was inevitable that he should have them, or should not have them, whichever happens to be true. Now in fact our common practical judgment is that human actions, like physical events, follow discoverable laws: this is only an inductive conclusion, but a well-supported one; in fact we are in the habit of tracing even how men's motives are produced by circumstances and by previous practices: we regard the "empirical self" as determined and postulate behind it a metaphysical self which is a true originator of action, to be the subject of moral judgments. This is indicated when we say "you ought to set about improving your character" for if it was the empirical self we were speaking of, it would *be* that character, though admittedly if one part of the character were already good it might set about reforming the rest. If we then start to regard the metaphysical self as determined, we must postulate a third self, and so on. When we say "you *ought* to go home" we imply that at some level in the series of selves a process which would determine the going home may or may not arise: this is a genuine origination of motion, not determined by anything else. An ultimate freedom, in this sense, is absolutely required for the full meaning of obligation: to see this we need only meditate on the common use of "ought." Now it may be argued that we are not absolutely certain that such freedom does not exist.

But now we turn to the other group of speakers. Even if such freedom did exist, it would be useless for morals. We say not only "you *ought* to go home" but also "*you* ought to go home." We ascribe the obligation to a person, and hold him responsible for acting or failing to act. From this point of view, we are not satisfied with a process that "just happens," which begins or does not begin by pure chance. The action must belong to the person, and this may be accounted for in either of two ways. There may be a self, an entity with some determinate character (which may be unknowable, but that does not matter) such that given that character the process "flows from it" inevitably: but this contradicts the previous requirement, that the action should be possible but not inevitable, and we are faced with an infinite regress, at no point in which can we stop and say "you (meaning a determinate character) ought to (implying can) go home." Alternatively the process may not "flow from" a self, but may be one of a group of originations of motion which together make up a self; the action belongs to the person as part to whole. Then either the different originations that occur as time passes are quite independent of one another, so that any one may be different and the rest unchanged—in which case there is no unity of the self, no real "you" to be held responsible—or else they exhibit a more or less unified character, and follow some kind of determinate law or mode of reaction to external stimulus, and again they are not true originations, but each one, given the rest, could not have occurred in any other way. In all this discussion there is no need for the determination to be causal or "mechanical": the argument may be applied to any form of determination that is postulated. Nor is it of any use to mix them, to suggest that we deny one kind of determination in our notion of obligation and assert another in our notion of responsibility. The *kind* of determination does not matter: the essential point, which our common notions both affirm and deny, is that the act is determined, that given the self and the circumstances, the act just will occur. The notion of obligation thus implies both freedom, and, through responsibility, which is a vital part of the notion, the negation of freedom, and cannot be objectively valid. We may wonder how it can even persist as a feeling; but it is easy not to attend to all aspects of the notion at once, and in any case we may well go on wanting what we know to be unattainable, we may regret what is past repair, whereas we cannot maintain as objective fact that these things ought or ought not to be. This demonstration leaves it possible that obligation, in an attenuated sense, may exist objectively. If we reject determinism, we may hold that certain events ought to happen, but it will be purely a matter of chance whether they do or not: it is nobody's business to bring them about. I am afraid that this concession will not satisfy the moralists, and that anyone who comes as far as this with us will abandon obligation altogether. But it should be noted as a logical possibility.

We may now sum up the progress that we have made. We have discovered how we can state the traditional view of moral sceptics without logical contradiction or denial of the observable facts of moral thinking, by saying that we have only moral feelings, but objectify these and think we are recognizing objective facts and qualities. But we were not sure how much of our moral thought was made up of these objectifications, whether there might not be, say, an objective quality of goodness, with which these objectifications have been confused. We have shown that obligation, as we commonly use the term, cannot be an objective fact, but our notion of it must be derived from objectification. The same is true of everything necessarily connected with it, the terms "should," "duty," and "right." Exhortation and recommendation can have no absolute validity when obligation is removed: we can only advise people how to attain what they already desire. With these we place those notions that bear plainly the marks of the process of objectification or of their emotional origin: the notion of value, the notion that goodness, if there is such an objective quality, has any necessary relation to desire, or to happiness and pleasure, since it is through desire that it is connected with these. Also, if there is such a quality, it will be such that we can recognize it without feeling impelled to approve of it or to pursue it. In fact, without going into further detail we may say that there may be an objective quality which we have confused with our objectifications of moral feelings, but if so it has few of the relations and other features that we have been in the habit of associating with goodness. But in any case we have shown that the great mass of what is called moral thought is, not nonsense, but error, the imagining of objective facts and qualities of external things where there exists nothing but our feelings of desire and approval.

1947

The Definition of Good

A. C. Ewing

One class of answer to the question how "good" is to be defined is given by the subjectivists. But, before we consider this type of answer, we must try to make clear to ourselves what could be meant by the "objectivity" of ethical judgments or of value judgments in general. It obviously does not mean that they ascribe value properties to physical objects. These clearly do not possess ethical qualities. It might indeed be held that they possessed the property of beauty and therefore the property of intrinsic goodness quite independently of being perceived. This view does not seem to me obviously false, but it is plain that most philosophers who have asserted the objectivity of value judgments did not wish to commit themselves to it, still less to maintain that all value judgments were objective in precisely the same sense as that in which judgments about physical objects are. We can therefore rule out at once the sense of "objective" as referring to what exists independently of being experienced. What then does "objective" mean when used in reference to ethics?

1. It may mean "claiming to be true." Obviously in this sense judgments about psychological events and dispositions are objective, though they do not refer to what exists independently of experience, and in this sense ethical judgments may be objective. To say they are is indeed to say no more than that they are judgments and not

A. C. Ewing, "The Definition of Good" from DEFINITION OF GOOD (New York: Macmillan, 1947). Reprinted with the permission of Routledge & Kegan Paul, Ltd.

merely something else which we have confused with judgments. But even this much is denied by some who maintain that so-called ethical judgments are only exclamations, commands, or wishes.

2. However, a person who admitted the occurrence of ethical judgments, but denied that they were ever in fact true or that we could ever have any justification for believing them to be true, would not usually be described as holding an objective view of ethics. So "objective" here may be taken as implying that ethical judgments in particular and value judgments in general are sometimes true and can be sometimes known or at least justifiably believed to be true. An objective view involves the rejection of scepticism in ethics.

3. But this would not by itself be sufficient to satisfy the holders of the view that ethical judgments are objective. Suppose "A is good" simply meant "I have a certain feeling about A." It would then be a judgment and could perfectly well be true and known to be true, yet anybody who maintained such a position would be said to be holding a subjective and not an objective view of ethics. The proposition that ethical judgments are objective, therefore, besides asserting that they are judgments, asserts of them a certain independence of the feelings or attitude of the person judging. They are not merely judgments about his feelings, or for that matter his thoughts. Even if partly based on feeling, they are not about the feeling itself but about something to which the feeling points, and something which cannot adequately be described in terms merely of the man's own psychology.

The view that "ethical judgments are objective" therefore excludes the following views: (a) that they are not really judgments at all, (b) that they are all false or that we are never justified in thinking them true, (c) that they are merely judgments about one's own psychological state or dispositions. Any of these three alternative views may be called "subjective."...

The simplest form of the subjectivist view is that according to which ethical judgments, though genuine judgments, assert only that the person who makes the judgment has or tends to have certain feelings. "This is good" or "right" on such a view becomes "I have [or tend to have] an emotion of approval on considering this." A number of incredibly paradoxical consequences would follow from the adoption of this view. Firstly, the judgments could not be false unless the person judging had made a mistake about his own psychology. Secondly, two different people would never mean the same thing when they made such a judgment, since each would mean "This is approved by *me*." Indeed the same person would never mean the same by it on two different occasions, because each time he would mean "I *now* feel [or tend to feel] approval of this."

Thirdly, if I judge something to be good and you judge it to be bad, our judgments would never be logically incompatible with each other. It is not a sufficient reply to point out that they can still be incompatible with each other in some different sense, for example in the sense that they express attitudes which are in conflict with each other or lead to incompatible policies. For we do not see merely that A's judgment "This is good" and B's judgment "This is bad" (in the corresponding sense of the word) lead to or express incompatible policies like A's judgment "I desire to further X" and B's judgment "I desire to oppose X." We see that the two judgments logically contradict each other so that it is logically impossible that they could both be true. No doubt, since "good" and "bad" can each be used in different senses, "this is bad" may not always contradict "this is good," because, for example, "good" may mean "instrumentally good" and "bad" may mean "intrinsically bad"; but at any rate they sometimes do so, and on the view under discussion they could, when asserted by different people, never do so.

Fourthly, no argument or rational discussion, nor indeed any citation of empirical facts, could be in any degree relevant to supporting or casting doubt on any ethical judgment unless it could be directed to showing that the person who makes the judgment has made a mistake about his own feelings or tendencies to have feelings. It is true that argument or fresh knowledge about the circumstances and likely consequences of an act might lead me to have different feelings about it and so judge it right while I had judged it wrong before, or vice versa; but it would not in any way indicate that my previous judgment was false.[1] The judgments would be different; but since they referred only to my feelings at different times they would not contradict each other any more than "I was ill on January 1" contradicts "I was well on February 1." Yet it is clear that argument can really cast doubt on propositions in ethics.

Fifthly, I could not, while asserting an ethical belief, conceive that I might possibly be wrong in this belief and yet be certain that I now feel (or tend to feel) disapproval. Since it is quite clear that I can conceive this in some cases at least, this argument provides another *reductio ad absurdum* of the theory. To think that an ethical belief now expressed by me may possibly be wrong is not the same as thinking that I may come in the future to have different feelings, for I think that the present judgment may be wrong and not a future one. To put the objection in another way, it would follow from the theory that to say "If I feel approval of A, A is always right [good]" is to utter a tautology. But it is not, it is a piece of gross conceit, if made in any ordinary context. Even if it were true that, if I feel approval of A, I shall always at the time judge A to be right (good), this is quite a different statement. I need not always be certain that my judgments are correct (unless judgment is so defined as to cover only cases of *knowledge*).

Sixthly, it would follow from the theory under discussion that, when I judge that Hitler was bad or acted wrongly, I am not really talking about Hitler at all but about my own psychology.

To me the consequences that I have mentioned are all quite incredible and constitute a fully sufficient *reductio ad absurdum* of the theory from which they are deduced. They hold whether it is applied both to "good" and to "right" or only to one of them. . . .

So let us now examine the case against the objectivity of ethical judgments. If it is conclusive we shall have to be subjectivists in the sense that we shall have to admit the impossibility of making any true or at least any justified ethical judgments, even if we do not admit that ethical judgments are of such a nature that they could not conceivably be true at all or true of anything but the mental state or dispositions of the speaker.

One argument is based on the striking differences in ethical views between different people. But the differences between the views of savages and those of modern scientists about eclipses, or between the views of different politicians as to the causes and likely effects of contemporary events, are as great as the differences between the views of savages and of Christians, or the views of democrats and of Nazis, as to ethics. Are we to conclude from this that the scientists are no more right than the savages or that the political events about which the disputes turn have not objectively any causes or effects? If we do not draw this conclusion here, why draw the corresponding conclusion about ethics? There are also various ways of explaining the differences of view that

[1] I am therefore quite unmoved by the elaborate discussion by C. L. Stevenson in *Ethics and Language* as to how argument can be relevant to ethical disagreements on a subjectivist view. It does not show it to be relevant in the sense in which we really see it to be relevant, but in some other sense. The book is no doubt a very able exposition of subjectivism for those who are already convinced, but it does not, as far as I can see, bring any real argument for it or avoid any of the objections that I have mentioned against it.

exist without casting doubt on the objectivity of ethics. In the first place, acts which bear the same name may be very different acts in different states of society, because the circumstances and the psychology of the people concerned are very different. So it might be the case that, for example, slavery or polygamy was right, as the course which involved least evil, in certain more primitive societies and wrong in ours. This is quite compatible with the objectivity of ethical judgments. The proposition that slavery was right in ancient Egypt would not contradict the proposition that it was wrong in the United States in 1850 A.D. Both we and the ancient Egyptians may be right in our ethical judgments. Let us, however, take cases where one party is wrong. Now it is important to note that differences in ethical beliefs are often due to differences of opinion as to matters of fact. If A and B differ as to the likely consequences of an action, they may well differ as to whether the action is right or wrong, and this is perhaps the most fertile source of disputes as to what is right. But it is not an ethical difference at all; it is a difference such as arises between rival scientific predictions based on inductive evidence. Differences or apparent differences of opinion of these two kinds obviously constitute no possible argument against the objectivity of ethics.

But there are also genuine ethical differences—that is, differences as to our judgments not of fact but of value. These may sometimes be explained by differences in people's experience of life. If I never experience A, I cannot realize the intrinsic goodness of A and may therefore wrongly subordinate it to something less good. And we must remember that what is intrinsically good is not a physical thing or a physical act, but the experience or state of mind associated with it. Even a long study of philosophical books would not qualify a person to pass a judgment on the intrinsic value of philosophy if he were hopelessly bad at the subject, because then, however many books he read, he would not have a genuinely philosophical experience. Two persons who differ as to the aesthetic value of a picture may really be judging about different things, their several experiences of it. Or at least their judgments will be based on different data. Other differences of view may be due to the misapplication of principles previously accepted, or to genuine intellectual confusions such as the philosopher or even the man of common sense who is not a philosopher could remove. For instance a man may confuse badness and wrongness and conclude or assume, for example, that, because he really sees lying to be always bad (an evil), he sees it to be always wrong, while it may be a case of choosing the lesser evil rather than the greater. Often a man will think that he knows intuitively P to be R when he really only sees it to be Q but confuses Q with R.

Or the judgment that something is good or bad on the whole may have been due to concentrating attention on one side of it while ignoring or underestimating the other sides, as, for instance, militarists concentrate their attention on the unselfish heroism which war brings out in men and forget or underestimate war's evils. Lesser degrees of such onesidedness it is impossible to avoid, and yet they may detrimentally influence ethical judgments. To decide what is right in a particular case is often a difficult matter of balancing the good or evil likely to be produced by one proposed act against that likely to be produced by others. For, even if we do not hold the view that the rightness of an act depends solely on its consequences, we cannot in any case deny that such balancing of the consequences should play the predominant part in at least many ethical decisions. Perhaps, if we foresaw all the consequences clearly as they would be in their factual character and could keep our attention fixed equally on them all, we should always be in agreement as to the degree in which they were good or evil as compared with the consequences of other possible acts. But, apart from the difficulty of estimating what the consequences of an act will be, it is practically impossible in cases which are at all complex to keep our attention sufficiently fixed at the same time on all the foreseeable consequences likely to be seriously relevant for good or evil, and so we are likely through lack of attention to underestimate the value or disvalue of some as compared to that of others.

The lack of attention I have mentioned is in some degree inevitable, but it is greatly enhanced by the influence of desire and prejudice. It is a commonplace that ethical mistakes are often due to non-intellectual factors. Whether these act only through affecting the attention or whether they can lead to mistaken valuations even in the presence of full attention to the object valued we need not discuss. Their influence is certainly not confined to ethical mistakes; we may note the different conclusions as to the factual consequences of a policy which members of different political parties may draw from the same evidence. There is in any case a large class of errors for which some form of "psychoanalysis" (I do not say necessarily the Freudian) is required rather than argument, and another (probably much larger) of which it can be said only that the person in question fell into error because he did not steadfastly will to seek the truth and therefore did not fix his attention on points which displeased him. The convictions of some people as to the objectivity of ethics appear to have been shaken by the fact that enthusiastic Nazis seem to have believed that it was their duty to do things which we are convinced are completely wrong, such as ill-treating the Jews; but is there any reason to think that these Nazis really wanted to arrive at the truth regarding the question whether it was right or wrong to send Jews to concentration camps? If not, we need not be so surprised that they did not attain the truth which they did not seek.

So it may well be the case that all differences in people's judgments whether certain actions are right or wrong or certain things good or bad are due to factors other than an irreducible difference in ethical intuition. But, even if they should not be, we must remember that ethical intuition, like our other capacities, is presumably a developing factor and therefore may be capable of error. But in any case we have said enough to show that great differences of opinion as to ethics are quite compatible with the objectivity of ethical judgments.

Differences between philosophers about the general theory of ethics are remarkably great; but experience shows that very wide philosophical differences are quite compatible with striking agreement as regards the kind of action judged right or wrong, just as radical differences between philosophers in their theory of perception and of physical objects are quite compatible with complete agreement in ordinary life as to what particular physical objects are in a particular place at a particular time. The differences between philosophers are differences not mainly as to their ethical judgments in concrete ethical situations, but as to the general theory explaining these. We may add that the differences between different peoples and different civilizations as to concrete ethical judgments are commonly exaggerated. David Livingstone says that nowhere had he need to teach the African savages at any rate the ethical, as opposed to the religious, portion of the Decalogue. But there is of course a great inconsistency (not only among savages) in confining to a limited group rules which demand universal extension.

Another argument is that ethical beliefs can be explained psychologically as having originated from non-ethical factors such as fear of punishment. Now there must be a psychological history of the origin of any beliefs, and there must have been a time when no ethical ideas or beliefs yet existed, both in the history of the individual and in the history of the race. But this does not prove that ethical beliefs originated solely from the pre-existing ideas through a sort of confusion and were not due to a genuine cognition of properties really present. There was also a time when there were no logical or mathematical ideas, but nobody would entertain a similar argument against logic or mathematics.

Further, to be sceptical about ethics on the strength of a theory as to the origin of ethical ideas would be to give up the more for the far less certain, indeed the extremely uncertain. For such a sceptical theory would rest on the psychology of children if applied to individual development, and the psychology of savages if applied to the evolutionary development of the race. But, owing to the impossibility of obtaining reliable introspective evidence, the psychology of children and savages, at least when we consider their higher mental processes or the beginnings of such, is speculative in the extreme. To quote from Broad, "Of all branches of empirical psychology that which is concerned with what goes on in the minds of babies must, from the nature of the case, be one of the most precarious. Babies, whilst they remain such, cannot tell us what their experiences are; and all statements made by grown persons about their own infantile experiences on the basis of ostensible memory are certainly inadequate and probably distorted. The whole of this part of psychology therefore is, and will always remain, a mere mass of speculations about infantile mental processes, put forward to explain certain features in the lives of grown persons and incapable in principle of any independent check or verification. Such speculations are of the weakest kind known to science."[2] The psychology of primitive savages is in an equally or almost equally weak position. Some of our ethical judgments, on the other hand, I should insist, are quite or almost as certain as any judgment, and, even if the reader is not prepared to go so far, he must admit that they are at any rate far more certain than could be any theory founded on the psychology of children and savages which explained them away. The same uncertainty must attach to any theory of ethics or analysis of ethical terms based on the way in which children learn the use of the terms. Such a theory is irrelevant unless it is based on a study of what children exactly have in mind and what their mental processes are when they use the words, and how can we possibly have a well founded idea of that when they cannot introspect or adequately report introspections?

Westermarck contends that objectivity is disproved by the fact that ethical judgments are based on emotion;[3] but he does not even try, as far as I can see, to disprove the view that emotions only provide a psychological condition in the absence of which we should not have been in a fit state ever to intuit the characteristic of goodness or the relation of obligation. I certainly should not admit that the emotion was normally or originally prior to at least a confused apprehension of good or evil, rightness or wrongness; but even if I, like some even among the objectivists and non-naturalists, admitted this and made the feeling of the emotion a necessary prior condition of the apprehension, Westermarck's conclusion would not follow. The making of an ethical judgment will in any case presuppose various psychological conditions, but it does not follow that the judgment must be about these conditions. Nobody would argue that ethical judgments must all really be about breathing because breathing is a necessary condition without which we could not have made the judgments. . . .

But probably the principal reason which makes people inclined to deny the objectivity of ethics is the fact that in ethical argument we are very soon brought to a point where we have to fall back on intuition, so that disputants are placed in a situation where there are just two conflicting intuitions between which there seem to be no means of deciding. However, it is not only ethics but all reasoning which presupposes intuition. I cannot argue A, ∴ B, ∴ C without seeing that A entails B and B entails C, and this must either be seen immediately or require a further argument. If it is seen

[2]*Mind,* Vol. LIII, No. 212, p. 354.
[3]*Ethical Relativity,* p. 60.

immediately, it is a case of intuition;[4] if it has to be established by a further argument, this means that another term, D, must be interpolated between A and B such that A entails D and D entails B, and similarly with B and C, but then the same question arises about A entailing D, so that sooner or later we must come to something which we see intuitively to be true, as the process of interpolation cannot go on *ad infinitum.* We cannot therefore, whatever we do, get rid of intuition if we are to have any valid inference at all. It may, however, be said that in subjects other than ethics people at any rate agree in their intuitions. But outside mathematics or formal logic this is by no means universally true. There is frequent disagreement about matters of fact as to what has happened or will happen or concerning the causes of something, and when we have exhausted the arguments on a given point in these matters there still remains a difference between the ways in which these arguments are regarded by the disputants. In any science where you cannot prove your conclusions but only make them more or less probable there will be different estimates as to the balance of probability. As in ethics you have to balance different values against each other in order to decide what you ought to do, so here you have to balance different probable arguments, and in order to do this you must rely at some point or other on an estimate of their strength which cannot itself be further justified by mediate reasoning. Yet, when everything has been said in the way of argument, people may not all agree. Some will attribute more weight to one consideration, others to another, as they do in ethical questions about what is the right action in a given case. Our decision as to which of two probable arguments is the stronger may be influenced by other arguments in turn; but in order to deal with the situation rationally we must also estimate the weight of these other arguments, so that in the last resort it is a matter of insight into their nature which cannot be settled by other arguments *ad infinitum.* Just as in a demonstrative argument you must see intuitively how each step follows from the preceding one, so in the case of a probable argument you must rely on estimates of the degree of probability given by the argument as compared to that given by arguments on the other side, and these estimates, unless the degree of probability can be mathematically calculated, must either be themselves intuitive or be deduced from other estimates which are intuitive. I do not wish to maintain that reasoning in these matters is altogether analogous to that which occurs in dealing with ethical questions, but at any rate it is the case here that, as in ethics, we are often confronted with a situation in which we either see or do not see, and cannot logically prove, that what we seem to see is true. Yet we cannot surely therefore conclude that the scientific or historical propositions under discussion are really only propositions about the state of mind of the people who assert them, or that they are neither true nor false, or that we have no justification whatever for believing any of them!

We must therefore have intuition, and in a subject where infallibility is not attainable intuitions will sometimes disagree. Some philosophers indeed prefer not to call them intuitions when they are wrong, but then the problem will be to distinguish real from ostensible intuitions, since people certainly sometimes think they see intuitively what is not true. Now Earl Russell says: "Since no way can be even imagined for deciding a difference as to values, the conclusion is forced upon us that the difference is one of tastes, not one as to any objective truth";[5] but what I have said shows that we can imagine plenty of ways. I have indicated that errors as to judgments of

[4]This proposition is not convertible: I include under "intuition" cases where some mediation is required but insight goes beyond anything that could be strictly proved by the mediation.

[5]*Religion and Science,* p. 250.

value may arise (a) from lack of the requisite experience, (b) from intellectual confusions of some sort, (c) from failure to attend adequately to certain aspects of the situation or of the consequences, or (d) from psychological causes such as those with which the psychoanalyst deals. Therefore to remove errors we may (a) supply the lacking experience, or failing this, if possible, describe it in a way which will make its nature clear to the other party; we may (b) dispel intellectual confusions by making adequate distinctions or exposing actual fallacies such as make a person think he has seen that A is C when he has really only seen that A is B and mistakenly identified B with C; we may (c) suggest the direction of attention to the neglected points, or we may (d) use psychological methods. And we shall, if we are wise, also look out to see whether we ourselves have tripped up in any of these ways. Further, even when inference cannot completely prove or disprove, we may use it to confirm or cast doubt on ostensible intuition. The large class of errors which result mainly from an unwillingness really to seek for the truth can hardly be used as an argument against objectivity, since they are due to the moral fault of the persons who are in error and could have been removed if the latter had tried. In these cases the trouble is not that there are no means of deciding but that the means are not used.

The methods I have suggested will not always be successful, but then is there any sphere in which human efforts always do succeed? Even the methodology of physical science cannot lay down rules which will guarantee that any scientist can make discoveries or show him in detail in advance how to prove to others the truth of the discoveries when made. I am not claiming that it is possible in practice to remove all ethical differences, but how do we know that it could not be done if there were a will on each side to listen to what the other had to say and an intelligence to discern the best methods to adopt in order to facilitate a decision? A person cannot be brought into agreement even with the established truths of science if he will not listen to what the scientist says, and there is no reason to think even with ethical intuition that there are not describable processes by which any cause of error can on principle be removed. I insert the words "on principle" simply because it will still often be the case that none of the disputants thinks of the right way of removing the error or that the person in error will not or cannot take it, as also occurs in disputes about questions of fact outside ethics.

Where the intuitive belief is due to non-intellectual factors of a kind which vitiate it, there seem to be two possibilities of cure. First, the person concerned may lose all tendency to hold the intuitive conviction when its alleged cause is clearly pointed out to him. The alleged cause is then in his case probably at least an essential part of the real cause. If, on the other hand, the intuitive belief remains unimpaired, and the man does not react to the causal explanation in a way which suggests that it has really touched a sore point, this is presumptive evidence that the explanation is mistaken. But, secondly, the cure from a false belief due to non-intellectual factors is more likely to arise because the man has been induced to approach the subject in a new spirit than merely because the true causation of the belief has been suggested to him. After all it is impossible to prove even to an unprejudiced person that such a causal theory as to the origin of a person's belief is really correct. How to induce a person to make such a new approach is a question not of logical argument but of practical psychology.

We must not think of intuition as something quite by itself, uninfluenced by inference; it is helped by inference but sees beyond what could be proved by inference. And, when intuitive ethical views differ, use may be made of inference to support one or other of the clashing views, especially by showing that it fits well into a coherent ethical system. This will not settle the question absolutely conclusively, but it can help toward settlement. Perhaps as the result of the inference one of the parties to the dispute may realize that he does not see by intuition what he claimed to see, but something rather different. It would thus be a great mistake to say that, when two men disagree on an ethical question, there is nothing to be done about it or that there is no scope in ethics for inference. No argument is available which could prove the subjectivity or fallaciousness of all ethics without establishing a similar conclusion about all other branches of study except mathematics and formal logic. . . .

1949

Fallacies in Moral Philosophy

Stuart Hampshire

1. In 1912 there appeared in *Mind* an article by the late Professor Prichard entitled "Does Moral Philosophy Rest on a Mistake?" I wish to ask the same question about contemporary moral philosophy, but to suggest different reasons for an affirmative answer. Most recent academic discussions of moral philosophy have directly or indirectly reflected the conception of the subject-matter of moral philosophy which is stated or implied in Professor Prichard's article; and this conception of the subject was in turn directly derived from Kant. Kant's influence has been so great, that it is now difficult to realize how revolutionary it was; yet I think that his main thesis, now generally accepted without question by philosophers as the starting-point of moral philosophy, had not been advocated, or even seriously entertained, by any philosopher who preceded him. I shall suggest that the *unbridgeable* separation between moral judgments and factual judgments, which Kant introduced, has had the effect, in association with certain logical assumptions, of leading philosophers away from the primary and proper questions of moral philosophy.[1]

What I shall summarily call the post-Kantian thesis, now so widely accepted without question, is: there is an unbridgeable logical gulf between sentences which

[1]Hume never denied that our moral judgments are based on arguments about matters of fact; he only showed that these arguments are not logically conclusive or deductive arguments.

Stuart Hampshire, "Fallacies in Moral Philosophy," *Mind* 58 (1949). Reprinted with the permission of Oxford University Press.

express statements of fact and sentences which express judgments of value and particularly moral judgments; this absolute logical independence, ignored or not clearly stated by Aristotle, must be the starting-point of moral philosophy, and constitutes its peculiar problem. Post-Kantian philosophers of different logical persuasions have, of course, given very different accounts of the logic and use of value judgments; but they have generally agreed in regarding the logical independence of moral and empirical beliefs as defining the main problem of ethics.

If one reads the Nichomachean Ethics after reading the works of (for example) Professor G. E. Moore or Sir David Ross or Professor Stevenson, one has the impression of confronting a wholly different subject. The first point of difference can be tentatively expressed by saying that Aristotle is almost entirely concerned to analyze the problems of the moral *agent,* while most contemporary moral philosophers seem to be primarily concerned to analyze the problems of the moral *judge* or critic. Aristotle describes and analyzes the processes of thought, or types of argument, which lead up to the *choice* of one course of action, or way of life, in preference to another, while most contemporary philosophers describe the arguments (or lack of arguments) which lead up to the acceptance or rejection of a moral *judgment about actions.* Aristotle's Ethics incidentally mentions the kind of arguments we use as spectators in justifying sentences which express moral praise and blame of actions already performed, while many contemporary moral philosophers scarcely mention any other kind of argument. Aristotle's principal question is—What sort of arguments do we use in practical deliberation about policies and courses of action and in choosing one kind of life in preference to another? What are the characteristic differences between moral and theoretical problems? The question posed by most contemporary moral philosophers seems to be—What do we mean by, and how (if at all) do we establish the truth of, sentences used to express moral judgments about our own or other people's actions?

The difference between these two approaches to the problems of moral philosophy emerges most clearly from the analogy between aesthetics and ethics to which allusion is made both in Aristotle's Ethics and also in most modern discussions of so-called value judgments (*e.g.* by Sir David Ross in "The Right and the Good" and by Professor Ayer in "Language, Truth and Logic"). For Aristotle (as for Plato) the aesthetic analogy which illuminates the problem of moral philosophy is the analogy between the artist or craftsman's characteristic procedures in designing and executing his work and the similar, but also different, procedures which we all use in designing and executing practical policies in ordinary life. For contemporary moral philosophers, largely preoccupied with elucidating sentences which express moral praise or blame (moral "judgments" in the sense in which a judge gives judgments), the relevant analogy is between sentences expressing moral praise or condemnation and sentences expressing aesthetic praise or condemnation. As aesthetics has become the study of the logic and language of aesthetic *criticism,* so moral philosophy has become largely the study of the logic and language of moral criticism.

No one will be inclined to dispute that the processes of thought which are characteristic of the artist or craftsman in conceiving and executing his designs, are essentially different from the processes of the critic who passes judgment on the artist's work; it is notorious that the processes involved in, and the gifts and training required for, the actual making of a work of art are different from those which are required for the competent appraisal of the work; the artist's problem is not the critic's problem. An aesthetician may choose—and in fact most modern aestheticians have chosen—to confine himself to an analysis of the characteristic arguments involved in arriving at a judgment about a work of art (theories of a special aesthetic emotion, of objective standards of taste, etc.). Alternatively he may analyze and characterize the creative process itself (theories of imagination, the relation of technique to conception, the formation of style, the nature of inspiration, etc.). He may decide that the two inquiries, though certainly distinguishable and separable, are in some respects complementary, or at least that there are some questions contained within the first which cannot be answered without a prior answer to the second. But, however complementary they may be, the first inquiry certainly does not include the second. Those who wish to distinguish more clearly the peculiar characteristics of artistic activity, will learn little or nothing from the typical aestheticians' discussions of the objective and subjective interpretations of critical aesthetic judgments. But it seems now to be generally assumed that to ask whether sentences expressing moral praise or blame are to be classified as true or false statements, or alternatively as mere expressions of feeling, is somehow a substitute for the analysis of the processes of thought by which as moral agents we decide what we ought to do and how we ought to behave. Unless this is the underlying assumption, it is difficult to understand why moral philosophers should concentrate attention primarily on the analysis of ethical terms as they are used in sentences expressing moral praise and blame; for we are not primarily interested in moral criticism, or even self-criticism, except in so far as it is directly or indirectly an aid to the solution of practical problems, to deciding what we ought to do in particular situations or types of situation; we do not normally perplex ourselves deeply in moral appraisal for its own sake, in allotting moral marks to ourselves or to other people. The typical moral problem is not a spectator's problem or a problem of classifying or describing conduct, but a problem of practical choice and decision.

But the aesthetic analogy may be misleading, in that the relation of the value judgments of the art critic to the characteristic problems of the artist or craftsman cannot be assumed to be the same as the relation of the sentences expressing moral praise or blame to the problems of the moral agent.[2] To press the analogy would be question-begging, although the validity of the analogy between the problems of ethics and aesthetics is so often assumed. Leaving aside the analogy, the issue is—Is the answer to the question "What are the distinguishing characteristics of sentences expressing moral praise or blame?" necessarily the same as the answer to the question "What are the distinguishing characteristics of moral problems as they present themselves to us as practical agents?" Unless these two questions are identical, or unless the first includes the second, much of contemporary moral philosophy is concerned with a relatively trivial side-issue, or is at the very least incomplete. My thesis is that the answer to the second question must contain the answer to the first, but that, if one tries to answer the first question without approaching it as part of the second, the answer will tend to be, not only incomplete, but positively misleading; and that the now most widely accepted philosophical interpretations of moral judgments, their logical status and peculiarities, are radically misleading for this reason. They purport to be logical characterizations of moral judgments and of the distinguishing features of moral arguments, but in these characterizations the *primary* use of moral judgments (= decisions) is largely or even entirely ignored.

[2]In so far as we now distinguish between the creative artist and the mere craftsman, a work of art by definition is not the answer to any problem; the artist is only said to have problems when conceived as a craftsman, that is, as having technical problems of devising means towards a given or presumed end. Where there is no problem posed, there can be no question of a right or wrong solution of it. Therefore the critic of poetry cannot be expected to show how the poem should be re-written; he describes, but he does not prescribe or make a practical judgment, as does the critic of conduct or technique. So the aesthetic analogy misleads in at least this respect; the valued critic of art excels in description and classification; he is not the artist's adviser, while moral or technical criticism is necessarily the giving of practical advice.

2. Suppose (what probably occurs occasionally in most people's experience) one is confronted with a difficult and untrivial situation in which one is in doubt what one ought to do, and then, after full consideration of the issues involved, one arrives at a conclusion. One's conclusion, reached after deliberation, expressed in the sentence "*x* is the best thing to do in these circumstances," is a pure or primary moral judgment (the solution of a practical problem). It is misleading to the point of absurdity to describe this sentence, as used in such a context, as meaningful only in the sense in which an exclamation is meaningful, or as having no literal significance, or as having the function merely of expressing and evoking feeling. It is also misleading to describe it as a statement about the agent's feeling or attitude; for such a description suggests that the judgment would be defended, if attacked, primarily by an appeal to introspection. It is surely misleading to describe the procedure by which such a judgment or decision is established as right as one of comparing degrees of moral emotion towards alternative courses of action. I am supposing (what is normal in such cases) that the agent has reasoned and argued about the alternatives, and am asserting that he would then justify his conclusion, if it were attacked, by reference to these arguments; and a statement about his own moral feelings or attitudes would not be, within the ordinary use of language, either a necessary or sufficient justification. Therefore the characterization of such judgments as purely, or even largely, reports of feelings or attitudes is at the least incomplete and misleadingly incomplete, because in this characterization the typical procedures of deliberation on which the judgment is based are suppressed or ignored. It is also paradoxical and misleading to introduce the word "intuition," as another group of post-Kantian philosophers have done, in describing the procedure by which such a judgment is arrived at, or by which it is justified and defended; for the force of the word "intuition" is to suggest that the ccnclusion is not established by any recognized form of argument, by any ratiocinative process involving a succession of steps which are logically criticizable; the word "intuition" carries the suggestion that we do not, or even cannot, deliberate and calculate in deciding what we ought to do; but we always can and often actually do deliberate and calculate.

If the procedure of practical deliberation does not conform, either in its intermediate steps or in the form of its conclusions, with any forms of argument acknowledged as respectable in logical text-books, this is a deficiency of the logical text-books. Or rather it is a mistake in the *interpretation* of text books of logic to assume that they provide, or that they are intended to provide, patterns of all forms of reasoning or argument which can properly be described as rational argument. Arguments may be, in the ordinary and wider sense, rational, without being included among the types of argument which are ordinarily studied by logicians, since logicians are generally concerned exclusively with the types of argument which are characteristic of the *a priori* and empirical sciences. There are other patterns of argument habitually used outside the sciences, which may be described as more or less rational in the sense that they are more or less strictly governed by recognized (though not necessarily formulated) rules of relevance. If one criticizes a sequence of sentences by saying that assertion or denial of the earlier members of the sequence is irrelevant to acceptance or rejection of their successors, then this sequence is being regarded as constituting an argument. Aristotle at least remarks that not all arguments are theoretical arguments, terminating in a conclusion which is intended as a statement, either factual or logically true; there are also practical arguments—he naturally says "syllogisms"—the form of which is similar in many respects to some types of theoretical argument, but which are also characteristically different in their form; in particular they differ in the form of their conclusion, which is not a theoretical or true-or-false statement, but has the distinctive form of a practical judgment, *e.g.* "this is the right action" or "this is the best thing to do," or "this ought to be done."

Even when sentences containing moral terms are used by spectators (not agents) in contexts in which they seem to be in fact associated with a purely emotional reaction to a decision or action, it is misleadingly incomplete to characterize them as having the logical force only, or largely, of expressions of, or statements about, the speaker's or writer's feelings or attitudes. If a purely critical and apparently emotional moral judgment of this kind is challenged and needs to be defended and justified, it will be justified by the same kind of arguments which one would have used as an agent in practical deliberation. If I am not prepared to produce such practical arguments, pointing to what ought to have been done, I shall admit that I am not making a genuine moral judgment, but merely expressing or reporting my own feelings; and I shall admit that it was misleading to use the form of sentence ordinarily associated with moral judgments, and not with expressions of feeling. Doubtless many sentences containing moral terms are ambiguous, and may be normally used both as expressions of practical judgments and as expressions of feeling; but the important point is that, if challenged about our intentions, we are required to *distinguish* between such uses; and our languages, by providing the distinctive quasi-imperative form of the practical judgment, enable us to distinguish. But moral philosophers, tacitly assuming that moral judgments must be descriptive statements, have represented a moral problem as a critic's or spectator's problem of proper classification and description.

If, following Aristotle, one begins by describing how moral problems differ both from technical and theoretical problems, one will have begun to answer the question about the distinctive nature of moral judgments, even in their purely critical use. But if one begins by separating them from their context in practical deliberation, and considers them as quasi-theoretical[3] expressions of moral praise and condemnation, the resulting characterization of them must be misleadingly incomplete.

3. The fact that moral judgments, in spite of the peculiarity of their form as practical judgments, are established by familiar patterns of argument, has been underemphasized by post-Kantian moral philosophers as a consequence of three connected logical doctrines: (*a*) the doctrine that so-called value judgments cannot be derived from factual judgments; (*b*) the doctrine that, although we deliberate and argue about the facts of moral situations (*e.g.* about the probable consequences of various possible actions), no further argument is possible when once the facts of the situation have been determined; we are thus left in every case of practical deliberation with (*c*) an ultimate moral judgment, which cannot be replaced by any statement of fact, or by an empirical statement of any kind, and which cannot itself be defended by further argument. From no consideration of facts, or accumulation of factual knowledge, can we ever deduce a moral judgment of the form "this ought to be done" or "this is the right action in these circumstances." Therefore all appeal to the procedure of deliberation is irrelevant to the real problem, which is the analysis or characterization of these *ultimate* moral judgments.

The fallacy in this position, as I have stated it, emerges in the words "derive" and "deduce." It is only in limiting cases that, in describing the logic of any class of sentences of ordinary discourse, one can reasonably expect to find another class of sentences from which the problem-sentences are logically deducible. Statements about

[3]To pose the problem of ethics as the problem of "ethical predicates" or "non-natural characteristics," is at the outset to suggest that moral judgments are to be interpreted as a peculiar kind of descriptive statement.

physical things cannot be deduced, or logically derived, from statements about sensations; statements about people's character or dispositions cannot be deduced, or logically derived from, statements about their behavior; yet in both cases the truth of the first kind of statement is established exclusively by reference to the second kind. In general, one kind of sentence may be established and defended exclusively by reference to another kind, without the first kind being deducible, or logically derivable, from the second. When as philosophers we ask how a particular kind of sentence is to be categorized or described, we are asking ourselves by what sort of arguments it is established and how we justify its use if it is disputed; to explain its logic and meaning is generally to describe and illustrate by examples the kind of sentences which are conventionally accepted as sufficient grounds for its assertion or rejection. So we may properly elucidate moral or practical judgments by saying that they are established and supported by arguments consisting of factual judgments of a particular range, while admitting that they are never strictly deducible, or in this sense logically derivable, from any set of factual judgments.

Certainly no practical judgment is logically deducible from any set of statements of fact; for if practical judgments were so deducible, they would be redundant; we could confine ourselves simply to factual or theoretical judgments; this is in effect what strict Utilitarians, such as Bentham, proposed that we should do. Bentham recommended the removal of distinctively moral terms from the language, so that moral problems would be replaced by technical problems, or problems of applied science. He made this proposal quite self-consciously and deliberately, wishing to introduce a science of morals, in which all moral problems would be experimentally decidable as technical problems. The distinctive form in which moral problems are posed and moral conclusions expressed disappears in his usage, precisely because he makes arguments about matters of fact *logically conclusive* in settling moral problems; and it is precisely to this *replacement* of moral terms that critics of strict Utilitarians have always objected (*e.g.* Professor G. E. Moore in *Principia Ethica*); they have argued that Utilitarians confuse the reasons on which moral judgments may be based with those judgments themselves; and this confusion arises from supposing that the reasons must be logically conclusive reasons, so that to accept the empirical premisses and to deny the moral conclusion is self-contradictory. But it does not follow from the fact that moral or practical judgments are not in their normal use so deducible that they must be described as ultimate, mysterious, and removed from the sphere of rational discussion. All argument is not deduction, and giving reasons in support of a judgment or statement is not necessarily, or even generally, giving logically conclusive reasons.

Once this assumption is removed, it is possible to reconsider, without philosophical prejudice, what is the difference and the relation between ordinary empirical statements and moral judgments as we actually use them when we are arguing with ourselves, or with others, about what we ought to do. It is important to consider examples of practical or moral problems which are neither trivial in themselves nor abstractly described; for it is only by reflecting on our procedure when confronted with what would ordinarily be called a genuine moral problem that the characteristic types of argument can be seen clearly deployed. A simplified variant of the situation presented in a recent novel[4] may serve the purpose. Suppose that I am convinced that if I continue to live, I cannot avoid inflicting great and indefinitely prolonged unhappiness on one or both of two people, and at the same time on myself; by committing suicide

[4]*The Heart of the Matter,* by Graham Greene.

without detection I can avoid this accumulation of unhappiness; I therefore decide, after careful deliberation, that the right or best thing to do is to commit suicide. This is a moral judgment of the primary kind. (Having reached this conclusion, I may of course in any particular case fail to act in accordance with it; as Aristotle points out, deciding *that* x is the best thing to do and deciding *to* do x are both distinguishable and separable.) Suppose that in this case the moral judgment, which is the conclusion of my deliberation, is challenged by someone who at the same time agrees with me in my assessment of all the facts of the situation; that is, he agrees with me about the probable consequences of all the possible courses of action, but does not agree with my conclusion that it is right to commit suicide. An argument develops; we each give our reasons for saying that suicide under these circumstances is right or wrong. However the argument may develop in detail, it will generally exhibit the following features. (1) Although it is assumed that my disputant agrees with me about the facts of this particular situation (probable consequences of various actions etc.), he will in his argument appeal to other facts or beliefs about the world, which are not strictly describable as beliefs about the facts of this particular situation. For instance, we might both recognize as relevant a dispute partly empirical and partly logical, about whether there is life after death, and whether the Christian dogmas on this subject are true or significant; or we may become involved in a largely historical argument about the social effects of suicide; and it would be recognized as pertinent to produce psychological arguments to the effect that intense unhappiness is often preferred to mere loneliness and *therefore* (and this "therefore" is not the sign of an entailment) it would be better not to desert the other two people involved. *The point is that it does not follow from the fact that two people are in agreement about the facts of a particular situation, but disagree in their moral judgment, that their disagreement is ultimate and admits of no further rational argument;* hence (2) our disagreement about the moral or practical conclusion, which is not a disagreement about the facts of the particular situation, is nevertheless, a disagreement to which empirical arguments, beliefs about an indefinitely wide range of matters of fact, are recognized to be relevant. If we are deliberating or arguing about whether suicide is right or wrong in these particular circumstances (or in any circumstances), then our psychological, historical and religious beliefs are always taken to be relevant parts of the argument. By representing so-called value judgments as ultimate and logically divorced from ordinary factual judgments, philosophers have implicitly or explicitly suggested that such sentences as "suicide is always wrong" or "suicide is wrong in these circumstances" cannot be defended or refuted by appeals to facts or to the empirical sciences. This paradox is a legacy of Kant's anxiety to underline as strongly as possible the difference between practical problems which are moral problems and those which are purely technical problems. Almost all previous philosophers—and most people without Kantian or other philosophical prejudices—have assumed accumulating knowledge, or changing beliefs arising out of the study of history, psychology, anthropology and other empirical sciences, to be relevant to their moral judgments; to be relevant, not in the sense that the falsity of moral judgments previously accepted as true can be *deduced* from some empirical propositions of history, psychology or any natural science, but in the sense in which (for example) propositions about somebody's conduct are relevant to propositions about his character; that is, previous moral judgments are shown to be groundless, the empirical propositions on which they were based having been contradicted as scientific or historical knowledge increases. The conflicting moral conclusions of a Marxist and a Christian Fundamentalist, or the differences which may arise even between two contemporary and similarly educated liberal unbelievers, will generally (but not always or necessarily) be shown in argument to rest on different empirical or at least corrigible beliefs about the constitution of the universe. Whenever we argue about any moral question which is not trivial, our beliefs and assumptions, however rudimentary and half-formulated, about psychological, sociological and probably theological questions are recognized as relevant, as logically involved in the nature of the dispute.

The result of the supposed argument about my judgment that suicide is the right policy in this particular circumstance might be that I am convinced that my judgment was wrong, and am persuaded that suicide is not the right policy. I might be persuaded to withdraw my original judgment, either because I have been made to recognize a fault in the logic of my previous argument, or because I have been persuaded to abandon admittedly relevant beliefs about matters of fact, or because my attention has been directed to new facts as being relevant to the decision, facts which I had known but the relevance of which I had previously overlooked. To direct attention to further known facts as relevant to a judgment is perhaps the most important effect and function of moral arguments or practical deliberation (*e.g.* of giving practical advice). It is misleading to speak of "the facts of a situation" in such a way as to suggest that there must be a closed set of propositions which, once established, precisely determine the situation.[5] The situations in which we must act or abstain from acting, are "open" in the sense that they cannot be uniquely described and finally circumscribed. Situations do not present themselves with their labels attached to them; if they did, practical problems would be conclusively soluble theoretical problems, the philosopher's dream; but *ἐν τῇ αἰσθήσει ἡ κρίσις*—the crux is in the labelling, or the decision depends on how we see the situation.

For these reasons the logical divorce between so-called judgments of value and factual judgments is misleading; for arguments about practical conclusions are arguments about facts. Our moral or practical judgments—"*x* is the right or best course of action (in these or in all circumstances)"—are corrigible by experience and observation; we feel certain about some, and very doubtful about others.

4. Certainly there may (logically) be cases in which we cannot attribute conflicting solutions of practical moral problems to conflicting beliefs about matters of fact; that is, two disputants, in giving their reasons for conflicting moral judgments, may be unable to find among their reasons any empirical proposition which is accepted by one of them and rejected by the other. It is logically possible that A and B should agree entirely *e.g.* about the effects of capital punishment, and furthermore should find no relevant differences in their general psychological or sociological or other beliefs, and yet disagree as to whether capital punishment should or should not now be abolished. However rare such situations may be (and I believe them to be much more rare than is commonly allowed) such so-called "ultimate" moral differences may occur. Both A and B, if they can claim to be making a moral judgment and not merely expressing their own feelings about, or attitudes towards, capital punishment, will be able to give the reasons which seem to them sufficient to justify their conclusion; but what is accepted by A as a sufficient reason for a practical conclusion is not accepted by B as a sufficient reason and *vice versa.* They may then argue further to ensure that each does recognize the reason which he is claiming to be sufficient in this case as

[5]The word "fact," here as always, is treacherous, involving the old confusion between the actual situation and the description of it; the situation is given, but not "the facts of the situation"; to state the facts is to analyze and interpret the situation. And just this is the characteristic difficulty of actual practical decisions, which disappears in the text-book cases, where the "relevant facts" are pre-selected. So the determining arguments are cut out of the text-book, and the gap is filled by "intuition" or feeling.

sufficient in other cases; but, when this consistency of use is once established, the argument must terminate. How is such an "ultimate" or irresoluble difference about a moral judgment properly described?

Compare this ultimate difference about the practical judgment with a similar ultimate difference about a theoretical judgment: if A and B were to disagree about whether somebody is intelligent, and yet find that they did not disagree about the facts (actual behavior) or probabilities (how he is likely to behave under hypothetical conditions) on which their judgment is based, they would describe their difference as a difference in the use of the word "intelligent"; they would say "you use a different criterion of intelligence, and so do not mean by "intelligent" exactly what I mean."[6] Similarly when it has been shown that A and B generally apply wholly or largely different tests in deciding whether something ought or ought not to be done, they might properly describe their so-called ultimate difference by saying that they do not both mean the same, or exactly the same, thing when they say that something ought or ought not to be done; and in most such cases of ultimate or irresoluble moral differences this is in fact what we do say—that different societies (and even different individuals within the same society) may have more or less different moral terminologies, which are not mutually translatable. But of practical judgments one cannot say that differences which are in principle irresoluble are *simply* terminological misunderstandings and in *no* sense genuine contradictions; for it is the distinguishing characteristic of practical judgments that they have a prescriptive or quasi-imperative force as part of their meaning. There is therefore one sense in which, when A says that capital punishment ought to be abolished and B says that it ought not, they are contradicting each other; their judgments contradict each other in the sense in which two conflicting commands or recommendations may be said to contradict each other. They can only argue about which of their prescriptions is right if they can agree on some common criteria of rightness. A, following the practice of all reforming moralists and many moral philosophers, may try to influence B's actions by giving moral reasons for preferring his own criteria of use to B's use; but in his advocacy of his own use of moral terms, he will be using his moral terms in his own way. The argument might have shown B that his conclusion was wrong in A's sense of "wrong" or even in his own sense of "wrong"; but no argument can show that B *must* use the criteria which A uses and so must attach the same meaning (in this sense) to moral terms as A. Between two consistently applied terminologies, whether in theoretical science or in moral decision, ultimately we must simply choose; we can give reasons for our choice, but not reasons for reasons for . . . *ad infinitum.*

5. We may find that many people do not deliberate and so can scarcely be said to make moral judgments, but simply act as they have been conditioned to act, and, when challenged, repeat the moral sentences which they have been taught to repeat or merely state or express personal feelings or attitudes. A second, and much smaller class, act generally, and even wholly, on impulse, in the sense that they do not propose practical problems to themselves or choose policies, but simply do whatever they feel inclined to do—and such people are to be distinguished from those who have *decided that* to act on impulse, or to do what one feels inclined to do, is the right policy; for this is to make a moral judgment. But the great majority of people for some part of their lives are think-

[6]"What do you mean by saying that he is intelligent?" is ordinarily interpreted as the same question as "what are your reasons for saying or why do you say, that he is intelligent?" Similarly, "What do you mean by saying that that was a wrong decision?" is the same question as "*Why* do you say that that was a wrong decision?" To find the different reasons in different cases is to find the meaning of "wrong," although no *one* set of reasons is *the* meaning.

ing about what is the best thing to do, sometimes reaching a conclusion and failing to act on it, sometimes reaching a conclusion which, in the light of corrections of their empirical beliefs or their logic, they later recognize to have been a wrong conclusion, and sometimes reaching a conclusion which they are prepared to defend by argument and acting in accordance with it.

"Thinking what is the best thing to do" describes a procedure which it is unprofitable, if not impossible, to analyze, or find a paraphrase for, in general terms without constant reference to specific cases. Aristotle begins by describing it as calculating means to a vaguely conceived end (happiness or well-doing), the nature of the end being more precisely determined by the means chosen as involved in its realization. But he progressively qualifies and complicates this schematic account in such a way as to suggest that to make a moral decision is not to choose means to an already decided end, but to choose a policy of means-to-end which is judged right or wrong as a whole. Practical problems are (as Kant emphasized and over-emphasized) sub-divisible into moral and purely technical problems; the choice of the most efficient means to an already determined end is not called a moral choice. It is the defining characteristic of a moral problem, that it requires an unconditional decision, the choice of an action or policy as a whole.

6. There is another and related logical fallacy, often implicitly assumed and not explicitly stated, which has led philosophers to describe moral or practical judgments as expressions or reports of feeling or as established by *a priori* intuitions, and to neglect their normal occurrence as the corrigible conclusions of arguments involving the facts of a particular situation and our general beliefs about the world; this is the fallacy of assuming that all literally significant sentences must correspond to something, or describe something. As ordinary empirical statements were said to correspond to facts, so some philosophers have introduced the word "values" in order that there should be something to which moral (and aesthetic) judgments can be said to correspond; we are said to "intuit" or to "apprehend" these values, these words being used to suggest an analogy with sense-perception. Other philosophers, wishing to define the world as the totality of facts, or as the objects of sense and introspection, have inferred that, as moral judgments cannot be said to correspond to anything in the external world, they must either correspond to something in the internal world (*i.e.* to feelings) or, failing that, that they cannot be admitted to be literally significant. The question "what do moral judgments correspond to?" or "what do they describe?" suggests itself particularly to those who are preoccupied with the critical use of these judgments as expressions of retrospective praise or blame; in so far as we relate them to practical deliberations and decisions, we come to recognize them as not descriptions of, but prescriptions for, actions. Practical judgments, no less than theoretical or descriptive statements, are in the natural sense of the words, literally significant, although they do not in the normal sense describe. If I say "this is (or would have been) the right action in these circumstances," this judgment can be significantly denied; but, as it is not a descriptive statement or statement of fact, the denial is not normally expressed in the form "it is *false* that this is the best action in these circumstances"; "true" and "false" are more naturally used with theoretical judgments and statements of fact.[7] Of course this distinction between true or false descriptive statements and right or wrong practical judgments is not absolute and clear; many sentences are partly descriptive and are partly expressions of practical judgments. But there is a distinction which emerges clearly in simple cases of pure moral judgments

[7]Although we can speak of believing that this is the right action we cannot speak of evidence that it is right. "Evidence" is tied to statements which are true or false.

and purely descriptive statements. One *can* describe somebody's behavior or character without making any moral judgment (*i.e.* prescription), even if in fact prescriptions and descriptions are often almost inextricably combined.

7. There is (I think) a widespread impression that the concentration of academic moral philosophers on the attempt to *define* ethical expressions—"good," "right," "ought," etc.,—as being the principal problem of moral philosophy has tended to make the subject sterile and unenlightening. One is inclined to say that it does not *matter* whether "right," as ordinarily used, is definable in terms of "good" or not. There is the feeling that the clarifications which one expects from the moral philosopher cannot be answered by verbal definitions or the discovery of paraphrases. And I think this apparently philistine impatience with the search for verbal definitions or equivalences has good logical grounds. If we wish to clarify our own or somebody else's use of moral terms, the discovery of verbal equivalences or paraphrases among these terms is not an answer, but, at the most, a preliminary step towards an answer. I can become clear about what somebody means by saying "this is the right action in these circumstances" only by finding out under what conditions he makes this judgment, and what reasons (and there may be many) he regards as sufficient to justify it. What we want to know, in clarifications of differences in our use of moral (or aesthetic) terms, is—What makes me (in the logical, not the causal sense) decide that this is the right action? There is no reason to expect a simple answer in terms of a single formula, *e.g.* "it is likely to increase happiness." But to search only for definitions or verbal equivalences is to assume that there must be a single sufficient reason from which I always and necessarily derive my judgment. This is another expression of the fundamental fallacy of thinking of analysis or clarification of the standard use of words or sentences as necessarily a matter of exhibiting deducibilities or entailments. If I am asked what I mean by saying of someone that he is intelligent, I explain my use of the word by describing specimens of the type of behavior to which I apply the word; I give some specimens of the types of statements about his behavior which would be taken as sufficient grounds for asserting or denying that he is intelligent. Similarly, one can only clarify the use of the principal moral (or aesthetic) terms—"good," "right," "ought," etc.—by describing specimens of conduct to which they are applied, that is, by quoting the different characteristics of actions which are normally and generally taken to be sufficient grounds for deciding that they are the right actions. The type of analysis which consists in defining, or finding synonyms for the moral terms of a particular language cannot illuminate the nature of moral decisions or practical problems; it is no more than local dictionary-making, or the elimination of redundant terms, which is useful only as a preliminary to the study of typical moral arguments. An informative treatise on ethics—or on the ethics of a particular society or person—would contain an accumulation of examples selected to illustrate the kind of decisions which are said to be right in various circumstances, and the reasons given and the arguments used in concluding that they are right. An uninformative treatise on ethics consists of specimens of moral sentences, separated from actual or imaginable contexts of argument about particular practical problems, and treated as texts for the definition of moral terms; and many academic text-books follow this pattern.

Summary—The four logically related fallacies underlying the typical post-Kantian approach to moral philosophy are (*a*) The assimilation of moral or practical judgments to descriptive statements, which is associated with concentration on the use or moral terms in sentences expressing a spectator's praise or blame; (*b*) the inference from the fact that moral or practical judgment cannot be logically derived from statements of fact that they cannot be based on, or established exclusively by reference to, beliefs about matters of fact; hence theories that moral judgments must be ultimate and irrational, that they are established by intuition or are not literally significant; (*c*) the assumption that all literally significant sentences must correspond to or describe something; moral decisions do not correspond to or describe anything, but they may, nevertheless, be said to be rational or irrational, right or wrong.[8] (*d*) The confusion between clarifying the use of ethical terms with discovering definitions of, or verbal equivalences between, these terms; the search for definitions is another expression of the old obsession of philosophers with entailment and deducibility as the only admissible relation between sentences in rational argument. To interpret "rational argument" so narrowly is, although misleading, not in itself fallacious; but if, on the basis of this arbitrary restriction, moral judgments are relegated to a logical limbo, labelled "emotive," the study of the characteristic logic of these sentences, and of the types of argument in which they occur, is obscured and suppressed.

[8]"I decided that *x* was the right thing to do" is a descriptive statement, true or false; but "*x* was the right thing to do" is a practical or moral judgment, right or wrong.

1949–1950

Egoism as a Theory of Human Motives

C. D. Broad

There seem *prima facie* to be a number of different kinds of ultimate desire which all or most men have. Plausible examples would be the desire to get pleasant experiences and to avoid unpleasant ones, the desire to get and exercise power over others, and the desire to do what is right and to avoid doing what is wrong. Very naturally philosophers have tried to reduce this plurality. They have tried to show that there is one and only one kind of ultimate desire, and that all other desires which seem at first sight to be ultimate are really subordinate to this. I shall call the view that there really are several different kinds of ultimate desire *Pluralism of Ultimate Desires;* and I shall call the view that there is really only one kind of ultimate desire *Monism of Ultimate Desires.* Even if a person were a pluralist about ultimate desires, he might hold that there are certain important features common to all the different kinds of ultimate desire.

Now much the most important theory on this subject is that all kinds of ultimate desire are *egoistic.* This is not in itself necessarily a monistic theory. For there might be several irreducibly different kinds of ultimate desire, even if they were all egoistic. Moreover, there might be several irreducibly different, though not necessarily unrelated, senses of the word "egoistic"; and some desires might be egoistic in one sense and some in another, even if all were egoistic in some sense. But the theory often takes the special form that the only kind of ultimate desire is the desire to get or to prolong

Being part of the Marett Memorial Lecture, 1949, delivered in Exeter College, Oxford.

pleasant experiences, and to avoid or to cut short unpleasant experiences, for oneself. That *is* a monistic theory. I shall call the wider theory *Psychological Egoism*, and this special form of it *Psychological Hedonism*. Psychological Egoism might be true, even though psychological hedonism were false; but, if psychological egoism be false, psychological hedonism cannot be true.

I shall now discuss Psychological Egoism. I think it is best to begin by enumerating all the kinds of desire that I can think of which might reasonably be called "egoistic" in one sense or another.

(1) Everyone has a special desire for the continued existence of himself in his present bodily life, and a special dread of his own death. This may be called *Desire for Self-preservation*. (2) Everyone desires to get and to prolong experiences of certain kinds, and to avoid and to cut short experiences of certain other kinds, because the former are pleasant to him and the latter unpleasant. This may be called *Desire for one's own Happiness*. (3) Everyone desires to acquire, keep, and develop certain mental and bodily powers and dispositions, and to avoid, get rid of, or check certain others. In general he wants to be or to become a person of a certain kind, and wants not to be or to become a person of certain other kinds. This may be called *Desire to be a Self of a certain kind*. (4) Everyone desires to feel certain kinds of emotion towards himself and his own powers and dispositions, and not to feel certain other kinds of reflexive emotion. This may be called *Desire for Self-respect*. (5) Everyone desires to get and to keep for himself the exclusive possession of certain material objects or the means of buying and keeping such objects. This may be called *Desire to get and to keep Property*. (6) Everyone desires to get and to exercise power over certain other persons, so as to make them do what he wishes, regardless of whether they wish it or not. This may be called *Desire for Self-assertion*. (7) Everyone desires that other persons shall believe certain things about him and feel certain kinds of emotion towards him. He wants to be noticed, to be respected by some, to be loved by some, to be feared by some, and so on. Under this head come the *Desire for Self-display, for Affection*, and so on.

Lastly, it must be noted that some desires, which are concerned primarily with other things or persons, either would not exist at all or would be very much weaker or would take a different form if it were not for the fact that those things or persons already stand in certain relations to oneself. I shall call such relations *egoistic motive-stimulants*. The following are among the most important of these. (i) The relation of ownership. If a person owns a house or a wife, *e.g.*, he feels a much stronger desire to improve the house or to make the woman happy than if the house belongs to another or the woman is married to someone else. (ii) Blood-relationship. A person desires, *e.g.*, the well-being of his own children much more strongly than that of other children. (iii) Relations of love and friendship. A person desires strongly, *e.g.*, to be loved and respected by those whom he loves. He may desire only to be feared by those whom he hates. And he may desire only very mildly, if at all, to be loved and respected by those to whom he feels indifferent. (iv) The relationship of being fellow-members of an institution to which one feels loyalty and affection. Thus, *e.g.*, an Englishman will be inclined to do services to another Englishman which he would not do for a foreigner, and an Old Etonian will be inclined to do services to another Old Etonian which he would not do for an Old Harrovian.

I think that I have now given a reasonably adequate list of motives and motive-stimulants which could fairly be called "egoistic" in some sense or other. Our next business is to try to classify them and to consider their inter-relations.

(1) Let us begin by asking ourselves the following question. Which of these motives could act on a person if he had been the only person or thing that had ever existed?

The answer is that he could still have had desires for *self-preservation,* for *his own happiness,* to be a *self of a certain kind,* and for *self-respect.* But he could not, unless he were under the delusion that there were other persons or things, have desires for *property,* for *self-assertion,* or for *self-display.* Nor could he have any of those desires which are stimulated by family or other alio-relative relationships. I shall call those desires, and only those, which could be felt by a person who knew or believed himself to be the only existent in the universe, *Self-confined.*

(2) Any desire which is not self-confined may be described as *extra-verted;* for the person who has such a desire is necessarily considering, not only himself and his own qualities, dispositions, and states, but also some other thing or person. If the desire is egoistic, it will also be *intro-verted;* for the person who has such a desire will also be considering himself and his relations to that other person or thing, and this will be an essential factor conditioning his experience. Thus a self-confined desire is purely introverted, whilst a desire which is egoistic but not self-confined is both intro-verted and extra-verted. Now we may subdivide desires of the latter kind into two classes, according as the primary emphasis is on the former or the latter aspect. Suppose that the person is concerned primarily with himself and his own acts and experiences, and that he is concerned with the other thing or person only or mainly as an object of these acts or experiences or as the other term in a relationship to himself. Then I shall call the desire *Self-centered.* I shall use the term *Self-regarding* to include both desires which are self-centered and those which are self-confined. Under the head of self-centered desires come the desire for *property,* for *self-assertion,* for *self-display,* and for *affection.*

(3) Lastly, we come to desires which are both intro-verted and extra-verted, but where the primary emphasis is on the other person or thing and its states. Here the relationship of the other person or thing to oneself acts as a strong egoistic motive-stimulant, but one's primary desire is that the other person or thing shall be in a certain state. I will call such desires *Other-regarding.* A desire which is other-regarding, but involves an egoistic motive-stimulant, may be described as *Self-referential.* The desire of a mother to render services to her own children which she would not be willing to render to other children is an instance of a desire which is other-regarding but self-referential. So, too, is the desire of a man to inflict suffering on one who has injured him or one whom he envies.

Having thus classified the various kinds of egoistic desire, I will now say something about their inter-relations.

(1) It is obvious that self-preservation may be desired as a necessary condition of one's own happiness; since one cannot acquire or prolong pleasant experiences unless one continues to exist. So the desire for self-preservation *may* be subordinate to the desire for one's own happiness. But it seems pretty clear that a person often desires to go on living even when there is no prospect that the remainder of his life will contain a balance of pleasant over unpleasant experiences. This attitude is expressed very strongly in the loathsome lines of Maecenas which Seneca has handed down to posterity:

Debilem facito manu, debilem pede coxo
tuber adstrue gibberum, lubricos quate dentes;
vita dum superest, bene est; banc mihi, vel acuta
si sedeam cruce, sustine.

(2) It is also obvious that property and power over others may be desired as a means to self-preservation or to happiness. So the desire to get and keep property, and the desire to get and exert power over others, *may* be subordinate to the desire for self-preservation or for one's own happiness. But it seems fairly certain that the former de-

sires are sometimes independent of the latter. Even if a person begins by desiring property or power only as a means—and it is very doubtful whether we always do begin in that way—it seems plain that he often comes to desire them for themselves, and to sacrifice happiness, security, and even life for them. Any miser, and almost any keen politician, provides an instance of this.

It is no answer to this to say that a person who desires power or property enjoys the experiences of getting and exercising power or of amassing and owning property, and then to argue that therefore his ultimate desire is to give himself those pleasant experiences. The premiss here is true, but the argument is self-stultifying. The experiences in question are pleasant to a person only in so far as he desires power or property. This kind of pleasant experience presupposes desires for something other than pleasant experiences, and therefore the latter desires cannot be derived from desire for that kind of pleasant experience.

Similar remarks apply to the desire for self-respect and the desire for self-display. If one already desires to feel certain emotions towards oneself, or to be the object of certain emotions in others, the experience of feeling those emotions or of knowing that others feel them towards one will be pleasant, because it will be the fulfilment of a pre-existing desire. But this kind of pleasure presupposes the existence of these desires, and therefore they cannot be derived from the desire for that kind of pleasure.

(3) Although the various kinds of egoistic desire cannot be reduced to a single ultimate egoistic desire, *e.g.* the desire for one's own happiness, they are often very much mixed up with each other. Take, *e.g.*, the special desire which a mother feels for the health, happiness, and prosperity of her children. This is predominantly other-regarding, though it is self-referential. The mother is directly attracted by the thought of her child as surviving, as having good dispositions and pleasant experiences, and as being the object of love and respect to other persons. She is directly repelled by the thought of him dying, or having bad dispositions or unpleasant experiences, or being the object of hatred or contempt to other persons. The desire is therefore other-regarding. It is self-referential, because the fact that it is *her* child and not another's acts as a powerful motive-stimulant. She would not be prepared to make the same sacrifices for the survival or the welfare of a child which was not her own. But this self-referential other-regarding motive is almost always mingled with other motives which are self-regarding. One motive which a woman has for wanting her child to be happy, healthy and popular is the desire that other women shall envy her as the mother of a happy, healthy and popular child. This motive is subordinate to the self-centered desire for self-display. Another motive, which may be present, is the desire not to be burdened with an ailing, unhappy and unpopular child. This motive is subordinate to the self-contained desire for one's own happiness. But, although the self-referential other-regarding motive is nearly always mixed with motives which are self-centered or self-confined, we cannot plausibly explain the behavior of many mothers on many occasions towards their children without postulating the other-regarding motive.

We can now consider the various forms which Psychological Egoism might take. The most rigid form is that all human motives are ultimately egoistic, and that all egoistic motives are ultimately of one kind. That one kind has generally been supposed to be the desire for one's own happiness, and so this form of Psychological Egoism may in practice be identified with Psychological Hedonism. This theory amounts to saying that the only ultimate motives are *self-confined,* and that the only ultimate self-confined motive is *desire for one's own happiness.*

I have already tried to show by examples that this is false. Among self-confined motives, *e.g.*, is the desire for self-preservation, and this cannot be reduced to desire for one's own happiness. Then, again, there are self-regarding motives which are self-centered but not self-confined, such as the desire for affection, for gratitude, for power over others, and so on. And, finally, there are motives which are self-referential but predominantly other-regarding, such as a mother's desire for her children's welfare or a man's desire to injure one whom he hates.

It follows that the only form of Psychological Egoism that is worth discussing is the following. It might be alleged that all ultimate motives are *either* self-confined *or* self-centered *or* other-regarding but self-referential, some being of one kind and some of another. This is a much more modest theory than, *e.g.* Psychological Hedonism. I think that it covers satisfactorily an immensely wide field of human motivation, but I am not sure that it is true without exception. I shall now discuss it in the light of some examples.

Case A. Take first the case of a man who does not expect to survive the death of his present body, and who makes a will, the contents of which will be known to no one during his lifetime.

(1) The motive of such a testator cannot possibly be the expectation of any experiences which he will enjoy after death through the provisions of his will being carried out; for he believes that he will have no more experiences after the death of his body. The only way in which this motive could be ascribed to such a man is by supposing that, although he is intellectually convinced of his future extinction, yet in practice he cannot help imagining himself as surviving and witnessing events which will happen after his death. I think that this kind of mental confusion is possible, and perhaps not uncommon; but I should doubt whether it is a plausible account of such a man's motives to say that they all involve this mistake.

(2) Can we say that his motive is the desire to enjoy during his life the pleasant experience of imagining the gratitude which the beneficiaries will feel towards him after his death? The answer is that this may well be *one* of his motives, but it cannot be primary, and therefore cannot be the only one. Unless he desired to be thought about in one way rather than another after his death, the present experience of imagining himself as becoming the object of certain retrospective thoughts and emotions on the part of the beneficiaries would be neither attractive nor repulsive to him.

(3) I think it is plain, then, that the ultimate motive of such a man cannot be desire for his own happiness. But it might be desire for power over others. For he may be said to be exercising this power when he makes his will, even though the effects will not begin until after his death.

(4) Can we say that his motive in making the will is simply to ensure that certain persons will think about him and feel towards him in certain ways after his death? In that case his motive would come under the head of self-display. (This must, of course, be distinguished from the question, already discussed, whether his motive might be to give himself the pleasant experience of imagining their future feelings of gratitude towards him.) The answer is that self-display, in a wide sense, may be a motive, and a very strong one, in making a will; but it could hardly be the sole motive. A testator generally considers the relative needs of various possible beneficiaries, the question whether a certain person would appreciate and take care of a certain picture or house or book, the question whether a certain institution is doing work which he thinks important, and so on. In so far as he is influenced by these considerations, his motives are other-regarding. But they may all be self-referential. In making his will he may desire to benefit persons only in so far as they are *his* relatives or friends. He may desire to benefit institutions only in so far as *he* is or has been a member of them. And so on. I think that it would be quite plausible to hold that the motives of such a

testator are all either self-regarding or self-referential, but that it would not be in the least plausible to say that they are all self-confined or that none of them are other-regarding.

Case B. Let us next consider the case of a man who subscribes anonymously to a certain charity. His motive cannot possibly be that of self-display. Can we say that his motive is to enjoy the pleasant experience of self-approval and of seeing an institution in which he is interested flourishing? The answer is, again, that these motives may exist and may be strong, but they cannot be primary and therefore cannot be his only motives. Unless he wants the institution to flourish, there will be nothing to attract him in the experience of seeing it flourish. And, unless he subscribes from some other motive than the desire to enjoy a feeling of self-approval, he will not obtain a feeling of self-approval. So here, again, it seems to me that some of his motives must be other-regarding. But it is quite possible that his other-regarding motives may all be self-referential. An essential factor in making him want to benefit this institution may be that it is *his* old college or that a great friend of *his* is at the head of it.

The question, then, that remains is this. Are there any cases in which it is reasonable to think that a person's motive is not egoistic in any of the senses mentioned? In practice, as we now see, this comes down to the question whether there are any cases in which an other-regarding motive is not stimulated by an egoistic motive-stimulus, *i.e.* whether there is any other-regarding motive which is not also and essentially self-referential.

Case C. Let us consider the case of a person who deliberately chooses to devote his life to working among lepers, in the full knowledge that he will almost certainly contract leprosy and die in a particularly loathsome way. This is not an imaginary case. To give the Psychological Egoist the longest possible run for his money I will suppose that the person is a Roman Catholic priest, who believes that his action may secure for him a place in heaven in the next world and a reputation for sanctity and heroism in this, that it may be rewarded posthumously with canonization, and that it will redound to the credit of the church of which he is an ordained member.

It is difficult to see what self-regarding or self-referential motives there could be *for* the action beside desire for happiness in heaven, desire to gain a reputation for sanctity and heroism and perhaps to be canonized after death, and desire to glorify the church of which one is a priest. Obviously there are extremely strong self-confined and self-centered motives *against* choosing this kind of life. And in many cases there must have been very strong self-referential other-regarding motives *against* it. For the person who made such a choice must sometimes have been a young man of good family and brilliant prospects, whose parents were heart-broken at his decision, and whose friends thought him an obstinate fool for making it.

Now there is no doubt at all that there was an other-regarding motive, viz., a direct desire to alleviate the sufferings of the lepers. No one who was not dying in the last ditch for an over-simple theory of human nature would deny this. The only questions that are worth raising about it are these. (1) Is this other-regarding motive stimulated by an egoistic motive-stimulus and thus rendered self-referential? (2) Suppose that this motive had not been supported by the various self-regarding and self-referential motives *for* deciding to go and work among the lepers, would it have sufficed, in presence of the motives *against* doing so, to ensure the choice that was actually made?

As regards the first question, I cannot see that there was any special pre-existing relationship between a young priest in Europe and a number of unknown lepers in Asia which might plausibly be held to act as an egoistic motive-stimulus. The lepers are neither his relatives nor his friends nor his benefactors nor members of any community or institution to which he belongs.

As regards the sufficiency of the other-regarding motive, whether stimulated egoistically or not, in the absence of all self-regarding motives tending in the same direction, no conclusive answer can be given. I cannot prove that a single person in the whole course of history *would* have decided to work among lepers, if all the motives against doing so had been present, whilst the hope of heaven, the desire to gain a reputation for sanctity and heroism, and the desire to glorify and extend one's church had been wholly absent. Nor can the Psychological Egoist prove that *no* single person would have so decided under these hypothetical conditions. Factors which cannot be eliminated cannot be shown to be necessary and cannot be shown to be superfluous; and there we must leave the matter.

I suspect that a Psychological Egoist might be tempted to say that the intending medical missionary found the experience of imagining the sufferings of the lepers intensely unpleasant, and that his primary motive for deciding to spend his life working among them was to get rid of this unpleasant experience. This, I think, is what Locke, *e.g.*, would have had to say in accordance with his theory of motivation. About this suggestion there are two remarks to be made.

(1) This motive cannot have been primary, and therefore cannot have been the only motive. Unless this person desired that the lepers should have their sufferings alleviated, there is no reason why the thought of their sufferings should be an unpleasant experience to him. A malicious man, *e.g.*, finds the thought of the sufferings of an enemy a very pleasant experience. This kind of pleasure presupposes a desire for the well-being or the ill-being of others.

(2) If his primary motive were to rid himself of the unpleasant experience of imagining the sufferings of the lepers, he could hardly choose a less effective means than to go and work among them. For the imagination would then be replaced by actual sense-perception; whilst, if he stayed at home and devoted himself to other activities, he would have a reasonably good chance of diverting his attention from the sufferings of the lepers. In point of fact one knows that such a person would reproach himself in so far as he managed to forget about the lepers. He would *wish* to keep them and their sufferings constantly in mind, as an additional stimulus to doing what he believes he ought to do, viz., to take active steps to help and relieve them.

In this connection it is important to notice the following facts. For most people the best way to realize the sufferings of strangers is to imagine oneself or one's parents or children or some intimate and beloved friend in the situation in which the stranger is placed. This, as we say, "brings home to one" his sufferings. A large proportion of the cruelty which decent people applaud or tolerate is applauded or tolerated by them only because they are either too stupid to put themselves imaginatively into the position of the victims or because they deliberately refrain from doing so. One important cause of their deliberately refraining is the notion of retributive justice, *i.e.*, the belief that these persons, or a group taken as a collective whole to which they belong, have *deserved* suffering by wrong-doing, and the desire that they shall get their deserts. Another important cause of this deliberate refrainment is the knowledge that one is utterly powerless to help the victims. However this may be, the fact that imagining oneself in their position is often a necessary condition of desiring to relieve the sufferings of strangers does not make that desire self-referential. Imagining oneself in their place is merely a condition for becoming vividly *aware of* their sufferings. Whether one will then desire to relieve them or to prolong them or will remain indifferent to them, depends on motives which are not primarily self-regarding or self-referential.

I will now summarize the results of this discussion.

(1) If Psychological Egoism asserts that all ultimate motives are self-confined; or that they are all either self-confined or self-centered, some being of one kind and some of the other; or that all self-confined motives can be reduced to the desire for one's own happiness; it is certainly false. It is not even a close approximation to the truth.

(2) If it asserts that all ultimate motives are either self-regarding or self-referential, some being of one kind and some of the other; and that all other-regarding motives require a self-referential stimulus, it is a close approximation to the truth. It is true, I think, that in most people and at most times other-regarding motives are very weak unless stimulated by a self-referential stimulus. As England's wisest and wittiest statesman put it in his inimitable way: "Temporal things will have their weight in the world, and, though zeal may prevail for a time and get the better in a skirmish, yet the war endeth generally on the side of flesh and blood, and will do so until mankind is another thing than it is at present."

(3) Nevertheless, Psychological Egoism, even in its most diluted form, is very doubtful if taken as a universal proposition. Some persons at some times are strongly influenced by other-regarding motives which cannot plausibly be held to be stimulated by a self-referential stimulus. It seems reasonable to hold that the presence of these other-regarding motives is *necessary* to account for their choice of the alternatives which they do choose, and for their persistence in the course which they have adopted, though this can never be conclusively established in any particular case. Whether it is also *sufficient* cannot be decided with certainty, for self-regarding and self-referential components are always present in one's total motive for choosing such an action.

I think that the summary which I have just given fairly represents the results of introspection and reflection on one's own and other men's voluntary actions. Yet Psychological Egoism in general and Psychological Hedonism in particular have seemed almost self-evident to many highly intelligent thinkers, and they do still seem highly plausible to nearly everyone when he first begins to speculate on human motivation. I believe that this depends, not on empirical facts, but on certain verbal ambiguities and misunderstandings. As so often happens in philosophy, clever people accept a false general principle on *a priori* grounds and then devote endless labor and ingenuity to explaining, or explaining away, plain facts which obviously conflict with it. A full discussion of the subject would require an analysis of the confusions which have made these theories seem so plausible; but this must be omitted here.

I must content myself with the following remarks in conclusion. I have tried to show that Psychological Egoism, in the only form in which it could possibly fit the facts of human life, is not a monistic theory of motives. On this extended interpretation of the theory the only feature common to all motives is that every motive which can *act on* a person has one or another of a large number of different kinds of special *reference to* that person. I have tried to show that this certainly covers a very wide field, but that it is by no means certain that there is even this amount of unity among *all* human motives. I think that Psychological Egoism is much the most plausible attempt to reduce the *prima facie* plurality of ultimate kinds of desire to a unity. If it fails, I think it is most unlikely that any alternative attempt on a different basis will succeed.

For my part I am inclined to accept an irreducibly pluralistic view of human motives. This does not, of course, entail that the present irreducible plurality of ultimate motives may not have evolved, in some sense of that highly ambiguous word, out of fewer, either in the history of each individual or in that of the human race. About that I express no opinion here and now.

Now, if Psychological Hedonism had been true, all conflict of motives would have been between motives of the *same kind.* It would always be of the form "Shall I go to the dentist and certainly be hurt now but probably avoid thereby frequent and prolonged toothache in future? Or shall I take the risk in order to avoid the certainty of being hurt by the dentist now?" On any pluralistic view there is also conflict between motives of irreducibly *different kinds, e.g.* between aversion to painful experience and desire to be thought manly, or between a desire to shine in conversation and aversion to hurting a sensitive person's feelings by a witty but wounding remark.

It seems to me plain that, in our ordinary moral judgments about ourselves and about others, we always unhesitatingly assume that there can be and often is conflict between motives of radically different kinds. Now I do not myself share that superstitious reverence for the beliefs of common sense which many contemporary philosophers profess. But I think that we must start from them, and that we ought to depart from them only when we find good reason to do so. If Psychological Hedonism, or any other monistic theory of motives had been true, we should have had to begin the study of Ethics by recognizing that most moral judgments which we pass on ourselves or on others are made under a profound misapprehension of the psychological facts and are largely vitiated thereby. If Psychological Hedonism, *e.g.*, had been true, the only ethical theory worth discussing would have been an egoistic form of Ethical Hedonism. For one cannot be under an obligation to attempt to do what is psychologically impossible. And, on the hypothesis of Psychological Hedonism, it is psychologically impossible for anyone ultimately to desire anything except to prolong or acquire experiences which he knows or expects to be pleasant and to cut short or avoid experiences which he knows or expects to be unpleasant. If it were still possible to talk of having duties at all, each person's duties would be confined within the limits which that psychological impossibility marks out. And it would clearly be impossible to suppose that any part of anyone's ultimate motive for doing any act is his belief that it would be right in the circumstances together with his desire to do what is right as such. For, if Psychological Hedonism were true, a desire to do what is right could not be ultimate; it must be subordinate to the desire to get or prolong pleasant experiences and to avoid or cut short unpleasant ones.

Now it is plain that such consequences as these conflict sharply with common-sense notions of morality. If we had been obliged to accept Psychological Egoism, in any of its narrower forms, on its merits, we should have had to say: "So much the worse for the common-sense notions of morality!" But, if I am right, the morality of common sense, with all its difficulties and incoherences, is immune at least to attacks from the basis of Psychological Egoism.

1949

The New Subjectivism in Ethics

Brand Blanshard

By the new subjectivism in ethics I mean the view that when anyone says "this is right" or "this is good," he is only expressing his own feeling, he is not asserting anything true or false, because he is not asserting or judging at all; he is really making an exclamation that expresses a favorable feeling.

This view has recently come into much favor. With variations of detail it is being advocated by Russell, Wittgenstein and Ayer in England, and by Carnap, Stevenson, Feigl, and others, in this country. Why is it that the theory has come into so rapid a popularity? Is it because moralism of insight have been making a fresh and searching examination of moral experience and its expression? No, I think not. A consideration of the names just mentioned suggests a truer reason. All these names belong roughly speaking, to a single school of thought in the theory of knowledge. If the new view has become popular in ethics, it is because certain persons who were at work in the theory of knowledge arrived at a new view there, and found, on thinking it out, that it required the new view in ethics; the view comes less from ethical analysis than from logical positivism.

As positivists, these writers held that every judgment belongs to one or other of two types. On the one hand, it may be *a priori* or necessary. But then it is always

Brand Blanshard, "The New Subjectivism in Ethics," *Philosophy and Phenomenological Research* 9 (1949). Reprinted with the permission of the publishers.

analytic, i.e., it unpacks in its predicate part or all of its subject. Can we safely say that 7 + 5 make 12? Yes, because 12 is what we mean by "7 + 5." On the other hand, the judgment may be empirical, and then, if we are to verify it, we can no longer look to our meanings only; it refers to sense experience and there we must look for its warrant. Having arrived at this division of judgments, the positivists raised the question where value judgments fall. The judgment that knowledge is good, for example, did not seem to be analytic; the value that knowledge might have did not seem to be part of our concept of knowledge. But neither was the statement empirical, for goodness was not a quality like red or squeaky that could be seen or heard. What were they to do, then with these awkward judgments of value? To find a place for them in their theory of knowledge would require them to revise the theory radically, and yet that theory was what they regarded as their most important discovery. It appeared that the theory could be saved in one way only. If it could be shown that judgments of good and bad were not judgments at all, that they asserted nothing true or false, but merely expressed emotions like "Hurrah" or "Fiddlesticks," then these wayward judgments would cease from troubling and weary heads could be at rest. This is the course the positivists took. They explained value judgments by explaining them away.

Now I do not think their view will do. But before discussing it, I should like to record one vote of thanks to them for the clarity with which they have stated their case. It has been said of John Stuart Mill that he wrote so clearly that he could be found out. This theory has been put so clearly and precisely that it deserves criticism of the same kind, and this I will do my best to supply. The theory claims to show by analysis that when we say, "That is good," we do not mean to assert a character of the subject of which we are thinking. I shall argue that we do mean to do just that.

Let us work through an example, and the simpler and commoner the better. There is perhaps no value statement on which people would more universally agree than the statement that intense pain is bad. Let us take a set of circumstances in which I happen to be interested on the legislative side and in which I think every one of us might naturally make such a statement. We come upon a rabbit that has been caught in one of the brutal traps in common use. There are signs that it has struggled for days to escape and that in a frenzy of hunger, pain, and fear, it has all but eaten off its own leg. The attempt failed: the animal is now dead. As we think of the long and excruciating pain it must have suffered, we are very likely to say: "It was a bad thing that the little animal should suffer so." The positivist tells us that when we say this we are only expressing our present emotion. I hold, on the contrary, that we mean to assert something of the pain itself, namely, that it was bad—bad when and as it occurred.

Consider what follows from the positivist view. On that view, nothing good or bad happened in the case until I came on the scene and made my remark. For what I express in my remark is something going on in me at the time, and that of course did not exist until I did come on the scene. The pain of the rabbit was not itself bad; nothing evil was happening when that pain was being endured; badness, in the only sense in which it is involved at all, waited for its appearance till I came and looked and felt. Now that this is at odds with our meaning may be shown as follows. Let us put to ourselves the hypothesis that we had not come on the scene and that the rabbit never was discovered. Are we prepared to say that in that case nothing bad occurred in the sense in which we said it did? Clearly not. Indeed we should say, on the contrary, that the accident of our later discovery made no difference whatever to the badness of the animal's pain, that it would have been every whit as bad whether a chance passer-by happened later to discover the body and feel repugnance or not. If so, then it is clear that in saying the suffering was bad we are not expressing our feelings only. We are saying that the pain was bad when and as it occurred and before anyone took an attitude toward it.

The first argument is thus an ideal experiment in which we use the method of difference. It removes our present expression and shows that the badness we meant would not be affected by this, whereas on positivist grounds it should be. The second argument applies the method in the reverse way. It ideally removes the past event, and shows that this would render false what we mean to say, whereas on positivist grounds it should not. Let us suppose that the animal did not in fact fall into the trap and did not suffer at all, but that we mistakenly believe it did, and say as before that its suffering was an evil thing. On the positivist theory, everything I sought to express by calling it evil in the first case is still present in the second. In the only sense in which badness is involved at all, whatever was bad in the first case is still present in its entirety, since all that is expressed in either case is a state of feeling, and that feeling is still there. And our question is, is such an implication consistent with what we meant? Clearly it is not. If anyone asked us, after we made the remark that the suffering was a bad thing, whether we should think it relevant to what we said to learn that the incident had never occurred and no pain had been suffered at all, we should say that it made all the difference in the world, that what we were asserting to be bad was precisely the suffering we thought had occurred back there, that if this had not occurred, there was nothing left to be bad, and that our assertion was in that case mistaken. The suggestion that in saying something evil had occurred we were after all making no mistake, because we had never meant anyhow to say anything about the past suffering, seems to me merely frivolous. If we did not mean to say this, why should we be so relieved on finding that the suffering had not occurred? On the theory before us, such relief would be groundless, for in that suffering itself there was nothing bad at all, and hence in its non-occurrence there would be nothing to be relieved about. The positivist theory would here distort our meaning beyond recognition.

So far as I can see, there is only one way out for the positivist. He holds that goodness and badness lie in feelings of approval or disapproval. And there is a way in which he might hold that badness did in this case precede our own feeling of disapproval without belonging to the pain itself. The pain in itself was neutral; but unfortunately the rabbit, on no grounds at all, took up toward this neutral object an attitude of disapproval, and that made it for the first time, and in the only intelligible sense, bad. This way of escape is theoretically possible, but since it has grave difficulties of its own and has not, so far as I know, been urged by positivists, it is perhaps best not to spend time over it.

I come now to a third argument, which again is very simple. When we come upon the rabbit and make our remark about its suffering being a bad thing, we presumably make it with some feeling; the positivists are plainly right in saying that such remarks do usually express feeling. But suppose that a week later we revert to the incident in thought and make our statement again. And suppose that the circumstances have now so changed that the feeling with which we made the remark in the first place has faded. The pathetic evidence is no longer before us; and we are now so fatigued in body and mind that feeling is, as we say, quite dead. In these circumstances, since what was expressed by the remark when first made is, on the theory before us, simply absent, the remark now expresses nothing. It is as empty as the word "Hurrah" would be when there was no enthusiasm behind it. And this seems to me untrue. When we repeat the remark that such suffering was a bad thing, the feeling with which we made it last week may be at or near the vanishing point, but if we were asked whether we meant to say what we did before, we should certainly answer Yes. We should say that we made our point with feeling the first time and little or no feeling the second time, but that it was the same point we were making. And if we can see that what we meant to say remains the same, while the feeling varies from intensity to near zero, it is not the feeling that we primarily meant to express.

I come now to a fourth consideration. We all believe that toward acts or effects of a certain kind one attitude is fitting and another not; but on the theory before us such a belief would not make sense. Broad and Ross have lately contended that this fitness is one of the main facts of ethics, and I suspect they are right. But that is not exactly my point. My point is this: whether there is such fitness or not, we all assume that there is, and if we do, we express in moral judgments more than the subjectivists say we do. Let me illustrate.

In his novel *The House of the Dead,* Dostoevsky tells of his experiences in a Siberian prison camp. Whatever the unhappy inmates of such camps are like today, Dostoevsky's companions were about as grim a lot as can be imagined. "I have heard stories," he writes, "of the most terrible, the most unnatural actions, of the most monstrous murders, told with the most spontaneous, childishly merry laughter." Most of us would say that in this delight at the killing of others or the causing of suffering there is something very unfitting. If we were asked why we thought so, we should say that these things involve great evil and are wrong, and that to take delight in what is evil or wrong is plainly unfitting. Now on the subjectivist view, this answer is ruled out. For before someone takes up an attitude toward death, suffering, or their infliction, they have no moral quality at all. There is therefore nothing about them to which an attitude of approval or condemnation could be fitting. They are in themselves neutral, and, so far as they get a moral quality, they get it only through being invested with it by the attitude of the onlooker. But if that is true, why is any attitude more fitting than any other? Would applause, for example, be fitting if, apart from the applause, there were nothing good to applaud? Would condemnation be fitting if, independently of the condemnation, there were nothing bad to condemn? In such a case, any attitude would be as fitting or unfitting as any other, which means that the notion of fitness has lost all point.

Indeed we are forced to go much farther. If goodness and badness lie in attitudes only and hence are brought into being by them, those men who greeted death and misery with childishly merry laughter are taking the only sensible line. If there is nothing evil in these things, if they get their moral complexion only from our feeling about them, why shouldn't they be greeted with a cheer? To greet them with repulsion would turn what before was neutral into something bad; it would needlessly bring badness into the world; and even on subjectivist assumptions that does not seem very bright. On the other hand, to greet them with delight would convert what before was neutral into something good; it would bring goodness into the world. If I have murdered a man and wish to remove the stain, the way is clear. It is to cry, "Hurrah for murder."

What is the subjectivist to reply? I can only guess. He may point out that the inflicting of death is *not* really neutral before the onlooker takes his attitude, for the man who inflicted the death no doubt himself took an attitude, and thus the act had a moral quality derived from this. But that makes the case more incredible still, for the man who did the act presumably approved it, and if so it was good in the only sense in which anything is good, and then our conviction that the laughter is unfit is more unaccountable still. It may be replied that the victim, too, had his attitude and that since this was unfavorable, the act was not unqualifiedly good. But the answer is plain. Let the killer be expert at his job; let him despatch his victim instantly before he has time to take an attitude, and then gloat about his perfect crime without ever telling anyone. Then, so far as I can see, his act will be good without any qualification. It would become bad only if someone found out about it and disliked it. And that would be a curiously irrational procedure, since the man's approving of his own killing is in itself just as neutral as the killing that it approves. Why then should anyone dislike it?

It may be replied that we can defend our dislike on this ground that, if the approval of killing were to go unchecked and spread, most men would have to live in insecurity and fear, and these things are undesirable. But surely this reply is not open; these things are not, on the theory, undesirable, for nothing is; in themselves they are neutral. Why then should I disapprove men's living in this state? The answer may come that if other men live in insecurity and fear, I shall in time be infected myself. But even in my own insecurity and fear there is, on the theory before us, nothing bad whatever, and therefore, if I disapprove them, it is without a shadow of ground and with no more fitness in my attitude than if I cordially cheered them. The theory thus conflicts with our judgments of fitness all along the line.

I come now to a fifth and final difficulty with the theory. It makes mistakes about values impossible. There is a whole nest of inter-connected criticisms here, some of which have been made so often that I shall not develop them again, such as that I can never agree or disagree in opinion with anyone else about an ethical matter, and that in these matters I can never be inconsistent with others or with myself. I am not at all content with the sort of analysis which says that the only contradictions in such cases have regard to facts and that contradictions about value are only differences of feeling. I think that if anyone tells me that having a bicuspid out without an anaesthetic is not a bad experience and I say it is a very nasty experience indeed, I am differing with him in opinion, and differing about the degree of badness of the experience. But without pressing this further, let me apply the argument in what is perhaps a fresh direction.

There is an old and merciful distinction that moralists have made for many centuries about conduct—the distinction between what is subjectively and what is objectively right. They have said that in any given situation there is some act which, in view of all the circumstances, would be the best act to do; and this is what would be objectively right. The notion of an objectively right act is the ground of our notion of duty: our duty is always to find and do this act if we can. But of course we often don't find it. We often hit upon and do acts that we think are the right ones, but we are mistaken; and then our act is only subjectively right. Between these two acts the disparity may be continual; Professor Prichard suggested that probably few of us in the course of our lives ever succeed in doing *the* right act.

Now so far as I can see, the new subjectivism would abolish this difference at a stroke. Let us take a case. A boy abuses his small brother. We should commonly say, "That is wrong, but perhaps he doesn't know any better. By reason of bad teaching and a feeble imagination, he may see nothing wrong in what he is doing, and may even be proud of it. If so, his act may be subjectively right, though it is miles away from what is objectively right." What concerns me about the new subjectivism is that it prohibits this distinction. If the boy feels this way about his act, then it is right in the only sense in which anything is right. The notion of an objective right lying beyond what he has discovered, and which he ought to seek and do is meaningless. There might, to be sure, be an act that would more generally arouse favorable feelings in others, but that would not make it right for him unless he thought of it and approved it, which he doesn't. Even if he did think of it, it would not be obligatory for him to feel about it in any particular way, since there is nothing in any act, as we have seen, which would make any feeling more suitable than any other.

Now if there is no such thing as an objectively right act, what becomes of the idea of duty? I have suggested that the idea of duty rests on the idea of such an act, since it is always our duty to find that act and do it if we can. But if whatever we feel approval for at the time is right, what is the point of doubting and searching further? Like the little girl in Boston who was asked if she would like to travel, we can answer, "Why should I travel when I'm already there?" If I am reconciled in feeling to my present act, no act I could discover by reflection could be better, and therefore why reflect or seek at all? Such a view seems to me to break the mainspring of duty, to destroy the motive for self-improvement, and to remove the ground for self-criticism. It may be replied that by further reflection I can find an act that would satisfy my feelings more widely than the present one, and that this is the act I should seek. But this reply means either that such general satisfaction is objectively better, which would contradict the theory, or else that, if at the time I don't feel it better, it isn't better, in which case I have no motive for seeking it. When certain self-righteous persons took an inflexible line with Oliver Cromwell, his very Cromwellian reply was, "Bethink ye, gentlemen, by the bowels of Christ, that ye may be mistaken." It was good advice. I hope nobody will take from me the privilege of finding myself mistaken. I should be sorry to think that the self of thirty years ago was as far along the path as the self of today, merely because he was a smug young jackanapes, or even that the paragon of today has as little room for improvement as would be allowed by his myopic complacency.

One final remark. The great problems of the day are international problems. Has the new subjectivism any bearing upon these problems? I think it has, and a somewhat sinister bearing. I would not suggest, of course, that those who hold the theory are one whit less public-spirited than others; surely there are few who could call themselves citizens of the world with more right (if "rights" have meaning any longer) than Mr. Russell. But Mr. Russell has confessed himself discontented with his ethical theory, and in view of his breadth of concern, one cannot wonder. For its general acceptance would, so far as one can see, be an international disaster. The assumption behind the old League and the new United Nations was that there is such a thing as right and wrong in the conduct of a nation, a right and wrong that do not depend on how it happens to feel at the time. It is implied, for example, that when Japan invaded Manchuria in 1931 she might be wrong, and that by discussion and argument she might be shown to be wrong. It was implied that when the Nazis invaded Poland they might be wrong, even though German public sentiment overwhelmingly approved it. On the theory before us, it would be meaningless to call these nations mistaken; if they felt approval for what they did, then it was right with as complete a justification as could be supplied for the disapproval felt by the rest of the world. In the present dispute between Russia and our own country over southeast Europe, it is nonsense to speak of the right or rational course for either of us to take; if with all the facts before the two parties, each feels approval for its own course, both attitudes are equally justified or unjustified; neither is mistaken; there is no common reason to which they can take an appeal; there are no principles by which an international court could pronounce on the matter; nor would there be any obligation to obey the pronouncement if it were made. This cuts the ground from under any attempt to establish one's case as right or anyone else's case as wrong. So if our friends the subjectivists still hold their theory after I have applied my little ruler to their knuckles, which of course they will, I have but one request to make of them: Do keep it from Mr. Molotov and Mr. Vishinsky.

1949

Ethical Intuitionism

P. F. Strawson

NORTH.—What is the trouble about moral facts? When someone denies that there is an objective moral order, or asserts that ethical propositions are pseudo-propositions, cannot I refute him (rather as Moore refuted those who denied the existence of the external world) by saying: "You know very well that Brown did wrong in beating his wife. You know very well that human affection is good and cruelty bad, that many actions are wrong and some are right"?

WEST.—Isn't the trouble about moral facts another case of trouble about knowing, about learning? We find out facts about the external world by looking and listening; about ourselves, by feeling; about other people, by looking and listening *and* feeling. When this is noticed, there arises a wish to say that the facts *are* what is seen, what is heard, what is felt; and, consequently, that moral facts fall into one of these classes. So those who have denied that there are "objective moral characteristics" have not wanted to deny that Brown's action was wrong or that keeping promises is right. They have wanted to point out that rightness and wrongness are a matter of what is felt in the heart, not of what is seen with the eyes or heard with the ears. They have wanted to emphasise the way in which "Promise-keeping is right" resembles "Going abroad is exciting," "Stories about mothers-in-law are comic," "Bombs are terrifying"; and differs from

P. F. Strawson, "Ethical Intuitionism," *Philosophy* 24 (1949). Reprinted with the permission of Cambridge University Press.

"Roses are red" and "Sea-water is salt." This does not prevent you from talking about the moral order, or the moral world, if you want to; but it warns you not to forget that the only access to the moral world is through remorse and approval and so on; just as the only access to the world of comedy is through laughter; and the only access to the coward's world is through fear.

NORTH.—I agree, of course, that we cannot see the goodness of something as we see its color, or identify rightness by the sense of touch; though I think you should add that the senses are indispensable as a means of our becoming aware of those characteristics upon which moral characteristics depend. You may be partly right, too, in saying that access to the moral world is obtained through experience of the moral emotions; for it may be that only when our moral feelings have been strongly stirred do we first become clearly aware of the characteristics which evoke these feelings. But these feelings are not identical with that awareness. "Goodness" does not stand to "feeling approval," "guilt" to "feeling guilty," "obligation" to "feeling bound," as "excitingness" stands to "being excited" and "humorousness" to "feeling amused." To use the jargon for a moment: moral characteristics and relations are non-empirical, and awareness of them is neither sensory nor introspectual. It is a different kind of awareness, which the specialists call "intuition": and it is only empiricist prejudice which prevents your acknowledging its existence. Once acknowledged, it solves our problems: and we see that while "Promise-keeping is right" differs from "The sea is salt," this is not because it resembles "Detective-stories are exciting"; it differs from *both* in being the report neither of a sensible nor an introspectible experience, but of an intuition. We may, perhaps, know some moral characteristics mediately, through others. ("Obligation" is, perhaps, definable in terms of "goodness.") But at least one such characteristic—rightness or goodness—is unanalyzable, and known by intuition alone. The fundamental cognitive situation in morals is that in which we intuit the rightness of a particular action or the goodness of a particular state of affairs. We see this moral characteristic as present in virtue of some other characteristics, themselves capable of being described in empirical terms, which the action or state of affairs possesses. (This is why I said that sense-perception is a necessary, though not a sufficient, condition of obtaining information about the moral order.) Our intuition, then, is not a bare intuition of the moral characteristic, but also the intuition of its dependence on some others: so that this fundamental situation yields us, by intuitive induction, knowledge of moral rules, generalizations regarding the right and the good, which we can apply in other cases, even when an actual intuition is lacking. So much do these rules become taken for granted, a part of our habitual moral life, that most of our everyday moral judgments involve merely an implicit reference to them[1]: a reference which becomes explicit only if the judgment is challenged or queried. Moral emotions, too, assume the character of habitual reactions. But emotions and judgments alike are grounded upon intuitions. Emotion may be the gatekeeper to the moral world; but intuition is the gate.

WEST.—Not so fast. I understand you to say that at least one fundamental moral characteristic—rightness or goodness—is unanalyzable. Perhaps both are. The experts are divided. In any case, the fundamental characteristic (or characteristics) can be known only by intuitive awareness of its presence in some particular contemplated action or state of affairs. There is, then, a kind of analogy between the word "right" (or "good") and the name of some simple sensible characteristic such as "red."[2] Just as everybody who understands the word "red" has seen some red things, so everybody

[1]Cf. D. Daiches Raphael, *The Moral Sense,* Chapters V and VI.
[2]Cf. G. E. Moore, *Principia Ethica,* p. 7 *et seq.*

who understands the word "right" or the word "good" has intuited the character, rightness, in some actions, or the character, goodness, in some states of affairs; and nobody who has not intuited these characters understands the words "right" or "good." But this is not quite enough, is it? In order for me to know *now* the meaning of an indefinable word, it is not enough that a certain perceptual or intuitional event should have occurred at some particular point in my history; for I might not only have forgotten the details of that event; I might have forgotten what *kind* of an event it was; I might not know *now* what it would be like for such an event to occur. If the word "red" expresses an indefinable visual concept, then it is self-contradictory to say: "I know what the word 'red' means, but I can't remember ever *seeing* red and I don't know what it would be *like* to see red." Similarly, if the word "right," or the word "good," expresses an indefinable intuitive concept, then it is self-contradictory to say: "I know what the word 'right' or the word 'good' means, but I can't remember ever *intuiting* rightness or goodness, and I don't know what it would be *like* to intuit rightness or goodness." If your theory is true, then this statement is a contradiction.

But it is not at all obvious to me that it is a contradiction. I should be quite prepared to assert that I understood the words "right" and "good," but that I couldn't remember ever intuiting rightness or goodness and that I couldn't imagine what it would be like to do so. And I think it is quite certain that I am not alone in this, but that there are a large number of people who are to be presumed capable of accurate reporting of their own cognitive experience, and who would find nothing self-contradictory in saying what I say. And if this is so, you are presented with a choice of two possibilities. The first is that the words "right" and "good" have quite a different meaning for one set of people from the meaning which they have for another set. But neither of us believes this. The second is that the intuitionist theory is a mistake; that the phrase "intuitional event having a moral characteristic as its object (or a part of its object)" is a phrase which describes nothing at all; or describes misleadingly the kind of emotional experience we both admit. There is no third possibility. It is no good saying: "All people who succeed in learning the meaning of moral words do as a matter of fact have moral intuitions, but unfortunately many people are inclined to forget them, to be quite unable to remember what they are like." True, there would be nothing self-contradictory in saying this: but it would simply be a variant of the first possibility; for I cannot be said to know *now* the meaning of a word expressing an intuitive concept unless I know now what it would be like to intuit the characteristic of which it is a concept. The trouble with your intuitionist theory is that, if true, it should be a truism. There should be no doubt about the occurrence of the distinctive experience of intuiting rightness (or goodness), and about its being the only way to learn the meaning of the primary moral words; just as there is no doubt about the occurrence of seeing red (or blue), and about this being the only way to learn the meaning of the primary color words. But there *is* doubt; and over against this doubt there rises a certainty: the certainty that we all know what it is to *feel* guilty, to *feel* bound, to *feel* approving.

NORTH.—What I have said *is* a truism; and that is its strength. It is not I who am inventing a mythical faculty, but you, irritated, perhaps, by the language of intuitionism, who are denying the obvious. When you said that you couldn't *imagine* what it would be like to have moral intuitions, isn't it clear that you wanted "intuiting a moral characteristic" to be like seeing a color or hearing a sound? Naturally you couldn't *imagine* anything of the sort. But I have already pointed out that moral characteristics are dependent on others of which the presence *is* ascertainable by looking and listening. You do not intuit rightness or goodness independently of the other features of the situation. You intuit *that* an action is (or would be) right, a state of affairs good, *because* it has (or would have) certain other empirically ascertainable qualities. The total content of your intuition includes the "because" clause. Of course, our ordinary moral judgments register unreflective reactions. Nevertheless "This act is right (or this state of affairs is good) because it has P, Q, R"—where "P, Q, R" stands for such empirically ascertainable qualities—expresses the type of fundamental cognitive situation in ethics, of which our normal judgments are copies, mediated by habit, but ready, if challenged, to become explicit as their original. Consider what happens when someone dissents from your opinion. You produce reasons. And this is not a matter of accounting for an emotional condition; but of bringing evidence in support of a verdict.

WEST.—When the jury brings in a verdict of guilty on a charge of murder, they do so because the facts adduced in evidence are of the kind covered by the definition of "murder." When the chemical analyst concludes that the material submitted for analysis is a salt, he does so because it exhibits the defining properties of a salt. The evidence is the sort of thing that is *meant* by "murder," by "salt." But the fundamental moral word, or words, you say, cannot be defined; their concepts are unanalyzable. So it cannot be in this way that the "because" clause of your ethical sentence functions as evidence. "X is a right action because it is a case of promise-keeping" does not work like "X is a salt because it is a compound of basic and acid radicals"; for, if "right" is indefinable, "X is right" does not *mean* "X is an act of promise-keeping or of relieving distress or of telling the truth or . . ."

When I say "It will be fine in the morning; for the evening sky is red," the evidence is of a different sort. For I might observe the fine morning without having noticed the state of the evening sky. But you have rightly stressed the point that there is no *independent* awareness of *moral* qualities: that they are always "seen" as dependent on those other features mentioned in the "because" clause. So it is not in this way, either, that the "because" clause of your ethical sentence functions as evidence. And there is no other way. Generally, we may say that whenever q is evidence for p, *either* q is the sort of thing we mean by "p" ("p" is definable in terms of "q") *or* we can have knowledge of the state of affairs described by "p" independently of knowledge of the state of affairs described by "q." But neither of these conditions is satisfied by the q, the "because" clause, of your ethical sentence.

The "because" clause, then, does not, as you said it did, constitute evidence for the ethical judgment. And this, it seems to me, should be a serious matter for you. For where is such evidence to be found? It is no good saying that, after all, the ethical judgments of other people (or your own at other times) may corroborate your own present judgment. They may agree with it; but their agreement strengthens the probability of your judgment only on the assumption that their moral intuitions tend on the whole to be correct. But the only possible evidence for the existence of a *tendency* to have correct intuitions is the correctness of *actual* intuitions. And it is precisely the correctness of actual intuitions for which we are seeking evidence, and failing to find it.

And evidence you must have, if your account of the matter is correct. You will scarcely say that ethical intuitions are infallible; for ethical disagreements may survive the resolution of factual disagreements. (You might, of course, say that *genuine* intuitions were infallible: then the problem becomes one of finding a criterion for distinguishing between the genuine ones and those false claimants that carry the same inner conviction.) So your use of the language of "unanalyzable predicates ascribed in moral judgment to particular actions and states of affairs" leads to contradiction. For to call such a judgment "non-infallible" would be meaningless unless there were some way of checking it; of confirming or confuting it, by producing evidence for or against it. But I have just shown that your account of these judgments is incompatible with the possibility of producing evidence for or against them. So, if your account is true, these judgments are both corrigible and incorrigible; and this is absurd.

But the absurdity points to the solution. Of course these judgments are corrigible: but not in the way in which the diagnosis of a doctor is corrigible; rather in the way in which the musical taste of a child is corrigible. Correcting them is not a matter of *producing evidence* for them or their contraries, though it is (partly) a matter of *giving reasons* for them or their contraries. We say, warningly, that ethical judgments are corrigible, because ethical disagreement sometimes survives the resolution of factual disagreement. We say, encouragingly, that ethical judgments are corrigible, because the resolution of factual disagreement sometimes leads to the resolution of ethical disagreement. But the one kind of agreement leads (when it *does* lead) to the other, not in the way in which agreed evidence leads to an agreed conclusion, but in the way in which common experience leads to sympathy. The two kinds of agreement, the two kinds of judgment, are as different as chalk from cheese. Ordinary language can accommodate the difference without strain: it is the pseudo-precise philosophical use of "judgment" which slurs over the difference and raises the difficulty. Is it not clear, then, what people have meant when they said that ethical disagreements were like disagreements in taste, in choice, in practical attitude?[3] Of course, as you said, when we produce our reasons, we are not often simply giving the causes of our emotional condition. But neither are we producing evidence for a verdict, for a moral diagnosis. We are using the facts to back our attitudes, to appeal to the capacity of others to feel as we feel, to respond as we respond.

NORTH.—I think I see now what you have been leaving out all the time. First, you accused me of inventing a mythical faculty to give us ethical knowledge. Then, when I pointed out that ethical qualities are not intuited out of all relation to other empirically ascertainable features of actions and states of affairs, but are intuited as dependent upon these, you twisted this dependence out of all recognition. You wanted to make it like the causal dependence of a psychological disposition upon some empirical feature of its object: as a child's fondness for strawberries depends upon their sweetness. But the connection between wrongness and giving pain to others is not an accident of our constitution; nor does its perception require any special faculty—but *simply that which we use in all our reasoning.* From the fact that an action involves inflicting needless pain upon others, *it follows* necessarily that the action is wrong, just as, from the fact that a triangle is equilateral, it follows necessarily that its angles are equal. This is the kind of dependence that we intuit; not an analytic dependence, but a synthetic entailment; and this is why the "because" clause of my ethical sentence does, after all, constitute evidence for the ascription of the moral characteristic.

I can anticipate the obvious objection. No moral rule, you will say, no moral generalization concerning the rightness of acts or the goodness of conditions, holds without exception. It is always possible to envisage circumstances in which the generalization breaks down. Or, if the generalization is so wide that no counter-example can be found, if it can be so interpreted as to cover every case, then it has become too wide: it has become tautologous, like "It is always right to do that which will have the best results on the whole," or intolerably vague, like "It is always right to treat people as ends in themselves" or "The greatest good is the greatest general welfare." It is plainly not with the help of such recipes as these that we find out what is right, what is good, in a particular case. There are no criteria for the meaning of "treating a man

[3]Cf. Charles Stevenson, *Ethics and Language,* Chapter I. See also his paper "The Emotive Meaning of Ethical Terms."

as an end," for "the greatest general welfare," which do not presuppose the narrower criteria of rightness and goodness of which I spoke and which seem always to have exceptions. All this is true. But it calls only for a trifling amendment to those narrower criteria. We cannot, for example, assert, as a necessary synthetic proposition, "All acts of promise-keeping are right" or "All states of aesthetic enjoyment are good." But we *can* assert, as a necessary synthetic proposition, "All acts of promise-keeping *tend as such* to be right (or have *prima facie* rightness)"[4] or "All states of aesthetic enjoyment *tend as such* to be good." And we derive our knowledge of such general necessary connections from seeing, in particular cases, that the rightness of an action, the goodness of a state, *follows from* its being an action or state of a certain kind.

WEST.—Your "trifling amendment" is a destructive one. When we say of swans that they tend to be white, we are not ascribing a certain quality, namely "tending to be white," to each individual swan. We are saying that the number of swans which are white exceeds the number of those which are not, that if anything is a swan, the chances are that it will be white. When we say "Welshmen tend to be good singers," we mean that most Welshmen sing well; and when we say, of an *individual* Welshman, that *he* tends to sing well, we mean that he sings well more often than not. In all such cases, we are talking of a *class* of things or occasions or events; and saying, not that *all* members of the class have the property *of tending-to-have* a certain characteristic, but that *most* members of the class do in fact have that characteristic. Nobody would accept the claim that a sentence of the form "*Most* As are Bs" expresses a necessary proposition. Is the claim made more plausible by re-writing the proposition in the form "*All* As *tend to be* Bs"?

But, waiving this point, there remains the difficulty that the need for such an amendment to our moral generalizations is incompatible with the account you gave of the way in which we come to know both the moral characteristics of individual actions and states, and the moral generalizations themselves. You said that we intuited the moral characteristic as *following from* some empirically ascertainable features of the action or state. True, if we did so, we should have implicitly learned a moral generalization: but it would be one asserting *without qualification* the entailment of the moral characteristic by these other features of the case. In other words, and to take your instance, if it *ever* follows, from the fact that an act has the empirically ascertainable features described by the phrase "being an act of promise-keeping," that the act is right, then it *always* follows, from the fact that an act is of this kind, that it has this moral quality. If, then, it is true that we intuit moral characteristics as thus "following from" others, it is false that the implied generalizations require the "trifling amendment"; and if it is true that they require the amendment, it is false that we so intuit moral characteristics.[5]

And this is all that need be said of that rationalist superstition according to which a quasi-logical necessity binds moral predicates to others. "Le coeur a ses raisons, que

[4]Ross, *Foundations of Ethics*, pp. 83–86; Broad, "Some of the Main Problems of Ethics," *Philosophy*, 1946, p. 117. [Reprinted in Herbert Feigl and Wilfrid Sellars, eds., *Reading in Philosophical Analysis*, Appleton-Century-Crofts, Inc., 1949.]

[5]One desperate expedient might occur to North. He might say that it is not the bare presence of the promise-keeping feature that entails the rightness of the act, but the presence of this feature, coupled with the absence of any features which would entail its wrongness. His general rules would then be, not of the form " 'x has ϕ' entails 'x is right,' " but of the form " 'x has ϕ and x has no ψ such that "x has ψ" entails "x is wrong" ' entails 'x is right.' " But the suggestion is inadmissible, since (i) the establishment of the general proposition "x has no ψ, etc." would require the enumeration of all those features which would make it wrong to keep a promise, and (ii) any rule of the form " 'x has ψ' entails 'x is wrong' " would require expansion in exactly the same way as the "right-making" rule; which would involve an infinite regress of such expansions. Besides having this *theoretical* defect, the suggested model is, of course, *practically* absurd.

la raison ne connaît pas": this is the whole truth of the matter: but your attention was so riveted to the first half of it that you forgot the second.

Looking for a logical nexus where there was none to be found, you overlooked the logical relations of the ethical words among themselves. And so you forgot what has often been pointed out: that for every expression containing the words "right" or "good," used in their ethical senses, it is always possible to find an expression with the same meaning, but containing, instead of these, the word "ought." The equivalences are various, and the variations subtle; but they are always to be found. For one to say, for example, "I know where the good lies, I know what the right course is; but I don't know the end I *ought* to aim at, the course I *ought* to follow" would be self-contradictory. "Right"-sentences, "good"-sentences are shorthand for "ought"-sentences. And this is enough in itself to explode the myth of unanalyzable characteristics designated by the indefinable predicates, "right" and "good." For "ought" is a *relational* word; whereas "right" and "good" are *predicative.* The simplest sentences containing "ought" are syntactically more complicated than the simplest sentences containing "right" or "good." And hence, since the equivalences of meaning hold, the various ethical usages of "right" and "good" *are all definable:* variously definable in terms of "ought."

Of course this last consideration alone is not decisive against intuitionism. If this were all, you could still re-form the ranks: taking your stand on an intuited unanalyzable non-natural *relation* of obligation, and admitting the definability of the ethical predicates in terms of this relation. But the objections I have already raised apply with equal force against this modified position; and, in other ways, its weakness is more obvious.[6]

NORTH.—Well, then, suppose we agree to bury intuitionism. What have you to offer in its place? Has any analysis of moral judgments in terms of feeling ever been suggested which was not monstrously paradoxical or artificial? Even the simplest ethical sentence obstinately resists translation: and not in the way in which "Life, like a dome of many-colored glass, Stains the white radiance of eternity" resists translation. For the ethical language is not the language of the poets, but the language of all the world. Somehow justice must be done both to this irreducible element of significance in ethical sentences, and to the community of knowledge of their correct, their appropriate, use. Intuitionism, at any rate, was a way of attempting to do this.

WEST.—Yes, intuitionism was a way of attempting to do this. It started from the fact that thousands and thousands of people can say, with perfect propriety: "I know that this is right, that is good"; and ended, as we have seen, by making it inexplicable how anybody could ever say such a thing. This was because of a failure to notice that the whole sentence, including the "I know," and not just the last word in the subordinate clause, is a unit of the ethical language; and, following upon this failure, a feverish

[6]E.g. There was a certain plausibility in saying "My feeling morally obliged to pursue such a course (or end) presupposes my believing that it is right (or good)," and thence concluding that this belief cannot be "reduced to" the feeling which it arouses. (For examples of this sort of argument, see Ross, *op. cit.*, pp. 261–262, and Broad, *op. cit.*, p. 115.) But the weakness of the reasoning is more clearly exposed when the sentence is re-written as "My feeling morally obliged to pursue it." The point is that "presupposes" and "believing" are both ambiguous. If "presupposes" means "causally requires" and "believing" is used in its ordinary sense, then it is obviously false that the beliefs which *occasion* such a feeling invariably include some belief which would be correctly described in these terms. (Compare: "My feeling frightened presupposes my believing that I am frightened.") But the argument begins to have weight against the "analyzability" of beliefs correctly so described only if they are invariably present as occasioning factors. If, on the other hand, "presupposes" means "logically requires," then "believing" might be used in a queer sense such that the sentence is *tautologically* true. But this result is secured only by defining "believing" (used in this sense) in terms of feeling (compare the sense in which "thinking *x* funny" means "being amused by *x*"): and this was precisely the result which North sought to avoid.

ransacking of the drawers of a Theory of Knowledge for an "I know" which would fit. (Do I, perhaps, work it out like the answer to a sum?)

The man who attempts to provide a translation sees more than this. He sees, at any rate, that the sentence must be treated as a unit. His error is to think that he can find a substitute, in a different language, which will serve the same purpose. So long as he confines himself to describing how, in what sort of circumstances, the sentence is used, he does valuable work. He errs when he talks as if to say how a sentence is used is the same as to use it. The man who says he can translate ethical sentences into feeling sentences makes the same sort of mistake as some who said they could (if they had time) translate material-object sentences into sentences about actual and possible sense-experiences. What they *mean*—the commentary they are making on the use of the ethical language or the material-object language—is correct. And it is precisely because the commentary would be incorrect as a translation that it is useful as a commentary. For it brings out the fact that the irreducibility of these languages arises from the systematic vagueness of the notation they use in comparison with that of the commentary-languages, and not from their being used to talk of, to describe, different things from those of which the commentary-languages talk. This descriptive vagueness is no defect: it is what makes these languages useful for the kinds of communication (and persuasion) for which they are severally required. But by being mistaken for something more than it is, it leads to one kind of metaphysics: the metaphysics of substance (the thing-in-itself), or of intuited unanalyzable ethical characteristics. And by being ignored altogether, it leads to another kind of metaphysics: the tough metaphysics of translation, the brutal suggestion that we could get along just as well without the ethical language. Neither metaphysics—neither the tender metaphysics of ultimacy, nor the tough metaphysics of reduction[7]—does justice to the facts: but the latter does them less injustice; for it doesn't seek to supplement them with a fairy-tale.

And so the alternative to intuitionism is not the provision of translations. For the communication and sharing of our moral experience, we must use the tools, the ethical language, we have. No sentences provided by the philosopher will take their place. His task is not to supply a new set of tools, but to describe what it is that is communicated and shared, and how the tools are used to do the work. And though the experience he describes is emotional experience, his descriptions are not like those of the psychologist. The psychologist is concerned with the relation of these experiences, to others of a different sort; the philosopher is concerned with their relation to the ordinary use of ethical language. Of course, then, it would be absurd for the philosopher to deny that some actions are right (fair, legitimate, etc.) and others wrong (unfair, illegitimate, etc.), and that we know this; and absurd to claim that we can say what such sentences say without using such words. For this *is* the language we use in sharing and shaping our moral experience; and the occurrence of experience so shared, so shaped, is not brought into question.

We are in the position of the careful phenomenalist; who, for all his emphasis on sense-experience, neither denies that there is a table in the dining-room, nor claims to be able to assert this without using such words as "dining-room" and "table." A phenomenalism as careful as this has been said to forfeit the right to be called a "philosophical doctrine."[8] Then let the title be reserved for the productions of those who rest in myth or paradox, and fail to complete that journey, from the familiar to the familiar,[9] which is philosophical analysis.

[7]Cf. Wisdom, "Metaphysics and Verification," *Mind,* 1938.
[8]Hardie, "The Paradox of Phenomenalism," *Proceedings of the Aristotelian Society,* 1945–46, p. 150.
[9]Wisdom.

1950

The Logic of Moral Reasoning

Stephen Toulmin

. . . [W]hat questions shall we expect to find arising in ethical contexts, and how are they to be answered?

2.1 QUESTIONS ABOUT THE RIGHTNESS OF ACTIONS

Consider, first, the simplest and commonest ethical question, "Is this the right thing to do?" We are taught when young to behave in ways laid down as appropriate to the situations we are in. Sometimes there is a doubt whether or no a proposed action conforms to the moral code. It is to resolve such doubts that we are taught to use the question, "Is this the right thing to do?," and, provided the code contains a relevant principle, the answer is "Yes" or "No," according as the proposed action does or does not conform. Questions like, "What is the right thing to do?," "What ought really to have been done?" and "Was this the correct decision?" do similar jobs, and can be understood in similar ways.

Stephen Toulmin, "The Logic of Moral Reasoning" from THE PLACE OF REASON IN ETHICS (New York: Cambridge University Press, 1950). Reprinted with the permission of the publishers.

In consequence, if someone complains, "That wasn't the thing to do" or "That was hardly the way of going about things, was it?," his remark may have a genuinely ethical force. And this remains the case, although the only *fact* at issue is whether the action in question belongs to a class of actions generally approved of in the speaker's community. Some people have been misled by this into arguing that many so-called "ethical" statements are just disguised statements of fact; that "what seems to be an ethical judgment is very often a factual classification of an action."[1] But this is a mistake. What makes us call a judgment "ethical" is the fact that it is used to harmonize people's actions (rather than to give a recognizable description of a state of affairs, for instance); judgments of the kind concerned are unquestionably "ethical" by this standard; and the fact that the action belongs to a certain class of actions is not so much the "disguised meaning of" as the "reason for" the ethical judgment.

Furthermore, the test for answering questions of this simple kind remains the accepted practice, even though the particular action may have unfortunate results. Suppose that I am driving along a winding, country road, and deliberately keep on the left-hand side going round the blind corners. It may happen that a driver going the other way is cutting his corners, so that we collide head-on; but this does not affect the propriety of my driving. My care to keep to the left remains "right," my decision not to take any risks on the corners remains "correct," in spite of the fact that the consequences, in the event, were unfortunate. Provided that I had no reason to expect such an upset, provided that I was not to know how the other man was behaving—knowledge which would have made a material difference to my decision, and would have taken my situation out of the straight-forward class to which the rule applies—the existence of the Rule of the Road is all that is needed to make my decision "correct."

2.2 REASONING ABOUT THE RIGHTNESS OF ACTIONS

This brings us to questions about one's "reasons" for a decision or an action.

If the policeman investigating the accident asks the other driver, "Why were you driving on the right-hand side of the road?," he will have to produce a long story in order to justify himself. If, however, I am asked why I was driving on the *left,* the only answer I can give is that the left-hand side is the one on which one *does* drive in England—that the Rule of the Road *is* to drive on the left.

Again, the schoolboy who gets his colors through favoritism may ask, "And why shouldn't I have been given them?" If he does so, his schoolfellows will point out that it is the practice (and in fact the whole point of colors) for them to go to the best cricketers; and that there were better cricketers to whom they could have been given. And this will be all the justification needed.

Finally, an example in which the logical structure of this type of "reasoning" is fully set out: suppose that I say, "I feel that I ought to take this book and give it back to Jones" (so reporting on my feelings). You may ask me, "But ought you really to do so?" (turning the question into an ethical one), and it is up to me to produce my "reasons," if I have any. To begin with, then, I may reply that I ought to take it back to him, "because I promised to let him have it back before midday"—so classifying my position as one of type S_1. "But ought you *really?,*" you may repeat. If you do, I can relate S_1 to a more general S_2, explaining, "I ought to, because I promised to let him have it back." And if

[1]Ayer, *Language, Truth and Logic* (2nd ed.), p. 21.

you continue to ask, "But why ought you really?," I can answer, in succession, "Because I ought to do whatever I promise him to do" (S_3), "Because I ought to do whatever I promise anyone to do" (S_4), and "Because anyone ought to do whatever he promises anyone else that he will do" or "Because it was a promise" (S_5). Beyond this point, however, the question cannot arise: there is no more general "reason" to be given beyond one which relates the action in question to an accepted social practice.

2.3 CONFLICTS OF DUTIES

This straightforward method of answering the questions, "Is this the right thing to do?" and "Why ought you to do that?," can apply only in situations to which a rule of action is unambiguously appropriate. The most interesting practical questions, however, always arise in those situations in which one set of facts drives us one way, and another pulls us in the opposite direction.

If the muck-heap at the bottom of my garden bursts into flames in midsummer, and someone says, "There's nothing to be surprised at in that: it's a simple case of spontaneous combustion. Surely you've heard of ricks burning in the same kind of way?," his explanation may satisfy me: the analogy between the burning of my muck-heap and the spontaneous combustion of a hayrick is close enough for it to be plausible. But, if it is late January, I may reject the explanation, and protest, "That's all very well in July or August, but not in midwinter: whoever heard of a hayrick catching fire with snow on the ground?," and, unless he can assure me that it does quite frequently happen, I shall continue to hanker after a different explanation.

In much the same way, the fact that I promised to let Jones have his book back will seem to me reason enough for taking it to him on time—if that is all that there is to it. But, if I have a critically ill relative in the house, who cannot be left, the issue is complicated. The situation is not sufficiently unambiguous for reasoning from the practice of promise-keeping to be conclusive: I may therefore argue, "That's all very well in the ordinary way, but not when I've got my grandmother to look after: whoever heard of risking someone else's life just to return a borrowed book?" Unless evidence is produced that the risks involved in breaking my promise to Jones are even greater than those attending my grandmother, if she is left alone, I shall conclude that it is my duty to remain with her.

Given two conflicting claims, that is to say, one has to weigh up, as well as one can, the risks involved in ignoring either, and choose "the lesser of the two evils." Appeal to a single current principle, though the primary test of the rightness of an action, cannot therefore be relied on as a universal test: where this fails, we are driven back upon our estimate of the probable consequences. And this is the case, not only where there is a conflict of duties, but also, for instance, in circumstances in which, although no matter of principle is involved, some action of ours can nevertheless meet another's need. Here again we naturally and rightly conclude that the action is one that we "ought" to perform, but we record in our usage the difference between such circumstances and those in which a matter of principle *is* involved: although we should say that we "ought" to perform the action, we should not usually say that we had a "moral obligation" to perform it, or even that it was our "duty." We here appeal to consequences in the absence of a relevant principle, or "duty."[2]

[2]We can, and sometimes do, employ the language of "duty" in this case also, by treating the reference to consequences as a reference to a completely general "duty" to help one another when in need. For our present purposes, the difference between these two ways of putting it is purely verbal.

So it comes about that we can, in many cases, justify an individual action by reference to its estimated consequences. Such a reference is no substitute for a principle, where any principle is at issue: but moral reasoning is so complex, and has to cover such a variety of types of situation, that no one logical test (such as "appeal to an accepted principle") can be expected to meet every case.

2.4 REASONING ABOUT THE JUSTICE OF SOCIAL PRACTICES

All these types of question are intelligible by reference to the primitive stage in the development of ethics. As soon as we turn to the second stage, however, there is room for questions of a radically different type.

Recall our analysis of "explanation." There I pointed out that, although on most occasions the question, "Is this really straight?," has a use, situations might be encountered in which the question, in its ordinary sense, simply cannot be asked. These occasions were of two kinds:

(i) those on which the criterion of straightness is itself questioned, within the framework of a particular theory, and

(ii) those on which the criteria of straightness used in alternative theories are found to be different.

The same kinds of situation arise (and, indeed, are more familiar) in ethics. To give an example of the first: so long as one confines oneself to a particular moral code, no more general "reason" can be given for an action than one which relates it to a practice (or principle) within that code. If an astronomer, who is discussing light-rays in outer space in terms of non-Euclidean geometry, is asked what reason he has for saying that they are straight, he can only reply, "Well, they just *are*": in the same way, if I am asked why one ought to keep a particular promise, all that I can say is, "Well, one just *ought*." Within the framework of a particular scientific theory, one can ask of most things, "Is *this* really straight?," but the *criterion* of straightness cannot be questioned: within the framework of a particular moral code, one can ask of most individual actions, "Is *this* really right?," but the *standards* of rightness cannot be questioned.

As an example of the second type of situation: the question, "Which is it really right to do—to have only one wife like a Christian, or to have anything up to four like the Mohammedans?," is odd in the same way as the question, "Is a light-ray going past the sun really straight, as a non-Euclidean theorist declares, or deflected, as a Euclidean theorist says?" If corresponding standards in two moral codes are found to be different, the question, "Which of these is really right?," cannot arise. Or rather (to put the same thing in another way), if the question *does* arise, it arises in a very different way, serves a different purpose, and requires an answer of a different sort.

What kind of purpose does it serves, and what kind of answer does it require? In science, if I insist on asking of the standard of straightness, "But is *it* really straight?," I am going outside the framework of that particular scientific theory. To question the standard is to question the theory—to criticize the theory *as a whole*—not to ask for an explanation of the phenomenon ostensibly under discussion (the properties of light-rays in outer space). So again in ethics: if I ask of the behavior prescribed in any standard of conduct, "Is *it* really right?," I am going outside the moral code; and my question is a criticism of the practice *as a practice*, not a request for a justification of a particular case of promise-keeping (or whatever it may be).

To question the rightness of a particular action is one thing: to question the justice of a practice *as a practice* is another. It is this second type of question which becomes intelligible when we turn to the second stage of development. If a society has a developing moral code, changes in the economic, social, political or psychological situation may lead people to regard the existing practices as unnecessarily restrictive, or as dangerously lax. If this happens, they may come to ask, for instance, "Is it right that women should be debarred from smoking in public?," or "Would it not be better if there were no mixed bathing after dark?," in each case questioning the practice concerned *as a whole*. The answer to be given will (remembering the function of ethics) be reached by estimating the probable consequences

(i) of retaining the present practice, and

(ii) of adopting the suggested alternative.

If, as a matter of fact, there is good reason to suppose that the sole consequences of making the proposed change would be to avoid some existing distresses, then, as a matter of ethics, there is certainly a good reason for making the change. As usual, however, the logically straightforward case is a comparatively uninteresting one: in practice, the interesting problems are those which arise when the happy consequences of the change are not so certain, or when they are likely to be accompanied by new, though perhaps less serious, distresses. And what stake may reasonably be risked for any particular likelihood of gain is something only to be settled with confidence—if then—by appeal to experience.

2.5 THE TWO KINDS OF MORAL REASONING

Two cautions are necessary. Although, as a matter of logic, it makes sense to discuss the justice of any social practice, some practices will in fact always remain beyond question. It is inconceivable (for instance) that any practice will ever be suggested, to replace promising and promise-keeping, which would be anything like as effective. Even in the most "advanced" stages of morality, therefore, promise-keeping will remain right.

Again, the fact that I can discuss the rightness of promise keeping as a practice, in this way, does not imply that there is any way of calling in question the rightness of keeping individual promises. In arguing that promise-keeping will remain right at all stages, "because its abolition would lead to suffering," I am doing something different in important respects from what I am doing, if I say that I ought to take this book back to Jones now, "because I promised to." I can justify the latter statement by pointing out that I am in any of the situations S_1 to S_5:[3] and such reasons will be acceptable in any community which expects promises to be fulfilled. But I cannot further justify it by saying, "Because one must not inflict avoidable suffering": this kind of reason is appropriate only when discussing whether a social practice should be retained or changed.

The two kinds of moral reasoning which we have encountered are, therefore, distinct. Each provides its own logical criteria—criteria which are appropriate to the criticism of individual actions, or social practices, but not both. It was this distinction between the "reasons" for an individual action and the "reasons" for a social practice which Socrates made as he waited for the hemlock: he was ready to die rather than repudiate it—refusing, when given the chance, to escape from the prison and so avoid execution. As an Athenian citizen, he saw that it was his duty (regardless of the actual consequences in his particular case) to respect the verdict and sentence of the court. To have escaped would have been to ignore this duty. By doing so, he would not merely

[3]See §II.2 above.

have questioned the justice of the verdict in his case: he would have renounced the Athenian constitution and moral code as a whole. This he was not prepared to do.

The history of Socrates illustrates the nature of the distinction, and the kind of situation in which it is important: the kind of situation in which it ceases to be of value can be seen from the story of Hampden and the "ship-money." It is those principles which we recognize as just which we have to respect most scrupulously: if we are prepared to dispute the justice of a principle, everything is altered. One of the most striking ways of disputing the justice of a principle is, indeed, by refusing to conform on a particular occasion: and such refusals give rise, in law and morality alike, to the notion of a "test case."

Over "test cases," the distinction between the two sorts of moral reasoning vanishes. In justifying the action concerned, one no longer refers to the current practice: it is the injustice of the accepted code, or the greater justice of some alternative proposal, which is now important. The justification of the action is made "a matter of principle" and the change in the logical criteria appropriate follows accordingly. In making an action a test case one must, however, take care that one's intentions are clear. If this is not done, the action may be criticized on the wrong level. It may be condemned, either by reference to the very principle it was intended to dispute, or as self-interested, or both; and the question of principle may go against one by default. There is an element of pathos about a test case which goes wrong for this reason; but those men whose protests are carried off successfully are often remembered as heroes.

2.6 THE LIMITED SCOPE OF COMPARISONS BETWEEN SOCIAL PRACTICES

The scope of ethical reasoning is limited as well as defined by the framework of activities in which it plays its part. We have already encountered one limitation: that, in unequivocal cases, once it has been shown that an action is in accordance with an established practice, there is no further room for the question, "But is this *really* the right thing to do?" The other questions which we have been discussing are, however, limited in similar ways, which we must now turn and consider.

Consider, first, the kinds of circumstance in which we question the rightness of a social practice. If, for example, it is regarded as disgusting for women to smoke in public, and I ask, "But ought they really to be debarred from doing so?," the nature of my inquiry is clear: I am suggesting that in future, when a lady lights a cigarette, people need not turn away in disapproval, look horrified, or cut her from their acquaintance. The change I propose is quite sufficiently indicated in my question for us to be able to discuss it as it stands, and even reach a decision about it, on its merits.

If, on the other hand, I ask, "Is it really right to have only one wife, like the Christians, or would it be better to have anything up to four, according to the old Mohammedan practice?," my question is a good deal less intelligible. In the first place, there seems to be a suggestion that we abandon our present practice in favor of an alternative one; but the exact nature of the change proposed is not clear; so how can one begin to estimate its probable consequences? Secondly, it is questionable whether the practices compared can be regarded as "alternatives" at all. The ramifications, both in Christian and in Muslim societies, of the institution of marriage, its relations to the institutions of property, of parenthood and so on, are so complex that there is no question of simply replacing the one institution by the other. Such different parts does the institution of "marriage" play in the ways of life of a Christian society and of a Muslim one that we might even feel it hardly right to describe Christian and Muslim marriage as being instances of the "same" institution at all.

The question, "Which of these institutions is 'right'?," is therefore an unreal one, and there is no conceivable way of answering it—as it stands. The only way of understanding it is to regard it as an even more general question, in a disguised form. As we saw, the question, "Is this the right thing to do?," when persisted in beyond a certain point, has to be understood as an inquiry about the justice of the social practice of which "this" is an instance—but an inquiry couched in an inappropriate form: so now the question, "Is it right for me to marry one wife or four?," has to be transformed, first into, "Is Christian marriage or Muslim marriage the better practice?"; and then again into, "Is the Christian or the Muslim *way of life* the better?"

When someone asks of two superficially similar institutions, from different ways of life, "Which is the better?," one may have to say that, by themselves, they are not comparable: all that can be compared are the ways of life *as wholes.* And *this* comparison is, if anything, a private one: which is to say, not that it *cannot* be reasoned about, but that, reason as you may, the final decision is personal. There is no magic wand which will turn the English social system into a Muslim one overnight: the only practical use for the question, "Which way of life is the better?," is in the service of a personal decision—for example, whether to remain here in our society, such as it is, or to go and live as an Arab tribesman in the desert.

In general, then, if one is to *reason* about social practices, the only occasions on which one can discuss the question which of two practices is the better are those on which they are genuine alternatives: when it would be practicable to change from one to the other *within one society.* Given this, the question, "Which is the better?," has the force of, "If we changed from one to the other, would the change have happy or unhappy consequences on the whole?" But, if this condition is not satisfied, there is, morally speaking, *no* reasoning about the question, and pretended arguments about the merits of rival systems—personal preferences apart—are of value only as rhetoric. . . .

2.7 THE LIMITS TO THE ANALYSIS OF ETHICAL CONCEPTS

Consider, secondly, the musty old conundrum over which moral philosophers have battled for so long: namely, whether the "real" analysis of "*X* is right" is "*X* is an instance of a rule of action (or maxim, or prima facie obligation)," or "*X* is the alternative which of all those open to us is likely to have the best results."[4] If the scope of ethical reasoning is limited by its function, does this question fall within or outside the limits?

To begin with, it must be clear from our discussion that, in talking of the "analysis" of "*X* is right," philosophers cannot be referring to the "meaning" of "*X* is right." The "meaning" of "*X* is right" is certainly neither of the alternatives proposed: it is "*X* is the thing to do in these circumstances, to encourage others to do in similar circumstances, etc. etc." To suppose otherwise is to be trapped into the "naturalistic fallacy"—that is to say, it is to confuse facts and values (the reasons for an ethical judgment, and the judgment itself), by attempting to express the "meaning" of an *ethical* judgment in *factual* form. The question which the "analysis" of "*X* is right" *can* answer is the question, "Which kinds of reason are required in order to show that something is right (i.e. the thing to do, to encourage others to do, etc.)—(i) that it is an instance of a rule of action, or (ii) that it is the alternative likely to have the best results?"

The answer, with comparatively little over-simplification, is that it depends upon the nature of the "thing." If it is an action which is an unambiguous instance of a maxim

[4] Cf. Broad, *Five Types of Ethical Theory,* pp. 206–7.

generally accepted in the community concerned, it will be right just because it *is* an instance of such a maxim; but, if it is an action over which there is a "conflict of duties," or is itself a principle (or social practice) as opposed to a particular action, it will be right or wrong according as its consequences are likely to be good or bad.

When we bear in mind the function of ethics, therefore, we see that the answer to the philosophers' question is, "Either, depending on the nature of the case." The question, in other words, falls within the logical limits set by the function of ethics—provided only that you are prepared to accept "Either" as an answer.

As a matter of history, philosophers have not been so prepared: they have tended to demand an "unequivocal" answer—. "The first" or "The second," and not "Either"—and to assume that either the "deontological" or the "teleological" answer must be "true," and the other "false."[5] But this is to mistake the nature of the problem. Questions presenting a pair of alternants, "Which is true—*A* or *B?*" are of two kinds: those to which the answer can sensibly be "Either" or "Neither," and those to which the only possible answers are "*A*" and "*B*." If I report to the police that I have seen a stolen car being driven along the Bath Road, and they ask me, "In which direction was it going?," the only positive answers I can give are "Eastwards" and "Westwards." I can, of course, say, "I didn't notice," but I *cannot* say "Either" or "Neither": if it was being driven along the Bath Road at all, it *must* have been going in the one direction or the other. This seems to be the kind of model which philosophers have had before them when attempting to answer their question, "Which is the analysis of "*X* is right"—*A* or *B?*" In any case, they have certainly overlooked the resemblance of their question to the other, verbally-similar type of question, represented in the extreme case by the algebraic query, "Which is the correct solution of the equation $x^2 - 5x + 6 = 0$, $x = 2$ or $x = 3$?"—the answer to which is, "Either, depending on the conditions of the particular problem."

If we must answer the philosophers' question about the "analysis" of "*X* is right," it will be along the lines of the algebraic query, rather than along those of the policeman's enquiry. It is, in fact, only as long as one is prepared to accept this kind of answer that the function of ethics leaves one room to ask the question at all.

2.8 THE LIMITS TO QUESTIONS ABOUT THE RIGHTNESS OF ACTIONS

Let us return, next, to the simplest and most primitive types of ethical question, "Is this the right thing to do?" and "Which of these actions ought I to do?" What limits are there to the circumstances in which we can ask these questions?

Once more we can get some guidance from the parallel between science and ethics. The question, "What is the scientific explanation of this?," can be answered in a great variety of circumstances, but one comes across some situations in which science cannot help to still the surprise which prompts the question. The instance I gave as an illustration of this was that of the family all of whom died on their birthdays. When, after the first two children have died on their birthdays, the third does also, you may well be surprised; but the fact that it happens is one to be accepted, not to be explained. None of

[5]And the consequences of this demand have been interesting, especially in the cases of the more honest and self-critical philosophers. Notice, for example, the comment made by A. E. Duncan-Jones on the second of the alternatives which I have quoted above (see *Mind,* n.s. XLII, p. 472): "I believe it in a peculiar way, so that sometimes the theory strikes me as undeniable and sometimes I am sceptical about it." This seems to me the kind of predicament into which a candid man is bound to find his way, if he demands an "unambiguous" answer to the present question.

the laws of nature, which we have developed as a summary of experience, could have led you to anticipate the event: none can now show you that it was to have been expected. There it is—and the pathologists cannot help you. The range of things for which it makes sense to talk of a "scientific explanation" is limited: there is a point up to which science can take you, but beyond that point it cannot go.

In ethics, too, the range of decisions for which it makes sense to talk of a "moral justification" is limited: again there is a point up to which morality can take you, but beyond which it cannot go. If you ask me, "Which of these two courses of action ought I to choose?," we can see which of the accepted social practices are relevant and, if no "matter of principle" is involved, estimate (as best we can) the effects which either course of action will have on the other members of the community. These considerations may lead us to rule out one of the two courses as "morally wrong"—that is, as one which, on moral grounds, you ought not to choose. But they may leave us where we were: no matter of principle may be involved, and the foreseeable consequences to others may be neither better nor worse in the one case than in the other. If this happens, and you persist in asking me, "But which *ought* I to choose?," I can only reply, "*Morally* speaking, there's nothing to choose between them, so there's no "ought" about it. It's entirely up to you now which you do."

The notions of "duty," of "obligation," of "morality," are derived from situations in which the conduct of one member of a community prejudices the interests of another, and are to be understood as part of the procedure for minimizing the effects of such conflicts. Provided that two courses of action are equally acceptable according to the established code, and their foreseeable effects on others are equally tolerable, the notions of "duty" and "obligation" no longer apply in their primitive senses. If one is to choose between the two courses of action, it is on grounds of a different kind, for "moral grounds" are no longer conclusive.

What kind of grounds will be relevant? It would be going beyond the scope of this book to discuss this question in detail, but we can take a quick look. At any given time, one can answer the question, "What, at this moment, do you wish to do?," and, if at that instant this wish were granted, one would, for the moment, be satisfied. (You do not have to be a psychologist to know this: it is just in the nature of a "wish.") But we soon find out that to get what we wish for each instant, quite apart from its effects on others, may bring no deep or lasting satisfaction. We therefore begin to bend our energies, less towards those things for which we have a momentary desire, and more towards other things—things which we expect to bring deeper and more lasting contentment. In doing so, we develop a "rule of life," a personal "code" with the help of which, when moral considerations are no longer relevant, we can choose between different courses of action. In developing this "rule of life," we have, of course, not only our own experience to guide us; we have the records which others have left of their attempts, failures and successes in the same quest, and the advice of friends and relatives to help us—or confuse us. Given all this mass of experience, we can now "reason" about proposed courses of action, even when moral considerations are no longer conclusive. At this stage, however, the decision must be a personal one. The argument will be of the form, "a_1, a_2, . . . (the reasons): so, if I were you, I should choose this course"; and the test of the argument concerns the future of the person concerned. If the course recommended was, as a matter of fact, likely to lead to his deepest and most permanent happiness, the advice was *good* advice—that is, advice worthy of acceptance: and, if the reasoning was such as to establish the true value of the advice, it was *good* reasoning—that is, reasoning worthy of notice.

Passing beyond the scope of "morality" means passing out of the reach of those principles which find their rightful place in "morality"—principles which can be formulated in terms independent of person and occasion. In the new field, every argument depends for its validity on an explicit or implicit "If I were you." Here the agent's "feelings" and "attitudes" enter in, not as the cardboard creatures of philosophical theory, but as logically indispensable participants. And if there is little space in a book of this kind to discuss this new field of argument, there is no reason to suppose that it is less worth discussing than those to which space has been given. It is simply a field in which less can be formalized; and therefore one in which the logician has less to contribute. Perhaps it is more important. Perhaps the chief value of discovering how much of the logic of ethics can be formalized lies in seeing why so much of it cannot—in seeing how (as E. M. Forster suggests in *Howards End*) the formal world of "moral principles," of "telegrams and anger," pales by comparison with the richer world of "personal relations." In some respects logic must be content to lag one step behind discovery: "form," at any rate, is created always after the event. "Moral principles" carry us only so far: it is only rarely that we can go all the way with their help. And when their job is done, the harder task remains of seeing the right answer to a question beginning "If you were me. . . ."

All this, though a matter of logic rather than of "empirical fact," was seen by Socrates and strikingly expressed by Plato. With his help, we can characterize, figuratively, the formal difference between the two kinds of reasoning relevant to the choice of an action. One is "reasoning on moral grounds," aimed at the Harmony of Society: the other, to which we turn when reasoning on moral grounds does not lead to a decision by itself, is concerned with each man's own Pursuit of the Good. And the Good?—

> The Good differs from everything else in a certain respect. . . . A creature that possesses it permanently, completely and absolutely, has never any need of anything else; its satisfaction is perfect.[6]

But this is not the end of the matter. The second type of reasoning about the choice of individual actions—that concerned with Happiness rather than with Harmony—has its counterpart in social ethics just as much as the first; and it is one which comes into the picture in similar circumstances. If we took a restricted view of "ethics," it might seem to be the case that, when the existing social practices were causing no positive hardship, so that people did not actually complain about them, then there was nothing to be said against them; and that the institutions were therefore "perfect"—by definition, as it were. This is a position which few people would wish to maintain. Over individual actions, to say that it does not matter what one decides to do, as long as it is within the moral code, is simply to shirk a proper decision—for often enough moral considerations do not take us all the way—and so also is it if one says that it does not matter what the present institutions and social practices are, as long as they do not cause positive and avoidable hardship. Certainly this is the first thing we must ask of our institutions; but, when we have satisfied ourselves about this, they are not necessarily exempt from all criticism. We can now inquire whether, if some specific change were made, the members of our community would lead fuller and happier lives. And again, if there are reasonable grounds for believing that they would, the change is surely justified.

One might naturally and properly argue that our definition of the "function" of ethics should take account of these considerations too. And we could extend it to do so, if we chose. It is important, however, if we are going to do so, to notice one thing: namely, that this *is* an extension. Our ideas of "right," of "justice," of "duty," of "obligation," are manifold: each word covers a genus of concepts. But some members of each

[6]*Philebus*, 60 B-C (tr. Hackforth); see *Plato's Examination of Pleasure*, p. 125.

genus are more characteristically ethical than others. "You ought to rest this afternoon, as you've a busy evening ahead of you," "You ought to hear his violin concerto," "You ought to visit him, if you promised to": these remarks all make use of the notion of "obligation," but only in the last of the three does it carry its full force. If you used instances of this last kind to teach someone the notion, you might expect him to recognize that the other uses were natural extensions of it; but you would never expect him to understand the full nature of "moral obligation" if given only instances of the first and second kinds—instances having hardly more force than that of "You'll enjoy his violin concerto if you hear it" and "If you don't rest this afternoon, you'll regret it later." The notions of "obligation," "right," "justice," "duty," and "ethics" apply in the first place where our actions or institutions may lead to avoidable misery for others; but it is a natural and familiar extension to use them also where the issue concerns the chance of deeper happiness for others, and even for ourselves.

2.9 IS ANY "JUSTIFICATION" OF ETHICS NEEDED?

In talking about the logic of ethical reasoning in the light of the function of ethics, I have tried to indicate two things:

(i) the different types of question which naturally arise in ethical contexts, and the ways in which they are answered; and
(ii) the limits of ethical reasoning—that is, the kinds of occasion on which questions and considerations of an ethical kind can no longer arise.

So far, however, I have not given an explicit answer to the question from which we set out: namely, "What is it, in an ethical discussion, that makes a reason a good reason, or an argument a valid argument?"

In previous chapters this question has always caused trouble. When discussing the objective doctrine of ethics, we found it impossible even to reach it without first mastering some highly mysterious arguments about "non-natural" properties; even more surprisingly, the advocates of the subjective and imperative doctrines tried to dismiss it as vain. But now we are in the opposite position. In this chapter, I have not attempted to give a "theory of ethics"; I have simply tried to describe the occasions, on which we are in fact prepared to call judgments "ethical" and decisions "moral," and the part which reasoning plays on such occasions. This description has led us to see how, in *particular types* of ethical question and argument, good reasoning is distinguished from bad, and valid argument from invalid—to be specific, by applying to individual judgments the test of principle, and to principles the test of general fecundity.

Now we have to ask, "Is any further answer needed? Given particular rules applicable to different kinds of ethical judgment and question, have we not all we want? And, if any more were needed, could it not be supplied from an account, more detailed and accurate than has been given, but of the same kind?"

I myself do not feel the need for any *general* answer to the question, "What makes some ethical reasoning 'good' and some ethical arguments 'valid'?": answers applicable to particular types of argument are enough. In fact, it seems to me that the demand for any such general answer (however it is to be obtained) must lead one to paradox . . . For either such a general answer will, in particular cases, be equivalent to the rules which we have found, or it will contradict them. In the first case, it can do one of two things. Either it can distort our account, so that one of the criteria alone seems important; or else it can point out, in a more or less roundabout way, the advantages—indeed, "the absolute necessity to the existence of society"[7]—of harmonious co-operation. Instead, however, it may contradict our results. What then? What if we try to adopt the new rules for criticizing arguments about conduct, which this general answer lays down?

If we do adopt these new criteria, then it will no longer be "ethical" reasoning, "moral" considerations, arguments from "duty" and questions about what we "ought" to do that we are criticizing: it will be questions, arguments and considerations of another kind—in fact, a different mode of reasoning. This can be shown quite quickly. For suppose that, far from radically changing our criteria, all that the new rules do is to select one of them as the *universal* criterion. If the test of principle is chosen, so that we are never to be allowed to question the pronouncements of those who administer the moral code, then it is not "morality" to which they apply—it is "authority," and authority of a kind which may reasonably be expected to develop rapidly into tyranny. And conversely, if the test of principle is itself ruled out in favor of a universal test of consequence (of the estimated effects on others), then we are faced with something which is no more "morality" than the other—it would now be better described as "expediency." But arguments from expediency and arguments from authority are no more "ethical" than experienced guess-work is "scientific." Consequently, even if all we do is to give up one or other of our present logical criteria, we turn ethics into something other than it is. And if this is the case there is no need for us to go on and consider more drastic alterations: they can be ruled out at once.

No doubt those philosophers who search for more general rules will not be satisfied. No doubt they will still feel that they want an explicit and unique answer to our central question. And no doubt they will object that, in all this, I have not even "justified" our using reason in ethics at all. "It's all very well your laying down the law about particular types of ethical argument," they will say; "but what is the justification for letting *any* reasoning affect how we decide to behave? Why *ought* one to do what is right, anyway?"

They are sufficiently answered by the peculiarity of their own questions. For let us consider what kind of answer they want when they ask, "Why ought one to do what is right?" There is no room *within* ethics for such a question. Ethical reasoning may be able to show why we ought to do this action as opposed to that, or advocate this social practice as opposed to that, but it is no help where there can be no choice. And their question does not present us with genuine alternatives at all. For, since the notions of "right" and of "obligation" originate in the same situations and serve similar purposes, it is a self-contradiction (taking "right" and "ought" in their simplest senses) to suggest that we "ought" to do anything but what is "right." This suggestion is as unintelligible as the suggestion that some emerald objects might not be green, and the philosophers' question is on a level with the question, "Why are all scarlet things red?" We can therefore parry it only with another question—"What else 'ought' one to do?"

Similar oddities are displayed by all their questions—as long as we take them literally. Ethics may be able to "justify" one of a number of courses of action, or one social practice as opposed to another: but it does not extend to the "justification" of all reasoning about conduct. One course of action can be opposed to another: one social practice can be opposed to another. But to what are we expected to oppose "ethics-as-a-whole"? There can be no discussion about the proposition, "Ethics is ethics"; any argument treating "ethics" as something other than it is must be false; and, if those who call for a "justification" of ethics want "the case for morality," as

[7]Hume, *Natural History of Religion,* § XIII, *ad fin.*

opposed to "the case for expediency," etc., then they are giving philosophy a job which is not its own. To show that you ought to choose certain actions is one thing: to make you *want to do* what you ought to do is another, and not a philosopher's task.

2.10 REASON AND SELF-LOVE

Hume ran sharply into this difficulty. He had, in fact, to confess (of a man in whom self-love overpowered the sense of right), "It would be a little difficult to find any [reasoning] which will appear to him satisfactory and convincing."[8] This confession of his was, however, a masterpiece of understatement. The difficulty he speaks of is no "little" one; indeed, it is an "absolute and insuperable" one, an "impossibility." But note the reason: it is not a *practical* impossibility at all, but a *logical* one. A man's ignoring all ethical arguments is just the kind of thing which would lead us to say that his self-love *had* overpowered his sense of right. As long, and only as long, as he continued to ignore all moral reasoning, we should say that his self-love continued in the ascendant: but once he began to accept such considerations as a guide to action, we should begin to think that "the sense of right" had won.

It is always possible that, when faced with a man whose self-love initially overpowered his sense of right, we might hit upon some reasoning which appeared to him "satisfactory and convincing." The result, however, would not be "a man in whom self-love was dominant, but who was satisfied and convinced by ethical reasoning" (for this is a contradiction in terms); it would be "a man in whom self-love was dominant, until reasoning beat it down and reinstated the sense of right."

There is, in this respect, an interesting parallel to be drawn between the notion of "rational belief" in science, and that of "reasonable belief" in ethics. We call the belief that (for instance) sulphonamides will control pneumonia a "rational belief," because it is arrived at by the procedure found reliable in clinical research. The same applies to any belief held as a result of a series of properly conducted scientific experiments. Any such belief is strengthened as a result of further confirmatory observations. These observations (we say) increase the "probability" of any hypothesis with which they are consistent: that is, they increase the degree of confidence with which it is rational to entertain the hypothesis. In practice, of course, we do not always adopt the most reliable methods of argument—we generalize hastily, ignore conflicting evidence, misinterpret ambiguous observations and so on. We know very well that there are reliable standards of evidence to be observed, but we do not always observe them. In other words, we are not always rational; for to be "rational" is to employ always these reliable, self-consistent methods of forming one's scientific beliefs, and to fail to be "rational" is to entertain the hypothesis concerned with a degree of confidence out of proportion to its "probability."[9]

As with the "rational" and the "probable," so with the "reasonable" and the "desirable" (the "desirable," that is, in its usual sense of what ought to be pursued): the belief that I ought to pay the bill which my bookshop has sent me is a "reasonable" belief, and the bookseller's demand for payment is a "reasonable" demand, because they represent a practice which has been found acceptable in such circumstances. Any ethical judgment, held as a result of properly interpreted moral experience, is also "reasonable." Any such judgment is strengthened by further experiences which confirm the

[8]Hume, *Enquiries* (ed. Selby-Bigge), p. 283.

[9]In connection with this discussion, see Ayer (op. cit. pp. 99–102), whose argument I paraphrase.

fecundity of the principle from which the judgment derives. Such experiences increase the "desirability" of the principle: that is, they increase the degree of conviction with which it is reasonable to advocate and act upon the principle. In practice, of course, we do not always adopt the most satisfactory methods of reaching moral decisions—we jump to conclusions, ignore the suffering of "inferior" people, misinterpret ambiguous experiences, and so on. We know very well that there are reliable standards to be observed in shaping our principles and institutions, but we do not always observe them. That is to say, we are not always reasonable; for to be "reasonable" is to employ these reliable, self-consistent methods in reaching all our moral decisions, and to fail to be "reasonable" is to advocate and act upon our principles with a degree of conviction out of proportion to their desirability.

Consider the light which this parallel throws on Hume's difficulties and on the "justification" of ethics. It is sometimes suggested that the "probability" of a hypothesis is just a matter of our confidence in it, as measured by our willingness to rely on it in practice. This account is over-simplified, for it would be completely acceptable only if we always related belief to observation in a "rational" way. "Probability" is, rather, a matter of the degree of confidence with which it is rational to adopt a hypothesis. In an analogous way, Hume's theory of ethics makes the "desirability" of a moral principle a matter of the conviction with which all fully-informed people do hold to it. This likewise would be true—provided that we always related our moral judgments to experience in a "reasonable" way. . . .

But this clears up the problem. The truth is that, if different people are to agree in their ethical judgments, it is not enough for them all to be fully informed. They must all be *reasonable,* too. (Even this may not be enough: when it comes to controversial questions, they may reasonably differ.) Unfortunately, people are not always reasonable. And this is a sad fact, which philosophers just have to accept. It is absurd and paradoxical of them to suppose that we need produce a "reasoned argument" capable of convincing the "wholly unreasonable," for this would be a self-contradiction.[10]

If, therefore, the request for a "justification" of ethics is equivalent to this demand, there is no room for a "justification"; and the question used to express this demand, "Why ought one to do what is right?," has no literal answer. There may yet be room for answers of a *different* kind: but, if there is, it is certainly not the business of a logician, and probably not the business of any kind of philosopher, to give them. . . .

[10]I should have thought it unnecessary to formulate such an obvious truth, had I not found it overlooked, in practice, by eminent philosophers. For instance, I recall a conversation with Bertrand Russell in which he remarked, as an objection to the present account of ethics, that it would not have convinced Hitler. But whoever supposed that it should? We do not prescribe logic as a treatment for lunacy, or expect philosophers to produce panaceas for psychopaths.

Part III

1951–1970

1951

Outline of a Decision Procedure for Ethics

John Rawls

1.1 The question with which we shall be concerned can be stated as follows: Does there exist a reasonable decision procedure which is sufficiently strong, at least in some cases, to determine the manner in which competing interests should be adjudicated, and, in instances of conflict, one interest given preference over another; and, further, can the existence of this procedure, as well as its reasonableness, be established by rational methods of inquiry? In order to answer both parts of this question in the affirmative, it is necessary to describe a reasonable procedure and then to evidence that it satisfies certain criteria. This I attempt to do beginning at 2.1 below.

1.2 It should be noted that we are concerned here only with the existence of a reasonable method, and not with the problem of how to make it psychologically effective in the settling of disputes. How much allegiance the method is able to gain is irrelevant for our present purposes.

1.3 The original question has been framed the way it is because the objectivity or the subjectivity of moral knowledge turns, not on the question whether ideal value entities exist or whether moral judgments are caused by emotions or whether there is a variety of moral codes the world over, but simply on the question: does there exist a reasonable method for validating and invalidating given or proposed moral rules and those decisions made on the basis of them? For to say of scientific knowledge that it is objective is to say that the propositions expressed therein may be evidenced to be true by a reasonable and reliable method, that is, by the rules and procedures of what we may call "inductive logic"; and, similarly, to establish the objectivity of moral rules, and the decisions based upon them, we must exhibit the decision procedure, which can be shown to be both reasonable and reliable, at least in some cases, for deciding between moral rules and lines of conduct consequent to them.

2.1 For the present, we may think of ethics as being more analogous to the study of inductive logic than to any other established inquiry. Just as in inductive logic we are concerned with discovering reasonable criteria which, when we are given a proposition, or theory, together with the empirical evidence for it, will enable us to decide the extent to which we ought to consider it to be true so in ethics we are attempting to find reasonable principles which, when we are given a proposed line of conduct and the situation in which it is to be carried out and the relevant interests which it effects, will enable us to determine whether or not we ought to carry it out and hold it to be just and right.

2.2 There is no way of knowing ahead of time how to find and formulate these reasonable principles. Indeed, we cannot even be certain that they exist, and it is well known that there are no mechanical methods of discovery. In what follows, however, a method will be described, and it remains for the reader to judge for himself to what extent it is, or can be, successful.

2.3 First it is necessary to define a class of competent moral judges as follows: All those persons having to a certain requisite degree each of the following characteristics, which can, if desired, be made more determinate:

(i) A competent moral judge is expected to have a certain requisite degree of intelligence, which may be thought of as that ability which intelligence tests are designed to measure. The degree of this ability required should not be set too high, on the assumption that what we call "moral insight" is the possession of the normally intelligent man as well as of the more brilliant. Therefore I am inclined to say that a competent moral judge need not be more than normally intelligent.

(ii) A competent judge is required to know those things concerning the world about him and those consequences of frequently performed actions, which it is reasonable to expect the average intelligent man to know. Further, a competent judge is expected to know, in all cases whereupon he is called to express his opinion, the peculiar facts of those cases. It should be noted that the kind of knowledge here referred to is to be distinguished from sympathetic knowledge discussed below.

(iii) A competent judge is required to be a reasonable man as this characteristic is evidenced by his satisfying the following tests: First, a reasonable man shows a willingness, if not a desire, to use the criteria of inductive logic in order to determine what is proper for him to believe. Second, a reasonable man, whenever he is confronted with a moral question, shows a disposition to find reasons for and against the possible lines of conduct which are open to him. Third, a reasonable man exhibits a desire to consider questions with an open mind, and consequently, while he may already have an opinion on some issue, he is always willing to reconsider it in the light of further evidence and reasons which may be presented to him in discussion. Fourth, a reasonable man knows, or tries to know, his own emotional, intellectual, and moral predilections and makes a conscientious effort to take them into account in weighing the merits of any question. He is not unaware of the influences of prejudice and bias even in his most sincere efforts to annul them; nor is he fatalistic about their effect so that he succumbs to them as being those factors which he thinks must sooner or later determine his decision.

(iv) Finally, a competent judge is required to have a sympathetic knowledge of those human interests which, by conflicting in particular cases, give rise to the need to make a moral decision. The presence of this characteristic is evidenced by the following: First, by the person's direct knowledge of those interests gained by experiencing, in his own life, the goods they represent. The more interests which a person can appreciate in terms of his own direct experience, the greater the extent to which he satisfies this first test. Yet it is obvious that no man can know all interests directly, and therefore the second test is that, should a person not be directly acquainted with an interest, his competency as a judge is seen, in part, by his capacity to give that interest an appraisal by means of an imaginative experience of it. This test also requires of a competent judge that he must not consider his own *de facto* preferences as the necessarily valid measure of the actual worth of those interests which come before him, but that he be both able and anxious to determine, by imaginative appreciation, what those interests mean to persons who share them, and to consider them accordingly. Third, a competent judge is required to have the capacity and the desire to lay before himself in imagination all the interests in conflict, together with the relevant facts of the case, and to bestow upon the appraisal of each the same care which he would give to it if that interest were his own. He is required to determine what he would think to be just and unjust if each of the interests were as thoroughly his own as they are in fact those of other persons, and to render his judgment on the case as he feels his sense of justice requires after he has carefully framed in his mind the issues which are to be decided.

2.4 Before considering the next step in the development of the method here adopted, it is necessary to make some comments on the previous remarks. First, the tests for defining and determining the class of competent moral judges are vague; that is, given a group of persons, there would be, in all probability, instances in which we could not decide whether a person is a competent moral judge or not. Yet we do recognize in everyday life the pattern of characteristics discussed above; we do think that certain individuals exhibit them to a comparatively pre-eminent degree, and these individuals we call "reasonable" or "impartial"; it is men of their character whom we want to decide any case in which our interests are at stake. Thus, while the foregoing tests are admittedly not precise, they do describe and select a recognized type of person; and those persons who do satisfy them beyond any reasonable doubt, will be called "competent moral judges."

Second, it is important to note that a competent judge has not been defined by what he says in particular cases, nor by what principles he expresses or adopts. Competence is determined solely by the possession of certain characteristics, some of which may be said to be capacities and achievements (intelligence and knowledge), while others may be said to be virtues (thus, the intellectual virtues of reasonableness). It will become clear in later sections why we cannot define a competent judge, at least at the beginning of our inquiry, as one who accepts certain principles. The reason is that we wish to say of some principles for adjudicating interests that one ground for accepting them as reasonable principles is that competent judges seem to apply them intuitively to decide moral issues. Obviously if a competent judge were defined as one who applies those principles, this reasoning would be circular. Thus a competent judge must not be defined in terms of what he says or by what principles he uses.

Third, one should note the kind of characteristics which have been used to define a competent moral judge: namely, those characteristics which, in the light of experience, show themselves as necessary conditions for the reasonable expectation that a given person may come to know something. Thus, we think of intelligence as being such a condition in all types of inquiry; and similarly with knowledge, since the more a man knows, the greater the likelihood of his success in further inquiry. Again, not only is it necessary to have certain abilities and achievements but, to be a good investigator, a person must develop those habits of mind and thought which we may call "intellectual virtues" (cf. 2.3 [iii]) Finally, there are those habits and capacities of thought and imagination which were described in connection with sympathetic knowledge of human interests. Just as intellectual capacities and virtues are found to foster the conditions necessary for successful inquiry of whatever type, so these habits and capacities are believed to be necessary for making fair decisions on moral issues. We may call them the "virtues of moral insight" with the understanding that they do not define either the content or the nature of moral insight, but, assuming it exists, simply represent those habits and capacities which secure the conditions under which we believe it most likely to assert itself effectively. Thus the defining characteristics of a competent judge have not been selected arbitrarily, but in each case there is a reason for choosing them which accords with the purpose of coming to know.

Finally, we can make these remarks clearer if we consider other methods of choosing the class of competent judges. It is one of the marks of an ideology that it violates the above criteria. Ideologies, of whatever type, claim a monopoly of the knowledge of truth and justice for some particular race, or social class, or institutional group, and competence is defined in terms of racial and/or sociological characteristics which have no known connection with coming to know. In the present method care has been exercised to select the class of competent moral judges according to those characteristics which are associated with coming to know something, and not by means of characteristics which are the privileged possession of any race, class, or group, but which can and often do belong, at least to certain degree, to men everywhere.

2.5 The next step in the development of our procedure is to define the class of considered moral judgments, the determining characteristics of which are as follows:

(i) It is required first that the judgment on a case be given under such conditions that the judge is immune from all of the reasonably foreseeable consequences of the judgment. For example, he will not be punished for deciding the case one way rather than another.

(ii) It is required that the conditions be such that the integrity of the judge can be maintained. So far as possible, the judge must not stand to gain in any immediate and personal way by his decision. These two tests are designed to exclude judgments wherein a person must weigh the merit of one of his own interests. The imposition of these conditions is justified on the grounds that fear and partiality are recognized obstructions in the determination of justice.

(iii) It is required that the case, on which the judgment is given, be one in which there is an actual conflict of interests. Thus, all judgments on hypothetical cases are excluded. In addition, it is preferable that the case be not especially difficult and be one that is likely to arise in ordinary life. These restrictions are desirable in order that the judgments in question be made in the effort to settle problems with which men are familiar and whereupon they have had an opportunity to reflect.

(iv) It is required that the judgment be one which has been preceded by a careful inquiry into the facts of the question at issue, and by a fair opportunity for all concerned to state their side of the case. This requirement is justified on the ground that it is only by chance that a just decision can be made without a knowledge of the relevant facts.

(v) It is required that the judgment be felt to be certain by the person making it. This characteristic may be called "certitude" and it is be sharply distinguished from certainty, which is a logical relation between a proposition, or theory, and its evidence. This test is justified on the ground that it seems more profitable to study those judgments which are felt to be correct than those which seem to be wrong or confused even to those who make them.

(vi) It is required that the judgment be stable, that is, that there be evidence that at other times and at other places competent judges have rendered the same judgment on similar cases, understanding similar cases to be those in which the relevant facts and the competing interests are similar. The stability must hold, by and large, over the class of competent judges and over their judgments at different times. Thus, if on similar cases of a certain type, competent judges decided one way one day, and another the next, or if a third of them decided one way, a third the opposite way, while the remaining third said they did not know how to decide the cases, then none of these judgments would be stable judgments, and therefore none would be considered judgments. These restrictions are justified on the grounds that it seems unreasonable to have any confidence that a judgment is correct if competent persons disagree about it.

(vii) Finally, it is required that the judgment be intuitive with respect to ethical principles, that is, that it should not be determined by a conscious application of principles so far as this may be evidenced by introspection. By the term "intuitive" I do not mean the same as that expressed by the terms "impulsive" and "instinctive." An intuitive judgment may be consequent to a thorough inquiry into the facts of the case, and it may follow a series of reflections on the possible effects of different decisions, and even the application of a common sense rule, e.g., promises ought to be kept. What is required is that the judgment not be determined by a systematic and conscious use of ethical principles. The reason for this restriction will be evident if one keeps in mind the aim of the present inquiry, namely, to describe a decision procedure whereby principles, by means of which we may justify specific moral decisions, may themselves be shown to be justifiable. Now part of this procedure will consist in showing that these principles are implicit in the considered judgments of competent judges. It is clear that if we allowed these judgments to be determined by a conscious and systematic application of these principles, then the method is threatened with circularity. We cannot test a principle honestly by means of judgments wherein it has been consciously and systematically used to determine the decision.

2.6 Up to this point I have defined, first, a class of competent judges and, second, a class of considered judgments. If competent judges are those persons most likely to make correct decisions, then we should take care to abstract those judgments of theirs which, from the conditions and circumstances under which they are made, are most likely to be correct. With the exception of certain requirements, which are needed to prevent circularity, the defining characteristics of considered judgments are such that they select those judgments most likely to be decided by the habits of thought and imagination deemed essential for a competent judge. One can say, then, that those judgments which are relevant for our present purposes are the considered judgments of competent judges as these are made from day to day on the moral issues which continually arise. No other judgments, for reasons previously stated, are of any concern.

3.1 The next step in the present method is as follows: once the class of considered judgments of competent judges has been selected, there remains to discover and formulate a satisfactory explication of the total range of these judgments. This process is understood as being a heuristic device which is likely to yield reasonable and justifiable principles.

3.2 The term "explication" is given meaning somewhat graphically as follows: Consider a group of competent judges making considered judgments in review of a set of cases which would be likely to arise in ordinary life. Then an explication of these judgments is defined to be a set of principles, such that, if any competent man were to apply them intelligently and consistently to the same cases under review, his judgments, made systematically nonintuitive by the explicit and conscious use of the principles, would be, nevertheless, identical, case by case, with the considered judgments of the group of competent judges. The range of an explication is specified by stating precisely those judgments which it is designed to explicate, and any given explication which successfully explicates its specified range is satisfactory.

3.3 The next objective, then, in the development of the present method is to discover and formulate an explication which is satisfactory, by and large, over the total range of the considered judgments of competent moral judges as they are made from day to day in ordinary life, and as they are found embodied in the many dictates of commonsense morality, in various aspects of legal procedure, and so on. If reasonable principles exist for deciding moral questions, there is a presumption that the principles of a satisfactory explication of the total range of the considered judgments of competent judges will at least approximate them. On the basis of this presumption the explication of these judgments is designed to be a heuristic device for discovering reasonable principles. Therefore, while explication is an empirical inquiry, it is felt that it is likely to be a way of finding reasonable and justifiable principles in view of the nature of the class of judgments which make up its range.

3.4 Since the concept of an explication may not be clear, I shall try to clarify it by stating some of the things that an explication is not. First, an explication is not an analysis of the meaning of the ethical terms used in the judgments constituting its range. An explication attempts to do nothing more than that explicitly stated above, and in no way concerns itself with the sense of ethical expressions or with their linguistic meaning.

Second, an explication is not concerned with what people intend to assert when they use ethical expressions or make moral judgments in particular cases.

Third, an explication is not a theory about the actual causes of the considered judgments of competent judges, and this fact, in addition to the restriction to a specified class of judgments, sharply distinguishes it from a psychological or a sociological study of moral judgments. The only sense in which explication, as here defined, is concerned with causes is that a satisfactory explication can be a cause, or could be a cause, of the judgments in its range, i.e., the explicit and conscious adoption of the principles of the explication would yield the same judgments. Since explication is not concerned with the actual causes of judgments, it is immaterial whether the judgments in its range are caused by the intuition of nonnatural ethical characteristics, or by the response of intentional feelings to directly experienced value qualities, or by emotional attitudes which may in turn have been caused by certain specifiable psychological and sociological determinants. Questions about the actual causes, while interesting, are irrelevant from the standpoint of the present method. That such questions are irrelevant is also clear from the fact, previously stated, that the objectivity or subjectivity of moral judgments depends not on their causes, in any of the senses just listed, but solely on whether a reasonable decision procedure exists which is sufficiently strong to decide, at least in some cases, whether a given decision, and the conduct consequent thereto, is reasonable.

Finally, there is only one way of showing an explication to be unsatisfactory, and that is to show that there exist considered judgments of competent judges on specifiable cases for which it either fails to yield any judgments at all or leads one to make judgments inconsistent with them. Conversely, the only way to show that an explication is satisfactory is to evidence that its explicit and conscious application can be, or could be, a cause of the judgments in its range.

3.5 Having noted some of the things that an explication is not, I consider some positive features thereof. First, an explication must be such that it can be applied intelligently by a competent judge; and since a competent judge is not required to have a special training in logic and mathematics, an explication either must be formulated or formulatable in ordinary language and its principles must be capable of an interpretation which the average competent man can grasp.

Second, an explication must be stated in the form of principles, the reason for this demand lying in the use of explication as a heuristic device. The typical form of a considered judgment is as follows: since *A, B, C,* . . ., and *M, N, O,* . . ., are the facts of the case and the interests in conflict, *M* is to be given preference over *N, O,* . . . A considered judgment does not provide any reasons for the decision. It simply states the felt preference in view of the facts of the case and the interests competing therein. The principles of an explication must be general directives, expressible in ordinary language, such that, when applied to specific cases, they yield the preferences expressed in considered judgments.

Finally, an explication, to be completely successful, must be comprehensive; that is, it must explicate, in view of the explication itself (for this proviso, see below, 4.3), all considered judgments; and it is expected to do this with the greatest possible simplicity and elegance. The requirement of simplicity means that, other things being equal, an explication is more or less satisfactory according to the number of principles which it uses; and although this demand is difficult to state precisely, it is clear that nothing is gained if we require a separate principle for each case or for each class of cases.

3.6 The attempt to discover a comprehensive explication may be thought of as the attempt to express the invariant in the considered judgments of competent judges in the sense that, given the wide variety of cases on which considered judgments are made at different times and places, the principles of explication are such that the conscious and systematic application of them could have been a common factor in the determination of the multiplicity of considered judgments as made on the wide variety of cases. Whether such an explication exists or not, one cannot know at present, and opinions vary; but the belief that such an explication does exist is perhaps a prerequisite for the finding of it, should it exist, for the reason that one who does not so believe is not likely to exert the great effort which is surely required to find it.

4.1 Perhaps the principal aim of ethics is the formulation of justifiable principles which may be used in cases wherein there are conflicting interests to determine which one of them should be given preference. Therefore it remains to consider what is meant by the terms "justifiable principle" and a "rational judgment" in a particular case.

4.2 Consider the simpler question first, namely, what is the test of whether a judgment in a particular case is rational? The answer is that a judgment in a particular case is evidenced to be rational by showing that, given the facts and the conflicting interests of the case, the judgment is capable of being explicated by a justifiable principle (or set of principles). Thus if the explicit and conscious adoption of a justifiable principle (or set of principles) can be, or could have been, the ground of the judgment, or if the judgment expresses that preference which justifiable principles would yield if applied to the case, then the judgment is rational. Clearly the justification of particular judgments, if the above is correct, depends upon the use of justifiable principles. But how do we know whether a principle is justifiable? Four criteria for answering this question are considered below.

4.3 In what follows we shall assume that a satisfactory and comprehensive explication of the considered judgments of competent judges is already known (note proviso under fourth test below). Now consider the question as to what reasons we can have for accepting these principles as justifiable.

The first reason for accepting them has already been touched upon: namely, since the principles explicate the considered judgments of competent judges, and since these judgments are more likely than any other judgments to represent the mature convictions of competent men as they have been worked out under the most favorable existing conditions, the invariant in what we call "moral insight," if it exists, is more likely to be approximated by the principles of a successful explication than by principles which a man might fashion out of his own head. Individual predilections will tend to be canceled out once the explication has included judgments of many persons made on a wide variety of cases. Thus the fact that the principles constitute a comprehensive explication of the considered judgments of competent judges is a reason for accepting them. That this should be so is understandable if we reflect, to take the contrary case, how little confidence we would have in principles which should happen to explicate the judgments of men under strong emotional or physical duress, or of those mentally ill. Hence the type of judgments which make up the range of the explication is the first ground for accepting the principles thereof.

Secondly, the reasonableness of a principle is tested by seeing whether it shows a capacity to become accepted by competent moral judges after they have freely weighed its merits by criticism and open discussion, and after each has thought it over and compared it with his own considered judgments. It is hoped that some principles will exhibit a capacity to win free and willing allegiance and be able to implement a gradual covergence of uncoerced opinion.

Thirdly, the reasonableness of a principle is tested by seeing whether it can function in existing instances of conflicting opinion, and in new cases causing difficulty, to yield a result which, after criticism and discussion, seems to be acceptable to all, or nearly all, competent judges, and to conform to their intuitive notion of a reasonable decision. For example, the problem of punishment has been a troublesome moral issue for some time, and if a principle or set of principles should be formulated which evidenced a capacity to settle this problem to the satisfaction of all, or nearly all, competent judges, then this principle, or set of principles, would meet this test in one possible instance of its application. In general, a principle evidences its reasonableness by being able to resolve moral perplexities which existed at the time of its formulation and which will exist in the future. This test is somewhat analogous to a test which we impose upon an empirical theory: namely, its ability to foresee laws and facts hitherto unknown, and to explain facts and laws hitherto unexplainable.

Finally, the reasonableness of a principle is tested by seeing whether it shows a capacity to hold its own (that is, to continue to be felt reasonable), against a subclass of the considered judgments of competent judges, as this fact may be evidenced by our intuitive conviction that the considered judgments are incorrect rather than the principle, when we confront them with the principle. A principle satisfies this test when a subclass of considered judgments, rather than the principle, is felt to be mistaken when the principle fails to explicate it. For example, it often happens that competent persons, in judging the moral worth of character, blame others in conflict with the rule that a man shall not be morally condemned for the possession of characteristics which would not have been otherwise even if he had so chosen. Frequently, however, when we point out that their judgments conflict with this rule, these persons, upon reflection, will decide that their judgments are incorrect, and acknowledge the principle. To the extent that principles exhibit this capacity to alter what we think to be our considered judgments in cases of conflict, they satisfy the fourth test. It is, of course, desirable, although not essential, that whenever a principle does successfully militate against what is taken to be a considered judgment, some convincing reason can be found to account for the anomaly. We should like to find that the once accepted intuitive conviction is actually caused by a mistaken belief as to a matter of fact of which we were unaware or fostered by what is admittedly a narrow bias of some kind. The rationale behind this fourth test is that while the considered judgments of competent judges are the most likely repository of the working out of men's sense of right and wrong, a more likely one, for example, than that of any particular individual's judgments alone, they may, nevertheless, contain certain deviations, or confusions, which are best discovered by comparing the considered judgments with principles which pass the first three tests and seeing which of the two tends to be felt incorrect in the light of reflection. The previous proviso (3.5) is to be understood in connection with the above discussion of the fourth test.

4.4 A principle is evidenced to be reasonable to the extent that it satisfies jointly all of the foregoing tests. In practice, however, we are wise if we expect less than this. We are not likely to find easily a comprehensive explication which convinces all competent judges, which resolves all existing difficulties, and which, should there be anomalies in the considered judgments themselves, always tends to overcome them. We should expect satisfactory explications of but delimited areas of the considered judgments. Ethics must, like any other discipline, work its way piece by piece.

4.5 It is worthwhile to note that the present method of evidencing the reasonableness of ethical principles is analogous to the method used to establish the reasonableness of the criteria of inductive logic. In the latter study what we attempt to do is to explicate the full variety of our intuitive judgments of credibility which we make in daily life and in science in connection with a proposition, or theory, given the evidence for it. In this way we hope to discover the principles of weighing evidence which are actually used and which seem to be capable of winning the assent of competent investigators. The principles so gained can be tested by seeing how well they can resolve our perplexity about how we ought to evaluate evidence in particular cases, and by how well they can stand up against what appear to be anomalous, but nevertheless settled, ways of appraising evidence, provided these anomalies exist. Thus each test above (4.3) has its parallel, or analogy, in the tests which are applied to inductive criteria. If we make the assumption that men have a capacity for knowing right and wrong, as they have for knowing what is true and false, then the present method is a likely way of developing a procedure for determining when we posses that knowledge; and we should be able to evidence the reasonableness of ethical principles in the same manner that we evidence the reasonableness of inductive criteria. On the other hand, just as the development of science and the method of science evidences the capacity to know what is true and false, so the actual formulation of ethical principles and the method whereby they can be tested, as this formulation is shown in the existence of satisfactory and reasonable explications, will evidence the capacity to know what is right and wrong as well as the validity of the objective distinction between the two. In the next sections I shall state what is designed to be such an explication.

5.1 In daily life we make moral judgments about at least three types of things: the moral worth of persons, the justice of actions, and the value of certain objects and activities. The explication below is designed to explicate our judgments on actions only. It will be necessary to make some preliminary definitions about goods and interests which will not be further discussed.

5.2 The class of things which are termed "goods" is held to fall into three subclasses: (i) good things, which are defined as being any physical objects which have a discernible capacity to satisfy, under specifiable conditions, one or more determinable needs, wants, or likings, e.g., food, clothes, houses. (ii) Good activities, which are defined as any activity which has a discernible capacity to satisfy, under specifiable conditions, one or more determinable needs, wants, or likings, e.g., the pursuit of knowledge, the creating and the contemplating of works of art, social fellowship. (iii) Enabling goods, which are defined as any object, or class of objects, or any activity or set of activities, whose use or exercise under specifiable circumstances tends to foster conditions under which goods of types (i) and (ii) may be produced, appropriated, or exercised.

The term "interest" is understood as follows: an interest is thought to be any need, want, or liking for some good, of any type; and in what follows, we are to think of this need, want, or liking as having been made articulate by means of an express claim before a body of competent judges (not of a legal, but of an ethical, court), and the claim is conceived of as asking for the possession of a good (if a thing), or as seeking the permission to exercise it (if an activity). Thus we may think of a claim as articulating an interest before a forum wherein its merits are to be weighed.

5.3 Next it is necessary to specify the kind of situation in which the problem of the justice of a decision and the action consequent thereto arises. This is done as follows: the problem of justice arises whenever it is the reasonably foreseeable consequence of the satisfaction of two or more claims of two or more persons that those claims, if given title, will interfere and conflict with one another. Hence the problem of the justice of actions, as a theoretical question, is essentially the problem of formulating reasonable principles for determining to which interests of a set of competing interests of two or more persons it is right to give preference.

5.4 It is required, further, to define a just state of affairs as follows: assuming that the principles just mentioned exist, then a state of affairs is just, if and only if, given the relevant interests in conflict prior to its establishment, those interests which are secured and satisfied within it are those which would be secured and satisfied within it if all those agents, who were instrumental in bringing it about, had intelligently applied those principles in order to determine their decisions and conduct. Otherwise a state of affairs is unjust. It can be seen from this definition that we cannot determine the justness of a situation by examining it at a single moment. We must know what interests were in existence prior to its establishment and in what manner its present characteristics have been determined by human action.

5.5 I shall now give a statement of what are hoped to be satisfactory principles of justice. The reasonableness of these principles is to be tested by the criteria discussed in 4.3. It should be said that the statement below is not intended to be more than provisionary. Little attention has been given to independence, simplicity, or elegance. These are luxuries which can only be had after a fruitful statement of the necessary principles has already been given.

(i) Each claim in a set of conflicting claims shall be evaluated by the same principles. Comment: This principle expresses one aspect of what is customarily meant in the parallel case at law wherein it is said that all men shall be equal before the law. It asserts nothing about the content of the principles, but only that, whatever the principles employed may be, the same ones shall be used for all the interests in conflict, and not one set for one interest, another set for another interest.

(ii) (a) Every claim shall be considered, on first sight, as meriting satisfaction. (b) No claim shall be denied possible satisfaction without a reason. (c) The only acceptable reason for denying a possible satisfaction to a claim, or for modifying it, shall be that its satisfaction has reasonably foreseeable consequences which interfere with the satisfaction of another claim, and the formulation of this rejection or modification is reasonable provided that it can be explicated by this, together with other, principles. Comment: This principle declares that the presumption is always in favor of a claim, and it specifies what kind of reasons are required to rebut this presumption.

(iii) (a) One claim shall not be denied, or modified, for the sake of another unless there is a reasonable expectation that the satisfaction of the one will directly and substantially interfere with the satisfaction of the other. (b) The phrase "reasonable expectation" shall be construed as referring to an expectation based upon beliefs which can be validated by evidence in view of the canons of inductive procedure. (c) The more worthy the claim the greater the tolerance which shall be allowed to its interference, or presumption of interference, with other interests, and vice versa. Comment: This principle may be thought of as a generalization of the so-called "clear and present danger" rule formulated to cover decisions regarding freedom of speech, etc.

(iv) (a) Given a group of competing claims, as many as possible shall be satisfied, so far as the satisfaction of them is consistent with other principles. (b) Before modifying one interest or sacrificing one interest to another, an attempt shall be made to find a way of securing the benefits of both, which, if successful, shall be followed.

(v) (a) If means of any kind are used for the purpose of securing an interest, it shall be reasonably demonstrable that they are designed to secure it. (b) If nonneutral means, that is, means whose employment effect some other interest or interests, are used for the purpose of securing an interest, then the appropriateness of using those means shall be determined by weighing the merits of all the interests effected in accordance with other principles. Comment: The phrase "reasonably demonstrable" is to be construed like the phrase "reasonable expectation" in (iii) (b).

(vi) (a) Claims shall be ordered according to their strength. (b) The strength of a claim depends directly and proportionately on the presence in the bearer of the claim of that characteristic which is relevant for the distribution, or the exercise, of the good. (c) Relevant characteristics are those specifiable needs, wants, and likings which the good thing or activity has a discernible capacity to satisfy under ascertainable conditions. Comment: This principle is designed to order a set of claims for a share in a particular good; and it asserts that relevant characteristics are those needs, wants, or likings whose satisfaction is ordinarily understood to be the purpose of appropriating or exercising a good. Thus, if the competing claims are for a share in a certain amount of food, then the relevant characteristic is the need for food. A test thereof should be devised, and the claims ordered accordingly. A nonrelevant characteristic for claims of this type would be the number of letters in the bearer's last name.

(vii) (a) Given a set of equal claims, as determined by their strength, all shall be satisfied equally, if that is possible. (b) Given a set of equal claims, if it is not possible to satisfy all of them, at least to some extent, then an impartially arbitrary method of choosing those to be satisfied shall be adopted. (c) Given a set of unequal claims, with subsets of equal claims which have been ordered according to (vi), then the claims shall be satisfied in that order; and, within subsets, (vii) (a) shall apply, if that is possible, otherwise (vii) (b). Comment: The term "impartially arbitrary" may be clarified as follows: Imagine a good of such a nature that it is impractical or impossible to divide it, and yet each of a number of persons has an equally strong claim on its possession or exercise. In such a case we would be directed to select one claim as meriting satisfaction by an impartially arbitrary method, e.g., by seeing who draws the highest card. This method is arbitrary because the characteristic of having drawn the highest card is not a relevant characteristic by (vi) (c). Yet the method is impartial because prior to the drawing of the cards each person has an equal chance to acquire in his person the characteristic arbitrarily taken to be relevant.

6.1 The above principles are offered as an explication of the considered judgments of competent judges made in situations involving the problem of the justice of actions. In addition, it is hoped that they will satisfy the tests of reasonableness stated in 4.3. Now it is obviously desirable to give an illustration of at least some of these principles, although space forbids any detailed discussion. The question is, how shall we illustrate them? Shall we use an imaginary example? The following considerations answer this question: just as epistemology is best studied by considering specific instances of intuitively acceptable knowledge, ethics is most profitably pursued by examining carefully instances of what seem to be intuitively acceptable and reasonable moral decisions; and just as the instances suitable for epistemology may often be found in the theories of the well-developed sciences, so instances suitable for ethics can be found in those decisions which seem to represent a well-established result of discussion on the part of moralists, jurists, and other persons who have given thought to the question at issue. Following this suggestion, I shall illustrate several principles by attempting to show that they yield an established result regarding freedom of speech and thought.

6.2 Consider the Inquisition, and recall that this institution justified its activity on the grounds that the teaching of heretics had the consequence of increasing the number of the damned and therefore of substantially interfering with the pre-eminent interests of other men in salvation. The difficulty is that there is no evidence, acceptable to the canons of inductive procedure, to support this belief, and therefore, by (iii), the proceedings of the Inquisition were unjust.

On the other hand, consider a person, or institution, adopting the rule that no one shall believe a proposition unless evidence, acceptable by the canons of inductive procedure, is known to exist as a ground for believing it, and suppose this person, or institution, takes repressive action accordingly. What are we to say of actions consequent to the adoption of this principle? We must hold that they are unjust on the grounds that (ii) is violated, since it is clear that believing propositions for which no evidence yet exists does not necessarily affect the interests of other persons. Consider the following two kinds of cases: First, it is generally recognized that hypotheses, presumed by the investigator to be true, but not known by evidence to be true, play an important part in scientific inquiry, yet no one believes that a scientist who believes such a hypothesis, and who labors to evidence it, is, at the early stage of inquiry, acting unjustly. Second, it is generally recognized that the articles of religious faiths are not usually establishable by evidence acceptable to inductive criteria. Believers themselves are often anxious to grant this point frequently on the grounds that otherwise faith would not be faith. Yet no one, believer or nonbeliever, is prepared to maintain that having religious beliefs is unjust, although some may think it mistaken. The having of such beliefs is an interest we respect, and a person is required to evidence his belief only when he proposes to take action on the basis of it which substantially interferes with the interests of other persons.

Thus, applied to the question of freedom of speech, thought, etc., principles (ii) and (iii) seem to yield what is an acceptable, and accepted, rule of justice: namely, each man may believe what he sees fit to believe, but not at the peril of another; and in an action wherein the interests of others are effected, a necessary condition for its being just is that the beliefs on which it is based are evidenced beyond any reasonable doubt.

It should be noted, in the light of this example, that we may think of rules, as opposed to principles, as maxims expressing the results of applying the principles of justice to recognized and frequently occurring types of cases. The justification for following a rule, or appealing to it in ordinary life, consists in showing that it is such a maxim. For brevity, however, we have omitted this intermediate step in discussing justification.

6.3 It is worthwhile to note how a decision with respect to a given set of conflicting interests, under given conditions, can be shown to be unjust. This is done by showing that the decision is not that decision which a competent and intelligent man would make if he used the stated principles of justice to determine his decision on the case, assuming here, for the sake of exposition, that these principles satisfy the tests in 4.3. To show that a given decision conflicts with what a principle would dictate is to give a reason for thinking it is unjust. To show this principle by principle and point by point, is to accumulate reasons against the decision and the conduct consequent thereto, so that, during the course of discussion, a decisive case may be made against it. The procedure is somewhat analogous to evidencing a proposition or theory in the real sciences, except that in moral discussions we try to validate or invalidate decisions and the action consequent thereto, given the circumstances and the interests in conflict (not acts of believing given a proposition or theory and its evidence), and the criteria we use are the principles of justice (and not the rules of inductive logic).

6.4 The manner of describing the decision procedure here advocated may have led the reader to believe that it claims to be a way of discovering justifiable ethical principles. There are, however, no precisely describable methods of discovery, and certainly the finding of a successful explication satisfying the tests of 4.3 will require at least some ingenuity. Therefore it is best to view the exposition as a description of the procedure of justification stated in reverse. Thus if a man were asked to justify his decision on a case, he should proceed as follows: first, he should show that, given the circumstances and the interests in conflict, his decision is capable of being explicated by the principles of justice. Second, he should evidence that these principles satisfy the tests in 4.3. If asked to proceed further, he should remark on the nature of considered judgments and competent judges and urge that one could hardly be expected to prefer judgments made under emotional duress, or in ignorance of the facts by unintelligent or mentally sick persons, and so on. Finally, he should stress that such considerations arise, if the demands for justification are pushed far enough, in validating inductive criteria as well as in justifying ethical principles. Provided an explication exists satisfying the tests in 4.3, moral actions can be justified in a manner analogous to the way in which decisions to believe a proposition, or theory, are justified.

6.5 Two possible objections remain to be considered. First, it may be said that, even if the foregoing decision procedure could be carried out in a particular case, the decision in question still would not be justified. To this I should say that we ought to inquire whether the person making the objection is not expecting too much. Perhaps he expects a justification procedure to show him how the decision is deducible from a synthetic a priori proposition. The answer to a person with such hopes is that they are logically impossible to satisfy and that all we should expect is that moral decisions and ethical principles are capable of the same sort of justification as decisions to believe and inductive criteria. Secondly, it may be said that a set of principles satisfying the tests of 4.3 does not exist. To this I should say that while it is obvious that moral codes and customs have varied in time, and change from place to place, yet when we think of a successful explication as representing the invariant in the considered judgments of competent judges, then the variation of codes and customs is not decisive against the existence of such an explication. Such a question cannot be decided by analysis or by talking about possibilities, but only by exhibiting explications which are capable of satisfying the tests which are properly applied to them. At some future time I hope to be able to offer something more constructive in this direction than the brief remarks in 5.5 and 6.2.

1952

Ethical Absolutism and the Ideal Observer

Roderick Firth

The moral philosophy of the first half of the twentieth century, at least in the English-speaking part of the world, has been largely devoted to problems concerning the analysis of ethical statements, and to correlative problems of an ontological or epistemological nature. This concentration of effort by many acute analytical minds has not produced any general agreement with respect to the solution of these problems; it seems likely, on the contrary, that the wealth of proposed solutions, each making some claim to plausibility, has resulted in greater disagreement than ever before, and in some cases disagreement about issues so fundamental that certain schools of thought now find it unrewarding, if not impossible, to communicate with one another. Moral philosophers of almost all schools seem to agree, however, that no major possibility has been neglected during this period, and that every proposed solution which can be adjudged at all plausible has been examined with considerable thoroughness. It is now common practice, for example, for the authors of books on moral philosophy to introduce their own theories by what purports to be a classification and review of all *possible* solutions to the basic problems of analysis; and in many cases, indeed, the primary defense of the author's own position seems to consist in the negative argument that his own position cannot fail to be correct because none of the others which he has mentioned is satisfactory.

Roderick Firth, "Ethical Absolutism and the Ideal Observer," *Philosophy and Phenomenological Research* 12, No. 3 (March 1952). Reprinted with the permission of the publishers.

There is one kind of analysis of ethical statements, however, which has certainly not been examined with the thoroughness that it deserves—the kind of analysis, namely, which construes ethical statements to be both absolutist and dispositional. In a paper entitled "Some Reflections on Moral-Sense Theories of Ethics,"[1] Broad has discussed a number of the most important features of this kind of analysis, and has even said that most competent persons would now agree that there are only two other theories about the meaning of ethical terms which are worth as much serious consideration. Yet there are many moral philosophers who leave no place for this kind of analysis in their classification of ethical theories, and many others who treat it unfairly by classifying it with less plausible proposals which are superficially similar. And what makes such carelessness especially unfortunate, is the fact that this kind of analysis seems to be capable of satisfying the major demands of certain schools of ethical thought which are ordinarily supposed to be diametrically opposed to one another. It is a kind of analysis, moreover, which may have been proposed and defended by several classical moralists;[2] and this is perhaps one good reason for giving it at least a small share of the attention which is now lavished on positions which are no more plausible.

The following discussion of absolutist dispositional analyses of ethical statements, is divided into two parts. In the first part I have discussed some of the important characteristics which are common to all analyses of this general form. In the second part I have discussed some of the problems which would have to be solved in working out a concrete analysis of this kind, and I have made certain proposals about the manner in which such an analysis can best be formulated.[3]

PART ONE: CHARACTERISTICS OF THE ANALYSIS

1. It Is Absolutist.

To explain the precise sense in which a dispositional analysis of ethical statements may be absolutist rather than relativist, it is helpful to begin by defining the two terms "relative statement" and "relativist analysis."

Speaking first about statements, we may say that any statement is relative if its meaning cannot be expressed without using a word or other expression which is egocentric. And egocentric expressions may be described as expressions of which the meaning varies systematically with the speaker. They are expressions which are ambiguous in abstraction from their relation to a speaker, but their ambiguity is conventional and systematic. They include the personal pronouns ("I," "you," etc.), the corresponding possessive adjectives ("my," "your," etc.), words which refer directly but relatively to spatial and temporal location ("this," "that," "here," "there," "now," "then," "past," "present," "future"), reflexive expressions such as "the person who is

[1]C.D. Broad, *Proceedings of the Aristotelian Society,* N.S. Vol. XLV, pp. 131–166.

[2]Adam Smith comes immediately to mind, but Hume can likewise be interpreted as accepting an absolutist dispositional analysis of "right." (*Vide,* e.g., F. C. Sharp, "Hume's Ethical Theory," *Mind,* N.S. Vol. XXX, pp. 53–56. But for a different interpretation of Hume, *vide* Broad, *Five Types of Ethical Theory,* pp. 84–93). It is even possible to make out a case for including Kant in this list. (*Vide* Part II of this paper on the subject of ethical impartiality.) Sidgwick, although he denied that "right" is analyzable, seems not unwilling to accept an absolutist dispositional analysis of "good." (*Methods of Ethics,* 4th ed., p. 112, last sentence.)

[3]In this connection I am much indebted to Professor R. B. Brandt, with whom I have discussed the problems of moral philosophy at great length. He is not, of course, responsible for my errors.

speaking," and the various linguistic devices which are used to indicate the tense of verbs. All of these egocentric expressions can apparently be defined in terms of the word "this."[4]

A moral philosopher is commonly called a relativist, and his analysis of ethical statements is said to be a relativist analysis, if he construes ethical statements to be relative. We may thus say, derivatively, that an analysis of ethical statements is relativist if it includes an egocentric expression, and if it is incompatible with any alternative analysis which does not include an egocentric expression.

It follows, therefore, that relativist analyses, no matter how much they may differ from one another, can always be conveniently and positively identified by direct inspection of their constituent expressions. Thus, to give a few examples, a philosopher is an ethical relativist if he believes that the meaning of ethical statements of the form "Such and such a particular act (x) is right" can be expressed by other statements which have any of the following forms: "*I* like x as much as any alternative to it," "*I* should (in fact) feel ashamed of myself if *I* did not feel approval towards x, and *I* wish that *other people* would too," "Most people *now* living would feel approval towards x if they knew what they really wanted," "If *I* should perceive or think about x and its alternatives, x would seem to *me* to be demanding to be performed," "x is compatible with the mores of the social group to which *the speaker* gives his primary allegiance," and "x will satisfy a maximum of the interests of people *now* living or who *will* live *in the future*." Each one of these possible analyses contains an egocentric expression (which I have italicized). And it is evident that if any of these analyses were correct, it would be possible for one person to say that a certain act is right, and for another person (provided, in some cases, that he is not a member of the same social group, nor living at the same time) to say that that very same act is not right, without logically contradicting each other. This familiar characteristic of all relativist analyses is not *definitive* of relativism; it is, however, a necessary *consequence* of the fact that relativist analyses contain egocentric expressions.

We may now define an absolutist analysis of ethical statements as one which is not relativist.[5] The kind of analysis which I propose to discuss in this paper, therefore, is one which does not include an egocentric expression. It is a kind of analysis, I suspect, which is closely associated with relativism in the minds of many philosophers, but it is unquestionably absolutist and implies that ethical statements are true or false, and consistent or inconsistent with one another, without special reference to the people who happen to be asserting them.

2. It Is Dispositional.

I shall say that a proposed analysis of ethical statements is dispositional if it construes ethical statements to assert that a certain being (or beings), either actual or hypothetical, is (or are) disposed to react to something in a certain way. To say that a certain being is disposed to react in a certain way is to say that the being in question would react in that way under certain specifiable conditions. Thus a dispositional analysis of an ethical

[4]*Vide* Bertrand Russell, *An Enquiry Into Meaning and Truth*, p. 134, and *Human Knowledge, Its Scope and Its Limits*, p. 92.

[5]It will be observed that according to these definitions a pure emotive theory of ethics is neither absolutist nor relativist. For absolutism and relativism are theories about the meaning of ethical *statements*, whereas a pure emotive theory denies, in effect, that there *are* any ethical statements (as contrasted with ethical exclamations, exhortations, etc.).

statement may always be formulated as a hypothetical statement of the kind which is commonly called a "contrary-to-fact conditional." A dispositional analysis of statements of the form "x is right," for example, might have the form: "Such and such a being, if it existed, would react to x in such and such a way if such and such conditions were realized."

During the past fifty years moral philosophers have given a good deal of attention to the evaluation of dispositional analyses which are *relativist,* and a comprehensive defense of one such relativist analysis can be found in the writings of Westermarck.[6] Westermarck believes, if I understand him, that the meaning of statements of the form "x is wrong," can be expressed by other statements of the form "The speaker tends to feel towards x (i.e., *would* feel in the absence of specifiable inhibiting factors), an emotion of disinterested moral disapproval which would be experienced by him as a quality or dynamic tendency in x." Although this analysis is considerably more sophisticated than many of the analyses which relativists have proposed, it is typical of a position to which absolutists have raised a number of closely-related, and by now very familiar, objections.

A dispositional analysis of ethical statements which was *absolutist* would not, of course, be open to the same objections. It would construe ethical statements in one of the following three ways: (1) as assertions about the dispositions of all *actual* (past, present, and future) beings of a certain kind; (2) as assertions about the dispositions of all *possible* beings of a certain kind (of which there might in fact exist only one or none at all), or (3) as assertions about the dispositions of a majority (or other fraction) of a number of beings (actual or possible) of a certain kind. It is evident that an analysis of any of these three types would include no egocentric expression, and would therefore construe ethical statements in such a way that they would be true or false, and consistent or inconsistent with one another, without special reference to the people who happen to be asserting them.

It is only the second of these three kinds of analysis which I propose to examine in this paper, for analyses of the other two types, it seems to me, are open to obvious and yet insuperable objections. An analysis of the first type would construe ethical statements to entail that there actually exists a being (perhaps God) whose dispositions are definitive of certain ethical terms. But this would mean that all ethical statements containing these ethical terms are necessarily false if such a being does *not* exist—a consequence which seems to be incompatible with what we intend to assert when we use ethical terms. And in my opinion an analysis of the third type would be even less plausible, because it would imply that ethical statements express judgments which can only be verified or refuted, at least theoretically, by statistical procedures. I shall not amplify these familiar arguments, however, since much of what I shall say about ethical analyses of the second type can be equally well applied to analyses of the other two types, and anyone who so wishes may easily make the necessary translations in reading the second part of this paper.

It will be convenient, throughout the following pages, to use the term "ideal observer" in speaking about a possible being of the kind referred to in an absolutist dispositional analysis. The adjective "ideal" is used here in approximately the same sense in which we speak of a perfect vacuum or a frictionless machine as ideal things; it is not intended to suggest that an ideal observer is necessarily *virtuous,* but merely that he is conceivable and that he has certain characteristics to an extreme degree. Perhaps it

[6] *Vide* especially *Ethical Relativity,* Ch. V. An equally interesting relativist dispositional analysis has been proposed by F. C. Sharp, *Ethics,* Appleton-Century, N.Y., 1928, Ch. VII.

would seem more natural to call such a being an ideal *judge*, but this term could be quite misleading if it suggested that the function of an ideal observer is to pass judgment on ethical issues. As an ideal observer, of course, it is sufficient that he be capable of reacting in a manner which will determine by definition whether an ethical judgment is true or false. And it is even conceivable, indeed, that an ideal observer, according to some analyses, should lack some of the characteristics which would make it *possible* for him to pass judgment on ethical issues—which would mean, of course, simply that he would not be able to judge the nature of his own dispositions.

Using the term "ideal observer," then, the kind of analysis which I shall examine in this paper is the kind which would construe statements of the form "x is P," in which P is some particular ethical predicate, to be identical in meaning with statements of the form: "Any ideal observer would react to x in such and such a way under such and such conditions."[7]

This formulation may draw attention to the fact that a dispositional analysis which is absolutist may nevertheless be extensionally equivalent to one that is relativist. For the egocentric expression in a relativist analysis is often qualified by reference to ideal conditions (described in if-clauses), and it is evident that each of these qualifications limits the respects in which one speaker could differ from another if the reactions of each were relevant to the truth of his own ethical statement. Westermarck, for example, analyzes ethical statements not by reference simply to the feeling which the speaker would actually have if confronted with a particular act or situation, but by reference to the feelings which he would have *if* he were impartial and *if* certain inhibiting factors (e.g., fatigue) were absent. And if a relativist were to continue to add such qualifications to his analysis, he might eventually reach a point at which *any* speaker who met all these qualifications would have all the characteristics which an absolutist might wish to attribute to an ideal observer. In that case ethical statements, when analyzed, would be contrary-to-fact conditionals of the form: "If I were an ideal observer I would react to x in such and such a way under such and such conditions." And if the specified characteristics of an ideal observer were sufficient to insure, in virtue of the laws of nature, that all ideal observers would react in the same way, it is evident that the truth value of ethical statements, so interpreted, would not differ from their truth value if interpreted absolutistically as statements about *any* ideal observer. Intentionally, however, the two analyses would still differ: the relativist, unlike the absolutist, would still maintain that the egocentric reference is essential, and by this he would imply, as we have seen, that two different speakers cannot make ethical assertions which are logically incompatible.

Let us now consider briefly some of the derivative characteristics of an analysis which is both absolutist and dispositional.

3. It Is Objectivist.

The adjectives "subjectivist" and "objectivist" are often used in a *logical* sense, and as synonyms, respectively, of the terms "relativist" and "absolutist"; in this sense, as we have seen, an analysis of the kind that we are discussing is objectivist. To avoid

[7]Lewis has proposed that dispositional analyses of "objectives statements" be formulated with a "probability qualification." (*Vide An Analysis of Knowledge and Valuation*, pp. 235–243.) If such a qualification were introduced into the analysis of ethical statements, an absolutist dispositional analysis would have the form: "Under such and such conditions an ideal observer would *in all probability* react in such and such a way." For simplicity I shall not consider this alternative, but none of the conclusions reached in this paper will be incompatible with the introduction of such a probability qualification.

duplication of meaning, however, I shall use the terms "subjectivist" and "objectivist" in a traditional *ontological* sense—in the sense in which Berkeley's analysis of all physical statements is subjectivist, and Descartes's analysis of some physical statements is objectivist. We may say, in this sense, that a proposed analysis of ethical statements is subjectivist if it construes ethical statements in such a way that they would all be false by definition if there existed no experiencing subjects (past, present, or future). An analysis may be called "objectivist," on the other hand, if it is not subjectivist. Thus it is evident that in this ontological sense, as well as in the logical sense, an analysis of the kind which we are discussing is objectivist: it construes ethical statements to be assertions about the reactions of an *ideal* observer—an observer who is conceivable but whose existence or non-existence is logically irrelevant to the truth or falsity of ethical statements.

This fact that a dispositional analysis is objectivist, is obviously a reflection of the fact that ethical statements, according to such an analysis, may always be formulated as conditional statements in the subjunctive mood; they may always be construed, in other words, as asserting that if such and such *were* the case, such and such *would* be the case. Hypothetical statements of this kind are commonly called "contrary-to-fact conditionals," but since they are sometimes used in such a way that they may be true even though they are not contrary to fact, they are perhaps more aptly referred to as "independent-of-fact conditionals." As used in an absolutist dispositional analysis, for example, such statements are not intended to imply *either* that there exists, *nor* that there does not exist, a being who satisfies the description of an ideal observer; they are intended to imply, on the contrary, that the existence or non-existence of such a being is *irrelevant* to the truth of the statement. Since the subjunctive conditional has exactly the same function whether the analysis is absolutist or relativist, it is evident that objectivism and absolutism are logically independent characteristics of an analysis of ethical statements; thus Westermarck's analysis is objectivist and relativist, whereas the one which we shall be examining is objectivist and absolutist.

The fact that an analysis of ethical statements is objectivist, moreover, is independent of all questions concerning the kinds of things to which ethical terms can be correctly applied. Thus it might in fact be true that the term "good" can be correctly applied only to conscious states, and hence that all ethical statements of the form "x is good" would in fact be false if there existed no experiencing subjects. And similarly, it might in fact always be false to say that a given act is wrong if neither that act, nor any of its alternatives, has any effect on the experience of conscious beings. But such facts would be entirely compatible with an objectivist *analysis* of ethical statements, for to say that an analysis is objectivist is to say merely that the existence of experiencing subjects is not essential *by definition* to the truth of ethical statements. This distinction is important because the term "subjectivist" is sometimes applied to hedonism and to certain forms of pluralistic utilitarianism, on the ground that these theories attribute value only to states of consciousness, or that they regard actual productivity of these valuable states as the sole determinant of the rightness or wrongness of an act. It is evident, however, that philosophers who support these theories should not be said to accept a subjectivist analysis of ethical statements unless they believe—as some of them, of course, do not—that ethical terms must be *defined* by reference to the experience of actual beings.

4. It Is Relational.

An analysis of ethical statements is *relational* if it construes ethical terms in such a way that to apply an ethical term to a particular thing (e.g., an act), is to assert that that thing is related in a certain way to some other thing, either actual or hypothetical. There is no doubt that an absolutist dispositional analysis is relational, since it construes ethical statements as asserting that a lawful relationship exists between certain reactions of an ideal observer and the acts or other things to which an ethical term may correctly be applied. But to avoid misunderstanding, this fact must be interpreted in the light of certain qualifying observations.

It should not be overlooked, in the first place, that if an absolutist dispositional analysis were correct, ethical statements would have the same form that statements about secondary qualities are often supposed to have. Not only phenomenalists and subjectivists, but many epistemological dualists, would agree that to say that a daffodil is yellow is to say something about the way the daffodil would appear to a certain kind of observer under certain conditions; and the analysis of ethical statements which we are considering is exactly analogous to this. Thus the sense in which an absolutist dispositional analysis is relational, is the very sense in which a great many philosophers believe that yellow is a relational property of physical objects; and to say that a statement of the form "x is right" is relational, therefore, is not necessarily to deny that the terms "right" and "yellow" designate equally simple properties.

But the analogy can be carried still further if a distinction is drawn between a relational and a non-relational sense of "yellow." Many philosophers believe that the adjective "yellow" has two meanings; they believe that it designates both a relational property of physical objects and a non-relational property of sense-data—a distinction corresponding roughly to the popular use of the terms "really yellow" and "apparently yellow." And it is quite possible not only that the term "right" is similarly ambiguous, but also that in one of its senses it designates a characteristic of human experience (apparent rightness) which in some important respect is just as simple and unanalyzable as the property of apparent yellowness. And thus we might even decide by analogy with the case of "yellow," that "really right" must be defined in terms of "apparently right"—i.e., that the experiencing of apparent rightness is an essential part of any ethically-significant reaction of an ideal observer.

And finally, it must be remembered that to call an absolutist analysis "relational," is not to imply that it construes the ethical properties of one thing to be dependent by definition on the *existence* of any other thing, either natural or supernatural. Since an ideal observer is a *hypothetical* being, no changes in the relationships of existent things would require us, for logical reasons alone, to attribute new ethical properties to any object, nor to revise any ethical judgment which we have previously made. For this reason an absolutist dispositional analysis is not open to one of the most familiar objections to relational analyses, namely, that such analyses construe the ethical properties of an object to be dependent on facts which seem quite clearly to be *accidental*—on the fact, for example, that certain actual people happen to have a certain attitude toward the object.[8]

5. It Is Empirical.

If we define the term "empirical" liberally enough so that the dispositional concepts of the natural sciences may properly be called empirical, there is no doubt that an absolutist dispositional analysis of ethical statements *might* be empirical. Such an analysis would be empirical, for example, if the defining characteristics of an ideal observer

[8]Since, according to an absolutist dispositional analysis, the truth or falsity of ethical statements is dependent on the laws of nature, ethical statements are not intuitively or logically necessary; they are necessary, however, in whatever sense of the laws of nature are necessary.

were psychological traits, and if the ethically-significant reactions of an ideal observer were feelings of desire, or emotions of approval and disapproval, or some other experiences accessible to psychological observation.

It might be somewhat less evident, however, that an absolutist dispositional analysis *must* be empirical. For most of the philosophers who maintain the ethical properties are non-natural, and that ethical truths are known by rational intuition, have admitted that ethical intuitions may be erroneous under certain unfavorable conditions, or else, if this is regarded as self-contradictory, that under certain conditions we may appear to be intuiting an ethical truth although in fact we are not.[9] And it might seem that to recognize the possibility of error in either of these two ways is to recognize a distinction between the property of apparent rightness and the property of real rightness—a distinction, as we have seen, which is sufficient to permit the formulation of an absolutist dispositional analysis.

On this issue, however, I think we must take the word of the rational intuitionists themselves, and if there is any one fact about which intuitionists agree, it is the fact that some ethical properties are neither introspectable nor analyzable. And from this fact it follows, necessarily, that their ethical theory is epistemologically dualist—i.e., that there is no formula, however complex, by which ethical statements can be translated into statements about experiences which confirm them. Intuitionists must admit, I believe, that they are able to assess the cognitive value of their ostensible intuitions by reference to the conditions under which these intuitions occur, and they must admit that they would not be able to do this unless they had some conception of an ideal observer. Thus Ewing lists[10] four factors which are responsible for false intuitions: (1) lack of experience, (2) intellectual confusions, (3) failure to attend adequately to certain aspects of the situation, (4) psychological causes "such as those with which the psychoanalyst deals." And the very fact that Ewing can compile such a list is proof that he has some conception of an ideal observer whose definition excludes these four factors. But this fact does not make intuitionism any less dualist, of course, for Ewing and other intuitionists will maintain that in formulating these ideal conditions they are merely formulating a *test* for the validity of an ethical statement, and not an analysis of the statement.[11]

Even though we conclude that an absolutist dispositional analysis must be empirical, however, there is still considerable room for disagreement about the precise nature of the ethically-significant reactions of an ideal observer. It seems clear that these reactions, if the analysis is to be at all plausible, must be defined in terms of the kind of moral experience which we take to be evidence, under ideal conditions, for the truth of our ethical judgments. It is important to observe that experiences of this kind—which we may properly call "moral data"—cannot be states of moral *belief*. An absolutist dispositional analysis, like any other analysis which grants cognitive meaning to ethical

[9]A. C. Ewing, for example, is willing to say that intuitions are sometimes false. (*Vide The Definition of Good,* pp. 27–9.) But Hastings Rashdall, for example, preferred to say that it is difficult to distinguish intuitions from "mere feelings or aversions which may be only prejudices due to inheritance or environment or superstition." (*Vide The Theory of Good and Evil,* Vol. I, pp. 211–213.)

[10]*Op. cit.,* p. 26.

[11]An empiricist could be expected to ask how the intuitionist can *know* that one particular set of conditions is preferable to another; for, if the intuitionist's position is correct, it is surely not inconceivable that any given pathological condition (e.g., any of "those with which the psychoanalyst deals") is especially conducive to, or even absolutely necessary for, correct intuiting. (Cf. Brandt, "The Significance of Differences of Ethical Opinion for Ethical Rationalism," *Philosophy and Phenomenological Research,* Vol. IV, No. 4, pp. 488–490.) If this creates a problem for the intuitionist, however, it is a kind of problem which he shares with epistemological dualists in general.

sentences, would permit us to say that we *do* have moral beliefs, and even that moral consciousness is *ordinarily* a state of belief. But if the ethically-significant reaction of an ideal observer were the belief (or judgment) that a certain act is right or wrong, it is evident that an absolutist dispositional analysis would be circular: it would contain the very ethical terms which it is intended to define.

In order to define an absolutist dispositional analysis, therefore, it is necessary to maintain that moral data are the moral experiences to which we appeal when *in doubt* about the correct solution of a moral problem, or when attempting to *justify* a moral belief. For the epistemic function of moral data, when defined in this way, will correspond to the function of color sensations in determining or justifying the belief that a certain material object is "really yellow." And in that case moral data could play the same role in the analysis of "right" that color sensations play in the analysis of "really yellow."

Now there are many debatable questions concerning the nature of moral data, and until these questions are answered it will not be possible to explain precisely what is meant by the "ethically-significant reactions" of an ideal observer. These questions are primarily psychological, however, and can easily be separated from other questions concerning the content of an absolutist dispositional analysis. And if it is possible to provide a satisfactory formulation of the other components of an absolutist dispositional analysis (especially the definition of "ideal observer") this formulation will be compatible with *any* phenomenological description of moral data.

One of the most salient differences of opinion, for example, concerning the nature of moral data, is the difference of opinion concerning what we may call their "phenomenal location." There are many philosophers, on the one hand, who maintain that moral data are primarily feelings, or emotions, or other elements of experience which appear in the deliberative consciousness of the moral judge as ostensible states of the judge himself. There seems to be a growing number of philosophers, on the other hand, who are equally empirical in their epistemology, but who maintain that the typical moral datum is an obligatoriness or "demand quality" which appears in the deliberative consciousness of the moral judge as an ostensible property of an envisaged act or goal.[12] But however important this difference of opinion may be, it is a difference of opinion about the nature of moral data and not about the logical or epistemological relationships between moral data and ethical statements; both of these positions are compatible, therefore, with the theory that ethical statements are statements about the dispositions of an ideal observer to experience moral data (whatever they may be) under certain specifiable conditions.

Whatever conclusion we might reach concerning the phenomenal location of moral data, it will still be necessary to distinguish very carefully between moral data themselves, which, under ideal conditions, are the *evidence* for moral beliefs, and the very similar experiences which may be the *consequences* of moral beliefs. This distinction would not be difficult to make if we were content to say that moral data are simply feelings of desire (or, correlatively, that moral data are "demand qualities" of *all* kinds). For there seems to be little reason to doubt that feelings of desire may occur in the absence of moral beliefs. But if we should wish to maintain, as many philosophers have done, that moral data are the emotions of moral approval and disapproval, it would be much harder to make the necessary distinction. As Broad has pointed out,

[12]*Vide, e.g.*, W. Köhler, *The Place of Value in a World of Facts*, Ch. III. Elsewhere ("Sense-data and the Percept Theory," *Mind*, Vol. LVIII, N. S., No. 232, and Vol. LIX, N.S., No. 233.) I have discussed in some detail the general philosophical significance of the view that such ostensible properties may be "objectively localized."

those emotions of approval and disapproval which we think of as specifically *moral* emotions, are the very ones "which appear *prima facie* to be felt towards persons or actions in respect of certain moral characteristics which they are believed to have."[13] So if these emotions are said to be the evidence for moral beliefs, there appears to be a vicious circle in the process by which moral beliefs are justified. And there appears to be a similar vicious circle in an absolutist dispositional analysis. For if moral emotions are experienced only as a consequence of moral beliefs or judgments, and if we refuse to attribute moral beliefs to an ideal observer in our analysis, then there is no reason to think that an ideal observer would experience any moral emotions at all. But if, on the other hand, we do attribute moral beliefs to an ideal observer, we should have to employ the very ethical terms (e.g., "right") which we are attempting to analyze. This fact, in one form or another, has provided the basis for many arguments in support of non-naturalist ethics.

But the difficulty, I believe, has been highly exaggerated. It cannot plausibly be denied that moral emotions are often (perhaps usually) felt as a consequence of moral beliefs—that we often feel approval, for example, toward those acts which we believe to be right. But this is merely to say, if an absolutist dispositional analysis is valid, that we often feel approval toward those acts which we think would produce approval in an ideal observer. The crucial question is whether it is possible to feel an emotion of moral approval toward an act when we are *in doubt* about whether it is right or wrong. And surely this *is* possible.[14] It is not uncommon, for example, to find ourselves feeling moral approval toward an act, and then to begin to wonder whether our reaction is *justified:* we might wonder, for example, whether we are sufficiently familiar with "the facts of the case" or whether our emotions are being unduly influenced by some selfish consideration. At such times we may continue to experience the emotion of moral approval although in doubt about the rightness of the act. We may even attempt to rationalize our emotion by persuading ourselves that the act is right. In rare cases, indeed, we may even continue to experience the emotion although convinced that our reaction is *not* justified. (This is sometimes the case, for example, when people feel approval toward an act of retribution.) Consequently, unless apparent facts of this kind can be discounted by subtle phenomenological analysis, there is no epistemological objection to defining the ethically significant reactions of an ideal observer in terms of moral emotions.

Whether or not this is the correct way to define these reactions, however, is a psychological question which I shall not consider in this paper. There are other, more fundamental, questions concerning the content of an absolutist dispositional analysis, and it is these to which the remaining part of this paper will be devoted.

PART TWO: THE CONTENT OF THE ANALYSIS

If it is possible to formulate a satisfactory absolutist and dispositional analysis of ethical statements, it must be possible, as we have seen, to express the meaning of statements of the form "x is right" in terms of other statements which have the form: "Any ideal observer would react to x in such and such a way under such and such conditions."

[13]"Some of the Main Problems of Ethics," *Philosophy,* Vol. XXI, No. 79, p. 115.

[14]I am assuming, of course, that an emotion of moral approval is not *defined* as an emotion of approval produced by a moral belief.

Thus even if we are not to discuss the nature of the ethically-significant reactions of an ideal observer in this paper, it might seem that we are nevertheless faced with two distinct questions: (1) What are the defining characteristics of an ideal observer? and (2) Under what conditions do the reactions of an ideal observer determine the truth or falsity of ethical statements? I believe, however, that the second of these questions can be treated as part of the first. For it is evident that the conditions under which the ethically-significant reactions of an ideal observer might occur, could be relevant to the meaning of ethical statements only if they could affect an ideal observer in such a way as to influence his ethically-significant reactions. And since the influence of any such relevant conditions must therefore be *indirect,* it would always be possible to insure precisely the same reactions by attributing suitable characteristics directly to the ideal observer. If, for example, the absence of certain emotional stimuli is thought to be a relevant and favorable condition, this fact could be taken into account simply by specifying that the ideal observer is by definition unresponsive to such emotional stimuli. I think it will soon become clear, moreover, that this procedure yields a type of analysis which comes closer to expressing what we actually intend to assert when we utter ethical statements. But even if I am mistaken about this, it will not be prejudicial to any basic problem if we assume, for simplicity, that the second question may be reduced to the first, namely, What are the defining characteristics of an ideal observer?

Before attempting to answer this question, however, there are a few remarks which I think should be made about the implications and methodology of any such attempt to define an ideal observer.

It is important, in the first place, to view any attempt of this kind in proper perspective. It would undoubtedly be difficult to arrive at a rational conclusion concerning the plausibility of absolutist dispositional analyses in general, without first experimenting with various concrete formulations. At the present stage in the history of moral philosophy, however, it would be especially unfortunate if the inadequacies of some particular formulation were to prejudice philosophers against absolutist dispositional analyses in general. Any plausible formulation is certain to be very complex, and there is no reason to suppose that philosophers could ever reach complete agreement concerning all the details of an adequate analysis. But this in itself should not prevent philosophers from agreeing that this general *form* of analysis is valid. Nor would it necessarily be irrational for a philosopher to decide that this general form is valid, although he is dissatisfied even with *his own* attempts to formulate a concrete analysis.[15]

Ethical words, moreover, like all other words, are probably used by different people, even in similar contexts, to express somewhat different meanings; and a correct analysis of one particular ethical statement, therefore, may not be a correct analysis of another statement which is symbolized in exactly the same way but asserted by a different person. This kind of ambiguity is a familiar obstacle to all philosophical analysis, but it causes unusual difficulties when we attempt to evaluate a proposed dispositional analysis of ethical statements. Any such analysis, if it is at all plausible, is certain to assign a number of complex characteristics to an ideal observer, and to refer to complex psychological phenomena in describing the nature of his ethically-significant reactions. And assuming that ethical statements *can* be analyzed in this manner, there is no good reason to believe that all human beings, no matter what the extent of their individual development, and no matter what their past social environment, could analyze their

[15]Cf. A. C. Ewing's statement (*The Definition of Good,* p. 43) that he can "see" in advance that nobody will ever be able to produce a satisfactory empirical analysis of ethical statements. Similarly a philosopher might "see" that *only* an empirical analysis which is absolutist and dispositional could be satisfactory.

ethical statements correctly by reference to precisely the same kind of ideal observer and precisely the same psychological phenomena. If there *are* any irreducible differences in the intended meaning of ethical statements, some of these differences might not be discoverable, and most of them might be so slight that they could not be held responsible for differences of opinion concerning the proper analysis of ethical statements. Some of these differences in meaning, on the other hand, might be sufficiently large to be reflected in the formulation of philosophical analyses of ethical statements. And there is consequently a clear sense in which philosophers may appear to disagree about the analysis of ethical statements, although in fact, because ethical words are somewhat ambiguous, they are analyzing different statements and hence not disagreeing at all.

It would be a serious mistake, however, to confuse the kind of ambiguity to which I have just referred with the kind of ambiguity which is definitive of a relativist analysis. The ambiguity which is definitive of relativism, as we have seen, is conventional, systematic, and characteristic only of statements which contain an egocentric expression. The kind of ambiguity which we have just been discussing, on the other hand, is accidental, unsystematic, and characteristic in some degree of all symbols. Thus it is not ordinarily the intention of an ethical absolutist to maintain that the words which we use to express ethical statements have a unique semiotical capacity—the capacity, namely, to express exactly the same meaning no matter who utters them; in fact even those absolutists who believe that ethical words express simple, unanalyzable, concepts, could scarcely maintain that there is any conclusive evidence to show that an ethical word, no matter who employs it, always expresses the *same* unanalyzable concept. The thesis maintained by the absolutist as such, is simply that ethical statements are not *conventionally* ambiguous in a manner which would require them to be analyzed by means of an egocentric expression; and this thesis is quite consistent, of course, with the proposition that ethical statements are *accidentally* ambiguous—perhaps even more ambiguous, indeed, than most other statements.

In the light of this distinction, then, it seems clear that if two philosophers believe that they are in perfect agreement concerning the meaning of ethical statements—i.e., if they believe that their ability to communicate is not limited by accidental ambiguity—they may still be either relativists or absolutists. If they are relativists, and related to one another spatially, temporally, and socially in certain ways, they will believe that neither of them could assert an ethical statement which is logically inconsistent with any ethical statement asserted by the other. If they are absolutists, however, they will believe that they *can* contradict each other in their ethical statements. Thus the absolutist, unlike the relativist, believes that nothing stands in the way of the expression of cognitive disagreement about ethical matters except the accidental ambiguity which is characteristic of all symbols. And since the absolutist can consistently admit that this accidental ambiguity may be sufficiently great to prevent philosophers from agreeing on a concrete analysis of ethical statements, the apparent inadequacy of any particular analysis, such as the one which I shall propose, should not be considered as proof that the general form of an absolutist dispositional analysis is unsatisfactory.

It should also be kept in mind that the kind of analysis which we are seeking is one which would be an analysis of ethical statements in the sense (and probably only in the sense) in which hypothetical statements about the way a daffodil would appear to a "normal" observer are said to constitute an analysis of the material object statement "This daffodil is yellow." To attempt an analysis of this sense of the word "analysis" would lead to difficult problems far beyond the scope of this paper. But two points may be mentioned. First, an analysis in this sense of the word is not required to be *prima facie* or "intuitively" equivalent to the analyzandum, and for this reason the surprising complexity of a proposed analysis is not a sufficient reason for rejecting it: thus the fact that a proposed analysis of "This daffodil is yellow" happens to refer to white light, a transparent medium, a neutral background, and a variety of physiological conditions of an observer, is not ordinarily thought to make the analysis unsatisfactory. And second, an analysis in this sense of the word is an analysis of the so-called "cognitive meaning" of ethical statements, and thus is not required to have the same emotive meaning as the analyzandum. Even if we should find a satisfactory analysis of ethical statements, therefore, we should still have to supplement this analysis by a theory of emotive meaning if we wished to take account of all the functions of ethical statements in actual discourse.

The method employed in formulating dispositional analyses—whether of "soluble" or "yellow" or "right"—is the method most aptly described as "pragmatic." In analyzing ethical statements, for example, we must try to determine the characteristics of an ideal observer by examining the procedures which we actually regard, implicitly or explicitly, as the rational ones for *deciding* ethical questions. These procedures, to mention just a few, might include religious exercises, the acquisition of certain kinds of factual information, appeals to a moral authority, and attempts to suppress one's emotions if they are thought to be prejudicial. Each of these procedures will suggest certain characteristics of an ideal observer, and there is reason to believe that the characteristics suggested by these various procedures will not be incompatible with one another: some of the characteristics which are likely to be attributed to a moral authority, for example, seem to be the very ones which we try to produce or to approximate in ourselves when we engage in religious exercises, or seek for factual information, or attempt to suppress emotions which we think are prejudicial.

This appeal to the procedures by which we judge or decide ethical questions, does not imply that the pragmatic method will force us to deny the important distinction, previously mentioned, between an ideal *observer* and an ideal *judge:* there is clearly no logical reason why a judge should have to *be* an ideal observer, or should even have to be closely similar to an ideal observer, in order to make correct judgments about the ethically-significant reactions of such a being. On the other hand, there cannot be much doubt that the ethically-significant reactions of an ideal observer must be psychological in nature, and that some of the evidence for the occurrence of these reactions could be directly accessible only to an ideal observer himself. It is for this epistemic reason that in practice we are likely to rate moral judges by reference to their similarity to an ideal observer. And it is to be expected, consequently, that any plausible description of an ideal observer will be a partial description of God, if God is conceived to be an infallible moral judge. But of course an ideal observer need not possess such characteristics as the power to create physical objects or even the power to reward and punish, if these characteristics appear to be irrelevant to God's capacities as a moral judge.

CHARACTERISTICS OF AN IDEAL OBSERVER

1. He Is Omniscient with Respect to Non-Ethical Facts.

We sometimes disqualify ourselves as judges of a particular ethical question on the ground that we are not sufficiently familiar with the facts of the case, and we regard one person as a better moral judge than another if, other things being equal, the one has a larger amount of relevant factual knowledge than the other. This suggests that an ideal observer must be characterized in part by reference to his knowledge of non-ethical facts. I say "non-ethical" because, as we have seen, the characteristics of an ideal observer must be determined by examining the procedures which we actually take to be the rational ones for deciding ethical questions; and there are many ethical questions (*viz.*, questions about "ultimate ethical principles") which cannot be decided by inference from ethical premises. This does not mean, of course, that an ideal observer (e.g., God) *cannot* have knowledge of ethical facts (facts, that is to say, about his own dispositions); it means merely that such knowledge is not *essential* to an ideal observer.

A difficulty seems to arise from the fact that in practice we evaluate the factual knowledge of a moral judge by reference to some standard of relevance, and regard one judge as better than another if, other things being equal, the one has more complete knowledge of all the facts which are *relevant*. But it is evident that a concept of relevance cannot be employed in *defining* an ideal observer. To say that a certain body of factual knowledge is not relevant to the rightness or wrongness of a given act, is to say, assuming that an absolutist dispositional analysis is correct, that the dispositions of an ideal observer toward the given act would be the same *whether or not* he possessed that particular body of factual knowledge or any part of it. It follows, therefore, that in order to explain what we mean by "relevant knowledge," we should have to employ the very concept of ideal observer which we are attempting to define.

Fortunately, however, we do not seem to think that a person is to any extent disqualified as a moral judge merely because he possesses factual information which we take to be *superfluous*. Our difficulty would be overcome, therefore, if we were simply to stipulate that an ideal observer is *omniscient* with respect to non-ethical facts, and so far as I can see the term "omniscient," when employed in this way, is neither extravagant nor mysterious. We apparently believe not only that the "facts of the case" are relevant to the objective rightness or wrongness of a particular act, but also that there is no point at which we could be logically certain that further information about matters of fact (e.g., further information about the consequences of the act), would be irrelevant. A satisfactory ethical analysis must be so formulated, therefore, that no facts are irrelevant *by definition* to the rightness or wrongness of any particular act. And this is the intent of the term "omniscient," for to say that an ideal observer is omniscient is to insure that no limits are put on the kinds or the quality of factual information which are available to influence his ethically-significant reactions.

Since omniscience implies complete knowledge of the *past* as well as the future, it might be wondered whether we are not being unnecessarily generous in attributing omniscience to the ideal observer. And it might seem that one's answer to this question will depend on one's views concerning the factors which determine whether an act is in fact right or wrong. Thus a philosopher whose position is not purely utilitarian (i.e., teleological), but to some extent deontological, might be expected to take one position; he might be expected to believe that certain events prior to the performance of an act (e.g., the making of contracts) are directly relevant to the objective rightness or wrongness of an act, in which case he would naturally wish to stipulate that the knowledge of an ideal observer extend to the past as well as the future. The typical utilitarian, on the other hand, believing that the past events are relevant only in so far as they affect the future, might be expected to deny that an ideal observer must have any knowledge about events occurring prior to the act which is being judged.

It seems clear, however, that this difference of opinion would exist only if the utilitarian wished to define rightness and wrongness in such a way that the thesis of utilitarianism followed analytically from his definitions, and most contemporary utilitarians maintain, I believe, that the thesis of utilitarianism is a synthetic proposition. What they would wish to say, therefore, if they accepted an absolutist dispositional analysis of ethical statements, is that an ideal observer, although he *is* by definition fully cognizant of all past events, would nevertheless have precisely the same ethically-significant reactions to a present act if by definition he were *not* cognizant of past events. Thus there is no reason why the utilitarian and the deontologist must disagree at this point about the analysis of ethical statements.

2. He Is Omnipercipient.

We sometimes disqualify ourselves as judges of certain ethical questions on the ground that we cannot satisfactorily imagine or visualize some of the relevant facts, and in general we regard one person as a better moral judge than another if, other things being equal, the one is better able to imagine or visualize the relevant facts. Practical moralists have often maintained that lack of imagination is responsible for many crimes, and some have suggested that our failure to treat strangers like brothers is in large part a result of our inability to imagine the joys and sorrows of strangers as vividly as those of our siblings. These facts seem to indicate that the ideal observer must be characterized by extraordinary powers of imagination.

The imaginal powers of the ideal observer, to be sure, are very closely related to his omniscience, and the word "omniscience" has sometimes been used to designate an unlimited imagination of perception. But however we may decide to use the word "omniscience," the important point is simply that it is not sufficient for an ideal observer to possess factual knowledge in a manner which will permit him to make true factual judgments. The ideal observer must be able, on the contrary, simultaneously to visualize all actual facts, and the consequences of all possible acts in any given situation, just as vividly as he would if he were actually perceiving them all. It is undoubtedly impossible for us to imagine the experience of a being capable of this kind of universal perception, but in making ethical decisions we sometimes attempt to visualize several alternative acts and their consequences in rapid succession, very much *as though* we wished our decision to be based on a simultaneous perception of the alternatives. And in view of this fact, and the others which I have mentioned, it seems necessary to attribute universal imagination to an ideal observer, thus guaranteeing that his ethically-significant reactions are forcefully and equitably stimulated.

3. He Is Disinterested.

We sometimes disqualify ourselves as judges of certain ethical questions on the ground that we cannot make ourselves impartial, and we regard one person as a better moral judge than another if, other things being equal, the one is more impartial than the other. This suggests that one of the defining characteristics of an ideal observer must be complete impartiality. But it is difficult to define the term "impartial" in a manner which will not make our analysis circular or be otherwise inconsistent with our purpose.

It is important, in the first place, not to confuse the impartiality of an ideal observer with the *uniformity* of his ethically-significant reactions. We are likely to think of a judge who is impartial as a judge who arrives at similar decisions in similar cases, and we may be tempted, therefore, to define an ideal observer as an observer whose ethically-significant reactions to two acts would always be the same if the two acts were alike in all ethically-relevant respects. But this will not do. For even if we could find a way to avoid circularity in defining "ethically-relevant respects," the characteristic which we should have analyzed would be more appropriately called "consistency" than "impartiality." And the fact that it is not self-contradictory to say that a person (e.g., a magistrate) is consistently partial, indicates that consistency and impartiality are not identical characteristics. Consistency, as we shall later see, *is* one of the characteristics of an ideal observer. But to say that an ideal observer is consistent is to say something about the uniformity of his ethically-significant reactions, whereas to say that he is impartial is to say something about the factors which *influence* his reactions.

When we try, however, to specify the kinds of factors which do and do not influence the decisions of an impartial judge, it is difficult to avoid interpreting the term "impartial" too broadly. For impartiality is so closely associated with the capacity for correct moral judgment, that we are likely to conclude that a judge lacks impartiality only if we believe that his decisions have been influenced by factors which *pervert* them—by factors, that is to say, which cause them to be incorrect. And whatever the justification for such reasoning may be when we are evaluating a moral judge, our analysis would evidently be circular if the term "impartial," as applied to an ideal observer, involved some concealed reference to a standard of correct moral judgment. It is difficulties of this kind which may have led Broad to remark that a philosopher who attempts this kind of dispositional analysis "is on a very slippery slope, and scarcely ever manages to avoid inconsistency. In defining his ideal he nearly always unwittingly introduces some characteristic which is in fact ethical, and thus fails . . . to define ethical characteristics in completely non-ethical terms."[16]

It is also difficult, on the other hand, to avoid interpreting the term "impartial" too narrowly. There is a familiar sense of this term, for example, which seems to be well represented by Bentham's maxim that every man should count for one and none for more than one. In this sense of the term a man would be impartial, in making a decision about his duty in a given situation, if he gave equal consideration to the welfare of each person who could be affected by his acts, regardless of how the person happened to be related to him.[17] And the maxim that we should treat all men as our brothers, has likewise been interpreted to imply a rule of impartiality in this sense—i.e., to imply that there are no special relationships which justify giving more consideration to one person than to another. But to analyze ethical statements by reference to this kind of impartiality, would rule out, by very definition of the words "right" and "wrong," the moral theory (held by Ross and others) that the rightness or wrongness of an act is determined in part by irreducible obligations arising directly from certain personal relationships; such an analysis would entail, for example, that there is never any moral justification, other things (including the value of the consequences) being equal, for making a decision which favors one's mother or friend or creditor at the expense of a greater benefit to someone else. Most philosophers would probably agree, however, that a correct analysis of ethical statements would not entail any particular conclusions concerning material questions of this sort. The solutions to such questions, they would agree, are synthetic and must not be prejudiced by our definitions.

Now it seems to me that a large part of what we mean when we say that an ideal judge is impartial, is that such a judge will not be influenced by interests of the kind which are commonly described as "particular"—interests, that is to say, which are directed toward a particular person or thing but not toward other persons or things of the same kind; and in so far as this is what we mean by "impartiality," we can define the term without falling into either of the errors which we have been considering. For to say

[16]*Five Types of Ethical Theory*, p. 263.

[17]Impartiality in this sense has sometimes been equated with distributive justice. *Vide*, e.g., Rashdall, *The Theory of Good and Evil*, Vol. I, Ch. VIII.

that an ideal observer is not influenced by particular interests, is to attribute to him a certain psychological characteristic which does not refer, either explicitly or implicitly, to a moral standard. Nor does it logically entail, on the other hand, either that an ideal observer would react favorably, or that he would react unfavorably, to an act which benefits one person at the expense of a greater benefit to another.

The term "particular interest," to be sure, is a difficult one to define, and raises problems about the nature of particularity which are beyond the scope of this paper; but I think that for present purposes it is not unreasonable to pass over these problems. Since ethical judgments are concerned, directly or indirectly, with acts, let us use "x" to denote the performance of a certain act by a certain agent. Let us first draw a distinction between the "essentially general properties" of x and the "essentially particular properties" of x. The properties of x which are essentially particular are those properties which cannot be defined without the use of proper names (which we may understand, for present purposes, to include egocentric particulars such as "I," "here," "now," and "this"); thus one of the essentially particular properties of x might be its tendency to increase the happiness of the citizens of the U.S.A. All other properties are essentially general; thus one of the essentially general properties of x might be its tendency to increase happiness. We may then say that a person has a positive particular interest in x if (1) he desires x, (2) he believes that x has a certain essentially particular property P, and (3) he would not desire x, or would desire it less intensely, if, his other beliefs remaining constant, he did not believe that x had this property P.

It may seem that this definition makes a variety of logical and ontological assumptions, some of which can be questioned. But I think that the intent of the definition is clear enough, and that the distinctions which it requires must be made, in one form or another, by any adequate logic and ontology. The definition is intended to represent the characteristic which we have in mind when we say that a moral judge who lacks impartiality is one who is tempted to "sacrifice principle"—i.e., to judge one act in a manner in which he would not wish to judge other acts which he thought to be of the same kind. And the definition proposes, in effect, that to say in this context that two acts are thought to be "of the same kind," is to say that they are thought to have the same essentially general properties. It is quite likely, of course, that we never actually believe that any two acts *do* have the same essentially general properties; it is for this reason, indeed, that we find it so easy to rationalize and "make exceptions" when judging acts which affect ourselves, our children, or our country. But this fact does not affect the usefulness of the definition, because part (3) is formulated hypothetically in the subjunctive mood: whether or not a person has a particular interest, is something to be decided by inferring, as best we can, how he *would* react *if* his beliefs were altered in certain ways.

It is important to observe that a person should not be said to have a particular interest in a certain act (x) merely because his interest in x is a result of his belief that x is related in a certain way to a *unique particular.* Let us suppose, for example, that Crito wanted Socrates to escape from prison because he thought that Socrates was the wisest man who would ever live. Let us suppose, for simplicity, that Crito did not want the wisest of men to be killed by his fellow human beings, and that this was his *sole* reason for wanting Socrates to escape. Now in this case it would surely be a mistake to maintain that Crito was necessarily influenced by a particular interest, for this would mean, if particular interests are excluded from an ideal observer, that the ethically-significant reactions of an ideal observer could *never* be influenced by the fact that a particular person or thing has a certain distinguishing property. And it is evident, I assume, that the ethical relevance or irrelevance of a fact of this sort cannot be decided merely by analyzing the meaning of ethical terms.

The crucial question about Crito's interest, therefore, is not whether it is an interest in the fate of a unique particular (Socrates), but whether the properties of Socrates which arouse this interest are essentially particular, i.e., properties which cannot be analyzed without the use of proper names. Two of the essentially particular properties which Crito might have attributed to Socrates are (A) being the wisest friend of Crito, and (B) being the most effective gad-fly in Athens. In a terminology suggested by Broad (following McTaggart), we may say that each of these is an "exclusive description" of Socrates. But Crito's interest, we are supposing, is a result of his belief that Socrates has the essentially general property (C) being wiser than any other man. In Broad's terminology this third property might also be an exclusive description of Socrates. But unlike the other two, this property is a "sufficient description," i.e., one which "refers to no merely designated particulars, but consists wholly of universals."[18] We may say, therefore, that Crito is interested in Socrates because of a certain sufficient description which he attributes to Socrates. For this reason his interest is not particular; it is an interest, so to speak, which he would have in *any* person whom he thought to be the wisest of all men. Interests of this kind, therefore, even though they are directed toward a particular person or thing, do not tend to make us impartial in our moral judgments.

Assuming now, that we have found a satisfactory definition of "particular interest," we must still decide how to use this term in our analysis. Shall we say that an ideal observer is completely lacking in particular interests? Or shall we say simply that his ethically-significant reactions are uninfluenced by such interests, leaving open the possibility, so far as our analysis is concerned, that such interests might be present but in some sense "suppressed"? At first thought the latter statement seems to be adequate to represent our concept of an impartial moral judge, for we often admire such a judge precisely because we believe that he does have particular interests but that his desire to be impartial has counteracted their influence. On further reflection it will be discovered, however, that we cannot explain what it means to say that a judge is uninfluenced by particular interests, except by reference, directly or indirectly, to the manner in which he *would* react *if* he had no particular interests. And this seems to imply that the first alternative is ultimately unavoidable if our analysis is to be complete. I think we must conclude, therefore, that an ideal observer is entirely lacking in particular interests—that he is, in this sense, *disinterested.*

4. He Is Dispassionate.

The concept of impartiality cannot be exhaustively analyzed in terms of interests, for an impartial judge, as ordinarily conceived, is a judge whose decisions are unaffected not only by his interests, but also by his emotions. This suggests that an ideal observer must be defined as a person who is in some sense dispassionate as well as disinterested. It is possible, to be sure, that the supposed effects of an emotion on our ethically-significant reactions, are always the effects of an accompanying or constituent interest; and if this were proved to our satisfaction, our conception of an ideal observer might be somewhat simplified. For our present purpose, however, this is irrelevant so long as it is generally believed that moral nearsightedness or blindness can be caused by the typically passional features of an emotion. We are searching for an analysis of ordinary ethical statements, and it is not to be expected that such an

[18]Broad, *Examination of McTaggart's Philosophy,* Vol. I, p. 178.

analysis will reflect all those distinctions, or just those distinctions, which would be required for an adequate system of psychology.

It is possible to construct a definition of the term "dispassionate" which will correspond, point by point, with our definition of the term "disinterested." Thus we can define a "particular emotion" as one which is directed toward an object only because the object is thought to have one or more essentially particular properties. And we can say that an ideal observer is dispassionate in the sense that he is incapable of experiencing emotions of this kind—such emotions as jealousy, self-love, personal hatred, and others which are directed towards particular individuals as such. At present this seems to me to be the most satisfactory way of defining the term "dispassionate" as applied to an ideal observer.

It would also be possible, however, to go a good deal further and to say that an ideal observer is incapable of experiencing any emotions at all, thus bringing our conception of an ideal observer closer to Kant's conception of a "purely rational being." There is no corresponding alternative open to us for the definition of "disinterested," because it seems unlikely that an ideal observer who had no interests at all would ever have any ethically-significant reactions. But the issue is not so clear with respect to emotions, especially if the moral datum, and hence the ethically-significant reactions of an ideal observer, can be defined in terms of a non-emotional, ostensibly objective, "demand quality."[19] And even those who believe that the moral datum is emotional, could maintain that an exception needs to be made only for moral approval and disapproval, or other emotions constituting the ethically-significant reactions of an ideal observer.

It might be maintained, to be sure, that there are certain emotions which are essential to an ideal observer, not because they constitute his ethically-significant reactions, but because they will influence these reactions in certain ways. And it should be observed that if this is an error, it is not a *logical* error, for precisely how an ideal observer should be defined can be determined only by analyzing the meaning of ethical statements. In fact, provided that we base our analysis on a direct examination of the meaning of ethical statements, it would not even be a logical mistake to attribute *virtues* to an ideal observer—to say, for example, that he has love and compassion for all human beings. It is true that love and compassion, assuming that they are truly virtues, are virtues only because of their relationship to certain ethically-significant reactions of an ideal observer—to those reactions, namely, by reference to which the ethical term "virtue" is defined; but virtues may be attributed to an ideal observer without circularity, of course, provided that we do not have to justify their attribution by reference to the fact that they are virtues. If, for example, the Christian conception of God has influenced our conception of an ideal observer, then, if an absolutist dispositional analysis is correct, it has influenced the very meaning of ethical statements. And if philosophers from a non-Christian culture have a somewhat different conception of an ideal observer, this fact implies nothing more surprising than that ethical statements possess the kind of ambiguity which I have called "accidental." Thus my reason for believing that it is not necessary to attribute such virtues as love and compassion to an ideal observer, is not that it would be a logical mistake to do so, but simply that I am not inclined to think that a man is necessarily a better moral judge, however superior as a person, merely because he possesses such virtues. The value of love and compassion to a judge, considered solely as a judge, seems to lie in the qualities of knowledge and disinterestedness which are so closely related to them; and these two qualities, as we have seen, can be independently attributed to an ideal observer.

[19] *Vide supra,* Part I, Section 5.

5. He Is Consistent.

Consistency is ordinarily regarded as one of the characteristics of a good judge, and this fact suggests that an ideal observer must be described in part as a being whose ethically-significant reactions are perfectly consistent with one another. But there are obstacles, as we shall see, to defining the relevant kind of consistency in a manner which avoids circularity and yet makes consistency an independent characteristic of an ideal observer.

When we say that the ethical decisions of a judge in two different cases are consistent with one another—or, correspondingly, that in two different situations the ethically-significant reactions of an ideal observer are consistent—we are evidently not passing judgment on the logic of any actual process of thought. There is an obvious sense, to be sure, in which a judge might accept consistent or inconsistent *premises* or use consistent or inconsistent *arguments* (either in reaching his decisions or in attempting to justify them); but when we assert that the two decisions of the judge are *themselves* consistent with one another, we intend to say something about a particular relationship between the two ethical statements which express the judge's final conclusions, and nothing, unless perhaps by insinuation, about the judge's processes of thought.

But it is also clear that we do not intend to say merely that these two ethical statements are *logically* consistent with one another. For since the two statements express ethical decisions about two different cases, they necessarily refer to different acts or events, and of course *any* two self-consistent statements are logically consistent with one another if they refer to different acts or events. Thus the kind of consistency which we have in mind must be "stronger" than logical consistency: we must mean to say that it is in some sense *possible* that the two statements are both true, but not merely that it is *logically* possible.

If this is so, however, the consistency or inconsistency of two ethical decisions must depend on the relationship of these decisions to certain general ethical principles which are conceived as restricting the "possible" combinations of ethical statements. And this conclusion is supported, I believe, by examination of the kind of reasoning which actually leads us to conclude that two decisions are consistent or inconsistent with one another. We might assert, for example, that a moral judge is inconsistent because in one case he decided in favor of act x rather than x′, whereas in another case he decided in favor of y rather than y′; and if we assert this, an analysis of our reasoning would probably show that we are assuming that it is possible for x to be the right act only if a certain ethical principle (*P*) is true, whereas it is possible for y to be the right act only if *P* is false.[20] Our judgment that the two decisions are inconsistent, therefore, is based on the assumption that there is no *other* valid ethical principle (a certain principle *Q*, for example) which could in some way take precedence over *P* in one of the two cases.[21] We are not, to be sure, committing ourselves either to the belief that *P* is true or to the belief that *P* is false. But we *are* assuming that the facts of the two cases are not different in some respect which is ethically crucial. And to assume even this is to presuppose at least one ethical proposition, namely, that there is no valid ethical principle (e.g., *Q*) which, together with *P*, could be used to justify *both* decisions.

[20]We might reason, for example, that x could be right only if we have a special obligation toward those who have suffered for our sake, whereas y could be right only if we do *not* have such an obligation. In some cases, of course, the principle *P* might itself be a complex conjunction of ethical principles.

[21]There are at least two kinds of cases in which a principle *Q* might be said to "take precedence over" a principle *P*: (1) Cases in which *P* and *Q* are conflicting principles, each representing a "claim" against the agent, and (2) cases in which *P* is simply an incomplete statement of a more completely qualified principle, *Q*.

I think we must conclude, therefore, that whenever we assert that the decisions of a moral judge in two different cases are consistent with one another, we are presupposing a certain amount of ethical knowledge. And this implies that our analysis would be circular if we made consistency of this kind one of the defining characteristics of an ideal observer.

There is, however, a much more limited kind of consistency which we might wish to attribute to an ideal observer. For if we agree that his ethically-significant reactions are stimulated by his imagination of a possible act, then, since an act may be imagined at any number of different times, there is nothing in our analysis up to this point which would logically require that an ideal observer always react in the same way even when he imagines one *particular* act (i.e., an act occurring at a particular time and place and hence having a certain particular set of alternatives). And if this appears to be a deficiency in our analysis, we could easily correct it by attributing a limited consistency to an ideal observer: we could define him, in part, as a being whose ethically-significant reactions to any particular act would always be exactly similar.

If we decide to do this, however, it is important to notice that consistency, when interpreted in this way, has a status very different from that of omniscience, disinterestedness, and the other defining characteristics of an ideal observer which we have so far considered. For according to the kind of absolutist analysis which we have been examining, ethical statements, as we have previously observed, are statements which depend for their truth or falsity on the existence of certain psychological laws; and if ethical statements are ever true, they are true only because we have defined an ideal observer in such a way that, in virtue of the relevant psychological laws, *any* ideal observer would react in the same way to a particular act. Thus in attributing omniscience, disinterestedness, and other such characteristics to an ideal observer, we are doing something of crucial importance for the kind of analysis which we are considering: we are eliminating from the personality of the ideal observer, so to speak, various factors which actually cause certain people to differ in their ethically-significant reactions from other people—such factors, for example, as selfish desires and ignorance of the facts of the case. And assuming that ethical statements *are* sometimes true, and absolutist dispositional analysis can be adequate only if such factors are completely eliminated from the personality of an ideal observer.

The characteristic of consistency, however, unlike omniscience, disinterestedness, and the others which we have discussed, does not eliminate some particular source of disagreement in ethical reactions. It is, on the contrary, a *consequence* of eliminating such disagreement, since any factor which could cause two different ideal observers to react in different ways to a particular act, could also cause one and the same ideal observer to react in different ways at different times. And this means, to put the matter bluntly, that if it is necessary to attribute consistency to an ideal observer in order to insure that he is psychologically incapable of reacting to the same act in different ways at different times, then we have simply failed to find all the *other* characteristics of an ideal observer which are necessary for the formulation of an adequate analysis. Thus an ideal observer will indeed be consistent if an adequate dispositional analysis can be formulated; but his consistency will be a derivative characteristic—a consequence of his other characteristics together with certain psychological laws.

6. In Other Respects He Is Normal.

An examination of the procedures by which we attempt to decide moral questions, reveals that there are a great many conditions which we recognize, though not always explicitly, to be favorable or unfavorable for making valid moral judgments. Mild bodily exercise such as walking, the presence of other people trying to make similar decisions, and certain kinds of esthetic stimuli, have all been regarded by some people as favorable conditions, whereas mental fatigue, distracting sensory stimuli, and lack of experience, are generally regarded as unfavorable. It seems likely, however, that our analysis will take all these special conditions into account if we attribute such general characteristics as omniscience and disinterestedness to an ideal observer.

It seems fairly clear, on the other hand, that no analysis in terms solely of such general, and highly ideal, characteristics, could be fully adequate to the meaning of ethical statements. For however ideal some of his characteristics may be, an ideal observer is, after all, a *person;* and whatever may be true of the future, our conception of the personality of an ideal observer has not yet undergone the refining processes which have enabled theologians, apparently with clear conscience, to employ the term "person" in exceedingly abstract ways. Most of us, indeed, can be said to have a conception of an ideal observer only in the sense that the characteristics of such a person are implicit in the procedures by which we compare and evaluate moral judges, and it seems doubtful, therefore, that an ideal observer can be said to lack any of the determinable properties of human beings.

The determinate properties of an ideal observer, however, except for the ideal characteristics which we have so far discussed, are apparently not capable of precise definition. We may employ the customary linguistic device, to be sure, and say that the properties of an ideal observer cannot vary beyond the limits of "normality," but there are a number of reasons why it does not seem to be possible to define these limits satisfactorily. It is evident, for example, that normality is a gestalt concept, and that a certain trait which in abstraction might properly be called abnormal, could nevertheless contribute to a total personality which falls within the bounds of normality. And this fact by itself is sufficient to destroy any hope of defining the term "normal" by continuing to add specific characteristics to the ones which we have already attributed to an ideal observer. This difficulty, however, and the others which prevent us from formulating a satisfactory definition of "normal," are practical rather than theoretical, and they do not tend in the slightest degree to disprove the thesis that ethical statements are statements about an ideal observer and his ethically-significant reactions. There are analogous difficulties, moreover, in formulating a dispositional analysis of the statement "This is (really) yellow"; and I have yet to find any convincing reason, indeed, for believing that "yellow" can be defined dispositionally although "right" cannot.

1954

The Point of View of Morality

Kurt Baier

Philosophical scepticism is often due to and supported by arguments based on confused epistemological theories. Scepticism in ethics is no exception. Consider sceptical views such as these: that the answers to moral questions are the unsupportable deliverances of our moral sense or intuition or flair, deliverances which unfortunately vary from age to age, from class to class, and even from person to person; or that they are merely the expressions of personal tastes, opinions, feelings or attitudes; or that they are the announcements of personal decisions, affirmations, choices or proposals. Philosophers usually come to hold such sceptical views because they have had before their minds questions which are not genuinely moral or, when they were genuinely moral, because their investigations of the ways in which we ordinarily go about answering moral questions were comparatively superficial. Repelled by the transparent attempts of many moral philosophers to assimilate moral to well-known "safe" questions and answers, such as mathematical, ordinary empirical or means-ends questions and answers, the sceptics over-emphasize the obvious differences. Opposition to the "safe" models leads them to adopt or think in terms of well-known "unsafe" ones, such as questions and answers in matters of taste, matters

Abridged version of a paper read to the Annual Congress of the A.A.P.P. in Melbourne in August, 1953.

Kurt Baier, "The Point of View of Morality," *Australasian Journal of Philosophy* (1954). Reprinted with the permission of the publishers.

of opinion, expressions of feelings and attitudes, and of decisions. The truth, however, is much more complicated.

Accordingly, I shall attempt to isolate one type of genuinely moral question and outline the appropriate procedure for answering it. It will then be seen that moral questions also have a "method of verification," although it is not the sort of empirical verification which in recent years has been taken as the only type deserving the name.

It will be granted that "What shall I do?" is sometimes a moral question. But obviously it is not the mere employment of these words themselves, not the form of the interrogative sentence in which they are employed, nor the ways in which these various employed words are severally used, that make it moral. This form of words constitutes a *moral* question only when it is *intended* as a moral question, i.e. when an answer of a certain sort is wanted, an answer that can stand up to certain complicated tests; in other words, when the questioner wants the person questioned first to consider and then to answer the question *from the point of view of morality.*

Let us be quite clear, in the first place, that not every question asked by means of these words is a moral question.

"What shall I do?" is not, for instance, a moral question when it is a request for instructions, as in the lieutenant's "What shall I do, Sir, shall I attack or wait for reinforcements?" This is not a moral question because the lieutenant, in asking for orders, is attempting to shift responsibility for what he is about to do on to his commanding officer. In moral cases, however, the agent himself is responsible for what he does. He cannot legitimately give the excuse "I acted on orders." Nor is it a moral question when asked by a pupil in the course of being taught. The learner wishing to know how to get on with his parking of the car, might ask the teacher, "What shall I do now?," but this is not necessarily a moral case either. When one asks for moral advice in a moral difficulty, one need not necessarily be a learner at all, not even a moral learner.

Nor is it a moral question when what one wants of the other person is that he should submit some suggestions or declare his own preferences in the matter, as when someone asks: "What shall I do? Shall I leave the key in the milk box or what?"

What, then, is it to ask a *moral* question by means of these words? We are nearer the typical case on those occasions when we are driven into raising this question by a practical problem which forces us to choose between alternative courses of action, as when I say "What shall I do? I must pay back. But there were no replies to my advertisement. So where can I get the money?" In such a case I can either answer my own question or I can seek guidance from other people. Both I myself and others must work out the answer by going through the process of deliberation. Everyone is in principle capable of deliberating on his own or on someone else's behalf. There is a symmetrical relation between the person who asks "What shall I do?" and the person whom he asks. Their roles might at any time be exchanged. There is no question of superordination or subordination. Both are surveying and weighing the considerations in favor of and against the possible alternatives. In asking for advice I am not necessarily asking for, and in giving it, I am not necessarily giving orders, instructions, or tuition. When I ask for advice I am asking the person to deliberate on my behalf, i.e. to survey the reasons or considerations relevant to the problem, though I am not necessarily asking him to *give* me these reasons. But I should think that he had not done what I asked him to do, if he had not surveyed and weighed the reasons, had not thought about my problem at all.

But not all advice, not all deliberation, is moral. It is only when I deliberate from the point of view of morality that my deliberation can be said to be moral. I am not considering the problem from this point of view unless I attempt to survey and weigh all the relevant moral considerations. I must here assume an understanding of what is by no means generally understood, namely, the nature of deliberation and of a consideration. All I have space to examine here are the questions, What is deliberation *from the point of view of morality?* and What are *moral* considerations?

Suppose I have wealthy relatives whose son wants a bicycle. Perhaps I could get the money I need by selling my bicycle to them. They would surely be prepared to pay a good price, for my bicycle is as good as new. It is an English racing bicycle and they know the boy would be very happy with it. The cost is of no importance to them.

So far, my deliberation was not from the point of view of morality at all, for I have merely asked myself whether the proposed line of conduct was likely to produce the effect desired. I cannot be said to have considered this question from the former point of view unless I ask myself whether there are *any moral objections to,* i.e. any moral considerations against my proposed line of conduct.

When would we say that there were such objections? There is a moral objection to a proposed line of conduct if it would constitute a breach of a moral rule. Determining whether a particular line of action does or does not constitute such a breach is a complicated business and we must not think that it can be done in one move. There are two main steps: first, finding out whether the contemplated act is forbidden, or incompatible with another act enjoined, by a moral rule of the agent's group; secondly, finding out whether this moral rule of the agent's group can stand up to the appropriate moral criticism.

1

Our first question, then, is whether the planned line of conduct is forbidden by a moral rule of the group, and this involves the further question, when we would say of a rule that it belonged to the morality of a given group.

A few preliminary remarks about the nature of this question will help. A given rule which is part of the way of life of a certain group may belong to its law, its religion, or its mores, and if to the mores, then either to that part of the mores which we call its etiquette, or to its manners, or its fashions and so on. That a rule belongs to the law of the group can be ascertained by a comparatively precise method, namely, by ascertaining whether the rule is a valid part of its legal system. That it belongs to the religion of the group can usually be determined by finding out whether it is contained in any of the sacred books. On the other hand, that a given rule belongs to the mores of the group cannot be determined in any of these comparatively precise and specific ways. The most obvious method of finding out would seem to be to see whether the rule in question is supported by one or the other of the types of social pressure by which the various parts of the mores are supported. For instance, the rule will be said to belong to the manners of the group if the person on account of its breach is called ill-mannered, ill-bred, impolite, rude, or some such epithet, *and is treated accordingly.*

What we want to know is how we can characterize those rules which must be said to belong to the morality of the group.

Now, briefly, my answer to this question is as follows. For a rule to belong to the morality of a given group it is not necessary that, like the Decalogue, it should forbid or enjoin or permit a certain definite line of conduct or one or the other out of a definite range of conduct. What is necessary is rather that it should be: (i) part of the mores of the group, (ii) supported by the characteristically moral pressure, (iii) universally teachable and therefore universalizable, (iv) not merely a taboo, (v) applied in accordance with certain principles of exception and modification, (vi) applied in accordance with certain principles of application whose prevalence is a condition of the group being said to have a morality.

If a rule satisfies all these conditions, then it must be said to belong to the morality of the group in question, it is a moral rule *of* that group. I now proceed to discuss these points in detail.

(i) I shall simply assume, without much further argument, that the moral rules of a group belong to its mores and not to its law or religion. Moral rules of a group cannot be laid down, amended, abrogated, abolished. If a legislator were to attempt to do that, the rules he lays down would become part of the law. If the legislator is divine, the law is Divine Law. Of course, a legislator may not actually make new law, but merely declare law what is already existing custom. But then he has made law what was previously custom. And if he declares law what is a moral rule, then the moral rule has received legal backing. The same line of behavior is now forbidden by a moral *and* by a legal rule. If it is morally wrong to break the law, then it is morally wrong to drive on the right, where the law forbids it. If it is morally wrong to disobey God, then it has been morally wrong to play tennis on Sunday ever since God prohibited it. In this sense only can the word of command or of law create moral rules. But no word of command or law can *create* the moral rule that it is morally wrong to break the law or disobey the word of God. A rule is part of the morality of a group in virtue of the moral convictions and pressures of the people of that group. A rule can become part of the morality of a group through propaganda, education, teaching, by hook or by crook, but not by word of command or law. A rule must become part of the living tradition of the group to become a moral rule *of* that group.

(ii) That a rule belongs to the mores of the group and not to its law or religion is not, however, sufficient. For it might still be merely a rule of etiquette or custom. Now it might be thought that all that was necessary was that the rule should be supported by the *specifically moral pressure.* If infringers of the rule are said to be immoral, wicked, wrongdoers, evil, morally bad, or some term implying one of these, and they are treated accordingly, then the rule is supported by the specifically moral pressure. Whatever may be the precise treatment meted out to those we think we rightly say are immoral, evil, wicked, etc., it is plain that we tend to condemn them, dissociate ourselves from them, perhaps would want to see them punished. Again, it is evidence that the rule is part of the morality of the group if rule-breakers feel guilty and experience remorse. It is evidence that the rule is not part of the group morality if group members feel merely regret or pleasure when infringing it. Finally, it is evidence that the rule belongs to the group morality if, on discovering that the rule is not part of the mores of another group, group members are shocked, outraged, indignant or horrified, and if they feel they must introduce this rule to the other group. Whereas, that they are quite unperturbed about this and don't feel driven to encourage them to adopt this rule, is evidence to the contrary.

Thus we can say that, although support of a rule by this sort of pressure is a necessary, it is not a sufficient condition of the rule belonging to the morality of the group.

(iii) A further condition which a rule must satisfy if it is to be said to belong to the morality of a given group, is that it must have been taught in a certain way. Three features of the teaching of moral rules are particularly important here. In the first place, moral rules must be taught to all children. Moral education is not the preserve of a certain privileged or oppressed caste or class within the group, nor of certain privileged or oppressed individuals. Secondly, children are made to understand that the breach of the moral rules is very serious and that infringers of moral rules are peculiarly reprehensible, horrible, and despicable. They are also taught that certain circumstances are extenuating and others aggravating and that in certain situations the rules need not be kept.

They are taught that everyone is expected to observe them and that everyone will be treated in the same way when breaking or when observing these rules. Lastly, these rules are taught quite openly to everybody and taught in a way which makes it clear that one may be proud of observing these rules, of encouraging others to observe them and teach them to their children, of disapproving of others for not observing them or not teaching them to their children.

From this last point about universal teaching there follow certain principles, often called principles of universalizability, which exclude rules with a certain content from being part of the morality of any group whatever, since they could not be taught in the way in which rules must be capable of being taught if they are to be called moral rules. That this is so, shows that certain rules (logically) could not be said to be moral rules of a group. Hence it is not necessary to invoke any sort of moral intuition to "see" whether they are true or false moral rules. This question does not arise at all.

Notice that these rules are not self-contradictory, but that their content is such that no one who understands the nature of morality could rationally wish them to belong to the morality of any group.

(*a*) No one could wish a rule to belong to the morality of a group if the rule embodied a principle that was *self-frustrating*. For surely it must be possible for moral rules to be observed by all members of the group. Each member of the group might for instance wish to adopt the rule, When you are down ask for help, but don't ever help another man when he is down. But if all members of the group adopted this principle, then their adopting the second half of it would frustrate what is *obviously* the point of adopting the first half, namely, to *get* help when one is down. Such a principle is not, in itself, self-contradictory. Any one person may for himself consistently adopt it. But it is clearly a parasitic principle. It is useful to anyone only if many people act on the opposite principle.

(*b*) The same is true of self-defeating rules. A principle is self-defeating if its point is defeated as soon as its adoption by someone is revealed by him, e.g. the principle, Give a promise even when you know or think that you can never keep it, or when you don't intend to keep it. Now, the very point of giving promises is to reassure and give a guarantee to the promisee. Hence any remark that throws doubt on the sincerity of the promiser will defeat the purpose of making a promise. But clearly to *say* that one gives promises even when one knows or thinks one cannot, or when one does not intend to keep them, is to raise such doubts. And to say that one acts on the above principle is to imply that one may well give promises in these cases. Hence to reveal that one acts on this principle will tend to defeat one's own purpose.

But it has already been said that moral rules must be capable of being taught openly. Yet this rule is self-defeating if it is taught openly, for then everyone would be known to act on it. Hence it cannot belong to the morality of any group.

(*c*) Lastly, there are some rules which it is literally impossible to teach in the way the moral rules of a group must be capable of being taught, e.g. the rule "Always assert what you don't think to be the case." Such *morally impossible* rules differ from self-frustrating and self-defeating rules in that the latter could have been taught in this way, although it would have been quite senseless to do so, whereas the former literally cannot be so taught.

The reason why this rule cannot be taught thus is that the only possible case of acting on this principle, doing so secretly, is ruled out by the conditions of moral teaching.

(i) Consider first someone secretly adopting this principle. His remarks will almost always mislead people, for *he will be taken to be saying what he thinks true,* and in most cases what he thinks true will be true. Thus, it will usually be the case that p when he says "not-p," and that not-p when he says "p," whereas people will take it that p when he says "p," and that not-p when he says "not-p." Thus communication between him and other people breaks down, since they will almost always be misled by him whether he wishes to mislead them or not. The possibility of communication depends on the possibility of a speaker's ability *at will* to say either what he thinks to be the case or what he does not think to be the case. Our speaker cannot communicate because by his principle he is forced to mislead his hearers.

Thus, anyone secretly adopting the principle, Always assert what you don't think to be the case, cannot communicate with others since he is bound to mislead them whether he wants to or not. Hence he cannot possibly teach the principle to anybody. And if he were to teach the principle without having adopted it himself, then although he would be understood, yet those who adopted it would not. At any rate, since moral teaching involves teaching rules such as the taught may openly avow to be observing, this case is ruled out. A principle which is taught for secret acceptance only, cannot be embodied in a *moral* rule of the group.

(ii) Of course, people might soon come to realize what is the matter with our man. They may discover that in order not to be misled by what he says, they only have to substitute "p" for "not-p" and vice versa. But if they do this then they have interpreted his way of speaking, not as a reversal of the general presumption that one says what one thinks is the case (not the opposite), but as a change of the use of "not." In his language, it will be said, "not" has become an affirmation sign, negation being effected by omitting it. Thus, if communication is to be possible, we must interpret as a change in usage what is intended as the reversal of the presumption that every assertion conveys what the assertor believes to be the case.

Thus, if everyone were, by accident, to adopt simultaneously and secretly our principle "Always assert what you think is not the case," then, for some time at least, communication would be impossible. If, on the other hand, it were adopted openly, then communication would be possible, but only if the adoption of this principle is accompanied by a change in the use of "not" which completely cancels the effect of the adoption of the principle. In that case, however, it can hardly be said that the principle has been adopted.

(iii) However, the case we are considering is neither (i) nor (ii). We are considering the case of the open teaching of the principle, Always assert what you don't think is the case, for open acceptance by everybody, which is not to be interpreted as a change in the use of "not." But this is nonsense. We cannot all openly tell one another that we are always going to mislead one another in a certain way and insist that we must continue to be misled, though we know how we could avoid being misled.

Thus, this principle could not be embodied in a rule belonging to the morality of any group.

These points are of some general interest in that they clarify some valuable points contained in Kant's doctrine of the Categorical Imperative. In particular they clarify the expression "can will" contained in the formulation "Act so that thou *canst will* thy maxim to become a universal law of nature." "Canst will" in one sense means what I have called "morally possible." That is to say, your maxim must be a formula which is morally possible, i.e. which is logically capable of being a rule belonging to the morality of some group, as the maxim "Always lie" is not. No one *can* wish that maxim to be a rule of some morality. To say that one is wishing it, is to contradict oneself. One cannot wish it any more than one can wish that time should move backwards.

The second sense of "can will" is that in which no rational person can will certain things. Self-frustrating and self-defeating moral rules are not morally impossible, they are merely senseless. No rational person could wish such rules to become part of any morality. That is to say, anyone wishing that they should would thereby expose himself to the charge of irrationality, like the person who wishes that he should never attain his ends or that he should (for no reason at all) be plagued by rheumatic pains throughout his life.

But the points made also show the weakness of Kant's doctrine. For while it is true that someone who acts on the maxim "Always lie" acts on a morally impossible one, it is not true that every liar necessarily acts on that maxim. For if he acts on a principle at all, it may e.g. be, Lie when it is the only way to avoid harming someone, or Lie when it is helpful to you and harmful to no one else, or Lie when it is entertaining and harmless, and so on. Maxims such as these can, of course, be willed in either of the senses explained.

(iv) That the rule should be taught in the way explained is a necessary but not a sufficient condition of the rule belonging to the morality of the group.

Suppose that a group had the rule "Don't pick your teeth after a meal" and that this rule was taught in the way explained and supported by the typically moral pressure. But suppose also that, provided you crossed the fingers of your left hand, it was all right to pick your teeth after a meal. I think we would not say that such a rule belonged to the morality of that group.

The reason is not far to seek. We would not call this a rule of their morality, because it is merely a taboo. We do not allow it to be one of their moral rules, because they allow exemption on irrational grounds. Of course, one would have to examine their beliefs further to be sure that this was irrational. It would not necessarily be irrational if they also thought and offered some reason for thinking that crossing one's fingers when picking one's teeth appeased the deity who was incensed by the picking of one's teeth. We would not call a system of taboos a morality, not only because of the frequently odd contents of taboos, but also because of the mechanical and irrational nature of the ways in which members can gain exemption.

(v) It might be thought that I have given the wrong reason for saying that the taboos of a group cannot be moral rules of that group; I should not have said "exemptions on the wrong grounds" but just "exemptions." For it is sometimes held that moral rules do not allow of exceptions at all. "Fiat iustitia ruat caelum." Yet we do not regard a man who kills another in self-defense or executioners carrying out death-sentences as murderers or even as wrong-doers. Theirs are justified killings. That we so regard them indicates more precisely the way we apply the rule "Never kill a man" by showing us one or the other of its legitimate exceptions. That we so interpret it does not show, as beginners usually think, that we do not really believe killing is wrong or that we have contradictory moral convictions, but it shows that, to speak technically, we think killing *prima facie* wrong, wrong other things being equal, wrong in the absence of special justifying factors.

What, then, are the required principles of making exceptions to a moral rule? It has been held that one of the principles is that one must never make an exception in one's own favor. This has been interpreted (and very naturally) as meaning "Never make an exception to a moral rule when doing so would be in your own interest." But this cannot be right, for I am at least as justified in killing a man in my own defense as I am in killing one in someone else's. And often it is just as immoral to make an exception when this is in someone else's interest, e.g. my wife's, my son's or my nephew's. In fact, it is quite unimportant in itself in whose favor the exception operates, so long as it was made legitimately, and it is made legitimately in the case of self-defense. The truth contained in this view is simply this, that I must not make exceptions to a moral rule *on the principle* that I will depart from the rule *whenever and simply because* doing so is in my interest or, for that matter, in that of someone else whom I wish to favor.

Generally speaking, we can say that a man is not treating a rule as moral unless he makes exceptions to the rule only in those cases which are themselves provided for by the rules of the morality of the group; that is to say, in our case, when the killing was by the hangman, in self-defense, of an enemy in war, and perhaps in mercy killing. But this is only rough, for it is not the case that we allow the morality of the group itself to provide for exceptions in any sorts of cases whatever. We would not, for instance, be satisfied to say that the rule, Never kill a human being, did belong to the morality of a group, if the rule was supported by the moral pressure, and if the making of exceptions on the grounds of self-interest was also supported by the moral pressure, as when a man is condemned for not killing another whose fortune he would have acquired.

(vi) The question we are trying to answer, "When would we say that a given rule was a moral rule of a given group?" or "When would we say that a given rule belonged to the morality of a given group?," does, of course, presuppose that the group has a morality. For otherwise the question could not arise. On the other hand, having moral rules is one of the conditions of a group being said to have a morality. It might, therefore, be thought that the group needed only one rule of the right sort, say, Thou shalt not kill, or Thou shalt not lie, in order to be said to have a morality.

But I think this would be a mistake. We have already seen that for any such rule to be said to belong to the morality of the group, it must be supported by the right sort of pressure, be taught in the right sort of way, and be applied in accordance with certain principles of exception. But even this is not enough. We would not say of a group that it had a morality, even if it had one or several such rules and had all the practices already mentioned unless, in addition, it applied these rules in accordance with certain very general principles. Only if it did so apply some rules would we say that the group had a morality, and only those which were so applied would be said to belong to the morality of the group. The principles I have in mind might be called principles of *differentiation* and of *priority*.

The supreme principle of the application of moral rules is that in the absence of morally relevant differences between people moral rules must be applied to everyone alike. If a group is to be said to have a morality, it must have certain rules of differentiation, i.e. rules which lay down what are to be regarded by group members as morally relevant differences.

We would be inclined to say of a group that it had no morality if its rules of differentiation deviated more than a certain amount from the true principles of differentiation. Just what these true principles are and just what this maximum amount of deviation is, I cannot say now. All I can do at present is to indicate what are our rules of differentiation. (More about this below, page 132 [p. 262 this volume].) Notice also that one of the grounds on which we grade different moralities as less or more civilized, more or less primitive, less or more advanced, is the amount by which they depart from what we regard as the true principles of differentiation.

The most obvious grounds recognized by our morality for differentiating between different people are these:

(i) Breach of a moral rule by someone and consequent forfeiture of the protection of certain moral rules. Thus a man who without provocation is attempting to kill another man cannot claim the protection of the moral rule, Thou shalt not kill. If the other man, in self-defense, kills him, then the killer cannot be said to be a murderer, as he otherwise might have to be.

(ii) Special effort (greater than standard) and consequent moral claims to special consideration. Thus a man who has worked hard on a common project is entitled to a greater return from the common proceeds than one who has been idle.

(iii) Greater or less need (than standard) and consequently fewer or more tasks, duties, jobs, obligations. Thus, a man with a large family or one who has lost his eyesight is entitled to special consideration, partly because his need is greater and partly because certain duties would be more onerous for him than for others.

(iv) Special undertakings freely entered into and consequently special obligations to carry these out. Thus, a man who has a job as a social worker is not entitled to the gratitude and reward to which another is entitled, who does the same thing without having entered into any undertakings.

The supreme *principle of priority* lays it down that when two rules clash, i.e. when a person, by doing one thing, would be breaking one rule and by not doing it, breaking another, he ought to observe the more important rule and break the less important. Rules of priority of a given group provide guidance for the most likely clashes of moral rules.

Thus, when I know that by lying to his pursuers about his whereabouts I can save the life of an innocent man endangered by them, I am in the position of having either to lie or to help increase the danger to someone's life. In making a moral decision on this, I am guided by moral rules of priority. Our morality lays it down, I think, that we should lie in order not to endanger the innocent man's life, rather than vice versa.

If a morality had no rules at all for those cases in which two or more moral rules clash, if people sometimes acted in one way and then in another and felt no need for a uniform settlement, then one would be inclined to say that the group had no morality.

This completes my explanation of the first step in answering the moral question "What shall I do?" Suppose our agent has found, in this way, that his proposed course was not forbidden by any moral rule of the group nor incompatible with any course of action required by such a rule. He has then found a (preliminary) positive answer to his moral question. Speaking in this preliminary way, there are no moral objections to doing what he is proposing to do. He can go ahead. What he is proposing to do is morally all right, is not something he morally ought not to do. If, on the other hand, he finds that this line of action is contrary to a moral rule of the group, then he has found a (preliminary) negative answer.

2

No doubt many people never go further than this. They are like Plato's well-behaved auxiliaries in never challenging the authority of those who have taught them what is right and wrong. But if there is to be moral progress there must be at least some who subject the morality of their group to rational scrutiny and attempt to reform it where it is found wanting. The view that our morality *needs* no criticism because it is the word of God Who revealed it to us is as detrimental to moral advance as the view that there is *no point* in criticizing it because the juggernaut of history is inexorably pushing it forward in its predetermined grooves, anyway.

Let us then try to understand what such criticism of a morality comes to. Suppose our questioner finds that his proposed line of conduct is contrary to a rule of this group morality. Suppose also that he is not satisfied to accept uncritically the morality of his group. He will then go on to ask a question which he might formulate in these words, "Granted that our morality forbids this course of action, is our morality right in forbidding it?" We all understand this question. Most of us have sometimes asked it. We all admit that at least a few of our moral convictions may be misguided. Most of us now suspect that certain views on poverty and private property widely held in England in the eighteenth century were wrong, and also the nineteenth century views on sex.

What, then, does such a critically-minded person ask? What sort of doubt is he raising about the rules of his group morality? In what ways can the rules of a group morality go wrong?

Consider, to begin with, the analogous case of the expression "religious rule." It is well to remember that the two most important senses of "religious rule" are not parallel to the two main senses of "legal rule," namely, "law" and "lawful rule." There is no sense of "religious rule" which corresponds to "lawful rule." We would not say of the rule "Don't pick your teeth in public" that it was in any sense religious, just because it was not irreligious; although we would say that this rule was legal just because it was not illegal, i.e. was lawful. "Moral rule" is in this respect like "religious rule" and *not* like "legal rule." "Don't pick your teeth in public" would no more be called a moral rule (because in our society it is not considered immoral) than it would be called a religious rule (because it is not irreligious).

There is, however, a sense of "religious rule" which is parallel to "legal rule" in the sense of "law." I think it would not be seriously misleading for our purposes if we said that no system of beliefs and rules could be called a religion if it did not contain either supernatural beliefs or prescribed rites or rules of worship. If we know that a group has a certain religion, we can then tell whether a given rule of a group belongs to its religion or not. In the case, for instance, of the Christian religion, it is easy to tell that a rule is religious, namely, if it is contained in one of the sacred books.

Even so, there are rather different sorts of rule in the Holy Scriptures.

(i) Thou shalt not make unto thee any graven image or any likeness of anything that is in the heaven above, or that is in the earth beneath, or that is in the water under the earth.

(ii) But if the ox were wont to push with his horn in time past, and it hath been testified to his owner, and he hath not kept him in, but that he hath killed a man or a woman; the ox shall be stoned, and his owner also shall be put to death.

Both these rules are religious rules, in a sense corresponding to that which makes certain rules legal rules, i.e. laws: being part of the system. But we must now take notice that there is another sense of "religious rule" in which they are not both religious rules. Rule (ii) about the ox is not, in this sense, religious, whereas clearly rule (i) is. Religious Jews would not feel that they were sinning if they broke the rule concerning the ox, but they would do so if they broke rule (i), even though both these rules are held to have been revealed by God on Mount Sinai.

We thus distinguish between those rules which are, as I shall say, *genuinely religious,* and those which merely happen to be *part of the religion of the group.* We may similarly distinguish between those moral rules of the group which are *genuinely moral* and those which merely happen to be *part of the morality of the group.*

Let us make this distinction a little clearer. As we have seen, a rule will be said to belong to the morality of the group (provided the group has a morality), if it is treated in all the important respects in the way in which a genuinely moral rule ought to be treated: if it is taught in the way indicated, if it is applied in accordance with the moral principles of making exceptions, if it passes the universalization tests, if rule-breakers are dealt with in the specifically moral way, and perhaps some other things.

On the other hand, even if a rule does satisfy all these conditions, we may still have misgivings about it. Take the rule "Don't eat beans" or "Don't walk under ladders." Like the rules "Don't kill a human being" or "Don't lie," these rules might satisfy all the conditions necessary in order to be said to belong to the morality of some group. But even when they satisfy these conditions, we think that they *ought not to* belong to any morality. The first of these rules may perhaps have a place in a treatise on health foods, and the second is a mere superstition. They may belong to, but neither belongs *in* a morality. How, then, do we distinguish the genuine from the spurious, among the rules actually belonging to the morality of a group?

Let us remember that doing this is the task of a *critic* of a morality. Hence we need to lay bare the standards employed in this task. There seem to me to be four ways of getting at these standards. (*A*) In the first place, we already have some idea of what point of view we actually adopt when we perform this task. We only need to remind ourselves of it and make it explicit. (*B*) Secondly, we have the paradigms of genuinely moral rules, such as "Don't kill any human being," "Don't lie," "Don't be cruel." With regard to these rules we are more certain to be right than with regard to any other rules and principles. Hence an examination of the characteristics of these rules as opposed to obviously spurious ones, like "Don't eat beans," will help us to work out the principles by which we distinguish between genuinely moral and spurious rules. (*C*) Thirdly, we already have a fair idea of some of the principles we are using in this job. (*D*) Lastly, we have some idea of the relative merit of moralities as a whole. We already grade them as primitive and advanced, crude and civilized, lower and higher, and so on. But since these gradings of whole moralities depend, at least to some extent, on whether a morality contains fewer or more of the genuinely moral rules than of the spurious ones, this too helps us to arrive at the truth. Arriving at the truth in this matter consists in following up these beginnings, pressing as far as possible the various implications contained in them, and making them consistent and sensible.

Ad (A). I take the following to be the point of view which we adopt when we perform the task of a critic of a morality. I shall call it the point of view of morality. We are adopting it if we regard the rules belonging to the morality of the group as designed to regulate the behavior of people all of whom are to be treated as equally important "centers" of cravings, impulses, desires, needs, aims, and aspirations; as people with ends of their own, all of which are entitled, *prima facie,* to be attained. (I take this to be the meaning of "treating them as ends in themselves and not merely as means to one's own ends.") The pursuits and wishes and ends of none of these goal-seekers are to be subordinated without special justification to those of any one or any group of them. From this point of view every one of these individuals is required to modify his impulsive behavior, his endeavors, and his plans by observing certain rules, the genuinely moral rules. These forbid any individual's pursuit, even that of his own greatest good, if it is at the expense of the legitimate pursuits of others, at the same time indicating whose pursuit has to be abandoned in the case of conflicts (e.g. "Don't kill anyone except in self-defense, etc."); or they direct or admit him to the performance of certain ministrations to or by others because of his either being in a certain social position (teacher, soldier, etc.), or his finding himself in certain social relations to others (female dependant, beneficiary), or having inflicted certain things on others or suffered them at their hands (maiming, deceiving someone, etc.).

It is worth noting that this point of view differs from that of an Enlightened Egoist. The latter regards other people as complicated and subtle organisms who tend to compete with him for the good things in life but who, if properly handled, can be made to serve him the better to attain his own ends. An Enlightened Egoist must be and is prepared for other people to be similarly engaged in the pursuit of their own good and for each to subordinate the good of others to his own, i.e. to pursue his own good whenever possible, even to the detriment of others.

The job of a critic of morality may also be confused with that of some sort of ideal legislator. For both moral rules and laws are rules for members of groups, both in the ideal case applying to all members alike, both varying from group to group inasmuch as the exigencies of life, the technical means and the social arrangements vary, and both designed to protect each individual in the pursuit of his own good (made possible within the framework of his society) from any interference and abuse of the social devices by others. But while there are these similarities, there also are decisive differences.

There are a number of quite different jobs to be performed in the field of law and in the field of morality. In the field of law a man may perform the task of a legal critic, of a legal reformer, or of a legislator. The job of legal critic is to examine the legal system of his group and to ferret out weaknesses and devise improvements. It is not his job to publicize the weaknesses or to campaign for their removal. That is the job of the legal reformer. The task of the legislator is to create new law. He merely uses the existing machinery of legislation. The job of the critic is the invention of improvements, the job of the reformer is the preparation of public opinion, the job of the legislator is the setting in motion of the legal machinery.

In the field of morality there are only two comparable jobs, that of the critic of a morality and of the moral reformer. For reasons already mentioned there could not be the job of a moral legislator. When public opinion has been swayed, the morality of the group has already been changed. The group is then ready for legal changes, but the actual legal changes have yet to come. Legal authority rests with the legislator, moral authority with the public.

The critic's job differs from that of the reformer in being theoretical rather than practical. A thinker can criticize the law or the morality of the Ancients, he cannot reform it. The critic may consider all sorts of past, present or future possibilities, the reformer considers only immediate practical future possibilities. There is no doubt that the institution of slavery was a shortcoming of the morality of the Ancients. There is considerable doubt whether the abolition of slavery should have been on the program of an ancient moral reformer.

There is a further important difference. Both the legal critic and the critic of morality may and should adopt the point of view of morality. But if the legal critic adopts it, he imposes on himself certain extraneous restrictions; if the critic of morality adopts it, he does not. If the legal critic does not adopt it, he may still be a legal critic; if the critic of morality does not adopt it, he cannot be a critic of morality. If the legal critic correctly criticizes law from the moral point of view, his criticisms will be morally justified, but they may be incompetent from the lawyers' point of view. If the critic of morality criticizes a morality from the point of view of morality, his criticism will be morally justified and that is all it needs to be.

It should now be clear what sort of a task it is to distinguish the genuine from the spurious among the rules actually belonging to the morality of a given group. It is the task of a critic of a morality. We all have this task in that, as moral beings, we are normally guided by the moral convictions of our group which we absorb in the course of our upbringing. It is our task as critics to examine this group morality, our task as moral reformers to attempt to bring about the removal of glaring inadequacies and needed improvements.

Ad (B). I have now completed my discussion of the point of view appropriate for a critic of the morality of his group. If my sketch of that point of view was accurate, it should enable us to say something about the principles governing the critic's work. In particular, if from the point of view of morality we look upon human beings as equally engaged in the pursuit of their legitimate interests, we would expect one of the principles by which we test group moralities to be this, that a genuine moral rule must be *for* *the good* of human beings. And since, from the point of view of morality, all are to be regarded equally, we would expect that the rules should *affect everyone alike.*

These points are confirmed independently, if we consider such, paradigms of moral rules as Thou shalt not kill, Thou shalt not be cruel, Thou shalt not break promises, Thou shalt not lie. It certainly would seem to be for the good of all human beings alike that rules like these are part of the morality of groups.

Ad (C). This can be seen more clearly if we turn to our third way of getting at the standards employed, in criticizing an existing morality, namely, the consideration of the principles which we actually find ourselves using in this job. If we investigated what more exactly is meant by saying that the inclusion of a certain rule in the morality of a given group is for the good of human beings alike, by trying it out in a number of individual cases, we find that the application of this general principle tallies with our actual practice as critics of a morality. When would a rule be said to be *for the good* of human beings?

(a) In the first place, a rule must *not* be harmful. But it will be said to be harmful if (i) acting in accordance with it is harmful to the agent (e.g. "If your eye offends you, pluck it out"); (ii) one man's acting on it is harmful to many people, including the agent (e.g. "If you want to have a really pleasant drive, get drunk first"); (iii) one man's acting in accordance with it is harmful to others but not to the agent (e.g. "If you can get away with it, cheat in business"); (iv) everybody's or many people's, but not a single person's acting in accordance with it, is generally detrimental (e.g. "Turn on the current during the restricted hours").

A few words must be said in explanation of cases (i) and (iv). In both cases the tests are tests of *rules,* not of *particular acts.* (i) says that a rule requiring of people behavior harmful to themselves is, other things being equal, not a genuinely moral rule even if it belongs to the morality of a group. But this must not be confused with the question whether a particular act harmful to the agent and known to him to be so, is morally wrong. Such an *act* would be morally wrong only if this sort of act, whether harmful or not, or if harming oneself in any manner whatsoever, were *contrary* to a genuine moral rule of that group. But this is the opposite of the case we are considering, namely, the case of a rule *enjoining* (not forbidding) what is harmful to the agent. A rule which forbids what is harmful to the agent may, of course, belong to the morality of a group.

It is characteristic e.g. of bourgeois morality that certain types of prudent behavior are regarded as virtues (the observation of moral rules) and certain imprudent ones as vices (contrary to moral rules forbidding what is harmful to *oneself*), e.g. taking exercise, saving money, working hard, on the one hand, and smoking, drinking, neglecting one's health on the other. It is not clear whether these types of behavior are so regarded because they tend to be harmful or useful, respectively, to the agent, or because they usually also tend to be harmful or useful *to others.* In my opinion, it is only if they really are harmful to others that these lines of action can rightly be regarded as vices.

An analogous distinction must be borne in mind when considering case (iv): there I have mentioned as reason for saying that a *rule* is not genuinely moral that everyone's or many people's acting in accordance with it would be generally detrimental. This too, is quite different from saying that *a particular line of conduct* is wrong because everyone's or many people's doing this sort of thing would be generally detrimental. In the notorious "landlady argument," "You can't use the iron just whenever you like, Miss Thompson; what if everybody were to do that!," the imaginary "universalization" does not test an existing moral rule—no one thinks of the rule, Use the iron whenever you like, as a rule of our morality—rather, it is supposed to be a test of a particular line of action. Let us be quite clear about the difference.

Suppose that there is a power shortage and that it is widely held that restrictions would be necessary if the supply is not to break down.

Take first the case of a society in which there are no regulations to cope with this. The legislator may then consider the imposition of restrictions on the use of electric appliances. Among *his* reasons for *introducing* this sort of legislation could be our argument in case (iv), namely, that if everybody or many people were to continue using these appliances at all times, the power supply would break down. If this is true, then it would be an excellent reason for introducing this piece of legislation and, unless there were reasons against doing so, the legislator would be to some extent to blame if he failed to do so.

In the absence of such legislation there would seem to be two possibilities: either the case is already covered by a moral rule of the group or it is not. In the first case it would clearly be morally wrong to use any electric appliances extensively. I am entitled to do so only if I have a special reason, as when I am ill and must have a radiator going continuously. In this case, if I really know that my turning on the radiator will not make any difference to the power supply, my justification for not observing the moral rule gains weight.

It may, of course, be difficult to decide whether the case is already covered by a rule or principle belonging to the morality of a given group. There is no doubt, for instance, that our morality does not contain the specific rule "Do not use electric appliances for more than an hour a day," although it does or did contain other similarly specific rules, such as "It is wrong for women to have careers of their own" or "It is wrong for young girls to use make-up." But it is not quite so obvious that our morality does not contain the rule "It is morally wrong to do that the doing of which by everyone or very many people (but not by one alone) would be harmful," which would cover our case. It may be said that we do have this rule because it is simply a specific case under the principle of fairness and we do have the principle of fairness, which in one of its forms runs as follows: "Take no unfair advantage, that is to say, no advantage which, in the circumstances, it would be harmful to grant to anyone and everyone." That our morality contains this principle can be seen from the fact that words like "shirking," "malingering," "not pulling one's weight" on the one hand and "taking more than one's fair share" on the other have negative "moral tone." It seems, therefore, reasonably certain that our morality contains the principle of fairness and that the general rule covering our example is a special application of it. If this is right, then it would be wrong by our moral standards to use the radiator in periods of known power shortage, whether or not there is a specific regulation prohibiting such use.

It would take too long to consider whether there could be moralities that contained no rules covering our case, and what we would say in such cases (if there were any) about the question whether, in the absence of specific legislation forbidding the use of radiators, it would be morally wrong to use them in times of known power shortage. All that can be said is that even if in such a society it could not be *shown* to be wrong, it would still *be* wrong, if it is true that the rule of fairness *ought* to belong to any morality whatsoever and if our case is covered by that rule.

But now consider the case where the appropriate legislation has already been introduced. Then it is (*prima facie*) morally wrong to infringe this legislation, since any *bona fide* law or regulation has the moral backing. One may argue with the legislator about the need for such regulations, but as a citizen one must obey them while they are in force. The reason for this is not that if everyone used his radiator the power supply would break down, but simply that there is a *bona fide* regulation against it. A citizen can, of course, agitate for the repeal of any piece of legislation, but until then he must (other things being equal) obey them, whether he thinks them necessary or unnecessary, good or bad laws.

It is, therefore, simply irrelevant to this issue that my own use of the radiator will make little or no difference. It is wrong to turn it on, even if I know that, because everybody else is law-abiding, no one else will do so and that, therefore, my doing so will make no difference. It is wrong to turn it on even if I know that everybody else will do so and that, therefore, the power supply will break down anyway. I have an excuse for breaking the regulation, if I have a special overriding ground for doing so, as when I am ill and must have warmth, but even then I should try to get a permit to do so. Here again my knowledge (if I know) that my turning on the radiator will make no difference, gives added force to my excuse for breaking the regulations.

Of course, all this holds only for valid *bona fide* laws and regulations. That a law or regulation is valid is determined by legal tests; that it is *bona fide* is not a legal matter. If a law enjoins what is known to be immoral because contrary to a moral principle of the group, then the law is not *bona fide*. In this case it is morally wrong to obey the law unless the consequences of disobeying it are morally worse than the consequences of obeying it. If, on the other hand, a law is wilfully unnecessary, i.e. such that everyone can see plainly that the law is unnecessary, as would be the case with the possible law "No women must smoke in the street" or "No New Australians must be served intoxicating liquor," then neither obeying it nor disobeying it while trying to avoid being caught is morally wrong. But this applies only to plainly wilfully unnecessary laws or plain chicaneries. If a law is in fact unnecessary, but it is still a highly disputable question whether it is unnecessary or if it is unnecessary, but not at all plainly so, then the law must be regarded as *bona fide* and, therefore, as morally binding.

(*b*) A further condition that must be satisfied if a rule is to be said to be for the good of human beings is that it must not impose any *unnecessary restrictions*. "Don't eat beans" is a rule which is unsuitable for inclusion on this score.

(*c*) Lastly, a rule is for the good of human beings if it promotes the good of some people, provided it does not violate any of the other conditions, especially of unjustifiably and necessarily harming or tending to harm some people. "Be kind to others," "Give to charity," "Be generous," "Help your aged parents" and so on belong in this group.

Here again, the difference between the justification of individual acts and of rules should be noted. It is wrong not to look after one's aged parents because there is in our morality a rule to that effect, and this rule is rightly part of our morality because it promotes the good of certain people and prevents harm to which they are exposed in the special conditions of our society. If the aged were cared for by the state and the rule ceased to be part of our morality, then it would no longer be morally wrong not to assist one's aged parents, although it might still not be wrong or might even be meritorious to do so.

On the other hand, it is not morally wrong not to be generous because no rule of our morality makes generosity compulsory. Generosity is merely meritorious. Or rather, we mean by "generosity" that amount of assistance to others which goes beyond that which is compulsory. As our moral and economic standards rise, more and more in the way of mutual assistance is required of us as a matter of course. Generosity and charity begin after that.

Ad (D). We can now turn to our last approach towards the standards of criticism of a morality: the grading of various different moralities. We say of some moralities that they are higher or lower, more or less advanced, more or less primitive or civilized, more or less developed or evolved than others. What are the standards in accordance with which we grade these?

The most obvious method of weighing moralities is according to the proportion of genuine over spurious moral rules. This is not a matter of mere counting, for some rules are more important than others: the rule "Don't kill any human being" is much more important than the rule "Don't be grumpy."

But there are other methods. We have seen above (p. 117) [p. 254 this volume] that a group in order to be clearly said to have a morality must have rules governing the making of exceptions to moral rules. We have distinguished above two sets of such rules, those concerning discrimination between different sets of people, and those governing conflicts between moral rules. We have mentioned the most obvious such rules of our morality, but have said nothing about what are the correct principles that should govern them. For obviously it is particularly in these fields that one morality differs from another. Racial theories, class and caste systems, nationalism, and so on are phenomena in which differences of rules of discrimination play an important part.

Take first the rules of discrimination. These are based on one basic principle, that of non-discrimination, i.e., the principle that all rules *qua* moral apply to everyone alike. That is to say, a moral rule must not discriminate between people, i.e. differentiate between them on morally irrelevant grounds, where a morally relevant ground of differentiation is one which reveals differences of moral desert. The system of these grounds of differentiation rests on the principle of equality, that to begin with, all other things being equal, i.e. unless there are some specific grounds for differentiation, all moral rules must, therefore, be equally applied to all.

But what can we say are the *correct* principles in accordance with which a group *should* recognize grounds of differentiation? I think we can say that those are correct which themselves satisfy all the tests which a genuine moral rule must satisfy.

We do, for instance, distinguish between parents and others in respect of what they owe their children because we think it *for the good of human beings* that someone in particular should have the responsibility for the care of the young and we think it most natural and, in our social set-up, best that the parents should have this responsibility.

The same thing is true, *mutatis mutandis,* of the rules of priority. These, too, must pass all the tests for genuine moral rules. If they pass these tests, then they are not merely rules of priority belonging to our group morality, but genuine rules of moral priority.

One more point in this connection. We have seen reason to think that if a group did not have any rules of differentiation or priority or if those it had were totally different from, perhaps contrary to the best ones, we would have reason to doubt whether the group in question had a morality at all. On the other hand, it is not necessary that these rules of discrimination and priority should be exactly in accordance with the best ones. Here there is the possibility of a gradual approximation to the ideal. It has often been pointed out that in the history of mankind we find a gradual extension of the application of rules of morality first to ever larger groups and then to people outside any particular group. Christianity, by the introduction of the notion of Equality in the eyes of God, All men being the children of God, All men being brothers, and so on, has contributed much to this spread. But we do not deny that a group has a morality simply because it does not extend the application of its moral rules equally to everyone.

We can thus say that there are certain minimal requirements which must be fulfilled if the group is to be said to have a morality at all. If these are fulfilled, we speak of varying degrees of perfection of a morality, depending on the degree of approximation to a certain ideal.

This completes the answer to our main question. We have seen that "What shall I do?" is a moral question if and only if it is asked with a view to getting an answer that can stand up to certain complicated tests. We have seen what these tests are. We make sure first that the proposed course of action is not contrary to a moral rule of the agent's group, and secondly that, if it is, this rule is not a genuine moral rule. Concerning the first step, we have seen that every member of a group that can be said to have a morality is taught the rules belonging to that morality. I have mentioned tests for telling whether a given rule does or does not belong to the morality of one's group, and tests for telling whether a rule is genuinely moral. With this information it is possible to answer the moral question "What shall I do?" One has to rely on one's moral education for supplying the first answer to whether or not a proposed line of conduct is contrary to a moral rule of the group. If one has found a rule which one has been taught as a moral rule of the group and to which the proposed line of conduct is contrary, then one can, by applying the tests I have mentioned, make sure whether it is *really wrong*. It is really morally wrong if it is contrary to a rule which is really a rule belonging to the morality of the group and which is also genuinely moral. I have said nothing about the more difficult cases when the line of conduct is contrary to a moral rule belonging to the group which is not genuinely moral (e.g. "No sports on Sundays"), and the case when it is contrary to a genuinely moral rule which is not part of the morality of the agent's group (e.g. "Don't discriminate against Jews").

Finally, it should be noticed that "What shall I do?" is a moral question asked by a particular agent belonging to a particular group, and cannot be answered *in abstracto*. On the other hand, the critical testing of moralities is done by means of standards and against principles which are not tied to any group. "What shall I do?," when it is a moral question, is asked from within a culture, but it involves the asking and answering of questions which would be the same in any culture context whatsoever. But this does not mean that these questions would receive the same answers in every culture context. "Parents, not the State, must look after children" may be a genuinely moral rule in one society but not in another, although the principles in accordance with which this is settled are the same in both cases.

How simple-minded it is to look for the one feature that marks off *the* moral judgment or utterance from other sorts. The moral agent asks moral questions and answers them with a view to doing something. The moral critic asks and answers the question whether a particular agent has acted in accordance with or contrary to the moral rules of his society, with a view to judging his moral merit. The critic of a morality, on the other hand, asks and answers the question whether any of its rules are spurious, or whether any genuine moral rules are missing, or perhaps whether this morality is more or less advanced or civilized than certain others. The moral reformer "sees" that certain rules belonging to the morality of his group are not genuinely moral rules, or that certain rules which would be genuinely moral rules, if they were part, are not part of the morality of his group, and advocates the necessary reform. Here "intuition" is the proper word to use.

But while all these people busy with all these different tasks are employing moral terms, moral arguments, and moral reasons, while they all engage in moral talk, it is surely absurd to think that they are all uttering quasi-imperatives or are all expressing or arousing specific emotions or attitudes or feelings, or that they are all trying to persuade someone to change his attitudes, or to give him moral advice, or pass moral judgment on him. Surely, they are sometimes doing one, sometimes another of these things.

1955

The Rational Imperatives

C. I. Lewis

From the start of these brief investigations we have had it in mind, as one desideratum, to approach the subject of ethics. In so short a study we could not hope, of course, to touch upon anything beyond what is most fundamental for the morally right or even to include more than suggestion of the fundamentals. Ethics is a most complex subject, and any attempt to reduce it to simple terms would be ill-judged and doomed to failure. What we have hoped is that it might illuminate problems of the moral to compare this category of the right with others and with the right in general.

What we seem to find is that the right at large concerns activities which are corrigible and determinable by decision, and hence are subject to deliberation and to critical assessment. In its connotation of the deliberate and deliberable, the right exhibits essential connection with the peculiarly human character of our mentality as cognitive and reflective. No manner of behavior wholly untouched by thinking could be right or wrong; and it is only such thinking as is bent upon the determination of fact and has the intent of some objective reference which is subject to normative assessment.

Since it is only such doing as is amenable to deliberation which could be right or wrong, criticized doing presumes thinking which may itself be criticized, as well as criticism of that which is brought about in the light of such thinking. For doing to be

C. I. Lewis, "The Rational Imperatives" from THE GROUND AND NATURE OF THE RIGHTS (New York: Columbia University Press, 1955). Reprinted with the permission of the publishers.

right in the fullest sense—objectively right, as we have called it—the thinking which underlies it must be consistent and cogent; characterized by that objectivity and integrity which summons all pertinent evidence and gives all items their due weight in conclusions drawn, as well as conforming to logical requirements.

What is additionally involved in the criticism and the justification of doing, beyond rightness of the thinking in the light of which it is determined, lies in the fact that doing alters the world about us and has consequences, in a sense in which thinking, if it could be completely separated from any physical bringing about, would have no consequences but leave the external world as it found it and as it will otherwise become. And what has import of the criticizable in such doing concerns the consequences of it as good or bad. If it were not for the qualities of good and bad in life and our possible effect upon them, there would be no point in doing, and it is at least doubtful that there would be any point in objective thinking. Broadly and loosely speaking, to do that the consequences of which are justifiably expected to be good rather than bad, is the objectively right way to act; and doing that which justified belief would indicate to have bad consequences rather than good, is the objectively wrong way to act. But the right and wrong in action are not determinable, simply and directly, by reference to good or bad consequences, because of the fact—amongst others—that what is justifiably believed may still be false, and what is justifiably disbelieved may still be true.

It is further pertinent to right and wrong that it is only *ways* of thinking and of doing which we can learn how to direct or govern, since it is only what characterizes more than one instance of activity which can be learned, or directed by any manner of knowing how. Activity is directable only as it answers to some generality, represents some mode, and hence is amenable to some formulatable rule of procedure. Consonantly all activities, in being criticizable only as governable modes of our self-direction, are likewise criticizable by reference to formulatable directives. It is by reference to such implicit or explicit directives of doing—directives themselves determined with included reference to the good or bad results of conforming to them—that right and wrong in doing are finally determinable.

The main modes in which the right or wrong of doing is assessed are the technical, the prudential, and that of justice as adjudged in the light of predictable consequences to all who are affected.

The technical critiques are the simplest, since they assume some species of desirable results, and presume this general desirability of them as antecedently determined fact. Thus a technical critique is critical of activity only in its relation to some such class of ends assumed as justifying that which will lead to realization of them. Its directives are the product of past experience indicating those modes of governing the technical activity which will, most reliably, produce such desirable, as against undesirable, results. The rightness of the directives themselves derives from this presumed goodness of the results and the reliability of achieving such results by following these directives, or from the unjustified character of expecting such good results if they are not heeded. Any imperativeness attaching to the technical rules is a matter of "if, as, and when"—if, as, and when the presumption that activity directed to the technical end is an otherwise justified decision of doing or choice of what to do. Kant called them hypothetical imperatives; and the sense in which that is appropriate will be evident.

However, as we noticed earlier, there is a kind of qualification to be observed here, especially if the term "technical" be extended to practice of the arts and professions. Such practice affects ends which are wider than the technical and is, so far forth, subject to criticism on moral grounds rather than on grounds relating to technical excellence or shortcoming. It is so that medical ethics is well-named; and the similar point is to be observed in the code governing the relation of the attorney to his clients, to his professional brethren, and to the courts. Such moral precepts as are peculiarly pertinent to the practice of a vocation may be collated with the critique of it as technically right or wrong but, strictly, they do not represent a part of the technical critique.

The prudential critique and the rules of prudence could be dealt with in the same manner as the technical: regardless of further considerations, one could surely say that determination of action by directives conformity to which will, as men have learned, reliably conduce to achievement of the doer's own good, is imperative if, as, and when the direction of action to this prudential end is an otherwise justified decision of what to do. And Kant so dealt with prudence, subsuming prudential rules and the prudential imperative under the hypothetical. But the prudential end, as he acknowledged, is happiness, the sum of all that men desire. And that concern, unlike any technical aim, is always with us and likely to be affected by any act whatever. Since any hypothetical directive becomes categorical when the "if" of it is satisfied, the prudential directives, whose "if" is that of wanting to be happy, have a force of "always" rather than of "when." In that sense, the prudential imperative is categorical rather than hypothetical. What Kant meant to insist upon is, of course, that although the prudential end is always desired, action by reference to it is far from being always justified, because the aim of prudence can be and should be overruled by that of justice when the two dictates are incompatible.

Granting, however, that justice has the precedent claim on action, there is still a further point of first importance. No concrete act can be so dictated by justice as to leave no feature of it undetermined and no remaining alternative of detail to be governed by prudence. I ought to pay my bill and satisfy my creditor; but payment by check or cash, today or the first of next month, may satisfy his just claim, and allow me justly to determine these alternatives by reference to any prudential consideration which may affect them. It lies in the fact that what any directive of right action will dictate is only a way of acting, and not some utterly specific doing, that prudence and justice, or any two diverse ends or grounds of right decision, may be coincidentally involved and be in whole or in part compatible. Furthermore, even when prudence is overruled, it still remains a valid concern, justly to be respected even though subordinated. As directive of such respect, the force of the prudential imperative, reflecting a pervasive and continuing concern, extends to every decision of action it could affect.

It is a shortcoming in ethics if the moralist, thinking to have elicited that overriding imperative to which any other must give way, forthwith dismisses directives of the right which are thus to be subordinated as if they had, in consequence, no significance for moral decisions of action and no import of the right and justified to do. It is even questionable to delimit the subject of morals by reference to any such categorical imperative which takes precedence. The total problem of right doing in any case, is of the same force and weight in all its parts; and to single out any one aspect as the moral import of it, and dismiss another aspect of the required decision as not a moral consideration, can be a prejudicial use of language. When it is not the whole of the specific act which need be dominated by the ruling requirement, the satisfaction of any which is subordinate remains as a valid demand of right doing calling for consideration in the decision to be taken. An act which is just to others but heedless of prudence is only partway justified and is a wrong way to act.

There is, moreover, a relation between prudence and justice by reason of which it is fair to say that justice presupposes validity of the prudential aim. Without individual interests there could be no group or social interests, and without the validity of self-interests, no validity of any social interest. Society, as Herbert Spencer observed, has no central consciousness and can enjoy or suffer only in the persons of its members. All social categories are derivative—which is not to deny that they are distinct. Furthermore, justice is not to be confused with altruism. If justice requires giving weight to the interest of another equally as to one's own, that equation is also reversible and requires that one's own interest be weighed equally with that of any other. I would not say that benevolence beyond the call of justice has no sanction. There are goods of benevolence which may accrue to the benevolent individual himself. He may identify his own good with the good of those he serves, and find in that a deep self-interest. On that point, I would express my impressment with the ethics of self-realization. But the man of good will beyond the limit of obligation makes a gift, and it is to be appreciated as such and not construed as a requirement of the moral.

Our remaining questions are principally two: first, that concerning any sanction of justice by which it may override a prudential aim which conflicts; and second, observing that determination of the right turns upon such rules or principles only as are *valid,* the question what distinguishes valid principles, genuinely imperative to heed, from directives which are not thus valid. To ask this second question is, of course, to ask for the *ground* of such validity.

I would here discuss these two together, because it appears to me that the sanction of justice is the most obscure of all questions of ethics and that any illumination of it through consideration of the ground of right in general, if that be possible, would be a welcome kind of help.

Time out of mind, men have sought to find and demonstrate an ultimate ground of the right. But the right is *sui generis:* if the formulation of it be a kind of fact, still it is fact of a kind which is like no other; and what is right cannot be proved right by summoning premises which themselves say nothing about right and wrong. If there are any first principles of right, or first principles of the various categories of the right—and it is, of course, such first or most comprehensive principles which we should seek—it lies in the nature of the case that the validity of them will be indemonstrable. How prove valid the most general of all formulations of any given sort?

How, for example, should we prove any principles of logic which are basic and comprehensive enough to stand as first? We cannot derive statements of the logical from premises which themselves say nothing about the logical. And if, *per impossible,* we could, we should still beg principles of logic as the only possible ground of correctness in this inference we make. Proof of a conclusion in logic calls not only for some assured premises of logic but also for demonstration of correctness in the proving. And proof of that kind of correctness can only be by appeal to logical principles, antecedently assured.

Or consider the question of demonstrating to a convinced Cynic the validity of the prudential aim so to act as to maximize the goodness realizable in a whole lifetime; or of proving this to one who holds the Benthamite principle of part-way prudence and is convinced that goods which are equally certain but more remote should weigh less heavily than nearer ones. We may truly say to one who flouts our correct principle of prudence, "You will be sorry someday"; but suppose he should answer, "So what? I'll be sorry when I get to it, but right now I'm having fun." We should be thrust back upon calling him perverse, silly, irrational; and these names would be appropriate, but they have no force of demonstration. Any attempt to induce recognition of principles of right as valid, can only appeal to some antecedent sense of such rightness which will, at some point, constrain any reasonable person to acknowledge them.

The ground of validity of imperatives must somehow lie in our human nature. Human nature calls for principles of right decision. The necessity of that acknowledgment, if it should be challenged, must lie finally in the fact that to decide is unavoidable.

Refusal to decide would be itself a decision. And one who in deciding should say, "I recognize no principles binding my decision," could be answered: "Let us be clear; just now you repudiate all principles, but that, I suppose, is only for the moment. Or do you repudiate principles, not by momentary whim, but as a matter of principle? Do you mean to make it a *principle* to have no principles?" He who adopts an active attitude constrains himself for the future. He who believes as true commits himself to continued belief so long as evidence remains the same, or otherwise, to acknowledge himself at fault in his belief. Consistency is first of attitude and prepared manner of response, and resistance to any changing whim of wishful thinking. The root of logic itself lies in the fact of decision, and decision as constraint upon future attitude.

Not only must we decide, and in decision find ourselves bound, but we must decide for some assignable reason. To decide but with no reason at all for so deciding, would be utterly to lose face with ourselves. That we must decide, and for a reason, is a distinctive feature of our human mentality. If we would put it in biological terms, we may observe that, having evolutionally outgrown exclusive government of our behavior by automatic response to stimuli and the way they make us feel, we are obliged to govern our doing, in part at least, by our thinking.

All thinking and, in consequence, all thoughtfully determined doing, exhibits two characteristics which are fundamental to the nature of it, namely, generality and objectivity. As we have already observed, generality is requisite because all learning and all knowing or knowing-how involves responding to a new and present situation in a manner reflective of the character of past like cases. Even the conditioned response of animals turns on that. And when thinking in part replaces such automatic response, it must still be general ways of thinking and ways of doing which we shall command and which will represent the modes in which any self-government is exercised. We must govern ourselves in definite ways which some elicitable rule could formulate.

What I would designate as objectivity is a character required by the fact that we live in time and the fact that it is the future only which can be affected—what is future in its impact on us, if not future in the occurrence of it. Thought and action are bent upon the future, to which alone any government or self-government can extend. That to which we must adapt is not immediate but something possible or to come and, so far as any activity is pertinent, possible to influence—possible to secure, to avert, to modify, or to prepare ourselves to meet. In our thinking, we must be impressed by something absent from the sensuously here and now and "realize" it as it will be when it comes. We must believe in what is not present but merely represented. And in our doing, we must respond to what is not felt but representationally intimated as we should respond if it were given with the poignancy of here and now. Only thus may we think as we shall later be satisfied to have thought and act so that later we shall not be sorry. However, to respond in this manner—directing ourselves to what is not immediate but with the same concern which we should have if we were immediately affected by it—requires on occasion some overriding of our animalish feeling which incites us to respond according to sensuous impact or emotive drive. That is the root of our sense of required constraint and of the imperative. And that is what is involved in our assignment of a reason for thinking or for deliberate doing. Our determination of the fact of what is absent from experience now, is what lies at the root of our reasoning. And our response governed by reference to non-immediate factualities, is our reasonable doing. To weigh the absent but represented in the *full-size* of it, and not in the measure of any presentational or emotive feeling which serves to intimate it, is to be objective. And to weigh it only in the measure of its immediate intimation as a present feeling, is to be subjective.

It is by reference to such objectivity in thought and action that, time out of mind, men have spoken of themselves as rational. And I see no reason to seek a different name for this distinctive feature of the human mentality. On this point, however, we have lived for two thousand years by ancient insights embedded in the idiom of our language; and in the process we may have come to substitute repetition of the familiar word for that self-understanding which the word was framed to convey. Perhaps it is time to replace the worn-out word by renewed grasp of the insight, and in terms which, conceivably, may better suit the context of the present. One thing we may need to observe is that the connotation of "reason" and "rationality" is not exclusively a reference to reasoning and valid inference. Correct inferring is only one side of this distinctive character of our mentality; only one aspect of being reasonable. A reason is a *consideration which justifies:* to have a sufficient reason for believing or for doing is to be justified in so deciding, and to have no reason is to be unjustified and non-rational or irrational.[1] It is recognition of imperatives as rational precepts which is the most general implication of human self-direction and self-constraint.

Let us try to suggest what lies at the root of all the imperatives of our thinking and doing as the Law of Objectivity: So conduct and determine your activities of thinking and of doing, as to conform any decision of them to the objective actualities, as cognitively signified to you in your representational apprehension of them, and not according to any impulsion or solicitation exercised by the affective quality of your present experience as immediate feeling merely.

Since so much of what should be decisive of thinking and of action concerns the future, let us add a corollary: Conduct yourself, with reference to those future eventualities which cognition advises that your activity may affect, as you would if these predictable effects of it were to be realized, at this moment of decision, with the poignancy of the here and now, instead of the less poignant feeling which representation of the future and possible may automatically arouse.

Does this Law of Objectivity have bearing upon that last and most difficult question concerning justice to others, and the sanction of it as imperative? In this connection, we may do well to remember that the distinctively human mentality and the potentialities of it are hardly to be well observed if examination be restricted to the human animal as an individual organism merely. That of which man is capable, by reason of his peculiar endowment, can only be fully discovered by observation of him in society and in the history of the civilization he creates. Man is the only animal which *has* a history, the only species whose history is modified by his apprehension of it. Individuals of other species each begin where the preceding generation began, and their behavior is modifiable only by what they individually experience. But the generations of men begin where the preceding generation left off, profiting by the cumulative social recollection of what past generations have suffered and achieved. It is a basic consideration for the valid imperatives of individual human action, that the possibility of that kind of evolution which man alone exhibits, and of that progressive amelioration and enrichment of individual life found only in the human species, is conditional upon the modification of individual behavior by social agencies. Indeed it requires modification of the individual mentality itself, as to its grasp and content, as an effect of social relations—relationships which themselves similarly evolve, and whose evolution is by the same instrumentalities. The peculiarly human kind of life is

[1]It may appear that "reason" in the sense of "a reason" has, as a second and unrelated meaning, the significance of "consideration which *explains,*" either as cause or as law. Let us note, however, that whatever explains provides a ground for crediting as veridical—believing—in case of doubt. We trust an apprehension which might otherwise be dubious in measure as we find, e.g., a known cause of phenomena of the type in question which accords with laws which are known.

That feature which is common to all senses of "reason" is connotation of subsumption of the individual case, or the particular, under some generality.

imperatively social. That fact is a datum for ethics. To do justice to that topic would need a book—and books have, of course, been devoted to it.

The basic imperative for individuals in their relations to one another, is simply the socially significant counterpart of what we have observed already: the dictate to govern one's activities affecting other persons, as one would if these effects of them were to be realized with the poignancy of the immediate—hence, in one's own person. The dictate is to respect other persons as the realities we representationally recognize them to be—as creatures whose gratifications and griefs have the same poignant factuality as our own; and as creatures who, like ourselves, find it imperative to govern themselves in the light of the cognitive apprehensions vouchsafed to them, by decisions which they themselves reach, and by reference to values discoverable to them.

Perhaps we should divide this most general of moral principles into two. It has one part which turns only upon recognition of other creatures as being, like ourselves, subject to enjoyment and suffering. The dictate so derived may be called the Law of Compassion. And this same general principle of objectivity has another part or bearing which is relevant only in the case of other creatures who are like us also in their cognitive capacities and, in consequence, in the necessity of governing their own behavior by deliberation, and of acting under constraint of the imperatives of rationality. The dictate which is correlative here, we may call the Law of Moral Equality.

It is plain that the Law of Compassion extends not only to other humans but to all conscious beings in measure of that sentience we attribute to them as the capacity to find their experience satisfying or feel pain. Indeed this dictate of compassion is peculiarly in point in relation to those who are not our peers, but may lie within our power to help or harm in ways in which they cannot equally help themselves, or defend themselves against our intentions toward them. It applies to our conduct toward the lower animals. And it is also pertinent whenever our doing may affect humans who do not so fully realize the powers latent in human nature, and in those circumstances in which normal individuals may still not be able to exercise their normal capacities to the full. Again, and obviously, it applies to our conduct toward the immature, whose capacities have not yet fully ripened and been trained by the experience of life. This Law of Compassion must, I think, remain as an indeterminate duty to respect all conscious life for what it is, insofar as we are able to discern the nature of it as sentient. The question so involved whether every creature that enjoys and suffers, and not humans only, is so far an end in itself, is an infrequent topic in Western ethics. I shall not attempt elaboration of it here, or formulation of the law itself except as a general obligation: Recognize, in your action affecting any sentient being, that claim on your compassion which comports with its capacity to enjoy and suffer. Perhaps we shall agree at least that it is imperative, in any connection, to cause no useless pain.

The Law of Moral Equality shows, in some sense, the obverse of the Law of Compassion. It is peculiarly relevant to moral dealing with our full peers, and dictates respect for others not only as ends in themselves but as entitled to full self-determination of their individual action, to some privacy of decision, and to freedom from coercion in their decisions taken, so long as they bring no harm to others and accord to others a like freedom. But the morally more important implication lies in the fact that this Law of Moral Equality is likewise the principle of Equality before the Moral Law; the law that there shall be no law for one which is not law for all. This principle has joint implication with the fact that all self-government is government of *ways* of acting and by reference to statable rule. Both respect for others as our peers in self-determination under recognized imperatives, and the fact that self-determination can be exercised only by reference to some generality formulatable as a directive, have the consequence that no precept is valid and no mode of action is justified except as it is valid in the case of others as in our own. No manner of thought or action is valid for any of us except as, in the same premises of circumstance and evidenced fact, it is valid for all of us. This, be it noted, covers omissions to do as well as doing, since a decision not to do is a decision of action.

I regret to think that, for accuracy, this principle of Equality before the Moral Law must be stated in terms which will sound pedantic: Take no decision of action which is member of any class of decisions of doing all members of which you would call upon others to avoid. That is, I think, the intent of recognizing our own acts as right to do toward others only if we likewise acknowledge them as right when done to us. The particular points here are two: first, that rightness under rule is a matter of the classification or modes of acts; and second, that an act is right only if it falls in no class interdicted by rule. It is not sufficient that it exhibit *some* justifiable mode of action—be classified as doing of *some* sort, or acting in *some* way, which is morally permissible. What is essential is that it *not* be doing of *any* sort or acting in *any* way which is morally forbidden.

Our pedantic manner of formulation is dictated for the avoidance of two difficulties. First, there is the difficulty that a specious moralizer or a fanatic may elevate his selfish preference or one-sided interest to the status of a moral precept if allowed to do so on the ground of *his* willingness to see some mode of action universally permitted or made universally mandatory. Employers might so be free to accept it as a universal precept that wages paid should be minimal; and employees, that profits should be nil. And every bigot, content to see his particular bigotry become universal, could so justify himself in uninhibited imposition of it on others. But paying minimal wages is *also* imposing near-starvation; elimination of profits is *also* expropriation of the fruits of individual labor and saving; and the imposition of any bigotry is *also* the imposition of private opinion on others—ways of acting which no employer, no employee, and no bigot could be content to see become universal.

Second, and somewhat similarly, our mode of formulation avoids those too easy generalizations often found as maxims but untrustworthy if applied without commonsense qualification, and hence dangerous in the hands of the injudicious or of puritanical rigorists. The classic examples are "Tell no lies" and "Do not steal" which, though hardly to be excelled for moral guidance in common practice, are out of place in dealing with madmen bent on murder.

No rule of action can do more than divide all acts to which it could find application into two subclasses; those which, under this rule, are permissible, and those which contravene it and are impermissible. But an act is wrong if it contravenes *any* rule of right doing. And it is right only if it contravenes *no* rule of right doing. An act is wrong if it is wrong in *any* way; is any wrong way of acting. And it is right only if it is right in *every* way; if it is an act which in all respects is right to do. But if it be said that there are rules which categorically oblige some act, in all its particulars, then the answer is simply that this is not so. If it be a categorical moral command to pay our debts, what it commands is, "Choose *some* act, *some* way of acting, which will liquidate your debt." It is of some importance to observe that even the moral law leaves those who lie under its command some freedom of moral choice. Thus, logically viewed, the significance of "Do right" is "Do no wrong"; "Do nothing you would call upon others universally to avoid."

These principles, we may think, are basic for ethics. But lest the impression should have been given that, on the ground of them alone, we could straightway proceed to solution of all the major ethical problems, let us barely mention one such problem—or nest of problems—which we should encounter soon.

The Law of Moral Equality does not delineate the *content* of justice. For that, there are further facts of our common human nature which must be adduced, and further principles also which are hardly immediate inferences from those we have considered. For instance, the egoist as well as the social utilitarian can plausibly claim conformity to the principle of Equality under the Moral Law. In claiming prudence as the solely valid sanction for decisions of his own action, he likewise recognizes the moral correctness of others in so deciding theirs. He claims that egoistic conduct is *just*. If there is a basic principle of morals which he affronts, it is the Law of Compassion. But a Bentham or a Hume would be sure to counter by the observation that compassion is a native human propensity and as rational and "selfish" to indulge in as any other. It is more plausible to suppose that universal egoism is contraindicated by the egoist's misapprehensions concerning the possibilities of a good life for anybody under conditions of uninhibited egoism. On that point, Hobbes seems more convincing; in such a state of nature life would be "nasty, brutish, and short."

But on the other hand, would life in a society of perfect altruists afford optimum conditions for individual happiness? Not, I should suppose, in view of our actual human nature. One of the major goods of life is liberty to decide private matters on private grounds, without paternalistic oversight, and with the privilege of making our own mistakes. We even—most of us—cherish some privilege of competition with our fellows, within the bounds of our over-all social cooperation; and we think that allowance, or even encouragement, of certain modes of competition is essential to progress and conducive to the general welfare. But a mode of activity is competitive only insofar as individual prudential ends are put in front of any equal consideration of the good of others affected, and only so far as the success of one participant or party militates against the like success of others.

The content of social justice, it is suggested, requires to be determined in view of additional premises concerning human nature and human good which are empirical generalizations rather than principles of the type so far cited. There may be also, contained in such considerations, the suggestion that any positive ethics may find itself in like case on other points. In particular, it may be suggested that the grounds of the cooperation of individuals in society, for the sake of the common good, and the ground on which dictates essential to the maintenance of effective cooperation are imperatives for individual conduct, would be among the problems to be so probed.

If, in conclusion, we look briefly to the general character of any ethic which should conform to the general conclusions here reached, we may observe that it would be of that type usually called naturalistic, so far as it is classified by reference to the thesis that no act can be determined as right or wrong without reference to consequences of it as good or bad. Also, it would be naturalistic in its interpretation of good and bad as matters of empirical fact and as significant, at bottom, of naturally found qualities of experience. It would, however, have a character frequently taken to be antithetic to naturalism; namely, in the thesis that right and wrong are nevertheless indeterminable except by reference of rules or principles—principles themselves including reference to the good or bad as essential to determining what specifically they dictate. It would likewise be liable to classification as antithetic to naturalism in its conclusion that these imperatives of right, and the validity of them, have no other determinable and final ground than that character of human nature by which it is called rational. However, if a view incorporating both sets of these features can be consistently maintained, then what so appears is that ethical naturalism and ethical rationalism (if "rationalism" is the right word here) are not in fact antithetic but complementary. Perhaps they are antithetic only for a naturalism which connotes nature short of human nature, or for a rationalism which interprets rationality as non-natural and significant of some transcendent world.

1955

Two Concepts of Rules

John Rawls

In this paper[1] I want to show the importance of the distinction between justifying a practice[2] and justifying a particular action falling under it, and I want to explain the logical basis of this distinction and how it is possible to miss its significance. While the distinction has frequently been made,[3] and is now becoming commonplace, there remains the task of explaining the tendency either to overlook it altogether, or to fail to appreciate its importance.

To show the importance of the distinction I am going to defend utilitarianism against those objections which have traditionally been made against it in connection with punishment and the obligation to keep promises. I hope to show that if one uses the distinction in question then one can state utilitarianism in a way which makes it a much

[1]This is a revision of a paper given at the Harvard Philosophy Club on April 30, 1954. . . .

[2]I use the word "practice" throughout as a sort of technical term meaning any form of activity specified by a system of rules which defines offices, roles, moves, penalties, defenses, and so on, and which gives the activity its structure. As examples one may think of games and rituals, trials and parliaments.

[3]The distinction is central to Hume's discussion of justice in *A Treatise of Human Nature,* Bk. III, pt. II, esp. secs. 2–4. It is clearly stated by John Austin in the second lecture of *Lectures on Jurisprudence* (4th ed.; London, 1873), i, 116ff. (1st ed., 1832). Also it may be argued that J. S. Mill took it for granted in *Utilitarianism;* on this point cf. J. O. Urmson, "The Interpretation of the Moral Philosophy of J. S. Mill," *Philosophical Quarterly,* vol. iii (1953). In addition to the arguments given by Urmson there are several clear statements of the distinction in *A System of Logic* (8th ed.; London, 1872), Bk. VI, ch. xii pars. 2, 3, 7. The

better explication of our considered moral judgments than traditional objections would seem to admit.[4] Thus the importance of the distinction is shown by the way it strengthens the utilitarian view regardless of whether that view is completely defensible or not.

To explain how the significance of the distinction may be overlooked, I am going to discuss two conceptions of rules. One of these conceptions conceals the importance of distinguishing between the justification of a rule or practice and the justification of a particular action falling under it. The other conception makes it clear why this distinction must be made and what is its logical basis.

1

The subject of punishment, in the sense of attaching legal penalties to the violation of legal rules, has always been a troubling moral question.[5] The trouble about it has not been that people disagree as to whether or not punishment is justifiable. Most people have held that, freed from certain abuses, it is an acceptable institution. Only a few have rejected punishment entirely, which is rather surprising when one considers all that can be said against it. The difficulty is with the justification of punishment: various arguments for it have been given by moral philosophers, but so far none of them has won any sort of general acceptance; no justification is without those who detest it. I hope to show that the use of the aforementioned distinction enables one to state the utilitarian view in a way which allows for the sound points of its critics.

For our purposes we may say that there are two justifications of punishment. What we may call the retributive view is that punishment is justified on the grounds that wrongdoing merits punishment. It is morally fitting that a person who does wrong should suffer in proportion to his wrongdoing. That a criminal should be punished follows from his guilt, and the severity of the appropriate punishment depends on the depravity of his act. The state of affairs where a wrongdoer suffers punishment is morally better than the state of affairs where he does not; and it is better irrespective of any of the consequences of punishing him.

What we may call the utilitarian view holds that on the principle that bygones are bygones and that only future consequences are material to present decisions, punishment is justifiable only by reference to the probable consequences of maintaining it as one of the devices of the social order. Wrongs committed in the past are, as such, not relevant considerations for deciding what to do. If punishment can be shown to promote effectively the interest of society it is justifiable, otherwise it is not.

I have stated these two competing views very roughly to make one feel the conflict between them: one feels the force of *both* arguments and one wonders how they

---

distinction is fundamental to J. D. Mabbott's important paper, "Punishment," *Mind*, n.s., vol. xlviii (April, 1939). More recently the distinction has been stated with particular emphasis by S. E. Toulmin in *The Place of Reason in Ethics* (Cambridge, 1950), see esp. ch. xi, where it plays a major part in his account of moral reasoning. Toulmin doesn't explain the basis of the distinction, nor how one might overlook its importance, as I try to in this paper, and in my review of his book (*Philosophical Review*, vol. lx [October, 1951]) as some of my criticisms show, I failed to understand the force of it. See also H. D. Aiken, "The Levels of Moral Discourse," *Ethics*, vol. lxii (1952); A. M. Quinton, "Punishment," *Analysis*, vol. xiv (June, 1954); and P. H. Nowell-Smith, *Ethics* (London, 1954), pp. 236–239, 271–273.

[4]On the concept of explication see the author's paper, *Philosophical Review*, vol. lx (April, 1951).

[5]While this paper was being revised, Quinton's appeared; footnote 3 supra. There are several respects in which my remarks are similar to his. Yet as I consider some further questions and rely on somewhat different arguments, I have retained the discussion of punishment and promises together as two test cases for utilitarianism.

can be reconciled. From my introductory remarks it is obvious that the resolution which I am going to propose is that in this case one must distinguish between justifying a practice as a system of rules to be applied and enforced, and justifying a particular action which falls under these rules; utilitarian arguments are appropriate with regard to questions about practices, while retributive arguments fit the application of particular rules to particular cases.

We might try to get clear about this distinction by imagining how a father might answer the question of his son. Suppose the son asks, "Why was *J* put in jail yesterday?" The father answers, "Because he robbed the bank at *B*. He was duly tried and found guilty. That's why he was put in jail yesterday." But suppose the son had asked a different question, namely, "Why do people put other people in jail?" Then the father might answer, "To protect good people from bad people" or "To stop people from doing things that would make it uneasy for all of us; for otherwise we wouldn't be able to go to bed at night and sleep in peace." There are two very different questions here. One question emphasizes the proper name: it asks why *J* was punished rather than someone else, or it asks what he was punished for. The other question asks why we have the institution of punishment: why do people punish one another rather than, say, always forgiving one another?

Thus the father says in effect that a particular man is punished, rather than some other man, because he is guilty, and he is guilty because he broke the law (past tense). In his case the law looks back, the judge looks back, the jury looks back, and a penalty is visited upon him for something he did. That a man is to be punished, and what his punishment is to be, is settled by its being shown that he broke the law and that the law assigns that penalty for the violation of it.

On the other hand we have the institution of punishment itself, and recommend and accept various changes in it, because it is thought by the (ideal) legislator and by those to whom the law applies that, as a part of a system of law impartially applied from case to case arising under it, it will have the consequence, in the long run, of furthering the interests of society.

One can say, then, that the judge and the legislator stand in different positions and look in different directions: one to the past, the other to the future. The justification of what the judge does, *qua* judge, sounds like the retributive view; the justification of what the (ideal) legislator does, *qua* legislator, sounds like the utilitarian view. Thus both views have a point (this is as it should be since intelligent and sensitive persons have been on both sides of the argument); and one's initial confusion disappears once one sees that these views apply to persons holding different offices with different duties, and situated differently with respect to the system of rules that make up the criminal law.[6]

One might say, however, that the utilitarian view is more fundamental since it applies to a more fundamental office, for the judge carries out the legislator's will so far as he can determine it. Once the legislator decides to have laws and to assign penalties for their violation (as things are there must be both the law and the penalty) an institution is set up which involves a retributive conception of particular cases. It is part of the concept of the criminal law as a system of rules that the application and enforcement of these rules in particular cases should be justifiable by arguments of a retributive character. The decision whether or not to use law rather than some other mechanism of social control, and the decision as to what laws to have and what penalties to assign, may

[6]Note the fact that different sorts of arguments are suited to different offices. One way of taking the differences between ethical theories is to regard them as accounts of the reasons expected in different offices.

be settled by utilitarian arguments; but if one decides to have laws then one has decided on something whose working in particular cases is retributive in form.[7]

The answer, then, to the confusion engendered by the two views of punishment is quite simple: one distinguishes two offices, that of the judge and that of the legislator, and one distinguishes their different stations with respect to the system of rules which make up the law; and then one notes that the different sorts of considerations which would usually be offered as reasons for what is done under the cover of these offices can be paired off with the competing justifications of punishment. One reconciles the two views by the time-honored device of making them apply to different situations.

But can it really be this simple? Well, this answer allows for the apparent intent of each side. Does a person who advocates the retributive view necessarily advocate, as an *institution,* legal machinery whose essential purpose is to set up and preserve a correspondence between moral turpitude and suffering? Surely not.[8] What retributionists have rightly insisted upon is that no man can be punished unless he is guilty, that is, unless he has broken the law. Their fundamental criticism of the utilitarian account is that, as they interpret it, it sanctions an innocent person's being punished (if one may call it that) for the benefit of society.

On the other hand, utilitarians agree that punishment is to be inflicted only for the violation of law. They regard this much as understood from the concept of punishment itself.[9] The point of the utilitarian account concerns the institution as a system of rules: utilitarianism seeks to limit its use by declaring it justifiable only if it can be shown to foster effectively the good of society. Historically it is a protest against the indiscriminate and ineffective use of the criminal law.[10] It seeks to dissuade us from assigning to penal institutions the improper, if not sacrilegious, task of matching suffering with moral turpitude. Like others, utilitarians want penal institutions designed so that, as far as humanly possible, only those who break the law run afoul of it. They hold that no official should have discretionary power to inflict penalties whenever he thinks it for the benefit of society; for on utilitarian grounds an institution granting such power could not be justified.[11]

The suggested way of reconciling the retributive and the utilitarian justifications of punishment seems to account for what both sides have wanted to say. There are, however, two further questions which arise, and I shall devote the remainder of this section to them.

[7]In this connection see Mabbott, op. cit., pp. 163–164.

[8]On this point see Sir David Ross, *The Right and the Good* (Oxford, 1930), pp. 57–60.

[9]See Hobbes's definition of punishment in *Leviathan,* ch. xxviii; and Bentham's definition in *The Principle of Morals and Legislation,* ch. xii, par. 36, ch. xv, par. 28, and in *The Rationale of Punishment* (London, 1830), Bk. I, ch. i. They could agree with Bradley that: "Punishment is punishment only when it is deserved. We pay the penalty, because we owe it, and for no other reason; and if punishment is inflicted for any other reason whatever than because it is merited by wrong, it is a gross immorality, a crying injustice, an abominable crime, and not what it pretends to be." *Ethical Studies* (2nd ed.; Oxford, 1927), pp. 26–27. Certainly by definition it isn't what it pretends to be. The innocent can only be punished by mistake; deliberate "punishment" of the innocent necessarily involves fraud.

[10]Cf. Leon Radzinowicz, *A History of English Criminal Law: The Movement for Reform 1750–1833* (London, 1948), esp. ch. xi on Bentham.

[11]Bentham discusses how corresponding to a punitory provision of a criminal law there is another provision which stands to it as an antagonist and which needs a name as much as the punitory. He calls it, as one might expect, the *anaetiosostic*, and of it he says: "The punishment of guilt is the object of the former one: the preservation of innocence that of the latter." In the same connection he asserts that it is never thought fit to give the judge the option of deciding whether a thief (that is, a person whom he believes to be a thief, for the judge's belief is what the question must always turn upon) should hang or not, and so the law writes the provision: "The judge shall not cause a thief to be hanged unless he have been duly convicted and sentenced in course of law" (*The Limits of Jurisprudence Defined,* ed. C. W. Everett [New York, 1945], pp. 238–239).

First, will not a difference of opinion as to the proper criterion of just law make the proposed reconciliation unacceptable to retributionists? Will they not question whether, if the utilitarian principle is used as the criterion, it follows that those who have broken the law are guilty in a way which satisfies their demand that those punished deserve to be punished? To answer this difficulty, suppose that the rules of the criminal law are justified on utilitarian grounds (it is only for laws that meet his criterion that the utilitarian can be held responsible). Then it follows that the actions which the criminal law specifies as offenses are such that, if they were tolerated, terror and alarm would spread in society. Consequently, retributionists can only deny that those who are punished deserve to be punished if they deny that such actions are wrong. This they will not want to do.

The second question is whether utilitarianism doesn't justify too much. One pictures it as an engine of justification which, if consistently adopted, could be used to justify cruel and arbitrary institutions. Retributionists may be supposed to concede that utilitarians *intend* to reform the law and to make it more humane; that utilitarians do not *wish* to justify any such thing as punishment of the innocent; and that utilitarians may appeal to the fact that punishment presupposes guilt in the sense that by punishment one understands an institution attaching penalties to the infraction of legal rules, and therefore that it is logically absurd to suppose that utilitarians in justifying *punishment* might also have justified punishment (if we may call it that) of the innocent. The real question, however, is whether the utilitarian, in justifying punishment, hasn't used arguments which commit him to accepting the infliction of suffering on innocent persons if it is for the good of society (whether or not one calls this punishment). More generally, isn't the utilitarian committed in principle to accepting many practices which he, as a morally sensitive person, wouldn't want to accept? Retributionists are inclined to hold that there is no way to stop the utilitarian principle from justifying too much except by adding to it a principle which distributes certain rights to individuals. Then the amended criterion is not the greatest benefit of society *simpliciter*, but the greatest benefit of society subject to the constraint that no one's rights may be violated. Now while I think that the classical utilitarians proposed a criterion of this more complicated sort, I do not want to argue that point here.[12] What I want to show is that there is *another* way of preventing the utilitarian principle from justifying too much, or at least of making it much less likely to do so: namely, by stating utilitarianism in a way which accounts for the distinction between the justification of an institution and the justification of a particular action falling under it.

I begin by defining the institution of punishment as follows: a person is said to suffer punishment whenever he is legally deprived of some of the normal rights of a citizen on the ground that he has violated a rule of law, the violation having been established by trial according to the due process of law, provided that the deprivation is carried out by the recognized legal authorities of the state, that the rule of law clearly specifies both the offense and the attached penalty, that the courts construe statutes strictly, and that the statute was on the books prior to the time of the offense.[13] This definition specifies what I shall understand by punishment. The question is whether utilitarian arguments may be found to justify institutions widely different from this and such as one would find cruel and arbitrary.

This question is best answered, I think, by taking up a particular accusation. Consider the following from Carritt:

[12]By the classical utilitarians I understand Hobbes, Hume, Bentham, J. S. Mill, and Sidgwick.

[13]All these features of punishment are mentioned by Hobbes; cf. *Leviathan*, ch. xxviii.

> . . . the utilitarian must hold that we are justified in inflicting pain always and only to prevent worse pain or bring about greater happiness. This, then, is all we need to consider in so-called punishment, which must be purely preventive. But if some kind of very cruel crime becomes common, and none of the criminals can be caught, it might be highly expedient, as an example, to hang an innocent man, if a charge against him could be so framed that he were universally thought guilty; indeed this would only fail to be an ideal instance of utilitarian "punishment" because the victim himself would not have been so likely as a real felon to commit such a crime in the future; in all other respects it would be perfectly deterrent and therefore felicific.[14]

Carritt is trying to show that there are occasions when a utilitarian argument would justify taking an action which would be generally condemned; and thus that utilitarianism justifies too much. But the failure of Carritt's argument lies in the fact that he makes no distinction between the justification of the general system of rules which constitutes penal institutions and the justification of particular applications of these rules to particular cases by the various officials whose job it is to administer them. This becomes perfectly clear when one asks who the "we" are of whom Carritt speaks. Who is this who has a sort of absolute authority on particular occasions to decide that an innocent man shall be "punished" if everyone can be convinced that he is guilty? Is this person the legislator, or the judge, or the body of private citizens, or what? It is utterly crucial to know who is to decide such matters, and by what authority, for all of this must be written into the rules of the institution. Until one knows these things one doesn't know what the institution is whose justification is being challenged; and as the utilitarian principle applies to the institution one doesn't know whether it is justifiable on utilitarian grounds or not.

Once this is understood it is clear what the countermove to Carritt's argument is. One must describe more carefully what the *institution* is which his example suggests, and then ask oneself whether or not it is likely that having this institution would be for the benefit of society in the long run. One must not content oneself with the vague thought that, when it's a question of *this* case, it would be a good thing if *somebody* did something even if an innocent person were to suffer.

Try to imagine, then, an institution (which we may call "telishment") which is such that the officials set up by it have authority to arrange a trial for the condemnation of an innocent man whenever they are of the opinion that doing so would be in the best interests of society. The discretion of officials is limited, however, by the rule that they may not condemn an innocent man to undergo such an ordeal unless there is, at the time, a wave of offenses similar to that with which they charge him and telish him for. We may imagine that the officials having the discretionary authority are the judges of the higher courts in consultation with the chief of police, the minister of justice, and a committee of the legislature.

Once one realizes that one is involved in setting up an *institution,* one sees that the hazards are very great. For example, what check is there on the officials? How is one to tell whether or not their actions are authorized? How is one to limit the risks involved in allowing such systematic deception? How is one to avoid giving anything short of complete discretion to the authorities to telish anyone they like? In addition to these considerations, it is obvious that people will come to have a very different attitude towards their penal system when telishment is adjoined to it. They will be uncertain as to whether a convicted man has been punished or telished. They will wonder whether or not they should feel sorry for him. They will wonder whether the same fate won't at any

[14] *Ethical and Political Thinking* (Oxford, 1947), p. 65.

time fall on them. If one pictures how such an institution would actually work, and the enormous risks involved in it, it seems clear that it would serve no useful purpose. A utilitarian justification for this institution is most unlikely.

It happens in general that as one drops off the defining features of punishment one ends up with an institution whose utilitarian justification is highly doubtful. One reason for this is that punishment works like a kind of price system: by altering the prices one has to pay for the performance of actions it supplies a motive for avoiding some actions and doing others. The defining features are essential if punishment is to work in this way; so that an institution which lacks these features, e.g., an institution which is set up to "punish" the innocent, is likely to have about as much point as a price system (if one may call it that) where the prices of things change at random from day to day and one learns the price of something after one has agreed to buy it.[15]

If one is careful to apply the utilitarian principle to the institution which is to authorize particular actions, then there is *less* danger of its justifying too much. Carritt's example gains plausibility by its indefiniteness and by its concentration on the particular case. His argument will only hold if it can be shown that there are utilitarian arguments which justify an institution whose publicly ascertainable offices and powers are such as to permit officials to exercise that kind of discretion in particular cases. But the requirement of having to build the arbitrary features of the particular decision into the institutional practice makes the justification much less likely to go through.

2

I shall now consider the question of promises. The objection to utilitarianism in connection with promises seems to be this: it is believed that on the utilitarian view when a person makes a promise the only ground upon which he should keep it, if he should keep it, is that by keeping it he will realize the most good on the whole. So that if one asks the question "Why should I keep *my* promise?" the utilitarian answer is understood to be that doing so in *this* case will have the best consequences. And this answer is said, quite rightly, to conflict with the way in which the obligation to keep promises is regarded.

Now of course critics of utilitarianism are not unaware that one defense sometimes attributed to utilitarians is the consideration involving the practice of promise-keeping.[16] In this connection they are supposed to argue something like this: it must be

[15]The analogy with the price system suggests an answer to the question how utilitarian considerations ensure that punishment is proportional to the offense. It is interesting to note that Sir David Ross, after making the distinction between justifying a penal law and justifying a particular application of it, and after stating that utilitarian considerations have a large place in determining the former, still holds back from accepting the utilitarian justification of punishment on the grounds that justice requires that punishment be proportional to the offense, and that utilitarianism is unable to account for this. Cf. *The Right and the Good*, pp. 61–62. I do not claim that utilitarianism can account for this requirement as Sir David might wish, but it happens, nevertheless, that if utilitarian considerations are followed penalties will be proportional to offenses in this sense: the order of offenses according to seriousness can be paired off with the order of penalties according to severity. Also the absolute level of penalties will be as low as possible. This follows from the assumption that people are rational (i.e., that they are able to take into account the "prices" the state puts on actions), the utilitarian rule that a penal system should provide a motive for preferring the less serious offense, and the principle that punishment as such is an evil. All this was carefully worked out by Bentham in *The Principles of Morals and Legislation*, chs. xiii–xv.

[16]Ross, *The Right and the Good*, pp. 37–39, and *Foundations of Ethics* (Oxford, 1939), pp. 92–94. I know of no utilitarian who has used this argument except W. A. Pickard-Cambridge in "Two Problems about Duty," *Mind*, n.s., xli (April, 1932), 153–157, although the argument goes with G. E. Moore's version of utilitarianism in *Principia Ethica* (Cambridge, 1903). To my knowledge it does not appear in the classical utilitarians; and if one interprets their view correctly this is no accident.

admitted that we feel strictly about keeping promises, more strictly than it might seem our view can account for. But when we consider the matter carefully it is always necessary to take into account the effect which our action will have on the practice of making promises. The promisor must weigh, not only the effects of breaking his promise on the particular case, but also the effect which his breaking his promise will have on the practice itself. Since the practice is of great utilitarian value, and since breaking one's promise always seriously damages it, one will seldom be justified in breaking one's promise. If we view our individual promises in the wider context of the practice of promising itself we can account for the strictness of the obligation to keep promises. There is always one very strong utilitarian consideration in favor of keeping them, and this will ensure that when the question arises as to whether or not to keep a promise it will usually turn out that one should, even where the facts of the particular case taken by itself would seem to justify one's breaking it. In this way the strictness with which we view the obligation to keep promises is accounted for.

Ross has criticized this defense as follows:[17] however great the value of the practice of promising, on utilitarian grounds, there must be some value which is greater, and one can imagine it to be obtainable by breaking a promise. Therefore there might be a case where the promisor could argue that breaking his promise was justified as leading to a better state of affairs on the whole. And the promisor could argue in this way no matter how slight the advantage won by breaking the promise. If one were to challenge the promisor his defense would be that what he did was best on the whole in view of all the utilitarian considerations, which in this case *include* the importance of the practice. Ross feels that such a defense would be unacceptable. I think he is right insofar as he is protesting against the appeal to consequences in general and without further explanation. Yet it is extremely difficult to weigh the force of Ross's argument. The kind of case imagined seems unrealistic and one feels that it needs to be described. One is inclined to think it would either turn out that such a case came under an exception defined by the practice itself, in which case there would not be an appeal to consequences in general on the particular case, or it would happen that the circumstances were so peculiar that the conditions which the practice presupposes no longer obtained. But certainly Ross is right in thinking that it strikes us as wrong for a person to defend breaking a promise by a general appeal to consequences. For a general utilitarian defense is not open to the promisor: it is not one of the defenses allowed by the practice of making promises.

Ross gives two further counterarguments.[18] First, he holds that it overestimates the damage done to the practice of promising by a failure to keep a promise. One who breaks a promise harms his own name certainly, but it isn't clear that a broken promise always damages the practice itself sufficiently to account for the strictness of the obligation. Second, and more important, I think, he raises the question of what one is to say of a promise which isn't known to have been made except to the promisor and the promisee, as in the case of a promise a son makes to his dying father concerning the handling of the estate.[19] In this sort of case the consideration relating to the practice

[17]Ross, *The Right and the Good*, pp. 38–39.

[18]Ross, ibid, p. 39. The case of the nonpublic promise is discussed again in *Foundations of Ethics*, pp. 95–96, 104–105. It occurs also in Mabbott, "Punishment," op. cit., pp. 155–157, and in A. I. Melden, "Two Comments on Utilitarianism," *Philosophical Review*, Ix (October, 1951), 519–523, which discusses Carritt's example in *Ethical and Political Thinking*, p. 64.

[19]Ross's example is described simply as that of two men dying alone where one makes a promise to the other. Carritt's example (cf. n. 17 supra) [Note 1. Ed] is that of two men at the North Pole. The example in the text is more realistic and is similar to Mabbott's. Another example is that of being told something in confidence by one who subsequently dies. Such cases need not be "desert-island arguments" as Nowell-Smith seems to believe (cf. his *Ethics*, pp. 239–244).

doesn't weigh on the promisor at all, and yet one feels that this sort of promise is as binding as other promises. The question of the effect which breaking it has on the practice seems irrelevant. The only consequence seems to be that one can break the promise without running any risk of being censured; but the obligation itself seems not the least weakened. Hence it is doubtful whether the effect on the practice ever weighs in the particular case; certainly it cannot account for the strictness of the obligation where it fails to obtain. It seems to follow that a utilitarian account of the obligation to keep promises cannot be successfully carried out.

From what I have said in connection with punishment, one can foresee what I am going to say about these arguments and counterarguments. They fail to make the distinction between the justification of a practice and the justification of a particular action falling under it, and therefore they fall into the mistake of taking it for granted that the promisor, like Carritt's official, is entitled without restriction to bring utilitarian considerations to bear in deciding whether to keep *his* promise. But if one considers what the practice of promising is one will see, I think, that it is such as not to allow this sort of general discretion to the promisor. Indeed, the point of the practice is to abdicate one's title to act in accordance with utilitarian and prudential considerations in order that the future may be tied down and plans coordinated in advance. There are obvious utilitarian advantages in having a practice which denies to the promisor, as a defense, any general appeal to the utilitarian principle in accordance with which the practice itself may be justified. There is nothing contradictory, or surprising, in this: utilitarian (or aesthetic) reasons might properly be given in arguing that the game of chess, or baseball, is satisfactory just as it is, or in arguing that it should be changed in various respects, but a player in a game cannot properly appeal to such considerations as reasons for his making one move rather than another. It is a mistake to think that if the practice is justified on utilitarian grounds then the promisor must have complete liberty to use utilitarian arguments to decide whether or not to keep his promise. The practice forbids this general defense; and it is a purpose of the practice to do this. Therefore what the above arguments presuppose—the idea that if the utilitarian view is accepted then the promisor is bound if, and only if, the application of the utilitarian principle to his own case shows that keeping it is best on the whole—is false. The promisor is bound because he promised: weighing the case on its merits is not open to him.[20]

Is this to say that in particular cases one cannot deliberate whether or not to keep one's promise? Of course not. But to do so is to deliberate whether the various excuses, exceptions and defenses, which are understood by, and which constitute an important part of, the practice, apply to one's own case.[21] Various defenses for not keeping one's promise are allowed, but among them there isn't the one that, on general utilitarian grounds, the promisor (truly) thought his action best on the whole, even though there may be the defense that the consequences of keeping one's promise would have been *extremely* severe. While there are too many complexities here to consider all the necessary details, one can see that the general defense isn't allowed if one asks the following question: what would one say of someone who, when asked why he broke his promise, replied simply that breaking it was best on the whole? Assuming that his reply is sincere, and that his belief was reasonable (i.e., one need not consider the possibility that he was mistaken), I think that one would question whether or not he knows what it means to say "I promise" (in the appropriate circumstances). It would

[20]What I have said in this paragraph seems to me to coincide with Hume's important discussion in the *Treatise of Human Nature*, Bk. III, pt. II, sec. 5; and also sec. 6, par. 8.

[21]For a discussion of these, see H. Sidgwick, *The Methods of Ethics* (6th ed.; London, 1901), Bk. III, ch. vi.

be said of someone who used this excuse without further explanation that he didn't understand what defenses the practice, which defines a promise, allows to him. If a child were to use this excuse one would correct him; for it is part of the way one is taught the concept of a promise to be corrected if one uses this excuse. The point of having the practice would be lost if the practice did allow this excuse.

It is no doubt part of the utilitarian view that every practice should admit the defense that the consequences of abiding by it would have been extremely severe; and utilitarians would be inclined to hold that some reliance on people's good sense and some concession to hard cases is necessary. They would hold that a practice is justified by serving the interests of those who take part in it; and as with any set of rules there is understood a background of circumstances under which it is expected to be applied and which need not—indeed which cannot—be fully stated. Should these circumstances change, then even if there is no rule which provides for the case, it may still be in accordance with the practice that one be released from one's obligation. But this sort of defense allowed by a practice must not be confused with the general option to weigh each particular case on utilitarian grounds which critics of utilitarianism have thought it necessarily to involve.

The concern which utilitarianism raises by its justification of punishment is that it may justify too much. The question in connection with promises is different: it is how utilitarianism can account for the obligation to keep promises at all. One feels that the recognized obligation to keep one's promise and utilitarianism are incompatible. And to be sure, they are incompatible if one interprets the utilitarian view as necessarily holding that each person has complete liberty to weigh every particular action on general utilitarian grounds. But must one interpret utilitarianism in this way? I hope to show that, in the sorts of cases I have discussed, one cannot interpret it in this way.

3

So far I have tried to show the importance of the distinction between the justification of a practice and the justification of a particular action falling under it by indicating how this distinction might be used to defend utilitarianism against two long-standing objections. One might be tempted to close the discussion at this point by saying that utilitarian considerations should be understood as applying to practices in the first instance and not to particular actions falling under them except insofar as the practices admit of it. One might say that in this modified form it is a better account of our considered moral opinions and let it go at that. But to stop here would be to neglect the interesting question as to how one can fail to appreciate the significance of this rather obvious distinction and can take it for granted that utilitarianism has the consequence that particular cases may always be decided on general utilitarian grounds.[22] I want to argue that this

[22]So far as I can see it is not until Moore that the doctrine is expressly stated in this way. See, for example, *Principia Ethica*, p. 147, where it is said that the statement "I am morally bound to perform this action" is identical with the statement "*This* action will produce the greatest possible amount of good in the Universe" (my italics). It is important to remember that those whom I have called the classical utilitarians were largely interested in social institutions. They were among the leading economists and political theorists of their day, and they were not infrequently reformers interested in practical affairs. Utilitarianism historically goes together with a coherent view of society, and is not simply an ethical theory, much less an attempt at philosophical analysis in the modern sense. The utilitarian principle was quite naturally thought of, and used, as a criterion for judging social institutions (practices) and as a basis for urging reforms. It is not clear, therefore, how far it is necessary to amend utilitarianism in its classical form. For a discussion of utilitarianism as an integral part of a theory of society, see L. Robbins, *The Theory of Economic Policy in English Classical Political Economy* (London, 1952).

mistake may be connected with misconceiving the logical status of the rules of practices; and to show this I am going to examine two conceptions of rules; two ways of placing them within the utilitarian theory.

The conception which conceals from us the significance of the distinction I am going to call the summary view. It regards rules in the following way: one supposes that each person decides what he shall do in particular cases by applying the utilitarian principle; one supposes further that different people will decide the same particular case in the same way and that there will be recurrences of cases similar to those previously decided. Thus it will happen that in cases of certain kinds the same decision will be made either by the same person at different times or by different persons at the same time. If a case occurs frequently enough one supposes that a rule is formulated to cover that sort of case. I have called this conception the summary view because rules are pictured as summaries of past decisions arrived at by the *direct* application of the utilitarian principle to particular cases. Rules are regarded as reports that cases of a certain sort have been found on *other* grounds to be properly decided in a certain way (although, of course, they do not *say* this).

There are several things to notice about this way of placing rules within the utilitarian theory.[23]

[23]This footnote should be read after sec. 3 and presupposes what I have said there. It provides a few references to statements by leading utilitarians of the summary conception. In general it appears that when they discussed the logical features of rules the summary conception prevailed and that it was typical of the way they talked about moral rules. I cite a rather lengthy group of passages from Austin as a full illustration.

John Austin in his *Lectures on Jurisprudence* meets the objection that deciding in accordance with the utilitarian principle case by case is impractical by saying that this is a misinterpretation of utilitarianism. According to the utilitarian view "... our conduct would conform to *rules* inferred from the tendencies of actions, but would not be determined by a direct resort to the principle of general utility. Utility would be the test of our conduct, ultimately, but not immediately: the immediate test of the rules to which our conduct would conform, but not the immediate test of specific or individual actions. Our rules would be fashioned on utility; our conduct, on our rules" (vol. 1, p. 116). As to how one decides on the tendency of an action he says: "If we would try the tendency of a specific or individual act, we must not contemplate the act as if it were single and insulated, but must look at the class of acts to which it belongs. We must suppose that acts of the class were generally done or omitted, and consider the probable effect upon the general happiness or good. We must guess the consequences which would follow, if the class of acts were general; and also the consequences which would follow, if they were generally omitted. We must then compare the consequences on the positive and negative sides, and determine on which of the two the *balance* of advantage lies. ... If we truly try the tendency of a specific or individual act, we try the tendency of the class to which that act belongs. The *particular* conclusion which we draw, with regard to the single act, implies a *general* conclusion embracing all similar acts. ... To the rules thus inferred, and lodged in the memory, our conduct would conform *immediately* if it were truly adjusted to utility" (ibid., p. 117). One might think that Austin meets the objection by stating the practice conception of rules; and perhaps he did intend to. But it is not clear that he has stated this conception. Is the generality he refers to of the statistical sort? This is suggested by the notion of tendency. Or does he refer to the utility of setting up a practice? I don't know; but what suggests the summary view is his subsequent remarks. He says: "To consider the specific consequences of single or individual acts, would *seldom* [my italics] consist with that ultimate principle" (ibid., p. 117). But would one ever do this? He continues: "... this being admitted, the necessity of pausing and calculating, which the objection in question supposes, is an imagined necessity. To preface each act or forbearance by a conjecture and comparison of consequences, were clearly *superfluous* [my italics] and mischievous. It were clearly superfluous, inasmuch as the *result of that process* [my italics] would be embodied in a known *rule*. It were clearly mischievous, inasmuch as the *true* result would be expressed by that rule, whilst the process would probably be faulty, if it were done on the spur of the occasion" (ibid., pp. 117–118). He goes on: "If our experience and observation of particulars were not *generalized*, our experience and observation of particulars would seldom avail us in *practice*. ... The inferences suggested to our minds by repeated experience and observation are, therefore, drawn into *principles*, or compressed into *maxims*. These we carry about us ready for use, and apply to individual cases promptly ... without reverting to the process by which they were obtained; or without recalling, and arraying before our minds, the numerous and intricate considerations of which they are *handy abridgments* [my

1. The point of having rules derives from the fact that similar cases tend to recur and that one can decide cases more quickly if one records past decisions in the form of rules. If similar cases didn't recur, one would be required to apply the utilitarian principle directly, case by case, and rules reporting past decisions would be of no use.

2. The decisions made on particular cases are logically prior to rules. Since rules gain their point from the need to apply the utilitarian principle to many similar cases, it follows that a particular case (or several cases similar to it) may exist whether or not there is a rule covering that case. We are pictured as recognizing particular cases prior to there being a rule which covers them, for it is only if we meet with a number of cases of a certain sort that we formulate a rule. Thus we are able to describe a particular case as a particular case of the requisite sort whether there is a rule regarding *that* sort of case or not. Put another way: what the *A*'s and the *B*'s refer to in rules of the form "Whenever *A* do *B*" may be described as *A*'s and *B*'s whether or not there is the rule "Whenever *A* do *B*," or whether or not there is any body of rules which makes up a practice of which that rule is a part.

---

italics]. . . . True theory is a *compendium* of particular truths. . . . Speaking then, generally, human conduct is inevitably *guided* [my italics] by *rules*, or by *principles* or *maxims* (ibid., pp. 117–118). I need not trouble to show how all these remarks incline to the summary view. Further, when Austin comes to deal with cases "of comparatively rare occurrence" he holds that specific considerations may outweigh the general. "Looking at the reasons from which we had inferred the rule, it were absurd to think it inflexible. We should therefore dismiss the *rule;* resort directly to the *principle* upon which our rules were fashioned; and calculate *specific* consequences to the best of our knowledge and ability" (ibid., pp. 120–121). Austin's view is interesting because it shows how one may come close to the practice conception and then slide away from it.

In *A System of Logic*, Bk. VI, ch. xii, par. 2, Mill distinguishes clearly between the position of judge and legislator and in doing so suggests the distinction between the two concepts of rules. However, he distinguishes the two positions to illustrate the difference between cases where one is to apply a rule already established and cases where one must formulate a rule to govern subsequent conduct. It's the latter case that interests him and he takes the "maxim of policy" of a legislator as typical of rules. In par. 3 the summary conception is very clearly stated. For example, he says of rules of conduct that they should be taken provisionally, as they are made for the most numerous cases. He says that they "point out" the manner in which it is least perilous to act; they serve as an "admonition" that a certain mode of conduct has been found suited to the most common occurrences. In *Utilitarianism*, ch. ii, par. 24, the summary conception appears in Mill's answer to the same objection Austin considered. Here he speaks of rules as "corollaries" from the principle of utility; these "secondary" rules are compared to "landmarks" and "direction-posts." They are based on long experience and so make it unnecessary to apply the utilitarian principle to each case. In par. 25 Mill refers to the task of the utilitarian principle in adjudicating between competing moral rules. He talks here as if one then applies the utilitarian principle directly to the particular case. On the practice view one would rather use the principle to decide which of the ways that make the practice consistent is the best. It should be noted that while in par. 10 Mill's definition of utilitarianism makes the utilitarian principle apply to morality, i.e., to the rules and precepts of human conduct, the definition in par. 2 uses the phrase "actions are right in *proportion* as they *tend* to promote happiness" [my italics] and this inclines towards the summary view. In the last paragraph of the essay "On the Definition of Political Economy," *Westminister Review* (October, 1836), Mill says that it is only in art, as distinguished from science, that one can properly speak of exceptions. In a question of practice, if something is fit to be done "in the majority of cases" then it is made the rule. "We may . . . in talking of art *unobjectionably* speak of the *rule* and the *exception*, meaning by the rule the cases in which there exists a preponderance . . . of inducements for acting in a particular way; and by the exception, the cases in which the preponderance is on the contrary side." These remarks, too, suggest the summary view.

In Moore's *Principia Ethica*, ch. v, there is a complicated and difficult discussion of moral rules. I will not examine it here except to express my suspicion that the summary conception prevails. To be sure, Moore speaks frequently of the utility of rules as generally followed, and of actions as generally practiced, but it is possible that these passages fit the statistical notion of generality which the summary conception allows. This conception is suggested by Moore's taking the utilitarian principle as applying directly to particular actions (pp. 147–148) and by his notion of a rule as something indicating which of the few alternatives likely to occur to anyone will generally produce a greater total good in the immediate future (p. 154). He talks of an "ethical law" as a prediction, and as a generalization (pp. 146, 155). The summary conception is also suggested by his discussion of exceptions (pp. 162–163) and of the force of examples of breaching a rule (pp. 163–164).

To illustrate this consider a rule, or maxim, which could arise in this way: suppose that a person is trying to decide whether to tell someone who is fatally ill what his illness is when he has been asked to do so. Suppose the person to reflect and then decide, on utilitarian grounds, that he should not answer truthfully; and suppose that on the basis of this and other like occasions he formulates a rule to the effect that when asked by someone fatally ill what his illness is, one should not tell him. The point to notice is that someone's being fatally ill and asking what his illness is, and someone's telling him, are things that can be described as such whether or not there is this rule. The performance of the action to which the rule refers doesn't require the stage-setting of a practice of which this rule is a part. This is what is meant by saying that on the summary view particular cases are logically prior to rules.

3. Each person is in principle always entitled to reconsider the correctness of a rule and to question whether or not it is proper to follow it in a particular case. As rules are guides and aids, one may ask whether in past decisions there might not have been a mistake in applying the utilitarian principle to get the rule in question, and wonder whether or not it is best in this case. The reason for rules is that people are not able to apply the utilitarian principle effortlessly and flawlessly; there is need to save time and to post a guide. On this view a society of rational utilitarians would be a society without rules in which each person applied the utilitarian principle directly and smoothly, and without error, case by case. On the other hand, ours is a society in which rules are formulated to serve as aids in reaching these ideally rational decisions on particular cases, guides which have been built up and tested by the experience of generations. If one applies this view to rules, one is interpreting them as maxims, as "rules of thumb"; and it is doubtful that anything to which the summary conception did apply would be called a *rule*. Arguing as if one regarded rules in this way is a mistake one makes while doing philosophy.

4. The concept of a *general* rule takes the following form. One is pictured as estimating on what percentage of the cases likely to arise a given rule may be relied upon to express the correct decision, that is, the decision that would be arrived at if one were to correctly apply the utilitarian principle case by case. If one estimates that by and large the rule will give the correct decision, or if one estimates that the likelihood of making a mistake by applying the utilitarian principle directly on one's own is greater than the likelihood of making a mistake by following the rule, and if these considerations held of persons generally, then one would be justified in urging its adoption as a general rule. In this way *general* rules might be accounted for on the summary view. It will still make sense, however, to speak of applying the utilitarian principle case by case, for it was by trying to foresee the results of doing this that one got the initial estimates upon which acceptance of the rule depends. That one is taking a rule in accordance with the summary conception will show itself in the naturalness with which one speaks of the rule as a guide, or as a maxim, or as a generalization from experience, and as something to be laid aside in extraordinary cases where there is no assurance that the generalization will hold and the case must therefore be treated on its merits. Thus there goes with this conception the notion of a particular exception which renders a rule suspect on a particular occasion.

The other conception of rules I will call the practice conception. On this view rules are pictured as defining a practice. Practices are set up for various reasons, but one of them is that in many areas of conduct each person's deciding what to do on utilitarian grounds case by case leads to confusion, and that the attempt to coordinate behavior by trying to foresee how others will act is bound to fail. As an alternative one realizes that what is required is the establishment of a practice, the specification of a new form of activity; and from this one sees that a practice necessarily involves the abdication of full liberty to act on utilitarian and prudential grounds. It is the mark of a practice that being taught how to engage in it involves being instructed in the rules which define it, and that appeal is made to those rules to correct the behavior of those engaged in it. Those engaged in a practice recognize the rules as defining it. The rules cannot be taken as simply describing how those engaged in the practice in fact behave: it is not simply that they act as if they were obeying the rules. Thus it is essential to the notion of a practice that the rules are publicly known and understood as definitive; and it is essential also that the rules of a practice can be taught and can be acted upon to yield a coherent practice. On this conception, then, rules are not generalizations from the decisions of individuals applying the utilitarian principle directly and independently to recurrent particular cases. On the contrary, rules define a practice and are themselves the subject of the utilitarian principle.

To show the important differences between this way of fitting rules into the utilitarian theory and the previous way, I shall consider the differences between the two conceptions on the points previously discussed.

1. In contrast with the summary view, the rules of practices are logically prior to particular cases. This is so because there cannot be a particular case of an action falling under a rule of a practice unless there is the practice. This can be made clearer as follows: in a practice there are rules setting up offices, specifying certain forms of action appropriate to various offices, establishing penalties for the breach of rules, and so on. We may think of the rules of a practice as defining offices, moves, and offenses. Now what is meant by saying that the practice is logically prior to particular cases is this: given any rule which specifies a form of action (a move), a particular action which would be taken as falling under this rule given that there is the practice would not be *described* as that sort of action unless there was the practice. In the case of actions specified by practices it is logically impossible to perform them outside the stage-setting provided by those practices, for unless there is the practice, and unless the requisite proprieties are fulfilled, whatever one does, whatever movements one makes, will fail to count as a form of action which the practice specifies. What one does will be described in some *other* way.

One may illustrate this point from the game of baseball. Many of the actions one performs in a game of baseball one can do by oneself or with others whether there is the game or not. For example, one can throw a ball, run, or swing a peculiarly shaped piece of wood. But one cannot steal a base, or strike out, or draw a walk, or make an error, or balk; although one can do certain things which appear to resemble these actions such as sliding into a bag, missing a grounder and so on. Striking out, stealing a base, balking, etc., are all actions which can only happen in a game. No matter what a person did, what he did would not be described as stealing a base or striking out or drawing a walk unless he could also be described as playing baseball, and for him to be doing this presupposes the rule-like practice which constitutes the game. The practice is logically prior to particular cases: unless there is the practice the terms referring to actions specified by it lack a sense.[24]

[24]One might feel that it is a mistake to say that a practice is logically prior to the forms of action it specifies on the grounds that if there were never any instances of actions falling under a practice then we should be strongly inclined to say that there wasn't the practice either. Blue-prints for a practice do not make a practice. That there is a practice entails that there are instances of people having been engaged and now being engaged in it (with suitable qualifications). This is correct, but it doesn't hurt the claim that any given particular instance of a form of action specified by a practice presupposes the practice. This isn't so on the summary picture, as each instance must be "there" prior to the rules, so to speak, as something from which one gets the rule by applying the utilitarian principle to it directly.

2. The practice view leads to an entirely different conception of the authority which each person has to decide on the propriety of following a rule in particular cases. To engage in a practice, to perform those actions specified by a practice, means to follow the appropriate rules. If one wants to do an action which a certain practice specifies then there is no way to do it except to follow the rules which define it. Therefore, it doesn't make sense for a person to raise the question whether or not a rule of a practice correctly applies to *his* case where the action he contemplates is a form of action defined by a practice. If someone were to raise such a question, he would simply show that he didn't understand the situation in which he was acting. If one wants to perform an action specified by a practice, the only legitimate question concerns the nature of the practice itself ("How do I go about making a will?").

This point is illustrated by the behavior expected of a player in games. If one wants to play a game, one doesn't treat the rules of the game as guides as to what is best in particular cases. In a game of baseball if a batter were to ask "Can I have four strikes?" it would be assumed that he was asking what the rule was; and if, when told what the rule was, he were to say that he meant that on this occasion he thought it would be best on the whole for him to have four strikes rather than three, this would be most kindly taken as a joke. One might contend that baseball would be a better game if four strikes were allowed instead of three; but one cannot picture the rules as guides to what is best on the whole in particular cases, and question their applicability to particular cases as particular cases.

3 and 4. To complete the four points of comparison with the summary conception, it is clear from what has been said that rules of practices are not guides to help one decide particular cases correctly as judged by some higher ethical principle. And neither the quasi-statistical notion of generality, nor the notion of a particular exception, can apply to the rules of practices. A more or less general rule of a practice must be a rule which according to the structure of the practice applies to more or fewer of the kinds of cases arising under it; or it must be a rule which is more or less basic to the understanding of the practice. Again, a particular case cannot be an exception to a rule of a practice. An exception is rather a qualification or a further specification of the rule.

It follows from what we have said about the practice conception of rules that if a person is engaged in a practice, and if he is asked why *he* does what *he* does, or if he is asked to defend what he does, then his explanation, or defense, lies in referring the questioner to the practice. He cannot say of *his* action, if it is an action specified by a practice, that he does it rather than some other because he thinks it is best on the whole.[25] When a man engaged in a practice is queried about his action he must assume that the questioner either doesn't know that he is engaged in it ("Why are you in a hurry to pay him?" "I promised to pay him today") or doesn't know what the practice is. One doesn't so much justify one's particular action as explain, or show, that it is in accordance with the practice. The reason for this is that it is only against the stage-setting of the practice that one's particular action is described as it is. Only by reference to the practice can one *say* what one is doing. To explain or to defend one's own action, as a particular action, one fits it into the practice which defines it. If this is not accepted it's a sign that a different question is being raised as to whether one is justified in accepting the practice, or in tolerating it. When the challenge is to the practice, citing the rules (saying what the practice is) is naturally to no avail. But when the challenge is to the particular action defined by the practice, there is nothing one can do but refer to the rules. Concerning particular actions

[25]A philosophical joke (in the mouth of Jeremy Bentham): "When I run to the other wicket after my partner has struck a good ball I do so because it is best on the whole."

there is only a question for one who isn't clear as to what the practice is, or who doesn't know that it is being engaged in. This is to be contrasted with the case of a maxim which may be taken as pointing to the correct decision on the case as decided on *other* grounds, and so giving a challenge on the case a sense by having it question whether these other grounds really support the decision on this case.

If one compares the two conceptions of rules I have discussed, one can see how the summary conception misses the significance of the distinction between justifying a practice and justifying actions falling under it. On this view rules are regarded as guides whose purpose it is to indicate the ideally rational decision on the given particular case which the flawless application of the utilitarian principle would yield. One has, in principle, full option to use the guides or to discard them as the situation warrants without one's moral office being altered in any way: whether one discards the rules or not, one always holds the office of a rational person seeking case by case to realize the best on the whole. But on the practice conception, if one holds an office defined by a practice then questions regarding one's actions in this office are settled by reference to the rules which define the practice. If one seeks to question these rules, then one's office undergoes a fundamental change: one then assumes the office of one empowered to change and criticize the rules, or the office of a reformer, and so on. The summary conception does away with the distinction of offices and the various forms of argument appropriate to each. On that conception there is one office and so no offices at all. It therefore obscures the fact that the utilitarian principle must, in the case of actions and offices defined by a practice, apply to the practice, so that general utilitarian arguments are not available to those who act in offices so defined.[26]

Some qualifications are necessary in what I have said. First, I may have talked of the summary and the practice conceptions of rules as if only one of them could be true of rules, and if true of any rules, then necessarily true of *all* rules. I do not, of course, mean this. (It is the critics of utilitarianism who make this mistake insofar as their arguments against utilitarianism presuppose a summary conception of the rules of practices.) Some rules will fit one conception, some rules the other; and so there are rules of practices (rules in the strict sense), and maxims and "rules of thumb."

Secondly, there are further distinctions that can be made in classifying rules, distinctions which should be made if one were considering other questions. The distinctions which I have drawn are those most relevant for the rather special matter I have discussed, and are not intended to be exhaustive.

Finally, there will be many border-line cases about which it will be difficult, if not impossible, to decide which conception of rules is applicable. One expects border-line cases with any concept, and they are especially likely in connection with such involved concepts as those of a practice, institution, game, rule, and so on. Wittgenstein has shown how fluid these notions are.[27] What I have done is to emphasize and sharpen two conceptions for the limited purpose of this paper.

[26]How do these remarks apply to the case of the promise known only to father and son? Well, at first sight the son certainly holds the office of promisor, and so he isn't allowed by the practice to weigh the particular case on general utilitarian grounds. Suppose instead that he wishes to consider himself in the office of one empowered to criticize and change the practice, leaving aside the question as to his right to move from his previously assumed office to another. Then he may consider utilitarian arguments as applied to the practice; but once he does this he will see that there are such arguments for not allowing a general utilitarian defense in the practice for this sort of case. For to do so would make it impossible to ask for and to give a kind of promise which one often wants to be able to ask for and to give. Therefore he will not want to change the practice, and so as a promisor he has no option but to keep his promise.

[27]*Philosophical Investigations* (Oxford, 1953), i, pars. 65–71, for example.

4

What I have tried to show by distinguishing between two conceptions of rules is that there is a way of regarding rules which allows the option to consider particular cases on general utilitarian grounds; whereas there is another conception which does not admit of such discretion except insofar as the rules themselves authorize it. I want to suggest that the tendency while doing philosophy to picture rules in accordance with the summary conception is what may have blinded moral philosophers to the significance of the distinction between justifying a practice and justifying a particular action falling under it; and it does so by misrepresenting the logical force of the reference to the rules in the case of a challenge to a particular action falling under a practice, and by obscuring the fact that where there is a practice, it is the practice itself that must be the subject of the utilitarian principle.

It is surely no accident that two of the traditional test cases of utilitarianism, punishment and promises, are clear cases of practices. Under the influence of the summary conception it is natural to suppose that the officials of a penal system, and one who has made a promise, may decide what to do in particular cases on utilitarian grounds. One fails to see that a general discretion to decide particular cases on utilitarian grounds is incompatible with the concept of a practice; and that what discretion one does have is itself defined by the practice (e.g., a judge may have discretion to determine the penalty within certain limits). The traditional objections to utilitarianism which I have discussed presuppose the attribution to judges, and to those who have made promises, of a plenitude of moral authority to decide particular cases on utilitarian grounds. But once one fits utilitarianism together with the notion of a practice, and notes that punishment and promising are practices, then one sees that this attribution is logically precluded.

That punishment and promising are practices is beyond question. In the case of promising this is shown by the fact that the form of words "I promise" is a performative utterance which presupposes the stage-setting of the practice and the proprieties defined by it. Saying the words "I promise" will only be promising given the existence of the practice. It would be absurd to interpret the rules about promising in accordance with the summary conception. It is absurd to say, for example, that the rule that promises should be kept could have arisen from its being found in past cases to be best on the whole to keep one's promise; for unless there were already the understanding that one keeps one's promises as part of the practice itself there couldn't have been any cases of promising.

It must, of course, be granted that the rules defining promising are not codified, and that one's conception of what they are necessarily depends on one's moral training. Therefore it is likely that there is considerable variation in the way people understand the practice, and room for argument as to how it is best set up. For example, differences as to how strictly various defenses are to be taken, or just what defenses are available, are likely to arise amongst persons with different backgrounds. But irrespective of these variations it belongs to the concept of the practice of promising that the general utilitarian defense is not available to the promisor. That this is so accounts for the force of the traditional objection which I have discussed. And the point I wish to make is that when one fits the utilitarian view together with the practice conception of rules, as one must in the appropriate cases, then there is nothing in that view which entails that there must be such a defense, either in the practice of promising, or in any other practice.

Punishment is also a clear case. There are many actions in the sequence of events which constitute someone's being punished which presuppose a practice. One can see this by considering the definition of punishment which I gave when discussing Carritt's criticism of utilitarianism. The definition there stated refers to such things as the normal rights of a citizen, rules of law, due process of law, trials and courts of law, statutes, etc., none of which can exist outside the elaborate stage-setting of a legal system. It is also the case that many of the actions for which people are punished presuppose practices. For example, one is punished for stealing, for trespassing and the like, which presuppose the institution of property. It is impossible to say what punishment is, or to describe a particular instance of it, without referring to offices, actions, and offenses specified by practices. Punishment is a move in an elaborate legal game and presupposes the complex of practices which make up the legal order. The same thing is true of the less formal sorts of punishment: a parent or guardian or someone in proper authority may punish a child, but no one else can.

There is one mistaken interpretation of what I have been saying which it is worthwhile to warn against. One might think that the use I am making of the distinction between justifying a practice and justifying the particular actions falling under it involves one in a definite social and political attitude in that it leads to a kind of conservatism. It might seem that I am saying that for each person the social practices of his society provide the standard of justification for his actions; therefore let each person abide by them and his conduct will be justified.

This interpretation is entirely wrong. The point I have been making is rather a logical point. To be sure, it has consequences in matters of ethical theory; but in itself it leads to no particular social or political attitude. It is simply that where a form of action is specified by a practice there is no justification possible of the particular action of a particular person save by reference to the practice. In such cases then action is what it is in virtue of the practice and to explain it is to refer to the practice. There is no inference whatsoever to be drawn with respect to whether or not one should accept the practices of one's society. One can be as radical as one likes but in the case of actions specified by practices the objects of one's radicalism must be the social practices and people's acceptance of them.

I have tried to show that when we fit the utilitarian view together with the practice conception of rules, where this conception is appropriate,[28] we can formulate it in a way which saves it from several traditional objections. I have further tried to show how the logical force of the distinction between justifying a practice and justifying an action falling under it is connected with the practice conception of rules and cannot be understood as long as one regards the rules of practices in accordance with the summary view. Why, when doing philosophy, one may be inclined to so regard them, I have not discussed. The reasons for this are evidently very deep and would require another paper.

[28]As I have already stated, it is not always easy to say where the conception is appropriate. Nor do I care to discuss at this point the general sorts of cases to which it does apply except to say that one should not take it for granted that it applies to many so-called "moral rules." It is my feeling that relatively few actions of the moral life are defined by practices and that the practice conception is more relevant to understanding legal and legal-like arguments than it is to the more complex sort of moral arguments. Utilitarianism must be fitted to different conceptions of rules depending on the case, and no doubt the failure to do this has been one source of difficulty in interpreting it correctly.

1956

Moral Perplexity

W. D. Falk

Every age has its moral perplexities, but our own seems to have more than its share. And this is not only so because the old days are always the good old days, though there may be something in this too. But it is fair to say that there is less agreement and more uncertainty about moral matters today than, let us say, in the late nineteenth century. There is more dispute about the rights and duties of parents and children, of husbands and wives, of individuals and the state. There is a rejection of ready-made rules, and, generally, an air of unsettlement.

And there is something else too, namely, a sense of uneasiness about the fact that we are so divided and unsure. We are used to believing that there is a right and wrong about choices and ways of life, and that right thinking, here as elsewhere, can discern truth and dispel error. But now there are not a few who feel that this view itself is on trial. What is added to our moral perplexities is perplexity about morals. People put this by saying that there is some radical error in the traditional view that "reason" can solve moral issues: according to some that "reason" can solve them at all, according to others that it can solve them unaided by religion. There was a time when Immanuel Kant could speak of the two great certainties, the starry heavens above us and the moral law, known by pure reason, within us. In our time both of these seem to be fading into the nebulae.

W. D. Falk, "Moral Perplexity," *Ethics* 66 (1956). Reprinted with the permission of The University of Chicago Press.

Such views are a measure of some people's bewilderment, but they need not be correct as a diagnosis. And one may look at the situation more soberly. Because one may say: There is after all no more to the moral condition of our time than could be expected from its character generally. Ours is a time which requires adaptation to big changes all-round. What were sound practices of public finance yesterday are so no longer today; and why should the same not apply to what used to be sound moral practices? Moral codes are rules of thumb for the advancement of individual and social welfare, and as they have been learned they may have to be unlearned. Consider our views on the relations between men and women. At a time when women have careers, when technology changes the economics of the household, medical science the care of the body, psychology our knowledge of mental hygiene, some traditional rules must lose their point, and new ways have to be evolved. This may not be easy and uncontroversial. But it involves none but practical problems. And there is no need for taking the birth pangs of adaptation for the crack of doom.

So one may have different views on the causes of our perplexities. One may attribute them simply to the complexities of a time of change, or to deeper causes, to errors or confusions about right thinking in moral matters. And what I want to discuss are these different diagnoses of the situation.

I might say straightaway that I think that our troubles are both on the practical and on the deeper philosophical level. And this should not be surprising. One cannot doubt that our time is setting us problems for conduct to which we have no ready answers, or which the answer of the past will no longer fit. And it is quite a usual feature of the growth of thought, whether in science or elsewhere, that with big new questions to solve one also has to query what sort of questions these are, and how to solve them. And this is why philosophical questions come up, because philosophy deals with the logic of questions. I might say here, by the way, that philosophers are much misunderstood people. They are either looked down on or admired more than they should be, much as a foreigner in conservative English society. Philosophers have not got a secret key to solving problems at which others fail. Their job is rather to assist question-solving when it gets bogged down in confusion about the questions and about the answers which they permit. This is why there is not really a separate animal in the academic zoo called "philosophy," over and above such creatures as history or physics or economics. Philosophy sits on all thought rather like the shell on the back of the tortoise; and where the tortoise goes there it goes, and as long as the tortoise keeps going it keeps going.

And now let us get on with the job. And here let me say first that not all moral disagreements lead to philosophical worries. Moral disagreements may have different origins, and this is the first point which we must note.

Many of them are simply about the best means toward achieving good ends. Take two parents who are disagreed on the upbringing of their children. Both will think that they should further their good, but one thinks that disciplinarian methods are right, and the other that they are plain wicked and wrong. This would be simply a disagreement about the means toward an agreed end, and, though there may be snags in practice, it is not in principle hard to solve. The facts about child development should decide who is right. And if there actually is much disagreement and uncertainty about this matter today, we may lay this at the door of a new science of infants still in its infancy. And many moral disputes are like this one. A dispute about the wrongness of gambling could be resolved by studying the effects of gambling on people's daily lives. The social effects of ownership will be relevant to disagreement about the right to property. And one could easily multiply examples, so much so that one may come to think that all moral disputes are of this kind. People have said: There is one ultimate end on which agreement can be presupposed: that, above all, we ought to do most good and least harm all-round; and all moral disputes are simply about the best means toward this end. And without doubt it would be a comfort if this were so. Because then, in the last resort, we could solve all moral problems with the aid of science. Psychology, medicine, sociology, economics tell us the story of what leads to what, of the effects of bashing children, of gambling, of private ownership. These sciences would then be our proper advisers on all matters of right and wrong.

Unfortunately this is too sweeping. And it is too sweeping because not all moral disputes arise from disagreement about the best means toward agreed ends. But before I turn to this, let me say that one may also easily underrate the importance of this view. Moral codes, like institutions in general, tend to settle in fixed grooves. We develop a jealous attachment to them. And when one feels most defensive about them, this is often the very moment for revising, "in a cool hour," as Bishop Butler said, what good or harm they really do. And to consult the findings of science at this point will not come amiss.

But, as I say, science cannot help us all the way, because there is another area of moral dispute which relates not to means but to ends. And let me first introduce this area, and then consider how it raises problems.

It seems so natural to say: There is one ultimate end, "above all, do most good and least harm all-round," and on this we are agreed. But, for several reasons, this is far too simple. For one, the formula is too vague. It says we ought to promote people's welfare. But when does a man really fare well? There are many constituents of a good life: freedom from want or fear, health and leisure, justice, freedom of self-expression. And not all of these can be realized to the same extent at the same time. One may have to choose between the one and the other, as, for instance, between economic security and freedom from restraints. So it follows that "do most good and least harm all-round" does not really relate to one ultimate end but to a family of such ends; and that there is a question for deciding in what order of priorities these ends should be realized.

Moreover, even if we are agreed on how to do most good all-round, can one really assume that everyone must be agreed on this as his first aim? I don't think that we can just presuppose this. Someone might come along and say: "Why this at all? Why concern myself with general good instead of my own?" And this raises the problem of convincing him in some way that the furtherance of general good is an end that he ought to make his own. So *the* ultimate moral premise may be a matter for dispute; and unless there is a way of supporting it, the whole edifice of obligations based on it will fall apart.

And, finally, it is also too simple to say that doing most good all-round is what everyone ought to attempt every time and above all. Because there are at any one moment many claimants for a good turn, and one cannot satisfy them all: there are ourselves and others, our children, parents, our group, the present generation and the next, and there is the good of mankind at large. We think that we have some obligation to further most good all-round, but that we have also got special obligations toward those near us, and that we have some rights ourselves. So, once more, there may be situations for choice: where we have to decide which of two conflicting ultimate claims should come first. Remember our example about the upbringing of children. Few parents will dispute that their children's good is their concern. But *how much so,* this is already another matter. It may be true that infinite patience will rear children free of hate and aggression. But to do so to perfection may also consume the time and energy of their parents. How much of their own lives, then, should parents make over to their children? This is no longer a question of means to ends. It is quite a different sort of question, one of deciding between legitimate and conflicting ends, of how to distribute one's good turns.

And now let us look at the moral perplexities of our time again. It is pretty plain that our major worries are in this area of ultimate ends and of decisions between them. There have been times when these issues were more concealed by a general consensus of opinion. But in our own time, all the devils of dissent and disorientation seem to be let loose. A Nazi will allow that the good of his children is his responsibility. He will allow high priority to the good of his group, far above that of his parents or friends or of any single individual. But he will deny that the good of other groups is his business; and nothing will persuade him of a right for everyone to be treated humanely. A pacifist will put the preservation of human life before everything else. A Communist will put social justice and economic security before freedom of decision or thought. And he will be far more ready than a liberal individualist would think right to sacrifice the good of the present generation to that of the next. These are all differences about moral premises. And when people apply these premises to daily life, then quite different choices will become right or wrong for them: with the effect that, as we are all in this, we become targets to one another of disapproval and dismay. Everyone feels that the other is wrongheaded beyond comprehension; and opportunities abound for feeling this way.

I said before that perplexity about morals is one of the signs of our time. It is the area of dissent which I have just indicated which is mainly responsible for this. Because dissent about first things raises the question of how to settle it. And on this question we find ourselves in a dilemma. As I said, everyone feels that the other is wrongheaded in placing his priorities where he does. And if the other really is wrongheaded, then there must be a right and a wrong in these matters, and a way of showing what it is. But, in practice, is there such a way? There are few who have not at some time tried and failed. We all know how disputes about first things begin in argument only to end in recrimination; and it is where words fail one that one resorts to bad language. But surely words should not fail one here. If the other is wrong, then there should be a way of putting him right. We have been taught, and believe, that by using "reason" we can put him right. But, as reason is understood, it does not seem to work.

And this is how the philosophical issue has come to be raised. Persistent failure at solving a problem suggests that one has got the wrong measure of it: that one expects too much or the wrong things. So out of the trials and tribulations of our daily experience we are being made to ask: "How can one decide the rights and wrongs of ultimate choices or ways of life at all?"

I must say a little about contemporary trends in response to this question. The keynote, as one would expect, is skepticism of reason. But different conclusions are drawn from this. A very fashionable view is to say that we fail to convince each other only because there is nothing to convince each other of: there just is no arguable right or wrong of ultimate choices. To some people independence ultimately matters more than security and to others not; to some the good of their children is far more important than personal achievement and to others less so. And this is all there is to it. There is no saying that one choice is more "proper" or "rational" than the other. There is no disputing of ultimate tastes. And the reason given is that if there were it should be possible to prove to people that they ought to choose one ultimate course rather than another: one should be able to offer a reason for this. And in the nature of the case, this is impossible. First things, like liberty or doing good to others, one values for themselves. And one cannot give people a reason for valuing things for themselves or for valuing one of them more than the other. Because the only reason for valuing things in themselves is in what they are, and if people don't want them knowing what they are, there is nothing to tell them that could convert them. Hume once said that "it was not against reason to prefer the scratching of my little finger to the destruction of the whole world." For if you asked "and why not?" there is nothing one could say. So in the matter of ultimate choices we must tolerate, or may bash, each other, but we must not be perplexed at making no headway with arguing.

One may find this "solution" a little hard to take, if not its tolerance too complacent to tolerate. And let me say that its logic is not as strong as it sounds. It is possible that one ultimate choice should be more right than another even if there is no argument from which to prove this because not all truths are known by a formal proof. One does not prove by argument that it is raining outside, one just goes and looks. And, maybe, that some ultimate choices are more proper for a human being than others is also something which everyone just has to see for himself. Supposing that one said: "You may not feel this now, but if you thought, you would not have it in your heart to stand by while others suffer." I cannot prove this to you, but it may be true of you, and you would be the one to check on it for yourself. And by saying that one ultimate choice may be more "proper" or "rational" than another, one may just mean this: that it would recommend itself more than the other to a human being who was thoughtful and sincere.

In fact, the main European tradition in ethics is built on a conception like this, and great hopes for a universal and objective ethics used to be pinned on it. Man, it was said, has the moral order in his own nature because he has both a social nature and can reflect. By reflection he can put it to himself what it is to do good or harm; his social nature enables him to respond to these ideas. So when guided by reflection any human being will find the obligation to doing good and not doing harm in his own heart. The right order of choices is laid down for all in their own natures, plain for everyone to see who will trouble to look into himself.

I am referring to this root conception of our ethical tradition because, as we are looking at contemporary trends, it is also under fire today. Its most challenging critic is Jean-Paul Sartre, the French existentialist. Sartre's ideas developed during the war, when Frenchmen were up against having to choose between collaboration and resistance, and where anyone might be in the sort of conflict which Sartre reports of one of his students: should he stay with his widowed mother whose life depended on him, or join the Free French in an uncertain gamble on doing some good for an anonymous cause? Here was the typical challenge to moral thinking: to solve conflict about ultimate ends and ways of life. And, according to Sartre, none of the traditional formulae will stand the test. Should the student do what will cause most good all-round? The calculus is impossible. And even if possible there would still be the choice between causing most good all-round and protecting his mother. Would it help him to consider which choice would be more right by being more properly human? Again, the formula is too wide and vague to meet the concrete case. Human nature is not uniform and fixed enough to allow expression only in one choice and not in any other. The conception of the human heart as a book of rules prescribing the same for all, if only consulted properly, is a metaphysical fiction. Should he then seek guidance from his personal feelings, scrutinize his motives, and decide on that which in truth matters to him most? Sartre will not let him have this way out either. One cannot ask: "Is it more proper for *me* to protect my mother or my country?" any more than one can ask: "Is it more proper for a human being to protect his mother or his country?" And one cannot ask this because it is an illusion that by reflection a man could find out about his true feelings so as to guide his choice by them. The only proof of one's true feelings is in the acting. One only knows oneself by what one has decided. And, therefore, in the situation of conflict *there is no known guide to turn to.* Man, Sartre concludes, is "deserted," he must choose in darkness, he must opt for his ultimate goals in default of any knowledge of a better or worse. All the consolation he has is that in freely committing himself one way or another he is not drifting but exercising his human power of cutting the Gordian knot.

This doctrine destroys the illusion that in every complex situation there is one choice which, for everyone alike and quite unmistakably, is more properly human than any other. But, if it has a point here, it does not stop at this. For it goes on to deny that not even in any more personal and more fallible sense could our ultimate choices be guided by any conception of a better or worse. We cannot wait to see on which side our Gordian knot is buttered. Moral thinking in the past was naive and hopeful enough to think that we could. But the conflicts of modern man have found this out.

One need not follow Sartre all the way, as we shall see in a moment. But even so it becomes clear that right choices of ultimate ends may often have no sure guide in reason. And not everyone will, like Sartre, accept this with stoic pride as the cross of human freedom. So it is not surprising that the present should show one more trend. The trust in reason as a guide to conduct has historically succeeded the view that reason in morals requires the backing of religion. The emancipation of morality from religion on the contemporary scale is a product of recent history. And now that the limits of reason have become more apparent, there are also voices which cry "we told you so." That reason fails us does not mean that there is no right or wrong for human choices; but it shows that we have forgotten to look for instruction in the right place. The true lesson of the present is that we must go back on the divorce of morals from religion.

And with this, the picture of the philosophical situation is complete. Skepticism of reason is its keynote. And if it leaves us with a problem, it is the problem of reassessing what part reason can play.

I should like to say some more about this. And I shall begin with a word about the last view, that return to religious authority is the key to the situation. This is a wide topic, and I cannot do it justice here. All I want to say is that in my opinion this solution would be no cure-all. Because morality, as we understand it, is logically independent of religious authority. And if the skeptics were right, and there were no better or worse in ultimate choices discernible by "reason," then religious authority could not mend things either.

Because how could any authority settle that well-doing is the right, and harm-doing the wrong, choice for a human being? One may say: "But if God says so, surely this should settle it." And, in a way, this is fair enough, for believers at any rate. But we must be clear about the sense in which this is to be taken. For some people will mean by this: "God settles the matter by *saying so,* by *commanding* us to choose in these ways." But this would not be to settle the matter in the required way. It might make people do good or avoid harm in obedience to an order. But it could not produce the conviction that this choice was a morally right one or produce actions which could be called "moral" because they flowed from this conviction. Because one understands by a morally right choice one which is justified purely on the merits of the case and one which one makes independently of anyone's "say-so." And one understands by moral conduct, conduct which is quite unforced from without, coming purely from the inner conviction that the action is right for one in itself. God's command as such, therefore, could not do in place of rational conviction of right or wrong. Morality, as we understand it, still stands or falls on the possibility of arriving at such a conviction independently of any authority.

But if it is said that, "if God says so, this should settle it," one may also mean something else: that what should settle it is that it is *God* who says so, rather than God *saying* so. For one will then be saying: "If God has given the command, then one must take it that he is commanding the right thing; and it is reasonable to take one's instructions from a superior being." And this would be fair enough. But, again, this is not a view which could do in place of an ability on our part to arrive at rational convictions. For, in the first place, it would presuppose that we can form these convictions. We could not even conceive of God as telling what ultimate choices are right for us unless we knew what it was like to distinguish by ourselves between a right or wrong choice. So if skepticism of reason were correct, this view of how God could support us in our ultimate choices would fall to the ground too. And, in the second place, God's support here could not replace independent thinking as much as one may hope. Because the divine rulings tend to be general, as general, in fact, as the general enjoinders to doing well or dealing justly, which one thinks have a plain support in reason too. And, like them, they still leave us without a sure guide when it comes to complex cases: to a choice like that of Sartre's student or to a problem like deciding on the right measure of liberty or social justice in the institution of a given society. Moreover, as the philosophers and divines of the eighteenth century used to stress, without the recourse to "right reason" and independent moral thinking, there would be no check on the interpretations of the divine will by fallible human minds.

I do not therefore think that, if skepticism were right, the return to religion, even if possible on a wide enough scale, could provide enough of a remedy; nor that our present bewilderment is, in the first place, due to confusions about the right place of religion in morals. The crucial question remains that of skepticism of reason. We must ask: How far is it really justified?

Skepticism often comes from the disappointment of misplaced expectations. There is no comfort in anything, because nothing is good enough to replace the lost hope. And Sartre's views illustrate this. He finds that there is no *sure* way of choosing between one's mother and one's country. So he concludes that there can be *no* way of choosing anything rather than anything else. But this is precisely what does not follow; and the truth, as I see it, is rather that the power of thought to guide ultimate choices is a matter of degree. Some of them are plainly right or wrong—for anyone who deserves the name of a human being. One would have to be a fiend not to have it in one to see that some thought must be given to the good or harm of others. But when it comes to concrete cases, and to matters of conflict, then the big certainties begin to evaporate. How *much* of one's own life is one to give to others? How *much* is one to prefer independence to security? How *much* the good of humankind to that of one's group? These are issues of a different kind, and this must be acknowledged. One has not got enough ground here for saying that only one choice and no other could be right for everyone who is properly human. But nor could one say that every natural basis for a better or worse choice has gone, but rather that the basis for choice has become more personal. One may still make these choices judiciously or not, be guided in them by impartial reflection and honest self-scrutiny, or follow one's blind leanings. For these are qualities of mind on which judiciousness in choice depend at all times. In hard cases they cannot be exercised easily; but this is not enough for saying with Sartre that there is no guide in them at all. If there is not always a choice which is the *one* that is properly human, there is always a properly human way of making one's choices.

We keep confusing ourselves when we call this the way of "reason," and this confusion accounts for much of our disorientation. The point is not that the right choice may not be called the one "guided by reason" but that "reason" may mean so many things. "Reason" makes one think of calculation, of deduction, of learning from experience. But the reason which can guide ultimate choices is none of these; and one draws attention to this when one says that "the good" need not be "the clever." The "reason" of the clever finds out about things unknown. But everyone knows what it is to do good or harm; and if people fail to take notice, then this is not for lack of knowledge. And yet one may say, if loosely, that it is for lack of "using reason." Because "using reason" may also mean "reminding oneself of what one knows already," "putting it to oneself clearly, vividly, and without reserve." And the properly human choice is the one which is directed by such reminders. In a thoughtless frame of mind one may not mind hurting others; if roused, one may even enjoy it. But if one reminds oneself, sympathetically and plainly, of what doing harm does, one will find that one's own nature will not let one. One finds that harm-doing could not be one's choice as a reflective and normal human being.

And the same principle applies to the more tricky choices between ultimate alternatives. I should say that even with as trivial a choice as that between lambs fry and Wiener schnitzel, one is not condemned, as Sartre will have it, to choose in darkness. Even here one may choose rashly or considerately, with one's eyes open or not, in order to elicit which alternative would truly deserve priority for one. And to choose considerately would here mean making quite clear to oneself the nature of the alternatives before one; presenting it to oneself that having the one would be forsaking the other; and eliciting one's response to the thought of still opting for the one even in full view of thereby sacrificing the other. A choice so determined will be the one more truly proper for one than any other; one which I can defend to myself and others; one to the thought of which I can hope to return ever afterward without self-reproach. And to choose between one's mother and one's country, between independence and security, between one's own good and that of others, is only harder and beset more by inner conflict, but in principle no different. Here, too, it is a matter of distinguishing between one's immediate leanings and the well-considered order of one's priorities: the one which sincere reflection on the competing alternatives would show one to express one's true evaluation, the one again with which one could afterward hope to live in peace.

But I want to emphasize that these cases also show more clearly what diverse qualities of mind right choice requires. Philosophers' talk about a simple and unique faculty of moral intuition has here done much to befog the truth. There is not one faculty, there are many qualities of mind which must cooperate. One must have experience of what one is choosing between. One cannot choose well between independence and security any more than between lambs fry and Wiener schnitzel if all one knows is the basic meaning of the words. One must know the savor of living the one as one must know the savor of eating the other. Experience of life and the chance of living it as well as the enterprise to seek it are conditions for making right choices. The real worth of things must be explored; it cannot be deduced. And with big issues like freedom or security this is just the difficulty. We cannot vary the balance of a social order just for the sake of deepening our experience, and if we put our money on trying the one, we easily destroy our chance of trying the other, perhaps even our fitness to try it. This is why it has been said that freedom is more easily lost than gained. Moreover, our own experience is not always enough. To be clear about the good or harm of others, one requires imagination as well, the ability to put oneself into the other fellow's shoes, to extend one's sympathies from the familiar to the unfamiliar by noticing a human being behind the curtain of color, age, class, and distance. This ability, as everyone knows, is not easily exercised; and failure to exercise it lies behind many of our disagreements about the ethics of group relations in the international field. (Though, I should hasten to add, not of all.) And then again right choice requires still another quality of mind. For in order to present the issues to ourselves effectively, we must also be able to relive in the imagination what we know already. One may know of three thousand flood victims and feel no compunction to help because, as Arthur Koestler once said, "statistics don't bleed"; and, one might add, not *unless one makes them bleed.* And, finally, merely to put the alternatives before one, as when one is choosing between oneself and another, may still not be enough—because one may also do this either halfheartedly or without reserve, with or without self-deceit. And only if done without reserve will one's proper choice come before one. Now one may follow custom and call this the "choice of reason." But, then, let us be quite clear that moral reason is not that of the scientist or mathematician, whose "reason" has in our time become the paradigm of all reason. One's proper choice is not found under the microscope or by calculation, but it can be found; and not by the exercise of one special faculty but, rather, by the whole man testing *himself* out against an *objective* view of the issues for choice.

I shall only say a little more by way of a summing up. I hope that I have shown why contemporary skepticism goes too far. It is not true that Sartre's student had nothing to guide him. It was up to him to be judicious about his choice or not. True enough, no one else could have *handed* him the answer: your conscience cannot tell me what I ought to do. But it is also needlessly tough to pretend that in matters like these there could be no answer, no helpful or critical exchange. One cannot prove how anyone ought to choose, but one need not therefore take everyone else's views on ultimate ends, or ways of life, in silence or leave each other confined to the ivory towers of our private consciences. The outsider may help from his experience to make the issues stand out more clearly; he may work on the other's imagination; he may prompt him to reflect in the right way; he may deflate his self-deceits by a calm "if you seriously feel that way, then go right ahead." One should not think that where there is no argument there can be no conversation.

This applies to small things and large, and our big contemporary disagreements about ways of life are not therefore beyond treatment. We do in fact fail in treating them. But then, rather than blame the instrument, we might blame our tardiness in using it in matters in which our interests, or our conceits, are involved.

But I said before that skepticism comes from the disappointment of misplaced expectations. And skeptical disorientation will remain a sign of our time until we have learned to accept moral thinking for what it is and with its limits. What everyone hopes for as a guide are rules by which to settle all cases, applicable with ease, and in the same way to everyone alike. Instead, what we have available is a procedure, calling on many and fallible qualities of mind; a procedure which yields some broad and fairly obvious answers, but which for the rest leaves us to puzzle things out for ourselves, with a margin for error and disagreement too wide for comfort. It may be that we still have to grow up to learn to accept this for a fact: there is no moral Santa Claus in pure reason.

And let me conclude with one gentle reminder. It would not be fair to blame philosophers or "sophists" for forcing this recognition on to us. For what is doing it are once more the circumstances of our time, and philosophers are at best their mouthpiece. Our circumstances are complicating the issues beyond the powers of any book of rules. Not every society has to choose between freedom and social welfare as hard as ours. In the days when economic laissez-faire was a working proposition, one could have freedom along with economic welfare without much of a need for choice, or so one could think. But today, with the new means for procuring economic welfare, we must choose. To choose one must think. And even if thinking came to no more than to having a heart and keeping one's head, it would not come to nothing.

1956

Good and Evil

P. T. Geach

My first task will be to draw a logical distinction between two sorts of adjectives, suggested by the distinction between *attributive* adjectives (e.g. "a red book") and *predicative* adjectives (e.g. "this book is red"); I shall borrow this terminology from the grammars. I shall say that in a phrase "an A B" ("A" being an adjective and "B" being a noun) "A" is a (logically) predicative adjective if the predication "is an A B" splits up logically into a pair of predications "is a B" and "is A"; otherwise I shall say that "A" is a (logically) attributive adjective. Henceforth I shall use the terms "predicative adjective" and "attributive adjective" always in my special logical sense, unless the contrary is shown by my inserting the adverb "grammatically."

There are familiar examples of what I call attributive adjectives. "Big" and "small" are attributive; "x is a big flea" does not split up into "x is a flea" and "x is big," nor "x is a small elephant" into "x is an elephant" and "x is small"; for if these analyses were legitimate, a simple argument would show that a big flea is a big animal and a small elephant a small animal. Again, the sort of adjective that the mediaevals called

Professor Geach has asked us to point out that in various respects this article no longer represents his present views. For his present position, see "Why Men Need the Virtues" and "Prudence," chapters 1 and 5 in his *The Virtues* (Cambridge University Press, 1977). See also "The Moral Law and the Law of God," essay 8 in his *God and the Soul* (Routledge Kegan Paul, 1969).

P. T. Geach, "Good and Evil," *Analysis* 17 (1956): 33–42. Reprinted with the permission of the author.

alienans is attributive; "x is a forged banknote" does not split up into "x is a banknote" and "x is forged," nor "x is the putative father of y" into "x is the father of y" and "x is putative." On the other hand, in the phrase "a red book" "red" is a predicative adjective in my sense, although not grammatically so, for "is a red book" logically splits up into "is a book" and "is red."

I can now state my first thesis about good and evil: "good" and "bad" are always attributive, not predicative, adjectives. This is fairly clear about "bad" because "bad" is something like an *alienans* adjective; we cannot safely predicate of a bad A what we predicate of an A, any more than we can predicate of a forged banknote or a putative father what we predicate of a banknote or a father. We actually call forged money "bad"; and we cannot infer e.g. that because food supports life bad food supports life. For "good" the point is not so clear at first sight, since "good" is not *alienans*—whatever holds true of an A as such holds true of a good A. But consider the contrast in such a pair of phrases as "red car" and "good car." I could ascertain that a distant object is a red car because I can see it is red and a keener-sighted but color-blind friend can see it is a car; there is no such possibility of ascertaining that a thing is a good car by pooling independent information that it is good and that it is a car. This sort of example shows that "good" like "bad" is essentially an attributive adjective. Even when "good" or "bad" stands by itself as a predicate, and is thus grammatically predicative, some substantive has to be understood; there is no such thing as being just good or bad, there is only being a good or bad so-and-so. (If I say that something is a good or bad *thing,* either "thing" is a mere proxy for a more descriptive noun to be supplied from the context; or else I am trying to use "good" or "bad" predicatively, and its being grammatically attributive is a mere disguise. The latter attempt is, on my thesis, illegitimate.)

We can indeed say *simpliciter* "A is good" or "A is bad," where "A" is a proper name; but this is an exception that proves the rule. For Locke was certainly wrong in holding that there is no nominal essence of individuals; the continued use of a proper name "A" always presupposes a continued reference to an individual as being the same X, where "X" is some common noun, and the "X" expresses the nominal essence of the individual called "A." Thus use of the proper name "Peter Geach" presupposes a continuing reference to the same *man;* use of "the Thames" a continuing reference to the same *river;* and so on. In modern logic books you often read that proper names have no meaning, in the sense of "meaning" in which common nouns are said to have meaning; or (more obscurely) that they have no "connotation." But consider the difference between the understanding that a man has of a conversation overheard in a country house when he knows that "Seggie" stands for a man, and what he has if he is uncertain whether "Seggie" stands for a man, a Highland stream, a village, or a dog. In the one case he knows *what* "Seggie" means, though not *whom;* in the other case he does not know *what* "Seggie" means and cannot follow the drift of the conversation. Well, then if the common noun "X" expresses the nominal essence of the individual called "A"; if *being the same X* is a condition whose fulfillment is presupposed by our still calling an individual "A"; then the meaning of "A is good/bad" said *simpliciter,* will be "A is a good/bad X." E.g. if "Seggie" stands for a man, "Seggie is good" said *simpliciter* will mean "Seggie is a good man," though context might make it mean "Seggie is a good deer-stalker," or the like.

The moral philosophers known as Objectivists would admit all that I have said as regards the ordinary uses of the terms "good" and "bad"; but they allege that there is an essentially different, predicative, use of the terms in such utterances as "pleasure is good" and "preferring inclination to duty is bad," and that this use alone is of philosophical importance. The ordinary uses of "good" and "bad" are for Objectivists just a complex tangle of ambiguities. I read an article once by an Objectivist exposing these ambiguities and the baneful effects they have on philosophers not forewarned of them. One philosopher who was so misled was Aristotle; Aristotle, indeed, did not talk English, but by a remarkable coincidence ἀγαθός had ambiguities quite parallel to those of "good." Such coincidences are, of course, possible; puns are sometimes translatable. But it is also possible that the uses of ἀγαθός and "good" run parallel because they express one and the same concept; that this is a philosophically important concept, in which Aristotle did well to be interested; and that the apparent dissolution of this concept into a mass of ambiguities results from trying to assimilate it to the concepts expressed by ordinary predicative adjectives. It is mere prejudice to think that either all things called "good" must satisfy some one condition, or the term "good" is hopelessly ambiguous. A philosopher who writes off most of the uses of "good" as trivial facts about the English language can, of course, with some plausibility, represent the remaining uses of "good" as all expressing some definite condition fulfilled by good things—e.g. that they either contain, or are conducive to, pleasure; or again that they satisfy desire. Such theories of goodness are, however, open to well-known objections; they are cases of the Naturalistic Fallacy, as Objectivists say. The Objectivists' own theory is that "good" in the selected uses they leave to the word does not supply an ordinary, "natural," description of things, but ascribes to them a simple and indefinable *non*-natural attribute. But nobody has ever given a coherent and understandable account of what it is for an attribute to be non-natural. I am very much afraid that the Objectivists are just playing fast and loose with the term "attribute." In order to assimilate "good" to ordinary predicative adjectives like "red" and "sweet" they call goodness an attribute; to escape undesired consequences drawn from the assimilation, they can always protest, "Oh no, not like that. Goodness isn't a *natural* attribute like redness and sweetness, it's a non-natural attribute." It is just as though somebody thought to escape the force of Frege's arguments that the number 7 is not a figure, by saying that it is a figure, only a non-natural figure, and that this is a possibility Frege failed to consider.

Moreover, can a philosopher offer philosophical utterances like "pleasure is good" as an *explanation* of how he means "good" to be taken in his discussions? "Forget the uses of 'good' in ordinary language" says the Objectivist; "in our discussion it shall mean what I mean by it in such typical remarks as 'pleasure is good.' You, of course, know just how I want you to take these. No, of course I cannot explain further: don't you know that 'good' in my sense is a simple and undefinable term?" But how can we be asked to take for granted at the outset that a peculiarly philosophical use of words necessarily means anything at all? Still less can we be expected at the outset to know what this use means.

I conclude that Objectivism is only the pretense of a way out of the Naturalistic Fallacy: it does not really give an account of how "good" differs in its logic from other terms, but only darkens counsel by words without knowledge.

What I have said so far would meet with general approval by contemporary ethical writers at Oxford (whom I shall henceforth call the Oxford Moralists); and I now have to consider their positive account of "good." They hold that the features of the term's use which I have described derive from its function's being primarily not descriptive at all but commendatory. "That is a good book" means something like "I recommend that book" or "choose that book." They hold, however, that although the primary force of "good" is commendation there are many cases where its force is purely descriptive—"Hutton was batting on a good wicket," in a newspaper report, would not mean "What a wonderful wicket Hutton was batting on. May you have such a wicket when you bat." The Oxford Moralists account for such cases by saying that here "good" is, so to say, in quotation marks; Hutton was batting on a "good" wicket, i.e. a wicket such as cricket fans would call "good," i.e. would commend and choose.

I totally reject this view that "good" has not a primarily descriptive force. Somebody who did not care two pins about cricket, but fully understood how the game worked (not an impossible supposition), could supply a purely descriptive sense for the phrase "good batting wicket" regardless of the tastes of cricket fans. Again if I call a man a good burglar or a good cut-throat I am certainly not commending him myself; one can imagine circumstances in which these descriptions would serve to guide another man's choice (e.g. if a commando leader were choosing burglars and cut-throats for a special job), but such circumstances are rare and cannot give the primary sense of the descriptions. It ought to be clear that calling a thing a good A does not influence choice unless the one who is choosing happens to want an A; and this influence on action is not the logically primary force of the word "good." "You have ants in your pants," which obviously has a primarily descriptive force, is far closer to affecting action than many uses of the term "good." And many uses of the word "good" have no reference to the tastes of a panel of experts or anything of the sort; if I say that a man has a good eye or a good stomach my remark has a very clear descriptive force and has no reference to any panel of eye or stomach fanciers.

So far as I can gather from their writings, the Oxford Moralists would develop two lines of objection against the view that "good" has a primarily descriptive force. First, if we avoid the twin errors of the Naturalistic Fallacy and of Objectivism we shall see that there is no one description, "natural" or "non-natural," to which all good things answer. The traits for which a thing is called "good" are different according to the kind of thing in question; a knife is called "good" if it is UVW, a stomach if it is XYZ, and so on. So, if "good" did have a properly descriptive force this would vary from case to case: "good" applied to knives would express the attributes UVW, "good" as applied to stomachs would express the attributes XYZ, and so on. If "good" is not to be merely ambiguous its primary force must be taken to be the unvarying commendatory force, not the indefinitely varying descriptive force.

This argument is a mere fallacy; it is another example of assimilating "good" to ordinary predicative adjectives, or rather it assumes that this assimilation would have to be all right if the force of "good" were descriptive. It would not in fact follow, even if "good" were an ordinary predicative adjective, that if "good knife" means the same as "knife that is UVW," "good" means the same as "UVW." "Triangle with all its sides equal" means the same as "triangle with three sides equal," but you cannot cancel out "triangle" and say that "with all its sides equal" means the same as "with three sides equal." In the case of "good" the fallacy is even grosser; it is like thinking that "square of" means the same as "double of" because "the square of 2" means the same as "the double of 2." This mathematical analogy may help to get our heads clear. There is no one number by which you can always multiply a number to get its square: but it does not follow either that "square of" is an ambiguous expression meaning sometimes "double of," sometimes "treble of," etc., or that you have to do something other than multiplying to find the square of a number; and, given a number, its square is determinate. Similarly, there is no one description to which all things called "good so-and-so's" answer; but it does not follow either that "good" is a very ambiguous expression or that calling a thing good is something different from describing it; and given the descriptive force of "A," the descriptive force of "a good A" does not depend upon people's tastes.

"But I could know what 'good hygrometer' meant without knowing what hygrometers were for; I could not, however, in that case be giving a definite descriptive force to 'good hygrometer' as opposed to 'hygrometer'; so 'good' must have commendatory not descriptive force." The reply to this objection (imitated from actual arguments of the Oxford Moralists) is that if I do not know what hygrometers are for, I do not really know what "hygrometer" means, and *therefore* do not really know what "good hygrometer" means; I merely know that I could find out its meaning by finding out what hygrometers were for—just as I know how I could find out the value of the square of the number of the people in Sark if I knew the number of people, and *so far* may be said to understand the phrase, "the square of the number of the people in Sark."

The Oxford Moralists' second line of objection consists in first asking whether the connection between calling a thing "a good A" and advising a man who wants an A to choose this one is analytic or empirical, and then developing a dilemma. It sounds clearly wrong to make the connection a mere empirical fact; but if we make it analytic, then "good" cannot have descriptive force, for from a mere description advice cannot be logically inferred.

I should indeed say that the connection is not merely empirical; but neither is it analytic. It belongs to the *ratio* of "want," "choose," "good," and "bad," that, normally, and other things being equal, a man who wants an A will choose a good A and will not choose a bad A—or rather will choose an A that he thinks good and will not choose an A that he thinks bad. This holds good whether the A's we are choosing between are knives, horses, or thieves; *quidquid appetitur, appetitur sub specie boni.* Since the qualifying phrase, "normally and other things being equal," is necessary for the truth of this statement, it is not an analytic statement. But the presence of these phrases does *not* reduce the statement to a mere rough empirical generalization: to think this would be to commit a crude empiricist fallacy, exposed once for all by Wittgenstein. Even if not all A's are B's, the statement that A's are normally B's may belong to the *ratio* of an A. Most chess moves are valid, most intentions are carried out, most statements are veracious; none of these statements is just a rough generalization, for if we tried to describe how it would be for most chess moves to be invalid, most intentions not to be carried out, most statements to be lies, we should soon find ourselves talking nonsense. We shall equally find ourselves talking nonsense if we try to describe a people whose custom it was, when they wanted A's, to choose A's they thought bad and reject A's they thought good. (And this goes for *all* interpretations of "A.")

There is, I admit, much more difficulty in passing from "man" to "good/bad/man," or from "human act" to "good/bad/human act," if these phrases are to be taken as purely descriptive and in senses determined simply by those of "man" and "human act." I think this difficulty could be overcome; but even so the Oxford Moralists could now deploy a powerful weapon of argument. Let us suppose that we have found a clear descriptive meaning for "good human act" and for "bad human act," and have shown that adultery answers to the description "bad human act." Why should this consideration deter an intending adulterer? By what logical step can we pass from the supposedly descriptive sentence "adultery is a bad human act" to the imperative "you must not commit adultery"? It is useless to say "It is your duty to do good and avoid doing evil"; either this is much the same as the unhelpful remark "It is good to do good and avoid doing evil," or else "It is your duty" is a smuggling in of an imperative force not conveyed by the terms "good" and "evil" which are *ex hypothesi* purely descriptive.

We must allow in the first place that the question, "Why should I?" or "Why shouldn't I?" is a reasonable question, which calls for an answer, not for abusive remarks about the wickedness of asking; and I think that the only relevant answer is an appeal to something the questioner *wants.* Since Kant's time people have supposed that there is another sort of relevant reply—an appeal not to inclination but to the Sense of Duty. Now indeed a man may be got by training into a state of mind in which "You *must* not" is a sufficient answer to "Why shouldn't I?"; in which, giving this answer to himself, or hearing it given by others, strikes him with a quite peculiar awe; in which, perhaps, he even thinks he "must not" ask why he "must not." (Cf. Lewis Carroll's juvenile poem "My Fairy," with its devastating "Moral: You mustn't.") Moral philosophers of the Objectivist school, like Sir David Ross, would call this "apprehension of one's obligations"; it does not worry them that, but for God's grace, this sort of training can make a man "apprehend" practically anything as his "obligations." (Indeed, they admire a man who does what he thinks he *must* do regardless of what he actually does; is he not acting from the Sense of Duty which is the highest motive?) But even if *ad hominem* "You mustn't" is a final answer to "Why shouldn't I?," it is no rational answer at all.

It can, I think, be shown that an action's being a good or bad human action is of itself something that touches the agent's desires. Although calling a thing "a good A" or "a bad A" does not of itself work upon the hearer's desires, it may be expected to do so if the hearer happens to be choosing an A. Now what a man cannot fail to be choosing is his manner of acting; so to call a manner of acting good or bad cannot but serve to guide action. As Aristotle says, acting well, *εὐπραξία*, is a man's aim *simpliciter*, *ἁπλῶς*, and *qua* man; other objects of choice are so only relatively, *προς τι*, or are the objects of a particular man, *τινός*[1]; but *any* man has to choose how to act, so calling an action good or bad does not depend for its effect as a suasion upon any individual peculiarities of desire.

I shall not here attempt to explicate the descriptive force of "good (bad) human action": but some remarks upon the logic of the phrase seem to be called for. In the first place, a tennis stroke or chess move is a human act. Are we to say, then, that the description "good tennis stroke" or "good chess move" is of itself something that must appeal to the agent's desire? Plainly not; but this is no difficulty. Although a tennis stroke or a chess move is a human act, it does not follow that a good tennis stroke or a good chess move is a good human act, because of the peculiar logic of the term "good"; so calling a tennis stroke or a chess move good is not *eo ipso* an appeal to what an agent must be wanting.

Secondly, though we can sensibly speak of a good or bad human act, we cannot sensibly speak of a good or bad event, a good or bad thing to happen. "Event," like "thing," is too empty a word to convey either a criterion of identity or a standard of goodness; to ask "Is this a good or bad thing (to happen)?" is as useless as to ask "Is this the same thing that I saw yesterday?" or "Is the same event still going on?," unless the emptiness of "thing" or "event" is filled up by a special context of utterance. Caesar's murder was a bad thing to happen to a living organism, a good fate for a man who wanted divine worship for himself, and again a good or bad act on the part of his murderers; to ask whether it was a good or bad event would be senseless.

Thirdly, I am deliberately ignoring the supposed distinction between the Right and the Good. In Aquinas there is no such distinction. He finds it sufficient to talk of good and bad human acts. When Ross would say that there is a morally good action but not a right act, Aquinas would say that a good human intention had issued in what was, in fact, a bad action; and when Ross would say that there was a right act but not a morally good action, Aquinas would say that there was a bad human act performed in circumstances in which a similar act with a different intention would have been a good one (e.g. giving money to a beggar for the praise of men rather than for the relief of his misery).

Since the English word "right" has an idiomatic predilection for the definite article—we speak of *a* good chess move but of *the* right move—people who think that

[1]E. N. 1139*b* 2–4.

doing right is something other than doing good will regard virtuous behavior as consisting, not just in doing good and eschewing evil, but in doing, on every occasion, *the* right act for the occasion. This speciously strict doctrine leads in fact to quite laxist consequences. A man who just keeps on doing good and eschewing evil, if he knows that adultery is an evil act, will decide that (as Aristotle says) there can be no deliberating when or how or with whom to commit adultery.[2] But a man who believes in discerning, on each occasion, *the* right act for the occasion, may well decide that on this occasion, all things considered, adultery is *the* right action. Sir David Ross explicitly tells us that on occasion *the* right act may be the judicial punishment of an innocent man "that the whole nation perish not": for in this case "the *prima facie* duty of consulting the general interest has proved more obligatory than the perfectly distinct *prima facie* duty of respecting the rights of those who have respected the rights of others."[3] (We must charitably hope that for him the words of Caiaphas that he quotes just had the vaguely hallowed associations of a Bible text, and that he did not remember whose judicial murder was being counselled.)[4]

I am well aware that much of this discussion is unsatisfying; some points on which I think I do see clear I have not been able to develop at proper length; on many points (e.g. the relation between desire and good, and the precise *ratio* of evil in evil acts), I certainly do not see clear. Moreover, though I have argued that the characteristic of being a good or bad human action is of itself bound to influence the agent's desires, I have not discussed whether an action of its nature bad is always and on all accounts to be avoided, as Aristotle thought. But perhaps, though I have not made everything clear, I have made some things clearer.

[2]E. N. 1107*a* 16.

[3]*The Right and the Good,* p. 61.

[4]Holding this notion of *the* right act, people have even held that some creative act would be *the* right act for a God—e.g. that a God would be obliged to create the best of all possible worlds, so that either this world of ours is the best possible or there is no good God. I shall not go further into this; it will be enough to say that what is to be expected of a good Creator is *a* good world, not *the* right world.

1956

Extreme and Restricted Utilitarianism

J. J. C. Smart

1

Utilitarianism is the doctrine that the rightness of actions is to be judged by their consequences. What do we mean by "actions" here? Do we mean particular actions or do we mean classes of actions? According to which way we interpret the word "actions" we get two different theories, both of which merit the appellation "utilitarian."

(1) If by "actions" we mean particular individual actions we get the sort of doctrine held by Bentham, Sidgwick, and Moore. According to this doctrine we test individual actions by their consequences, and general rules, like "keep promises," are mere rules of thumb which we use only to avoid the necessity of estimating the probable consequences of our actions at every step. The rightness or wrongness of keeping a promise on a particular occasion depends only on the goodness or badness of the consequences of keeping or of breaking the promise on that particular occasion. Of course part of the consequences of breaking the promise, and a part to which we will normally ascribe decisive importance, will be the weakening of faith in the institution of promising. However, if the goodness of the consequences of breaking the rule is *in toto* greater than

Based on a paper read to the Victorian Branch of the Australasian Association of Psychology and Philosophy, October, 1955.

J. J. C. Smart, "Extreme and Restricted Utilitarianism" from ESSAYS METAPHYSICAL AND MORAL (Oxford: Basil Blackwell, 1987). Originally in *Philosophical Quarterly* 6 (1956). Reprinted with the permission of Blackwell Publishers.

the goodness of the consequences of keeping it, then we must break the rule, irrespective of whether the goodness of the consequences of *everybody's* obeying the rule is or is not greater than the consequences of *everybody's* breaking it. To put it shortly, rules do not matter, save *per accidens* as rules of thumb and as *de facto* social institutions with which the utilitarian has to reckon when estimating consequences. I shall call this doctrine "extreme utilitarianism."

(2) A more modest form of utilitarianism has recently become fashionable. The doctrine is to be found in Toulmin's book *The Place of Reason in Ethics,* in Nowell-Smith's *Ethics* (though I think Nowell-Smith has qualms), in John Austin's *Lectures on Jurisprudence* (Lecture II), and even in J. S. Mill, if Urmson's interpretation of him is correct (*Philosophical Quarterly,* Vol. 3, pp. 33–39, 1953). Part of its charm is that it appears to resolve the dispute in moral philosophy between intuitionists and utilitarians in a way which is very neat. The above philosophers hold, or seem to hold, that moral rules are more than rules of thumb. In general the rightness of an action is *not* to be tested by evaluating its consequences but only by considering whether or not it falls under a certain rule. Whether the rule is to be considered an acceptable moral rule, is, however, to be decided by considering the consequences of adopting the rule. Broadly, then, actions are to be tested by rules and rules by consequences. The only cases in which we must test an individual action directly by its consequences are *(a)* when the action comes under two different rules, one of which enjoins it and one of which forbids it, and *(b)* when there is no rule whatever that governs the given case. I shall call this doctrine "restricted utilitarianism."

It should be noticed that the distinction I am making cuts across, and is quite different from, the distinction commonly made between hedonistic and ideal utilitarianism. Bentham was an extreme hedonistic utilitarian and Moore an extreme ideal utilitarian, and Toulmin (perhaps) could be classified as a restricted ideal utilitarian. A hedonistic utilitarian holds that the goodness of the consequences of an action is a function only of their pleasurableness and an ideal utilitarian, like Moore, holds that pleasurableness is not even a necessary condition of goodness. Mill seems, if we are to take his remarks about higher and lower pleasures seriously, to be neither a pure hedonistic nor a pure ideal utilitarian. He seems to hold that pleasurableness is a necessary condition for goodness, but that goodness is a function of other qualities of mind as well. Perhaps we can call him a quasi-ideal utilitarian. When we say that a state of mind is good I take it that we are expressing some sort of *rational preference.* When we say that it is pleasurable I take it that we are saying that it is enjoyable, and when we say that something is a higher pleasure I take it that we are saying that it is more truly, or more deeply, enjoyable. I am doubtful whether "more deeply enjoyable" does not just mean "more enjoyable, even though not more enjoyable on a first look," and so I am doubtful whether quasi-ideal utilitarianism, and possibly ideal utilitarianism too, would not collapse into hedonistic utilitarianism on a closer scrutiny of the logic of words like "preference," "pleasure," "enjoy," "deeply enjoy," and so on. However, it is beside the point of the present paper to go into these questions. I am here concerned only with the issue between extreme and restricted utilitarianism and am ready to concede that both forms of utilitarianism can be either hedonistic or non-hedonistic.

The issue between extreme and restricted utilitarianism can be illustrated by considering the remark "But suppose everyone did the same" (Cf. A. K. Stout's article in *The Australasian Journal of Philosophy,* Vol. 32, pp. 1–29). Stout distinguishes two forms of the universalization principle, the causal forms and the hypothetical form. To say that you ought not to do an action A because it would have bad results if everyone (or many people) did action A may be merely to point out that while the action A would otherwise be the optimific one, nevertheless when you take into account that doing A will probably cause other people to do A too, you can see that A is not, on a broad view, really optimific. If this causal influence could be avoided (as may happen in the case of a secret desert island promise) then we would disregard the universalization principle. This is the causal form of the principle. A person who accepted the universalization principle in its hypothetical form would be one who was concerned only with what would happen *if* everyone did the action A: he would be totally unconcerned with the question of whether in fact everyone would do the action A. That is, he might say that it would be wrong not to vote because it would have bad results if everyone took this attitude, and he would be totally unmoved by arguments purporting to show that my refusing to vote has no effect whatever on other people's propensity to vote. Making use of Stout's distinction, we can say that an extreme utilitarian would apply the universalization principle in the causal form, while a restricted utilitarian would apply it in the hypothetical form.

How are we to decide the issue between extreme and restricted utilitarianism? I wish to repudiate at the outset that milk and water approach which describes itself sometimes as "investigating what is implicit in the common moral consciousness" and sometimes as "investigating how people ordinarily talk about morality." We have only to read the newspaper correspondence about capital punishment or about what should be done with Formosa to realize that the common moral consciousness is in part made up of superstitious elements, of morally bad elements, and of logically confused elements. I address myself to good hearted and benevolent people and so I hope that if we rid ourselves of the logical confusion the superstitious and morally bad elements will largely fall away. For even among good hearted and benevolent people it is possible to find superstitious and morally bad reasons for moral beliefs. These superstitious and morally bad reasons hide behind the protective screen of logical confusion. With people who are not logically confused but who are openly superstitious or morally bad I can of course do nothing. That is, our ultimate pro-attitudes may be different. Nevertheless I propose to rely on *my own* moral consciousness and to appeal to *your* moral consciousness and to forget about what people ordinarily say. "The obligation to obey a rule," says Nowell-Smith (*Ethics*, p. 239), "does not, *in the opinion of ordinary men*" (my italics), "rest on the beneficial consequences of obeying it in a particular case." What does this prove? Surely it is more than likely that ordinary men are confused here. Philosophers should be able to examine the question more rationally.

2

For an extreme utilitarian moral rules are rules of thumb. In practice the extreme utilitarian will mostly guide his conduct by appealing to the rules ("do not lie," "do not break promises," etc.) of common sense morality. This is not because there is anything sacrosanct in the rules themselves but because he can argue that probably he will most often act in an extreme utilitarian way if he does not think as a utilitarian. For one thing, actions have frequently to be done in a hurry. Imagine a man seeing a person drowning. He jumps in and rescues him. There is no time to reason the matter out, but usually this will be the course of action which an extreme utilitarian would recommend if he did reason the matter out. If, however, the man drowning had been drowning in a river near Berchtesgaden in 1938, and if he had had the well known black forelock and moustache of Adolf Hitler, an extreme utilitarian would, if he had time, work out the probability of the man's being the villainous dictator, and if the probability were high enough he would, on extreme utilitarian grounds, leave him to drown. The rescuer, however, has not time. He trusts to his instincts and dives in and rescues the man. And this trusting to instincts and to moral rules can be justified on extreme utilitarian grounds. Furthermore, an extreme utilitarian who knew that the drowning man was Hitler would nevertheless praise the rescuer, not condemn him. For by praising the man he is strengthening a courageous and benevolent disposition of mind, and in general this disposition has great positive utility. (Next time, perhaps, it will be Winston Churchill that the man saves!) We must never forget that an extreme utilitarian may praise actions which he knows to be wrong. Saving Hitler was wrong, but it was a member of a class of actions which are generally right, and the motive to do actions of this class is in general an optimific one. In considering questions of praise and blame it is not the expediency of the praised or blamed action that is at issue, but the expediency of the praise. It can be expedient to praise an inexpedient action and inexpedient to praise an expedient one.

Lack of time is not the only reason why an extreme utilitarian may, on extreme utilitarian principles, trust to rules of common sense morality. He knows that in particular cases where his own interests are involved his calculations are likely to be biased in his own favor. Suppose that he is unhappily married and is deciding whether to get divorced. He will in all probability greatly exaggerate his own unhappiness (and possibly his wife's) and greatly underestimate the harm done to his children by the break up of the family. He will probably also underestimate the likely harm done by the weakening of the general faith in marriage vows. So probably he will come to the correct extreme utilitarian conclusion if he does not in this instance think as an extreme utilitarian but trusts to common sense morality.

There are many more and subtle points that could be made in connection with the relation between extreme utilitarianism and the morality of common sense. All those that I have just made and many more will be found in Book IV Chapters 3–5 of Sidgwick's *Methods of Ethics*. I think that this book is the best book ever written on ethics, and that these chapters are the best chapters of the book. As they occur so near the end of a very long book they are unduly neglected. I refer the reader, then, to Sidgwick for the classical exposition of the relation between (extreme) utilitarianism and the morality of common sense. One further point raised by Sidgwick in this connection is whether an (extreme) utilitarian ought on (extreme) utilitarian principles to propagate (extreme) utilitarianism among the public. As most people are not very philosophical and not good at empirical calculations, it is probable that they will most often act in an extreme utilitarian way if they do not try to think as extreme utilitarians. We have seen how easy it would be to misapply the extreme utilitarian criterion in the case of divorce. Sidgwick seems to think it quite probable that an extreme utilitarian should not propagate his doctrine too widely. However, the great danger to humanity comes nowadays on the plane of public morality—not private morality. There is a greater danger to humanity from the hydrogen bomb than from an increase of the divorce rate, regrettable though that might be, and there seems no doubt that extreme utilitarianism makes for good sense in international relations. When France walked out of the United Nations because she did not wish Morocco discussed, she said that she was within her rights because Morocco and Algiers are part of her metropolitan territory and nothing to do with U.N. This was clearly a legalistic if not superstitious argument. We should not be concerned with the so-called "rights" of France or any other country but with whether the cause of humanity would best be served by discussing Morocco in U.N. (I am not saying that the answer to this is "Yes." There are good grounds for supposing that more harm than good would come by such a discussion.) I myself have no hesitation in saying that on extreme utilitarian principles we ought to propagate extreme utilitarianism as widely as possible. But Sidgwick had respectable reasons for suspecting the opposite.

The extreme utilitarian, then, regards moral rules as rules of thumb and as sociological facts that have to be taken into account when deciding what to do, just as facts of any other sort have to be taken into account. But in themselves they do not justify any action.

3

The restricted utilitarian regards moral rules as more than rules of thumb for short-circuiting calculations of consequences. Generally, he argues, consequences are not relevant at all when we are deciding what to do in a particular case. In general, they are relevant only to deciding what rules are good reasons for acting in a certain way in particular cases. This doctrine is possibly a good account of how the modern unreflective twentieth century Englishman often thinks about morality, but surely it is monstrous as an account of how it is most rational to think about morality. Suppose that there is a rule *R* and that in 99% of cases the best possible results are obtained by acting in accordance with *R*. Then clearly *R* is a useful rule of thumb; if we have not time or are not impartial enough to assess the consequences of an action it is an extremely good bet that the thing to do is to act in accordance with *R*. But is it not monstrous to suppose that if we *have* worked out the consequences and if we have perfect faith in the impartiality of our calculations, and if we *know* that in this instance to break *R* will have better results than to keep it, we should nevertheless obey the rule? Is it not to erect *R* into a sort of idol if we keep it when breaking it will prevent, say, some avoidable misery? Is not this a form of superstitious rule-worship (easily explicable psychologically) and not the rational thought of a philosopher?

The point may be made more clearly if we consider Mill's comparison of moral rules to the tables in the nautical almanac (*Utilitarianism*, Everyman Edition, pp. 22–23). This comparison of Mill's is adduced by Urmson as evidence that Mill was a restricted utilitarian, but I do not think that it will bear this interpretation at all. (Though I quite agree with Urmson that many other things said by Mill are in harmony with restricted rather than extreme utilitarianism. Probably Mill had never thought very much about the distinction and was arguing for utilitarianism, restricted or extreme, against other and quite non-utilitarian forms of moral argument.) Mill says: "Nobody argues that the art of navigation is not founded on astronomy, because sailors cannot wait to calculate the Nautical Almanac. Being rational creatures, they go out upon the sea of life with their minds made up on the common questions of right and wrong, as well as on many of the far more difficult questions of wise and foolish. . . . Whatever we adopt as the fundamental principle of morality, we require subordinate principles to apply it by." Notice that this is, as it stands, only an argument for subordinate principles as rules of thumb. The example of the nautical almanac is misleading because the information given in the almanac is in all cases the same as the information one would get if one made a long and laborious calculation from the original astronomical data on which the almanac is founded. Suppose, however, that astronomy were different. Suppose that the behavior of the sun, moon and planets was very nearly as it is now, but that on rare occasions there were peculiar irregularities and discontinuities, so that the almanac gave us rules of the form "in 99% of cases where the observations are such and such you can deduce that your position is so and so." Furthermore, let us suppose that there were methods which enabled us, by direct and laborious calculation from the original astronomical data, not using the rough and ready tables of the almanac, to get our correct position in 100% of cases. Seafarers might use the almanac because they never had time for the long calculations and they were content with a 99% chance of success in calculating their positions. Would it not be absurd, however, if they *did* make the direct calculation, and finding that it disagreed with the almanac calculation, nevertheless they ignored it and stuck to the almanac conclusion? Of course the case would be altered if there were a high enough probability of making slips in the direct calculation: then we might stick to the almanac result, liable to error though we knew it to be, simply because the direct calculation would be open to error for a different reason, the fallibility of the computer. This would be analogous to the case of the extreme utilitarian who abides by the conventional rule against the dictates of his utilitarian calculations simply because he thinks that his calculations are probably affected by personal bias. But if the navigator were sure of his direct calculations would he not be foolish to abide by his almanac? I conclude, then, that if we change our suppositions about astronomy and the almanac (to which there are no exceptions) to bring the case into line with that of morality (to whose rules there are exceptions), Mill's example loses its appearance of supporting the restricted form of utilitarianism. Let me say once more that I am not here concerned with how ordinary men think about morality but with how they ought to think. We could quite well imagine a race of sailors who acquired a superstitious reverence for their almanac, even though it was only right in 99% of cases, and who indignantly threw overboard any man who mentioned the possibility of a direct calculation. But would this behavior of the sailors be rational?

Let us consider a much discussed sort of case in which the extreme utilitarian might go against the conventional moral rule. I have promised to a friend, dying on a desert island from which I am subsequently rescued, that I will see that his fortune (over which I have control) is given to a jockey club. However, when I am rescued I decide that it would be better to give the money to a hospital, which can do more good with it. It may be argued that I am wrong to give the money to the hospital. But why? *(a)* The hospital can do more good with the money than the jockey club can. *(b)* The present case is unlike most cases of promising in that no one except me knows about the promise. In breaking the promise I am doing so with complete secrecy and am doing nothing to weaken the general faith in promises. That is, a factor, which would normally keep the extreme utilitarian from promise breaking even in otherwise unoptimific cases, does not at present operate. *(c)* There is no doubt a slight weakening in my own character as an habitual promise keeper, and moreover psychological tensions will be set up in me every time I am asked what the man made me promise him to do. For clearly I shall have to say that he made me promise to give the money to the hospital, and, since I am an habitual truth teller, this will go very much against the grain with me. Indeed I am pretty sure that in practice I myself would keep the promise. But we are not discussing what my moral habits would probably make me do; we are discussing what I ought to do. Moreover, we must not forget that even if it would be most rational of me to give the money to the hospital it would also be most rational of you to punish or condemn me if you did, most improbably, find out the truth (e.g. by finding a note washed ashore in a bottle). Furthermore, I would agree that though it was most rational of me to give the money to the hospital it would be most rational of you to condemn me for it. We revert again to Sidgwick's distinction between the utility of the action and the utility of the praise of it.

Many such issues are discussed by A. K. Stout in the article to which I have already referred. I do not wish to go over the same ground again, especially as I think that Stout's arguments support my own point of view. It will be useful, however, to consider one other example that he gives. Suppose that during hot weather there is an edict that no water must be used for watering gardens. I have a garden and I reason that most people are sure to obey the edict, and that as the amount of water that I use will be by itself negligible no harm will be done if I use the water secretly. So I do use the water, thus producing some lovely flowers which give happiness to various people. Still, you may say, though the action was perhaps optimific, it was unfair and wrong.

There are several matters to consider. Certainly my action should be condemned. We revert once more to Sidgwick's distinction. A right action may be rationally condemned. Furthermore, this sort of offense is normally found out. If I have a wonderful garden when everybody else's is dry and brown there is only one explanation. So if I water my garden I am weakening my respect for law and order, and as this leads to bad results an extreme utilitarian would agree that I was wrong to water the garden. Suppose now that the case is altered and that I can keep the thing secret: there is a secluded part of the garden where I grow flowers which I give away anonymously to a home for old ladies. Are you still so sure that I did the wrong thing by watering my garden? However, this is still a weaker case than that of the hospital and the jockey club. There will be tensions set up within myself: my secret knowledge that I have broken the rule will make it hard for me to exhort others to keep the rule. These psychological ill effects in myself may be not inconsiderable: directly and indirectly they may lead to harm which is at least of the same order as the happiness that the old ladies get from the flowers. You can see that on an extreme utilitarian view there are two sides to the question.

So far I have been considering the duty of an extreme utilitarian in a predominantly non-utilitarian society. The case is altered if we consider the extreme utilitarian who lives in a society every member, or most members, of which can be expected to reason as he does. Should he water his flowers now? (Granting, what is doubtful, that in the case already considered he would have been right to water his flowers.) As a first approximation, the answer is that he should not do so. For since the situation is a completely symmetrical one, what is rational for him is rational for others. Hence, by a *reductio ad absurdum* argument, it would seem that watering his garden would be rational for none. Nevertheless, a more refined analysis shows that the above argument is not quite correct, though it is correct enough for practical purposes. The argument considers each person as confronted with the choice either of watering his garden or of not watering it. However there is a third possibility, which is that each person should, with the aid of a suitable randomizing device, such as throwing dice, give himself a certain probability of watering his garden. This would be to adopt what in the theory of games is called "a mixed strategy." If we could give numerical values to the private benefit of garden watering and to the public harm done by 1, 2, 3, etc., persons using the water in this way, we could work out a value of the probability of watering his garden that each extreme utilitarian should give himself. Let a be the value which each extreme utilitarian gets from watering his garden, and let $f(1), f(2), f(3)$, etc., be the public harm done by exactly 1, 2, 3, etc., persons respectively watering their gardens. Suppose that p is the probability that each person gives himself of watering his garden. Then we can easily calculate, as functions of p, the probabilities that exactly 1, 2, 3, etc., persons will water their gardens. Let these probabilities be $p_1, p_2, \ldots p_n$. Then the total net probable benefit can be expressed as

$$V = p_1\,(a - f(1)) + p_2\,(2a - f(2)) + \ldots p_n\,(na - f(n))$$

Then if we know the function $f(x)$ we can calculate the value of p for which $(dV/dp) = 0$. This gives the value of p which it would be rational for each extreme utilitarian to adopt. The present argument does not of course depend on a perhaps unjustified assumption that the values in question are measurable, and in a practical case such as that of the garden watering we can doubtless assume that *p* will be so small that we can take it near enough as equal to zero. However the argument is of interest for the theoretical underpinning of extreme utilitarianism, since the possibility of a mixed strategy is usually neglected by critics of utilitarianism, who wrongly assume that the only relevant and symmetrical alternatives are of the form "everybody does *X*" and "nobody does *X*."

I now pass on to a type of case which may be thought to be the trump card of restricted utilitarianism. Consider the rule of the road. It may be said that since all that matters is that everyone should do the same it is indifferent which rule we have, "go on the left hand side" or "go on the right hand side." Hence the only *reason* for going on the left hand side in British countries is that this is the rule. Here the rule does seem to be a reason, in itself, for acting in a certain way. I wish to argue against this. The rule in itself is not a reason for our actions. We would be perfectly justified in going on the right hand side if *(a)* we knew that the rule was to go on the left hand side, and *(b)* we were in a country peopled by super-anarchists who always on principle did the opposite of what they were told. This shows that the rule does not give us a reason for acting so much as an indication of the probable actions of others, which helps us to find out what would be our own most rational course of action. If we are in a country not peopled by anarchists, but by non-anarchist extreme Utilitarians, we expect, other things being equal, that they will keep rules laid down for them. Knowledge of the rule enables us to predict their behavior and to harmonize our own actions with theirs. The rule "keep to the left hand side," then, is not a logical *reason* for action but an anthropological *datum* for planning actions.

I conclude that in every case if there is a rule *R* the keeping of which is in general optimific, but such that in a special sort of circumstances the optimific behavior is to break *R*, then in these circumstances we should break *R*. Of course we must consider all the less obvious effects of breaking *R*, such as reducing people's faith in the moral order, before coming to the conclusion that to break *R* is right: in fact we shall rarely come to such a conclusion. Moral rules, on the extreme utilitarian view, are rules of thumb only, but they are not bad rules of thumb. But if we *do* come to the conclusion that we should break the rule and if we have weighed in the balance our own fallibility and liability to personal bias, what good reason remains for keeping the rule? I can understand "it is optimific" as a reason for action, but why should "it is a member of a class of actions which are usually optimific" or "it is a member of a class of actions which as a class are more optimific than any alternative general class" be a good reason? You might as well say that a person ought to be picked to play for Australia just because all his brothers have been, or that the Australian team should be composed entirely of the Harvey family because this would be better than composing it entirely of any other family. The extreme utilitarian does not appeal to artificial feelings, but only to our feelings of benevolence, and what better feelings can there be to appeal to? Admittedly we can have a pro-attitude to anything, even to rules, but such artificially begotten pro-attitudes smack of superstition. Let us get down to realities, human happiness and misery, and make these the objects of our pro-attitudes and anti-attitudes.

The restricted utilitarian might say that he is talking only of *morality,* not of such things as rules of the road. I am not sure how far this objection, if valid, would affect my argument, but in any case I would reply that as a philosopher I conceive of ethics as the study of how it would be *most rational* to act. If my opponent wishes to restrict the word "morality" to a narrower use he can have the word. The fundamental question is the question of rationality of action *in general.* Similarly if the restricted utilitarian were to appeal to ordinary usage and say "it might be most rational to leave Hitler to drown but it would surely not be *wrong* to rescue him," I should again let him have the words "right" and "wrong" and should stick to "rational" and "irrational." We already saw that it would be rational to praise Hitler's rescuer, even though it would have been most rational not to have rescued Hitler. In ordinary language, no doubt, "right" and "wrong" have not only the meaning "most rational to do" and "not most rational to do" but also have the meaning "praiseworthy" and "not praiseworthy." Usually to the utility of an action corresponds utility of praise of it, but as we saw, this is not always so. Moral language could thus do with tidying up, for example by reserving "right" for "most rational" and "good" as an epithet of praise for the motive from which the action sprang. It would be more becoming in a philosopher to try to iron out illogicalities in moral language and to make suggestions for its reform than to use it as a court of appeal whereby to perpetuate confusions.

One last defense of restricted utilitarianism might be as follows. "Act optimifically" might be regarded as itself one of the rules of our system (though it would be odd to say that this rule was justified by its optimificality). According to Toulmin (*The Place of Reason in Ethics*, pp. 146–8) if "keep promises," say, conflicts with another rule we are allowed to argue the case on its merits, as if we were extreme utilitarians. If "act optimifically" is itself one of our rules then there will always be a conflict of rules whenever to keep a rule is not itself optimific. If this is so, restricted utilitarianism collapses into extreme utilitarianism. And no one could read Toulmin's book or Urmson's article on Mill without thinking that Toulmin and Urmson are of the opinion that they have thought of a doctrine which does *not* collapse into extreme utilitarianism, but which is, on the contrary, an improvement on it.

1957

Ultimate Principles and Ethical Egoism

Brian Medlin

I believe that it is now pretty generally accepted by professional philosophers that ultimate ethical principles must be arbitrary. One cannot derive conclusions about what should be merely from accounts of what is the case; one cannot decide how people ought to behave merely from one's knowledge of how they do behave. To arrive at a conclusion in ethics one must have at least one ethical premiss. This premiss, if it be in turn a conclusion, must be the conclusion of an argument containing at least one ethical premiss. And so we can go back, indefinitely but not for ever. Sooner or later, we must come to at least one ethical premiss which is not deduced but baldly asserted. Here we must be a-rational; neither rational nor irrational, for here there is no room for reason even to go wrong.

But the triumph of Hume in ethics has been a limited one. What appears quite natural to a handful of specialists appears quite monstrous to the majority of decent intelligent men. At any rate, it has been my experience that people who are normally rational resist the above account of the logic of moral language, not by argument—for that can't be done—but by tooth and nail. And they resist from the best motives. They see the philosopher wantonly unravelling the whole fabric of morality. If our ultimate principles are arbitrary, they say, if those principles came out of thin air, then anyone can hold

Brian Medlin, "Ultimate Principles and Ethical Egoism," *Australasian Journal of Philosophy* (1957). Reprinted with the permission of the publishers.

any principle he pleases. Unless moral assertions are statements of fact about the world and either true or false, we can't claim that any man is wrong, whatever his principles may be, whatever his behavior. We have to surrender the luxury of calling one another scoundrels. That this anxiety flourishes because its roots are in confusion is evident when we consider that we don't call people scoundrels, anyhow, for being mistaken about their facts. Fools, perhaps, but that's another matter. Nevertheless, it doesn't become us to be high-up. The layman's uneasiness, however irrational it may be, is very natural and he must be reassured.

People cling to objectivist theories of morality from moral motives. It's a very queer thing that by doing so they often thwart their own purposes. There are evil opinions abroad, as anyone who walks abroad knows. The one we meet with most often, whether in pub or parlor, is the doctrine that everyone should look after himself. However refreshing he may find it after the high-minded pomposities of this morning's editorial, the good fellow knows this doctrine is wrong and he wants to knock it down. But while he believes that moral language is used to make statements either true or false, the best he can do is to claim that what the egoist says is false. Unfortunately, the egoist can claim that it's true. And since the supposed fact in question between them is not a publicly ascertainable one, their disagreement can never be resolved. And it is here that even good fellows waver, when they find they have no refutation available. The egoist's word seems as reliable as their own. Some begin half to believe that perhaps it is possible to supply an egoistic basis for conventional morality, some that it may be impossible to supply any other basis. I'm not going to try to prop up our conventional morality, which I fear to be a task beyond my strength, but in what follows I do want to refute the doctrine of ethical egoism. I want to resolve this disagreement by showing that what the egoist says is inconsistent. It is true that there are moral disagreements which can never be resolved, but this isn't one of them. The proper objection to the man who says "Everyone should look after his own interests regardless of the interests of others" is not that he isn't speaking the truth, but simply that he isn't speaking.

We should first make two distinctions. This done, ethical egoism will lose much of its plausibility.

1. UNIVERSAL AND INDIVIDUAL EGOISM

Universal egoism maintains that everyone (including the speaker) ought to look after his own interests and to disregard those of other people except in so far as their interests contribute towards his own.

Individual egoism is the attitude that the egoist is going to look after himself and no one else. The egoist cannot promulgate that he is going to look after himself. He can't even preach that he *should* look after himself and preach this alone. When he tries to convince me that he should look after himself, he is attempting so to dispose me that I shall approve when he drinks my beer and steals Tom's wife. I cannot approve of his looking after himself and himself alone without so far approving of his achieving his happiness, regardless of the happiness of myself and others. So that when he sets out to persuade me that he should look after himself regardless of others, he must also set out to persuade me that I should look after him regardless of myself and others. Very small chance he has! And if the individual egoist cannot promulgate his doctrine without enlarging it, what he has is no doctrine at all.

A person enjoying such an attitude may believe that other people are fools not to look after themselves. Yet he himself would be a fool to tell them so. If he did tell them, though, he wouldn't consider that he was giving them *moral* advice. Persuasion to the effect that one should ignore the claims of morality because morality doesn't pay, to the effect that one has insufficient selfish motive and, therefore, insufficient motive for moral behavior is not moral persuasion. For this reason I doubt that we should call the individual egoist's attitude an ethical one. And I don't doubt this in the way someone may doubt whether to call the ethical standards of Satan "ethical" standards. A malign morality is none the less a morality for being malign. But the attitude we're considering is one of mere contempt for all moral considerations whatsoever. An indifference to morals may be wicked, but it is not a perverse morality. So far as I am aware, most egoists imagine that they are putting forward a doctrine in ethics, though there may be a few who are prepared to proclaim themselves individual egoists. If the good fellow wants to know how he should justify conventional morality to an individual egoist, the answer is that he shouldn't and can't. Buy your car elsewhere, blackguard him whenever you meet, and let it go at that.

2. CATEGORICAL AND HYPOTHETICAL EGOISM

Categorical egoism is the doctrine that we all ought to observe our own interests, *because that is what we ought to do.* For the categorical egoist the egoistic dogma is the ultimate principle in ethics.

The hypothetical egoist, on the other hand, maintains that we all ought to observe our own interests, because . . . If we want such and such an end, we must do so and so (look after ourselves). The hypothetical egoist is not a real egoist at all. He is very likely an unwitting utilitarian who believes mistakenly that the general happiness will be increased if each man looks wisely to his own. Of course, a man may believe that egoism is enjoined on us by God and he may therefore promulgate the doctrine and observe it in his conduct, not in the hope of achieving thereby a remote end, but simply in order to obey God. But neither is *he* a real egoist. He believes, ultimately, that we should obey God, even should God command us to altruism.

An ethical egoist will have to maintain the doctrine in both its universal and categorical forms. Should he retreat to hypothetical egoism he is no longer an egoist. Should he retreat to individual egoism his doctrine, while logically impregnable, is no longer ethical, no longer even a doctrine. He may wish to quarrel with this and if so, I submit peacefully. Let him call himself what he will, it makes no difference. I'm a philosopher, not a rat-catcher, and I don't see it as my job to dig vermin out of such burrows as individual egoism.

Obviously something strange goes on as soon as the ethical egoist tries to promulgate his doctrine. What is he doing when he urges upon his audience that they should each observe his own interests and those interests alone? Is he not acting contrary to the egoistic principle? It cannot be to his advantage to convince them, for seizing always their own advantage they will impair his. Surely if he does believe what he says, he should try to persuade them otherwise. Not perhaps that they should devote themselves to his interests, for they'd hardly swallow that; but that everyone should devote himself to the service of others. But is not to believe that someone should act in a certain way to try to persuade him to do so? Of course, we don't always try to persuade people to act as we think they should act. We may be lazy, for instance. But in so far as we believe that Tom should do so and so, we have a tendency to induce him to do so and so. Does it make sense to say: "Of course you should do this, but for goodness' sake don't"? Only where we mean: "You should do this for certain reasons, but here are even more persuasive reasons for not doing it." If the egoist believes ultimately that others should mind themselves alone, then, he must persuade them accordingly. If he doesn't persuade them, he is no universal egoist. It certainly makes sense to say: "I know very well that Tom should act in such and such a way. But I know also that it's not to my advantage that he should so act. So I'd better dissuade him from it." And this is just what the egoist must say, if he is to consider his own advantage and disregard everyone else's. That is, he must behave as an individual egoist, if he is to be an egoist at all.

He may want to make two kinds of objection here:

1. That it will not be to his disadvantage to promulgate the doctrine, provided that his audience fully understand what is to their ultimate advantage. This objection can be developed in a number of ways, but I think that it will always be possible to push the egoist into either individual or hypothetical egoism.
2. That it is to the egoist's advantage to preach the doctrine if the pleasure he gets out of doing this more than pays for the injuries he must endure at the hands of his converts. It is hard to believe that many people would be satisfied with a doctrine which they could only consistently promulgate in very special circumstances. Besides, this looks suspiciously like individual egoism in disguise.

I shall say no more on these two points because I want to advance a further criticism which seems to me at once fatal and irrefutable.

Now it is time to show the anxious layman that we have means of dealing with ethical egoism which are denied him; and denied him by just that objectivism which he thinks essential to morality. For the very fact that our ultimate principles must be arbitrary means they can't be anything we please. Just because they come out of thin air they can't come out of hot air. Because these principles are not propositions about matters of fact and cannot be deduced from propositions about matters of fact, they must be the fruit of our own attitudes. We assert them largely to modify the attitudes of our fellows but by asserting them we express our own desires and purposes. This means that we cannot use moral language cavalierly. Evidently, we cannot say something like "All human desires and purposes are bad." This would be to express our own desires and purposes, thereby committing a kind of absurdity. Nor, I shall argue, can we say "Everyone should observe his own interests regardless of the interests of others."

Remembering that the principle is meant to be both universal and categorical, let us ask what kind of attitude the egoist is expressing. Wouldn't that attitude be equally well expressed by the conjunction of an infinite number of avowals thus?—

I want myself to come out on top	and	I don't care about Tom, Dick, Harry . . .
and		and
I want Tom to come out on top	and	I don't care about myself, Dick, Harry . . .
and		and
I want Dick to come out on top	and	I don't care about myself, Tom, Harry . . .
and		and
I want to Harry to come out on top	and	I don't care about myself, Dick, Tom . . .
etc.		etc.

From this analysis it is obvious that the principle expressing such an attitude must be inconsistent.

But now the egoist may claim that he hasn't been properly understood. When he says "Everyone should look after himself and himself alone," he means "Let each man do what he wants regardless of what anyone else wants." The egoist may claim that what he values is merely that he and Tom and Dick and Harry should each do what he wants and not care about what anyone else may want and that this doesn't involve his principle in any inconsistency. Nor need it. But even if it doesn't, he's no better off. Just what does he value? Is it the well-being of himself, Tom, Dick and Harry or merely their going on in a certain way regardless of whether or not this is going to promote their well-being? When he urges Tom, say, to do what he wants, is he appealing to Tom's self-interest? If so, his attitude can be expressed thus:

I want myself to be happy and I want Tom to be happy	and	I want myself not to care about Tom, Dick, Harry . . .

We need go no further to see that the principle expressing such an attitude must be inconsistent. I have made this kind of move already. What concerns me now is the alternative position the egoist must take up to be safe from it. If the egoist values merely that people should go on in a certain way, regardless of whether or not this is going to promote their well-being, then he is not appealing to the self-interest of his audience when he urges them to regard their own interests. If Tom has any regard for himself at all, the egoist's blandishments will leave him cold. Further, the egoist doesn't even have his own interest in mind when he says that, like everyone else, he should look after himself. A funny kind of egoism this turns out to be.

Perhaps now, claiming that he is indeed appealing to the self-interest of his audience, the egoist may attempt to counter the objection of the previous paragraph. He may move into "Let each man do what he wants and let each man disregard what others want when their desires clash with his own." Now his attitude may be expressed thus:

I want everyone to be happy	and	I want everyone to disregard the happiness of others when their happiness clashes with his own.

The egoist may claim justly that a man can have such an attitude and also that in a certain kind of world such a man could get what he wanted. Our objection to the egoist has been that his desires are incompatible. And this is still so. If he and Tom and Dick and Harry did go on as he recommends by saying "Let each man disregard the happiness of others, when their happiness conflicts with his own," then assuredly they'd all be completely miserable. Yet he wants them to be happy. He is attempting to counter this by saying that it is merely a fact about the world that they'd make one another miserable by going on as he recommends. The world could conceivably have been different. For this reason, he says, this principle is not inconsistent. This argument may not seem very compelling, but I advance it on the egoist's behalf because I'm interested in the reply to it. For now we don't even need to tell him that the world isn't in fact like that. (What it's like makes no difference.) Now we can point out to him that he is arguing not as an egoist but as a utilitarian. He has slipped into hypothetical egoism to save his principle from inconsistency. If the world were such that we always made ourselves and others happy by doing one another down, then we could find good utilitarian reasons for urging that we should do one another down.

If, then, he is to save his principle, the egoist must do one of two things. He must give up the claim that he is appealing to the self-interest of his audience, that he has even his own interest in mind. Or he must admit that, in the conjunction on page 116 [p. 320 this volume], although "I want everyone to be happy" refers to ends, nevertheless "I want everyone to disregard the happiness of others when their happiness conflicts with his own" can refer only to means. That is, his so-called ultimate principle is really compounded of a principle and a moral rule subordinate to that principle. That is, he is really a utilitarian who is urging everyone to go on in a certain way so that everyone may be happy. A utilitarian, what's more, who is ludicrously mistaken about the nature of the world. Things being as they are, his moral rule is a very bad one. Things being as they are, it can only be deduced from his principle by means of an empirical premiss which is manifestly false. Good fellows don't need to fear him. They may rest easy that the world is and must be on their side and the best thing they can do is be good.

It may be worth pointing out that objections similar to those I have brought against the egoist can be made to the altruist. The man who holds that the principle "Let everyone observe the interests of others" is both universal and categorical can be compelled to choose between two alternatives, equally repugnant. He must give up the claim that he is concerned for the well-being of himself and others. Or he must admit that, though "I want everyone to be happy" refers to ends, nevertheless "I want everyone to disregard his own happiness when it conflicts with the happiness of others" can refer only to means.

I have said from time to time that the egoistic principle is inconsistent. I have not said it is contradictory. This for the reason that we can, without contradiction, express inconsistent desires and purposes. To do so is not to say anything like "Goliath was ten feet tall and not ten feet tall." Don't we all want to eat our cake and have it too? And when we say we do we aren't asserting a contradiction. We are not asserting a contradiction whether we be making an avowal of our attitudes or stating a fact about them. We all have conflicting motives. As a utilitarian exuding benevolence I want the man who mows my landlord's grass to be happy, but as a slug-a-bed I should like to see him scourged. None of this, however, can do the egoist any good. For we assert our ultimate principles not only to express our own attitudes but also to induce similar attitudes in others, to dispose them to conduct themselves as we wish. In so far as their desires conflict, people don't know what to do. And, therefore, no expression of incompatible desires can ever serve for an ultimate principle of human conduct.

1958

Saints and Heroes

J. O. Urmson

Moral philosophers tend to discriminate, explicitly or implicitly, three types of action from the point of view of moral worth. First, they recognize actions that are a duty, or obligatory, or that we ought to perform, treating these terms as approximately synonymous; second, they recognize actions that are right in so far as they are permissible from a moral standpoint and not ruled out by moral considerations, but that are not morally required of us, like the lead of this or that card at bridge; third, they recognize actions that are wrong, that we ought not to do. Some moral philosophers, indeed, could hardly discriminate even these three types of action consistently with the rest of their philosophy; Moore, for example, could hardly recognize a class of morally indifferent actions, permissible but not enjoined, since it is to be presumed that good or ill of some sort will result from the most trivial of our actions. But most moral philosophers recognize these three types of action and attempt to provide a moral theory that will make intelligible such a threefold classification.

To my mind this threefold classification, or any classification that is merely a variation on or elaboration of it, is totally inadequate to the facts of morality; any moral theory that leaves room only for such a classification will in consequence also be inad-

J. O. Urmson, "Saints and Heroes" from ESSAYS IN MORAL PHILOSOPHY, edited by A. I. Melde (Seattle, WA: University of Washington Press, 1958). Reprinted with the permission of the publishers.

equate. My main task in this paper will be to show the inadequacy of such a classification by drawing attention to two of the types of action that most conspicuously lie outside such a classification; I shall go on to hazard some views on what sort of theory will most easily cope with the facts to which I draw attention, but the facts are here the primary interest.

We sometimes call a person a saint, or an action saintly, using the word "saintly" in a purely moral sense with no religious implications; also we sometimes call a person a hero or an action heroic. It is too clear to need argument that the words "saint" and "hero" are at least normally used in such a way as to be favorably evaluative; it would be impossible to claim that this evaluation is always moral, for clearly we sometimes call a person a saint when evaluating him religiously rather than morally and may call a person the hero of a game or athletic contest in which no moral qualities were displayed, but I shall take it that no formal argument is necessary to show that at least sometimes we use both words for moral evaluation.

If "hero" and "saint" can be words of moral evaluation, we may proceed to the attempt to make explicit the criteria that we implicitly employ for their use in moral contexts. It appears that we so use them in more than one type of situation, and that there is a close parallel between the ways in which the two terms "hero" and "saint" are used; we shall here notice three types of situation in which they are used which seem to be sufficiently different to merit distinction. As the first two types of situation to be noticed are ones that can be readily subsumed under the threefold classification mentioned above, it will be sufficient here to note them and pass on to the third type of situation, which, since it cannot be subsumed under that classification, is for the purposes of this paper the most interesting.

A person may be called a saint (1) if he does his duty regularly in contexts in which inclination, desire, or self-interest would lead most people not to do it, and does so as a result of exercising abnormal self-control; parallel to this a person may be called a hero (1) if he does his duty in contexts in which terror, fear, or a drive to self-preservation would lead most men not to do it, and does so by exercising abnormal self-control. Similarly for actions: an action may be called saintly (1) if it is a case of duty done by virtue of self-control in a context in which most men would be led astray by inclination or self-interest, and an action may be called heroic (1) if it is a case of duty done by virtue of self-control in a context in which most men would be led astray by fear or a drive for self-preservation. The only difference between the saintly and the heroic in this sort of situation is that the one involves resistance to desire and self-interest; the other, resistance to fear and self-preservation. This is quite a clear difference, though there may be marginal cases, or cases in which motives were mixed, in which it would be equally appropriate to call an action indifferently saintly or heroic. It is easy to give examples of both the heroic and the saintly as distinguished above: the unmarried daughter does the saintly deed of staying at home to tend her ailing and widowed father; the terrified doctor heroically stays by his patients in a plague-ridden city.

A person may be called a saint (2) if he does his duty in contexts in which inclination or self-interest would lead most men not to do it, not, as in the previous paragraph, by abnormal self-control, but without effort; parallel to this a person may be called a hero (2) if he does his duty in contexts in which fear would lead most men not to do it, and does so without effort. The corresponding accounts of a saintly (2) or heroic (2) action can easily be derived. Here we have the conspicuously virtuous deed, in the Aristotelian sense, as opposed to the conspicuously self-controlled, encratic deed of the previous paragraph. People thus purged of temptation or disciplined against fear may be rare, but Aristotle thought there could be such; there is a tendency today to think of such people as merely lucky or unimaginative, but Aristotle thought more highly of them than of people who need to exercise self-control.

It is clear that, in the two types of situation so far considered, we are dealing with actions that fall under the concept of duty. Roughly, we are calling a person saintly or heroic because he does his duty in such difficult contexts that most men would fail in them. Since for the purposes of this paper I am merely conceding that we do use the terms "saintly" and "heroic" in these ways, it is unnecessary here to spend time arguing that we do so use them or in illustrating such uses. So used, the threefold classification of actions whose adequacy I wish to deny can clearly embrace them. I shall therefore pass immediately to a third use of the terms "heroic" and "saintly" which I am not merely willing to concede but obliged to establish.

I contend, then, that we may also call a person a saint (3) if he does actions that are far beyond the limits of his duty, whether by control of contrary inclination and interest or without effort; parallel to this we may call a person a hero (3) if he does actions that are far beyond the bounds of his duty, whether by control of natural fear or without effort. Such actions are saintly (3) or heroic (3). Here, as it seems to me, we have the hero or saint, heroic or saintly deed, par excellence; until now we have been considering but minor saints and heroes. We have considered the, certainly, heroic action of the doctor who does his duty by sticking to his patients in a plague-stricken city; we have now to consider the case of the doctor who, no differently situated from countless other doctors in other places, volunteers to join the depleted medical forces in that city. Previously we were considering the soldier who heroically does his duty in the face of such dangers as would cause most to shirk—the sort of man who is rightly awarded the Military Medal in the British Army; we have now to consider the case of the soldier who does more than his superior officers would ever ask him to do—the man to whom, often posthumously, the Victoria Cross is awarded. Similarly, we have to turn from saintly self-discipline in the way of duty to the dedicated, self-effacing life in the service of others which is not even contemplated by the majority of upright, kind, and honest men, let alone expected of them.

Let us be clear that we are not now considering cases of natural affection, such as the sacrifice made by a mother for her child; such cases may be said with some justice not to fall under the concept of morality but to be admirable in some different way. Such cases as are here under consideration may be taken to be as little bound up with such emotions as affection as any moral action may be. We may consider an example of what is meant by "heroism" (3) in more detail to bring this out.

We may imagine a squad of soldiers to be practicing the throwing of live hand grenades; a grenade slips from the hand of one of them and rolls on the ground near the squad; one of them sacrifices his life by throwing himself on the grenade and protecting his comrades with his own body. It is quite unreasonable to suppose that such a man must be impelled by the sort of emotion that he might be impelled by if his best friend were in the squad; he might only just have joined the squad; it is clearly an action having moral status. But if the soldier had not thrown himself on the grenade would he have failed in his duty? Though clearly he is superior in some way to his comrades, can we possibly say that they failed in their duty by not trying to be the one who sacrificed himself? If he had not done so, could anyone have said to him, "You ought to have thrown yourself on that grenade"? Could a superior have decently ordered him to do it? The answer to all these questions is plainly negative. We clearly have here a case of a moral action, a heroic action, which cannot be subsumed under the classification whose inadequacy we are exposing.

But someone may not be happy with this conclusion, and for more respectable reasons than a desire to save the traditional doctrine. He may reason as follows: in so far as that soldier had time to feel or think at all, he presumably felt that he ought to do that deed; he considered it the proper thing to do; he, if no one else, might have reproached himself for failing to do his duty if he had shirked the deed. So, it may be argued, if an act presents itself to us in the way this act may be supposed to have presented itself to this soldier, then it is our duty to do it; we have no option. This objection to my thesis clearly has some substance, but it involves a misconception of what is at issue. I have no desire to present the act of heroism as one that is naturally regarded as optional by the hero, as something he might or might not do; I concede that he might regard himself as being obliged to act as he does. But if he were to survive the action only a modesty so excessive as to appear false could make him say, "I only did my duty," for we know, and he knows, that he has done more than duty requires. Further, though he might say to himself that so to act was a duty, he could not say so even beforehand to anyone else, and no one else could ever say it. Subjectively, we may say, at the time of action, the deed presented itself as a duty, but it was not a duty.

Another illustration, this time of saintliness, may help. It is recorded by Bonaventura that after Francis of Assisi had finished preaching to the birds on a celebrated occasion his companions gathered around him to praise and admire. But Francis himself was not a bit pleased; he was full of self-reproach that he had hitherto failed in what he now considered to be his duty to preach to the feathered world. There is indeed no degree of saintliness that a suitable person may not come to consider it to be his duty to achieve. Yet there is a world of difference between this failure to have preached hitherto to the birds and a case of straightforward breach of duty, however venial. First, Francis could without absurdity reproach himself for his failure to do his duty, but it would be quite ridiculous for anyone else to do so, as one could have done if he had failed to keep his vows, for example. Second, it is not recorded that Francis ever reproached anyone else for failure to preach to the birds as a breach of duty. He could claim this action for himself as a duty and could perhaps have exhorted others to preach to the birds; but there could be no question of reproaches for not so acting.

To sum up on this point, then, it seems clear that there is no action, however quixotic, heroic, or saintly, which the agent may not regard himself as obliged to perform, as much as he may feel himself obliged to tell the truth and to keep his promises. Such actions do not present themselves as optional to the agent when he is deliberating; but, since he alone can call such an action of his a duty, and then only from the deliberative viewpoint, only for himself and not for others, and not even for himself as a piece of objective reporting, and since nobody else can call on him to perform such an act as they can call on him to tell the truth and to keep his promises, there is here a most important difference from the rock-bottom duties which are duties for all and from every point of view, and to which anyone may draw attention. Thus we need not deny the points made by our imaginary objector in order to substantiate the point that some acts of heroism and saintliness cannot be adequately subsumed under the concept of duty.

Let us then take it as established that we have to deal in ethics not with a simple trichotomy of duties, permissible actions, and wrong actions, or any substantially similar conceptual scheme, but with something more complicated. We have to add at least the complication of actions that are certainly of moral worth but that fall outside the notion of a duty and seem to go beyond it, actions worthy of being called heroic or saintly. It should indeed be noted that heroic and saintly actions are not the sole, but merely conspicuous, cases of actions that exceed the basic demands of duty; there can be cases of disinterested kindness and generosity, for example, that are clearly more than basic duty requires and yet hardly ask for the high titles, "saintly" and "heroic." Indeed, every case of "going the second mile" is a case in point, for it cannot be one's duty to go the second mile in the same basic sense as it is to go the first—otherwise it could be argued first that it is one's duty to go two miles and therefore that the spirit of the rule of the second mile requires that one go altogether four miles, and by repetition one could establish the need to go every time on an infinite journey. It is possible to go just beyond one's duty by being a little more generous, forbearing, helpful, or forgiving than fair dealing demands, or to go a very long way beyond the basic code of duties with the saint or the hero. When I here draw attention to the heroic and saintly deed, I do so merely in order to have conspicuous cases of a whole realm of actions that lie outside the trichotomy I have criticized and therefore, as I believe, outside the purview of most ethical theories.

Before considering the implications for ethics of the facts we have up to now been concerned to note, it might be of value to draw attention to a less exalted parallel to these facts. If we belong to a club there will be rules of the club, written or unwritten, calling upon us to fulfill certain basic requirements that are a condition of membership, and that may be said to be the duties of membership. It may perhaps be such a basic requirement that we pay a subscription. It will probably be indifferent whether we pay this subscription by check or in cash—both procedures will be "right"—and almost certainly it will be quite indifferent what sort of hat we wear at the meetings. Here, then, we have conformity to rule which is the analogue of doing one's duty, breach of rule which is the analogue of wrongdoing, and a host of indifferent actions, in accordance with the traditional trichotomy. But among the rule-abiding members of such a club what differences there can be! It is very likely that there will be one, or perhaps two or three, to whose devotion and loyal service the success of the club is due far more than to the activities of all the other members together; these are the saints and the heroes of the clubs, who do more for them by far than any member could possibly be asked to do, whose many services could not possibly be demanded in the rules. Behind them come a motley selection, varying from the keen to the lukewarm, whose contributions vary in value and descend sometimes to almost nothing beyond what the rules demand. The moral contribution of people to society can vary in value in the same way.

So much, then, for the simple facts to which I have wished to draw attention. They are simple facts and, unless I have misrepresented them, they are facts of which we are all, in a way, perfectly well aware. It would be absurd to suggest that moral philosophers have hitherto been unaware of the existence of saints and heroes and have never even alluded to them in their works. But it does seem that these facts have been neglected in their general, systematic accounts of morality. It is indeed easy to see that on some of the best-known theories there is no room for such facts. If for Moore, and for most utilitarians, any action is a duty that will produce the greatest possible good in the circumstances, for them the most heroic self-sacrifice or saintly self-forgetfulness will be duties on all fours with truth-telling and promise-keeping. For Kant, beyond the counsels of prudence and the rules of skill, there is only the categorical imperative of duty, and every duty is equally and utterly binding on all men; it is true that he recognizes the limiting case of the holy will, but the holy will is not a will that goes beyond duty but a will that is beyond morality through being incapable of acting except in accordance with the imperative. The nearest to an equivalent to a holy will in the cases we have been noting is the saintly will in the second sense we distinguished—the will that effortlessly does its duty when most would fail—but this is not a true parallel and in any case does not fall within the class of moral actions that go beyond duty to which our attention is primarily given. It is also true that Kant recognized virtues and talents as having conditional value, but not moral value, whereas the acts of heroism and saintliness we have considered have full moral worth, and their value is as unconditional as anyone could wish. Without committing ourselves to a scholarly examination of Kant's ethical works, it is surely evident that Kant could not consistently do justice to the facts before us. Intuitionism seems to me so obscurantist that I should not wish to prophesy what an intuitionist might feel himself entitled to say; but those intuitionists with whose works I am acquainted found their theories on an intuition of the fitting, the prima facie duty or the claim; the act that has this character to the highest degree at any time is a duty. While they recognize greater and lesser, stronger and weaker, claims, this is only in order to be able to deal with the problem of the conflict of duties; they assign no place to the act that, while not a duty, is of high moral importance.

Simple utilitarianism, Kantianism, and intuitionism, then, have no obvious theoretical niche for the saint and the hero. It is possible, no doubt, to revise these theories to accommodate the facts, but until so modified successfully they must surely be treated as unacceptable, and the modifications required might well detract from their plausibility. The intuitionists, for example, might lay claim to the intuition of a nonnatural characteristic of saintliness, of heroism, of decency, of sportingness, and so on, but this would give to their theory still more the appearance of utilizing the advantages of theft over honest toil.

Thus as moral theorists we need to discover some theory that will allow for both absolute duties, which, in Mill's phrase, can be exacted from a man like a debt, to omit which is to do wrong and to deserve censure, and which may be embodied in formal rules or principles, and also for a range of actions which are of moral value and which an agent may feel called upon to perform, but which cannot be demanded and whose omission cannot be called wrongdoing. Traditional moral theories, I have suggested, fail to do this. It would be well beyond the scope of this paper, and probably beyond my capacity, to produce here and now a full moral theory designed to accommodate all these facts, including the facts of saintliness and heroism. But I do think that of all traditional theories utilitarianism can be most easily modified to accommodate the facts, and would like before ending this paper to bring forward some considerations tending to support this point of view.

Moore went to great pains to determine exactly the nature of the intrinsically good, and Mill to discover the *summum bonum,* Moore's aim being to explain thereby directly the rightness and wrongness of particular actions and Mill's to justify a set of moral principles in the light of which the rightness or wrongness of particular actions can be decided. But, though there can be very tricky problems of duty, they do not naturally present themselves as problems whose solution depends upon an exact determination of an ultimate end; while the moral principles that come most readily to mind—truth-telling; promise-keeping; abstinence from murder, theft, and violence; and the like—make a nice discrimination of the supreme good seem irrelevant. We do not need to debate whether it is Moore's string of intrinsic goods or Mill's happiness that is achieved by conformity to such principles; it is enough to see that without them social life would be impossible and any life would indeed be solitary, poor, nasty, brutish, and short. Even self-interest (which some have seen as the sole foundation of morality) is sufficient ground to render it wise to preach, if not to practice, such principles. Such considerations as these, which are not novel, have led some utilitarians to treat avoidance of the *summum malum* rather than the achievement of the *summum bonum* as the foundation of morality. Yet to others this has seemed, with some justification, to assign to morality too ignoble a place.

But the facts we have been considering earlier in this paper are surely relevant at this point. It is absurd to ask just what ideal is being served by abstinence from murder; but on the other hand nobody could see in acts of heroism such as we have been considering a mere avoidance of antisocial behavior. Here we have something more gracious, actions that need to be inspired by a positive ideal. If duty can, as Mill said, be exacted from persons as a debt, it is because duty is a minimum requirement for living together; the positive contribution of actions that go beyond duty could not be so exacted.

It may, however, be objected that this is a glorification of the higher flights of morality at the expense of duty, toward which an unduly cynical attitude is being taken. In so far as the suggestion is that we are forgetting how hard the way of duty may be and that doing one's duty can at times deserve to be called heroic and saintly, the answer is that we have mentioned this and acknowledge it; it is not forgotten but irrelevant to the point at issue, which is the place of duty in a moral classification of actions, not the problem of the worth of moral agents. But I may be taken to be acquiescing in a low and circumscribed view of duty which I may be advised to enlarge. We should, it may be said, hitch our wagons to the stars and not be content to say: you must do this and that as duties, and it would be very nice if you were to do these other things but we do not expect them of you. Is it perhaps only an imperfect conception of duty which finds it not to comprise the whole of morality? I want to examine this difficulty quite frankly, and to explain why I think that we properly recognize morality that goes beyond duty; for it seems to me incontestable that properly or improperly we do so.

No intelligent person will claim infallibility for his moral views. But allowing for this one must claim that one's moral code is ideal so far as one can see; for to say, "I recognize moral code A but see clearly that moral code B is superior to it," is but a way of saying that one recognizes moral code B but is only prepared to live up to moral code A. In some sense, then, everybody must be prepared to justify his moral code as ideal; but some philosophers have misunderstood this sense. Many philosophers have thought it necessary, if they were to defend their moral code as ideal, to try to show that it had a superhuman, a priori validity. Kant, for example, tried to show that the moral principles he accepted were such as any rational being, whether man or angel, must inevitably accept; the reputedly empiricist Locke thought that it must be possible to work out a deductive justification of moral laws. In making such claims such philosophers have unintentionally done morality a disservice; for their failure to show that the moral code was ideal in the sense of being a rationally justifiable system independent of time, place, circumstance, and human nature has led many to conclude that there can be no justification of a moral code, that moral codes are a matter of taste or convention.

But morality, I take it, is something that should serve human needs, not something that incidentally sweeps man up with itself, and to show that a morality was ideal would be to show that it best served man—man as he is and as he can be expected to become, not man as he would be if he were perfectly rational or an incorporeal angel. Just as it would be fatuous to build our machines so that they would give the best results according to an abstract conception of mechanical principles, and is much more desirable to design them to withstand to some extent our ham-fistedness, ignorance, and carelessness, so our morality must be one that will work. In the only sense of "ideal" that is of importance in action, it is part of the ideal that a moral code should actually help to contribute to human well-being, and a moral code that would work only for angels (for whom it would in any case be unnecessary) would be a far from ideal moral code for human beings. There is, indeed, a place for ideals that are practically unworkable in human affairs, as there is a place for the blueprint of a machine that will never go into production; but it is not the place of such ideals to serve as a basic code of duties.

If, then, we are aiming at a moral code that will best serve human needs, a code that is ideal in the sense that a world in which such a code is acknowledged will be a better place than a world in which some other sort of moral code is acknowledged, it seems that there are ample grounds why our code should distinguish between basic rules, summarily set forth in simple rules and binding on all, and the higher flights of morality of which saintliness and heroism are outstanding examples. These grounds I shall enumerate at once.

1. It is important to give a special status of urgency, and to exert exceptional pressure, in those matters in which compliance with the demands of morality by all is indispensable. An army without men of heroic valor would be impoverished, but without general attention to the duties laid down in military law it would become a mere rabble. Similarly, while life in a world without its saints and heroes would be impoverished, it would only be poor and not necessarily brutish or short as when basic duties are neglected.

2. If we are to exact basic duties like debts, and censure failure, such duties must be, in ordinary circumstances, within the capacity of the ordinary man. It would be silly for us to say to ourselves, our children and our fellow men, "This and that you and everyone else must do," if the acts in question are such that manifestly but few could bring themselves to do them, though we may ourselves resolve to try to be of that few. To take a parallel from positive law, the prohibition laws asked too much of the American people and were consequently broken systematically; and as people got used to breaking the law a general lowering of respect for the law naturally followed; it no longer seemed that a law was something that everybody could be expected to obey. Similarly in Britain the gambling laws, some of which are utterly unpractical, have fallen into contempt as a body. So, if we were to represent the heroic act of sacrificing one's life for one's comrades as a basic duty, the effect would be to lower the degree of urgency and stringency that the notion of duty does in fact possess. The basic moral code must not be in part too far beyond the capacity of the ordinary men on ordinary occasions, or a general breakdown of compliance with the moral code would be an inevitable consequence; duty would seem to be something high and unattainable, and not for "the likes of us." Admirers of the Sermon on the Mount do not in practice, and could not, treat failure to turn the other cheek and to give one's cloak also as being on all fours with breaches of the Ten Commandments, however earnestly they themselves try to live a Christian life.

3. A moral code, if it is to be a code, must be formulable, and if it is to be a code to be observed it must be formulable in rules of manageable complexity. The ordinary man has to apply and interpret this code without recourse to a Supreme Court or House of Lords. But one can have such rules only in cases in which a type of action that is reasonably easy to recognize is almost invariably desirable or undesirable, as killing is almost invariably undesirable and promise-keeping almost invariably desirable. Where no definite rule of manageable complexity can be justified, we cannot work on that moral plane on which types of action can be enjoined or condemned as duty or crime. It has no doubt often been the case that a person who has gone off to distant parts to nurse lepers has thereby done a deed of great moral worth. But such an action is not merely too far beyond average human capacity to be regarded as a duty, as was insisted in (2) above; it would be quite ridiculous for everyone, however circumstanced, to be expected to go off and nurse lepers. But it would be absurd to try to formulate complicated rules to determine in just what circumstances such an action is a duty. This same point can readily be applied to such less spectacular matters as excusing legitimate debts or nursing sick neighbors.

4. It is part of the notion of a duty that we have a right to demand compliance from others even when we are interested parties. I may demand that you keep your promises to me, tell me the truth, and do me no violence, and I may reproach you if you transgress. But however admirable the tending of strangers in sickness may be it is not a basic duty, and we are not entitled to reproach those to whom we are strangers if they do not tend us in sickness; nor can I tell you, if you fail to give me a cigarette when I have run out, that you have failed in your duty to me, however much you may subsequently reproach yourself for your meanness if you do so fail. A line must be drawn between what we can expect and demand from others and what we can merely hope for and receive with gratitude when we get it; duty falls on one side of this line, and other acts with moral value on the other, and rightly so.

5. In the case of basic moral duties we act to some extent under constraint. We have no choice but to apply pressure on each other to conform in these fundamental matters; here moral principles are like public laws rather than like private ideals. But free choice of the better course of action is always preferable to action under pressure, even when the pressure is but moral. When possible, therefore, it is better that pressure should not be applied and that there should be encouragement and commendation for performance rather than outright demands and censure in the event of non-performance. There are no doubt degrees in this matter. Some pressure may reasonably be brought to persuade a person to go some way beyond basic duty in the direction of kindliness and forbearance, to be not merely a just man but also not too hard a man. But, while there is nothing whatever objectionable in the idea of someone's being pressed to carry out such a basic duty as promise-keeping, there is something horrifying in the thought of pressure being brought on him to perform an act of heroism. Though the man might feel himself morally called upon to do the deed, it would be a moral outrage to apply pressure on him to do such a deed as sacrificing his life for others.

These five points make it clear why I do not think that the distinction of basic duty from other acts of moral worth, which I claim to detect in ordinary moral thought, is a sign of the inferiority of our everyday moral thinking to that of the general run of moral theorists. It in no way involves anyone in acquiescing in a second best. No doubt from the agent's point of view it is imperative that he should endeavor to live up to the highest ideals of behavior that he can think of, and if an action falls within the ideal it is for him irrelevant whether or not it is a duty or some more supererogatory act. But it simply does not follow that the distinction is in every way unimportant, for it is important that we should not demand ideal conduct from others in the way in which we must demand basic morality from them, or blame them equally for failures in all fields. It is not cynicism to make the minimum positive demands upon one's fellow men; but to characterize an act as a duty is so to demand it.

Thus we may regard the imperatives of duty as prohibiting behavior that is intolerable if men are to live together in society and demanding the minimum of cooperation toward the same end; that is why we have to treat compliance as compulsory and dereliction as liable to public censure. We do not need to ask with Bentham whether push-pin is as good as poetry, with Mill whether it is better to be Socrates dissatisfied or a fool satisfied, or with Moore whether a beautiful world with no one to see it would have intrinsic worth; what is and what is not tolerable in society depends on no such nice discrimination. Utilitarians, when attempting to justify the main rules of duty in terms of a *summum bonum,* have surely invoked many different types of utilitarian justification, ranging from the avoidance of the intolerable to the fulfillment of the last detail of a most rarefied ideal.

Thus I wish to suggest that utilitarianism can best accommodate the facts to which I have drawn attention; but I have not wished to support any particular view about the supreme good or the importance of pleasure. By utilitarianism I mean only a theory that moral justification of actions must be in terms of results. We can be content to say that duty is mainly concerned with the avoidance of intolerable results, while other forms of moral behavior have more positive aims.

To summarize, I have suggested that the trichotomy of duties, indifferent actions, and wrongdoing is inadequate. There are many kinds of action that involve going beyond duty proper, saintly and heroic actions being conspicuous examples of such kinds of action. It has been my main concern to note this point and to ask moral philosophers to theorize in a way that does not tacitly deny it, as most traditional theories have. But I have also been so rash as to suggest that we may look upon our duties as basic requirements to be universally demanded as providing the only tolerable basis of social life. The higher flights of morality can then be regarded as more positive contributions that go beyond what is universally to be exacted; but while not exacted publicly they are clearly equally pressing *in foro interno* on those who are not content merely to avoid the intolerable. Whether this should be called a version of utilitarianism, as I suggest, is a matter of small moment.

1958

Justice as Fairness

John Rawls

I. It might seem at first sight that the concepts of justice and fairness are the same, and that there is no reason to distinguish them, or to say that one is more fundamental than the other. I think that this impression is mistaken. In this paper I wish to show that the fundamental idea in the concept of justice is fairness; and I wish to offer an analysis of the concept of justice from this point of view. To bring out the force of this claim, and the analysis based upon it, I shall then argue that it is this aspect of justice for which utilitarianism, in its classical form, is unable to account, but which is expressed, even if misleadingly, by the idea of the social contract.

To start with I shall develop a particular conception of justice by stating and commenting upon two principles which specify it, and by considering the circumstances and conditions under which they may be thought to arise. The principles defining this conception, and the conception itself, are, of course, familiar. It may be possible, however, by using the notion of fairness as a framework, to assemble and to look at them in a new way. Before stating this conception, however, the following preliminary matters should be kept in mind.

An abbreviated version of this paper (less than one-half the length) was presented in a symposium with the same title at the American Philosophical Association, Eastern Division, December 28, 1957, and appeared in the *Journal of Philosophy*, LIV, 653–662.

Throughout I consider justice only as a virtue of social institutions, or what I shall call practices.[1] The principles of justice are regarded as formulating restrictions as to how practices may define positions and offices, and assign thereto powers and liabilities, rights and duties. Justice as a virtue of particular actions or of persons I do not take up at all. It is important to distinguish these various subjects of justice, since the meaning of the concept varies according to whether it is applied to practices, particular actions, or persons. These meanings are, indeed, connected, but they are not identical. I shall confine my discussion to the sense of justice as applied to practices, since this sense is the basic one. Once it is understood, the other senses should go quite easily.

Justice is to be understood in its customary sense as representing but *one* of the many virtues of social institutions, for these may be antiquated, inefficient, degrading, or any number of other things, without being unjust. Justice is not to be confused with an all-inclusive vision of a good society; it is only one part of any such conception. It is important, for example, to distinguish that sense of equality which is an aspect of the concept of justice from that sense of equality which belongs to a more comprehensive social ideal. There may well be inequalities which one concedes are just, or at least not unjust, but which, nevertheless, one wishes, on other grounds, to do away with. I shall focus attention, then, on the usual sense of justice in which it is essentially the elimination of arbitrary distinctions and the establishment, within the structure of a practice, of a proper balance between competing claims.

Finally, there is no need to consider the principles discussed below as *the* principles of justice. For the moment it is sufficient that they are typical of a family of principles normally associated with the concept of justice. The way in which the principles of this family resemble one another, as shown by the background against which they may be thought to arise, will be made clear by the whole of the subsequent argument.

2. The conception of justice which I want to develop may be stated in the form of two principles as follows: first, each person participating in a practice, or affected by it, has an equal right to the most extensive liberty compatible with a like liberty for all; and second, inequalities are arbitrary unless it is reasonable to expect that they will work out for everyone's advantage, and provided the positions and offices to which they attach, or from which they may be gained, are open to all. These principles express justice as a complex of three ideas: liberty, equality, and reward for services contributing to the common good.[2]

The term "person" is to be construed variously depending on the circumstances. On some occasions it will mean human individuals, but in others it may refer to nations, provinces, business firms, churches, teams, and so on. The principles of justice apply in

[1]I use the word "practice" throughout as a sort of technical term meaning any form of activity specified by a system of rules which defines offices, roles, moves, penalties, defenses, and so on, and which gives the activity its structure. As examples one may think of games and rituals, trials and parliaments, markets and systems of property. I have attempted a partial analysis of the notion of a practice in a paper "Two Concepts of Rules," *Philosophical Review*, LXIV (1955), 3–32.

[2]These principles are, of course, well-known in one form or another and appear in many analyses of justice even where the writers differ widely on other matters. Thus if the principle of equal liberty is commonly associated with Kant (see *The Philosophy of Law*, tr. by W. Hastie, Edinburgh, 1887, pp. 56 f.), it may be claimed that it can be also be found in J. S. Mill's *On Liberty* and elsewhere, and in many other liberal writers. Recently H. L. A. Hart has argued for something like it in his paper "Are There Any Natural Rights?," *Philosophical Review*, LXIV (1955), 175–191. The injustice of inequalities which are not won in return for a contribution to the common advantage is, of course, widespread in political writings of all sorts. The conception of justice here discussed is distinctive, if at all, only in selecting these two principles in this form; but for another similar analysis, see the discussion by W. D. Lamont, *The Principles of Moral Judgment* (Oxford, 1946), ch. v.

all these instances, although there is a certain logical priority to the case of human individuals. As I shall use the term "person," it will be ambiguous in the manner indicated.

The first principle holds, of course, only if other things are equal: that is, while there must always be a justification for departing from the initial position of equal liberty (which is defined by the pattern of rights and duties, powers and liabilities, established by a practice), and the burden of proof is placed on him who would depart from it, nevertheless, there can be, and often there is, a justification for doing so. Now, that similar particular cases, as defined by a practice, should be treated similarly as they arise, is part of the very concept of a practice; it is involved in the notion of an activity in accordance with rules.[3] The first principle expresses an analogous conception, but as applied to the structure of practices themselves. It holds, for example, that there is a presumption against the distinctions and classifications made by legal systems and other practices to the extent that they infringe on the original and equal liberty of the persons participating in them. The second principle defines how this presumption may be rebutted.

It might be argued at this point that justice requires only an equal liberty. If, however, a greater liberty were possible for all without loss or conflict, then it would be irrational to settle on a lesser liberty. There is no reason for circumscribing rights unless their exercise would be incompatible, or would render the practice defining them less effective. Therefore no serious distortion of the concept of justice is likely to follow from including within it the concept of the greatest equal liberty.

The second principle defines what sorts of inequalities are permissible; it specifies how the presumption laid down by the first principle may be put aside. Now by inequalities it is best to understand not *any* differences between offices and positions, but differences in the benefits and burdens attached to them either directly or indirectly, such as prestige and wealth, or liability to taxation and compulsory services. Players in a game do not protest against there being different positions, such as batter, pitcher, catcher, and the like, nor to there being various privileges and powers as specified by the rules; nor do the citizens of a country object to there being the different offices of government such as president, senator, governor, judge, and so on, each with their special rights and duties. It is not differences of this kind that are normally thought of as inequalities, but differences in the resulting distribution established by a practice, or made possible by it, of the things men strive to attain or avoid. Thus they may complain about the pattern of honors and rewards set up by a practice (e.g., the privileges and salaries of government officials) or they may object to the distribution of power and wealth which results from the various ways in which men avail themselves of the opportunities allowed by it (e.g., the concentration of wealth which may develop in a free price system allowing large entrepreneurial or speculative gains).

It should be noted that the second principle holds that an inequality is allowed only if there is reason to believe that the practice with the inequality, or resulting in it, will work for the advantage of *every* party engaging in it. Here it is important to stress that *every* party must gain from the inequality. Since the principle applies to practices, it implies that the representative man in every office or position defined by a practice, when he views it as a going concern, must find it reasonable to prefer his condition and prospects with the inequality to what they would be under the practice without it. The principle excludes, therefore, the justification of inequalities on the grounds that the disadvantages of those in

[3]This point was made by Sidgwick, *Methods of Ethics*, 6th ed. (London, 1901), Bk. III, ch. v, sec. 1. It has recently been emphasized by Sir Isaiah Berlin in a symposium, "Equality," *Proceedings of the Aristotelian Society*, n.s. LVI (1955–56), 305 f.

one position are outweighed by the greater advantages of those in another position. This rather simple restriction is the main modification I wish to make in the utilitarian principle as usually understood. When coupled with the notion of a practice, it is a restriction of consequence,[4] and one which some utilitarians, e.g., Hume and Mill, have used in their discussions of justice without realizing apparently its significance, or at least without calling attention to it.[5] Why it is a significant modification of principle, changing one's conception of justice entirely, the whole of my argument will show.

Further, it is also necessary that the various offices to which special benefits or burdens attach are open to all. It may be, for example, to the common advantage, as just defined, to attach special benefits to certain offices. Perhaps by doing so the requisite talent can be attracted to them and encouraged to give its best efforts. But any offices having special benefits must be won in a fair competition in which contestants are judged on their merits. If some offices were not open, those excluded would normally be justified in feeling unjustly treated, even if they benefited from the greater efforts of those who were allowed to compete for them. Now if one can assume that offices are open, it is necessary only to consider the design of practices themselves and how they jointly, as a system, work together. It will be a mistake to focus attention on the varying relative positions of particular persons, who may be known to us by their proper names, and to require that each such change, as a once for all transaction viewed in isolation, must be in itself just. It is the system of practices which is to be judged, and judged from a general point of view: unless one is prepared to criticize it from the standpoint of a representative man holding some particular office, one has no complaint against it.

3. Given these principles one might try to derive them from a priori principles of reason, or claim that they were known by intuition. These are familiar enough steps and, at least in the case of the first principle, might be made with some success. Usually, however, such arguments, made at this point, are unconvincing. They are not likely to lead to an understanding of the basis of the principles of justice, not at least as principles of justice. I wish, therefore, to look at the principles in a different way.

[4]In the paper referred to above, footnote 2, I have tried to show the importance of taking practices as the proper subject of the utilitarian principle. The criticisms of so-called "restricted utilitarianism" by J. J. C. Smart, "Extreme and Restricted Utilitarianism," *Philosophical Quarterly*, VI (1956), 344–354, and by H. J. McCloskey, "An Examination of Restricted Utilitarianism," *Philosophical Review*, LXVI (1957), 466–485, do not affect my argument. These papers are concerned with the very general proposition, which is attributed (with what justice I shall not consider) to S. E. Toulmin and P. H. Nowell-Smith (and in the case of the latter paper, also, apparently, to me); namely, the proposition that particular moral actions are justified by appealing to moral rules, and moral rules in turn by reference to utility. But clearly I meant to defend no such view. My discussion of the concept of rules as maxims is an explicit rejection of it. What I did argue was that, in the *logically special* case of practices (although actually quite a common case) where the rules have special features and are not moral rules at all but legal rules or rules of games and the like (except, perhaps, in the case of promises), there is a peculiar force to the distinction between justifying particular actions and justifying the system of rules themselves. Even then I claimed only that restricting the utilitarian principle to practices as defined strengthened it. I did not argue for the position that this amendment alone is sufficient for a complete defense of utilitarianism as a general theory of morals. In this paper I take up the question as to how the utilitarian principle itself must be modified, but here, too, the subject of inquiry is not all of morality at once, but a limited topic, the concept of justice.

[5]It might seem as if J. S. Mill, in paragraph 36 of Chapter V of *Utilitarianism*, expressed the utilitarian principle in this modified form, but in the remaining two paragraphs of the chapter, and elsewhere, he would appear not to grasp the significance of the change. Hume often emphasizes that *every* man must benefit. For example, in discussing the utility of general rules, he holds that they are requisite to the "well-being of every individual"; from a stable system of property "every individual person must find himself a gainer in balancing the account. . . ." "Every member of society is sensible of this interest; everyone expresses this sense to his fellows along with the resolution he has taken of squaring his actions by it, on the conditions that others will do the same." *A Treatise of Human Nature*, Bk. III, Pt. II, Section II, paragraph 22.

Imagine a society of persons amongst whom a certain system of practices is *already* well established. Now suppose that by and large they are mutually self-interested; their allegiance to their established practices is normally founded on the prospect of self-advantage. One need not assume that, in all senses of the term "person," the persons in this society are mutually self-interested. If the characterization as mutually self-interested applies when the line of division is the family, it may still be true that members of families are bound by ties of sentiment and affection and willingly acknowledge duties in contradiction to self-interest. Mutual self-interestedness in the relations between families, nations, churches, and the like, is commonly associated with intense loyalty and devotion on the part of individual members. Therefore, one can form a more realistic conception of this society if one thinks of it as consisting of mutually self-interested families, or some other association. Further, it is not necessary to suppose that these persons are mutually self-interested under all circumstances, but only in the usual situations in which they participate in their common practices.

Now suppose also that these persons are rational: they know their own interests more or less accurately; they are capable of tracing out the likely consequences of adopting one practice rather than another; they are capable of adhering to a course of action once they have decided upon it; they can resist present temptations and the enticements of immediate gain; and the bare knowledge or perception of the difference between their condition and that of others is not, within certain limits and in itself, a source of great dissatisfaction. Only the last point adds anything to the usual definition of rationality. This definition should allow, I think, for the idea that a rational man would not be greatly downcast from knowing, or seeing, that others are in a better position than himself, unless he thought their being so was the result of injustice, or the consequence of letting chance work itself out for no useful common purpose, and so on. So if these persons strike us as unpleasantly egoistic, they are at least free in some degree from the fault of envy.[6]

Finally, assume that these persons have roughly similar needs and interests, or needs and interests in various ways complementary, so that fruitful cooperation amongst them is possible; and suppose that they are sufficiently equal in power and ability to guarantee that in normal circumstances none is able to dominate the others. This condition (as well as the others) may seem excessively vague; but in view of the conception of justice to which the argument leads, there seems no reason for making it more exact here.

Since these persons are conceived as engaging in their common practices, which are already established, there is no question of our supposing them to come together to deliberate as to how they will set these practices up for the first time. Yet we can imagine that from time to time they discuss with one another whether any of them has a legitimate complaint against their established institutions. Such discussions are perfectly natural in any normal society. Now suppose that they have settled on doing this in the following way. They first try to arrive at the principles by which complaints, and so practices themselves, are to be judged. Their procedure for this is to let each person propose the principles upon which he wishes his complaints to be tried with the understanding that, if acknowledged, the complaints of others will be similarly tried, and that

[6]It is not possible to discuss here this addition to the usual conception of rationality. If it seems peculiar, it may be worth remarking that it is analogous to the modification of the utilitarian principle which the argument as a whole is designed to explain and justify. In the same way that the satisfaction of interests, the representative claims of which violate the principles of justice, is not a reason for having a practice (see sec. 7), unfounded envy, within limits, need not to be taken into account.

no complaints will be heard at all until everyone is roughly of one mind as to how complaints are to be judged. They each understand further that the principles proposed and acknowledged on this occasion are binding on future occasions. Thus each will be wary of proposing a principle which would give him a peculiar advantage, in his present circumstances, supposing it to be accepted. Each person knows that he will be bound by it in future circumstances the peculiarities of which cannot be known, and which might well be such that the principle is then to his disadvantage. The idea is that everyone should be required to make *in advance* a firm commitment, which others also may reasonably be expected to make, and that no one be given the opportunity to tailor the canons of a legitimate complaint to fit his own special condition, and then to discard them when they no longer suit his purpose. Hence each person will propose principles of a general kind which will, to a large degree, gain their sense from the various applications to be made of them, the particular circumstances of which being as yet unknown. These principles will express the conditions in accordance with which each is the least unwilling to have his interests limited in the design of practices, given the competing interests of the others, on the supposition that the interests of others will be limited likewise. The restrictions which would so arise might be thought of as those a person would keep in mind if he were designing a practice in which his enemy were to assign him his place.

The two main parts of this conjectural account have a definite significance. The character and respective situations of the parties reflect the typical circumstances in which questions of justice arise. The procedure whereby principles are proposed and acknowledged represents constraints, analogous to those of having a morality, whereby rational and mutually self-interested persons are brought to act reasonably. Thus the first part reflects the fact that questions of justice arise when conflicting claims are made upon the design of a practice and where it is taken for granted that each person will insist, as far as possible, on what he considers his rights. It is typical of cases of justice to involve persons who are pressing on one another their claims, between which a fair balance or equilibrium must be found. On the other hand, as expressed by the second part, having a morality must at least imply the acknowledgment of principles as impartially applying to one's own conduct as well as to another's, and moreover principles which may constitute a constraint, or limitation, upon the pursuit of one's own interests. There are, of course, other aspects of having a morality: the acknowledgment of moral principles must show itself in accepting a reference to them as reasons for limiting one's claims, in acknowledging the burden of providing a special explanation, or excuse, when one acts contrary to them, or else in showing shame and remorse and a desire to make amends, and so on. It is sufficient to remark here that having a morality is analogous to having made a firm commitment in advance; for one must acknowledge the principles of morality even when to one's disadvantage.[7] A man whose moral judgments always coincided with his interests could be suspected of having no morality at all.

Thus the two parts of the foregoing account are intended to mirror the kinds of circumstances in which questions of justice arise and the constraints which having a

[7]The idea that accepting a principle as a moral principle implies that one generally acts on it, failing a special explanation, has been stressed by R. M. Hare, *The Language of Morals* (Oxford, 1952). His formulation of it needs to be modified, however, along the lines suggested by P. L. Gardiner, "On Assenting to a Moral Principle," *Proceedings of the Aristotelian Society,* n.s. LV (1955), 23–44. See also C. K. Grant, "Akrasia and the Criteria of Assent to Practical Principles," *Mind,* LXV (1956), 400–407, where the complexity of the criteria for assent is discussed.

morality would impose upon persons so situated. In this way one can see how the acceptance of the principles of justice might come about, for given all these conditions as described, it would be natural if the two principles of justice were to be acknowledged. Since there is no way for anyone to win special advantages for himself, each might consider it reasonable to acknowledge equality as an initial principle. There is, however, no reason why they should regard this position as final; for if there are inequalities which satisfy the second principle, the immediate gain which equality would allow can be considered as intelligently invested in view of its future return. If, as is quite likely, these inequalities work as incentives to draw out better efforts, the members of this society may look upon them as concessions to human nature: they, like us, may think that people ideally should want to serve one another. But as they are mutually self-interested, their acceptance of these inequalities is merely the acceptance of the relations in which they actually stand, and a recognition of the motives which lead them to engage in their common practices. *They* have no title to complain of one another. And so provided that the conditions of the principle are met, there is no reason why they should not allow such inequalities. Indeed, it would be short-sighted of them to do so, and could result, in most cases, only from their being dejected by the bare knowledge, or perception, that others are better situated. Each person will, however, insist on an advantage to himself, and so on a common advantage, for none is willing to sacrifice anything for the others.

These remarks are not offered as a proof that persons so conceived and circumstanced would settle on the two principles, but only to show that these principles could have such a background, and so can be viewed as those principles which mutually self-interested and rational persons, when similarly situated and required to make in advance a firm commitment, could acknowledge as restrictions governing the assignment of rights and duties in their common practices, and thereby accept as limiting their rights against one another. The principles of justice may, then, be regarded as those principles which arise when the constraints of having a morality are imposed upon parties in the typical circumstances of justice.

4. These ideas are, of course, connected with a familiar way of thinking about justice which goes back at least to the Greek Sophists, and which regards the acceptance of the principles of justice as a compromise between persons of roughly equal power who would enforce their will on each other if they could, but who, in view of the equality of forces amongst them and for the sake of their own peace and security, acknowledge certain forms of conduct insofar as prudence seems to require. Justice is thought of as a pact between rational egoists the stability of which is dependent on a balance of power and a similarity of circumstances.[8] While the previous account is

[8]Perhaps the best known statement of this conception is that given by Glaucon at the beginning of Book II of Plato's *Republic*. Presumably it was, in various forms, a common view among the Sophists; but that Plato gives a fair representation of it is doubtful. See K. R. Popper, *The Open Society and Its Enemies*, rev. ed. (Princeton, 1950), pp. 112–118. Certainly Plato usually attributes to it a quality of manic egoism which one feels must be an exaggeration; on the other hand, see the Melian Debate in Thucydides, *The Peloponnesian War*, Book V, ch. VII, although it is impossible to say to what extent the views expressed there reveal any current philosophical opinion. Also in this tradition are the remarks of Epicurus on justice in *Principal Doctrines*, XXXI–XXXVIII. In modern times elements of the conception appear in a more sophisticated form in Hobbes *The Leviathan* and in Hume *A Treatise of Human Nature*, Book III, Pt. II, as well as in the writings of the school of natural law such as Pufendorf's *De jure naturae et gentium*. Hobbes and Hume are especially instructive. For Hobbes's argument see Howard Warrender's *The Political Philosophy of Hobbes* (Oxford, 1957). W. J. Baumol's *Welfare Economics and the Theory of the State* (London, 1952), is valuable in showing the wide applicability of Hobbes's fundamental idea (interpreting his natural law as principles of prudence), although in this book it is traced back only to Hume's *Treatise*.

connected with this tradition, and with its most recent variant, the theory of games,[9] it differs from it in several important respects which, to forestall misinterpretations, I will set out here.

First, I wish to use the previous conjectural account of the background of justice as a way of analyzing the concept. I do not want, therefore, to be interpreted as assuming a general theory of human motivation: when I suppose that the parties are mutually self-interested, and are not willing to have their (substantial) interests sacrificed to others, I am referring to their conduct and motives as they are taken for granted in cases where questions of justice ordinarily arise. Justice is the virtue of practices where there are assumed to be competing interests and conflicting claims, and where it is supposed that persons will press their rights on each other. That persons are mutually self-interested in certain situations and for certain purposes is what gives rise to the question of justice in practices covering those circumstances. Amongst an association of saints, if such a community could really exist, the disputes about justice could hardly occur; for they would all work selflessly together for one end, the glory of God as defined by their common religion, and reference to this end would settle every question of right. The justice of practices does not come up until there are several different parties (whether we think of these as individuals, associations, or nations and so on, is irrelevant) who do press their claims on one another, and who do regard themselves as representatives of interests which deserve to be considered. Thus the previous account involves no general theory of human motivation. Its intent is simply to incorporate into the conception of justice the relations of men to one another which set the stage for questions of justice. It makes no difference how wide or general these relations are, as this matter does not bear on the analysis of the concept.

Again, in contrast to the various conceptions of the social contract, the several parties do not establish any particular society or practice; they do not covenant to obey a particular sovereign body or to accept a given constitution.[10] Nor do they, as in the theory of games (in certain respects a marvelously sophisticated development of this tradition), decide on individual strategies adjusted to their respective circumstances in the game. What the parties do is to *jointly* acknowledge certain *principles* of appraisal relating to their common *practices* either as already established or merely proposed. They accede to standards of judgment, not to a given practice; they do not make any specific agreement, or bargain, or adopt a particular strategy. The subject of their acknowledgment is, therefore, very general indeed; it is simply the acknowledgment of certain principles of judgment, fulfilling certain general conditions, to be used in criticizing the arrangement of their common affairs. The relations of mutual self-interest between the parties who are similarly circumstanced mirror the conditions under which questions of justice arise, and the procedure by which the principles of judgment are proposed and acknowledged reflects the constraints of having a morality. Each aspect, then, of the preceding hypothetical account serves the purpose of bringing out a feature of the notion of justice. One could, if one liked, view the principles of justice as the "solution" of this highest order "game" of adopting, subject to the procedure described, principles of argument for all coming particular "games" whose peculiarities one can in no way foresee. But this comparison, while no doubt helpful, must

[9]See J. von Neumann and O. Morgenstern, *The Theory of Games and Economic Behavior*, 2nd ed. (Princeton, 1947). For a comprehensive and not too technical discussion of the developments since, see R. Duncan Luce and Howard Raiffa, *Games and Decisions: Introduction and Critical Survey* (New York, 1957). Chs. VI and XIV discuss the developments most obviously related to the analysis of justice.

[10]For a general survey see J. W. Gough, *The Social Contract*, 2nd ed. (Oxford, 1957), and Otto von Gierke, *The Development of Political Theory*, tr. by B. Freyd (London, 1939), Pt. II, ch. II.

not obscure the fact that this highest order "game" is of a special sort.[11] Its significance is that its various pieces represent aspects of the concept of justice.

Finally, I do not, of course, conceive the several parties as necessarily coming together to establish their common practices for the first time. Some institutions may, indeed, be set up *de novo;* but I have framed the preceding account so that it will apply when the full complement of social institutions already exists and represents the result of a long period of development. Nor is the account in any way fictitious. In any society where people reflect on their institutions they will have an idea of what principles of justice would be acknowledged under the conditions described, and there will be occasions when questions of justice are actually discussed in this way. Therefore if their practices do not accord with these principles, this will affect the quality of their social relations. For in this case there will be some recognized situations wherein the parties are mutually aware that one of them is being forced to accept what the other would concede is unjust. The foregoing analysis may then be thought of as representing the actual quality of relations between persons as defined by practices accepted as just. In such practices the parties will acknowledge the principles on which it is constructed, and the general recognition of this fact shows itself in the absence of resentment and in the sense of being justly treated. Thus one common objection to the theory of the social contract, its apparently historical and fictitious character, is avoided.

5. That the principles of justice may be regarded as arising in the manner described illustrates an important fact about them. Not only does it bring out the idea that justice is a primitive moral notion in that it arises once the concept of morality is imposed on mutually self-interested agents similarly circumstanced, but it emphasizes that, fundamental to justice, is the concept of fairness which relates to right dealing between persons who are cooperating with or competing against one another, as when one speaks of fair games, fair competition, and fair bargains. The question of fairness arises when free persons, who have no authority over one another, are engaging in a joint activity and amongst themselves settling or acknowledging the rules which define it and which determine the respective shares in its benefits and burdens. A practice will strike

[11]The difficulty one gets into by a mechanical application of the theory of games to moral philosophy can be brought out by considering among several possible examples, R. B. Braithwaite's study, *Theory of Games as a Tool for the Moral Philosopher* (Cambridge, 1955). On the analysis there given, it turns out that the fair division of playing time between Matthew and Luke depends on their preferences, and these in turn are connected with the instruments they wish to play. Since Matthew has a threat advantage over Luke, arising purely from the fact that Matthew, the trumpeter, prefers both of them playing at once to neither of them playing, whereas Luke, the pianist, prefers silence to cacophony, Matthew is alloted 26 evenings of play to Luke's 17. If the situation were reversed, the threat advantage would be with Luke. See pp. 36 f. But now we have only to suppose that Matthew is a jazz enthusiast who plays the drums, and Luke a violinist who plays sonatas, in which case it will be fair, on this analysis, for Matthew to play whenever and as often as he likes, assuming, of course, as it is plausible to assume, that he does not care whether Luke plays or not. Certainly something has gone wrong. To each according to his threat advantage is hardly the principle of fairness. What is lacking is the concept of morality, and it must be brought into the conjectural account in some way or other. In the text this is done by the form of the procedure whereby principles are proposed and acknowledged (Section 3). If one starts directly with the particular case as known, and if one accepts as given and definitive the preferences and relative positions of the parties, whatever they are, it is impossible to give an analysis of the moral concept of fairness. Braithwaite's use of the theory of games, insofar as it is intended to analyze the concept of fairness, is, I think, mistaken. This is not, of course, to criticize in any way the theory of games as a mathematical theory, to which Braithwaite's book certainly contributes, nor as an analysis of how rational (and amoral) egoists might behave (and so as an analysis of how people sometimes actually do behave). But it is to say that if the theory of games is to be used to analyze moral concepts, its formal structure must be interpreted in a special and general manner as indicated in the text. Once we do this, though, we are in touch again with a much older tradition.

the parties as fair if none feels that, by participating in it, they or any of the others are taken advantage of, or forced to give in to claims which they do not regard as legitimate. This implies that each has a conception of legitimate claims which he thinks it reasonable for others as well as himself to acknowledge. If one thinks of the principles of justice as arising in the manner described, then they do define this sort of conception. A practice is just or fair, then, when it satisfies the principles which those who participate in it could propose to one another for mutual acceptance under the aforementioned circumstances. Persons engaged in a just, or fair, practice can face one another openly and support their respective positions, should they appear questionable, by reference to principles which it is reasonable to expect each to accept.

It is this notion of the possibility of mutual acknowledgment of principles by free persons who have no authority over one another which makes the concept of fairness fundamental to justice. Only if such acknowledgment is possible can there be true community between persons in their common practices; otherwise their relations will appear to them as founded to some extent on force. If, in ordinary speech, fairness applies more particularly to practices in which there is a choice whether to engage or not (e.g., in games, business competition), and justice to practices in which there is no choice (e.g., in slavery), the element of necessity does not render the conception of mutual acknowledgment inapplicable, although it may make it much more urgent to change unjust than unfair institutions. For one activity in which one can always engage is that of proposing and acknowledging principles to one another supposing each to be similarly circumstanced; and to judge practices by the principles so arrived at is to apply the standard of fairness to them.

Now if the participants in a practice accept its rules as fair, and so have no complaint to lodge against it, there arises a prima facie duty (and a corresponding prima facie right) of the parties to each other to act in accordance with the practice when it falls upon them to comply. When any number of persons engage in a practice, or conduct a joint undertaking according to rules, and thus restrict their liberty, those who have submitted to these restrictions when required have the right to a similar acquiescence on the part of those who have benefited by their submission. These conditions will obtain if a practice is correctly acknowledged to be fair, for in this case all who participate in it will benefit from it. The rights and duties so arising are special rights and duties in that they depend on previous actions voluntarily undertaken, in this case on the parties having engaged in a common practice and knowingly accepted its benefits.[12] It is not, however, an obligation which presupposes a deliberate performative act in the sense of a promise, or contract, and the like.[13] An unfortunate mistake of proponents of the idea of the social contract was to suppose that political obligation does require some such act, or at least to use language which suggests it. It is sufficient that one has knowingly participated in and accepted the benefits of a practice acknowledged to be fair. This prima facie obligation may, of course, be overridden: it may happen, when it comes one's turn to follow a rule, that other considerations will justify not doing so. But one cannot, in general, be released from this obligation by denying the justice of the practice only when it falls on one to obey. If a person rejects a practice, he should, so far as possible, declare his intention in advance, and avoid participating in it or enjoying its benefits.

[12]For the definition of this prima facie duty, and the idea that it is a special duty, I am indebted to H. L. A. Hart. See his paper "Are There Any Natural Rights?," *Philosophical Review,* LXIV (1955), 185 f.

[13]The sense of "performative" here is to be derived from J. L. Austin's paper in the symposium, "Other Minds," *Proceedings of the Aristotelian Society,* Supplementary Volume (1946), pp. 170–174.

This duty I have called that of fair play, but it should be admitted that to refer to it in this way is, perhaps, to extend the ordinary notion of fairness. Usually acting unfairly is not so much the breaking of any particular rule, even if the infraction is difficult to detect (cheating), but taking advantage of loop-holes or ambiguities in rules, availing oneself of unexpected or special circumstances which make it impossible to enforce them, insisting that rules be enforced to one's advantage when they should be suspended, and more generally, acting contrary to the intention of a practice. It is for this reason that one speaks of the sense of fair play: acting fairly requires more than simply being able to follow rules; what is fair must often be felt, or perceived, one wants to say. It is not, however, an unnatural extension of the duty of fair play to have it include the obligation which participants who have knowingly accepted the benefits of their common practice owe to each other to act in accordance with it when their performance falls due; for it is usually considered unfair if someone accepts the benefits of a practice but refuses to do his part in maintaining it. Thus one might say of the tax-dodger that he violates the duty of fair play: he accepts the benefits of government but will not do his part in releasing resources to it; and members of labor unions often say that fellow workers who refuse to join are being unfair: they refer to them as "free riders," as persons who enjoy what are the supposed benefits of unionism, higher wages, shorter hours, job security, and the like, but who refuse to share in its burdens in the form of paying dues, and so on.

The duty of fair play stands beside other prima facie duties such as fidelity and gratitude as a basic moral notion; yet it is not to be confused with them.[14] These duties are all clearly distinct, as would be obvious from their definitions. As with any moral duty, that of fair play implies a constraint on self-interest in particular cases; on occasion it enjoins conduct which a rational egoist strictly defined would not decide upon. So while justice does not require of anyone that he sacrifice his interests in that *general position* and procedure whereby the principles of justice are proposed and acknowledged, it may happen that in particular situations, arising in the context of engaging in a practice, the duty of fair play will often cross his interests in the sense that he will be required to forgo particular advantages which the peculiarities of his circumstances might permit him to take. There is, of course, nothing surprising in this. It is simply the consequence of the firm commitment which the parties may be supposed to have made, or which they would make, in the general position, together with the fact that they have participated in and accepted the benefits of a practice which they regard as fair.

Now the acknowledgment of this constraint in particular cases, which is manifested in acting fairly or wishing to make amends, feeling ashamed, and the like, when one has evaded it, is one of the forms of conduct by which participants in a common practice exhibit their recognition of each other as persons with similar interests and capacities. In the same way that, failing a special explanation, the criterion for the recognition of suffering is helping one who suffers, acknowledging the duty of fair play is a necessary part of the criterion for recognizing another as a person with similar interests

[14]This, however, commonly happens. Hobbes, for example, when invoking the notion of a "tacit covenant," appeals not to the natural law that promises should be kept but to his fourth law of nature, that of gratitude. On Hobbes's shift from fidelity to gratitude, see Warrender, *op. cit.*, pp. 51–52, 233–237. While it is not a serious criticism of Hobbes, it would have improved his argument had he appealed to the duty of fair play. On his premises he is perfectly entitled to do so. Similarly Sidgwick thought that a principle of justice, such as every man ought to receive adequate requital for his labor, is like gratitude universalized. See *Methods of Ethics*, Bk. III, ch. v, Sec. 5. There is a gap in the stock of moral concepts used by philosophers into which the concept of the duty of fair play fits quite naturally.

and feelings as oneself.[15] A person who never under any circumstances showed a wish to help others in pain would show, at the same time, that he did not recognize that they were in pain; nor could he have any feelings of affection or friendship for anyone; for having these feelings implies, failing special circumstances, that he comes to their aid when they are suffering. Recognition that another is a person in pain shows itself in sympathetic action; this primitive natural response of compassion is one of those responses upon which the various forms of moral conduct are built.

Similarly, the acceptance of the duty of fair play by participants in a common practice is a reflection in each person of the recognition of the aspirations and interests of the others to be realized by their joint activity. Failing a special explanation, their acceptance of it is a necessary part of the criterion for their recognizing one another as persons with similar interests and capacities, as the conception of their relations in the general position supposes them to be. Otherwise they would show no recognition of one another as persons with similar capacities and interests, and indeed, in some cases perhaps hypothetical, they would not recognize one another as persons at all, but as complicated objects involved in a complicated activity. To recognize another as a person one must respond to him and act towards him in certain ways; and these ways are intimately connected with the various prima facie duties. Acknowledging these duties in *some* degree, and so having the elements of morality, is not a matter of choice, or of intuiting moral qualities, or a matter of the expression of feelings or attitudes (the three interpretations between which philosophical opinion frequently oscillates); it is simply the possession of one of the forms of conduct in which the recognition of others as persons is manifested.

These remarks are unhappily obscure. Their main purpose here, however, is to forestall, together with the remarks in Section 4, the misinterpretation that, on the view presented, the acceptance of justice and the acknowledgment of the duty of fair play depend in every day life solely on there being a *de facto* balance of forces between the parties. It would indeed be foolish to underestimate the importance of such a balance in securing justice; but it is not the only basis thereof. The recognition of one another as persons with similar interests and capacities engaged in a common practice must, failing a special explanation, show itself in the acceptance of the principles of justice and the acknowledgment of the duty of fair play.

The conception at which we have arrived, then, is that the principles of justice may be thought of as arising once the constraints of having a morality are imposed upon rational and mutually self-interested parties who are related and situated in a special way. A practice is just if it is in accordance with the principles which all who participate in it might reasonably be expected to propose or to acknowledge before one another when they are similarly circumstanced and required to make a firm commitment in advance without knowledge of what will be their peculiar condition, and thus when it meets standards which the parties could accept as fair should occasion arise for them to debate its merits. Regarding the participants themselves, once persons knowingly engage in a practice which they acknowledge to be fair and accept the benefits of doing

[15] I am using the concept of criterion here in what I take to be Wittgenstein's sense. See *Philosophical Investigations* (Oxford, 1953); and Norman Malcolm's review, "Wittgenstein's *Philosophical Investigations*," *Philosophical Review*, LXIII (1954), 543–547. That the response of compassion, under appropriate circumstances, is part of the criterion for whether or not a person understands what "pain" means, is, I think, in the *Philosophical Investigations*. The view in the text is simply an extension of this idea. I cannot, however, attempt to justify it here. Similar thoughts are to be found, I think, in Max Scheler, *The Nature of Sympathy*, tr. by Peter Heath (New Haven, 1954). His way of writing is often so obscure that I cannot be certain.

so, they are bound by the duty of fair play to follow the rules when it comes their turn to do so, and this implies a limitation on their pursuit of self-interest in particular cases.

Now one consequence of this conception is that, where it applies, there is no moral value in the satisfaction of a claim incompatible with it. Such a claim violates the conditions of reciprocity and community amongst persons, and he who presses it, not being willing to acknowledge it when pressed by another, has no grounds for complaint when it is denied; whereas he against whom it is pressed can complain. As it cannot be mutually acknowledged it is a resort to coercion; granting the claim is possible only if one party can compel acceptance of what the other will not admit. But it makes no sense to concede claims the denial of which cannot be complained of in preference to claims the denial of which can be objected to. Thus in deciding on the justice of a practice it is not enough to ascertain that it answers to wants and interests in the fullest and most effective manner. For if any of these conflict with justice, they should not be counted, as their satisfaction is no reason at all for having a practice. It would be irrelevant to say, even if true, that it resulted in the greatest satisfaction of desire. In tallying up the merits of a practice one must toss out the satisfaction of interests the claims of which are incompatible with the principles of justice.

6. The discussion so far has been excessively abstract. While this is perhaps unavoidable, I should now like to bring out some of the features of the conception of justice as fairness by comparing it with the conception of justice in classical utilitarianism as represented by Bentham and Sidgwick, and its counterpart in welfare economics. This conception assimilates justice to benevolence and the latter in turn to the most efficient design of institutions to promote the general welfare. Justice is a kind of efficiency.[16]

Now it is said occasionally that this form of utilitarianism puts no restrictions on what might be a just assignment of rights and duties in that there might be circumstances which, on utilitarian grounds, would justify institutions highly offensive to our ordinary sense of justice. But the classical utilitarian conception is not totally unprepared for this objection. Beginning with the notion that the general happiness can be represented by a social utility function consisting of a sum of individual utility functions with identical weights (this being the meaning of the maxim that each counts for one and no more than one),[17] it is commonly assumed that the utility functions of indi-

[16]While this assimilation is implicit in Bentham's and Sidgwick's moral theory, explicit statements of it as applied to justice are relatively rare. One clear instance in *The Principles of Morals and Legislation* occurs in ch. x, footnote 2 to section XL: ". . . justice, in the only sense in which it has a meaning, is an imaginary personage, feigned for the convenience of discourse, whose dictates are the dictates of utility, applied to certain particular cases. Justice, then, is nothing more than an imaginary instrument, employed to forward on certain occasions, and by certain means, the purposes of benevolence. The dictates of justice are nothing more than a part of the dictates of benevolence, which, on certain occasions, are applied to certain subjects. . . ." Likewise in *The Limits of Jurisprudence Defined*, ed. by C. W. Everett (New York, 1945), pp. 117 f., Bentham criticizes Grotius for denying that justice derives from utility; and in *The Theory of Legislation*, ed. by C. K. Ogden (London, 1931), p. 3, he says that he uses the words "just" and "unjust" along with other words "simply as collective terms including the ideas of certain pains or pleasures." That Sidgwick's conception of justice is similar to Bentham's is admittedly not evident from his discussion of justice in Book III, ch. v of *Methods of Ethics*. But it follows, I think, from the moral theory he accepts. Hence C. D. Broad's criticisms of Sidgwick in the matter of distributive justice in *Five Types of Ethical Theory* (London, 1930), pp. 249–253, do not rest on a misinterpretation.

[17]This maxim is attributed to Bentham by J. S. Mill in *Utilitarianism*, ch. v, paragraph 36. I have not found it in Bentham's writings, nor seen such a reference. Similarly James Bonar, *Philosophy and Political Economy* (London, 1893), p. 234 n. But it accords perfectly with Bentham's ideas. See the hitherto unpublished manuscript in David Baumgardt, *Bentham and the Ethics of Today* (Princeton, 1952), Appendix IV. For example, "the total value of the stock of pleasure belonging to the whole community is to be obtained by multiplying the number expressing the value of it as respecting any one person, by the number expressing the multitude of such individuals" (p. 556).

viduals are similar in all essential respects. Differences between individuals are ascribed to accidents of education and upbringing, and they should not be taken into account. This assumption, coupled with that of diminishing marginal utility, results in a prima facie case for equality, e.g., of equality in the distribution of income during any given period of time, laying aside indirect effects on the future. But even if utilitarianism is interpreted as having such restrictions built into the utility function, and even if it is supposed that these restrictions have in practice much the same result as the application of the principles of justice (and appear, perhaps, to be ways of expressing these principles in the language of mathematics and psychology), the fundamental idea is very different from the conception of justice as fairness. For one thing, that the principles of justice should be accepted is interpreted as the contingent result of a higher order administrative decision. The form of this decision is regarded as being similar to that of an entrepreneur deciding how much to produce of this or that commodity in view of its marginal revenue, or to that of someone distributing goods to needy persons according to the relative urgency of their wants. The choice between practices is thought of as being made on the basis of the allocation of benefits and burdens to individuals (these being measured by the present capitalized value of their utility over the full period of the practice's existence), which results from the distribution of rights and duties established by a practice.

Moreover, the individuals receiving these benefits are not conceived as being related in any way: they represent so many different directions in which limited resources may be allocated. The value of assigning resources to one direction rather than another depends solely on the preferences and interests of individuals as individuals. The satisfaction of desire has its value irrespective of the moral relations between persons, say as members of a joint undertaking, and of the claims which, in the name of these interests, they are prepared to make on one another;[18] and it is this value which is to be taken into account by the (ideal) legislator who is conceived as adjusting the rules of the system from the center so as to maximize the value of the social utility function.

It is thought that the principles of justice will not be violated by a legal system so conceived provided these executive decisions are correctly made. In this fact the principles of justice are said to have their derivation and explanation; they simply express the most important general features of social institutions in which the administrative problem is solved in the best way. These principles have, indeed, a special urgency because, given the facts of human nature, so much depends on them; and this explains

[18]An idea essential to the classical utilitarian conception of justice. Bentham is firm in his statement of it: "It is only upon that principle [the principle of asceticism], and not from the principle of utility, that the most abominable pleasure which the vilest of malefactors ever reaped from his crime would be reprobated, if it stood alone. The case is, that it never does stand alone; but is necessarily followed by such a quantity of pain (or, what comes to the same thing, such a chance for a certain quantity of pain) that the pleasure in comparison of it, is as nothing: and this is the true and sole, but perfectly sufficient, reason for making it a ground for punishment" (*The Principles of Morals and Legislation,* ch. II, sec. iv. See also ch. X, sec. X, footnote I). The same point is made in *The Limits of Jurisprudence Defined,* pp. 115 f. Although much recent welfare economics, as found in such important works as I. M. D. Little, *A Critique of Welfare Economics,* 2nd ed. (Oxford, 1957) and K. J. Arrow, *Social Choice and Individual Values* (New York, 1951), dispenses with the idea of cardinal utility, and use instead the theory of ordinal utility as stated by J. R. Hicks, *Value and Capital,* 2nd ed. (Oxford, 1946), Pt. I, it assumes with utilitarianism that individual preferences have value as such, and so accepts the idea being criticized here. I hasten to add, however, that this is no objection to it as a means of analyzing economic policy, and for that purpose it may, indeed, be a necessary simplifying assumption. Nevertheless it is an assumption which cannot be made in so far as one is trying to analyze moral concepts, especially the concept of justice, as economists would, I think, agree. Justice is usually regarded as a separate and distinct part of any comprehensive criterion of economic policy. See, for example, Tibor Scitovsky, *Welfare and Competition* (London, 1952), pp. 59–69, and Little, *op. cit.,* ch. VII.

the peculiar quality of the moral feelings associated with justice.[19] This assimilation of justice to a higher order executive decision, certainly a striking conception, is central to classical utilitarianism; and it also brings out its profound individualism, in one sense of this ambiguous word. It regards persons as so many *separate* directions in which benefits and burdens may be assigned; and the value of the satisfaction or dissatisfaction of desire is not thought to depend in any way on the moral relations in which individuals stand, or on the kinds of claims which they are willing, in the pursuit of their interests, to press on each other.

7. Many social decisions are, of course, of an administrative nature. Certainly this is so when it is a matter of social utility in what one may call its ordinary sense: that is, when it is a question of the efficient design of social institutions for the use of common means to achieve common ends. In this case either the benefits and burdens may be assumed to be impartially distributed, or the question of distribution is misplaced, as in the instance of maintaining public order and security or national defense. But as an interpretation of the basis of the principles of justice, classical utilitarianism is mistaken. It *permits* one to argue, for example, that slavery is unjust on the grounds that the advantages to the slaveholder as slaveholder do not counterbalance the disadvantages to the slave and to society at large burdened by a comparatively inefficient system of labor. Now the conception of justice as fairness, when applied to the practice of slavery with its offices of slaveholder and slave, would not allow one to consider the advantages of the slaveholder in the first place. As that office is not in accordance with principles which could be mutually acknowledged, the gains accruing to the slaveholder, assuming them to exist, cannot be counted as in *any* way mitigating the injustice of the practice. The question whether these gains outweigh the disadvantages to the slave and to society cannot arise, since in considering the justice of slavery these gains have no weight at all which requires that they be overridden. Where the conception of justice as fairness applies, slavery is *always* unjust.

I am not, of course, suggesting the absurdity that the classical utilitarians approved of slavery. I am only rejecting a type of argument which their view allows them to use in support of their disapproval of it. The conception of justice as derivative from efficiency implies that judging the justice of a practice is always, in principle at least, a matter of weighing up advantages and disadvantages, each having an intrinsic value or disvalue as the satisfaction of interests, irrespective of whether or not these interests necessarily involve acquiescence in principles which could not be mutually acknowledged. Utilitarianism cannot account for the fact that slavery is always unjust, nor for the fact that it would be recognized as irrelevant in defeating the accusation of injustice for one person to say to another, engaged with him in a common practice and debating its merits, that nevertheless it allowed of the greatest satisfaction of desire. The charge of injustice cannot be rebutted in this way. If justice were derivative from a higher order executive efficiency, this would not be so.

But now, even if it is taken as established that, so far as the ordinary conception of justice goes, slavery is always unjust (that is, slavery by definition violates commonly recognized principles of justice), the classical utilitarian would surely reply that these principles, as other moral principles subordinate to that of utility, are only generally correct. It is simply for the most part true that slavery is less efficient than other institutions; and while common sense may define the concept of justice so that slavery is unjust, nevertheless, where slavery would lead to the greatest satisfaction of desire, it is not wrong. Indeed, it is then right, and for the very same reason that justice, as ordinar-

[19]See J. S. Mill's argument in *Utilitarianism*, ch. v, pars. 16–25.

ily understood, is usually right. If, as ordinarily understood, slavery is always unjust, to this extent the utilitarian conception of justice might be admitted to differ from that of common moral opinion. Still the utilitarian would want to hold that, as a matter of moral principle, his view is correct in giving no special weight to considerations of justice beyond that allowed for by the general presumption of effectiveness. And this, he claims, is as it should be. The every day opinion is morally in error, although, indeed, it is a useful error, since it protects rules of generally high utility.

The question, then, relates not simply to the analysis of the concept of justice as common sense defines it, but the analysis of it in the wider sense as to how much weight considerations of justice, as defined, are to have when laid against other kinds of moral considerations. Here again I wish to argue that reasons of justice have a *special* weight for which only the conception of justice as fairness can account. Moreover, it belongs to the concept of justice that they do have this special weight. While Mill recognized that this was so, he thought that it could be accounted for by the special urgency of the moral feelings which naturally support principles of such high utility. But it is a mistake to resort to the urgency of feeling; as with the appeal to intuition, it manifests a failure to pursue the question far enough. The special weight of considerations of justice can be explained from the conception of justice as fairness. It is only necessary to elaborate a bit what has already been said as follows.

If one examines the circumstances in which a certain tolerance of slavery is justified, or perhaps better, excused, it turns out that these are of a rather special sort. Perhaps slavery exists as an inheritance from the past and it proves necessary to dismantle it piece by piece; at times slavery may conceivably be an advance on previous institutions. Now while there may be some excuse for slavery in special conditions, it is never an excuse for it that it is sufficiently advantageous to the slaveholder to outweigh the disadvantages to the slave and to society. A person who argues in this way is not perhaps making a wildly irrelevant remark; but he is guilty of a moral fallacy. There is disorder in his conception of the ranking of moral principles. For the slaveholder, by his own admission, has no moral title to the advantages which he receives as a slaveholder. He is no more prepared than the slave to acknowledge the principle upon which is founded the respective positions in which they both stand. Since slavery does not accord with principles which they could mutually acknowledge, they each may be supposed to agree that it is unjust: it grants claims which it ought not to grant and in doing so denies claims which it ought not to deny. Amongst persons in a general position who are debating the form of their common practices, it cannot, therefore, be offered as a reason for a practice that, in conceding these very claims that ought to be denied, it nevertheless meets existing interests more effectively. By their very nature the satisfaction of these claims is without weight and cannot enter into any tabulation of advantages and disadvantages.

Furthermore, it follows from the concept of morality that, to the extent that the slaveholder recognizes his position vis-a-vis the slave to be unjust, he would not choose to press his claims. His not wanting to receive his special advantages is one of the ways in which he shows that he thinks slavery is unjust. It would be fallacious for the legislator to suppose, then, that it is a ground for having a practice that it brings advantages greater than disadvantages, if those for whom the practice is designed, and to whom the advantages flow, acknowledge that they have no moral title to them and do not wish to receive them.

For these reasons the principles of justice have a special weight; and with respect to the principle of the greatest satisfaction of desire, as cited in the general position amongst those discussing the merits of their common practices, the principles of justice have an absolute weight. In this sense they are not contingent; and this is why their force is greater than can be accounted for by the general presumption (assuming that there is one) of the effectiveness, in the utilitarian sense, of practices which in fact satisfy them.

If one wants to continue using the concepts of classical utilitarianism, one will have to say, to meet this criticism, that at least the individual or social utility functions must be so defined that no value is given to the satisfaction of interests the representative claims of which violate the principles of justice. In this way it is no doubt possible to include these principles within the form of the utilitarian conception; but to do so is, of course, to change its inspiration altogether as a moral conception. For it is to incorporate within it principles which cannot be understood on the basis of a higher order executive decision aiming at the greatest satisfaction of desire.

It is worth remarking, perhaps, that this criticism of utilitarianism does not depend on whether or not the two assumptions, that of individuals having similar utility functions and that of diminishing marginal utility, are interpreted as psychological propositions to be supported or refuted by experience, or as moral and political principles expressed in a somewhat technical language. There are, certainly, several advantages in taking them in the latter fashion.[20] For one thing, one might say that this is what Bentham and others really meant by them, as least as shown by how they were used in arguments for social reform. More importantly, one could hold that the best way to defend the classical utilitarian view is to interpret these assumptions as moral and political principles. It is doubtful whether, taken as psychological propositions, they are true of men in general as we know them under normal conditions. On the other hand, utilitarians would not have wanted to propose them merely as practical working principles of legislation, or as expedient maxims to guide reform, given the egalitarian sentiments of modern society.[21] When pressed they might well have invoked the idea of a more or less equal capacity of men in relevant respects if given an equal chance in a just society. But if the argument above regarding slavery is correct, then granting these assumptions as moral and political principles makes no difference. To view individuals as equally fruitful lines for the allocation of benefits, even as a matter of moral principle, still leaves the mistaken notion that the satisfaction of desire has value in itself irrespective of the relations between persons as members of a common practice, and irrespective of the claims upon one another which the satisfaction of interests represents. To see the error of this idea one must give up the conception of justice as an executive decision altogether and refer to the notion of justice as fairness: that participants in a common practice be regarded as having an original and equal liberty and that their common practices be considered unjust unless they accord with principles which persons so circumstanced and related could freely acknowledge before one another, and so could accept as fair. Once the emphasis is put upon the concept of the mutual recognition of principles by participants in a common practice the rules of which are to define their several relations and give form to their claims on one another, then it is clear that the granting of a claim the principle of which could not be acknowledged by each in the general position (that is, in the position in which the parties propose and acknowledge principles

[20]See D. G. Ritchie, *Natural Rights* (London, 1894), pp. 95 ff., 249 ff. Lionel Robbins has insisted on this point on several occasions. See *An Essay on the Nature and Significance of Economic Science*, 2nd ed. (London, 1935), pp. 134–143, "Interpersonal Comparisons of Utility: A Comment," *Economic Journal*, XLVIII (1938), 635–641, and more recently, "Robertson on Utility and Scope," *Economica*, n.s. XX (1953), 108 f.

[21]As Sir Henry Maine suggested Bentham may have regarded them. See *The Early History of Institutions* (London, 1875), pp. 398 ff.

before one another) is not a reason for adopting a practice. Viewed in this way, the background of the claim is seen to exclude it from consideration; that it can represent a value in itself arises from the conception of individuals as separate lines for the assignment of benefits, as isolated persons who stand as claimants on an administrative or benevolent largesse. Occasionally persons do so stand to one another; but this is not the general case, nor, more importantly, is it the case when it is a matter of the justice of practices themselves in which participants stand in various relations to be appraised in accordance with standards which they may be expected to acknowledge before one another. Thus however mistaken the notion of the social contract may be as history, and however far it may overreach itself as a general theory of social and political obligation, it does express, suitably interpreted, an essential part of the concept of justice.[22]

8. By way of conclusion I should like to make two remarks: first, the original modification of the utilitarian principle (that it require of practices that the offices and positions defined by them be equal unless it is reasonable to suppose that the representative man in *every* office would find the inequality to his advantage), slight as it may appear at first sight, actually has a different conception of justice standing behind it. I have tried to show how this is so by developing the concept of justice as fairness and by indicating how this notion involves the mutual acceptance, from a general position, of the principles on which a practice is founded, and how this in turn requires the exclusion from consideration of claims violating the principles of justice. Thus the slight alteration of principle reveals another family of notions, another way of looking at the concept of justice.

Second, I should like to remark also that I have been dealing with the *concept* of justice. I have tried to set out the kinds of principles upon which judgments concerning the justice of practices may be said to stand. The analysis will be successful to the degree that it expresses the principles involved in these judgments when made by competent persons upon deliberation and reflection.[23] Now every people may be supposed to have the concept of justice, since in the life of every society there must be at least some relations in which the parties consider themselves to be circumstanced and related as the concept of justice as fairness requires. Societies will differ from one another not in having or in failing to have this notion but in the range of cases to which they apply it and in the emphasis which they give to it as compared with other moral concepts.

A firm grasp of the concept of justice itself is necessary if these variations, and the reasons for them, are to be understood. No study of the development of moral ideas and of the differences between them is more sound than the analysis of the fundamental

[22]Thus Kant was not far wrong when he interpreted the original contract merely as an "Idea of Reason"; yet he still thought of it as a *general* criterion of right and as providing a general theory of political obligation. See the second part of the essay, "On the Saying 'That may be right in theory but has no value in practice' " (1793), in *Kant's Principles of Politics,* tr. by W. Hastie (Edinburgh, 1891). I have drawn on the contractarian tradition not for a general theory of political obligation but to clarify the concept of justice.

[23]For a further discussion of the idea expressed here, see my paper, "Outline of a Decision Procedure for Ethics," in the *Philosophical Review,* LX (1951), 177–197. For an analysis, similar in many respects but using the notion of the ideal observer instead of that of the considered judgment of a competent person, see Roderick Firth, "Ethical Absolutism and the Ideal Observer," *Philosophy and Phenomenological Research,* XII (1952), 317–345. While the similarities between these two discussions are more important than the differences, an analysis based on the notion of a considered judgment of a competent person, as it is based on a kind of judgment, may prove more helpful in understanding the features of moral judgment than an analysis based on the notion of an ideal observer, although this remains to be shown. A man who rejects the conditions imposed on a considered judgment of a competent person could no longer profess to *judge* at all. This seems more fundamental than his rejecting the conditions of observation, for these do not seem to apply, in an ordinary sense, to making a moral judgment.

moral concepts upon which it must depend. I have tried, therefore, to give an analysis of the concept of justice which should apply generally, however large a part the concept may have in a given morality, and which can be used in explaining the course of men's thoughts about justice and its relations to other moral concepts. How it is to be used for this purpose is a large topic which I cannot, of course, take up here. I mention it only to emphasize that I have been dealing with the concept of justice itself and to indicate what use I consider such an analysis to have.

1958

Modern Moral Philosophy

G. E. M. Anscombe

I will begin by stating three theses which I present in this paper. The first is that it is not profitable for us at present to do moral philosophy; that should be laid aside at any rate until we have an adequate philosophy of psychology, in which we are conspicuously lacking. The second is that the concepts of obligation, and duty—*moral* obligation and *moral* duty, that is to say—and of what is *morally* right and wrong, and of the *moral* sense of "ought," ought to be jettisoned if this is psychologically possible; because they are survivals, or derivatives from survivals, from an earlier conception of ethics which no longer generally survives, and are only harmful without it. My third thesis is that the differences between the well-known English writers on moral philosophy from Sidgwick to the present day are of little importance.

Anyone who has read Aristotle's *Ethics* and has also read modern moral philosophy must have been struck by the great contrasts between them. The concepts which are prominent among the moderns seem to be lacking, or at any rate buried or far in the background, in Aristotle. Most noticeably, the term "moral" itself, which we have by direct inheritance from Aristotle, just doesn't seem to fit, in its modern sense, into an account of

This paper was originally read to the Voltaire Society in Oxford

Elizabeth Anscombe, "Modern Moral Philosophy," *Philosophy* 33, No. 124 (January 1958). Reprinted with the permission of G. E. M. Anscombe.

Aristotelian ethics. Aristotle distinguishes virtues as moral and intellectual. Have some of what he calls "intellectual" virtues what *we* should call a "moral" aspect? It would seem so; the criterion is presumably that a failure in an "intellectual" virtue—like that of having good judgment in calculating how to bring about something useful, say in municipal government—may be *blameworthy.* But—it may reasonably be asked—cannot *any* failure be made a matter of blame or reproach? Any derogatory criticism, say of the workmanship of a product or the design of a machine, can be called blame or reproach. So we want to put in the word "morally" again: sometimes such a failure may be *morally* blameworthy, sometimes not. Now has Aristotle got this idea of *moral* blame, as opposed to any other? If he has, why isn't it more central? There are some mistakes, he says, which are causes, not of involuntariness in actions but of scoundrelism, and for which a man is blamed. Does this mean that there is a *moral* obligation not to make certain intellectual mistakes? Why doesn't he discuss obligation in general, and this obligation in particular? If someone professes to be expounding Aristotle and talks in a modern fashion about "moral" such-and-such he must be very imperceptive if he does not constantly feel like someone whose jaws have somehow got out of alignment: the teeth don't come together in a proper bite.

We cannot, then, look to Aristotle for any elucidation of the modern way of talking about "moral" goodness, obligation, etc. And all the best-known writers on ethics in modern times, from Butler to Mill, appear to me to have faults as thinkers on the subject which make it impossible to hope for any direct light on it fiom them. I will state these objections with the brevity which their character makes possible.

Butler exalts conscience, but appears ignorant that a man's conscience may tell him to do the vilest things.

Hume defines "truth" in such a way as to exclude ethical judgments from it, and professes that he has proved that they are so excluded. He also implicitly defines "passion" in such a way that aiming at anything is having a passion. His objection to passing from "is" to "ought" would apply equally to passing from "is" to "owes" or from "is" to "needs." (However, because of the historical situation, he has a point here, which I shall return to.)

Kant introduces the idea of "legislating for oneself," which is as absurd as if in these days, when majority votes command great respect, one were to call each reflective decision a man made a *vote* resulting in a majority, which as a matter of proportion is overwhelming, for it is always 1–0. The concept of legislation requires superior power in the legislator. His own rigoristic convictions on the subject of lying were so intense that it never occurred to him that a lie could be relevantly described as anything but just a lie (e.g. as "a lie in such-and-such circumstances"). His rule about universalizable maxims is useless without stipulations as to what shall count as a relevant description of an action with a view to constructing a maxim about it.

Bentham and Mill do not notice the difficulty of the concept "pleasure." They are often said to have gone wrong through committing the "naturalistic fallacy"; but this charge does not impress me, because I do not find accounts of it coherent. But the other point—about pleasure—seems to me a fatal objection from the very outset. The ancients found this concept pretty baffling. It reduced Aristotle to sheer babble about "the bloom on the cheek of youth" because, for good reasons, he wanted to make it out both identical with and different from the pleasurable activity. Generations of modern philosophers found this concept quite unperplexing, and it reappeared in the literature as a problematic one only a year or two ago when Ryle wrote about it. The reason is simple: since Locke, pleasure was taken to be some sort of internal impression. But it was superficial, if that was the right account of it, to make it the point of actions. One might adapt something Wittgenstein said about "meaning" and say "Pleasure cannot be an internal impression, for no internal impression could have the consequences of pleasure."

Mill also, like Kant, fails to realize the necessity for stipulation as to relevant descriptions, if his theory is to have content. It did not occur to him that acts of murder and theft could be otherwise described. He holds that where a proposed action is of such a kind as to fall under some one principle established on grounds of utility, one must go by that; where it falls under none or several, the several suggesting contrary views of the action, the thing to do is to calculate particular consequences. But pretty well any action can be so described as to make it fall under a variety of principles of utility (as I shall say for short) if it falls under any.

I will now return to Hume. The features of Hume's philosophy which I have mentioned, like many other features of it, would incline me to think that Hume was a mere—brilliant—sophist; and his procedures are certainly sophistical. But I am forced, not to reverse, but to add to, this judgment by a peculiarity of Hume's philosophizing: namely that although he reaches his conclusions—with which he is in love—by sophistical methods, his considerations constantly open up very deep and important problems. It is often the case that in the act of exhibiting the sophistry one finds oneself noticing matters which deserve a lot of exploring: the obvious stands in need of investigation as a result of the points that Hume pretends to have made. In this, he is unlike, say, Butler. It was already well known that conscience could dictate vile actions; for Butler to have written disregarding this does not open up any new topics for us. But with Hume it is otherwise: hence he is a very profound and great philosopher, in spite of his sophistry. For example:

Suppose that I say to my grocer "Truth consists in *either* relations of ideas, as that 20s. = £1, *or* matters of fact, as that I ordered potatoes, you supplied them, and you sent me a bill. So it doesn't apply to such a proposition as that I *owe* you such-and-such a sum."

Now if one makes this comparison, it comes to light that the relation of the facts mentioned to the description "X owes Y so much money" is an interesting one, which I will call that of being "brute relative to" that description. Further, the "brute" facts mentioned here themselves have descriptions relatively to which *other* facts are "brute"—as, e.g., *he had potatoes carted to my house* and *they were left there* are brute facts relative to "he supplied me with potatoes." And the fact *X owes Y money* is in turn "brute" relative to other descriptions—e.g. "X is solvent." Now the relation of "relative bruteness" is a complicated one. To mention a few points: if xyz is a set of facts brute relative to a description A, then xyz is a set out of a range some set among which holds if A holds; but the holding of some set among these does not necessarily entail A because exceptional circumstances can always make a difference; and what are exceptional circumstances relatively to A can generally only be explained by giving a few diverse examples, and *no* theoretically adequate provision can be made for exceptional circumstances, since a further special context can theoretically always be imagined that would reinterpret any special context. Further, though in normal circumstances, xyz would be a justification for A, that is not to say that A just comes to the same as "xyz"; and also there is apt to be an institutional context which gives its point to the description A, of which institution A is of course not itself a description. (E.g. the statement that I give someone a shilling is not a description of the institution of money or of the currency of this country.) Thus, though it would be ludicrous to pretend that there can be no such thing as a transition from, e.g., "is" to "owes," the character of the transition is in fact rather interesting and comes to light as a result of reflecting on Hume's arguments.[1]

That I owe the grocer such-and-such a sum would be one of a set of facts which would be "brute" in relation to the description "I am a bilker." "Bilking" is of course a

[1]The above two paragraphs are an abstract of a paper "On Brute Facts," *Analysis*, 18, 3 (1958).

species of "dishonesty" or "injustice." (Naturally the consideration will not have any effect on my actions unless I want to commit or avoid acts of injustice.)

So far, in spite of their strong associations, I conceive "bilking," "injustice" and "dishonesty" in a merely "factual" way. That I can do this for "bilking" is obvious enough; "justice" I have no idea how to define, except that its sphere is that of actions which relate to someone else, but "injustice," its defect, can for the moment be offered as a generic name covering various species. E.g.: "bilking," "theft" (which is relative to whatever property institutions exist), "slander," "adultery," "punishment of the innocent."

In present-day philosophy an explanation is required how an unjust man is a bad man, or an unjust action a bad one; to give such an explanation belongs to ethics; but it cannot even be begun until we are equipped with a sound philosophy of psychology. For the proof that an unjust man is a bad man would require a positive account of justice as a "virtue." This part of the subject-matter of ethics is, however, completely closed to us until we have an account of what *type of characteristic* a virtue is—a problem, not of ethics, but of conceptual analysis—and how it relates to the actions in which it is instanced: a matter which I think Aristotle did not succeed in really making clear. For this we certainly need an account at least of what a human action is at all, and how its description as "doing such-and-such" is affected by its motive and by the intention or intentions in it; and for this an account of such concepts is required.

The terms "should" or "ought" or "needs" relate to good and bad: e.g. machinery needs oil, or should or ought to be oiled, in that running without oil is bad for it, or it runs badly without oil. According to this conception, of course, "should" and "ought" are not used in a special "moral" sense when one says that a man should not bilk. (In Aristotle's sense of the term "moral" [ἠθικός], they are being used in connection with a *moral* subject-matter: namely that of human passions and [non-technical] actions.) But they have now acquired a special so-called "moral" sense—i.e. a sense in which they imply some absolute verdict (like one of guilty/not guilty on a man) on what is described in the "ought" sentences used in certain types of context: not merely the contexts that *Aristotle* would call "moral"—passions and actions—but also some of the contexts that he would call "intellectual."

The ordinary (and quite indispensable) terms "should," "needs," "ought," "must"—acquired this special sense by being equated in the relevant contexts with "is obliged," or "is bound," or "is required to," in the sense in which one can be obliged or bound by law, or something can be required by law.

How did this come about? The answer is in history: between Aristotle and us came Christianity, with its *law* conception of ethics. For Christianity derived its ethical notions from the Torah. (One might be inclined to think that a law conception of ethics could arise only among people who accepted an allegedly divine positive law; that this is not so is shown by the example of the Stoics, who also thought that whatever was involved in conformity to human virtues was required by divine law.)

In consequence of the dominance of Christianity for many centuries, the concepts of being bound, permitted, or excused became deeply embedded in our language and thought. The Greek word "ἁμαρτάνειν," the aptest to be turned to that use, acquired the sense "sin," from having meant "mistake," "missing the mark," "going wrong." The Latin *peccatum* which roughly corresponded to ἁμάρτημα was even apter for the sense "sin," because it was already associated with "culpa"—"guilt"—a juridical notion. The blanket term "illicit," "unlawful," meaning much the same as our blanket term "wrong," explains itself. It is interesting that Aristotle did not have such a blanket term. He has blanket terms for wickedness—"villain," "scoundrel"; but of course a man is not a villain or a scoundrel by the performance of one bad action, or a few bad actions. And he has terms like "disgraceful," "impious"; and specific terms signifying defect of the relevant virtue, like "unjust"; but no term corresponding to "illicit." The extension of this term (i.e. the range of its application) could be indicated in his terminology only by a quite lengthy sentence: that is "illicit" which, whether it is a thought or a consented-to passion or an action or an omission in thought or action, is something contrary to one of the virtues the lack of which shows a man to be bad *qua* man. That formulation would yield a concept co-extensive with the concept "illicit."

To have a *law* conception of ethics is to hold that what is needed for conformity with the virtues failure in which is the mark of being bad *qua* man (and not merely, say, *qua* craftsman or logician)—that what is needed for *this,* is required by divine law. Naturally it is not possible to have such a conception unless you believe in God as a law-giver; like Jews, Stoics, and Christians. But if such a conception is dominant for many centuries, and then is given up, it is a natural result that the concepts of "obligation," of being bound or required as by a law, should remain though they had lost their root; and if the word "ought" has become invested in certain contexts with the sense of "obligation," it too will remain to be spoken with a special emphasis and a special feeling in these contexts.

It is as if the notion "criminal" were to remain when criminal law and criminal courts had been abolished and forgotten. A Hume discovering this situation might conclude that there was a special sentiment, expressed by "criminal," which alone gave the word its sense. So Hume discovered the situation in which the notion "obligation" survived, and the notion "ought" was invested with that peculiar force having which it is said to be used in a "moral" sense, but in which the belief in divine law had long since been abandoned: for it was substantially given up among Protestants at the time of the Reformation.[2] The situation, if I am right, was the interesting one of the survival of a concept outside the framework of thought that made it a really intelligible one.

When Hume produced his famous remarks about the transition from "is" to "ought," he was, then, bringing together several quite different points. One I have tried to bring out by my remarks on the transition from "is" to "owes" and on the relative "bruteness" of facts. It would be possible to bring out a different point by enquiring about the transition from "is" to "needs"; from the characteristics of an organism to the environment that it needs, for example. To say that it needs that environment is not to say, e.g., that you want it to have that environment, but that it won't flourish unless it has it. Certainly, it all depends whether you *want* it to flourish! as Hume would say. But what "all depends" on whether you want it to flourish is whether the fact that it needs that environment, or won't flourish without it, has the slightest influence on your actions, Now *that* such-and-such "ought" to be or "is needed" is supposed to have an influence on your actions: from which it seemed natural to infer that to judge that it "ought to be" was in fact to grant what you judged "ought to be" influence on your actions. And no amount of truth as to what *is* the case could possibly have a logical claim to have influence on your actions. (It is not judgment as such that sets us in motion; but our judgment on how to get or do something we *want.*) Hence it *must* be impossible to infer "needs" or "ought to be" from "is." But in the case of a

[2]They did not deny the existence of divine law; but their most characteristic doctrine was that it was given, not to be obeyed, but to show man's incapacity to obey it, even by grace; and this applied not merely to the ramified prescriptions of the Torah, but to the requirements of "natural divine law." Cf. in this connection the decree of Trent against the teaching that Christ was only to be trusted in as mediator, not obeyed as legislator.

plant, let us say, the inference from "is" to "needs" is certainly not in the least dubious. It is interesting and worth examining; but not at all fishy. Its interest is similar to the interest of the relation between brute and less brute facts: these relations have been very little considered. And while you can contrast "what it needs" with "what it's got"—like contrasting *de facto* and *de iure*—that does not make its needing this environment less of a "truth."

Certainly in the case of what the plant needs, the thought of a need will only affect action if you want the plant to flourish. Here, then, there is no necessary connection between what you can judge the plant "needs" and what you want. But there is some sort of necessary connection between what you think *you* need, and what you want. The connection is a complicated one; it is possible *not* to want something that you judge you need. But, e.g., it is not possible never to want *anything* that you judge you need. This, however, is not a fact about the meaning of the word "to need," but about the phenomenon of *wanting*. Hume's reasoning, we might say, in effect, leads one to think it must be about the word "to need," or "to be good for."

Thus we find two problems already wrapped up in the remark about a transition from "is" to "ought"; now supposing that we had clarified the "relative bruteness" of facts on the one hand, and the notions involved in "needing," and "flourishing" on the other—there would *still* remain a third point. For, following Hume, someone might say: Perhaps you have made out your point about a transition from "is" to "owes" and from "is" to "needs": but only at the cost of showing "owes" and "needs" sentences to express a *kind* of truths, a *kind* of facts. And it remains impossible to infer "*morally ought*" from "is" sentences.

This comment, it seems to me, would be correct. This word "ought," having become a word of mere mesmeric force, could not, in the character of having that force, be inferred from anything whatever. It may be objected that it could be inferred from other "morally ought" sentences: but that cannot be true. The appearance that this is so is produced by the fact that we say "All men are ϕ" and "Socrates is a man" implies "Socrates is ϕ." But here "ϕ" is a dummy predicate. We mean that if you substitute a real predicate for "ϕ" the implication is valid. A real predicate is required; not just a word containing no intelligible thought: a word retaining the suggestion of force, and apt to have a strong psychological effect, but which no longer signifies a real concept at all.

For its suggestion is one of a *verdict* on my action, according as it agrees or disagrees with the description in the "ought" sentence. And where one does not think there is a judge or a law, the notion of a verdict may retain its psychological effect, but not its meaning. Now imagine that just this word "verdict" *were* so used—with a characteristically solemn emphasis—as to retain its atmosphere but not its meaning, and someone were to say: "For a *verdict*, after all, you need a law and a judge." The reply might be made: "Not at all, for if there were a law and a judge who gave a verdict, the question for us would be whether accepting that verdict is something that there is a *Verdict* on." This is an analogue of an argument which is so frequently referred to as decisive: If someone does have a divine law conception of ethics, all the same, he has to agree that he has to have a judgment that he *ought* (morally ought) to obey the divine law; so his ethic is in exactly the same position as any other: he merely has a "practical major premise"[3]: "Divine law ought to be obeyed" where someone else has, e.g., "The greatest happiness principle ought to be employed in all decisions."

I should judge that Hume and our present-day ethicists had done a considerable

[3]As it is absurdly called. Since major premise = premise containing the term which is predicate in the conclusion, it is a solecism to speak of it in the connection with practical reasoning.

service by showing that no content could be found in the notion "morally ought"; if it were not that the latter philosophers try to find an alternative (very fishy) content and to retain the psychological force of the term. It would be most reasonable to drop it. It has no reasonable sense outside a law conception of ethics; they are not going to maintain such a conception; and you can do ethics without it, as is shown by the example of Aristotle. It would be a great improvement if, instead of "morally wrong," one always named a genus such as "untruthful," "unchaste," "unjust." We should no longer ask whether doing something was "wrong," passing directly from some description of an action to this notion; we should ask whether, e.g., it was unjust; and the answer would sometimes be clear at once.

I now come to the epoch in modern English moral philosophy marked by Sidgwick. There is a startling change that seems to have taken place between Mill and Moore. Mill assumes, as we saw, that there is no question of calculating the particular consequences of an action such as murder or theft; and we saw too that his position was stupid, because it is not at all clear how an action *can* fall under just one principle of utility. In Moore and in subsequent academic moralists of England we find it taken to be pretty obvious that "the right action" is the action which produces the best possible consequences (reckoning among consequences the intrinsic values ascribed to certain kinds of act by some "Objectivists"[4]). Now it follows from this that a man does well, subjectively speaking, if he acts for the best in the particular circumstances according to his judgment of the total consequences of this particular action. I say that this follows, not that any philosopher has said precisely that. For discussion of these questions can of course get extremely complicated: e.g. it can be doubted whether "such-and-such is the right action" is a satisfactory formulation, on the grounds that things have to exist to have predicates—so perhaps the best formulation is "I am obliged"; or again, a philosopher may deny that "right" is a "descriptive" term, and then take a roundabout route through linguistic analysis to reach a view which comes to the same thing as "the right action is the one productive of the best consequences" (e.g. the view that you frame your "principles" to effect the end you choose to pursue, the connection between "choice" and "best" being supposedly such that choosing reflectively means that you choose how to act so as to produce the best consequences); further, the roles of what are called "moral principles" and of the "motive of duty" have to be described; the differences between "good" and "morally good" and "right" need to be explored, the special characteristics of "ought" sentences investigated. Such discussions generate an appearance of significant diversity of views where what is really significant is an overall similarity. The overall similarity is made clear if you consider that every one of the best known English academic moral philosophers has put out a philosophy according to which, e.g., it is not possible to hold that it cannot be right to kill the innocent as a means to any end whatsoever and that someone who thinks otherwise is in error. (I have to mention both points; because Mr. Hare, for example, while teaching a philosophy which would encourage a person to judge that killing the innocent would be what he "ought" to choose for over-riding purposes would also teach, I think, that if a man chooses to make avoiding killing the innocent for any purpose his "supreme practical principle," he cannot be impugned for error: that just is his "principle." But with that qualification, I think it can be seen that the point I have mentioned holds good of every

[4] Oxford Objectivists of course distinguish between "consequences" and "intrinsic values" and so produce a misleading appearance of not being "consequentialists." But they do not hold—and Ross explicitly denies—that the gravity of, e.g., procuring the condemnation of the innocent is such that it cannot be outweighed by, e.g., national interest. Hence their distinction is of no importance.

single English academic moral philosopher since Sidgwick.) Now this is a significant thing: for it means that all these philosophies are quite incompatible with the Hebrew-Christian ethic. For it has been characteristic of that ethic to teach that there are certain things forbidden whatever *consequences* threaten, such as choosing to kill the innocent for any purpose, however good; vicarious punishment; treachery (by which I mean obtaining a man's confidence in a grave matter by promises of trustworthy friendship and then betraying him to his enemies); idolatry; sodomy; adultery; making a false profession of faith. The prohibition of certain things simply in virtue of their description as such-and-such identifiable kinds of action, regardless of any further consequences, is certainly not the whole of the Hebrew-Christian ethic; but it is a noteworthy feature of it; and if every academic philosopher since Sidgwick has written in such a way as to exclude this ethic, it would argue a certain provinciality of mind not to see this incompatibility as the most important fact about these philosophers, and the differences between them as somewhat trifling by comparison.

It is noticeable that none of these philosophers displays any consciousness that there is such an ethic, which he is contradicting: it is pretty well taken for obvious among them all that a prohibition such as that on murder does not operate in face of some consequences. But of course the strictness of the prohibition has as its point *that you are not to be tempted by fear or hope of consequences.*

If you notice the transition from Mill to Moore, you will suspect that it was made somewhere by someone; Sidgwick will come to mind as a likely name; and you will in fact find it going on, almost casually, in him. He is rather a dull author; and the important things in him occur in asides and footnotes and small bits of argument which are not concerned with his grand classification of the "methods of ethics." A divine law theory of ethics is reduced to an insignificant variety by a footnote telling us that "the best theologians" (God knows whom he meant) tell us that God is to be obeyed in his capacity of a *moral* being. *ἦ φορτικός ὁ ἔπαινος*; one seems to hear Aristotle saying: "Isn't the praise vulgar?"[5]—But Sidgwick *is* vulgar in that kind of way: he thinks, for example, that humility consists in underestimating your own merits—i.e. in a species of untruthfulness; and that the ground for having laws against blasphemy was that it was offensive to believers; and that to go accurately into the virtue of purity is to offend against its canons, a thing he reproves "medieval theologians" for not realizing.

From the point of view of the present enquiry, the most important thing about Sidgwick was his definition of intention. He defines intention in such a way that one must be said to intend any foreseen consequences of one's voluntary action. This definition is obviously incorrect, and I dare say that no one would be found to defend it now. He uses it to put forward an ethical thesis which would now be accepted by many people: the thesis that it does not make any difference to a man's responsibility for something that he foresaw, that he felt no desire for it, either as an end or as a means to an end. Using the language of intention more correctly, and avoiding Sidgwick's faulty conception, we may state the thesis thus: it does not make any difference to a man's responsibility for an effect of his action which he can foresee, that he does not intend it. Now this sounds rather edifying; it is I think quite characteristic of very bad degenerations of thought on such questions that they sound edifying. We can see what it amounts to by considering an example. Let us suppose that a man has a responsibility for the maintenance of some child. Therefore deliberately to withdraw support from it is a bad sort of thing for him to do. It would be bad for him to withdraw its maintenance because he didn't want to maintain it any longer; *and* also bad for him to withdraw it because by

[5]E. N. 1178b16.

doing so he would, let us say, compel someone else to do something. (We may suppose for the sake of argument that compelling that person to do that thing is in itself quite admirable.) But now he has to choose between doing something disgraceful and going to prison; if he goes to prison, it will follow that he withdraws support from the child. By Sidgwick's doctrine, there is no difference in his responsibility for ceasing to maintain the child, between the case where he does it for its own sake or as a means to some other purpose, and when it happens as a foreseen and unavoidable consequence of his going to prison rather than do something disgraceful. It follows that he must weigh up the relative badness of withdrawing support from the child and of doing the disgraceful thing; and it may easily be that the disgraceful thing is in fact a less vicious action than intentionally withdrawing support from the child would be; if then the fact that withdrawing support from the child is a side effect of his going to prison does not make any difference to his responsibility, this consideration will incline him to do the disgraceful thing; which can still be pretty bad. And of course, once he has started to look at the matter in this light, the only reasonable thing for him to consider will be the consequences and not the intrinsic badness of this or that action. So that, given that he judges reasonably that no *great* harm will come of it, he can do a much more disgraceful thing than deliberately withdrawing support from the child. And if his calculations turn out in fact wrong, it will appear that he was not responsible for the consequences, because he did not foresee them. For in fact Sidgwick's thesis leads to its being quite impossible to estimate the badness of an action except in the light of *expected* consequences. But if so, then *you* must estimate the badness in the light of the consequences *you* expect; and so it will follow that you can exculpate yourself from the *actual* consequences of the most disgraceful actions, so long as you can make out a case for not having foreseen them. Whereas I should contend that a man is responsible for the bad consequences of his bad actions, but gets no credit for the good ones; and contrariwise is not responsible for the bad consequences of good actions.

The denial of *any* distinction between foreseen and intended consequences, as far as responsibility is concerned, was not made by Sidgwick in developing any one "method of ethics"; he made this important move on behalf of everybody and just on its own account; and I think it plausible to suggest that *this* move on the part of Sidgwick explains the difference between old-fashioned Utilitarianism and that *consequentialism,* as I name it, which marks him and every English academic moral philosopher since him. By it, the kind of consideration which would formerly have been regarded as a temptation, the kind of consideration urged upon men by wives and flattering friends, was given a status by moral philosophers in their theories.

It is a necessary feature of consequentialism that it is a shallow philosophy. For there are always borderline cases in ethics. Now if you are either an Aristotelian, or a believer in divine law, you will deal with a borderline case by considering whether doing such-and-such in such-and-such circumstances is, say, murder, or is an act of injustice; and according as you decide it is or it isn't, you judge it to be a thing to do or not. This would be the method of casuistry; and while it may lead you to stretch a point on the circumference, it will not permit you to destroy the center. But if you are a consequentialist, the question "What is it right to do in such-and-such circumstances?" is a stupid one to raise. The casuist raises such a question only to ask "Would it be *permissible* to do so-and-so?" or "Would it be permissible *not* to do so-and-so?" Only if it would *not* be permissible *not* to do so-and-so could he say "*This* would be *the* thing to do."[6] Otherwise, though he may speak *against* some action, he

[6]Necessarily a rare case: for the positive precepts, e.g. "Honor your parents," hardly ever prescribe, and seldom even necessitate, any particular action.

cannot prescribe any—for in an *actual* case, the circumstances (beyond the ones imagined) might suggest all sorts of possibilities, and you can't know in advance what the possibilities are going to be. Now the consequentialist has no footing on which to say "This would be permissible, this not"; because by his own hypothesis, it is the consequences that are to decide, and he has no business to pretend that he can lay it down what possible twists a man could give doing this or that; the most he can say is: a man must not *bring about* this or that; he has no right to say he will, in an actual case, bring about such-and-such unless he does so-and-so. Further, the consequentialist, in order to be imagining borderline cases at all, has of course to assume some sort of law or standard according to which this is a borderline case, Where then does he get the standard from? In practice the answer invariably is: from the standards current in his society or his circle. And it has in fact been the mark of all these philosophers that they have been extremely conventional; they have nothing in them by which to revolt against the conventional standards of their sort of people; it is impossible that they should be profound. But the chance that a whole range of conventional standards will be decent is small.—Finally, the point of considering hypothetical situations, perhaps very improbable ones, *seems* to be to elicit from yourself or someone else a hypothetical decision to do something of a bad kind. I don't doubt this has the effect of predisposing people—who will never get into the situations for which they have made hypothetical choices—to consent to similar bad actions, or to praise and flatter those who do them, so long as their crowd does so too, when the desperate circumstances imagined don't hold at all.

Those who recognize the origins of the notions of "obligation" and of the emphatic, "moral," *ought,* in the divine law conception of ethics, but who reject the notion of a divine legislator, sometimes look about for the possibility of retaining a law conception without a divine legislator. This search, I think, has some interest in it. Perhaps the first thing that suggests itself is the "norms" of a society. But just as one cannot be impressed by Butler when one reflects what conscience can tell people to do, so, I think, one cannot be impressed by this idea if one reflects what the "norms" of a society can be like. That legislation can be "for oneself" I reject as absurd; whatever you do "for yourself" may be admirable; but is not legislating. Once one sees this, one may say: I have to frame my own rules, and these are the best I can frame, and I shall go by them until I know something better: as a man might say "I shall go by the customs of my ancestors." Whether this leads to good or evil will depend on the *content* of the rules or of the customs of one's ancestors. If one is lucky it will lead to good. Such an attitude would be hopeful in this at any rate: it seems to have in it some Socratic doubt where, from having to fall back on such expedients, it should be clear that Socratic doubt is good; in fact rather generally it must be good for anyone to think "Perhaps in some way I can't see, I may be on a bad path, perhaps I am hopelessly wrong in some essential way".—The search for "norms" might lead someone to look for laws of nature, as if the universe were a legislator; but in the present day this is not likely to lead to good results; it might lead one to eat the weaker according to the laws of nature, but would hardly lead anyone nowadays to notions of justice the pre-Socratic feeling about justice as comparable to the balance or harmony which kept things going is very remote to us.

There is another possibility here: "obligation" may be contractual. Just as we look at the law to find out what a man subject to it is required by it to do, so we look at a contract to find out what the man who has made it is required by it to do. Thinkers, admittedly remote from us, might have the idea of a *foedus rerum,* of the universe not as a legislator but as the embodiment of a contract. Then if you could find out what the contract was, you would learn your obligations under it. Now, you cannot be under a law unless it has been promulgated to you; and the thinkers who believed in "natural divine law" held that it was promulgated to every grown man in his knowledge of good and evil. Similarly you cannot be in a contract without having contracted, i.e. given signs of entering upon the contract. Just possibly, it might be argued that the use of language which one makes in the ordinary conduct of life amounts in some sense to giving the signs of entering into various contracts. If anyone had this theory, we should want to see it worked out. I suspect that it would be largely formal; it might be possible to construct a system embodying the law (whose status might be compared to that of "laws" of logic): "what's sauce for the goose is sauce for the gander," but hardly one descending to such particularities as the prohibition on murder or sodomy. Also, while it is clear that you can be subject to a law that you do not acknowledge and have not thought of as law, it does not seem reasonable to say that you can enter upon a contract without knowing that you are doing so; such ignorance is usually held to be destructive of the nature of a contract.

It might remain to look for "norms" in human virtues: just as *man* has so many teeth, which is certainly not the average number of teeth men have, but is the number of teeth for the species, so perhaps the species *man*, regarded not just biologically, but from the point of view of the activity of thought and choice in regard to the various departments of life—powers and faculties and use of things needed—"has" such-and-such virtues: and this "man" with the complete set of virtues is the "norm," as "man" with, e.g., a complete set of teeth is a norm. But in *this* sense "norm" has ceased to be roughly equivalent to "law." In *this* sense the notion of a "norm" brings us nearer to an Aristotelian than a law conception of ethics. There is, I think, no harm in that; but if someone looked in this direction to give "norm" a sense, then he ought to recognize what has happened to the notion "norm," which he wanted to mean "law—without bringing God in"—it has ceased to mean "law" at all; and *so* the notions of "moral obligation," "the moral ought," and "duty" are best put on the Index, if he can manage it.

But meanwhile—is it not clear that there are several concepts that need investigating simply as part of the philosophy of psychology and,—as I should recommend—*banishing ethics totally* from our minds? Namely—to begin with: "action," "intention," "pleasure," "wanting." More will probably turn up if we start with these. Eventually it might be possible to advance to considering the concept "virtue"; with which, I suppose, we should be beginning some sort of a study of ethics.

I will end by describing the advantages of using the word "ought" in a non-emphatic fashion, and not in a special "moral" sense; of discarding the term "wrong" in a "moral" sense, and using such notions as "unjust."

It is possible, if one is allowed to proceed just by giving examples, to distinguish between the intrinsically unjust, and what is unjust given the circumstances. To arrange to get a man judicially punished for something which it can be clearly seen he has not done is intrinsically unjust. This might be done, of course, and often has been done, in all sorts of ways; by suborning false witnesses, by a rule of law by which something is "deemed" to be the case which is admittedly not the case as a matter of fact, and by open insolence on the part of the judges and powerful people when they more or less openly say: "A fig for the fact that you did not do it; we mean to sentence you for it all the same." What is unjust given, e.g., normal circumstances is to deprive people of their ostensible property without legal procedure, not to pay debts, not to keep contracts, and a host of other things of the kind. Now, the circumstances can clearly make a great deal of difference in estimating the justice or injustice of such procedures as these; and these circumstances may *sometimes* include expected consequences; for example, a man's claim to a bit of property can become a nullity when its seizure and use can avert some obvious disaster: as, e.g., if you could use a machine of his to produce an explosion in which it would be destroyed, but by means of which you could divert a flood or make a gap which a fire could not jump. Now this certainly does not mean that what would ordinarily be an act of injustice, but is not intrinsically unjust, can always be rendered just by a reasonable calculation of better consequences; far from it; but the problems that would be raised in an attempt to draw a boundary line (or boundary area) here are obviously complicated. And while there are certainly some general remarks which ought to be made here, and some boundaries that can be drawn, the decision on particular cases would for the most part be determined κατόν όρθον λόγον "according to what's reasonable."—E.g. that *such-and-such* a delay of payment of a *such-and-such* debt to a person *so* circumstanced, on the part of a person *so* circumstanced, would or would not be unjust, is really only to be decided "according to what's reasonable"; and for this there can *in principle* be no canon other than giving a few examples. That is to say, while it is because of a big gap in philosophy that we can give no general account of the concept of virtue and of the concept of justice, but have to proceed using the concepts, only by giving examples; still there is an area where it is not because of any gap, but is in principle the case, that there is no account except by way of examples: and that is where the canon is "what's reasonable": which of course is *not* a canon.

That is all I wish to say about what is just in some circumstances, unjust in others; and about the way in which expected consequences can play a part in determining what is just. Returning to my example of the intrinsically unjust: if a procedure *is* one of judicially punishing a man for what he is clearly understood not to have done, there can be absolutely no argument about the description of this as unjust. No circumstances, and no expected consequences, which do *not* modify the description of the procedure as one of judicially punishing a man for what he is known not to have done can modify the description of it as unjust. Someone who attempted to dispute this would only be pretending not to know what "unjust" means: for this is a paradigm case of injustice.

And here we see the superiority or the term "unjust" over the terms "morally right" and "morally wrong." For in the context of English moral philosophy since Sidgwick it appears legitimate to discuss whether it *might* be "morally right" in some circumstances to adopt that procedure; but it cannot be argued that the procedure would in any circumstances be just.

Now I am not able to do the philosophy involved—and I think that no one in the present situation of English philosophy *can* do the philosophy involved—but it is clear that a good man is a just man; and a just man is a man who habitually refuses to commit or participate in any unjust actions for fear of any consequences, or to obtain any advantage, for himself or anyone else. Perhaps no one will disagree. But, it will be said, what *is* unjust is sometimes determined by expected consequences; and certainly that is true. But there are cases where it is not: now if someone says, "I agree, but all this wants a lot of explaining," then he is right, and, what is more, the situation at present is that we can't do the explaining; we lack the philosophic equipment. But if someone really thinks, *in advance,*[7] that it is open to question whether such an action as procuring the

[7]If he thinks it in the concrete situation, he is of course merely a normally tempted human being. In discussion when this paper was read, as was perhaps to be expected, this case was produced: a government is required to have an innocent man tried, sentenced and executed under threat of a "hydrogen bomb war." It would seem strange to me to have much hope of so averting a war threatened by such men as made this demand. But the most important thing about the way in which cases like this are invented in discussions, is the assumption that only two courses are open: here, compliance and open defiance. No one can say in advance of such a situation what the possibilities are going to be—e.g. that there is none of stalling by a feigned willingness to comply, accompanied by a skillfully arranged "escape" of the victim.

judicial execution of the innocent should be quite excluded from consideration—I do not want to argue with him; he shows a corrupt mind.

In such cases our moral philosophers seek to impose a dilemma upon us. "If we have a case where the term 'unjust' applies purely in virtue of a factual description, can't one raise the question whether one sometimes conceivably ought to do injustice? If 'what is unjust' is determined by consideration of whether it is *right* to do so-and-so in such-and-such circumstances, then the question whether it is 'right' to commit injustice can't arise, just because 'wrong' has been built into the definition of injustice. But if we have a case where the description 'unjust' applies purely in virtue of the facts, without bringing 'wrong' in, then the question can arise whether one 'ought' perhaps to commit an injustice, whether it might not be 'right' to? And of course 'ought' and 'right' are being used in their *moral* senses here. Now either you must decide what is 'morally right' in the light of certain *other* 'principles,' or you make a 'principle' about *this* and decide that an injustice is never 'right'; but even if you do the latter you are going beyond the facts; you are making a decision that you will not, or that it is wrong to, commit injustice. But in either case, *if* the term 'unjust' is determined simply by the facts, it is not the term 'unjust' that determines that the term 'wrong' applies, but a decision that injustice is *wrong,* together with the diagnosis of the 'factual' description as entailing injustice. But the man who makes an absolute decision that injustice is 'wrong' has no footing on which to criticize someone who does *not* make that decision as judging falsely."

In this argument "wrong" of course is explained as meaning "morally wrong," and all the atmosphere of the term is retained while its substance is guaranteed quite null. Now let us remember that "morally wrong" is the term which is the heir of the notion "illicit," or "what there is an obligation *not* to do"; which belongs in a divine law theory or ethics. Here it really does add something to the description "unjust" to say there is an obligation not to do it; for what obliges is the divine law—as rules oblige in a game. So if the divine law obliges not to commit injustice by forbidding injustice, it really does add something to the description "unjust" to say there is an obligation not to do it. And it is because "morally wrong" is the heir of this concept, but an heir that is cut off from the family of concepts from which it sprang, that "morally wrong" *both* goes beyond the mere factual description "unjust" *and* seems to have no discernible content except a certain compelling force, which I should call purely psychological. And such is the force of the term that philosophers actually suppose that the divine law notion can be dismissed as making no essential difference even if it is held—*because* they think that a "practical principle" running "I *ought* (i.e. am morally obliged) to obey divine laws" is required for the man who believes in divine laws. But actually this notion of obligation is a notion which only operates in the context of law. And I should be inclined to congratulate the present-day moral philosophers on depriving "morally ought" of its now delusive appearance of content, if only they did not manifest a detestable desire to retain the atmosphere of the term.

It may be possible, if we are resolute, to discard the notion "morally ought," and simply return to the ordinary "ought," which, we ought to notice, is such an extremely frequent term of human language that it is difficult to imagine getting on without it. Now if we do return to it, can't it reasonably be asked whether one might ever need to commit injustice, or whether it won't be the best thing to do? Of course it can. And the answers will be various. One man—a philosopher—may say that since justice is a virtue, and injustice a vice, and virtues and vices are built up by the performances of the action in which they are instanced, an act of injustice will tend to make a man bad; and essentially the flourishing of a man *qua* man consists in his being good (e.g. in virtues); but for any

X to which such terms apply, X needs what makes it flourish, so a man needs, or ought to perform, only virtuous actions; and even if, as it must be admitted may happen, he flourishes less, or not at all, in inessentials, by avoiding injustice, his life is spoiled in essentials by not avoiding injustice—so he still needs to perform only just actions. That is roughly how Plato and Aristotle talk; but it can be seen that philosophically there is a huge gap, at present unfillable as far as we are concerned, which needs to be filled by an account of human nature, human action, the type of characteristic a virtue is, and above all of human "flourishing." And it is the last concept that appears the most doubtful. For it is a bit much to swallow that a man in pain and hunger and poor and friendless is "flourishing," as Aristotle himself admitted. Further, someone might say that one at least needed to stay alive to "flourish." Another man unimpressed by all that will say in a hard case "What we need is such-and-such, which we won't get without doing this (which is unjust)—so this is what we ought to do." Another man, who does not follow the rather elaborate reasoning of the philosophers, simply says "I know it is in any case a disgraceful thing to say that one had better commit this unjust action." The man who believes in divine laws will say perhaps "It is forbidden, and however it looks, it cannot be to anyone's profit to commit injustice"; he like the Greek philosophers can think in terms of "flourishing." If he is a Stoic, he is apt to have a decidedly strained notion of what "flourishing consists" in; if he is a Jew or Christian, he need not have any very distinct notion: the way it will profit him to abstain from injustice is something that he leaves it to God to determine, himself only saying "It can't do me any good to go against his law." (But he also hopes for a great reward in a new life later on, e.g. at the coming of Messiah; but in this he is relying on special promises.)

It is left to modern moral philosophy—the moral philosophy of all the well-known English ethicists since Sidgwick—to construct systems according to which the man who says "We need such-and-such, and will only get it this way" *may* be a virtuous character: that is to say, it is left open to debate whether such a procedure as the judicial punishment of the innocent may not in some circumstances be the "right" one to adopt; and though the present Oxford moral philosophers would accord a man *permission* to "make it his principle" not to do such a thing, they teach a philosophy according to which the particular consequences of such an action *could* "morally" be taken into account by a man who was debating what to do; and if they were such as to conflict with his "ends," it might be a step in his moral education to frame a moral principle under which he "managed" (to use Mr. Nowell-Smith's phrase[8]) to bring the action; or it might be a new "decision of principle," making which was an advance in the formation of his moral thinking (to adopt Mr. Hare's conception), to decide: in such-and-such circumstances one ought to procure the judicial condemnation of the innocent. And that is my complaint.

[8] *Ethics,* p. 308.

1958–1959

Moral Beliefs

Philippa Foot

To many people it seems that the most notable advance in moral philosophy during the past fifty years or so has been the refutation of naturalism; and they are a little shocked that at this late date such an issue should be reopened. It is easy to understand their attitude: given certain apparently unquestionable assumptions, it would be about as sensible to try to reintroduce naturalism as to try to square the circle. Those who see it like this have satisfied themselves that they know in advance that any naturalistic theory must have a catch in it somewhere, and are put out at having to waste more time exposing an old fallacy. This paper is an attempt to persuade them to look critically at the premises on which their arguments are based.

It would not be an exaggeration to say that the whole of moral philosophy, as it is now widely taught, rests on a contrast between statements of fact and evaluations, which runs something like this: "The truth or falsity of statements of fact is shown by means of evidence; and what counts as evidence is laid down in the meaning of the expressions occurring in the statement of fact. (For instance, the meaning of 'round' and 'flat' made Magellan's voyages evidence for the roundness rather than the flatness of the Earth; someone who went on questioning whether the evidence was evidence could eventually be shown to have made some linguistic mistake.) It follows

Philippa Foot, "Moral Beliefs," *Proceedings of the Aristotelian Society* 59 (1958–9).

that no two people can make the same statement and count completely different things as evidence; in the end one at least of them could be convicted of linguistic ignorance. It also follows that if a man is given good evidence for a factual conclusion he cannot just refuse to accept the conclusion on the ground that in his scheme of things this evidence is not evidence at all. With evaluations, however, it is different. An evaluation is not connected logically with the factual statements on which it is based. One man may say that a thing is good because of some fact about it, and another may refuse to take that fact as any evidence at all, for nothing is laid down in the meaning of 'good' which connects it with one piece of 'evidence' rather than another. It follows that a moral eccentric could argue to moral conclusions from quite idiosyncratic premises; he could say, for instance, that a man was a good man because he clasped and unclasped his hands, and never turned N. N. E. after turning S. S. W. He could also reject someone else's evaluation simply by denying that his evidence was evidence at all.

"The fact about 'good' which allows the eccentric still to use this term without falling into a morass of meaninglessness, is its 'action-guiding' or 'practical' function. This it retains; for like everyone else he considers himself bound to choose the things he calls 'good' rather than those he calls 'bad.' Like the rest of the world he uses 'good' in connection only with a 'pro-attitude'; it is only that he has pro-attitudes to quite different things, and therefore calls them good."

There are here two assumptions about "evaluations," which I will call assumption (1) and assumption (2).

Assumption (1) is that some individual may, without logical error, base his beliefs about matters of value entirely on premises which no one else would recognize as giving any evidence at all. Assumption (2) is that, given the kind of statement which other people regard as evidence for an evaluative conclusion, he may refuse to draw the conclusion because *this* does not count as evidence for *him.*

Let us consider assumption (1). We might say that this depends on the possibility of keeping the meaning of "good" steady through all changes in the facts about anything which are to count in favor of its goodness. (I do not mean, of course, that a man can make changes as fast as he chooses; only that, whatever he has chosen, it will not be possible to rule him out of order.) But there is a better formulation, which cuts out trivial disputes about the meaning which "good" happens to have in some section of the community. Let us say that the assumption is that the evaluative function of "good" can remain constant through changes in the evaluative principle; on this ground it could be said that even if no one can call a man *good* because he clasps and unclasps his hands, he can commend him or express his *pro-attitude* towards him, and if necessary can invent a new moral vocabulary to express his unusual moral code.

Those who hold such a theory will naturally add several qualifications. In the first place, most people now agree with Hare, against Stevenson, that such words as "good" only apply to individual cases through the application of general principles, so that even the extreme moral eccentric must accept principles of commendation. In the second place "commending," "having a pro-attitude," and so on, are supposed to be connected with doing and choosing, so that it would be impossible to say, e.g., that a man was a good man only if he lived for a thousand years. The range of evaluation is supposed to be restricted to the range of possible action and choice. I am not here concerned to question these supposed restrictions on the use of evaluative terms, but only to argue that they are not enough.

The crucial question is this. Is it possible to extract from the meaning of words such as "good" some element called "evaluative meaning" which we can think of as externally related to its objects? Such an element would be represented, for instance, in the rule that when any action was "commended" the speaker must hold himself bound to accept an imperative "let me do these things." This is externally related to its object because, within the limitation which we noticed earlier, to possible actions, it would make sense to think of anything as the subject of such "commendation." On this hypothesis a moral eccentric could be described as commending the clasping of hands as the action of a good man, and we should not have to look for some background to give the supposition sense. That is to say, on this hypothesis the clasping of hands could be commended without any explanation; it could be what those who hold such theories call "an ultimate moral principle."

I wish to say that this hypothesis is untenable, and that there is no describing the evaluative meaning of "good," evaluation, commending, or anything of the sort, without fixing the object to which they are supposed to be attached. Without first laying hands on the proper object of such things as evaluation, we shall catch in our net either something quite different such as accepting an order or making a resolution, or else nothing at all.

Before I consider this question, I shall first discuss some other mental attitudes and beliefs which have this internal relation to their object. By this I hope to clarify the concept of internal relation to an object, and incidentally, if my examples arouse resistance, but are eventually accepted, to show how easy it is to overlook an internal relation where it exists.

Consider, for instance, pride.

People are often surprised at the suggestion that there are limits to the things a man can be proud of, about which indeed he can feel pride. I do not know quite what account they want to give of pride; perhaps something to do with smiling and walking with a jaunty air, and holding an object up where other people can see it; or perhaps they think that pride is a kind of internal sensation, so that one might naturally beat one's breast and say "pride is something I feel *here*." The difficulties of the second view are well known; the logically private object cannot be what a name in the public language is the name of.[1] The first view is the more plausible, and it may seem reasonable to say that given certain behavior a man can be described as showing that he is proud of something, whatever that something may be. In one sense this is true, and in another sense not. Given any description of an object, action, personal characteristic, etc., it is not possible to rule it out as an object of pride. Before we can do so we need to know what would be said about it by the man who is to be proud of it, or feels proud of it; but if he does not hold the right beliefs about it then whatever his attitude is it is not pride. Consider, for instance, the suggestion that someone might be proud of the sky or the sea: he looks at them and what he feels is *pride,* or he puffs out his chest and gestures with *pride* in their direction. This makes sense only if a special assumption is made about his beliefs, for instance that he is under some crazy delusion and believes that he has saved the sky from falling, or the sea from drying up. The characteristic object of pride is something seen (*a*) as in some way a man's own, and (*b*) as some sort of achievement or advantage; without this object pride cannot be described. To see that the second condition is necessary, one should try supposing that a man happens to feel proud because he has laid one of his hands on the other, three times in an hour. Here again the supposition that it is pride that he feels will make perfectly good sense if a special background is filled in. Perhaps he is ill, and it is an achievement even to do this; perhaps this gesture has some

[1]See Wittgenstein, *Philosophical Investigations,* especially §§243–315.

religious or political significance, and he is a brave man who will so defy the gods or the rulers. But with no special background there can be no pride, not because no one could psychologically speaking feel pride in such a case, but because whatever he did feel could not logically be pride. Of course, people can see strange things as achievements, though not just anything, and they can identify themselves with remote ancestors, and relations, and neighbors, and even on occasions with Mankind. I do not wish to deny there are many far-fetched and comic examples of pride.

We could have chosen many other examples of mental attitudes which are internally related to their object in a similar way. For instance, fear is not just trembling, and running, and turning pale; without the thought of some menacing evil no amount of this will add up to fear. Nor could anyone be said to feel dismay about something he did not see as bad; if his thoughts about it were that it was altogether a good thing, he could not say that (oddly enough) what he felt about it was dismay. "How odd, I feel dismayed when I ought to be pleased" is the prelude to a hunt for the adverse aspect of the thing, thought of as lurking behind the pleasant facade. But someone may object that pride and fear and dismay are feelings or emotions and therefore not a proper analogy for "commendation," and there will be an advantage in considering a different kind of example. We could discuss, for instance, the belief that a certain thing is dangerous, and ask whether this could logically be held about anything whatsoever. Like "this is good," "this is dangerous" is an assertion, which we should naturally accept or reject by speaking of its truth or falsity; we seem to support such statements with evidence, and moreover there may seem to be a "warning function" connected with the word "dangerous" as there is supposed to be a "commending function" connected with the word "good." For suppose that philosophers, puzzled about the property of dangerousness, decided that the word did not stand for a property at all, but was essentially a practical or action-guiding term, used for *warning*. Unless used in an "inverted comma sense" the word "dangerous" was used to warn, and this meant that anyone using it in such a sense committed himself to avoiding the things he called dangerous, to preventing other people from going near them, and perhaps to running in the opposite direction. If the conclusion were not obviously ridiculous, it would be easy to infer that a man whose application of the term was different from ours throughout might say that the oddest things were dangerous without fear of disproof; the idea would be that he could still be described as "thinking them dangerous," or at least as "warning," because by his attitude and actions he would have fulfilled the conditions for these things. This is nonsense because without its proper object *warning*, like *believing dangerous*, will not be there. It is logically impossible to warn about anything not thought of as threatening evil, and for danger we need a particular kind of serious evil such as injury or death.

There are, however, some differences between thinking a thing dangerous and feeling proud, frightened or dismayed. When a man says that something is dangerous he must support his statement with a special kind of evidence; but when he says that he feels proud or frightened or dismayed the description of the object of his pride or fright or dismay does not have quite this relation to his original statement. If he is shown that the thing he was proud of was not his after all, or was not after all anything very grand, he may have to say that his pride was not justified, but he will not have to take back the statement that he was proud. On the other hand, someone who says that a thing is dangerous, and later sees that he made a mistake in thinking that an injury might result from it, has to go back on his original statement and admit that he was wrong. In neither case, however, is the speaker able to go on as before. A man who discovered that it was not his pumpkin but someone else's which had won the prize could only say that he still felt proud, if he could produce some other ground for pride. It is in this way that even feelings are logically vulnerable to facts.

It will probably be objected against these examples that for part of the way at least they beg the question. It will be said that indeed a man can be proud only of something he thinks a good action, or an achievement, or a sign of noble birth; as he can feel dismay only about something which he sees as bad, frightened at some threatened evil; similarly he can warn only if he is also prepared to speak, for instance, of injury. But this will limit the range of possible objects of those attitudes and beliefs only if the range of these terms is limited in its turn. To meet this objection I shall discuss the meaning of "injury" because this is the simplest case. Anyone who feels inclined to say that anything could be counted as an achievement, or as the evil of which people were afraid, or about which they felt dismayed, should just try this out. I wish to consider the proposition that anything could be thought of as dangerous, because if it causes injury it is dangerous, and anything could be counted as an injury. I shall consider bodily injury because this is the injury connected with danger; it is not correct to put up a notice by the roadside reading "Danger!" on account of bushes which might scratch a car. Nor can a substance be labelled "dangerous" on the ground that it can injure delicate fabrics; although we can speak of the danger that it may do so, that is not the use of the word which I am considering here.

When a body is injured it is changed for the worse in a special way, and we want to know which changes count as injuries. First of all, it matters how an injury comes about; e.g., it cannot be caused by natural decay. Then it seems clear that not just any kind of thing will do, for instance, any unusual mark on the body, however much trouble a man might take to have it removed. By far the most important class of injuries are injuries to a part of the body, counting as injuries because there is interference with the function of that part; injury to a leg, an eye, an ear, a hand, a muscle, the heart, the brain, the spinal cord. An injury to an eye is one that affects, or is likely to affect, its sight; an injury to a hand one which makes it less well able to reach out and grasp, and perform other operations of this kind. A leg can be injured because its movements and supporting power can be affected; a lung because it can become too weak to draw in the proper amount of air. We are most ready to speak of an injury where the function of a part of the body is to perform a characteristic operation, as in these examples. We might hesitate to say that a skull can be injured, and might prefer to speak of damage to it, since although there is indeed a function (a protective function) there is no operation. But thinking of the protective function of the skull we may want to speak of injury here. In so far as the concept of *injury* depends on that of *function* it is narrowly limited, since not even every use to which a part of the body is put will count as its function. Why is it that, even if it is the means by which they earn their living, we would never consider the removal of the dwarf's hump or the bearded lady's beard as a bodily injury? It will be tempting to say that these things are disfigurements, but this is not the point; if we suppose that a man who had some invisible extra muscle made his living as a court jester by waggling his ears, the ear would not have been injured if this were made to disappear. If it were natural to men to communicate by movements of the ear, then ears would have the function of signalling (we have no word for this kind of "speaking") and an impairment of this function would be an injury; but things are not like this. This court jester would use his ears to make people laugh, but this is not the function of ears.

No doubt many people will feel impatient when such facts are mentioned, because they think that it is quite unimportant that this or that *happens* to be the case, and it seems to them arbitrary that the loss of the beard, the hump, or the ear muscle would not be called an injury. Isn't the loss of that by which one makes one's living a pretty catastrophic loss? Yet it seems quite natural that these are not counted as injuries if one thinks about the conditions of human life, and contrasts the loss of a special ability to make people gape or laugh with the ability to see, hear, walk, or pick things up. The first is only needed for one very special way of living; the other in any foreseeable future for any man. This restriction seems all the more natural when we observe what other threats besides that of injury can constitute danger: of death, for instance, or mental derangement. A shock which could cause mental instability or impairment of memory would be called dangerous, because a man needs such things as intelligence, memory, and concentration as he needs sight or hearing or the use of hands. Here we do not speak of injury unless it is possible to connect the impairment with some physical change, but we speak of danger because there is the same loss of a capacity which any man needs.

There can be injury outside the range we have been considering; for a man may sometimes be said to have received injuries where no part of his body has had its function interfered with. In general, I think that any blow which disarranged the body in such a way that there was lasting pain would inflict an injury, even if no other ill resulted, but I do not know of any other important extension of the concept.

It seems therefore that since the range of things which can be called injuries is quite narrowly restricted, the word "dangerous" is restricted in so far as it is connected with injury. We have the right to say that a man cannot decide to call just anything dangerous, however much he puts up fences and shakes his head.

So far I have been arguing that such things as pride, fear, dismay, and the thought that something is dangerous have an internal relation to their object, and hope that what I mean is becoming clear. Now we must consider whether those attitudes or beliefs which are the moral philosopher's study are similar, or whether such things as "evaluation" and "thinking something good" and "commendation" could logically be found in combination with any object whatsoever. All I can do here is to give an example which may make this suggestion seem implausible, and to knock away a few of its supports. The example will come from the range of trivial and pointless actions such as we were considering in speaking of the man who clasped his hands three times an hour, and we can point to the oddity of the suggestion that this can be called a good action. We are bound by the terms of our question to refrain from adding any special background, and it should be stated once more that the question is about what can count in favour of the goodness or badness of a man or an action, and not what could be, or be thought, good or bad with a special background. I believe that the view I am attacking often seems plausible only because the special background is surreptitiously introduced.

Someone who said that clasping the hands three times in an hour was a good action would first have to answer the question "How do you mean?" For the sentence "this is a good action" is not one which has a clear meaning. Presumably, since our subject is moral philosophy, it does not here mean "that was a good thing to do" as this might be said of a man who had done something sensible in the course of any enterprise whatever; we are to confine our attention to "the moral use of 'good.'" I am not clear that it makes sense to speak of "a moral use of 'good,'" but we can pick out a number of cases which raise moral issues. It is because these are so diverse and because "this is a good action" does not pick out any one of them, that we must ask "How do you mean?" For instance, some things that are done to fulfil a duty, such as the duty of parents to children or children to parents. I suppose that when philosophers speak of good actions they would include these. Some come under the heading of a virtue such as charity, and they will be included too. Others again are actions which require the virtues of courage or temperance, and here the moral aspect is due to the fact that they are done in spite of fear or the temptation of pleasure; they must indeed be done for the sake of some real or fancied good, but not necessarily what philosophers would want to call a moral good. Courage is not *particularly* concerned with saving other people's lives, or temperance with leaving them their share of the food and drink, and the goodness of *what is done* may here be all kinds of usefulness. It is because there are these very diverse cases included (I suppose) under the expression "a good action" that we should refuse to consider applying it without asking what is meant, and we should now ask what is intended when someone is supposed to say that "clasping the hands three times in an hour is a good action." Is it supposed that this action fulfils a duty? Then in virtue of what does a man have this duty, and to whom does he owe it? We have promised not to slip in a special background, but he cannot possibly have a *duty* to clasp his hands unless such a background exists. Nor could it be an act of charity, for it is not thought to do anyone any good, nor again a gesture of humility unless a special assumption turns it into this. The action could be courageous, but only if it were done both in the face of fear and for the sake of a good; and we are not allowed to put in special circumstances which could make this the case.

I am sure that the following objection will now be raised. "Of course clasping one's hands three times in an hour cannot be brought under one of the virtues which we recognize, but that is only to say that is not a good action by our current moral code. It is logically possible that in a quite different moral code quite different virtues should be recognized, for which we have not even got a name." I cannot answer this objection properly, for that would need a satisfactory account of the concept of a virtue. But anyone who thinks it would be easy to describe a new virtue connected with clasping the hands three times in an hour should just try. I think he will find that he has to cheat, and suppose that in the community concerned the clasping of hands has been given some special significance, or is thought to have some special effect. The difficulty is obviously connected with the fact that without a special background there is no possibility of answering the question "What's the point?" It is no good saying that there would be a point in doing the action because the action was a morally good action: the question is how it can be given any such description if we cannot first speak about the point. And it is just as crazy to suppose that we can call *anything* the point of doing something without having to say what the point of *that* is. In clasping one's hands one may make a slight sucking noise, but what is the point of that? It is surely clear that moral virtues must be connected with human good and harm, and that it is quite impossible to call anything you like good or harm. Consider, for instance, the suggestion that a man might say he had been harmed because a bucket of water had been taken out of the sea. As usual it would be possible to think up circumstances in which this remark would make sense; for instance, when coupled with a belief in magical influences; but then the harm would consist in what was done by the evil spirits, not in the taking of the water from the sea. It would be just as odd if someone were supposed to say that harm had been done to him because the hairs of his head had been reduced to an even number.[2]

I conclude that assumption (1) is very dubious indeed, and that no one should be allowed to speak as if we can understand "evaluation" "commendation" or "pro-attitude," whatever the actions concerned.

[2]In face of this sort of example many philosophers take refuge in the thicket of aesthetics. It would be interesting to know if they are willing to let their whole case rest on the possibility that there might be aesthetic objections to what was done.

2

I propose now to consider what was called Assumption (2), which said that a man might always refuse to accept the conclusion of an argument about values, because what counted as evidence for other people did not count for him. Assumption (2) could be true even if Assumption (1) were false, for it might be that once a particular question of values—say a moral question—had been accepted, any disputant was bound to accept particular pieces of evidence as relevant, the same pieces as everyone else, but that he could always refuse to draw any moral conclusions whatsoever or to discuss any questions which introduced moral terms. Nor do we mean "he might refuse to draw the conclusion" in the trivial sense in which anyone can perhaps refuse to draw *any* conclusion; the point is that any statement of value always seems to go beyond any statement of fact, so that he might have a reason for accepting the factual premises but refusing to accept the evaluative conclusion. That this is so seems to those who argue in this way to follow from the practical implication of evaluation. When a man uses a word such as "good" in an "evaluative" and not an "inverted comma" sense, he is supposed to commit his will. From this it has seemed to follow inevitably that there is a logical gap between fact and value; for is it not one thing to say that a thing is so, and another to have a particular attitude towards its being so; one thing to see that certain effects will follow from a given action, and another to care? Whatever account was offered of the essential feature of evaluation—whether in terms of feelings, attitudes, the acceptance of imperatives or what not—the fact remained that with an evaluation there was a committal in a new dimension, and that this was not guaranteed by any acceptance of facts.

I shall argue that this view is mistaken; that the practical implication of the use of moral terms has been put in the wrong place, and that if it is described correctly the logical gap between factual premises and moral conclusion disappears.

In this argument it will be useful to have as a pattern the practical or "action-guiding" force of the word "injury," which is in some, though not all, ways similar to that of moral terms. It is clear I think that an injury is necessarily something bad and therefore something which as such anyone always has a reason to avoid, and philosophers will therefore be tempted to say that anyone who uses "injury" in its full "action-guiding" sense commits himself to avoiding the things he calls injuries. They will then be in the usual difficulties about the man who says he knows he ought to do something but does not intend to do it; perhaps also about weakness of the will. Suppose that instead we look again at the kinds of things which count as injuries, to see if the connection with the will does not start here. As has been shown, a man is injured whenever some part of his body, in being damaged, has become less well able to fulfil its ordinary function. It follows that he suffers a disability, or is liable to do so; with an injured hand he will be less well able to pick things up, hold on to them, tie them together or chop them up, and so on. With defective eyes there will be a thousand other things he is unable to do, and in both cases we should naturally say that he will often be unable to get what he wants to get or avoid what he wants to avoid.

Philosophers will no doubt seize on the word "want," and say that if we suppose that a man happens to want the things which an injury to his body prevents him from getting, we have slipped in a supposition about a "pro-attitude" already; and that anyone who does not happen to have these wants can still refuse to use "injury" in its prescriptive, or "action-guiding" sense. And so it may seem that the only way to make a *necessary* connection between "injury" and the things that are to be avoided, is to say that it is used in an "action-guiding sense" only when applied to something the speaker intends to avoid. But we should look carefully at the crucial move in that argument, and query the suggestion that someone might happen not to want anything for which he would need the use of hands or eyes. Hands and eyes, like ears and legs, play a part in so many operations that a man could only be said not to need them if he had no wants at all. That such people exist, in asylums, is not to the present purpose at all; the proper use of his limbs is something a man has reason to want if he wants anything.

I do not know just what someone who denies this proposition could have in mind. Perhaps he is thinking of changing the facts of human existence, so that merely wishing, or the sound of the voice, will bring the world to heel? More likely he is proposing to rig the circumstances of some individual's existence within the framework of the ordinary world, by supposing for instance that he is a prince whose servant will sow and reap and fetch and carry for him, and so use their hands and eyes in his service that he will not need the use of his. Let us suppose that such a story could be told about a man's life; it is wildly implausible, but let us pretend that it is not. It is clear that in spite of this we could say that any man had a reason to shun injury; for even if at the end of his life it could be said that by a strange set of circumstances he had never needed the use of his eyes, or his hands, this could not possibly be foreseen. Only by once more changing the facts of human existence, and supposing every vicissitude foreseeable, could such a supposition be made.

This is not to say that an injury might not bring more incidental gain than necessary harm; one has only to think of times when the order has gone out that able-bodied men are to be put to the sword. Such a gain might even, in some peculiar circumstances, be reliably foreseen, so that a man would have even better reason for seeking than for avoiding injury. In this respect the word "injury" differs from terms such as "injustice"; the practical force of "injury" means only that anyone has *a* reason to avoid injuries, not that he has an overriding reason to do so.

It will be noticed that this account of the "action-guiding" force of "injury" links it with reasons for acting rather than with actually doing something. I do not think, however, that this makes it a less good pattern for the "action-guiding" force of moral terms. Philosophers who have supposed that actual action was required if "good" were to be used in a sincere evaluation have got into difficulties over weakness of will, and they should surely agree that enough has been done if we can show that any man has reason to aim at virtue and avoid vice. But is this impossibly difficult if we consider the kinds of things that count as virtue and vice? Consider, for instance, the cardinal virtues, prudence, temperance, courage and justice. Obviously any man needs prudence, but does he not also need to resist the temptation of pleasure when there is harm involved? And how could it be argued that he would never need to face what was fearful for the sake of some good? It is not obvious what someone would mean if he said that temperance or courage were not good qualities, and this not because of the "praising" sense of these *words*, but because of the things that courage and temperance are.

I should like to use these examples to show the artificiality of the notions of "commendation" and of "pro-attitudes" as these are commonly employed. Philosophers who talk about these things will say that after the facts have been accepted—say that X is the kind of man who will climb a dangerous mountain, beard an irascible employer for a rise in pay, and in general face the fearful for the sake of something he thinks worth while—there remains the question of "commendation" or "evaluation." If the word "courage" is used they will ask whether or not the man who speaks of another as having courage is supposed to have commended him. If we say "yes" they will insist that the judgment about courage *goes beyond the facts*, and might therefore be rejected by someone who refused to do so; if we say "no" they will argue that "courage" is being used in a purely descriptive or "inverted comma sense," and that we have not got an example of the evaluative use of language which is the moral philosopher's special study. What sense can be made, however, of the question "does he commend?" What is this extra element which is supposed to be present or absent after the facts have been settled? It is not a matter of liking the man who has courage, or of thinking him altogether good, but of "commending him for his courage." How are we supposed to do that? The answer that will be given is that we only commend someone else in speaking of him as courageous if we accept the imperative "let me be courageous" for ourselves. But this is quite unnecessary. I can speak of someone else as having the virtue of courage, and of course recognize it as a virtue in the proper sense, while knowing that I am a complete coward, and making no resolution to reform. I know that I should be better off if I were courageous, and so have a reason to cultivate courage but I may also know that I will do nothing of the kind.

If someone were to say that courage was not a virtue he would have to say that it was not a quality by which a man came to act well. Perhaps he would be thinking that someone might be worse off for his courage, which is true, but only because an incidental harm might arise. For instance, the courageous man might have underestimated a risk, and run into some disaster which a cowardly man would have avoided because he was not prepared to take any risk at all. And his courage, like any other virtue, could be the cause of harm to him because possessing it he fell into some disastrous state of pride.[3] Similarly, those who question the virtue of temperance are probably thinking not of the virtue itself but of men whose temperance has consisted in resisting pleasure for the sake of some illusory good, or those who have made this virtue their pride.

But what, it will be asked, of justice? For while prudence, courage and temperance are qualities which benefit the man who has them, justice seems rather to benefit others, and to work to the disadvantage of the just man himself. Justice as it is treated here, as one of the cardinal virtues, covers all those things owed to other people: it is under injustice that murder, theft and lying come, as well as the withholding of what is owed for instance by parents to children and by children to parents, as well as the dealings which would be called unjust in everyday speech. So the man who avoids injustice will find himself in need of things he has returned to their owner, unable to obtain an advantage by cheating and lying; involved in all those difficulties painted by Thrasymachus in the first book of the Republic, in order to show that injustice is more profitable than justice to a man of strength and wit. We will be asked how, on our theory, justice can be a virtue and injustice a vice, since it will surely be difficult to show that any man whatsoever must need to be just as he needs the use of his hands and eyes, or needs prudence, courage and temperance?

Before answering this question I shall argue that if it cannot be answered, then justice can no longer be recommended as a virtue. The point of this is not to show that it must be answerable, since justice is a virtue, but rather to suggest that we should at least consider the possibility that justice is not a virtue. This suggestion was taken seriously by Socrates in the Republic, where it was assumed by everyone that if Thrasymachus could establish his premise—that injustice was more profitable than justice—his conclusion would follow: that a man who had the strength to get away with injustice had reason to follow this as the best way of life. It is a striking fact about modern moral philosophy that no one sees any difficulty in accepting Thrasymachus' premise and rejecting his conclusion, and it is because Nietzsche's position is at this point much closer to that of Plato that he is remote from academic moralists of the present day.

[3]Cp. Aquinas, *Summa Theologica*, I–II, q. 55, Art. 4.

In the Republic it is assumed that if justice is not a good to the just man, moralists who recommend it as a virtue are perpetrating a fraud. Agreeing with this, I shall be asked where exactly the fraud comes in; where the untruth that justice is profitable to the individual is supposed to be told? As a preliminary answer we might ask how many people are prepared to say frankly that injustice is more profitable than justice? Leaving aside, as elsewhere in this paper, religious beliefs which might complicate the matter, we will suppose that some tough atheistical character has asked "Why should I be just?" (Those who believe that this question has something wrong with it can employ their favorite device for sieving out "evaluating meaning," and suppose that the question is "Why should I be 'just'?") Are we prepared to reply "As far as you are concerned you will be better off if you are unjust, but it matters to the rest of us that you should be just, so we are trying to get you to be just"? He would be likely to enquire into our methods, and then take care not to be found out, and I do not think that many of those who think that it is not necessary to show that justice is profitable to the just man would easily accept that there was nothing more they could say.

The crucial question is: "Can we give anyone, strong or weak, a reason why he should be just?"—and it is no help at all to say that since "just" and "unjust" are "action-guiding words" no one can even ask "Why should I be just?" Confronted with that argument the man who wants to do unjust things has only to be careful to avoid the *word,* and he has not been given a reason why he should not do the things which other people call "unjust." Probably it will be argued that he has been given a reason so far as anyone can ever be given a reason for doing or not doing anything, for the chain of reasons must always come to an end somewhere, and it may seem that one may always reject the reason which another man accepts. But this is a mistake; some answers to the question "why should I?" bring the series to a close and some do not. Hume showed how *one* answer closed the series in the following passage:

"Ask a man *why he uses exercise;* he will answer, *because he desires to keep his health.* If you then enquire, *why he desires health,* he will readily reply, *because sickness is painful.* If you push your enquiries farther, and desire a reason *why he hates pain,* it is impossible he can ever give any. This is an ultimate end, and is never referred to any other object." (*Enquiries,* Appendix I, V.) Hume might just as well have ended this series with boredom: sickness often brings boredom, and no one is required to give a reason why he does not want to be bored, any more than he has to give a reason why he does want to pursue what interests him. In general, anyone is given a reason for acting when he is shown the way to something he wants; but for some wants the question "Why do you want that?" will make sense, and for others it will not.[4] It seems clear that in this division justice falls on the opposite side from pleasure and interest and such things. "Why shouldn't I do that?" is not answered by the words "because it is unjust" as it is answered by showing that the action will bring boredom, loneliness, pain, discomfort or certain kinds of incapacity, and this is why it is not true to say that "it's unjust" gives a reason in so far as any reasons can ever be given. "It's unjust" gives a reason only if the nature of justice can be shown to be such that it is necessarily connected with what a man wants.

This shows why a great deal hangs on the question of whether justice is or is not a good to the just man, and why those who accept Thrasymachus' premise and reject his conclusion are in a dubious position. They recommend justice to each man, as something he has a reason to follow, but when challenged to show why he should do so they

[4]For an excellent discussion of reasons for action, see G. E. M. Anscombe, *Intention* §34–40.

will not always be able to reply. This last assertion does not depend on any "selfish theory of human nature" in the philosophical sense. It is often possible to give a man a reason for acting by showing him that someone else will suffer if he does not; someone else's good may really be more to him than his own. But the affection which mothers feel for children, and lovers for each other, and friends for friends, will not take us far when we are asked for reasons why a man should be just; partly because it will not extend far enough, and partly because the actions dictated by benevolence and justice are not always the same. Suppose that I owe someone money; ". . . what if he be my enemy, and has given me just cause to hate him? What if he be a vicious man, and deserves the hatred of all mankind? What if he be a miser, and can make no use of what I would deprive him of? What if he be a profligate debauchee, and would rather receive harm than benefit from large possessions?"[5] Even if the general practice of justice could be brought under the motive of universal benevolence—the desire for the greatest happiness of the greatest number—many people certainly do not have any such desire. So that if justice is only to be recommended on these grounds a thousand tough characters will be able to say that they have been given no reason for practicing justice, and many more would say the same if they were not too timid or too stupid to ask questions about the code of behavior which they have been taught. Thus, given Thrasymachus' premise Thrasymachus' point of view is reasonable; we have no particular reason to admire those who practice justice through timidity or stupidity.

It seems to me, therefore, that if Thrasymachus' thesis is accepted things cannot go on as before; we shall have to admit that the belief on which the status of justice as a virtue was founded is mistaken, and if we still want to get people to be just we must recommend justice to them in a new way. We shall have to admit that injustice is more profitable than justice, at least for the strong, and then do our best to see that hardly anyone can get away with being unjust. We have, of course, the alternative of keeping quiet, hoping that for the most part people will follow convention into a kind of justice, and not ask awkward questions, but this policy might be overtaken by a vague scepticism even on the part of those who do not know just what is lacking; we should also be at the mercy of anyone who was able and willing to expose our fraud.

Is it true, however, to say that justice is not something a man needs in his dealings with his fellows, supposing only that he be strong? Those who think that he can get on perfectly well without being just should be asked to say exactly how such a man is supposed to live. We know that he is to practice injustice whenever the unjust act would bring him advantage; but what is he to say? Does he admit that he does not recognize the rights of other people, or does he pretend? In the first case even those who combine with him will know that on a change of fortune, or a shift of affection, he may turn to plunder them, and he must be as wary of their treachery as they are of his. Presumably the happy unjust man is supposed, as in Book II of the Republic, to be a very cunning liar and actor, combining complete injustice with the appearance of justice: he is prepared to treat others ruthlessly, but pretends that nothing is further from his mind. Philosophers often speak as if a man could thus hide himself even from those around him, but the supposition is doubtful, and in any case the price in vigilance would be colossal. If he lets even a few people see his true attitude he must guard himself against them; if he lets no one into the secret he must always be careful in case the least spontaneity betray him. Such facts are important because the need a man has for justice in dealings with other men depends on the fact that they are men and not inanimate objects

[5]Hume, *Treatise* Book III, Part II, Sect. 1.

or animals. If a man only needed other men as he needs household objects, and if men could be manipulated like household objects, or beaten into a reliable submission like donkeys, the case would be different. As things are, the supposition that injustice is more profitable than justice is very dubious, although like cowardice and intemperance it might turn out incidentally to be profitable.

The reason why it seems to some people so impossibly difficult to show that justice is more profitable than injustice is that they consider in isolation particular just acts. It is perfectly true that if a man is just it follows that he will be prepared, in the event of very evil circumstances, even to face death rather than to act unjustly—for instance, in getting an innocent man convicted of a crime of which he has been accused. For him it turns out that his justice brings disaster on him, and yet like anyone else he had good reason to be a just and not an unjust man. He could not have it both ways and while possessing the virtue of justice hold himself ready to be unjust should any great advantage accrue. The man who has the virtue of justice is not ready to do certain things, and if he is too easily tempted we shall say that he was ready after all.

1960

What If Everyone Did That?

Colin Strang

I want to discuss the force and validity of the familiar type of ethical argument epitomized in my title. A typical example of it would be: "If everyone refrained from voting the result would be disastrous, therefore *you* ought to vote." Now since the argument is addressed to the person concerned simply *qua* member of the class of people entitled to vote, it could be addressed with equal force to any member or all members of that class indifferently; so the conclusion might just as validly be: "therefore *everyone* ought to vote."

There is no doubt that this argument has some force. People *are* sometimes impressed by it. But it is not nearly so obvious that it is a valid one, i.e. that they *ought* to be impressed by it.

One way of not being impressed by it is to reply: "Yes, but everyone *won't* refrain from voting, so there will be no disaster, so it's all right for me not to vote." But this reply is beside the point. The argument never claimed that this one abstention would lead to disaster, nor did it claim that universal abstention (which *would* be disastrous) would occur; indeed it implied, on each point, the very opposite. This brings out the important fact that the argument does not appeal to the consequences of the action it condemns and so is not of a utilitarian type, but that it is applicable, if anywhere, just where utilitarian arguments do *not* apply.

Colin Strang, "What If Everyone Did That?," *Durham University Journal* (1960). Reprinted with the permission of *The Durham University Journal*, Department of English Studies, Durham, England.

The objector, who remains unimpressed, will continue: "Granted that my first objection is beside the point, I still can't see how you get from your premiss to your conclusion. Your premiss is, roughly: "Everyone's non-voting is to be deplored," and your conclusion is: "Everyone's voting is obligatory." Why should it be irrational to accept the premiss but deny the conclusion? In any case the validity of the argument cannot depend on its form alone. Plenty of arguments of the very same form are plainly invalid. For instance; if everyone switched on their electric fires at 9 A.M. sharp there would be a power breakdown, therefore no one should; furthermore, this argument applies not only to 9 A.M. but to all times, so no one should ever switch on an electric fire. Again, if everyone taught philosophy whole-time we should all starve, so no one should; or if everyone built houses or did anything else whatever (bar farming) whole-time, we should all starve; and if everyone farmed we would be without clothes or shelter and would die of exposure in winter, so no one should farm. It rather looks, on your kind of argument, as if every whole-time activity is forbidden to everyone. Conversely, if no one farmed we would all starve, so everyone should farm; if no one made clothes we would all die of exposure, so everyone ought to make clothes—and so on. So it also looks, on your kind of argument, as if all sorts of part-time activity are obligatory on everybody. You surely do not mean to commit yourself to enjoining self-sufficiency and condemning specialization? What I want to know is why some arguments of this form are valid (as you claim) while others are not (as you must admit)."

In face of this kind of objection the obvious move is to place certain restrictions on the use of arguments of this form, and to show that only those satisfying certain conditions are valid while the rest are not. This is in fact the move adopted in two recent treatments of this problem: one is by A. C. Ewing (*Philosophy,* January 1953), and the other by M. G. Singer (*Mind,* July 1955). These two are independent, since Singer makes no mention of Ewing; and Ewing, incidentally, regards himself as doing pioneer work in the subject, being able to quote only one previous treatment of it (C. D. Broad, *International Journal of Ethics,* 1915–16). But the restrictions these two wish to impose on the argument seem to me *ad hoc;* they fail to explain why the argument is valid in the remaining cases, and it is just this that I aim to discover.

Compare the voting case with this one: "If everyone here refuses to dig a latrine the camp will be insanitary, therefore everyone ought to dig one." Surely the conclusion we want is, rather: "therefore *someone* ought to dig one." In the voting case, on the other hand, given the premiss "If everyone refused to vote there would be no government," the conclusion "therefore someone ought to vote" clearly will not do; and even the conclusion "therefore everyone ought to vote" is hardly cogent on the reasonable assumption that a 10% abstention will do no harm. If the argument is to be at all cogent it must make some reference to the percentage vote (say n%) needed, thus: "If more than (100 − n)% of the electorate abstained, there would be no government"; this allows us to draw an acceptable conclusion, i.e. "therefore n% of the electorate (not just one of them, nor all of them) ought to vote." So n% must vote to avert anarchy and one must dig to avert disease. But our argument has gained in cogency and precision (being now of a simple utilitarian kind) only at the expense of being no longer effective, or even seemingly so, against the defaulter. He will reply: "All right, so n% ought to vote (someone ought to dig), but why me?" However, there is hope yet for the moralist. To the retort "Why me?" the argument may not suggest any obvious reply; but the retort itself does suggest the counter-retort "Why not you?," to which again there is no obvious reply. An impasse is thus reached in which the moralist cannot say why the defaulter should vote or dig, and the defaulter cannot say why he should not. Evidently it was a mistake to amend the original argument, and yet there seemed to be something wrong with it as it stood; and yet, as it stood, it still seemed to be giving an answer, however obscurely, to the baffling question "Why me?": "Because if *everyone* did that . . ."

To return to the camp: certainly it is agreed by all members of the party that some digging ought to be done, and it is also agreed that the duty does not lie on anyone outside the party. But just where it lies within the party is hard to say. It does not lie on everyone, nor on anyone in particular. Where then? Whatever the answer to that apparently pressing question may be, we all know what would in fact happen. Someone would volunteer, or a leader would allot duties, or the whole party would cast lots. Or, if the thing to be done were not a once-and-for-all job like digging latrines but a daily routine like washing up, they might take it in turns.

Although various acceptable answers to the question how the duties are to be allotted are readily listed, they leave us quite in the dark as to just *who* ought to dig, wash up, etc. That question hardly seems to arise. In the absence of an argumentative defaulter there is no call to think up reasons why I or you should do this or that or reasons why I or you should not, and we are left with the defaulter's "Why me?" and the moralist's "Why not you?" unanswered.

Our enquiry has made little progress, but the fog is beginning to lift from the territory ahead. We are evidently concerned with communities of people and with things that must be done, or not done, if the community is to be saved from damage or destruction; and we want to know whose duty it is to do, or not to do, these things. The complexity of the problem is no longer in doubt. (1) There are some things that need doing once, some that need doing at regular intervals, and some that need doing all the time. (2) Some things need doing by one person, some by a number of people which can be roughly estimated, and some by as many as possible. (3) In practice, who shall do what (though not who *ought* to do what) is determined by economic factors, or by statutory direction (e.g. service with the armed forces in war, paying income tax), or merely by people's inclinations generally, i.e. when enough people are inclined to do the thing anyway.

Somewhere in this territory our quarry has its lair. The following dialogue between defaulter and moralist on the evasion of income tax and military service begins the hunt. Our first steps are taken on already familiar ground:

DEFAULTER: £100 is a drop in the ocean to the exchequer. No one will suffer from their loss of £100, but it means a good deal to me.

MORALIST: But what if everyone did that and offered the same excuse?

D.: But the vast majority won't, so no one will suffer.

M.: Still, would you say it was *in order* for anyone whatever to evade tax and excuse himself on the same grounds as you do?

D.: Certainly.

M.: So it would be quite in order for *everyone* to do the same and offer the same excuse?

D.: Yes.

M.: Even though disaster would ensue for the exchequer and for everyone?

D.: Yes. The exchequer would no more miss my £100 if *everyone* evaded than they would if only I evaded. They wouldn't miss anyone's individual evasion. What they would miss would be the aggregate £1,000,000,000 or so, and that isn't my default or yours or anyone's. So even if everyone evades it is still all right for me to evade; and if it's all right for me to evade it's all right for everyone to evade.

M.: You seem now to be in the paradoxical position of saying that if everyone evaded it would be disastrous, and yet no one would be to blame.

D.: Paradoxical, perhaps, but instructive. I am not alarmed. Let me recur to one of your previous questions: you asked whether it would be in order for all to evade and give the same excuse. I now want to reply: No, it would not be in order, but only in the sense that it would be disastrous; but it *would* be in order in the sense that each person's grounds for evasion would still be as valid as they would have been if he had been the *only* evader and no disaster had ensued. In other words, none of the defaulters would be to blame for the disaster—and certainly not one of them would blame himself: on the contrary, each one would argue that had he paid he would have been the only one to pay and thus lost his £100 without doing himself or anyone else any good. He would have been a mug to pay.

M.: But surely there can't be a disaster of this kind for which no one is to blame.

D.: If anyone is to blame it is the person whose job it is to circumvent evasion. If too few people vote, then it should be made illegal not to vote. If too few people volunteer, then you must introduce conscription. If too many people evade taxes, then you must tighten up your system of enforcement. My answer to your "If everyone did that" is "Then someone had jolly well better see to it that they don't"; it doesn't impress me as a reason why *I* should, however many people do or don't.

M.: But surely you are being inconsistent here. Take the case of evading military service.

D.: You mean not volunteering in time of crisis, there being no conscription? I do that too.

M.: Good. As I was saying, aren't you being inconsistent? You think *both* that it is all right not to volunteer even if too few other people volunteer (because one soldier more or less could make no difference), *and* think that you ought to be conscripted.

D.: But that is not at all inconsistent. Look: the enemy threatens, a mere handful volunteer, and the writing is on the wall; my volunteering will not affect the outcome, but conscript me with the rest to stay the deluge and I will come without a murmur. In short, no good will come of my volunteering, but a great good will come of a general conscription which gathers me in with the rest. There is no inconsistency. I should add that my volunteering would in fact do positive harm: all who resist and survive are to be executed forthwith. There will be one or two heroes, but I did not think you were requiring me to be heroic.

M.: I confirm that I was not, and I concede that your position is not inconsistent, however unedifying. As I see it, the nub of your position is this: Given the premiss "if everyone did that the result would be disastrous" you cannot conclude "therefore *you* oughtn't" but only "therefore someone ought to see to it that they don't." If you are right, the "if everyone did" argument, as usually taken, is invalid. But then we are left with the question: Whence does it derive its apparent force?

D.: Whence, indeed?

(*interval*)

M.: Suppose when you give your justification for evading ("no one will miss *my* contribution") I reply: But don't you think it *unfair* that other people should bear the burden which you shirk and from the bearing of which by others you derive benefit for yourself?

D.: Well, yes, it is rather unfair. Indeed you make me feel a little ashamed; but I wasn't prepared, and I'm still not, to let your pet argument by without a fight. Just where does fairness come into it?

M.: I think I can see. Let me begin by pushing two or three counters from different points on the periphery of the problem with the hope that they will meet at the center. First, then: if someone is morally obliged (or permitted or forbidden) to do some particular thing, then there is a reason why he is so obliged. Further, if someone is obliged to do something for a particular reason, then anyone else whatever is equally obliged provided the reason applies to him also. The reason why a particular person is obliged to do something will be expressible in general terms, and could be expressed by describing some class to which he belongs. My principle then reads as follows: If someone is obliged to do something *just because* he is a member of a certain class, then any other member of that class will be equally obliged to do that thing. You yourself argued, remember, that any member of the class of people whose contribution would not be missed (here I allude to your reason for evasion) was no less entitled to evade than you.

D.: Agreed.

M.: My second counter now comes into play. "Fairness," you will agree, is a moral term like "rightness." An act is unfair if it results in someone getting a greater or lesser share of something (whether pleasant or unpleasant) than he ought to get—more or less than his fair share, as we say.

Now there are a number of things, burdensome or otherwise, which need to be done if the community is not to suffer. But who precisely is to do them? Why me? Why not me? You will also agree, I hope, to the wide principle that where the thing to be done is burdensome the burden should be fairly distributed?

D.: Certainly. I seldom dispute a truism. But in what does a fair distribution consist?

M.: In other words: given two people and a burden, how much of it ought each to bear? I say: *unless there is some reason why one should bear more or less of it than the other, they should both bear the same amount.* This is my Fairness Principle. It concerns both the fair allocation of the burden to some class of community members and the fair distribution of it within that class (and this may mean dividing the class into sub-classes of "isophoric" members): there must always be a *reason* for treating people differently. For instance, people who are unfit or above or below a certain age are exempted or excluded from military service, and for good reasons; women are exempted or excluded from certain kinds of military service, for what Plato regarded as bad reasons; those with more income pay more tax, while those with more children pay less, and for good reasons—and so on. You will have noticed that the typical complaint about unfair dealing begins with a "why": "Why did they charge me more than him?" (unfair distribution), or "Why should married couples be liable for so much surtax?" (unfair allocation). The maxim governing differential treatment, i.e. which is behind the reasons given for it, seems to be: From each according to his resources, to each according to his need. You might argue that my principle about equal burdens is no more than a special case of this maxim. But that principle is all I need for my argument and all I insist on; I shall not stick my neck out further than necessary.

D.: It is not, thus far, too dangerously exposed, I think.

M.: Good. We are now ready to move a little nearer to the core of the problem. But first compare the two principles I have advanced. The first was: if a thing is obligatory etc. for one person, then it is obligatory etc. for anyone in the same class (i.e. the class relevant to the reason given). This is a license to argue from one member of a class to all its members; we will call it the Universalization Principle (U-Principle). The second, which is my Fairness Principle, is: A burden laid on a particular class is to be shared equally by all its members, unless there is reason to the contrary. This, in contrast to the first, is a license to argue from the class itself to each of its members. I take it, by the way, that these two principles are independent, that neither follows from the other.

D.: Granted, granted. I am impatient to know what light all this throws on your "if everyone did" argument.

M.: I am coming to that. You will remember that you used the U-Principle yourself to argue that if it's all right for you to evade it's all right for everyone else. But it was no use to me in pressing my case, and we can now see why: it argues from one to all, and there was no *one* to argue from. Nor, of course, could I argue from the consequences of your act. "Why me?" you asked, and I had then no reply. But I did at least have a retort: "Why not you?" Now it seems to me that it is just my Fairness Principle that lies behind the effectiveness of this retort, for by it you can be shown to have a duty in cases like this unless you can show that you have not. You would have to show, in the military service example, that you were not a member of the class on which the duty of military service is normally (and we will assume, fairly) regarded as lying. But you cannot show this: you cannot claim to be under age or over age or blind or lame. All you claim is that you have a certain property, the property of being one whose contribution won't be missed, which is shared by every other member of the military class; and this claim, so far from being a good reason for not volunteering, now stands revealed as no reason at all.

D.: Still, you didn't dispute my point that the blame for a disaster following upon wholesale evasion lay upon those whose duty it was, or in whose power it lay, to prevent such evasion.

M.: You certainly had a point, but I can see now that you made too much of it. I concede that the authorities failed in their duty, but then the military class as a whole failed in theirs too. The duty of both was ultimately the same, to ensure the safety of the state, just as the duty of wicket-keeper and long-stop is the same, to save byes. To confine the blame to the authorities is like saying that it's all right to burn the house down so long as it's insured or that the mere existence of a police force constitutes a general license to rob banks. As for the individual defaulter, you wanted to absolve him from all blame—a claim which seemed at once plausible and paradoxical: plausible because he was not, as you rightly pointed out, to blame for the disaster (it was not his duty to prevent that, since it was not in his power to do so); paradoxical because he was surely to blame for *something,* and we now know what for: failure to bear his share of the burden allotted to his class.

D.: Maybe, but it still seems to me that if I volunteer and others don't I shall be taking on an unfair share of it, and *that* can't be fair. Then again if I don't volunteer I shall be doing less than my share, and *that* can't be fair either. Whichever I do, there's something wrong. And that can't be right.

M.: There are two mistakes here. Whichever you do there's something wrong, but nothing unfair; the only wrong is people failing in their duty. Fairness is an attribute of distributions, and whether you volunteer or not neither you nor anyone else are distributing anything. Nor, for that matter, are fate or circumstances, for they are not persons. That is your first mistake. Your second is this: you talk as if the lone volunteer will necessarily do more than his fair share. He may, but he needn't. If he does, that is his own look out: *volenti non fit iniuria.*

D.: It's more dangerous to fight alone than as one among many. How can he ration the danger?

M.: He can surrender or run away. Look, he isn't expected to be heroic or to do, or even attempt, the impossible. If two are needed to launch and man the lifeboat, the lone volunteer can only stand and wait: *he also* serves. The least a man can do is offer and hold himself ready, though sometimes it is also the most he can do.

D.: Let it be so. But I am still in trouble about one thing: suppose I grant all you say about fairness and the defaulter, I'm still not clear why you choose to make your point against him in just the mysterious way you do, i.e. by fixing him with your glittering eye and beginning "If everyone did that."

M.: It is a little puzzling, isn't it? But not all that puzzling. After all, the premiss states and implies a good deal: (1) It states that wholesale evasion will have such and such results; (2) it states or implies that the results will be bad; (3) it implies strongly that a duty to prevent them must lie *somewhere;* (4) it implies that the duty does not lie solely on the person addressed (otherwise a quite different kind of argument would apply); (5) it implies, rather weakly, that nevertheless the person addressed has no better excuse for doing nothing about it than anyone else has. The conclusion is then stated that he ought to do something about it. A gap remains, to be sure; but it can't be a very big one, or people wouldn't, as they sometimes do, feel the force of the argument, however obscurely. The "Why me?" retort brings out implication (4), while the "Why not you?" counter-retort brings out implication (5); and we didn't really have very far to go from there.

The argument is clearly elliptical and needs filling out with some explicit reference to the Fairness Principle. I would formalize it as follows:

Unless such and such is done, undesirable consequences X will ensue;
the burden of preventing X lies upon class Y as a whole;
each member of class Y has a *prima facie* duty to bear an equal share of the burden by doing Z;
you are a member of class Y;
therefore you have a *prima facie* duty to do Z.

I have introduced the notion of a *prima facie* duty at this late stage to cover those cases where only a few members of class Y are required to do Z and it would be silly to put them all to work. In the latrine case only one person needs to dig, and in America only a small proportion of fit persons are required for short-term military service. In such cases it is considered fair to select the requisite number by lot. Until the lot is cast I must hold myself ready; if I am selected my *prima facie* duty becomes an actual duty; if I am spared, it lapses. Why selection by lot should be a fair method I leave you to work out for yourself.

Notice that the argument only holds if the thing to be done is burdensome. Voting isn't really very burdensome; indeed a lot of people seem to enjoy it, and this accounts for the weakness of the argument in this application. If the thing to be done were positively enjoyable one might even have to invoke the Fairness Principle against over-indulgence.

Notice, finally, that the argument doesn't apply unless there is a fairly readily isolable class to which a burden can be allotted. This rules out the farming and such like cases. You can't lay it down that the burden of providing food for the nation (if it *is* a burden) lies on the farmers (i.e. the class that provides food for the nation), for that is a tautology, or perhaps it implies the curious proposition that everyone *ought* to be doing the job he *is* doing. Might one say instead that *everyone* has a *prima facie* duty to farm, but that the duty lapses when inclination, ability and economic reward conspire to select a sufficient farming force? Far-fetched, I think. The matter might be pursued, but only at the risk of tedium. Well, are you satisfied?

D.: Up to a point. Your hypothesis obviously calls for a lot more testing yet. But I have carried the burden a good deal further than my fair share of the distance; let others take it from here.

1963

A Moral Argument

R. M. Hare

And as ye would that men should do to you, do ye also to them likewise.

St. Luke vi. 31

6.1. Historically, one of the chief incentives to the study of ethics has been the hope that its findings might be of help to those faced with difficult moral problems. That this is still a principal incentive for many people is shown by the fact that modern philosophers are often reproached for failing to make ethics relevant to morals.[1] This is because one of the main tenets of many recent moral philosophers has been that the most popular method by which it was sought to bring ethics to bear on moral problems was not feasible—namely the method followed by the group of theories loosely known as "naturalist."

The method of naturalism is so to characterize the *meanings* of the key moral terms that, given certain factual premises, not themselves moral judgments, moral conclusions can be deduced from them. If this could be done, it was thought that it would

Prof. Hare has asked us to point out that the argument contained herein is set out more fully in chaps. 5 and 6 of his *Moral Thinking* (Oxford: 1981).

[1]I have tried to fill in some of the historical background of these reproaches, and to assess the justification for them, in my article in *The Philosophy of C. D. Broad*, ed. P. Schilpp.

be of great assistance to us in making moral decisions; we should only have to find out the nonmoral facts, and the moral conclusion as to what we ought to do would follow. Those who say that it cannot be done leave themselves the task of giving an alternative account of moral reasoning.

Naturalism seeks to make the findings of ethics *relevant* to moral decisions by making the former not morally *neutral.* It is a very natural assumption that if a statement of ethics is relevant to morals, then it cannot be neutral as between different moral judgments; and naturalism is a tempting view for those who make this assumption. Naturalistic definitions are not morally neutral, because with their aid we could show that statements of nonmoral facts *entailed* moral conclusions. And some have thought that unless such an entailment can be shown to hold, the moral philosopher has not made moral reasoning possible.

One way of escaping this conclusion is to say that the relation linking a set of nonmoral premises with a moral conclusion is not one of entailment, but that some other logical relation, peculiar to morals, justifies the inference. This is the view put forward, for example, by Mr. Toulmin.[2] Since I have argued elsewhere against this approach, I shall not discuss it here. Its advocates have, however, hit upon an important insight: that moral reasoning does not necessarily proceed by way of *deduction* of moral conclusions from nonmoral premises. Their further suggestion, that therefore it makes this transition by means of some other, peculiar, nondeductive kind of inference, is not the only possibility. It may be that moral reasoning is not, typically, any kind of "straightline" or "linear" reasoning from premises to conclusion.

6.2. A parallel from the philosophy of science will perhaps make this point clear. It is natural to suppose that what the scientist does is to reason from premises, which are the data of observation, to conclusions, which are his "scientific laws," by means of a special sort of inference called "inductive." Against this view, Professor Popper has forcibly argued that in science there are no inferences other than deductive; the typical procedure of scientists to propound hypotheses, and then look for ways of testing them—i.e. experiments which, if they are false, will show them to be so. A hypothesis which, try as we may, we fail to falsify, we accept provisionally, though ready to abandon it if, after all, further experiment refutes it; and of those that are so accepted we rate highest the ones which say most, and which would, therefore, be most likely to have been falsified if they were false. The only inferences which occur in this process are deductive ones, from the truth of certain observations to the falsity of a hypothesis. There is no reasoning which proceeds from the data of observation to the *truth* of a hypothesis. Scientific inquiry is rather a kind of *exploration,* or looking for hypotheses which will stand up to the test of experiment.[3]

We must ask whether moral reasoning exhibits any similar features. I want to suggest that it too is a kind of exploration, and not a kind of linear inference, and that the only inferences which take place in it are deductive. What we are doing in moral reasoning is to look for moral judgments and moral principles which, when we have considered their logical consequences and the facts of the case, we can still accept. As we shall see, this approach to the problem enables us to reject the assumption, which seemed so natural, that ethics cannot be relevant to moral decisions without ceasing to be neutral. This is because we are not going to demand any inferences in our reasoning

[2]S. E. Toulmin, *The Place of Reason in Ethics,* esp. pp. 38–60. See my review in *Philosophical Quarterly,* I (1950–51), 372, and *Language of Morals* 3.4.

[3]K. R. Popper, *The Logic of Scientific Discovery* (esp. pp. 32 f.). See also his article in C. A. Mace, ed., *British Philosophy in the Mid-Century,* p. 155.

other than deductive ones, and because none of these deductive inferences rely for their validity upon naturalistic definitions of moral terms.

Two further parallels may help to make clear the sense in which ethics is morally neutral. In the kind of scientific reasoning just described, mathematics plays a major part, for many of the deductive inferences that occur are mathematical in character. So we are bound to admit that mathematics is relevant to scientific inquiry. Nevertheless, it is also neutral, in the sense that no discoveries about matters of physical fact can be made with the aid of mathematics alone, and that no mathematical inference can have a conclusion which says more, in the way of prediction of observations, than its premises implicitly do.

An even simpler parallel is provided by the rules of games. The rules of a game are neutral as between the players, in the sense that they do not, by themselves, determine which player is going to win. In order to decide who wins, the players have to play the game in accordance with the rules, which involves their making, themselves, a great many individual decisions. On the other hand, the "neutrality" of the rules of a game does not turn it into a game of chance, in which the bad player is as likely to win as the good.

Ethical theory, which determines the meanings and functions of the moral words, and thus the "rules" of the moral "game," provides only a clarification of the conceptual framework within which moral reasoning takes place; it is therefore, in the required sense, neutral as between different moral opinions. But it is highly relevant to moral reasoning because, as with the rules of a game, there could be no such thing as moral reasoning without this framework, and the framework dictates the form of the reasoning. It follows that naturalism is not the only way of providing for the possibility of moral reasoning; and this may, perhaps, induce those who have espoused naturalism as a way of making moral thought a rational activity to consider other possibilities.

The rules of moral reasoning are, basically, two, corresponding to the two features of moral judgments which I argued for in the first of this book [*Freedom and Reason*], prescriptivity and universalizability. When we are trying, in a concrete case, to decide what we ought to do, what we are looking for (as I have already said) is an action to which we can commit ourselves (prescriptivity) but which we are at the same time prepared to accept as exemplifying a principle of action to be prescribed for others in like circumstances (universalizability). If, when we consider some proposed action, we find that, when universalized, it yields prescriptions which we cannot accept, we reject this action as a solution to our moral problem—if we cannot universalize the prescription, it cannot become an "ought."

It is to be noticed that, troublesome as was the problem of moral weakness when we were dealing theoretically with the logical character of the moral concepts, it cannot trouble us here. For if a person is going to reason seriously at all about a moral question, he has to presuppose that the moral concepts are going, in his reasoning, to be used prescriptively. One cannot start a moral argument about a certain proposal on the basis that, whatever the conclusion of it, it makes no difference to what anybody is to do. When one has arrived at a conclusion, one may then be too weak to put it into practice. But *in arguing* one has to discount this possibility; for, as we shall see, to abandon the prescriptivity of one's moral judgments is to unscrew an essential part of the logical mechanism on which such arguments rely. This is why, if a person were to say "Let's have an argument about this grave moral question which faces us, but let's not think of any conclusion we may come to as requiring anybody to *do* one thing rather than another," we should be likely to accuse him of flippancy, or worse.

6.3. I will now try to exhibit the bare bones of the theory of moral reasoning that I wish to advocate by considering a very simple (indeed oversimplified) example. As we shall see, even this very simple case generates the most baffling complexities; and so we may be pardoned for not attempting anything more difficult to start with.

The example is adapted from a well-known parable.[4] A owes money to B, and B owes money to C, and it is the law that creditors may exact their debts by putting their debtors into prison. B asks himself, "Can I say that I ought to take this measure against A in order to make him pay?" He is no doubt *inclined* to do this, or *wants* to do it. Therefore, if there were no question of universalizing his prescriptions, he would assent readily to the *singular* prescription "Let me put A into prison." . . . But when he seeks to turn this prescription into a moral judgment, and says, "I *ought* to put A into prison because he will not pay me what he owes," he reflects that this would involve accepting the principle "Anyone who is in my position ought to put his debtor into prison if he does not pay." But then he reflects that C is in the same position of unpaid creditor with regard to himself (B), and that the cases are otherwise identical; and that if anyone in this position ought to put his debtors into prison, then so ought C to put him (B) into prison. And to accept the moral prescription "C ought to put me into prison" would commit him (since, as we have seen, he must be using the word "ought" prescriptively) to accepting the singular prescription "Let C put me into prison"; and this he is not ready to accept. But if he is not, then neither can he accept the original judgment that he (B) ought to put A into prison for debt. Notice that the whole of this argument would break down if "ought" were not being used both universalizably *and prescriptively;* for if it were not being used prescriptively, the step from "C ought to put me into prison" to "Let C put me into prison" would not be valid.

The structure and ingredients of this argument must now be examined. We must first notice an analogy between it and the Popperian theory of scientific method. What has happened is that a provisional or suggested moral principle has been rejected because one of its particular consequences proved unacceptable. But an important difference between the two kinds of reasoning must also be noted; it is what we should expect, given that the data of scientific observation are recorded in descriptive statements, whereas we are here dealing with prescriptions. What knocks out a suggested hypothesis, on Popper's theory, is a singular statement of fact: the hypothesis has the consequence that p; but not-p. Here the logic is just the same, except that in place of the observation statements "p" and "not-p" we have the singular *prescriptions* "Let C put B into prison for debt" and its contradictory. Nevertheless, given that B is disposed to reject the first of these prescriptions, the argument against him is just as cogent as in the scientific case.

We may carry the parallel further. Just as science, seriously pursued, is the search for hypotheses and the testing of them by the attempt to falsify their particular consequences, so morals, as a serious endeavor, consists in the search for principles and the testing of them against particular cases. Any rational activity has its discipline, and this is the discipline of moral thought: to test the moral principles that suggest themselves to us by following out their consequences and seeing whether we can accept *them.*

No argument, however, starts from nothing. We must therefore ask what we have to have before moral arguments of the sort of which I have given a simple example can proceed. The first requisite is that the facts of the case should be given; for all moral discussion is about some particular set of facts, whether actual or supposed. Secondly we have the logical framework provided by the meaning of the word "ought" (i.e. prescriptivity and universalizability, both of which we saw to be necessary). Because moral

[4] Matthew XVIII. 23.

judgments have to be universalizable, B cannot say that he ought to put A into prison for debt without committing himself to the view that C, who is *ex hypothesi* in the same position *vis-à-vis* himself, ought to put *him* into prison; and because moral judgments are prescriptive, this would be, in effect, prescribing to C to put him into prison; and this he is unwilling to do, since he has a strong inclination not to go to prison. This inclination gives us the third necessary ingredient in the argument: if B were a completely apathetic person, who literally did not mind what happened to himself or to anybody else, the argument would not touch him. The three necessary ingredients which we have noticed, then, are (1) facts; (2) logic; (3) inclinations. These ingredients enable us, not indeed to arrive at an evaluative conclusion, but to *reject* an evaluative proposition. We shall see later that these are not, in all cases, the only necessary ingredients.

6.4. In the example which we have been using, the position was deliberately made simpler by supposing that B actually stood to some other person in exactly the same relation as A does to him. Such cases are unlikely to arise in practice. But it is not necessary for the force of the argument that B should *in fact* stand in this relation to anyone; it is sufficient that he should consider hypothetically such a case, and see what would be the consequences in it of those moral principles between whose acceptance and rejection he has to decide. Here we have an important point of difference from the parallel scientific argument, in that the crucial case which leads to rejection of the principle can itself be a supposed, not an observed, one. That hypothetical cases will do as well as actual ones is important, since it enables us to guard against a possible misinterpretation of the argument which I have outlined. It might be thought that what moves B is the *fear* that C will actually do to him as he does to A—as happens in the gospel parable. But this fear is not only irrelevant to the moral argument; it does not even provide a particularly strong nonmoral motive unless the circumstances are somewhat exceptional. C may, after all, not find out what B has done to A; or C's moral principles may be different from B's, and independent of them, so that what moral principle B accepts makes no difference to the moral principles on which C acts.

Even, therefore, if C did not exist, it would be no answer to the argument for B to say "But in my case there is no fear that anybody will ever be in a position to do to me what I am proposing to do to A." For the argument does not rest on any such fear. All that is essential to it is that B should disregard the fact that he plays the particular role in the situation which he does, without disregarding the inclinations which people have in situations of this sort. In other words, he must be prepared to give weight to A's inclinations and interests as if they were his own. This is what turns selfish prudential reasoning into moral reasoning. It is much easier, psychologically, for B to do this if he is actually placed in a situation like A's *vis-à-vis* somebody else; but this is not necessary, provided that he has sufficient imagination to envisage what it is like to be A. For our first example, a case was deliberately chosen in which little imagination was necessary; but in most normal cases a certain power of imagination and readiness to use it is a fourth necessary ingredient in moral arguments, alongside those already mentioned, viz. logic (in the shape of universalizability and prescriptivity), the facts, and the inclinations or interests of the people concerned.

It must be pointed out that the absence of even one of these ingredients may render the rest ineffective. For example, impartiality by itself is not enough. If, in becoming impartial, B became also completely dispassionate and apathetic, and moved as little by other people's interests as by his own, then, as we have seen, there would be nothing to make him accept or reject one moral principle rather than another. That is why those who, like Adam Smith and Professor Kneale, advocate what have been called "Ideal Observer Theories" of ethics, sometimes postulate as their imaginary ideal observer not merely an impartial spectator, but an impartially *sympathetic* spectator.[5] To take another example, if the person who faces the moral decision has no imagination, then even the fact that someone can do the very same thing to him may pass him by. If, again, he lacks the readiness to universalize, then the vivid imagination of the sufferings which he is inflicting on others may only spur him on to intensify them, to increase his own vindictive enjoyment. And if he is ignorant of the material facts (for example about what is likely to happen to a person if one takes out a writ against him), then there is nothing to tie the moral argument to particular choices.

6.5. The best way of testing the argument which we have outlined will be to consider various ways in which somebody in B's position might seek to escape from it. There are indeed a number of such ways; and all of them may be successful, at a price. It is important to understand what the price is in each case. We may classify these maneuvers which are open to B into two kinds. There are first of all the moves which depend on his using the moral words in a different way from that on which the argument relied. We saw that for the success of the argument it was necessary that "ought" should be used universalizably and prescriptively. If B uses it in a way that is either not prescriptive or not universalizable, then he can escape the force of the argument, at the cost of resigning from the kind of discussion that we thought we were having with him. We shall discuss these two possibilities separately. Secondly, there are moves which can still be made by B, even though he is using the moral words in the same way as we are. We shall examine three different sub-classes of these.

Before dealing with what I shall call the *verbal* maneuvers in detail, it may be helpful to make a general remark. Suppose that we are having a simple mathematical argument with somebody, and he admits, for example, that there are five eggs in this basket, and six in the other, but maintains that there are a dozen eggs in the two baskets taken together; and suppose that this is because he is using the expression "a dozen" to mean "eleven." It is obvious that we cannot compel him logically to admit that there are not a dozen eggs, in *his* sense of "dozen." But it is equally obvious that this should not disturb us. For such a man only appears to be dissenting from us. His dissent is only apparent, because the proposition which his words express is actually consistent with the conclusion which we wish to draw; he *says* "There are a dozen eggs"; but he *means* what we should express by saying "There are eleven eggs"; and this we are not disputing. It is important to remember that in the moral case also the dissent may be only apparent, if the words are being used in different ways, and that it is no defect in a method of argument if it does not make it possible to prove a conclusion to a person when he is using words in such a way that the conclusion does not follow.

It must be pointed out, further (since this is a common source of confusion), that in this argument nothing whatever hangs upon our *actual* use of words in common speech, any more than it does in the arithmetical case. That we use the sound "dozen" to express the meaning that we customarily do use it to express is of no consequence for the argument about the eggs; and the same may be said of the sound "ought." There is, however, something which I, at any rate, customarily express by the sound "ought,"

[5]It will be plain that there are affinities, though there are also differences, between this type of theory and my own. For such theories see W. C. Kneale, *Philosophy*, XXV (1950), 162; R. Firth and R. B. Brandt, *Philosophy and Phenomenological Research*, XII (1951–52), 317, and XV (1954–55), 407, 414, 422; and J. Harrison, *Aristotelian Society*, supp. vol. XXVIII (1954), 132. Firth, unlike Kneale, says that the observer must be "dispassionate," but see Brandt, op. cit., p. 411 n. For a shorter discussion see Brandt, *Ethical Theory*, p. 173. Since for many Christians God occupies the role of "ideal observer," the moral judgments which they make may be expected to coincide with those arrived at by the method of reasoning which I am advocating.

whose character is correctly described by saying that it is a universal or universalizable prescription. I hope that what I customarily express by the sound "ought" is the same as what most people customarily express by it; but if I am mistaken in this assumption, I shall still have given a correct account, so far as I am able, of that which I express by this sound.[6] Nevertheless, this account will interest other people mainly in so far as my hope that they understand the same thing as I do by "ought" is fulfilled; and since I am moderately sure that this is indeed the case with many people, I hope that I may be of use to them in elucidating the logical properties of the concept which they thus express.

At this point, however, it is of the utmost importance to stress that the fact that two people express the same thing by "ought" does not entail that they share the same moral opinions. For the formal, logical properties of the word "ought" (those which are determined by its *meaning*) are only one of the four factors (listed earlier) whose combination governs a man's moral opinion on a given matter. Thus ethics, the study of the logical properties of the moral words, remains morally neutral (its conclusions neither are substantial moral judgments, nor entail them, even in conjunction with factual premises); its bearing upon moral questions lies in this, that it makes logically impossible certain combinations of moral and other prescriptions. Two people who are using the word "ought" in the same way may yet disagree about what ought to be done in a certain situation, either because they differ about the facts, or because one or other of them lacks imagination, or because their different inclinations make one reject some singular prescription which the other can accept. For all that, ethics (i.e. the logic of moral language) is an immensely powerful engine for producing moral agreement; for if two people are willing to use the moral word "ought," and to use it in the same way (viz. the way that I have been describing), the other possible sources of moral disagreement are all eliminable. People's inclinations about most of the important matters in life tend to be the same (very few people, for example, like being starved or run over by motorcars); and, even when they are not, there is a way of generalizing the argument . . . , which enables us to make allowance for differences in inclinations. The facts are often, given sufficient patience, ascertainable. Imagination can be cultivated. If these three factors are looked after, as they can be, agreement on the use of "ought" is the only other necessary condition for producing moral agreement, at any rate in typical cases. And, if I am not mistaken, this agreement in use is already there in the discourse of anybody with whom we are at all likely to find ourselves arguing; all that is needed is to to think clearly, and so make it evident.

After this methodological digression, let us consider what is to be done with the man who professes to be using "ought" in some different way from that which I have described—because he is not using it prescriptively, or not universalizably. For the reasons that I have given, if he takes either of these courses, he is no longer in substantial moral disagreement with us. Our apparent moral disagreement is really only verbal; for although, as we shall see shortly, there may be a residuum of substantial disagreement, this cannot be moral.[7]

Let us take first the man who is using the word "ought" prescriptively, but not universalizably. He can say that he ought to put his debtor into prison, although he is not prepared to agree that his creditor ought to put *him* into prison. We, on the other hand, since we are not prepared to admit that our creditors in these circumstances ought to put

[6]Cf. Moore, *Principia Ethica*, p. 6.

[7]Strictly, we should say "evaluative"; but for the reason given on p. 130 [p. 386 this volume], we can ignore the nonevaluative moral judgments mentioned on pp. 26 f. [of *Freedom and Reason*] and in *Language of Morals* 11.3.

us into prison, cannot say that we ought to put our debtors into prison. So there is an appearance of substantial moral disagreement, which is intensified by the fact that, since we are both using the word "ought" prescriptively, our respective views will lead to different particular actions. Different *singular* prescriptions about what to do are (since both our judgments are prescriptive) derivable from what we are respectively saying. But this is not enough to constitute a moral disagreement. For that, we should have to differ, not only about what *is* to be done in some particular case, but about some universal principle concerning what *ought* to be done in cases of a certain sort; and since B is (on the hypothesis considered) advocating no such universal principle, he is saying nothing with which we can be in moral or evaluative disagreement. Considered purely as prescriptions, indeed, our two views are in substantial disagreement; but the moral, evaluative (i.e. the *universal* prescriptive) disagreement is only verbal, because, when the expression of B's view is understood as he means it, the view turns out not to be a view about the morality of the action at all. So B, by this maneuver, can go on prescribing to himself to put A into prison, but has to abandon the claim that he is justifying the action morally, as we understand the word "morally." One may, of course, use any word as one pleases, at a price. But he can no longer claim to be giving that sort of justification of his action for which, as I think, the common expression is "moral justification."

I need not deal at length with the second way in which B might be differing from us in his use of "ought," viz. by not using it prescriptively. If he were not using it prescriptively, it will be remembered, he could assent to the singular prescription "Let not C put me into prison for debt," and yet assent also to the nonprescriptive moral judgment "C ought to put me into prison for debt." And so his disinclination to be put into prison for debt by C would furnish no obstacle to his saying that he (B) ought to put A into prison for debt. And thus he could carry out his own inclination to put A into prison with apparent moral justification. The justification would be, however, only apparent. For if B is using the word "ought" nonprescriptively, then "I ought to put A into prison for debt" does not entail the singular prescription "Let me put A into prison for debt"; the "moral" judgment becomes quite irrelevant to the choice of what to do. There would also be the same lack of substantial moral disagreement as we noticed in the preceding case. B would not be disagreeing with us other than verbally, so far as the moral question is concerned (though there might be points of *factual* disagreement between us, arising from the *descriptive* meaning of our judgments). The "moral" disagreement could be only verbal, because whereas we should be dissenting from the universalizable prescription "B ought to put A into prison for debt," *this* would not be what B was expressing, though the words he would be using would be the same. For B would not, by these words, be expressing a prescription at all.

6.6. So much for the ways (of which my list may well be incomplete) in which B can escape from our argument by using the word "ought" in a different way from us. The remaining ways of escape are open to him even if he is using "ought" in the same way as we are, viz. to express a universalizable prescription.

We must first consider that class of escape routes whose distinguishing feature is that B, while using the moral words in the same way as we are, refuses to make positive moral judgments at all in certain cases. There are two main variations of this maneuver. B may either say that it is indifferent, morally, whether he imprisons A or not; or he may refuse to make any moral judgment at all, even one of indifference, about the case. It will be obvious that if he adopts either of these moves, he can evade the argument as so far set out. For that argument only forced him to *reject* the moral judgment "I ought to imprison A for debt." It did not force him to assent to any moral judgment; in particular, he remained free to assent, either to the judgment that he ought not to imprison A for debt (which is the one that we want him to accept) or to the judgment that it is neither the case that he ought, nor the case that he ought not (that it is, in short, indifferent); and he remained free, also, to say "I am just not making any moral judgments at all about this case."

We have not yet, however, exhausted the arguments generated by the demand for universalizability, provided that the moral words are being used in a way which allows this demand. For it is evident that these maneuvers could, in principle, be practiced in any case whatever in which the morality of an act is in question. And this enables us to place B in a dilemma. Either he practices this maneuver in *every* situation in which he is faced with a moral decision; or else he practices it only *sometimes.* The first alternative, however, has to be subdivided; for "every situation" might mean "every situation in which he himself has to face a moral decision regarding one of his own actions," or it might mean "every situation in which a moral question arises for him, whether about his own actions or about somebody else's." So there are three courses that he can adopt: (1) He either refrains altogether from making moral judgments, or makes none except judgments of indifference (that is to say, he either observes a complete moral silence, or says "Nothing matters morally"; either of these two positions might be called a sort of amoralism); (2) He makes moral judgments in the normal way about other people's actions, but adopts one or other of the kinds of amoralism, just mentioned, with regard to his own; (3) He expresses moral indifference, or will make no moral judgment at all, with regard to *some* of his own actions and those of other people, but makes moral judgments in the normal way about others.

Now it will be obvious that in the first case there is nothing that we can do, and that this should not disturb us. Just as one cannot win a game of chess against an opponent who will not make any moves—and just as one cannot argue mathematically with a person who will not commit himself to any mathematical statements—so moral argument is impossible with a man who will make no moral judgments at all, or—which for practical purposes comes to the same thing—makes only judgments of indifference. Such a person is not entering the arena of moral dispute, and therefore it is impossible to contest with him. He is compelled also—and this is important—to abjure the protection of morality for his own interests.

In the other two cases, however, we have an argument left. If a man is prepared to make positive moral judgments about other people's actions, but not about his own, or if he is prepared to make them about some of his own decisions, but not about others, then we can ask him on what principle he makes the distinction between these various cases. This is a particular application of the demand for universalizability. He will still have left to him the ways of escape from this demand which are available in all its applications, and which we shall consider later. But there is no way of escape which is available in this application, but not in others. He must either produce (or at least admit the existence of) some principle which makes him hold different moral opinions about apparently similar cases, or else admit that the judgments he is making are not moral ones. But in the latter case, he is in the same position, in the present dispute, as the man who will not make any moral judgments at all; he has resigned from the contest.

In the particular example which we have been considering, we supposed that the cases of B and of C, his own creditor, were identical. The demand for universalization therefore compels B to make the same moral judgment, whatever it is, about both cases. He has therefore, unless he is going to give up the claim to be arguing morally, either to say that neither he nor C ought to exercise their legal rights to imprison their debtors; or that both ought (a possibility to which we shall recur in the next section); or that it is indifferent whether they do. But the last alternative leaves it open to B and C to do what they like in the matter; and we may suppose that, though B himself would like to have this freedom, he will be unwilling to allow it to C. It is as unlikely that he will *permit* C to put him (B) into prison as that he will *prescribe* it. We may say, therefore, that while move (1), described above, constitutes an abandonment of the dispute, moves (2) and (3) really add nothing new to it.

6.7. We must next consider a way of escape which may seem much more respectable than those which I have so far mentioned. Let us suppose that B is a firm believer in the rights of property and the sanctity of contracts. In this case he may say roundly that debtors ought to be imprisoned by their creditors whoever they are, and that, specifically, C ought to imprison him (B), and he (B) ought to imprison A. And he may, unlike the superficially similar person described earlier, be meaning by "ought" just what we usually mean by it—i.e. he may be using the word prescriptively, realizing that in saying that C ought to put him into prison, he is prescribing that C put him in prison. B, in this case, is perfectly ready to go to prison for his principles, in order that the sanctity of contracts may be enforced. In real life, B would be much more likely to take this line if the situation in which he himself played the role of debtor were not actual but only hypothetical; but this, as we saw earlier, ought not to make any difference to the argument.

We are not yet, however, in a position to deal with this escape route. All we can do is to say why we cannot now deal with it, and leave this loose end to be picked up later. B, if he is sincere in holding the principle about the sanctity of contracts (or any other universal moral principle which has the same effect in this particular case), may have two sorts of grounds for it. He may hold it on utilitarian grounds, thinking that, unless contracts are rigorously enforced, the results will be so disastrous as to outweigh any benefits that A, or B himself, may get from being let off. This could, in certain circumstances, be a good argument. But we cannot tell whether it is, until we have generalized the type of moral argument which has been set out in this chapter, to cover cases in which the interests of more than two parties are involved. As we saw, it is only the interests of A and B that come into the argument as so far considered (the interests of the third party, C, do not need separate consideration, since C was introduced only in order to show B, if necessary fictionally, a situation in which the roles were reversed; therefore C's interests, being a mere replica of B's, will vanish, as a separate factor, once the A/B situation, and the moral judgments made on it, are universalized). But if utilitarian grounds of the sort suggested are to be adduced, they will bring with them a reference to all the other people whose interests would be harmed by laxity in the enforcement of contracts. This escape route, therefore, if this is its basis, introduces considerations which cannot be assessed until we have generalized our form of argument to cover "multilateral" moral situations. At present, it can only be said that if B can show that leniency in the enforcement of contracts would really have the results he claims for the community at large, he might be justified in taking the severer course. This will be apparent after we have considered in some detail an example (that of the judge and the criminal) which brings out these considerations even more clearly.

On the other hand, B might have a quite different, nonutilitarian kind of reason for adhering to his principle. He might be moved, not by any weight which he might attach to the interests of other people, but by the thought that to enforce contracts of this sort is necessary in order to conform to some moral or other *ideal* that he has espoused. Such ideals might be of various sorts. He might be moved, for example, by an ideal of abstract justice, of the *fiat justitia, ruat caelum* variety. We have to distinguish such an ideal of justice, which pays no regard to people's interests, from that which is concerned merely to do justice *between* people's interests. It is very important, if considerations of justice are introduced into a moral argument, to know of which sort they are. Justice of the second kind can perhaps be accommodated within a moral view which it is not misleading to call utilitarian. . . . But this is not true of an ideal of the first kind. It is characteristic of this sort of nonutilitarian ideals that, when they are introduced into moral arguments, they render ineffective the appeal to universalized self-interest which is the foundation of the argument that we have been considering. This is because the person who has wholeheartedly espoused such an ideal (we shall call him the "fanatic") does not mind if people's interests—even his own—are harmed in the pursuit of it.

It need not be justice which provides the basis of such an escape route as we are considering. Any moral ideal would do, provided that it were pursued regardless of other people's interests. For example, B might be a believer in the survival of the fittest, and think that, in order to promote this, he (and everyone else) ought to pursue their own interests by all means in their power and regardless of everyone else's interests. This ideal might lead him, in this particular case, to put A in prison, and he might agree that C ought to do the same to him, if he were not clever enough to avoid this fate. He might think that universal obedience to such a principle would maximize the production of supermen and so make the world a better place. If these were his grounds, it is possible that we might argue with him factually, showing that the universal observance of the principle would not have the results he claimed. But we might be defeated in this factual argument if he had an ideal which made him call the world "a better place" when the jungle law prevailed; he could then agree to our factual statements, but still maintain that the condition of the world described by us as resulting from the observance of his principle would be better than its present condition. In this case, the argument might take two courses. If we could get him to imagine himself in the position of the weak, who went to the wall in such a state of the world, we might bring him to realize that to hold his principle involved prescribing that things should be done to him, in hypothetical situations, which he could not sincerely prescribe. If, so, then the argument would be on the rails again, and could proceed on lines which we have already sketched. But he might stick to his principle and say "If I were weak, then I ought to go to the wall." If he did this, he would be putting himself beyond the reach of what we shall call "golden rule" or "utilitarian" arguments by becoming what we shall call a "fanatic." Since a great part of the rest of this book [*Freedom and Reason*] will be concerned with people who take this sort of line, it is unnecessary to pursue their case further at this point.

6.8. The remaining maneuver that B might seek to practice is probably the commonest. It is certainly the one which is most frequently brought up in philosophical controversies on this topic. This consists in a fresh appeal to the facts—i.e. in asserting that there are in fact morally relevant differences between his case and that of others. In the example which we have been considering, we have artificially ruled out this way of escape by assuming that the case of B and C is exactly similar to that of A and B; from this it follows *a fortiori* that there are no morally relevant differences. Since the B/C case may be a hypothetical one, this condition of exact similarity can always be fulfilled, and therefore this maneuver is based on a misconception of the type of argument against which it is directed. Nevertheless it may be useful, since this objection is so commonly raised, to deal with it at this point, although nothing further will be added thereby to what has been said already.

It may be claimed that no two actual cases would ever be exactly similar; there would always be some differences, and B might allege that some of these were morally relevant. He might allege, for example, that, whereas his family would starve if C put him into prison, this would not be the case if he put A into prison, because A's family would be looked after by A's relatives. If such a difference existed, there might be nothing logically disreputable in calling it morally relevant, and such arguments are in fact often put forward and accepted.

The difficulty, however, lies in drawing the line between those arguments of this sort which are legitimate, and those which are not. Suppose that B alleges that the fact that A has a hooked nose or a black skin entitles him, B, to put him in prison, but that C ought not to do the same thing to him, B, because his nose is straight and his skin white. Is this an argument of equal logical respectability? Can I say that the fact that I have a mole in a particular place on my chin entitles me to further my own interests at others' expense, but that they are forbidden to do this by the fact that they lack this mark of natural preeminence?

The answer to this maneuver is implicit in what has been said already about the relevance, in moral arguments, of hypothetical as well as of actual cases. The fact that no two actual cases are ever identical has no bearing on the problem. For all we have to do is to imagine an identical case in which the roles are reversed. Suppose that my mole disappears, and that my neighbor grows one in the very same spot on his chin. Or, to use our other example, what does B say about a hypothetical case in which he has a black skin or a hooked nose, and A and C are both straight nosed and white skinned? Since this is the same argument, in essentials, as we used at the very beginning, it need not be repeated here. B is in fact faced with a dilemma. Either the property of his own case, which he claims to be morally relevant, is a properly universal property (i.e. one describable with out reference to individuals), or it is not. If it is a universal property, then, because of the meaning of the word "universal," it is a property which might be possessed by another case in which he played a different role (though in fact it may not be); and we can therefore ask him to ignore the fact that it is he himself who plays the role which he does in this case. This will force him to count as morally relevant only those properties which he is prepared to allow to be relevant even when other people have them. And this rules out all the attractive kinds of special pleading. On the other hand, if the property in question is not a properly universal one, then he has not met the demand for universalizability, and cannot claim to be putting forward a moral argument at all.

6.9. It is necessary, in order to avoid misunderstanding, to add two notes to the foregoing discussion. The misunderstanding arises through a too literal interpretation of the common forms of expression—which constantly recur in arguments of this type—"How would you like it if . . .?" and "Do as you would be done by." Though I shall later, for convenience, refer to the type of arguments here discussed as "golden rule" arguments, we must not be misled by these forms of expression.

First of all, we shall make the nature of the argument clearer if, when we are asking B to imagine himself in the position of his victim, we phrase our question, never in the form "What *would* you say, or feel, or think, or how *would* you like it, if you were he?" but always in the form "What *do* you say (*in propria persona*) about a hypothetical case in which you are in your victim's position?" The importance of this way of phrasing the question is that, if the question were put in the first way, B might reply "Well, of course, if anybody did this to me I should resent it very much and make all sorts of adverse moral judgments about the act; but this has absolutely no bearing on the validity of the moral opinion which I am *now* expressing." To involve him in contradiction, we have to show that he *now* holds an opinion about the hypothetical case which is inconsistent with his opinion about the actual case.

The second thing which has to be noticed is that the argument, as set out, does not involve any sort of deduction of a moral judgment, or even of the negation of a moral judgment, from a factual statement about people's inclinations, interests, etc. We are not saying to B "You are as a matter of fact averse to this being done to you in a hypothetical case; and from this it follows logically that you ought not to do it to another." Such a deduction would be a breach of Hume's Law ("No 'ought' from an 'is'"), to which I have repeatedly declared my adherence (*Language of Morals* 2.5). The point is, rather, that because of his aversion to its being done to him in the hypothetical case, he cannot accept the singular *prescription* that in the hypothetical case it should be done to him; and this, because of the logic of "ought," precludes him from accepting the moral judgment that he ought to do likewise to another in the actual case. It is not a question of a factual statement about a person's inclinations being inconsistent with a moral judgment; rather, his inclinations being what they are, he cannot assent sincerely to a certain singular prescription, and if he cannot do this, he cannot assent to a certain universal prescription which entails it, when conjoined with factual statements about the circumstances whose truth he admits. Because of this entailment, if he assented to the factual statements and to the universal prescription, but refused (as he must, his inclinations being what they are) to assent to the singular prescription, he would be guilty of a logical inconsistency.

If it be asked what the relation is between his aversion to being put in prison in the hypothetical case, and his inability to accept the hypothetical singular prescription that if he were in such a situation he should be put into prison, it would seem that the relation is not unlike that between a belief that the cat is on the mat, and an inability to accept the proposition that the cat is not on the mat. Further attention to this parallel will perhaps make the position clearer. Suppose that somebody advances the hypothesis that cats never sit on mats, and that we refute him by pointing to a cat on a mat. The logic of our refutation proceeds in two stages. Of these, the second is: "Here is a cat sitting on a mat, so it is not the case that cats never sit on mats." This is a piece of logical deduction! and to it, in the moral case, corresponds the step from "Let this not be done to me" to "It is not the case that I ought to do it to another in similar circumstances." But in both cases there is a first stage whose nature is more obscure, and different in the two cases, though there is an analogy between them.

In the "cat" case, it is logically possible for a man to look straight at the cat on the mat, and yet believe that there is no cat on the mat. But if a person with normal eyesight and no psychological aberrations does this, we say that he does not understand the meaning of the words, "The cat is on the mat." And even if he does not have normal eyesight, or suffers from some psychological aberration (such as phobia of cats, say, that he just *cannot* admit to himself that he is face to face with one), yet, if we can convince him that everyone else can see a cat there, he will have to admit that there *is* a cat there, or be accused of misusing the language.

If, on the other hand, a man says "But I *want* to be put in prison, if ever I am in that situation," we can, indeed, get as far as accusing him of having eccentric desires; but we cannot, when we have proved to him that nobody else has such a desire, face him with the choice of either saying, with the rest, "Let this not be done to me," or else being open to the accusation of not understanding what he is saying. For it is not an incorrect use of words to want eccentric things. Logic does not prevent me wanting to be put in a gas chamber if a Jew. It is perhaps true that I logically cannot want for its own sake an experience which I think of as *unpleasant;* for to say that I think of it as unpleasant may be logically inconsistent with saying that I want it for its own sake. If this is so, it is because "unpleasant" is a prescriptive expression. But "to be put in prison" and "to be put in a gas chamber if a Jew," are not prescriptive expressions; and therefore these things can be wanted without offense to logic. It is, indeed, in the logical possibility of wanting *anything* (neutrally described) that the "freedom" which is alluded to in my title essentially consists. And it is this, as we shall see, that lets by the person whom I shall call the "fanatic."

There is not, then, a complete analogy between the man who says "There is no cat on the mat" when there is, and the man who wants things which others do not. But there is a partial analogy, which, having noticed this difference, we may be able to isolate. The analogy is between two relations: the relations between, in both cases, the "mental state" of these men and what they say. If I believe that there is a cat on the mat I cannot sincerely say that there is not; and, if I want not to be put into prison more than I want anything else, I cannot sincerely say "Let me be put into prison." When, therefore, I said above "His inclinations being what they are, he cannot assent sincerely to a certain singular prescription," I was making an analytic statement (although the "cannot" is not a logical "cannot"); for if he were to assent sincerely to the prescription, that would entail *ex vi terminorum* that his inclinations had changed—in the very same way that it is analytically true that, if the other man were to say sincerely that there was a cat on the mat, when before he had sincerely denied this, he must have changed his belief.

If, however, instead of writing "His inclinations being what they are, he cannot . . . ," we leave out the first clause and write simply "He cannot . . . ," the statement is no longer analytic; we are making a statement about his psychology which might be false. For it is logically possible for inclinations to change; hence it is possible for a man to come sincerely to hold an ideal which requires that he himself should be sent to a gas chamber if a Jew. That is the price we have to pay for our freedom. But, as we shall see, in order for reason to have a place in morals it is not necessary for us to close this way of escape by means of a logical barrier; it is sufficient that, men and the world being what they are, we can be very sure that hardly anybody is going to take it with his eyes open. And when we are arguing with one of the vast majority who are not going to take it, the reply that somebody else *might* take it does not help his case against us. In this respect, all moral arguments are *ad hominem.*[8]

[8]The above discussion may help to atone for what is confused or even wrong in *Language of Morals* 3.3 (p. 42). The remarks there about the possibility or impossibility of accepting certain moral principles gave the impression of creating an impasse; I can, however, plead that in *Language of Morals* 4.4 (p. 69) there appeared a hint of the way out which is developed in this book [*Freedom and Reason*].

1964

G. E. Moore on the Naturalistic Fallacy

Casimir Lewy

G. E. Moore's literary remains contain very little concerning ethics; but they include an unfinished draft (in manuscript) of what was intended to be a preface to the second edition of *Principia Ethica.* For various reasons it seems to me highly probable that this was written in 1920 or 1921; but in the end Moore abandoned the idea of a second edition, and in 1922 *Principia* was reprinted without any alterations, except for the correction of a few misprints and grammatical mistakes and the inclusion of a prefatory note of seven lines.

Owing to the fact that the draft is unfinished and in parts very fragmentary, the task of preparing it for publication would be a very difficult one, though I may possibly attempt it in the future. What I want to do today is first to give a synopsis, or rather a reconstruction, of what seem to me to be the main points of the unpublished preface (which from now on I shall simply call "the Preface"), and secondly to discuss independently one particular aspect of the subject.

Casimir Lewy, "G. E. Moore on the Naturalistic Fallacy," *The Proceedings of the British Academy* Volume L, 1964 *Lectures and Memoirs* (read 11 November 1964). Reprinted with the permission of The British Academy.

1

Moore begins by pointing out that there are several senses of the word "good," and that in *Principia* he was concerned with only one of them. He does not now think, however, that this sense can be called *the* ordinary sense of the word, even if any one sense of it is commoner than any other. But he thinks that the sense in question can be specified by saying that it is *the* sense which has a unique and fundamentally important relation to the conceptions of right and wrong. *What* the relation in question *is,* he proposes, he says, to discuss later; but in fact no such discussion is included in the Preface.

He goes on to ask, however, what are the main things that he wished to say in *Principia* about the concept which is expressed by the word "good," when the word is used in this sense. The first thing he wished to say, he continues, is that Good[1] is simple in the sense of being indefinable or unanalyzable. Is this proposition true?, he asks. He still thinks it is probably true, but he is not certain, for it seems to him that possibly "right" is unanalyzable, and Good is to be analyzed partly in terms of "right." But whether Good is analyzable or not does not seem to him now nearly as important as it did when he wrote *Principia.* If Good *were* unanalyzable, it would follow that it could not be identical with any such property as "is desired" or "is a state of pleasure," since these *are* analyzable; but it would be a great mistake to suppose that, as he implied in *Principia,* the fact that Good is not identical with any such property *rests* on the contention that Good is unanalyzable.

He says that in the passage in *Principia* (§§ 6–14) in which he asserted that Good was unanalyzable, he made another assertion which must not be confused with it, though he did so confuse it, namely, the assertion ". . . good is good, and that is the end of the matter" (*Principia,* p. 6). What, he asks, did he mean by this? Clearly, he meant to assert about Good what Bishop Butler, in the passage which Moore quoted on his title-page, asserted to be true of everything, namely, that it is what it is, and not another thing. In other words, he meant to assert that Good is Good, and nothing else whatever.

But this, Moore now says, may mean *either* "Good is different from everything other than Good" *or* "Good is different from everything which we express by any word or phrase other than the word 'good.' " The first is wholly trivial and unimportant; and that Good is unanalyzable cannot possibly follow from it, since the property of being different from every property that is different from it, is a property which must belong to every property without exception, analyzable and unanalyzable alike. And for the same reason it cannot possibly follow from it that certain particular properties such as "is a state of pleasure" or "is desired" are different from Good. For even if Good were identical with, say, "is desired," Good would still be different from every property which was different from it.

The second assertion, however—that Good is different from everything which we express by any word or phrase other than the word "good"—is far from being trivial. If it were true, it would really follow that Good was different from any such property as "is a state of pleasure" or "is desired." And also, if it were true, it would afford at least a strong presumption that Good was unanalyzable. For "where a word expresses an *analyzable* property, that property is generally also sometimes expressed by a phrase, made up of several words, which point out elements which enter into its analysis, and, in that sense, 'contain an analysis' of it." So that if Good were analyzable, it would

[1] As Moore himself does in the Preface, I shall write *Good,* with a capital *G* but without quotes, when I talk about the concept, and not the word. But (again like Moore) I shall not adopt this device in connection with other concepts.

probably be sometimes expressed by some such complex phrase—a phrase, therefore, different from the mere word "good." Indeed Moore thinks that this fact probably partly explains how he was led to identify such obviously different propositions as "Good is Good, and nothing else whatever" and "Good is unanalyzable." For we have just seen that if the former proposition be understood as asserting that Good is different from any property expressed by any phrase other than the word "good," this proposition, if true, would at least afford a strong presumption that Good was unanalyzable. And he may have supposed—he continues—that, conversely, from the fact that Good was unanalyzable, it would follow that it could not be expressed by any phrase other than "good." He may have supposed so owing to his perceiving that if Good were unanalyzable, it could not be expressed by any phrase which *contained an analysis* of it, but failing to perceive the distinction between expressing the meaning of a word in other words which *contain an analysis* of it, and expressing its meaning by giving a synonym.

But the fact that there is this distinction is fatal to the truth of the proposition we are now considering. It may be true that Good is unanalyzable, and therefore cannot be expressed by other words which contain an analysis of it: but it is certainly not true that it cannot be expressed by any other words at all. For instance (quite apart from the obvious fact that there are languages other than English), the word "desirable" is sometimes used as a synonym for "good."

Moore therefore concludes that the assertion "Good is Good, and nothing else whatever" is either merely trivial or else obviously false.

But this is not the end of the matter. For Moore also thinks that the examples which he gave in *Principia* do suggest to most people's minds that what he really meant to assert was that Good was not identical with any property belonging to a *particular class;* and *this* assertion still seems to him both true and important. But what is the class in question? Moore says in effect that he can only describe this class by saying that it is the class of all those properties which are either natural or metaphysical; and what he really wanted to assert, he says, was that Good was not identical with any natural or metaphysical property.

He admits that in *Principia* he confused natural objects (or events) with a certain kind of property which may belong to them. He actually confused a particular event, which consists in somebody's being pleased, with the property which we ascribe to it when we say that it is "a state of pleasure"—just as he confused a particular patch of yellow with the property of being yellow. And he also admits that he confused *parts* of natural objects with *properties* of such objects.

For these and other reasons his attempts to define a "natural property" were, he says, hopelessly confused. The nearest he came to suggesting a correct definition in *Principia* was on p. 40, where he said that to identify Good with any natural property resulted in replacing ethics by one of the natural sciences (including psychology). This now suggests to him the following definitions. A "natural" property is a property with which it is the business of the natural sciences or of psychology to deal, or which can be completely defined in terms of such. A "metaphysical" property is a property which stands to some supersensible object in the same relation in which natural properties stand to natural objects.

Moore now points out that the proposition that Good is not identical with any natural or metaphysical property (as now defined)—which is what he really wished to assert in *Principia*—neither implies nor is implied by the proposition that Good is unanalyzable. For it might plainly be true, even if Good *were* analyzable; and, on the other hand, even if Good were *un*analyzable, Good might still be identical with some natural property, since many such properties may be unanalyzable. At the same time, he says, if Good is not identical with any natural or metaphysical property, it does follow that, if it is analyzable at all, it involves in its analysis *some* unanalyzable notion which is not natural or metaphysical. That some unanalyzable notion of this sort, he says, is involved in ethics was certainly a part of what he wished to assert when he asserted that Good was unanalyzable. Only he did not see that this was a far more important and less doubtful assertion than that Good itself was the unanalyzable notion in question.

Of course Moore realizes that his new definitions—and it would perhaps be better to call them "explanations" rather than "definitions"—are still not fully satisfactory. It is clear that he intended to return to the topic in a later part of the Preface; but he never in fact came to write it.

There are, however, still some pages of the Preface which are of considerable interest, and of special relevance to our subject. It will have been noticed that so far the expression "the naturalistic fallacy" has not been introduced, although it is obvious that what Moore meant by it is very closely connected with the propositions we have been considering. But he now explicitly raises the question: What *is* "the naturalistic fallacy"? And he says that the most important mistake which he made in his discussion of the matter in *Principia* was exactly analogous to the chief of those which he made in his assertions about Good. In the latter case, as we have seen, he confused the three entirely different propositions "Good is not identical with any property other than itself"; "Good is not identical with any analyzable property"; and "Good is not identical with any natural or metaphysical property." In the case of the naturalistic fallacy, he goes on, he similarly confused the three entirely different propositions (1) "So-and-so is identifying Good with some property other than Good;" (2) "So-and-so is identifying Good with some *analyzable* property;" and (3) "So-and-so is identifying Good with some *natural or metaphysical* property."

He points out that he sometimes implies that to say of a man that he is committing the naturalistic fallacy is to say (1) of him; sometimes that it is to say (2) of him; and sometimes that it is to say (3) of him.

But in addition to this, his main mistake, he also made, he says, two further mistakes. First, he sometimes talked (*Principia,* p. 14) as if to commit the naturalistic fallacy was to suppose that in, for example, "This is good," the word "is" always expresses identity between the thing called "this" and Good. And secondly, he confused (A) "To say that so-and-so is committing the naturalistic fallacy is to say that he is holding, with respect to some property of a certain kind, the *view* that that property is identical with Good," and (B) "To say that so-and-so is committing the naturalistic fallacy is to say that he is *confusing* some property of a certain kind with Good." But the operation mentioned in (A) is quite different from that mentioned in (B).

Finally, Moore admits that he feels doubtful whether either of these two operations could properly be called the commission of a fallacy, for the simple reason that to commit a fallacy seems properly to mean to make a certain kind of *inference;* whereas the mere confusion of two properties, or the holding of a view with regard to them, seems not to be a process of inference at all.

Moore ends this part of the Preface by saying that if he still wished to use the term "naturalistic fallacy," he would define it as follows: "So-and-so is committing the naturalistic fallacy" means "He is *either* confusing Good with a natural or metaphysical property *or* holding it to be identical with such a property *or* making an inference *based* upon such a confusion." And he would also expressly point out that in so using the term "fallacy" he was using it in an extended, and perhaps improper, sense.

This concludes my synopsis, or reconstruction, of the Preface, or rather of that part of it which it is possible to reconstruct, for the rest is in a very incomplete state indeed. And it will, I think, have been seen that many of the criticisms made of Moore's treatment of the naturalistic fallacy and related topics in the 1930's and 1940's were fully anticipated by him many years earlier.

2

I now wish to discuss independently one particular aspect of the subject. In the Preface, it will be recalled, Moore says that he still believes it to be true and important to assert that Good is not identical with any natural or metaphysical property. But he neither produces any new arguments for this assertion nor makes any comments on the arguments which he gave in *Principia.* I wish now to examine in some detail two passages in the book which contain such arguments. The first occurs in § 13 (pp. 15–16), and runs as follows:

> The hypothesis that disagreement about the meaning of good is disagreement with regard to the correct analysis of a given whole, may be most plainly seen to be incorrect by consideration of the fact that, whatever definition be offered, it may be always asked, with significance, of the complex so defined, whether it is itself good. To take, for instance, one of the more plausible, because one of the more complicated of such proposed definitions, it may easily be thought, at first sight, that to be good may mean to be that which we desire to desire. Thus if we apply this definition to a particular instance and say "When we think that A is good, we are thinking that A is one of the things which we desire to desire," our proposition may seem quite plausible. But, if we carry the investigation further, and ask ourselves "Is it good to desire to desire A?" it is apparent, on a little reflection, that this question is itself as intelligible, as the original question "Is A good?"—that we are, in fact, now asking for exactly the same information about the desire to desire A, for which we formerly asked with regard to A itself. But it is also apparent that the meaning of this second question cannot be correctly analyzed into "Is the desire to desire A one of the things which we desire to desire?": we have not before our minds anything so complicated as the question "Do we desire to desire to desire to desire A?" Moreover anyone can easily convince himself by inspection that the predicate of this proposition—"good"—is positively different from the notion of "desiring to desire" which enters into its subject: "That we should desire to desire A is good" is *not* merely equivalent to "That A should be good is good." It may indeed be true that what we desire to desire is always also good; perhaps, even the converse may be true: but it is very doubtful whether this is the case, and the mere fact that we understand very well what is meant by doubting it, shows clearly that we have two different notions before our minds.

The second passage occurs a little later (p. 38). Moore there says that he will discuss certain theories which claim that only a single kind of thing is good. He thinks that such theories rest on the naturalistic fallacy, and goes on as follows:

> That a thing should be good, it has been thought, *means* that it possesses this single property: and hence (it is thought) only what possesses this property is good. The inference seems very natural; and yet what is meant by it is self-contradictory. For those who make it fail to perceive that their conclusion "what possesses this property is good" is a significant proposition: that it does not mean either "what possesses this property, possesses this property" or "the word 'good' denotes that a thing possesses this property." And yet, if it does *not* mean one or other of these two things, the inference contradicts its own premise.

It will have been noticed that Moore speaks in these passages as if he were showing that Good is not analyzable at all; but what I chiefly wish to discuss is the question whether he has shown that Good is not identical with the property of being one of the things which we desire to desire—that is, with the property which he takes as an example in the first passage. Moreover, I cannot hope to say here all that ought to be said about these passages. In particular, I cannot consider all the different arguments which they contain and which are not clearly distinguished from each other. All I can do is to try to reformulate and discuss what seems to me to be the chief of these arguments.

I think I can do this most clearly with the help of an analogy. Let us suppose that we are concerned, not with Good, but with the concept of being a brother. Suppose that someone asserts that to be a brother is to be a male sibling—or, to use the terminology that Moore himself often used in later life—that the concept of being a brother is identical with the concept of being a male sibling. Now what follows from this proposition? So far as I can see, one thing which certainly follows from it is that the proposition "John is a brother" is identical with the proposition "John is a male sibling." Similarly, in Moore's case, if to be good is to be one of the things which we desire to desire, it follows that any proposition of the form "*x* is good" is identical with the corresponding proposition of the form "*x* is one of the things which we desire to desire." It follows, for instance, that the proposition "A is good" (and we must now assume that "A" is a name or description of a thing or state of things) is identical with the proposition "A is one of the things which we desire to desire."

Consequently, Moore could have argued against the identification of Good with the property of being one of the things which we desire to desire, by pointing out that even if at first it may seem plausible to suppose that these two propositions are identical, yet further reflection makes it apparent that they are *not* identical.

But this is not what he does. He obviously thought that he had a more complicated but more convincing argument. For what he asks us to consider are not the two propositions I have just mentioned, but the completely different propositions "It is good to desire to desire A" and "The desire to desire A is one of the things which we desire to desire." And he says that it is apparent on reflection that *these* propositions are not identical.

Let me put the matter in terms of questions rather than propositions. Moore could have argued that the question (1) "Is A good?" is quite different from the question (2) "Is A one of the things which we desire to desire?" Yet if to be good is to be one of the things which we desire to desire, these questions are identical. But what he in fact says is that the question (3) "Is it good to desire to desire A?" is quite different from the question (4) "Is the desire to desire A one of the things which we desire to desire?"

But though the latter questions are more complicated than the former, they are no better. For on the view he is discussing, just as (1) and (2) are identical, so are (3) and (4). And it is no plainer that (3) and (4) are *not* identical than it is that (1) and (2) are not identical. Similarly, on the view in question, the proposition (3A) "It is good that we desire to desire A" *is* identical with the proposition (3B) "It is good that A is good" (and each of them is identical with the proposition "We desire to desire to desire to desire A"). And again, it is no plainer that (3A) and (3B) are *not* identical than it is that "A is good" and "A is one of the things which we desire to desire" are not identical.

Did Moore, then, have at the back of his mind some other questions, even more complicated? I think that the second passage which I have quoted makes it fairly clear that he did, and that they were (5) "Is A, which is one of the things which we desire to desire, good?," and (6) "Is A, which is one of the things which we desire to desire, one of the things which we desire to desire?" And I think that he confused (5) with (3), and (6) with (4).

Unfortunately, each of these last two questions—(5) and (6)—is capable of at least two totally different interpretations. Question (5) may mean *either* "Is it the case that A is good if and only if it is one of the things which we desire to desire?"—where the expression "if and only if" is used truth-functionally;[2] *or* "Is it the case that to say that A is good is the same thing as to say that A is one of the things which we desire to desire?" More generally, the question of which (5) is merely a particular example may mean *either* "Is it the case that a thing is good if and only if it is one of the things which we desire to desire?" (where the expression "if and only if" is used truth-functionally); *or* "Is it the case that to be good is to be one of the things which we desire to desire?" An affirmative answer to the *first* question would be given by the proposition "It *is* the case that a thing is good if and only if it is one of the things which we desire to desire," which is logically equivalent to the proposition (α) "A thing is good if and only if it is one of the things which we desire to desire." An affirmative answer to the *second* question would be given by the proposition "It *is* the case that to be good is to be one of the things which we desire to desire," which is logically equivalent to the proposition (β) "To be good is to be one of the things which we desire to desire."

Similarly, the question of which (6) is merely a particular example may mean *either* "Is it the case that a thing is one of the things which we desire to desire if and only if it is one of the things which we desire to desire?" (where "if and only if" is used truth-functionally); *or* "Is it the case that to be one of the things which we desire to desire is to be one of the things which we desire to desire?" An affirmative answer to the *first* question would be given by the proposition "It *is* the case that a thing is one of the things which we desire to desire if and only if it is one of the things which we desire to desire," which is logically equivalent to (γ) "A thing is one of the things which we desire to desire if and only if it is one of the things which we desire to desire." On the other hand, an affirmative answer to the *second* question would be given by the proposition "It *is* the case that to be one of the things which we desire to desire is to be one of the things which we desire to desire," which is logically equivalent to the proposition (δ) "To be one of the things which we desire to desire is to be one of the things which we desire to desire."

For the sake of simplicity, I will now again speak in terms of propositions rather than questions. The main point I now wish to make is that there is a fundamental difference between (α) and (γ) on the one hand, and (β) and (δ) on the other. For the truth-value (that is, the truth or falsity) of (α) would not be altered if we substituted for any expression which occurs in the sentence which I have used to express (α), another expression with the same extension (that is, another expression which applies to exactly the same things); and the same is true of (γ). But this is not true either of (β) or of (δ). In current logical terminology, whilst the sentences which I have used to express (α) and (γ) are *extensional*, those I have used to express (β) and (δ) are *not* extensional.

It is clear that at the time Moore wrote *Principia* (1903), he did not see this distinction; and he therefore failed to distinguish (α) from (β), and (γ) from (δ). But (α) *is* quite different from (β), and (γ) *is* quite different from (δ). Consequently, we get two different interpretations of Moore's argument.

First, we can interpret him as arguing that to be good is not the same as to be one of the things which we desire to desire, because, if it were, then (β) would be identical with (δ); and maintaining, further, that it is apparent on reflection that (β) is *not* identi-

[2]That is to say, in such a way that the question can also be expressed by asking "Are the two propositions 'A is good' and 'A is one of the things which we desire to desire' either *both* true or *both* false?"

cal with (δ). If interpreted in this way, the argument seems to me to be completely invalid. For in the same kind of way it would be possible to show with regard to any concept whatever that it is unanalyzable—in other words, that it is simple. For instance, we could show that to be a brother is not the same thing as to be a male sibling, because, if it were, then the proposition "To be a brother is to be a male sibling" would be identical with the proposition "To be a male sibling is to be a male sibling." Yet it is clear on reflection that these propositions are *not* identical.

In other words, Moore's argument, in this interpretation, would be a particular instance of what he himself later in life called the "Paradox of Analysis." He was never fully satisfied with any solution of it, and said different things about it at different times. But I have no doubt at all, on the basis of a large number of discussions which I have had with him on the subject over a period of many years, that his considered view was that whatever may be the *complete* solution, it was essential to hold that (in the example I have just given) to be a brother *is* to be a male sibling, and that yet the proposition "To be a brother is to be a male sibling" is *not* identical with the proposition "To be a male sibling is to be a male sibling." And he therefore held that from "To be a brother is to be a male sibling," the identity of these propositions does *not* follow. I think that this is right; and if so, then his *Principia* argument, in the interpretation I am now considering, is clearly invalid.

We must now, however, discuss my second interpretation. Here we should interpret Moore as arguing that to be good is not the same as to be one of the things which we desire to desire, because, if it were, then (a) would be identical with (γ); and maintaining, further, that it is apparent on reflection that (a) is *not* identical with (γ). Now *this* argument seems to me to be perfectly valid. For, although I once succeeded in so confusing myself as to deny it, I now think it undeniable that *if* to be good is to be one of the things which we desire to desire, then (a) *is* identical with (γ). Yet it is absolutely clear that (a) is *not* identical with (γ). And that (a) is not identical with (γ) follows from something which is also absolutely clear, namely, that it is logically possible to doubt (a) *without* doubting (γ); and each of these things follows from something which is also absolutely clear, namely, that whilst (γ) is a necessary proposition, (a) is a contingent proposition.

Moreover, it is *not* possible to use this kind of argument to show with regard to any concept whatever, that it is unanalyzable. Indeed, if to be a brother is to be a male sibling, then the proposition "A creature is a brother if and only if it is a male sibling" is identical with the proposition "A creature is a male sibling if and only if it is a male sibling" (where in both sentences "if and only if" is used truth-functionally). But *these* propositions *are* identical.

Of course, Moore's argument, in the present interpretation, may be said to be "begging the question." For a person who holds that to be good is to be one of the things which we desire to desire, may admit that if this is so, then (a) is identical with (γ); and he may then go on to assert that (a) *is* identical with (γ). This is true: but I think we can all see that a person who asserted *this*, would be mistaken.

It seems to me obvious that any theory which identifies Good with a concept which is not itself at least partly ethical, can be refuted in an analogous way. I think therefore that for all his mistakes, Moore can fairly be said to have found a means of refuting any such theory.

1964

How to Derive "Ought" from "Is"

John Searle

1

It is often said that one cannot derive an "ought" from an "is." This thesis, which comes from a famous passage in Hume's *Treatise,* while not as clear as it might be, is at least clear in broad outline: there is a class of statements of fact which is logically distinct from a class of statements of value. No set of statements of fact by themselves entails any statement of value. Put in more contemporary terminology, no set of *descriptive* statements can entail an *evaluative* statement without the addition of at least one evaluative premise. To believe otherwise is to commit what has been called the naturalistic fallacy.

I shall attempt to demonstrate a counterexample to this thesis.[1] It is not of course to be supposed that a single counterexample can refute a philosophical thesis, but in the present instance if we can present a plausible counterexample and can in addition give some account or explanation of how and why it is a counterexample, and if we can further offer a theory to back up our counterexample—a theory which will generate an indefinite number of counterexamples—we may at the very least cast considerable light on the original thesis; and possibly, if we can do all these things, we may even incline

Earlier versions of this paper were read before the Stanford Philosophy Colloqium and the Pacific Division of the American Philosophical Association. I am indebted to many people for helpful comments and criticisms, especially Hans Herzberger, Arnold Kaufmann, Benson Mates, A. I. Melden, and Dagmar Searle.

[1]In its modern version. I shall not be concerned with Hume's treatment of the problem.

ourselves to the view that the scope of that thesis was more restricted than we had originally supposed. A counterexample must proceed by taking a statement or statements which any proponent of the thesis would grant were purely factual or "descriptive" (they need not actually contain the word "is") and show how they are logically related to a statement which a proponent of the thesis would regard as clearly "evaluative." (In the present instance it will contain an "ought.")[2]

Consider the following series of statements:

1. Jones uttered the words "I hereby promise to pay you, Smith, five dollars."
2. Jones promised to pay Smith five dollars.
3. Jones placed himself under (undertook) an obligation to pay Smith five dollars.
4. Jones is under an obligation to pay Smith five dollars.
5. Jones ought to pay Smith five dollars.

I shall argue concerning this list that the relation between any statement and its successor, while not in every case one of "entailment," is nonetheless not just a contingent relation; and the additional statements necessary to make the relationship one of entailment do not need to involve any evaluative statements, moral principles, or anything of the sort.

Let us begin. How is (1) related to (2)? In certain circumstances, uttering the words in quotation marks in (1) is the act of making a promise. And it is a part of or a consequence of the meaning of the words in (1) that in those circumstances uttering them is promising. "I hereby promise" is a paradigm device in English for performing the act described in (2), promising.

Let us state this fact about English usage in the form of an extra premise:

(1a) Under certain conditions *C* anyone who utters the words (sentence) "I hereby promise to pay you, Smith, five dollars" promises to pay Smith five dollars.

What sorts of things are involved under the rubric "conditions *C*"? What is involved will be all those conditions, those states of affairs, which are necessary and sufficient conditions for the utterance of the words (sentence) to constitute the successful performance of the act of promising. The conditions will include such things as that the speaker is in the presence of the hearer Smith, they are both conscious, both speakers of English, speaking seriously. The speaker knows what he is doing, is not under the influence of drugs, not hypnotized or acting in a play, not telling a joke or reporting an event, and so forth. This list will no doubt be somewhat indefinite because the boundaries of the concept of a promise, like the boundaries of most concepts in a natural language, are a bit loose.[3] But one thing is clear; however loose the boundaries may be, and however difficult it may be to decide marginal cases, the conditions under which a man who utters "I hereby promise" can correctly be said to have made a promise are straightforwardly empirical conditions.

So let us add as an extra premise the empirical assumption that these conditions obtain.

[2]If this enterprise succeeds, we shall have bridged the gap between "evaluative" and "descriptive" and consequently have demonstrated a weakness in this very terminology. At present, however, my strategy is to play along with the terminology, pretending that the notions of evaluative and descriptive are fairly clear. At the end of the paper I shall state in what respects I think they embody a muddle.

[3]In addition the concept of a promise is a member of a class of concepts which suffer from looseness of a peculiar kind, viz. defeasibility. Cf. H. L. A. Hart, "The Ascription of Responsibility and Rights," *Logic and Language*, First Series, ed. by A. Flew (Oxford, 1951).

1b. Conditions C obtain.

From (1), (1a), and (1b) we derive (2). The argument is of the form: If *C* then (if *U* then *P*): *C* for conditions, *U* for utterance, *P* for promise. Adding the premises *U* and *C* to this hypothetical we derive (2). And as far as I can see, no moral premises are lurking in the logical woodpile. More needs to be said about the relation of (1) to (2), but I reserve that for later.

What is the relation between (2) and (3)? I take it that promising is, by definition, an act of placing oneself under an obligation. No analysis of the concept of promising will be complete which does not include the feature of the promiser placing himself under or undertaking or accepting or recognizing an obligation to the promisee, to perform some future course of action, normally for the benefit of the promisee. One may be tempted to think that promising can be analyzed in terms of creating expectations in one's hearers, or some such, but a little reflection will show that the crucial distinction between statements of intention on the one hand and promises on the other lies in the nature and degree of commitment or obligation undertaken in promising.

I am therefore inclined to say that (2) entails (3) straight off, but I can have no objection if anyone wishes to add—for the purpose of formal neatness—the tautological premise:

2a. All promises are acts of placing oneself under (undertaking) an obligation to do the thing promised.

How is (3) related to (4)? If one has placed oneself under an obligation, then, other things being equal, one is under an obligation. That I take it also is a tautology. Of course it is possible for all sorts of things to happen which will release one from obligations one has undertaken and hence the need for the *ceteris paribus* rider. To get an entailment between (3) and (4) we therefore need a qualifying statement to the effect that:

3a. Other things are equal.

Formalists, as in the move from (2) to (3), may wish to add the tautological premise:

3b. All those who place themselves under an obligation are, other things being equal, under an obligation.

The move from (3) to (4) is thus of the same form as the move from (1) to (2): If *E* then (if *PUO* then *UO*): *E* for other things are equal, *PUO* for place under obligation and *UO* for under obligation. Adding the two premises *E* and *PUO* we derive *UO*.

Is (3a), the *ceteris paribus* clause, a concealed evaluative premise? It certainly looks as if it might be, especially in the formulation I have given it, but I think we can show that, though questions about whether other things are equal frequently involve evaluative considerations, it is not logically necessary that they should in every case. I shall postpone discussion of this until after the next step.

What is the relation between (4) and (5)? Analogous to the tautology which explicates the relation of (3) and (4) there is here the tautology that, other things being equal, one ought to do what one is under an obligation to do. And here, just as in the previous case, we need some premise of the form:

4a. Other things are equal.

We need the *ceteris paribus* clause to eliminate the possibility that something extraneous to the relation of "obligation" to "ought" might interfere.[4] Here, as in the previous two steps, we eliminate the appearance of enthymeme by pointing out that the apparently suppressed premise is tautological and hence, though formally neat, it is redundant. If, however, we wish to state it formally, this argument is of the same form as the move from (3) to (4): If *E* then (if *UO* then *O*); *E* for other things are equal, *UO* for under obligation, *O* for ought. Adding the premises *E* and *UO* we derive *O*.

Now a word about the phrase "other things being equal" and how it functions in my attempted derivation. This topic and the closely related topic of defeasibility are extremely difficult and I shall not try to do more than justify my claim that the satisfaction of the condition does not necessarily involve anything evaluative. The force of the expression "other things being equal" in the present instance is roughly this. Unless we have some reason (that is, unless we are actually prepared to give some reason) for supposing the obligation is void (step 4) or the agent ought not to keep the promise (step 5), then the obligation holds and he ought to keep the promise. It is not part of the force of the phrase "other things being equal" that in order to satisfy it we need to establish a universal negative proposition to the effect that no reason could ever be given by anyone for supposing the agent is not under an obligation or ought not to keep the promise. That would be impossible and would render the phrase useless. It is sufficient to satisfy the condition that no reason to the contrary can in fact be given.

If a reason is given for supposing the obligation is void or that the promiser ought not to keep a promise, then characteristically a situation calling for an evaluation arises. Suppose, for example, we consider a promised act wrong, but we grant that the promiser did undertake an obligation. Ought he to keep the promise? There is no established procedure for objectively deciding such cases in advance, and an evaluation (if that is really the right word) is in order. But unless we have some reason to the contrary, the *ceteris paribus* condition is satisfied, no evaluation is necessary, and the question whether he ought to do it is settled by saying "he promised." It is always an open possibility that we may have to make an evaluation in order to derive "he ought" from "he promised," for we may have to evaluate a counterargument. But an evaluation is not logically necessary in every case, for there may as a matter of fact be no counterarguments. I am therefore inclined to think that there is nothing necessarily evaluative about the *ceteris paribus* condition, even though deciding whether it is satisfied will frequently involve evaluations.

But suppose I am wrong about this: would that salvage the belief in an unbridgeable logical gulf between "is" and "ought"? I think not, for we can always rewrite my steps (4) and (5) so that they include the *ceteris paribus* clause as part of the conclusion. Thus from our premises we would then have derived "Other things being equal Jones ought to pay Smith five dollars," and that would still be sufficient to refute the tradition, for we would still have shown a relation of entailment between descriptive and evaluative statements. It was not the fact that extenuating circumstances can void obligations that drove philosophers to the naturalistic fallacy; it was rather a theory of language, as we shall see later on.

We have thus derived (in as strict a sense of "derive" as natural languages will admit of) an "ought" from an "is." And the extra premises which were needed to make the

[4]The *ceteris paribus* clause in this step excludes somewhat different sorts of cases from those excluded in the previous step. In general we say, "He undertook an obligation, but nonetheless he is not (now) under an obligation" when the obligation has been *removed*, e.g., if the promisee says, "I release you from your obligation." But we say, "He is under an obligation, but nonetheless ought not to fulfill it" in cases where the obligation is *overridden* by some other considerations, e.g., a prior obligation.

derivation work were in no cause moral or evaluative in nature. They consisted of empirical assumptions, tautologies, and descriptions of word usage. It must be pointed out also that the "ought" is a "categorical" not a "hypothetical" ought. (5) does not say that Jones ought to pay up if he wants such and such. It says he ought to pay up, period. Note also that the steps of the derivation are carried on in the third person. We are not concluding "I ought" from "I said 'I promise,'" but "he ought" from "he said 'I promise.'"

The proof unfolds the connection between the utterance of certain words and the speech act of promising and then in turn unfolds promising into obligation and moves from obligation to "ought." The step from (1) to (2) is radically different from the others and requires special comment. In (1) we construe "I hereby promise . . ." as an English phrase having a certain meaning. It is a consequence of that meaning that the utterance of that phrase under certain conditions is the act of promising. Thus by presenting the quoted expressions in (1) and by describing their use in (1a) we have as it were already invoked the institution of promising. We might have started with an even more ground-floor premise than (1) by saying:

1b. **ʒones uttered the phonetic sequence: /ai + hirbai + pramis + təpei + yu + smiθ + faiv + dalərz/**

We would then have needed extra empirical premises stating that this phonetic sequence was associated in certain ways with certain meaningful units relative to certain dialects.

The moves from (2) to (5) are relatively easy. We rely on definitional connections between "promise," "obligate," and "ought," and the only problem which arises is that obligations can be overridden or removed in a variety of ways and we need to take account of that fact. We solve our difficulty by adding further premises to the effect that there are no contrary considerations, that other things are equal.

2

In this section I intend to discuss three possible objections to the derivation.

First Objection

Since the first premise is descriptive and the conclusion evaluative, there must be a concealed evaluative premise in the description of the conditions in (1b).

So far, this argument merely begs the question by assuming the logical gulf between descriptive and evaluative which the derivation is designed to challenge. To make the objection stick, the defender of the distinction would have to show how exactly (1b) must contain an evaluative premise and what sort of premise it might be. Uttering certain words in certain conditions just *is* promising and the description of these conditions needs no evaluative element. The essential thing is that in the transition from (1) to (2) we move from the specification of a certain utterance of words to the specification of a certain speech act. The move is achieved because the speech act is a conventional act; and the utterance of the words, according to the conventions, constitutes the performance of just that speech act.

A variant of this first objection is to say: all you have shown is that "promise" is an evaluative, not a descriptive, concept. But this objection again begs the question and in the end will prove disastrous to the original distinction between descriptive and evaluative. For that a man uttered certain words and that these words have the meaning they do are surely objective facts. And if the statement of these two objective facts plus a description of the conditions of the utterance is sufficient to entail the statement (2) which the objector alleges to be an evaluative statement (Jones promised to pay Smith five dollars), then an evaluative conclusion is derived from descriptive premises without even going through steps (3), (4), and (5).

Second Objection

Ultimately the derivation rests on the principle that one ought to keep one's promises and that is a moral principle, hence evaluative.

I don't know whether "one ought to keep one's promises" is a "moral" principle, but whether or not it is, it is also tautological; for it is nothing more than a derivation from the two tautologies:

All promises are (create, are undertakings of, are acceptances of) obligations,

and

One ought to keep (fulfil) one's obligations.

What needs to be explained is why so many philosophers have failed to see the tautological character of this principle. Three things I think have concealed its character from them.

The first is a failure to distinguish external questions about the institution of promising from internal questions asked within the framework of the institution. The questions "Why do we have such an institution as promising?" and "Ought we to have such institutionalized forms of obligation as promising?" are external questions asked about and not within the institution of promising. And the question "Ought one to keep one's promises?" can be confused with or can be taken as (and I think has often been taken as) an external question roughly expressible as "Ought one to accept the institution of promising?" But taken literally, as an internal question, as a question about promises and not about the institution of promising, the question "Ought one to keep one's promises?" is as empty as the question "Are triangles three-sided?" To recognize something as a promise is to grant that, other things being equal, it ought to be kept.

A second fact which has clouded the issue is this. There are many situations, both real and imaginable, where one ought not to keep a promise, where the obligation to keep a promise is overridden by some further considerations, and it was for this reason that we needed those clumsy *ceteris paribus* clauses in our derivation. But the fact that obligations can be overridden does not show that there were no obligations in the first place. On the contrary. And these original obligations are all that is needed to make the proof work.

Yet a third factor is the following. Many philosophers still fail to realize the full force of saying that "I hereby promise" is a performative expression. In uttering it one performs but does not describe the act of promising. Once promising is seen as a speech act of a kind different from describing, then it is easier to see that one of the features of the act is the undertaking of an obligation. But if one thinks the utterance of "I promise" or "I hereby promise" is a peculiar kind of description—for example, of one's mental state—then the relation between promising and obligation is going to seem very mysterious.

Third Objection

The derivation uses only a factual or inverted-commas sense of the evaluative terms employed. For example, an anthropologist observing the behavior and attitudes of the

Anglo-Saxons might well go through these derivations, but nothing evaluative would be included. Thus step (2) is equivalent to "He did what they call promising" and step (5) to "According to them he ought to pay Smith five dollars." But since all of the steps (2) to (5) are in *oratio obliqua* and hence disguised statements of fact, the fact-value distinction remains unaffected.

This objection fails to damage the derivation, for what it says is only that the steps *can* be reconstructed as in *oratio obliqua,* that we can construe them as a series of external statements, that we can construct a parallel (or at any rate related) proof about reported speech. But what I am arguing is that, taken quite literally, without any *oratio obliqua* additions or interpretations, the derivation is valid. That one can construct a similar argument which would fail to refute the fact-value distinction does not show that this proof fails to refute it. Indeed it is irrelevant.

3

So far I have presented a counterexample to the thesis that one cannot derive an "ought" from an "is" and considered three possible objections to it. Even supposing what I have said so far is true, still one feels a certain uneasiness. One feels there must be some trick involved somewhere. We might state our uneasiness thus: How can my granting a mere fact about a man, such as the fact that he uttered certain words or that he made a promise, commit *me* to the view that *he* ought to do something? I now want briefly to discuss what broader philosophic significance my attempted derivation may have, in such a way as to give us the outlines of an answer to this question.

I shall begin by discussing the grounds for supposing that it cannot be answered at all.

The inclination to accept a rigid distinction between "is" and "ought," between descriptive and evaluative, rests on a certain picture of the way words relate to the world. It is a very attractive picture, so attractive (to me at least) that it is not entirely clear to what extent the mere presentation of counterexamples can challenge it. What is needed is an explanation of how and why this classical empiricist picture fails to deal with such counterexamples. Briefly, the picture is constructed something like this: first we present examples of so-called descriptive statements ("my car goes eighty miles an hour," "Jones is six feet tall," "Smith has brown hair"), and we contrast them with so-called evaluative statements ("my car is a good car," "Jones ought to pay Smith five dollars," "Smith is a nasty man"). Anyone can see that they are different. We articulate the difference by pointing out that for the descriptive statements the question of truth or falsity is objectively decidable, because to know the meaning of the descriptive expressions is to know under what objectively ascertainable conditions the statements which contain them are true or false. But in the case of evaluative statements the situation is quite different. To know the meaning of the evaluative expressions is not by itself sufficient for knowing under what conditions the statements containing them are true or false, because the meaning of the expressions is such that the statements are not capable of objective or factual truth or falsity at all. Any justification a speaker can give of one of his evaluative statements essentially involves some appeal to attitudes he holds, to criteria of assessment he has adopted, or to moral principles by which he has chosen to live and judge other people. Descriptive statements are thus objective, evaluative statements subjective, and the difference is a consequence of the different sorts of terms employed.

The underlying reason for these differences is that evaluative statements perform a completely different job from descriptive statements. Their job is not to describe any features of the world but to express the speaker's emotions, to express his attitudes, to praise or condemn, to laud or insult, to commend, to recommend, to advise, and so forth. Once we see the different jobs the two perform, we see that there must be a logical gulf between them. Evaluative statements must be different from descriptive statements in order to do their job, for if they were objective they could no longer function to evaluate. Put metaphysically, values cannot lie in the world, for if they did they would cease to be values and would just be another part of the world. Put in the formal mode, one cannot define an evaluative word in terms of descriptive words, for if one did, one would no longer be able to use the evaluative word to commend, but only to describe. Put yet another way, any effort to derive an "ought" from an "is" must be a waste of time, for all it could show even if it succeeded would be that the "is" was not a real "is" but only a disguised "ought" or, alternatively, that the "ought" was not a real "ought" but only a disguised "is."

This summary of the traditional empirical view has been very brief, but I hope it conveys something of the power of this picture. In the hands of certain modern authors, especially Hare and Nowell-Smith, the picture attains considerable subtlety and sophistication.

What is wrong with this picture? No doubt many things are wrong with it. In the end I am going to say that one of the things wrong with it is that it fails to give us any coherent account of such notions as commitment, responsibility, and obligation.

In order to work toward this conclusion I can begin by saying that the picture fails to account for the *different types* of "descriptive" statements. Its paradigms of descriptive statements are such utterances as "my car goes eighty miles an hour," "Jones is six feet tall," "Smith has brown hair," and the like. But it is forced by its own rigidity to construe "Jones got married," "Smith made a promise," "Jackson has five dollars," and "Brown hit a home run" as descriptive statements as well. It is so forced, because whether or not someone got married, made a promise, has five dollars, or hit a home run is as much a matter of objective fact as whether he has red hair or brown eyes. Yet the former kind of statement (statements containing "married," "promise," and so forth) seem to be quite different from the simple empirical paradigms of descriptive statements. How are they different? Though both kinds of statements state matters of objective fact, the statements containing words such as "married," "promise," "home run," and "five dollars" state facts whose existence presupposes certain institutions: a man has five dollars, given the institution of money. Take away the institution and all he has is a rectangular bit of paper with green ink on it. A man hits a home run only given the institution of baseball; without the institution he only hits a sphere with a stick. Similarly, a man gets married or makes a promise only within the institutions of marriage and promising. Without them, all he does is utter words or makes gestures. We might characterize such facts as institutional facts, and contrast them with noninstitutional, or brute, facts: that a man has a bit of paper with green ink on it is a brute fact, that he has five dollars is an institutional fact.[5] The classical picture fails to account for the differences between statements of brute fact and statements of institutional fact.

The word "institution" sounds artificial here, so let us ask: what sorts of institutions are these? In order to answer that question I need to distinguish between two different kinds of rules or conventions. Some rules regulate antecedently existing forms of behavior. For example, the rules of polite table behavior regulate eating, but eating exists independently of these rules. Some rules, on the other hand, do not merely regulate but create or define new forms of behavior: the rules of chess, for example, do not merely regulate an antecedently existing activity called playing chess; they, as it were, create the possibility of or define that activity. The activity of playing chess is

[5]For a discussion of this distinction see G. E. M. Anscombe, "Brute Facts," *Analysis* (1958).

constituted by action in accordance with these rules. Chess has no existence apart from these rules. The distinction I am trying to make was foreshadowed by Kant's distinction between regulative and constitutive principles, so let us adopt his terminology and describe our distinction as a distinction between regulative and constitutive rules. Regulative rules regulate activities whose existence is independent of the rules; constitutive rules constitute (and also regulate) forms of activity whose existence is logically dependent on the rules.[6]

Now the institutions that I have been talking about are systems of constitutive rules. The institutions of marriage, money, and promising are like the institutions of baseball or chess in that they are systems of such constitutive rules or conventions. What I have called institutional facts are facts which presuppose such institutions.

Once we recognize the existence of and begin to grasp the nature of such institutional facts, it is but a short step to see that many forms of obligations, commitments, rights, and responsibilities are similarly institutionalized. It is often a matter of fact that one has certain obligations, commitments, rights, and responsibilities, but it is a matter of institutional, not brute, fact. It is one such institutionalized form of obligation, promising, which I invoked above to derive an "ought" from an "is." I started with a brute fact, that a man uttered certain words, and then invoked the institution in such a way as to generate institutional facts by which we arrived at the institutional fact that the man ought to pay another man five dollars. The whole proof rests on an appeal to the constitutive rule that to make a promise is to undertake an obligation.

We are now in a position to see how we can generate an indefinite number of such proofs. Consider the following vastly different example. We are in our half of the seventh inning and I have a big lead off second base. The pitcher whirls, fires to the shortstop covering, and I am tagged out a good ten feet down the line. The umpire shouts, "Out!" I, however, being a positivist, hold my ground. The umpire tells me to return to the dugout. I point out to him that you can't derive an "ought" from an "is." No set of descriptive statements describing matters of fact, I say, will entail any evaluative statements to the effect that I should or ought to leave the field. You just can't get orders or recommendations from facts alone. What is needed is an evaluative major premise. I therefore return to and stay on second base (until I am carried off the field). I think everyone feels my claims here to be preposterous, and preposterous in the sense of logically absurd. Of course you can derive an "ought" from an "is," and though to actually set out the derivation in this case would be vastly more complicated than in the case of promising, it is in principle no different. By undertaking to play baseball I have committed myself to the observation of certain constitutive rules.

We are now also in a position to see that the tautology that one ought to keep one's promises is only one of a class of similar tautologies concerning institutionalized forms of obligation. For example, "one ought not to steal" can be taken as saying that to recognize something as someone else's property necessarily involves recognizing his right to dispose of it. This is a constitutive rule of the institution of private property.[7]

[6]For a discussion of a related distinction see J. Rawls, "Two Concepts of Rules," *Philosophical Review,* LXIV (1955).

[7]Proudhon said: "Property is theft." If one tries to take this as an internal remark it makes no sense. It was intended as an external remark attacking and rejecting the institution of private property. It gets its air of paradox and its force by using terms which are internal to the institution in order to attack the institution.

Standing on the deck of some institutions one can tinker with constitutive rules and even throw some other institutions overboard. But could one throw all institutions overboard (in order perhaps to avoid ever having to derive an "ought" from an "is")? One could not and still engage in those forms of behavior we consider characteristically human. Suppose Proudhon had added (and tried to live by): "Truth is a lie, marriage is infidelity, language is uncommunicative, law is a crime," and so on with every possible institution.

"One ought not to tell lies" can be taken as saying that to make an assertion necessarily involves undertaking an obligation to speak truthfully. Another constitutive rule. "One ought to pay one's debts" can be construed as saying that to recognize something as a debt is necessarily to recognize an obligation to pay it. It is easy to see how all these principles will generate counterexamples to the thesis that you cannot derive an "ought" from an "is."

My tentative conclusions, then, are as follows:

1. The classical picture fails to account for institutional facts.
2. Institutional facts exist within systems of constitutive rules.
3. Some systems of constitutive rules involve obligations, commitments, and responsibilities.
4. Within those systems we can derive "ought's" from "is's" on the model of the first derivation.

With these conclusions we now return to the question with which I began this section: How can my stating a fact about a man, such as the fact that he made a promise, commit me to a view about what he ought to do? One can begin to answer this question by saying that for me to state such an institutional fact is already to invoke the constitutive rules of the institution. It is those rules that give the word "promise" its meaning. But those rules are such that to commit myself to the view that Jones made a promise involves committing myself to what he ought to do (other things being equal).

If you like, then, we have shown that "promise" is an evaluative word, but since it is also purely descriptive, we have really shown that the whole distinction needs to be reexamined. The alleged distinction between descriptive and evaluative statements is really a conflation of at least two distinctions. On the one hand there is a distinction between different kinds of speech acts, one family of speech acts including evaluations, another family including descriptions. This is a distinction between different kinds of illocutionary force.[8] On the other hand there is a distinction between utterances which involve claims objectively decidable as true or false and those which involve claims not objectively decidable, but which are "matters of personal decision" or "matters of opinion." It has been assumed that the former distinction is (must be) a special case of the latter, that if something has the illocutionary force of an evaluation, it cannot be entailed by factual premises. Part of the point of my argument is to show that this contention is false, that factual premises can entail evaluative conclusions. If I am right, then the alleged distinction between descriptive and evaluative utterances is useful only as a distinction between two kinds of illocutionary force, describing and evaluating, and it is not even very useful there, since if we are to use these terms strictly, they are only two among hundreds of kinds of illocutionary force; and utterances of sentences of the form (5)—"Jones ought to pay Smith five dollars"—would not characteristically fall in either class.

[8]See J. L. Austin, *How to Do Things with Words* (Cambridge, Mass., 1962), for an explanation of this notion.

1967

Some Merits of One Form of Rule-Utilitarianism

Richard B. Brandt

1. Utilitarianism is the thesis that the moral predicates of an act—at least its objective rightness or wrongness, and sometimes also its moral praiseworthiness or blameworthiness—are functions in some way, direct or indirect, of consequences for the welfare of sentient creatures, and of nothing else. Utilitarians differ about what precise function they are; and they differ about what constitutes welfare and how it is to be measured. But they agree that all one needs to know, in order to make moral appraisals correctly, is the consequences of certain things for welfare.

Utilitarianism is thus a normative ethical thesis and not, at least not necessarily, a metaethical position—that is, a position about the meaning and justification of ethical statements. It is true that some utilitarians have declared that the truth of the normative thesis follows, given the ordinary, or proper, meaning of moral terms such as "right." I shall ignore this further, metaethical claim. More recently some writers have suggested something very similar, to the effect that our concept of "morality" is such that we could not call a system of rules a "moral system" unless it were utilitarian in some sense.

A revised version of a paper presented to a conference on moral philosophy held at the University of Colorado in October, 1965.

Richard B. Brandt, "Some Merits of One Form of Rule-Utilitarianism," *University of Colorado Studies* (1967). Reprinted with the permission of the author and the University Press of Colorado.

This latter suggestion is of special interest to us, since the general topic of the present conference is "the concept of morality," and I wish to comment on it very briefly. It is true that there is a connection between utilitarianism and the concept of morality; at least I believe—and shall spell out the contention later—that utilitarianism cannot be explained, at least in its most plausible form, without making use of the concept of "morality" and, furthermore, without making use of an analysis of this concept. But the reverse relationship does not hold: it is not true that the concept "morality" is such that we cannot properly call a system of rules a morality unless it is a thoroughly utilitarian system, although possibly we would not call a system of rules a "morality" if it did not regulate at all the forms of conduct which may be expected to do good or harm to sentient persons. One reason why it is implausible to hold that any morality is necessarily utilitarian is that any plausible form of utilitarianism will be a rather complex thesis, and it seems that the concept of morality is hardly subtle enough to entail anything so complex—although, of course, such reasoning does not exclude the possibility of the concept of morality entailing some simple and unconvincing form of utilitarianism. A more decisive reason, however, is that we so use the term "morality" that we can say consistently that the morality of a society contains some prohibitions which considerations of utility do not support, or are not even thought to support: for example, some restrictions on sexual behavior. (Other examples are mentioned later.) Thus there is no reason to think that only a utilitarian code could properly be called a "moral code" or a "morality," as these are ordinarily used.

In any case, even if "nonutilitarian morality" (or "right, but harmful") were a contradiction in terms, utilitarianism as a normative thesis would not yet be established; for it would be open to a nonutilitarian to advocate changing the meaning of "morality" (or "right") in order to allow for his normative views. There is, of course, the other face of the coin: even if, as we actually use the term "morality" (or "right"), the above expressions are not contradictions in terms, it might be a good and justifiable thing for people to be taught to use words so that these expressions would become self-contradictory. But if there are good reasons for doing the last, presumably there are good and convincing reasons for adopting utilitarianism as a normative thesis, without undertaking such a roundabout route to the goal. I shall, therefore, discuss utilitarianism as a normative thesis, without supposing that it can be supported by arguing that a nonutilitarian morality is a contradiction in terms.

2. If an analysis of concepts like "morally wrong" and "morality" and "moral code" does not enable us to establish the truth of the utilitarian thesis, the question arises what standard a normative theory like utilitarianism has to meet in order for a reasonable presumption to be established in its favor. It is well known that the identity and justification of any such standard can be debated at length. In order to set bounds to the present discussion, I shall state briefly the standard I shall take for granted for purposes of the present discussion. Approximately this standard would be acceptable to a good many writers on normative ethics. However this may be, it would be agreed that it is worth knowing whether some form of utilitarianism meets this standard better than any other form of utilitarian theory, and it is this question which I shall discuss.

The standard which I suggest an acceptable normative moral theory has to meet is this: The theory must contain no unintelligible concepts or internal inconsistencies; it must not be inconsistent with known facts; it must be capable of precise formulation so that its implications for action can be determined; and—most important—its implications must be acceptable to thoughtful persons who have had reasonably wide experience, when taken in the light of supporting remarks that can be made, and when compared with the implications of other clearly statable normative theories. It is not required that the implications of a satisfactory theory be consonant with the uncriticized moral intuitions of intelligent and experienced people, but only with those intuitions which stand in the light of supporting remarks, etc. Furthermore, it is not required of an acceptable theory that the best consequences would be produced by people adopting that theory, in contrast to other theories by which they might be convinced. (The theory might be so complex that it would be a good thing if most people did not try their hand at applying it to concrete situations!) It may be a moving *ad hominem* argument, if one can persuade an act-utilitarian that it would have bad consequences for people to try to determine the right act according to that theory, and to live by their conclusions; but such a showing would not be a reasonable ground for rejecting that normative theory.

3. Before turning to the details of various types of utilitarian theory, it may be helpful to offer some "supporting remarks" which will explain some reasons why some philosophers are favorably disposed toward a utilitarian type of normative theory.

(a) The utilitarian principle provides a clear and definite procedure for determining which acts are right or wrong (praiseworthy or blameworthy), by observation and the methods of science alone and without the use of any supplementary intuitions (assuming that empirical procedures can determine when something maximizes utility), for all cases, including the complex ones about which intuitions are apt to be mute, such as whether kleptomanic behavior is blameworthy or whether it is right to break a confidence in certain circumstances. The utilitarian presumably frames his thesis so as to conform with enlightened intuitions which are clear, but his thesis, being general, has implications for all cases, including those about which his intuitions are not clear. The utilitarian principle is like a general scientific theory, which checks with observations at many points, but can also be used as a guide to beliefs on matters inaccessible to observation (like the behavior of matter at absolute zero temperature).

Utilitarianism is not the only normative theory with this desirable property; egoism is another, and, with some qualifications, so is Kant's theory.

(b) Any reasonably plausible normative theory will give a large place to consequences for welfare in the moral assessment of actions, for this consideration enters continuously and substantially into ordinary moral thinking. Theories which ostensibly make no appeal of this sort either admit utilitarian considerations by the back door, or have counter-intuitive consequences. Therefore the ideal of simplicity leads us to hope for the possibility of a pure utilitarian theory. Moreover, utilitarianism avoids the necessity of weighing disparate things such as justice and utility.

(c) If a proposed course of action does not raise moral questions, it is generally regarded as rational, and its agent well advised to perform it, if and only if it will maximize expectable utility for the agent. In a similar vein, it can be argued that society's "choice" of an institution of morality is rational and well advised, if and only if having it will maximize expectable social utility—raise the expectable level of the average "utility curve" of the population. If morality is a system of traditional and arbitrary constraints on behavior, it cannot be viewed as a rational institution. But it can be, if the system of morality is utilitarian. In that case the institution of morality can be recommended to a person of broad human sympathies, as an institution which maximizes the expectation of general welfare; and to a selfish person, as an institution which, in the absence of particular evidence about his own case, may be expected to maximize his own expectation of welfare (his own welfare being viewed as a random sample from the population). To put it in other words, a utilitarian morality can be "vindicated" by appeal either to the humanity or to the selfishness of human beings.

To say this is not to deny that nonutilitarian moral principles may be capable of vindication in a rather similar way. For instance, to depict morality as an institution which fosters human equality is to recommend it by appeal to something which is perhaps as deep in man as his sympathy or humanity.[1]

4. The type of utilitarianism on which I wish to focus is a form of rule-utilitarianism, as contrasted with act-utilitarianism. According to the latter type of theory (espoused by Sidgwick and Moore), an act is objectively right if no other act the agent could perform would produce better consequences. (On this view, an act is blameworthy if and only if it is right to perform the act of blaming or condemning it; the principles of blameworthiness are a special case of the principle of objectively right actions.) Act-utilitarianism is hence a rather atomistic theory: the rightness of a single act is fixed by its effects on the world. Rule-utilitarianism, in contrast, is the view that the rightness of an act is fixed, not by its relative utility, but by the utility of having a relevant moral rule, or of most or all members of a certain class of acts being performed.

The implications of act-utilitarianism are seriously counter-intuitive, and I shall ignore it except to consider whether some ostensibly different theories really are different.

5. Rule-utilitarianisms may be divided into two main groups, according as the rightness of a particular act is made a function of ideal rules in some sense, or of the actual and recognized rules of a society. The variety of theory I shall explain more fully is of the former type.

According to the latter type of theory, a person's moral duties or obligations in a particular situation are determined, with some exceptions, solely by the moral rules, or institutions, or practices prevalent in the society, and not by what rules (etc.) it would ideally be best to have in the society. (It is sometimes held that actual moral rules, practices, etc., are only a necessary condition of an act's being morally obligatory or wrong.) Views roughly of this sort have been held in recent years by A. MacBeath, Stephen Toulmin, John Rawls, P. F. Strawson, J. O. Urmson, and B. J. Diggs. Indeed, Strawson says in effect that for there to be a moral obligation on one is just for there to be a socially sanctioned demand on him, in a situation where he has an interest in the system of demands which his society is wont to impose on its members, and where such demands are generally acknowledged and respected by members of his society.[2] And Toulmin asserts that when a person asks, "Is this the right thing to do?" what he is normally asking is whether a proposed action "conforms to the moral code" of his group, "whether the action in question belongs to a class of actions generally approved of in the agent's community." In deliberating about the question what is right to do, he says, "there is no more general 'reason' to be given beyond one which related the action . . . to an accepted social practice."[3]

So far the proposal does not appear to be a form of utilitarianism at all. The theory is utilitarian, however, in the following way: it is thought that what is relevant for a decision whether to try to change moral codes, institutions, etc., or for a justification of them, is the relative utility of the code, practice, etc. The recognized code or practice determines the individual's moral obligations in a particular case; utility of the code or

[1]It would not be impossible to combine a restricted principle of utility with a morality of justice or equality. For instance, it might be said that an act is right only if it meets a certain condition of justice, and also if it is one which, among all the just actions open to the agent, meets a requirement of utility as well as any other.

[2]P. F. Strawson, "Social Morality and Individual Ideal," *Philosophy,* XXXVI (1961), 1–17.

[3]Stephen Toulmin, *An Examination of the Place of Reason in Ethics* (Cambridge University Press, 1950), pp. 144–45. See various acute criticisms, with which I mostly agree, in Rawls's review, *Philosophical Review,* LX (1951), 572–80.

practice determines whether it is justified or ought to be changed. Furthermore, it is sometimes held that utilitarian considerations have some relevance to the rightness of a particular action. For instance, Toulmin thinks that in case the requirements of the recognized code or practice conflict in a particular case, the individual ought (although strictly, he is not morally obligated) to do what will maximize utility in the situation, and that in case an individual can relieve the distress of another, he ought (strictly, is not morally obligated) to do so, even if the recognized code does not require him to.[4]

This theory, at least in some of its forms or parts, has such conspicuously counterintuitive implications that it fails to meet the standard for a satisfactory normative theory. In general, we do not believe that an act's being prohibited by the moral code of one's society is sufficient to make it morally wrong. Moral codes have prohibited such things as work on the Sabbath, marriage to a divorced person, medically necessary abortion, and suicide; but we do not believe it was really wrong for persons living in a society with such prohibitions, to do these things.[5]

Neither do we think it a necessary condition of an act's being wrong that it be prohibited by the code of the agent's society, or of an act's being obligatory that it be required by the code of his society. A society may permit a man to have his wife put to death for infidelity, or to have a child put to death for almost any reason; but we still think such actions wrong. Moreover, a society may permit a man absolute freedom in divorcing his wife, and recognize no obligations on his part toward her; but we think, I believe, that a man has some obligations for the welfare of a wife of thirty years' standing (with some qualifications), whatever his society may think.[6]

Some parts of the theory in some of its forms, however, appear to be correct. In particular, the theory in some forms implies that, if a person has a certain recognized obligation in an institution or practice (e.g., a child to support his aged parent, a citizen to pay his taxes), then he morally does have this obligation, with some exceptions, irrespective of whether in an ideal institution he would or would not have. This we do roughly believe, although we need not at the same time accept the reasoning which has been offered to explain how the fact of a practice or institution leads to the moral obligation. The fact that the theory seems right in this would be a strong point in its favor if charges were correct that "ideal" forms of rule-utilitarianism necessarily differ at this point. B. J. Diggs, for instance, has charged that the "ideal" theories imply that:

> one may freely disregard a rule if ever he discovers that action on the rule is not maximally felicific, and in this respect makes moral rules like "practical maxims." . . . It deprives so-

[4]Toulmin and Rawls sometimes go further, and suggest that a person is morally free to do something which the actual code or practice of his society prohibits, if he is convinced that the society would be better off if the code or practice were rewritten so as to permit that sort of thing, and he is prepared to live according to the ideally revised code. If their theory were developed in this direction, it need not be different from some "ideal" forms of rule-utilitarianism, although, as stated, the theory makes the recognized code the standard for moral obligations, with exceptions granted to individuals who hold certain moral opinions. See Toulmin, op. cit., pp. 151–52, and Rawls, "Two Concepts of Rules," *Philosophical Review,* LXIV (1955), 28–29, especially ftnt. 25. It should be noticed that Rawls's proposal is different from Toulmin's in an important way. He is concerned with only a segment of the moral code, the part which can be viewed as the rules of practices. As he observes, this may be only a small part of the moral code.

[5]Does a stranger living in a society have a moral obligation to conform to its moral code? I suggest we think that he does not, unless it is the right moral code or perhaps at least he thinks it is, although we think that offense he might give to the feelings of others should be taken into account, as well as the result his nonconformity might have in weakening regard for moral rules in general.

[6]It is a different question whether we should hold offenders in such societies seriously morally blameworthy. People cannot be expected to rise much above the level of recognized morality, and we condemn them little when they do not.

cial and moral rules of their authority and naturally is in sharp conflict with practice. On this alternative rule-utilitarianism collapses into act-utilitarianism. Surely it is a mistake to maintain that a set of rules, thought to be ideally utilitarian or felicific, is the criterion of right action. . . . If we are presented with a list [of rules], but these are not rules in practice, the most one could reasonably do is to try to get them adopted.[7]

I believe, however, and shall explain in detail later that this charge is without foundation.

6. Let us turn now to "ideal" forms of rule-utilitarianism, which affirm that whether it is morally obligatory or morally right to do a certain thing in a particular situation is fixed, not by the actual code or practice of the society (these may be indirectly relevant, as forming part of the situation), but by some "ideal" rule—that is, by the utility of having a certain general moral rule, or by the utility of all or most actions being performed which are members of a relevant class of actions.

If the rightness of an act is fixed by the utility of a relevant rule (class), are we to say that the rule (class) which qualifies must be the optimific rule (class), the one which maximizes utility, or must the rule (class) meet only some less stringent requirement (e.g., be better than the absence of any rule regulating the type of conduct in question)? And, if it is to be of the optimific type, are all utilities to be counted, or perhaps only "negative" utilities, as is done when it is suggested that the rule (class) must be the one which minimizes suffering?[8]

The simplest proposal—that the rule (class) which qualifies is the one that maximizes utility, with all utilities, whether "positive" or "negative," being counted—also seems to me to be the best, and it is the one I shall shortly explain more fully. Among the several possible theories different from this one I shall discuss briefly only one, which seems the most plausible of its kind, and is at least closely similar to the view defended by Professor Marcus Singer.

According to this theory, an action (or inaction) at time t in circumstances C is wrong if and only if, were everyone in circumstances C to perform a relevantly similar action, harm would be done—meaning by "doing harm" that affected persons would be made worse off by the action (or inaction) than they already were at time t. (I think it is not meant that the persons must be put in a state of "negative welfare" in some sense, but simply made worse off than they otherwise would have been.) Let us suppose a person is deciding whether to do A in circumstances C at t. The theory, then, implies the following: (1) If everyone doing A in circumstances C would make people worse off than they already were at t (A can be inaction, such as failing to pull a drowning man from the water) whereas some other act would not make them so, then it is wrong for anyone to do A. (2) If everyone doing A would not make people worse off, then even if everyone doing something else would make them better off, it is not wrong to do A. (3) If everyone doing A would make people worse off, but if there is no alternative act, the performance of which by everyone would avoid making people worse off, then it is right to do A, even though doing A would make people relatively much worse off than they would have been made by the performance of some other action instead. The "optimific rule" theory, roughly, would accept (1), but reject (2) and (3).

[7] "Rules and Utilitarianism," *American Philosophical Quarterly*, I (1964), 32–44.

[8] In a footnote to Chapter 9 of *The Open Society*, Professor Popper suggested that utilitarianism would be more acceptable if its test were minimizing suffering rather than maximizing welfare, to which J. J. C. Smart replied (*Mind*, 1958, pp. 542–43) that the proposal implies that we ought to destroy all living beings, as the surest way to eliminate suffering. It appears, however, that Professor Popper does not seriously advocate what seemed to be the position of the earlier footnote (Addendum to fourth edition, p. 386).

Implication (3) of the theory strikes me as clearly objectionable; I am unable to imagine circumstances in which we should think it not morally incumbent on one to avoid very bad avoidable consequences for others, even though a situation somewhat worse than the status quo could not be avoided. Implication (2) is less obviously dubious. But I should think we do have obligations to do things for others, when we are not merely avoiding being in the position of making them worse off. For instance, if one sees another person at a cocktail party, standing by himself and looking unhappy, I should suppose one has some obligation to make an effort to put him at his ease, even though doing nothing would hardly make him worse off than he already is.

Why do proponents of this view, like Professor Singer, prefer his view to the simpler, "maximize utility" form of rule-utilitarianism? This is not clear. One objection sometimes raised is that an optimific theory implies that every act is morally weighty and none morally indifferent. And one may concede that this is a consequence of some forms of utilitarianism, even rule-utilitarianism of the optimific variety; but we shall see that it is by no means a consequence of the type of proposal described below. For the theory below will urge that an action is not morally indifferent only if it falls under some prescription of an optimific moral code, and, since there are disadvantages in a moral code regulating actions, optimific moral codes will prohibit or require actions of a certain type only when there are significant utilitarian reasons for it. As a consequence, a great many types of action are morally indifferent, according to the theory. Professor Singer also suggests that optimific-type theories have objectionable consequences for state-of-nature situations;[9] we may postpone judgment on this until we have examined these consequences of the theory here proposed, at a later stage. Other objections to the optimizing type of rule-utilitarianism with which I am familiar either confuse rule-utilitarianism with act-utilitarianism, or do not distinguish among the several possible forms of optimizing rule-utilitarianisms.

7. I propose, then, that we tentatively opt for an "ideal" rule-utilitarianism, of the "maximizing utility" variety. This decision, however, leaves various choices still to be made, between theories better or worse fitted to meet various problems. Rather than attempt to list alternatives, and explain why one choice rather than another between them would work out better, I propose to describe in some detail the type of theory which seems most plausible. I shall later show how this theory meets the one problem to which the "actual rule" type theories seemed to have a nice solution; and I shall discuss its merits, as compared with another quite similar type of theory which has been suggested by Jonathan Harrison and others.

The theory I wish to describe is rather similar to one proposed by J. D. Mabbott in his 1953 British Academy lecture, "Moral Rules." It is also very similar to the view defended by J. S. Mill in *Utilitarianism,* although Mill's formulation is ambiguous at some points, and he apparently did not draw some distinctions he should have drawn. (I shall revert to this historical point.)

For convenience I shall refer to the theory as the "ideal moral code" theory. The essence of it is as follows: Let us first say that a moral code is "ideal" if its currency in a particular society would produce at least as much good per person (the total divided by the number of persons) as the currency of any other moral code. (Two different codes might meet this condition, but, in order to avoid complicated formulations, the following discussion will ignore this possibility.) Given this stipulation for the meaning of "ideal," the Ideal Moral Code theory consists in the assertion of the following thesis: *An act is right if and only if it would not be prohibited by the moral code ideal for the*

[9]M. G. Singer, *Generalization in Ethics* (New York: Alfred A. Knopf, Inc., 1961), p. 192.

society; and an agent is morally blameworthy (praiseworthy) for an act if, and to the degree that, the moral code ideal in that society would condemn (praise) him for it. It is a virtue of this theory that it is a theory both about objective rightness and about moral blameworthiness (praiseworthiness) of actions, but the assertion about blameworthiness will be virtually ignored in what follows.

8. In order to have a clear proposal before us, however, the foregoing summary statement must be filled out in three ways: (1) by explaining what it is for a moral code to have currency; (2) by making clear what is the difference between the rules of a society's moral code and the rules of its institutions; and (3) by describing how the relative utility of a moral code is to be estimated.

First, then, the notion of a moral code having currency in a society.

For a moral code to have currency in a society, two things must be true. First, a high proportion of the adults in the society must subscribe to the moral principles, or have the moral opinions, constitutive of the code. Exactly how high the proportion should be, we can hardly decide on the basis of the ordinary meaning of "the moral code"; but probably it would not be wrong to require at least ninety per cent agreement. Thus, if at least ninety per cent of the adults subscribe to principle A, and ninety per cent to principle B, etc., we may say that a code consisting of A and B (etc.) has currency in the society, provided the second condition is met. Second, we want to say that certain principles A, B, etc. belong to the moral code of a society only if they are recognized as such. That is, it must be that a large proportion of the adults of the society would respond correctly if asked, with respect to A and B, whether most members of the society subscribed to them. (It need not be required that adults base their judgments on such good evidence as recollection of moral discussions; it is enough if for some reason the correct opinion about what is accepted is widespread.) It is of course possible for certain principles to constitute a moral code with currency in a society even if some persons in the society have no moral opinions at all, or if there is disagreement, e.g., if everyone in the society disagrees with every other person with respect to at least one principle.

The more difficult question is what it is for an individual to subscribe to a moral principle or to have a moral opinion. What is it, then, for someone to think sincerely that any action of the kind F is wrong? (1) He is to some extent motivated to avoid actions which he thinks are F, and often, if asked why he does not perform such an action when it appears to be to his advantage, offers, as one of his reasons, that it is F. In addition, the person's motivation to avoid F-actions does not derive entirely from his belief that F-actions on his part are likely to be harmful to him or to persons to whom he is somehow attached. (2) If he thinks he has just performed an F-action, he feels guilty or remorseful or uncomfortable about it, unless he thinks he has some excuse—unless, for instance, he knows that at the time of action he did not think his action would be an F-action. "Guilt" (etc.) is not to be understood as implying some special origin such as interiorization of parental prohibitions, or as being a vestige of anxiety about punishment. It is left open that it might be an unlearned emotional response to the thought of being the cause of the suffering of another person. Any feeling which must be viewed simply as anxiety about anticipated consequences, for one's self or person to whom one is attached, is not, however, to count as a "guilt" feeling. (3) If he believes that someone has performed an F-action, he will tend to admire him less as a person, unless he thinks that the individual has a good excuse. He thinks that action of this sort, without excuse, reflects on character—this being spelled out, in part, by reference to traits like honesty, respect for the rights of others, and so on. (4) He thinks that these attitudes of his are correct or well justified, in some sense, but with one restriction: it is not enough if he thinks that what justifies them is simply the fact that they are shared by all or most members of his society. This restriction corresponds with our distinction between a moral conviction and something else. For instance, we are inclined to think no moral attitude is involved if an Englishman disapproves of something but says that his disapproval is justified by the fact that it is shared by "well-bred Englishmen." In such cases we are inclined to say that the individual subscribes only to a custom, or to a rule of etiquette or manners. On the other hand, if the individual thinks that what justifies his attitude unfavorable to F-actions is that F-actions are contrary to the will of God (and the individual's attitude is not merely a prudential one), or inconsistent with the welfare of mankind, or contrary to human nature, we are disposed to say the attitude is a moral attitude and the opinion expressed a moral one. And the same if he thinks his attitude justified, but can give no reason. There are perhaps other restrictions we should make on acceptable justifications (perhaps to distinguish a moral code from a code of honor), and other types of justification we should wish to list as clearly acceptable (perhaps an appeal to human equality).

9. It is important to distinguish between the moral code of a society and its institutions, or the rules of its institutions. It is especially important for the Ideal Moral Code theory, for this theory involves the conception of a moral code ideal for a society in the context of its institutions, so that it is necessary to distinguish the moral code which a society does or might have from its institutions and their rules. The distinction is also one we actually do make in our thinking, although it is blurred in some cases. (For instance, is "Honor thy father and thy mother" a moral rule, or a rule of the family institution, in our society?)[10]

An institution is a set of positions or statuses, with which certain privileges and jobs are associated. (We can speak of these as "rights" and "duties" if we are careful to explain that we do not mean moral rights and duties.) That is, there are certain, usually nameable, positions which consist in the fact that anyone who is assigned to the position is expected to do certain things, and at the same time is expected to have certain things done for him. The individuals occupying these positions are a group of cooperating agents in a system which as a whole is thought to have the aim of serving certain ends. (E.g., a university is thought to serve the ends of education, research, etc.) The rules of the system concern jobs that must be done in order that the goals of the institution be achieved; they allocate the necessary jobs to different positions. Take, for instance, a university. There are various positions in it: the presidency, the professorial ranks, the registrars, librarians, etc. It is understood that one who occupies a certain post has certain duties, say teaching a specified number of classes or spending time working on research in the case of the instructing staff. Obviously the university cannot achieve its ends unless certain persons do the teaching, some tend to the administration, some do certain jobs in the library, and so on. Another such system is the family. We need not speculate on the "purpose" of the family, whether it is primarily a device for producing a new generation, etc. But it is clear that when a man enters marriage, he takes a position to which certain jobs are attached, such as providing support for the family to the best of his ability, and to which also certain rights are attached, such as exclusive sexual rights with his wife, and the right to be cared for should he become incapacitated.

[10]The confusion is compounded by the fact that terms like "obligation" and "duty" are used sometimes to speak about moral obligations and duties, and sometimes not. The fact that persons have a certain legal duty in certain situations is a rule of the legal institutions of the society; a person may not have a moral duty to do what is his legal duty. The fact that a person has an obligation to invite a certain individual to dinner is a matter of manners or etiquette, and at least may not be a matter of moral obligation. See R. B. Brandt, "The Concepts of Duty and Obligation," *Mind,* LXXIII (1964), especially 380–84.

If an "institution" is defined in this way, it is clear that the moral code of a society cannot itself be construed as an institution, nor its rules as rules of an institution. The moral code is society-wide, so if we were to identify its rules as institutional rules, we should presumably have to say that everyone belongs to this institution. But what is the "purpose" of society as a whole? Are there any distinctions of status, with rights and duties attached, which we could identify as the "positions" in the moral system? Can we say that moral rules consist in the assignment of jobs in such a way that the aims of the institution may be achieved? It is true that there is a certain analogy: society as a whole might be said to be aiming at the good life for all, and the moral rules of the society might be viewed as the rules with which all must conform in order to achieve this end. But the analogy is feeble. Society as a whole is obviously not an organization like a university, an educational system, the church, General Motors, etc.; there is no specific goal in the achievement of which each position has a designated role to play. Our answer to the above questions must be in the negative: morality is not an institution in the explained sense; nor are moral rules institutional expectations or rules.

The moral code of a society may, of course, have implications that bear on institutional rules. For one thing, the moral code may imply that an institutional system is morally wrong and ought to be changed. Moreover, the moral code may imply that a person has also a moral duty to do something which is his institutional job. For instance, it may be a moral rule that a person ought to do whatever he has undertaken to do, or that he ought not to accept the benefits of a position without performing its duties. Take for instance the rules, "A professor should meet his classes" or "Wives ought to make the beds." Since the professor has undertaken to do what pertains to his office, and the same for a wife, and since these tasks are known to pertain to the respective offices, the moral rule that a person is morally bound (with certain qualifications) to do what he has undertaken to do implies, in context, that the professor is morally bound to meet his classes and the wife to make the beds, other things being equal (viz., there being no contrary moral obligations in the situation). But these implications are not themselves part of the moral code. No one would say that a parent had neglected to teach his child the moral code of the society if he had neglected to teach him that professors must meet classes, and that wives must make the beds. A person becomes obligated to do these things only by participating in an institution, by taking on the status of professor or wife. Parents do not teach children to have guilt feelings about missing classes, or making beds. The moral code consists only of more general rules, defining what is to be done in certain types of situations in which practically everyone will find himself. ("Do what you have promised!")

Admittedly some rules can be both moral and institutional: "Take care of your father in his old age" might be both an institutional rule of the family organization and also a part of the moral code of a society. (In this situation, one can still raise the question whether this moral rule is optimific in a society with that institutional rule; the answer could be negative.)

It is an interesting question whether "Keep your promises" is a moral rule, an institutional rule (a rule of an "institution" of promises), or both. Obviously it is a part of the moral code of western societies. But is it also a rule of an institution? There are difficulties in the way of affirming that it is. There is no structure of cooperating individuals with special functions, which serves to promote certain aims. Nor, when one steps into the "role" of a promisor, does one commit one's self to any specific duties; one fixes one's own duties by what one promises. Nor, in order to understand what one is committing one's self to by promising, need one have any knowledge of any system of expectations prevalent in the society. A three-year-old, who has never heard of any duties incumbent on promisors, can tell his friends, who wish to play baseball that afternoon, that he will bring the ball and bat, and that they need give no thought to the availability of these items. His invitation to rely on him for something needed for their common enjoyment, and his assurance that he will do something and his encouraging them thereby to set their minds at rest, *is* to make a promise. No one need suppose that the promisor is stepping into a socially recognized position, with all the rights and duties attendant on the same, although it is true he has placed himself in a position where he will properly be held responsible for the disappointment if he fails, and where inferences about his reliability as a person will properly be drawn if he forgets, or worse, if it turns out he was never in a position to perform. The bindingness of a promise is no more dependent on a set of expectations connected with an institution, than is the wrongness of striking another person without justifying reason.

Nevertheless, if one thinks it helpful to speak of a promise as an institution or a practice, in view of certain analogies (promisor and promisee may be said to have rights and duties like the occupants of roles in an institution, and there is the ritual word "promise" the utterance of which commits the speaker to certain performances), there is no harm in this. The similarities and dissimilarities are what they are, and as long as these are understood it seems to make little difference what we say. Nevertheless, even if making a promise is participating in a practice or institution, there is still the *moral* question whether one is morally bound to perform, and in what conditions, and for what reasons. This question is left open, given the institution is whatever it is—as is the case with all rules of institutions.

10. It has been proposed above that an action is right if and only if it would not be prohibited by the moral code ideal for the society in which it occurs, where a moral code is taken to be "ideal" if and only if its currency would produce at least as much good per person as the currency of any other moral code.[11] We must now give more attention to the conception of an ideal moral code, and how it may be decided when a given moral code will produce as much good per person as any other. We may, however, reasonably bypass the familiar problems of judgments of comparative utilities, especially when different persons are involved, since these problems are faced by all moral theories that have any plausibility. We shall simply assume that rough judgments of this sort are made and can be justified.

(a) We should first notice that, as "currency" has been explained above, a moral code could not be current in a society if it were too complex to be learned or applied. We may therefore confine our consideration to codes simple enough to be absorbed by human beings, roughly in the way in which people learn actual moral codes.

(b) We have already distinguished the concept of an institution and its rules from the concept of a moral rule, or rule of the moral code. (We have, however, pointed out that in some cases a moral rule may prescribe the same thing that is also an institutional expectation. But this is not a necessary situation, and a moral code could condemn an institutional expectation.) Therefore, in deciding how much good the currency of a specific moral system would do, we consider the institutional setting as it is, as part of the situation. We are asking which moral code would produce the most good in the long run in this setting. One good to be reckoned, of course, might be that the currency of a given moral code would tend to change the institutional system.

[11]Some utilitarians have suggested that the right act is determined by the total net intrinsic good produced. This view can have embarrassing consequences for problems of population control. The view here advocated is that the right act is determined by the per person, average, net intrinsic good produced.

(c) In deciding which moral code will produce the most per person good, we must take into account the probability that certain types of situation will arise in the society. For instance, we must take for granted that people will make promises and subsequently want to break them, that people will sometimes assault other persons in order to achieve their own ends, that people will be in distress and need the assistance of others, and so on. We may not suppose that, because an ideal moral code might have certain features, it need not have other features because they will not be required; for instance, we may not suppose, on the ground that an ideal moral system would forbid everyone to purchase a gun, that such a moral system needs no provisions about the possession and use of guns—just as our present moral and legal codes have provisions about self-defense, which would be unnecessary if everyone obeyed the provision never to assault anyone.

It is true that the currency of a moral code with certain provisions might bring about a reduction in certain types of situation, e.g., the number of assaults or cases of dishonesty. And the reduction might be substantial, if the moral code were current which prohibited these offenses very strongly. (We must remember that an ideal moral code might differ from the actual one not only in what it prohibits or enjoins, but also in how strongly it prohibits or enjoins.) But it is consistent to suppose that a moral code prohibits a certain form of behavior very severely, and yet that the behavior will occur, since the "currency" of a moral code requires only ninety per cent subscription to it, and a "strong" subscription, on the average, permits a great range from person to person. In any case there must be doubt whether the best moral code will prohibit many things very severely, since there are serious human costs in severe prohibitions: the burden of guilt feelings, the traumas caused by the severe criticism by others which is a part of having a strong injunction in a code, the risks of any training process which would succeed in interiorizing a severe prohibition, and so on.

(d) It would be a great oversimplification if, in assessing the comparative utility of various codes, we confined ourselves merely to counting the benefits of people doing (refraining from doing) certain things, as a result of subscribing to a certain code. To consider only this would be as absurd as estimating the utility of some feature of a legal system by attending only to the utility of people behaving in the way the law aims to make them behave—and overlooking the fact that the law only reduces and does not eliminate misbehavior, as well as the disutility of punishment to the convicted, and the cost of the administration of criminal law. In the case of morals, we must weigh the benefit of the improvement in behavior as a result of the restriction built into conscience, against the cost of the restriction—the burden of guilt feelings, the effects of the training process, etc. There is a further necessary refinement. In both law and morals we must adjust our estimates of utility by taking into account the envisaged system of excuses. That *mens rea* is required as a condition of guilt in the case of most legal offenses is most important; and it is highly important for the utility of a moral system whether accident, intent, and motives are taken into account in deciding a person's liability to moral criticism. A description of a moral code is incomplete until we have specified the severity of condemnation (by conscience or the criticism of others) to be attached to various actions, along with the excuses to be allowed as exculpating or mitigating.

II. Philosophers have taken considerable interest in the question what implications forms of rule-utilitarianism have for the moral relevance of the behavior of persons other than the agent. Such implications, it is thought, bring into focus the effective difference between any form of rule-utilitarianism, and act-utilitarianism. In particular, it has been thought that the implications of rule-utilitarianisms for two types of situation are especially significant: (a) for situations in which persons are generally violating the recognized moral code, or some feature of it; and (b) for situations in which, because the moral code is generally respected, maximum utility would be produced by violation of the code by the agent. An example of the former situation (sometimes called a "state of nature" situation) would be widespread perjury in making out income tax declarations. An example of the latter situation would be widespread conformity to the rule forbidding walking on the grass in a park.

What are the implications of the suggested form of rule-utilitarianism for these types of situation? Will it prescribe conduct which is not utility maximizing in these situations? If it does, it will clearly have implications discrepant with those of act-utilitarianism—but perhaps unpalatable to some people.

It is easy to see how to go about determining what is right or wrong in such situations, on the above described form of rule-utilitarianism—it is a question of what an "ideal" moral code would prescribe. But it is by no means easy to see where a reasonable person would come out, after going through such an investigation. Our form of rule-utilitarianism does not rule out, as morally irrelevant, reference to the behavior of other persons; it implies that the behavior of others is morally relevant precisely to the extent to which an optimific moral code (the one the currency of which is optimific) would take it into account. How far, then, we might ask, would an optimific moral code take into account the behavior of other persons, and what would its specific prescriptions be for the two types of situations outlined?

It might be thought, and it has been suggested, that an ideal moral code could take no cognizance of the behavior of other persons, and in particular of the possibility that many persons are ignoring some prohibitions of the code, sometimes for the reason, apparently, that it is supposed that a code of behavior would be self-defeating if it prescribed for situations of its own breach, on a wide scale. It is a sufficient answer to this suggestion, to point out that our actual moral code appears to contain some such prescriptions. For instance, our present code seems to permit, for the case in which almost everyone is understating his income, that others do the same, on the ground that otherwise they will be paying more than their fair share. It is, of course, true that a code simple enough to be learned and applied cannot include prescriptions for all possible types of situation involving the behavior of other persons; but it can contain some prescriptions pertinent to some general features of the behavior of others.

Granted, then, that an ideal moral code may contain some special prescriptions which pay attention to the behavior of other persons, how in particular will it legislate for special situations such as the examples cited above? The proper answer to this question is that there would apparently be no blanket provision for all cases of these general types, and that a moral agent faced with such a concrete situation would have to think out what an ideal moral code would imply for his type of concrete situation. Some things do seem clear. An ideal moral code would not provide that a person is permitted to be cruel in a society where most other persons are cruel; there could only be loss of utility in any special provision permitting that. On the other hand, if there is some form of cooperative activity which enhances utility only if most persons cooperate, and non-participation in which does not reduce utility when most persons are not cooperating, utility would seem to be maximized if the moral code somehow permitted all to abstain—perhaps by an abstract formula stating this very condition. (This is on the assumption that the participation by some would not, by example, eventually bring about the participation of most or all.) Will there be any types of situation for which an ideal moral code would prescribe infringement of a generally respected moral code, by a few, when a few infringements (provided there are not many) would maximize utility? The possibility of this is not ruled out. Obviously there will be some regulations for emergencies; one may cut across park grass in order to rush a heart-attack victim to a hospital. And there will be rules making special exceptions when considerable utility is involved; the boy with no other place to play may use the grass in the park. But, when an agent has no special claim which others could not make, it is certainly not clear that ideal moral rules will make him an exception on the ground that some benefit will come to him, and that restraint by him is unnecessary in view of the cooperation of others.

The implications of the above form of rule-utilitarianism, for these situations, are evidently different from those of act-utilitarianism.[12]

12. The Ideal Moral Code theory is very similar to the view put forward by J. S. Mill in *Utilitarianism.*

Mill wrote that his creed held that "actions are right in proportion as they tend to promote happiness; wrong as they tend to produce the reverse of happiness." Mill apparently did not intend by this any form of act-utilitarianism. He was—doubtless with much less than full awareness—writing of act-*types,* and what he meant was that an act of a certain type is morally obligatory (wrong) if and only if acts of that type tend to promote happiness (the reverse). Mill supposed that it is known that certain kinds of acts, e.g., murder and theft, promote unhappiness, and that therefore we can say, with exceptions only for very special circumstances, that murder and theft are wrong. Mill recognized that there can be a discrepancy between the tendency of an act-type, and the probable effects, in context, of an individual act. He wrote: "In the case of abstinences, indeed—of things which people forbear to do from moral considerations, though the consequences in the particular case might be beneficial—, it would be unworthy of an intelligent agent not to be consciously aware that the action is of a class which, if practiced generally, would be generally injurious, and that this is the ground of the obligation to abstain from it."[13] Moreover, he specifically denied that one is morally obligated to perform (avoid) an act just on the ground that it can be expected to produce good consequences; he says that "there is no case of moral obligation in which some secondary principle is not involved." (op. cit., p. 33).

It appears, however, that Mill did not quite think that it is morally obligatory to perform (avoid) an act according as its general performance would promote (reduce) happiness in the world. For he said (p. 60) that "We do not call anything wrong unless we mean to imply that a person ought to be punished in some way or other for doing it—if not by law, by the opinion of his fellow creatures; if not by opinion, by the reproaches of his own conscience. This seems the real turning point of the distinction between morality and simple expediency." The suggestion here is that it is morally obligatory to perform (avoid) an act according as it is beneficial to have a system of sanctions (with what this promises in way of performance), whether formal, informal (criticism by others), or internal (one's own conscience), for enforcing the performance (avoidance) of the type of act in question. This is very substantially the Ideal Moral Code theory.

Not that there are no differences. Mill is not explicit about details, and the theory outlined above fills out what he actually said. Moreover, Mill noticed that an act can fall under more than one secondary principle and that the relevant principles may give conflicting rulings about what is morally obligatory. In such a case, Mill thought, what one

[12]The above proposal is different in various respects from that set forth in the writer's "Toward a Credible Form of Utilitarianism," in Castaneda and Nakhnikian, *Morality and the Language of Conduct,* 1963. The former paper did not make a distinction between institutional rules and moral rules. (The present paper, of course, allows that both may contain a common prescription.) A result of these differences is that the present theory is very much simpler, and avoids some counter-intuitive consequences which some writers have pointed out in criticism of the earlier proposal.

[13]*Utilitarianism* (New York: Library of Liberal Arts, 1957), p. 25.

ought to do (but it is doubtful whether he believed there is a strict moral obligation in this situation) is what will maximize utility in the concrete situation. This proposal for conflicts of "ideal moral rules" is not a necessary part of the Ideal Moral Code theory as outlined above.

13. It is sometimes thought that a rule-utilitarianism rather like Mill's cannot differ in its implication about what is right or wrong from the act-utilitarian theory. This is a mistake.

The contention would be correct if two dubious assumptions happened to be true. The first is that one of the rules of an optimific moral code will be that a person ought always to do whatever will maximize utility. The second is that, when there is a conflict between the rules of an optimific code, what a person ought to do is to maximize utility. For then either the utilitarian rule is the only one that applies (and it always will be relevant), in which case the person ought to do what the act-utilitarian directs; or if there is a conflict among the relevant rules, the conflict resolving principle takes over, and this, of course, prescribes exactly what act-utilitarianism prescribes. Either way, we come out where the act-utilitarian comes out.

But there is no reason at all to suppose that there will be a utilitarian rule in an optimific moral code. In fact, obviously there will not be. It is true that there should be a directive to relieve the distress of others, when this can be done, say at relatively low personal cost; and there should be a directive not to injure other persons, except in special situations. And so on. But none of this amounts to a straight directive to do the most good possible. Life would be chaotic if people tried to observe any such moral requirement.

The second assumption was apparently acceptable to Mill. But a utilitarian principle is by no means the only possible conflict resolving principle. For if we say, with the Ideal Moral Code theory, that what is right is fixed by the content of the moral system with maximum utility, the possibility is open that the utility maximizing moral system will contain some rather different device for resolving conflicts between lowest-level moral rules. The ideal system might contain several higher-level conflict resolving principles, all different from Mill's. Or, if there is a single one, it could be a directive to maximize utility; it could be a directive to do what an intelligent person who had fully interiorized the rest of the ideal moral system would feel best satisfied with doing; and so on. But the final court of appeal need not be an appeal to direct utilities. Hence the argument that Mill-like rule-utilitarianism must collapse into direct utilitarianism is doubly at fault.[14]

In fact, far from "collapsing" into act-utilitarianism, the Ideal Moral Code theory appears to avoid the serious objections which have been leveled at direct utilitarianism. One objection to the latter view is that it implies that various immoral actions (murdering one's elderly father, breaking solemn promises) are right or even obligatory if only they can be kept secret. The Ideal Moral Code theory has no such implication. For it obviously would not maximize utility to have a moral code which condoned secret murders or breaches of promise. W. D. Ross criticized act-utilitarianism on the ground that it ignored the personal relations important in ordinary morality, and he listed a half-dozen types of moral rule which he thought captured the main themes of thoughtful

[14]Could some moral problems be so unique that they would not be provided for by the set of rules it is best for the society to have? If so, how should they be appraised morally? Must there be some appeal to rules covering cases most closely analogous, as seems to be the procedure in law? If so, should we say that an act is right if it is not prohibited, either explicitly or by close analogy, by an ideal moral code? I shall not attempt to answer these questions.

morality: obligations of fidelity, obligations of gratitude, obligations to make restitution for injuries, obligations to help other persons, to avoid injuring them, to improve one's self, and to bring about a just distribution of good things in life. An ideal moral code, however, would presumably contain substantially such rules in any society, doubtless not precisely as Ross stated them. So the rule-utilitarian need not fail to recognize the personal character of morality.

14. In contrast to the type of theory put forward by Toulmin and others, the Ideal Moral Code theory has the advantage of implying that the moral rules recognized in a given society are not necessarily morally binding. They are binding only in so far as they maximize welfare, as contrasted with other possible moral rules. Thus if, in a given society, it is thought wrong to work on the Sabbath, to perform socially desirable abortions, or to commit suicide, it does not follow, on the Ideal Moral Code theory, that these things are necessarily wrong. The question is whether a code containing such prohibitions would maximize welfare. Similarly, according to this theory, a person may act wrongly in doing certain things which are condoned by his society.

A serious appeal of theories like Toulmin's is, however, their implications for institutional obligations. For instance, if in society A it is a recognized obligation to care for one's aged father, Toulmin's theory implies that it really is a moral obligation for a child in that society to care for his aged parent (with some qualifications); whereas if in society B it is one's recognized obligation not to care for one's aged father, but instead for one's aged maternal uncle, his theory implies that it really is the moral obligation of a person in that society to care for his aged maternal uncle—even if a better institutional system would put the responsibilities in different places. This seems approximately what we do believe.

The Ideal Moral Code theory, however, has much the same implications. According to it, an institutional system forms the setting within which the best (utility maximizing) moral code is to be applied, and one's obligation is to follow the best moral rules in that institutional setting—not to do what the best moral rules would require for some other, more ideal, setting.

Let us examine the implications of the Ideal Moral Code theory by considering a typical example. Among the Hopi Indians, a child is not expected to care for his father (he is always in a different clan), whereas he is expected to care for his mother, maternal aunt, and maternal uncle, and so on up the female line (all in the same clan). It would be agreed by observers that this system does not work very well. The trouble with it is that the lines of institutional obligation and the lines of natural affection do not coincide, and, as a result, an elderly male is apt not to be cared for by anyone.

Can we show that an "ideal moral code" would call on a young person to take care of his maternal uncle, in a system of this sort? (It might also imply he should try to change the system, but that is another point.) One important feature of the situation of the young man considering whether he should care for his maternal uncle is that, the situation including the expectations of others being what it is, if he does nothing to relieve the distress of his maternal uncle, it is probable that it will not be relieved. His situation is very like that of the sole observer of an automobile accident; he is a mere innocent bystander, but the fact is that if he does nothing, the injured persons will die. So the question for us is whether an ideal moral code will contain a rule that, if someone is in a position where he can relieve serious distress, and where it is known that in all probability it will not be relieved if he does not do so, he should relieve the distress. The answer seems to be that it will contain such a rule: we might call it an "obligation of humanity." But there is a second, and more important point. Failure of the young person to provide for his maternal uncle would be a case of unfairness or free riding. For the family system operates like a system of insurance; it provides one with various sorts of privileges or protections, in return for which one is expected to make certain payments, or accept the risk of making certain payments. Our young man has already benefited by the system, and stands to benefit further; he has received care and education as a child, and later on his own problems of illness and old age will be provided for. On the other hand, the old man, who has (we assume) paid such premiums as the system calls on him to pay in life, is now properly expecting, in accordance with the system, certain services from a particular person whom the system designates as the one to take care of him. Will the ideal moral code require such a person to pay the premium in such a system? I suggest that it will, and we can call the rule in question an "obligation of fairness."[15] So, we may infer that our young man will have a moral obligation to care for his maternal uncle, on grounds both of humanity and fairness.

We need not go so far as to say that such considerations mean that an ideal moral code will underwrite morally every institutional obligation. An institution may be grossly inequitable; or some part of it may serve no purpose at all but rather be injurious (as some legal prohibitions may be). But I believe we can be fairly sure that Professor Diggs went too far in saying that a system of this sort "deprives social and moral rules of their authority and naturally is in sharp conflict with practice" and that it "collapses into act-utilitarianism."

15. It may be helpful to contrast the Ideal Moral Code theory with a rather similar type of rule-utilitarianism, which in some ways is simpler than the Ideal Moral Code theory, and which seems to be the only form of rule-utilitarianism recognized by some philosophers. This other type of theory is suggested in the writings of R. F. Harrod, Jonathan Harrison, perhaps John Hospers and Marcus Singer, although, as I shall describe it, it differs from the exact theory proposed by any of these individuals, in more or less important ways.

The theory is a combination of act-utilitarianism with a Kantian universalizability requirement for moral action. It denies that an act is necessarily right if it will produce

[15]See John Rawls, in "Justice as Fairness," *Philosophical Review*, LXVII (1958), 164–94, especially 179–84.

It seems to be held by some philosophers that an ideal moral code would contain no rule of fairness. The line of argument seems to be as follows: Assume we have an institution involving cooperative behavior for an end which will necessarily be of benefit to all in the institution. Assume further that the cooperative behavior required is burdensome. Assume finally that the good results will be produced even if fewer than all cooperate—perhaps ninety per cent is sufficient. It will then be to an individual's advantage to shirk making his contribution, since he will continue to enjoy the benefits. Shirking on the part of some actually maximizes utility, since the work is burdensome, and the burdensome effort of those who shirk (provided there are not too many) is useless.

I imagine that it would be agreed that, in this sort of system, there should be an agreed and known rule for exempting individuals from useless work. (E.g., someone who is ill would be excused.) In the absence of this, a person should feel free to excuse himself for good and special reason. Otherwise, I think we suppose everyone should do his share, and that it is not a sufficient reason for shirking, to know that enough are cooperating to produce the desired benefits. Let us call this requirement, of working except for special reason (etc.) a "rule of fairness."

Would an ideal moral code contain a rule of fairness? At least, there could hardly be a public rule permitting people to shirk while a sufficient number of others work. For what would the rule be? It would be all too easy for most people to believe that a sufficient number of others were working (like the well-known difficulty in farm planning, that if one plants what sold at a good price the preceding year, one is apt to find that prices for that product will drop, since most other farmers have the same idea). Would it even be a good idea to have a rule to the effect that if one absolutely knows that enough others are working, one may shirk? This seems highly doubtful.

Critics of rule-utilitarianism seem to have passed from the fact that the best system would combine the largest product with the least effort, to the conclusion that the best moral code would contain a rule advising not to work when there are enough workers already. This is a non sequitur.

consequences no worse than would any other action the agent might perform; rather, it affirms that an act is right if and only if universal action on the "maxim" of the act would not produce worse consequences than universal action on some other maxim on which the agent could act. Or, instead of talking of universal action on the "maxim" of the act in question, we can speak of all members of the class of relevantly similar actions being performed; then the proposal is that an action is right if and only if universal performance of the class of relevantly similar acts would not have worse consequences than universal performance of the class of acts relevantly similar to some alternative action the agent might perform. Evidently it is important how we identify the "maxim" of an act or the class of "relevantly similar" acts.

One proceeds as follows. One may begin with the class specified by the properties one thinks are the morally significant ones of the act in question. (One could as well start with the class defined by all properties of the act, if one practically could do this!) One then enlarges the class by omitting from its definition those properties which would not affect the average utility which would result from all the acts in the class being performed. (The total utility might be affected simply by enlarging the size of the class; merely enlarging the class does not affect the average utility.) Conversely, one must also narrow any proposed class of "relevantly similar" acts if it is found that properties have been omitted from the specification of it, the presence of which would affect the average utility which would result if all the acts in the class were performed. The relevant class must not be too large, because of omission of features which define subclasses with different utilities; or too small, because of the presence of features which make no difference to the utilities.

An obvious example of an irrelevant property is that of the agent having a certain name (in most situations), or being a certain person. On the other hand, the fact that the agent wants (does not want) to perform a certain act normally is relevant to the utility of the performance of that act.

So much by way of exposition of the theory.

For many cases this theory and the Ideal Moral Code theory have identical implications. For, when it is better for actions of type A to be performed in a certain situation than for actions of any other type to be performed, it will often be a good thing to have type A actions prescribed by the moral code, directly or indirectly.

The theory also appears more simple than the Ideal Moral Code theory. In order to decide whether a given act is right or wrong we are not asked to do anything as grand as decide what some part of an ideal moral code would be like, but merely whether it would be better, or worse, for all in a relevant class of acts to be performed, as compared with some other relevant class. Thus it offers simple answers to questions such as whether one should vote ("What if nobody did?"), pick wildflowers along the road ("What if everyone did?"), join the army in wartime, or walk on the grass in a park.[16] Furthermore, the theory has a simple way of dealing with conflicts of rules: one determines whether it would be better, or worse, for all members of the more complex class

[16]One should not, however, overemphasize the simplicity. Whether one should vote in these circumstances is not decided by determining that it would have bad consequences if no one voted at all. It is a question whether it would be the best thing for all those people to vote (or not vote) in the class of situations relevantly similar to this one. It should be added, however, that if I am correct in my (below) assessment of the identity of this theory with act-utilitarianism, in the end it is simple, on the theory, to answer these questions.

It hardly seems that an ideal moral code would contain prescriptions as specific as rules about these matters. But the implications for such matters would be fairly direct if, as suggested above, an ideal moral code would contain a principle enjoining fairness, i.e., commanding persons to do their share in common enterprises (or restraints), when everyone benefits if most persons do their share, when persons find doing their share a burden, and when it is not essential that everyone do his share although it is essential that most do so, for the common benefit to be realized.

(about which the rules conflict) of actions to be performed (e.g., promises broken in the situation where the breach would save a life).

In one crucial respect, however, the two theories are totally different. For, in contrast with the Ideal Moral Code theory, this theory implies that exactly those acts are objectively right which are objectively right on the act-utilitarian theory. Hence the implications of this theory for action include the very counter-intuitive ones which led its proponents to seek an improvement over act-utilitarianism.

It must be conceded that this assessment of the implications of the theory is not yet a matter of general agreement,[17] and depends on a rather complex argument. In an earlier paper (loc. cit.) I argued that the theory does have these consequences, although my statement of the theory was rather misleading. More recently Professor David Lyons has come to the same conclusion, after an extensive discussion in which he urges that the illusion of a difference between the consequences of this theory and those of act-utilitarianism arises because of failure to notice certain important features of the context of actions, primarily the relative frequency of similar actions at about the same time, and "threshold effects" which an action may have on account of these features.[18]

It may be worthwhile to draw attention to the features of the Ideal Moral Code theory which avoid this particular result. In the first place, the Ideal Moral Code theory sets a limit to the number and complexity of the properties which define a class of morally similar actions. For, on this theory, properties of an act make a difference to its rightness, only if a moral principle referring to them (directly or indirectly) can be learned as part of the optimific moral code. Actual persons, with their emotional and intellectual limitations, are unable to learn a moral code which incorporates all the distinctions the other theory can recognize as morally relevant; and even if they could learn it, it would not be utility maximizing for them to try to apply it. In the second place, we noted that to be part of a moral code a proscription must be public, believed to be part of what is morally disapproved of by most adults. Thus whereas some actions (e.g., some performed in secret) would be utility maximizing, the Ideal Moral Code theory may imply that they are wrong, because it would be a bad thing for it to be generally recognized that a person is free to do that sort of thing.

16. I do not know of any reason to think that the Ideal Moral Code theory is a less plausible normative moral theory than any other form of utilitarianism. Other types of rule-utilitarianism are sufficiently like it, however, that it might be that relatively minor changes in formulation would make their implications for conduct indistinguishable from those of the Ideal Moral Code theory.

Two questions have not here been discussed. One is whether the Ideal Moral Code theory is open to the charge that it implies that some actions are right which are unjust in such an important way that they cannot be right. The second question is one a person would naturally wish to explore if he concluded that the right answer to the first question is affirmative: it is whether a rule-utilitarian view could be combined with some other principles like a principle of justice in a plausible way, without loss of all the features which make utilitarianism attractive. The foregoing discussion has not been intended to provide an answer to these questions.

[17]See, for instance, the interesting paper by Michael A. G. Stocker, "Consistency in Ethics," *Analysis* Supplement, XXV (January 1965), 116–22.

[18]David Lyons, *Forms and Limits of Utilitarianism* (Oxford: Clarendon Press, 1965).

1967

Morality and Advantage

David Gauthier

I

Hume asks, rhetorically, "what theory of morals can ever serve any useful purpose, unless it can show, by a particular detail, that all the duties which it recommends, are also the true interest of each individual?"[1] But there are many to whom this question does not seem rhetorical. Why, they ask, do we speak the language of morality, impressing upon our fellows their duties and obligations, urging them with appeals to what is right and good, if we could speak to the same effect in the language of prudence, appealing to considerations of interest and advantage? When the poet, Ogden Nash, is moved by the muse to cry out:

> O Duty,
> Why hast thou not the visage of a sweetie or a cutie?[2]

we do not anticipate the reply:

> O Poet,
> I really am a cutie and I think you ought to know it.

[1]David Hume, *An Enquiry Concerning the Principles of Morals,* sec. IX, pt. II.
[2]Ogden Nash, "Kind of an Ode to Duty."

The belief that duty cannot be reduced to interest, or that morality may require the agent to subordinate all considerations of advantage, is one which has withstood the assaults of contrary-minded philosophers from Plato to the present. Indeed, were it not for the conviction that only interest and advantage can motivate human actions, it would be difficult to understand philosophers contending so vigorously for the identity, or at least compatibility, of morality with prudence.

Yet if morality is not true prudence it would be wrong to suppose that those philosophers who have sought some connection between morality and advantage have been merely misguided. For it is a truism that we should all expect to be worse off if men were to substitute prudence, even of the most enlightened kind, for morality in all of their deliberations. And this truism demands not only some connection between morality and advantage, but a seemingly paradoxical connection. For if we should all expect to suffer, were men to be prudent instead of moral, then morality must contribute to advantage in a unique way, a way in which prudence—following reasons of advantage—cannot.

Thomas Hobbes is perhaps the first philosopher who tried to develop this seemingly paradoxical connection between morality and advantage. But since he could not admit that a man might ever reasonably subordinate considerations of advantage to the dictates of obligation, he was led to deny the possibility of real conflict between morality and prudence. So his argument fails to clarify the distinction between the view that claims of obligation reduce to considerations of interest and the view that claims of obligation promote advantage in a way in which considerations of interest cannot.

More recently, Kurt Baier has argued that "being moral is following rules designed to overrule self-interest whenever it is in the interest of everyone alike that everyone should set aside his interest."[3] Since prudence is following rules of (enlightened) self-interest, Baier is arguing that morality is designed to overrule prudence when it is to everyone's advantage that it do so—or, in other words, that morality contributes to advantage in a way in which prudence cannot.[4]

Baier does not actually demonstrate that morality contributes to advantage in this unique and seemingly paradoxical way. Indeed, he does not ask how it is possible that morality should do this. It is this possibility which I propose to demonstrate.

II

Let us examine the following proposition, which will be referred to as "the thesis": *Morality is a system of principles such that it is advantageous for everyone if everyone accepts and acts on it, yet acting on the system of principles requires that some persons perform disadvantageous acts.*[5]

What I wish to show is that this thesis *could be true,* that morality could possess those characteristics attributed to it by the thesis. I shall not try to show that the thesis is true—indeed, I shall argue in Section V that it presents at best an inadequate conception of morality. But it is plausible to suppose that a modified form of the thesis states a necessary, although not a sufficient, condition for a moral system.

[3]Kurt Baier, *The Moral Point of View: A Rational Basis of Ethics* (Ithaca, 1958), p. 314.

[4]That this, and only this, is what he is entitled to claim may not be clear to Baier, for he supposes his account of morality to answer the question "Why should we be moral?," interpreting "we" distributively. This, as I shall argue in Sec. IV, is quite mistaken.

[5]The thesis is not intended to state Baier's view of morality. I shall suggest in Sec. V that Baier's view would require substituting "everyone can expect to benefit" for "it is advantageous to everyone." The thesis is stronger and easier to discuss.

Two phrases in the thesis require elucidation. The first is "advantageous for everyone." I use this phrase to mean that *each* person will do better if the system is accepted and acted on than if *either* no system is accepted and acted on *or* a system is accepted and acted on which is similar, save that it never requires any person to perform disadvantageous acts.

Clearly, then, the claim that it is advantageous for everyone to accept and act on the system is a very strong one; it may be so strong that no system of principles which might be generally adopted could meet it. But I shall consider in Section V one among the possible ways of weakening the claim.

The second phrase requiring elucidation is "disadvantageous acts." I use this phrase to refer to acts which, in the context of their performance, would be less advantageous to the performer than some other act open to him in the same context. The phrase does not refer to acts which merely impose on the performer some short-term disadvantage that is recouped or outweighed in the long run. Rather it refers to acts which impose a disadvantage that is never recouped. It follows that the performer may say to himself, when confronted with the requirement to perform such an act, that it would be better *for him* not to perform it.

It is essential to note that the thesis, as elucidated, does not maintain that morality is advantageous for everyone in the sense that each person will do *best* if the system of principles is accepted and acted on. Each person will do better than if no system is adopted, or than if the one particular alternative mentioned above is adopted, but not than if any alternative is adopted.

Indeed, for each person required by the system to perform some disadvantageous act, it is easy to specify a better alternative—namely, the system modified so that it does not require *him* to perform any act disadvantageous to himself. Of course, there is no reason to expect such an alternative to be better than the moral system for everyone, or in fact for anyone other than the person granted the special exemption.

A second point to note is that each person must gain more from the disadvantageous acts performed by others than he loses from the disadvantageous acts performed by himself. If this were not the case, then some person would do better if a system were adopted exactly like the moral system save that it never requires *any* person to perform disadvantageous acts. This is ruled out by the force of "advantageous for everyone."

This point may be clarified by an example. Suppose that the system contains exactly one principle. Everyone is always to tell the truth. It follows from the thesis that each person gains more from those occasions on which others tell the truth, even though it is disadvantageous to them to do so, than he loses from those occasions on which he tells the truth even though it is disadvantageous to him to do so.

Now this is not to say that each person gains by telling others the truth in order to ensure that in return they tell him the truth. Such gains would merely be the result of accepting certain short-term disadvantages (those associated with truth-telling) in order to reap long-term benefits (those associated with being told the truth). Rather, what is required by the thesis is that those disadvantages which a person incurs in telling the truth, when he can expect neither short-term nor long-term benefits to accrue to him from truth-telling, are outweighed by those advantages he receives when others tell him the truth when they can expect no benefits to accrue to them from truth-telling.

The principle enjoins truth-telling in those cases in which whether one tells the truth or not will have no effect on whether others tell the truth. Such cases include those in which others have no way of knowing whether or not they are being told the truth. The thesis requires that the disadvantages one incurs in telling the truth in these cases are less than the advantages one receives in being told the truth by others in parallel cases; and the thesis requires that this holds for everyone.

Thus we see that although the disadvantages imposed by the system on any person are less than the advantages secured him through the imposition of disadvantages on others, yet the disadvantages are real in that incurring them is *unrelated* to receiving the advantages. The argument of long-term prudence, that I ought to incur some immediate disadvantage *so that* I shall receive compensating advantages later on, is entirely inapplicable here.

III

It will be useful to examine in some detail an example of a system which possesses those characteristics ascribed by the thesis to morality. This example, abstracted from the field of international relations, will enable us more clearly to distinguish, first, conduct based on immediate interest; second, conduct which is truly prudent; and third, conduct which promotes mutual advantage but is not prudent.

A and *B* are two nations with substantially opposed interests, who find themselves engaged in an arms race against each other. Both possess the latest in weaponry, so that each recognizes that the actual outbreak of full-scale war between them would be mutually disastrous. This recognition leads *A* and *B* to agree that each would be better off if they were mutually disarming instead of mutually arming. For mutual disarmament would preserve the balance of power between them while reducing the risk of war.

Hence *A* and *B* enter into a disarmament pact. The pact is advantageous for both if both accept and act on it, although clearly it is not advantageous for either to act on it if the other does not.

Let *A* be considering whether or not to adhere to the pact in some particular situation, whether or not actually to perform some act of disarmament. *A* will quite likely consider the act to have disadvantageous consequences. *A* expects to benefit, not by its own acts of disarmament, but by *B*'s acts. Hence if *A* were to reason simply in terms of immediate interest, *A* might well decide to violate the pact.

But *A*'s decision need be neither prudent nor reasonable. For suppose first that *B* is able to determine whether or not *A* adheres to the pact. If *A* violates, then *B* will detect the violation and will then consider what to do in the light of *A*'s behavior. It is not to *B*'s advantage to disarm alone; *B* expects to gain, not by its own acts of disarmament, but by *A*'s acts. Hence *A*'s violation, if known to *B*, leads naturally to *B*'s counter-violation. If this continues, the effect of the pact is entirely undone, and *A* and *B* return to their mutually disadvantageous arms race. *A*, foreseeing this when considering whether or not to adhere to the pact in the given situation, must therefore conclude that the truly prudent course of action is to adhere.

Now suppose that *B* is unable to determine whether or not *A* adheres to the pact in the particular situation under consideration. If *A* judges adherence to be in itself disadvantageous, then it will decide, both on the basis of immediate interest and on the basis of prudence, to violate the pact. Since *A*'s decision is unknown to *B*, it cannot affect whether or not *B* adheres to the pact, and so the advantage gained by *A*'s violation is not outweighed by any consequent loss.

Therefore if *A* and *B* are prudent they will adhere to their disarmament pact whenever violation would be detectable by the other, and violate the pact whenever violation would not be detectable by the other. In other words, they will adhere openly and violate secretly. The disarmament pact between *A* and *B* thus possesses two of the characteristics ascribed by the thesis to morality. First, accepting the pact and acting on it is more advantageous for each than making no pact at all. Second, in so far as the pact stipulates that each must disarm even when disarming is undetectable by the other, it requires each to perform disadvantageous acts—acts which run counter to considerations of prudence.

One further condition must be met if the disarmament pact is to possess those characteristics ascribed by the thesis to a system of morality. It must be the case that the requirement that each party perform disadvantageous acts be essential to the advantage conferred by the pact; or, to put the matter in the way in which we expressed it earlier, both *A* and *B* must do better to adhere to this pact than to a pact which is similar save that it requires no disadvantageous acts. In terms of the example, *A* and *B* must do better to adhere to the pact than to a pact which stipulates that each must disarm only when disarming is detectable by the other.

We may plausibly suppose this condition to be met. Although *A* will gain by secretly retaining arms itself, it will lose by *B*'s similar acts, and its losses may well outweigh its gains. *B* may equally lose more by *A*'s secret violations than it gains by its own. So, despite the fact that prudence requires each to violate secretly, each may well do better if both adhere secretly than if both violate secretly. Supposing this to be the case, the disarmament pact is formally analogous to a moral system, as characterized by the thesis. That is, acceptance of and adherence to the pact by *A* and *B* is more advantageous for each, either than making no pact at all or than acceptance of and adherence to a pact requiring only open disarmament, and the pact requires each to perform acts of secret disarmament which are disadvantageous.

Some elementary notation, adapted for our purposes from the mathematical theory of games, may make the example even more perspicuous. Given a disarmament pact between *A* and *B*, each may pursue two pure strategies—adherence and violation. There are, then, four possible combinations of strategies, each determining a particular outcome. These outcomes can be ranked preferentially for each nation; we shall let the numerals 1 to 4 represent the ranking from first to fourth preference. Thus we construct a simple matrix,[6] in which *A*'s preferences are stated first:

		B	
		adheres	*violates*
A	adheres	2, 2	4, 1
	violates	1, 4	3, 3

The matrix does not itself show that agreement is advantageous to both, for it gives only the rankings of outcomes given the agreement. But it is plausible to assume that *A* and *B* would rank mutual violation on a par with no agreement. If we assume this, we can then indicate the value to each of making and adhering to the pact by reference to the matrix.

The matrix shows immediately that adherence to the pact is not the most advantageous possibility for either, since each prefers the outcome, if it alone violates, to the outcome of mutual adherence. It shows also that each gains less from its own vio-

[6]Those familiar with the theory of games will recognize the matrix as a variant of the Prisoner's Dilemma. In a more formal treatment, it would be appropriate to develop the relation between morality and advantage by reference to the Prisoner's Dilemma. This would require reconstructing the disarmament pact and the moral system as proper games. Here I wish only to suggest the bearing of game theory on our enterprise.

lations than it loses from the other's, since each ranks mutual adherence above mutual violation.

Let us now use the matrix to show that, as we argued previously, public adherence to the pact is prudent and mutually advantageous, whereas private adherence is not prudent although mutually advantageous. Consider first the case when adherence—and so violation—are open and public.

If adherence and violation are open, then each knows the strategy chosen by the other, and can adjust its own strategy in the light of this knowledge—or, in other words, the strategies are interdependent. Suppose that each initially chooses the strategy of adherence. *A* notices that if it switches to violation it gains—moving from 2 to 1 in terms of preference ranking. Hence immediate interest dictates such a switch. But it notices further that if it switches, then *B* can also be expected to switch—moving from 4 to 3 on its preference scale. The eventual outcome would be stable, in that neither could benefit from switching from violation back to adherence. But the eventual outcome would represent not a gain for *A* but a loss—moving from 2 to 3 on its preference scale. Hence prudence dictates no change from the strategy of adherence. This adherence is mutually advantageous; *A* and *B* are in precisely similar positions in terms of their pact.

Consider now the case when adherence and violation are secret and private. Neither nation knows the strategy chosen by the other, so the two strategies are independent. Suppose *A* is trying to decide which strategy to follow. It does not know *B*'s choice. But it notices that if *B* adheres, then it pays *A* to violate, attaining 1 rather than 2 in terms of preference ranking. If *B* violates, then again it pays *A* to violate, attaining 3 rather than 4 on its preference scale. Hence, no matter which strategy *B* chooses, *A* will do better to violate, and so prudence dictates violation.

B of course reasons in just the same way. Hence each is moved by considerations of prudence to violate the pact, and the outcome assigns each rank 3 on its preference scale. This outcome is mutually disadvantageous to *A* and *B*, since mutual adherence would assign each rank 2 on its preference scale.

If *A* and *B* are both capable only of rational prudence, they find themselves at an impasse. The advantage of mutual adherence to the agreement when violations would be secret is not available to them, since neither can find it in his own over-all interest not to violate secretly. Hence, strictly prudent nations cannot reap the maximum advantage possible from a pact of the type under examination.

Of course, what *A* and *B* will no doubt endeavor to do is eliminate the possibility of secret violations of their pact. Indeed, barring additional complications, each must find it to his advantage to make it possible for the other to detect his own violations. In other words, each must find it advantageous to ensure that their choice of strategies is interdependent, so that the pact will always be prudent for each to keep. But it may not be possible for them to ensure this, and to the extent that they cannot, prudence will prevent them from maximizing mutual advantage.

IV

We may now return to the connection of morality with advantage. Morality, if it is a system of principles of the type characterized in the thesis, requires that some persons perform acts genuinely disadvantageous to themselves, as a means to greater mutual advantage. Our example shows sufficiently that such a system is possible, and indicates more precisely its character. In particular, by an argument strictly parallel to that which we have pursued, we may show that men who are merely prudent will not perform the required disadvantageous acts. But in so violating the principles of morality, they will disadvantage themselves. Each will lose more by the violations of others than he will gain by his own violations.

Now this conclusion would be unsurprising if it were only that no man can gain if he alone is moral rather than prudent. Obviously such a man loses, for he adheres to moral principles to his own disadvantage, while others violate them also to his disadvantage. The benefit of the moral system is not one which any individual can secure for himself, since each man gains from the sacrifices of others.

What is surprising in our conclusion is that no man can ever gain if he is moral. Not only does he not gain by being moral if others are prudent, but he also does not gain by being moral if others are moral. For although he now receives the advantage of others' adherence to moral principles, he reaps the disadvantage of his own adherence. As long as his own adherence to morality is independent of what others do (and this is required to distinguish morality from prudence), he must do better to be prudent.

If all men are moral, all will do better than if all are prudent. But any one man will always do better if he is prudent than if he is moral. There is no real paradox in supposing that morality is advantageous, even though it requires the performance of disadvantageous acts.

On the supposition that morality has the characteristics ascribed to it by the thesis, is it possible to answer the question "Why should we be moral?" where "we" is taken distributively, so that the question is a compendious way of asking, for each person, "Why should I be moral?" More simply, is it possible to answer the question "Why should I be moral?"

I take it that this question, if asked seriously, demands a reason for being moral other than moral reasons themselves. It demands that moral reasons be shown to be reasons for acting by a noncircular argument. Those who would answer it, like Baier, endeavor to do so by the introduction of considerations of advantage.

Two such considerations have emerged from our discussion. The first is that if all are moral, all will do better than if all are prudent. This will serve to answer the question "Why should we be moral?" if this question is interpreted rather as "Why should we all be moral—rather than all being something else?" If we must all be the same, then each person has a reason—a prudential reason—to prefer that we all be moral.

But, so interpreted, "Why should we be moral?" is not a compendious way of asking, for each person, "Why should I be moral?" Of course, if everyone is to be whatever I am, then I should be moral. But a general answer to the question "Why should I be moral?" cannot presuppose this.

The second consideration is that any individual always does better to be prudent rather than moral, provided his choice does not determine other choices. But in so far as this answers the question "Why should I be moral?" it leads to the conclusion "I should not be moral." One feels that this is not the answer which is wanted.

We may put the matter otherwise. The individual who needs a reason for being moral which is not itself a moral reason cannot have it. There is nothing surprising about this; it would be much more surprising if such reasons could be found. For it is more than apparently paradoxical to suppose that considerations of advantage could ever of themselves justify accepting a real disadvantage.

V

I suggested in Section II that the thesis, in modified form, might provide a necessary, although not a sufficient, condition for a moral system. I want now to consider how one might characterize the man who would qualify as moral according to the thesis—I shall call him the "moral" man—and then ask what would be lacking from this characterization, in terms of some of our commonplace moral views.

The rationally prudent man is incapable of moral behavior, in even the limited sense defined by the thesis. What difference must there be between the prudent man and the "moral" man? Most simply, the "moral" man is the prudent but trustworthy man. I treat trustworthiness as the capacity which enables its possessor to adhere, and to judge that he ought to adhere, to a commitment which he has made, without regard to considerations of advantage.

The prudent but trustworthy man does not possess this capacity completely. He is capable of trustworthy behavior only in so far as he regards his *commitment* as advantageous. Thus he differs from the prudent man just in the relevant respect; he accepts arguments of the form "If it is advantageous for me to agree[7] to do *x*, and I do agree to do *x*, then I ought to do *x*, whether or not it then proves advantageous for me to do *x*."

Suppose that *A* and *B*, the parties to the disarmament pact, are prudent but trustworthy. *A*, considering whether or not secretly to violate the agreement, reasons that its advantage in making and keeping the agreement, provided *B* does so as well, is greater than its advantage in not making it. If it can assume that *B* reasons in the same way, then it is in a position to conclude that it ought not to violate the pact. Although violation would be advantageous, consideration of this advantage is ruled out by *A*'s trustworthiness, given the advantage in agreeing to the pact.

The prudent but trustworthy man meets the requirements implicitly imposed by the thesis for the "moral" man. But how far does this "moral" man display two characteristics commonly associated with morality—first, a willingness to make sacrifices, and second, a concern with fairness?

Whenever a man ignores his own advantage for reasons other than those of greater advantage, he may be said to make some sacrifice. The "moral" man, in being trustworthy, is thus required to make certain sacrifices. But these are extremely limited. And—not surprisingly, given the general direction of our argument—it is quite possible that they limit the advantages which the "moral" man can secure.

Once more let us turn to our example. *A* and *B* have entered into a disarmament agreement and, being prudent but trustworthy, are faithfully carrying it out. The government of *A* is now informed by its scientists, however, that they have developed an effective missile defense, which will render *A* invulnerable to attack by any of the weapons actually or potentially at *B*'s disposal, barring unforeseen technological developments. Furthermore, this defense can be installed secretly. The government is now called upon to decide whether to violate its agreement with *B*, install the new defense, and, with the arms it has retained through its violation, establish its dominance over *B*.

A is in a type of situation quite different from that previously considered. For it is not just that *A* will do better by secretly violating its agreement. *A* reasons not only that it will do better to violate no matter what *B* does, but that it will do better if both violate than if both continue to adhere to the pact. *A* is now in a position to gain from abandoning the agreement; it no longer finds mutual adherence advantageous.

We may represent this new situation in another matrix:

[7]The word "agree" requires elucidation. It is essential not to confuse an advantage in agreeing to do *x* with an advantage in saying that one will do *x*. If it is advantageous for me to agree to do *x*, then there is some set of actions open to me which includes both saying that I will do *x* and doing *x*, and which is more advantageous to me than any se' of actions open to me which does not include saying that I will do *x*. On the other hand, if it is advantageous for me to say that I will do *x*, then there is some set of actions open to me which includes saying that I will do *x*, and which is more advantageous to me than any set which does not include saying that I will do *x*. But this set need not include doing *x*.

		B	
		adheres	*violates*
A	adheres	3, 2	4, 1
	violates	1, 4	2, 3

We assume again that the ranking of mutual violation is the same as that of no agreement. Now had this situation obtained at the outset, no agreement would have been made, for *A* would have had no reason to enter into a disarmament pact. And of course had *A* expected this situation to come about, no agreement—or only a temporary agreement—would have been made; *A* would no doubt have risked the short-term dangers of the continuing arms race in the hope of securing the long-run benefit of predominance over *B* once its missile defense was completed. On the contrary, *A* expected to benefit from the agreement, but now finds that, because of its unexpected development of a missile defense, the agreement is not in fact advantageous to it.

The prudent but trustworthy man is willing to carry out his agreements, and judges that he ought to carry them out, in so far as he considers them advantageous. *A* is prudent but trustworthy. But is *A* willing to carry out its agreement to disarm, now that it no longer considers the agreement advantageous?

If *A* adheres to its agreement in this situation, it makes a sacrifice greater than any advantage it receives from the similar sacrifices of others. It makes a sacrifice greater in kind than any which can be required by a mutually advantageous agreement. It must, then, possess a capacity for trustworthy behavior greater than that ascribed to the merely prudent but trustworthy man (or nation). This capacity need not be unlimited; it need not extend to a willingness to adhere to any commitment no matter what sacrifice is involved. But it must involve a willingness to adhere to a commitment made in the expectation of advantage, should that expectation be disappointed.

I shall call the man (or nation) who is willing to adhere, and judges that he ought to adhere, to his prudentially undertaken agreements even if they prove disadvantageous to him, the trustworthy man. It is likely that there are advantages available to trustworthy men which are not available to merely prudent but trustworthy men. For there may be situations in which men can make agreements which each expects to be advantageous to him, provided he can count on the others' adhering to it whether or not their expectation of advantage is realized. But each can count on this only if all have the capacity to adhere to commitments regardless of whether the commitment actually proves advantageous. Hence, only trustworthy men who know each other to be such will be able rationally to enter into, and so to benefit from, such agreements.

Baier's view of morality departs from that stated in the thesis in that it requires trustworthy, and not merely prudent but trustworthy, men. Baier admits that "a person might do better for himself by following enlightened self-interest rather than morality."[8] This admission seems to require that morality be a system of principles which each person may expect, initially, to be advantageous to him, if adopted and adhered to by everyone, but not a system which actually is advantageous to everyone.

Our commonplace moral views do, I think, support the view that the moral man must be trustworthy. Hence, we have established one modification required in the thesis, if it is to provide a more adequate set of conditions for a moral system.

But there is a much more basic respect in which the "moral" man falls short of our expectations. He is willing to temper his single-minded pursuit of advantage only by

[8]Baier, *op. cit.*, p. 314.

accepting the obligation to adhere to prudentially undertaken commitments. He has no real concern for the advantage of others, which would lead him to modify his pursuit of advantage when it conflicted with the similar pursuits of others. Unless he expects to gain, he is unwilling to accept restrictions on the pursuit of advantage which are intended to equalize the opportunities open to all. In other words, he has no concern with fairness.

We tend to think of the moral man as one who does not seek his own well-being by means which would deny equal well-being to his fellows. This marks him off clearly from the "moral" man, who differs from the prudent man only in that he can overcome the apparent paradox of prudence and obtain those advantages which are available only to those who can display real restraint in their pursuit of advantage.

Thus a system of principles might meet the conditions laid down in the thesis without taking any account of considerations of fairness. Such a system would contain principles for ensuring increased advantage (or expectation of advantage) to everyone, but no further principle need be present to determine the distribution of this increase.

It is possible that there are systems of principles which, if adopted and adhered to, provide advantages which strictly prudent men, however rational, cannot attain. These advantages are a function of the sacrifices which the principles impose on their adherents.

Morality may be such a system. If it is, this would explain our expectation that we should all be worse off were we to substitute prudence for morality in our deliberations. But to characterize morality as a system of principles advantageous to all is not to answer the question "Why should I be moral?" nor is it to provide for those considerations of fairness which are equally essential to our moral understanding.

Part IV

1971–1993

1972

Morality as a System of Hypothetical Imperatives

Philippa Foot

There are many difficulties and obscurities in Kant's moral philosophy, and few contemporary moralists will try to defend it all. Many, for instance, agree in rejecting Kant's derivation of duties from the mere form of the law expressed in terms of a universally legislative will. Nevertheless, it is generally supposed, even by those who would not dream of calling themselves his followers, that Kant established one thing beyond doubt—namely, the necessity of distinguishing moral judgments from hypothetical imperatives. That moral judgments cannot be hypothetical imperatives has come to seem an unquestionable truth. It will be argued here that it is not.

In discussing so thoroughly Kantian a notion as that of the hypothetical imperative, one naturally begins by asking what Kant himself meant by a hypothetical imperative, and it may be useful to say a little about the idea of an imperative as this appears in Kant's works. In writing about imperatives Kant seems to be thinking at least as much of statements about what ought to be or should be done, as of injunctions expressed in the imperative mood. He even describes as an imperative the assertion that it would be "good to do or refrain from doing something"[1] and explains that for a will that "does not always do something simply because it is presented to it as a good thing to do" this has the force of a command of reason. We may therefore think of Kant's imperatives as statements to the effect that something ought to be done or that it would be good to do it.

[1]*Foundations of the Metaphysics of Morals,* Sec. II, trans. by L. W. Beck.

The distinction between hypothetical imperatives and categorical imperatives, which plays so important a part in Kant's ethics, appears in characteristic form in the following passages from the *Foundations of the Metaphysics of Morals:*

> All imperatives command either hypothetically or categorically. The former present the practical necessity of a possible action as a means to achieving something else which one desires (or which one may possibly desire). The categorical imperative would be one which presented an action as of itself objectively necessary, without regard to any other end.[2]
>
> If the action is good only as a means to something else, the imperative is hypothetical; but if it is thought of as good in itself, and hence as necessary in a will which of itself conforms to reason as the principle of this will, the imperative is categorical.[3]

The hypothetical imperative, as Kant defines it, "says only that the action is good to some purpose" and the purpose, he explains, may be possible or actual. Among imperatives related to actual purposes Kant mentions rules of prudence, since he believes that all men necessarily desire their own happiness. Without committing ourselves to this view it will be useful to follow Kant in classing together as "hypothetical imperatives" those telling a man what he ought to do because (or if) he wants something and those telling him what he ought to do on grounds of self-interest. Common opinion agrees with Kant in insisting that a moral man must accept a rule of duty whatever his interests or desires.[4]

Having given a rough description of the class of Kantian hypothetical imperatives it may be useful to point to the heterogeneity within it. Sometimes what a man should do depends on his passing inclination, as when he wants his coffee hot and should warm the jug. Sometimes it depends on some long-term project, when the feelings and inclinations of the moment are irrelevant. If one wants to be a respectable philosopher one should get up in the mornings and do some work, though just at that moment when one should do it the thought of being a respectable philosopher leaves one cold. It is true nevertheless to say of one, at that moment, that one wants to be a respectable philosopher,[5] and this can be the foundation of a desire-dependent hypothetical imperative. The term "desire" as used in the original account of the hypothetical imperative was meant as a grammatically convenient substitute for "want," and was not meant to carry any implication of inclination rather than long-term aim or project. Even the word "project," taken strictly, introduces undesirable restrictions. If someone is devoted to his family or his country or to any cause, there are certain things he wants, which may then be the basis of hypothetical imperatives, without either inclinations or projects being quite what is in question. Hypothetical imperatives should already be appearing as extremely diverse; a further important distinction is between those that concern an individual and those that concern a group. The desires on which a hypothetical imperative is dependent may be those of one man, or may be taken for granted as belonging to a number of people engaged in some common project or sharing common aims.

Is Kant right to say that moral judgments are categorical, not hypothetical, imperatives? It may seem that he is, for we find in our language two different uses of

[2]Ibid.

[3]Ibid.

[4]According to the position sketched here we have three forms of hypothetical imperative: "If you want x you should do y," "Because you want x you should do y," and "Because x is in your interest you should do y." For Kant the third would automatically be covered by the second.

[5]To say that at that moment one wants to be a respectable philosopher would be another matter. Such a statement requires a special connection between the desire and the moment.

words such as "should" and "ought," apparently corresponding to Kant's hypothetical and categorical imperatives, and we find moral judgments on the "categorical" side. Suppose, for instance, we have advised a traveller that he should take a certain train, believing him to be journeying to his home. If we find that he has decided to go elsewhere, we will most likely have to take back what we said: the "should" will now be unsupported and in need of support. Similarly, we must be prepared to withdraw our statement about what he should do if we find that the right relation does not hold between the action and the end—that it is either no way of getting what he wants (or doing what he wants to do) or not the most eligible among possible means. The use of "should" and "ought" in moral contexts is, however, quite different. When we say that a man should do something and intend a moral judgment we do not have to back up what we say by considerations about his interests or his desires; if no such connection can be found the "should" need not be withdrawn. It follows that the agent cannot rebut an assertion about what, morally speaking, he should do by showing that the action is not ancillary to his interests or desires. Without such a connection the "should" does not stand unsupported and in need of support;[6] the support that *it* requires is of another kind.[7]

There is, then, one clear difference between moral judgments and the class of "hypothetical imperatives" so far discussed. In the latter "should" is "used hypothetically," in the sense defined, and if Kant were merely drawing attention to this piece of linguistic usage his point would easily be proved. But obviously Kant meant more than this; in describing moral judgments as non-hypothetical—that is, categorical imperatives—he is ascribing to them a special dignity and necessity which this usage cannot give. Modern philosophers follow Kant in talking, for example, about the "unconditional requirement" expressed in moral judgments. These, they say, tell us what we have to do whatever our interests or desires, and by their inescapability they are distinguished from hypothetical imperatives.

The problem is to find proof for this further feature of moral judgments. If anyone fails to see the gap that has to be filled it will be useful to point out to him that we find "should" used non-hypothetically in some non-moral statements to which no one attributes the special dignity and necessity conveyed by the description "categorical imperative." For instance, we find this non-hypothetical use of "should" in sentences enunciating rules of etiquette, as, for example, that an invitation in the third person should be answered in the third person, where the rule does not *fail to apply* to someone who has his own good reasons for ignoring this piece of nonsense, or who simply does not care about what, from the point of view of etiquette, he should do. Similarly, there is a non-hypothetical use of "should" in contexts where something like a club rule is in question. The club secretary who has told a member that he should not bring ladies into the smoking-room does not say, "Sorry, I was mistaken" when informed that this member is resigning tomorrow and cares nothing about his reputation in the club. Lacking a connection with the agent's desires or interests, this "should" does not stand "unsupported and in need of support"; it requires only the backing of the rule. The use of "should" is therefore "non-hypothetical" in the sense defined.

[6] I am here going back on something I said in an earlier article ("Moral Beliefs" [*Proceedings of the Aristotelian Society,* Volume 59, 1958–59. Reprinted in Foot, *Virtues and Vices and Other Essays in Moral Philosophy.* Berkeley, Ca.: Univ. of California Press, 1978]) where I thought it necessary to show that virtue must benefit the agent. I believe the rest of the article can stand.

[7] Op. cit. [*Virtues and Vices*], p. 119. See also Foot, "Moral Arguments" [*Mind,* Volume 67, 1958. Reprinted in *Virtues and Vices,* p. 105].

It follows that if a hypothetical use of "should" gave a hypothetical imperative, and a non-hypothetical use of "should" a categorical imperative, then "should" statements based on rules of etiquette, or rules of a club would be categorical imperatives. Since this would not be accepted by defenders of the categorical imperative in ethics, who would insist that these other "should" statements give hypothetical imperatives, they must be using this expression in some other sense. We must therefore ask what they mean when they say that "You should answer . . . in the third person" is a hypothetical imperative. Very roughly the idea seems to be that one may reasonably ask why anyone should bother about what should (from the point of view of etiquette) be done, and that such considerations deserve no notice unless reason is shown. So although people give as their reason for doing something the fact that it is required by etiquette, we do not take this consideration as *in itself giving us reason to act.* Considerations of etiquette do not have any automatic reason-giving force, and a man might be right if he denied that he had reason to do "what's done."

This seems to take us to the heart of the matter, for, by contrast, it is supposed that moral considerations necessarily give reasons for acting to any man. The difficulty is, of course, to defend this proposition which is more often repeated than explained. Unless it is said, implausibly, that all "should" or "ought" statements give reasons for acting, which leaves the old problem of assigning a special categorical status to moral judgment, we must be told what it is that makes the moral "should" relevantly different from the "shoulds" appearing in normative statements of other kinds.[8] Attempts have sometimes been made to show that some kind of irrationality is involved in ignoring the "should" of morality: in saying "Immoral—so what?" as one says "Not *comme il faut*—so what?" But as far as I can see these have all rested on some illegitimate assumption, as, for instance, of thinking that the amoral man, who agrees that some piece of conduct is immoral but takes no notice of that, is inconsistently disregarding a rule of conduct that he has accepted; or again of thinking it inconsistent to desire that others will not do to one what one proposes to do to them. The fact is that the man who rejects morality because he sees no reason to obey its rules can be convicted of villainy but not of inconsistency. Nor will his action necessarily be irrational. Irrational actions are those in which a man in some way defeats his own purposes, doing what is calculated to be disadvantageous or to frustrate his ends. Immorality does not *necessarily* involve any such thing.

It is obvious that the normative character of moral judgment does not guarantee its reason-giving force. Moral judgments are normative, but so are judgments of manners, statements of club rules, and many others. Why should the first provide reasons for acting as the others do not? In every case it is because there is a background of teaching that the non-hypothetical "should" can be used. The behavior is required, not

[8]To say that moral considerations are *called* reasons is blatantly to ignore the problem.

In the case of etiquette or club rules it is obvious that the non-hypothetical use of "should" has resulted in the loss of the usual connection between what one should do and what one has reason to do. Someone who objects that in the moral case a man cannot be justified in restricting his practical reasoning in this way, since every moral "should" gives reasons for acting, must face the following dilemma. Either it is possible to create reasons for acting simply by putting together any silly rules and introducing a non-hypothetical "should," or else the non-hypothetical "should" does not necessarily imply reasons for acting. If it does not necessarily imply reasons for acting we may ask why it is supposed to do so in the case of morality. Why cannot the indifferent amoral man say that for him "$should_m$" gives no reason for acting, treating "$should_m$" as most of us treat "$should_e$"? Those who insist that "$should_m$" is categorical in this second "reason-giving" sense do not seem to realize that they never prove this to be so. They sometimes say that moral considerations "just do" give reasons for acting, without explaining why some devotee of etiquette could not say the same about the rules of etiquette.

simply recommended, but the question remains as to why we should do what we are required to do. It is true that moral rules are often enforced much more strictly than the rules of etiquette, and our reluctance to press the non-hypothetical "should" of etiquette may be one reason why we think of the rules of etiquette as hypothetical imperatives. But are we then to say that there is nothing behind the idea that moral judgments are categorical imperatives but the relative stringency of our moral teaching? I believe that this may have more to do with the matter than the defenders of the categorical imperative would like to admit. For if we look at the kind of thing that is said in its defense we may find ourselves puzzled about what the words can even mean unless we connect them with the feelings that this stringent teaching implants. People talk, for instance, about the "binding force" of morality, but it is not clear what this means if not that we *feel* ourselves unable to escape. Indeed the "inescapability" of moral requirements is often cited when they are being contrasted with hypothetical imperatives. No one, it is said, escapes the requirements of ethics by having or not having particular interests or desires. Taken in one way this only reiterates the contrast between the "should" of morality and the hypothetical "should," and once more places morality alongside of etiquette. Both are inescapable in that behavior does not cease to offend against either morality or etiquette because the agent is indifferent to their purposes and to the disapproval he will incur by flouting them. But morality is supposed to be inescapable in some special way and this may turn out to be merely the reflection of the way morality is taught. Of course, we must try other ways of expressing the fugitive thought. It may be said, for instance, that moral judgments have a kind of necessity since they tell us what we "must do" or "have to do" whatever our interests and desires. The sense of this is, again, obscure. Sometimes when we use such expressions we are referring to physical or mental compulsion. (A man has to go along if he is pulled by strong men and he has to give in if tortured beyond endurance.) But it is only in the absence of such conditions that moral judgments apply. Another and more common sense of the words is found in sentences such as "I caught a bad cold and had to stay in bed" where a penalty for acting otherwise is in the offing. The necessity of acting morally is not, however, supposed to depend on such penalties. Another range of examples, not necessarily having to do with penalties, is found where there is an unquestioned acceptance of some project or role, as when a nurse tells us that she has to make her rounds at a certain time, or we say that we have to run for a certain train.[9] But these too are irrelevant in the present context, since the acceptance condition can always be revoked.

No doubt it will be suggested that it is in some other sense of the words "have to" or "must" that one has to or must do what morality demands. But why should one insist that there must be such a sense when it proves so difficult to say what it is? Suppose that what we take for a puzzling thought were really no thought at all but only the reflection of our *feelings* about morality? Perhaps it makes no sense to say that we "have to" submit to the moral law, or that morality is "inescapable" in some special way. For just as one may feel as if one is falling without believing that one is moving downward, so one may feel as if one has to do what is morally required without believing oneself to be under physical or psychological compulsion, or about to incur a penalty if one does not comply. No one thinks that if the word "falling" is used in a statement reporting one's sensations it must be used in a special sense. But this kind of mistake may be involved in looking for the special sense in which one "has to" do what morality demands. There is no difficulty about the idea that we feel we *have to* behave morally, and given the

[9] I am grateful to Rogers Albritton for drawing my attention to this interesting use of expressions such as "have to" or "must."

psychological conditions of the learning of moral behavior it is natural that we should have such feelings. What we cannot do is quote them in support of the doctrine of the categorical imperative. It seems, then, that in so far as it is backed up by statements to the effect that the moral law *is* inescapable, or that we *do* have to do what is morally required of us, it is uncertain whether the doctrine of the categorical imperative even makes sense.

The conclusion we should draw is that moral judgments have no better claim to be categorical imperatives than do statements about matters of etiquette. People may indeed follow either morality or etiquette without asking why they should do so, but equally well they may not. They may ask for reasons and may reasonably refuse to follow either if reasons are not to be found.

It will be said that this way of viewing moral considerations must be totally destructive of morality, because no one could ever act morally unless he accepted such considerations as in themselves sufficient reason for action. Actions that are truly moral must be done "for their own sake," "because they are right," and not for some ulterior purpose. This argument we must examine with care, for the doctrine of the categorical imperative has owed much to its persuasion.

Is there anything to be said for the thesis that a truly moral man acts "out of respect for the moral law" or that he does what is morally right because it is morally right? That such propositions are not prima facie absurd depends on the fact that moral judgment concerns itself with a man's reasons for acting as well as with what he does. Law and etiquette require only that certain things are done or left undone, but no one is counted as charitable if he gives alms "for the praise of men," and one who is honest only because it pays him to be honest does not have the virtue of honesty. This kind of consideration was crucial in shaping Kant's moral philosophy. He many times contrasts acting out of respect for the moral law with acting from an ulterior motive, and what is more from one that is self-interested. In the early *Lectures on Ethics* he gave the principle of truth-telling under a system of hypothetical imperatives as that of not lying *if it harms one* to lie. In the *Metaphysics of Morals* he says that ethics cannot start from the ends which a man may propose to himself, since these are all "selfish."[10] In the *Critique of Practical Reason* he argues explicitly that when acting not out of respect for moral law but "on a material maxim" men do what they do for the sake of pleasure or happiness.

> All material practical principles are, as such, of one and the same kind and belong under the general principle of self love or one's own happiness.[11]

Kant, in fact, was a psychological hedonist in respect of all actions except those done for the sake of the moral law, and this faulty theory of human nature was one of the things preventing him from seeing that moral virtue might be compatible with the rejection of the categorical imperative.

If we put this theory of human action aside, and allow as ends the things that seem to be ends, the picture changes. It will surely be allowed that quite apart from thoughts of duty a man may care about the suffering of others, having a sense of identification with them, and wanting to help if he can. Of course he must want not the reputation of charity, nor even a gratifying role helping others, but, quite simply, their good. If this is what he does care about, then he will be attached to the end proper to the virtue of charity and a comparison with someone acting from an ulterior motive (even a respectable

[10] Pt. II, Introduction, sec. II.

[11] Immanuel Kant, *Critique of Practical Reason*, trans. L. W. Beck, p. 133.

ulterior motive) is out of place. Nor will the conformity of his action to the rule of charity be merely contingent. Honest action may happen to further a man's career; charitable actions do not *happen* to further the good of others.[12]

Can a man accepting only hypothetical imperatives possess other virtues besides that of charity? Could he be just or honest? This problem is more complex because there is no end related to such virtues as the good of others is related to charity. But what reason could there be for refusing to call a man a just man if he acted justly because he loved truth and liberty, and wanted every man to be treated with a certain respect? And why should the truly honest man not follow honesty for the sake of the good that honest dealing brings to men? Of course, the usual difficulties can be raised about the rare case in which no good is foreseen from an individual act of honesty. But it is not evident that a man's desires could not give him reason to act honestly even here. He wants to live openly and in good faith with his neighbors; it is not all the same to him to lie and conceal.

If one wants to know whether there could be a truly moral man who accepted moral principles as hypothetical rules of conduct, as many people accept rules of etiquette as hypothetical rules of conduct, one must consider the right kind of example. A man who demanded that morality should be brought under the heading of self-interest would not be a good candidate, nor would anyone who was ready to be charitable or honest only so long as he felt inclined. A cause such as justice makes strenuous demands, but this is not peculiar to morality, and men are prepared to toil to achieve many ends not endorsed by morality. That they are prepared to fight so hard for moral ends—for example, for liberty and justice—depends on the fact that these are the kinds of ends that arouse devotion. To sacrifice a great deal for the sake of etiquette one would need to be under the spell of the emphatic "ought." One could hardly be devoted to behaving *comme il fault.*

In spite of all that has been urged in favour of the hypothetical imperative in ethics, I am sure that many people will be unconvinced and will argue that one element essential to moral virtue is still missing. This missing feature is the recognition of a *duty* to adopt those ends which we have attributed to the moral man. We have said that he *does* care about others, and about causes such as liberty and justice; that it is on this account that he will accept a system of morality. But what if he never cared about such things, or what if he ceased to care? Is it not the case that he *ought* to care? This is exactly what Kant would say, for though at times he sounds as if he thought that morality is not concerned with ends, at others he insists that the adoption of ends such as the happiness of others is itself dictated by morality.[13] How is this proposition to be regarded by one who rejects all talk about the binding force of the moral law? He will agree that a moral man has moral ends and cannot be indifferent to matters such as suffering and injustice. Further, he will recognize in the statement that one *ought* to care about these things a correct application of the non-hypothetical moral "ought" by which society is apt to voice its demands. He will not, however, take the fact that he ought to have certain ends as in itself reason to adopt them. If he himself is a moral man then he cares about such things, but not "because he ought." If he is an amoral man he may deny that he has any reason to trouble his head over this or any other moral demand. Of course he may be mistaken, and his life as well as others' lives may be most sadly spoiled by his selfishness. But this is not what is urged by those who think they can close the matter by

[12]It is not, of course, necessary that charitable actions should *succeed* in helping others; but when they do so they do not *happen* to do so, since that is necessarily their aim. (Footnote added, 1977.)

[13]See, e.g., *The Metaphysics of Morals,* pt. II, sec. 30.

an emphatic use of "ought." My argument is that they are relying on an illusion, as if trying to give the moral "ought" a magic force.[14]

This conclusion may, as I said, appear dangerous and subversive of morality. We are apt to panic at the thought that we ourselves, or other people, might stop caring about the things we do care about, and we feel that the categorical imperative gives us some control over the situation. But it is interesting that the people of Leningrad were not struck by the thought that only the *contingent* fact that other citizens shared their loyalty and devotion to the city stood between them and the Germans during the terrible years of the siege. Perhaps we should be less troubled than we are by fear of defection from the moral cause; perhaps we should even have less reason to fear it if people thought of themselves as volunteers banded together to fight for liberty and justice and against inhumanity and oppression. It is often felt, even if obscurely, that there is an element of deception in the official line about morality. And while some have been persuaded by talk about the authority of the moral law, others have turned away with a sense of distrust.[15]

[14]See G. E. M. Anscombe, "Modern Moral Philosophy," *Philosophy* (1958). My view is different from Miss Anscombe's, but I have learned from her.

[15]So many people have made useful comments on drafts of this article that I despair of thanking them all. Derek Parfit's help has been sustained and invaluable, and special thanks are also due to Barry Stroud.

An earlier version of this paper was read at the Center for Philosophical Exchange, Brockport, N.Y., and published in *Philosophical Exchange* (Summer 1971). Footnote 8 is mostly from this paper, and I add here some other paragraphs that may throw light on the present paper.

My own view is that while there are ends within ethics which one should adopt (as e.g. that one's children get a good education) there are difficulties about saying that one "ought" to take account of the general good. For either the "ought" means "morally ought" or "ought from a moral point of view" or else it does not. If it does we have a tautological principle. If it does not the problem is to know what is being said. By hypothesis a prudential "ought" is not intended here, or one related to others of the agent's contingent ends. Nor do we have the "ought" and "ought not" operating within the system of etiquette, or some system of institutional rules. This "ought"—the one in the sentence "One ought to be moral"—is supposed to be free floating and unsubscripted, and I have never found anyone who could explain the use of the word in such a context. (They are apt to talk about the expressing of resolves, or of decisions, but it is then not clear why we need the "ought" terminology when "I resolve" and "I've decided" are already in use.) My own conclusion is that "One ought to be moral" makes no sense at all unless the "ought" has the moral subscript, giving a tautology, or else relates morality to some other system such as prudence or etiquette. I am, therefore putting forward quite seriously a theory that disallows the possibility of saying that a man ought (free unsubscripted "ought") to have ends other than those he does have e.g. that the uncaring, amoral man ought to care about the relief of suffering or the protection of the weak. In my view we must start from the fact that some people do care about such things, and even devote their lives to them; they may therefore talk about what should be done presupposing such common aims. These things are necessary, but only subjectively and conditionally necessary, as Kant would put it.

Kant would of course object that I am treating men as if, in the army of duty, they were volunteers, and this is exactly my thought. Why does Kant so object to the idea that those who are concerned about morality are joining together with like-minded people to fight against injustice and oppression, or to try to relieve suffering, and that they do so because, caring about such things, they are ready to volunteer in the cause? Kant says that there is a kind of conceit involved in such a conception. Why does he think this? He supposes that in so viewing the matter (in seeing ourselves as volunteers) we are forgetting our nature as human beings, members of the phenomenal as well as the noumenal world, whose will may be determined by the moral law but also by desire, so that we do not automatically act as a being with a holy will would act, and are beings for whom the dictates of reason take the form of a command. Let us agree that a human being doesn't necessarily have moral ends, and that even when he does his inclination may be stronger than his moral resolves. Both of these things being true a man could be mistaken either in supposing that his concern for others could not fail, or in supposing that by merely following his inclinations he could serve moral causes with no need for resolution or self-discipline. We have already pointed out that a morality of hypothetical imperatives is not a morality of inclination; resolution and self-discipline being at least as necessary to achieve moral ends as to achieve anything else. So let us consider the other suggestion, that the supporter of the hypothetical imperative is failing to recognize that the desires of even the most moral of men could always change. This charge should be denied. One who supports the hypothetical imperative does not forget that desires might change; he has simply given up trying to deal, in advance, with such a contingency by saying to himself that he would still be under command. That this seems hard to accept is the fact that lies, I think, at the heart of Kantianism in ethics, and to the neo-Kantianism of those who accept his strictures on the hypothetical imperative though rejecting the rest of his theory. It will seem to many impossible that one should have nothing to say about the case where moral concerns have vanished, except of course, to note the character of the man concerned, and in the case of other people, to take what measures one can to stop them from doing harm. Perhaps the greatest fear is of a change in oneself; one wants as it were to make sure one is stuck with the idea of acting morally whatever one's concerns have become. The move betrays a lack of confidence which oddly does not often trouble people when their devotion is to causes other than those of morality.

These suggestions are, of course, directly relevant to Kant's arguments against the hypothetical imperative, for the same problems arise about the meaning of the things that he says. What, for instance, does it mean to say that moral rules are categorical commands? In the first place they are not commands at all, neither commands of men nor commands of God; or rather if they are commands of God it is not as commanded by God that they are in Kant's sense categorical commands. (This he says explicitly.) What we actually have are rules of conduct adopted by certain societies, and individuals within these societies; and Kant is saying that these rules are universally valid. But when we put it this way, in terms of rules, the difficulty of understanding the notion of universal validity is apparent. (It can no longer mean that everyone is commanded, which shows that there is some point in denying Kant the picturesque language of commands.) Kant's thought seems to be that moral rules are universally valid in that they are inescapable, that no one can contract out of morality, and above all that no one can say that as he does not happen to care about the ends of morality, morality does not apply to him. This thought about inescapability is very important, and we should pause to consider it. It is perhaps Kant's most compelling argument against the hypothetical imperative, and the one that may make Kantians of us all.

There is, of course, a sense in which morality is inescapable. Consider, for instance, moral epithets such as "dishonest," "unjust," "uncharitable"; these do not cease to apply to a man because he is indifferent to the ends of morality: they may indeed apply to him because of his indifference. He is judged by the criteria of morality when moral character is in question, and Kant is indeed right in saying that these criteria are independent of his desires. (*Contrast* a word such as "rash.") No one can escape the application of the moral terms by pleading his indifference. Nor can he escape them by turning to ways of life in which he can be counted as being neither morally good or morally bad, as he can escape being a good or a bad husband by simply not marrying, or a good or bad carpenter by refusing to take up the tools. In this sense, then, morality is inescapable, but this can be accepted, and insisted on, by Kant's opponent, the defender of the hypothetical imperative. The latter may also agree that the application of such epithets will often be the vehicle for the expression of opposition, disgust or hatred. It has already been agreed that with our present "non-hypothetical" use of "should" in moral contexts the application of the moral "should" is also inescapable. But someone who thinks that significant concessions have now been made to Kant must answer the following question. Has anything been said about the inescapability of morality which could not also be said about the inescapability of etiquette? For just as a man is immoral if he does certain things, despite his indifference to the nature and result of his actions, so he is rude or unmannerly, or one who does what is "not done," whatever his views about etiquette. Since no one says that the rules of etiquette are categorical imperatives the task must be to explain the additional inescapability belonging to morality.

We must return, therefore, to the difficulty of discovering what Kant can have meant by saying that moral rules have objective necessity, are categorical commands, are universally valid, or are binding upon the will of every free agent. Nothing that we have yet considered has given Kant what he wants, and one cannot, I think, avoid the following conclusion. Kant's argument that moral rules have a peculiar and dignified status depends wholly upon his attempt to link moral action with rationality through the mere concept of the form of law and the principle of universalizability, as interpreted by him. In acting morally Kant thinks that we do as reason dictates. In acting immorally we are acting irrationally, and if this is not how Kant puts it, it is what he must show in order to make his point, if it could be proved, then any man, whatever his desires, could be shown to have reason to act morally, since one has reason to do what it is rational to do. The difficulty, as everyone knows, is to accept Kant's arguments purporting to show that morally bad actions are those whose maxim could not belong to a universally legislative will, and moreover that action according to such maxims is irrational action. These difficulties have been argued *ad nauseam,* and I shall not repeat the arguments here. All I would claim to have shown is that no one who rejects Kant's attempts to derive morality from reason has been given any reason to reject the hypothetical imperative in morals. It is commonly believed that even if Kant has not shown the connection between reason and morality he has at least destroyed the hypothetical imperative. I have urged that, on the contrary, there is no valid argument against the hypothetical imperative to be found in Kant should the argument from reason fail. (Footnote added in 1977.)

1973

A Critique of Utilitarianism

Bernard Williams

No one can hold that everything, of whatever category, that has value, has it in virtue of its consequences. If that were so, one would just go on for ever, and there would be an obviously hopeless regress. That regress would be hopeless even if one takes the view, which is not an absurd view, that although men set themselves ends and work towards them, it is very often not really the supposed end, but the effort towards it on which they set value—that they travel, not really in order to arrive (for as soon as they have arrived they set out for somewhere else), but rather they choose somewhere to arrive, in order to travel. Even on that view, not everything would have consequential value; what would have non-consequential value would in fact be travelling, even though people had to think of travelling as having the consequential value, and something else—the destination—the non-consequential value.

If not everything that has value has it in virtue of consequences, then presumably there are some types of thing which have non-consequential value, and also some particular things that have such value because they are instances of those types. Let us say,

Bernard Williams, "A Critique of Utilitarianism" from UTILITARIANISM: For and Against, edited by J. J. C. Smart and Bernard Williams (New York: Cambridge University Press, 1973). Reprinted with the permission of the author and Cambridge University Press.

using a traditional term, that anything that has that sort of value, has *intrinsic* value.[1] I take it to be the central idea of consequentialism that the only kind of thing that has intrinsic value is states of affairs, and that anything else that has value has it because it conduces to some intrinsically valuable state of affairs.

How much, however, does this say? Does it succeed in distinguishing consequentialism from anything else? The trouble is that the term "state of affairs" seems altogether too permissive to exclude anything: may not the obtaining of absolutely anything be represented formally as a state of affairs? A Kantian view of morality, for instance, is usually thought to be opposed to consequentialism, if any is; at the very least, if someone were going to show that Kantianism collapsed into consequentialism, it should be the product of a long and unobvious argument, and not just happen at the drop of a definition. But on the present account it looks as though Kantianism can be made instantly into a kind of consequentialism—a kind which identifies the states of affairs that have intrinsic value (or at least intrinsic moral value) as those that consist of actions being performed for duty's sake.[2] We need something more to our specification if it is to be the specification of anything distinctly consequentialist.

The point of saying that consequentialism ascribes intrinsic value to states of affairs is rather to *contrast* states of affairs with other candidates for having such value: in particular, perhaps, actions. A distinctive mark of consequentialism might rather be this, that it regards the value of actions as always consequential (or, as we may more generally say, derivative), and not intrinsic. The value of actions would then lie in their causal properties, of producing valuable states of affairs; or if they did not derive their value in this simple way, they would derive it in some more roundabout way, as for instance by being expressive of some motive, or in accordance with some rule, whose operation in society conduced to desirable states of affairs. (The lengths to which such indirect derivations can be taken without wrecking the point of consequentialism is something we shall be considering later.)

To insist that what has intrinsic value are states of affairs and not actions seems to come near an important feature of consequentialism. Yet it may be that we have still not hit exactly what we want, and that the restriction is now too severe. Surely *some* actions, compatible with consequentialism, might have intrinsic value? This is a question which has a special interest for utilitarianism, that is to say, the form of consequentialism concerned particularly with happiness. Traditionally utilitarians have tended to regard happiness or, again, pleasure, as experiences or sensations which were related to actions and activity as effect to cause; and, granted that view, utilitarianism will indeed see the value of all action as derivative, intrinsic value being reserved for the experiences of happiness. But that view of the relations between action and either pleasure or happiness is widely recognized to be inadequate. To say that a man finds certain actions or activity pleasant, or that they make him happy, or that he finds his happiness in them, is certainly not always to say that they induce certain sensations in him, and in the case of happiness, it is doubtful whether that is ever what is meant. Rather it means such things (among others) as that he enjoys doing these things for their own sake. It would trivialize the discussion of utilitarianism to tie it by definition to inadequate conceptions of happiness or pleasure, and we must be able to recognize as versions of utilitarianism those which, as most modern versions do, take as central some notion such as *satisfac-*

[1]The terminology of things "being valuable," "having intrinsic value," etc., is not meant to beg any questions in general value-theory. Non-cognitive theories, such as Smart's, should be able to recognize the distinctions made here.

[2]A point noted by Smart, p. 13 [*Utilitarianism: For and Against*].

tion, and connect that criterially with such matters as the activities which a man will freely choose to engage in. But the activities which a man engages in for their own sake are activities in which he finds intrinsic value. So any specification of consequentialism which logically debars action or activity from having intrinsic value will be too restrictive even to admit the central case, utilitarianism, so soon as that takes on a more sophisticated and adequate conception of its basic value of happiness.

So far then, we seem to have one specification of consequentialism which is too generous to exclude anything, and another one which is too restrictive to admit even the central case. These difficulties arise from either admitting without question actions among desirable states of affairs, or blankly excluding all actions from the state of affairs category. This suggests that we shall do better by looking at the interrelations between states of affairs and actions.

It will be helpful, in doing this, to introduce the notion of the *right* action for an agent in given circumstances. I take it that in any form of direct consequentialism, and certainly in act-utilitarianism, the notion of the right action in given circumstances is a maximizing notion:[3] the right action is that which out of the actions available to the agent brings about or represents the highest degree of whatever it is the system in question regards as intrinsically valuable—in the central case, utilitarianism, this is of course happiness. In this argument, I shall confine myself to direct consequentialism, for which "right action" is unqualifiedly a maximizing notion.

The notion of the right action as that which, of the possible alternatives, maximizes the good (where this embraces, in unfavorable circumstances, minimizing the bad), is an objective notion in this sense, that it is perfectly possible for an agent to be ignorant or mistaken, and non-culpably ignorant or mistaken, about what is the right action in the circumstances. Thus the assessment by others of whether the agent did, in this sense, do the right thing, is not bounded by the agent's state of knowledge at the time, and the claim that he did the wrong thing is compatible with recognizing that he did as well as anyone in his state of knowledge could have done.[4] It might be suggested that, contrary to this, we have already imported the subjective conditions of action in speaking of the best of the actions *available to him:* if he is ignorant or misinformed, then the actions which might seem to us available to him were not in any real sense available. But this would be an exaggeration; the notion of availability imports some, but not all, kinds of subjective condition. Over and above the question of actions which, granted his situation and powers, were physically not available to him, we might perhaps add that a course of action was not really available to an agent if his historical, cultural or psychological situation was such that it could not possibly occur to him. But it is scarcely reasonable to extend the notion of unavailability to actions which merely did not occur to him; and surely absurd to extend it to actions which did occur to him, but where he was misinformed about their consequences.

If then an agent does the right thing, he does the best of the alternatives available to him (where that, again, embraces the least bad: we shall omit this rider from now on). Standardly, the action will be right in virtue of its causal properties, of maximally conducing to good states of affairs. Sometimes, however, the relation of the action to the good state of affairs may not be that of cause to effect—the good state of affairs may be constituted, or partly constituted, by the agent's doing that act (as when under utilitarianism he just enjoys doing it, and there is no project available to him more productive of happiness for him or anyone else).

[3]Cf. Smart's definition, p. 45 [*Utilitarianism: For and Against*].

[4]In Smart's terminology, the "rational thing": pp. 46–7 [*Utilitarianism: For and Against*].

Although this may be so under consequentialism, there seems to be an important difference between this situation and a situation of an action's being right for some non-consequentialist reason, as for instance under a Kantian morality. This difference might be brought out intuitively by saying that for the consequentialist, even a situation of this kind in which the action itself possesses intrinsic value is one in which the rightness of the act is derived from the goodness of a certain state of affairs—the act is right *because* the state of affairs which consists in its being done is better than any other state of affairs accessible to the agent; whereas for the non-consequentialist it is sometimes, at least, the other way round, and a state of affairs which is better than the alternatives is so because it consists of the right act being done. This intuitive description of the difference has something in it, but it needs to be made more precise.

We can take a step towards making it more precise, perhaps, in the following way. Suppose *S* is some particular concrete situation. Consider the statement, made about some particular agent

(1) In *S*, he did the right thing in doing *A*.

For consequentialists, (1) implies a statement of the form

(2) The state of affairs *P* is better than any other state of affairs accessible to him; where a state of affairs being "accessible" to an agent means that it is a state of affairs which is the consequence of, or is constituted by, his doing an act available to him (for that, see above); and *P* is a state of affairs accessible to him only in virtue of his doing *A*.[5]

Now in the exceptional case where it is just his doing *A* which carries the intrinsic value, we get for (2)

(3) The state of affairs which consists in his doing *A* is better than any other state of affairs accessible to him.

It was just the possibility of this sort of case which raised the difficulty of not being able to distinguish between a sophisticated consequentialism and non-consequentialism. The question thus is: if (3) is what we get for consequentialism in this sort of case, is it what a non-consequentialist would regard as implied by (1)? If so, we still cannot tell the difference between them. But the answer in fact seems to be "no."

There are two reasons for this. One reason is that a non-consequentialist, though he must inevitably be able to attach a sense to (1), does not have to be able to attach a sense to (3) at all, while the consequentialist, of course, attaches a sense to (1) only because he attaches a sense to (3). Although the non-consequentialist is concerned with right actions—such as the carrying out of promises—he may have no general way of comparing states of affairs from a moral point of view at all. Indeed, we shall see later and in greater depth than these schematic arguments allow, that the emphasis on the necessary comparability of situations is a peculiar feature of consequentialism in general, and of utilitarianism in particular.

A different kind of reason emerges if we suppose that the non-consequentialist does admit, in general, comparison between states of affairs. Thus, we might suppose that some non-consequentialist would consider it a better state of things in which more, rather than fewer, people kept their promises, and kept them for non-consequentialist reasons. Yet consistently with that he could accept, in a particular case, all of the following: that *X* would do the right thing only if he kept his promise; that keeping his promise would involve (or consist in) doing *A;* that several other people would, as a

[5]"Only" here may seem a bit strong: but I take it that it is not an unreasonable demand on an account of his doing *the* right thing in *S* that his action is uniquely singled out from the alternatives. A further detail: one should strictly say, not that (1) implies a statement of the form (2), but that (1) implies *that there is* a true statement of that form.

matter of fact, keep their promises (and for the right reasons) if and only if *X* did not do *A*. There are all sorts of situations in which this sort of thing would be true: thus it might be the case that an effect of *X*'s doing *A* would be to provide some inducement to these others which would lead them to break promises which otherwise they would have kept. Thus a non-consequentialist can hold both that it is a better state of affairs in which more people keep their promises, and that the right thing for *X* to do is something which brings it about that fewer promises are kept. Moreover, it is very obvious what view of things goes with holding that. It is one in which, even though from some abstract point of view one state of affairs is better than another, it does not follow that a given agent should regard it as his business to bring it about, even though it is open to him to do so. More than that, it might be that he could not properly regard it as his business. If the goodness of the world were to consist in people's fulfilling their obligations, it would by no means follow that one of my obligations was to bring it about that other people kept their obligations.

Of course, no sane person could really believe that the goodness of the world just consisted in people keeping their obligations. But that is just an example, to illustrate the point that under non-consequentialism (3) does not, as one might expect, follow from (1). Thus even allowing some actions to have intrinsic value, we can still distinguish consequentialism. A consequentialist view, then, is one in which a statement of the form (2) follows from a statement of the form (1). A non-consequentialist view is one in which this is not so—not even when the (2)-statement takes the special form of (3).

This is not at all to say that the alternative to consequentialism is that one has to accept that there are some actions which one should always do, or again some which one should never do, *whatever the consequences:* this is a much stronger position than any involved, as I have defined the issues, in the denial of consequentialism. All that is involved, on the present account, in the denial of consequentialism, is that with respect to some type of action, there are some situations in which that would be the right thing to do, even though the state of affairs produced by one's doing that would be worse than some other state of affairs accessible to one. The claim that there is a type of action which is right *whatever the consequences* can be put by saying that with respect to some type of action, assumed as being adequately specified, then *whatever* the situation may (otherwise) be, that will be the right thing to do, *whatever* other state of affairs might be accessible to one, however much better it might be than the state of affairs produced by one's doing this action.

If that somewhat Moorean formulation has not hopelessly concealed the point, it will be seen that this second position—the *whatever the consequences* position—is very much stronger than the first, the mere rejection of consequentialism. It is perfectly consistent, and it might be thought a mark of sense, to believe, while not being a consequentialist, that there was no type of action which satisfied this second condition: that if an adequate (and non–question-begging) specification of a type of action has been given in advance, it is always possible to think of some situation in which the consequences of doing the action so specified would be so awful that it would be right to do something else.

Of course, one might think that there just *were* some types of action which satisfied this condition; though it seems to me obscure how one could have much faith in a list of such actions unless one supposed that it had supernatural warrant. Alternatively, one might think that while logically there was a difference between the two positions, in social and psychological fact they came to much the same thing, since so soon (it might be claimed) as people give up thinking in terms of certain things being right or wrong whatever the consequences, they turn to thinking in purely consequential terms. This might be offered as a very general proposition about human thought, or (more plausibly) as a sociological proposition about certain situations of social change, in which utilitarianism (in particular) looks the only coherent alternative to a dilapidated set of values. At the level of language, it is worth noting that the use of the word "*absolute*" mirrors, and perhaps also assists, this association: the claim that no type of action is "absolutely right"—leaving aside the sense in which it means that the rightness of anything depends on the value-system of a society (the confused doctrine of relativism)—can mean either that no type of action is right-whatever-its-consequences, or, alternatively, that "it all depends on the consequences," that is, in each case the decision whether an action is right is determined by its consequences.

A particular sort of psychological connection—or in an old-fashioned use of the term, a "moral" connection—between the two positions might be found in this. If people do not regard certain things as "absolutely out," then they are prepared to start thinking about extreme situations in which what would otherwise be out might, exceptionally, be justified. They will, if they are to get clear about what they believe, be prepared to compare different extreme situations and ask what action would be justified in them. But once they have got used to that, their inhibitions about thinking of everything in consequential terms disappear: the difference between the extreme situations and the less extreme, presents itself no longer as a difference between the exceptional and the usual, but between the greater and the less—and the consequential thoughts one was prepared to deploy in the greater it may seem quite irrational not to deploy in the less. *A fortiori,* someone might say: but he would have already had to complete this process to see it as a case of *a fortiori.*

One could regard this process of adaptation to consequentialism, moreover, not merely as a blank piece of psychological association, but as concealing a more elaborate structure of thought. One might have the idea that the *unthinkable* was itself a moral category; and in more than one way. It could be a feature of a man's moral outlook that he regarded certain courses of action as unthinkable, in the sense that he would not entertain the idea of doing them: and the witness to that might, in many cases, be that they simply would not come into his head. Entertaining certain alternatives, regarding them indeed as *alternatives,* is itself something that he regards as dishonorable or morally absurd. But, further, he might equally find it unacceptable to consider what to do in certain conceivable situations. Logically, or indeed empirically conceivable they may be, but they are not to him morally conceivable, meaning by that that their occurrence as situations presenting him with a choice would represent not a special problem in his moral world, but something that lay beyond its limits. For him, there are certain situations so monstrous that the idea that the processes of moral rationality could yield an answer in them is insane: they are situations which so transcend in enormity the human business of moral deliberation that from a moral point of view it cannot matter any more what happens. Equally, for him, to spend time thinking what one would decide if one were in such a situation is also insane, if not merely frivolous.

For such a man, and indeed for anyone who is prepared to take him seriously, the demand, in Herman Kahn's words, to *think the unthinkable* is not an unquestionable demand of rationality, set against a cowardly or inert refusal to follow out one's moral thoughts. Rationality he sees as a demand not merely on him, but on the situations in, and about, which he has to think; unless the environment reveals minimum sanity, it is insanity to carry the decorum of sanity into it. Consequentialist rationality, however, and in particular utilitarian rationality, has no such limitations: making the best of a bad job is one of its maxims, and it will have something to say even on the difference between massacring seven million, and massacring seven million and one.

There are other important questions about the idea of the morally unthinkable, which we cannot pursue here. Here we have been concerned with the role it might play in someone's connecting, by more than a mistake, the idea that there was nothing which was right whatever the consequences, and the different idea that everything depends on consequences. While someone might, in this way or another, move from one of those ideas to the other, it is very important that the two ideas are different: especially important in a world where we have lost traditional reasons for resisting the first idea, but have more than enough reasons for fearing the second.

3. NEGATIVE RESPONSIBILITY: AND TWO EXAMPLES

Although I have defined a state of affairs being *accessible* to an agent in terms of the actions which are *available* to him,[6] nevertheless it is the former notion which is really more important for consequentialism. Consequentialism is basically indifferent to whether a state of affairs consists in what I do, or is produced by what I do, where that notion is itself wide enough to include, for instance, situations in which other people do things which I have made them do, or allowed them to do, or encouraged them to do, or given them a chance to do. All that consequentialism is interested in is the idea of these doings being *consequences* of what I do, and that is a relation broad enough to include the relations just mentioned, and many others.

Just what the relation is, is a different question, and at least as obscure as the nature of its relative, cause and effect. It is not a question I shall try to pursue; I will rely on cases where I suppose that any consequentialist would be bound to regard the situations in question as consequences of what the agent does. There are cases where the supposed consequences stand in a rather remote relation to the action, which are sometimes difficult to assess from a practical point of view, but which raise no very interesting question for the present enquiry. The more interesting points about consequentialism lie rather elsewhere. There are certain situations in which the causation of the situation, the relation it has to what I do, is in no way remote or problematic in itself, and entirely justifies the claim that the situation is a consequence of what I do: for instance, it is quite clear, or reasonably clear, that if I do a certain thing, this situation will come about, and if I do not, it will not. So from a consequentialist point of view it goes into the calculation of consequences along with any other state of affairs accessible to me. Yet from some, at least, non-consequentialist points of view, there is a vital difference between some such situations and others: namely, that in some a vital link in the production of the eventual outcome is provided by *someone else's* doing something. But for consequentialism, all causal connections are on the same level, and it makes no difference, so far as that goes, whether the causation of a given state of affairs lies through another agent, or not.

Correspondingly, there is no relevant difference which consists *just* in one state of affairs being brought about by me, without intervention of other agents, and another being brought about through the intervention of other agents; although some genuinely causal differences involving a difference of value may correspond to that (as when, for instance, the other agents derive pleasure or pain from the transaction), that kind of difference will already be included in the specification of the state of affairs to be produced. Granted that the states of affairs have been adequately described in causally and

[6]See last section, p. 87 [p. 458 this volume].

evaluatively relevant terms, it makes no further comprehensible difference who produces them. It is because consequentialism attaches value ultimately to states of affairs, and its concern is with what states of affairs the world contains, that it essentially involves the notion of *negative responsibility:* that if I am ever responsible for anything, then I must be just as much responsible for things that I allow or fail to prevent, as I am for things that I myself, in the more everyday restricted sense, bring about.[7] Those things also must enter my deliberations, as a responsible moral agent, on the same footing. What matters is what states of affairs the world contains, and so what matters with respect to a given action is what comes about if it is done, and what comes about if it is not done, and those are questions not intrinsically affected by the nature of the causal linkage, in particular by whether the outcome is partly produced by other agents.

The strong doctrine of negative responsibility flows directly from consequentialism's assignment of ultimate value to states of affairs. Looked at from another point of view, it can be seen also as a special application of something that is favored in many moral outlooks not themselves consequentialist—something which, indeed, some thinkers have been disposed to regard as the essence of morality itself: a principle of impartiality. Such a principle will claim that there can be no relevant difference from a moral point of view which consists just in the fact, not further explicable in general terms, that benefits or harms accrue to one person rather than to another—"it's me" can never in itself be a morally comprehensible reason.[8] This principle, familiar with regard to the reception of harms and benefits, we can see consequentialism as extending to their production: from the moral point of view, there is no comprehensible difference which consists just in my bringing about a certain outcome rather than someone else's producing it. That the doctrine of negative responsibility represents in this way the extreme of impartiality, and abstracts from the identity of the agent, leaving just a locus of causal intervention in the world—that fact is not merely a surface paradox. It helps to explain why consequentialism can seem to some to express a more serious attitude than non-consequentialist views, why part of its appeal is to a certain kind of high-mindedness. Indeed, that is part of what is wrong with it.

For a lot of the time so far we have been operating at an exceedingly abstract level. This has been necessary in order to get clearer in general terms about the differences between consequentialist and other outlooks, an aim which is important if we want to know what features of them lead to what results for our thought. Now, however, let us look more concretely at two examples, to see what utilitarianism might say about them, what we might say about utilitarianism and, most importantly of all, what would be implied by certain ways of thinking about the situations. The examples are inevitably schematized, and they are open to the objection that they beg as many questions as they illuminate. There are two ways in particular in which examples in moral philosophy tend to beg important questions. One is that, as presented, they arbitrarily cut off and restrict the range of alternative courses of action—this objection might particularly be made against the first of my two examples. The second is that they inevitably present one with the situation as a going concern, and cut off questions about how the agent got into it, and correspondingly about moral considerations which might flow from that: this objection might

[7]This is a fairly modest sense of "responsibility," introduced merely by one's ability to reflect on, and decide, what one ought to do. This presumably escapes Smart's ban (p. 54) on the notion of "the responsibility" as "a piece of metaphysical nonsense"—his remarks seem to be concerned solely with situations of interpersonal blame. For the limitations of that, see, section 6 (pp. 123 ff.) [*Utilitarianism: For and Against*].

[8]There is a tendency in some writers to suggest that it is not a comprehensible reason at all. But this, I suspect, is due to the overwhelming importance those writers ascribe to the moral point of view.

perhaps specially arise with regard to the second of my two situations. These difficulties, however, just have to be accepted, and if anyone finds these examples cripplingly defective in this sort of respect, then he must in his own thought rework them in richer and less question-begging form. If he feels that no presentation of any imagined situation can ever be other than misleading in morality, and that there can never be any substitute for the concrete experienced complexity of actual moral situations, then this discussion, with him, must certainly grind to a halt: but then one may legitimately wonder whether every discussion with him about conduct will not grind to a halt, including any discussion about the actual situations, since discussion about how one would think and feel about situations somewhat different from the actual (that is to say, situations to that extent imaginary) plays an important role in discussion of the actual.

(1) George, who has just taken his Ph.D. in chemistry, finds it extremely difficult to get a job. He is not very robust in health, which cuts down the number of jobs he might be able to do satisfactorily. His wife has to go out to work to keep them, which itself causes a great deal of strain, since they have small children and there are severe problems about looking after them. The results of all this, especially on the children, are damaging. An older chemist, who knows about this situation, says that he can get George a decently paid job in a certain laboratory, which pursues research into chemical and biological warfare. George says that he cannot accept this, since he is opposed to chemical and biological warfare. The older man replies that he is not too keen on it himself, come to that, but after all George's refusal is not going to make the job or the laboratory go away; what is more, he happens to know that if George refuses the job, it will certainly go to a contemporary of George's who is not inhibited by any such scruples and is likely if appointed to push along the research with greater zeal than George would. Indeed, it is not merely concern for George and his family, but (to speak frankly and in confidence) some alarm about this other man's excess of zeal, which has led the older man to offer to use his influence to get George the job . . . George's wife, to whom he is deeply attached, has views (the details of which need not concern us) from which it follows that at least there is nothing particularly wrong with research into CBW. What should he do?

(2) Jim finds himself in the central square of a small South American town. Tied up against the wall are a row of twenty Indians, most terrified, a few defiant, in front of them several armed men in uniform. A heavy man in a sweat-stained khaki shirt turns out to be the captain in charge and, after a good deal of questioning of Jim which establishes that he got there by accident while on a botanical expedition, explains that the Indians are a random group of the inhabitants who, after recent acts of protest against the government, are just about to be killed to remind other possible protestors of the advantages of not protesting. However, since Jim is an honored visitor from another land, the captain is happy to offer him a guest's privilege of killing one of the Indians himself. If Jim accepts, then as a special mark of the occasion, the other Indians will be let off. Of course, if Jim refuses, then there is no special occasion, and Pedro here will do what he was about to do when Jim arrived, and kill them all. Jim, with some desperate recollection of schoolboy fiction, wonders whether if he got hold of a gun, he could hold the captain, Pedro and the rest of the soldiers to threat, but it is quite clear from the set-up that nothing of that kind is going to work: any attempt at that sort of thing will mean that all the Indians will be killed, and himself. The men against the wall, and the other villagers, understand the situation, and are obviously begging him to accept. What should he do?

To these dilemmas, it seems to me that utilitarianism replies, in the first case, that George should accept the job, and in the second, that Jim should kill the Indian. Not only does utilitarianism give these answers but, if the situations are essentially as described and there are no further special factors, it regards them, it seems to me, as *obviously* the right answers. But many of us would certainly wonder whether, in (1), that could possibly be the right answer at all; and in the case of (2), even one who came to think that perhaps that was the answer, might well wonder whether it was obviously the answer. Nor is it just a question of the rightness or obviousness of these answers. It is also a question of what sort of considerations come into finding the answer. A feature of utilitarianism is that it cuts out a kind of consideration which for some others makes a difference to what they feel about such cases: a consideration involving the idea, as we might first and very simply put it, that each of us is specially responsible for what *he* does, rather than for what other people do. This is an idea closely connected with the value of integrity. It is often suspected that utilitarianism, at least in its direct forms, makes integrity as a value more or less unintelligible. I shall try to show that this suspicion is correct. Of course, even if that is correct, it would not necessarily follow that we should reject utilitarianism; perhaps, as utilitarians sometimes suggest, we should just forget about integrity, in favor of such things as a concern for the general good. However, if I am right, we cannot merely do that, since the reason why utilitarianism cannot understand integrity is that it cannot coherently describe the relations between a man's projects and his actions.

4. TWO KINDS OF REMOTER EFFECT

A lot of what we have to say about this question will be about the relations between my projects and other people's projects. But before we get on to that, we should first ask whether we are assuming too hastily what the utilitarian answers to the dilemmas will be. In terms of more direct effects of the possible decisions, there does not indeed seem much doubt about the answer in either case; but it might be said that in terms of more remote or less evident effects counterweights might be found to enter the utilitarian scales. Thus the effect on George of a decision to take the job might be invoked, or its effect on others who might know of his decision. The possibility of there being more beneficent labors in the future from which he might be barred or disqualified, might be mentioned; and so forth. Such effects—in particular, possible effects on the agent's character, and effects on the public at large—are often invoked by utilitarian writers dealing with problems about lying or promise-breaking, and some similar considerations might be invoked here.

There is one very general remark that is worth making about arguments of this sort. The certainty that attaches to these hypotheses about possible effects is usually pretty low; in some cases, indeed, the hypothesis invoked is so implausible that it would scarcely pass if it were not being used to deliver the respectable moral answer, as in the standard fantasy that one of the effects of one's telling a particular lie is to weaken the disposition of the world at large to tell the truth. The demands on the certainty or probability of these beliefs as beliefs about particular actions are much milder than they would be on beliefs favoring the unconventional course. It may be said that this is as it should be, since the presumption must be in favor of the conventional course: but that scarcely seems a *utilitarian* answer, unless utilitarianism has already taken off in the direction of not applying the consequences to the particular act at all.

Leaving aside that very general point, I want to consider now two types of effect that are often invoked by utilitarians, and which might be invoked in connection with these imaginary cases. The attitude or tone involved in invoking these effects may sometimes seem peculiar; but that sort of peculiarity soon becomes familiar in utilitarian discussions, and indeed it can be something of an achievement to retain a sense of it.

First, there is the psychological effect on the agent. Our descriptions of these situations have not so far taken account of how George or Jim will be after they have taken the one course or the other; and it might be said that if they take the course which seemed at first the utilitarian one, the effects on them will be in fact bad enough and extensive enough to cancel out the initial utilitarian advantages of that course. Now there is one version of this effect in which, for a utilitarian, some confusion must be involved, namely that in which the agent feels bad, his subsequent conduct and relations are crippled and so on, *because he thinks that he has done the wrong thing*—for if the balance of outcomes was as it appeared to be *before* invoking this effect, then he has not (from the utilitarian point of view) done the wrong thing. So that version of the effect, for a rational and utilitarian agent, could not possibly make any difference to the assessment of right and wrong. However, perhaps he is not a thoroughly rational agent, and is disposed to have bad feelings, whichever he decided to do. Now such feelings, which are from a strictly utilitarian point of view irrational—nothing, a utilitarian can point out, is advanced by having them—cannot, consistently, have any great weight in a utilitarian calculation. I shall consider in a moment an argument to suggest that they should have no weight at all in it. But short of that, the utilitarian could reasonably say that such feelings should not be encouraged, even if we accept their existence, and that to give them a lot of weight is to encourage them. Or, at the very best, even if they are straightforwardly and without any discount to be put into the calculation, their weight must be small: they are after all (and at best) one man's feelings.

That consideration might seem to have particular force in Jim's case. In George's case, his feelings represent a larger proportion of what is to be weighed, and are more commensurate in character with other items in the calculation. In Jim's case, however, his feelings might seem to be of very little weight compared with other things that are at stake. There is a powerful and recognizable appeal that can be made on this point: as that a refusal by Jim to do what he has been invited to do would be a kind of self-indulgent squeamishness. That is an appeal which can be made by other than utilitarians—indeed, there are some uses of it which cannot be consistently made by utilitarians, as when it essentially involves the idea that there is something dishonorable about such self-indulgence. But in some versions it is a familiar, and it must be said a powerful, weapon of utilitarianism. One must be clear, though, about what it can and cannot accomplish. The most it can do, so far as I can see, is to invite one to consider how seriously, and for what reasons, one feels that what one is invited to do is (in these circumstances) wrong, and in particular, to consider that question from the utilitarian point of view. When the agent is not seeing the situation from a utilitarian point of view, the appeal cannot force him to do so; and if he does come round to seeing it from a utilitarian point of view, there is virtually nothing left for the appeal to do. If he does not see it from a utilitarian point of view, he will not see his resistance to the invitation, and the unpleasant feelings he associates with accepting it, *just* as disagreeable experiences of his; they figure rather as emotional expressions of a thought that to accept would be wrong. He may be asked, as by the appeal, to consider whether he is right, and indeed whether he is fully serious, in thinking that. But the assertion of the appeal, that he is being self-indulgently squeamish, will not itself answer that question, or even help to answer it, since it essentially tells him to regard his feelings just as unpleasant experiences of his, and he cannot, by doing that, answer the question they pose when they are precisely not so regarded, but are regarded as indications[9] of what he thinks is right and wrong. If he does come round fully to the utilitarian point of view then of course he will

[9]On the non-cognitivist meta-ethic in terms of which Smart presents his utilitarianism, the term "indications" here would represent an understatement.

regard these feelings just as unpleasant experiences of his. And once Jim—at least—has come to see them in that light, there is nothing left for the appeal to do, since *of course* his feelings, so regarded, are of virtually no weight at all in relation to the other things at stake. The "squeamishness" appeal is not an argument which adds in a hitherto neglected consideration. Rather, it is an invitation to consider the situation, and one's own feelings, from a utilitarian point of view.

The reason why the squeamishness appeal can be very unsettling, and one can be unnerved by the suggestion of self-indulgence in going against utilitarian considerations, is not that we are utilitarians who are uncertain what utilitarian value to attach to our moral feelings, but that we are partially at least not utilitarians, and cannot regard our moral feelings merely as objects of utilitarian value. Because our moral relation to the world is partly given by such feelings, and by a sense of what we can or cannot "live with," to come to regard those feelings from a purely utilitarian point of view, that is to say, as happenings outside one's moral self, is to lose a sense of one's moral identity; to lose, in the most literal way, one's integrity. At this point utilitarianism alienates one from one's moral feelings; we shall see a little later how, more basically, it alienates one from one's actions as well.

If, then, one is really going to regard one's feelings from a strictly utilitarian point of view, Jim should give very little weight at all to his; it seems almost indecent, in fact, once one has taken that point of view, to suppose that he should give any at all. In George's case one might feel that things were slightly different. It is interesting, though, that one reason why one might think that—namely that one person principally affected is his wife—is very dubiously available to a utilitarian. George's wife has some reason to be interested in George's integrity and his sense of it; the Indians, quite properly, have no interest in Jim's. But it is not at all clear how utilitarianism would describe that difference.

There is an argument, and a strong one, that a strict utilitarian should give not merely small extra weight, in calculations of right and wrong, to feelings of this kind, but that he should give absolutely no weight to them at all. This is based on the point, which we have already seen, that if a course of action is, before taking these sorts of feelings into account, utilitarianly preferable, then bad feelings about that kind of action will be from a utilitarian point of view irrational. Now it might be thought that even if that is so, it would not mean that in a utilitarian calculation such feelings should not be taken into account; it is after all a well-known boast of utilitarianism that it is a realistic outlook which seeks the best in the world as it is, and takes any form of happiness or unhappiness into account. While a utilitarian will no doubt seek to diminish the incidence of feelings which are utilitarianly irrational—or at least of disagreeable feelings which are so—he might be expected to take them into account while they exist. This is without doubt classical utilitarian doctrine, but there is good reason to think that utilitarianism cannot stick to it without embracing results which are startlingly unacceptable and perhaps self-defeating.

Suppose that there is in a certain society a racial minority. Considering merely the ordinary interests of the other citizens, as opposed to their sentiments, this minority does no particular harm; we may suppose that it does not confer any very great benefits either. Its presence is in those terms neutral or mildly beneficial. However, the other citizens have such prejudices that they find the sight of this group, even the knowledge of its presence, very disagreeable. Proposals are made for removing in some way this minority. If we assume various quite plausible things (as that programs to change the majority sentiment are likely to be protracted and ineffective) then even if the removal would be unpleasant for the minority, a utilitarian calculation might well end up favoring this step, especially if the minority were a rather small minority and the majority were very severely prejudiced, that is to say, were made very severely uncomfortable by the presence of the minority.

A utilitarian might find that conclusion embarrassing; and not merely because of its nature, but because of the grounds on which it is reached. While a utilitarian might be expected to take into account certain other sorts of consequences of the prejudice, as that a majority prejudice is likely to be displayed in conduct disagreeable to the minority, and so forth, he might be made to wonder whether the unpleasant experiences of the prejudiced people should be allowed, *merely as such,* to count. If he does count them, merely as such, then he has once more separated himself from a body of ordinary moral thought which he might have hoped to accommodate; he may also have started on the path of defeating his own view of things. For one feature of these sentiments is that they are from the utilitarian point of view itself irrational, and a thoroughly utilitarian person would either not have them, or if he found that he did tend to have them, would himself seek to discount them. Since the sentiments in question are such that a rational utilitarian would discount them in himself, it is reasonable to suppose that he should discount them in his calculations about society; it does seem quite unreasonable for him to give just as much weight to feelings—considered just in themselves, one must recall, as experiences of those that have them—which are essentially based on views which are from a utilitarian point of view irrational, as to those which accord with utilitarian principles. Granted this idea, it seems reasonable for him to rejoin a body of moral thought in other respects congenial to him, and discount those sentiments, just considered in themselves, totally, on the principle that no pains or discomforts are to count in the utilitarian sum which their subjects have just because they hold views which are by utilitarian standards irrational. But if he accepts that, then in the cases we are at present considering no extra weight at all can be put in for bad feelings of George or Jim about their choices, if those choices are, leaving out those feelings, on the first round utilitarianly rational.

The psychological effect on the agent was the first of two general effects considered by utilitarians, which had to be discussed. The second is in general a more substantial item, but it need not take so long, since it is both clearer and has little application to the present cases. This is the *precedent effect.* As Burke rightly emphasized, this effect can be important: that one morally *can* do what someone has actually done, is a psychologically effective principle, if not a deontically valid one. For the effect to operate, obviously some conditions must hold on the publicity of the act and on such things as the status of the agent (such considerations weighed importantly with Sir Thomas More); what these may be will vary evidently with circumstances.

In order for the precedent effect to make a difference to a utilitarian calculation, it must be based upon a confusion. For suppose that there is an act which would be the best in the circumstances, except that doing it will encourage by precedent other people to do things which will not be the best things to do. Then the situation of those other people must be relevantly different from that of the original agent; if it were not, then in doing the same as what would be the best course for the original agent, they would necessarily do the best thing themselves. But if the situations are in this way relevantly different, it must be a confused perception which takes the first situation, and the agent's course in it, as an adequate precedent for the second.

However, the fact that the precedent effect, if it really makes a difference, is in this sense based on a confusion, does not mean that it is not perfectly real, nor that it is to be discounted: social effects are by their nature confused in this sort of way. What it does emphasize is that calculations of the precedent effect have got to be realistic, involving considerations of how people are actually likely to be influenced. In the present examples, however, it is very implausible to think that the precedent effect could be invoked to make any difference to the calculation. Jim's case is extraordinary enough, and it is hard to imagine who the recipients of the effect might be supposed to be; while George is not in a sufficiently public situation or role for the question to arise in that form, and in any case one might suppose that the motivations of others on such an issue were quite likely to be fixed one way or another already.

No appeal, then, to these other effects is going to make a difference to what the utilitarian will decide about our examples. Let us now look more closely at the structure of those decisions.

5. INTEGRITY

The situations have in common that if the agent does not do a certain disagreeable thing, someone else will, and in Jim's situation at least the result, the state of affairs after the other man has acted, if he does, will be worse than after Jim has acted, if Jim does. The same, on a smaller scale, is true of George's case. I have already suggested that it is inherent in consequentialism that it offers a strong doctrine of negative responsibility: if I know that if I do *X*, O_1 will eventuate, and if I refrain from doing *X*, O_2 will, and that O_2 is worse than O_1, then I am responsible for O_2 if I refrain voluntarily from doing *X*. "You could have prevented it," as will be said, and truly, to Jim, if he refuses, by the relatives of the other Indians. (I shall leave the important question, which is to the side of the present issue, of the obligations, if any, that nest round the word "know": how far does one, under utilitarianism, have to research into the possibilities of maximally beneficent action, including prevention?)

In the present cases, the situation of O_2 includes another agent bringing about results worse than O_1. So far as O_2 has been identified up to this point—merely as the worse outcome which will eventuate if I refrain from doing *X*—we might equally have said that what that other brings about is O_2; but that would be to underdescribe the situation. For what occurs if Jim refrains from action is not solely twenty Indians dead, but *Pedro's killing twenty Indians*, and that is not a result which Pedro brings about, though the death of the Indians is. We can say: what one does is not included in the outcome of what one does, while what another does can be included in the outcome of what one does. For that to be so, as the terms are now being used, only a very weak condition has to be satisfied: for Pedro's killing the Indians to be the outcome of Jim's refusal, it only has to be causally true that if Jim had not refused, Pedro would not have done it.

That may be enough for us to speak, in some sense, of Jim's responsibility for that outcome, if it occurs; but it is certainly not enough, it is worth noticing, for us to speak of Jim's *making* those things happen. For granted this way of their coming about, he could have made them happen only by making Pedro shoot, and there is no acceptable sense in which his refusal makes Pedro shoot. If the captain had said on Jim's refusal, "you leave me with no alternative," he would have been lying, like most who use that phrase. While the deaths, and the killing, may be the outcome of Jim's refusal, it is misleading to think, in such a case, of Jim having an *effect* on the world through the medium (as it happens) of Pedro's acts; for this is to leave Pedro out of the picture in his essential role of one who has intentions and projects, projects for realizing which Jim's refusal would leave an opportunity. Instead of thinking in terms of supposed effects of Jim's projects on Pedro, it is more revealing to think in terms of the effects of Pedro's projects on Jim's decision. This is the direction from which I want to criticize the notion of negative responsibility.

There are of course other ways in which this notion can be criticized. Many have hoped to discredit it by insisting on the basic moral relevance of the distinction between action and inaction, between intervening and letting things take their course. The distinction is certainly of great moral significance, and indeed it is not easy to think of any moral outlook which could get along without making some use of it. But it is unclear, both in itself and in its moral applications, and the unclarities are of a kind which precisely cause it to give way when, in very difficult cases, weight has to be put on it. There is much to be said in this area, but I doubt whether the sort of dilemma we are considering is going to be resolved by a simple use of this distinction. Again, the issue of negative responsibility can be pressed on the question of how limits are to be placed on one's apparently boundless obligation, implied by utilitarianism, to improve the world. Some answers are needed to that, too—and answers which stop short of relapsing into the bad faith of supposing that one's responsibilities could be adequately characterized just by appeal to one's roles.[10] But, once again, while that is a real question, it cannot be brought to bear directly on the present kind of case, since it is hard to think of anyone supposing that in Jim's case it would be an adequate response for him to say that it was none of his business.

What projects does a utilitarian agent have? As a utilitarian, he has the general project of bringing about maximally desirable outcomes; how he is to do this at any given moment is a question of what causal levers, so to speak, are at that moment within reach. The desirable outcomes, however, do not just consist of agents carrying out *that* project; there must be other more basic or lower-order projects which he and other agents have, and the desirable outcomes are going to consist, in part, of the maximally harmonious realization of those projects ("in part," because one component of a utilitarianly desirable outcome may be the occurrence of agreeable experiences which are not the satisfaction of anybody's projects). Unless there were first-order projects, the general utilitarian project would have nothing to work on, and would be vacuous. What do the more basic or lower-order projects comprise? Many will be the obvious kinds of desires for things for oneself, one's family, one's friends, including basic necessities of life, and in more relaxed circumstances, objects of taste. Or there may be pursuits and interests of an intellectual, cultural or creative character. I introduce those as a separate class not because the objects of them lie in a separate class, and provide—as some utilitarians, in their churchy way, are fond of saying—"higher" pleasures. I introduce them separately because the agent's identification with them may be of a different order. It does not have to be: cultural and aesthetic interests just belong, for many, along with any other taste; but some people's commitment to these kinds of interests just is at once more thoroughgoing and serious than their pursuit of various objects of taste, while it is more individual and permeated with character than the desire for the necessities of life.

Beyond these, someone may have projects connected with his support of some cause: Zionism, for instance, or the abolition of chemical and biological warfare. Or there may be projects which flow from some more general disposition towards human conduct and character, such as a hatred of injustice, or of cruelty, or of killing.

It may be said that this last sort of disposition and its associated project do not count as (logically) "lower-order" relative to the higher-order project of maximizing desirable outcomes; rather, it may be said, it is itself a "higher-order" project. The vital question is not, however, how it is to be classified, but whether it and similar projects are to count among the projects whose satisfaction is to be included in the maximizing

[10]For some remarks bearing on this, see *Morality*, the section on "Goodness and roles," and Cohen's article there cited.

sum, and, correspondingly, as contributing to the agent's happiness. If the utilitarian says "no" to that, then he is almost certainly committed to a version of utilitarianism as absurdly superficial and shallow as Benthamite versions have often been accused of being. For this project will be discounted, presumably, on the ground that it involves, in the specification of its object, the mention of other people's happiness or interests: thus it is the kind of project which (unlike the pursuit of food for myself) presupposes a reference to other people's projects. But that criterion would eliminate any desire at all which was not blankly and in the most straightforward sense egoistic.[11] Thus we should be reduced to frankly egoistic first-order projects, and—for all essential purposes—the one second-order utilitarian project of maximally satisfying first-order projects. Utilitarianism has a tendency to slide in this direction, and to leave a vast hole in the range of human desires, between egoistic inclinations and necessities at one end, and impersonally benevolent happiness-management at the other. But the utilitarianism which has to leave this hole is the most primitive form, which offers a quite rudimentary account of desire. Modern versions of the theory are supposed to be neutral with regard to what sorts of things make people happy or what their projects are. Utilitarianism would do well then to acknowledge the evident fact that among the things that make people happy is not only making other people happy, but being taken up or involved in any of a vast range of projects, or—if we waive the evangelical and moralizing associations of the word—commitments. One can be committed to such things as a person, a cause, an institution, a career, one's own genius, or the pursuit of danger.

Now none of these is itself the *pursuit of happiness:* by an exceedingly ancient platitude, it is not at all clear that there could be anything which was just that, or at least anything that had the slightest chance of being successful. Happiness, rather, requires being involved in, or at least content with, something else.[12] It is not impossible for utilitarianism to accept that point: it does not have to be saddled with a naïve and absurd philosophy of mind about the relation between desire and happiness. What it does have to say is that if such commitments are worth while, then pursuing the projects that flow from them, and realizing some of those projects, will make the person for whom they are worthwhile, happy. It may be that to claim that is still wrong: it may well be that a commitment can make sense to a man (can make sense of his life) without his supposing that it will make him *happy.*[13] But that is not the present point; let us grant to utilitarianism that all worthwhile human projects must conduce, one way or another, to happiness. The point is that even if that is true, it does not follow, nor could it possibly be true, that those projects are themselves projects of pursuing happiness. One has to believe in, or at least want, or quite minimally, be content with, other things, for there to be anywhere that happiness can come from.

Utilitarianism, then, should be willing to agree that its general aim of maximizing happiness does not imply that what everyone is doing is just pursuing happiness. On the contrary, people have to be pursuing other things. What those other things may be, utilitarianism, sticking to its professed empirical stance, should be prepared just to find out.

[11]On the subject of egoistic and non-egoistic desires, see "Egoism and altruism," in *Problems of the Self* (Cambridge University Press, London, 1973).

[12]This does not imply that there is no such thing as the project of pursuing pleasure. Some writers who have correctly resisted the view that all desires are desires for pleasure, have given an account of pleasure so thoroughly adverbial as to leave it quite unclear how there could be a distinctively hedonist way of life at all. Some room has to be left for that, though there are important difficulties both in defining it and living it. Thus (particularly in the case of the very rich) it often has highly ritual aspects, apparently part of a strategy to counter boredom.

[13]For some remarks on this possibility, see *Morality,* section on "What is morality about?"

No doubt some possible projects it will want to discourage, on the grounds that their being pursued involves a negative balance of happiness to others: though even there, the unblinking accountant's eye of the strict utilitarian will have something to put in the positive column, the satisfactions of the destructive agent. Beyond that, there will be a vast variety of generally beneficent or at least harmless projects; and some no doubt, will take the form not just of tastes or fancies, but of what I have called "commitments." It may even be that the utilitarian researcher will find that many of those with commitments, who have really identified themselves with objects outside themselves, who are thoroughly involved with other persons, or institutions, or activities or causes, are actually happier than those whose projects and wants are not like that. If so, that is an important piece of utilitarian empirical lore.

When I say "happier" here, I have in mind the sort of consideration which any utilitarian would be committed to accepting: as for instance that such people are less likely to have a break-down or commit suicide. Of course that is not all that is actually involved, but the point in this argument is to use to the maximum degree utilitarian notions, in order to locate a breaking point in utilitarian thought. In appealing to this strictly utilitarian notion, I am being more consistent with utilitarianism than Smart is. In his struggles with the problem of the brain-electrode man, Smart (p. 22) [*Utilitarianism: For and Against*] commends the idea that "happy" is a partly evaluative term, in the sense that we call "happiness" those kinds of satisfaction which, as things are, we approve of. But *by what standard* is this surplus element of approval supposed, from a utilitarian point of view, to be allocated? There is no source for it, on a strictly utilitarian view, except further degrees of satisfaction, but there are none of those available, or the problem would not arise. Nor does it help to appeal to the fact that we dislike in prospect things which we like when we get there, for from a utilitarian point of view it would seem that the original dislike was merely irrational or based on an error. Smart's argument at this point seems to be embarrassed by a well-known utilitarian uneasiness, which comes from a feeling that it is not respectable to ignore the "deep," while not having anywhere left in human life to locate it.[14]

Let us now go back to the agent as utilitarian, and his higher-order project of maximizing desirable outcomes. At this level, he is committed only to that: what the outcome will actually consist of will depend entirely on the facts, on what persons with what projects and what potential satisfactions there are within calculable reach of the causal levers near which he finds himself. His own substantial projects and commitments come into it, but only as one lot among others—they potentially provide one set of satisfactions among those which he may be able to assist from where he happens to be. He is the agent of the satisfaction system who happens to be at a particular point at a particular time: in Jim's case, our man in South America. His own decisions as a utilitarian agent are a function of all the satisfactions which he can affect from where he is: and this means that the projects of others, to an indeterminately great extent, determine his decision.

This may be so either positively or negatively. It will be so positively if agents within the causal field of his decision have projects which are at any rate harmless, and so should be assisted. It will equally be so, but negatively, if there is an agent within the causal field whose projects are harmful, and have to be frustrated to maximize desirable outcomes. So it is with Jim and the soldier Pedro. On the utilitarian view, the undesirable projects of other people as much determine, in this negative way, one's decisions as

[14]One of many resemblances in spirit between utilitarianism and high-minded evangelical Christianity.

the desirable ones do positively: if those people were not there, or had different projects, the causal nexus would be different, and it is the actual state of the causal nexus which determines the decision. The determination to an indefinite degree of my decisions by other people's projects is just another aspect of my unlimited responsibility to act for the best in a causal framework formed to a considerable extent by their projects.

The decision so determined is, for utilitarianism, the right decision. But what if it conflicts with some project of mine? This, the utilitarian will say, has already been dealt with: the satisfaction to you of fulfilling your project, and any satisfactions to others of your so doing, have already been through the calculating device and have been found inadequate. Now in the case of many sorts of projects, that is a perfectly reasonable sort of answer. But in the case of projects of the sort I have called "commitments," those with which one is more deeply and extensively involved and identified, this cannot just by itself be an adequate answer, and there may be no adequate answer at all. For, to take the extreme sort of case, how can a man, as a utilitarian agent, come to regard as one satisfaction among others, and a dispensable one, a project or attitude round which he has built his life, just because someone else's projects have so structured the causal scene that that is how the utilitarian sum comes out?

The point here is not, as utilitarians may hasten to say, that if the project or attitude is that central to his life, then to abandon it will be very disagreeable to him and great loss of utility will be involved. I have already argued in section 4 that it is not like that; on the contrary, once he is prepared to look at it like that, the argument in any serious case is over anyway. The point is that he is identified with his actions as flowing from projects and attitudes which in some cases he takes seriously at the deepest level, as what his life is about (or, in some cases, this section of his life—seriousness is not necessarily the same as persistence). It is absurd to demand of such a man, when the sums come in from the utility network which the projects of others have in part determined, that he should just step aside from his own project and decision and acknowledge the decision which utilitarian calculation requires. It is to alienate him in a real sense from his actions and the source of his action in his own convictions. It is to make him into a channel between the input of everyone's projects, including his own, and an output of optimific decision; but this is to neglect the extent to which *his* actions and *his* decisions have to be seen as the actions and decisions which flow from the projects and attitudes with which he is most closely identified. It is thus, in the most literal sense, an attack on his integrity.[15]

These sorts of considerations do not in themselves give solutions to practical dilemmas such as those provided by our examples; but I hope they help to provide other ways of thinking about them. In fact, it is not hard to see that in George's case, viewed from this perspective, the utilitarian solution would be wrong. Jim's case is different, and harder. But if (as I suppose) the utilitarian is probably right in this case, that is not to be found out just by asking the utilitarian's questions. Discussions of it—and I am not going to try to carry it further here—will have to take seriously the distinction between my killing someone, and its coming about because of what I do that someone else kills them: a distinction based, not so much on the distinction between action and inaction, as on the distinction between my projects and someone else's projects. At least it

[15]Interestingly related to these notions is the Socratic idea that courage is a virtue particularly connected with keeping a clear sense of what one regards as most important. They also centrally raise questions about the value of pride. Humility, as something beyond the real demand of correct self-appraisal, was specially a Christian virtue because it involved subservience to God. In a secular context it can only represent subservience to other men and their projects.

will have to start by taking that seriously, as utilitarianism does not; but then it will have to build out from there by asking why that distinction seems to have less, or a different, force in this case than it has in George's. One question here would be how far one's powerful objection to killing people just is, in fact, an application of a powerful objection to their being killed. Another dimension of that is the issue of how much it matters that the people at risk are actual, and there, as opposed to hypothetical, or future, or merely elsewhere.[16]

There are many other considerations that could come into such a question, but the immediate point of all this is to draw one particular contrast with utilitarianism: that to reach a grounded decision in such a case should not be regarded as a matter of just discounting one's reactions, impulses and deeply held projects in the face of the pattern of utilities, nor yet merely adding them in—but in the first instance of trying to understand them.

Of course, time and circumstances are unlikely to make a grounded decision, in Jim's case at least, possible. It might not even be decent. Instead of thinking in a rational and systematic way either about utilities or about the value of human life, the relevance of the people at risk being present, and so forth, the presence of the people at risk may just have its effect. The significance of the immediate should not be underestimated. Philosophers, not only utilitarian ones, repeatedly urge one to view the world *sub specie aeternitatis,*[17] but for most human purposes that is not a good *species* to view it under. If we are not agents of the universal satisfaction system, we are not primarily janitors of any system of values, even our own: very often, we just act, as a possibly confused result of the situation in which we are engaged. That, I suspect, is very often an exceedingly good thing. . . .

[16]For a more general discussion of this issue see Charles Fried, *An Anatomy of Values* (Harvard University Press, Cambridge, Mass., 1970), Part Three.

[17]Cf. Smart, p. 63 [*Utilitarianism: For and Against*].

1973

Later Selves and Moral Principles

Derek Parfit

I shall first sketch different views about the nature of personal identity, then suggest that the views support different moral claims.

I

Most of us seem to have certain beliefs about our own identity. We seem for instance to believe that, whatever happens, any future person must be either us, or someone else.

These beliefs are like those that some of us have about a simpler fact. Most of us now think that to be a person, as opposed to a mere animal, is just to have certain more specific properties, such as rationality. These are matters of degree. So we might say that the fact of personhood is just the fact of having certain other properties, which are had to different degrees.

There is a different view. Some of us believe that personhood is a further, deep, fact, and cannot hold to different degrees.

I have been helped in writing this by T. Nagel; also by S. Blackburn, E. Borowitz, S. Clark, L. Francis, H. Frankfurt, J. Griffin, R. M. Hare, S. Lukes, J. Mackie, A. Orenstein, C. Peacocke, A. Rorty, A. Ryan, S. Shoemaker, D. Thomas, R. Walker, and others.

Derek Parfit, "Later Selves and Moral Principles" from PHILOSOPHY AND PERSONAL RELATIONS, edited by A. Montefiore (London: Routledge & Kegan Paul, 1973). Reprinted with the permission of the author.

This second view may be confused with some trivial claims. Personhood is, in a sense, a further fact. And there is a sense in which all persons are equally persons.

Let us first show how these claims may be trivial. We can use a different example. There is a sense in which all our relatives are equally our relatives. We can use the phrase "related to" so that what it means has no degrees; on this use, parents and remote cousins are as much relatives. It is obvious, though, that kinship has degrees. This is shown in the phrase "closely related to": remote cousins are, as relatives, less close. I shall summarize such remarks in the following way. On the above use, the fact of being someone's relative has in its *logic* no degrees. But in its *nature*—in what it involves—it does have degrees. So the fact's logic hides its nature. Hence the triviality of the claim that all our relatives are equally our relatives. (The last few sentences may be wrongly worded,[1] but I hope that the example suggests what I mean.)

To return to the claims about personhood. These were: that it is a further fact, and that all persons are equally persons. As claims about the fact's logic, these are trivial. Certain people think the claims profound. They believe them to be true of the fact's nature.

The difference here can be shown in many ways. Take the question, "When precisely does an embryo become a person?" If we merely make the claims about the fact's logic, we shall not believe that this question must have a precise answer.[2] Certain people do believe this. They believe that any embryo must either be, or not be, a complete person. Their view goes beyond the "logical claims." It concerns the nature of personhood.

We can now return to the main argument. About the facts of both personhood and personal identity, there are two views. According to the first, these facts have a special nature. They are further facts, independent of certain more specific facts; and in every case they must either hold completely, or completely fail to hold. According to the second view, these facts are not of this nature. They consist in the holding of the more specific facts; and they are matters of degree.

Let us name such opposing views. I shall call the first kind "Simple" and the second "Complex."

Such views may affect our moral principles, in the following way. If we change from a Simple to a Complex View, we acquire two beliefs: we decide that a certain fact is in its nature less deep, and that it sometimes holds to reduced degrees. These beliefs may have two effects: the first belief may weaken certain principles, and the second give the principles a new scope.

Take the views about personhood. An ancient principle gives to the welfare of people absolute precedence over that of mere animals. If the difference between people and mere animals is in its nature less deep, this principle can be more plausibly denied. And if embryos are not people, and become them only by degrees, the principle forbidding murder can be more plausibly given less scope.[3]

I have not defended these claims. They are meant to parallel what I shall defend in the case of the two views about personal identity.

[1]But compare "*de dicto*" versus "*de re*."

[2]We might say, "The concept of a person is too vague to yield such an answer."

[3]Here is another example. Some of those who dislike all Jews seem to take Jewishness to be a special, deep property, equally possessed by all Jews. If they lose this belief, their attitude may be both weakened and reduced in scope. They may dislike "typical Jews" less, and untypical Jews not at all.

II

We must first sketch these views. It will help to revive a comparison. What is involved in the survival of a nation are just certain continuities, such as those of a people and a political system. When there is a weakening of these continuities, as there was, say, in the Norman Conquest, it may be unclear whether a nation survives. But there is here no problem. And the reason is that the survival of a nation just involves these continuities. Once we know how the continuities were weakened, we need not ask, as a question about an independent fact, "Did a nation cease to exist?" There is nothing left to know.

We can add the following remarks. Though identity has no degrees,[4] these continuities are matters of degree. So the identity of nations over time is only in its logic "all-or-nothing"; in its nature it has degrees.

The identity of people over time is, according to the "Complex View," comparable.[5] It consists in bodily and psychological continuity. These, too, are matters of degree. So we can add the comparable remark. The identity of people over time is only in its logic "all-or-nothing"; in its nature it has degrees.

How do the continuities of bodies and minds have degrees? We can first dismiss bodies, since they are morally trivial.[6] Let us next call "direct" the psychological relations which hold between: the memory of an experience and this experience, the intention to perform some later action and this action, and different expressions of some lasting character-trait. We can now name two general features of a person's life. One, "connectedness," is the holding, over time, of particular "direct" relations. The other, "continuity," is the holding of a chain of such relations. If, say, I cannot now remember some earlier day, there are no "connections of memory" between me now and myself on that day. But there may be "continuity of memory." This there is if, on every day between, I remembered the previous day.

Of these two general relations, I define "continuous with" so that, in its logic, it has no degrees. It is like "related to" in the use on which all our relatives are equally our relatives. But "connectedness" has degrees. Between different parts of a person's life, the connections of memory, character, and intention are—in strength and number—more or less. ("Connected to" is like "closely related to"; different relatives can be more or less close.)

We can now restate the Complex View. What is important in personal identity are the two relations we have just sketched. One of these, continuity, is in its logic all-or-nothing. But it just involves connectedness, which clearly has degrees. In its nature, therefore, continuity holds to different degrees. So the fact of personal identity also, in its nature, has degrees.

To turn to the Simple View. Here the fact is believed to be, in its nature, all-or-nothing. This it can only be if it does not just consist in (bodily and) psychological continuity—if it is, in its nature, a further fact. To suggest why: These continuities hold, over time, to different degrees. This is true in actual cases, but is most clearly true in some imaginary cases. We can imagine cases where the continuities between each of us

[4]The thing of which X is true can only be, or not be, the thing of which Y is true.

[5]Cf. Hume: "I cannot compare the soul more properly to anything than to a republic or commonwealth." (Hume, Book I, Part IV, Section 6, p. 261.)

[6]They cannot be so dismissed in a full account. The Complex View is not identical to Hume's view. It is even compatible with physicalism. See, for example, Quinton (1962), and Quinton (1972), pp. 88–102.

and a future person hold to every possible degree.[7] Suppose we think, in imagining these cases, "Such a future person must be either, and quite simply, *me,* or *someone else.*" (Suppose we think, "Whatever happens, any future experience must be either *wholly* mine, or *not* mine at *all.*") If the continuities can hold to every degree, but the fact of our identity must hold completely or not at all, then this fact cannot consist in these continuities. It must be a further, independent, fact.

It is worth repeating that the Simple View is about the nature of personal identity, not its logic. This is shown by the reactions most of us have to various so-called "problem cases."[8] These reactions also show that even if, on the surface, we reject the Simple View, at a deeper level we assume it to be true.[9]

We can add this—rough—test of our assumptions. Nations are in many ways unlike people; for example, they are not organisms. But if we take the Complex View, we shall accept this particular comparison: the survival of a person, like that of a nation, is a matter of degree. If instead we reject this comparison, we take the Simple View.

One last preliminary. We can use "I," and the other pronouns, so that they cover only the part of our lives to which, when speaking, we have the strongest psychological connections. We assign the rest of our lives to what we call our "other selves." When, for instance, we have undergone any marked change in character, or conviction, or style of life, we might say, "It was not *I* who did that, but an earlier self."

Such talk can become natural. To quote three passages:

> Our dread of a future in which we must forego the sight of faces, the sound of voices, that we love, friends from whom we derive today our keenest joys, this dread, far from being dissipated, is intensified, if to the grief of such a privation we reflect that there will be added what seems to us now in anticipation an even more cruel grief: not to feel it as a grief at all—to remain indifferent: for if that should occur, our self would then have changed. It would be in a real sense the death of ourself, a death followed, it is true, by a resurrection, but in a different self, the life, the love of which are beyond the reach of those elements of the existing self that are doomed to die.[10]

> It is not because other people are dead that our affection for them grows faint, it is because we ourself are dying. Albertine had no cause to rebuke her friend. The man who was usurping his name had merely inherited it. . . . My new self, while it grew up in the shadow of the old, had often heard the other speak of Albertine; through that other self . . . it thought that it knew her, it found her attractive . . . but this was merely an affection at second hand.[11]

[7]Here are two (crude) ranges of cases. In the first, different proportions of the cells in our brains and bodies will be replaced by exact duplicates. At the start of this range, where there is no replacement, there is full bodily continuity; at the end, where there is complete (simultaneous) "replacement," there is no bodily continuity. In the second range, the duplication is progressively less accurate. At the start of this range, where there are perfect duplicates, there is full psychological continuity; at the end, where there are no duplicates, there is none. In the first case of the first range there is clearly personal identity. In the last case of the second range there is clearly no identity. But the two ranges can be super-imposed to form a smooth spectrum. It is unbelievable that, at a precise point on the spectrum, identity would suddenly disappear. If we grant its psycho-physical assumptions, the spectrum seems to show that our identity over time could *imaginably* hold to any degree. This prepares the ground for the claim that it *actually* holds to reduced degrees.

[8]The main such reaction is the belief that these cases pose problems. (Cf. our reaction to the question, "When, precisely, does an embryo become a person?") Among the "problem" cases would be those described in note 7, or in Williams.

[9]That we are inclined to this view is shown in Williams. That the view is false I began to argue in Parfit (1971).

[10]Proust (1967), p. 349. (I have slightly altered the translation.)

[11]Proust (1949), p. 249.

> Nadya had written in her letter: "When you return. . . ." But that was the whole horror: that there would be no *return*. . . . A new, unfamiliar person would walk in bearing the name of her husband, and she would see that the man, her beloved, for whom she had shut herself up to wait for fourteen years, no longer existed. . . .[12]

Whether we are inclined to use such talk will depend upon our view about the nature of personal identity. If we take the Simple View, we shall not be so inclined, for we shall think it deeply true that all the parts of a person's life are as much parts of his life. If we take the Complex View, we shall be less impressed by this truth. It will seem like the truth that all the parts of a nation's history are as much parts of its history. Because this latter truth is superficial, we at times subdivide such a history into that of a series of successive nations, such as Anglo-Saxon, Medieval, or Post-Imperial England.[13] The connections between these, though similar in kind, differ in degree. If we take the Complex View, we may also redescribe a person's life as the history of a series of successive selves. And the connections between these we shall also claim to be similar in kind, different in degree.[14]

III

We can now turn to our question. Do the different views tend to support different moral claims?

I have space to consider only three subjects: desert, commitment, and distributive justice. And I am forced to oversimplify, and to distort. So it may help to start with some general remarks.

My suggestions are of this form: "The Complex View supports certain claims." By "supports" I mean both "makes more plausible" and "helps to explain." My suggestions thus mean: "If the true view is the Complex, not the Simple, View, certain claims are more plausible.[15] We may therefore[16] be, on the Complex View, more inclined to make these claims."

I shall be discussing two kinds of case: those in which the psychological connections are as strong as they ever are, and those in which they are markedly weak. I choose these kinds of case for the following reason. If we change from the Simple to the Complex View, we believe (I shall claim) that our identity is in its nature less deep, and that it sometimes holds to reduced degrees. The first of these beliefs covers every case, even those where there are the strongest connections. But the second of the two beliefs only covers cases where there are weak connections. So the two kinds of case provide separate testing-grounds for the two beliefs.

[12]Solzhenitsyn, p. 232. (Curiously, Solzhenitsyn, like Keats [p. 322], seems to attach weight not just to psychological but to *cellular* change. Cf. Hume.)

[13]Someone might say, "These are not successive nations. They are just stages of a single nation." What about Prussia, Germany, and West Germany? We *decide* what counts as the same nation.

[14]Talk about successive selves can be easily misunderstood. It is intended *only* to imply the weakening of psychological connections. It does *not* report the discovery of a new type of thing. We should take the question, "When did that self end?" as like the question, "What marked the end of medieval England?" Cf. note 24. (There is of course another use of "earlier self" which, because it equates "self" and "person," does not distinguish successive selves.)

[15]I do not mean "more plausible than their denials"; I mean "than they would be if the Simple View were true."

[16]The implied factual assumption surely holds for *some* of us.

Let us start with the cases of weak connection. And our first principle can be that we deserve to be punished for certain crimes.

We can suppose that, between some convict now and himself when he committed some crime, there are only weak psychological connections. (This will usually be when conviction takes place after many years.) We can imply the weakness of these connections by calling the convict, not the criminal, but his later self.[17]

Two grounds for detaining him would be unaffected. Whether a convict should be either reformed, or preventively detained, turns upon his present state, not his relation to the criminal. A third ground, deterrence, turns upon a different question. Do potential criminals care about their later selves? Do they care, for instance, if they do not expect to be caught for many years? If they do, then detaining their later selves could perhaps deter.

Would it be deserved? Locke thought that if we forget our crimes we deserve no punishment.[18] Geach considers this view "morally repugnant."[19] Mere loss of memory does seem to be insufficient. Changes of character would appear to be more relevant. The subject is, though, extremely difficult. Claims about desert can be plausibly supported with a great variety of arguments. According to some of these loss of memory would be important. And according to most the nature and cause of any change in character would need to be known.

I have no space to consider these details, but I shall make one suggestion. This appeals to the following assumption. When some morally important fact holds to a lesser degree, it can be more plausibly claimed to have less importance—even, in extreme cases, none.

I shall not here defend this assumption. I shall only say that most of us apply the assumption to many kinds of principle. Take, for example, the two principles that we have special duties to help our relatives, or friends. On the assumption, we might claim that we have less of a special duty to help our less close relatives, or friends, and, to those who are very distant, none at all.

My suggestion is this. If the assumption is acceptable, and the Complex View correct, it becomes more plausible to make the following claim: when the connections between convicts and their past criminal selves are less, they deserve less punishment; if they are very weak, they perhaps deserve none. This claim extends the idea of "diminished responsibility." It does not appeal to mental illness, but instead treats a later self like a sane accomplice. Just as a man's deserts correspond to the degree of his complicity with some criminal, so his deserts, now, for some past crime correspond to the degree of connectedness between himself now and himself when committing that crime.[20]

[17]Talk about successive selves can be used, like this, merely to imply the weakness of psychological connections. It can also be used to assign moral or emotional significance to such a weakness. This "evaluative" use I have sketched elsewhere, in Parfit (1972). It is the "descriptive" use which I need here. On this use, if a convict says, "It was only my past self," all that he implies is the weakening in connections. On the "evaluative" use, his claim suggests that, because of this weakening, he does not now deserve to be punished for his crime. Since the questions I am asking here all concern whether such a weakening *does* have such significance, it is the "descriptive" use which I here employ. The "evaluative" use begs these questions.

[18]Locke, Book II, chapter XXVII, section 26. (Cf. also the "Defense of Mr. Locke's Opinion" in certain editions of Locke's *Works* [e.g., 11th edn, vol. 3].)

[19]Geach, p. 4.

[20]If we are tempted to protest, "But it was just as much *his* crime," we seem to be taking the Simple View. The comparable claim, "Every accomplice is just as much an accomplice" is, in the sense in which it is true, clearly trivial. (See Parfit [1972].) (It is perhaps worth repeating that the Complex View deals with our relations at certain times, to ourselves at other times. The convict and criminal are, timelessly, the same person. But the convict's present self and his past self are not the same, any more than Roman and Victorian Britain are the same.)

If we add the further assumption that psychological connections are, in general, weaker over longer periods,[21] the claim provides a ground for Statutes of Limitations. (They of course have other grounds.)

IV

We can next consider promises. There are here two identities involved. The first is that of the person who, once, made a promise. Let us suppose that between this person now and himself then there are only weak connections. Would this wipe away his commitment? Does a later self start with a clean slate?

On the assumption that I gave, the Complex View supports the answer, "yes." Certain people think that only short-term promises carry moral weight. This belief becomes more plausible on the Complex View.

The second relevant identity is that of the person who received the promise. There is here an asymmetry. The possible effect of the Complex View could be deliberately blocked. We could ask for promises of this form: "I shall help you, and all your later selves." If the promises that I *receive* take this form, they cannot be plausibly held to be later undermined by any change in *my* character, or by any other weakening, over the rest of *my* life, in connectedness.

The asymmetry is this: similar forms cannot so obviously stay binding on the *maker* of a promise. I might say, "I, and all my later selves, shall help you." But it is plausible to reply that I can only bind my present self. This is plausible because it is like the claim that I can only bind myself. No one, though, denies that I can promise you that I shall help someone else. So I can clearly promise you that I shall help your later selves.

Such a promise may indeed seem especially binding. Suppose that you change faster than I do. I may then regard myself as committed, not to you, but to your earlier self. I may therefore think that you cannot waive my commitment. (It would be like a commitment, to someone now dead, to help his children. We cannot be released from such commitments.)

Such a case would be rare. But an example may help the argument. Let us take a nineteenth-century Russian who, in several years, should inherit vast estates. Because he has socialist ideals, he intends, now, to give the land to the peasants. But he knows that in time his ideals may fade. To guard against this possibility, he does two things. He first signs a legal document, which will automatically give away the land, and which can only be revoked with his wife's consent. He then says to his wife, "If I ever change my mind, and ask you to revoke the document, promise me that you will not consent." He might add, "I regard my ideals as essential to me. If I lose these ideals, I want you to think that *I* cease to exist. I want you to regard your husband, then, not as me, the man who asks you for this promise, but only as his later self. Promise me that you would not do what he asks."

This plea seems understandable.[22] And if his wife made this promise, and he later asked her to revoke the document, she might well regard herself as in no way released from her commitment. It might seem to her as if she has obligations to two different people. She might think that to do what her husband now asks would be to betray the young man whom she loved and married. And she might regard what her husband now says as unable to acquit her of disloyalty to this young man—of disloyalty to her husband's earlier self.

[21] This is only generally true. Old men, for instance, can be closer to themselves in childhood than to themselves in youth.

[22] It involves the new use of pronouns, and of the word "man," to refer to one out of a series of selves.

Such an example may seem not to require the distinction between successive selves. Suppose that I ask you to promise me never to give me cigarettes, even if I beg you for them. You might think that I cannot, in begging you, simply release you from this commitment. And to think this you need not deny that it is I to whom you are committed.

This seems correct. But the reason is that addiction clouds judgment. Similar examples might involve extreme stress or pain, or (as with Odysseus, tied to the mast) extraordinary temptation. When, though, nothing clouds a person's judgment, most of us believe that the person to whom we are committed can always release us. He can always, if in sound mind, waive our commitment. We believe this whatever the commitment may be. So (on this view) the content of a commitment cannot stop its being waived.

To return to the Russian couple. The man's ideals fade, and he asks his wife to revoke the document. Though she promised him to refuse, he declares that he now releases her from this commitment. We have sketched two ways in which she might think that she is not released. She might, first, take her husband's change of mind as proof that he cannot now make considered judgments. But we can suppose that she has no such thought. We can also suppose that she shares our view about commitment. If so, she will only believe that her husband is unable to release her if she thinks that it is, in some sense, not *he* to whom she is committed. We have sketched such a sense. She may regard the young man's loss of his ideals as involving his replacement by a later self.

The example is of a quite general possibility. We may regard some events within a person's life as, in certain ways, like birth or death. Not in all ways, for beyond these events the person has earlier or later selves. But it may be only one out of the series of selves which is the object of some of our emotions, and to which we apply some of our principles.[23]

The young Russian socialist regards his ideals as essential to his present self. He asks his wife to promise to this present self not to act against these ideals. And, on this way of thinking, she can never be released from her commitment. For the self to whom she is committed would, in trying to release her, cease to exist.

The way of thinking may seem to be within our range of choice. We can indeed choose when to *speak* of a new self, just as we can choose when to speak of the end of Medieval England. But the way of speaking would express beliefs. And the wife in our example cannot choose her beliefs. That the young man whom she loved and married has, in a sense, ceased to exist, that her middle-aged and cynical husband is at most the later self of this young man—these claims may seem to her to express more of the truth than the simple claim, "but they are the same person." Just as we can give a more accurate description if we divide the history of Russia into that of the Empire and of the Soviet Union, so it may be more accurate to divide her husband's life into that of two successive selves.[24]

V

I have suggested that the Complex View supports certain claims. It is worth repeating that these claims are at most more plausible on the Complex View (more, that is, than on the Simple View). They are not entailed by the Complex View.

[23] I have here moved from the use of talk about successive selves which is merely "descriptive," which merely implies the weakening of connections, to the use which is also "evaluative," which assigns to such a weakening certain kinds of significance. It may seem confusing to allow these different uses, but they cannot be sharply distinguished. The "merely descriptive" use lies at the end-point of a spectrum.

[24] If we take the Complex View, we might add: "It would be even more accurate to abandon talk about 'selves,' and to describe actions, thoughts, and experiences in a quite 'impersonal' way. (Cf. Strawson,

We can sometimes show this in the following way. Some claims make sense when applied to successive generations. Such claims can obviously be applied to successive selves. For example, it perhaps makes sense to believe that we inherit the commitments of our parents. If so, we can obviously believe that commitments are inherited by later selves.

Other claims may be senseless when applied to generations. Perhaps we cannot intelligibly think that we deserve to be punished for all our parents' crimes. But even if this is so, it should still make sense to have the comparable thought about successive selves. No similarity in the form of two relations could force us to admit that they are morally equivalent, for we can always appeal to the difference in their content.

There are, then, no entailments. But there seldom are in moral reasoning. So the Complex View may still support certain claims. Most of us think that our children are neither bound by our commitments, nor responsible for all we do. If we take the Complex View, we may be more inclined to think the same about our later selves. And the correctness of the view might make such beliefs more defensible.

VI

What, next, of our present selves? What of the other kind of case, where there are the strongest psychological connections? Here it makes no difference to believe that our identity has, in its nature, degrees, for there is here the strongest degree. But in the change to the Complex View we acquire a second new belief. We decide that our identity is in its nature less deep, or involves less. This belief applies to every case, even those where there are the strongest connections.

It is worth suggesting why there must be this second difference between the two views. On the Complex View, our identity over time just involves bodily and psychological continuity. On the Simple View, it does not just involve these continuities; it is in its nature a further fact. If we stop believing that it is a further fact, then (by arithmetic) we believe that it involves less. There is still the bare possibility that we thought

---

pp. 81–4). If these are not ascribed to any 'subject,' their various interconnections can then be directly specified. But the concept of a 'subject of experience,' like that of a nation, is an abbreviatory device of enormous convenience. If we remember that it is just this, and nothing more, it can be safely used" (Cf. Mill, p. 252. Those who disagree, see note 57). These remarks may *not* apply to the concept of a persisting object. This may be essential to the spatio-temporal framework. But observed objects do not require observers. They require observations.

Here is another way in which the move from "person" to "successive self" may help to express the truth. Suppose that, in middle age, the Russian wife asks herself, "Do I love my husband?" If it is asked in this form, she may find the question baffling. She may then realize that there is someone she loves—her husband's earlier self. (The object of love can be in the past. We can love the dead.) Cf. Solzhenitsyn, p. 393:

> Innokenty felt sorry for her and agreed to come. . . . He felt sorry, not for the wife he lived with and yet did not live with these days, the wife he was going to leave again soon, but for the blond girl with the curls hanging down to her shoulders, the girl he had known in the tenth grade. . . .

Cf. also Nabokov, p. 64.

> They said the only thing this Englishman loved in the world was Russia. Many people could not understand why he had not remained there. Moon's reply to questions of that kind would invariably be: "Ask Robertson" (the orientalist) "why he did not stay in Babylon." The perfectly reasonable objection would be raised that Babylon no longer existed. Moon would nod with a sly, silent smile. He saw in the Bolshevist insurrection a certain clear-cut finality. While he willingly allowed that, by-and-by, after the primitive phases, some civilization might develop in the "Soviet Union," he nevertheless maintained that Russia was concluded and unrepeatable. . . .

the further fact superficial.[25] But it seems to most of us peculiarly deep.[26] This is why, if we change to the Complex View, we believe that our identity is in its nature less deep.

Would this belief affect our principles? If it has effects, they would not be confined to the special cases where there are only weak psychological connections. They would hold in every case. The effects would not be that we give certain principles a different scope. They would be that we give the principles a different weight.

Such effects could be defended on the following assumption. When some morally important fact is seen to be less deep, it can be plausibly claimed to be less important. As the limiting case, it becomes more plausible to claim that it has no importance. (This assumption is a variant of the one I used earlier.) The implications are obvious. The principles of desert and commitment presuppose that personal identity is morally important. On the assumption I have just sketched, the Complex View supports the claim that it is—because less deep—less important. So it may tend to weaken these principles.

I shall not here discuss these possible effects. I shall only say that the principle of commitment seems to be the less threatened by this weakening effect. The reason may be that, unlike the principle of desert, it is a conventional or "artificial" principle. This may shield it from a change of view about the facts.[27]

I shall now turn to my last subject, distributive justice. Here the consequences of a change to the Complex View seem harder to assess. The reason is this: in the case of the principles of desert and commitment, both the possible effects, the weakening and the change in scope, are in theory pro-utilitarian. (Since these principles compete with the principle of utility, it is obviously in theory pro-utilitarian if they are weakened.[28] And their new scope would be a reduced scope. This should also be pro-utilitarian.[29]) Since both the possible effects would be in the same direction, we can make this general claim: if the change of view has effects upon these principles, these effects would be pro-utilitarian. In the case of distributive justice, things are different. Here, as I shall argue, the two possible effects seem to be in opposite directions. So there is a new question: which is the more plausible combined effect? My reply will again be: pro-utilitarian.

VII

Before defending this claim, I shall mention two related claims. These can be introduced in the following way.

[25]As, for example, Leibniz may have done. See the remark that Shoemaker quotes in Care, p. 127. Locke sometimes held a similar view. (I refer to his claim that "whether it be the same identical substance, which always thinks in the same person . . . matters not at all.")

[26]As Williams suggests. Cf. Bayle's reply to Leibniz quoted by Chisholm in Care, p. 139; and, for other statements, Geach, pp. 1–29, Penelhum, closing chapters (both implicit), Butler, pp. 385 ff., Reid, Essay III, chs 4 and 6, and Chisholm (more explicit).

[27]We should perhaps add the obvious remark that the principle of desert seems itself to be more threatened by a change of view, not about personal identity, but about psychological causation.

[28]That it may in practice be anti-utilitarian is, for instance, emphasized in Sidgwick (1901), Book IV, ch. V. (In Sidgwick [1902], p. 114, he writes, "It may be—I think it is—true that Utilitarianism is only adapted for practical use by human beings at an advanced stage of intellectual development.")

[29]There are some exceptions. If, for instance, we hold the principle of desert in its "negative" form (cf. Hart), its receiving less scope may in theory seem anti-utilitarian. Useful punishments might be ruled out on the ground that they are no longer deserved. But this would in practice be a minor point. (And there seems to be no corresponding point about commitment.)

Utilitarians reject distributive principles. They aim for the greatest net sum of benefits minus burdens, whatever its distribution. Let us say they "maximize."

There is, here, a well-known parallel. When we can affect only one person, we accept maximization. We do not believe that we ought to give a person fewer happy days so as to be more fair in the way we spread them out over the parts of his life. There are, of course, arguments for spreading out enjoyments. We remain fresh, and have more to look forward to. But these arguments do not count against maximization; they remind us how to achieve it.

When we can affect several people, utilitarians make similar claims. They admit new arguments for spreading out enjoyments, such as that which appeals to relative deprivation. But they treat equality as a mere means, not a separate aim.

Since their attitude to sets of lives is like ours to single lives, utilitarians disregard the boundaries between lives. We may ask, "Why?"

Here are three suggestions.—Their approach to morality leads them to overlook these boundaries.—They believe that the boundaries are unimportant, because they think that sets of lives are like single lives.—They take the Complex View.

The first suggestion has been made by Rawls. It can be summarized like this. Utilitarians tend to approach moral questions as if they were impartial observers. When they ask themselves, as observers, what is right, or what they prefer, they tend to *identify* with *all* the affected people. This leads them to ignore the fact that *different* people are affected, and so to reject the claims of justice.[30]

In the case of some utilitarians, Rawls's explanation seems sufficient.[31] Let us call these the "identifying observers." But there are others who in contrast always seem "*detached* observers." These utilitarians do not seem to overlook the distinction between people.[32] And, as Rawls remarks, there is no obvious reason why observers who remain *detached* cannot adopt the principles of justice. If we approach morality in a quite detached way—if we do not think of ourselves as potentially involved[33]—we may, I think, be somewhat more inclined to reject these principles.[34] But this particular approach to moral questions does not itself seem a sufficient explanation for utilitarian beliefs.

The Complex View may provide a different explanation. These two are quite compatible. Utilitarians may both approach morality as observers, and take the Complex View. (The explanations may indeed be mutually supporting.)

To turn to the remaining explanation. Utilitarians treat sets of lives in the way that we treat single lives. It has been suggested, not that they ignore the difference between

[30]Rawls, p. 27, and pp. 185–9.

[31]Rawls mentions C. I. Lewis (Rawls, p. 188); but the explanation cannot hold for him, for he insists upon the claims of justice (Lewis, pp. 553–4). The explanation may seem to apply to Hare; see Hare (1963), p. 123; but p. 121 suggests that it does not. In Mackaye, pp. 129–30 and p. 189 seem to fit; but again, pp. 146–50 point the other way.

[32]Among the many utilitarians who clearly remain detached is Sidgwick. To quote a typical sentence: "I as a disengaged spectator should like him to sacrifice himself to the general good: but I do not expect him to do it, any more than I should do it myself in his place." (Sidgwick [1901], pp. XVII–XVIII.) Sidgwick ended the first edition of his book with the word "failure" mostly because he assigned such weight to the distinction between people. (See, for example [1901], p. 404, or [1902], p. 67, or the remark in *Mind* [1889], pp. 483–4, "The distinction between any one individual and another is real, and fundamental." [Sidgwick's own view about personal identity is hard to judge. In (1901), pp. 418–19, he appears to disclaim one form of the Complex View. In *Mind* (1883), p. 326, he admits a Kantian claim about the necessity of the 'permanent, identical self'. Perhaps (like Kant himself?) he was torn between the two views.])

[33]As we do if we are either contracting agents (Rawls), or universal prescribers (Hare).

[34]As the contrast between the two halves of the first quotation in note 32 may suggest. For a different suggestion, see Hare (1972) and (1973).

people, but that they actually believe that a group of people is like a super-person. This suggestion is, in a sense, the reverse of mine. It imputes a different view about the facts. And it can seem the more plausible.

Let us start with an example. Suppose that we must choose whether to let some child undergo some hardship. If he does, this will either be for his own greater benefit in adult life, or for the similar benefit of someone else. Does it matter which?

Most of us would answer: "Yes. If it is for the child's own benefit, there can at least be no unfairness." We might draw the general conclusion that failure to relieve useful burdens is more likely to be justified if they are for a person's *own* good.

Utilitarians, confusingly, could accept this conclusion. They would explain it in a different way. They might, for instance, point out that such burdens are in general easier to bear.

To block this reply, we can suppose that the child in our example cannot be cheered up in this way. Let us next ignore other such arguments.[35] This simplifies the disagreement. Utilitarians would say: "Whether it is right to let the child bear the burden only depends upon how great the benefit will be. It does not depend upon who benefits. It would make no moral difference if the benefit comes, not to the child himself, but to someone else." Non-utilitarians might reply: "On the contrary, if it comes to the child himself this helps to justify the burden. If it comes to someone else, that is unfair."

We can now ask: do the two views about the nature of personal identity tend to support different sides in this debate?

Part of the answer seems clear. Non-utilitarians think it a morally important fact that it be the child himself who, as an adult, benefits. This fact, if it seems more important on one of the views, ought to do so on the Simple View, for it is on this view that the identity between the child and the adult is in its nature deeper. On the Complex View, it is less deep, and holds, over adolescence, to reduced degrees. If we take the Complex View, we may compare the lack of connections between the child and his adult self to the lack of connections between different people. That it will be *he* who receives the benefit may thus seem less important. We might say, "It will not be *he*. It will only be his adult self."

The Simple View seems, then, to support the non-utilitarian reply. Does it follow that the Complex View tends to support utilitarian beliefs? Not directly. For we might say, "Just as it would be unfair if it is someone else who benefits, so if it won't be he, but only his adult self, that would also be unfair."

The point is a general one. If we take the Complex View, we may regard the (rough) subdivisions within lives as, in certain ways, like the divisions between lives. We may therefore come to treat alike two kinds of distribution: within lives, and between lives. But there are two ways of treating these alike. We can apply distributive principles to both, or to neither.

Which of these might we do? I claim that we may abandon these principles. Someone might object: "If we do add, to the divisions between lives, subdivisions within lives, the effects could only be these. The principles that we now apply to the divisions we come to apply to the sub-divisions. (If, to use your own example, we believe that our sons do not inherit our commitments, we may come to think the same about our later selves.)

"The comparable effect would now be this. We demand fairness to later selves. We *extend* distributive principles. You instead claim that we may abandon these principles. Since this is *not* the comparable effect, your claim must be wrong."

[35]Such as those which appeal to the undermining of the general sense of security, or to pessimism about the "acceptance-utility" of utilitarian beliefs.

The objection might be pressed. We might add: "If we did abandon these principles, we should be moving in reverse. We should not be treating parts of one life as we now treat different lives, but be treating different lives as we now treat one life. This, the reverse effect, could only come from the reverse comparison. Rather than thinking that a person's life is like the history of a nation, we must be thinking that a nation—or indeed any group—is like a person."

To review the argument so far. Treating alike single people and groups may come from accepting some comparison between them. But there are two ways of treating them alike. We can demand fairness even within single lives, or reject this demand in the case of groups. And there are two ways of taking this comparison. We can accept the Complex View and compare a person's life to the history of a group, or accept the reverse view and compare groups to single people.

Of these four positions, I had matched the Complex View with the abandonment of fairness. The objection was that it seemed to be better matched with the demand for fairness even within lives. And the rejection of this demand, in the case of groups, seemed to require what I shall call "the Reverse View."

My reply will be this. Disregard for the principles of fairness could perhaps be supported by the Reverse View. But it does not have to be. And in seeing why we shall see how it may be supported by the Complex View.

Many thinkers have believed that a society, or nation, is like a person. This belief seems to weaken the demand for fairness. When we are thought to be mere parts of a social organism, it can seem to matter less how we are each treated.[36]

If the rejection of fairness has to be supported in this way, utilitarians can be justly ignored. This belief is at best superficially true when held about societies. And to support utilitarian views it would have to be held about the whole of mankind, where it is absurd.

Does the rejection of fairness need such support? Certain writers think that it does. Gauthier, for instance, suggests that to suppose that we should maximize for mankind "is to suppose that mankind is a super-person."[37] This suggestion seems to rest on the following argument. "We are free to maximize within one life only because it is *one* life.[38] So we could only be free to maximize over different lives if they are like parts of a single life."

Given this argument, utilitarians would, I think, deny the premise. They would deny that it is the unity of a life which, within this life, justifies maximization. They can then think this justified over different lives without assuming mankind to be a super-person.

The connection with the Complex View is, I think, this. It is on this view, rather than the Simple View, that the premise is more plausibly denied. That is how the Complex View may support utilitarian beliefs.

To expand these remarks. There are two kinds of distribution: within lives, and between lives. And there are two ways of treating these alike. We can apply distributive principles to both, or to neither.

Utilitarians apply them to neither. I suggest that this may be (in part) because they take the Complex View. An incompatible suggestion is that they take the Reverse View.

[36]Cf. the claim of Espinas, that society "is a living being like an individual" (Perry, p. 402). Good Hegelians do not argue in this way.

[37]Gauthier, p. 126.

[38]Someone might say: "No. We are free, here, because it is not a moral matter what we do with our own lives." This cannot be right, for we are allowed to maximize within the life of *someone else*. (Medicine provides examples. Doctors are allowed to maximize on behalf of their unconscious patients.)

My suggestion may seem clearly wrong if we overlook the following fact. There are two routes to the abandonment of distributive principles. We may give them no scope, or instead give them no weight.

Suppose we assume that the only route is the change in scope.[39] Then it may indeed seem that utilitarians must either be assuming that any group of people is like a single person (Gauthier's suggestion), or at least be forgetting that it is not (Rawls's suggestion).

I shall sketch the other route. Utilitarians may not be denying that distributive principles have scope. They may be denying that they have weight. This, the second of the kinds of effect that I earlier distinguished, *may* be supported by the Complex View.

The situation, more precisely, may be this. If the Complex View supports a change in the scope of distributive principles, it perhaps supports giving them more scope. It perhaps supports their extension even within single lives. But the other possible effect, the weakening of these principles, may be the more strongly supported. That is how the net effect may be pro-utilitarian.

This suggestion differs from the other two in the following way. Rawls remarks that the utilitarian attitude seems to involve "conflating all persons into one."[40] This remark also covers Gauthier's suggestion. But the attitude may derive, not from the conflation of persons, but from their (partial) disintegration. It may rest upon the view that a person's life is less deeply integrated than we mostly think. Utilitarians may be treating benefits and burdens, not as if they all came within the same life, but as if it made no moral difference where they came. This belief may be supported by the view that the unity of each life, and hence the difference between lives, is in its nature less deep.[41]

VIII

I shall next sketch a brief defense of this suggestion. And I shall start with a new distributive principle. Utilitarians believe that benefits and burdens can be freely weighed against each other, even if they come to different people. This is frequently denied.

We must first distinguish two kinds of weighing. The claim that a certain burden "factually outweighs" another is the claim that it is greater. The claim that it "morally outweighs" the other is the claim that we should relieve it even at the cost of failing to relieve the other. Similar remarks apply to the weighing of benefits against burdens, and against each other.

Certain people claim that burdens cannot even *factually* outweigh each other if they come to different people. (They claim that the sense of "greater than" can only be provided by a single person's preferences.) I am here concerned with a different claim.[42] At its boldest this is that the burdens and benefits of different people cannot be *morally* weighed. I shall consider one part of this claim. This goes: "Someone's

[39]As Rawls seems to do. Cf. his remark: "the utilitarian extends to society the principle of choice for one man" (p. 28, and elsewhere, e.g. p. 141). The assumption here is that the route to utilitarianism is a change in the scope, not of distributive principles, but of their correlative: our freedom to ignore these principles.

[40]p. 27; cf. p. 191; cf. also Nagel, p. 134.

[41]The utilitarian attitude is *impersonal.* Rawls suggests that it "mistakes impersonality for impartiality" (p. 190). I suggest that it may in part derive from a view about the nature of persons. This suggestion, unlike his, may be no criticism. For as he writes "the correct regulative principle for anything depends upon the nature of that thing" (p. 29).

[42]The possibility of "factual weighing" over different lives can, I think, be shown with an argument which appeals to the Complex View. But the argument would have to be long.

burden cannot be morally outweighed by mere benefits to someone else." I say "mere" benefits, because the claim is not intended to deny that it *can* be right to let a person bear a burden so as to benefit another. Such acts may, for instance, be required by justice. What the claim denies is that such acts can be justified solely upon utilitarian grounds. It denies that a person's burden can be morally outweighed by *mere* benefits to someone else.

This claim often takes qualified forms. It can be restricted to great burdens, or be made to require that the net benefit be proportionately great.[43] I shall here discuss the simplest form, for my remarks could be adapted to the other forms. Rawls puts the claim as follows: "The reasoning which balances the gains and losses of different persons . . . is excluded."[44] So I shall call this the "objection to balancing."

This objection rests in part on a different claim. This goes: "Someone's burden cannot be *compensated* by benefits to someone else." This second claim is, with qualifications,[45] clearly true. We cannot say, "On the contrary, our burdens can be compensated by benefits to anyone else, even a total stranger."

Not only is this second claim clearly true; its denial is in no way supported by the Complex View. So if the change to this view has effects upon this claim, they would be these. We might, first, extend the claim even within single lives. We might say, in the example that I gave, "The child's burden cannot be compensated by benefits to his adult self." This claim would be like the claims that we are sometimes not responsible for, nor bound by, our earlier selves. It would apply to certain parts of one life what we now believe about different lives. It would therefore seem to be, as a change in scope, in the right direction.[46]

We might, next, give the claim less weight. Our ground would be the one that I earlier gave. Compensation presupposes personal identity. On the Complex View, we may think that our identity is, because less deep, less morally important. We may therefore think that the fact of compensation is itself less morally important. Though it cannot be denied, the claim about compensation may thus be given less weight.[47]

[43]Cf. Perry, p. 674: "We do not . . . balance one man's loss against a million's gain. We acknowledge that there are amounts or degrees of value associated with each party, between which it is impossible to discriminate." This claim seems to be slightly qualified. (It is not wholly clear whether Perry is objecting *only* to *moral* weighing.)

[44]p. 28. I omit the words "as if they were one person," for I am asking whether this reasoning must involve this assumption.

[45]The main such qualification is to exclude cases where the first person wants the second to receive the benefit.

[46]It seems worth mentioning here an idea of Nagel's. Like Rawls, Nagel claims that if we imagine that we are going to *be* all of the affected parties, we may then ignore the claims of justice. He then suggests that this is only so if our future lives are to be had *seriatim.* "We can [instead] imagine a person splitting into several persons. . . . This provides a sense in which an individual might expect to become *each* of a number of different persons—not in series, but simultaneously." (Nagel, pp. 141–2; cf. Rawls, pp. 190–1.) *This* model, he believes, "renders plausible the extremely strict position that there can be no interpersonal compensation for sacrifice." Why? How can it make a difference whether the person's future lives are to be lived in series, or concurrently? The relation between the person now and the future lives is, in either case, the same. (It is "as good as survival"; see Parfit [1971], pp. 4–10.) Nagel suggests an answer: "*Each* of [the] lives would in a sense be his unique life, without deriving any compensatory or supplementary experiences, good or bad, by seepage from the other unique lives he is leading at the time." This, of course, is the *utilitarian* answer. It treats *pure* compensation as of no value. It suggests that compensation only matters when it actually has good effects (when it produces "compensatory . . . supplementary experiences"). The disagreement seems to disappear!

[47]This distinction bears on the "Is–Ought" debate. That it is unjust to punish the innocent cannot be denied; but the claim can be given no weight. We might say, "It is just as *bad* to punish the guilty."

If we now return to the objection to balancing, things are different. The concept of "greater moral weight" does not presuppose personal identity.[48] So this objection can be denied; and the Complex View seems to support this denial.

The denial might be put like this: "Our burdens cannot indeed be *compensated* by mere benefits to someone else. But they may be *morally outweighed* by such benefits. It may still be right to give the benefits rather than relieve the burdens. Burdens are morally outweighed by benefits if they are factually outweighed by these benefits. All that is needed is that the benefits be greater than the burdens. It is unimportant, in itself, to whom both come."

This is the utilitarian reply.[49] I shall next suggest why the Complex View seems, more than the Simple View, to support this reply.

The objection to balancing rests in part on the claim about compensation. On the Complex View, this claim can more plausibly be thought less important. If we take this view, we may (we saw) think both that there is less scope for compensation and that it has less moral weight. If the possibilities of compensation are, in these two ways, less morally important, there would then be less support for the objection to balancing. It would be more plausible to make the utilitarian reply.

The point can be made in a different way. Even those who object to balancing think it justified to let us bear burdens for our own good. So their claim must be that a person's burden, while it can be morally outweighed by benefits to him, cannot ever be outweighed by mere benefits to others. This is held to be so even if the benefits are far greater than the burden. The claim thus gives to the boundaries between lives—or to the fact of non-identity—overwhelming significance. It allows within the same life what, for different lives, it totally forbids.

This claim seems to be more plausible on the Simple View. Since identity is, here, thought to involve more, non-identity could plausibly seem more important. On the Simple View, we are impressed by the truth that all of a person's life is as much his life. If we are impressed by this truth—by the unity of each life—the boundaries between lives will seem to be deeper. This supports the claim that, in the moral calculus, these boundaries cannot be crossed. On the Complex View, we are less impressed by this truth. We regard the unity of each life as in its nature less deep, and as a matter of degree. We may therefore think the boundaries between lives to be less like those between, say, the squares on a chess-board,[50] and to be more like those between different countries. They may then seem less morally decisive.[51]

[48]It might do so, indirectly, if we cannot even *factually* weigh over different lives, and adopt utility as our only principle. No one (that I know) holds this position.

[49]It would be their reply to the many arguments in which the objection to balancing and the claim about compensation are intertwined. Cf. Rawls's phrase "cannot be justified by, or compensated for, by . . ." (p. 61), and similar remarks on pp. 14–15, p. 287, and elsewhere. Perry writes: "The happiness of a million somehow fails utterly to compensate or even to mitigate the torture of one." This undeniable remark he seems to equate with the objection to balancing (Perry, p. 671).

[50]Cf: "The difference between self and another is as plain as the difference between black and white." (Hobhouse, p. 51.)

[51]Someone might object: "On the Complex View, we may claim that the parts of each life are less deeply unified; but we do not claim that there is more unity between lives. So the boundaries between lives are, on this view, just as deep." We could answer: "Not so. Take for comparison the fact of personhood. We may decide that to be a person, as opposed to a mere animal, is not in its nature a further fact, beyond the fact of having certain more specific properties, but that it just consists in this fact. This belief is not itself the belief that we are more like mere animals than we thought. But it still removes a believed difference. So it makes the boundaries between us and mere animals less deep. Similar remarks apply to the two views about personal identity."

IX

We can now turn to different principles, for example that of equal distribution. Most of us give such principles only *some* weight. We think, for instance, that unequal distribution can be justified if it brings an overall gain in social welfare. But we may insist that the gain be proportionately great.[52]

We do not, in making such claims, forbid utilitarian policies. We allow that every gain in welfare has moral value. But we do restrain these policies. We insist that it also matters *who* gains. Certain distributions are, we claim, morally preferable. We thus claim that we ought to favor the worst off, and to incline towards equality.

Utilitarians would reply: "These claims are of course plausible. But the policies they recommend are the very policies which tend to increase total welfare. This coincidence suggests[53] that we ought to change our view about the status of these claims. We should regard them, not as checks upon, but as guides to, utilitarian policy. We should indeed value equal distribution. But the value lies in its typical effects."

This reply might be developed in the following way. Most of us believe that a mere difference in *when* something happens, if it does not affect the nature of what happens, cannot be morally significant. Certain answers to the question "When?" are of course important. We cannot ignore the timing of events. And it is even plausible to claim that if, say, we are planning when to give or to receive benefits, we should aim for an equal distribution over time. But we aim for this only because of its effects. We do not believe that the equality of benefit at different times is, as such, morally important.

Utilitarians might say: "If it does not, as such, matter *when* something happens, why does it matter *to whom* it happens? Both of these are mere differences in position. What is important is the nature of what happens. When we choose between social policies, we need only be concerned with how *great* the benefits will be. *Where* they come, whether in space, or in time, or as between people, has in itself no importance."

Part of the disagreement is, then, this. Non-utilitarians take the question "Who?" to be quite unlike the question "When?" If they are asked for the simplest possible description of the morally relevant facts, they will sometimes give them in a form which is tenseless; but it will always be personal. They will say, "Someone gains, the same person loses, someone else gains. . . ." Utilitarians would instead say, "A gain, a loss, another gain. . . ."

There are many different arguments for and against these two positions. We are only asking: would a change to the Complex View tend to support either one?

It would seem so. On the Simple View, it is more plausible to insist upon the question "Who?" On the Complex View, it is more plausible to compare this to the question "When?," and to present the moral data in the second, or "impersonal," form.[54]

[52]These are examples of what both Sidgwick and Rawls would call "the intuitionism of Common Sense." I cannot here discuss Rawls's principles, or his "contractual" argument. (I should point out that a contractual argument for the principles of justice seems to be in no way weakened by the Complex View. But alongside the contractual argument, Rawls suggests another: that these principles are required by the *plurality* of persons (cf. p. 29). This is the argument which, however strong, seems to me less strong on the Complex View.)

[53]See, for instance, Sidgwick (1901), p. 425 (or indeed pp. 199–457).

[54]I am here claiming that the Complex View tends to weaken distributive principles. What of the other possible effect, the change in scope? Might we demand fair shares for successive selves? *Perhaps*. (Cf. Findlay, p. 239.) But the demand would, I think (and for various reasons), be rare. And the argument in the text only requires the following claim: the weakening of distributive principles would be more supported than the widening in their scope. The effects of the former would outweigh the effects of the latter. As the limiting case, if we give distributive principles no weight, nothing follows from a change in their scope.

It may help to return to our comparison. Most of us believe that the existence of a nation does not involve anything more than the existence of associated people. We do not deny the reality of nations. But we do deny that they are separately, or independently, real. They are entirely composed of associated people.[55]

This belief seems to support certain moral claims. If there is nothing to a nation but its citizens, it is less plausible to regard the nation as itself a (primary) object of duties, or possessor of rights. It is more plausible to focus upon the citizens, and to regard them less as citizens, more as people. We may therefore, on this view, think a person's nationality less morally important.[56]

On the Complex View, we hold similar beliefs. We regard the existence of a person as, in turn, involving nothing more than the occurrence of interrelated mental and physical events. We do not, of course, deny the reality of people (our own reality!). And we agree that we are not, strictly, series of events—that we are not thoughts, but thinkers, not actions, but agents. But we consider this a fact of grammar. And we do deny that we are not just conceptually distinct from our bodies, actions, and experiences, but also separately real. We deny that the identity of a person, of the so-called "subject" of mental and physical events, is a further, deep, fact, independent of the facts about the interrelations between these events.[57]

This belief may support similar claims. We may, when thinking morally, focus less upon the person, the subject of experience, and instead focus more upon the experiences themselves. Just as we often ignore whether people come from the same or different nations, so we may more often ignore whether experiences come within the same or different lives.

Take, for example, the relief of suffering. Suppose that we can only help one of two people. We shall achieve more if we help the first; but it is the second who, in the past, suffered more.

Those who believe in fair shares may decide to help the second person. This will be less effective; so the amount of suffering in the two people's lives will, in sum, be greater; but the amounts in each life will be made more equal.

If we take the Complex View, we may reject this line of thought. We may decide to do the most we can to relieve suffering. To suggest why, we can vary the example. Suppose that we can only help one of two nations. Here again, the one that we can help most is the one whose history was, in earlier centuries, the more fortunate. Most of us would not believe that it could be right to allow mankind to suffer more, so that its suffering could be more equally divided between the histories of different nations.

On the Complex View, we compare the lives of people to the histories of nations. We may therefore think the same about them too. We may again decide to aim for the least possible suffering, whatever its distribution.[58]

[55]This is ontological reductionism. It may not require the truth of analytical reductionism (or "methodological individualism"). See, for instance, Strawson, p. 201, Dummett, p. 242, and Kripke, p. 271. I have no space to pursue this point here.

[56]We could, of course, still claim that the fact of being associated-in-a-nation has supreme importance. But this claim, though possible, may still be less supported by this view. This it will be if the independent reality, which this view denies would have helped to support the claim.

[57]Someone might object: "The comparison fails. The interrelations between citizens could in theory be described without mentioning nations. The interrelations between mental and physical events could *not* in theory be described without mentioning the 'subject of experience.' " This seems to me false. The difference is only one of practical convenience. (See Parfit [1971], section III, for a very brief statement.) But even if the comparison *does* fail in this respect, it would still hold in the respects which are morally important.

[58]Someone might object: "This reasoning only applies to the demand for equal distribution as between entire lives. But we might make the demand in a form which ignores both the past and the future. We might

X

We can next explain what, earlier, may have seemed puzzling. Besides the Complex View, which compares people to nations, I mentioned a reverse view, which compares nations to people. How can these be different?

It will help to introduce two more terms. With respect to many types of thing, we may take one of two views. We may believe that the existence of this type of thing does not involve anything more than the existence of certain other (interrelated) things. Such a view can be called "atomistic." We may instead believe that the things in question have a quite separate existence, over and above that of these other things. Such a view can be called "holistic."

One example of an atomistic view is the one we mostly take about nations. Most of us do not (here and now) believe that there is more to nations than associated people. On the other hand, we mostly do seem to assume that there is more to us than a series of mental and physical events. We incline to what I call the Simple View. Most of us are therefore atomists about nations, holists about people.

It is the difference between these common views which explains the two comparisons. The claim that X is like Y typically assumes the common view of Y. We shall therefore say "People are like nations" if we are atomists about both. We shall instead say "Nations are like people" if we are holists about both. Either way, we assume one of the common views and deny the other.[59]

We can end by considering a remark in Rawls. There is, he writes, "a curious anomaly":[60]

> It is customary to think of utilitarianism as individualistic, and certainly there are good reasons for this. The utilitarians . . . held that the good of society is constituted by the advantages enjoyed by individuals. Yet utilitarianism is not individualistic . . . in that . . . it applies to society the principle of choice for one man.

Our account suggests an explanation. Individualists claim that the welfare of society only consists in the welfare of its members, and that the members have rights to fair shares.

Suppose that we are holists about society. We believe that the existence of society transcends that of its members. This belief threatens the first of the individualist claims. It supports the view that the welfare of society also transcends that of its members. This in turn threatens the second claim, for in the pursuit of a transcendent social goal, fair shares may seem less important. Social holists may thus reject both of the individualist claims.

Utilitarians reject the second claim, but accept the first. This would indeed be anomalous if their attitude to these claims rested upon social holism. If this were their ground, we should expect them to reject *both* claims.

We have sketched a different ground. Rather than being holists about society, utilitarians may be atomists about people. This dissolves the anomaly. For they are also atomists about society, and this double atomism seems to support the two positions Rawls describes. If we are atomists about society, we can then more plausibly accept

---

value equal distribution as between people (or 'successive selves') at any given time." True. But this new demand seems, on reflection, implausible. Why the restriction to the *same* (given) time? How can simultaneity have intrinsic moral weight? (The new demand may, of course, have good effects. This is here irrelevant.)

[59]I am here forced (by lack of space) into gross oversimplification. There are many intermediate views. To give one example: if we are atomists about organisms, we shall find it easier to compare nations to organisms. For some of the complexities see Perry, p. 400 onwards and Hobhouse.

[60]Rawls, p. 29.

the first of the individualist claims, *viz,* that the welfare of society only consists in that of its members.[61] If we are also atomists about people, we can then more plausibly reject the second claim, the demand for fair shares. We may tend to focus less upon the person, the subject of experience, and instead focus more upon the experiences themselves. We may then decide that it is only the nature of what happens which is morally important, not to whom it happens. We may thus decide that it is always right to increase benefits and reduce burdens, whatever their distribution.[62]

"Utilitarianism," Rawls remarks, "does not take seriously the distinction between persons."[63] If "the separateness of persons . . . is *the* basic fact for morals,"[64] this is a grave charge. I have tried to show how one view about the nature of persons may provide *some* defense.[65]

BIBLIOGRAPHY

ANSCHUTZ, R. P., *The Philosophy of J. S. Mill,* Oxford, Clarendon Press, 1953.
BUTLER, JOSEPH, "Of Personal Identity," appendix to *The Analogy of Natural Religion,* vol. 1, ed. W. E. Gladstone, Oxford, Frowde, 1897.
CARE, N. and GRIMM, R. H., *Perception and Personal Identity,* Cleveland, Press of Case-Western Reserve University, 1967.
CHISHOLM, R., "Problems of Identity," in *Identity and Individuation,* ed. M. K. Munitz, New York University Press, 1971.
DUMMETT, M., "The Reality of the Past," *Proceedings of the Aristotelian Society,* 69, 1968–9.
FINDLAY, J., *Values and Intentions,* London, Allen & Unwin, 1961.
GAUTHIER, D., *Practical Reasoning,* Oxford, Clarendon Press, 1963.
GEACH, P. T., *God and the Soul,* London, Routledge & Kegan Paul, 1969.
HARE, R. M. (1963), *Freedom and Reason,* Oxford, Clarendon Press.
HARE, R. M. (1972), "Rules of War and Moral Reasoning," *Philosophy and Public Affairs,* winter.
HARE, R. M. (1973), review of Rawls in *Philosophical Quarterly.*
HART, H. L. A., *Punishment and Responsibility,* Oxford, Clarendon Press, 1968.
HOBHOUSE, L. T., *The Metaphysical Theory of the State,* London, Allen & Unwin, 1918.
HUME, DAVID, "A Treatise of Human Nature," 1740.
KEATS, JOHN, *Letters,* ed. R. Gittings, London, Oxford University Press, 1970.
KRIPKE, S., "Naming and Necessity," in *Semantics of Natural Language,* eds. D. Davidson and G. Harman, Dordrecht, Reidel, 1972.
LEWIS, C. I., *An Analysis of Knowledge and Valuation,* La Salle, Illinois, Open Court, 1962.
LOCKE, JOHN, *Essay Concerning Human Understanding,* 1690.
LUKES, S., *Individualism,* Oxford, Blackwell, 1973.
MACKAYE, J., *The Economy of Happiness,* Boston, Little, Brown, 1906.

[61]Cf.: "As the public body is every individual collected, so the public good is the collected good of those individuals" (Thomas Paine, quoted in Lukes, p. 49). Sidgwick remarks that while we commend "one man dying for his country . . . it would be absurd that all should: there would be no country to die for." (1902, p. 79.) We might still deny that "the public good is merely a . . . collection of private goods" on the ground that "men desire for their own sake" irreducibly public goods (Plamenatz, p. 251). But this claim still appeals to personal desires.

[62]The Complex View seems also to support other utilitarian claims, such as that the welfare of a person just consists in the quality of his experiences, or (to give a variant) in the fulfillment of his various particular desires. Cf. the remark in Anschutz (pp. 19–20) that "Bentham's principle of individualism," unlike Mill's, "is entirely transitional," since "Bentham is saying that . . . as a community is reducible to the individuals who are said to be its members, so also are the individuals reducible, at least for the purposes of morals and legislation, to the pleasures and pains which they are said to suffer."

[63]Rawls, p. 27; cf. Nagel, p. 134.

[64]Findlay, p. 393; cf. p. 294.

[65]I have not claimed that it could provide a sufficient defense.

MILL, J. S., *An Examination of Sir William Hamilton's Philosophy,* London, Longmans, 1872.
NABOKOV, V., *Glory,* London, Weidenfeld & Nicolson, 1971.
NAGEL, T., *The Possibility of Altruism,* Oxford, Clarendon Press, 1970.
PARFIT, D. (1971), "Personal Identity," *Philosophical Review,* January.
PARFIT, D. (1972), "On 'The Importance of Self-Identity'," *Journal of Philosophy,* 21 October.
PENELHUM, T., *Survival and Disembodied Existence,* London, Routledge & Kegan Paul, 1970.
PERRY, R., *General Theory of Value,* Cambridge, Mass., Harvard University Press, 1950.
PLAMENATZ, J., *Man and Society,* vol. 2, London, Longmans, 1963.
PROUST, MARCEL (1949), *The Sweet Cheat Gone,* trans. by C. K. Scott Moncrieff, London, Chatto & Windus.
PROUST, MARCEL (1967), *Within a Budding Grove,* vol. 1, trans. by C. K. Scott Moncrieff, London, Chatto & Windus.
QUINTON, A. M. (1962), "The Soul," *Journal of Philosophy,* 59.
QUINTON, A. M. (1972), *On the Nature of Things,* London, Routledge & Kegan Paul.
RAWLS, J., *A Theory of Justice,* Cambridge, Mass., Harvard University Press, 1971.
REID, JOSEPH, *Essays on the Intellectual Powers of Man,* Essay III., chs IV and VI.
SIDGWICK, HENRY (1901), *Methods of Ethics,* sixth edition, London, Macmillan.
SIDGWICK, HENRY (1902), *The Ethics of Green, Spencer, and Martineau,* London, Macmillan.
SOLZHENITSYN, A., *The First Circle,* New York, Bantam Books, 1969.
STRAWSON, P. F., *Individuals,* London, Methuen, 1959.
WILLIAMS, B. A. O., "The Self and the Future," *Philosophical Review,* 1970.

1974
The Experience Machine
Robert Nozick

. . . Suppose there were an experience machine that would give you any experience you desired. Superduper neuropsychologists could stimulate your brain so that you would think and feel you were writing a great novel, or making a friend, or reading an interesting book. All the time you would be floating in a tank, with electrodes attached to your brain. Should you plug into this machine for life, preprogramming your life's experiences? If you are worried about missing out on desirable experiences, we can suppose that business enterprises have researched thoroughly the lives of many others. You can pick and choose from their large library or smorgasbord of such experiences, selecting your life's experiences for, say, the next two years. After two years have passed, you will have ten minutes or ten hours out of the tank, to select the experiences of your *next* two years. Of course, while in the tank you won't know that you're there; you'll think it's all actually happening. Others can also plug in to have the experiences they want, so there's no need to stay unplugged to serve them. (Ignore problems such as who will service the machines if everybody plugs in.) Would you plug in? *What else can matter to us, other than how our lives feel from the inside?* Nor should you refrain because of the few moments of distress between the moment you've decided and the moment you're plugged. What's a few moments of distress compared to a lifetime of bliss (if that's what you choose), and why feel any distress at all if your decision *is* the best one?

What does matter to us in addition to our experiences? First, we want to *do* certain things, and not just have the experience of doing them. In the case of certain experiences, it is only because first we want to do the actions that we want the experiences of doing them or thinking we've done them. (But *why* do we want to do the activities rather than merely to experience them?) A second reason for not plugging in is that we want to *be* a certain way, to be a certain sort of person. Someone floating in a tank is an indeterminate blob. There is no answer to the question of what a person is like who has long been in the tank. Is he courageous, kind, intelligent, witty, loving? It's not merely that it's difficult to tell; there's no way he is. Plugging into the machine is a kind of suicide. It will seem to some, trapped by a picture, that nothing about what we are like can matter except as it gets reflected in our experiences. But should it be surprising that what *we are* is important to us? Why should we be concerned only with how our time is filled, but not with what we are?

Thirdly, plugging into an experience machine limits us to a man-made reality, to a world no deeper or more important than that which people can construct. There is no *actual* contact with any deeper reality, though the experience of it can be simulated. Many persons desire to leave themselves open to such contact and to a plumbing of deeper significance.[1] This clarifies the intensity of the conflict over psychoactive drugs, which some view as mere local experience machines, and others view as avenues to a deeper reality; what some view as equivalent to surrender to the experience machine, others view as following one of the reasons *not* to surrender!

We learn that something matters to us in addition to experience by imagining an experience machine and then realizing that we would not use it. We can continue to imagine a sequence of machines each designed to fill lacks suggested for the earlier machines. For example, since the experience machine doesn't meet our desire to *be* a certain way, imagine a transformation machine which transforms us into whatever sort of person we'd like to be (compatible with our staying us). Surely one would not use the transformation machine to become as one would wish, and thereupon plug into the experience machine![2] So something matters in addition to one's experiences *and* what one is like. Nor is the reason merely that one's experiences are unconnected with what one is like. For the experience machine might be limited to provide only experiences possible to the sort of person plugged in. Is it that we want to make a difference in the world? Consider then the result machine, which produces in the world any result you would produce and injects your vector input into any joint activity. We shall not pursue here the fascinating details of these or other machines. What is most disturbing about them is

[1]Traditional religious views differ on the *point* of contact with a transcendent reality. Some say that contact yields eternal bliss or Nirvana, but they have not distinguished this sufficiently from merely a *very* long run on the experience machine. Others think it is intrinsically desirable to do the will of a higher being which created us all, though presumably no one would think this if we discovered we had been created as an object of amusement by some superpowerful child from another galaxy or dimension. Still others imagine an eventual merging with a higher reality, leaving unclear its desirability, or where that merging leaves us.

[2]Some wouldn't use the transformation machine at all; it seems like *cheating*. But the one-time use of the transformation machine would not remove all challenges; there would still be obstacles for the new us to overcome, a new plateau from which to strive even higher. And is this plateau any the less earned or deserved than that provided by genetic endowment and early childhood environment? But if the transformation machine could be used indefinitely often, so that we could accomplish anything by pushing a button to transform ourselves into someone who could do it easily, there would remain no limits we *need* to strain against or try to transcend. Would there be anything left *to do?* Do some theological views place God outside of time because an omniscient omnipotent being couldn't fill up his days?

their living of our lives for us. Is it misguided to search for *particular* additional functions beyond the competence of machines to do for us? Perhaps what we desire is to live (an active verb) ourselves, in contact with reality. (And this, machines cannot do *for* us.) Without elaborating on the implications of this, which I believe connect surprisingly with issues about free will and causal accounts of knowledge, we need merely note the intricacy of the question of what matters *for people* other than their experiences. Until one finds a satisfactory answer, and determines that this answer does not *also* apply to animals, one cannot reasonably claim that only the felt experiences of animals limit what we may do to them.

1974

The "Is–Ought" Problem Resolved

Alan Gewirth

When I told one of my philosophical friends the title of this paper, he suggested that I make a slight addition, so that the title would read: "The 'Is–Ought' Problem Resolved—Again?" Indeed, I agree with his implied conviction that on certain interpretations of it the "Is–Ought" Problem has already been resolved several times; and I wish to emphasize that these resolutions and the polemical exchanges generated by them have done much to sharpen the issues. Nevertheless, I also maintain that the real "Is–Ought" Problem has not yet been resolved. I therefore want to do three main things in this paper. First, I shall present what I take to be the real "Is–Ought" Problem and shall indicate why it is the real one. Second, I shall review the main recent attempts to resolve the Problem and shall show that none of these has succeeded so far as the real "Is–Ought" Problem is concerned. Third, I shall give my resolution of this real Problem.

Alan Gewirth, "The 'Is/Ought' Problem Resolved." Presidential Address delivered before the 72nd Annual Western Meeting of The American Philosophical Association, St. Louis, 4/26/74. Appeared in *Proceedings and Addresses of the APA* 47 (1973–74): 34–61. Reprinted with the permission of The American Philosophical Association.

I

First, then, what is the real "Is–Ought" Problem? It will come as no surprise that the Problem is concerned with moral "oughts." After all, it was in the context of a discussion of the basis of "moral distinctions" that Hume wrote his famous passage about the need for explaining and justifying the transition from "is" to "ought" as copulas of propositions.[1] And in the introduction to a recent anthology devoted to the subject, the editor writes that the "Is–Ought" Problem is "the central problem in moral philosophy."[2]

Now the word "moral" is used in several different senses. While taking account of these differences, I shall focus on certain paradigm cases of what are undeniably moral "ought"-judgments which persons have sought to derive from "is"-statements. These judgments are of two main kinds. One kind sets forth negative moral duties to refrain from inflicting serious harm on other persons. Their paradigm uses have been of this form: "A intends to do X to B in order to gratify A's inclinations although he knows this will bring only great suffering to B; therefore, A ought not to do X to B." The other kind sets forth positive duties to perform certain actions for the benefit of other persons, especially where the latter would otherwise suffer serious harm. Their paradigm uses have been of this sort: "B is drowning and A by throwing him a rope can rescue him; therefore A ought to throw the rope to B"; or "B is starving while A has plenty of food; therefore A ought to give some food to B"; and so forth. In addition to such individual moral duties, persons have also sought to derive more specifically sociopolitical moral "oughts" from "is"-statements; for example, "That society is characterized by great inequalities of wealth and power; therefore it ought to be changed"; or "This state respects civil liberties; therefore we ought to that extent to support it"; and so forth.

The "oughts" presented in these judgments have five important formal and material characteristics, which will constitute five interrelated conditions or tests that must be satisfied by any solution of the real "Is–Ought" Problem. First, the "oughts" are moral ones in the sense that they take positive account of the interests of other persons as well as the agent or speaker, especially as regards the distribution of what is considered to be basic well-being. It is this well-being, indicated in the antecedent "is"-statements, that provides the reasons for the actions urged in the "ought"-judgments.

Second, these "oughts" are prescriptive in that their users advocate or seek to guide or influence actions, which they set forth as required by the facts presented in the antecedents. Although not all uses of "ought" are prescriptive, such advocacy marks the unconditional use of "ought" as in the above cases, where the antecedent empirical statements serve not to qualify or restrict the "oughts" but rather to indicate the facts or reasons which make them mandatory.

Third, the "oughts" are egalitarian in that they require that at least basic well-being be distributed equally as between the agent addressed and his potential recipients, or as among the members of a society. Although such egalitarianism is sometimes made part of the definition of "moral," and I shall myself sometimes use "moral" to include both this and the prescriptiveness just mentioned, it seems best to distinguish these considerations, since there may, after all, be non-egalitarian moralities.

A fourth important characteristic of these "oughts" is that they are determinate. By this I mean that the actions they prescribe have definite contents such that the opposite contents cannot be obtained by the same mode of derivation. Thus, in my above

[1]*Treatise of Human Nature,* III. i. 1 (ed. Selby-Bigge, pp. 469–470).
[2]W. D. Hudson, ed., *The Is–Ought Question* (London: Macmillan and Co., 1969), p. 11.

examples, the "oughts" require, respectively, rescuing, feeding, not harming; at the same time they are opposite-excluding in that one cannot, by the mode of derivation in question, obtain as conclusions "oughts" which permit or require not rescuing, not feeding, or harming.

A fifth characteristic of these "oughts," which to some extent encompasses some of the other characteristics, is that they are categorical, not merely hypothetical. By this characteristic, which applies more directly to the individual "ought"-judgments, I mean that the requirements set forth therein are normatively overriding and ineluctable or necessary, in that their bindingness cannot be removed by, and hence is not contingent on or determined by, variable, escapable features either of the persons addressed or of their social relations. These escapable, non-determining features include the self-interested desires of the persons addressed, their variable choices, opinions, and attitudes, and institutional rules whose obligatoriness may itself be doubtful or variable.

Now it is with "ought"-judgments having these five characteristics of being moral, prescriptive, egalitarian, determinate, and categorical that the real "Is–Ought" Problem is concerned. The Problem is this: how can "ought"-judgments having these five characteristics be logically derived from, or be justified on the basis of, premisses which state empirical facts? As this question suggests, a sixth condition which must be satisfied by any solution of the real "Is–Ought" Problem is that of non-circularity, especially in the respect that the premisses from which the "ought"-conclusions are derived must not themselves be moral or prescriptive. The resolution of the Problem calls not only for presenting a derivation which satisfies these six conditions but also for a theory which adequately explains why this derivation is successful and why previous attempts at derivation have been unsuccessful. There may indeed be problems about deriving from empirical statements "ought"-judgments which lack one or more of these five characteristics; but they are not the real "Is-Ought" Problem, not only because, having fewer conditions to satisfy, they are easier to resolve, but also because they necessarily fail to cope with the issue of justifying categorical moral "ought"-judgments, judgments which bear on the most basic requirements of how persons ought to live in relation to one another.

It is the decisive importance of this issue of justification that makes the real "Is–Ought" Problem at once so central and so difficult for moral philosophy. There is a familiar sequence of considerations at this point. The moral "ought"-judgments of the sort I mentioned above are not self-evident; hence if they are to be justified at all they must be derived in some way from other statements. These other, justifying statements must themselves be either moral or non-moral (where "moral" here includes also the characteristics of prescriptiveness and categoricalness). If the justifying statements are moral ones, then there recurs the question of how *they* are to be justified, since they too are not self-evident, and the question continues to recur as we mount through more general moral rules and principles. If, on the other hand, the statements from which the moral "ought"-judgments are to be derived are non-moral ones, such as the empirical statements that figured in my paradigm cases, then there is the difficulty that the "ought"-judgments are not derivable from those statements either inductively or deductively, unless we define "ought" in empirical terms; and such a definition raises many questions of adequacy, including how the "ought"-judgments can pass the tests of prescriptiveness and categoricalness. But it seems clear that if the moral "ought"-judgments cannot in any way be justified on the basis of empirical and logical considerations, i.e. by logical derivation from "is"-statements, then they cannot be definitively justified at all. Hence the crucial importance of the real "Is–Ought" Problem.

I shall use the expressions *external model* and *internal model* to distinguish the two chief positions on this issue. The external model holds that "ought" is external to "is" in that there is a basic logical gap between them: "ought" cannot be correctly defined in terms of empirical and logical considerations alone, nor can these considerations constitute determinate criteria of "ought" because any facts adduced as such criteria must ultimately reflect personal and hence variable decisions; consequently, "ought" cannot be logically derived from "is." The internal model upholds the opposite position. The external model asserts also that "ought"-judgments are not self-evident, so it concludes that they are not capable of any definitive justification at all; they reflect decisions or attitudes to which, at least at an ultimate level, questions of justification are inapplicable. Although logical gaps of some sort have also been held to underlie various other philosophical Problems—for example, in the Problem of Induction there is the logical gap between particular observation-statements and general laws, and in the Mind–Body Problem there is the logical gap between statements about bodily movements and statements about intentional human actions—the "is–ought" gap is declared by the external model to be much wider than any of these others, for while both sides of the other gaps fall within the "is," the "is-ought" gap involves a difference between "is" and something belonging to an entirely separate category.

The current status of the debate between the external and internal models is as follows. Some of the main arguments for the external model's categorial separation of "is" from "ought" have been refuted, but the refutations have not gone far enough to resolve the real "Is–Ought" Problem. I now want to show this briefly in two phases: first, by considering three of the most familiar arguments for the external model's logical gap, and second by reviewing seven recent attempts to derive "ought" from "is."

II

One argument for the gap is that there is a basic difference in function between empirical statements and moral "ought"-judgments, in that while the former only describe something, the latter, being prescriptive, take a stand for or against something by advocating or guiding action, so that they cannot be derived from what is non-prescriptive. To this it has been replied that empirical statements may also be used to guide or influence actions. This reply, however, makes the serious concession that such guidance occurs only when the person uttering or hearing the empirical statement has a want or desire to which the fact presented in the statement bears some means-end or other causal relation, as, for example, in the statement "There is a cobra curled up right behind you." This point hence does not satisfy the condition of categoricalness; for, as we saw above, categorical moral "oughts" present requirements for action which are normatively binding even when the person addressed has no such related self-interested want or desire.

A second familiar argument for the gap is that moral "ought"-judgments, unlike empirical statements, have no truth-value and hence cannot follow logically from statements having truth-value. In addition to the noncognitivist position that moral "oughts" express feelings or commands but not beliefs, an important basis of this argument goes back to the classical doctrine of modern philosophy and science according to which the "is," the world of fact, consists only in material particles moving according to physical laws, so that it contains no moral "oughts" and hence nothing to which categorical moral "ought"-judgments can correspond or by reference to which they can be proved or disproved. This classical doctrine superseded the teleological conceptions of ancient and medieval thinkers, which were repeated in other terms in the theories of Hegel. Marx, and Spencer that human history or the whole evolutionary process progressively fulfills moral criteria.

Recent replies to the truth-value gap argument have renewed this teleological emphasis on a more restricted scale by pointing out that there are institutional facts, means-end relations, and eudaemonist conditions which serve to provide correspondence-correlates for "ought"-judgments. Other replies have contended, first, that sentences need not have truth-values in order to figure in logical relations; second, that the truth-value argument takes a too narrow view of truth since, for example, negative and hypothetical statements are admittedly capable of being true or false without there being facts in the world to which they correspond; and third, that moral "ought"-judgments have many characteristics regularly taken as conditions of being propositions having truth-value—for example, they are expressed in the indicative mood, they are asserted, denied, believed, disbelieved, questioned, and argued for and against; and such arguments often appeal to empirical facts which are held to provide reasons for believing or disbelieving the judgments.[3]

These replies to the truth-value argument, while sound, do not go far enough to satisfy the conditions of the real "Is–Ought" Problem. Insofar as the replies construe categorical moral "ought"-judgments as having truth-value by virtue of correspondence, they have not shown to what the judgments must correspond in order to be true. Both institutional facts and means-end relations fail in this respect, for, as I shall indicate more fully below, they do not satisfy the conditions of categoricalness and determinacy. And if instead of a correspondence requirement for the truth of statements we adopt an epistemological requirement, such as that there must at least in principle be ways of confirming or disconfirming the statements, then it has not yet been shown how categorical moral "ought"-judgments, or at least the most basic ones, are to be confirmed or disconfirmed. Hence, there is as yet no definitive warrant for holding that they are susceptible of truth or falsity.

A third familiar argument for the external model declares that "ought" cannot be logically derived from "is" because whatever is in the conclusion must be in the premisses and there is no "ought" in the premisses. This argument is easily refutable by a consideration of non-syllogistic modes of inference. But, as I shall go on to show, this refutation does little to resolve the real "Is–Ought" Problem, for the derivations it authorizes do not satisfy the condition of determinacy.

I shall now briefly review seven recent attempts to derive "ought" from "is." The derivations fall into two groups, formal and material, in that the first four, unlike the last three, do not depend on the specific contents assigned to the "oughts."

The four formal derivations clearly fail the test of determinacy, and hence are of little or no help in resolving the real "Is–Ought" Problem. First, the *truth-functional* derivation applies such rules as that a false proposition materially implies any proposition, and any proposition materially implies the disjunction of itself with any other proposition. Thus, the false proposition "There is no one in this room" materially implies both "We ought to rescue drowning persons" and "We ought not to rescue drowning persons."

[3]For an important recent statement of a teleological approach to moral judgments which utilizes ontological doctrines of Aristotle and Aquinas, see Henry B. Veatch, *For an Ontology of Morals* (Evanston, Ill.: Northwestern University Press, 1971). Other recent arguments for the truth-value of moral judgments can be found in A. C. Ewing, *Second Thoughts in Moral Philosophy* (London: Routledge and Kegan Paul, 1959), ch. 2; Robert J. Fogelin, *Evidence and Meaning* (London: Routledge and Kegan Paul, 1967), p. 135; Jonathan Harrison, *Our Knowledge of Right and Wrong* (London: George Allen and Unwin, 1971), pp. 251 ff.; Alan B. White, *Truth* (London: Macmillan Press, 1970), pp. 57–65; Kurt Baier, *The Moral Point of View* (Ithaca, N.Y.: Cornell University Press, 1958), pp. 173–186; Kai Nielsen, "On Moral Truth," *American Philosophical Quarterly*, Monograph Series No. 1 (1968), pp. 9–25.

Second, the *immediate inference by added determinant* derives an "ought"-conclusion from a subject–predicate "is"-statement by adding some deontic qualification to both the subject and the predicate.[4] Thus on the one hand we have: "Jones is a millionaire; therefore, if all millionaires ought to help the weak, Jones ought to help the weak." But by the same mode of derivation we also have: "Jones is a millionaire; therefore, if all millionaires ought to refrain from helping the weak, Jones ought to refrain from helping the weak."

Third, there is the *"ought"–"can"* derivation, which, assuming the familiar principle that "ought" implies "can," argues by contraposition that if some person cannot perform some action, then it is not the case that he ought to perform it.[5] Since this mode of derivation puts no restrictions on the "ought"-judgments with which one begins other than the ability of the agent, it also fails the test of determinacy.

Fourth, there is the *ideal procedural* derivation, which begins from facts or purported facts about mental procedures having certain ideal intellectual or emotional characteristics, and then argues that moral "oughts" are derived either from the procedures themselves or from the results of applying them. The mental procedures in question are characterized as emerging from an "ideal observer" or some similar source, and the characteristics embodied in these procedures include being fully informed, free, imaginative, calm, willing to universalize, reflecting as fully as possible upon all the relevant facts, and so forth.[6]

Now all these modes of derivation suffer from indeterminacy. For there is no assurance that two persons, reflecting as fully as possible upon all the same facts or otherwise using these mental procedures, will arrive at the same moral "ought"-judgments. And if, to ward off this indeterminacy, we include among the ideal procedural traits such egalitarian moral features as impartiality and sympathy, then the condition of noncircularity is violated.

I turn now to the material "is–ought" derivations. Each of these rests on a version of the internal model whereby "ought" is internal to "is," in that either "ought" is defined in terms of empirical and logical properties or such properties constitute purportedly determinate criteria of "ought." More specifically, "ought" here means: necessitated or required by reasons stemming from some structured context. A context is structured when it is constituted by laws or rules which determine certain existential or practical necessities. The context in question need not be a practical or even a human one; it may, for example, be the context of physical nature. Thus in such an inference as, "It is lightning, therefore it ought to thunder," the "ought" means that, given the occurrence of lightning, it is required or necessary that thunder also occur, this necessity stemming from the law-governed context of physical nature. The descriptive causal laws of this context furnish directly or indirectly the major premisses for this derivation of "ought" from "is."[7]

[4]For the first two derivations, see A. N. Prior, "The Autonomy of Ethics," *Australasian Journal of Philosophy*, vol. 18 (1960), pp. 199 ff.; George I. Mavrodes, "On Deriving the Normative from the Non-Normative," *Papers of the Michigan Academy of Science, Arts, and Letters*, vol. 53 (1968), pp. 353 ff.

[5]See David Rynin, "The Autonomy of Morals," *Mind*, vol. 66 (1957), p. 313; George I. Mavrodes, " 'Is' and 'Ought' " *Analysis*, vol. 28 (1964), pp. 42 ff.; K. E. Tranoy, " 'Ought' Implies 'Can': A Bridge from Fact to Norm," *Ratio*, vol. 14 (1972).

[6]See Roderick Firth, "Ethical Absolutism and the Ideal Observer," *Philosophy and Phenomenological Research*, vol. 12 (1951), pp. 317 ff.; Richard B. Brandt, *Ethical Theory* (Englewood Cliffs, N.J.: Prentice-Hall, 1959), ch. 10; Paul W. Taylor, *Normative Discourse* (Englewood Cliffs, N.J.: Prentice-Hall, 1961), ch. 6.

[7]For similar views of the "univocity" of "ought" in theoretical and practical contexts, see especially Roger Wertheimer, *The Significance of Sense* (Ithaca, N.Y.: Cornell University Press, 1972), ch. 3. See also Joseph Margolis, *Values and Conduct* (Oxford: Clarendon Press, 1971), ch. 3; Glen O. Allen. "The Is–Ought Question Reformulated and Answered." *Ethics*, vol. 82 (1972), pp. 184 ff.

In the practical sphere, similarly, there are various structured contexts which contain requirements for action. These requirements, however, consist not in existential necessities expressible in descriptive predictions of what must occur regardless of human action; they consist rather in directive rules as to what actions must be performed if certain values or purposes are to be achieved, the fulfillment of the rules being contingent on human decision. The contexts constituted by these rules, nevertheless, are factual ones in that they consist in ordered relations whose existence can be ascertained empirically. Three such contexts have figured especially prominently in recent "is–ought" derivations: the contexts of means-end connections, of institutional rules, and of eudaemonist conditions, i.e. the conditions of human well-being. In each of these contexts, a statement of the form "A ought to do X" means that there is a requirement that A do X stemming from the structure of that context, i.e. from what must be done by A if one of his ends is to be fulfilled or if he is to participate in some institution with its rules or if he is to promote his or others' well-being. And in each case the derivation of "ought" from "is" goes through because the general structure of the respective contexts is presupposed as supplying the relevant major premisses.

From this brief characterization we can see three sharp limitations of these material "is–ought" derivations, which prevent them from resolving the real "Is–Ought" Problem. First, the derived "oughts" are only hypothetical, not categorical. For the derivations are of the form: *If* the respective practical contexts with their requirements are accepted, *then* such and such actions ought to be done. Hence, the requirements represented by the derived "oughts" are only intra-contextual; their obligatoriness is contingent on persons' variable choices or decisions to accept the context in question, or on some independent justification of the context itself as setting forth valid requirements for action. Second, by the same token, "ought" as it figures in the internal model as so far explicated is not necessarily prescriptive. For to say that "ought" means what is required by some structured context is not to say that the speaker who uses such an "ought" necessarily accepts this requirement as binding either on himself or on his hearers; for he may not accept or commit himself to the context. Third, there arises, as a consequence, what I shall call the *dilemma of commitment.* The person who is deriving "ought" from "is" within one of these practical contexts either does or does not choose to accept or commit himself to the context with its requirements. If he does choose to commit himself, then the "ought" he will derive will indeed be prescriptive, i.e. it will carry his endorsement or advocacy; but the derivation will be circular in that he will simply be resuming in the conclusion a commitment or advocacy which he had already chosen to make in the premiss. The derivation will hence be not from "is" to "ought" but rather from prescriptive "ought" to prescriptive "ought." If, on the other hand, the person making the derivation does not choose to commit himself to the context with its requirements, then his derivation will not be circular; but then the "ought" he derives will not be prescriptive, for it will not carry his advocacy or endorsement of the requirement he derives from the context. None of the three main recent material "is–ought" derivations is able to resolve this dilemma, so I shall not refer to it again in discussing them; nor shall I repeat the other limitations just mentioned.

I wish, however, briefly to look further at each of these derivations in order to note some other difficulties, especially in connection with determinacy. The fifth derivation, that of *means-end,* proceeds from the two "is"-premisses that a person wants to achieve some end or purpose and that his performing a certain action is the only means to his achieving this end; from these it infers the conclusion that the person ought to perform the action.[8] This derivation, as indicated above, goes through because there is assumed from the context some such major premiss as, "One ought to do that which is the necessary and sufficient means to achieving one's end." But the derivation does not satisfy the condition of categoricalness, not only for the general reason already given but also because it makes the requiredness of the specific "ought" to be contingent on the variable wants or desires of the person addressed, so that he can evade its requirement by shifting his wants or ends. Also, the derivation does not satisfy the condition of determinacy, for by this mode of argument one could infer either that one ought or that one ought not to feed starving persons or rescue drowning persons, depending upon one's own selfish wants in the matter.

The sixth mode of derivation, which I shall call the *institutional,* begins from "is"-statements describing institutional facts about ways in which persons participate in institutions having certain requirements or rules, and it concludes with "ought"-judgments that the persons in question have certain obligations by virtue of this participation. The most famous examples of this institutional derivation in the recent literature have been concerned with the institutions of promising and of buying and selling. The argument has been that if one participates in these institutions by making a promise or a purchase, then, by virtue of the rules of the respective institutions, one is obligated to keep the promise or to pay for what one buys, and so forth.[9] Again, certain relevant major premisses are assumed from the context.

This derivation also fails the test of determinacy. One could, by the same mode of derivation, infer diametrically opposed "oughts." For example, if one participates in the institution of constitutional democracy then one ought to support civil liberties, but if one participates in the institution of dictatorship then one ought to oppose such liberties, and if one participates in the institution of slavery then one ought to regard some humans as other humans' property, and so forth.[10] If, to ward off this indeterminacy, one stipulates that only those arrangements are to be considered institutions which are voluntarily accepted or agreed upon by all their participants, then this would not only restrict unduly the concept of an institution, but it would also violate the condition of non-circularity. For now the derivation would not begin from a morally neutral "is"-statement, since the initial presumption would be that the institution in question fulfills the moral requirement of not being coercively imposed on its participants. Similarly, if we try further to avoid the indeterminacy of the institutional derivation by beginning from the institution of morality itself, or from "the moral point of view," and building into it such egalitarian moral requirements as that the good of everyone alike is to be promoted or that the ends of all persons are to be harmonized so far as possible, this would again violate the condition of non-circularity, since its starting-point would not be morally neutral.

The seventh and last mode of derivation to be considered I shall call the *eudaemonist,* from the Greek word for well-being. This assumes that the meaning or criterion of the moral "ought" is to be found in the context of human well-being, so that "A morally ought to do X" means that doing X is required for the attainment of human

[8]See Max Black, "The Gap between 'Is' and 'Should,'" *Philosophical Review,* vol. 73 (1964), pp. 165 ff.: also G. H. von Wright, "Practical Inference." *ibid.*, vol. 72 (1963), pp. 159 ff.

[9]See John Searle, "How to Derive 'Ought' from 'Is,'" *Philosophical Review,* vol. 73 (1964), pp. 43 ff.; Searle, *Speech Acts* (Cambridge: University Press, 1969), pp. 132–136 and ch. 8; G. E. M. Anscombe, "On Brute Facts," *Analysis,* vol. 18 (1958), pp. 69 ff.

[10]See my "Obligation: Political, Legal, Moral," *Nomos,* vol. XII (1970), pp. 55 ff.

well-being or for the avoidance of ill-being. With this definition, one can argue deductively from the factual premiss that certain actions are necessary for human well-being to the conclusion that those actions morally ought to be performed.[11]

This mode of derivation is, however, circular because its premisses about what constitutes human well-being or harm, far from being straightforwardly factual or descriptive, represent moral commitments about what is worth striving for or what interests of persons other than the agent are worth promoting. Consider, for example, the moral disagreements between religionists and secularists, between pacifists and militarists, between romantics and practical-minded persons, and so forth; and in addition there is the dispute between teleologists and deontologists over whether moral "oughts" are tied to any considerations of well-being at all. Because of such disputes, the eudaemonist derivation does not yield determinate "oughts." Nor are the "oughts" categorical, since their content depends on persons' variable opinions about what constitutes well-being and morality. Moreover, the eudaemonist derivation fails to cope with the crucial moral problem of distribution, of *whose* well-being ought to be promoted and whose harm avoided.[12]

I conclude, then, that while these recent "is–ought" derivations have made valuable contributions, none has succeeded in resolving the real "Is–Ought" Problem.

III

In this final section I want to show how "ought"-judgments which are categorical, determinate, prescriptive, egalitarian, and moral can be logically and non-circularly derived from "is"-statements which describe empirical facts about the world. I shall do this by presenting a certain version of what I have called the internal model. But my version differs in important respects from those considered above. The main bases of these differences comprise two interrelated points, one about the context, the other about method.

The factual context within which my argument will proceed is that of the generic features of action. This context is both logically prior to and more invariable and inescapable than the other contexts appealed to in the attempted material "is–ought" derivations considered above. In those derivations, as we have seen, there were two sorts of variabilities, each of which made the "ought"-conclusions hypothetical rather than categorical. The arguments went as follows: Given a certain structured context, certain actions are necessary or required by that context. The necessities here were hence hypothetical in that, while one had first to accept the respective contexts as normatively binding, as justifiably setting forth requirements for action, this acceptance was not itself necessary, but was rather a matter of one's choice. I shall call this the acceptance-variability of the respective contexts. In addition, the specific contents of each context could vary; that is, even if one accepted the context in general, one might adopt different ends, participate in different institutions, have different conceptions of well-being, and these diversities generated quite different and even opposed "ought"-conclusions. I shall call this the content-variability of the respective contexts. So there was a double

[11]See Philippa Foot, "Moral Arguments," *Mind*, vol. 67 (1958), pp. 502 ff.; "Moral Beliefs," *Proceedings of the Aristotelian Society*, vol. 59 (1958–59), pp. 83 ff.

[12]For some of these objections, see D. Z. Phillips, "On Morality's Having a Point," in Hudson, *op. cit.*, pp. 228 ff. These difficulties, as well as the dilemma of commitment presented above, are not taken account by Peter Singer, "The Triviality of the Debate over "Is–Ought" and the Definition of 'Moral,'" *American Philosophical Quarterly*, vol. 10 (1973), pp. 51 ff.

hypotheticalness in these arguments, and this accounted for their failure to satisfy the conditions of categoricalness and determinacy.

In the context of the generic features of action, on the other hand, neither of these variabilities is found. There is no acceptance-variability, for it is not open to any person intentionally to evade or reject the context of action. To be sure, one might try to carry out such rejection by intentionally committing suicide, ingesting sleep-inducing drugs, selling oneself into slavery, and so forth. But not only would this intentional removal of oneself from the context of action obviously carry a crushing price, but moreover the very acts of taking these evading steps would themselves be actions, and hence the necessary conditions of actions, their generic features, would be fulfilled in the very process of removing oneself from further involvement in the context of action. Similarly, if one views actions in terms of their generic features there is no content-variability in the context of actions; for although actions may, of course, be of many different sorts, they all have certain generic features in common, features which are necessarily exhibited by any instance of action, and these necessary features logically generate certain requirements or "oughts" regardless of the specific differences of kinds of action. Because of this lack of acceptance-variability and content-variability, the "oughts" derived from the context of the generic features of action have a necessity which enables them to satisfy the conditions of categoricalness and determinacy. I shall, in fact, try to show that the relation of the theory of action to moral philosophy is much closer and more substantive than has hitherto been thought.

It is to be noted that I am here using the word "action" in a quite strict sense. In this sense, human movements or behaviors are not actions if they occur from one or more of the following kinds of cause: (a) direct compulsion by someone or something external to the person; (b) causes internal to the person, such as reflexes, ignorance, or disease, which decisively contribute, in ways beyond his control, to the occurrence of the behavior; (c) indirect compulsion whereby the person's choice to emit some behavior is forced by someone else's coercion. In contrast to such behaviors, actions in the strict sense have the generic features of being voluntary and purposive. By "voluntary" I mean that the agent occurrently or dispositionally controls his behavior by his unforced choice, knowing the various proximate circumstances of his action. By "purposive" I mean that the agent intends to do what he does, envisaging some purpose or goal which may consist either in the performance of the action itself or in some outcome of that performance; in either case, insofar as it is the purpose of his action the agent regards it as some sort of good. These generic features also mean that actions are characterized by freedom and relative well-being on the part of the agent: by freedom in virtue of their uncoerced character and the agent's control over them; by well-being in the relative sense that the agent's purpose is to do or obtain something he regards as good, although not necessarily good in terms either of morality or even of his own self-interest.

The direct relevance of action in the strict sense to the "Is–Ought" Problem can be seen from the fact that "ought"-judgments are primarily concerned with action in this sense. When it is said, not only in moral or political precepts but also in prudential, technical, institutional, and other practical precepts, that some person ought to do something, the assumption of the speaker, at least prospectively, is that the person addressed is an actual or potential agent who can control his behavior with a view to achieving the objective set forth in the precept, and that the agent will set some sort of preferred priority either on this objective or on the ones for which he would otherwise act. As this last point indicates, actions in the strict sense include behaviors whereby agents may violate as well as fulfill moral, political, and other practical precepts, and they also include behaviors which are indifferent in relation to such precepts.

In addition to this consideration, the direct rational justification for focusing on the generic features of action is that, being invariable, they impose themselves on every agent, as against the particular contents of his actions which vary with his different and possibly arbitrary inclinations, and also that, being necessary to all action, they take priority for the agent over the particular purposes for which he may contingently act.

Before proceeding to the derivation, I must say something about the method I shall follow. Philosophers have, of course, dealt with and disagreed over the nature of their operations and results; in this regard they have used such phrases as "rational reconstruction," "conceptual analysis," "criteriological connection," "phenomenological description," "inductive generalization," and so forth. I cannot, of course, deal with this issue here. But in order to facilitate understanding of what I shall try to do, I should point out that I shall use what I call a dialectically necessary method. My method is dialectical in a sense closely related to that referred to in the Socratic dialogues and in Aristotle: that is, it begins from assumptions, statements, or claims made by protagonists—in this case, the agent—and it examines what these logically imply. The method is dialectically necessary, however, in that the assumptions or claims in question are necessarily made by agents; they reflect not some protagonist's variable opinions, interests, or ideals but rather the necessary structure of purposive action as viewed by the agent. One aspect of this necessity has already been suggested in my statements about the invariability of the context of the generic features of action. On the basis of these necessary contents, I shall show that every agent is logically committed to making or at least accepting certain determinate, categorical moral "ought"-judgments. Although I shall characterize the steps leading to this logical commitment as entailments, my argument will not be materially affected if the connections in question are interpreted in some less stringent way, so long as their necessary connection with the context of the generic features of action is kept in view.

It will constitute no objection to my use of this method that agents do not necessarily perform speech acts or make linguistic utterances. For on the basis of their actions certain thought-contents can be attributed to them in either direct or indirect discourse. If we see someone running very hard in order to catch a bus, we can safely infer, without stopping him and asking him, that he thinks it is worth his effort to try to catch that bus, just as if we see someone reading a book with avid interest we don't have to see whether he is moving his lips in order to attribute to him such a judgment as, "It is worth my attention reading this book," according to whatever criterion of worth is involved in his purpose of reading. Moreover, although there is in general a difference between entailment-relations among propositions and relations of belief of those propositions—if p entails q, this does not entail that someone's believing that p entails his believing that q—nevertheless I shall here attribute to the agent belief in or acceptance of certain propositions on the basis of their being entailed by other propositions he accepts. The justification for this is that the entailments in question are so direct that awareness of them can safely be attributed to any person who is sufficiently rational to be able to control his behavior by his unforced choice with a view to achieving his purposes.

Enough of preliminaries. I shall now undertake to show how "ought"-judgments having the five required characteristics are logically derivable from "is"-statements which describe the occurrence of actions in the strict sense defined above. Although the argument will involve various complexities, some of which I have treated in detail elsewhere, I can indicate enough of the main lines in what follows.

To begin with, that purposive actions occur or that some person performs an action is an empirical fact which can be stated in descriptive, empirical propositions regardless of whether the statements are made by the agent himself or by other persons.

As made by the agent himself, the statement may be put formally as, "I do X for purpose E." Although there has been an abortive attempt to argue that assertions of the performance or occurrence of actions are ascriptive rather than descriptive in that they make moral or legal judgments about the agent's responsibility, this attempt has, by general agreement, been definitively refuted.[13] And although some utterances of this form are performatory in Austin's sense, most are not. In a somewhat different direction we can also disregard here Cartesian doubts about the possibility of empirically ascertaining that the choices and purposes involved in action are in fact occurrently or dispositionally present. This disregard is especially warranted because, in accordance with my dialectical method, I shall be considering actions as they are viewed and referred to by the agent himself.

From this empirical premiss, the agent's statement that he performs an action, the derivation will now proceed in four main steps. The first step involves the point that action as viewed by the agent has, in virtue of its purposiveness, a certain evaluative element. To see this, we must note that action is not a mere physical occurrence in which the entities concerned make no choices and guide themselves for the sake of no purposes. Nor is the agent's attitude toward his action merely a passive or contemplative one; the action is not something that happens to him from causes beyond his control. On the contrary, the agent's relation to the action he brings about is conative and evaluative, for he acts for some purpose which seems to him to be good. In acting, the agent envisages more or less clearly some preferred outcome, some objective or goal which he wants to achieve, where such wanting may be either intentional or inclinational. This goal is regarded by the agent as worth aiming at or pursuing; for if he did not so regard it he would not unforcedly choose to move from quiescence or non-action to action with a view to achieving the goal. This conception of worth constitutes a valuing on the part of the agent; he regards the object of his action as having at least sufficient value to merit his acting to attain it, according to whatever criteria are involved in his action. These criteria of value need not be moral nor even hedonic; they run the full range of the purposes for which the agent acts. Now "value" in this broad sense is synonymous with "good" in a similarly broad sense encompassing a wide range of nonmoral as well as moral criteria. Hence, since the agent values, at least instrumentally, the purposes or objects for which he acts, it can also be said that he regards these objects as at least instrumentally good according to whatever criteria lead him to try to achieve his purpose. He may, of course, also regard his purpose as bad on other criteria, and he may regret the narrow range of alternatives open to him among which he chooses. Still, so long as his choice is not forced, by the very fact that he chooses to act he shows that he regards his action as worth performing and hence as good at least relatively to his not acting at all or to his acting for other purposes which are open to him. The presence of choice and purpose in action thus gives it a structure such that, from the standpoint of the agent, "I do X for purpose E" entails "X and E are good." Since the latter statement is a value-judgment, or at least the function of such a judgment, to this extent from the standpoint of the agent the "fact-value" gap, even if not the "is–ought" gap, is already bridged in action.

The agent's positive evaluative judgment extends not only to his particular action and purpose but also to the generic features which characterize all his actions. Since his action is a means to attaining something he regards as good, even if this is only the performance of the action itself, he regards as good the voluntariness or freedom which is

[13]See H. L. A. Hart, "The Ascription of Rights and Responsibilities," *Proceedings of the Aristotelian Society*, vol. 49 (1948–49); P. T. Geach, "Ascriptivism," *Philosophical Review*, vol. 69 (1960), pp. 221 ff.; Hart, *Punishment and Responsibility* (Oxford: Clarendon Press, 1968), Preface.

an essential feature of his action, for without this he would not be able to act for any purpose at all. He also regards as good those basic aspects of his well-being which are the necessary conditions both of the existence and of the success of all his actions, and which hence are not relative to his particular purposes and not subject to the disagreements that we saw earlier attach to different interpretations of well-being as a whole. This basic well-being comprises certain physical and psychological dispositions ranging from life and physical integrity to a feeling of confidence as to the general possibility of attaining one's goals.

In connection with this point, it should be noted that whereas the eudaemonist derivation considered above, like other naturalistic doctrines, left itself open to the objection that what it regards as well-being is not really good or is not considered good by some persons, my present argument does not incur this objection. For, being dialectical, the argument proceeds from within the standpoint of the agent himself and his own purposes and conceptions of well-being, whatever they may be. But as against the means-end derivation considered above, my argument, being dialectically *necessary,* does not depend for its direct content upon the contingent and variable purposes which different persons may have and the means required for these; it depends rather upon the necessary means which are required for any purposive actions, and which any agent must therefore regard as good. Thus, because freedom and basic well-being are at least instrumentally necessary to all the agent's actions for purposes, from the agent's standpoint his statement, "I do X for purpose E" entails not only "X and E are good" but also "My freedom and basic well-being are good as the necessary conditions of all my actions."

From this first main step there follows a second, bearing on justifications and right-claims. In virtue of his positive evaluations the agent regards himself as justified in performing his actions and in having the freedom and basic well-being which generically figure in all his actions, and he implicitly makes a corresponding right-claim. To regard something as justified on some criterion is to hold that its rightness is or can be established according to that criterion, and to have toward it a corresponding attitude of endorsement. Now an important, even if not the only, basis of an action's being right from the standpoint of its agent is that he regards it as having a good purpose. The agent therefore regards his action as justified by this goodness. But, *a fortiori,* he especially regards himself as justified in having freedom and basic well-being, since these are the necessary conditions of all his actions and hence of any purposes or goals he may attain or pursue through action.

This justificatory attitude takes the logical form of a claim on the part of the agent that he has a right to perform his actions and to have freedom and basic well-being. Even if there is not in every case a correct inference from an agent's regarding X as good to his claiming a right to X, the inference does hold from within the agent's standpoint insofar as X consists in freedom and basic well-being, because of the strategic relation of these goods to all his purposive actions. In the case of every claim to have a right to X, a necessary condition is that X seem directly or indirectly good to the claimant, and a sufficient condition is that he regard X as a basic good such as is required for his pursuit of any other goods. For it is central to the concept of a right, at least where it is advanced as a claim by individuals, that its primary, even if not its only, application is to the proximate prerequisites of any purposive actions, since without the direct capacity for such action the claimant, beyond making the claim itself, would not be able to move toward anything he regards as good. It is this elemental aspect of right-claims that seems to me to underlie Jefferson's asserting as self-evident that all men have inalienable rights to life, liberty, and the pursuit of happiness. Put in the dialectically necessary terms I am using here, this says that since every agent regards as basic goods the freedom and basic well-being which are the proximate necessary conditions of his acting for the achievement of any of his purposes, and since the criterion of claiming justifications and rights, so far as the agent is concerned, consists in the first instance in such proximate necessary conditions, it follows that any agent must claim, at least implicitly, that he has a right to freedom and basic well-being. And this right-claim is prescriptive: it carries the agent's advocacy or endorsement.

According to this second main step, then, action as viewed by the agent has a normative as well as an evaluative structure, in that it involves right-claims as well as judgments of good. From the agent's standpoint, his judgment "My freedom and basic well-being are good as the necessary conditions of all my actions" entails "I have a right to freedom and basic well-being."[14] This second step is, of course, crucial for the "is–ought" derivation, since the normative concept of having a right either already is, or is directly translatable into, a deontic concept. Nevertheless, in order to show how all five conditions of the real "Is–Ought" Problem are to be satisfied, I must go through two further steps.

The third main step involves the consideration that, given the agent's claim that he has a right to freedom and basic well-being, he is logically committed to a generalization of this right-claim to all prospective agents and hence to all persons. To see this, we must note that every right-claim is made on behalf of some person or group with an at least implicit recognition of the description or sufficient reason which is held to ground the right. This description or sufficient reason may be quite general or quite particular, but in any case the person who claims some right must admit, on pain of contradiction, that this right also belongs to any other persons to whom that description or reason applies. This necessity is an exemplification of the logical principle of universalizability: if some predicate P belongs to some subject S because S has the property Q (where the "because" is that of sufficient reason or condition), then P must also belong to all other subjects $S_1, S_2, \ldots, S_n$ which have Q. If one denies this implication in the case of some individual, such as S_1, which has Q, then one contradicts oneself, for in saying that P belongs to S because S has Q one implies that all Q is P, but in denying this in the case of S_1, which has Q, one says that some Q is not P.

The crucial question in the present context concerns the description or sufficient reason which the agent adduces as decisively relevant in claiming that he has a right to freedom and basic well-being. Many philosophers have held that there is no logical limit in this respect, that any agent can choose whatever description or sufficient reason he likes without committing any logical error. He may claim that he has the rights in question because and only because, for example, he is white or male or American or a philosopher or an atheist, or for that matter because he is named Wordsworth Donisthorpe or because he was born on such and such a date at such and such a place, and so forth. And, of course, depending on the property he adduces as a sufficient reason for his right-claim, he will be logically required to grant only that these rights belong to all other persons who have this property, including, at the extreme, the class consisting only of one member, himself.

In opposition to this view, I hold that the agent logically must adduce only a certain description or sufficient reason as the ground of his claim that he has a right to freedom and basic well-being. This description or sufficient reason is that he is a prospective agent who has purposes he wants to fulfill. If the agent adduces anything

[14]For more detailed arguments for the above two steps, see my "The Normative Structure of Action." *Review of Metaphysics*, vol. 25 (1971), pp. 238 ff.

less general than this as his exclusive justifying description, then, by the preceding argument, he can be shown to contradict himself. Let us designate by the letter *R* such a more restrictive description. Examples of *R* would include, "My name is Wordsworth Donisthorpe" and the other descriptions just mentioned. Now let us ask the agent whether, while being an agent, he would still claim to have the rights of freedom and basic well-being even if he were not *R*. If he answers yes, then he contradicts his assertion that he has these rights only insofar as he is *R*. He would hence have to admit that he is mistaken in restricting his justificatory description to *R*. But if he answers no, i.e. if he says that while being an agent he would not claim these rights if he were not *R*, then he can be shown to contradict himself with regard to the generic features of action. For, as we have seen, it is necessarily true of every agent both that he requires freedom and basic well-being in order to act and that he hence implicitly claims the right to have freedom and basic well-being. For an agent not to claim these rights would mean that he does not act for purposes he regards as good at all and that he does not regard his actions, with their necessary conditions of freedom and basic well-being, as justified by the goodness of his purpose. But this in turn would mean that he is not an agent, which contradicts the initial assumption. Thus, to avoid contradicting himself, the agent must admit that he would claim to have the rights of freedom and basic well-being even if he were not *R*, and hence that the description or sufficient reason for which he claims these rights is not anything less general than that he is a prospective agent who has purposes he wants to fulfill.[15]

It is also this generality that explains why, in the necessary description or sufficient reason of his having these rights, I have referred to a "prospective agent who has purposes he wants to fulfill." For the agent claims these rights not only in his present action with its particular purpose but in all his actions. To restrict to his present purpose his reason for claiming the rights of freedom and basic well-being would be to overlook the fact that he regards these as goods in respect of all his actions and purposes, not only his present one.

Since, then, the agent, in order to avoid contradicting himself, must claim that he has the rights of freedom and basic well-being for the sufficient reason that he is a prospective agent who has purposes he wants to fulfill, he logically must accept the generalization that all prospective agents who have purposes they want to fulfill, and hence all persons, have the rights of freedom and basic well-being. This generalization is a direct application of the principle of universalizability; and if the agent denies the generalization, then, as we have seen, he contradicts himself. For on the one hand in holding, as he logically must, that he has the rights of freedom and basic well-being because he is a prospective purposive agent, he implies that all prospective purposive agents have these rights; but on the other hand he holds that some prospective purposive agent does not have these rights.

I shall henceforth refer to the agent who avoids such contradictions, and who hence accepts the opposed logically necessary statements, as a "rational agent." It will be noted that this is the minimal and most basic sense of "rational" as applied to persons and that its criterion is a purely logical one, involving consistency or the avoidance of self-contradiction. Thus we have seen that, by virtue of accepting the statement "I have a right to freedom and basic well-being," the rational agent must also accept "I have these rights for the sufficient reason that I am a prospective purposive agent," and hence

[15] I have presented this and related arguments more fully in "The Justification of Egalitarian Justice," *American Philosophical Quarterly*, vol. 8 (1971), pp. 331 ff., and in *Moral Rationality*, The Lindley Lecture for 1972 (University of Kansas, 1972).

that "All prospective purposive agents have a right to freedom and basic well-being." The rational agent must therefore advocate or endorse these rights for all other persons on the same ground as he advocates them for himself.

The fourth and final main step moves directly from this generalized right-claim to a correlative "ought"-judgment. For all rights are logically correlative with at least negative duties or "oughts," in that for any person A to have a right to have or do something X entails that all other persons ought to refrain from interfering either with A's having or doing X or at least with A's trying to have or do X. Hence, since the agent logically had to admit that "All prospective purposive agents have a right to freedom and basic well-being," he must also logically accept the "ought"-judgment, "I ought to refrain from interfering with the freedom and basic well-being of all prospective purposive agents," and hence of all persons. Interference with their freedom would constitute coercion; interference with their basic well-being would constitute basic harm. Thus we have seen that from the initial empirical premise, "I do X for purpose E," there logically follows the "ought"-judgment, "I ought to refrain from coercing other persons or inflicting basic harm on them." The agent is logically compelled to admit these "oughts," on pain of contradiction.

The general principle of these "oughts" or duties may be expressed as the following precept addressed to every agent: *Apply to your recipient the same generic features of action that you apply to yourself.* I shall call this the *Principle of Generic Consistency (PGC),* since it combines the formal consideration of consistency, as found in the above universalization argument, with the material consideration of the generic features of action, including the right-claims which the agent necessarily makes. The *PGC* is an egalitarian universalist moral principle since it requires an equal distribution of the most basic rights of action. It says to every agent that just as, in acting, he necessarily applies to himself and claims as rights for himself the generic features of action, voluntariness or freedom and purposiveness at least in the sense of basic well-being, so he ought to apply these same generic features to all the recipients of his actions by allowing them also to have freedom and basic well-being and hence by refraining from coercing them or inflicting basic harm on them. This means that the agent ought to be impartial as between himself and other persons when the latter's freedom and basic well-being are at stake, so that he ought to respect other persons' freedom and basic well-being as well as his own. And as we have seen, if the agent denies or violates this principle, then he contradicts himself.

The *PGC* has as direct or indirect logical consequences egalitarian moral "ought"-judgments of the paradigmatic sort that I presented at the outset. Given the *PGC,* there directly follows the negative duty not to inflict serious gratuitous harm on other persons. There also directly follows the positive duty to perform such actions as rescuing drowning persons or feeding starving persons, especially when this can be done at relatively little cost to oneself. For the *PGC* prohibits inflicting basic harms on other persons; but to refrain from performing such actions as rescuing and feeding in the circumstances described would be to inflict basic harms on the persons in need and would hence violate the impartiality required by the *PGC.* It would mean that while the agent participates in the situation voluntarily and with basic well-being, not to mention his other purposes, he prevents his recipients from doing so. Although there is indeed a distinction between causing a basic harm to occur and merely permitting it to occur by one's inaction, such intentional inaction in the described circumstances is itself an action that interferes with the basic well-being of the persons in need. For it prevents, by means under the agent's control and with his knowledge, the occurrence of transactions which would remove the basic harms in question.

The *PGC* also has as its indirect consequences sociopolitical moral "ought"-judgments requiring actions in support of civil liberties and in opposition to great inequalities of wealth and power. While I do not have the time now to go into such institutional applications, the general point is that since the *PGC* requires an equal distribution of the most basic rights of action, freedom and basic well-being, it also requires legal, political, and economic institutions which foster such libertarian and egalitarian rights, and it hence requires actions which support such institutions. Unlike the direct institutional derivations considered earlier, if the obligations grounded in various institutions are to be justified, then the institutions themselves must first be justifiable through the *PGC*.[16] And it is by rules based on such justified institutions that conflicts arising from agents' use of their freedom are to be resolved.

This, then, concludes my argument. So far as concerns the particular paradigmatic moral "ought"-judgments which I presented at the outset, I have not derived them directly from their antecedent "is"-statements about B's starving and so forth; rather I have treated these combinations as enthymemes having such specific "ought"-premisses as: "Whenever some person is starving and someone else can relieve him at no comparable cost to himself, he ought to do so." These "ought"-premisses, however, follow from the *PGC*, and the *PGC* in turn follows, through the steps I have indicated, from the "is"-statement made by the agent that he performs actions for purposes. Hence, the particular moral "ought"-judgments have been derived, through several intermediate steps, from an empirical "is"-statement.

I have here presented, then, a complex version of what I have called the internal model of the relation between "ought" and "is." I have not directly defined "ought" in terms of "is"; rather, I have held that the application of "ought" is entailed by the correlative concept of having a right. The agent's application of this concept, in turn, has been derived from the concept of goods which are the necessary conditions of all his actions, since he necessarily claims that he has a right to at least these goods. And the agent's application of the concept of good, finally, has been derived from his acting for purposes. Since the agent's assertion that he acts for purposes is an empirical, descriptive statement, I have in this indirect way derived "ought" from "is." Whether the derivation is at each point definitional or is rather of some other non-arbitrary sort does not materially affect my argument, so long as its necessary relation to the context of action is recognized.

If this derivation has been successful, if it constitutes a resolution of the real "Is–Ought" Problem, then the "ought"-judgments which I have derived have the five characteristics indicated in my first section. Let us examine whether this is so. We have already seen that the *PGC* and the more specific "ought"-judgments that follow from it are moral and egalitarian. They are also prescriptive, since they follow logically from the agent's prescriptive claim that he has a right to freedom and basic well-being. And they are determinate, for they rule out the coercion and basic harm which we saw were permitted by other "is–ought" derivations.

It may be questioned, however, whether the condition of categoricalness has been satisfied. The objection would be that there is a conflict between the categorical and the dialectical. Since my argument has been dialectical in that it proceeds from within the standpoint of the agent, including the evaluations and right-claims he makes, the *PGC* and the ensuing "ought"-judgments I have derived are valid, so holds the objection, only relatively to the agent's standpoint, but not absolutely. Even if the agent is logi-

[16]For fuller discussion of how institutional obligations are derived from the *PGC*, see my "Obligation: Political, Legal, Moral," *op. cit.*, (above, n. 10). See also my "Categorial Consistency in Ethics," *Philosophical Quarterly*, vol. 17 (1967), pp. 289 ff.

cally compelled to uphold certain "ought"-judgments, given his initial statement that he performs actions for purposes, this does not establish that those judgments are really correct or binding. Hence, their "oughts" are not categorical.

My reply to this objection is that the dialectically *necessary* aspect of my method gives the "ought"-conclusions a more than contingent or hypothetical status. Since moral "oughts" apply only or primarily to the context of action and hence to agents, to have shown that certain "ought"-judgments logically must be granted by all agents, on pain of contradiction, is to give the judgments an absolute status since their validity is logically ineluctable within the whole context of their possible application. It will be recalled that in my original specification I said that for "ought"-judgments to be categorical the normative bindingness of the requirements they set forth cannot be removed or evaded by variable, escapable features of the persons addressed, including their self-interested desires or their contingent choices, opinions, and attitudes. This condition of categoricalness is fulfilled by the *PGC*'s "ought"-judgment.

This necessity also explicates the respect in which moral judgments have truth-value. The *PGC* and the moral judgments that follow from it are true in that they correspond to the concept of a rational agent, for they indicate what logically must be admitted by such an agent. As I noted above, the criterion of "rational" here is a purely logical one.

Finally, what of the condition of non-circularity? Although my argument began from the agent's empirical statements that he performs actions, I then pointed out that actions as viewed by him have certain ineluctable evaluative and normative elements. Doesn't this mean that I have reached a normative or at least a prescriptive "ought"-conclusion only by putting normativeness or prescriptiveness into my premiss about action? It was this question that figured in the "dilemma of commitment" that I presented above. Now an assumption of this dilemma was that for any person who undertakes to derive "ought" from "is" within some context, it is open to him to choose or to refrain from choosing to commit himself to that context with its requirements. As we have seen, however, it is impossible intentionally to refrain from committing oneself to the context of the generic features of action, for any such refraining would itself exhibit those features. Hence, the "ought" which is derived within that context is prescriptive; but nevertheless the derivation is not circular, because the derived "ought" reflects not a dispensable choice or commitment but rather a necessity which is not subject to any choice or decision on the part of the agent. The objector hence cannot say, "You've reached a commitment or prescription in the conclusion only because you've already chosen to put the commitment or prescription into your premiss;" for the latter commitment in the premiss is not one that the deriver has *chosen* or has *put into* the premiss. Rather, the commitment is there in the nature of the case, and all he is doing is recognize it; but he cannot evade it. In any event, as already noted, the initial premiss of the derivation is the agent's empirical statement that he performs actions for purposes; and the prescriptiveness of the moral "ought"-conclusion is accounted for more specifically by the advocacy embodied in his right-claim together with its logical generalization.

What I have tried to show here, then, is that the "is" of the performance of actions having the generic features logically generates the "ought" of categorical moral judgments; or, in other words, that the fact of being a purposive agent logically requires, on pain of self-contradiction, an acknowledgment that one ought to act in certain basic moral ways. To summarize: Because actions are conative and value-pursuing, they commit the agent to advocate or endorse for himself the rights of freedom and basic well-being which are the proximate necessary prerequisites of all his acting; hence, he makes judgments which fulfill the condition of prescriptiveness. Because the agent must advocate these rights for general reasons stemming from his simply being a prospective purposive agent, his advocacy must logically be extended to all other persons; hence, his judgments fulfill the conditions of being moral and egalitarian. And because this extension is based on the generic and hence inescapable features of action, it logically cannot be evaded or reversed regardless of any variable desires, choices, or attitudes on the part of the agent; hence, his judgments fulfill the conditions of determinacy and categoricalness. In this way, then, by an analysis of the generic features of action and their normative implications, I have argued that the real "Is–Ought" Problem is resolved.

1975

Moral Relativism Defended

Gilbert Harman

My thesis is that morality arises when a group of people reach an implicit agreement or come to a tacit understanding about their relations with one another. Part of what I mean by this is that moral judgments—or, rather, an important class of them—make sense only in relation to and with reference to one or another such agreement or understanding. This is vague, and I shall try to make it more precise in what follows. But it should be clear that I intend to argue for a version of what has been called moral relativism.

In doing so, I am taking sides in an ancient controversy. Many people have supposed that the sort of view which I am going to defend is obviously correct—indeed, that it is the only sort of account that could make sense of the phenomenon of morality. At the same time there have also been many who have supposed that moral relativism is confused, incoherent, and even immoral, at the very least obviously wrong.

Most arguments against relativism make use of a strategy of dissuasive definition; they define moral relativism as an inconsistent thesis. For example, they define it as the assertion that *(a)* there are no universal moral principles and *(b)* one ought to act in accordance with the principles of one's own group, where this latter principle, *(b), is* supposed to be a universal moral principle.[1] It is easy enough to show that this version of

[1]Bernard Williams, *Morality: An Introduction to Ethics* (New York, 1972), pp. 20–21; Marcus Singer, *Generalization in Ethics* (New York, 1961), p. 332.

moral relativism will not do, but that is no reason to think that a defender of moral relativism cannot find a better definition.

My moral relativism is a soberly logical thesis—a thesis about logical form, if you like. Just as the judgment that something is large makes sense only in relation to one or another comparison class, so too, I will argue, the judgment that it is wrong of someone to do something makes sense only in relation to an agreement or understanding. A dog may be large in relation to chihuahuas but not large in relation to dogs in general. Similarly, I will argue, an action may be wrong in relation to one agreement but not in relation to another. Just as it makes no sense to ask whether a dog is large, period, apart from any relation to a comparison class, so too, I will argue, it makes no sense to ask whether an action is wrong, period, apart from any relation to an agreement.

There is an agreement, in the relevant sense, if each of a number of people intends to adhere to some schedule, plan, or set of principles, intending to do this on the understanding that the others similarly intend. The agreement or understanding need not be conscious or explicit; and I will not here try to say what distinguishes moral agreements from, for example, conventions of the road or conventions of etiquette, since these distinctions will not be important as regards the purely logical thesis that I will be defending.

Although I want to say that certain moral judgments are made in relation to an agreement, I do not want to say this about all moral judgments. Perhaps it is true that all moral judgments are made in relation to an agreement; nevertheless, that is not what I will be arguing. For I want to say that there is a way in which certain moral judgments are relative to an agreement but other moral judgments are not. My relativism is a thesis only about what I will call "inner judgments," such as the judgment that someone ought or ought not to have acted in a certain way or the judgment that it was right or wrong of him to have done so. My relativism is not meant to apply, for example, to the judgment that someone is evil or the judgment that a given institution is unjust.

In particular, I am not denying (nor am I asserting) that some moralities are "objectively" better than others or that there are objective standards for assessing moralities. My thesis is a soberly logical thesis about logical form.

I. INNER JUDGMENTS

We make inner judgments about a person only if we suppose that he is capable of being motivated by the relevant moral considerations. We make other sorts of judgment about those who we suppose are not susceptible of such motivation. Inner judgments include judgments in which we say that someone should or ought to have done something or that someone was right or wrong to have done something. Inner judgments do not include judgments in which we call someone (literally) a savage or say that someone is (literally) inhuman, evil, a betrayer, a traitor, or an enemy.

Consider this example. Intelligent beings from outer space land on Earth, beings without the slightest concern for human life and happiness. That a certain course of action on their part might injure one of us means nothing to them; that fact by itself gives them no reason to avoid the action. In such a case it would be odd to say that nevertheless the beings ought to avoid injuring us or that it would be wrong for them to attack us. Of course we will want to resist them if they do such things and we will make negative judgments about them; but we will judge that they are dreadful enemies to be repelled and even destroyed, not that they should not act as they do.

Similarly, if we learn that a band of cannibals has captured and eaten the sole survivor of a shipwreck, we will speak of the primitive morality of the cannibals and may call them savages, but we will not say that they ought not to have eaten their captive.

Again, suppose that a contented employee of Murder, Incorporated was raised as a child to honor and respect members of the "family" but to have nothing but contempt for the rest of society. His current assignment, let us suppose, is to kill a certain bank manager, Bernard J. Ortcutt. Since Ortcutt is not a member of the "family," the employee in question has no compunction about carrying out his assignment. In particular, if we were to try to convince him that he should not kill Ortcutt, our argument would merely amuse him. We would not provide him with the slightest reason to desist unless we were to point to practical difficulties, such as the likelihood of his getting caught. Now, in this case it would be a misuse of language to say of him that he ought not to kill Ortcutt or that it would be wrong of him to do so, since that would imply that our own moral considerations carry some weight with him, which they do not. Instead we can only judge that he is a criminal, someone to be hunted down by the police, an enemy of peace-loving citizens, and so forth.

It is true that we can make certain judgments about him using the word "ought." For example, investigators who have been tipped off by an informer and who are waiting for the assassin to appear at the bank can use the "ought" of expectation to say, "He ought to arrive soon," meaning that on the basis of their information one would expect him to arrive soon. And, in thinking over how the assassin might carry out his assignment, we can use the "ought" of rationality to say that he ought to go in by the rear door, meaning that it would be more rational for him to do that than to go in by the front door. In neither of these cases is the moral "ought" in question.

There is another use of "ought" which is normative and in a sense moral but which is distinct from what I am calling the moral "ought." This is the use which occurs when we say that something ought or ought not to be the case. It ought not to be the case that members of Murder, Incorporated go around killing people; in other words, it is a terrible thing that they do so.[2] The same thought can perhaps be expressed as "They ought not to go around killing people," meaning that it ought not to be the case that they do, not that they are wrong to do what they do. The normative "ought to be" is used to assess a situation; the moral "ought to do" is used to describe a relation between an agent and a type of act that he might perform or has performed.

The sentence "They ought not to go around killing people" is therefore multiply ambiguous. It can mean that one would not expect them to do so (the "ought" of expectation), that it is not in their interest to do so (the "ought" of rationality), that it is a bad thing that they do so (the normative "ought to be"), or that they are wrong to do so (the moral "ought to do"). For the most part I am here concerned only with the last of these interpretations.

The word "should" behaves very much like "ought to." There is a "should" of expectation ("They should be here soon"), a "should" of rationality ("He should go in by the back door"), a normative "should be" ("They shouldn't go around killing people like that"), and the moral "should do" ("You should keep that promise"). I am of course concerned mainly with the last sense of "should."

"Right" and "wrong" also have multiple uses; I will not try to say what all of them are. But I do want to distinguish using the word "wrong" to say that a particular

[2]Thomas Nagel has observed that often, when we use the evaluative "ought to be" to say that something ought to be the case, we imply that someone ought to do something or ought to have done something about it. To take his example, we would not say that a certain hurricane ought not to have killed fifty people just on the ground that it was a terrible thing that the hurricane did so; but we might say this if we had in mind that the deaths from the hurricane would not have occurred except for the absence of safety or evacuation procedures which the authorities ought to have provided.

situation or action is wrong from using the word to say that it is wrong *of someone* to do something. In the former case, the word "wrong" is used to assess an act or situation. In the latter case it is used to describe a relation between an agent and an act. Only the latter sort of judgment is an inner judgment. Although we would not say concerning the contented employee of Murder, Incorporated mentioned earlier that it was wrong *of him* to kill Ortcutt, we could say that *his action* was wrong and we could say that it is wrong that there is so much killing.

To take another example, it sounds odd to say that Hitler should not have ordered the extermination of the Jews, that it was wrong of him to have done so. That sounds somehow "too weak" a thing to say. Instead we want to say that Hitler was an evil man. Yet we can properly say, "Hitler ought not to have ordered the extermination of the Jews," if what we mean is that it ought never to have happened; and we can say without oddity that what Hitler did was wrong. Oddity attends only the inner judgment that Hitler was wrong to have acted in that way. That is what sounds "too weak."

It is worth noting that the inner judgments sound too weak not because of the enormity of what Hitler did but because we suppose that in acting as he did he shows that he could not have been susceptible to the moral considerations on the basis of which we make our judgment. He is in the relevant sense beyond the pale and we therefore cannot make inner judgments about him. To see that this is so, consider, say, Stalin, another mass-murderer. We can perhaps imagine someone taking a sympathetic view of Stalin. In such a view, Stalin realized that the course he was going to pursue would mean the murder of millions of people and he dreaded such a prospect; however, the alternative seemed to offer an even greater disaster—so, reluctantly and with great anguish, he went ahead. In relation to such a view of Stalin, inner judgments about Stalin are not as odd as similar judgments about Hitler. For we might easily continue the story by saying that, despite what he hoped to gain, Stalin should not have undertaken the course he did, that it was wrong of him to have done so. What makes inner judgments about Hitler odd, "too weak," is not that the acts judged seem too terrible for the words used but rather that the agent judged seems beyond the pale—in other words beyond the motivational reach of the relevant moral considerations.

Of course, I do not want to deny that for various reasons a speaker might pretend that an agent is or is not susceptible to certain moral considerations. For example, a speaker may for rhetorical or political reasons wish to suggest that someone is beyond the pale, that he should not be listened to, that he can be treated as an enemy. On the other hand, a speaker may pretend that someone is susceptible to certain moral considerations in an effort to make that person or others susceptible to those considerations. Inner judgments about one's children sometimes have this function. So do inner judgments made in political speeches that aim at restoring a lapsed sense of morality in government.

II. THE LOGICAL FORM OF INNER JUDGMENTS

Inner judgments have two important characteristics. First, they imply that the agent has reasons to do something. Second, the speaker in some sense endorses these reasons and supposes that the audience also endorses them. Other moral judgments about an agent, on the other hand, do not have such implications; they do not imply that the agent has reasons for acting that are endorsed by the speaker.

If someone *S* says that *A* (morally) ought to do *D, S* implies that *A* has reasons to do *D* and *S* endorses those reasons—whereas if *S* says that *B* was evil in what *B* did, *S* does not imply that the reasons *S* would endorse for not doing what *B* did were reasons for *B* not to do that thing; in fact, *S* implies that they were not reasons for *B*.

Let us examine this more closely. If *S* says that (morally) *A* ought to do *D*, *S* implies that *A* has reasons to do *D* which *S* endorses. I shall assume that such reasons would have to have their source in goals, desires, or intentions that *S* takes *A* to have and that *S* approves of *A*'s having because *S* shares those goals, desires, or intentions. So, if *S* says that (morally) *A* ought to do *D*, there are certain motivational attitudes *M* which *S* assumes are shared by *S*, *A*, and *S*'s audience.

Now, in supposing that reasons for action must have their source in goals, desires, or intentions, I am assuming something like an Aristotelian or Humean account of these matters, as opposed, for example, to a Kantian approach which sees a possible source of motivation in reason itself.[3] I must defer a full-scale discussion of the issue to another occasion. Here I simply assume that the Kantian approach is wrong. In particular, I assume that there might be no reasons at all for a being from outer space to avoid harm to us; that, for Hitler, there might have been no reason at all not to order the extermination of the Jews; that the contented employee of Murder, Incorporated might have no reason at all not to kill Ortcutt; that the cannibals might have no reason not to eat their captive. In other words, I assume that the possession of rationality is not sufficient to provide a source for relevant reasons, that certain desires, goals, or intentions are also necessary. Those who accept this assumption will, I think, find that they distinguish inner moral judgments from other moral judgments in the way that I have indicated.

Ultimately, I want to argue that the shared motivational attitudes *M* are intentions to keep an agreement (supposing that others similarly intend). For I want to argue that inner moral judgments are made relative to such an agreement. That is, I want to argue that, when *S* makes the inner judgment that *A* ought to do *D*, *S* assumes that *A* intends to act in accordance with an agreement which *S* and *S*'s audience also intend to observe. In other words, I want to argue that the source of the reasons for doing *D* which *S* ascribes to *A* is *A*'s sincere intention to observe a certain agreement. I have not yet argued for the stronger thesis, however. I have argued only that *S* makes his judgment relative to *some* motivational attitudes *M* which *S* assumes are shared by *S*, *A*, and *S*'s audience.

Formulating this as a logical thesis, I want to treat the moral "ought" as a four-place predicate (or "operator"), "Ought (*A*, *D*, *C*, *M*)," which relates an agent *A*, a type of act *D*, considerations *C*, and motivating attitudes *M*. The relativity to considerations *C* can be brought out by considering what are sometimes called statements of prima-facie obligation, "Considering that you promised, you ought to go to the board meeting, but considering that you are the sole surviving relative, you ought to go to the funeral; all things considered, it is not clear what you ought to do."[4] The claim that there is *this* relativity, to considerations, is not, of course, what makes my thesis a version of moral relativism, since any theory must acknowledge relativity to considerations. The relativity to considerations does, however, provide a model for a coherent interpretation of moral relativism as a similar kind of relativity.

It is not as easy to exhibit the relativity to motivating attitudes as it is to exhibit the relativity to considerations, since normally a speaker who makes a moral "ought" judgment intends the relevant motivating attitudes to be ones that the speaker shares with the agent and the audience, and normally it will be obvious what attitudes these are. But sometimes a speaker does invoke different attitudes by invoking a morality the speaker does not share. Someone may say, for example, "As a Christian, you ought to turn the other cheek; I, however, propose to strike back." A spy who has been found out by a friend might say, "As a citizen, you ought to turn me in, but I hope that you will

[3]For the latter approach, see Thomas Nagel, *The Possibility of Altruism* (Oxford, 1970).
[4]See Donald Davidson, "Weakness of Will," in Joel Feinberg (ed.), *Moral Concepts* (Oxford, 1969).

not." In these and similar cases a speaker makes a moral "ought" judgment that is explicitly relative to motivating attitudes that the speaker does not share.

In order to be somewhat more precise, then, my thesis is this. "Ought *(A, D, C, M)*" means roughly that, given that *A* has motivating attitudes *M* and given *C, D* is the course of action for *A* that is supported by the best reasons. In judgments using this sense of "ought," *C* and *M* are often not explicitly mentioned but are indicated by the context of utterance. Normally, when that happens, *C* will be "all things considered" and *M* will be attitudes that are shared by the speaker and audience.

I mentioned that inner judgments have two characteristics. First, they imply that the agent has reasons to do something that are capable of motivating the agent. Second, the speaker endorses those reasons and supposes that the audience does too. Now, any "Ought *(A, D, C, M)*" judgment has the first of these characteristics, but as we have just seen a judgment of this sort will not necessarily have the second characteristic if made with explicit reference to motivating attitudes not shared by the speaker. If reference is made either implicitly or explicitly (for example, through the use of the adverb "morally") to attitudes that are shared by the speaker and audience, the resulting judgment has both characteristics and is an inner judgment. If reference is made to attitudes that are not shared by the speaker, the resulting judgment is not an inner judgment and does not represent a full-fledged moral judgment on the part of the speaker. In such a case we have an example of what has been called an inverted-commas use of "ought."[5]

III. MORAL BARGAINING

I have argued that moral "ought" judgments are relational, "Ought (*A, D, C, M*)," where *M* represents certain motivating attitudes. I now want to argue that the attitudes *M* derive from an agreement. That is, they are intentions to adhere to a particular agreement on the understanding that others also intend to do so. Really, it might be better for me to say that I put this forward as a hypothesis, since I cannot pretend to be able to prove that it is true. I will argue, however, that this hypothesis accounts for an otherwise puzzling aspect of our moral views that, as far as I know, there is no other way to account for.

I will use the word "intention" in a somewhat extended sense to cover certain dispositions or habits. Someone may habitually act in accordance with the relevant understanding and therefore may be disposed to act in that way without having any more or less conscious intention. In such a case it may sound odd to say that he *intends* to act in accordance with the moral understanding. Nevertheless, for present purposes I will count that as his having the relevant intention in a dispositional sense.

I now want to consider the following puzzle about our moral views, a puzzle that has figured in recent philosophical discussion of issues such as abortion. It has been observed that most of us assign greater weight to the duty not to harm others than to the duty to help others. For example, most of us believe that a doctor ought not to save five of his patients who would otherwise die by cutting up a sixth patient and distributing his healthy organs where needed to the others, even though we do think that the doctor has a duty to try to help as many of his patients as he can. For we also think that he has a stronger duty to try not to harm any of his patients (or anyone else) even if by so doing he could help five others.[6]

[5]R. M. Hare, *The Language of Morals* (Oxford, 1952), pp. 164–168.

[6]Philippa Foot, "Abortion and the Doctrine of Double Effect," in James Rachels (ed.), *Moral Problems* (New York, 1971).

This aspect of our moral views can seem very puzzling, especially if one supposes that moral feelings derive from sympathy and concern for others. But the hypothesis that morality derives from an agreement among people of varying powers and resources provides a plausible explanation. The rich, the poor, the strong, and the weak would all benefit if all were to try to avoid harming one another. So everyone could agree to that arrangement. But the rich and the strong would not benefit from an arrangement whereby everyone would try to do as much as possible to help those in need. The poor and weak would get all of the benefit of this latter arrangement. Since the rich and the strong could foresee that they would be required to do most of the helping and that they would receive little in return, they would be reluctant to agree to a strong principle of mutual aid. A compromise would be likely and a weaker principle would probably be accepted. In other words, although everyone could agree to a strong principle concerning the avoidance of harm, it would not be true that everyone would favor an equally strong principle of mutual aid. It is likely that only a weaker principle of the latter sort would gain general acceptance. So the hypothesis that morality derives from an understanding among people of different powers and resources can explain (and, according to me, does explain) why in our morality avoiding harm to others is taken to be more important than helping those who need help.

By the way, I am here only trying to *explain* an aspect of our moral views. I am not therefore *endorsing* that aspect. And I defer until later a relativistic account of the way in which aspects of our moral view can be criticized "from within."

Now we need not suppose that the agreement or understanding in question is explicit. It is enough if various members of society knowingly reach an agreement in intentions—each intending to act in certain ways on the understanding that the others have similar intentions. Such an implicit agreement is reached through a process of mutual adjustment and implicit bargaining.

Indeed, it is essential to the proposed explanation of this aspect of our moral views to suppose that the relevant moral understanding is thus the result of *bargaining*. It is necessary to suppose that, in order to further our interests, we form certain conditional intentions, hoping that others will do the same. The others, who have different interests, will form somewhat different conditional intentions. After implicit bargaining, some sort of compromise is reached.

Seeing morality in this way as a compromise based on implicit bargaining helps to explain why our morality takes it to be worse to harm someone than to refuse to help someone. The explanation requires that we view our morality as an implicit agreement about what to do. This sort of explanation could not be given if we were to suppose, say, that our morality represented an agreement only about the facts (naturalism). Nor is it enough simply to suppose that our morality represents an agreement in attitude, if we forget that such agreement can be reached, not only by way of such principles as are mentioned, for example, in Hare's "logic of imperatives,"[7] but also through bargaining. According to Hare, to accept a general moral principle is to intend to do something.[8] If we add to his theory that the relevant intentions can be reached through implicit bargaining, the resulting theory begins to look like the one that I am defending.

Many aspects of our moral views can be given a utilitarian explanation. We could account for these aspects, using the logical analysis I presented in the previous section of this paper, by supposing that the relevant "ought" judgments presuppose shared attitudes of sympathy and benevolence. We can equally well explain them by supposing

[7]R. M. Hare, *op. cit.* and *Freedom and Reason* (Oxford, 1963).
[8]*The Language of Morals*, pp. 18–20, 168–169.

that considerations of utility have influenced our implicit agreements, so that the appeal is to a shared intention to adhere to those agreements. Any aspect of morality that is susceptible of a utilitarian explanation can also be explained by an implicit agreement, but not conversely. There are aspects of our moral views that seem to be explicable only in the second way, on the assumption that morality derives from an agreement. One example, already cited, is the distinction we make between harming and not helping. Another is our feeling that each person has an inalienable right of self-defense and self-preservation. Philosophers have not been able to come up with a really satisfactory utilitarian justification of such a right, but it is easily intelligible on our present hypothesis, as Hobbes observed many years ago. You cannot, except in very special circumstances, rationally form the intention not to try to preserve your life if it should ever be threatened, say, by society or the state, since you know that you cannot now control what you would do in such a situation. No matter what you now decided to do, when the time came, you would ignore your prior decision and try to save your life. Since you cannot now intend to do something later which you now know that you would not do, you cannot now intend to keep an agreement not to preserve your life if it is threatened by others in your society.[9]

This concludes the positive side of my argument that what I have called inner moral judgments are made in relation to an implicit agreement. I now want to argue that this theory avoids difficulties traditionally associated with implicit agreement theories of morality.

IV. OBJECTIONS AND REPLIES

One traditional difficulty for implicit agreement theories concerns what motivates us to do what we have agreed to do. It will, obviously, not be enough to say that we have implicitly agreed to keep agreements, since the issue would then be why we keep *that* agreement. And this suggests an objection to implicit agreement theories. But the apparent force of the objection derives entirely from taking an agreement to be a kind of ritual. To agree in the relevant sense is not just to say something; it is to intend to do something—namely, to intend to carry out one's part of the agreement on the condition that others do their parts. If we agree in this sense to do something, we intend to do it and intending to do it is already to be motivated to do it. So there is no problem as to why we are motivated to keep our agreements in this sense.

We do believe that in general you ought not to pretend to agree in this sense in order to trick someone else into agreeing. But that suggests no objection to the present view. All that it indicates is that *our* moral understanding contains or implies an agreement to be open and honest with others. If it is supposed that this leaves a problem about someone who has not accepted our agreement—"What reason does *he* have not to pretend to accept our agreement so that he can then trick others into agreeing to various things?"—the answer is that such a person may or may not have such a reason. If someone does not already accept something of our morality it may or may not be possible to find reasons why he should.

A second traditional objection to implicit agreement theories is that there is not a perfect correlation between what is generally believed to be morally right and what actually is morally right. Not everything generally agreed on is right and sometimes

[9]Cf. Thomas Hobbes, *Leviathan* (Oxford, 1957, *inter alia*), Pt. I, Ch. 14, "Of the First and Second Natural Laws, And of Contracts."

courses of action are right that would not be generally agreed to be right. But this is no objection to my thesis. My thesis is not that the implicit agreement from which a morality derives is an agreement in moral judgment; the thesis is rather that moral judgments make reference to and are made in relation to an agreement in intentions. Given that a group of people have agreed in this sense, there can still be disputes as to what the agreement implies for various situations. In my view, many moral disputes are of this sort. They presuppose a basic agreement and they concern what implications that agreement has for particular cases.

There can also be various things wrong with the agreement that a group of people reach, even from the point of view of that agreement, just as there can be defects in an individual's plan of action even from the point of view of that plan. Given what is known about the situation, a plan or agreement can in various ways be inconsistent, incoherent, or self-defeating. In my view, certain moral disputes are concerned with internal defects of the basic moral understanding of a group, and what changes should be made from the perspective of that understanding itself. This is another way in which moral disputes make sense with reference to and in relation to an underlying agreement.

Another objection to implicit agreement theories is that not all agreements are morally binding—for example, those made under complusion or from a position of unfair disadvantage, which may seem to indicate that there are moral principles prior to those that derive from an implicit agreement. But, again, the force of the objection derives from an equivocation concerning what an agreement is. The principle that compelled agreements do not obligate concerns agreement in the sense of a certain sort of ritual indicating that one agrees. My thesis concerns a kind of agreement in intentions. The principle about compelled agreements is part of, or is implied by, our agreement in intentions. According to me it is only with reference to some such agreement in intentions that a principle of this sort makes sense.

Now it may be true our moral agreement in intentions also implies that it is wrong to compel people who are in a greatly inferior position to accept an agreement in intentions that they would not otherwise accept, and it may even be true that there is in our society at least one class of people in an inferior position who have been compelled thus to settle for accepting a basic moral understanding, aspects of which they would not have accepted had they not been in such an inferior position. In that case there would be an incoherence in our basic moral understanding and various suggestions might be made concerning the ways in which this understanding should be modified. But this moral critique of the understanding can proceed from that understanding itself rather than from "prior" moral principles.

In order to fix ideas, let us consider a society in which there is a well-established and long-standing tradition of hereditary slavery. Let us suppose that everyone accepts this institution, including the slaves. Everyone treats it as in the nature of things that there should be such slavery. Furthermore, let us suppose that there are also aspects of the basic moral agreement which speak against slavery. That is, these aspects together with certain facts about the situation imply that people should not own slaves and that slaves have no obligation to acquiesce in their condition. In such a case, the moral understanding would be defective, although its defectiveness would presumably be hidden in one or another manner, perhaps by means of a myth that slaves are physically and mentally subhuman in a way that makes appropriate the sort of treatment elsewhere reserved for beasts of burden. If this myth were to be exposed, the members of the society would then be faced with an obvious incoherence in their basic moral agreement and might come eventually to modify their agreement so as to eliminate its acceptance of slavery.

In such a case, even relative to the old agreement it might be true that slave owners ought to free their slaves, that slaves need not obey their masters, and that people ought to work to eliminate slavery. For the course supported by the best reasons, given that one starts out with the intention of adhering to a particular agreement, may be that one should stop intending to adhere to certain aspects of that agreement and should try to get others to do the same.

We can also (perhaps—but see below) envision a second society with hereditary slavery whose agreement has no aspects that speak against slavery. In that case, even if the facts of the situation were fully appreciated, no incoherence would appear in the basic moral understanding of the society and it would not be true in relation to that understanding that slave owners ought to free their slaves, that slaves need not obey their masters, and so forth. There might nevertheless come a time when there were reasons of a different sort to modify the basic understanding, either because of an external threat from societies opposed to slavery or because of an internal threat of rebellion by the slaves.

Now it is easier for us to make what I have called inner moral judgments about slave owners in the first society than in the second. For we can with reference to members of the first society invoke principles that they share with us and, with reference to those principles, we can say of them that they ought not to have kept slaves and that they were immoral to have done so. This sort of inner judgment becomes increasingly inappropriate, however, the more distant they are from us and the less easy it is for us to think of our moral understanding as continuous with and perhaps a later development of theirs. Furthermore, it seems appropriate to make only non-inner judgments of the slave owners in the second society. We can say that the second society is unfair and unjust, that the slavery that exists is wrong, that it ought not to exist. But it would be inappropriate in this case to say that it was morally wrong of the slave owners to own slaves. The relevant aspects of our moral understanding, which we would invoke in moral judgments about them, are not aspects of the moral understanding that exists in the second society. (I will come back to the question of slavery below.)

Let me turn now to another objection to implicit agreement theories, an objection which challenges the idea that there is an agreement of the relevant sort. For, if we have agreed, when did we do it? Does anyone really remember having agreed? How did we indicate our agreement? What about those who do not want to agree? How do they indicate that they do not agree and what are the consequences of their not agreeing? Reflection on these and similar questions can make the hypothesis of implicit agreement seem too weak a basis on which to found morality.

But once again there is equivocation about agreements. The objection treats the thesis as the claim that morality is based on some sort of ritual rather than an agreement in intentions. But, as I have said, there is an agreement in the relevant sense when each of a number of people has an intention on the assumption that others have the same intention. In this sense of "agreement," there is no given moment at which one agrees, since one continues to agree in this sense as long as one continues to have the relevant intentions. Someone refuses to agree to the extent that he or she does not share these intentions. Those who do not agree are outside the agreement; in extreme cases they are outlaws or enemies. It does not follow, however, that there are no constraints on how those who agree may act toward those who do not, since for various reasons the agreement itself may contain provisions for dealing with outlaws and enemies.

This brings me to one last objection, which derives from the difficulty people have in trying to give an explicit and systematic account of their moral views. If one actually agrees to something, why is it so hard to say what one has agreed? In response I can say only that many understandings appear to be of this sort. It is often possible to recognize what is in accordance with the understanding and what would violate it without being able to specify the understanding in any general way. Consider, for example, the understanding that exists among the members of a team of acrobats or a symphony orchestra.

Another reason why it is so difficult to give a precise and systematic specification of any actual moral understanding is that such an understanding will not in general be constituted by absolute rules but will take a vaguer form, specifying goals and areas of responsibility. For example, the agreement may indicate that one is to show respect for others by trying where possible to avoid actions that will harm them or interfere with what they are doing; it may indicate the duties and responsibilities of various members of the family, who is to be responsible for bringing up the children, and so forth. Often what will be important will be not so much exactly what actions are done as how willing participants are to do their parts and what attitudes they have—for example, whether they give sufficient weight to the interests of others.

The vague nature of moral understandings is to some extent alleviated in practice. One learns what can and cannot be done in various situations. Expectations are adjusted to other expectations. But moral disputes arise nonetheless. Such disputes may concern what the basic moral agreement implies for particular situations; and, if so, that can happen either because of disputes over the facts or because of a difference in basic understanding. Moral disputes may also arise concerning whether or not changes should be made in the basic agreement. Racial and sexual issues seem often to be of this second sort; but there is no clear line between the two kinds of dispute. When the implications of an agreement for a particular situation are considered, one possible outcome is that it becomes clear that the agreement should be modified.

Moral reasoning is a form of practical reasoning. One begins with certain beliefs and intentions, including intentions that are part of one's acceptance of the moral understanding in a given group. In reasoning, one modifies one's intentions, often by forming new intentions, sometimes by giving up old ones, so that one's plans become more rational and coherent—or, rather, one seeks to make all of one's attitudes coherent with each other.

The relevant sort of coherence is not simply consistency. It is something very like the explanatory coherence which is so important in theoretical reasoning. Coherence involves generality and lack of arbitrariness. Consider our feelings about cruelty to animals. Obviously these do not derive from an agreement that has been reached with animals. Instead it is a matter of coherence. There is a prima-facie arbitrariness and lack of generality in a plan that involves avoiding cruelty to people but not to animals.

On the other hand, coherence in this sense is not the only relevant factor in practical reasoning. Another is conservatism or inertia. A third is an interest in satisfying basic desires or needs. One tries to make the least change that will best satisfy one's desires while maximizing the overall coherence of one's attitudes. Coherence by itself is not an overwhelming force. That is why our attitudes towards animals are weak and wavering, allowing us to use them in ways we would not use people.

Consider again the second hereditary slave society mentioned above. This society was to be one in which no aspects of the moral understanding shared by the masters spoke against slavery. In fact that is unlikely, since there is *some* arbitrariness in the idea that people are to be treated in different ways depending on whether they are born slave or free. Coherence of attitude will no doubt speak at least a little against the system of slavery. The point is that the factors of conservatism and desire might speak more strongly in favor of the *status quo,* so that, all things considered, the slave owners might have no reason to change their understanding.

One thing that distinguishes slaves from animals is that slaves can organize and threaten revolt, whereas animals cannot. Slaves can see to it that both coherence and desire oppose conservatism, so that it becomes rational for the slave owners to arrive at a new, broader, more coherent understanding, one which includes the slaves.

It should be noted that coherence of attitude provides a constant pressure to widen the consensus and eliminate arbitrary distinctions. In this connection it is useful to recall ancient attitudes toward foreigners, and the ways people used to think about "savages," "natives," and "Indians." Also, recall that infanticide used to be considered as acceptable as we consider abortion to be. There has been a change here in our moral attitudes, prompted, I suggest, largely by considerations of coherence of attitude.

Finally, I would like to say a few brief words about the limiting case of group morality, when the group has only one member; then, as it were, a person comes to an understanding with himself. In my view, a person can make inner judgments in relation to such an individual morality only about himself. A familiar form of pacifism is of this sort. Certain pacifists judge that it would be wrong of them to participate in killing, although they are not willing to make a similar judgment about others. Observe that such a pacifist is unwilling only to make *inner* moral judgments about others. Although he is unwilling to judge that those who do participate are wrong to do so, he is perfectly willing to say that it is a bad thing that they participate. There are of course many other examples of individual morality in this sense, when a person imposes standards on himself that he does not apply to others. The existence of such examples is further confirmation of the relativist thesis that I have presented.

My conclusion is that relativism can be formulated as an intelligible thesis, the thesis that morality derives from an implicit agreement and that moral judgments are in a logical sense made in relation to such an agreement. Such a theory helps to explain otherwise puzzling aspects of our own moral views, in particular why we think that it is more important to avoid harm to others than to help others. The theory is also partially confirmed by what is, as far as I can tell, a previously unnoticed distinction between inner and non-inner moral judgments. Furthermore, traditional objections to implicit agreement theories can be met.[10]

[10]Many people have given me good advice about the subjects discussed in this paper, which derives from a larger study of practical reasoning and morality. I am particularly indebted to Donald Davidson, Stephen Schiffer, William Alston, Frederick Schick, Thomas Nagel, Walter Kaufmann, Peter Singer, Robert Audi, and the editors of the *Philosophical Review*.

1976

The Schizophrenia of Modern Ethical Theories

Michael Stocker

Modern ethical theories, with perhaps a few honorable exceptions, deal only with reasons, with values, with what justifies. They fail to examine motives and the motivational structures and constraints of ethical life. They not only fail to do this, they fail as ethical theories by not doing this—as I shall argue in this paper. I shall also attempt two correlative tasks: to exhibit some constraints that motivation imposes on ethical theory and life; and to advance our understanding of the relations between reason and motive.

One mark of a good life is a harmony between one's motives and one's reasons, values, justifications. Not to be moved by what one values—what one believes good, nice, right, beautiful, and so on—bespeaks a malady of the spirit. Not to value what moves one also bespeaks a malady of the spirit. Such a malady, or such maladies, can properly be called *moral schizophrenia*—for they are a split between one's motives and one's reasons. (Here and elsewhere, "reasons" will stand also for "values" and "justifications.")

An extreme form of such schizophrenia is characterized, on the one hand, by being moved to do what one believes bad, harmful, ugly, abasing; on the other, by being

I wish to thank all those who have heard or read various versions of this paper and whose comments have greatly encouraged and helped me.

Michael Stocker, "The Schizophrenia of Modern Ethical Theories," *The Journal of Philosophy* 73, No. 14 (August 12, 1976). Reprinted with the permission of the author and *The Journal of Philosophy*.

disgusted, horrified, dismayed by what one wants to do. Perhaps such cases are rare. But a more modest schizophrenia between reason and motive is not, as can be seen in many examples of weakness of the will, indecisiveness, guilt, shame, self-deception, rationalization, and annoyance with oneself.

At the very least, we should be moved by our major values and we should value what our major motives seek. Should, that is, if we are to lead a good life. To repeat, such harmony is a mark of a good life. Indeed, one might wonder whether human life—good or bad—is possible without some such integration.

This is not, however, to say that in all cases it is better to have such harmony. It is better for us if self-seeking authoritarians feel fettered by their moral upbringing; better, that is, than if they adopt the reason of their motives. It would have been far better for the world and his victims had Eichmann not wanted to do what he thought he should do.[1]

Nor is this to say that in all areas of endeavor such harmony is necessary or even especially conducive to achieving what is valued. In many cases, it is not. For example, one's motives in fixing a flat tire are largely irrelevant to getting under way again. (In many such cases, one need not even value the intended outcome.)

Nor is this even to say that in all "morally significant" areas such harmony is necessary or especially conducive to achieving what is valued. Many morally significant jobs, such as feeding the sick, can be done equally well pretty much irrespective of motive. And, as Ross, at times joined by Mill, argues, for a large part of ethics, there simply is no philosophical question of harmony or disharmony between value and motive: you can do what is right, obligatory, your duty no matter what your motive for so acting. If it is your duty to keep a promise, you fulfill that duty no matter whether you keep the promise out of respect for duty, fear of losing your reputation, or whatever. What motivates is irrelevant so far as rightness, obligatoriness, duty are concerned.

Notwithstanding the very questionable correctness of this view so far as rightness, obligatoriness, duty are concerned,[2] there remain at least two problems. The first is that even here there is still a question of harmony. What sort of life would people have who did their duties but never or rarely wanted to? Second, duty, obligation, and rightness are only one part—indeed, only a small part, a dry and minimal part—of ethics. There is the whole other area of the values of personal and interpersonal relations and activities; and also the area of moral goodness, merit, virtue. In both, motive is an essential part of what is valuable; in both, motive and reason must be in harmony for the values to be realized.

For this reason and for the reason that such harmony is a mark of a good life, any theory that ignores such harmony does so at great peril. Any theory that makes difficult, or precludes, such harmony stands, if not convicted, then in need of much and powerful defense. What I shall now argue is that modern ethical theories—those theories prominent in the English-speaking philosophical world—make such harmony impossible.

CRITICISM OF MODERN ETHICS

Reflection on the complexity and vastness of our moral life, on what has value, shows that recent ethical theories have by far overconcentrated on duty, rightness, and obliga-

[1]It might be asked what is better for such people, to have or lack this harmony, given their evil motives or values; in which way they would be morally better. Such questions may not be answerable.

[2]See my "Act and Agent Evaluations," *Review of Metaphysics,* XXVII, 1, 105 (September 1973): 42–61.

tion.[3] This failure—of overconcentrating—could not have been tolerated but for the failure of not dealing with motives or with the relations of motives to values. (So too, the first failure supports and explains the second.) In this second failure, we find a far more serious defect of modern ethical theories than such overconcentration: they necessitate a schizophrenia between reason and motive in vitally important and pervasive areas of value, or alternatively they allow us the harmony of a morally impoverished life, a life deeply deficient in what is valuable. It is not possible for moral people, that is, people who would achieve what is valuable, to act on these ethical theories, to let them comprise their motives. People who do let them comprise their motives will, for that reason, have a life seriously lacking in what is valuable.

These theories are, thus, doubly defective. As ethical theories, they fail by making it impossible for a person to achieve the good in an integrated way. As theories of the mind, of reasons and motives, of human life and activity, they fail, not only by putting us in a position that is psychologically uncomfortable, difficult, or even untenable, but also by making us and our lives essentially fragmented and incoherent.

The sort of disharmony I have in mind can be brought out by considering a problem for egoists, typified by hedonistic egoists. Love, friendship, affection, fellow feeling, and community are important sources of personal pleasure. But can such egoists get these pleasures? I think not—not so long as they adhere to the motive of pleasure-for-self.

The reason for this is not that egoists cannot get together and decide, as it were, to enter into a love relationship. Surely they can (leaving aside the irrelevant problems about deciding to do such a thing). And they can do the various things calculated to bring about such pleasure: have absorbing talks, make love, eat delicious meals, see interesting films, and so on, and so on.

Nonetheless, there is something necessarily lacking in such a life: love. For it is essential to the very concept of love that one care for the beloved, that one be prepared to act for the sake of the beloved. More strongly, one must care for the beloved and act for that person's sake as a final goal; the beloved, or the beloved's welfare or interest, must be a final goal of one's concern and action.

To the extent that my consideration for you—or even my trying to make you happy—comes from my desire to lead an untroubled life, a life that is personally pleasing for me, I do not act for your sake. In short, to the extent that I act in various ways toward you with the final goal of getting pleasure—or, more generally, good—for myself, I do not act for your sake.

When we think about it this way, we may get some idea of why egoism is often claimed to be essentially lonely. For it is essentially concerned with external relations with others, where, except for their effects on us, one person is no different from, nor more important, valuable, or special than any other person or even any other thing. The individuals as such are not important, only their effects on us are; they are essentially replaceable, anything else with the same effects would do as well. And this, I suggest, is intolerable personally. To think of yourself this way, or to believe that a person you love thinks of you this way, is intolerable. And for conceptual, as well as psychological, reasons it is incompatible with love.

It might be suggested that it is rather unimportant to have love of this sort. But this would be a serious error. The love here is not merely modern-romantic or sexual. It is also the love among members of a family, the love we have for our closest friends,

[3]See *ibid.* and my "Rightness and Goodness: Is There a Difference?," *American Philosophical Quarterly*, X, 2 (April 1973): 87–98.

and so on. Just what sort of life would people have who never "cared" for anyone else, except as a means to their own interests? And what sort of life would people have who took it that no one loved them for their own sake, but only for the way they served the other's interest?

Just as the notion of doing something for the sake of another, or of caring for the person for that person's sake, is essential for love, so too is it essential for friendship and all affectionate relations. Without this, at best we could have good relations, friendly relations. And similarly, such caring and respect is essential for fellow feeling and community.

Before proceeding, let us contrast this criticism of egoism with a more standard one. My criticism runs as follows: Hedonistic egoists take their own pleasure to be the sole justification of acts, activities, ways of life; they should recognize that love, friendship, affection, fellow feeling, and community are among the greatest (sources of) personal pleasures. Thus, they have good reason, on their own grounds, to enter such relations. But they cannot act in the ways required to get those pleasures, those great goods, if they act on their motive of pleasure-for-self. They cannot act for the sake of the intended beloved, friend, and so on; thus, they cannot love, be or have a friend, and so on. To achieve these great personal goods, they have to abandon that egoistical motive. They cannot embody their reason in their motive. Their reasons and motives make their moral lives schizophrenic.

The standard criticism of egoists is that they simply cannot achieve such nonegoistical goods, that their course of action will, as a matter of principle, keep them from involving themselves with others in the relevant ways, and so on. This criticism is not clearly correct. For there may be nothing inconsistent in egoists' adopting a policy that will allow them to forget, as it were, that they are egoists, a policy that will allow and even encourage them to develop such final goals and motives as caring for another for that person's own sake. Indeed, as has often been argued, the wise egoist would do just this.

Several questions should be asked of this response: would the transformed person still be an egoist? Is it important, for the defense of egoism, that the person remain an egoist? Or is it important only that the person live in a way that would be approved of by an egoist? It is, of course, essential to the transformation of the person from egoistical motivation to caring for others that the person-as-egoist lose conscious control of him/herself. This raises the question of whether such people will be able to check up and see how their transformed selves are getting on in achieving egoistically approved goals. Will they have a mental alarm clock which wakes them up from their nonegoistical transforms every once in a while, to allow them to reshape these transforms if they are not getting enough personal pleasure—or, more generally, enough good? I suppose that this would not be impossible. But it hardly seems an ideal, or even a very satisfactory, life. It is bad enough to have a private personality, which you must hide from others; but imagine having a personality that you must hide from (the other parts of) yourself. Still, perhaps this is possible. If it is, then it seems that egoists may be able to meet this second criticism. But this does not touch my criticism: that they will not be able to embody their reason in their motives; that they will have to lead a bifurcated, schizophrenic life to achieve what is good.

This might be thought a defect of only such ethical theories as egoism. But consider those utilitarianisms which hold that an act is right, obligatory, or whatever if and only if it is optimific in regard to pleasure and pain (or weighted expectations of them). Such a view has it that the only good reason for acting is pleasure vs. pain, and thus should highly value love, friendship, affection, fellow feeling, and community. Suppose, now, you embody this utilitarian reason as your motive in your actions and thoughts toward someone. Whatever your relation to that person, it is necessarily not love (nor is it friendship, affection, fellow feeling, or community). The person you supposedly love engages your thought and action not for him/herself, but rather as a source of pleasure.

The problem is not simply that pleasure is taken to be the only good, the only right-making feature. To see this, consider G. E. Moore's formalistic utilitarianism, which tells us to maximize goodness, without claiming to have identified all the goods. If, as I would have it and as Moore agrees, love relations and the like are goods, how could there be any disharmony here? Would it not be possible to embody Moore's justifying reason as a motive and still love? I do not think so.

First, if you try to carry on the relationship for the sake of goodness, there is no essential commitment even to that activity, much less to the persons involved. So far as goodness is involved, you might as well love as ski or write poetry or eat a nice meal or. . . Perhaps it would be replied that there is something special about that good, the good of love—treating it now not qua good but qua what is good or qua this good. In such a case, however, there is again an impersonality so far as the individuals are concerned. Any other person who would elicit as much of this good would be as proper an object of love as the beloved. To this it might be replied that it is that good which is to be sought—with emphasis on the personal and individual features, the features that bind these people together. But now it is not clear in what sense goodness is being sought, nor that the theory is still telling us to maximize goodness.[4] True, the theory tells us to bring about this good, but now we cannot separate what is good, the love, from its goodness. And this simply is not Moore's utilitarianism.

Just as egoism and the above sorts of utilitarianisms necessitate a schizophrenia between reason and motive—and just as they cannot allow for love, friendship, affection, fellow feeling, and community—so do current rule utilitarianisms. And so do current deontologies.

What is lacking in these theories is simply—or not so simply—the person. For, love, friendship, affection, fellow feeling, and community all require that the other person be an essential part of what is valued. The person—not merely the person's general values nor even the person-qua-producer-or-possessor-of-general-values—must be valued. The defect of these theories in regard to love, to take one case, is not that they do not value love (which, often, they do not) but that they do not value the beloved. Indeed, a person who values and aims at simply love, that is, love-in-general or even love-in-general-exemplified-by-this-person "misses" the intended beloved as surely as does an adherent of the theories I have criticized.

The problem with these theories is not, however, with *other*-people-as-valuable. It is simply—or not so simply—with *people*-as-valuable. Just as they would do *vis-à-vis* other people, modern ethical theories would prevent each of us from loving, caring for, and valuing ourself—as opposed to loving, caring for, and valuing our general values or ourself-qua-producer-or-possessor-of-general-values. In these externality-ridden theories, there is as much a disappearance or nonappearance of the self as of other

[4]Taking love and people-in-certain-relations as intrinsically valuable helps show mistaken various views about acting rationally (or well). First, maximization: i.e., if you value "item" *C* and if state *S* has more *C* than does *S′*, you act rationally only if you choose *S*—unless *S′*, has more of other items you value than does *S*, or your cost in getting *S*, as opposed to *S′*, is too high, or you are not well enough informed. Where *C* is love (and indeed where *C* is many, if not most, valuable things), this does not hold—not even if all the values involved are self-regarding. Second, paying attention to value differences, being alive to them and their significance for acting rationally: just consider a person who (often) checks to see whether a love relation with another person would be "better" than the present love.

people. Their externality-ridden universes of what is intrinsically valuable are not solipsistic; rather, they are devoid of all people.[5]

It is a truism that it is difficult to deal with people as such. It is difficult really to care for them for their own sake. It is psychically wearing and exhausting. It puts us in too open, too vulnerable a position. But what must also be looked at is what it does to us—taken individually and in groups as small as a couple and as large as society—to view and treat others externally, as essentially replaceable, as mere instruments or repositories of general and non-specific value; and what it does to us to be treated, or believe we are treated, in these ways.

At the very least, these ways are dehumanizing. To say much more than this would require a full-scale philosophical anthropology showing how such personal relations as love and friendship are possible, how they relate to larger ways and structures of human life, and how they—and perhaps only they—allow for the development of those relations which are constitutive of a human life worth living: how, in short, they work together to produce the fullness of a good life, a life of eudaimonia.

Having said this, it must be acknowledged that there are many unclarities and difficulties in the notion of valuing a person, in the notion of a person-as-valuable. When we think about this—e.g., what and why we value—we seem driven either to omitting the person and ending up with a person-qua-producer-or-possessor-of-general-values or with a person's general values, or to omitting them and ending up with a bare particular ego.

In all of this, perhaps we could learn from the egoists. Their instincts, at least, must be to admit themselves, each for self, into their values. At the risk of absurdity—indeed, at the risk of complete loss of appeal of their view—what they find attractive and good about good-for-self must be, not only the good, but also and preeminently the for-self.

At this point, it might help to restate some of the things I have tried to do and some I have not. Throughout I have been concerned with what sort of motives people can have if they are to be able to realize the great goods of love, friendship, affection, fellow feeling, and community. And I have argued that, if we take as motives, embody in our motives, those various things which recent ethical theories hold to be ultimately good or right, we will, of necessity, be unable to have those motives. Love, friendship, affection, fellow feeling, and community, like many other states and activities, essentially contain certain motives and essentially preclude certain others; among those precluded we find motives comprising the justifications, the goals, the goods of those ethical theories most prominent today. To embody in one's motives the values of current ethical theories is to treat people externally and to preclude love, friendship, affection, fellow feeling, and community—both with others and with oneself. To get these great goods while holding those current ethical theories requires a schizophrenia between reason and motive.

I have not argued that if you have a successful love relationship, friendship, . . . , then you will be unable to achieve the justifications, goals, goods posited by those theories. You can achieve them, but not by trying to live the theory directly. Or, more exactly, to to the extent that you live the theory directly, to that extent you will fail to achieve its goods.

So far I have urged the charge of disharmony, bifurcation, schizophrenia only in regard to the personal relationships of love, friendship, affection, fellow feeling, and

[5]Moore's taking friendship to be an intrinsic good is an exception to this. But if the previous criticism of Moore holds, his so taking friendship introduces serious strains, verging on inconsistencies, into his theory.

community. The importance of these is, I would think, sufficient to carry the day. However, let us look at one further area: inquiry, taken as the search for understanding, wisdom. Although I am less sure here, I also think that many of the same charges apply.

Perhaps the following is only a special case, but it seems worth considering. You have been locked up in a psychiatric hospital, and are naturally most eager to get out. You ask the psychiatrist when you will be released; he replies, "Pretty soon." You find out that, instead of telling patients what he really believes, he tells them what he believes is good for them to hear (good for them to believe he believes). Perhaps you could "crack his code," by discovering his medical theories and his beliefs about you. Nonetheless, your further conversations—if they can be called that—with him are hardly the model of inquiry. I am not so unsure that we would be in a different position when confronted with people who engage in inquiry for their own sake, for God's glory, for the greatest pleasure, or even for the greatest good. Again, we might well be able to crack their codes—e.g., we could find out that someone believes his greatest chance for academic promotion is to find out the truth in a certain area. Nonetheless . . .

(Is the residual doubt "But what if he comes to believe that what is most pleasing to the senior professors will gain promotion; and how can we tell what he really believes?" of any import here? And is it essentially different from "But what if he ceases to value truth as such; and how can we tell what he really values?" Perhaps if understanding, not "mere knowledge," is the goal, there is a difference.)

It might be expected that, in those areas explicitly concerned with motives and their evaluation, ethical theories would not lead us into this disharmony or the corresponding morally defective life. And to some extent this expectation is met. But even in regard to moral merit and demerit, moral praise- and blameworthiness, the moral virtues and vices, the situation is not wholly dissimilar. Again, the problem of externality and impersonality, and the connected disharmony, arises.

The standard view has it that a morally good intention is an essential constituent of a morally good act. This seems correct enough. On that view, further, a morally good intention is an intention to do an act for the sake of its goodness or rightness. But now, suppose you are in a hospital, recovering from a long illness. You are very bored and restless and at loose ends when Smith comes in once again. You are now convinced more than ever that he is a fine fellow and a real friend—taking so much time to cheer you up, traveling all the way across town, and so on. You are so effusive with your praise and thanks that he protests that he always tries to do what he thinks is his duty, what he thinks will be best. You at first think he is engaging in a polite form of self-deprecation, relieving the moral burden. But the more you two speak, the more clear it becomes that he was telling the literal truth: that it is not essentially because of you that he came to see you, not because you are friends, but because he thought it his duty, perhaps as a fellow Christian or Communist or whatever, or simply because he knows of no one more in need of cheering up and no one easier to cheer up.

Surely there is something lacking here—and lacking in moral merit or value. The lack can be sheeted home to two related points: again, the wrong sort of thing is said to be the proper motive; and, in this case at least, the wrong sort of thing is, again, essentially external.[6]

[6]For a way to evade this problem, see my "Morally Good Intentions," *The Monist*, LIV, 1 (January 1970): 124–141, where it is argued that goodness and rightness need not be the object of a morally good intention, but rather that various goods or right acts can be.

SOME QUESTIONS AND CONCLUDING REMARKS

I have assumed that the reasons, values, justifications of ethical theories should be such as to allow us to embody them in our motives and still act morally and achieve the good. But why assume this? Perhaps we should take ethical theories as encouraging indirection—getting what we want by seeking something else: e.g., some say the economic well-being of all is realized, not by everyone's seeking it but by everyone's seeking his/her own well-being. Or perhaps we should take ethical theories as giving only indices, not determinants, of what is right and good.

Theories of indirection have their own special problems. There is always a great risk that we will get the something else, not what we really want. There are, also, these two related problems. A theory advocating indirection needs to be augmented by another theory of motivation, telling us which motives are suitable for which acts. Such a theory would also have to explain the connections, the indirect connections, between motive and real goal.

Second, it may not be very troubling to talk about indirection in such large-scale and multi-person matters as the economics of society. But in regard to something of such personal concern, so close to and so internal to a person as ethics, talk of indirection is both implausible and baffling. Implausible in that we do not seem to act by indirection, at least not in such areas as love, friendship, affection, fellow feeling, and community. In these cases, our motive has to do directly with the loved one, the friend, . . . , as does our reason. In doing something for a loved child or parent, there is no need to appeal to, or even think of, the reasons found in contemporary ethical theories. Talk of indirection is baffling, in an action- and understanding-defeating sense, since, once we begin to believe that there is something beyond such activities as love which is necessary to justify them, it is only by something akin to self-deception that we are able to continue them.

One partial defense of these ethical theories would be that they are not intended to supply what can serve as both reasons and motives; that they are intended only to supply indices of goodness and rightness, not determinants. Formally, there may be no problems in taking ethical theories this way. But several questions do arise. Why should we be concerned with such theories, theories that cannot be acted on? Why not simply have a theory that allows for harmony between reason and motive? A theory that gives determinants? And indeed, will we not need to have such a theory? True, our pre-analytic views might be sufficient to judge among index theories; we may not need a determinant theory to pick out a correct index theory. But will we not need a determinant theory to know why the index is correct, why it works, to know what is good about what is so indexed?[7]

Another partial defense of recent theories would be that, first, they are concerned almost entirely with rightness, obligation, and duty, and not with the whole of ethics;

[7]Taking contemporary theories to be index theories would help settle one of the longest-standing disputes in ethical philosophy—a dispute which finds Aristotle and Marx on the winning side and many if not most contemporary ethicists on the other. The dispute concerns the relative explanatory roles of pleasure and good activity and good life. Put crudely, many utilitarians and others have held that an activity is good only because and insofar as it is productive of pleasure; Aristotle and Marx hold of at least many pleasures that if they are good this is because they are produced by good activity. The problem of immoral pleasures has seemed to many the mo·t important test case for this dispute. To the extent that my paper is correct, we have another way to settle the dispute. For, if I am correct, pleasure cannot be what makes all good activity, good even prescinding from immoral pleasures. It must be activity, such as love and friendship, which make some pleasures good.

and, second, that within this restricted area, they do not suffer from disharmony or schizophrenia. To some extent this defense, especially its second point, has been dealt with earlier. But more should be said. It is perhaps clear enough by now that recent ethicists have ignored large and extremely important areas of morality—e.g., that of personal relations and that of merit. To this extent, the first point of the defense is correct. What is far from clear, however, is whether these theories were advanced only as partial theories, or whether it was believed by their proponents that duty and so on were really the whole, or at least the only important part, of ethics.

We might be advised to forget past motivation and belief, and simply look at these theories and see what use can be made of them. Perhaps they were mistaken about the scope and importance of duty and so on. Nonetheless they could be correct about the concepts involved. In reply, several points should be made. First, they were mistaken about these concepts, as even a brief study of supererogation and self-regarding notions would indicate. Second, these theories are dangerously misleading; for they can all too readily be taken as suggesting that all of ethics can be treated in an external, legislation-model, index way. (On "legislation-model" see below.) Third, the acceptance of such theories as partial theories would pose severe difficulties of integration within ethical theory. Since these theories are so different from those concerning, e.g., personal relations, how are they all to be integrated? Of course, this third point may not be a criticism of these theories of duty, but only a recognition of the great diversity and complexity of our moral life.[8]

In conclusion, it might be asked how contemporary ethical theories come to require either a stunted moral life or disharmony, schizophrenia. One cluster of (somewhat speculative) answers surrounds the preeminence of duty, rightness, and obligation in these theories. This preeminence fits naturally with theories developed in a time of diminishing personal relations; of a time when the ties holding people-together and easing the frictions of their various enterprises were less and less affection; of a time when commercial relations superseded family (or family like) relations; of a time of growing individualism. It also fits naturally with a major concern of those philosophers: legislation. When concerned with legislation, they were concerned with duty, rightness, obligation. (Of course, the question then is, Why were they interested in legislation, especially of this sort? To some small extent this has been answered, but no more will be said on this score.) When viewing morality from such a legislator's point of view, taking such legislation to be the model, motivation too easily becomes irrelevant. The legislator wants various things done or not done; it is not important why they are done or not done; one can count on and know the actions, but not the motives. (This is also tied up with a general devaluing of our emotions and emotional possibilities—taking emotions to be mere feelings or urges, without rational or cognitive content or constraint; and taking us to be pleasure-seekers and pain-avoiders—forgetting or denying that love, friendship, affection, fellow feeling, and desire for virtue are extremely strong movers of people.) Connected with this is the legislative or simply the third-person's-eye view, which assures us that others are getting on well if they are happy, if they are

[8]Part of this complexity can be seen as follows: Duty seems relevant in our relations with our loved ones and friends, only when our love, friendship, and affection lapse. If a family is "going well," its members "naturally" help each other; that is, their love, affection, and deep friendship are sufficient for them to care for and help one another (to put it a bit coolly). Such "feelings" are at times worn thin. At these times, duty may have to be looked to or called upon (by the agent or by others) to get done at least a modicum of those things which love would normally provide. To some rough extent, the frequency with which a family member acts out of duty, instead of love, toward another in the family is a measure of the lack of love the first has for the other. But this is not to deny that there are duties of love, friendship, and the like.

doing what gives them pleasure, and the like. The effect guarantees the cause—in the epistemic sense. (One might wonder whether the general empiricist confusion of *ratio cognescendi* and *ratio essendi* is at work here.)

These various factors, then, may help explain this rather remarkable inversion (to use Marx's notion): of taking the "effect," pleasure and the like, for the "cause," good activity.

Moore's formalistic utilitarianism and the traditional views of morally good action also suffer from something like an inversion. Here, however, it is not causal, but philosophical. It is as if these philosophers have taken it that, because these various good things can all be classified as good, their goodness consists in this, rather than conversely. The most general classification seems to have been reified and itself taken as the morally relevant goal.

These inversions may help answer a question which afflicts this paper: Why have I said that contemporary ethics suffers from schizophrenia, bifurcation, disharmony? Why have I not claimed simply that these theories are mistaken in their denomination of what is good and bad, right- and wrong-making? For it is clear enough that, if we aim for the wrong goal, then (in all likelihood) we will not achieve what we really want, what is good, and the like. My reason for claiming more than a mere mistake is that the mistake is well reasoned; it is closely related to the truth, it bears many of the features of the truth. To take only two examples (barring bad fortune and bad circumstances), good activity does bring about pleasure; love clearly benefits the lover. There is, thus, great plausibility in taking as good what these theories advance as good. But when we try to act on the theories, try to embody their reasons in our motives—as opposed to simply seeing whether our or others' lives would be approved of by the theories—then in a quite mad way, things start going wrong. The personalities of loved ones get passed over for their effects, moral action becomes self-stultifying and self-defeating. And perhaps the greatest madnesses of all are—and they stand in a vicious interrelation—first, the world is increasingly made such as to make these theories correct; and, second, we take these theories to be correct and thus come to see love, friendship, and the like only as possible, and not very certain, sources of pleasure or whatever. We mistake the effect for the cause and when the cause-seen-as-effect fails to result from the effect-seen-as-cause, we devalue the former, relegating it, at best, to good as a means and embrace the latter, wondering why our chosen goods are so hollow, bitter, and inhumane.

1976

Truth, Invention, and the Meaning of Life

David Wiggins

TRUTH, INVENTION, AND THE MEANING OF LIFE

Nul n'est besoin d'espérer pour entreprendre, ni de réussir pour persévérer.

William the Silent

Eternal survival after death completely fails to accomplish the purpose for which it has always been intended. Or is some riddle solved by my surviving for ever? Is not this eternal life as much of a riddle as our present life?

Wittgenstein

1. Even now, in an age not much given to mysticism, there are people who ask "What is the meaning of life?" Not a few of them make the simple "unphilosophical" assumption that there is something to be known here. (One might say that they are "cognitivists" with regard to this sort of question.) And most of these same people make the equally unguarded assumption that the whole issue of life's meaning presupposes some positive answer to the question whether it can be plainly and straightforwardly

David Wiggins, "Truth, Invention, and the Meaning of Life" (revised) from NEEDS, VALUES, TRUTH, Second Edition. Originally in *Proceedings of the British Academy* (read 24 November 1976). Reprinted with the permission of the author, The British Academy, and Blackwell Publishers, Ltd.

true that this or that thing or activity or pursuit is good, has value, or is worth something. And then, what is even harder, they suppose that questions like that of life's meaning must be among the central questions of moral philosophy.

The question of life's having a meaning and the question of truth are not at the centre of moral philosophy as we now have it. The second is normally settled by something bordering on stipulation,[1] and the first is under suspicion of belonging in the same class as "What is the greatest good of the greatest number?" or "What is the will?" or "What holds the world up?" This is the class of questions not in good order, or best not answered just as they stand.

If there is a semantical crux about this sort of occurrence of the word "meaning," then all logical priority attaches to it; and no reasonable person could pretend that a perfectly straightforward purport attaches to the idea of life's meaning something. But logical priority is not everything; and, most notably, the order of logical priority is not always or necessarily the same as the order of discovery. Someone who was very perplexed or very persistent would be well within his rights to insist that, where a question has been asked as often as this one has, a philosopher must make what he can of it: and that, if the sense really is obscure, then he must find what significance the effort to frame an answer is apt to *force* upon the question.

In what follows, I try to explore the possibility that the question of truth and the question of life's meaning are among the most fundamental questions of moral philosophy. The outcome of the attempt may perhaps indicate that, unless we want to continue to think of moral philosophy as the casuistry of emergencies, these questions and the other questions that they bring to our attention are a better focus for ethics and metaethics than the textbook problem "What [under this or that or the other circumstance] shall I do?" My finding will be that the question of life's meaning does, as the untheoretical suppose, lead into the question of truth—and conversely. Towards the end I shall also claim to uncover the possibility that philosophy has put happiness in the place that should have been occupied in moral philosophy by meaning. This is a purely theoretical claim, but if it is correct, it is not without consequences; and if (as some say) weariness and dissatisfaction have issued from the direct pursuit of happiness as such, then it is not without all explanatory power.

2. I have spoken in favor of the direct approach, but it is impossible to reach out to the perplexity for which the question of meaning is felt to stand without first recording the sense that, during relatively recent times, there has been some shift in the way the question of life's meaning is seen, and in the kind of answer it is felt to require. Here is an answer made almost exactly two hundred years ago, two years before the death of Voltaire:

> We live in this world to compel ourselves industriously to enlighten one another by means of reasoning and to apply ourselves always to carrying forward the sciences and the arts. (W. A. Mozart to Padre Martini: letter of 4 December 1776.)[2]

What we envy here is the specificity, and the certainty of purpose. But, even as we feel envy, it is likely that we want to rejoice in our freedom to disbelieve in that which provided the contingent foundation of the specificity and certainty. I make this remark, not because I think that we ought to believe in what Mozart and Padre Martini believed in, but in outright opposition to the hope that some relatively painless accommodation can

[1]In 1976, at the time of speaking, the remark stood in less need of qualification than it does now.

[2]Compare the composer's choice of expression on the occasion of his father's birthday anniversary in 1777: "I wish you as many years as are needed to have nothing left to do in music."

be made between the freedom and the certainty. The foundation of what we envy was the now (I think) almost unattainable conviction that there exists a God whose purpose ordains certain specific duties for all men, and appoints particular men to particular roles or vocations.

That conviction was not only fallible: there are many who would say that it was positively dangerous—and that the risk it carried was that, if the conviction were false, then one might prove to have thrown one's life away. It is true that in the cases we are considering, "throwing one's life away" seems utterly the wrong thing to say of the risk carried by the conviction. It seems wrong even for the aspects of these men's lives that were intimately conditioned by the belief in God. But if one doubts that God exists, then it is one form of the problem of meaning to justify not wanting to speak here of throwing a life away. It is a terrible thing to try to live a life without believing in *anything*. But surely that doesn't mean that just any old set of concerns and beliefs will do, provided one *could* live a life by them. Surely if any old set would do, that is the same as life's being meaningless.

If we envy the certainty of the 1776 answer, then most likely this is only one of several differences that we see between our own situation and the situation of those who lived before the point at which Darwin's theory of evolution so confined the scope of the religious imagination. History has not yet carried us to the point where it is impossible for a description of such differences to count as exaggerated. But they are formidable. And, for the sake of the clarity of what is to come, I must pause to express open dissent from two comments that might be made about them.

First, someone more interested in theory than in what it was like to be alive then and what it is like now may try to diminish the differences that we sense, by arguing from the accessibility to both eighteenth and twentieth centuries of a core notion of God, a notion that he may say persists in the concept of God championed by modern theologians. To this use of their ideas I object that, whatever gap it is which lies between 1776 and 1976, such notions as *God as the ground of our being* cannot bridge it. For recourse to these exemplifies a tendency towards an *a priori* conception of God which, even if the eighteenth century had had it, most of the men of that age would have hastened to amplify with a more hazardous *a posteriori* conception. Faith in God conceived *a posteriori* was precisely the cost of the particularity and definiteness of the certainty that we envy.

The other thing someone might say is that, in one crucial respect, our situation is not different from a late Enlightenment situation, because there is a conceptually determined need in which the eighteenth century stood and in which we stand equally. This, it might be said, is the need for commitment. In the eighteenth-century case, this extra thing was commitment to submission to God's purpose. . . . Faced however with this second comment, one might wonder how someone could come to the point of recognizing or even suspecting that it was God's purpose that he should be a composer (say) and yet be indifferent to that. Surely no extra anything, over and above some suspicion that this or that is God's purpose, is required to create the concern we should expect to find that that suspicion would have implanted in him. On the other hand, if this extra thing were supplied, then it would bring too much. For the commitment to submission seems to exclude rebellion; and rebellion against what is taken as God's purpose has never been excluded by the religious attitude as such.

What then are the similarities and the differences between the eighteenth-century orientation and our own orientation upon the meaning of life? It seems that the similarities that persist will hold between the conceptual scheme with which they in that century confronted the world of everyday experience and the scheme with which we, in spite of our thoroughgoing acceptance of natural science, confront it: and the dissimilarities will relate to the specificity and particularity of the focus of the various concerns in which their world-view involved them and our world-view involves us. For us there is less specificity and much less focus.

If this is still a dark statement, it is surely not so dark as to obscure the relationship between this difference between them and us and a cognate difference that will have signalled its presence and importance so soon as I prepared to approach the divide between the eighteenth and twentieth centuries by reference to the purposive or practical certainty of individual men. Unless we are Marxists, we are much more resistant in the second half of the twentieth century than eighteenth- or nineteenth-century men knew how to be against attempts to locate the meaning of human life or human history in mystical or metaphysical conceptions—in the emancipation of mankind, or progress, or the onward advance of Absolute Spirit. It is not that we have lost interest in emancipation or progress themselves. But, whether temporarily or permanently, we have more or less abandoned the idea that the importance of emancipation or progress (or a correct conception of spiritual advance) is that these are marks by which our minute speck in the universe can distinguish itself as the spiritual focus of the cosmos. Perhaps that is what makes the question of the meaning we can find in life so difficult and so desolate for us.

With these bare and inadequate historical assertions, however, the time is come to go straight to a modern philosophical account of the matter. There are not very many to choose from.

3. The account I have taken is that given in Chapter 18 of Richard Taylor's book *Good and Evil*—an account rightly singled out for praise by the analytical philosopher who reviewed the book for the *Philosophical Review.*[3]

Taylor's approach to the question whether life has any meaning is first to "bring to our minds a clear image of meaningless existence," and then determine what would need to be inserted into the meaningless existence so depicted in order to make it not meaningless. Taylor writes:

> A perfect image of meaninglessness of the kind we are seeking is found in the ancient myth of Sisyphus. Sisyphus, it will be remembered, betrayed divine secrets to mortals, and for this he was condemned by the gods to roll a stone to the top of the hill, the stone then immediately to roll back down, again to be pushed to the top by Sisyphus, to roll down once more, and so on again and again, *forever.*

Two ways are then mentioned in which this meaninglessness could be alleviated or removed. First:

> . . . if we supposed that these stones . . . were assembled [by Sisyphus] at the top of the hill . . . in a beautiful and enduring temple, then . . . his labors would have a point, something would come of them all . . .

That is one way. But Taylor is not in the end disposed to place much reliance in this species of meaning, being more impressed by a second mode of enrichment.

> Suppose that the gods, as an afterthought, waxed perversely merciful by implanting in [Sisyphus] a strange and irrational impulse . . . to roll stones . . . To make this more graphic, suppose they accomplish this by implanting in him some substance that has this effect on

[3]See Richard Taylor, *Good and Evil* (New York: Macmillan, 1970). The review was by Judith Jarvis Thomson, *Philosophical Review* vol. 81, 1973, p. 113.

> his character and drives . . . This little afterthought of the gods . . . was . . . merciful. For they have by this device managed to give Sisyphus precisely what he wants—by making him want precisely what they inflict on him. However it may appear to us, Sisyphus' . . . life is now filled with mission and meaning, and he seems to himself to have been given an entry to heaven . . . The *only* thing that has happened is this: Sisyphus has been reconciled to [his existence] . . . He has been led to embrace it. Not, however, by reason or persuasion, but by nothing more rational than the potency of a new substance in his veins . . .

So much for meaninglessness, and two ways of alleviating it. Meaninglessness, Taylor says,

> is essentially endless pointlessness, and meaningfulness is therefore the opposite. Activity, and even long drawn out and repetitive activity, has a meaning if it has some significant culmination, some more or less lasting end that can be considered to have been the direction and purpose of the activity.

That is the temple-building option, of course.

> But the descriptions so far also provide something else; namely, the suggestion of how an existence that is objectively meaningless, in this sense, can nevertheless acquire a meaning for him whose existence it is.

This "something else" is the option of implanting in Sisyphus the *impulse* to push what he has to push. Here Taylor turns aside to compare, in point of meaninglessness or meaningfulness, the condition of Sisyphus and the lives of various animals, working from the lower to the higher animals—cannibalistic blindworms, the cicada, migratory birds, and so on up to ourselves. His verdict is that the point of any living thing's life is evidently nothing but life itself.

> This life of the world thus presents itself to our eyes as a vast machine, feeding on itself, running on and on forever to nothing. And we are part of that life. To be sure, we are not just the same, but the differences are not so great as we like to think; many are merely invented and none really cancels meaninglessness . . . We are conscious of our activity. Our goals, whether in any significant sense we choose them or not, are things of which we are at least partly aware and can . . . appraise . . . Men have a history, as other animals do not. [Still] . . . if we think that, unlike Sisyphus', [our] labors do have a point, that they culminate in something lasting and, independently of our own deep interests in them, very worthwhile, then we simply have not considered the thing closely enough . . . For [Sisyphus' temple] to make any difference it had to be a temple that would at least endure, adding beauty to the world for the remainder of time. Our achievements . . . , those that do last, like the sandswept pyramids, soon become mere curiosities, while around them the rest of mankind continues its perpetual toting of rocks, only to see them roll down . . .

Here is a point that obsesses the author. Paragraph upon paragraph is devoted to describing the lamentable but undoubted impermanence (futility *sub specie aeternitatis*) of the architectural or built monuments of human labour. It is not entirely clear that the same effect could have been contrived if the gradual accumulation of scientific understanding or the multiplication of the sublime utterances of literature or music had been brought into the argument. What is clear is that Taylor is committed to a strong preference for the second method of enriching Sisyphus' life—that is the compulsion caused by the substance put into Sisyphus' veins. For as for the first method, and temple-building for the sake of the temple,

> Suppose . . . that after ages of dreadful toil, all directed at this final result [Sisyphus] did at last complete his temple, [so] that now he could say his work was done, and he could rest

> and forever enjoy the result. Now what? What picture now presents itself to our minds? It is precisely the picture of infinite boredom! Of Sisyphus doing nothing ever again, but contemplating what he has already wrought and can no longer add anything to, and contemplating it for eternity! Now in this picture we have a meaning for Sisyphus' existence, a point for his prodigious labor, because we have put it there; yet, at the same time, that which is really worthwhile seems to have slipped away entirely.

The final reckoning would appear to be this: (a) a lasting end or *telos* could constitute a purpose for the work; but (b) there is no permanence; and (c), even if there were such permanence, its point would be effectively negated by boredom with the outcome of the work. And so we are thrown inexorably into the arms of the other and second sort of meaning.

> We can reintroduce what has been resolutely pushed aside in an effort to view our lives and human existence with objectivity; namely, our own wills, our deep interest in what we find ourselves doing . . . Even the glow worms . . . whose cycles of existence over the millions of years seem so pointless when looked at by us, will seem utterly different to us if we can somehow try to view their existence from within. . . . If the philosopher is apt to see in this a pattern similar to the unending cycles of the existence of Sisyphus, and to despair, then it is indeed because the meaning and point he is seeking is not there—but mercifully so. The meaning of life is from within us, it is not bestowed from without, and it far exceeds in its beauty and permanence any heaven of which men have ever dreamed or yearned for.

4. Connoisseurs of twentieth-century ethical theory in its Anglo-Saxon and Continental variants will not be slow to see the affinities of this account. Practitioners of the first of these kinds are sometimes singled out for their failure to say anything about such questions as the meaning of life. But, if the affinities are as strong as I think, then, notwithstanding Taylor's philosophical distance from his contemporaries, what we have just unearthed has a strong claim to be their secret doctrine of the meaning of life.

Consider first the sharp supposedly unproblematic distinction, reinforced by the myth as told and retold here, between what we discover already there in the world—the facts, including the gods' enforcement of their sentence—and what is invented or, by thinking or willing, somehow *put into* or *spread onto* the factual world—namely the values.[4] Nobody who knows the philosophical literature on value will be surprised by Taylor's variant on the myth. . . . Here, however, at the point where the magic stuff is to be injected into the veins of Sisyphus, I must digress for the sake of what is to come, in order to explain the deliberate way in which I shall use the word "value."

I propose that we distinguish between *evaluations* (typically recorded by such forms as "x is good," "bad," "beautiful," "ugly," "ignoble," "brave," "just," "mischievous," "malicious," "worthy," "honest," "corrupt," "disgusting," "amusing," "diverting," "boring," *etc.*—no restrictions at all on the category of x) and *directive* or *deliberative* (or *practical*) *judgments* (*e.g.* "I must ψ," "I ought to ψ," "it would be best, all things considered, for me to ψ," *etc.*).[5] It is true that between these there is an important no-man's-land (comprising, *e.g.*, general judgments of the strongly deprecatory or commendatory kind about vices and virtues, and general or particular statements

[4]On the differences between discovery and invention, and on some abuses of the distinction, see William Kneale, "The Idea of Invention," *Proceedings of the British Academy* vol. 39, 1955.

[5]Note that this is not a distinction whose rationale is originally *founded* in a difference in the motivating force of judgments of the two classes, even if such a difference may be forthcoming from the distinction. In both cases, the thinking that p is arguably derivative from the *finding* that p.

about actions that it is ignoble or inhuman or unspeakably wicked to do or not to do).[6] But the fact that many other kinds of judgment lie between pure valuations and pure directives is no objection; and it does nothing to obstruct the discrimination I seek to effect between the fact–value distinction and the is–ought or is–must distinction. The unavailability of any well-grounded notion of the factual that will make the fact–value distinction an exclusive distinction can only promote our interest in the possibility of there being some *oughts* or *musts* that will not count as a case of an *is*. If we then conceive of a distinction between *is* and *must* as corresponding to the distinction between appreciation and decision and at the same time emancipate ourselves from a limited and absurd idea of what *is*, then there can be a new verisimilitude in our several accounts of all these things.[7]

This being proposed as the usage of the word "value" to be adhered to in this paper, let us return now to Sisyphus and the body of doctrine that is illustrated by Taylor's version of his story. At one moment Sisyphus sees his task as utterly futile and degrading: a moment later, supposedly without any initiating change in his cognitive appreciation, we are told that he sees his whole life as infinitely rewarding. What I was about to say before the digression was that there is only one philosophy of value that can even attempt to accommodate this possibility.

Consider next Taylor's account of the escape from meaninglessness—or what he might equally well have followed the Existentialists in calling *absurdity*. Taylor's mode of escape is simply a variation on the habitual philosophical reaction to the perception of the real or supposed meaninglessness of human existence. As a method for escape it is co-ordinate with every other proposal that is known, suicide (always one recognized way), scorn or defiance (Albert Camus), resignation or drift (certain orientally influenced positions), various kinds of commitment (R. M. Hare and J.-P. Sartre), and what may be the most recently enlisted member of this équipe, which is irony.[8]

Again, few readers of *Freedom and Reason* will fail to recognize in Sisyphus, after the injection of the gods' substance into his veins, a Mark I, stone-rolling model of R. M. Hare's further elaborated, rationally impregnable "fanatic."[9] As for the mysterious substance itself, surely this is some extra oomph, injected afterwards *ad libitum*, that will enable Sisyphus' factual judgments about stone-rolling to take on "evaluative meaning."

Finally, nor has nineteenth- or twentieth-century Utilitarianism much to fear from Taylor's style of fable-telling. For the *locus* or origin of all value has been firmly confined within the familiar area of psychological states conceived in independence of what they are directed to.[10]

In order to have a name, I shall call Taylor's and all similar accounts non-cognitive accounts of the meaning of life. This choice of name is not inappropriate if it helps to signal the association of these accounts with a long-standing philosophical tendency

[6]For some purposes, judgments that philosophers describe as judgments of *prima facie* obligation (better *pro tanto* obligation) might almost, or without excessive distortion be assimilated to valuational judgments.

[7]See below, §§6 and 10. In the language of note 20, ad fin, my own view is that the fact–value distinction is not like a *bat/elephant* distinction, but like an *animal/elephant* distinction. On the other hand, if §11 is right, then the *is/must* distinction is more like a *mammal/carnivore* distinction. For this possibility, see the diagram (p. 108) [p. 552 this volume] illustrating overlap of concept extensions.

[8]See Thomas Nagel, "The Absurd" in *Journal of Philosophy* vol. 68, 1971.

[9]R. M. Hare, *Freedom and Reason* (Oxford University Press, 1963). I mean that Sisyphus is the *stuff* of which the fanatic is made.

[10]For efforts in the direction of a better account of some of these states, see below §6.

to strive for descriptions of the human condition by which will and intellect-cum-perception are kept separate and innocent of all insider transactions. The intellect supplies uncontaminated factual perception, deduction, and means–end reasoning. Ends are supplied (in this picture) by feeling or will, which are not conceived either as percipient or as determinants in any interesting way of perception.

What I shall argue next is that, in spite of the well-tried familiarity of these ideas, the non-cognitive account depends for its whole plausibility upon abandoning at the level of theory the inner perspective that it commends as the only possible perspective upon life's meaning. This is a kind of incoherence, and one that casts some doubt upon the distinction of the inside and the outside viewpoints. I also believe that, once we break down the supposed distinction between the inner or participative and the outer, supposedly objective, viewpoints, there will be a route by which we can advance—though not to anything like the particularity of the moral certainty that we began by envying.

5. Where the non-cognitive account essentially depends on the existence and availability of the inner view, it is a question of capital importance whether the non-cognitivist's account of the inner view makes such sense of our condition as it actually has for us from the inside.

The first ground for suspecting distortion is that, if the non-cognitive view is put in the way Taylor puts it, then it seems to make too little difference to the meaningfulness of life how well or badly our strivings are apt to turn out. Stone-rolling for its own sake, and stone-rolling for successful temple building, and stone-rolling for temple building that will be frustrated—all seem to come to much the same thing. I object that that is not how it feels to most people. No doubt there are "committed" individuals like William the Silent or the doctor in Camus' *La Peste* who will constitute exceptions to my claim. But in general, the larger the obstacles nature or other people put in our way, and the more truly hopeless the prospect, the less point most of us will feel anything has. "Where there is no hope, there is no endeavor" as Samuel Johnson observed. In the end point is partly dependent on expectation of outcome; and expectation is dependent on past outcomes. So point is not independent of outcome.

The non-cognitivist may make two replies here. The first is that, in so far as the outcome is conceived by the agent as crucial for the value of the activity, the activity is merely instrumental and must lead back to other activities that are their own outcome. And these he will say are what matter. But in opposition to this,

a. I shall show in due course how activities that can be regarded as "their own goals" typically depend on valuations that non-cognitivism makes bad sense of (§6 below);
b. I shall question whether all activities that have a goal independent of the activity itself are perceived by their agents as only derivatively meaningful (§13 below).

The non-cognitivists' second reply will be directed against the objection that he makes it matter too little how well or badly our strivings turn out. Is it not a point on *his* side that the emptier and worse worlds where one imagines everything having even less point than it has now are worlds where the will itself will falter? To this I say Yes, I hear the reply. But if the non-cognitive view was to make the sense of our condition that we attribute to it, then something needed to be written into the non-cognitive account about what kinds of object will engage with the will as important. And it is still unclear at this stage how much room can be found within non-cognitivism for the will's own distinctions between good and bad reasons for caring about anything as important. Objectively speaking (once "we disengage our wills"), any reason is as good or as bad as any other reason, it seems to say. For on the non-cognitive account, life is *objectively* meaningless. So, by the non-cognitivist's lights, it must appear that whatever the will chooses to treat as a good reason to engage itself is, for the will, a good reason. But the will itself, taking the inner view, picks and chooses, deliberates, weighs, and tests its own concerns. It craves objective reasons; and often it could not go forward unless it thought it had them. The extension of the concept *objective* is quite different on the inner view from the extension assigned to it by the outer view. And the rationale for determining the extension is different also.

There is here an incoherence. To avoid it without flying in the face of what we think we know already about the difference between meaning and meaninglessness, the disagreement between the inner and the outer views must be softened somehow. The trouble is that, if we want to preserve any of the distinctive emphases of Taylor's and similar accounts, then we are bound to find that, for purposes of the validation of any given concern, the non-cognitive view always readdresses the problem to the inner perspective *without itself adopting that perspective.* It cannot adopt the inner perspective because, according to the picture that the non-cognitivist paints of these things, the inner view has to be unaware of the outer one, and has to enjoy essentially illusory notions of objectivity, importance, and significance: whereas the outer view has to hold that life is objectively meaningless. The non-cognitivist mitigates the outrageousness of so categorical a denial of meaning as the outer view issues by pointing to the availability of the participant perspective. But the most that he can do is to point to it. Otherwise the theorist is himself engulfed by a view that he must maintain to be false.

So much for the first distortion I claim to find in non-cognitivism and certain inconclusive defenses of that approach. There is also a second distortion.

To us there seems to be an important difference between the life of the cannibalistic blindworms that Taylor describes and the life of (say) a basking seal or a dolphin at play, creatures that are conscious, can rest without sleeping, can adjust the end to the means as well as the means to the end, and can take in far more about the world than they have the immediate or instrumental need to take in. There also seems to us to be a difference, a different difference, between the life of seals or dolphins and the life of human beings living in communities with a history. And there is even a third difference, which as participants we insist upon, between the life of a man who contributes something to a society with a continuing history and a life lived on the plan of a southern pig-breeder who (in the economics textbooks, if not in real life) buys more land to grow more corn to feed more hogs to buy more land, to grow more corn to feed more hogs . . . The practical concerns of this man are at once regressive and circular. And we are keenly interested, on the inner view, in the difference between these concerns and non-circular practical reasonings or life plans.

For the inner view, this difference undoubtedly exists. If the outside view is right to commend the inside view, then the outside view must pay some heed to the differences that the inner view perceives. But needing to depreciate them, it cannot accord them an importance that is commensurate with the weight that the non-cognitive theory of life's meaning thrusts upon the inner view. "The differences are merely invented," Taylor has to say, "and none really cancels the kind of meaninglessness we found in Sisyphus."

To the participant it may seem that it is far harder to explain what is so good about buying more land to grow more corn to feed more hogs to buy more land, to grow more corn to feed more hogs . . . than it is to explain what is good about digging a ditch with a man whom one likes, or helping the same man to talk or drink the sun down the sky. It might seem to a participant that the explanation of the second sort of thing, so far from having nowhere to go but round and round in circles, fans out into a whole arborescence of concerns; that, unlike any known explanation of what is so good about breeding hogs to buy more land to breed more hogs . . . , it can be pursued backwards and outwards to take in all the concerns of a whole life. But on the non-cognitive view of the inner view there is no way to make these differences stick. They count for so little that it is a mystery why the non-cognitivist doesn't simply say: life is meaningless; and that's all there is to it. If only he would make that pronouncement, we should know where we were.

But why do the differences just mentioned count for so little for the non-cognitivist? Because they all arise from subjective or anthropocentric considerations, and what is subjective or anthropocentric is not by the standards of the outer view objective. (Taylor insists that to determine whether something matters, we have to view it "independently of our own deep interest.") I shall come back to this when I reconstruct the non-cognitive view; but let me point out immediately the *prima facie* implausibility of the idea that the distinction between objectivity and non-objectivity (which appears to have to do with the existence of publicly accepted and rationally criticizable standards of argument, or of ratiocination towards truth) should coincide with the distinction between the anthropocentric and the non-anthropocentric (which concerns orientation towards human interests or a human point of view). The distinctions are not without conceptual links, but the *prima facie* appearance is that a matter that is anthropocentric may be either more objective or less objective, or (at the limit) *merely* subjective.[11] This is how things will appear until we have an argument to prove rigorously the mutual coincidence of independently plausible accounts of the anthropocentric/non-anthropocentric distinction, the non-objective/objective distinction, and the subjective/non-subjective distinction.[12]

The third and last distortion of experience I find in Taylor's presentation of non-cognitivism I shall try to convey by an anecdote. Two or three years ago, when I went to see some film at the Academy Cinema, the second feature of the evening was a documentary film about creatures fathoms down on the ocean-bottom. When it was over, I turned to my companion and asked, "What is it about these films that makes one feel so utterly desolate?" Her reply was: "apart from the fact that so much of the film was about sea monsters eating one another, the unnerving thing was that nothing down there ever seemed to *rest*." As for play, disinterested curiosity, or merely contemplating, she could have added, these seemed inconceivable.

At least about the film we had just seen, these were just the points that needed to be made—untrammelled by all pseudo-philosophical inhibitions, which are irrelevant in any case to the "inner" or participant perspective. And the thought the film leads to is this. If we can project upon a form of life nothing but the pursuit of life itself, if we find there no non-instrumental concerns and no interest in the world considered as lasting longer than the animal in question will need the world to last in order to sustain the an-

[11]For an independent account of the subjective, see Essay V [of *Needs, Values, Truth,* 2d ed. (Basil Blackwell Ltd., 1991)].

[12]A similar observation needs to be entered about all the other distinctions that are in the offing here—the distinctions between the neutral and the committed, the neutral and the biased, the descriptive and the prescriptive, the descriptive and the evaluative, the quantifiable and the unquantifiable, the absolute and the relative, the scientific and the unscientific, the not essentially contestable and the essentially contestable, the verifiable or falsifiable and the neither verifiable nor falsifiable, the factual and the normative. . . . In common parlance, and in sociology and economics—even in political science, which should know better—these distinctions are used almost interchangeably. But they are different. Each of these contrasts has its own rationale. An account of all of them would be a contribution not only to philosophy but to life.

imal's own life; then the form of life must be to some considerable extent alien to us.[13] Any adequate description of the point we can attach to our form of life must do more than treat our appetitive states in would-be isolation from their relation to the things they are directed at.

For purposes of his eventual philosophical destination, Richard Taylor had to forge an intimate and direct link between contemplation, permanence, and boredom. But, at least on the inner view, the connection between these things is at once extremely complex and relatively indirect.[14] And, once one has seen the final destination towards which it is Taylor's design to move the whole discussion, then one sees in a new light his obsession with monuments. Surely these are his hostages for the objects of psychological states in general; and all such objects are due to be in some sense discredited. (Discredited on the outer view, or accorded a stultifyingly indiscriminate tolerance on the outer account of the inner view.) And one comprehends all too well Taylor's sour grapes insistence on the impermanence of monuments—as if by this he could reduce to nil the philosophical (as opposed, he might say, to subjective) importance of all the objects of psychological states, longings, lookings, reverings, contemplatings, or whatever.

6. Leaving many questions still dangling, I shall conclude discussion of the outer account of the inner perspective with a general difficulty, and a suggestion.

There is a tendency, in Utilitarian writings and in the writings of economists,[15] to locate all ultimate or intrinsic value in human appetitive states.[16] They are contrasted (as we also see Taylor contrasting them for his purposes) with everything else in the world. According to this sort of view, the value of anything that is not a psychological state derives from the psychological state or states for which it is an actual or potential object. See here what Bentham says in *An Introduction to the Principles of Morals and Legislation:*

> Strictly speaking, nothing can be said to be good or bad, but either in itself; which is the case only with pain or pleasure; or on account of its effects; which is the case only with things that are the causes or preventives of pain and pleasure.

[13]Here, I think, or in this neighborhood, lies the explanation of the profound unease that some people feel at the systematic and unrelenting exploitation of nature and animals which is represented by factory farming, by intensive livestock rearing, or by the mindless spoliation of non-renewable resources. This condemnation of evil will never be understood till it is distinguished by its detractors from its frequent, natural, but only contingent concomitant—the absolute prohibition of all killing not done in self-defense.

[14]On permanence, *cf.* Wittgenstein *Tractatus Logico-Philosophicus* 6.4312 quoted *ad init.;* F. P. Ramsey, "Is there anything to discuss?," *Foundations of Mathematics and other Essays* (London, 1931):

> I apply my perspective not merely to space but also to time. In time the world will cool and everything will die; but that is a long time off still and its percent value at compound discount is almost nothing. Nor is the present less valuable because the future will be blank.

[15]*Cf.* Wilfred Beckerman, *New Statesman,* 21 June 1974, p. 880.

> The second, and real question is: at what rate should we use up resources in order to maximize the welfare of human beings . . . Throughout existence man has made use of the environment, and the only valid question for those who attach—as I do (in accordance with God's first injunction to Adam)—*complete and absolute priority to human welfare* is what rate of use provides the maximum welfare for humans, including future generations.

I quote this relatively guarded specimen to illustrate the hazards of making too easy a distinction between human welfare on the one side and the environment on the other. But it also illustrates the purely ornamental role which has devolved upon the Hebrew scriptures. They constitute matter for the literary decoration of sentiments formed and apprehended by quite different methods of divination. It is irrelevant for instance that the world-view given voice in the first chapters of *Genesis* is perceptibly more complicated than the one Beckerman expresses.

[16]Or in the case of vegetarian utilitarian writings, to locate all ultimate value in conscious animal appetitive states.

One has only to put the matter like this, however, to be troubled by a curious instability. Since nothing at all can count for the outer view as inherently or intrinsically good, the doctrine must belong to the inner or inside view. But, as experienced, the inner view too will reject this view of value. For, adopting that inner view,[17] and supposing with Bentham that certain conscious states are good in themselves, we must take these states as they appear to the inner view. But then one cannot say without radical misconception that these states are all that is intrinsically valuable. For (a) many of these conscious states have intentional objects; (b) many of the conscious states in which intrinsic value supposedly resides are strivings *after* objects that are not states, or are contemplations *of* objects that are not themselves states; and (c) it is of the essence of these conscious states, experienced as strivings or contemplations or whatever, to accord to their intentional objects a non-instrumental value. For from the inside of lived experience, and by the scale of value that that imposes, the shape of an archway or the sound of the lapping of the sea against the shore at some place at some time may appear to be of an altogether different order of importance from the satisfaction that some human being once had from his breakfast.[18]

The participant, with the going concepts of the objective and the worth while, descries certain external properties in things and states of affairs. And the presence there of these properties is what invests them with importance in his eyes. The one thing that properties cannot be, at least for him, is mere projections resulting from a certain kind of efficacy in the causation of satisfaction. For no appetitive or aesthetic or contemplative state can see its own object as having a value that is derivative in the special way that is required by the thesis that all non-instrumental value resides in human states of satisfaction. But, if that is right, then the outer view cannot rely for its credibility upon the meaning that the inner view perceives in something. To see itself and its object in the alien manner of the outer view, the state as experienced would have to be prepared to suppose that it, the state, could just as well have lighted on any other object (even any other kind of object), provided only that the requisite attitudes could have been induced. But in this conception of such states we are entitled to complain that nothing remains that we can recognize, or that the inner perspective will not instantly disown.[19]

[17]Perhaps some one individual man's inner view. For here and only here could it be held to be perfectly or fully obvious that the special goodness in themselves of certain of his pleasurable states is something simply above or beyond argument for him. Beyond that point—notwithstanding utilitarian explanations of the superfluity of argument on something so allegedly evident—it is less obvious to him.

[18]This feature of experience is of course lamented by thinkers who seek to make moral philosophy out of (("formal value theory" + moral earnestness) + some values of the theorist's own, generalized and thereby tested) + applications. But the feature is part of what is given in the phenomenology of some of the very same "satisfaction" experiences that are the starting-point of the utilitarians themselves. And there is nothing to take fright at in this feature of them, inconsistent though it is with absurd slogans of the literally absolute priority of human welfare.

[19]An example will make these claims clearer perhaps. A man comes at dead of night to a hotel in a place where he has never been before. In the morning he stumbles out from his darkened room and, following the scent of coffee out of doors, he finds a sunlit terrace looking out across a valley on to a range of blue mountains in the half-distance. The sight of them—a veritable vale of Tempe—entrances him. In marvelling at the valley and mountains he thinks only how overwhelmingly beautiful they are. The value of the state depends on the value attributed to the object. But the theory I oppose says all non-instrumental value resides here in the man's own state, and in the like states of others who are actually so affected by the mountains. The more numerous such states are, the greater, presumably, the theory holds, is the "realized" value of the mountains. The theory says that the whole actual value of the beauty of the valley and mountains is dependent upon arranging for the full exploitation of the capacity of these things to produce such states in human beings. (Exploitation now begun and duly recorded in Paul Jennings's Wordsworthian emendation: "I wandered lonely as a crowd.") What I am saying about the theory is simply that it is untrue to the actual experience of the object-directed states that are the starting-point of that theory.

I promised to conclude the critique of non-cognitivism with a suggestion about values. It is this: no attempt to make sense of the human condition can really succeed if it treats the objects of psychological states as unequal partners or derivative elements in the conceptual structure of values and states and their objects. This is far worse than Aristotle's opposite error:

> We desire the object because it seems good to us, rather than the object's seeming good to us because we desire it. *Metaphysics,* 1072a29

Spinoza appears to have taken this sentence as it stood and deliberately negated it (*Ethics,* part III, proposition 9, note). But maybe it is the beginning of real wisdom to see that we may have to side against both Aristotle and Spinoza here and ask: "Why should the *because* not hold both ways round?" Surely an adequate account of these matters will have to treat psychological states and their objects as equal and reciprocal partners, and is likely to need to see the identifications of the states and of the properties under which the states subsume their objects as interdependent. (If these interdependencies are fatal to the distinction of inner and outer, we are already in a position to be grateful for that.)

Surely it can be true both that we desire *x* because we think *x* good, and that *x* is good because *x* is such that we desire *x*. It does not count against the point that the explanation of the "because" is different in each direction. Nor does it count against the particular anti-non-cognitivist position that is now emerging in opposition to non-cognitivism that the second "because" might have to be explained in some such way as this: such desiring by human beings directed in this way is one part of what is required for there to be such a thing as the perspective from which the non-instrumental goodness of *x* is there to be perceived.

There is an analogy for this suggestion. We may see a pillar-box as red because it is red. But also pillar-boxes, painted as they are, *count* as red only because there actually exists a perceptual apparatus (*e.g.* our own) that discriminates, and learns on the direct basis of experience to group together, all and only the actually red things. Not every sentient animal that sees a red postbox sees it as red. But this in no way impugns the idea that redness is an external, monadic property of a postbox. "Red postbox" is not short for "red to human beings postbox." Red is not a relational property. (It is certainly not relational in the way in which "father of" is relational, or "moves" is relational on a Leibniz-Mach view of space.) All the same, it is in one interesting sense a *relative* property. For the category of color is an anthropocentric category. The category corresponds to an interest that can only take root in creatures with something approaching our own sensory apparatus.

Philosophy has dwelt nearly exclusively on differences between "good" and "red" or "yellow." I have long marvelled at this.[20] For there resides in the combined

[20]Without of course wishing to deny the difference that good is "attributive" to a marked degree, whereas color words are scarcely attributive at all, I think that, in these familiar discussions, philosophers have misdescribed the undoubted fact that, because there is no standing interest to which yellowness answers, "yellow" is not such as to be *cut out* (by virtue of standing for what it stands for) to commend a thing or evaluate it favorably. But, surely, if there were such a standing interest, "yellow" would be at least as well suited to commend as "sharp" or "beautiful" or even "just" are.

Against the suggestion that axiological predicates are a species of predicate not clearly marked off from the factual, there is a trick the non-cognitivist always plays and he ought not to be allowed to play. He picks himself a "central case" of a descriptive predicate, and a "central case" of a valuational predicate. Then he remarks how very different the predicates he has picked are. But what on earth can that show? Nobody thinks you could prove a bat was not an animal by contrasting some bat (a paradigm case of a bat) with some elephant (a paradigm case of an animal). Nothing can come clear from such procedures in advance of explana-

objectivity and anthropocentricity of color a striking analogy to illuminate not only the externality that human beings attribute to the properties by whose ascription they evaluate things, people, and actions, but also the way in which the quality *by* which the thing qualifies as good and the desire *for* the thing are equals—are "made for one another" so to speak. Compare the way in which the quality by which a thing counts as funny and the mental set that is presupposed to being amused by it are made for one another.

7. The time has come to sort out the non-cognitive theory to accommodate these findings and expel contradiction. But it is possible that I have not convinced you that any sorting out is necessary, and that you have found more coherent than I have allowed it to be the non-cognitivist's use of the idea of perspective, and of different and incompatible perspectives.

Perspective is not a form of illusion, distortion, or delusion. All the different perspectives of a single array of objects are perfectly consistent with one another. Given a set of perspectives, we can recover, if only they be reliably collected, a unified true account of the shape, spatial relations, and relative dimensions of the objects in the array. If we forget these platitudes then we may think it is much more harmless than it really is that the so-called outer and inner perspectives should straightforwardly contradict one another. There is nothing whatever in the idea of a perspective to license this scandalous idea—no more than the truism that two perspectives may include or exclude different aspects will create the license to think that the participant and external views, as the noncognitivist has described them, may unproblematically conflict over whether a certain activity or pursuit is really (or objectively) worth while or not.[21]

There are several different reasons then why the non-cognitivist theory must be redeployed, if it is to continue to be taken seriously. The traditional twentieth-century way

---

tion of the point of the contrast. In the present case the point of the factual/non-factual distinction has not been explained; and it has to be explained without begging the question in favor of the non-cognitivist, who picked the quarrel in the first place. What was the nature or rationale of the difference which was by these means to have been demonstrated? Till it is explained there must remain all the following possibilities:

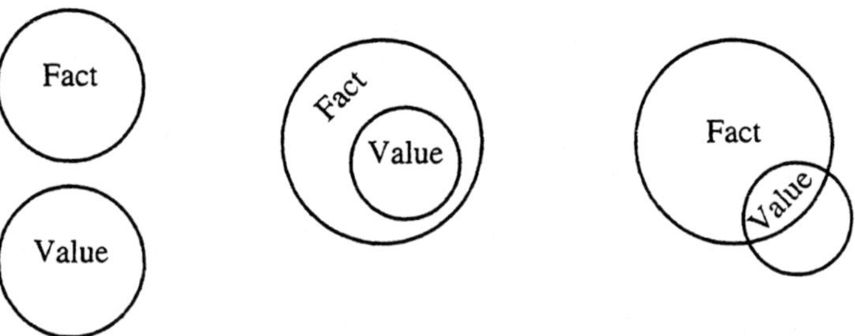

It would be unfair to say there have been no attempts at all to elucidate the point of the fact–value contrast as exclusive. Wittgenstein tried (unsuccessfully) to explain it so in his "Lecture on Ethics," *Philosophical Review* vol. 74, 1965, p. 6. And prescriptivists explain it as exclusive by reference to the link they allege holds between evaluation and action. But, although there is some such link between deliberative judgment and action, the required link does not hold between evaluation and action. That was one part of the point of the contrast I proposed at the beginning of §4.

[21]Still less does the language of perspective license the supposition that the philosopher who answers the question of the meaning of life could make a virtue out of committing himself to neither, or neither and both perspectives. Does he think of himself as one who somehow looks at everything from no perspective at all? For the closest approximation he could coherently conceive of attaining to this aspiration, see § 10 below.

of amending the theory to secure its self-consistency would have been *meta-ethics*, conceived as an axiologically neutral branch of "logic." Meta-ethics is not as neutral as was supposed. But it may be that it is still the best way for us to understand ourselves better.

Let us take the language of practice or morals as an object language. Call it L. The theorist's duty is then to discover, and to explain in the meta-language which is his own language, both a *formal theory* and a more discursive *informal theory* of L-utterances, not least L-utterances concerning what is worth while or a good thing to do with one's life. In place of philosophical analysis, let him concentrate on the informal elucidation of such judgments, then study the assertibility predicate in its application to various types of moral judgment and in each case determine its approximation there to genuine truth.

What does this involve? First, and this is the humble formal task that is presupposed to his more distinctively ethical aspirations, the theorist needs to be able to say, or assume that someone can say, what each of the sentences of the object language means. To achieve this, a procedure is needed for parsing L-sentences into their primitive semantic components, and an axiom is required for each primitive component accounting for its particular contribution to assertion conditions. Then, given any L-sentence s, the axioms can be deployed to derive a pairing of s with an assertion condition p, the pairing being stated in the meta-language by a theorem in the form:

s is assertible if and only if *p*.

Moral philosophy as we now know it makes many sophisticated claims about meaning and meanings, all hard to assess. Compared with everything that would be involved in making those assessments, what we are assuming here is minimal. What we are assuming is only that the informal remarks the moral theorist hopes to make about the status of this, that, or the other judgment in L will presuppose that such a biconditional can be constructed for each sentence of L. These assertion conditions give the meaning of the judgments he wants to comment upon. If no such principled understanding of what they mean may be thought of as obtainable, then (whatever other treasures he possesses) he cannot even count on the first thing.

I speak of *assertion* conditions as that by which meaning is given, and not yet of *truth* conditions, but only because within this meta-ethical framework the non-cognitivist's most distinctive non-formal thesis is likely to be the denial that the assertibility of a value judgment or of a deliberative judgment can amount to anything as objective as we suppose truth to be. To do justice to this denial of his, we leave undecided—as Dummett in one way and Davidson and McDowell in another have shown to be possible—the relationship of truth and assertibility.[22] In this way we arrange matters so that it can turn out—as it does for empirical or scientific utterances—that truth is a special case of assertibility; but it is not theoretically excluded that, for certain classes of judgments, assertibility should fall short of truth. The matter is left open, and it is for meta-ethics and the informal theory that is built around the formal theory to close it. I come now to this informal theory.

[22]See M. A. E. Dummett, *Frege: Philosophy of Language* (London: Duckworth, 1973) and John McDowell, "Bivalence and Verificationism" in *Truth and Meaning: Essays in Semantics* (Oxford University Press, 1972), edited by Gareth Evans and John McDowell. McDowell shows how we can build up an independent account of what a semantical predicate F will have to be like if the sentences of an object language are to be interpreted by means of equivalences which will say what the object language sentences mean. His way of showing that it can be a *discovery*, so to speak, that it is the truth predicate which fulfils the requirements on F is prefigured at p. 210 of Donald Davidson, "Truth and Meaning," *Synthèse* vol. 17, 1967.

Adapting Tarski's so-called "Convention T" to the purposes of the formal theory, we may say now that the meta-language has a materially adequate definition of the predicate "assertible" just in case it has as consequences all sentences obtained from the schema "*s* is assertible if and only if *p*" by substituting for "*s*" a name of any sentence of L and substituting for "*p*" the translation or interpretation of this sentence in the meta-language.[23] So if the ethical theorist is to erect a theory of objectivity, subjectivity, relativism, or whatever upon these foundations, then the next thing we need to say some more about is how a theory of L-assertibility is to be constrained in order to ensure that the sentence used on the right-hand side of any particular equivalence that is entailed by the theory of assertibility should indeed interpret or translate the sentence mentioned on the left. What is *interpretation* or *translation* in this context? If we can supply this constraint then, as a bonus, we shall understand far better the respective roles of participant and theorist and what assertibility would have to amount to.

It seems obvious that the only way to by-pass Tarski's explicit use of the word "translation" is by reference to what Davidson has called radical interpretation.[24] A promising proposal is this. Rewrite convention T to state that the meta-language possesses an empirically correct definition of "assertible" just in case the semantical axioms, in terms of which the definition of assertibility is given, all taken together, entail a set Σ of equivalences "*s* is assertible just in case *p*," one equivalence for each sentence of L, with the following overall property: a theorist who employs the condition *p* with which each sentence *s* is mated in a Σ-equivalence, and who employs the equivalence to interpret utterances of *s*, is in the best position he can be to make the *best possible overall sense* there is to be made of L-speakers. This goal sets a real constraint—witness the fact that the theorist may test his theory, try it out as a way of making sense of his subjects, even as he constructs it. By "making sense of them" would be meant ascribing to the speakers of L, on the strength of their linguistic and other actions, an intelligible collection of beliefs, needs, and concerns. That is a collection that diminishes to the bare minimum the need for the interpreter to ascribe inexplicable error or inexplicable irrationality to them.[25] By "interpreting an utterance of *s*" is intended here: saying what it is that *s* is used to say.

[23]See p. 187 of A. Tarski, "The Concept of Truth in Formalized Languages," in *Logic, Semantics, and Metamathematics* (Oxford University Press, 1956). For my present doubts that there is anything to be gained, except an expository point, by the fabrication of a predicate of semantic assessment that is independent of "true" in the fashion that "assertible" might seem to promise to be, see Essay IV, §18 following [*Needs, Values, Truth*].

[24]See D. Davidson, "Radical Interpretation," *Dialectica* vol. 27, 1973. The original problem is of course Quine's. See W. V. Quine, *Word and Object* (Cambridge, Mass: MIT Press, 1960). Davidson's own conception has been progressively refined by many philosophers, notably by Richard Grandy, Donald Davidson, Christopher Peacocke, Gareth Evans, and John McDowell.

[25]See Richard Grandy, "Reference, Meaning, and Belief," *Journal of Philosophy* vol. 70, 1973: John McDowell, *op. cit.* The requirement that we diminish to the minimum the theoretical need to postulate inexplicable error or irrationality is a precondition of trying to project any interpretation at all upon alien speakers. It was phrased by Davidson in another way, and called by him the requirement of charity. The replacement given here is closer to what has been dubbed by Richard Grandy the requirement of *humanity*. The further alterations reflect the belief that philosophy must desist from the systematic destruction of the sense of the word "want," and that what Davidson calls "primary reasons" must be diversified to embrace a wider and more diverse class of affective states than *desire*. (For a little more on these points, see now my *Sameness and Substance* [Oxford: Blackwell, 1980], Longer Note 6.36.)

Note that, even though we must for purposes of radical interpretation project upon L-speakers our own notions of rationality (and there is no proof they are the sole possible), and even though we take all the advantage we can of the fact that the speakers of the object-language are like us in being men, there is no guarantee that there must be a unique best theory of the assertibility conditions of their utterances. It has not been excluded that there might be significant disagreement between interpreters who have made equally good overall sense of the shared life of speakers of L, but at some points rejected one another's interpretations of L.

This general description is intended to pass muster for the interpretation of a totally alien language. But now suppose that we envisage the object-language and meta-language both being English. Then we can turn radical interpretation to advantage in order to envisage ourselves as occupying simultaneously the roles of theorist or interpreter and subject or participant. That will be to envisage ourselves as engaged in an attempt to understand ourselves.

Whether we think of things in this way or not, it is very important to note how essentially similar are the positions of the linguistic theorist and his subjects. The role of the theorist is only to *supplement,* for theoretical purposes, the existing understanding of L-speakers. It is true that, subject to the constraint upon which the whole exercise of interpretation itself rests—namely sufficient agreement in beliefs, concerns, and conceptions of what is rational and what is not—the theorist need not have exactly the same beliefs as his subjects. But the descriptions of the world that are available to him are essentially the same sorts of description as those available to his subjects. He uses the very same sort of sentence to describe the conditions under which *s* is assertible as the sentence *s* itself: and the meta-language is at no descriptive distance from the object-language. If the theorist believes his own semantic theory, then he is committed to be ready to put his mind where his mouth is at least once for each sentence *s* of the object-language, in a statement of assertion conditions for *s* in which he himself uses either *s* or a faithful translation of *s.* It follows that the possibility simply does not exist for the theorist to stand off entirely from the language of his subjects or from the viewpoint that gives this its sense. He has to begin at least by embracing—or by making as if to embrace—the very same commitments and world-view as the ordinary speakers of the object language. (This is not to say that having understood them, he cannot then back off from that world-view. What requires careful statement is how he is to do so.)

8. Even if this will be a disappointment to those who have supposed that, by means of meta-ethics, the theorist of value could move straight to a position of complete neutrality, it faces us in the right direction for the reconstitution of the non-cognitive theory. In fact the framework I have been proposing precisely enables him to register his own distinctive point. He can do so in at least two distinctive ways. The first accepts and the second actually requires that framework.

First, using the language of his subjects but thinking (as a moralist like a Swift or an Aristophanes should, or as any moral theorist may) a bit harder than the generality of his subjects, he may try to make them look at themselves; and he may prompt them to see their own pursuits and concerns in unaccustomed ways. There is an optical metaphor that is much more useful here than that of perspective. Staying within the participant perspective, what the theorist may do is *lower the level of optical resolution.* Suppressing irrelevancies and trivialities, he may perceive, and then persuade others to perceive, the capriciousness of some of the discriminations we unthinkingly engage in; or the obtuseness of some of the assimilations that we are content with. Again, rather differently but placing the non-cognitivist closer within reach of his own hobby-horse, he may direct the attention of his audience to what Aurel Kolnai called "the incongruities of ordinary practice."[26] Here Kolnai alluded to the irremovable disproportion between how heroic is the effort that it is biologically instinct in us to put into the pursuit of certain of our concerns, and how "finite, limited, transient, perishable, tiny, tenuous" we ourselves and our goods and satisfactions all are. To lower the level of resolution, not down to the point where human concerns themselves are invisible—we shall come to that—but to the point where both the disproportion and its terms are manifest, is a precondition of human (as opposed to merely animal) resilience, of humor, of

[26]"The Utopian Mind" (unpublished typescript), p. 77.

sense of proportion, of sanity even. It is the traditional function of the moralist who is a participant and of the satirist (who may want not to be). But this way of seeing is not the seeing of the total meaninglessness that Taylor spoke of. Nor, in the existentialist philosopher's highly technical sense, is it the perception of absurdity. For the participant perspective can contain together both the perception of incongruity and a nice appreciation of the limited but not necessarily infinitesimal importance of this or that particular object or concern. (It is not perfectly plain what Kolnai thought about the affinity of existentialist absurdity and incongruity—the manuscript is a fragment—but, if Kolnai had doubted the compatibility of the perceptions of incongruity and importance, I think I could have convinced him by a very Kolnaistic point. The disproportion between our effort and our transience is a fugitive quantity. It begins to disappear as soon as one is properly impressed by it. For it is only to us or our kind that our own past or future efforts can seem heroic.)

So much then for the non-cognitivist's first way of making his chief point. It will lead to nothing radical enough for him. The second way to make his point is to abstract it from the long sequence of preposterous attempts at traditional philosophical analysis of *good, ought, right, etc.* in terms of pleasure or feeling or approval . . . , and to transform it into an informal observation concerning the similarity or difference between the status of assertibility enjoyed by evaluative judgments and practical judgments, on the one hand, and the status of plain, paradigmatic, or canonical truth enjoyed by (for example) historical or geographical judgments on the other hand.[27]

What then is plain truth? Well, for purposes of the comparison, perhaps it will be good enough to characterize it by what may be called the truisms of plain truth. These truisms I take to be (1) the primacy of truth as a dimension for the assessment of judgments: (2) the answerability of truth to evidenced argument that will under favorable conditions converge upon agreement whose proper explanation involves that very truth; and (3) the independence of truth both from our will and from our own limited means of recognizing the presence or absence of the property in a statement. (2) and (3) together suggest the truism (4) that every truth is true in virtue of something. We shall expect further (5) that every plain truth is compatible with every other plain truth. Finally, a putative further truism (6*) requires the complete determinacy of truth and of all questions whose answers can aspire to that status.[28]

Does the assertibility of evaluative judgments and/or deliberative judgments come up to this standard? If we press this question within the framework just proposed, the non-cognitivist's distinctive doctrine becomes the contention that the answer is *no*. The question can be pressed from a point that is well within reach. We do not need to pretend to be outside our own conceptual scheme, or at a point that ought to have been both inaccessible and unthinkable.[29] The question is one we can pursue by working with informal elucidations of truth and assertibility that can be fruitfully constrained by the project of radical interpretation.[30] And as regards the apparent incoherence of Taylor's non-cognitivism, we can supersede the separate outer and inner perspectives by a common perspective that is accessible to both theorist and participant. Suppose it is asserted that this, that, or the other thing is worth doing, and that the assertion is made on the

[27]See in this connection Essay IV [*Needs, Values, Truth*].

[28]These formulations are superseded by the statement of the marks of truth given in §5 of Essay IV [*Needs, Values, Truth*]. (6*) does not survive there, for reasons that emerge in §10 below.

[29]Compare the manner in which we could ascertain from within the space that we occupy certain of the geometrical properties of that very space: e.g., discover whether all equilateral triangles we encounter, of whatever size, are in fact similar triangles. If not, then the space is non-Euclidean.

[30]Cp. Essay IV, §4 [*Needs, Values, Truth*].

best sort of grounds known to participant or theorist. Or suppose that a man dies declaring that his life has been marvelously worth while. The non-cognitive theory is first and foremost a theory not about the meaning but about the *status* of those remarks: that their assertibility is not plain truth and reflects no fact of the matter. What is more, this is precisely the suspicion that sometimes troubles and perplexes the untheoretical participant who is moved to ask the questions from which we began this inquiry. Finally, let it be noticed, and put down to the credit of the framework being commended, that within this it was entirely predictable that the question would be there to be asked.

9. The non-cognitivist's answer to the question can now be considered under two separate heads, value judgments (strict valuations) in general (this §) and deliberative judgments in general (§ 11).

For the non-cognitive critique of the assertibility predicate as it applies to value judgments I propose to employ a formulation given by Bernard Williams in "The Truth in Relativism," *Proceedings of the Aristotelian Society* (1974/5).

Relativism will be true, Williams says, just in case there are or can be systems of beliefs S_1 and S_2 such that:

1. S_1 and S_2 are distinct and to some extent self-contained;
2. Adherents of S_1 can understand adherents of S_2;
3. S_1 and S_2 exclude one another—by (a) being comparable and (b) returning divergent yes/no answers to at least one question identifying some action or object type which is the locus of disagreement under some agreed description;
4. S_1 and S_2 do not (for us here now, say) stand in real confrontation because, whichever of S_1 and S_2 is ours, the question of whether the other one is right lacks the relation to our concerns "which alone gives any point or substance to appraisal: the only real questions of appraisal [being] about real options" (p. 255). "For we recognize that there can be many systems S which have insufficient relation to our concerns for our [own] judgments to have any grip on them."

If this is right then the non-cognitivist critique of valuations comes to this. Their mere assertibility as such lacks one of the truistic properties of plain truth: for an assertible valuation may fail even under favorable conditions to command agreement (*cf.* truism (2) §8). Again, there is nothing in the assertibility property itself to guarantee that all one by one assertible evaluations are *jointly* assertible (*cf.* truism (5)). Nor is it clear that where there is disagreement there is always something or other at issue (*cf.* truism (4)). For truth on the other hand we expect and demand all of this.

The participant will find this disturbing, even discouraging. But is Williams right about the compatibility of his four conditions?[31] He mentions among other things undifferentiated judgments of "right" and "wrong," "ought" and "ought not." Here, where the point of agreement or disagreement or opting one way or another lies close to action, and radical interpretation is correspondingly less problematical, I think he is on strong ground. We can make good sense of conditions (2) and (3) being satisfied together. We can easily imagine condition (4) being satisfied. But for valuations in the

[31]Both for Williams's purposes and for ours—which is the status of the assertibility concept as it applies to value judgments, and then as it applies (§11) to deliberative or practical judgments—we have to be able to convert a relativism such as this, concerning as it does overall systems S_1 and S_2, into a relativism concerning this or that particular judgment or class of judgments identifiable and reidentifiable across S_1 and S_2. Williams requires this in order that disagreement shall be focused. I require it in order to see whether it is possible to distinguish judgments in S_1 or S_2 whose assertibility conditions coincide with plain truth from other judgments where this is dubious.

strict and delimited sense, such as "brave," "dishonest," "ignoble," "just," "malicious," "priggish," there is a real difficulty. The comparability condition (3) requires that radical interpretation be possible. But radical interpretation requires the projection by one person upon another of a collection of beliefs, desires, and concerns that differ from the interpreter's own only in a fashion that the interpreter can describe and, to some extent, explain: and the remoter the link between the word to be interpreted and action, and (which is different) the more special the flavor of the word, the more detailed and delicate the projection that has to be possible to anchor interpretation. Evaluations raise both of these problems at once. (And one of the several factors that make the link between strict valuations and action so remote is something that Williams himself has prominently insisted upon in other connections—the plurality, mutual irreducibility, and incommensurability of goods.) The more feasible interpretation is here, the smaller must be the distance between the concerns of interpreter and subject.[32] But then the harder condition (4) is to satisfy.

In the theoretical framework of radical interpretation we shall suddenly see the point of Wittgenstein's dictum (*Philosophical Investigations,* §242) "If language is to be a means of communication there must be agreement not only in definitions but, queer as this may sound, agreement in judgments also."[33]

10. The difficulty the non-cognitivist is having in pressing his claim at this point is scarcely a straightforward vindication of cognitivism. If the case for the coincidence of truth and assertibility in evaluative judgments is made in the terms of §9, then truth itself is in danger of coming in the process to seem a fairly parochial thing. It is strange to be driven to the conclusion that the more idiosyncratic the customs of a people, the more inscrutable their form of life, and the more special and difficult their language to interpret, the smaller the problem of the truth status of their evaluations.

It would be natural for someone perplexed by the question of the meaning of life to insist at this point that we shall not have found what it takes for individual lives to have the meaning we attribute to them unless we link meaning with rationality. He will say that the threat of relativism does not depend on Williams's condition (3) in Section VIII being satisfied. The threat is rather that, contrary to the tenor of §5, the reasons that impress us as good reasons have no foundation in reason at all. Or as Hume states the point in a famous passage of the First Appendix to the *Inquiry concerning the Principles of Morals:*

> It appears evident that the ultimate ends of human actions can never, in any case, be accounted for by *reason,* but recommend themselves entirely to the sentiments and affections of mankind, without any dependence on the intellectual faculties. Ask a man *why he uses exercise;* he will answer, *because he desires to keep his health.* If you then enquire, *why he desires health,* he will readily reply, *because sickness is painful.* If you push your enquiries farther, and desire a reason *why he hates pain,* it is impossible he can ever give any. This is an ultimate end, and is never referred to any other object.
>
> Perhaps to your second question, *why he desires health,* he may also reply, that *it is necessary for the exercise of his calling.* If you ask, *why he is anxious on that head,* he will answer, *because he desires to get money.* If you demand *Why? It is the instrument of pleasure,* says he. And beyond this it is an absurdity to ask for a reason. It is impossible there

[32]There are valuations which are so specific, and so special in their point, that interpretation requires interpreter and subject to have in some area of concern the very same interests and the same precise focus. But specificity is only one part of the problem.

[33]*Cf.* §241 and the rest of §242. *Cf.* also p. 223 (*passim*): "If a lion could talk, we couldn't understand him."

> can be a progress *in infinitum;* and that one thing can always be a reason why another is desired. Something must be desirable on its own account, and because of its immediate accord or agreement with human sentiment and affection.

Not only is it pointless to hope to discover *a rational* foundation in human sentiment and affection. It is not even as if human sentiment and affection will *effectively* determine the difference between the worth while and the not worth while. Each culture, and each generation in each culture, confronts the world in a different way and reacts to it in a different way.

This scepticism pointedly ignores all the claims I made earlier, in §5. Rallying to their support, I ask: What does this scepticism show about our own judgments of significance or importance? After all there is no such thing as a rational creature of no particular neuro-physiological formation or a rational man of no particular historical formation. And even if, inconceivably, there were such, why should we care about what this creature would find compelling? It is not in this make-believe context that we are called upon to mount a critique of our own conceptions of the objective, the true, and the worth while.

So much seems to hang on this, but the reply comes so close to simply repeating the words of the relativist whom it is meant to challenge, that there is no alternative but to illustrate what happens when we do try to think of rationality in the absolute impersonal or cosmic fashion that it seems our interlocutor requires.

It is interesting that, so far as rationality in theoretical beliefs is concerned, it is by no means impossible for us to conceive of thinking in the impersonal way. Suppose we take a Peircean view of Science as discovering that which is destined, the world being what it is, to be ultimately agreed by all who investigate.[34] Let "all" mean "all actual or possible intelligent beings competent, whatever their conceptual scheme, to look for the fundamental explanatory principles of the world." Then think of all these theories gradually converging through isomorphism towards identity. Cosmic rationality in belief will then consist in conforming one's beliefs so far as possible to the truths that are destined to survive in this process of convergence.[35]

Perhaps this is all make-believe. (Actually I think it isn't.) But the important thing is that, if we identify properties across all theories that converge upon what are destined to be agreed upon (by us or any other determined natural researchers) as the fundamental principles of nature, then the only non-logical, non-mathematical predicates we shall not discard from the language of rational belief are those which, in one guise or another, will always pull their weight in all explanatorily adequate theories of the world. As a result, and corresponding to predicates fit and not fit so to survive, we

[34]*Cf.* C. S. Peirce: "How to Make Our Ideas Clear," *Popular Science Monthly* vol. 12, 1878, pp. 286–302.

> Different minds may set out with the most antagonistic views, but the progress of investigations carries them by a force outside themselves to one and the same conclusion. This activity of thought by which we are carried, not where we wish but to a foreordained goal, is like the operation of destiny. No modification of the point of view taken, no selection of other facts for study, no natural bent of mind even, can enable a man to escape the predestinate opinion. This great law is embodied in the conception of truth and reality. The opinion which is fated to be ultimately agreed to by all who investigate is what we mean by the truth, and the object represented in this opinion is the real. That is the way I would explain reality.

[35]Inasmuch as there is a reality which dictates the way a scientific theory has to be in order that what happens in the world be explained by the theory, the difficulties of radical interpretation, attempted against the background of the truth about the world and the unwaveringly constant desire of speakers of the language to understand the material world, are at their slightest. Or so the upholder of a modest realism might maintain.

shall have a wonderful contrast between the primary qualities of nature and all other qualities. We can then make for ourselves a fact–value distinction that has a real and definite point. We can say that no value predicate stands for any real primary quality, and that the real properties of the world, the properties which inhere in the world *however it is viewed,* are the primary qualities.[36]

This is a very stark view. It expresses what was an important element of truth in the "external" perspective. Seeing the world in this way, one sees no meaning in anything.[37] But it is evidently absurd to try to reduce the sharpness of the viewpoint by saying that meaning can be introduced into the world thus seen by the addition of human commitment. Commitment to what? This Peircean conceptual scheme *articulates* nothing that it is humanly possible to care about. It does not even have the expressive resources to pick out the extensions of predicates like "red," "chair," "person," "famine." . . . For none of these has a strong claim to be factual by the scientific criterion. The distinction of fact and value we reach here, at the very limit of our understanding of scientific understanding, cannot be congruent with what the non-cognitivists intended as their distinction. It is as dubious as ever that there is anything for them to have intended. Starting out with the idea that value properties are mental projections, they have discovered that, if value properties are mental projections, then, except for the primary qualities, all properties are mental projections.

We come now to practical rationality for all conceivable rational agents. (Cosmically valid practical rationality.) The idea here would be, I suppose, that to be serious about objective reasons, or why anything matters, one must try to ascend closer to the viewpoint of an impersonal intelligence;[38] and that the properties of such an intelligence should be determinable *a priori.* A great deal of time and effort has been channelled into this effort. It might have been expected that the outcome would be the transformation of the bareness of our conception of an impersonal intelligence into the conception of an impersonal intelligence of great bareness. What was not so plainly to be expected was that the most elementary part of the subject should immediately collide—as it has—with a simple and (within the discipline thus *a priori* conceived) unanswerable paradox—the so-called "Prisoner's Dilemma."[39] What underlies the paradox

[36]One should talk here also of the fundamental physical constants. *Cf.* B. A. W. Russell, *Human Knowledge* (London, 1948), p. 41:

> These constants appear in the fundamental equations of physics . . . it should be observed that we are much more certain of the importance of these constants than we are of this or that interpretation of them. Planck's constant, in its brief history since 1900, has been represented in various ways, but its numerical value has not been affected . . . Electrons may disappear completely from modern physics but *e* [charge] and *m* [mass] are pretty certain to survive. In a sense it may be said that the discovery and measurement of these constants is what is most solid in modern physics.

[37]*Cf.* Tolstoy, *Anna Karenina,* Penguin, p. 820: "[Levin was] stricken with horror, not so much at death, as at life, without the least conception of its origin, its purpose, its reason, its nature. The organism, its decay, the indestructibility of matter, the law of the conservation of energy, evolution, were the terms that had superseded those of his early faith." This is a description of what might pass as one stage in the transition we have envisaged as completed.

[38]Compare Thomas Nagel "The Absurd," note 8, *op. cit.,* pp. 720 and 722, "the philosophical judgment [of absurdity] contrasts the pretensions of life with a larger context in which *no* standards can be discovered, rather than with a context from which alternative overriding standards may be applied."

[39]I take this as a "paradox" in the following sense: a general principle of decision-theoretic prudence, generalizable to any agent whatever caught in the relevant circumstances, will lead in a wide variety of applications to what must be agreed by everybody to be a situation which is worse than it might have been for each participant if he had not acted on the generalizable principle.

To say this is not to "solve" the paradox. It cannot be solved. But it could only be accounted a real paradox if there were some antecedent grounds to suppose that it *should* have been possible to construct an *a*

(or the idea that there *is* here some paradox) is the supposition that it is simply obvious that an *a priori* theory of rational action ought to be possible—that some cosmic peg must exist on which we can fasten a set of concerns clearly and unproblematically identified *independently* of all ideals of agency and rationality themselves. First you have a set of projects; then you think of a way that they might be best brought about. That was the picture. But, in a new guise, it was nothing other than the absurd idea that all deliberation is really of means.[40]

11. I conclude that there is no such thing as a pure *a priori* theory of rationality conceived in isolation from what it is for us as we are to have a reason: and that even if there were such a thing, it would always have been irrelevant to finding a meaning in life, or seeing anything as worthwhile. What we need is to define non-cognitivist relativism in a way that is innocent of all dependence on a contrast between our rationality and some purer rationality, yet restates the point we found in Taylor.

It now says: Perhaps all strict valuations of the more specific and interesting kind have the interesting property that the interpretation of the value predicate itself presupposes a shared viewpoint, and a set of concerns common between interpreter and subject. Let it be admitted that the exclusive fact–value distinction then fails. If a cognitivist insists, nothing need prevent him from exploiting the collapse of that distinction in order to redescribe in terms of a shift or wandering of the "value–focus" all the profound changes in valuation that have occurred in history, when the Greek world became the Christian world, or the Christian world the Renaissance world. The relativist will not forbid the cognitivist to say with Nicolai Hartmann, as John Findlay reports him, that these changes were all by-products of an intense consciousness of new values, whose swimming into focus pushed out the old: that such newly apprehended values were not really new, only hitherto ignored.[41]

All this the non-cognitivist may let pass as harmless, however eccentrically expressed; and may in less colorful language himself assert. He may even allow *totidem verbis* that, just as the world cannot be prised by us away from our manner of conceiving it, so our manner of conceiving it cannot be prised apart from our concerns themselves.[42] Again, it is open to him to assert the compatibility of anthropocentricity with

---

priori theory of rationality or prudence such that "rational (A)" is incompatible with "rational (not-A)," and such that that rationality is definable both independently of morality and ideals of agency and in such a way as to have independent leverage in these ancient disputes. (*Cf.* Plato, *Republic,* 445a.)

For an illuminating account of some of the asymmetries it is rational to expect between an *a priori* theory of belief and an *a priori* theory of practical reasonableness, see Ronald de Sousa, "The Good and the True," *Mind* vol. 83, 1974.

[40] That practically all interesting deliberation relates to ends and their practical specification in the light of actually or potentially available constituents, and that the place of means-ends reasoning is subordinate in practical reason, is argued by A. T. Kolnai, "Deliberation is of Ends," *Proceedings of the Aristotelian Society* (1962), and in Essay VI, a divergent interpretation of Aristotle's thought on this point, but an account similar to Kolnai's of the problem itself.

[41] See J. N. Findlay, *Axiological Ethics* (London: Macmillan, 1970). *Cf.* William James, *Talks to Teachers on Psychology: and to Students on some of Life's Ideals* (Longman, Green & Co., 1899), p. 299.

> In this solid and tridimensional sense, so to call it, those philosophers are right who contend that the world is a standing thing with no progress, no real history. The changing conditions of history touch only the surface of the show. The altered equilibriums and redistributions only diversify our opportunities and open chances to us for new ideals. But, with each new ideal that comes into life, the chance for a life based on some old ideal will vanish; and he would needs be a presumptuous calculator who should with confidence say that the total sum of significance is positively and absolutely greater at any one epoch than at any other of the world.

[42] *Cf.* A. J. Ayer, *The Central Questions of Philosophy* (London: Macmillan, 1974), p. 235: "we have seen that the world cannot be prised away from our manner of conceiving it."

the only thing that there is for us to mean by objectivity, and to concede that the differences between higher and lower forms of life are not fictitious. They are even objective, he will say, if you use the word "objective" like that. But here he will stick. Where he will not back down from Taylor's original position is in respect of Taylor's denial that these differences are *decisive.* Such differences may be important to us. But they depend for their significance upon a framework that is a free construct, not upon something fashioned in a manner that is answerable to how anything really is.

Here at last we approach the distinctive nucleus of non-cognitivism (married, without the consent of either, to Williams's relativism). What the new position will say is that, in so far as anything matters, and in so far as human life has the meaning we think it has, that possibility is rooted in something that is arbitrary, contingent, unreasoned, objectively non-defensible—and not one whit the less arbitrary, contingent and indefensible by virtue of the fact that the unconstrained inventive processes underlying it have been gradual, unconscious, and communal. Our form of life—or that in our form of life which gives individual lives a meaning—is not something that we as a species ever (as we say) found or discovered. It is not something that we can criticize or regulate or adjust with an eye to what is true or correct or reasonable. Even within the going enterprise of existing concerns and deliberations, it would be a sad illusion to suppose that the judgment that this or that is worthwhile, or that life is worth living (or worth leaving), would be simply and plainly true. That sort of *terra firma* is simply not to be had.

The doctrine thus reconstructed from the assets of bankrupted or naïve non-cognitivism I shall call the doctrine of cognitive underdetermination. Unlike the positions it descends from, this position does not contradict itself. It is consistent with its own rationale. It can be explained without entering at all into the difficulties and ineffabilities of cultural relativism. It can even be stated in a manner innocent of the commoner confusions between the idea that morality and culture are constructs and a more questionable idea, that the references (content/truth-value) of the judgments that these things make possible are constructs. (A sort of sense reference confusion.)

Suppose someone says: "For me it is neither here nor there that I cannot prise my way of seeing the world apart from my concerns. This does nothing to answer my complaint that there is not *enough* meaning in the world. My life doesn't add up. Nothing matters sufficiently to me. My concerns themselves are too unimportant, too scattered, and too disparate." Equally devastatingly to the naïve cognitivism that the doctrine of cognitive underdetermination bids us abandon, another one may say he finds that the objects of his concern beckon to him too insistently, too cruelly beguilingly, from too many different directions. "I have learned that I cannot strive after all of these objects, or minister even to most of the concerns that stand behind them. To follow more than a minute subset is to be doomed to be frustrated in all. The mere validity—if it were valid—of the total set from which I am to choose one subset would provide no guarantee at all that any subset I can actually have will *add up* to anything that means anything to me."

It is the undetermination theorist's role to comment here that things can never add up for the complainant who finds too frustratingly much, or for the complainant who finds too inanely little, unless each of us supplies something extra, some conception of his own, to make sense of things for *himself.*

The problem of living a life, he may say, is to realize or respect a long and incomplete or open-ended list of concerns which are always at the limit conflicting. The claims of all true beliefs (about how the world is) are reconcilable. Everything true must be consistent with everything else that is true (*cf.* truism (5) of §8). But not all the claims of all rational concerns or even of all moral concerns (that the world *be* thus or so) need be actually reconcilable. When we judge that this is what we must do now,[43] or that that is what we'd better do, or that our life must now take one direction rather than another direction, we are not fitting truths (or even probabilities) into a pattern where a discrepancy proves that we have mistaken a falsehood for a truth.[44] Often we have to make a practical choice that another rational agent might understand through and through, not fault or even disagree with, but (as Winch has stressed)[45] make differently himself; whereas, if there is disagreement over what is factually true and two rational men have come to different conclusions, then we think it has to be theoretically possible to uncover some discrepancy in their respective views of the evidence. In matters of fact, we suppose that, if two opposing answers to a yes/no question are equally good, then they might as well have been equally bad. But in matters of practice, we are grateful for the existence of alternative answers. The choice between them is then up to us. Here is our freedom. But here too is the bareness of the world we inhabit. If there were practical truth it would have to violate the third and fifth truisms of truth ((3) and (5) of §8 above). In living a life there is no truth, and there is nothing *like* plain truth, for us to aim at. Anybody who supposes that the assertibility of "I must do this" or the assertibility of "This is the way for me to live, not that" consists in their plain truth is simply deluded.

Aristotle wrote (*NE* 1094a23): "Will not knowledge of the good have a great influence on life? Shall we not, like archers who have a mark to aim at, be more likely to hit upon the right thing?" But in reality there is no such thing as *The Good,* no such thing as knowledge of it, and nothing fixed independently of ourselves to aim at. Or that is what is implied by the thesis of cognitive underdetermination.

12. If there is any common ground to be discovered in modern literature and one broad stream of modern philosophy it is here. What philosophers, even philosophers of objectivist formation, have constantly stressed is the absence of the unique solutions and unique determinations of the practical that naïve cognitivism would have predicted.[46] They have thus supplied the theoretical basis for what modern writers (not excluding modern writers who have believed in God) have felt rather as a void in our experience of the apprehension of value, and have expressed not so much

[43]I have put "*must,*" because *must* and *must not,* unlike *ought* and *ought not,* are genuine contraries.

[44]See B. A. O. Williams, "Consistency and Realism," *Proceedings of the Aristotelian Society Supplementary Volume,* 1966 and *cf.* J. N. Findlay, *op. cit.*, pp. 74–5:

> What is good [Hartmann tells us] necessarily lies in a large number of incompatible directions, and it is intrinsically impossible that all of these should be followed out into realization. One cannot, for example, achieve pure simplicity and variegated richness in the same thing or occasion, and yet both incontestably make claims upon us . . . in practice we sacrifice one good to another, or we make compromises and accommodations . . . such practical accommodations necessarily override the claims of certain values and everywhere consummate something that in some respect [ideally] ought not to be . . . a man [ideally should] be as wise as a serpent and gentle as a dove, but that does not mean that . . . it is *possible* for him to be both of them.

[45]Peter Winch, "The Universalizability of Moral Judgments," *Monist* vol. 49, 1965.

[46]The plurality and mutual irreducibility of things good has been stressed by F. Brentano (*Origins of Our Knowledge of Right and Wrong,* see especially para. 32); by N. Hartmann (see J. Findlay, *op. cit.*); by Isaiah Berlin, see, for instance, *Four Essays on Liberty* (Oxford University Press, 1969), Introduction p. XLIX; by A. T. Kolnai and B. A. O. Williams (*op. cit.*). See also Leszek Kolakowski, "In Praise of Inconsistency" in *Marxism and Beyond* (London, 1969); Stuart Hampshire, *Morality and Pessimism* (Cambridge University Press, 1972); and Essay VII [of *Needs, Values, Truth*].

in terms of the plurality and mutual irreducibility of goods as in terms of the need for an organizing focus or meaning or purpose that we ourselves *bring* to life. The mind is not only a receptor: it is a projector.[47]

At the end of *Anna Karenina* Levin says to himself: "I shall still lose my temper with Ivan the coachman, I shall still embark on useless discussions and . . . express my opinions inopportunely; there will still be the same wall between the sanctuary of my inmost soul and other people, even my wife . . . but my life now, my whole life, independently of anything that can happen to me, every minute of it is no longer meaningless as it was before, but has a positive meaning of goodness with which I have the power to invest it."

However remote such declarations may appear from the language of the non-cognitivist philosopher, this need for autonomous making or investing of which Levin speaks is one part of what, in my presentation of him, the non-cognitive philosopher means by cognitive underdetermination. The familiar idea is that we do not discover a meaning for life or strictly find one: we have to make do with an artifact or construct or projection—something as it were invented.[48] And, whereas discovery is answerable to truth, invention and construction are not. From this he concludes that a limited and low-grade objectivity is the very best one could hope for in predications of meaning or significance.

The non-cognitivist takes two steps here and the assessment of the second step concerning objectivity depends markedly on the notion of truth that is employed at the first. What is this notion, we need to know, and to what extent does the cognitivist's position depend upon a naïve and precritical understanding of it? Give or take a little—subtract perhaps the more indeterminate among subjunctive conditionals—the precritical notion of truth covers empirical judgments fairly well. But it consorts less well with conceptions of truth or assertibility defended in mathematics by mathematical intuitionists or mathematical constructivists. It is well worth remarking that, for someone who wanted to combine objectivity with a doctrine of qualified cognitivism or of underdetermination, there might be no better model than Wittgenstein's normative conception of the objectivity of mathematics; and no better exemplar than Wittgenstein's extended description of how a continuing cumulative process of making or constructing can amount to the creation of a shared form of life that is constitutive of rationality itself, furnishing proofs that are not compulsions but procedures

[47]For the seed of this idea in Plotinus' theory of cognition and for its transplantation and subsequent growth, see M. H. Abrams, *The Mirror and the Lamp* (Oxford University Press, 1953), Plotinus, *Ennead*, IV. 6.2–3: "The mind affirms something not contained within impression: this is the characteristic of a power—within its allotted sphere to act." "The mind gives radiance to the objects of sense out of its own store."

[48]For a remarkable expression of the non-cognitivist's principal point and some others, see Aldous Huxley, *Do As You Will* (London, 1929), p. 101:

> The purpose of life, outside the mere continuance of living (already a most noble and beautiful end), is the purpose we put into it. Its meaning is whatever we may choose to call the meaning. Life is not a crossword puzzle, with an answer settled in advance and a prize for the ingenious person who noses it out. The riddle of the universe has as many answers as the universe has living inhabitants. Each answer is a working hypothesis, in terms of which the answerer experiments with reality. The best answers are those which permit the answerer to live most fully, the worst are those which condemn him to partial or complete death. . . . Every man has an inalienable right to the major premiss of his philosophy of life.

If anything need be added to this, presumably it is only that, concerning what 'living most fully' is for each man, the final authority must be the man himself. There is something right with this; but there is something wrong with it too.

to guide our conceptions, explaining, without explaining away, our sense that sometimes we have no alternative but to infer this from that.[49]

Perhaps this is a million miles from ethics. Or perhaps Wittgenstein's philosophy of mathematics is completely unsuccessful. But if the subject-matter of moral philosophy had any of the features that Wittgenstein attributed to the sort of subject-matter he thought he was treating, then the issue whether the assertibility of practical judgments was truth, and did or did not sufficiently approximate to the truth of statements universally agreed to be factual, might become relatively unimportant.[50] We could measure the distance, assess its importance, and think how to live with it. (Is there an independent case for tampering in certain ways with the received truisms of truth? Or should we leave them to define an ideal that practical judgment must fall far short of? How important really is the shortfall?)

Of course, if practical judgments were candidates to be accounted simply true, then what made them true, unlike valuations,[51] could not be the world itself, whatever that is.[52] But, saying what they say, the world is not really what they purport to characterize. (Compare what Wittgenstein, whether rightly or wrongly, wanted to say about statements of arithmetic.) In the assertibility (or truth) of mathematical statements we see what perhaps we can never see in the assertibility of empirical (such as geographical or historical) statements: the compossibility of objectivity, discovery, *and* invention.

If we combine Wittgenstein's conception of mathematics with the constructivist or intuitionist views that are its cousins, then we find an illuminating similarity. One cannot get more out of the enterprise of making than one has in one way or another put there. ("What if someone were to reply to a question: 'So far there is no such thing as an answer to this question'?" *Remarks on the Foundations of Mathematics, IV. 9.*) And at any given moment one will have put less than everything into it. So however many determinations have been made, we never have a reason to think we have reached a point where no more decisions or determinations will be needed. No general or unrestricted affirmation is possible of the law of excluded middle. But then anyone who wishes to defend the truth status for practical judgments is released from claiming that every practical ques-

[49] *Cf.* L. Wittgenstein, *Remarks on the Foundation of Mathematics* (Oxford: Blackwell, 1956), III–30.

[50] There is a cheap victory to be won even here of course. For it has proved much easier to achieve convergence or reflective equilibrium within our culture about the value of, say, civil liberty than about how exactly printing extra bank-notes will act upon conditions of economic recession. But this is not the point I am making.

[51] Note that the distinction proposed at §4 between evaluation and practical judgment is observed both here and throughout this essay.

[52] Everything would be the wrong way round. *Cf.* B. A. O. Williams, "Consistency and Realism" (*op. cit.*, n. 44), p. 19:

> the line on one side of which consistency plays its peculiarly significant role is the line between the theoretical and the practical, the line between discourse which (to use a now familiar formula) has to fit the world, and discourse which the world must fit. With discourse that is practical in these terms, we can see why . . . consistency . . . should admit of exception and should be connected with coherence notions of a less logical character.

This whole passage suggests something important, not only about statements of what ideally should be, but also about deliberative judgments,—namely that the exigencies of having to decide what to believe are markedly dissimilar from the exigencies of having to decide how to act. What the argument does *not* show is that the only truth there could be in a practical judgment is a peculiar truth which transposes the onus of match on to the world. (Still less that, if one rejects that idea, then the onus of match would be from the sentence or its annexed action to an *ideal* world.) Williams has illuminatingly glossed (1) precisely why truth in a practical judgment would not be like that; (2) the reasons why "Ought (A)" and "Ought (not-A)" are actually consistent; and (3) why "must (A)" (which *is* inconsistent with "must (not-A)") is only strictly assertible or true if A is the unique thing you must here do.

tion already has an answer. For reasons both independent of the practical and helpful to its pretensions, we may doubt how mandatory it ever was to enter into the system of ideas and preconceptions that issues in such declarations as truism (6*) of §8 above.

I shall break off from these large questions with two points of comparison and contrast.

(i) It seems that in the sphere of the practical we may know for certain that there exist absolutely undecidable questions—*e.g.,* cases where the situation is so calamitous or the choices so insupportable that nothing could count as *the* morally reasonable answer. In mathematics, on the other hand, it appears to be an undecidable question even how much sense attaches to the idea of an absolutely undecidable question. This is a potentially important discrepancy between the two subject matters. If we insist upon the actuality of some absolute undecidability in the practical sphere, then we shall burst the bounds of ordinary, plain truth. To *negate* the law of excluded middle is to import a contradiction into the intuitionist logic which our comparison makes the natural choice for practical judgments. The *denial* of "((A would be right) or not (A would be right))" contradicts the intuitionist theorem "(not (not (p or not p))).

(ii) If a man makes an arithmetical mistake he may collide with a brick wall or miss a train. He may bankrupt himself. For each calculation there is some risk, and for each risk a clear mark of the worst's having befallen us. There is nothing so definite with practical judgments. But surely it is begging the question to require it. Equally, it is begging the question to shrug this off without another word.

13. Let us review what has been found, before trying to advance further.

However rarely or often practical judgments attain truth, and whatever is the extent and importance of cognitive underdetermination, we have found no overwhelming reason to deny all objectivity to practical judgments. That practical questions might have more than one answer, and that there is not always an ordering of better or worse answers, is no reason to conclude that good and bad answers cannot be argumentatively distinguished.

It is either false or senseless to deny that what valuational predicates stand for are properties in a world. It is neither here nor there that these value properties are not primary qualities, provided that they be objectively discriminable and can impinge upon practical appreciation and judgment. No extant argument shows that they cannot.

Individual human lives can have more or less point in a manner partially dependent upon the disposition in the world of these value properties. The naïve non-cognitivist has sometimes given the impression that the way we give point to our lives is as if by blindfolding ourselves and attaching to something—anything—some free-floating commitment, a commitment that is itself sustained by the mere fact of our animal life. But that was a mistake. There is no question here of blindfolding. And that is not what is said or implied by the reconstructed doctrine of cognitive underdetermination.

In as much as invention and discovery are distinguishable, and in so far as either of these ideas properly belongs here, life's having a point may depend as much upon something contributed by the person whose life it is as it depends upon something discovered. Or it may depend upon what the owner of the life brings to the world in order to see the world in such a way as to discover meaning. This cannot happen unless world and person are to some great extent reciprocally suited. And unluckily, all claims of human adaptability notwithstanding, those things are often not well suited to one another.

14. To get beyond here, something now needs to be said about the connection of meaning and happiness. In most moral philosophy, the requirement to treat meaning is commuted into the requirement to specify the end; and the end is usually identified with happiness. One thing that has seemed to make this identification plausible is the apparent correctness of the claim that happiness is the state of one's life having a point or meaning. But on any natural account of the relation of point and end, this claim is actually inconsistent with the equation "Happiness = The End." (Unless happiness can consist in simply having happiness as one's end.) It is also worth observing that, in the very special cases where it is straightforward to say what the point of someone's life is, we may say what he stands for, or may describe his life's work. (I choose these cases not because I think they are specially central but because they are specially clear.) The remarkable thing is that these specifications are not even categorically of a piece with happiness. That does not prove that happiness is *never* the point. The works of practical moralists are replete, however, with warnings of the difficulty or futility of making happiness the aim. If they are right then, by the same token, it would be futile to make it the point.

The misidentification—if misidentification it is—of happiness and end has had a long history. The first fully systematic equation of the end, the good for man, and happiness is Aristotle's. The lamentable and occasionally comical effects of this are much palliated by the close observation and good sense that Aristotle carried to the *specification* of happiness. And it may be said in Aristotle's defense that the charge of misidentification of happiness and the good for man is captious, because his detailed specification of *eudaimonia* can perfectly well stand in—if this be what is required—as a description of the point of human existence: also that Aristotle meant by *eudaimonia* not exactly happiness but a certain kind of success. But that is too quick. Unless we want to walk the primrose path to the trite and solemn conclusion that a meaningful life is just a sum (*cf. Nicomachean Ethics,* 1097b17) of activities worthwhile in themselves, or self-complete (in the sense of *Metaphysics,* 1048b17), the question is worth taking some trouble over. Not only is this proposition trite and solemn. Read in the way Aristotle intended it is absurd.

Out of good nature a man helps his neighbor dig a drainage ditch. The soil is hard but not impossibly intractable, and together the two of them succeed in digging the ditch. The man who offers to help sees what he is doing in helping dig the ditch as worthwhile. In so far as meaning is an issue for him, he may see the episode as all of a piece with a life that has meaning. He would not see it so, and he would not have taken on the task, if it were impossible. In the case as we imagine it, the progress of the project is integral to his pleasure in it. But so equally is the fact that he likes his neighbor and enjoys working with him (provided it be on projects that it is within their joint powers to complete).

Shall we say here that the man's helping dig the ditch is instrumental and has the meaning or importance it has for the helper only derivatively? Derivatively from what, on the non-cognitivist view? Or shall we say that the ditch-digging is worthwhile in itself? But it isn't. It is end-directed. If we cannot say either of these things, can we cut the Gordian knot by saying both? In truth, the embracing of the end depends on the man's feeling for the task of helping someone he likes. But his feeling for the project of helping equally depends on the existence and attainability of the end of digging the ditch.

This is not to deny that Aristotle's doctrine can be restored to plausibility if we allow the meaning of the particular life that accommodates the activity to *confer* intrinsic worth upon the activity. But this is to reverse Aristotle's procedure (which is the only procedure available to a pure cognitivist). And I doubt we have to choose (*cf.* §6). At its modest and most plausible best the doctrine of cognitive underdetermination can say that we need to be able to think in both directions, down from point to the human activities that answer to it, and up from activities whose intrinsic worth can be demonstrated by Aristotle's consensual method to forms of life in which we are capable by nature of finding point.[53]

15. It might be interesting and fruitful to pick over the wreckage of defunct and discredited ethical theories and see what their negligence of the problem of life's having a meaning contributed to their ruin. I have little to report under this head. But it does seem plain that the failure of naturalistic theories, theories reductively identifying the Good or the End with some natural reality, has been bound up with the question of meaning. Surely the failure of all the reductive naturalisms of the nineteenth century—Pleasure and Pain Utilitarianism, Marxism, Evolutionary Ethics—was precisely the failure to discover in brute nature itself (either in the totality of future pleasures or in the supposedly inevitable advance of various social or biological cum evolutionary processes), anything that the generality of untheoretical men could find reason to invest with overwhelming *importance.* These theories offered nothing that could engage in the right way with human concerns or give point or focus to anyone's life. (This is the cognitivist version of a point that ought to be attributed to David Hume.)

Naturalistic theories have been replaced in our own time by Prescriptivism, Emotivism, Existentialism, and Neutral (satisfaction-based) Utilitarianism. It is misleading to speak of them together. The second and third have had important affinities with moral Pyrrhonism. The first and fourth are very careful and, in the promotion of formal or second-order goods such as equality, tolerance, or consistency, rather earnest. But it is also misleading not to see these positions together.

Suppose that, when pleasure and absence of pain give place in an ethical theory to unspecified merely determinable satisfaction (and when the last drop of mentality is squeezed from the revealed preference theory which is the economic parallel of philosophical Utilitarianism), someone looks to modern Utilitarianism for meaning or happiness. The theory points him towards the greatest satisfaction of human beings' desires. He might embrace that end, if he could understand what that satisfaction consisted in. He might if he could see from his own case what satisfaction consisted in. But that is very likely where he started—unless, more wisely, he started closer to the real issue and was asking himself where he should look to find a point for his life. But, so far as either question is concerned, the theory has crossed out the infantile proposal "pleasure and lack of pain,"[54] and distorted and degraded (in description if not in fact) the complexity of the structure within which a man might have improved upon the childish answer for himself. For all questions of ends, all problems about what constitutes the attainment of

[53]Surely neither the consensual method nor the argued discussion of such forms would be possible in the absence of the shared neurophysiology that makes possible such community of concepts and such agreement as exists in evaluative and deliberative judgments. Nor would there be such faint prospects as there are of attaining reflective equilibrium or finding a shared mode of criticism. But nature plays only a causal and enabling role here, not the unconvincing speaking part assigned to it by Ethical Naturalism and by Aristotelian Eudaemonism. Aristotle qualified by the addition "in a complete life" (1098a16) the equation *eudaimonia = activity of soul in accordance with virtue.* And, tempering somewhat the *sum of goods* conception, he could agree with my strictures on the idea that the philosopher describes a meaning for life by building upwards from the special condition of its meaninglessness. But, as J. L. Austin used to complain, "If *life* comes in at all, it should not come into Aristotle's argument as an afterthought." And no help is to be had here from Aristotle's idea that, just as an eye has a function f such that the eye's goodness in respect of f = the good *for* the eye, so a man has his function. Eye:body::man:what? *Cf.* 1194b12. What is it for a man to find some function f that he can *embrace as his,* as giving his life meaning? Nature does not declare.

[54]For the thought that this might be literally infantile, I am indebted indirectly to Bradley and directly to Richard Wollheim, "The Good Self and the Bad Self," *Proceedings of the British Academy,* 1975.

given human ends, and all perplexities of meaning, have been studiously but fallaciously transposed by this theory into questions of instrumental means. But means to what? The theory is appreciably further than the nineteenth-century theory was from a conceptual appreciation of the structure of values and focused unfrustrated concerns presupposed to a man's finding a point in his life; and of the need to locate correctly happiness, pleasure, and a man's conception of his own unfolding life within that structure.

If we look to existentialism, we find something curiously similar. Going back to the formation of some of these ideas, I found André Maurois's description in *Call No Man Happy* (trans. Lindley: Cape; London, 1943, p. 43) of his teacher Alain (Emile-Auguste Chartier):

> what I cannot convey by words is the enthusiasm inspired in us by this search, boldly pursued with such a guide; the excitement of those classes which are entered with the persistent hope of discovering, that very morning, the secret of life, and from which one departed with the joy of having understood that perhaps there was no such secret but that nevertheless it was possible to be a human being and to be so with dignity and nobility. When I read in *Kim* the story of the Lama who sought so piously for the River of the Arrow, I thought of *our* search.

What goes wrong here—and remember that Alain was teacher not only of Maurois but also of Sartre—goes wrong even in the question "What is *the* meaning of life?" We bewitch ourselves to think that we are looking for some one thing like the Garden of the Hesperides, the Holy Grail . . . Then finding nothing like that in the world, no one thing from which all values can be derived and no one focus by which all other concerns can be organized, we console ourselves by looking inwards, but again for some one substitute thing, one thing in us now instead of the world. Of course if the search is conducted in this way it is more or less inevitable that the one consolation will be *dignity* or *nobility* or *commitment:* or more spectatorially *irony, resignation, scorn* . . . But, warm though its proper place is for each of these—important though each of them is in its own non-substitutive capacity—it would be better to go back to the "the" in the original question; and to interest ourselves afresh in what everybody knows about—the set of concerns he actually has, their objects, and the focus he has formed or seeks to bring to bear upon these: also the prospects of purifying, redeploying or extending this set.[55]

Having brought the matter back to this place, how can a theorist go on? I think he must continue from the point where I myself ought to have begun if the products of philosophy itself had not obstructed the line of sight: laboring within an intuitionism or moral phenomenology as tolerant of low-grade non-behavioral evidence as is literature (but more obsessively elaborative of the commonplace, and more theoretical, in the interpretive sense, than literature), he has to appreciate and describe the working day complexity of what is experientially involved in seeing a point in living. It is no use to take a going moral theory—Utilitarianism or whatever it is—and paste on to it such *postscripta* as the Millian insight "It really is of importance not only what men do, but what manner of men they are that do it": or the insight that to see a point in living a man has to be such that he can like himself: or to try to superimpose upon the theory the structure that we have complained that Utilitarianism degrades. If

[55]*Cf.* Williams, "Persons, Character and Morality" (pp. 208ff.), in Amelie Rorty (ed.), *The Identities of Persons* (University of California Press, 1976):

> The categorical desires which propel one forward do not have to be even very evident to consciousness, let alone grand or large; one good testimony to one's existence having a point is that the question of its point does not arise, and the propelling concerns may be of a relatively everyday kind such as certainly provide the ground of many sorts of happiness (*cf.* p. 209).

life's having a point is at all central to moral theory then room must be made for these things right from the very beginning. The phenomenological account I advocate would accommodate all these things in conjunction with (1) ordinary anthropocentric objectivity, (2) the elements of value-focus and discovery, and (3) the element of invention that it is the non-cognitivist's conspicuous distinction to have imported into the argument.

Let us not underestimate what would have been done if this work were realized. But ought the theorist to be able to do more? Reluctant though I am to draw any limits to the potentiality or enterprise of discursive reason, I see no reason why he should. Having tamed non-cognitivism and made of it a doctrine of cognitive underdetermination, which allows the world to impinge upon but not to determine the point possessed by individual lives, and which sees value properties not as created but as *lit up* by the focus that the one who lives the life brings to the world; and, having described what finding meaning is, it will not be for the theorist as such to insist on intruding himself further. As Bradley says in *Appearance and Reality* (450):

> If to show theoretical interest in morality and religion is taken as setting oneself up as a teacher or preacher, I would rather leave these subjects to whoever feels that such a character suits him.

1976

Moral Luck

Thomas Nagel

Kant believed that good or bad luck should influence neither our moral judgment of a person and his actions, nor his moral assessment of himself.

> The good will is not good because of what it effects or accomplishes or because of its adequacy to achieve some proposed end; it is good only because of its willing, i.e., it is good of itself. And, regarded for itself, it is to be esteemed incomparably higher than anything which could be brought about by it in favor of any inclination or even of the sum total of all inclinations. Even if it should happen that, by a particularly unfortunate fate or by the niggardly provision of a stepmotherly nature, this will should be wholly lacking in power to accomplish its purpose, and if even the greatest effort should not avail it to achieve anything of its end, and if there remained only the good will (not as a mere wish but as the summoning of all the means in our power), it would sparkle like a jewel in its own right, as something that had its full worth in itself. Usefulness or fruitlessness can neither diminish nor augment this worth.[1]

He would presumably have said the same about a bad will: whether it accomplishes its evil purposes is morally irrelevant. And a course of action that would be condemned if

[1] *Foundations of the Metaphysics of Morals,* first section, third paragraph.

Tom Nagel, "Moral Luck," *Proceedings of the Aristotelian Society* 50 (1976).

it had a bad outcome cannot be vindicated if by luck it turns out well. There cannot be moral risk. This view seems to be wrong, but it arises in response to a fundamental problem about moral responsibility to which we possess no satisfactory solution.

The problem develops out of the ordinary conditions of moral judgment. Prior to reflection it is intuitively plausible that people cannot be morally assessed for what is not their fault, or for what is due to factors beyond their control. Such judgment is different from the evaluation of something as a good or bad thing, or state of affairs. The latter may be present in addition to moral judgment, but when we blame someone for his actions we are not merely saying it is bad that they happened, or bad that he exists: we are judging *him,* saying he is bad, which is different from his being a bad thing. This kind of judgment takes only a certain kind of object. Without being able to explain exactly why, we feel that the appropriateness of moral assessment is easily undermined by the discovery that the act or attribute, no matter how good or bad, is not under the person's control. While other evaluations remain, this one seems to lose its footing. So a clear absence of control, produced by involuntary movement, physical force, or ignorance of the circumstances, excuses what is done from moral judgment. But what we do depends in many more ways than these on what is not under our control—what is not produced by a good or a bad will, in Kant's phrase. And external influences in this broader range are not usually thought to excuse what is done from moral judgment, positive or negative.

Let me give a few examples, beginning with the type of case Kant has in mind. Whether we succeed or fail in what we try to do nearly always depends to some extent on factors beyond our control. This is true of murder, altruism, revolution, the sacrifice of certain interests for the sake of others—almost any morally important act. What has been done, and what is morally judged, is partly determined by external factors. However jewel-like the goodwill may be in its own right, there is a morally significant difference between rescuing someone from a burning building and dropping him from a twelfth-story window while trying to rescue him. Similarly, there is a morally significant difference between reckless driving and manslaughter. But whether a reckless driver hits a pedestrian depends on the presence of the pedestrian at the point where he recklessly passes a red light. What we do is also limited by the opportunities and choices with which we are faced, and these are largely determined by factors beyond our control. Someone who was an officer in a concentration camp might have led a quiet and harmless life if the Nazis had never come to power in Germany. And someone who led a quiet and harmless life in Argentina might have become an officer in a concentration camp if he had not left Germany for business reasons in 1930.

I shall say more later about these and other examples. I introduce them here to illustrate a general point. Where a significant aspect of what someone does depends on factors beyond his control, yet we continue to treat him in that respect as an object of moral judgment, it can be called moral luck. Such luck can be good or bad. And the problem posed by this phenomenon, which led Kant to deny its possibility, is that the broad range of external influences here identified seems on close examination to undermine moral assessment as surely as does the narrower range of familiar excusing conditions. If the condition of control is consistently applied, it threatens to erode most of the moral assessments we find it natural to make. The things for which people are morally judged are determined in more ways than we at first realize by what is beyond their control. And when the seemingly natural requirement of fault or responsibility is applied in light of these facts, it leaves few pre-reflective moral judgments intact. Ultimately, nothing or almost nothing about what a person does seems to be under his control.

Why not conclude, then, that the condition of control is false—that it is an initially plausible hypothesis refuted by clear counter-examples? One could in that case look instead for a more refined condition which picked out the *kinds* of lack of control that really undermine certain moral judgments, without yielding the unacceptable conclusion derived from the broader condition, that most or all ordinary moral judgments are illegitimate.

What rules out this escape is that we are dealing not with a theoretical conjecture but with a philosophical problem. The condition of control does not suggest itself merely as a generalization from certain clear cases. It seems *correct* in the further cases to which it is extended beyond the original set. When we undermine moral assessment by considering new ways in which control is absent, we are not just discovering what *would* follow given the general hypothesis, but are actually being persuaded that in itself the absence of control is relevant in these cases too. The erosion of moral judgment emerges not as the absurd consequence of an over-simple theory, but as a natural consequence of the ordinary idea of moral assessment, when it is applied in view of a more complete and precise account of the facts. It would therefore be a mistake to argue from the unacceptability of the conclusions to the need for a different account of the conditions of moral responsibility. The view that moral luck is paradoxical is not a *mistake,* ethical or logical, but a perception of one of the ways in which the intuitively acceptable conditions of moral judgment threaten to undermine it all.

It resembles the situation in another area of philosophy, the theory of knowledge. There too conditions which seem perfectly natural, and which grow out of the ordinary procedures for challenging and defending claims to knowledge, threaten to undermine all such claims if consistently applied. Most skeptical arguments have this quality: they do not depend on the imposition of arbitrarily stringent standards of knowledge, arrived at by misunderstanding, but appear to grow inevitably from the consistent application of ordinary standards.[2] There is a substantive parallel as well, for epistemological skepticism arises from consideration of the respects in which our beliefs and their relation to reality depend on factors beyond our control. External and internal causes produce our beliefs. We may subject these processes to scrutiny in an effort to avoid error, but our conclusions at this next level also result, in part, from influences which we do not control directly. The same will be true no matter how far we carry the investigation. Our beliefs are always, ultimately, due to factors outside our control, and the impossibility of encompassing those factors without being at the mercy of others leads us to doubt whether we know anything. It looks as though, if any of our beliefs are true, it is pure biological luck rather than knowledge.

Moral luck is like this because while there are various respects in which the natural objects of moral assessment are out of our control or influenced by what is out of our control, we cannot reflect on these facts without losing our grip on the judgments.

There are roughly four ways in which the natural objects of moral assessment are disturbingly subject to luck. One is the phenomenon of constitutive luck—the kind of person you are, where this is not just a question of what you deliberately do, but of your inclinations, capacities, and temperament. Another category is luck in one's circumstances—the kind of problems and situations one faces. The other two have to do with the causes and effects of action: luck in how one is determined by antecedent circumstances, and luck in the way one's actions and projects turn out. All of them present a common problem. They are all opposed by the idea that one cannot be more culpable or estimable for anything than one is for that fraction of it which is under one's control. It seems irrational to take or dispense credit or blame for matters over which a person has

[2]See Thompson Clarke, "The Legacy of Skepticism," *Journal of Philosophy,* LXIX, no. 20 (November 9, 1972), 754–69.

no control, or for their influence on results over which he has partial control. Such things may create the conditions for action, but action can be judged only to the extent that it goes beyond these conditions and does not just result from them.

Let us first consider luck, good and bad, in the way things turn out. Kant, in the above-quoted passage, has one example of this in mind, but the category covers a wide range. It includes the truck driver who accidentally runs over a child, the artist who abandons his wife and five children to devote himself to painting,[3] and other cases in which the possibilities of success and failure are even greater. The driver, if he is entirely without fault, will feel terrible about his role in the event, but will not have to reproach himself. Therefore this example of agent-regret[4] is not yet a case of *moral* bad luck. However, if the driver was guilty of even a minor degree of negligence—failing to have his brakes checked recently, for example—then if that negligence contributes to the death of the child, he will not merely feel terrible. He will blame himself for the death. And what makes this an example of moral luck is that he would have to blame himself only slightly for the negligence itself if no situation arose which required him to brake suddenly and violently to avoid hitting a child. Yet the *negligence* is the same in both cases, and the driver has no control over whether a child will run into his path.

The same is true at higher levels of negligence. If someone has had too much to drink and his car swerves onto the sidewalk, he can count himself morally lucky if there are no pedestrians in its path. If there were, he would be to blame for their deaths, and would probably be prosecuted for manslaughter. But if he hurts no one, although his recklessness is exactly the same, he is guilty of a far less serious legal offense and will certainly reproach himself and be reproached by others much less severely. To take another legal example, the penalty for attempted murder is less than that for successful murder—however similar the intentions and motives of the assailant may be in the two cases. His degree of culpability can depend, it would seem, on whether the victim happened to be wearing a bullet-proof vest, or whether a bird flew into the path of the bullet—matters beyond his control.

Finally, there are cases of decision under uncertainty—common in public and in private life. Anna Karenina goes off with Vronsky, Gauguin leaves his family, Chamberlain signs the Munich agreement, the Decembrists persuade the troops under their command to revolt against the czar, the American colonies declare their independence from Britain, you introduce two people in an attempt at match-making. It is tempting in all such cases to feel that some decision must be possible, in the light of what is known at the time, which will make reproach unsuitable no matter how things turn out. But this is not true; when someone acts in such ways he takes his life, or his moral position, into his hands, because how things turn out determines what he has done. It is possible *also* to assess the decision from the point of view of what could be known at the time, but this is not the end of the story. If the Decembrists had succeeded

[3]Such a case, modelled on the life of Gauguin, is discussed by Bernard Williams in "Moral Luck" *Proceedings of the Aristotelian Society,* supplementary vol. L (1976), 115–35 (to which the original version of this essay was a reply). He points out that though success or failure cannot be predicted in advance, Gauguin's most basic retrospective feelings about the decision will be determined by the development of his talent. My disagreement with Williams is that his account fails to explain why such retrospective attitudes can be called moral. If success does not permit Gauguin to justify himself to others, but still determines his most basic feelings, that shows only that his most basic feelings need not be moral. It does not show that morality is subject to luck. If the retrospective judgment were moral, it would imply the truth of a hypothetical judgment made in advance, of the form "If I leave my family and become a great painter, I will be justified by success; if I don't become a great painter, the act will be unforgivable."

[4]Williams' term (*ibid.*).

in overthrowing Nicholas I in 1825 and establishing a constitutional regime, they would be heroes. As it is, not only did they fail and pay for it, but they bore some responsibility for the terrible punishments meted out to the troops who had been persuaded to follow them. If the American Revolution had been a bloody failure resulting in greater repression, then Jefferson, Franklin and Washington would still have made a noble attempt, and might not even have regretted it on their way to the scaffold, but they would also have had to blame themselves for what they had helped to bring on their compatriots. (Perhaps peaceful efforts at reform would eventually have succeeded.) If Hitler had not overrun Europe and exterminated millions, but instead had died of a heart attack after occupying the Sudetenland, Chamberlain's action at Munich would still have utterly betrayed the Czechs, but it would not be the great moral disaster that has made his name a household word.[5]

In many cases of difficult choice the outcome cannot be foreseen with certainty. One kind of assessment of the choice is possible in advance, but another kind must await the outcome, because the outcome determines what has been done. The same degree of culpability or estimability in intention, motive, or concern is compatible with a wide range of judgments, positive or negative, depending on what happened beyond the point of decision. The *mens rea* which could have existed in the absence of any consequences does not exhaust the grounds of moral judgment. Actual results influence culpability or esteem in a large class of unquestionably ethical cases ranging from negligence through political choice.

That these are genuine moral judgments rather than expressions of temporary attitude is evident from the fact that one can say *in advance* how the moral verdict will depend on the results. If one negligently leaves the bath running with the baby in it, one will realize, as one bounds up the stairs toward the bathroom, that if the baby has drowned one has done something awful, whereas if it has not one has merely been careless. Someone who launches a violent revolution against an authoritarian regime knows that if he fails he will be responsible for much suffering that is in vain, but if he succeeds he will be justified by the outcome. I do not mean that *any* action can be retroactively justified by history. Certain things are so bad in themselves, or so risky, that no results can make them all right. Nevertheless, when moral judgment does depend on the outcome, it is objective and timeless and not dependent on a change of standpoint produced by success or failure. The judgment after the fact follows from an hypothetical judgment that can be made beforehand, and it can be made as easily by someone else as by the agent.

From the point of view which makes responsibility dependent on control, all this seems absurd. How is it possible to be more or less culpable depending on whether a child gets into the path of one's car, or a bird into the path of one's bullet? Perhaps it is true that what is done depends on more than the agent's state of mind or intention. The problem then is, why is it not irrational to base moral assessment on what people do, in this broad sense? It amounts to holding them responsible for the contributions of fate as well as for their own—provided they have made some contribution to begin with. If we look at cases of negligence or attempt, the pattern seems to be that overall culpability corresponds to the product of mental or intentional fault and the seriousness of the outcome. Cases of decision under uncertainty are less easily explained in this way, for it seems that the overall judgment can even shift from positive to negative depending on

[5]For a fascinating but morally repellent discussion of the topic of justification by history, see Maurice Merleau-Ponty, *Humanisme et Terreur* (Paris: Gallimard, 1947), translated as *Humanism and Terror* (Boston: Beacon Press, 1969).

the outcome. But here too it seems rational to subtract the effects of occurrences subsequent to the choice, that were merely possible at the time, and concentrate moral assessment on the actual decision in light of the probabilities. If the object of moral judgment is the *person,* then to hold him accountable for what he has done in the broader sense is akin to strict liability, which may have its legal uses but seems irrational as a moral position.

The result of such a line of thought is to pare down each act to its morally essential core, an inner act of pure will assessed by motive and intention. Adam Smith advocates such a position in *The Theory of Moral Sentiments,* but notes that it runs contrary to our actual judgments.

> But how well soever we may seem to be persuaded of the truth of this equitable maxim, when we consider it after this manner, in abstract, yet when we come to particular cases, the actual consequences which happen to proceed from any action, have a very great effect upon our sentiments concerning its merit or demerit, and almost always either enhance or diminish our sense of both. Scarce, in any one instance, perhaps, will our sentiments be found, after examination, to be entirely regulated by this rule, which we all acknowledge ought entirely to regulate them.[6]

Joel Feinberg points out further that restricting the domain of moral responsibility to the inner world will not immunize it to luck. Factors beyond the agent's control, like a coughing fit, can interfere with his decisions as surely as they can with the path of a bullet from his gun.[7] Nevertheless the tendency to cut down the scope of moral assessment is pervasive, and does not limit itself to the influence of effects. It attempts to isolate the will from the other direction, so to speak, by separating out constitutive luck. Let us consider that next.

Kant was particularly insistent on the moral irrelevance of qualities of temperament and personality that are not under the control of the will. Such qualities as sympathy or coldness might provide the background against which obedience to moral requirements is more or less difficult, but they could not be objects of moral assessment themselves, and might well interfere with confident assessment of its proper object—the determination of the will by the motive of duty. This rules out moral judgment of many of the virtues and vices, which are states of character that influence choice but are certainly not exhausted by dispositions to act deliberately in certain ways. A person may be greedy, envious, cowardly, cold, ungenerous, unkind, vain, or conceited, but *behave* perfectly by a monumental effort of will. To possess these vices is to be unable to help having certain feelings under certain circumstances, and to have strong spontaneous impulses to act badly. Even if one controls the impulses, one still has the vice. An envious person hates the greater success of others. He can be morally condemned as envious even if he congratulates them cordially and does nothing to denigrate or spoil their success. Conceit, likewise, need not be displayed. It is fully present in someone who cannot help dwelling with secret satisfaction on the superiority of his own achievements, talents, beauty, intelligence, or virtue. To some extent such a quality may be the product of earlier choices; to some extent it may be amenable to change by current actions. But it is largely a matter of constitutive bad fortune. Yet people are morally condemned for such qualities, and esteemed for others equally beyond control of the will: they are assessed for what they are *like.*

[6] Pt II, sect. 3, Introduction, para. 5.

[7] "Problematic Responsibility in Law and Morals," in Joel Feinberg, *Doing and Deserving* (Princeton: Princeton University Press, 1970).

To Kant this seems incoherent because virtue is enjoined on everyone and therefore must in principle be possible for everyone. It may be easier for some than for others, but it must be possible to achieve it by making the right choices, against whatever temperamental background.[8] One may want to have a generous spirit, or regret not having one, but it makes no sense to condemn oneself or anyone else for a quality which is not within the control of the will. Condemnation implies that you should not be like that, not that it is unfortunate that you are.

Nevertheless, Kant's conclusion remains intuitively unacceptable. We may be persuaded that these moral judgments are irrational, but they reappear involuntarily as soon as the argument is over. This is the pattern throughout the subject.

The third category to consider is luck in one's circumstances, and I shall mention it briefly. The things we are called upon to do, the moral tests we face, are importantly determined by factors beyond our control. It may be true of someone that in a dangerous situation he would behave in a cowardly or heroic fashion, but if the situation never arises, he will never have the chance to distinguish or disgrace himself in this way, and his moral record will be different.[9]

A conspicuous example of this is political. Ordinary citizens of Nazi Germany had an opportunity to behave heroically by opposing the regime. They also had an opportunity to behave badly, and most of them are culpable for having failed this test. But it is a test to which the citizens of other countries were not subjected, with the result that even if they, or some of them, would have behaved as badly as the Germans in like circumstances, they simply did not and therefore are not similarly culpable. Here again one is morally at the mercy of fate, and it may seem irrational upon reflection, but our ordinary moral attitudes would be unrecognizable without it. We judge people for what they actually do or fail to do, not just for what they would have done if circumstances had been different.[10]

This form of moral determination by the actual is also paradoxical, but we can begin to see how deep in the concept of responsibility the paradox is embedded. A person can be morally responsible only for what he does; but what he does results from a

[8]"if nature has put little sympathy in the heart of a man, and if he, though an honest man, is by temperament cold and indifferent to the sufferings of others, perhaps because he is provided with special gifts of patience and fortitude and expects or even requires that others should have the same—and such a man would certainly not be the meanest product of nature—would not he find in himself a source from which to give himself a far higher worth than he could have got by having a good-natured temperament?" (*Foundations of the Metaphysics of Morals,* first section, eleventh paragraph).

[9]Cf. Thomas Gray, 'Elegy Written in a Country Churchyard':

Some mute inglorious Milton here may rest,
Some Cromwell, guiltless of his country's blood.

An unusual example of circumstantial moral luck is provided by the kind of moral dilemma with which someone can be faced through no fault of his own, but which leaves him with nothing to do which is not wrong. See chapter 5; and Bernard Williams, "Ethical Consistency," *Proceedings of the Aristotelian Society,* supplementary vol. XXXIX (1965), reprinted in *Problems of the Self* (Cambridge: Cambridge University Press, 1973), pp. 166–86.

[10]Circumstantial luck can extend to aspects of the situation other than individual behavior. For example, during the Vietnam War even U.S. citizens who had opposed their country's actions vigorously from the start often felt compromised by its crimes. Here they were not even responsible; there was probably nothing they could do to stop what was happening, so the feeling of being implicated may seem unintelligible. But it is nearly impossible to view the crimes of one's own country in the same way that one views the crimes of another country, no matter how equal one's lack of power to stop them in the two cases. One *is* a citizen of one of them, and has a connection with its actions (even if only through taxes that cannot be withheld)—that one does not have with the other's. This makes it possible to be ashamed of one's country, and to feel a victim of moral bad luck that one was an American in the 1960s.

great deal that he does not do; therefore he is not morally responsible for what he is and is not responsible for. (This is not a contradiction, but it is a paradox.)

It should be obvious that there is a connection between these problems about responsibility and control and an even more familiar problem, that of freedom of the will. That is the last type of moral luck I want to take up, though I can do no more within the scope of this essay than indicate its connection with the other types.

If one cannot be responsible for consequences of one's acts due to factors beyond one's control, or for antecedents of one's acts that are properties of temperament not subject to one's will, or for the circumstances that pose one's moral choices, then how can one be responsible even for the stripped-down acts of the will itself, if *they* are the product of antecedent circumstances outside of the will's control?

The area of genuine agency, and therefore of legitimate moral judgment, seems to shrink under this scrutiny to an extensionless point. Everything seems to result from the combined influence of factors, antecedent and posterior to action, that are not within the agent's control. Since he cannot be responsible for them, he cannot be responsible for their results—though it may remain possible to take up the aesthetic or other evaluative analogues of the moral attitudes that are thus displaced.

It is also possible, of course, to brazen it out and refuse to accept the results, which indeed seem unacceptable as soon as we stop thinking about the arguments. Admittedly, if certain surrounding circumstances had been different, then no unfortunate consequences would have followed from a wicked intention, and no seriously culpable act would have been performed; but since the circumstances were *not* different, and the agent *in fact* succeeded in perpetrating a particularly cruel murder, *that* is what he did, and that is what he is responsible for. Similarly, we may admit that if certain antecedent circumstances had been different, the agent would never have developed into the sort of person who would do such a thing; but since he *did* develop (as the inevitable result of those antecedent circumstances) into the sort of swine he is, and into the person who committed such a murder, *that* is what he is blameable for. In both cases one is responsible for what one actually does—even if what one actually does depends in important ways on what is not within one's control. This compatibilist account of our moral judgments would leave room for the ordinary conditions of responsibility—the absence of coercion, ignorance, or involuntary movement—as part of the determination of what someone has done—but it is understood not to exclude the influence of a great deal that he has not done.[11]

The only thing wrong with this solution is its failure to explain how skeptical problems arise. For they arise not from the imposition of an arbitrary external requirement, but from the nature of moral judgment itself. Something in the ordinary idea of what someone does must explain how it can seem necessary to subtract from it anything that merely happens—even though the ultimate consequence of such subtraction is that nothing remains. And something in the ordinary idea of knowledge must explain why it seems to be undermined by any influences on belief not within the control of the subject—so that knowledge seems impossible without an impossible foundation in autonomous reason. But let us leave epistemology aside and concentrate on action, character, and moral assessment.

[11]The corresponding position in epistemology would be that knowledge consists of true beliefs formed in certain ways, and that it does not require all aspects of the process to be under the knower's control, actually or potentially. Both the correctness of these beliefs and the process by which they are arrived at would therefore be importantly subject to luck. The Nobel Prize is not awarded to people who turn out to be wrong, no matter how brilliant their reasoning.

The problem arises, I believe, because the self which acts and is the object of moral judgment is threatened with dissolution by the absorption of its acts and impulses into the class of events. Moral judgment of a person is judgment not of what happens to him, but of him. It does not say merely that a certain event or state of affairs is fortunate or unfortunate or even terrible. It is not an evaluation of a state of the world, or of an individual as part of the world. We are not thinking just that it would be better if he were different, or did not exist, or had not done some of the things he has done. We are judging *him,* rather than his existence or characteristics. The effect of concentrating on the influence of what is not under his control is to make this responsible self seem to disappear, swallowed up by the order of mere events.

What, however, do we have in mind that a person must *be* to be the object of these moral attitudes? While the concept of agency is easily undermined, it is very difficult to give it a positive characterization. That is familiar from the literature on Free Will.

I believe that in a sense the problem has no solution, because something in the idea of agency is incompatible with actions being events, or people being things. But as the external determinants of what someone has done are gradually exposed, in their effect on consequences, character, and choice itself, it becomes gradually clear that actions are events and people things. Eventually nothing remains which can be ascribed to the responsible self, and we are left with nothing but a portion of the larger sequence of events, which can be deplored or celebrated, but not blamed or praised.

Though I cannot define the idea of the active self that is thus undermined, it is possible to say something about its sources. There is a close connection between our feelings about ourselves and our feelings about others. Guilt and indignation, shame and contempt, pride and admiration are internal and external sides of the same moral attitudes. We are unable to view ourselves simply as portions of the world, and from inside we have a rough idea of the boundary between what is us and what is not, what we do and what happens to us, what is our personality and what is an accidental handicap. We apply the same essentially internal conception of the self to others. About ourselves we feel pride, shame, guilt, remorse—and agent-regret. We do not regard our actions and our characters merely as fortunate or unfortunate episodes—though they may also be that. We cannot *simply* take an external evaluative view of ourselves—of what we most essentially are and what we do. And this remains true even when we have seen that we are not responsible for our own existence, or our nature, or the choices we have to make, or the circumstances that give our acts the consequences they have. Those acts remain ours and we remain ourselves, despite the persuasiveness of the reasons that seem to argue us out of existence.

It is this internal view that we extend to others in moral judgment—when we judge *them* rather than their desirability or utility. We extend to others the refusal to limit ourselves to external evaluation, and we accord to them selves like our own. But in both cases this comes up against the brutal inclusion of humans and everything about them in a world from which they cannot be separated and of which they are nothing but contents. The external view forces itself on us at the same time that we resist it. One way this occurs is through the gradual erosion of what we do by the subtraction of what happens.[12]

The inclusion of consequences in the conception of what we have done is an acknowledgment that we are parts of the world, but the paradoxical character of moral

[12]See P. F. Strawson's discussion of the conflict between the objective attitude and personal reactive attitudes in "Freedom and Resentment," *Proceedings of the British Academy,* 1962, reprinted in *Studies in the Philosophy of Thought and Action,* ed. P. F. Strawson (London: Oxford University Press, 1968), and in P. F. Strawson, *Freedom and Resentment and Other Essays* (London: Methuen, 1974).

luck which emerges from this acknowledgment shows that we are unable to operate with such a view, for it leaves us with no one to be. The same thing is revealed in the appearance that determinism obliterates responsibility. Once we see an aspect of what we or someone else does as something that happens, we lose our grip on the idea that it has been done and that we can judge the doer and not just the happening. This explains why the absence of determinism is no more hospitable to the concept of agency than is its presence—a point that has been noticed often. Either way the act is viewed externally, as part of the course of events.

The problem of moral luck cannot be understood without an account of the internal conception of agency and its special connection with the moral attitudes as opposed to other types of value. I do not have such an account. The degree to which the problem has a solution can be determined only by seeing whether in some degree the incompatibility between this conception and the various ways in which we do not control what we do is only apparent. I have nothing to offer on that topic either. But it is not enough to say merely that our basic moral attitudes toward ourselves and others are determined by what is actual; for they are also threatened by the sources of that actuality, and by the external view of action which forces itself on us when we see how everything we do belongs to a world that we have not created.

1978

Virtues and Vices

Philippa Foot

I

For many years the subject of the virtues and vices was strangely neglected by moralists working within the school of analytic philosophy. The tacitly accepted opinion was that a study of the topic would form no part of the fundamental work of ethics; and since this opinion was apparently shared by philosophers such as Hume, Kant, Mill, G. E. Moore, W. D. Ross, and H. A. Prichard, from whom contemporary moral philosophy has mostly been derived, perhaps the neglect was not so surprising after all. However that may be, things have recently been changing. During the past ten or fifteen years several philosophers have turned their attention to the subject; notably H. W. von Wright and Peter Geach. Von Wright devoted a not at all perfunctory chapter to the virtues in his book *The Varieties of Goodness*[1] published in 1963, and Peter

I am indebted to friends in many universities for their help in forming my views on this subject; and particularly to John Giuliano of UCLA, whose unpublished work on the unity of the virtues I have consulted with profit, and to Rosalind Hurtshouse who commented on a draft of the middle period.

[1]H. W. von Wright, The *Varieties of Goodness* (London, 1963).

Philippa Foot, "Virtues and Vices" from VIRTUES AND VICES AND OTHER ESSAYS IN MORAL PHILOSOPHY (Berkeley, CA: University of California Press, 1979). Reprinted with the permission of the author.

Geach's book called *The Virtues*[2] appeared in 1977. Meanwhile a number of interesting articles on the topic have come out in the journals.

In spite of this recent work, it is best when considering the virtues and vices to go back to Aristotle and Aquinas. I myself have found Plato less helpful, because the individual virtues and vices are not so clearly or consistently distinguished in his work. It is certain, in any case, that the most systematic account is found in Aristotle, and in the blending of Aristotelian and Christian philosophy found in St. Thomas. By and large Aquinas followed Aristotle—sometimes even heroically—where Aristotle gave an opinion, and where St. Thomas is on his own, as in developing the doctrine of the theological virtues of faith, hope and charity, and in his theocentric doctrine of happiness, he still uses an Aristotelian framework where he can: as for instance in speaking of happiness as man's last end. However, there are different emphases and new elements in Aquinas's ethics: often he works things out in far more detail than Aristotle did, and it is possible to learn a great deal from Aquinas that one could not have got from Aristotle. It is my opinion that the *Summa Theologica* is one of the best sources we have for moral philosophy, and moreover that St. Thomas's ethical writings are as useful to the atheist as to the Catholic or other Christian believer.

There is, however, one minor obstacle to be overcome when one goes back to Aristotle and Aquinas for help in constructing a theory of virtues, namely a lack of coincidence between their terminology and our own. For when we talk about the virtues we are not taking as our subject everything to which Aristotle gave the name *aretē* or Aquinas *virtus,* and consequently not everything called a virtue in translations of these authors. "The virtues" to us are the moral virtues whereas *aretē* and *virtus* refer also to arts, and even to excellences of the speculative intellect whose domain is theory rather than practice. And to make things more confusing we find some dispositions called moral virtues in translations from the Greek and Latin, although the class of virtues that Aristotle calls *aretai ēthikai* and Aquinas *virtutes morales* does not exactly correspond with our class of moral virtues. For us there are four cardinal moral virtues: courage, temperance, wisdom and justice. But Aristotle and Aquinas call only three of these virtues moral virtues; practical wisdom (Aristotle's *phronēsis* and Aquinas's *prudentia*) they class with the intellectual virtues, though they point out the close connections between practical wisdom and what they call moral virtues; and sometimes they even use *aretē* and *virtus* very much as we use "virtue."

I will come back to Aristotle and Aquinas, and shall indeed refer to them frequently in this paper. But I want to start by making some remarks, admittedly fragmentary, about the concept of a moral virtue as we understand the idea.

First of all it seems clear that virtues are, in some general way, beneficial. Human beings do not get on well without them. Nobody can get on well if he lacks courage, and does not have some measure of temperance and wisdom, while communities where justice and charity are lacking are apt to be wretched places to live, as Russia was under the Stalinist terror, or Sicily under the Mafia. But now we must ask to whom the benefit goes, whether to the man who has the virtue or rather to those who have to do with him? In the case of some of the virtues the answer seems clear. Courage, temperance and wisdom benefit both the man who has these dispositions and other people as well; and moral failings such as pride, vanity, worldliness, and avarice harm both their possessor and others, though chiefly perhaps the former. But what about the virtues of charity and justice? These are directly concerned with the welfare of others, and with what is owed to them; and since each may require sacrifice of interest on the part of the virtuous man

[2] Peter Geach, *The Virtues* (Cambridge, 1977).

both may seem to be deleterious to their possessor and beneficial to others. Whether in fact it is so has, of course, been a matter of controversy since Plato's time or earlier. It is a reasonable opinion that on the whole a man is better off for being charitable and just, but this is not to say that circumstances may not arise in which he will have to sacrifice everything for charity or justice.

Nor is this the only problem about the relation between virtue and human good. For one very difficult question concerns the relation between justice and the common good. Justice, in the wide sense in which it is understood in discussions of the cardinal virtues, and in this paper, has to do with that to which someone has a right—that which he is owed in respect of non-interference and positive service—and rights may stand in the way of the pursuit of the common good. Or so at least it seems to those who reject utilitarian doctrines. This dispute cannot be settled here, but I shall treat justice as a virtue independent of charity, and standing as a possible limit on the scope of that virtue.

Let us say then, leaving unsolved problems behind us, that virtues are in general beneficial characteristics, and indeed ones that a human being needs to have, for his own sake and that of his fellows. This will not, however, take us far towards a definition of a virtue, since there are many other qualities of a man that may be similarly beneficial, as for instance bodily characteristics such as health and physical strength, and mental powers such as those of memory and concentration. What is it, we must ask, that differentiates virtues from such things?

As a first approximation to an answer we might say that while health and strength are excellences of the body, and memory and concentration of the mind, it is the will that is good in a man of virtue. But this suggestion is worth only as much as the explanation that follows it. What might we mean by saying that virtue belongs to the will?

In the first place we observe that it is primarily by his intentions that a man's moral dispositions are judged. If he does something unintentionally this is usually irrelevant to our estimate of his virtue. But of course this thesis must be qualified, because failures in performance rather than intention may show a lack of virtue. This will be so when, for instance, one man brings harm to another without realizing he is doing it, but where his ignorance is itself culpable. Sometimes in such cases there will be a previous act or omission to which we can point as the source of the ignorance. Charity requires that we take care to find out how to render assistance where we are likely to be called on to do so, and thus, for example, it is contrary to charity to fail to find out about elementary first aid. But in an interesting class of cases in which it seems again to be performance rather than intention that counts in judging a man's virtue there is no possibility of shifting the judgment to previous intentions. For sometimes one man succeeds where another fails not because there is some specific difference in their previous conduct but rather because his heart lies in a different place; and the disposition of the heart is part of virtue.

Thus it seems right to attribute a kind of moral failing to some deeply discouraging and debilitating people who say, without lying, that they mean to be helpful; and on the other side to see virtue *par excellence* in one who is prompt and resourceful in doing good. In his novel *A Single Pebble* John Hersey describes such a man, speaking of a rescue in a swift flowing river

> It was the head tracker's marvellous swift response that captured my admiration at first, his split second solicitousness when he heard a cry of pain, his finding in mid-air, as it were, the only way to save the injured boy. But there was more to it than that. His action, which could not have been mulled over in his mind, showed a deep, instinctive love of life, a compassion, an optimism, which made me feel very good . . .

What this suggests is that a man's virtue may be judged by his innermost desires as well as by his intentions; and this fits with our idea that a virtue such as generosity lies as much in someone's attitudes as in his actions. Pleasure in the good fortune of others is, one thinks, the sign of a generous spirit; and small reactions of pleasure and displeasure often the surest signs of a man's moral disposition.

None of this shows that it is wrong to think of virtues as belonging to the will; what it does show is that "will" must here be understood in its widest sense, to cover what is wished for as well as what is sought.

A different set of considerations will, however, force us to give up any simple statement about the relation between virtue and will, and these considerations have to do with the virtue of wisdom. Practical wisdom, we said, was counted by Aristotle among the intellectual virtues, and while our *wisdom* is not quite the same as *phronēsis* or *prudentia* it too might seem to belong to the intellect rather than the will. Is not wisdom a matter of knowledge, and how can knowledge be a matter of intention or desire? The answer is that it isn't, so that there is good reason for thinking of wisdom as an intellectual virtue. But on the other hand wisdom has special connections with the will, meeting it at more than one point.

In order to get this rather complex picture in focus we must pause for a little and ask what it is that we ourselves understand by wisdom: what the wise man knows and what he does. Wisdom, as I see it, has two parts. In the first place the wise man knows the means to certain good ends; and secondly he knows how much particular ends are worth. Wisdom in its first part is relatively easy to understand. It seems that there are some ends belonging to human life in general rather than to particular skills such as medicine or boatbuilding, ends having to do with such matters as friendship, marriage, the bringing up of children, or the choice of ways of life; and it seems that knowledge of how to act well in these matters belongs to some people but not to others. We call those who have this knowledge wise, while those who do not have it are seen as lacking wisdom. So, as both Aristotle and Aquinas insisted, wisdom is to be contrasted with cleverness because cleverness is the ability to take the right steps to any end, whereas wisdom is related only to good ends, and to human life in general rather than to the ends of particular arts.

Moreover, we should add, there belongs to wisdom only that part of knowledge which is within the reach of any ordinary adult human being: knowledge that can be acquired only by someone who is clever or who has access to special training is not counted as part of wisdom, and would not be so counted even if it could serve the ends that wisdom serves. It is therefore quite wrong to suggest that wisdom cannot be a moral virtue because virtue must be within the reach of anyone who really wants it and some people are too stupid to be anything but ignorant even about the most fundamental matters of human life. Some people are wise without being at all clever or well informed: they make good decisions and they know, as we say, "what's what."

In short wisdom, in what we called its first part, is connected with the will in the following ways. To begin with it presupposes good ends: the man who is wise does not merely know *how* to do good things such as looking after his children well, or strengthening someone in trouble, but must also want to do them. And then wisdom, in so far as it consists of knowledge which anyone can gain in the course of an ordinary life, is available to anyone who really wants it. As Aquinas put it, it belongs "to a power under the direction of the will."[3]

[3]Aquinas, *Summa Theologica*, 1a2ae Q.56 a.3.

The second part of wisdom, which has to do with values, is much harder to describe, because here we meet ideas which are curiously elusive, such as the thought that some pursuits are more worthwhile than others, and some matters trivial and some important in human life. Since it makes good sense to say that most men waste a lot of their lives in ardent pursuit of what is trivial and unimportant it is not possible to explain the important and the trivial in terms of the amount of attention given to different subjects by the average man. But I have never seen, or been able to think out, a true account of this matter, and I believe that a complete account of wisdom, and of certain other virtues and vices must wait until this gap can be filled. What we can see is that one of the things a wise man knows and a foolish man does not is that such things as social position, and wealth, and the good opinion of the world, are too dearly bought at the cost of health or friendship or family ties. So we may say that a man who lacks wisdom "has false values," and that vices such as vanity and worldliness and avarice are contrary to wisdom in a special way. There is always an element of false judgment about these vices, since the man who is vain for instance sees admiration as more important than it is, while the worldly man is apt to see the good life as one of wealth and power. Adapting Aristotle's distinction between the weak-willed man (the *akratēs*) who follows pleasure though he knows, in some sense, that he should not, and the licentious man (the *akolastos*) who sees the life of pleasure as the good life,[4] we may say that moral failings such as these are never purely "akratic." It is true that a man may criticize himself for his worldliness or vanity or love of money, but then it is his values that are the subject of his criticism.

Wisdom in this second part is, therefore, partly to be described in terms of apprehension, and even judgment, but since it has to do with a man's attachments it also characterizes his will.

The idea that virtues belong to the will, and that this helps to distinguish them from such things as bodily strength or intellectual ability has, then, survived the consideration of the virtue of wisdom, albeit in a fairly complex and slightly attenuated form. And we shall find this idea useful again if we turn to another important distinction that must be made, namely that between virtues and other practical excellences such as arts and skills.

Aristotle has sometimes been accused, for instance by von Wright, of failing to see how different virtues are from arts or skills;[5] but in fact one finds, among the many things that Aristotle and Aquinas say about this difference, the observation that seems to go the heart of the matter. In the matter of arts and skills, they say, voluntary error is preferable to involuntary error, while in the matter of virtues (what we call virtues) it is the reverse.[6] The last part of the thesis is actually rather hard to interpret, because it is not clear what is meant by the idea of involuntary viciousness. But we can leave this aside and still have all we need in order to distinguish arts or skills from virtues. If we think, for instance, of someone who deliberately makes a spelling mistake (perhaps when writing on the blackboard in order to explain this particular point) we see that this does not in any way count against his skill as a speller: "I did it deliberately" rebuts an accusation of this kind. And what we can say without running into any difficulties is that there is no comparable rebuttal in the case of an accusation relating to lack of virtue. If a man acts unjustly or uncharitably, or in a cowardly or intemperate manner, "I

[4]Aristotle, *Nicomachean Ethics*, especially bk. VII.
[5]von Wright op. cit. chapter VIII.
[6]Aristotle op. cit. 1140 b 22–25. Aquinas op. cit. 1a2ae Q.57 a.4.

did it deliberately" cannot on any interpretation lead to exculpation. So, we may say, a virtue is not, like a skill or an art, a mere capacity: it must actually engage the will.

II

I shall now turn to another thesis about the virtues, which I might express by saying that they are *corrective,* each one standing at a point at which there is some temptation to be resisted or deficiency of motivation to be made good. As Aristotle put it, virtues are about what is difficult for men, and I want to see in what sense this is true, and then to consider a problem in Kant's moral philosophy in the light of what has been said.

Let us first think about courage and temperance. Aristotle and Aquinas contrasted these virtues with justice in the following respect. Justice was concerned with operations and courage and temperance with passions.[7] What they meant by this seems to have been, primarily, that the man of courage does not fear immoderately nor the man of temperance have immoderate desires for pleasure, and that there was no corresponding moderation of a passion implied in the idea of justice. This particular account of courage and temperance might be disputed on the ground that a man's courage is measured by his action and not by anything as uncontrollable as fear; and similarly that the temperate man who must on occasion refuse pleasures need not *desire* them any less than the intemperate man. Be that as it may (and something will be said about it later) it is obviously true that courage and temperance have to do with particular springs of action as justice does not. Almost any desire can lead a man to act unjustly, not even excluding the desire to help a friend or to save a life, whereas a cowardly act must be motivated by fear or a desire for safety, and an act of intemperance by a desire for pleasure, perhaps even for a particular range of pleasures such as those of eating or drinking or sex. And now, going back to the idea of virtues as correctives one may say that it is only because fear and the desire for pleasure often operate as temptations that courage and temperance exist as virtues at all. As things are we often want to run away not only where that is the right thing to do but also where we should stand firm; and we want pleasure not only where we should seek pleasure but also where we should not. If human nature had been different there would have been no need of a corrective disposition in either place, as fear and pleasure would have been good guides to conduct throughout life. So Aquinas says, about the passions

> They may incite us to something against reason, and so we need a curb, which we name *temperance.* Or they may make us shirk a course of action dictated by reason, through fear of dangers or hardships. Then a person needs to be steadfact and not run away from what is right; and for this *courage* is named.[8]

As with courage and temperance so with many other virtues: there is, for instance, a virtue of industriousness only because idleness is a temptation; and of humility only because men tend to think too well of themselves. Hope is a virtue because despair too is a temptation; it might have been that no one cried that all was lost except where he could really see it to be so, and in this case there would have been no virtue of hope.

With virtues such as justice and charity it is a little different, because they correspond not to any particular desire or tendency that has to be kept in check but rather to a deficiency of motivation; and it is this that they must make good. If people were as

[7][Rightly or wrongly, Aquinas attributed this doctrine to] Aristotle. [See] op. cit. 1a2ae Q.60 a.2.
[8]Aquinas op. cit. 1a2ae Q.61 a.3.

much attached to the good of others as they are to their own good there would no more be a general virtue of benevolence than there is a general virtue of self-love. And if people cared about the rights of others as they care about their own rights no virtue of justice would be needed to look after the matter, and rules about such things as contracts and promises would only need to be made public, like the rules of a game that everyone was eager to play.

On this view of the virtues and vices everything is seen to depend on what human nature is like, and the traditional catalogue of the two kinds of dispositions is not hard to understand. Nevertheless it may be defective, and anyone who accepts the thesis that I am putting forward will feel free to ask himself where the temptations and deficiencies that need correcting are really to be found. It is possible, for example, that the theory of human nature lying behind the traditional list of the virtues and vices puts too much emphasis on hedonistic and sensual impulses, and does not sufficiently take account of less straightforward inclinations such as the desire to be put upon and dissatisfied, or the unwillingness to accept good things as they come along.

It should now be clear why I said that virtues should be seen as correctives; and part of what is meant by saying that virtue is about things that are difficult for men should also have appeared. The further application of this idea is, however, controversial, and the following difficulty presents itself: that we both are and are not inclined to think that the harder a man finds it to act virtuously the more virtue he shows if he does act well. For on the one hand great virtue is needed where it is particularly hard to act virtuously; yet on the other it could be argued that difficulty in acting virtuously shows that the agent is imperfect in virtue: according to Aristotle, to take pleasure in virtuous action is the mark of true virtue, with the self-mastery of the one who finds virtue difficult only a second best. How then is this conflict to be decided? Who shows most courage, the one who wants to run away but does not, or the one who does not even want to run away? Who shows most charity, the one who finds it easy to make the good of others his object, or the one who finds it hard?

What is certain is that the thought that virtues are corrective does not constrain us to relate virtue to difficulty in each individual man. Since men in general find it hard to face great dangers or evils, and even small ones, we may count as courageous those few who without blindness or indifference are nevertheless fearless even in terrible circumstances. And when someone has a natural charity or generosity it is, at least part of the virtue that he has; if natural virtue cannot be the whole of virtue this is because a kindly or fearless disposition could be disastrous without justice and wisdom, and these virtues have to be learned, not because natural virtue is too easily acquired. I have argued that the virtues can be seen as correctives in relation to human nature in general but not that each virtue must present a difficulty to each and every man.

Nevertheless many people feel strongly inclined to say that it is for moral effort that moral praise is to be bestowed, and that in proportion as a man finds it easy to be virtuous so much the less is he to be morally admired for his good actions. The dilemma can be resolved only when we stop talking about difficulties standing in the way of virtuous action as if they were of only one kind. The fact is that some kinds of difficulties do indeed provide an occasion for much virtue, but that others rather show that virtue is incomplete.

To illustrate this point I shall first consider an example of honest action. We may suppose for instance that a man has an opportunity to steal, in circumstances where stealing is not morally permissible, but that he refrains. And now let us ask our old question. For one man it is hard to refrain from stealing and for another man it is not: which shows the greater virtue in acting as he should? It is not difficult to see in this case that it makes all the difference whether the difficulty comes from circumstances, as that a man is poor, or that his theft is unlikely to be detected, or whether it comes from something that belongs to his own character. The fact that a man is *tempted* to steal is something about him that shows a certain lack of honesty: of the thoroughly honest man we say that it "never entered his head," meaning that it was never a real possibility for him. But the fact that he is poor is something that makes the occasion more *tempting,* and difficulties of this kind make honest action all the more virtuous.

A similar distinction can be made between different obstacles standing in the way of charitable action. Some circumstances, as that great sacrifice is needed, or that the one to be helped is a rival, give an occasion on which a man's charity is severely tested. Yet in given circumstances of this kind it is the man who acts easily rather than the one who finds it hard who shows the most charity. Charity is a virtue of attachment, and that sympathy for others which makes it easier to help them is part of the virtue itself.

These are fairly simple cases, but I am not supposing that it is always easy to say where the relevant distinction is to be drawn. What, for instance, should we say about the emotion of fear as an obstacle to action? Is a man more courageous if he fears much and nevertheless acts, or if he is relatively fearless? Several things must be said about this. In the first place it seems that the emotion of fear is not a necessary condition for the display of courage; in face of a great evil such as death or injury a man may show courage even if he does not tremble. On the other hand even irrational fears may give an occasion for courage: if someone suffers from claustrophobia or a dread of heights he may require courage to do that which would not be a courageous action for others. But not all fears belong from this point of view to the circumstances rather than to a man's character. For while we do not think of claustrophobia or a dread of heights as features of character, a general timorousness may be. Thus, although pathological fears are not the result of a man's choices and values some fears may be. The fears that count against a man's courage are those that we think he could overcome, and among them, in a special class, those that reflect the fact that he values safety too much.

In spite of problems such as these, which have certainly not all been solved, both the distinction between different kinds of obstacles to virtuous action, and the general idea that virtues are correctives, will be useful in resolving a difficulty in Kant's moral philosophy closely related to the issues discussed in the preceding paragraphs. In a passage in the first section of the *Groundwork of the Metaphysics of Morals* Kant notoriously tied himself into a knot in trying to give an account of those actions which have as he put it "positive moral worth." Arguing that only actions done out of a sense of duty have this worth he contrasts a philanthropist who "takes pleasure in spreading happiness around him" with one who acts out of respect for duty, saying that the actions of the latter but not the former have moral worth. Much scorn has been poured on Kant for this curious doctrine, and indeed it does seem that something has gone wrong, but perhaps we are not in a position to scoff unless we can give our own account of the idea on which Kant is working. After all it does seem that he is right in saying that some actions are in accordance with duty, and even required by duty, without being the subjects of moral praise, like those of the honest trader who deals honestly in a situation in which it is in his interest to do so.

It was this kind of example that drove Kant to his strange conclusion. He added another example, however, in discussing acts of self-preservation; these he said, while they normally have no positive moral worth, may have it when a man preserves his life not from inclination but without inclination and from a sense of duty. Is he not right in saying that acts of self-preservation normally have no moral significance but that they may have it, and how do we ourselves explain this fact?

To anyone who approaches this topic from a consideration of the virtues the solution readily suggests itself. Some actions are in accordance with virtue without requiring virtue for their performance, whereas others are both in accordance with virtue and such as to show possession of a virtue. So Kant's trader was dealing honestly in a situation in which the virtue of honesty is not required for honest dealing, and it is for this reason that his action did not have "positive moral worth." Similarly, the care that one ordinarily takes for one's life, as for instance on some ordinary morning in eating one's breakfast and keeping out of the way of a car on the road, is something for which no virtue is required. As we said earlier there is no general virtue of self-love as there is a virtue of benevolence or charity, because men are generally attached sufficiently to their own good. Nevertheless in special circumstances virtues such as temperance, courage, fortitude, and hope may be needed if someone is to preserve his life. Are these circumstances in which the preservation of one's own life is a duty? Sometimes it is so, for sometimes it is what is owed to others that should keep a man from destroying himself, and then he may act out of a sense of duty. But not all cases in which acts of self-preservation show virtue are like this. For a man may display each of the virtues just listed even where he does not do any harm to others if he kills himself or fails to preserve his life. And it is this that explains why there may be a moral aspect to suicide which does not depend on possible injury to other people. It is not that suicide is "always wrong," whatever that would mean, but that suicide is *sometimes* contrary to virtues such as courage and hope.

Let us now return to Kant's philanthropists, with the thought that it is action that is in accordance with virtue and also displays a virtue that has moral worth. We see at once that Kant's difficulties are avoided, and the happy philanthropist reinstated in the position which belongs to him. For charity is, as we said, a virtue of attachment as well as action, and the sympathy that makes it easier to act with charity is part of the virtue. The man who acts charitably out of a sense of duty is not to be undervalued, but it is the other who most shows virtue and therefore to the other that most moral worth is attributed. Only a detail of Kant's presentation of the case of the dutiful philanthropist tells on the other side. For what he actually said was that this man felt no sympathy and took no pleasure in the good of others because "his mind was clouded by some sorrow of his own," and this is the kind of circumstance that increases the virtue that is needed if a man is to act well.

III

It was suggested above that an action with "positive moral worth," or as we might say a positively good action, was to be seen as one which was in accordance with virtue, by which I mean contrary to no virtue, and moreover one for which a virtue was required. Nothing has so far been said about another case, excluded by the formula, in which it might seem that an act displaying one virtue was nevertheless contrary to another. In giving this last description I am thinking not of two virtues with competing claims, as if what were required by justice could nevertheless be demanded by charity, or something of that kind, but rather of the possibility that a virtue such as courage or temperance or industry which overcomes a special temptation, might be displayed in an act of folly or villainy. Is this something that we must allow for, or is it only good or innocent actions which can be acts of these virtues? Aquinas, in his definition of virtue, said that virtues can produce only good actions, and that they are dispositions "of which no one can make bad use,"[9] except when they are treated as objects, as in being the subject of

[9]Aquinas op. cit. 1a2ae Q.56 a.5.

hatred or pride. The common opinion nowadays is, however, quite different. With the notable exception of Peter Geach hardly anyone sees any difficulty in the thought that virtues may sometimes be displayed in bad actions. Von Wright, for instance, speaks of the courage of the villain as if this were a quite unproblematic idea, and most people take it for granted that the virtues of courage and temperance may aid a bad man in his evil work. It is also supposed that charity may lead a man to act badly, as when someone does what he has no right to do, but does it for the sake of a friend.

There are, however, reasons for thinking that the matter is not as simple as this. If a man who is willing to do an act of injustice to help a friend, or for the common good, is supposed to act out of charity, and he so acts where a just man will not, it should be said that the unjust man has more charity than the just man. But do we not think that someone not ready to act unjustly may yet be perfect in charity, the virtue having done its whole work in prompting a man to do the acts that are permissible? And is there not more difficulty than might appear in the idea of an act of injustice which is nevertheless an act of courage? Suppose for instance that a sordid murder were in question, say a murder done for gain or to get an inconvenient person out of the way, but that this murder had to be done in alarming circumstances or in the face of real danger; should we be happy to say that such an action was an act of courage or a courageous act? Did the murderer, who certainly acted boldly, or with intrepidity, if he did the murder, also act courageously? Some people insist that they are ready to say this, but I have noticed that they like to move over to a murder for the sake of conscience, or to some other act done in the course of a villainous enterprise but whose immediate end is innocent or positively good. On their hypothesis, which is that bad acts can easily be seen as courageous acts or acts of courage, my original example should be just as good.

What are we to say about this difficult matter? There is no doubt that the murderer who murdered for gain was *not a coward*: he did not have a second moral defect which another villain might have had. There is no difficulty about this because it is clear that one defect may neutralize another. As Aquinas remarked, it is better for a blind horse if it is slow.[10] It does not follow, however, that an act of villainy can be courageous; we are inclined to say that it "took courage," and yet it seems wrong to think of courage as equally connected with good actions and bad.

One way out of this difficulty might be to say that the man who is ready to pursue bad ends does indeed have courage, and shows courage in his action, but that in him courage is not a virtue. Later I shall consider some cases in which this might be the right thing to say, but in this instance it does not seem to be. For unless the murderer consistently pursues bad ends his courage will often result in good; it may enable him to do many innocent or positively good things for himself or for his family and friends. On the strength of an individual bad action we can hardly say that in him courage is not a virtue. Nevertheless there is something to be said even about the individual action to distinguish it from one that would readily be called an act of courage or a courageous act. Perhaps the following analogy may help us to see what it is. We might think of words such as "courage" as naming characteristics of human beings in respect of a certain power, as words such as "poison" and "solvent" and "corrosive" so name the properties of physical things. The power to which virtue-words are so related is the power of producing good action, and good desires. But just as poisons, solvents and corrosives do not always operate characteristically, so it could be with virtues. If P (say arsenic) is a poison it does not follow that P acts as a poison wherever it is found. It is quite natural to say on occasion "P does not act as a poison here" though P is a poison and it is P that is acting here. Similarly

[10]Aquinas op. cit. Ia2ae Q.58 a.4.

courage is not operating as a virtue when the murderer turns his courage, which is a virtue to bad ends. Not surprisingly the resistance that some of us registered was not to the expression "the courage of the murderer" or to the assertion that what he did "took courage" but rather to the description of that action as an act of courage or a courageous act. It is not that the action *could* not be so described, but that the fact that courage does not here have its characteristic operation is a reason for finding the description strange.

In this example we were considering an action in which courage was not operating as a virtue, without suggesting that in that agent it generally failed to do so. But the latter is also a possibility. If someone is both wicked and foolhardy this may be the case with courage, and it is even easier to find examples of a general connection with evil rather than good in the case of some other virtues. Suppose, for instance, that we think of someone who is over-industrious, or too ready to refuse pleasure, and this is characteristic of him rather than something we find on one particular occasion. In this case the virtue of industry, or the virtue of temperance, has a systematic connection with defective action rather than good action; and it might be said in either case that the virtue did not operate as a virtue in this man. Just as we might say in a certain setting "P is not a poison here" though P is a poison and P is here, so we might say that industriousness, or temperance, is not a virtue in some. Similarly in a man habitually given to wishful thinking, who clings to false hopes, hope does not operate as a virtue and we may say that it is not a virtue in him.

The thought developed in the last paragraph, to the effect that not every man who has a virtue has something that is a virtue in him, may help to explain a certain discomfort that one may feel when discussing the virtues. It is not easy to put one's finger on what is wrong, but it has something to do with a disparity between the moral ideals that may seem to be implied in our talk about the virtues, and the moral judgments that we actually make. Someone reading the foregoing pages might, for instance, think that the author of this paper always admired most those people who had all the virtues, being wise and temperate as well as courageous, charitable, and just. And indeed it is sometimes so. There are some people who do possess all these virtues and who are loved and admired by all the world, as Pope John XXIII was loved and admired. Yet the fact is that many of us look up to some people whose chaotic lives contain rather little of wisdom or temperance, rather than to some others who possess these virtues. And while it may be that this is just romantic nonsense I suspect that it is not. For while wisdom always operates as a virtue, its close relation prudence does not, and it is prudence rather than wisdom that inspires many a careful life. Prudence is not a virtue in everyone, any more than industriousness is, for in some it is rather an over-anxious concern for safety and propriety, and a determination to keep away from people or situations which are apt to bring trouble with them; and by such defensiveness much good is lost. It is the same with temperance. Intemperance can be an appalling thing, as it was with Henry VIII of whom Wolsey remarked that

> rather than he will either miss or want any part of his will or appetite, he will put the loss of one half of his realm in danger.

Nevertheless in some people temperance is not a virtue, but is rather connected with timidity or with a grudging attitude to the acceptance of good things. Of course what is best is to live boldly yet without imprudence or intemperance, but the fact is that rather few can manage that.

1980

Moral Dilemmas and Consistency

Ruth Barcan Marcus

I want to argue that the existence of moral dilemmas, even where the dilemmas arise from a categorical principle or principles, need not and usually does not signify that there is some inconsistency (in a sense to be explained) in the set of principles, duties, and other moral directives under which we define our obligations either individually or socially. I want also to argue that, on the given interpretation, consistency of moral principles or rules does not entail that moral dilemmas are resolvable in the sense that acting with good reasons in accordance with one horn of the dilemma erases the original obligation with respect to the other. The force of this latter claim is not simply to indicate an intractable fact about the human condition and the inevitability of guilt. The point to be made is that, although dilemmas are not settled without residue, the recognition of their reality has a dynamic force. It motivates us to arrange our lives and institutions with a view to avoiding such conflicts. It is the underpinning for a second-order regulative principle: that as rational agents with some control of our lives and institutions, we ought to conduct our lives and arrange our institutions so as to minimize predicaments of moral conflict.

This paper was written during my tenure as a Fellow at the Center for the Advanced Study of the Behavioral Sciences. I am grateful to Robert Stalnaker for his illuminating comments. A version of the paper was delivered on January 17, 1980, at Wayne State University as the Gail Stine Memorial Lecture.

Ruth Barcan Marcus, "Moral Dilemmas and Consistency," *The Journal of Philosophy* 77, No. 3 (March 1980). Reprinted with the permission of the author and *The Journal of Philosophy.*

I

Moral dilemmas have usually been presented as predicaments for individuals. Plato, for example, describes a case in which the return of a cache of arms has been promised to a man who, intent on mayhem, comes to claim them. Principles of promise keeping and benevolence generate conflict. One does not lack for examples. It is safe to say that most individuals for whom moral principles figure in practical reasoning have confronted dilemmas, even though these more commonplace dilemmas may lack the poignancy and tragic proportions of those featured in biblical, mythological, and dramatic literature. In the one-person case there are principles in accordance with which one ought to do x and one ought to do y, where doing y requires that one refrain from doing x; i.e., one ought to do not-x. For the present rough-grained discussion, the one-person case may be seen as an instance of the n-person case under the assumption of shared principles. Antigone's sororal (and religious) obligations conflict with Creon's obligations to keep his word and preserve the peace. Antigone is obliged to arrange for the burial of Polyneices; Creon is obliged to prevent it. Under generality of principles they are each obliged to respect the obligations of the other.

It has been suggested that moral dilemmas, on their face, seem to reflect some kind of inconsistency in the principles from which they derive. It has also been supposed that such conflicts are products of a plurality of principles and that a single-principled moral system does not generate dilemmas.

In the introduction to the *Metaphysics of Morals* Kant[1] says, "Because however duty and obligation are in general concepts that express the objective practical necessity of certain actions . . . it follows . . . that a conflict of duties and obligations is inconceivable (*obligationes non colliduntor*)." More recently John Lemmon,[2] citing a familiar instance of dilemma, says, "It may be argued that our being faced with this moral situation merely reflects an implicit inconsistency in our existing moral code; we are forced, if we are to remain both moral and logical, by the situation to restore consistency to our code by adding exception clauses to our present principles or by giving priority to one principle over another, or by some such device. The situation is as it is in mathematics: there, if an inconsistency is revealed by derivation, we are compelled to modify our axioms; here, if an inconsistency is revealed in application, we are forced to revise our principles." Donald Davidson,[3] also citing examples of conflict, says, "But then unless we take the line that moral principles *cannot* conflict in application to a case, we must give up the concept of the nature of practical reason we have so far been assuming. For how can premises, all of which are true (or acceptable) entail a contradiction? It is astonishing that in contemporary moral philosophy this problem has received little attention and no satisfactory treatment."

The notion of inconsistency which views dilemmas as evidence for inconsistency seems to be something like the following. We have to begin with a set of one or more moral principles which we will call a *moral code*. To count as a principle in such a code, a precept must be of a certain generality; that is, it cannot be tied to specific individuals

[1]Immanuel Kant, *The Metaphysical Elements of Justice:* Part I of the *Metaphysics of Morals*, translated by John Ladd (Indianapolis: Bobbs-Merrill, 1965), p. 24.

[2]"Deontic Logic and the Logic of Imperatives," *Logique et Analyse*, VIII, 29 (April 1965): 39–61. Lemmon originally presented his paper at a symposium of the Western Division meeting of the American Philosophical Association in May 1964. My unpublished comments on that occasion contain some of the ideas here presented.

[3]"How Is Weakness of the Will Possible?," in Joel Feinberg, ed., *Moral Concepts* (New York: Oxford, 1970), p. 105.

at particular times or places, except that on any occasion of use it takes the time of that occasion as a zero coordinate. The present rough-grained discussion does not require that a point be made of the distinction between categorical moral principles and conditional moral principles, which impose obligations upon persons in virtue of some condition, such as that of being a parent, or a promise-maker or contractee. For our purposes we may think of categorical principles as imposing obligations in virtue of one's being a person and a member of a moral community.

In the conduct of our lives, actual circumstances may arise in which a code mandates a course of action. Sometimes, as in dilemmas, incompatible actions *x* and *y* are mandated; that is, the doing of *x* precludes the doing of *y; y* may in fact be the action of refraining from doing *x*. The underlying view that takes dilemmas as evidence of inconsistency is that a code is consistent if it applies without conflict to all actual—or, more strongly—to all possible cases. Those who see a code as the foundation of moral reasoning and adopt such a view of consistency argue that the puzzle of dilemmas can be resolved by elaboration of the code: by hedging principles with exception clauses, or establishing a rank ordering of principles, or both, or a procedure of assigning weights, or some combination of these. We need not go into the question of whether exception clauses can be assimilated to priority rankings, or priority rankings to weight assignments. In any case, there is some credibility in such solutions, since they fit some of the moral facts. In the question of whether to return the cache of arms, it is clear (except perhaps to an unregenerate Kantian) that the principle requiring that the promise be kept is overridden by the principle requiring that we protect human lives. Dilemmas, it is concluded, are merely apparent and not real. For, with a complete set of rules and priorities or a complete set of riders laying out circumstances in which a principle does not apply, in each case one of the obligations will be vitiated. What is incredible in such solutions is the supposition that we could arrive at a complete set of rules, priorities, or qualifications which would, in every possible case, unequivocally mandate a single course of action; that where, on any occasion, doing *x* conflicts with doing *y*, the rules with qualifications or priorities will yield better clear reasons for doing one than for doing the other.

The foregoing approach to the problem of moral conflict—ethical formalism—attempts to dispel the reality of dilemmas by expanding or elaborating on the code. An alternative solution, that of moral intuitionism, denies that it is possible to arrive at an elaboration of a set of principles which will apply to all particular circumstances. W. D. Ross,[4] for example, recognizes that estimates of the stringency of different prima facie principles can sometimes be made, but argues that no general universally applicable rules for such rankings can be laid down. However, the moral intuitionists *also* dispute the reality of moral dilemmas. Their claim is that moral codes are only guides; they are not the only and ultimate ground of decision making. Prima facie principles play an important heuristic role in our deliberations, but not as a set of principles that can tell us how we ought to act in all particular circumstances. That ultimate determination is a matter of intuition, albeit rational intuition. Moral dilemmas are prima facie, not real conflicts. In apparent dilemmas there *is* always a correct choice among the conflicting options; it is only that, and here Ross quotes Aristotle, "the decision rests with perception." For Ross, those who are puzzled by moral dilemmas have failed to see that the problem is epistemological and not ontological, or real. Faced with a dilemma generated by prima facie principles, *uncertainty* is increased as to whether, in choosing *x* over *y*, we have in fact done the right thing. As Ross puts it, "Our judgments about our actual

[4]*The Right and the Good* (New York: Oxford, 1930), p. 41.

duty in concrete situations, have none of the certainty that attaches to our recognition of general principles of duty. . . . Where a possible act is seen to have two characteristics in virtue of one of which it is prima facie right and in virtue of the other prima facie wrong we are well aware that we are not certain whether we ought or ought not to do it. Whether we do it or not we are taking a moral risk" (30). For Ross, as well as the formalist, it is only that we may be uncertain of the right way. To say that dilemma is evidence of inconsistency is to confuse inconsistency with uncertainty. There *is* only one right way to go, and hence no problem of inconsistency.

There are, as we see, points of agreement between the formalist and the intuitionist as here described. Both claim that the appearance of dilemma and inconsistency flows from prima facie principles and that dilemmas can be resolved by supplementation. They differ in the nature of the supplementation.[5] They further agree that it is the multiplicity of principles which generates the prima facie conflicts; that if there were one rule or principle or maxim, there would be no conflicts. Quite apart from the unreasonableness of the belief that we can arrive ultimately at a single moral principle, such proposed single principles have played a major role in moral philosophy, Kant's categorical imperative and various versions of the principle of utility being primary examples. Setting aside the casuistic logical claim that a single principle can always be derived by conjunction from a multiplicity, it can be seen that the single-principle solution is mistaken. There is always the analogue of Buridan's ass. Under the single principle of promise keeping, I might make two promises in all good faith and reason that they will not conflict, but then they do, as a result of circumstances that were unpredictable and beyond my control. All other considerations may balance out. The lives of identical twins are in jeopardy, and, through force of circumstances, I am in a position to save only one. Make the situation as symmetrical as you please. A single-principled framework is not necessarily unlike the code with qualifications or priority rule, in that it would appear that, however strong our wills and complete our knowledge, we might be faced with a moral choice in which there are no moral grounds for favoring doing x over y.

Kant imagined that he had provided a single-principled framework from which all maxims flowed. But Kantian ethics is notably deficient in coping with dilemmas. Kant seems to claim that they don't really arise, and we are provided with no moral grounds for their resolution.

It is true that unregenerate act utilitarianism is a plausible candidate for dilemma-free principle or conjunction of principles, but not because it can be framed as a single principle. It is rather that attribution of rightness or wrongness to certain kinds of acts *per se* is ruled out whether they be acts of promise keeping or promise breaking, acts of trust or betrayal, of respect or contempt. One might, following Moore, call such attributes "non-natural kinds," and they enter into all examples of moral dilemmas. The attribute of having maximal utility as usually understood is not such an attribute. For to the unregenerate utilitarian it is not features of an act *per se* which make it right. The only thing to be counted is certain consequences, and, for any given action, one can imagine possible circumstances, possible worlds if you like, in each of which the action will be assigned different values—depending on different outcomes in those worlds. In the unlikely cases where in fact two conflicting courses of action have the same utility, it is open to the act utilitarian to adopt a procedure for deciding, such as tossing a coin.

[5]For the formalist, priority rankings (like Rawls's lexical ordering), or weights permitting some computation, or qualifications of principles to take care of all problematic cases, are supposed possible. For the intuitionist it is intuitive "seeing" in each case which supplements prima facie principles.

In suggesting that, in all examples of dilemma, we are dealing with attributions of rightness *per se* independent of consequences is not to say that principles of utility do not enter into moral dilemmas. It is only that such conflicts will emerge in conjunction with non-utilitarian principles. Indeed, such conflicts are perhaps the most frequently debated examples, but not, as we have seen, the only ones. I would like to claim that it is a better fit with the moral facts that all dilemmas are real, even where the reasons for doing *x* outweigh, and in whatever degree, the reasons for doing *y*. That is, wherever circumstances are such that an obligation to do *x* and an obligation to do *y* cannot as a matter of circumstance be fulfilled, the obligations to do each are not erased, even though they are unfulfillable. Mitigating circumstances may provide an explanation, an excuse, or a defense, but I want to claim that this is not the same as denying one of the obligations altogether.

We have seen that one of the motives for denying the reality of moral dilemmas is to preserve, on some notion of consistency, the consistency of our moral reasoning. But other not unrelated reasons have been advanced for denying their reality which have to do with the notion of guilt. If an agent ought to do *x*, then he is guilty if he fails to do it. But if, however strong his character and however good his will and intentions, meeting other equally weighted or overriding obligations precludes his doing *x*, then we cannot assign guilt, and, if we cannot, then it is incoherent to suppose that there is an obligation. Attendant feelings of the agent are seen as mistaken or misplaced.

That argument has been rejected by Bas van Fraassen[6] on the ground that normative claims about when we ought to assign guilt are not part of the analysis of the concept of guilt, for if it were, such doctrines as that of "original sin" would be rendered incoherent. The Old Testament assigns guilt to three or four generations of descendants of those who worship false gods. Or consider the burden of guilt borne by all the descendants of the house of Atreus, or, more recently, the readiness of many Germans to assume a burden of guilt for the past actions of others. There are analogous converse cases, as in the assumption of guilt by parents for actions of adult children. Having presented the argument. I am not wholly persuaded that a strong case can be made for the coherence of such doctrines. However, the situation faced by agents in moral dilemmas is not parallel. Where moral conflict occurs, there is a genuine sense in which both what is done and what fails to be done are, before the actual choice among irreconcilable alternatives, within the agent's range of options. But, as the saying goes—and it is not incoherent—you are damned if you do and you are damned if you don't.

I will return to the question of the reality of moral dilemmas, but first let me propose a definition of consistency for a moral code which is compatible with that claim.

[6]"Values and the Heart's Command," this JOURNAL, LXX, 1 (Jan. 11, 1973): 5–19. Van Fraassen makes the point that such a claim would make *the* doctrine of "original sin" incoherent. As I see it, there are at least three interesting doctrines, one of them very likely true, which could qualify as doctrines of original sin. One of them, which I call "inherited guilt," is the doctrine that some of the wrongful actions of some persons are such that other persons, usually those with some special connection to the original sinners, are also judged to be sinners; their feelings of guilt are appropriate, their punishment "deserved," and so on. Such is the case described in Exodus and Deuteronomy here mentioned. A second notion of original sin is to be found in the account of the Fall. Here it is suggested that, however happy our living arrangements, however maximal the welfare state, we will each of us succumb to some temptation. There is universality of sin because of universality of weakness of will, but specific sins are neither inherited by nor bequeathed to others.

A third candidate supposes the reality and inevitability, for each of us, of moral dilemma. Here we do not inherit the sins of others, nor need we be weak of will. The circumstances of the world conspire against us. However perfect our will, the contingencies are such that situations arise where, if we are to follow one right course of action, we will be unable to follow another.

II

Consistency, as defined for a set of meaningful sentences or propositions, is a property that such a set has if it is possible for all of the members of the set to be true, in the sense that contradiction would not be a logical consequence of supposing that each member of the set is true. On that definition "grass is white" and "snow is green" compose a consistent set although false to the facts. There is a possible set of circumstances in which those sentences are true, i.e., where snow is green and grass is white. Analogously we can define a set of rules as consistent if there is some possible world in which they are all obeyable in all circumstances in *that* world. (Note that I have said "obeyable" rather than "obeyed" for I want to allow for the partition of cases where a rule-governed action fails to be done between those cases where the failure is a personal failure of the agent—an imperfect will in Kant's terms—and those cases where "external" circumstances prevent the agent from meeting conflicting obligations. To define consistency relative to a kingdom of ends, a deontically perfect world in which all actions that ought to be done are done, would be too strong; for that would require both perfection of will *and* the absence of circumstances that generate moral conflict.) In such a world, where all rules are obeyable, persons intent on mayhem have not been promised or do not simultaneously seek the return of a cache of arms. Sororal obligations such as those of Antigone do not conflict with obligations to preserve peace, and so on. Agents may still fail to fulfill obligations.

Consider, for example, a silly two-person card game. (This is the partial analogue of a two-person dilemma. One can contrive silly games of solitaire for the one-person dilemma.) In the two-person game the deck is shuffled and divided equally, face down between two players. Players turn up top cards on each play until the cards are played out. Two rules are in force: black cards trump red cards, and high cards (ace high) trump lower-valued cards without attention to color. Where no rule applies, e.g., two red deuces, there is indifference and the players proceed. We could define the winner as the player with the largest number of tricks when the cards are played out. There is an inclination to call such a set of rules inconsistent. For suppose the pair turned up is a red ace and a black deuce; who trumps? This is not a case of rule indifference as in a pair of red deuces. Rather, two rules apply, and both cannot be satisfied. But, on the definition here proposed, the rules are consistent in that there are possible circumstances where, in the course of playing the game, the dilemma would not arise and the game would proceed to a conclusion. It is possible that the cards be so distributed that, when a black card is paired with a red card, the black card happens to be of equal or higher value. Of course, with shuffling, the likelihood of dilemma-free circumstances is small. But we could have invented a similar game where the likelihood of proceeding to a conclusion without dilemma is greater. Indeed a game might be so complex that its being dilemmatic under any circumstances is very small and may not even be known to the players.[7] On the proposed definition, rules are consistent if there are possible circumstances in which no conflict will emerge. By

[7]There is a question whether, given such rules, the "game" is properly described as a game. Wittgenstein says "Let us suppose that the game [which I have invented] is such that whoever begins can always win by a particular simple trick. But this has not been realized;—so it is a game. Now someone draws our attention to it—and it stops being a game." *Remarks on the Foundations of Mathematics*, ed., G. H. von Wright *et al.*, translated by G. E. M. Anscombe (Oxford: Blackwell, 1956), II 78, p. 100e. Wittgenstein is pointing to that canon of a game which requires that both players have some opportunity to win. The canon that rules out dilemmatic rules is that the game must be playable to a conclusion. (I am beholden to Robert Fogelin for reminding me of this quotation.)

extension, a set of rules is inconsistent if there are *no* circumstances, no possible world, in which all the rules are satisfiable.[8]

A pair of offending rules which generates inconsistency as *here* defined provides *no* guide to action under any circumstance. Choices are thwarted whatever the contingencies. Well, a critic might say, you have made a trivial logical point. What pragmatic difference is there between the inconsistent set of rules and a set, like those of the game described above, where there is a likelihood of irresolvable dilemma? A code is, after all, supposed to guide action. If it allows for conflicts without resolution, if it tells us in some circumstances that we ought to do x and we ought to do y even though x and y are incompatible in those circumstances, that is tantamount to telling us that we ought to do x and we ought to refrain from doing x and similarly for y. The code has failed us as a guide. If it is not inconsistent, then it is surely deficient, and, like the dilemma-provoking game, in need of repair.

But the logical point is not trivial, for there are crucial disanalogies between games and the conduct of our lives. It is part of the canon of the family of games of chance like the game described, that the cards must be shuffled. The distribution of the cards must be "left to chance." To stack the deck, like loading the dice, is to cheat. But, presumably, the moral principles we subscribe to are, whatever their justification, not justified merely in terms of some canon for games. Granted, they must be guides to action and hence not totally defeasible. But consistency in our sense is surely only a necessary but not a sufficient condition for a set of moral rules. Presumably, moral principles have some ground; we adopt principles when we have reasons to believe that they serve to guide us in right action. Our interest is not merely in having a playable game whatever the accidental circumstances, but in doing the right thing to the extent that it is possible. We want to maximize the likelihood that in all circumstances we can act in accordance with each of our rules. To that end, our alternative as moral agents, individually and collectively, as contrasted with the card-game players, is to try to stack the deck so that dilemmas do not arise.

Given the complexity of our lives and the imperfection of our knowledge, the occasions of dilemma cannot always be foreseen or predicted. In playing games, when we are faced with a conflict of rules we abandon the game or invent new playable rules; dissimilarly, in the conduct of our lives we do not abandon action, and there may be no justification for making new rules to fit. We proceed with choices as best we can. Priority rules and the like assist us in those choices and in making the best of predicaments. But, if we do make the best of a predicament, and make a choice, to claim that one of the conflicting obligations has thereby been erased is to claim that it would be mistaken to feel guilt or remorse about having failed to act according to that obligation. So the agent would be said to believe falsely that he is guilty, since his obligation was vitiated and his feelings are inappropriate. But that is false to the facts. Even where priorities are clear and overriding and even though the burden of guilt may be appropriately small, explanations and excuses are in order. But in such tragic cases as that described by Jean-Paul Sartre[9] where the choice to be made by the agent is between

[8]Bernard Williams, in *Problems of the Self* (New York: Cambridge, 1977), chs. 11 and 12, also recognizes that the source of some apparent inconsistencies in imperatives and rules is to be located in the contingency of their simultaneous inapplicability on a given occasion.

[9]Sartre in "Existentialism Is a Humanism" describes a case where a student is faced with a decision between joining the Free French forces and remaining with his mother. He is her only surviving son and her only consolation. Sartre's advice was that "No rule of general morality can show you what you ought to do." His claim is that in such circumstances "nothing remains but to trust our instincts." But what is "trust" here?

abandoning a wholly dependent mother and not becoming a freedom fighter, it is inadequate to insist that feelings of guilt about the rejected alternative are mistaken and that assumption of guilt is inappropriate. Nor is it puritanical zeal which insists on the reality of dilemmas and the appropriateness of the attendant feelings. For dilemmas, when they occur, are data of a kind. They are to be taken into account in the future conduct of our lives. If we are to avoid dilemmas we must be motivated to do so. In the absence of associated feelings, motivation to stack the deck, to arrange our lives and institutions so as to minimize or avoid dilemma is tempered or blunted.

Consider, for example, the controversies surrounding nonspontaneous abortion. Philosophers are often criticized for inventing bizarre examples and counterexamples to make a philosophical point. But no contrived example can equal the complexity and the puzzles generated by the actual circumstances of fetal conception, parturation, and ultimate birth of a human being. We have an organism, internal to and parasitic upon a human being, hidden from view but relentlessly developing into a human being, which at some stage of development can live, with nurture, outside of its host. There are arguments that recognize competing claims: the right to life of the fetus (at some stage) versus the right of someone to determine what happens to his body. Arguments that justify choosing the mother over the fetus (or vice-versa) where their survival is in competition. Arguments in which fetuses that are defective are balanced against the welfare of others. Arguments in which the claims to survival of others will be said to override survival of the fetus under conditions of great scarcity. There are even arguments that deny prima facie conflicts altogether on some metaphysical grounds, such as that the fetus is not a human being or a person until quickening, or until it has recognizable human features, or until its life can be sustained external to its host, or until birth, or until after birth when it has interacted with other persons. Various combinations of such arguments are proposed in which the resolution of a dilemma is seen as more uncertain, the more proximate the fetus is to whatever is defined as being human or being a person. What all the arguments seem to share is the assumption that there is, despite uncertainty, a resolution without residue; that there is a correct set of metaphysical claims, principles, and priority rankings of principles which will justify the choice. Then, given the belief that one choice is justified, assignment of guilt relative to the overridden alternative is seen as inappropriate, and feelings of guilt or pangs of conscience are viewed as, at best, sentimental. But as one tries to unravel the tangle of arguments, it is clear that to insist that there is in every case a solution without residue is false to the moral facts.

John Rawls,[10] in his analysis of moral sentiments, says that it is an essential characteristic of a moral feeling that an agent, in explaining the feeling, "invokes a moral concept and its associated principle. His (the agent's) account of his feeling

---

Does our action reveal to us that we subscribe to a priority principle or that in the absence of some resolving principles we may just as well follow our inclination? In any case to describe our feelings about the rejected alternative as "regret" seems inadequate. See Walter Kaufmann, ed., *Existentialism from Dostoevsky to Sartre* (New York: Meridian, 1956), pp. 295–298.

[10]*A Theory of Justice* (Cambridge, Mass.: Harvard, 1971), pp. 481–483. Rawls's claim is that such sensations, to be properly describable as "guilt feelings" and not something resembling such feelings, must occur in the broader context of beliefs, strivings, acknowledgments, and readiness to accept outcomes, and cannot be detached from that context. He rejects the possibility that there are such "pure" sensations that can occur independent of the broader context. This is partially, perhaps, an empirical claim about identifying sameness of feeling. The theater-goer might claim that he does feel guilty because he has the same feeling he has when he acknowledges that he is guilty, that what remains is to give an account of when such feelings of guilt are justified. Still, Rawls's analysis seems to me to be a better account.

makes reference to an acknowledged right or wrong." Where those ingredients are absent, as, for example, in the case of someone of stern religious background who claims to feel guilty when attending the theater although he no longer believes it is wrong, Rawls wants to say that such a person has certain sensations of uneasiness and the like which resemble those he has when he feels guilty, but, since he is not apologetic for his behavior, does not resolve to absent himself from the theater, does not agree that negative sanctions are deserved, he experiences not a feeling of guilt, but only something like it. Indeed, it is the feeling which needs to be explained; it is not the action which needs to be excused. For, says Rawls, in his discussion of moral feelings and sentiments, "When plagued by feelings of guilt . . . a person wishes to act properly in the future and strives to modify his conduct accordingly. He is inclined to admit what he has done, to acknowledge and accept reproofs and penalties." Guilt qua feeling is here defined not only in terms of sensations but also in terms of the agent's disposition to acknowledge, to have wishes and make resolutions about future actions, to accept certain outcomes, and the like. Where an agent acknowledges conflicting obligations, unlike the theater-goer who acknowledges no obligation, there is sufficient overlap with dilemma-free cases of moral failure to warrant describing the associated feelings where present as guilt, and where absent as appropriate to an agent with moral sensibility. Granted that, unlike agents who fail to meet their obligations simpliciter, the agent who was confronted with a dilemma may finally act on the best available reasons. Still, with respect to the rejected alternative he acknowledges a wrong in that he recognizes that it was within his power to do otherwise. He may be apologetic and inclined to explain and make excuses. He may sometimes be inclined to accept external reproofs and penalties. Not perhaps those which would be a consequence of a simple failure to meet an obligation but rather like the legal cases in which mitigating circumstances evoke a lesser penalty—or reproof.[11]

Even if, as Rawls supposes, or hopes (but as seems to me most unlikely), a complete set of rules and priorities were possible which on rational grounds would provide a basis for choosing among competing claims in all cases of moral conflict that actually arise, it is incorrect to suppose that the feeling evoked on such occasions, if it is evoked, only resembles guilt, and that it is inappropriate on such occasions to ascribe guilt. *Legal* ascriptions of guilt require sanctions beyond the pangs of conscience and self-imposed reproofs. In the absence of clear external sanctions, legal guilt is normally not ascribable. But that is one of the many distinctions between the legal and the moral.

Most important, an agent in a predicament of conflict will also "wish to act properly in the future and strive to modify his actions accordingly." He will strive to arrange his own life and encourage social arrangements that would prevent, to the extent that it is possible, future conflicts from arising. To deny the appropriateness or correctness of ascriptions of guilt is to weaken the impulse to make such arrangements.[12]

[11]To insist that "regret" is appropriate rather than "guilt" or "remorse" is false to the facts. It seems inappropriate, for example, to describe as "regret" the common feelings of guilt that women have in cases of abortion even where they believe (perhaps mistakenly) that there was moral justification in such an undertaking.

[12]Bernard Williams ["Politics and Moral Character," in Stuart Hampshire, ed., *Public and Private Morality* (New York: Cambridge, 1978), pp. 54–74] discusses the question in the context of politics and the predicament of "dirty hands." He argues that, where moral ends of politics justify someone in public life lying, or misleading, or using others, "the moral disagreeableness of these acts is not merely cancelled." In particular, we would not want, as our politicians, those "practical politicians" for whom the disagreeableness does not arise.

III

I have argued that the consistency of a set of moral rules, even in the absence of a complete set of priority rules, is not incompatible with the reality of moral dilemmas. It would appear, however, that at least some versions of the principle "'ought' implies 'can' " are being denied; for dilemmas are circumstances where, for a pair of obligations, if one is satisfied then the other cannot be. There is, of course, a range of interpretations of the precept resulting from the various interpretations of "ought," "can," and "implies." Some philosophers who recognize the reality of dilemmas have rejected the precept that "'ought' implies 'can'"; some have accepted it.[13] If we interpret the "can" of the precept as "having the ability in this world to bring about," then, as indicated above, in a moral dilemma, "ought" *does* imply "can" for *each* of the conflicting obligations, *before* either one is met. And after an agent has chosen one of the alternatives, there is still something which he ought to have done and could have done and which he did not do. "Can," like "possible," designates a modality that cannot always be factored out of a conjunction. Just as "possible *P* and possible *Q*" does not imply "possible both *P* and *Q*," so "*A* can do *x* and *A* can do *y*" does not imply "*A* can do both *x* and *y*." If the precept "'ought' implies 'can'" is to be preserved, it must also be maintained that "ought" designates a modality that cannot be factored out of a conjunction. From "*A* ought to do *x*" and "*A* ought to do *y*" it does not follow that "*A* ought to do *x* and *y*." Such a claim is of course a departure from familiar systems of deontic logic.

The analysis of consistency and dilemmas advanced in this paper suggests a second-order principle which relates "ought" and "can" and which provides a plausible gloss of the Kantian principle "Act so that thou canst will thy maxim to become a universal law of nature." As Kant understood laws of nature, they are, taken together, universally and jointly applicable in all particular circumstances. It is such a second-order principle that has been violated when we knowingly make conflicting promises. It is such a second-order principle that has, for example, been violated when someone knowingly and avoidably conducts himself in such a way that he is confronted with a choice between the life of a fetus, the right to determine what happens to one's body, and benefits to others. To will maxims to become universal laws we must will the means, and among those means are the conditions for their compatibility. One ought to act in such a way that, if one ought to do *x* and one ought to do *y*, then one can do both *x* and *y*. But the second-order principle is regulative. This second-order "ought" does *not* imply "can."[14] There is no reason to suppose, this being the actual world, that we can, individually or collectively, however holy our wills or rational our strategies, succeed in foreseeing and wholly avoiding such conflict. It is not merely failure of will, or failure of reason, which thwarts moral maxims from becoming universal laws. It is the contingencies of this world.

[13]For example, John Lemmon, in "Moral Dilemmas," *Philosophical Review,* LXXI, 2 (April 1962): 139–158, p. 150, rejects the principle that "ought" implies "can." Van Fraassen, *op. cit.*, pp. 12/3, accepts it, as does Bernard Williams seemingly in *Problems of the Self, op. cit.*, pp. 179–184. Van Fraassen and Williams see that such acceptance requires modification of the principle of factoring for the deontic "ought." There are other received principles of deontic logic which will have to be rejected, but they will be discussed in a subsequent paper. It should also be noted that, in "Ethical Consistency" and "Consistency and Realism" in *Problems of the Self,* Williams also articulates the contingent source of dilemmas and argues for their "reality."

[14]See fn 13. The reader is reminded that, on the present analysis, "ought" is indexical in the sense that applications of principles on given occasions project into the future. They concern bringing something about.

IV

Where does that leave us? I have argued that all dilemmas are real in a sense I hope has been made explicit. Also that there is no reason to suppose on considerations of consistency that there *must* be principles which, on moral grounds, will provide a sufficient ordering for deciding all cases. But, it may be argued, when confronted with what are *apparently* symmetrical choices undecidable on moral grounds, agents do, finally, choose. That is sometimes understood as a way in which, given good will, an agent makes explicit the rules under which he acts. It is the way an agent discovers a priority principle under which he orders his actions. I should like to question that claim.

A frequently quoted remark of E. M. Forster[15] is "if I had to choose between betraying my country and betraying my friend, I hope I should have the courage to betray my country." One could of course read that as if Forster had made manifest some priority rule: that certain obligations to friends override obligations to nation. But consider a remark of A. B. Worster, "if I had to choose between betraying my country and betraying my friend, I hope I should have the courage to betray my friend." Both recognize a dilemma, and one can read Worster as subscribing to a different priority rule and, to that extent, a different set of rules from Forster's. But is that the only alternative? Suppose Forster had said that, morally, Worster's position is as valid as his own. That there was no moral reason for generalizing his own choice to all. That there was disagreement between them not about moral principles but rather about the kind of persons they wished to be and the kind of lives they wished to lead. Forster may not want Worster for a friend; a certain possibility of intimacy may be closed to them which perhaps Forster requires in a friend. Worster may see in Forster a sensibility that he does not admire. But there is no reason to suppose that such appraisals are or must be moral appraisals. Not all questions of value are moral questions, and it may be that not all moral dilemmas are resolvable by principles for which moral justification can be given.

[15] *Two Cheers for Democracy* (London: E. Arnold, 1939).

1980

Value

Thomas Nagel

1. Whether values can be objective depends on whether an interpretation of objectivity can be found that allows us to advance our knowledge of what to do, what to want, and what things provide reasons for and against action. Last week [*The Tanner Lectures on Human Values*] I argued that the physical conception of objectivity was not able to provide an understanding of the mind, but that another conception was available which allowed external understanding of at least some *aspects* of mental phenomena. A still different conception is required to make sense of the objectivity of values, for values are neither physical nor mental. And even if we find a conception, it must be applied with care. Not all values are likely to prove to be objective in any sense.

Let me say in advance that my discussion of values and reasons in this lecture and the next will be quite general. I shall be talking largely about what determines whether something has value, or whether someone has a reason to do or want something. I shall say nothing about how we pass from the identification of values and reasons to a conclusion as to what should be *done*. That is of course what makes reasons important; but I shall just assume that values do often provide the basis for such conclusions, without trying to describe even in outline how the full process of practical

Thomas Nagel, "Value," THE TANNER LECTURES ON HUMAN VALUES, Volume 1, edited by Sterling McMurrin (Salt Lake City: University of Utah Press, 1980). Reprinted with the permission of the publishers.

reasoning works. I am concerned here only with the general question, whether values have an objective foundation at all.

In general, as I said last time, objectivity is advanced when we step back, detach from our earlier point of view toward something, and arrive at a new view of the whole that is formed by including ourselves and our earlier viewpoint in what is to be understood.

In theoretical reasoning this is done by forming a new conception of reality that includes ourselves as components. This involves an alteration, or at least an extension, of our beliefs. Whether the effort to detach will actually result in an increase of understanding depends on the creative capacity to form objective ideas which is called into action when we add ourselves to the world and start over.

In the sphere of values or practical reasoning, the problem is somewhat different. As in the theoretical case, in order to pursue objectivity we must take up a new, comprehensive viewpoint after stepping back and including our former perspective in what is to be understood. But in this case the new viewpoint will be *not* a new set of *beliefs,* but a new, or extended, set of *values.* If objectivity means anything here, it will mean that when we detach from our individual perspective and the values and reasons that seem acceptable from within it, we can sometimes arrive at a new conception which may endorse some of the original reasons but will reject some as subjective appearances and add others. This is what is usually meant by an objective, disinterested view of a practical question.

The basic step of placing ourselves and our attitudes within the world to be considered is familiar, but the form of the result—a new set of values, reasons, and motives—is different. In order to discover whether there are any objective values or reasons we must try to arrive at *normative* judgments, with *motivational content,* from an impersonal standpoint: a standpoint outside of our lives. We cannot use a *non-normative* criterion of objectivity: for *if* any values are objective, they are objective *values,* not objective anything else.

2. There are many opinions about whether what we have reason to do or want can be determined from a detached standpoint toward ourselves and the world. They range all the way from the view that objectivity has *no* place in this domain except what is inherited from the objectivity of those theoretical and factual elements that play a role in practical reasoning, to the view that objectivity applies here, but with a nihilistic result: i.e., that nothing is objectively right or wrong because objectively nothing matters. In between are many positive objectifying views which claim to get some definite results from a detached standpoint. Each of them is criticized by adherents of opposing views either for trying to force too much into a single objective framework or for according too much or too little respect to divergent subjective points of view.

Here as elsewhere there is a direct connection between the goal of objectivity and the belief in *realism.* The most basic idea of practical objectivity is arrived at by a practical analogue of the rejection of solipsism or idealism in the theoretical domain. Just as realism about the facts leads us to seek a detached point of view from which reality can be discerned and appearance corrected, so realism about values leads us to seek a detached point of view from which it will be possible to correct inclination and to discern what we really should do, or want. Practical objectivity means that practical reason can be understood and even engaged in by the objective self.

This assumption, though powerful, is not yet an ethical position. It merely marks the place which an ethical position will occupy if we can make any sense of the subject. It says that the world of reasons, including my reasons, does not exist only from my point of view. I am in a world whose properties are to a certain extent independent of what I think, and if I have reasons to act it is because the person who I am has those reasons, in virtue of his condition and circumstances. One would expect those reasons to be understandable from outside. Here as elsewhere objectivity is a form of understanding not necessarily available for all of reality. But it is reasonable at least to look for such understanding over as wide an area as possible.

3. It is important not to lose sight of the dangers of *false* objectification, which too easily elevate personal tastes and prejudices into cosmic values. But initially, at least, it is natural to look for some objective account of those reasons that appear from one's own point of view.

In fact those reasons usually present themselves with some pretensions of objectivity to begin with, just as perceptual appearances do. When two things look the same size to me, they look at least initially as if they *are* the same size. And when I want to take aspirin because it will cure my headache, I believe at least initially that this *is* a reason for me to take aspirin, that it can be recognized as a reason from outside, and that if I failed to take it into account, that would be a mistake, and others could recognize this.

The ordinary process of deliberation, aimed at finding out what I have reason to do, assumes that the question has an answer. And in difficult cases especially, deliberation is often accompanied by the belief that I may not *arrive* at that answer. I do not assume that the correct answer is just whatever will result or has resulted from consistent application of deliberative methods—even assuming perfect information about the facts. In deliberation we are trying to arrive at conclusions that are correct in virtue of something *independent* of our arriving at them. If we arrive at a conclusion, we believe that it would have been correct even if we *hadn't* arrived at it. And we can also acknowledge that we might be *wrong,* since the process of reasoning doesn't guarantee the correctness of the result. So the pursuit of an objective account of practical reasons has its basis in the realist claims of ordinary practical reasoning. In accordance with pretheoretical judgment we adopt the working hypothesis that there are reasons which may diverge from actual motivation even under conditions of perfect information—as reality can diverge from appearance—and then consider what form these reasons take. I shall say more about the general issue of realism later on. But first I want to concentrate on the process of thought by which, against a realist background, one might try to arrive at objective conclusions about reasons for action. In other words, if there really are values, how is objective knowledge of them possible?

In this inquiry no particular hypothesis occupies a privileged position, and it is certain that some of our starting points will be abandoned as we proceed. However, one condition on reasons obviously presents itself for consideration: a condition of generality. This is the condition that if something provides a reason for a particular individual to do something, then there is a general form of that reason which applies to anyone else in comparable circumstances. What count as comparable circumstances depends on the general form of the reason. This condition is not tautological. It is a rather strong condition which may be false, or true only for some kinds of reasons. But the search for generality is a natural beginning.

4. There is more than one type of generality, and no reason to assume that a single form will apply to every kind of reason or value. In fact I think that the choice among types of generality defines some of the central issues of contemporary moral theory.

One respect in which reasons may vary is in their *breadth.* A general principle may apply to everyone but be quite specific in content, and it is an open question to what extent narrower principles of practical reasons (don't lie; develop your talents) can be subsumed under broader ones (don't hurt others; consider your long-term interests), or even at the limit under a single widest principle from which all the rest derive. Reasons may be general, in other words, without forming a unified system that always provides a method for arriving at determinate conclusions about what one should do.

A second respect in which reasons vary is in their *relativity to the agent*, the person for whom they are reasons. The distinction between reasons that are relative to the agent and reasons that are not is an extremely important one. I shall follow Derek Parfit in using the terms "agent-relative" and "agent-neutral" to mark this distinction. (Formerly I used the terms "subjective" and "objective," but those terms are here reserved for other purposes.)

If a reason can be given a general form which does *not* include an essential reference to the person to whom it applies, it is an *agent-neutral* reason. For example, if it is a reason for *anyone* to do or want something that it would reduce the amount of wretchedness in the world, then that is an agent-neutral reason.

If on the other hand the general form of a reason *does* include an essential reference to the person to whom it applies, it is an *agent-relative* reason. For example, if it is a reason for anyone to do or want something that it would be in *his* interest, then that is an agent-relative reason. In such a case, if something were in Jones's interest but contrary to Smith's, Jones would have reason to want it to happen and Smith would have the *same* reason to want it *not* to happen. (Both agent-relative and agent-neutral reasons are objective, since both can be understood from outside the viewpoint of the individual who has them.)

A third way in which reasons may vary is in their degree of externality, or independence of the interests of sentient beings. Most of the apparent reasons that initially present themselves to us are intimately connected with interests and desires, our own or those of others, and often with experiential satisfaction. But it is conceivable that some of these interests give evidence that their objects have intrinsic value independent of the satisfaction that anyone may derive from them or of the fact that anyone wants them—independent even of the existence of beings who can take an interest in them. I shall call a reason *internal* if it depends on the existence of an interest or desire in someone, and *external* if it does not. External reasons were believed to exist by Plato, and more recently by G. E. Moore, who believed that aesthetic value provided candidates for this kind of externality.

These three types of variation cut across one another. Formally, a reason may be narrow, external, and agent-relative (don't eat pork, keep your promises), or broad, internal, and agent-neutral (promote happiness), or internal and agent-relative (promote your own happiness). There may be other significant dimensions of variation. I want to concentrate on these because they locate the main controversies about what ethics is. Reasons and values that can be described in these terms provide the material for objective judgments. If one looks at human action and its conditions from outside and considers whether some normative principles are plausible, these are the forms they will take.

The actual *acceptance* of a general normative judgment will have motivational implications, for it will commit you under some circumstances to the acceptance of reasons to want and do things *yourself.*

This is most clear when the objective judgment is that something has *agent-neutral* value. That means *anyone* has reason to want it to happen—*and that includes someone considering the world in detachment from the perspective of any particular person within it.* Such a judgment has motivational content even before it is brought back down to the particular perspective of the individual who has accepted it objectively.

Agent-relative reasons are different. An objective judgment that some kind of thing has *agent-relative* value commits us only to believing that someone has reason to want and pursue it if it is related to him in the right way (being in *his* interest, for example). Someone who accepts this judgment is not committed to wanting it to *be the case* that people in general are influenced by such reasons. The judgment commits him to wanting something only when its implications are drawn *for the individual person he happens to be.* With regard to others, the content of the objective judgment concerns only what *they* should do or want.

I believe that judgments of both these kinds, as well as others, are evoked from us when we take up an objective standpoint. And I believe such judgments can be just as true and compelling as objective factual judgments about the real world that contains us.

5. When we take the step to objectivity in practical reasoning by detaching from our own point of view, the question we must ask ourselves is this: What reasons for action can be said to apply to people when we regard them from a standpoint detached from the values of any particular person?

The simplest answer, and one that some people would give, is "None." But that is not the only option. The suggested classification of types of generality provides a range of alternative hypotheses. It also provides some flexibility of response, for with regard to any reason that may appear to a particular individual to exist subjectively, the corresponding objective judgment may be that it does not exist at all, or that it corresponds to an agent-neutral, external value, or anything in between.

The choice among these hypotheses, plus others not yet imagined, is difficult, and there is no general method of making it any more than there is a general method of selecting the most plausible objective account of the facts on the basis of the appearances. The only "method," here or elsewhere, is to try to generate hypotheses and then to consider which of them seems most reasonable, in light of everything else one is fairly confident of.

This is not quite empty, for it means at least that logic alone can settle nothing. We do *not* have to be shown that the denial of some kind of objective values is *self-contradictory* in order to be reasonably led to accept their existence. There is no constraint to pick the weakest or narrowest or most economical principle consistent with the initial data that arise from individual perspectives. Our admission of reasons beyond these is determined *not* by logical entailment, but by what we cannot help believing, or at least finding most plausible among the alternatives.

In this respect it is no different from anything else: theoretical knowledge does not arise by deductive inference from the appearances either. The main difference is that our objective thinking about practical reasons is very primitive, and has difficulty taking even the first step. Philosophical skepticism and idealism about values are much more popular than their metaphysical counterparts. Nevertheless I believe they are no more correct. I shall argue that although no *single* objective principle of practical reason like egoism or utilitarianism covers everything, the acceptance of some objective values is unavoidable—not because the alternative is inconsistent but because it is not *credible.* Someone who, as in Hume's example, prefers the destruction of the whole world to the scratching of his finger, may not be involved in a *contradiction* or in any false *expectations,* but he is unreasonable nonetheless (to put it mildly), and anyone else not in the grip of an overly narrow conception of what reasoning is would regard his preference as objectively wrong.

6. But even if it is unreasonable to deny that anyone ever objectively has a reason to do anything, it is not easy to find positive objective principles that *are* reasonable. I am going to attempt to defend a few in the rest of this lecture and the next. But I want to acknowledge in advance that it is not easy to follow the objectifying impulse without distorting individual life and personal relations. We want to be able to understand and accept the way we live from outside, but it may not always follow that we should control our lives from inside by the terms of that external understanding. Often the objective viewpoint will not be suitable as a replacement for the subjective, but will coexist with it, setting a standard with which the subjective is constrained not to clash. In deciding what to do, for example, we should not reach a result different from what we could decide objectively that that *person* should do—but we need not arrive at the result in the same way from the two standpoints.

Sometimes, also, the objective standpoint will allow us to judge how people should *be* or should *live,* without permitting us to translate this into a judgment about what they have *reasons* to do. For in some respects it is better to live and act not for reasons, but because we cannot help it. This is especially true of close personal relations. Here the objective standpoint cannot be brought into the perspective of *action* without destroying precisely what it affirms the value of. Nevertheless the possibility of this objective affirmation is important. We should be *able* to view our lives from outside without extreme dissociation or distaste, and the extent to which we should live without *considering* the objective point of view or even any reasons *at all* is itself *determined* largely from that point of view.

It is also possible that some idiosyncratic individual grounds of action, or the values of strange communities, will prove objectively inaccessible. To take an example in our midst: I don't think that people who want to be able to run twenty-six miles without stopping are irrational, but their reasons can be understood only from the perspective of a value system that is completely alien to me, and will I hope remain so. A correct objective view will have to allow for such pockets of unassimilable subjectivity, which need not clash with objective principles but won't be affirmed by them either. Many aspects of personal taste will come in this category, if, as I think, they cannot all be brought under a general hedonistic principle.

But the most difficult and interesting problems of accommodation appear where objectivity *can* be employed as a standard, but we have to decide *how.* Some of the problems are these: To what extent should an objective view admit *external* values? To what extent should it admit *internal* but *agent-neutral* values? To what extent should the reasons to respect the interests of *others* take an *agent-relative* form? To what extent is it legitimate for each person to give priority to his own interests? These are all questions about the proper form of generality for different kinds of practical reasoning, and the proper relation between objective principles and the deliberations of individual agents. I shall return to some of them later, but there is a great deal that I shall not get to.

I shall not, for example, discuss the question of external values, i.e., values which may be *revealed* to us by the attractiveness of certain things, but whose existence is independent of the existence of any interests or desires. I am not sure whether there are any such values, though the objectifying tendency produces a strong impulse to believe that there are, especially in aesthetics where the object of interest is external and the interest seems perpetually capable of criticism in light of further attention to the object.

What I shall discuss is the proper form of *internal* values or reasons—those which depend on interests or desires. They can be objectified in more than one way, and I believe different forms of objectification are appropriate for different cases.

7. I plan to take up some of these complications in the next lecture. Let me begin, however, with a case for which I think the solution is simple: that of pleasure and pain. I am not an ethical hedonist, but I think pleasure and pain are very important, and they have a kind of neutrality that makes them fit easily into ethical thinking—unlike preferences or desires, for example, which I shall discuss later on.

I mean the kinds of pleasure and pain that do not depend on activities or desires which *themselves* raise questions of justification and value. Many pleasures and pains are just sensory experiences in relation to which we are fairly passive, but toward which we feel involuntary desire or aversion. Almost everyone takes the avoidance of his own pain and the promotion of his own pleasure as subjective reasons for action in a fairly simple way; they are not backed up by any further reasons. On the other hand if someone pursues pain or avoids pleasure, these idiosyncracies usually *are* backed up by further reasons, like guilt or sexual masochism. The question is, what sort of general value, if any, ought to be assigned to pleasure and pain when we consider these facts from an objective standpoint?

It seems to me that the least plausible hypothesis is the zero position, that pleasure and pain have no value of any kind that can be objectively recognized. That would mean that looking at it from outside, you couldn't even say that someone had a reason not to put his hand on a hot stove. Try looking at it from the outside and see whether you can manage to withhold that judgment.

But I want to leave this position aside, because what really interests me is the choice between two other hypotheses, both of which admit that people have reason to avoid their own pain and pursue their own pleasure. They are the fairly obvious general hypotheses formed by assigning (a) agent-relative or (b) agent-neutral value to those experiences. If the avoidance of pain has only agent-relative value, then people have reason to avoid their own pain, but not to avoid the pain of others (unless other kinds of reasons come into play). If the avoidance of pain has agent-neutral value as well, then *anyone* has a reason to want *any* pain to stop, whether or not it is his. From an objective standpoint, which of these hypotheses is more plausible? Is the value of sensory pleasure and pain agent-relative or agent-neutral?

I believe it is agent-neutral, at least in part. That is, I believe pleasure is a good thing and pain is a bad thing, and that the most reasonable objective principle which admits that each of us has reason to pursue his own pleasure and avoid his own pain will acknowledge that these are not the only reasons present. This is a normative claim. Unreasonable, as I have said, does not mean inconsistent.

In arguing for this claim, I am somewhat handicapped by the fact that I find it self-evident. It is therefore difficult for me to find something still more certain with which to back it up. But I shall try to say what is wrong with rejecting it, and with the reasons that may lie behind its rejection. What would it be to really *accept* the alternative hypothesis that pleasure and pain are not impersonally good or bad? If I accept this hypothesis, assuming at the same time that each person has reason to seek pleasure and avoid pain for *himself,* then when I regard the matter objectively the result is very peculiar. I will have to believe that I have a reason to take aspirin for a headache, but that there *is no reason* for me to *have* an aspirin. And I will have to believe the same about anyone else. From an objective standpoint I must judge that everyone has reason to pursue a type of result that is *impersonally valueless,* that has value only to *him.*

This needs to be explained. If agent-neutral reasons are not ruled out of consideration from the start (and one would need reasons for that), why do we not have evidence of them here? The avoidance of pain is not an individual project, expressing the agent's personal values. The desire to make pain stop is simply *evoked* in the person who feels it. He may decide for various reasons not to stop it, but in the first instance he doesn't have to *decide* to want it to stop: he just does. He wants it to go away because it's *bad:* it is not *made* bad by his deciding that he wants it to go away. And I believe that when we think about it objectively, concentrating on what pain is *like,* and ask ourselves whether it is (a) not bad at all, (b) bad only for its possessor, or (c) bad *period,* the third answer is the one that needs to be argued *against,* not the one that needs to be argued *for.* The philosophical problem here is to get rid of the obstacles to the admission of the obvious. But first they have to be identified.

Consider how *strange* is the question posed by someone who wants a justification for altruism about such a basic matter as this. Suppose he and some other people have been admitted to a hospital with severe burns after being rescued from a fire. "I understand how *my* pain provides *me* with a reason to take an analgesic," he says, "and I understand how my groaning neighbor's pain gives *him* a reason to take an analgesic; but how does *his* pain give *me* any reason to want him to be given an analgesic? How can *his* pain give *me* or anyone else looking at it from outside a reason?"

This question is *crazy.* As an expression of puzzlement, it has that characteristic philosophical craziness which indicates that something very fundamental has gone wrong. This shows up in the fact that the *answer* to the question is *obvious,* so obvious that to ask the question is obviously a philosophical act. The answer is that pain is *awful.* The pain of the man groaning in the next bed is just as awful as yours. That's your reason to want him to have an analgesic.

Yet to many philosophers, when they think about the matter theoretically, this answer seems not to be available. The pain of the person in the next bed is thought to need major external help before it can provide me with a reason for wanting or doing anything: otherwise it can't get its hooks into me. Since most of these people are perfectly aware of the force such considerations actually have for them, justifications of some kind are usually found. But they take the form of working *outward* from the desires and interests of the individual for whom reasons are being sought. The burden of proof is thought always to be on the claim that he has reason to care about anything that is not *already* an object of his interest.

These justifications are unnecessary. They plainly falsify the real nature of the case. My reason for wanting my neighbor's pain to cease is just that it's awful, and I know it.

8. What is responsible for this demand for justification with its special flavor of philosophical madness? I believe it is something rather deep, which doesn't surface in the ordinary course of life: an inappropriate sense of the burden of proof. Basically, we are being asked for a demonstration of the *possibility* of real impersonal values, on the assumption that they are *not* possible unless such a general proof can be given.

But I think this is wrong. We can already *conceive* of such a possibility, and once we take the step of thinking about what reality, if any, there is in the domain of practical reason, it becomes a possibility we are bound to consider, that we cannot help considering. If there really are *reasons,* not just motivational pushes and pulls, and if agent-neutral reasons are among the kinds we can conceive of, then it becomes an obvious possibility that physical pain is simply bad: that even from an impersonal standpoint there is reason to want it to stop. When we view the matter objectively, this is one of the general positions that naturally suggests itself.

And once this is seen as a *possibility,* it becomes difficult *not* to accept it. It becomes a hypothesis that has to be *dislodged* by anyone who wishes to claim, for example, that all reasons are agent-relative. The question is, what are the alternatives, once we take up the objective standpoint? We must think *something.* If there is room in the realistic conception of reasons for agent-neutral values, then it is unnatural *not* to ascribe agent-neutral badness to burn pains. That is the natural conclusion from the fact that anyone who has a burn pain and is therefore closest to it wants acutely to be rid of it, and requires no indoctrination or training to want this. This evidence does not *entail* that burn pains are impersonally bad. It is logically conceivable that there is nothing bad about them at all, or that they provide only agent-relative reasons to their possessors to want them to go away. But to take such hypotheses seriously we would need justifications of a kind that seem totally unavailable in this case.

What could possibly show us that acute physical pain, which everyone finds horrible, is in reality not impersonally bad at all, so that except from the point of view of the sufferer it doesn't in itself matter? Only a very remarkable and farfetched picture of the value of a cosmic order beyond our immediate grasp, in which pain played an essential part which made it good or at least neutral—or else a demonstration that there can *be* no agent-neutral values. But I take it that neither of these is available: the first because the Problem of Evil has not been solved, the second because the absence of a logical demonstration that there *are* agent-neutral values is not a demonstration that there are *not* agent-neutral values.

My position is this. No demonstration is necessary in order to allow us to *consider* the possibility of agent-neutral reasons: the possibility simply *occurs* to us once we take up an objective stance. And there is no mystery about how an individual could have a reason to want something independently of its relation to his particular interests or point of view, because beings like ourselves are not *limited* to the particular point of view that goes with their personal position inside the world. They are also, as I have put it earlier, *objective selves:* they cannot *help* forming an objective conception of the world with themselves in it; they cannot help trying to arrive at judgments of *value* from that standpoint; they cannot help asking whether, from that standpoint, in abstraction from who in the world they are, they have any reason to want anything to be the case or not—any reason to want anything to happen or not.

Agent-neutral reasons do not have to find a miraculous source in our personal lives, because we are not *merely* personal beings: we are also importantly and essentially viewers of the world *from nowhere within it*—and in this capacity we remain open to judgments of value, both general and particular. The possibility of agent-neutral values is evident as soon as we begin to think from this standpoint about the reality of any reasons whatever. If we acknowledge the possibility of realism, then we cannot rule out agent-neutral values in advance.

Realism is therefore the fundamental issue. If there really are values and reasons, then it should be possible to expand our understanding of them by objective investigation, and there is no reason to rule out the natural and compelling objective judgment that pain is impersonally bad and pleasure impersonally good. So let me turn now to the abstract issue of realism about values.

9. Like the presumption that things exist in an external world, the presumption that there are real values and reasons can be defeated in individual cases, if a purely subjective account of the appearances is more plausible. And like the presumption of an external world, its complete falsity is not self-contradictory. The reality of values, agent-neutral or otherwise, is not *entailed* by the totality of appearances any more than the reality of a physical universe is. But if either of them is recognized as a possibility, then its reality in detail can be confirmed by appearances, at least to the extent of being rendered more plausible than the alternatives. So a lot depends on whether the possibility of realism is admitted in the first place.

It is very difficult to argue for such a possibility. Sometimes there will be arguments against it, which one can try to refute. Berkeley's argument against the conceivability of a world independent of experience is an example. But what is the result when such an argument is refuted? Is the possibility in a stronger position? I believe so: in general, there is no way to prove the possibility of realism; one can only refute impossibility arguments, and the more often one does this the more confidence one may have in the realist alternative. So to consider the merits of an admission of realism about value, we have to consider the reasons against it. I shall discuss three. They have been picked for their apparent capacity to convince people.

The first argument depends on the question-begging assumption that if values are real, they must be real objects of some other kind. John Mackie, for example, in his recent book *Ethics,* denies the objectivity of values by saying that they are not part of the fabric of the world, and that if they were, they would have to be "entities or qualities or relations of a very strange sort, utterly different from anything else in the universe."[1] Apparently he has a very definite picture of what the universe is like, and assumes that realism about value would require crowding it with extra entities, qualities, or relations—things like Platonic Forms or Moore's non-natural qualities. But this assumption is not correct. The impersonal badness of pain is not some mysterious further property that all pains have, but just the fact that there is reason for anyone capable of viewing the world objectively to want it to *stop,* whether it is his or someone else's. The view that values are real is not the view that they are real occult entities or properties, but that they are real *values:* that our claims about value and about what people have reason to do may be *true* or *false* independently of our beliefs and inclinations. No *other* kinds of truths are involved. Indeed, no other kinds of truths *could* imply the reality of values.[2]

The second argument I want to consider is not, like the first, based on a misinterpretation of moral objectivity. Instead, it tries to represent the unreality of values as an objective *discovery.* The argument is that if claims of value have to be objectively correct or incorrect, and if they are not reducible to any *other* kind of objective claim, then we can just *see* that all positive value claims must be false. Nothing has any objective value, because objectively nothing matters at all. If we push the claims of objective detachment to their logical conclusion, and survey the world from a standpoint completely detached from all interests, we discover that there is *nothing*—no values left of any kind: things can be said to matter at all only to individuals within the world. The result is objective nihilism.

I don't deny that the objective standpoint tempts one in this direction. But I believe this can seem like the required conclusion only if one makes the mistake of assuming that objective judgments of value must emerge from the detached standpoint *alone.* It is true that with nothing to go on but a conception of the world from nowhere, one would have no way of telling whether anything had value. But an objective view has more to go on, for its data include the appearance of value to individuals with particular perspectives, including oneself. In this respect practical reason is no different from anything else. Starting from a pure idea of a possible reality and a very impure set of appearances, we try to fill in the idea of reality so as to make some partial sense of the appearances, using objectivity as a method. To find out what the world is like from outside we have to approach it from within: it is no wonder that the same is true for ethics.

[1]J. L. Mackie, *Ethics* (Harmondsworth, Middlesex: Penguin Books, 1977), p. 38.

[2]In discussion, Mackie claimed that I had misrepresented him, and that his disbelief in the reality of values and reasons does not depend on the assumption that to be real they must be strange *entities* or *properties.* As he says in his book, it applies directly to reasons themselves. For whatever they are they are not needed to explain anything that happens, and there is consequently no reason to believe in their existence. But I would reply that this raises the same issue. It begs the question to assume that *explanatory* necessity is the test of reality in this area. The claim that certain reasons exist is a normative claim, not a claim about the best explanation of anything. To assume that only what has to be included in the best explanatory picture of the world is real, is to assume that there are no irreducibly normative truths.

There is much more to be said on both sides of this issue, and I hope I have not misrepresented Mackie in this short footnote.

And indeed, when we take up the objective standpoint, the problem is not that values seem to disappear but that there seem to be too many of them, coming from every life and drowning out those that arise from our own. It is just as easy to form desires from an objective standpoint as it is to form beliefs. Probably easier. Like beliefs, these desires and evaluations must be criticized and justified partly in *terms* of the appearances. But they are not just further appearances, any more than the beliefs about the world which arise from an impersonal standpoint are just further appearances.

The third type of argument against the objective reality of values is an empirical argument. It is also perhaps the most common. It is intended not to rule out the possibility of real values from the start, but rather to demonstrate that even if their *possibility* is admitted, we have no reason to believe that there are any. The claim is that if we consider the wide cultural variation in normative beliefs, the importance of social pressure and other psychological influences to their formation, and the difficulty of settling moral disagreements, it becomes highly implausible that they are anything but pure appearances.

Anyone offering this argument must admit that not every psychological factor in the explanation of an appearance shows that the appearance corresponds to nothing real. Visual capacities and elaborate training play a part in explaining the physicist's perception of a cloud-chamber track, or a student's coming to believe a proposition of geometry, but the path of the particle and the truth of the proposition also play an essential part in these explanations. So far as I know, no one has produced a general account of the kinds of psychological explanation that discredit an appearance. But some skeptics about ethics feel that because of the way we acquire moral beliefs and other impressions of value, there are grounds for confidence that no real, objective values play a part in the explanation.

I find the popularity of this argument surprising. The fact that morality is socially inculcated and that there is radical disagreement about it across cultures, over time, and even within cultures at a time is a poor reason to conclude that values have no objective reality. Even where there is truth, it is not always easy to discover. Other areas of knowledge are taught by social pressure, many truths as well as falsehoods are believed without rational grounds, and there is wide disagreement about scientific and social facts, especially where strong interests are involved which will be affected by different answers to a disputed question. This last factor is present throughout ethics to a uniquely high degree: it is an area in which one would expect extreme variation of belief and radical disagreement however objectively real the subject actually was. For comparably motivated disagreements about matters of fact, one has to go to the heliocentric theory, the theory of evolution, the Dreyfus case, the Hiss case, and the genetic contribution to racial differences in I.Q.

Although the methods of ethical reasoning are rather primitive, the degree to which agreement can be achieved and social prejudices transcended in the face of strong pressures suggests that something real is being investigated, and that part of the explanation of the appearances, both at simple and at complex levels, is that we perceive, often inaccurately, that certain reasons for action exist, and go on to infer, often erroneously, the general form of the principles that best accounts for those reasons.

The controlling conception that supports these efforts at understanding, in ethics as in science, is realism, or the possibility of realism. Without being sure that we will find one, we look for an account of what reasons there really are, an account that can be objectively understood.

I have not discussed all the possible arguments against realism about values, but I have tried to give general reasons for skepticism about such arguments. It seems to me that they tend to be supported by a narrow preconception of what there *is,* and that this is essentially question-begging.

10. Let me close this lecture by indicating what I plan to discuss next week. So far I have been arguing against skepticism, and in favor of realism and the pursuit of objectivity in the domain of practical reason. But if realism is admitted as a possibility, one is quickly faced with the opposite of the problem of skepticism. This is the problem of over-objectification: the temptation to interpret the objectivity of reasons in too strong and unitary a way.

In ethics, as in metaphysics, the allure of objectivity is very great: there is a persistent tendency in both areas to seek a *single, complete* objective account of reality—in the area of value that means a search for the most objective possible account of all reasons for action: the account acceptable from a maximally detached standpoint.

This idea underlies the fairly common moral assumption that the only real values are agent-neutral values, and that someone can really have a reason to do something only if there is an agent-neutral reason for it to *happen.* That is the essence of consequentialism: the only reason for anyone to do anything is that it would be better in itself, considering the world as a whole, if he did it. (The idea also finds a reflection in Professor Hare's view about the only kind of judgment that moral language can be used to express: for his claim that moral judgments are universally *prescriptive* means that they depend on what one would *want to happen,* considering the question from all points of view—rather than on what one would think people had *reason to do,* considering the question in this way. Consequently, any principle that was *moral* in his sense would have to be *agent-neutral.*)

In the next lecture I shall try to explain why ethics has to be based not only on agent-neutral values like those that attach to pleasure and pain. We can no more assume that all reasons are agent-neutral than that all reality is physical. I argued earlier that not everything there is can be gathered into a uniform conception of the universe from nowhere within it. If certain perspectives evidently exist which cannot be analyzed in physical terms, we must modify our idea of objective reality to include them. If that is not enough, we must admit to reality some things that cannot be objectively understood. Similarly, if certain reasons for action which appear to exist cannot be accommodated within a purely agent-neutral system—or even perhaps within a general but agent-relative system—then we may have to modify our realist idea of value and practical reason accordingly. I don't mean to suggest that there is no conflict here. The opposition between objective reasons and subjective inclinations may be severe, and may require us to change our lives. I mean only that the truth, if there is any, will be arrived at by the exploration of this conflict rather than by the automatic victory of the most transcendent standpoint. In the conduct of life, of all places, the rivalry between the view from within and the view from without must be taken seriously.

1981

The Nature of the Virtues

Alasdair MacIntyre

One response to the history which I have narrated so far might well be to suggest that even within the relatively coherent tradition of thought which I have sketched there are just too many different and incompatible conceptions of a virtue for there to be any real unity to the concept or indeed to the history. Homer, Sophocles, Aristotle, the New Testament and medieval thinkers differ from each other in too many ways. They offer us different and incompatible lists of the virtues; they give a different rank order of importance to different virtues; and they have different and incompatible theories of the virtues. If we were to consider later Western writers on the virtues, the list of differences and incompatibilities would be enlarged still further; and if we extended our enquiry to Japanese, say, or American Indian cultures, the differences would become greater still. It would be all too easy to conclude that there are a number of rival and alternative conceptions of the virtues, but, even within the tradition which I have been delineating, no single core conception.

The case for such a conclusion could not be better constructed than by beginning from a consideration of the very different lists of items which different authors in different times and places have included in their catalogues of virtues. Some of these catalogues—Homer's, Aristotle's and the New Testament's—I have already noticed at greater or lesser length. Let me at the risk of some repetition recall some of their key features and then introduce for further comparison the catalogues of two later Western writers, Benjamin Franklin and Jane Austen.

The first example is that of Homer. At least some of the items in a Homeric list of the *aretai* would clearly not be counted by most of us nowadays as virtues at all, physical strength being the most obvious example. To this it might be replied that perhaps we ought not to translate the word *aretê* in Homer by our word "virtue," but instead by our word "excellence"; and perhaps, if we were so to translate it, the apparently surprising difference between Homer and ourselves would at first sight have been removed. For we could allow without any kind of oddity that the possession of physical strength is the possession of an excellence. But in fact we would not have removed, but instead would merely have relocated, the difference between Homer and ourselves. For we would now seem to be saying that Homer's concept of an *aretê,* an excellence, is one thing and that our concept of a virtue is quite another since a particular quality can be an excellence in Homer's eyes, but not a virtue in ours and *vice versa.*

But of course it is not that Homer's list of virtues differs only from our own; it also notably differs from Aristotle's. And Aristotle's of course also differs from our own. For one thing, as I noticed earlier, some Greek virtue-words are not easily translated into English or rather out of Greek. Moreover consider the importance of friendship as a virtue in Aristotle's list—how different from us! Or the place of *phronêsis*—how different from Homer and from us! The mind receives from Aristotle the kind of tribute which the body receives from Homer. But it is not just the case that the difference between Aristotle and Homer lies in the inclusion of some items and the omission of others in their respective catalogues. It turns out also in the way in which those catalogues are ordered, in which items are ranked as relatively central to human excellence and which marginal.

Moreover the relationship of virtues to the social order has changed. For Homer the paradigm of human excellence is the warrior; for Aristotle it is the Athenian gentleman. Indeed according to Aristotle certain virtues are only available to those of great riches and of high social status; there are virtues which are unavailable to the poor man, even if he is a free man. And those virtues are on Aristotle's view ones central to human life; magnanimity—and once again, any translation of *megalopsuchia* is unsatisfactory—and munificence are not just virtues, but important virtues within the Aristotelian scheme.

At once it is impossible to delay the remark that the most striking contrast with Aristotle's catalogue is to be found neither in Homer's nor in our own, but in the New Testament's. For the New Testament not only praises virtues of which Aristotle knows nothing—faith, hope and love—and says nothing about virtues such as *phronêsis* which are crucial for Aristotle, but it praises at least one quality as a virtue which Aristotle seems to count as one of the vices relative to magnanimity, namely humility. Moreover since the New Testament quite clearly sees the rich as destined for the pains of Hell, it is clear that the key virtues cannot be available to them; yet they *are* available to slaves. And the New Testament of course differs from both Homer and Aristotle not only in the items included in its catalogue, but once again in its rank ordering of the virtues.

Turn now to compare all three lists of virtues considered so far—the Homeric, the Aristotelian, and the New Testament's—with two much later lists, one which can be compiled from Jane Austen's novels and the other which Benjamin Franklin constructed for himself. Two features stand out in Jane Austen's list. The first is the importance that she allots to the virtue which she calls "constancy," a virtue about which I shall say more in a later chapter [of *After Virtue*]. In some ways constancy plays a role in Jane Austen analogous to that of *phronêsis* in Aristotle; it is a virtue the possession of which is a prerequisite for the possession of other virtues. The second is the fact that what Aristotle treats as the virtue of agreeableness (a virtue for which he says there is no name) she treats as only the simulacrum of a genuine virtue—the genuine virtue in question is the one she calls amiability. For the man who practices agreeableness does so from considerations of honor and expediency, according to Aristotle; whereas Jane Austen thought it possible and necessary for the possessor of that virtue to have a certain real affection for people as such. (It matters here that Jane Austen is a Christian.) Remember that Aristotle himself had treated military courage as a simulacrum of true courage. Thus we find here yet another type of disagreement over the virtues; namely, one as to which human qualities are genuine virtues and which mere simulacra.

In Benjamin Franklin's list we find almost all the types of difference from at least one of the catalogues we have considered and one more. Franklin includes virtues which are new to our consideration such as cleanliness, silence and industry; he clearly considers the drive to acquire itself a part of virtue, whereas for most ancient Greeks this is the vice of *pleonexia;* he treats some virtues which earlier ages had considered minor as major; but he also redefines some familiar virtues. In the list of thirteen virtues which Franklin compiled as part of his system of private moral accounting, he elucidates each virtue by citing a maxim obedience to which *is* the virtue in question. In the case of chastity the maxim is "Rarely use venery but for health or offspring—never to dullness, weakness or the injury of your own or another's peace or reputation." This is clearly not what earlier writers had meant by "chastity."

We have therefore accumulated a startling number of differences and incompatibilities in the five stated and implied accounts of the virtues. So the question which I raised at the outset becomes more urgent. If different writers in different times and places, but all within the history of Western culture, include such different sets and types of items in their lists, what grounds have we for supposing that they do indeed aspire to list items of one and the same kind, that there is any shared concept at all? A second kind of consideration reinforces the presumption of a negative answer to this question. It is not just that each of these five writers lists different and differing kinds of items; it is also that each of these lists embodies, is the expression of a different theory about what a virtue is.

In the Homeric poems a virtue is a quality the manifestation of which enables someone to do exactly what their well-defined social role requires. The primary role is that of the warrior king and that Homer lists those virtues which he does becomes intelligible at once when we recognize that the key virtues therefore must be those which enable a man to excel in combat and in the games. It follows that we cannot identify the Homeric virtues until we have first identified the key social roles in Homeric society and the requirements of each of them. The concept of *what anyone filling such-and-such a role ought to do* is prior to the concept of a virtue; the latter concept has application only via the former.

On Aristotle's account matters are very different. Even though some virtues are available only to certain types of people, nonetheless virtues attach not to men as inhabiting social roles, but to man as such. It is the *telos* of man as a species which determines what human qualities are virtues. We need to remember however that although Aristotle treats the acquisition and exercise of the virtues as means to an end, the relationship of means to end is internal and not external. I call a means internal to a given end when the end cannot be adequately characterized independently of a characterization of the means. So it is with the virtues and the *telos* which is the good life for man on Aristotle's account. The exercise of the virtues is itself a crucial component of the good life for man. This distinction between internal and external means to an end is not drawn by Aristotle himself in the *Nicomachean Ethics,* as I noticed earlier, but it is an essential distinction to be drawn if we are to understand what Aristotle intended. The distinction *is* drawn explicitly by Aquinas in the course of his defense of St. Augustine's definition of a virtue, and it is clear that Aquinas understood that in drawing it he was maintaining an Aristotelian point of view.

The New Testament's account of the virtues, even if it differs as much as it does in content from Aristotle's—Aristotle would certainly not have admired Jesus Christ and he would have been horrified by St. Paul—does have the same logical and conceptual structure as Aristotle's account. A virtue is, as with Aristotle, a quality the exercise of which leads to the achievement of the human *telos.* The good for man is of course a supernatural and not only a natural good, but supernature redeems and completes nature. Moreover the relationship of virtues as means to the end which is human incorporation in the divine kingdom of the age to come is internal and not external, just as it is in Aristotle. It is of course this parallelism which allows Aquinas to synthesize Aristotle and the New Testament. A key feature of this parallelism is the way in which the concept of *the good life for man* is prior to the concept of a virtue in just the way in which on the Homeric account the concept of a social role was prior. Once again it is the way in which the former concept is applied which determines how the latter is to be applied. In both cases the concept of a virtue is a secondary concept.

The intent of Jane Austen's theory of the virtues is of another kind. C. S. Lewis has rightly emphasized how profoundly Christian her moral vision is and Gilbert Ryle has equally rightly emphasized her inheritance from Shaftesbury and from Aristotle. In fact her views combine elements from Homer as well, since she is concerned with social roles in a way that neither the New Testament nor Aristotle are. She is therefore important for the way in which she finds it possible to combine what are at first sight disparate theoretical accounts of the virtues. But for the moment any attempt to assess the significance of Jane Austen's synthesis must be delayed. Instead we must notice the quite different style of theory articulated in Benjamin Franklin's account of the virtues.

Franklin's account, like Aristotle's, is teleological; but unlike Aristotle's, it is utilitarian. According to Franklin in his *Autobiography* the virtues are means to an end, but he envisages the means-ends relationship as external rather than internal. The end to which the cultivation of the virtues ministers is happiness, but happiness understood as success, prosperity in Philadelphia and ultimately in heaven. The virtues are to be useful and Franklin's account continuously stresses utility as a criterion in individual cases: "Make no expense but to do good to others or yourself; i.e. waste nothing," "Speak not but what may benefit others or yourself. Avoid trifling conversation" and, as we have already seen, "Rarely use venery but for health or offspring. . . ." When Franklin was in Paris he was horrified by Parisian architecture: "Marble, porcelain and gilt are squandered without utility."

We thus have at least three very different conceptions of a virtue to confront: a virtue is a quality which enables an individual to discharge his or her social role (Homer); a virtue is a quality which enables an individual to move towards the achievement of the specifically human *telos,* whether natural or supernatural (Aristotle, the New Testament and Aquinas); a virtue is a quality which has utility in achieving earthly and heavenly success (Franklin). Are we to take these as three different rival accounts of the same thing? Or are they instead accounts of three different things? Perhaps the moral structures in archaic Greece, in fourth-century Greece, and in eighteenth-century Pennsylvania were so different from each other that we should treat them as embodying quite different concepts, whose difference is initially disguised from us by the historical accident of an inherited vocabulary which misleads us by linguistic resemblance long after conceptual identity and similarity have failed. Our initial question has come back to us with redoubled force.

Yet although I have dwelt upon the *prima facie* case for holding that the differences and incompatibilities between different accounts at least suggest that there is no single, central, core conception of the virtues which might make a claim for universal allegiance, I ought also to point out that each of the five moral accounts which I have sketched so summarily does embody just such a claim. It is indeed just this feature of those accounts that makes them of more than sociological or antiquarian interest. Every one of these accounts claims not only theoretical, but also an institutional hegemony. For Odysseus the Cyclopes stand condemned because they lack agriculture, an *agora* and *themis*. For Aristotle the barbarians stand condemned because they lack the *polis* and are therefore incapable of politics. For New Testament Christians there is no salvation outside the apostolic church. And we know that Benjamin Franklin found the virtues more at home in Philadelphia than in Paris and that for Jane Austen the touchstone of the virtues is a certain kind of marriage and indeed a certain kind of naval officer (that is, a certain kind of *English* naval officer).

The question can therefore now be posed directly: are we or are we not able to disentangle from these rival and various claims a unitary core concept of the virtues of which we can give a more compelling account than any of the other accounts so far? I am going to argue that we can in fact discover such a core concept and that it turns out to provide the tradition of which I have written the history with its conceptual unity. It will indeed enable us to distinguish in a clear way those beliefs about the virtues which genuinely belong to the tradition from those which do not. Unsurprisingly perhaps it is a complex concept, different parts of which derive from different stages in the development of the tradition. Thus the concept itself in some sense embodies the history of which it is the outcome.

One of the features of the concept of a virtue which has emerged with some clarity from the argument so far is that it always requires for its application the acceptance for some prior account of certain features of social and moral life in terms of which it has to be defined and explained. So in the Homeric account the concept of a virtue is secondary to that of *a social role,* in Aristotle's account it is secondary to that of *the good life for man* conceived as the *telos* of human action and in Franklin's much later account it is secondary to that of utility. What is it in the account which I am about to give which provides in a similar way the necessary background against which the concept of a virtue has to be made intelligible? It is in answering this question that the complex, historical, multi-layered character of the core concept of virtue becomes clear. For there are no less than three stages in the logical development of the concept which have to be identified in order, if the core conception of a virtue is to be understood, and each of these stages has its own conceptual background. The first stage requires a background account of what I shall call a practice, the second an account of what I have already characterized as the narrative order of a single human life and the third an account a good deal fuller than I have given up to now of what constitutes a moral tradition. Each later stage presupposes the earlier, but not *vice versa.* Each earlier stage is both modified by and reinterpreted in the light of, but also provides an essential constituent of each later stage. The progress in the development of the concept is closely related to, although it does not recapitulate in any straightforward way, the history of the tradition of which it forms the core.

In the Homeric account of the virtues—and in heroic societies more generally—the exercise of a virtue exhibits qualities which are required for sustaining a social role and for exhibiting excellence in some well-marked area of social practice: to excel is to excel at war or in the games, as Achilles does, in sustaining a household, as Penelope does, in giving counsel in the assembly, as Nestor does, in the telling of a tale, as Homer himself does. When Aristotle speaks of excellence in human activity, he sometimes though not always, refers to some well-defined type of human practice: flute-playing, or war, or geometry. I am going to suggest that this notion of a particular type of practice as providing the arena in which the virtues are exhibited and in terms of which they are to receive their primary, if incomplete, definition is crucial to the whole enterprise of identifying a core concept of the virtues. I hasten to add two *caveats* however.

The first is to point out that my argument will not in any way imply that virtues are *only* exercised in the course of what I am calling practices. The second is to warn that I shall be using the word "practice" in a specially defined way which does not completely agree with current ordinary usage, including my own previous use of that word. What am I going to mean by it?

By a "practice" I am going to mean any coherent and complex form of socially established cooperative human activity through which goods internal to that form of activity are realized in the course of trying to achieve those standards of excellence which are appropriate to, and partially definitive of, that form of activity, with the result that human powers to achieve excellence, and human conceptions of the ends and goods involved, are systematically extended. Tic-tac-toe is not an example of a practice in this sense, nor is throwing a football with skill; but the game of football is, and so is chess. Bricklaying is not a practice; architecture is. Planting turnips is not a practice; farming is. So are the enquiries of physics, chemistry and biology, and so is the work of the historian, and so are painting and music. In the ancient and medieval worlds the creation and sustaining of human communities—of households, cities, nations—is generally taken to be a practice in the sense in which I have defined it. Thus the range of practices is wide: arts, sciences, games, politics in the Aristotelian sense, the making and sustaining of family life, all fall under the concept. But the question of the precise range of practices is not at this stage of the first importance. Instead let me explain some of the key terms involved in my definition, beginning with the notion of goods internal to a practice.

Consider the example of a highly intelligent seven-year-old child whom I wish to teach to play chess, although the child has no particular desire to learn the game. The child does however have a very strong desire for candy and little chance of obtaining it. I therefore tell the child that if the child will play chess with me once a week I will give the child 50 cents worth of candy; moreover I tell the child that I will always play in such a way that it will be difficult, but not impossible, for the child to win and that, if the child wins, the child will receive an extra 50 cents worth of candy. Thus motivated the child plays and plays to win. Notice however that, so long as it is the candy alone which provides the child with a good reason for playing chess, the child has no reason not to cheat and every reason to cheat, provided he or she can do so successfully. But, so we may hope, there will come a time when the child will find in those goods specific to chess, in the achievement of a certain highly particular kind of analytical skill, strategic imagination and competitive intensity, a new set of reasons, reasons now not just for winning on a particular occasion, but for trying to excel in whatever way the game of chess demands. Now if the child cheats, he or she will be defeating not me, but himself or herself.

There are thus two kinds of good possibly to be gained by playing chess. On the one hand there are those goods externally and contingently attached to chess-playing and to other practices by the accidents of social circumstance—in the case of the imaginary child candy, in the case of real adults such goods as prestige, status and money. There are always alternative ways for achieving such goods, and their achievement is never to be had *only* by engaging in some particular kind of practice. On the other hand there are the goods internal to the practice of chess which cannot be had in any way but by playing chess or some other game of that specific kind. We call them internal for two reasons: first, as I have already suggested, because we can only specify them in terms of chess or some other game of that specific kind and by means of examples from such games (otherwise the meagerness of our vocabulary for speaking of such goods forces us into such devices as my own resort to writing of "a certain highly particular kind of"); and secondly because they can only be identified and recognized by the experience of participating in the practice in question. Those who lack the relevant experience are incompetent thereby as judges of internal goods.

This is clearly the case with all the major examples of practices: consider for example—even if briefly and inadequately—the practice of portrait painting as it developed in Western Europe from the late middle ages to the eighteenth century. The successful portrait painter is able to achieve many goods which are in the sense just defined external to the practice of portrait painting—fame, wealth, social status, even a measure of power and influence at courts upon occasion. But those external goods are not to be confused with the goods which are internal to the practice. The internal goods are those which result from an extended attempt to show how Wittgenstein's dictum "The human body is the best picture of the human soul" (*Investigations,* p. 178e) might be made to become true by teaching us "to regard . . . the picture on our wall as the object itself (the men, landscape and so on) depicted there" (p. 205e) in a quite new way. What is misleading about Wittgenstein's dictum as it stands is its neglect of the truth in George Orwell's thesis "At fifty everyone has the face he deserves." What painters from Giotto to Rembrandt learnt to show was how the face at any age may be revealed as the face that the subject of a portrait deserves.

Originally in medieval paintings of the saints the face was an icon; the question of a resemblance between the depicted face of Christ or St. Peter and the face that Jesus or Peter actually possessed at some particular age did not even arise. The antithesis to this iconography was the relative naturalism of certain fifteenth-century Flemish and German painting. The heavy eyelids, the coifed hair, the lines around the mouth undeniably represent some particular woman, either actual or envisaged. Resemblance has usurped the iconic relationship. But with Rembrandt there is, so to speak, synthesis: the naturalistic portrait is now rendered as an icon, but an icon of a new and hitherto inconceivable kind. Similarly in a very different kind of sequence mythological faces in a certain kind of seventeenth-century French painting become aristocratic faces in the eighteenth century. Within each of these sequences at least two different kinds of good internal to the painting of human faces and bodies are achieved.

There is first of all the excellence of the products, both the excellence in performance by the painters and that of each portrait itself. This excellence—the very verb "excel" suggests it—has to be understood historically. The sequences of development find their point and purpose in a progress towards and beyond a variety of types and modes of excellence. There are of course sequences of decline as well as of progress, and progress is rarely to be understood as straightforwardly linear. But it is in participation in the attempts to sustain progress and to respond creatively to problems that the second kind of good internal to the practices of portrait painting is to be found. For what the artist discovers within the pursuit of excellence in portrait painting—and what is true of portrait painting is true of the practice of the fine arts in general—is the good of a certain kind of life. That life may not constitute the whole of life for someone who is a painter by a very long way or it may at least for a period, Gauguin-like, absorb him or her at the expense of almost everything else. But it is the painter's living out of a greater or lesser part of his or her life *as a painter* that is the second kind of good internal to painting. And judgment upon these goods requires at the very least the kind of competence that is only to be acquired either as a painter or as someone willing to learn systematically what the portrait painter has to teach.

A practice involves standards of excellence and obedience to rules as well as the achievement of goods. To enter into a practice is to accept the authority of those standards and the inadequacy of my own performance as judged by them. It is to subject my own attitudes, choices, preferences and tastes to the standards which currently and partially define the practice. Practices of course, as I have just noticed, have a history: games, sciences and arts all have histories. Thus the standards are not themselves immune from criticism, but nonetheless we cannot be initiated into a practice without accepting the authority of the best standards realized so far. If, on starting to listen to music, I do not accept my own incapacity to judge correctly, I will never learn to hear, let alone to appreciate, Bartok's last quartets. If, on starting to play baseball, I do not accept that others know better than I when to throw a fast ball and when not, I will never learn to appreciate good pitching let alone to pitch. In the realm of practices the authority of both goods and standards operates in such a way as to rule out all subjectivist and emotivist analyses of judgment. De gustibus *est* disputandum.

We are now in a position to notice an important difference between what I have called internal and what I have called external goods. It is characteristic of what I have called external goods that when achieved they are always some individual's property and possession. Moreover characteristically they are such that the more someone has of them, the less there is for other people. This is sometimes necessarily the case, as with power and fame, and sometimes the case by reason of contingent circumstance as with money. External goods are therefore characteristically objects of competition in which there must be losers as well as winners. Internal goods are indeed the outcome of competition to excel, but it is characteristic of them that their achievement is a good for the whole community who participate in the practice. So when Turner transformed the seascape in painting or W. G. Grace advanced the art of batting in cricket in a quite new way their achievement enriched the whole relevant community.

But what does all or any of this have to do with the concept of the virtues? It turns out that we are now in a position to formulate a first, even if partial and tentative definition of a virtue: *A virtue is an acquired human quality the possession and exercise of which tends to enable us to achieve those goods which are internal to practices and the lack of which effectively prevents us from achieving any such goods.* Later this definition will need amplification and amendment. But as a first approximation to an adequate definition it already illuminates the place of the virtues in human life. For it is not difficult to show for a whole range of key virtues that without them the goods internal to practices are barred to us, but not just barred to us generally, barred in a very particular way.

It belongs to the concept of a practice as I have outlined it—and as we are all familiar with it already in our actual lives, whether we are painters or physicists or quarterbacks or indeed just lovers of good painting or first-rate experiments or a well-thrown pass—that its goods can only be achieved by subordinating ourselves within the practice in our relationship to other practitioners. We have to learn to recognize what is due to whom; we have to be prepared to take whatever self-endangering risks are demanded along the way; and we have to listen carefully to what we are told about our own inadequacies and to reply with the same carefulness for the facts. In other words we have to accept as necessary components of any practice with internal goods and standards of excellence the virtues of justice, courage and honesty. For not to accept these, to be willing to cheat as our imagined child was willing to cheat in his or her early days at chess, so far bars us from achieving the standards of excellence or the goods internal to the practice that it renders the practice pointless except as a device for achieving external goods.

We can put the same point in another way. Every practice requires a certain kind of relationship between those who participate in it. Now the virtues are those goods by reference to which, whether we like it or not, we define our relationships to those other people with whom we share the kind of purposes and standards which inform practices. Consider an example of how reference to the virtues has to be made in certain kinds of human relationship.

A, B, C, and D are friends in that sense of friendship which Aristotle takes to be primary: they share in the pursuit of certain goods. In my terms they share in a practice. D dies in obscure circumstances, A discovers how D died and tells the truth about it to B while lying to C. C discovers the lie. What A cannot then intelligibly claim is that he stands in the same relationship of friendship to both B and C. By telling the truth to one and lying to the other he has partially defined a difference in the relationship. Of course it is open to A to explain this difference in a number of ways; perhaps he was trying to spare C pain or perhaps he is simply cheating C. But some difference in the relationship now exists as a result of the lie. For their allegiance to each other in the pursuit of common goods has been put in question.

Just as, so long as we share the standards and purposes characteristic of practices, we define our relationship to each other, whether we acknowledge it or not, by reference to standards of truthfulness and trust, so we define them too by reference to standards of justice and of courage. If A, a professor, gives B and C the grades that their papers deserve, but grades D because he is attracted by D's blue eyes or is repelled by D's dandruff, he has defined his relationship to D differently from his relationship to the other members of the class, whether he wishes it or not. Justice requires that we treat others in respect of merit or desert according to uniform and impersonal standards; to depart from the standards of justice in some particular instance defines our relationship with the relevant person as in some way special or distinctive.

The case with courage is a little different. We hold courage to be a virtue because the care and concern for individuals, communities and causes which is so crucial to so much in practices requires the existence of such a virtue. If someone says that he cares for some individual, community or cause, but is unwilling to risk harm or danger on his, her or its own behalf, he puts in question the genuineness of his care and concern. Courage, the capacity to risk harm or danger to oneself, has its role in human life because of this connection with care and concern. This is not to say that a man cannot genuinely care and also be a coward. It is in part to say that a man who genuinely cares and has not the capacity for risking harm or danger has to define himself, both to himself and to others, as a coward.

I take it then that from the standpoint of those types of relationship without which practices cannot be sustained truthfulness, justice and courage—and perhaps some others—are genuine excellences, are virtues in the light of which we have to characterize ourselves and others, whatever our private moral standpoint or our society's particular codes may be. For this recognition that we cannot escape the definition of our relationships in terms of such goods is perfectly compatible with the acknowledgment that different societies have and have had different codes of truthfulness, justice and courage. Lutheran pietists brought up their children to believe that one ought to tell the truth to everybody at all times, whatever the circumstances or consequences, and Kant was one of their children. Traditional Bantu parents brought up their children not to tell the truth to unknown strangers, since they believed that this could render the family vulnerable to witchcraft. In our culture many of us have been brought up not to tell the truth to elderly great-aunts who invite us to admire their new hats. But each of these codes embodies an acknowledgment of the virtue of truthfulness. So it is also with varying codes of justice and of courage.

Practices then might flourish in societies with very different codes; what they could not do is flourish in societies in which the virtues were not valued, although institutions and technical skills serving unified purposes might well continue to flourish. (I shall have more to say about the contrast between institutions and technical skills mobilized for a unified end, on the one hand, and practices on the other, in a moment.) For the kind of cooperation, the kind of recognition of authority and of achievement, the kind of respect for standards and the kind of risk-taking which are characteristically involved in practices demand for example fairness in judging oneself and others—the kind of fairness absent in my example of the professor, a ruthless truthfulness without which fairness cannot find application—the kind of truthfulness absent in my example of A, B, C, and D—and willingness to trust the judgments of those whose achievement in the practice give them an authority to judge which presupposes fairness and truthfulness in those judgments, and from time to time the taking of self-endangering and even achievement-endangering risks. It is no part of my thesis that great violinists cannot be vicious or great chess-players mean-spirited. Where the virtues are required, the vices also may flourish. It is just that the vicious and mean-spirited necessarily rely on the virtues of others for the practices in which they engage to flourish and also deny themselves the experience of achieving those internal goods which may reward even not very good chess-players and violinists.

To situate the virtues any further within practices it is necessary now to clarify a little further the nature of a practice by drawing two important contrasts. The discussion so far I hope makes it clear that a practice, in the sense intended, is never just a set of technical skills, even when directed towards some unified purpose and even if the exercise of those skills can on occasion be valued or enjoyed for their own sake. What is distinctive in a practice is in part the way in which conceptions of the relevant goods and ends which the technical skills serve—and every practice does require the exercise of technical skills—are transformed and enriched by these extensions of human powers and by that regard for its own internal goods which are partially definitive of each particular practice or type of practice. Practices never have a goal or goals fixed for all time—painting has no such goal nor has physics—but the goals themselves are transmuted by the history of the activity. It therefore turns out not to be accidental that every practice has its own history and a history which is more and other than that of the improvement of the relevant technical skills. This historical dimension is crucial in relation to the virtues.

To enter into a practice is to enter into a relationship not only with its contemporary practitioners, but also with those who have preceded us in the practice, particularly those whose achievements extended the reach of the practice to its present point. It is thus the achievement, and *a fortiori* the authority, of a tradition which I then confront and from which I have to learn. And for this learning and the relationship to the past which it embodies the virtues of justice, courage and truthfulness are prerequisite in precisely the same way and for precisely the same reasons as they are in sustaining present relationships within practices.

It is not only of course with sets of technical skills that practices ought to be contrasted. Practices must not be confused with institutions. Chess, physics and medicine are practices; chess clubs, laboratories, universities and hospitals are institutions. Institutions are characteristically and necessarily concerned with what I have called external goods. They are involved in acquiring money and other material goods; they are structured in terms of power and status, and they distribute money, power and status as rewards. Nor could they do otherwise if they are to sustain not only themselves, but also the practices of which they are the bearers. For no practices can survive for any length of time unsustained by institutions. Indeed so intimate is the relationship of practices to institutions—and consequently of the goods external to the goods internal to the practices in question—that institutions and practices characteristically form a single causal order in which the ideals and the creativity of the practice are always vulnerable to the acquisitiveness of the institution, in which the cooperative care for common goods of the practice is always vulnerable to the competitiveness of the institution. In this context the essential function of the virtues is clear. Without them, without justice, courage and truthfulness, practices could not resist the corrupting power of institutions.

Yet if institutions do have corrupting power, the making and sustaining of forms of human community—and therefore of institutions—itself has all the characteristics of a practice, and moreover of a practice which stands in a peculiarly close relationship to the exercise of the virtues in two important ways. The exercise of the virtues is itself apt to require a highly determinate attitude to social and political issues; and it is always within some particular community with its own specific institutional forms that we learn or fail to learn to exercise the virtues. There is of course a crucial difference between the way in which the relationship between moral character and political community is envisaged from the standpoint of liberal individualist modernity and the way in which that relationship was envisaged from the standpoint of the type of ancient and medieval tradition of the virtues which I have sketched. For liberal individualism a community is simply an arena in which individuals each pursue their own self-chosen conception of the good life, and political institutions exist to provide that degree of order which makes such self-determined activity possible. Government and law are, or ought to be, neutral between rival concepts as of the good life for man, and hence, although it is the task of government to promote law-abidingness, it is on the liberal view no part of the legitimate function of government to inculcate any one moral outlook.

By contrast, on the particular ancient and medieval view which I have sketched political community not only requires the exercise of the virtues for its own sustenance, but it is one of the tasks of parental authority to make children grow up so as to be virtuous adults. The classical statement of this analogy is by Socrates in the *Crito.* It does not of course follow from an acceptance of the Socratic view of political community and political authority that we ought to assign to the modern state the moral function which Socrates assigned to the city and its laws. Indeed the power of the liberal individualist standpoint partly derives from the evident fact that the modern state is indeed totally unfitted to act as moral educator of any community. But the history of how the modern state emerged is of course itself a moral history. If my account of the complex relationship of virtues to practices and to institutions is correct, it follows that we shall be unable to write a true history of practices and institutions unless that history is also one of the virtues and vices. For the ability of a practice to retain its integrity will depend on the way in which the virtues can be and are exercised in sustaining the institutional forms which are the social bearers of the practice. The integrity of a practice causally requires the exercise of the virtues by at least some of the individuals who embody it in their activities; and conversely the corruption of institutions is always in part at least an effect of the vices.

The virtues are of course themselves in turn fostered by certain types of social institution and endangered by others. Thomas Jefferson thought that only in a society of small farmers could the virtues flourish; and Adam Ferguson with a good deal more sophistication saw the institutions of modern commercial society as endangering at least some traditional virtues. It is Ferguson's type of sociology which is the empirical counterpart of the conceptual account of the virtues which I have given, a sociology which aspires to lay bare the empirical, causal connection between virtues, practices and institutions. For this kind of conceptual account has strong empirical implications; it provides an explanatory scheme which can be tested in particular cases. Moreover my thesis has empirical content in another way; it does entail that without the virtues there could be a recognition only of what I have called external goods and not at all of internal goods in the context of practices. And in any society which recognized only external goods competitiveness would be the dominant and even exclusive feature. We have a brilliant portrait of such a society in Hobbes's account of the state of nature; and Professor Turnbull's report of the fate of the Ik suggests that social reality does in the most horrifying way confirm both my thesis and Hobbes's.

Virtues then stand in a different relationship to external and to internal goods. The possession of the virtues—and not only of their semblance and simulacra—is necessary to achieve the latter; yet the possession of the virtues may perfectly well hinder us in achieving external goods. I need to emphasize at this point that external goods genuinely are goods. Not only are they characteristic objects of human desire, whose allocation is what gives point to the virtues of justice and of generosity, but no one can despise them altogether without a certain hypocrisy. Yet notoriously the cultivation of truthfulness, justice and courage will often, the world being what it contingently is, bar us from being rich or famous or powerful. Thus although we may hope that we can not only achieve the standards of excellence and the internal goods of certain practices by possessing the virtues *and* become rich, famous and powerful, the virtues are always a potential stumbling block to this comfortable ambition. We should therefore expect that, if in a particular society the pursuit of external goods were to become dominant, the concept of the virtues might suffer first attrition and then perhaps something near total effacement, although simulacra might abound.

The time has come to ask the question of how far this partial account of a core conception of the virtues—and I need to emphasize that all that I have offered so far is the first stage of such an account—is faithful to the tradition which I delineated. How far, for example, and in what ways is it Aristotelian? It is—happily—not Aristotelian in two ways in which a good deal of the rest of the tradition also dissents from Aristotle. First, although this account of the virtues is teleological, it does not require any allegiance to Aristotle's metaphysical biology. And secondly, just because of the multiplicity of human practices and the consequent multiplicity of goods in the pursuit of which the virtues may be exercised—goods which will often be contingently incompatible and which will therefore make rival claims upon our allegiance—conflict will not spring solely from flaws in individual character. But it was just on these two matters that Aristotle's account of the virtues seemed most vulnerable; hence if it turns out to be the case that this socially teleological account can support Aristotle's general account of the virtues as well as does his own biologically teleological account, these differences from Aristotle himself may well be regarded as strengthening rather than weakening the case for a generally Aristotelian standpoint.

There are at least three ways in which the account that I have given *is* clearly Aristotelian. First it requires for its completion a cogent elaboration of just those distinctions and concepts which Aristotle's account requires: voluntariness, the distinction between the intellectual virtues and the virtues of character, the relationship of both to natural abilities and to the passions and the structure of practical reasoning. On every one of these topics something very like Aristotle's view has to be defended, if my own account is to be plausible.

Secondly my account can accommodate an Aristotelian view of pleasure and enjoyment, whereas it is interestingly irreconcilable with any utilitarian view and more particularly with Franklin's account of the virtues. We can approach these questions by considering how to reply to someone who, having considered my account of the differences between goods internal to and goods external to a practice enquired into which class, if either, does pleasure or enjoyment fall? The answer is, "Some types of pleasure into one, some into the other."

Someone who achieves excellence in a practice, who plays chess or football well or who carries through an enquiry in physics or an experimental mode in painting with success, characteristically enjoys his achievement and his activity in achieving. So does someone who, although not breaking the limit of achievement, plays or thinks or acts in a way that leads towards such a breaking of limit. As Aristotle says, the enjoyment of the activity and the enjoyment of achievement are not the ends at which the agent aims, but the enjoyment supervenes upon the successful activity in such a way that the activity achieved and the activity enjoyed are one and the same state. Hence to aim at the one is to aim at the other; and hence also it is easy to confuse the pursuit of excellence with the pursuit of enjoyment *in this specific sense.* This particular confusion is harmless enough; what is not harmless is the confusion of enjoyment *in this specific sense* with other forms of pleasure.

For certain kinds of pleasure are of course external goods along with prestige, status, power and money. Not all pleasure is the enjoyment supervening upon achieved activity; some is the pleasure of psychological or physical states independent of all activity. Such states—for example that produced on a normal palate by the closely successive and thereby blended sensations of Colchester oyster, cayenne pepper and Veuve Cliquot—may be sought as external goods, as external rewards which may be purchased by money or received in virtue of prestige. Hence the pleasures are categorized neatly and appropriately by the classification into internal and external goods.

It is just this classification which can find no place within Franklin's account of the virtues which is framed entirely in terms of external relationships and external goods. Thus although by this stage of the argument it is possible to claim that my account does capture a conception of the virtues which is at the core of the particular ancient and medieval tradition which I have delineated, it is equally clear that there is more than one possible conception of the virtues and that Franklin's standpoint and indeed any utilitarian standpoint is such that to accept it will entail rejecting the tradition and *vice versa.*

One crucial point of incompatibility was noted long ago by D. H. Lawrence. When Franklin asserts, "Rarely use venery but for health or offspring . . . ," Lawrence replies, "Never *use* venery." It is of the character of a virtue that in order that it be effective in producing the internal goods which are the rewards of the virtues it should be exercised without regard to consequences. For it turns out to be the case that—and this is in part at least one more empirical factual claim—although the virtues are just those qualities which tend to lead to the achievement of a certain class of goods, nonetheless unless we practice them irrespective of whether in any particular set of contingent circumstances they will produce those goods or not, we cannot possess them at all. We cannot be genuinely courageous or truthful and be so only on occasion. Moreover, as we have seen, cultivation of the virtues always may and often does hinder the achievement of those external goods which are the mark of worldly success. The road to success in Philadelphia and the road to heaven may not coincide after all.

Furthermore we are now able to specify one crucial difficulty for *any* version of utilitarianism—in addition to those which I noticed earlier. Utilitarianism cannot accommodate the distinction between goods internal to and goods external to a practice.

Not only is that distinction marked by none of the classical utilitarians—it cannot be found in Bentham's writings nor in those of either of the Mills or of Sidgwick—but internal goods and external goods are not commensurable with each other. Hence the notion of summing goods—and *a fortiori* in the light of what I have said about kinds of pleasure and enjoyment the notion of summing happiness—in terms of one single formula or conception of utility, whether it is Franklin's or Bentham's or Mill's, makes no sense. Nonetheless we ought to note that although *this* distinction is alien to J. S. Mill's thought, it is plausible and in no way patronizing to suppose that something like this is the distinction which he was trying to make in *Utilitarianism* when he distinguished between "higher" and "lower" pleasures. At the most we can say "something like this"; for J. S. Mill's upbringing had given him a limited view of human life and powers, had unfitted him, for example, for appreciating games just because of the way it had fitted him for appreciating philosophy. Nonetheless the notion that the pursuit of excellence in a way that extends human powers is at the heart of human life is instantly recognizable as at home in not only J. S. Mill's political and social thought, but also in his and Mrs. Taylor's life. Were I to choose human exemplars of certain of the virtues as I understand them, there would of course be many names to name, those of St. Benedict and St. Francis of Assisi and St. Theresa *and* those of Frederick Engels and Eleanor Marx and Leon Trotsky among them. But that of John Stuart Mill would have to be there as certainly as any other.

Thirdly my account is Aristotelian in that it links evaluation and explanation in a characteristically Aristotelian way. From an Aristotelian standpoint to identify certain actions as manifesting or failing to manifest a virtue or virtues is never only to evaluate; it is also to take the first step towards explaining why those actions rather than some others were performed. Hence for an Aristotelian quite as much as for a Platonist the fate of a city or an individual can be explained by citing the injustice of a tyrant or the courage of its defenders. Indeed without allusion to the place that justice and injustice, courage and cowardice play in human life very little will be genuinely explicable. It follows that many of the explanatory projects of the modern social sciences, a methodological canon of which is the separation of "the facts"—this conception of the "the facts" is the one which I delineated in Chapter 7 [*After Virtue*]—from all evaluation, are bound to fail. For the fact that someone was or failed to be courageous or just cannot be recognized as "a fact" by those who accept that methodological canon. The account of the virtues which I have given is completely at one with Aristotle's on this point. But now the question may be raised: your account may be in many respects Aristotelian, but is it not in some respects false? Consider the following important objection.

I have defined the virtues partly in terms of their place in practices. But surely, it may be suggested, some practices—that is, some coherent human activities which answer to the description of what I have called a practice—are evil. So in discussion by some moral philosophers of this type of account of the virtues it has been suggested that torture and sadomasochistic sexual activities might be examples of practices. But how can a disposition be a virtue if it is the kind of disposition which sustains practices and some practices issue in evil? My answer to this objection falls into two parts.

First I want to allow that there *may* be practices—in the sense in which I understand the concept—which simply *are* evil. I am far from convinced that there are, and I do not in fact believe that either torture or sadomasochistic sexuality answer to the description of a practice which my account of the virtues employs. But I do not want to rest my case on this lack of conviction, especially since it is plain that as a matter of contingent fact many types of practice may on particular occasions be productive of evil. For the range of practices includes the arts, the sciences and certain types of intellectual and athletic games. And it is at once obvious that any of these may under certain conditions be a source of evil: the desire to excel and to win can corrupt, a man may be so engrossed by his painting that he neglects his family, what was initially an honorable resort to war can issue in savage cruelty. But what follows from this?

It certainly is not the case that my account entails *either* that we ought to excuse or condone such evils *or* that whatever flows from a virtue is right. I do have to allow that courage sometimes sustains injustice, that loyalty has been known to strengthen a murderous aggressor and that generosity has sometimes weakened the capacity to do good. But to deny this would be to fly in the face of just those empirical facts which I invoked in criticizing Aquinas' account of the unity of the virtues. That the virtues need initially to be defined and explained with reference to the notion of a practice thus in no way entails approval of all practices in all circumstances. That the virtues—as the objection itself presupposed—*are* defined not in terms of good and right practices, but of practices, does not entail or imply that practices as actually carried through at particular times and places do not stand in need of moral criticism. And the resources for such criticism are not lacking. There is in the first place no inconsistency in appealing to the requirements of a virtue to criticize a practice. Justice may be initially defined as a disposition which in its particular way is necessary to sustain practices; it does not follow that in pursuing the requirements of a practice violations of justice are not to be condemned. Moreover I already pointed out in Chapter 12 [*After Virtue*] that a morality of virtues requires as its counterpart a conception of moral law. Its requirements too have to be met by practices. But, it may be asked, does not all this imply that more needs to be said about the place of practices in some larger moral context? Does not this at least suggest that there is more to the core concept of a virtue than can be spelled out in terms of practices? I have after all emphasized that the scope of any virtue in human life extends beyond the practices in terms of which it is initially defined. What then is the place of the virtues in the larger arenas of human life?

I stressed earlier that any account of the virtues in terms of practices could only be a partial and first account. What is required to complement it? The most notable difference so far between my account and any account that could be called Aristotelian is that although I have in no way restricted the exercise of the virtues to the context of practices, it is in terms of practices that I have located their point and function. Whereas Aristotle locates that point and function in terms of the notion of a type of whole human life which can be called good. And it does seem that the question "What would a human being lack who lacked the virtues?" must be given a kind of answer which goes beyond anything which I have said so far. For such an individual would not merely fail *in a variety of particular ways* in respect of the kind of excellence which can be achieved through participation in practices and in respect of the kind of human relationship required to sustain such excellence. His own life *viewed as a whole* would perhaps be defective; it would not be the kind of life which someone would describe in trying to answer the question "What is the best kind of life for this kind of man or woman to live?" And that question cannot be answered without at least raising Aristotle's own question, "What is the good life for man?" Consider three ways in which human life informed only by the conception of the virtues sketched so far would be defective.

It would be pervaded, first of all, by *too many* conflicts and *too much* arbitrariness. I argued earlier that it is a merit of an account of the virtues in terms of a multiplicity of goods that it allows for the possibility of tragic conflict in a way in which Aristotle's does not. But it may also produce even in the life of someone who is virtuous and disciplined too many occasions when one allegiance points in one direction, another in another. The claims of one practice may be incompatible with another in such a way that one may find oneself oscillating in an arbitrary way, rather than making rational choices. So it seems to have been with T. E. Lawrence. Commitment to sustaining the kind of community in which the virtues can flourish may be incompatible with the devotion which a particular practice—of the arts, for example—requires. So there may be tensions between the claims of family life and those of the arts—the problem that Gauguin solved or failed to solve by fleeing to Polynesia, or between the claims of politics and those of the arts—the problem that Lenin solved or failed to solve by refusing to listen to Beethoven.

If the life of the virtues is continuously fractured by choices in which one allegiance entails the apparently arbitrary renunciation of another, it may seem that the goods internal to practices do after all derive their authority from our individual choices; for when different goods summon in different and in incompatible directions, "I" have to choose between their rival claims. The modern self with its criterionless choices apparently reappears in the alien context of what was claimed to be an Aristotelian world. This accusation might be rebutted in part by returning to the question of why both goods and virtues do have authority in our lives and repeating what was said earlier in this chapter. But this reply would only be partly successful; the distinctively modern notion of choice would indeed have reappeared, even if with a more limited scope for its exercise than it has usually claimed.

Secondly, without an overriding conception of the *telos* of a whole human life, conceived as a unity, our conception of certain individual virtues has to remain partial and incomplete. Consider two examples. Justice, on an Aristotelian view, is defined in terms of giving each person his or her due or desert. To deserve well is to have contributed in some substantial way to the achievement of those goods, the sharing of which and the common pursuit of which provide foundations for human community. But the goods internal to practices, including the goods internal to the practice of making and sustaining forms of community, need to be ordered and evaluated in some way if we are to assess relative desert. Thus any substantive application of an Aristotelian concept of justice requires an understanding of goods and of the good that goes beyond the multiplicity of goods which inform practices. As with justice, so also with patience. Patience is the virtue of waiting attentively without complaint, but not of waiting thus for anything at all. To treat patience as a virtue presupposes some adequate answer to the question: waiting for what? Within the context of practices a partial, although for many purposes adequate, answer can be given: the patience of a craftsman with refractory material, of a teacher with a slow pupil, of a politician in negotiations, are all species of patience. But what if the material is just too refractory, the pupil too slow, the negotiations too frustrating? Ought we always at a certain point just to give up in the interests of the practice itself? The medieval exponents of the virtue of patience claimed that there are certain types of situation in which the virtue of patience requires that I do not ever give up on some person or task, situations in which, as they would have put it, I am required to embody in my attitude to that person or task something of the patient attitude of God towards his creation. But this could only be so if patience served some overriding good, some *telos* which warranted putting other goods in a subordinate place. Thus it turns out that the content of the virtue of patience depends upon how we order various goods in a hierarchy and *a fortiori* on whether we are able rationally so to order these particular goods.

I have suggested so far that unless there is a *telos* which transcends the limited goods of practices by constituting the good of a whole human life, the good of a human life conceived as a unity, it will *both* be the case that a certain subversive arbitrariness will invade the moral life *and* that we shall be unable to specify the context of certain virtues adequately. These two considerations are reinforced by a third: that there is at least one virtue recognized by the tradition which cannot be specified at all except with reference to the wholeness of a human life—the virtue of integrity or constancy. "Purity of heart," said Kierkegaard, "is to will one thing." This notion of singleness of purpose in a whole life can have no application unless that of a whole life does. . . .

1981

Persons, Character and Morality

Bernard Williams

I

Much of the most interesting recent work in moral philosophy has been of basically Kantian inspiration; Rawls' own work[1] and those to varying degrees influenced by him such as Richards[2] and Nagel[3] are very evidently in the debt of Kant, while it is interesting that a writer such as Fried[4] who gives evident signs of being pulled away from some characteristic features of this way of looking at morality nevertheless, I shall suggest later, tends to get pulled back into it. This is not of course a very pure Kantianism, and still less is it an expository or subservient one. It differs from Kant among other things in making no demands on a theory of noumenal freedom, and also, importantly, in admitting considerations of a general empirical character in determining fundamental moral demands, which Kant at least supposed himself not to be doing. But allowing for those and many other important differences, the inspiration is there and the similarities

[1]John Rawls, *A Theory of Justice* (Oxford, 1972).
[2]D. A. J. Richards, *A Theory of Reasons for Action* (Oxford, 1971).
[3]Thomas Nagel, *The Possibility of Altruism* (Oxford, 1970).
[4]Charles Fried, *An Anatomy of Values* (Cambridge, Mass., 1970).

Bernard Williams, "Persons, Character and Morality" from MORAL LUCK (New York: Cambridge University Press, 1981). Reprinted with the permission of the author and Cambridge University Press.

both significant and acknowledged. They extend far beyond the evident point that both the extent and the nature of opposition to Utilitarianism resembles Kant's: though it is interesting that in this respect they are more Kantian than a philosophy which bears an obvious but superficial formal resemblance to Kantianism, namely Hare's. Indeed, Hare now supposes that when a substantial moral theory is elicited from his philosophical premisses, it turns out to be a version of Utilitarianism. This is not merely because the universal and prescriptive character of moral judgments lays on the agent, according to Hare, a requirement of hypothetical identification with each person affected by a given decision—so much is a purely Kantian element. It is rather that each identification is treated just as yielding "acceptance" or "rejection" of a certain prescription, and they in turn are construed solely in terms of satisfactions, so that the outputs of the various identifications can, under the usual Utilitarian assumptions, be regarded additively.

Among Kantian elements in these outlooks are, in particular, these: that the moral point of view is basically different from a non-moral, and in particular self-interested, point of view, and by a difference of kind; that the moral point of view is specially characterized by its impartiality and its indifference to any particular relations to particular persons, and that moral thought requires abstraction from particular circumstances and particular characteristics of the parties, including the agent, except in so far as these can be treated as universal features of any morally similar situation; and that the motivations of a moral agent, correspondingly, involve a rational application of impartial principle and are thus different in kind from the sorts of motivations that he might have for treating some particular persons (for instance, though not exclusively, himself) differently because he happened to have some particular interest towards them. Of course, it is not intended that these demands should exclude other and more intimate relations nor prevent someone from acting in ways demanded by and appropriate to them: that is a matter of the relations of the moral point of view to other points of view. But I think it is fair to say that included among the similarities of these views to Kant's is the point that like his they do not make the question of the relations between those points of view at all easy to answer. The deeply disparate character of moral and of non-moral motivation, together with the special dignity or supremacy attached to the moral, make it very difficult to assign to those other relations and motivations the significance or structural importance in life which some of them are capable of possessing.

It is worth remarking that this detachment of moral motivations and the moral point of view from the level of particular relations to particular persons, and more generally from the level of all motivations and perceptions other than those of an impartial character, obtains even when the moral point of view is itself explained in terms of the self-interest under conditions of ignorance of some abstractly conceived contracting parties, as it is by Rawls, and by Richards, who is particularly concerned with applying directly to the characterization of the moral interest, the structure used by Rawls chiefly to characterize social justice. For while the contracting parties are pictured as making some kind of self-interested or prudential choice of a set of rules, they are entirely abstract persons making this choice in ignorance of their own particular properties, tastes, and so forth; and the self-interested choice of an abstract agent is intended to model precisely the moral choice of a concrete agent, by representing what he would choose granted that he made just the kinds of abstraction from his actual personality, situation and relations which the Kantian picture of moral experience requires.

Some elements in this very general picture serve already to distinguish the outlook in question from Utilitarianism. Choices made in deliberate abstraction from empirical information which actually exists are necessarily from a Utilitarian point of view irrational, and to that extent the formal structure of the outlook, even allowing the admission of *general* empirical information, is counter-Utilitarian. There is a further point of difference with Utilitarianism, which comes out if one starts from the fact that there is one respect at least in which Utilitarianism itself requires a notable abstraction in moral thought, an abstraction which in this respect goes even further than the Kantians': if Kantianism abstracts in moral thought from the identity of persons, Utilitarianism strikingly abstracts from their separateness. This is true in more than one way. First, as the Kantian theorists have themselves emphasized, persons lose their separateness as beneficiaries of the Utilitarian provisions, since in the form which maximizes total utility, and even in that which maximizes average utility, there is an agglomeration of satisfactions which is basically indifferent to the separateness of those who have the satisfactions; this is evidently so in the total maximization system, and it is only superficially not so in the average maximization system, where the agglomeration occurs before the division. Richards,[5] following Rawls, has suggested that the device of the ideal observer serves to model the agglomeration of these satisfactions: equivalent to the world could be one person, with an indefinite capacity for happiness and pain. The Kantian view stands opposed to this; the idea of the contractual element, even between these shadowy and abstract participants, is in part to make the point that there are limitations built in at the bottom to permissible trade-offs between the satisfactions of individuals.

A second aspect of the Utilitarian abstraction from separateness involves agency.[6] It turns on the point that the basic bearer of value for Utilitarianism is the *state of affairs,* and hence, when the relevant causal differences have been allowed for, it cannot make any further difference who produces a given state of affairs: if S1 consists of my doing something, together with consequences, and S2 consists of someone else doing something, with consequences, and S2 comes about just in case S1 does not, and S1 is better than S2, then I should bring about S1, however *prima facie* nasty S1 is. Thus, unsurprisingly, the doctrine of negative responsibility has its roots at the foundation of Utilitarianism; and whatever projects, desires, ideals, or whatever I may have as a particular individual, as a Utilitarian agent my action has to be the output of *all* relevant causal items bearing on the situation, including all projects and desires within causal reach, my own and others. As a Utilitarian agent, I am just the representative of the satisfaction system who happens to be near certain causal levers at a certain time. At this level, there is abstraction not merely from the identity of agents, but, once more, from their separateness, since a conceivable extension or restriction of the causal powers of a given agent could always replace the activities of some other agent, so far as Utilitarian outcomes are concerned, and an outcome allocated to two agents as things are could equivalently be the product of one agent, or three, under a conceivable redistribution of causal powers.

In this latter respect also the Kantian outlook can be expected to disagree. For since we are concerned not just with outcomes, but at a basic level with actions and policies, *who* acts in a given situation makes a difference, and in particular I have a particular responsibility for *my* actions. Thus in more than one way the Kantian outlook emphasizes something like the separateness of agents, and in that sense makes less of

[5]Richards, op. cit., p. 87 al; cf. Rawls, op. cit., p. 27; also Nagel, op. cit., p. 134. This is not the only, nor perhaps historically the soundest, interpretation of the device: cf. Derek Parfit, "Later Selves and Moral Principles," in A. Montefiore, ed., *Philosophy and Personal Relations* (London, 1973), pp. 149–50 and nn. 30–4.

[6]For a more detailed account, see "A Critique of Utilitarianism," in J. J. C. Smart and B. Williams, *Utilitarianism: For and Against* (Cambridge, 1973).

an abstraction than Utilitarianism does (though, as we have seen, there are other respects, with regard to causally relevant empirical facts, in which its abstraction is greater). But now the question arises, of whether the honourable instincts of Kantianism to defend the individuality of individuals against the agglomerative indifference of Utilitarianism can in fact be effective granted the impoverished and abstract character of persons as moral agents which the Kantian view seems to impose. Findlay has said "the separateness of persons . . . is . . . the basic fact for morals,"[7] and Richards hopes to have respected that fact.[8] Similarly Rawls claims that impartiality does not mean impersonality.[9] But it is a real question, whether the conception of the individual provided by the Kantian theories is in fact enough to yield what is wanted, even by the Kantians; let alone enough for others who, while equally rejecting Utilitarianism, want to allow more room than Kantianism can allow for the importance of individual character and personal relations in moral experience.

II

I am going to take up two aspects of this large subject. They both involve the idea that an individual person has a set of desires, concerns or, as I shall often call them, projects, which help to constitute a *character*. The first issue concerns the connection between that fact and the man's having a reason for living at all. I approach this through a discussion of some work by Derek Parfit; though I touch on a variety of points in this, my overriding aim is to emphasize the basic importance for our thought of the ordinary idea of a self or person which undergoes changes of character, as opposed to an approach which, even if only metaphorically, would dissolve the person, under changes of character, into a series of "selves."

In this section I am concerned just with the point that each person has a character, not with the point that different people have different characters. That latter point comes more to the fore on the second issue, which I take up in part III, and which concerns personal relations. Both issues suggest that the Kantian view contains an important misrepresentation.

First, then, I should like to comment on some arguments of Parfit which explore connections between moral issues and a certain view of personal identity: a view which, he thinks, might offer, among other things, "some defense"[10] of the Utilitarian neglect of the separateness of persons. This view Parfit calls the "Complex View." This view takes seriously the idea that relations of psychological connectedness (such as memory and persistence of character and motivation) are what really matter with regard to most questions which have been discussed in relation to personal identity. The suggestion is that morality should take this seriously as well, and that there is more than one way of its doing so. Psychological connectedness (unlike the surface logic of personal identity) admits of degrees. Let us call the relevant properties and relations which admit of degrees, *scalar* items. One of Parfit's aims is to make moral thought reflect more directly the scalar character of phenomena which underlie personal identity. In particular, in those cases in which the scalar relations hold in reduced degree, this fact should receive recognition in moral thought.

[7]Findlay, *Values and Intentions* (London, 1961), pp. 235–6.
[8]Richards, op. cit., p. 87.
[9]Rawls, op. cit., p. 190.
[10]Parfit, op. cit., p. 160, his emphasis. In what follows and elsewhere in this chapter I am grateful to Parfit for valuable criticisms of an earlier draft.

Another, and more general, consequence of taking the Complex View is that the matter of personal identity may appear altogether less deep, as Parfit puts it, than if one takes the Simple View, as he calls that alternative view which sees as basically significant the all-or-nothing logic of personal identity. If the matter of personal identity appears less deep, the *separateness* of persons, also, may come to seem less an ultimate and specially significant consideration for morality. The connection between those two thoughts is not direct, but there is more than one indirect connection between them.[11]

So far as the problems of *agency* are concerned, Parfit's treatment is not going to help Utilitarianism. His loosening of identity is diachronic, by reference to the weakening of psychological connectedness over time: where there is such weakening to a sufficient degree, he is prepared to speak of "successive selves," though this is intended only as a *façon de parler.*[12] But the problems that face Utilitarianism about agency can arise with any agent whose projects stretch over enough time, and are sufficiently grounded in character, to be in any substantial sense *his* projects, and that condition will be satisfied by something that is, for Parfit, even *one* self. Thus there is nothing in this degree of dissolution of the traditional self which can help over agency.

In discussing the issues involved in making moral thought reflect more directly the scalar nature of what underlies personal identity, it is important to keep in mind that the talk of "past selves," "future selves" and generally "several selves" is only a convenient fiction. Neglect of this may make the transpositions in moral thought required by the Complex View seem simpler and perhaps more inviting than they are, since they may glide along on what seems to be a mere multiplication, in the case of these new "selves," of familiar interpersonal relations. We must concentrate on the scalar facts. But many moral notions show a notable resistance to reflecting the scalar: or, rather, to reflecting it in the right way. We may take the case of promising, which Parfit has discussed.[13] Suppose that I promise to *A* that I will help him in certain ways in three years time. In three years time a person appears, let us say *A*★, whose memories, character etc., bear some, but a rather low, degree of connectedness to *A*'s. How am I to mirror these scalar facts in my thought about whether, or how, I am to carry out my promise?

Something, first, should be said about the promise itself. "*You*" was the expression it used: "I will help *you,*" and it used that expression in such a way that it covered both the recipient of these words and the potential recipient of the help. This was not a promise that could be carried out (or, more generally, honored) by helping anyone else, or indeed by doing anything except helping that person I addressed when I said "you"—thus the situation is not like that with some promises to the dead (those where there is still something one can do about it).[14] If there is to be any action of mine which is to count as honoring that promise, it will have to be action which consists in now helping *A*★. How am I to mirror, in my action and my thought about it, *A*★'s scalar relations to *A?*

There seem to be only three ways in which they could be so mirrored, and none seems satisfactory. First, the action promised might itself have some significant scalar dimension, and it might be suggested that this should vary with my sense of the proximity or remoteness of *A*★ from *A*. But this will not do: it is clearly a lunatic idea that if I promised to pay *A* a sum of money, then my obligation is to pay *A*★ some money, but

[11]Parfit develops one such connection in the matter of distributive justice: pp. 148ff. In general it can be said that one very natural correlate of being impressed by the separateness of several persons' lives is being impressed by the peculiar unity of one person's life.

[12]Ibid., n. 14, pp. 161–2.

[13]Ibid., pp. 144 ff.

[14]Ibid., p. 144 fin.

a smaller sum. A more serious suggestion would be that what varies with the degree of connectedness of $A^\star$ to A is the degree of stringency of the obligation to do what was promised. While less evidently dotty, it is still, on reflection, dotty; thus, to take a perhaps unfair example, it seems hard to believe that if someone had promised to marry A, they would have an obligation to marry $A^\star$, only an obligation which came lower down the queue.

What, in contrast, is an entirely familiar sort of thought is, last of all, one that embodies degrees of doubt or obscurity whether a given obligation (of fixed stringency) applies or not. Thus a secret agent might think that he was obliged to kill the man in front of him if and only if that man was Martin Bormann; and be in doubt whether he should kill this man, because he was in doubt whether it was Bormann. (Contrast the two analogously dotty types of solution to this case: that, at any rate, he is obliged to wound him; or, that he is obliged to kill him, but it has a lower priority than it would have otherwise.) But this type of thought is familiar at the cost of not really embodying the scalar facts; it is a style of thought appropriate to uncertainty about a matter of all-or-nothing and so embodies in effect what Parfit calls the Simple View, that which does not take seriously the scalar facts to which the Complex View addresses itself.

These considerations do not, of course show that there are no ways of mirroring the Complex View in these areas of moral thought, but they do suggest that the displacements required are fairly radical. It is significant that by far the easiest place in which to find the influence of the scalar considerations is in certain *sentiments,* which themselves have a scalar dimension—here we can see a place where the Complex View and Utilitarianism easily fit together. But the structure of such sentiments is not adequate to produce the structure of all moral thought. The rest of it will have to be more radically adapted, or abandoned, if the Complex View is really to have its effect.

One vitally important item which is in part (though only in part) scalar is a man's concern for (what commonsense would call) his own future. That a man should have some interest now in what he will do or undergo later, requires that he have some desires or projects or concerns now which relate to those doings or happenings later; or, as a special case of that, that some very general desire or project or concern of his now relate to desires or projects which he will have then. The limiting case, at the basic physical level, is that in which he is merely concerned with future pain, and it may be that that concern can properly reach through any degree of psychological discontinuity.[15] But even if so, it is not our present concern, since the mere desire to avoid physical pain is not adequate to constitute a character. We are here concerned with more distinctive and structured patterns of desire and project, and there are possible psychological changes in these which could be predicted for a person and which would put his future after such changes beyond his present interest. Such a future would be, so to speak, over the horizon of his interest, though of course if the future picture could be filled in as a *series* of changes leading from here to there, he might recapture an interest in the outcome.

In this connection, to take the language of "future selves" at all literally would be deeply misleading: it would be to take the same facts twice over. My concern for my descendants or other relatives may be, as Parfit says, to some degree proportional to their remoteness from me; equally, my concern for other persons in general can vary with the degree to which their character is congenial to my own, their projects sympathetic to my outlook. The two considerations, of proximity and congeniality, evidently

[15]Cf. "The Self and the Future," in *Problems of the Self* (Cambridge, 1973).

interact—ways in which they can reinforce or cancel one another are, for instance, among the commonplaces of dynastic fiction. But the proximity of Parfitian "later selves" to me, their ancestor, just consists of the relations of their character and interests to my present ones. I cannot first identify a later self "descendant," and then consider the relations of his character to mine, since it is just the presence or lack of these relations which in good part determines his proximity and even his existence as a separate self.

Thus if I take steps now to hinder what will or may predictably be my future projects, as in Parfit's Russian nobleman case,[16] it would be a case of double vision to see this as my treating my future self as another person, since, spelled out, that would have to mean, treating my future self as another person *of whose projects I disapprove;* and therein lies the double vision. To insist here that what I would be doing is to hinder *my own* future projects (where it is understood that that is not necessarily a foolish thing to do) is to keep hold on a number of deeply important facts. One is that to contemplate, or expect, or regard as probable, such changes in my own character is different from my relation to them in someone else (still more, of course, from my attitude to the mere *arrival* of someone else with a different character). The question must arise, how prediction is, in my own case, related to acquiescence, and special and obscure issues arise about the range of methods that it could be appropriate or rational for a man to use to prevent or deflect predicted changes in his own character. Thought about those issues must take as basic the *he* for whom these changes would be changes in *his* character.

Relatedly, there is the question of why I should regard my present projects and outlook as having more authority than my future ones. I do *not* mean by that the question, why I should not distribute consideration equally over my whole life: I shall later touch on the point that it is a mistake of Kantians (and perhaps of some kinds of Utilitarians too) to think it *a priori* evident that one rationally should do that. I mean rather the question of how, in the supposed type of example, I evaluate the two successive outlooks. Why should I hinder my future projects from the perspective of my present values rather than inhibit my present projects from the perspective of my future values? It is not enough in answer to that to say that evidently present action must flow from present values. If the future prospect were of something now identified as a growth in enlightenment, present action would try to hinder present projects in its interest. For that to be so, there indeed would have to be now some dissatisfaction with one's present values, but that consideration just turns attention, in the Russian nobleman case, to the corresponding question, of why the young man is so unquestioningly satisfied with his present values. He may have, for instance, a theory of degeneration of the middle-aged, but then he should reflect that, when middle-aged, he will have a theory of the naiveté of the young.

I am not saying that there are no answers to any of these questions, or that there is no way out of this kind of diachronic relativism. The point is that if it is true that this man will change in these ways, it is only by understanding his present projects *as the projects of one who will so change* that he can understand them even as his present projects; and if he knows that he will so change, then it is only through such an understanding that he could justifiably give his present values enough authority to defeat his future values, as he clear-headedly conceives them to be. If he clear-headedly knows that his present projects are solely the projects of his youth, how does he know that they are not *merely* that, unless he has some view which makes sense of, among other things,

[16]Parfit, op. cit., pp. 145ff.

his own future? One cannot even start on the important questions of how this man, so totally identified with his present values, will be related to his future without them, if one does not take as basic the fact that it is his own future that he will be living through without them.

This leads to the question of why we go on at all.

It might be wondered why, unless we believe in a possibly hostile after-life, or else are in a muddle which the Epicureans claimed to expose, we should regard death as an evil.[17] One answer to that is that we desire certain things; if one desires something, then to that extent one has reason to resist the happening of anything which prevents one getting it, and death certainly does that, for a large range of desires. Some desires are admittedly contingent on the prospect of one's being alive, but not all desires can be in that sense conditional, since it is possible to imagine a person rationally contemplating suicide, in the face of some predicted evil, and if he decides to go on in life, then he is propelled forward into it by some desire (however general or inchoate) which cannot operate conditionally on his being alive, since it settles the question of whether he is going to be alive. Such a desire we may call a categorical desire. Most people have many categorical desires, which do not depend on the assumption of the person's existence, since they serve to prevent that assumption's being questioned, or to answer the question if it is raised. Thus one's pattern of interests, desires and projects not only provide the reason for an interest in what happens within the horizon of one's future, but also constitute the conditions of there being such a future at all.

Here, once more, to deal in terms of later selves who were like descendants would be to misplace the heart of the problem. Whether to commit suicide, and whether to leave descendants, are two separate decisions: one can produce children before committing suicide. A person might even choose deliberately to do that, for comprehensible sorts of reasons; or again one could be deterred, as by the thought that one would not be there to look after them. Later selves, however, evade all these thoughts by having the strange property that while they come into existence only with the death of their ancestor, the physical death of their ancestor will abort them entirely. The analogy seems unhelpfully strained, when we are forced to the conclusion that the failure of all my projects, and my consequent suicide, would take with me all my "descendants," although they are in any case a kind of descendants who arise only with my ceasing to exist. More than unhelpfully, it runs together what are two quite different questions: whether, my projects having failed, I should cease to exist, and whether I shall have descendants whose projects may be quite different from mine and are in any case largely unknown. The analogy makes every question of the first kind involve a question of the second kind, and thus obscures the peculiar significance of the first question to the theory of the self. If, on the other hand, a man's future self is not another self, but the future of his self, then it is unproblematic why it should be eliminated with the failure of that which might propel him into it. The primacy of one's ordinary self is given, once more, by the thought that it is precisely what will not be in the world if one commits suicide.

The language of "later selves," too literally taken, could exaggerate in one direction the degree to which my relation to some of my own projects resembles my relation to the projects of others. The Kantian emphasis on moral impartiality exaggerates it in quite another, by providing ultimately too slim a sense in which any projects are mine at all. This point once more involves the idea that my present projects are the condition of

[17]The argument is developed in more detail in *Problems of the Self*, pp. 82ff.

my existence,[18] in the sense that unless I am propelled forward by the conatus of desire, project and interest, it is unclear why I should go on at all: the world, certainly, as a kingdom of moral agents, has no particular claim on my presence or, indeed, interest in it. (That kingdom, like others, has to respect the natural right to emigration.) Now the categorical desires which propel one on do not have to be even very evident to consciousness, let alone grand or large; one good testimony to one's existence having a point is that the question of its point does not arise, and the propelling concerns may be of a relatively everyday kind such as certainly provide the ground of many sorts of happiness. Equally, while these projects may present *some* conflicts with the demands of morality, as Kantianly conceived, these conflicts may be fairly minor; after all—and I do not want to deny or forget it—these projects, in a normally socialized individual, have in good part been formed within, and formed by, dispositions which constitute a commitment to morality. But, on the other hand, the possibility of radical conflict is also there. A man may have, for a lot of his life or even just for some part of it, a *ground* project or set of projects which are closely related to his existence and which to a significant degree give a meaning to his life.

I do not mean by that they provide him with a life-plan, in Rawls' sense. On the contrary, Rawls' conception, and the conception of practical rationality, shared by Nagel, which goes with it, seems to me rather to imply an external view of one's own life, as something like a given rectangle that has to be optimally filled in.[19] This perspective omits the vital consideration already mentioned, that the continuation and size of this rectangle is up to me; so, slightly less drastically, is the question of how much of it I care to cultivate. The correct perspective on one's life is *from now*. The consequences of that for practical reasoning (particularly with regard to the relevance of proximity or remoteness in time of one's objective), is a large question which cannot be pursued here; here we need only the idea of a man's ground projects providing the motive force which propels him into the future, and gives him a reason for living.

For a project to play this ground role, it does not have to be true that if it were frustrated or in any of various ways he lost it, he would have to commit suicide, nor does he have to think that. Other things, or the mere hope of other things, may keep him going. But he may feel in those circumstances that he might as well have died. Of course, in general a man does not have one separable project which plays this ground role: rather, there is a nexus of projects, related to his conditions of life, and it would be the loss of all or most of them that would remove meaning.

Ground projects do not have to be selfish, in the sense that they are just concerned with things for the agent. Nor do they have to be self-centered, in the sense that the creative projects of a Romantic artist could be considered self-centered (where it has to be *him*, but not *for* him). They may certainly be altruistic, and in a very evident sense moral, projects; thus he may be working for reform, or justice, or

[18]We can note the consequence that present projects are the condition of future ones. This view stands in opposition to Nagel's: as do the formulations used above, p. 10. But while, as Nagel says, taking a rational interest in preparing for the realization of my later projects does not require that they be my present projects, it seems nevertheless true that it presupposes my having some present projects which directly or indirectly reach out to a time when those later projects will be my projects.

[19]It is of course a separate question what the criteria of optimality are, but it is not surprising that a view which presupposes that no risks are taken with the useful area of the rectangle should also favor a very low risk strategy in filling it: cf. Rawls (on prudential rationality in general), op. cit., p. 422: "we have the guiding principle that a rational individual is always to act so that he need never blame himself no matter how things finally transpire." Cf. also the passages cited in Rawls' footnote. . . .

general improvement. There is no contradiction in the idea of a man's dying for a ground project—quite the reverse, since if death really is necessary for the project, then to live would be to live with it unsatisfied, something which, if it really is his ground project, he has no reason to do.

That a man's projects were altruistic or moral would not make them immune to conflict with impartial morality, any more than the artist's projects are immune. Admittedly *some* conflicts are ruled out by the projects sincerely being *those* projects; thus a man devoted to the cause of curing injustice in a certain place, cannot just insist on his plan for doing that over others', if convinced that theirs will be as effective as his (something it may be hard to convince him of). For if he does insist on that, then we learn that his concern is not merely that injustice be removed, but that *he* remove it—not necessarily a dishonorable concern, but a different one. Thus some conflicts are ruled out by the project being not self-centered. But not all conflicts: thus his selfless concern for justice may do havoc to quite other commitments.

A man who has such a ground project will be required by Utilitarianism to give up what it requires in a given case just if that conflicts with what he is required to do as an impersonal utility-maximizer when all the causally relevant considerations are in. That is a quite absurd requirement.[20] But the Kantian, who can do rather better than that, still cannot do well enough. For impartial morality, if the conflict really does arise, must be required to win; and that cannot necessarily be a reasonable demand on the agent. There can come a point at which it is quite unreasonable for a man to give up, in the name of the impartial good ordering of the world of moral agents, something which is a condition of his having any interest in being around in that world at all. Once one thinks about what is involved in having a character, one can see that the Kantians' omission of character is a condition of their ultimate insistence on the demands of impartial morality, just as it is a reason for finding inadequate their account of the individual.

III

All this argument depends on the idea of one person's having a character, in the sense of having projects and categorical desires with which that person is identified; nothing has yet been said about different persons having different characters. It is perhaps important, in order to avoid misunderstanding, to make clear a way in which difference of character does *not* come into the previous argument. It does not come in by way of the man's thinking that only if he affirms these projects will they be affirmed, while (by contrast) the aims of Kantian morality can be affirmed by anyone. Though that thought could be present in some cases, it is not the point of the argument. The man is not pictured as thinking that he will have earned his place in the world, if his project is affirmed: that a distinctive contribution to the world will have been made, if his distinctive project is carried forward. The point is that he wants these things, finds his life bound up with them, and that they propel him forward, and thus they give him a reason for living his life. But that is compatible with these drives, and this life, being much like others'. They give him, distinctively, a reason for living this life, in the sense that he has no desire to give up and make room for others, but they do not require him to lead a *distinctive* life. While this is so, and the point has some importance, nevertheless the interest and substance of most of the discussion depends on its in fact being the case that people have dissimilar characters and projects. Our *general* view of these matters,

[20]Cf. "A Critique of Utilitarianism," sections 3–5.

and the significance given to individuality in our own and others' lives, would certainly change if there were not between persons indefinitely many differences which are important to us. The level of description is of course also vital for determining what is the same or different. A similar description can be given of two people's dispositions, but the concrete detail be perceived very differently—and it is a feature of our experience of persons that we can perceive and be conscious of an indefinitely fine degree of difference in concrete detail (though it is only in certain connections and certain cultures that one spends much time rehearsing it).

One area in which *difference* of character directly plays a role in the concept of moral individuality is that of personal relations, and I shall close with some remarks in this connection. Differences of character give substance to the idea that individuals are not inter-substitutable. As I have just argued, a particular man so long as he is propelled forward does not need to assure himself that he is unlike others, in order not to feel substitutable, but in his personal relations to others the idea of difference can certainly make a contribution, in more than one way. To the thought that his friend cannot just be equivalently replaced by another friend, is added both the thought that he cannot just be replaced himself, and also the thought that he and his friend are different from each other. This last thought is important to us as part of our view of friendship, a view thus set apart from Aristotle's opinion that a good man's friend was a duplication of himself. This I suspect to have been an Aristotelian, and not generally a Greek, opinion. It is connected with another feature of his views which seems even stranger to us, at least with regard to any deeply committed friendship, namely that friendship for him has to be minimally *risky*—one of his problems is indeed to reconcile the role of friendship with his unappetizing ideal of self-sufficiency. Once one agrees that a three-dimensional mirror would not represent the ideal of friendship, one can begin to see both how some degree of difference can play an essential role, and, also, how a commitment or involvement with a particular other person might be one of the kinds of project which figured basically in a man's life in the ways already sketched—something which would be mysterious or even sinister on an Aristotelian account.

For Kantians, personal relations at least presuppose moral relations, and some are rather disposed to go further and regard them as a *species* of moral relations, as in the richly moralistic account given by Richards[21] of one of the four main principles of supererogation which would be accepted in "the Original Position" (that is to say, adopted as a moral limitation):

> a principle of mutual love requiring that people should not show personal affection and love to others on the basis of arbitrary physical characteristics alone, but rather on the basis of traits of personality and character related to acting on moral principles.

This righteous absurdity is no doubt to be traced to a feeling that love, even love based on "arbitrary physical characteristics," is something which has enough power and even authority to conflict badly with morality unless it can be brought within it from the beginning, and evidently that is a sound feeling, though it is an optimistic Kantian who thinks that much will be done about that by the adoption of this principle in the Original Position. The weaker view, that love and similar relations presuppose moral relations, in the sense that one could love someone only if one also had to them the moral relations one has to all people, is less absurd, but also wrong. It is of course true that loving someone involves some relations of the kind that morality requires or imports more generally, but it does not follow from that that one cannot have them in a particular case

[21]Richards, op. cit., p. 94.

unless one has them generally in the way the moral person does. Someone might be concerned about the interests of someone else, and even about carrying out promises he made to that person, while not very concerned about these things with other persons. To the extent (whatever it may be) that loving someone involves showing some of the same concerns in relation to them that the moral person shows, or at least thinks he ought to show, elsewhere, the lover's relations will be examples of moral relations, or at least resemble them, but this does not have to be because they are *applications to this case* of relations which the lover, *qua* moral person, more generally enters into. (That might not be the best description of the situation even if he *is* a moral person who enters into such relations more generally.)

However, once morality is there, and also personal relations to be taken seriously, so is the possibility of conflict. This of course does not mean that if there is some friendship with which his life is much involved, then a man must prefer any possible demand of that over other, impartial, moral demands. That would be absurd, and also a pathological kind of friendship, since both parties exist in the world and it is part of the sense of their friendship that it exists in the world. But the possibility of conflict with substantial moral claims of others is there, and it is not only in the outcome. There can also be conflict with moral demands on how the outcome is arrived at: the situation may not have been subjected to an impartial process of resolution, and this fact itself may cause unease to the impartial moral consciousness. There is an example of such unease in a passage by Fried. After an illuminating discussion of the question why, if at all, we should give priority of resources to actual and present sufferers over absent or future ones, he writes:[22]

> surely it would be absurd to insist that if a man could, at no risk or cost to himself, save one or two persons in equal peril, and one of those in peril was, say, his wife, he must treat both equally, perhaps by flipping a coin. One answer is that where the potential rescuer occupies no office such as that of captain of a ship, public health official or the like, the occurrence of the accident may itself stand as a sufficient randomizing event to meet the dictates of fairness, so he may prefer his friend, or loved one. Where the rescuer does occupy an official position, the argument that he must overlook personal ties is not unacceptable.

The most striking feature of this passage is the direction in which Fried implicitly places the onus of proof: the fact that coin-flipping would be inappropriate raises some question to which an "answer" is required, while the resolution of the question by the rescuer's occupying an official position is met with what sounds like relief (though it remains unclear what that rescuer does when he "overlooks personal ties"—does *he* flip a coin?). The thought here seems to be that it is unfair to the second victim that, the first being the rescuer's wife, they never even get a chance of being rescued; and the answer (as I read the reference to the "sufficient randomizing event") is that at another level it is sufficiently fair—although in this disaster this rescuer has a special reason for saving the other person, it might have been another disaster in which another rescuer had a special reason for saving them. But, apart from anything else, that "might have been" is far too slim to sustain a reintroduction of the notion of fairness. The "random" element in such events, as in certain events of tragedy, should be seen not so much as affording a justification, in terms of an appropriate application of a lottery, as being a reminder that some situations lie beyond justifications.

[22]Fried, op. cit., p. 227. [Note 1981] Fried has perhaps now modified the view criticized here. He has himself used the idea of friendship as creating special moral relations, but in a connection where, it seems to me, it is out of place: for criticism, see chapter 4 [of *Moral Luck*].

But has anything yet shown that? For even if we leave behind thoughts of higher-order randomization, surely *this* is a justification on behalf of the rescuer, that the person he chose to rescue was his wife? It depends on how much weight is carried by "justification": the consideration that it was his wife is certainly, for instance, an explanation which should silence comment. But something more ambitious than this is usually intended, essentially involving the idea that moral principle can legitimate his preference, yielding the conclusion that in situations of this kind it is at least all right (morally permissible) to save one's wife. (This could be combined with a variety of higher-order thoughts to give it a rationale; rule-Utilitarians might favor the idea that in matters of this kind it is best for each to look after his own, like house insurance.) But this construction provides the agent with one thought too many: it might have been hoped by some (for instance, by his wife) that his motivating thought, fully spelled out, would be the thought that it was his wife, not that it was his wife and that in situations of this kind it is permissible to save one's wife.

Perhaps others will have other feelings about this case. But the point is that somewhere (and if not in this case, where?) one reaches the necessity that such things as deep attachments to other persons will express themselves in the world in ways which cannot at the same time embody the impartial view, and that they also run the risk of offending against it.

They run that risk if they exist at all; yet unless such things exist, there will not be enough substance or conviction in a man's life to compel his allegiance to life itself. Life has to have substance if anything is to have sense, including adherence to the impartial system; but if it has substance, then it cannot grant supreme importance to the impartial system, and that system's hold on it will be, at the limit, insecure.

It follows that moral philosophy's habit, particularly in its Kantian forms, of treating persons in abstraction from character is not so much a legitimate device for dealing with one aspect of thought, but is rather a misrepresentation, since it leaves out what both limits and helps to define that aspect of thought. Nor can it be judged solely as a theoretical device: this is one of the areas in which one's conception of the self, and of oneself, most importantly meet.

1982

Contractualism and Utilitarianism

T. M. Scanlon

Utilitarianism occupies a central place in the moral philosophy of our time. It is not the view which most people hold; certainly there are very few who would claim to be act utilitarians. But for a much wider range of people it is the view towards which they find themselves pressed when they try to give a theoretical account of their moral beliefs. Within moral philosophy it represents a position one must struggle against if one wishes to avoid it. This is so in spite of the fact that the implications of act utilitarianism are wildly at variance with firmly held moral convictions, while rule utilitarianism, the most common alternative formulation, strikes most people as an unstable compromise.

The wide appeal of utilitarianism is due, I think, to philosophical considerations of a more or less sophisticated kind which pull us in a quite different direction than our first order moral beliefs. In particular, utilitarianism derives much of its appeal from alleged difficulties about the foundations of rival views. What a successful alternative to

I am greatly indebted to Derek Parfit for patient criticism and enormously helpful discussion of many earlier versions of this paper. Thanks are due also to the many audiences who have heard parts of those versions delivered as lectures and kindly responded with helpful comments. In particular, I am indebted to Marshall Cohen, Ronald Dworkin, Owen Fiss, and Thomas Nagel for valuable criticism.

T. M. Scanlon, "Contractualism and Utilitarianism" from UTILITARIANISM AND BEYOND, edited by Amartya Sen and Bernard Williams (New York: Cambridge University Press, 1981). Reprinted with the permission of the author and Cambridge University Press.

utilitarianism must do, first and foremost, is to sap this source of strength by providing a clear account of the foundations of non-utilitarian moral reasoning. In what follows I will first describe the problem in more detail by setting out the questions which a philosophical account of the foundations of morality must answer. I will then put forward a version of contractualism which, I will argue, offers a better set of responses to these questions than that supplied by straightforward versions of utilitarianism. Finally I will explain why contractualism, as I understand it, does not lead back to some utilitarian formula as its normative outcome.

Contractualism has been proposed as the alternative to utilitarianism before, notably by John Rawls in *A Theory of Justice* (Rawls 1971). Despite the wide discussion which this book has received, however, I think that the appeal of contractualism as a foundational view has been underrated. In particular, it has not been sufficiently appreciated that contractualism offers a particularly plausible account of moral motivation. The version of contractualism that I shall present differs from Rawls' in a number of respects. In particular, it makes no use, or only a different and more limited kind of use, of his notion of choice from behind a veil of ignorance. One result of this difference is to make the contrast between contractualism and utilitarianism stand out more clearly.

I

There is such a subject as moral philosophy for much the same reason that there is such a subject as the philosophy of mathematics. In moral judgments, as in mathematical ones, we have a set of putatively objective beliefs in which we are inclined to invest a certain degree of confidence and importance. Yet on reflection it is not at all obvious what, if anything, these judgments can be about, in virtue of which some can be said to be correct or defensible and others not. This question of subject matter, or the grounds of truth, is the first philosophical question about both morality and mathematics. Second, in both morality and mathematics it seems to be possible to discover the truth simply by thinking or reasoning about it. Experience and observation may be helpful, but observation in the normal sense is not the standard means of discovery in either subject. So, given any positive answer to the first question—any specification of the subject matter or ground of truth in mathematics or morality—we need some compatible epistemology explaining how it is possible to discover the facts about this subject matter through something like the means we seem to use.

Given this similarity in the questions giving rise to moral philosophy and to the philosophy of mathematics, it is not surprising that the answers commonly given fall into similar general types. If we were to interview students in a freshman mathematics course many of them would, I think, declare themselves for some kind of conventionalism. They would hold that mathematics proceeds from definitions and principles that are either arbitrary or instrumentally justified, and that mathematical reasoning consists in perceiving what follows from these definitions and principles. A few others, perhaps, would be realists or platonists according to whom mathematical truths are a special kind of non-empirical fact that we can perceive through some form of intuition. Others might be naturalists who hold that mathematics, properly understood, is just the most abstract empirial science. Finally there are, though perhaps not in an average freshman course, those who hold that there are no mathematical facts in the world "outside of us," but that the truths of mathematics are objective truths about the mental constructions of which we are capable. Kant held that pure mathematics was a realm of objective mind-dependent truths, and Brouwer's mathematical Intuitionism is another theory of this type (with the important difference that it offers grounds for the warranted assertability of mathematical judgments rather than for their truth in the classical sense). All of these positions have natural correlates in moral philosophy. Intuitionism of the sort espoused by W. D. Ross is perhaps the closest analogue to mathematical platonism, and Kant's theory is the most familiar version of the thesis that morality is a sphere of objective, mind-dependent truths.

All of the views I have mentioned (with some qualification in the case of conventionalism) give positive (i.e. non-sceptical) answers to the first philosophical question about mathematics. Each identifies some objective, or at least intersubjective, ground of truth for mathematical judgments. Outright scepticism and subjective versions of mind-dependence (analogues of emotivism or prescriptivism) are less appealing as philosophies of mathematics than as moral philosophies. This is so in part simply because of the greater degree of intersubjective agreement in mathematical judgment. But it is also due to the difference in the further questions that philosophical accounts of the two fields must answer.

Neither mathematics nor morality can be taken to describe a realm of facts existing in isolation from the rest of reality. Each is supposed to be connected with other things. Mathematical judgments give rise to predictions about those realms to which mathematics is applied. This connection is something that a philosophical account of mathematical truth must explain, but the fact that we can observe and learn from the correctness of such predictions also gives support to our belief in objective mathematical truth. In the case of morality the main connection is, or is generally supposed to be, with the will. Given any candidate for the role of subject matter of morality we must explain why anyone should care about it, and the need to answer this question of motivation has given strong support to subjectivist views.

But what must an adequate philosophical theory of morality say about moral motivation? It need not, I think, show that the moral truth gives anyone who knows it a reason to act which appeals to that person's present desires or to the advancement of his or her interests. I find it entirely intelligible that moral requirement might correctly apply to a person even though that person had no reason of either of these kinds for complying with it. Whether moral requirements give those to whom they apply reasons for compliance of some third kind is a disputed question which I shall set aside. But what an adequate moral philosophy must do, I think, is to make clearer to us the nature of the reasons that morality does provide, at least to those who are concerned with it. A philosophical theory of morality must offer an account of these reasons that is, on the one hand, compatible with its account of moral truth and moral reasoning and, on the other, supported by a plausible analysis of moral experience. A satisfactory moral philosophy will not leave concern with morality as a simple special preference, like a fetish or a special taste, which some people just happen to have. It must make it understandable why moral reasons are ones that people can take seriously, and why they strike those who are moved by them as reasons of a special stringency and inescapability.

There is also a further question whether susceptibility to such reasons is compatible with a person's good or whether it is, as Nietzsche argued, a psychological disaster for the person who has it. If one is to defend morality one must show that it is not disastrous in this way, but I will not pursue this second motivational question here. I mention it only to distinguish it from the first question, which is my present concern.

The task of giving a philosophical explanation of the subject matter of morality differs both from the task of analysing the meaning of moral terms and from that of finding the most coherent formulation of our first order moral beliefs. A maximally coherent ordering of our first order moral beliefs could provide us with a valuable kind of explanation: it would make clear how various, apparently disparate moral notions, precepts and judgments are related to one another, thus indicating to what degree conflicts between them are fundamental and to what degree, on the other hand, they can be resolved or explained away. But philosophical inquiry into the subject matter of morality takes a more external view. It seeks to explain what kind of truths moral truths are by describing them in relation to other things in the world and in relation to our particular concerns. An explanation of how we can come to know the truth about morality must be based on such an external explanation of the kind of things moral truths are rather than on a list of particular moral truths, even a maximally coherent list. This seems to be true as well about explanations of how moral beliefs can give one a reason to act.[1]

Coherence among our first-order moral beliefs—what Rawls has called narrow reflective equilibrium[2]—seems unsatisfying[3] as an account of moral truth or as an account of the basis of justification in ethics just because, taken by itself, a maximally coherent account of our moral beliefs need not provide us with what I have called a philosophical explanation of the subject matter of morality. However internally coherent our moral beliefs may be rendered, the nagging doubt may remain that there is nothing to them at all. They may be merely a set of socially inculcated reactions, mutually consistent perhaps but not judgments of a kind which can properly be said to be correct or incorrect. A philosophical theory of the nature of morality can contribute to our confidence in our first order moral beliefs chiefly by allaying these natural doubts about the subject. Insofar as it includes an account of moral epistemology, such a theory may guide us towards new forms of moral argument, but it need not do this. Moral argument of more or less the kind we have been familiar with may remain as the only form of justification in ethics. But whether or not it leads to revision in our modes of justification, what a good philosophical theory should do is to give us a clearer understanding of what the best forms of moral argument amount to and what kind of truth it is that they can be a way of arriving at. (Much the same can be said, I believe, about the contribution which philosophy of mathematics makes to our confidence in particular mathematical judgments and particular forms of mathematical reasoning.)

Like any thesis about morality, a philosophical account of the subject matter of morality must have some connection with the meaning of moral terms: it must be plausible to claim that the subject matter described is in fact what these terms refer to at least in much of their normal use. But the current meaning of moral terms is the product of many different moral beliefs held by past and present speakers of the language, and this meaning is surely compatible with a variety of moral views and with a variety of views about the nature of morality. After all, moral terms are used to express many different views of these kinds, and people who express these views are not using moral terms incorrectly, even though what some of them say must be mistaken. Like a first-order moral judgment, a philosophical characterization of the subject matter of morality is a substantive claim about morality, albeit a claim of a different kind.

While a philosophical characterization of morality makes a kind of claim that differs from a first-order moral judgment, this does not mean that a philosophical theory of morality will be neutral between competing normative doctrines. The adoption of a philosophical thesis about the nature of morality will almost always have some effect

[1]Though here the ties between the nature of morality and its content are more important. It is not clear that an account of the nature of morality which left its content *entirely* open could be the basis for a plausible account of moral motivation.

[2]See Rawls 1974–5, p. 8; and Daniels 1979 pp. 257–8. How closely the process of what I am calling philosophical explanation will coincide with the search for "wide reflective equilibrium" as this is understood by Rawls and by Daniels is a further question which I cannot take up here.

[3]For expression of this dissatisfaction see Singer 1974 and Brandt 1979, pp. 16–21.

on the plausibility of particular moral claims, but philosophical theories of morality vary widely in the extent and directness of their normative implications. At one extreme is intuitionism, understood as the philosophical thesis that morality is concerned with certain non-natural properties. Rightness, for example, is held by Ross[4] to be the property of "fittingness" or "moral suitability." Intuitionism holds that we can identify occurrences of these properties, and that we can recognize as self-evident certain general truths about them, but that they cannot be further analyzed or explained in terms of other notions. So understood, intuitionism is in principle compatible with a wide variety of normative positions. One could, for example, be an intuitionistic utilitarian or an intuitionistic believer in moral rights, depending on the general truths about the property of moral rightness which one took to be self-evident.

The other extreme is represented by philosophical utilitarianism. The term "utilitarianism" is generally used to refer to a family of specific normative doctrines—doctrines which might be held on the basis of a number of different philosophical theses about the nature of morality. In this sense of the term one might, for example, be a utilitarian on intuitionist or on contractualist grounds. But what I will call "philosophical utilitarianism" is a particular philosophical thesis about the subject matter of morality, namely the thesis that the only fundamental moral facts are facts about individual well-being.[5] I believe that this thesis has a great deal of plausibility for many people, and that, while some people are utilitarians for other reasons, it is the attractiveness of philosophical utilitarianism which accounts for the widespread influence of utilitarian principles.

It seems evident to people that there is such a thing as individuals' being made better or worse off. Such facts have an obvious motivational force; it is quite understandable that people should be moved by them in much the way that they are supposed to be moved by moral considerations. Further, these facts are clearly relevant to morality as we now understand it. Claims about individual well-being are one class of valid starting points for moral argument. But many people find it much harder to see how there could be any other, independent starting points. Substantive moral requirements independent of individual well-being strike people as intuitionist in an objectionable sense. They would represent "moral facts" of a kind it would be difficult to explain. There is no problem about recognizing it as a fact that a certain act is, say, an instance of lying or of promise breaking. And a utilitarian can acknowledge that such facts as these often have (derivative) moral significance: they are morally significant because of their consequences for individual well-being. The problems, and the charge of "intuitionism," arise when it is claimed that such acts are wrong in a sense that is not reducible to the fact that they decrease individual well-being. How could this independent property of moral wrongness be understood in a way that would give it the kind of importance and motivational force which moral considerations have been taken to have? If one accepts the idea that there are no moral properties having this kind of intrinsic significance, then philosophical utilitarianism may seem to be the only tenable account of morality. And once philosophical utilitarianism is accepted, some form of normative utilitarianism seems to be forced on us as the correct first-order moral theory. Utilitarianism thus has, for many people, something like the status which Hilbert's Formalism and Brouwer's Intuitionism have for their believers. It is a view which seems to be forced on us by the need to give a philosophically defensible account of the

[4]Ross 1939 pp. 52–4, 315.

[5]For purposes of this discussion I leave open the important questions of which individuals are to count and how "well-being" is to be understood. Philosophical utilitarianism will retain the appeal I am concerned with under many different answers to these questions.

subject. But it leaves us with a hard choice: we can either abandon many of our previous first-order beliefs or try to salvage them by showing that they can be obtained as derived truths or explained away as useful and harmless fictions.

It may seem that the appeal of philosophical utilitarianism as I have described it is spurious, since this theory must amount either to a form of intuitionism (differing from others only in that it involves just one appeal to intuition) or else to definitional naturalism of a kind refuted by Moore and others long ago. But I do not think that the doctrine can be disposed of so easily. Philosophical utilitarianism is a philosophical thesis about the nature of morality. As such, it is on a par with intuitionism or with the form of contractualism which I will defend later in this paper. None of these theses need claim to be true as a matter of definition; if one of them is true it does not follow that a person who denies it is misusing the words "right," "wrong" and "ought." Nor are all these theses forms of intuitionism, if intuitionism is understood as the view that moral facts concern special non-natural properties, which we can apprehend by intuitive insight but which do not need or admit of any further analysis. Both contractualism and philosophical utilitarianism are specifically incompatible with this claim. Like other philosophical theses about the nature of morality (including, I would say, intuitionism itself), contractualism and philosophical utilitarianism are to be appraised on the basis of their success in giving an account of moral belief, moral argument and moral motivation that is compatible with our general beliefs about the world: our beliefs about what kinds of things there are in the world, what kinds of observation and reasoning we are capable of, and what kinds of reasons we have for action. A judgment as to which account of the nature of morality (or of mathematics) is most plausible in this general sense is just that: a judgment of overall plausibility. It is not usefully described as an insight into concepts or as a special intuitive insight of some other kind.

If philosophical utilitarianism is accepted then some form of utilitarianism appears to be forced upon us as a normative doctrine, but further argument is required to determine which form we should accept. If all that counts morally is the well-being of individuals, no one of whom is singled out as counting for more than the others, and if all that matters in the case of each individual is the degree to which his or her well-being is affected, then it would seem to follow that the basis of moral appraisal is the goal of maximising the *sum*[6] of individual well-being. Whether this standard is to be applied to the criticism of individual actions, or to the selection of rules or policies, or to the inculcation of habits and dispositions to act is a further question, as is the question of how "well-being" itself is to be understood. Thus the hypothesis that much of the appeal of utilitarianism as a normative doctrine derives from the attractiveness of philosophical utilitarianism explains how people can be convinced that some form of utilitarianism must be correct while yet being quite uncertain as to which form it is, whether it is "direct" or "act" utilitarianism or some form of indirect "rule" or "motive" utilitarianism. What these views have in common, despite their differing normative consequences, is the identification of the same class of fundamental moral facts.

II

If what I have said about the appeal of utilitarianism is correct, then what a rival theory must do is to provide an alternative to philosophical utilitarianism as a conception of the

[6] "Average Utilitarianism" is most plausibly arrived at through quite a different form of argument, one more akin to contractualism. I discuss one such argument in section IV below.

subject matter of morality. This is what the theory which I shall call contractualism seeks to do. Even if it succeeds in this, however, and is judged superior to philosophical utilitarianism as an account of the nature of morality, normative utilitarianism will not have been refuted. The possibility will remain that normative utilitarianism can be established on other grounds, for example as the normative outcome of contractualism itself. But one direct and, I think, influential argument for normative utilitarianism will have been set aside.

To give an example of what I mean by contractualism, a contractualist account of the nature of moral wrongness might be stated as follows.

> An act is wrong if its performance under the circumstances would be disallowed by any system of rules for the general regulation of behavior which no one could reasonably reject as a basis for informed, unforced general agreement.

This is intended as a characterization of the kind of property which moral wrongness is. Like philosophical utilitarianism, it will have normative consequences, but it is not my present purpose to explore these in detail. As a contractualist account of one moral notion, what I have set out here is only an approximation, which may need to be modified considerably. Here I can offer a few remarks by way of clarification.

The idea of "informed agreement" is meant to exclude agreement based on superstition or false belief about the consequences of actions, even if these beliefs are ones which it would be reasonable for the person in question to have. The intended force of the qualification "reasonably," on the other hand, is to exclude rejections that would be unreasonable *given* the aim of finding principles which could be the basis of informed, unforced general agreement. Given this aim, it would be unreasonable, for example, to reject a principle because it imposed a burden on you when every alternative principle would impose much greater burdens on others. I will have more to say about grounds for rejection later in the paper.

The requirement that the hypothetical agreement which is the subject of moral argument be unforced is meant not only to rule out coercion, but also to exclude being forced to accept an agreement by being in a weak bargaining position, for example because others are able to hold out longer and hence to insist on better terms. Moral argument abstracts from such considerations. The only relevant pressure for agreement comes from the desire to find and agree on principles which no one who had this desire could reasonably reject. According to contractualism, moral argument concerns the possibility of agreement among persons who are all moved by this desire, and moved by it to the same degree. But this counter-factual assumption characterizes only the agreement with which morality is concerned, not the world to which moral principles are to apply. Those who are concerned with morality look for principles for application to their imperfect world which they could not reasonably reject, and which others in this world, who are not now moved by the desire for agreement, could not reasonably reject should they come to be so moved.[7]

The contractualist account of moral wrongness refers to principles "which no one could reasonably reject" rather than to principles "which everyone could reasonably accept" for the following reason.[8] Consider a principle under which some people will suffer severe hardships, and suppose that these hardships are avoidable. That is, there are alternative principles under which no one would have to bear comparable

[7]Here I am indebted to Gilbert Harman for comments which have helped me to clarify my statement of contractualism.

[8]A point I owe to Derek Parfit.

burdens. It might happen, however, that the people on whom these hardships fall are particularly self-sacrificing, and are willing to accept these burdens for the sake of what they see as the greater good of all. We would not say, I think, that it would be unreasonable of them to do this. On the other hand, it might not be unreasonable for them to refuse these burdens, and, hence, not unreasonable for someone to reject a principle requiring him to bear them. If this rejection would be reasonable, then the principle imposing these burdens is put in doubt, despite the fact that some particularly self-sacrificing people could (reasonably) accept it. Thus it is the reasonableness of rejecting a principle, rather than the reasonableness of accepting it, on which moral argument turns.

It seems likely that many non-equivalent sets of principles will pass the test of non-rejectability. This is suggested, for example, by the fact that there are many different ways of defining important duties, no one of which is more or less "rejectable" than the others. There are, for example, many different systems of agreement-making and many different ways of assigning responsibility to care for others. It does not follow, however, that any action allowed by at least one of these sets of principles cannot be morally wrong according to contractualism. If it is important for us to have *some* duty of a given kind (some duty of fidelity to agreements, or some duty of mutual aid) of which there are many morally acceptable forms, then one of these forms needs to be established by convention. In a setting in which one of these forms *is* conventionally established, acts disallowed by it will be wrong in the sense of the definition given. For, given the need for such conventions, one thing that could not be generally agreed to would be a set of principles allowing one to disregard conventionally established (and morally acceptable) definitions of important duties. This dependence on convention introduces a degree of cultural relativity into contractualist morality. In addition, what a person can reasonably reject will depend on the aims and conditions that are important in his life, and these will also depend on the society in which he lives. The definition given above allows for variation of both of these kinds by making the wrongness of an action depend on the circumstances in which it is performed.

The partial statement of contractualism which I have given has the abstract character appropriate in an account of the subject matter of morality. On its face, it involves no specific claim as to which principles could be agreed to or even whether there is a unique set of principles which could be the basis of agreement. One way, though not the only way, for a contractualist to arrive at substantive moral claims would be to give a technical definition of the relevant notion of agreement, e.g. by specifying the conditions under which agreement is to be reached, the parties to this agreement and the criteria of reasonableness to be employed. Different contractualists have done this in different ways. What must be claimed for such a definition is that (under the circumstances in which it is to apply) what it describes is indeed the kind of unforced, reasonable agreement at which moral argument aims. But contractualism can also be understood as an informal description of the subject matter of morality on the basis of which ordinary forms of moral reasoning can be understood and appraised without proceeding via a technical notion of agreement.

Who is to be included in the general agreement to which contractualism refers? The scope of morality is a difficult question of substantive morality, but a philosophical theory of the nature of morality should provide some basis for answering it. What an adequate theory should do is to provide a framework within which what seem to be relevant arguments for and against particular interpretations of the moral boundary can be carried out. It is often thought that contractualism can provide no plausible basis for an answer to this question. Critics charge either that contractualism provides no answer at all, because it must begin with some set of contracting parties taken as given, or that contractualism suggests an answer which is obviously too restrictive, since a contract requires parties who are able to make and keep agreements and who are each able to offer the others some benefit in return for their cooperation. Neither of these objections applies to the version of contractualism that I am defending. The general specification of the scope of morality which it implies seems to me to be this: morality applies to a being if the notion of justification to a being of that kind makes sense. What is required in order for this to be the case? Here I can only suggest some necessary conditions. The first is that the being have a good, that is, that there be a clear sense in which things can be said to go better or worse for that being. This gives partial sense to the idea of what it would be reasonable for a trustee to accept on the being's behalf. It would be reasonable for a trustee to accept at least those things that are good, or not bad, for the being in question. Using this idea of trusteeship we can extend the notion of acceptance to apply to beings that are incapable of literally agreeing to anything. But this minimal notion of trusteeship is too weak to provide a basis for morality, according to contractualism. Contractualist morality relies on notions of what it would be reasonable to accept, or reasonable to reject, which are essentially comparative. Whether it would be unreasonable for me to reject a certain principle, given the aim of finding principles which no one with this aim could reasonably reject, depends not only on how much actions allowed by that principle might hurt me in absolute terms but also on how that potential loss compares with other potential losses to others under this principle and alternatives to it. Thus, in order for a being to stand in moral relations with us it is not enough that it have a good, it is also necessary that its good be sufficiently similar to our own to provide a basis for some system of comparability. Only on the basis of such a system can we give the proper kind of sense to the notion of what a trustee could reasonably reject on a being's behalf.

But the range of possible trusteeship is broader than that of morality. One could act as a trustee for a tomato plant, a forest or an ant colony, and such entities are not included in morality. Perhaps this can be explained by appeal to the requirement of comparability: while these entities have a good, it is not comparable to our own in a way that provides a basis for moral argument. Beyond this, however, there is in these cases insufficient foothold for the notion of justification *to* a being. One further minimum requirement for this notion is that the being constitute a point of view; that is, that there be such a thing as what it is like to be that being, such a thing as what the world seems like to it. Without this, we do not stand in a relation to the being that makes even hypothetical justification to *it* appropriate.

On the basis of what I have said so far contractualism can explain why the capacity to feel pain should have seemed to many to count in favor of moral status: a being which has this capacity seems also to satisfy the three conditions I have just mentioned as necessary for the idea of justification to it to make sense. If a being can feel pain, then it constitutes a center of consciousness to which justification can be addressed. Feeling pain is a clear way in which the being can be worse off; having its pain alleviated a way in which it can be benefited; and these are forms of weal and woe which seem directly comparable to our own.

It is not clear that the three conditions I have listed as necessary are also sufficient for the idea of justification to a being to make sense. Whether they are, and, if they are not, what more may be required, are difficult and disputed questions. Some would restrict the moral sphere to those to whom justifications could in principle be communicated, or to those who can actually agree to something, or to those who have the capacity to understand moral argument. Contractualism as I have stated it does not settle these issues at once. All I claim is that it provides a basis for argument about them which is at least as plausible as that offered by rival accounts of the nature of morality. These proposed restrictions on the scope of morality are naturally understood as debatable claims about the conditions under which the relevant notion of justification makes sense, and the arguments commonly offered for and against them can also be plausibly understood on this basis.

Some other possible restrictions on the scope of morality are more evidently rejectable. Morality might be restricted to those who have the capacity to observe its constraints, or to those who are able to confer some reciprocal benefit on other participants. But it is extremely implausible to suppose that the beings excluded by these requirements fall entirely outside the protection of morality. Contractualism as I have formulated it[9] can explain why this is so: the absence of these capacities alone does nothing to undermine the possibility of justification to a being. What it may do in some cases, however, is to alter the justifications which are relevant. I suggest that whatever importance the capacities for deliberative control and reciprocal benefit may have is as factors altering the duties which beings have and the duties others have towards them, not as conditions whose absence suspends the moral framework altogether.

III

I have so far said little about the normative content of contractualism. For all I have said, the act utilitarian formula might turn out to be a theorem of contractualism. I do not think that this is the case, but my main thesis is that whatever the normative implications of contractualism may be it still has distinctive content as a philosophical thesis about the nature of morality. This content—the difference, for example, between being a utilitarian because the utilitarian formula is the basis of general agreement and being a utilitarian on other grounds—is shown most clearly in the answer that a contractualist gives to the first motivational question.

Philosophical utilitarianism is a plausible view partly because the facts which it identifies as fundamental to morality—facts about individual well-being—have obvious motivational force. Moral facts can motivate us, on this view, because of our sympathetic identification with the good of others. But as we move from philosophical utilitarianism to a specific utilitarian formula as the standard of right action, the form of motivation that utilitarianism appeals to becomes more abstract. If classical utilitarianism is the correct normative doctrine then the natural source of moral motivation will be a tendency to be moved by changes in aggregate well-being, however these may be composed. We must be moved in the same way by an aggregate gain of the same magnitude whether it is obtained by relieving the acute suffering of a few people or by bringing tiny benefits to a vast number, perhaps at the expense of moderate discomfort for a few. This is very different from sympathy of the familiar kind toward particular individuals, but a utilitarian may argue that this more abstract desire is what

[9]On this view (as contrasted with some others in which the notion of a contract is employed) what is fundamental to morality is the desire for reasonable agreement, not the pursuit of mutual advantage. See section V below. It should be clear that this version of contractualism can account for the moral standing of future persons who will be better or worse off as a result of what we do now. It is less clear how it can deal with the problem presented by future people who would not have been born but for actions of ours which also made the conditions in which they live worse. Do such people have reason to reject principles allowing these actions to be performed? This difficult problem, which I cannot explore here, is raised by Derek Parfit in Parfit 1976.

natural sympathy becomes when it is corrected by rational reflection. This desire has the same content as sympathy—it is a concern for the good of others—but it is not partial or selective in its choice of objects.

Leaving aside the psychological plausibility of this even-handed sympathy, how good a candidate is it for the role of moral motivation? Certainly sympathy of the usual kind is one of the many motives that can sometimes impel one to do the right thing. It may be the dominant motive, for example, when I run to the aid of a suffering child. But when I feel convinced by Peter Singer's article[10] on famine, and find myself crushed by the recognition of what seems a clear moral requirement, there is something else at work. In addition to the thought of how much good I could do for people in drought-stricken lands, I am overwhelmed by the further, seemingly distinct thought that it would be wrong for me to fail to aid them when I could do so at so little cost to myself. A utilitarian may respond that his account of moral motivation cannot be faulted for not capturing this aspect of moral experience, since it is just a reflection of our non-utilitarian moral upbringing. Moreover, it must be groundless. For what kind of fact could this supposed further fact of moral wrongness be, and how could it give us a further, special reason for acting? The question for contractualism, then, is whether it can provide a satisfactory answer to this challenge.

According to contractualism, the source of motivation that is directly triggered by the belief that an action is wrong is the desire to be able to justify one's actions to others on grounds they could not reasonably[11] reject. I find this an extremely plausible account of moral motivation—a better account of at least my moral experience than the natural utilitarian alternative—and it seems to me to constitute a strong point for the contractualist view. We all might like to be in actual agreement with the people around us, but the desire which contractualism identifies as basic to morality does not lead us simply to conform to the standards accepted by others whatever these may be. The desire to be able to justify one's actions to others on grounds they could not reasonably reject will be satisfied when we know that there is adequate justification for our action even though others in fact refuse to accept it (perhaps because they have no interest in finding principles which we and others could not reasonably reject). Similarly, a person moved by this desire will not be satisfied by the fact that others accept a justification for his action if he regards this justification as spurious.

One rough test of whether you regard a justification as sufficient is whether you would accept that justification if you were in another person's position. This connection between the idea of "changing places" and the motivation which underlies morality explains the frequent occurrence of "Golden Rule" arguments within different systems of morality and in the teachings of various religions. But the thought experiment of changing places is only a rough guide; the fundamental question is what would it be unreasonable to reject as a basis for informed, unforced, general agreement. As Kant observed,[12] our different individual points of view, taken as they are, may in general by simply irreconcilable. "Judgmental harmony" requires the construction of a genuinely interpersonal form of justification which is nonetheless something that each individual could agree to. From this interpersonal standpoint, a certain amount of how things look from another person's point of view, like a certain amount of how they look from my own, will be counted as bias.

[10]Singer 1972.

[11]Reasonably, that is, given the desire to find principles which others similarly motivated could not reasonably reject.

[12]Kant 1785, section 2, footnote 14.

I am not claiming that the desire to be able to justify one's actions to others on grounds they could not reasonably reject is universal or "natural." "Moral education" seems to me plausibly understood as a process of cultivating this desire and shaping it, largely by learning what justifications others are in fact willing to accept, by finding which ones you yourself find acceptable as you confront them from a variety of perspectives, and by appraising your own and others' acceptance or rejection of these justifications in the light of greater experience.

In fact it seems to me that the desire to be able to justify one's actions (and institutions) on grounds one takes to be acceptable is quite strong in most people. People are willing to go to considerable lengths, involving quite heavy sacrifices, in order to avoid admitting the unjustifiability of their actions and institutions. The notorious insufficiency of moral motivation as a way of getting people to do the right thing is not due to simple weakness of the underlying motive, but rather to the fact that it is easily deflected by self-interest and self-deception.

It could reasonably be objected here that the source of motivation I have described is not tied exclusively to the contractualist notion of moral truth. The account of moral motivation which I have offered refers to the idea of a justification which it would be unreasonable to reject, and this idea is potentially broader than the contractualist notion of agreement. For let *M* be some non-contractualist account of moral truth. According to *M,* we may suppose, the wrongness of an action is simply a moral characteristic of that action in virtue of which it ought not to be done. An act which has this characteristic, according to *M,* has it quite independently of any tendency of informed persons to come to agreement about it. However, since informed persons are presumably in a position to recognize the wrongness of a type of action, it would seem to follow that if an action is wrong then such persons would agree that it is not to be performed. Similarly, if an act is not morally wrong, and there is adequate moral justification to perform it, then there will presumably be a moral justification for it which an informed person would be unreasonable to reject. Thus, even if *M,* and not contractualism, is the correct account of moral truth, the desire to be able to justify my actions to others on grounds they could not reasonably reject could still serve as a basis for moral motivation.

What this shows is that the appeal of contractualism, like that of utilitarianism, rests in part on a qualified scepticism. A non-contractualist theory of morality can make use of the source of motivation to which contractualism appeals. But a moral argument will trigger this source of motivation only in virtue of being a good justification for acting in a certain way, a justification which others would be unreasonable not to accept. So a non-contractualist theory must claim that there are moral properties which have justificatory force quite independent of their recognition in any ideal agreement. These would represent what John Mackie has called instances of intrinsic "to-be-doneness" and "not-to-be-doneness."[13] Part of contractualism's appeal rests on the view that, as Mackie puts it, it is puzzling how there could be such properties "in the world." By contrast, contractualism seeks to explain the justificatory status of moral properties, as well as their motivational force, in terms of the notion of reasonable agreement. In some cases the moral properties are themselves to be understood in terms of this notion. This is so, for example, in the case of the property of moral wrongness, considered above. But there are also right- and wrong-making properties which are themselves independent of the contractualist notion of agreement. I take the property of being an act of killing for the pleasure of doing so to be a wrong-making property of this kind. Such

[13]Mackie 1977, p. 42.

properties are wrong-making because it would be reasonable to reject any set of principles which permitted the acts they characterize. Thus, while there are morally relevant properties "in the world" which are independent of the contractualist notion of agreement, these do not constitute instances of intrinsic "to-be-doneness" and "not-to-be-doneness": their moral relevance—their force in justifications as well as their link with motivation—is to be explained on contractualist grounds.

In particular, contractualism can account for the apparent moral significance of facts about individual well-being, which utilitarianism takes to be fundamental. Individual well-being will be morally significant, according to contractualism, not because it is intrinsically valuable or because promoting it is self-evidently a right-making characteristic, but simply because an individual could reasonably reject a form of argument that gave his well-being no weight. This claim of moral significance is, however, only approximate, since it is a further difficult question exactly how "well-being" is to be understood and in what ways we are required to take account of the well-being of others in deciding what to do. It does not follow from this claim, for example, that a given desire will always and everywhere have the same weight in determining the rightness of an action that would promote its satisfaction, a weight proportional to its strength or "intensity." The right-making force of a person's desires is specified by what might be called a conception of morally legitimate interests. Such a conception is a product of moral argument; it is not given, as the notion of individual well-being may be, simply by the idea of what it is rational for an individual to desire. Not everything for which I have a rational desire will be something in which others need concede me to have a legitimate interest which they undertake to weigh in deciding what to do. The range of things which may be objects of my rational desires is very wide indeed, and the range of claims which others could not reasonably refuse to recognize will almost certainly be narrower than this. There will be a tendency for interests to conform to rational desire—for those conditions making it rational to desire something also to establish a legitimate interest in it—but the two will not always coincide.

One effect of contractualism, then, is to break down the sharp distinction, which arguments for utilitarianism appeal to, between the status of individual well-being and that of other moral notions. A framework of moral argument is required to define our legitimate interests and to account for their moral force. This same contractualist framework can also account for the force of other moral notions such as rights, individual responsibility and procedural fairness.

IV

It seems unlikely that act utilitarianism will be a theorem of the version of contractualism which I have described. The positive moral significance of individual interests is a direct reflection of the contractualist requirement that actions be defensible to each person on grounds he could not reasonably reject. But it is a long step from here to the conclusion that each individual must agree to deliberate always from the point of view of maximum aggregate benefit and to accept justifications appealing to this consideration alone. It is quite possible that, according to contractualism, *some* moral questions may be properly settled by appeal to maximum aggregate well-being, even though this is not the sole or ultimate standard of justification.

What seems less improbable is that contractualism should turn out to coincide with some form of "two-level" utilitarianism. I cannot fully assess this possibility here. Contractualism does share with these theories the important features that the defense of individual actions must proceed via a defense of principles that would allow those acts.

But contractualism differs from *some* forms of two level utilitarianism in an important way. The role of principles in contractualism is fundamental; they do not enter merely as devices for the promotion of acts that are right according to some other standard. Since it does not establish two potentially conflicting forms of moral reasoning, contractualism avoids the instability which often plagues rule utilitarianism.

The fundamental question here, however, is whether the principles to which contractualism leads must be ones whose general adoption (either ideally or under some more realistic conditions) would promote maximum aggregate well-being. It has seemed to many that this must be the case. To indicate why I do not agree I will consider one of the best known arguments for this conclusion and explain why I do not think it is successful. This will also provide an opportunity to examine the relation between the version of contractualism I have advocated here and the version set forth by Rawls.

The argument I will consider, which is familiar from the writings of Harsanyi[14] and others, proceeds via an interpretation of the contractualist notion of acceptance and leads to the principle of maximum average utility. To think of a principle as a candidate for unanimous agreement I must think of it not merely as acceptable to *me* (perhaps in virtue of my particular position, my tastes, etc.) but as acceptable[15] to others as well. To be relevant, my judgment that the principle is acceptable must be impartial. What does this mean? To judge impartially that a principle is acceptable is, one might say, to judge that it is one which you would have reason to accept no matter who you were. That is, and here is the interpretation, to judge that it is a principle which it would be rational to accept if you did not know which person's position you occupied and believed that you had an equal chance of being in any of these positions. ("Being in a person's position" is here understood to mean being in his objective circumstances and evaluating these from the perspective of his tastes and preferences.) But, it is claimed, the principle which it would be rational to prefer under these circumstances—the one which would offer the chooser greatest expected utility—would be that principle under which the average utility of the affected parties would be highest.

This argument might be questioned at a number of points, but what concerns me at present is the interpretation of impartiality. The argument can be broken down into three stages. The first of these is the idea that moral principles must be impartially acceptable. The second is the idea of choosing principles in ignorance of one's position (including one's tastes, preferences, etc.). The third is the idea of rational choice under the assumption that one has an equal chance of occupying anyone's position. Let me leave aside for the moment the move from stage two to stage three, and concentrate on the first step, from stage one to stage two. There is a way of making something like this step which is, I think, quite valid, but it does not yield the conclusion needed by the argument. If I believe that a certain principle, *P*, could not reasonably be rejected as a basis for informed, unforced general agreement, then I must believe not only that it is something which it would be reasonable for me to accept but something which it would be reasonable for others to accept as well, insofar as we are all seeking a ground for general agreement. Accordingly, I must believe that I would have reason to accept *P* no matter which social position I were to occupy (though, for reasons mentioned above, I

[14]See Harsanyi 1955, sec. IV. He is there discussing an argument which he presented earlier in Harsanyi 1953.

[15]In discussing Harsanyi and Rawls I will generally follow them in speaking of the acceptability of principles rather than their unrejectability. The difference between these, pointed out above, is important only within the version of contractualism I am presenting; accordingly, I will speak of rejectability only when I am contrasting my own version with theirs.

may not believe that I *would* agree to *P* if I were in some of these positions). Now it may be thought that no sense can be attached to the notion of choosing or agreeing to a principle in ignorance of one's social position, especially when this includes ignorance of one's tastes, preferences, etc. But there is at least a minimal sense that might be attached to this notion. If it would be reasonable for everyone to choose or agree to *P*, then my knowledge that I have reason to do so need not depend on my knowledge of my particular position, tastes, preferences, etc. So, insofar as it makes any sense at all to speak of choosing or agreeing to something in the absence of this knowledge, it could be said that I have reason to choose or agree to those things which everyone has reason to choose or agree to (assuming, again, the aim of finding principles on which all could agree). And indeed, this same reasoning can carry us through to a version of stage three. For if I judge *P* to be a principle which everyone has reason to agree to, then it could be said that I would have reason to agree to it if I thought that I had an equal chance of being anybody, or indeed, if I assign any other set of probabilities to being one or another of the people in question.

But it is clear that this is not the conclusion at which the original argument aimed. That conclusion concerned what it would be rational for a self-interested person to choose or agree to under the assumption of ignorance or equal probability of being anyone. The conclusion we have reached appeals to a different notion: the idea of what it would be unreasonable for people to reject given that they are seeking a basis for general agreement. The direction of explanation in the two arguments is quite different. The original argument sought to explain the notion of impartial acceptability of an ethical principle by appealing to the notion of rational self-interested choice under special conditions, a notion which appears to be a clearer one. My revised argument explains how *a* sense might be attached to the idea of choice or agreement in ignorance of one's position given some idea of what it would be unreasonable for someone to reject as a basis for general agreement. This indicates a problem for my version of contractualism: it may be charged with failure to explain the central notion on which it relies. Here I would reply that my version of contractualism does not seek to explain this notion. It only tries to describe it clearly and to show how other features of morality can be understood in terms of it. In particular, it does not try to explain this notion by reducing it to the idea of what would maximize a person's self-interested expectations if he were choosing from a position of ignorance or under the assumption of equal probability of being anyone.

The initial plausibility of the move from stage one to stage two of the original argument rests on a subtle transition from one of these notions to the other. To believe that a principle is morally correct one must believe that it is one which all could reasonably agree to and none could reasonably reject. But my belief that this is the case may often be distorted by a tendency to take its advantage to me more seriously than its possible costs to others. For this reason, the idea of "putting myself in another's place" is a useful corrective device. The same can be said for the thought experiment of asking what I could agree to in ignorance of my true position. But both of these thought experiments are devices for considering more accurately the question of what *everyone* could reasonably agree to or what no one could reasonably reject. That is, they involve the pattern of reasoning exhibited in my revised form of the three-stage argument, not that of the argument as originally given. The question, what would maximize the expectations of a single self-interested person choosing in ignorance of his true position, is a quite different question. This can be seen by considering the possibility that the distribution with the highest average utility, call it *A*, might involve extremely low utility levels for some people, levels much lower than the minimum anyone would enjoy under a more equal distribution.

Suppose that *A* is a principle which it would be rational for a self-interested chooser with an equal chance of being in anyone's position to select. Does it follow that no one could reasonably reject *A?* It seems evident that this does not follow.[16] Suppose that the situation of those who would fare worst under *A,* call them the Losers, is extremely bad, and that there is an alternative to *A,* call it *E,* under which no one's situation would be nearly as bad as this. Prima facie, the losers would seem to have a reasonable ground for complaint against *A.* Their objection may be rebutted, by appeal to the sacrifices that would be imposed on some other individual by the selection of *E* rather than *A.* But the mere fact that *A* yields higher average utility, which might be due to the fact that many people do very slightly better under *A* than under *E* while a very few do much worse, does not settle the matter.

Under contractualism, when we consider a principle our attention is naturally directed first to those who would do worst under it. This is because if anyone has reasonable grounds for objecting to the principle it is *likely* to be them. It does not follow, however, that contractualism always requires us to select the principle under which the expectations of the worse off are highest. The reasonableness of the Losers' objection to *A* is not established simply by the fact that they are worse off under *A* and no-one would be this badly off under *E.* The force of their complaint depends also on the fact that their position under *A* is, in absolute terms, very bad, and would be significantly better under *E.* This complaint must be weighed against those of individuals who would do worse under *E.* The question to be asked is, is it unreasonable for someone to refuse to put up with the Losers' situation under *A* in order that someone else should be able to enjoy the benefits which he would have to give up under *E?* As the supposed situation of the Loser under *A* becomes better, or his gain under *E* smaller in relation to the sacrifices required to produce it, his case is weakened.

One noteworthy feature of contractualist argument as I have presented it so far is that it is non-aggregative: what are compared are individual gains, losses and levels of welfare. How aggregative considerations can enter into contractualist argument is a further question too large to be entered into here.

I have been criticizing an argument for Average Utilitarianism that is generally associated with Harsanyi, and my objections to this argument (leaving aside the last remarks about maximin) have an obvious similarity to objections raised by Rawls.[17] But the objections I have raised apply as well against some features of Rawls' own argument. Rawls accepts the first step of the argument I have described. That is, he believes that the correct principles of justice are those which "rational persons concerned to advance their interests" would accept under the conditions defined by his Original Position, where they would be ignorant of their own particular talents, their conception of the good, and the social position (or generation) into which they were born. It is the second step of the argument which Rawls rejects, i.e. the claim that it would be rational for persons so situated to choose those principles which would offer them greatest expected utility under the assumption that they have an equal chance of being anyone in the society in question. I believe, however, that a mistake has already been made once the first step is taken.

[16]The discussion which follows has much in common with the contrast between majority principles and unanimity principles drawn by Thomas Nagel in "Equality," Chapter 8 of Nagel 1979. I am indebted to Nagel's discussion of this idea.

[17]For example, the intuitive argument against utilitarianism on page 14 of Rawls 1971 and his repeated remark that we cannot expect some people to accept lower standards of life for the sake of the higher expectations of others.

This can be brought out by considering an ambiguity in the idea of acceptance by persons "concerned to advance their interests." On one reading, this is an essential ingredient in contractual argument; on another it is avoidable and, I think, mistaken. On the first reading, the interests in question are simply those of the members of society to whom the principles of justice are to apply (and by whom those principles must ultimately be accepted). The fact that they have interests which may conflict; and which they are concerned to advance, is what gives substance to questions of justice. On the second reading, the concern "to advance their interests" that is in question is a concern of the parties to Rawls' Original Position, and it is this concern which determines, in the first instance,[18] what principles of justice they will adopt. Unanimous agreement among these parties, each motivated to do as well for himself as he can, is to be achieved by depriving them of any information that could give them reason to choose differently from one another. From behind the veil of ignorance, what offers the best prospects for one will offer the best prospects for all, since no-one can tell what would benefit him in particular. Thus the choice of principles can be made, Rawls says, from the point of view of a single rational individual behind the veil of ignorance.

Whatever rules of rational choice this single individual, concerned to advance his own interests as best he can, is said to employ, this reduction of the problem to the case of a single person's self-interested choice should arouse our suspicion. As I indicated in criticizing Harsanyi, it is important to ask whether this single individual is held to accept a principle because he judges that it is one he could not reasonably reject whatever position he turns out to occupy, or whether, on the contrary, it is supposed to be acceptable to a person in any social position because it would be the rational choice for a single self-interested person behind the veil of ignorance. I have argued above that the argument for average utilitarianism involves a covert transition from the first pattern of reasoning to the second. Rawls' argument also appears to be of this second form; his defence of his two principles of justice relies, at least initially, on claims about what it would be rational for a person, concerned to advance his own interests, to choose behind a veil of ignorance. I would claim, however, that the plausibility of Rawls' arguments favoring his two principles over the principle of average utility is preserved, and in some cases enhanced, when they are interpreted as instances of the first form of contractualist argument.

Some of these arguments are of an informal moral character. I have already mentioned his remark about the unacceptability of imposing lower expectations on some for the sake of the higher expectations of others. More specifically, he says of the parties to the Original Position that they are concerned "to choose principles the consequences of which they are prepared to live with whatever generation they turn out to belong to"[19] or, presumably, whatever their social position turns out to be. This is a clear statement of the first form of contractualist argument. Somewhat later he remarks, in favor of the two principles, that they "are those a person would choose for the design of a society in which his enemy is to assign him a place."[20] Rawls goes on to dismiss this remark, saying that the parties "should not reason from false premises,"[21] but it is worth asking why it seemed a plausible thing to say in the first place. The reason, I take it, is this. In a

[18]Though they must then check to see that the principles they have chosen will be stable, not produce intolerable strains of commitment, and so on. As I argue below, these further considerations can be interpreted in a way that brings Rawls' theory closer to the version of contractualism presented here.

[19]Rawls 1971, p. 137.

[20]Rawls 1971, p. 152.

[21]Rawls 1971, p. 153.

contractualist argument of the first form, the object of which is to find principles acceptable to each person, assignment by a malevolent opponent is a thought experiment which has a heuristic role like that of a veil of ignorance: it is a way of testing whether one really does judge a principle to be acceptable from all points of view or whether, on the contrary, one is failing to take seriously its effect on people in social positions other than one's own.

But these are all informal remarks, and it is fair to suppose that Rawls' argument, like the argument for average utility, is intended to move from the informal contractualist idea of principles "acceptable to all" to the idea of rational choice behind a veil of ignorance, an idea which is, he hopes, more precise and more capable of yielding definite results. Let me turn then to his more formal arguments for the choice of the Difference Principle by the parties to the Original Position. Rawls cites three features of the decision faced by parties to the Original Position which, he claims, make it rational for them to use the maximum rule and, therefore, to select his Difference Principle as a principle of justice. These are (1) the absence of any objective basis for estimating probabilities, (2) the fact that some principles could have consequences for them which "they could hardly accept" while (3) it is possible for them (by following maximin) to ensure themselves of a minimum prospect, advances above which, in comparison, matter very little.[22] The first of these features is slightly puzzling, and I leave it aside. It seems clear, however, that the other considerations mentioned have at least as much force in an informal contractualist argument about what all could reasonably agree to as they do in determining the rational choice of a single person concerned to advance his interests. They express the strength of the objection that the "losers" might have to a scheme that maximized average utility at their expense, as compared with the counter-objections that others might have to a more egalitarian arrangement.

In addition to this argument about rational choice, Rawls invokes among "the main grounds for the two principles" other considerations which, as he says, use the concept of contract to a greater extent.[23] The parties to the Original Position, Rawls says, can agree to principles of justice only if they think that this agreement is one that they will actually be able to live up to. It is, he claims, more plausible to believe this of his two principles than of the principle of average utility, under which the sacrifices demanded ("the strains of commitment") could be much higher. A second, related claim is that the two principles of justice have greater psychological stability than the principle of average utility. It is more plausible to believe, Rawls claims, that in a society in which they were fulfilled people would continue to accept them and to be motivated to act in accordance with them. Continuing acceptance of the principle of average utility, on the other hand, would require an exceptional degree of identification with the good of the whole on the part of those from who sacrifices were demanded.

These remarks can be understood as claims about the "stability" (in a quite practical sense) of a society founded on Rawls' two principles of justice. But they can also be seen as an attempt to show that a principle arrived at via the second form of contractualist reasoning will also satisfy the requirements of the first form, i.e. that it is something no one could reasonably reject. The question "Is the acceptance of this principle an agreement you could actually live up to?" is, like the idea of assignment by one's worst enemy, a thought experiment through which we can use our own reactions to test our judgment that certain principles are ones that no one could reasonably reject. General principles of human psychology can also be invoked to this same end.

[22]Rawls 1971, p. 154.
[23]Rawls 1971, sec. 29, pp. 175ff.

Rawls' final argument is that the adoption of his two principles gives public support to the self-respect of individual members of society, and "give a stronger and more characteristic interpretation of Kant's idea"[24] that people must be treated as ends, not merely as means to the greater collective good. But, whatever difference there may be here between Rawls' two principles of justice and the principle of average utility, there is at least as sharp a contrast between the two patterns of contractualist reasoning distinguished above. The connection with self-respect, and with the Kantian formula, is preserved by the requirement that principles of justice be ones which no member of the society could reasonably reject. This connection is weakened when we shift to the idea of a choice which advances the interests of a single rational individual for whom the various individual lives in a society are just so many different possibilities. This is so whatever decision rule this rational chooser is said to employ. The argument from maximin seems to preserve this connection because it reproduces as a claim about rational choice what is, in slightly different terms, an appealing moral argument.

The "choice situation" that is fundamental to contractualism as I have described it is obtained by beginning with "mutually disinterested" individuals with full knowledge of their situations and adding to this (not, as is sometimes suggested, benevolence but) a desire on each of their parts to find principles which none could reasonably reject insofar as they too have this desire. Rawls several times considers such an idea in passing.[25] He rejects it in favor of his own idea of mutually disinterested choice from behind a veil of ignorance on the ground that only the latter enables us to reach definite results: "if in choosing principles we required unanimity even where there is full information, only a few rather obvious cases could be decided."[26] I believe that this supposed advantage is questionable. Perhaps this is because my expectations for moral argument are more modest than Rawls'. However, as I have argued, almost all of Rawls' own arguments have at least as much force when they are interpreted as arguments within the form of contractualism which I have been proposing. One possible exception is the argument from maximin. If the Difference Principle were taken to be generally applicable to decisions of public policy, then the second form of contractualist reasoning through which it is derived would have more far reaching implications than the looser form of argument by comparison of losses, which I have employed. But these wider applications of the principle are not always plausible, and I do not think that Rawls intends it to be applied so widely. His intention is that the Difference Principle should be applied only to major inequalities generated by the basic institutions of a society, and this limitation is a reflection of the special conditions under which he holds maximin to be the appropriate basis for rational choice: some choices have outcomes one could hardly accept, while gains above the minimum one can assure one's self matter very little, and so on. It follows, then, that in applying the Difference Principle—in identifying the limits of its applicability—we must fall back on the informal comparison of losses which is central to the form of contractualism I have described.

V

I have described this version of contractualism only in outline. Much more needs to be said to clarify its central notions and to work out its normative implications. I hope that

[24]Rawls 1971, p. 183.

[25]E.g. Rawls 1971, pp. 141, 148, although these passages may not clearly distinguish between this alternative and an assumption of benevolence.

[26]Rawls 1971, p. 141.

I have said enough to indicate its appeal as a philosophical theory of morality and as an account of moral motivation. I have put forward contractualism as an alternative to utilitarianism, but the characteristic feature of the doctrine can be brought out by contrasting it with a somewhat different view.

It is sometimes said[27] that morality is a device for our mutual protection. According to contractualism, this view is partly true but in an important way incomplete. Our concern to protect our central interests will have an important effect on what we could reasonably agree to. It will thus have an important effect on the content of morality if contractualism is correct. To the degree that this morality is observed, these interests will gain from it. If we had no desire to be able to justify our actions to others on grounds they could reasonably accept, the hope of gaining this protection would give us reason to try to instil this desire in others, perhaps through mass hypnosis or conditioning, even if this also meant acquiring it ourselves. But given that we have this desire already, our concern with morality is less instrumental.

The contrast might be put as follows. On one view, concern with protection is fundamental, and general agreement becomes relevant as a means or a necessary condition for securing this protection. On the other, contractualist view, the desire for protection is an important factor determining the content of morality because it determines what can reasonably be agreed to. But the idea of general agreement does not arise as a means of securing protection. It is, in a more fundamental sense, what morality is about.

[27]In different ways by G. J. Warnock in Warnock 1971, and by J. L. Mackie in Mackie 1977. See also Richard Brandt's remarks on justification in Chapter X of Brandt 1979.

1986

Morality's Demands and Their Limits

Samuel Scheffler

If an otherwise plausible normative moral theory makes unusually heavy demands of individual agents, what is the appropriate response to that theory? Here are four possibilities. The first is to say that the theory is unacceptable, and that we should seek a less demanding one. The second is to say that certain areas of human life are simply not subject to moral assessment or moral demands, so that the theory may be acceptable provided its scope is construed as restricted, with the severity of its demands limited in consequence. The third response holds that morality itself is excessively demanding, so that while the theory in question may be entirely acceptable as a theory of what morality requires, morality itself deserves less respect than it usually receives. And the fourth response denies that a showing of extreme demandingness constitutes a criticism of any kind. Morality demands what it demands, and if people find it hard to live up to those demands, that just shows that people are not, in general, morally very good.

Of these four responses, the first two both accept the idea that what morality demands is limited by considerations having to do with the individual agent's psychology and well-being. They disagree about whether the limitations are built into the content of morality or whether they operate instead as restrictions on its scope, but they agree that

[P]resented in an APA symposium on The Limits of Ethical Theory, December 30, 1986. . . .

Samuel Scheffler, "Morality's Demands and Their Limits," *The Journal of Philosophy* 83, No. 10 (October 1986). Reprinted with the permission of the author and *The Journal of Philosophy*.

there *are* limitations. The third and fourth responses, by contrast, deny this. Morality demands what it demands, they assert, and it may in fact demand a great deal. Of course we may find it hard to satisfy the demands of morality. So much the worse for morality, says the third response. So much the worse for us, says the fourth.

I

In the space available, I must confine myself almost exclusively to the issue posed by the choice between the first two responses. If one believes that the demands of morality are limited by considerations having to do with the effects of those demands on individual agents, then are the relevant limitations best thought of as part of the content of morality, or as restrictions on its scope?

Critics of the first response may say that the idea of responding to an excessively demanding moral theory by substituting a less demanding one has an intolerably moralistic cast. Although a less demanding theory would permit things that a more demanding theory would forbid, there are some cases, it may be said, in which the point is *not* that agents are *morally permitted* to do what the more demanding theory forbids, but rather that the issue of moral permissibility simply doesn't arise. Two kinds of examples are frequently mentioned. First there are acts that are said to be too trivial to be subject to moral evaluation. It would strike us as fatuous, for instance, to claim that I was morally justified in brushing my teeth this morning. Examples of the second kind are cases in which a failure to perform some act would be extremely costly, either to the agent himself or to someone dear to him. Thus Bernard Williams discusses a case in which a man can, at no cost to himself, save the life of either but not both of two people, one of whom is his wife and one of whom is a stranger.[1] It would be wrong, Williams says, to claim that the man is *morally justified* in saving his wife precisely because she is his wife. We should instead see this as a situation that "lie[s] beyond justifications."[2]

Why exactly may it seem intolerably moralistic to think of acts of these two types as morally permissible? There is a clue in Williams's response, when discussing the case just mentioned, to the question whether the fact that one of the people is the man's wife might not provide a justification for saving her instead of the stranger.

> It depends on how much weight is carried by "justification": . . . something . . . ambitious . . . is usually intended, essentially involving the idea that moral principle can legitimate his preference, yielding the conclusion that in situations of this kind it is at least all right (morally permissible) to save one's wife . . . But this construction provides the agent with one thought too many: it might have been hoped by some (for instance, by his wife) that his motivating thought, fully spelled out, would be the thought that it was his wife, not that it was his wife and that in situations of this kind it is permissible to save one's wife (p. 18).

Williams assumes that if we deem it morally permissible for the man to save his wife precisely because she *is* his wife, we are then committed to a further view about what the man's "motivating thought" should be when he acts: his motivating thought

[1] See "Persons, Character and Morality," in *Moral Luck* (New York: Cambridge, 1981), pp. 1–19.

[2] *Ibid.*, p. 18. For purposes of this discussion, I am interpreting the claim that the situation is beyond justifications as meaning that the man's act of saving his wife excludes moral assessment: the issue of moral justification does not arise here. Whether or not this is the best interpretation of Williams's considered views on the matter, it represents a theoretically important position, and one to which Williams himself seems drawn at least sometimes.

should be that, under the circumstances, it is morally permissible for him to save his wife. Given this assumption, the view that it is permissible for the man to save his wife does indeed seem intolerably moralistic. Similarly, the view that it was permissible for me to brush my teeth this morning certainly seems objectionable if it commits me to the additional claim that I ought to have been motivated in brushing my teeth by the thought that it was permissible for me to do so. However, Williams's assumption is implausible, and he provides no support for it.[3] Thus the charge that the first response is excessively moralistic may itself be unsupported insofar as it depends on a generalized form of that assumption. Of course, the most that we accomplish if we succeed in rebutting that charge is to eliminate some of the motivation for the second response. It remains to supply some positive reason for preferring one response or the other.

II

Consider again trivial actions. There certainly seems to be some plausibility to the claim that some acts are not important enough to warrant moral assessment. This is partly because it can seem hard to imagine what—other than philosophical discussion—would lead anyone actually to say, or even to think, that, for example, it was morally permissible for me to brush my teeth this morning. It may seem hard to supply that evaluative proposition with a plausible setting in ordinary human thought and discourse. But suppose that, as I began to brush, some food lodged in the windpipe of the person in the next room. Through the open door I saw the person trying vainly to dislodge the food. I realized what was happening, I am expert in the use of the Heimlich maneuver, and I knew that there was nobody else in a position to help. If I nevertheless proceeded to brush merrily away, then I presumably did something morally unacceptable. This suggests that, when we agreed that my brushing my teeth this morning seemed too trivial to warrant moral assessment, we were assuming that nobody was choking to death in the next room as I was brushing and that there was no comparable emergency that I was in a comparably good position to respond to. More generally, the judgment that a particular act is "too trivial" to warrant moral evaluation implicitly depends on an assessment not only of the act itself, but also of the consequences of the act, the alternatives available to the agent, and their consequences. For ease of discussion, and not as a claim with any independent meaning, we can summarize this by saying that such a judgment always depends implicitly on an assessment of the act and its context.

Thus the judgment that a particular act is too trivial to warrant moral evaluation always depends on an assessment of the act and its context. And for any given act that is said to be too trivial, we can imagine a change of context that would render it suitable for moral evaluation. If these two points are correct, I can see no basis for distinguishing between acts that are morally permissible and those which are too trivial to warrant moral evaluation. For there is no relevant difference between the kind of assessment that issues in judgments of triviality and the kind that issues in judgments of moral permissibility, prohibition, and requirement. Both consist in assessment of the act and its context, and both are sensitive to the same sorts of feature. It is tempting to conclude that a judgment of triviality constitutes a disguised form of moral judgment, for it appears to depend on an assessment of the act and its context which is indistinguishable from moral assessment. At the very least, the distinction between those acts which are morally per-

[3]For related criticism, see Barbara Herman, "Integrity and Impartiality," *The Monist*, LXVI, 2 (April 1983): 233–250.

missible and those which are too trivial to evaluate seems to multiply categories needlessly, for it is unclear what the putative distinction comes to. In each case, the acts in question are regarded as acceptable, in the sense that they are neither morally required nor morally prohibited. Assignment of an act to either category depends on the same kind of assessment of the act and its context; and the same sorts of changes in context would lead to reassignment of acts from either of these categories to one of the others.

Similar considerations apply to cases like those Williams discusses. Anyone familiar with the contemporary philosophical art of counterexample construction will be able to supply a context in which the man's saving his wife would be, shall we say, morally dubious. The man's wife, whom he loathes and has recently sued for divorce, is a notorious and sadistic mass murderer who will be missed by nobody. The stranger, on the other hand, is a brilliant and saintly medical researcher who, in addition to being the sole source of support for five small and adorable children plus two aged and admirable parents, has just discovered a cure for cancer but has not yet had a chance to write it down. You get the idea. Any judgment that a particular act is "beyond justifications," like a judgment of triviality, implicitly depends on an assessment of the act and its context which appears indistinguishable from moral assessment. And for any given act that is thought to be beyond justifications, we can imagine a change in context that would render it suitable for moral evaluation. So it is not clear what the distinction between acts that are beyond justifications and acts that are morally permissible really comes to.

A further point. I have been discussing the idea that, in the original example, where, we have been assuming, the wife is not a loathsome murderer and the stranger is not a saintly medical researcher, the man's saving of his wife is beyond justifications. And I have argued that that judgment depends implicitly on a kind of assessment of the act and its context that is indistinguishable from moral assessment. But beyond that, it is also the case that *other* acts available to the same agent at the same time seem uncontroversially subject to moral assessment. (What if he saved the stranger and let his wife die? Or what if he sat by, whistling and twiddling his thumbs, and watched them *both* die? What if he pulled out a gun and shot them both?) If that is right, then the claim that the original act does not admit of moral assessment comes to seem even less plausible, to me at any rate.

III

Considerations such as these lead me to prefer the first response to the demandingness criticism over the second. They also provide support for the idea that morality is *pervasive,* in the sense that no voluntary human action is in principle resistant to moral assessment (although of course one or another of the familiar excusing conditions may apply). The suggestion that morality is pervasive neither entails nor is entailed by the more frequently discussed claim that morality is *overriding,* where that is understood as meaning that it can never be rational knowingly to do what morality forbids. More generally, morality may be seen as having any combination of the following properties: *pervasiveness, overridingness,* and, as I shall refer to it, *stringency,* the property of being very demanding within whatever domain it applies.[4]

[4]It is easy to become confused about the difference between stringency and overridingness, for the following reason. In assessing what individuals ought morally to do, virtually any moral theory will say that considerations of the agent's own interests are sometimes *overridden* by other considerations, so that what one morally ought to do sometimes differs from what would maximally advance one's own interests. Since stringent theories see this happening more often than nonstringent theories, stringency can be identified with the

Nevertheless, people's attitudes toward any one of these properties may be affected by their beliefs about the others. For example, some who believe that morality is overriding may for that very reason be inclined to resist the suggestion that it is pervasive, feeling that the authority of morality is so great within its domain that that domain must be limited if people are to have sufficient opportunity to pursue personal projects and commitments. Of course, this concern is likely to be greatest when morality is also thought of as stringent, and then it may help to explain the appeal of what I have been calling the "second response." And it is likely to diminish if stringency is rejected, so that morality itself is construed as permitting people to devote substantial attention to personal projects. Or, to take another example, some who deny that morality is stringent may for that reason be inclined to *accept* the suggestion that it is overriding. They may feel that morality as they understand it already gives people's personal projects all the weight they can rationally have, so that, in any conflict that nevertheless arises between morality and personal concerns, the balance of reasons must always favor morality.[5] However, they are not committed to this view. The claim of overridingness remains an independent thesis, which those who deny that morality is stringent can accept or reject.

IV

One reaction to an unusually demanding moral theory is to deny that morality has the property of stringency and, hence, to conclude that the theory in question cannot be acceptable. That, in effect, is what I have been calling the "first response." Another reaction is to deny that morality is pervasive, so mitigating the severity of the theory's demands. That is what I have been calling the "second response." Still another reaction is to deny that morality is overriding, and so to challenge its authority, while allowing that the theory in question may be perfectly acceptable as a theory of what morality requires. That is what the third response does. Only the fourth response is compatible with the view that morality has all three properties: overridingness, pervasiveness, and stringency.

I have defended the first response as against the second: defended the denial of stringency over the denial of pervasiveness as an expression of the idea that there are limits to the demands of morality. I have not said anything about the choice among the first, third, and fourth responses. Whereas the first response thinks of limits to morality's demands as built into its content, the third response sees limits to morality's authority but not to its demands, and the fourth invokes limits to neither. We should be clear: the first response thinks of limits to morality's *demands* as built into its content, but it sees morality's *role* as *less* limited than the other two responses do. That is, it sees morality as properly accommodating the interests and perspective of the individual agent in a way that they do not, whereas they see morality as more disengaged from the standpoint of the agent than it does. For my part, I find the broader construal of morality's role attractive. To defend it, however, one would have to locate it within a more comprehensive understanding of the complex relations between the requirements of morality and the living of an actual human life: an understanding, in other words, both of how and why the content of morality is constrained

relatively frequent overriding of the agent's interests in arriving at over-all moral verdicts. However the "claim of overridingness," as I am understanding it, is the very different idea that, *given* an over-all verdict about what one morally ought to do, one cannot rationally defy it. The claim that morality is overriding in this sense is clearly distinct from and independent of the claim that it is stringent.

[5] See Thomas Nagel, *The View from Nowhere* (New York: Oxford, 1986), ch. 10.

by considerations of the agent's psychology and well-being, and of the ways in which it is appropriate for morality to enter into an agent's life, and to impinge on his or her thought, deliberation, feeling, and action.

One final word. In this paper, I have approached questions about the limits of morality's demands through a discussion of some alternative responses to very demanding moral theories. This will seem appropriate only if one believes that the idea of a "moral theory" has a legitimate role to play in our thinking about morality. Although I am sympathetic to some of the doubts that have been expressed about that idea, I do nevertheless think that it has such a role. Those who disagree may see questions about the demandingness of moral theories and questions about the demands of morality as less closely related.

1986

Moral Realism

Peter Railton

Among contemporary philosophers, even those who have not found skepticism about empirical science at all compelling have tended to find skepticism about morality irresistible. For various reasons, among them an understandable suspicion of moral absolutism, it has been thought a mark of good sense to explain away any appearance of objectivity in moral discourse. So common has it become in secular intellectual culture to treat morality as subjective or conventional that most of us now have difficulty imagining what it might be like for there to be facts to which moral judgments answer.

Undaunted, some philosophers have attempted to establish the objectivity of morality by arguing that reason, or science, affords a foundation for ethics. The history of such attempts hardly inspires confidence. Although rationalism in ethics has retained adherents long after other rationalisms have been abandoned, the powerful philosophical currents that have worn away at the idea that unaided reason might afford a standpoint from which to derive substantive conclusions show no signs of slackening. And ethical naturalism has yet to find a plausible synthesis of the empirical and the normative: the more it has given itself over to descriptive accounts of the origin of norms, the less has it retained recognizably moral force; the more it has undertaken to provide a

Peter Railton, "Moral Realism," *Philosophical Review* 95, No. 2 (April 1986).

recognizable basis for moral criticism or reconstruction, the less has it retained a firm connection with descriptive social or psychological theory.[1]

In what follows, I will present in a programmatic way a form of ethical naturalism that owes much to earlier theorists, but that seeks to effect a more satisfactory linkage of the normative to the empirical. The link cannot, I believe, be effected by proof. It is no more my aim to refute moral skepticism than it is the aim of contemporary epistemic naturalists to refute Cartesian skepticism. The naturalist in either case has more modest aspirations. First, he seeks to provide an analysis of epistemology or ethics that permits us to see how the central evaluative functions of this domain could be carried out within existing (or prospective) empirical theories. Second, he attempts to show how traditional nonnaturalist accounts rely upon assumptions that are in some way incoherent, or that fit ill with existing science. And third, he presents to the skeptic a certain challenge, namely, to show how a skeptical account of our epistemic or moral practices could be as plausible, useful, or interesting as the account the naturalist offers, and how a skeptical reconstruction of such practices—should the skeptic, as often he does, attempt one—could succeed in preserving their distinctive place and function in human affairs. I will primarily be occupied with the first of these three aspirations.

One thing should be said at the outset. Some may be drawn to, or repelled by, moral realism out of a sense that it is the view of ethics that best expresses high moral earnestness. Yet one can be serious about morality, even to a fault, without being a moral realist. Indeed, a possible objection to the sort of moral realism I will defend here is that it may not make morality serious enough.

I. SPECIES OF MORAL REALISM

Such diverse views have claimed to be—or have been accused of being—realist about morality, that an initial characterization of the position I will defend is needed before proceeding further. Claims—and accusations—of moral realism typically extend along some or all of the following dimensions. Roughly put: (1) Cognitivism—Are moral judgments capable of truth and falsity? (2) Theories of truth—If moral judgments do have truth values, in what sense? (3) Objectivity—In what ways, if any, does the existence of moral properties depend upon the actual or possible states of mind of intelligent beings? (4) Reductionism—Are moral properties reducible to, or do they in some weaker sense supervene upon, nonmoral properties? (5) Naturalism—Are moral properties natural properties? (6) Empiricism—Do we come to know moral facts in the same way we come to know the facts of empirical science, or are they revealed by reason or by some special mode of apprehension? (7) Bivalence—Does the principle of the excluded middle apply to moral judgments? (8) Determinateness—Given whatever procedures we have for assessing moral judgments, how much of morality is likely to be determinable? (9) Categoricity—Do all rational agents necessarily have some reason to obey moral imperatives? (10) Universality—Are moral imperatives applicable to all rational agents, even (should such exist) those who lack a reason to comply with them? (11) Assessment of existing moralities—Are present moral beliefs approximately true, or do prevailing moral intuitions in some other sense constitute privileged data? (12) Relativism—Does the truth or warrant of moral judgments depend directly upon individually- or socially-adopted norms or practices? (13) Pluralism—Is there a uniquely

[1]Nineteenth-century evolutionary naturalism affords an example of the former, Dewey—and, on at least one reading, perhaps Mill as well—an example of the latter.

good form of life or a uniquely right moral code, or could different forms of life or moral codes be appropriate in different circumstances?

Here, then, are the approximate coordinates of my own view in this multidimensional conceptual space. I will argue for a form of moral realism which holds that moral judgments can bear truth values in a fundamentally non-epistemic sense of truth; that moral properties are objective, though relational; that moral properties supervene upon natural properties, and may be reducible to them; that moral inquiry is of a piece with empirical inquiry; that it cannot be known *a priori* whether bivalence holds for moral judgments or how determinately such judgments can be assessed; that there is reason to think we know a fair amount about morality, but also reason to think that current moralities are wrong in certain ways and could be wrong in quite general ways; that a rational agent may fail to have a reason for obeying moral imperatives, although they may nonetheless be applicable to him; and that, while there are perfectly general criteria of moral assessment, nonetheless, by the nature of these criteria no one kind of life is likely to be appropriate for all individuals and no one set of norms appropriate for all societies and all times. The position thus described might well be called "stark, raving moral realism," but for the sake of syntax, I will colorlessly call it "moral realism." This usage is not proprietary. Other positions, occupying more or less different coordinates, may have equal claim to either name.

II. THE FACT/VALUE DISTINCTION

Any attempt to argue for a naturalistic moral realism runs headlong into the fact/value distinction. Philosophers have given various accounts of this distinction, and of the arguments for it, but for present purposes I will focus upon several issues concerning the epistemic and ontological status of judgments of value as opposed to judgments of fact.

Perhaps the most frequently heard argument for the fact/value distinction is epistemic: it is claimed that disputes over questions of value can persist even after all rational or scientific means of adjudication have been deployed, hence, value judgments cannot be cognitive in the sense that factual or logical judgments are. This claim is defended in part by appeal to the instrumental (hypothetical) character of reason, which prevents reason from dictating ultimate values. In principle, the argument runs, two individuals who differ in ultimate values could, without manifesting any rational defect, hold fast to their conflicting values in the face of any amount of argumentation or evidence. As Ayer puts it, "we find that argument is possible on moral questions only if some system of values is presupposed."[2]

One might attempt to block this conclusion by challenging the instrumental conception of rationality. But for all its faults and for all that it needs to be developed, the instrumental conception seems to me the clearest notion we have of what it is for an agent to have reasons to act. Moreover, it captures a central normative feature of reason-giving, since we can readily see the commending force for an agent of the claim that a given act would advance his ends. It would be hard to make much sense of someone who sincerely claimed to have certain ends and yet at the same time insisted that they could not provide him even *prima facie* grounds for action. (Of course, he might also believe that he has other, perhaps countervailing, grounds.)

Yet this version of the epistemic argument for the fact/value distinction is in difficulty even granting the instrumental conception of rationality. From the standpoint of in-

[2]A. J. Ayer, *Language, Truth, and Logic* (New York: Dover, 1952), p. 111.

strumental reason, belief-formation is but one activity among others: to the extent that we have reasons for engaging in it, or for doing it one way rather than another, these are at bottom a matter of its contribution to our ends.[3] What it would be rational for an individual to believe on the basis of a given experience will vary not only with respect to his other beliefs, but also with respect to what he desires.[4] From this it follows that no amount of mere argumentation or experience could force one on pain of irrationality to accept even the factual claims of empirical science. The long-running debate over inductive logic well illustrates that rational choice among competing hypotheses requires much richer and more controversial criteria of theory choice than can be squeezed from instrumental reason alone. Unfortunately for the contrast Ayer wished to make, we find that argument is possible on scientific questions only if some system of values is presupposed.

However, Hume had much earlier found a way of marking the distinction between facts and values without appeal to the idea that induction—or even deduction—could require a rational agent to adopt certain beliefs rather than others when this would conflict with his contingent ends.[5] For Hume held the thesis that morality is practical, by which he meant that if moral facts existed, they would necessarily provide a reason (although perhaps not an overriding reason) for moral action to all rational beings, regardless of their particular desires. Given this thesis as a premise, the instrumental conception of rationality can clinch the argument after all, for it excludes the possibility of categorical reasons of this kind. By contrast, Hume did not suppose it to be constitutive of logic or science that the facts revealed by these forms of inquiry have categorical force for rational agents, so the existence of logical and scientific facts, unlike the existence of moral facts, is compatible with the instrumental character of reason.

Yet this way of drawing the fact/value distinction is only as compelling as the claim that morality is essentially practical in Hume's sense.[6] Hume is surely right in claiming there to be an intrinsic connection, no doubt complex, between valuing something and having some sort of positive attitude toward it that provides one with an instrumental reason for action. We simply would disbelieve someone who claimed to value honesty and yet never showed the slightest urge to act honestly when given an easy opportunity. But this is a fact about the connection between the values *embraced by* an individual and his reasons for action, not a fact showing a connection between moral evaluation and rational motivation.

[3]In saying this, I am insisting that questions about what it would be rational to believe belong to practical rather than theoretical reason. While results of theoretical reason—for example, conclusions of deductive inferences—are in general relevant to questions about rational belief, they are not determinative apart from the agent's practical reasons.

[4]Of course, individual belief-formation is not typically governed by explicit means–end reasoning, but rather by habits of belief-formation and tendencies to invest varying degrees of confidence in particular kinds of beliefs. If we accept an instrumental account of rationality, then we can call such habits rational from the standpoint of the individual to the extent that they fit into a constellation of attitudes and tendencies that promote his ends. This matter will arise again in Section IV.

[5]Neither these remarks, nor those in subsequent paragraphs, are meant to be a serious exegesis of Hume's arguments, which admit of interpretations other than the one suggested here. I mean only to capture certain features of what I take Hume's arguments to be, for example, in Book III, Part I, Section I of *A Treatise of Human Nature*, edited by L. A. Selby-Bigge (Oxford: Clarendon, 1973), esp. pp. 465–466, and in Appendix I of *An Inquiry Concerning the Principles of Morals*, edited by C. W. Hendel (Indianapolis: Bobbs-Merrill, 1957), esp. pp. 111–112.

[6]Philippa Foot has questioned this thesis, although her way of posing and arguing the question differs enough from mine that I cannot judge whether she would be in agreement with the argument that follows. See her *Virtues and Vices* (Berkeley: University of California Press, 1978), especially Essay XI. The presentation of the issues here owes its main inspiration to William K. Frankena's distinction between the rational and the moral points of view.

Suppose for example that we accept Hume's characterization of justice as an artificial virtue directed at the general welfare. This is in a recognizable sense an evaluative or normative notion—"a value" in the loose sense in which this term is used in such debates—yet it certainly does not follow from its definition that every rational being, no matter what his desires, who believes that some or other act is just in this sense will have an instrumental reason to perform it. A rational individual may fail to value justice for its own sake, and may have ends contrary to it. In Hume's discussion of our "interested obligation" to be just, he seems to recognize that in the end it may not be possible to show that a "sensible knave" has a reason to be just. Of course, Hume held that the rest of us—whose hearts rebel at Sensible Knave's attitude that he may break his word, cheat, or steal whenever it suits his purposes—have reason to be just, to deem Knave's attitude unjust, and to try to protect ourselves from his predations.[7]

Yet Knave himself could say, perhaps because he accepts Hume's analysis of justice, "Yes, my attitude is unjust." And by Hume's own account of the relation of reason and passion, Knave could add "But what is that to me?" without failing to grasp the content of his previous assertion. Knave, let us suppose, has no doubts about the intelligibility or reality of "the general welfare," and thinks it quite comprehensible that people attach great significance in public life to the associated notion of justice. He also realizes that for the bulk of mankind, whose passions differ from his, being just is a source and a condition of much that is most worthwhile in life. He thus understands that appeals to justice typically have motivating force. Moreover, he himself uses the category of justice in analyzing the social world, and he recognizes—indeed, his knavish calculations take into account—the distinction between those individuals and institutions that truly are just, and those that merely appear just or are commonly regarded as just. Knave does view a number of concepts with wide currency—religious ones, for example—as mere fictions that prey on weak minds, but he does not view justice in this way. Weak minds and moralists have, he thinks, surrounded justice with certain myths—that justice is its own reward, that once one sees what is just one will automatically have a reason to do it, and so on. But then, he thinks that weak minds and moralists have likewise surrounded wealth and power with myths—that the wealthy are not truly happy, that the powerful inevitably ride for a fall, and so on—and he does not on this account doubt whether there are such things as wealth and power. Knave is glad to be free of prevailing myths about wealth, power, and justice; glad, too, that he is free in his own mind to pay as much or as little attention to any of these attributes as his desires and circumstances warrant. He might, for example, find Mae West's advice convincing: diamonds are very much worth acquiring, and "goodness ha[s] nothing to do with it."

We therefore must distinguish the business of saying what an individual values from the business of saying what it is for him to make measurements against the criteria of a species of evaluation that he recognizes to be genuine.[8]

To deny Hume's thesis of the practicality of moral judgment, and so remove the ground of his contrast between facts and values, is not to deny that morality has an action-guiding character. Morality surely can remain prescriptive within an instrumental framework, and can recommend itself to us in much the same way that, say, epistemology does: various significant and enduring—though perhaps not universal—human ends can be advanced if we apply certain evaluative criteria to our

[7]See the *Inquiry Concerning the Principles of Morals*, Sec. IX, Pt. II, pp. 102–103.

[8]The ancient criticism of non-cognitivism that it has difficulty accounting for the difference between moral value and other sorts of desirability (so that Hume can speak in one breath of our approval of a man's "good offices" and his "well-contrived apartment"), gains some vitality in the present context. To account for

actions. That may be enough to justify to ourselves our abiding concern with the epistemic or moral status of what we do.[9]

By arguing that reason does not compel us to adopt particular beliefs or practices apart from our contingent, and variable, ends, I may seem to have failed to negotiate my way past epistemic relativism, and thus to have wrecked the argument for moral realism before it has even left port. Rationality does go relative when it goes instrumental, but epistemology need not follow. The epistemic warrant of an individual's belief may be disentangled from the rationality of his holding it, for epistemic warrant may be tied to an external criterion—as it is for example by causal or reliabilist theories of knowledge.[10] It is part of the naturalistic realism that informs this essay to adopt such a criterion of warrant. We should not confuse the obvious fact that in general our ends are well served by reliable causal mechanisms of belief-formation with an internalist claim to the effect that reason requires us to adopt such means. Reliable mechanisms have costs as well as benefits, and successful pursuit of some ends—Knave would point to religious ones, and to those of certain moralists—may in some respects be incompatible with adoption of reliable means of inquiry.

This rebuttal of the charge of relativism invites the defender of the fact/value distinction to shift to ontological ground. Perhaps facts and values cannot be placed on opposite sides of an epistemological divide marked off by what reason and experience can compel us to accept. Still, the idea of reliable causal mechanisms for moral learning, and of moral facts "in the world" upon which they operate, is arguably so bizarre that I may have done no more than increase my difficulties.

III. VALUE REALISM

The idea of causal interaction with moral reality certainly would be intolerably odd if moral facts were held to be *sui generis;*[11] but there need be nothing odd about causal mechanisms for learning moral facts if these facts are constituted by natural facts, and that is the view under consideration. This response will remain unconvincing, however, until some positive argument for realism about moral facts is given. So let us turn to that task.

What might be called "the generic stratagem of naturalistic realism" is to postulate a realm of facts in virtue of the contribution they would make to the *a posteriori* explanation of certain features of our experience. For example, an external world is posited to explain the coherence, stability, and intersubjectivity of sense-experience. A

---

such differences it is necessary to have a contentful way of characterizing criteria of moral assessment so that moral approval does not reduce to "is valued by the agent." (Such a characterization will be offered in Section IV.) Value *sans phrase* is a generic, and not necessarily moral, notion. One sometimes hears it said that generic value becomes moral in character when we reach that which the agent prizes above all else. But this would invest pets and mementos with moral value, and have the peculiar effect of making amoralism a virtual conceptual impossibility. It seems more plausible to say that not all value is moral value, and that the highest values for an individual need not be, nor need they even seem to him to be, moral values. Once we turn to questions of duty, the situation should be clearer still: moral theorists have proposed quite different relations among the categories of moral rightness, moral goodness, and non-moral goodness, and it seems implausible to say that deeming an act or class of actions morally right is necessarily equivalent to viewing it personally as valuable *sans phrase.*

[9]The character of moral imperatives receives further discussion in Section V.

[10]Such theories are suitably externalist when, in characterizing the notions of *reliability* or *warrant-conferring causal process,* they employ an account of truth that does not resolve truth into that which we have reason to believe—for example, a nontrivial correspondence theory.

[11]Or if moral facts were supposed to be things of a kind to provide categorical reasons for action. However, this supposition is simply Hume's thesis of practicality in ontological garb.

moral realist who would avail himself of this stratagem must show that the postulation of moral facts similarly can have an explanatory function. The stratagem can succeed in either case only if the reality postulated has these two characteristics:

1. *independence:* it exists and has certain determinate features independent of whether we think it exists or has those features, independent, even, of whether we have good reason to think this;
2. *feedback:* it is such—and we are such—that we are able to interact with it, and this interaction exerts the relevant sort of shaping influence or control upon our perceptions, thought, and action.

These two characteristics enable the realist's posit to play a role in the explanation of our experience that cannot be replaced without loss by our mere *conception* of ourselves or our world. For although our conceptual scheme mediates even our most basic perceptual experiences, an experience-transcendent reality has ways of making itself felt without the permission of our conceptual scheme—causally. The success or failure of our plans and projects famously is not determined by expectation alone. By resisting or yielding to our worldly efforts in ways not anticipated by our going conceptual scheme, an external reality that is never directly revealed in perception may nonetheless significantly influence the subsequent evolution of that scheme.

The realist's use of an external world to explain sensory experience has often been criticized as no more than a picture. But do we even have a picture of what a realist explanation might look like in the case of values?[12] I will try to sketch one, filling in first a realist account of non-moral value—the notion of something being desirable for someone, or good for him.[13]

Consider first the notion of someone's *subjective interests*—his wants or desires, conscious or unconscious. Subjective interest can be seen as a secondary quality, akin to taste. For me to take a subjective interest in something is to say that it has a positive *valence* for me, that is, that in ordinary circumstances it excites a positive attitude or inclination (not necessarily conscious) in me. Similarly, for me to say that I find sugar sweet is to say that in ordinary circumstances sugar excites a certain gustatory sensation in me. As secondary qualities, subjective interest and perceived sweetness supervene upon primary qualities of the perceiver, the object (or other phenomenon) perceived, and the surrounding context: the perceiver is so constituted that this sort of object in this sort of context will excite that sort of sensation. Call this complex set of relational, dispositional, primary qualities the *reduction basis* of the secondary quality.

We have in this reduction basis an objective notion that corresponds to, and helps explain, subjective interests. But it is not a plausible foundation for the notion of non-moral goodness, since the subjective interests it grounds have insufficient normative force to capture the idea of desirableness. My subjective interests frequently reflect ignorance, confusion, or lack of consideration, as hindsight attests. The fact that I am now

[12]J. L. Mackie, in *Ethics: Inventing Right and Wrong* (Harmondsworth, Middlesex: Penguin, 1977), and Gilbert Harman, in *The Nature of Morality: An Introduction to Ethics* (New York: Oxford University Press, 1977), both challenge moral realism in part by questioning its capacity to explain. Nicholas L. Sturgeon, in "Moral Explanations," David Copp and David Zimmerman, eds., *Morality, Reason and Truth: New Essays in the Foundations of Ethics* (Totowa, N.J.: Rowman and Allanhead, 1984), takes the opposite side, using arguments different from those offered below.

[13]A full-scale theory of value would, I think, show the concept of someone's good to be slightly different from the concept of what is desirable for him. However, this difference will not affect the argument made here.

so constituted that I desire something which, had I better knowledge of it, I would wish I had never sought, does not seem to recommend it to me as part of my good.

To remedy this defect, let us introduce the notion of an *objectified subjective interest* for an individual A, as follows.[14] Give to an actual individual A unqualified cognitive and imaginative powers, and full factual and nomological information about his physical and psychological constitution, capacities, circumstances, history, and so on. *A* will have become *A+*, who has complete and vivid knowledge of himself and his environment, and whose instrumental rationality is in no way defective. We now ask *A+* to tell us not what *he* currently wants, but what he would want his non-idealized self *A* to want—or, more generally, to seek—were he to find himself in the actual condition and circumstances of *A*.[15] Just as we assumed there to be a reduction basis for an individual A's actual subjective interests, we may assume there to be a reduction basis for his objectified subjective interests, namely, those facts about A and his circumstances that *A+* would combine with his general knowledge in arriving at his views about what he would want to want were he to step into *A*'s shoes.

For example, Lonnie, a traveler in a foreign country, is feeling miserable. He very much wishes to overcome his malaise and to settle his stomach, and finds he has a craving for the familiar: a tall glass of milk. The milk is desired by Lonnie, but is it also desirable for him? Lonnie-Plus can see that what is wrong with Lonnie, in addition to homesickness, is dehydration, a common affliction of tourists, but one often not detectable from introspective evidence. The effect of drinking hard-to-digest milk would be to further unsettle Lonnie's stomach and worsen his dehydration. By contrast, Lonnie-Plus can see that abundant clear fluids would quickly improve Lonnie's physical condition—which, incidentally, would help with his homesickness as well. Lonnie-Plus can also see just how distasteful Lonnie would find it to drink clear liquids, just what would happen were Lonnie to continue to suffer dehydration, and so on. As a result of this information, Lonnie-Plus might then come to desire that were he to assume Lonnie's place, he would want to drink clear liquids rather than milk, or at least want to act in such a way that a want of this kind would be satisfied. The reduction basis of this objectified interest includes facts about Lonnie's circumstances and constitution, which determine, among other things, his existing tastes and his ability to acquire certain new tastes, the consequences of continued dehydration, the effects and availability of various sorts of liquids, and so on.

[14]It was some work by Richard C. Jeffrey on epistemic probability that originally suggested to me the idea of objectifying subjective interests. See note 17. I have since benefited from Richard B. Brandt's work on "rational desire," although I fear that what I will say contains much that he would regard as wrong-headed. See *A Theory of the Good and the Right* (Oxford: Clarendon, 1979), Part I.

[15]We ask this question of *A+*, rather than what *A+* wants for himself, because we are seeking the objectified subjective interests of *A*, and the interests of *A+* might be quite different owing to the changes involved in the idealization of *A*. For example, *A+* presumably does not want any more information for himself—there is no more to be had and he knows this. Yet it might still be true that *A+* would want to want more knowledge were he to be put in the place of his less well-informed self, *A*. It may as a psychological matter be impossible for *A+* to set aside entirely his desires *in his present circumstances* with regard to himself or to *A* in considering what he would want to want were he to be put *in the place of* his less-than-ideal self. This reveals a measurement problem for objective interests: giving an individual the information and capacities necessary to "objectify" his interests may perturb his psychology in ways that alter the phenomenon we wish to observe. Such difficulties attend even the measurement of subjective interests, since instruments for sampling preferences (indeed, mere acts of reflection upon one's preferences) tend to affect the preferences expressed. For obvious reasons, interference effects come with the territory. Though not in themselves sufficient ground for skepticism about subjective or objective interests, these measurement problems show the need for a "perturbation theory," and for caution about attributions of interests that are inattentive to interference effects.

Let us say that this reduction basis is the constellation of primary qualities that make it be the case that the Lonnie has a certain *objective interest.*[16] That is, we will say that Lonnie has an objective interest in drinking clear liquids in virtue of this complex, relational, dispositional set of facts. Put another way, we can say that the reduction basis, not the fact that Lonnie-Plus would have certain wants, is the truth-maker for the claim that this is an objective interest of Lonnie's. The objective interest thus explains why there is a certain objectified interest, not the other way around.[17]

Let us now say that X is *non-morally good for A* if and only if *X* would satisfy an objective interest of *A*.[18] We may think of *A*+'s views about what he would want to want were he in *A*'s place as generating a ranking of potential objective interests of *A,* a ranking that will reflect what is better or worse for *A* and will allow us to speak of *A*'s actual wants as better or worse approximations of what is best for him. We may also decompose *A*+'s views into *prima facie* as opposed to "on balance" objective interests of *A*, the former yielding the notion of "*a* good for *A*," the latter, of "*the* good for *A*."[19] This

[16]"Interest" is not quite the word wanted here, for in ordinary language we may speak of a want where we would not speak of a corresponding interest. See Brian Barry, *Political Argument* (London: Routledge and Kegan Paul, 1965), especially Chapter X, for discussion. A more accurate, but overly cumbersome, expression would be "positive-valence-making characteristic."

[17]Suppose for a moment, contrary to what was urged above, that there is a workable notion of epistemic probability that determines rational degrees of belief independent of the contingent goals of the epistemic agent. Perhaps then the following analogy will be helpful. Consider a physically random process, such as alpha-decay. We can ask an individual what subjective probability he would assign to an event consisting in a certain rate of decay for a given sample of uranium; we can also ask what rational degree of belief the individual would assign to this event were he to become ideally informed about the laws of physics and the relevant initial conditions. Call the latter rational degree of belief the *objectified subjective probability* of the event, and suppose it to be equal to one fifth. (Compare Richard C. Jeffrey, *The Logic of Decision* (New York: McGraw-Hill, 1964), pp. 190–196.) But now consider the physical facts that, in conjunction with the laws of quantum mechanics, ground the idealized individual's judgment. Call these the *reduction basis* of that judgment. This reduction basis is a complex set of primary qualities that can be said to bring it about that the event in question has an *objective probability* of one fifth. (It should be said that it is not part of Jeffrey's approach to posit such objective probabilities.) The existence of this objective probability can explain why an ideally informed individual would select an objectified subjective probability equal to one fifth, but the probability judgment of an ideally informed individual cannot explain why the objective probability is one fifth—that is a matter of the laws of physics. Similarly, the existence of an individual's objective interest can explain why his ideally informed self would pick out for his less-informed self a given objectified subjective interest, but not *vice versa.*

[18]More precisely, we may say that X is non-morally good for *A* at time *t* if and only if *X* would satisfy an objective interest of *A* the reduction basis of which exists at *t*. Considerations about the evolution of interests over time raise a number of issues that cannot be entered into here.

[19]*A*+, putting himself in *A*'s place, may find several different sets of wants equally appealing, so that several alternatives could be equal-best for *A* in this sense. This would not make the notion of "the good for *A*" problematic, just pluralistic. However, a more serious question looms. Is there sufficient determinacy in the specification of *A*+'s condition, or in the psychology of desire, to make the notion of objective interest definite enough for my purposes? Without trying to say how definite *that* might be, let me suggest two ways in which an answer to the worry about definiteness might begin. (1) It seems that we do think that there are rather definite answers to questions about how an individual A's desires would change were his beliefs to change in certain limited ways. If Lonnie were to learn the consequences of drinking milk, he would no longer want his desire for milk to be effective. But a large change in belief can be accomplished piecemeal, by a sequence of limited changes in belief. Thus, if (admittedly, a big "if") *order* of change is not in the end significant, then the facts and generalizations that support counterfactuals about limited changes might support an extrapolation all the way to *A*+. (2) Beliefs and desires appear to co-vary systematically. Typically, we find that individuals who differ markedly in their desires—for example, about careers or style of life—differ markedly, and characteristically, in their beliefs; as individuals become more similar in their beliefs, they tend to become more similar in their desires. This suggests that if (another big "if") the characterization given of *A*+ fixes the entire content of his beliefs in a definite way (at least, given a choice of language), then his desires may be quite comprehensively fixed as well. If we had in hand a general theory of the co-variation of beliefs and desires, then we could appeal directly to this theory—plus facts about *A*—to ground the counterfactuals needed to characterize *A*'s objectified interests, eliminating any essential reference to the imaginary individual *A*+.

seems to me an intuitively plausible account of what someone's non-moral good consists in: roughly, what he would want himself to seek if he knew what he were doing.[20]

Moreover, this account preserves what seems to me an appropriate link between non-moral value and motivation. Suppose that one desires *X*, but wonders whether *X* really is part of one's good. This puzzlement typically arises because one feels that one knows too little about *X*, oneself, or one's world, or because one senses that one is not being adequately rational or reflective in assessing the information one has—perhaps one suspects that one has been captivated by a few salient features of *X* (or repelled by a few salient features of its alternatives). If one were to learn that one would still want oneself to want *X* in the circumstances were one to view things with full information and rationality, this presumably would reduce the force of the original worry. By contrast, were one to learn that when fully informed and rational one would want oneself *not* to want *X* in the circumstances, this presumably would add force to it. Desires being what they are, a reinforced worry might not be sufficient to remove the desire for *X*. But if one were to become genuinely and vividly convinced that one's desire for *X* is in this sense not supported by full reflection upon the facts, one presumably would feel this to be a count against acting upon the desire. This adjustment of desire to belief might not in a given case be required by reason or logic; it might be "merely psychological." But it is precisely such psychological phenomena that naturalistic theories of value take as basic.

In what follows, we will need the notion of intrinsic goodness, so let us say that *X* is *intrinsically non-morally good for A* just in case *X* is in *A*'s objective interest without reference to any other objective interest of *A*. We can in an obvious way use the notion of objective intrinsic interest to account for all other objective interests. Since individuals and their environments differ in many respects, we need not assume that everyone has the same objective intrinsic interests. *A fortiori,* we need not assume that they have the same objective instrumental interests. We should, however, expect that when personal and situational similarities exist across individuals—that is, when there are similarities in reduction bases—there will to that extent be corresponding similarities in their interests.

It is now possible to see how the notion of non-moral goodness can have explanatory uses. For a start, it can explain why one's actual desires have certain counterfactual features, for example, why one would have certain hypothetical desires rather than others were one to become fully informed and aware. Yet this sort of explanatory use—following as it does directly from the definition of objective interest—might well be thought unimpressive unless some other explanatory functions can be found.

Consider, then, the difference between Lonnie and Tad, another traveler in the same straits, but one who, unlike Lonnie, wants to drink clear liquids, and proceeds to do so. Tad will perk up while Lonnie remains listless. We can explain this difference by noting that although both Lonnie and Tad acted upon their wants, Tad's wants better reflected his interests. The congruence of Tad's wants with his interests may be fortuitous,

[20]The account may, however, yield some counterintuitive results. Depending upon the nature and circumstances of given individuals, they might have objective interests in things we find wrong or repulsive, and that do not seem to us part of a good life. We can explain a good deal of our objection to certain desires—for example, those involving cruelty—by saying that they are not *morally* good; others—for example, those of a philistine nature—by saying that they are not *aesthetically* valuable; and so on. It seems to me preferable to express our distaste for certain ends in terms of specific categories of value, rather than resort to the device of saying that such ends could under no circumstances be part of anyone's non-moral good. People, or at least some people, might be put together in a way that makes some not-very-appetizing things essential to their flourishing, and we do not want to be guilty of wishful thinking on this score. (There will be wishful thinking enough before we are through.)

or it may be that Tad knows he is dehydrated and knows the standard treatment. In the latter case we would ordinarily say that the explanation of the difference in their condition is that Tad, but not Lonnie, "knew what was good for him."

Generally, we can expect that what $A+$ would want to want were he in A's place will correlate well with what would permit A to experience physical or psychological well-being or to escape physical or psychological ill-being. Surely our well- or ill-being are among the things that matter to us most, and most reliably, even on reflection.[21] Appeal to degrees of congruence between A's wants and his interests thus will often help to explain facts about how satisfactory he finds his life. Explanation would not be preserved were we to substitute "believed to be congruent" for "are (to such-and-such a degree) congruent," since, as cases like Lonnie's show, even if one were to convince oneself that one's wants accurately reflected one's interests, acting on these wants might fail to yield much satisfaction.

In virtue of the correlation to be expected between acting upon motives that congrue with one's interests and achieving a degree of satisfaction or avoiding a degree of distress, one's objective interests may also play an explanatory role in the *evolution* of one's desires. Consider what I will call the *wants/interests mechanism,* which permits individuals to achieve selfconscious and unselfconscious learning about their interests through experience. In the simplest sorts of cases, trial and error leads to the selective retention of wants that are satisfiable and lead to satisfactory results for the agent.

For example, suppose that Lonnie gives in to his craving and drinks the milk. Soon afterwards, he feels much worse. Still unable to identify the source of his malaise and still in the grips of a desire for the familiar, his attention is caught by a green-and-red sign in the window of a small shop he is moping past: "7-Up," it says. He rushes inside and buys a bottle. Although it is lukewarm, he drinks it eagerly. "Mmm," he thinks, "I'll have another." He buys a second bottle, and drains it to the bottom. By now he has had his fill of tepid soda, and carries on. Within a few hours, his mood is improving. When he passes the store again on the way back to his hotel, his pleasant association with drinking 7-Up leads him to buy some more and carry it along with him. That night, in the dim solitude of his room, he finds the soda's reassuringly familiar taste consoling, and so downs another few bottles before finally finding sleep. When he wakes up the next morning, he feels very much better. To make a dull story short: the next time Lonnie is laid low abroad, he may have some conscious or unconscious, reasoned or superstitious, tendency to seek out 7-Up. Unable to find that, he might seek something quite like it, say, a local lime-flavored soda, or perhaps even the *agua mineral con gaz* he had previously scorned. Over time, as Lonnie travels more and suffers similar malaise, he regularly drinks clearish

[21]To put the matter in more strictly naturalistic terms, we can expect that evolution will have favored organisms so constituted that those behaviors requisite to their survival and flourishing are associated with positive internal states (such as pleasure) and those opposed to survival or flourishing with negative states (such as pain). "Flourishing" here, even if understood as mere reproductive fitness, is not a narrow notion. In order for beings such as humans to be reproductively successful, they must as phenotypes have lives that are psychologically sustainable, internally motivating, and effectively social; lives, moreover, that normally would engage in a wide range of their peculiarly human capacities. Humankind could hardly have been a success story even at the reproductive level were not pursuit of the sorts of things that characteristically have moved humans to action associated with existences of this kind. However, it must be kept in mind that most human evolution occurred under circumstances different in important ways from the present. It therefore is quite possible that the interaction of evolved human motivational potentials with existing circumstances will produce incongruities between what we tend to aim at, or to be driven by, and what would produce the greatest pleasure for us. That is one reason for doubting hedonism as a theory of motivation.

liquids and regularly feels better, eventually developing an actual desire for such liquids—and an aversion to other drinks, such as milk—in such circumstances.

Thus have Lonnie's desires evolved through experience to conform more closely to what is good for him, in the naturalistic sense intended here. The process was not one of an ideally rational response to the receipt of ideal information, but rather of largely unreflective experimentation, accompanied by positive and negative associations and reinforcements. There is no guarantee that the desires "learned" through such feedback will accurately or completely reflect an individual's good. Still less is there any guarantee that, even when an appropriate adjustment in desire occurs, the agent will comprehend the origin of his new desires or be able to represent to himself the nature of the interests they reflect. But then, it is a quite general feature of the various means by which we learn about the world that they may fail to provide accurate or comprehending representations of it. My ability to perceive and understand my surroundings coexists with, indeed draws upon the same mechanisms as, my liability to deception by illusion, expectation, or surface appearance.

There are some broad theoretical grounds for thinking that something like the wants/interests mechanism exists and has an important role in desire-formation. Humans are creatures motivated primarily by wants rather than instincts. If such creatures were unable through experience to conform their wants at all closely to their essential interests—perhaps because they were no more likely to experience positive internal states when their essential interests are met than when they are not—we could not expect long or fruitful futures for them. Thus, if humans in general did not come to want to eat the kinds of food necessary to maintain some degree of physical well-being, or to engage in the sorts of activities or relations necessary to maintain their sanity, we would not be around today to worry whether we can know what is good for us. Since creatures as sophisticated and complex as humans have evolved through encounters with a variety of environments, and indeed have made it their habit to modify their environments, we should expect considerable flexibility in our capacity through experience to adapt our wants to our interests. However, this very flexibility makes the mechanism unreliable: our wants may at any time differ arbitrarily much from our interests; moreover, we may fail to have experiences that would cause us to notice this, or to undergo sufficient feedback to have much chance of developing new wants that more nearly approximate our interests. It is entirely possible, and hardly infrequent, that an individual live out the course of a normal life without ever recognizing or adjusting to some of his most fundamental interests. Individual limitations are partly remedied by cultural want-acquiring mechanisms, which permit learning and even theorizing over multiple lives and life-spans, but these same mechanisms also create a vast potential for the inculcation of wants at variance with interests.

The argument for the wants/interests mechanism has about the same status, and the same breezy plausibility, as the more narrowly biological argument that we should expect the human eye to be capable of detecting objects the size and shape of our predators or prey. It is not necessary to assume anything approaching infallibility, only enough functional success to hold our own in an often inhospitable world.[22]

[22]"Functional success" rather than "representational accuracy" for the following reason. Selection favors organisms that have some-or-other feature that happens in their particular environment to contribute to getting their needs met. Whether that feature will be an accurate representational capacity cannot be settled by an argument of this kind. Of course, it would be a very great coincidence if beings who rely as heavily upon representations as we do were able to construct only grossly inaccurate representations while at the same time managing successfully in a range of environments over a long period of time. But such coincidences cannot be ruled out.

Thus far the argument has concerned only those objective interests that might be classified as needs, but the wants/interests mechanism can operate with respect to any interest—even interests related to an individual's particular aptitudes or social role—whose frustration is attended even indirectly by consciously or unconsciously unsatisfactory results for him. (To be sure, the more indirect the association the more unlikely that the mechanism will be reliable.) For example, the experience of taking courses in both mathematics and philosophy may lead an undergraduate who thought himself cut out to be a mathematician to come to prefer a career in philosophy, which would in fact better suit his aptitudes and attitudes. And a worker recently promoted to management from the shop floor may find himself less inclined to respond to employee grievances than he had previously wanted managers to be, while his former co-workers may find themselves less inclined to confide in him than before.

If a wants/interests mechanism is postulated, and if what is non-morally good for someone is a matter of what is in his objective interest, then we can say that objective value is able to play a role in the explanation of subjective value of the sort the naturalistic realist about value needs. These explanations even support some qualified predictions: for example, that, other things equal, individuals will ordinarily be better judges of their own interests than third parties; that knowledge of one's interests will tend to increase with increased experience and general knowledge; that people with similar personal and social characteristics will tend to have similar values; and that there will be greater general consensus upon what is desirable in those areas of life where individuals are most alike in other regards (for example, at the level of basic motives), and where trial-and-error mechanisms can be expected to work well (for example, where esoteric knowledge is not required). I am in no position to pronounce these predictions correct, but it may be to their credit that they accord with widely-held views.

It should perhaps be emphasized that although I speak of the objectivity of value, the value in question is human value, and exists only because humans do. In the sense of old-fashioned theory of value, this is a relational rather than absolute notion of goodness. Although relational, the relevant facts about humans and their world are objective in the same sense that such non-relational entities as stones are: they do not depend for their existence or nature merely upon our conception of them.[23]

Thus understood, objective interests are supervenient upon natural and social facts. Does this mean that they cannot contribute to explanation after all, since it should always be possible in principle to account for any particular fact that they purport to explain by reference to the supervenience basis alone? If mere supervenience were grounds for denying an explanatory role to a given set of concepts, then we would have to say that chemistry, biology, and electrical engineering, which clearly supervene upon physics, lack explanatory power. Indeed, even outright reducibility is no ground for doubting explanatoriness. To establish a relation of reduction between, for example, a chemical phenomenon such as valence and a physical model of the atom does nothing to suggest that there is no such thing as valence, or that generalizations involving valence cannot support explanations. There can be no issue here of ontological economy

[23]Although some elements of their reduction basis depend upon our past choices, our objective interests are not therefore subjective in a sense damaging to the present argument. After all, such unproblematically objective facts about us as our weight, income, and spatial location depend in the same way upon past choices. The point is not that our subjective interests have no role in shaping the reduction basis of our objective interests, but rather that they can affect our objective interests only in virtue of their actual (rather than merely desired) effects upon this reduction basis, just as they can affect our weight, income, or spatial location only in virtue of actual (rather than merely desired) effects upon our displacement, employment, or movement.

or eschewing unnecessary entities, as might be the case if valence were held to be something *sui generis,* over and above any constellation of physical properties. The facts described in principles of chemical valence are genuine, and permit a powerful and explanatory systematization of chemical combination; the existence of a successful reduction to atomic physics only bolsters these claims.

We are confident that the notion of chemical valence is explanatory because proffered explanations in terms of chemical valence insert explananda into a distinctive and well-articulated nomic nexus, in an obvious way increasing our understanding of them. But what comparably powerful and illuminating theory exists concerning the notion of objective interest to give us reason to think—whether or not strict reduction is possible—that proffered explanations using this notion are genuinely informative?

I would find the sort of value realism sketched here uninteresting if it seemed to me that no theory of any consequence could be developed using the category of objective value. But in describing the wants/interests mechanism I have already tried to indicate that such a theory may be possible. When we seek to explain why people act as they do, why they have certain values or desires, and why sometimes they are led into conflict and other times into cooperation, it comes naturally to common sense and social science alike to talk in terms of people's interests. Such explanations will be incomplete and superficial if we remain wholly at the level of subjective interests, since these, too, must be accounted for.[24]

IV. NORMATIVE REALISM

Suppose everything said thus far to have been granted generously. Still, I would as yet have no right to speak of *moral* realism, for I have done no more than to exhibit the possibility of a kind of realism with regard to non-moral goodness, a notion that perfect moral skeptics can admit. To be entitled to speak of moral realism I would have to show realism to be possible about distinctively moral value, or moral norms. I will concentrate on moral norms—that is, matters of moral rightness and wrongness—although the argument I give may, by extension, be applied to moral value. In part, my reason is that normative realism seems much less plausible intuitively than value realism. It therefore is not surprising that many current proposals for moral realism focus essentially upon value—and sometimes only upon what is in effect non-moral value. Yet on virtually any conception of morality, a moral theory must yield an account of rightness.

Normative moral realism is implausible on various grounds, but within the framework of this essay, the most relevant is that it seems impossible to extend the generic strategy of naturalistic realism to moral norms. Where is the place in explanation for facts about what *ought* to be the case—don't facts about the way things *are* do all the explaining there is to be done? Of course they do. But then, my naturalistic moral real-

[24]In a similar way, it would be incomplete and superficial to explain why, once large-scale production became possible, the world's consumption of refined sugar underwent such explosive development, by mentioning only the fact that people liked its taste. Why, despite wide differences in traditional diet and acquired tastes, has sugar made such inroads into human consumption? Why haven't the appearance and promotion of other equally cheap foodstuffs produced such remarkable shifts in consumption? Why, even in societies where sugar is recognized as a health hazard, does consumption of sugars, often in concealed forms, continue to climb? Facts about the way we are constituted, about the rather singular ways sugar therefore affects us, and about the ways forms of production and patterns of consumption co-evolved to generate both a growing demand and an expanding supply, must supplement a theory that stops at the level of subjective preferences. See Sidney W. Mintz, *Sweetness and Power: The Place of Sugar in Modern History* (New York: Viking, 1985) for relevant discussion.

ism commits me to the view that facts about what ought to be the case are facts of a special kind about the way things are. As a result, it may be possible for them to have a function within an explanatory theory. To see how this could be, let me first give some examples of explanations outside the realm of morality that involve naturalized norms.

"Why did the roof collapse?—For a house that gets the sort of snow loads that one did, the rafters ought to have been 2×8's at least, not 2×6's." This explanation is quite acceptable, as far as it goes, yet it contains an "ought." Of course, we can remove this "ought" as follows: "If a roof of that design is to withstand the snow load that one bore, then it must be framed with rafters at least 2×8 in cross-section." An architectural "ought" is replaced by an engineering "if . . . then . . . ." This is possible because the "ought" clearly is hypothetical, reflecting the universal architectural goal of making roofs strong enough not to collapse. Because the goal is contextually fixed, and because there are more or less definite answers to the question of how to meet it, and moreover because the explanandum phenomenon is the result of a process that selects against instances that do not attain that goal, the "ought"-containing account conveys explanatory information.[25] I will call this sort of explanation *criterial:* we explain why something happened by reference to a relevant criterion, given the existence of a process that in effect selects for (or against) phenomena that more (or less) closely approximate this criterion. Although the criterion is defined naturalistically, it may at the same time be of a kind to have a regulative role in human practice—in this case, in house-building.

A more familiar sort of criterial explanation involves norms of individual rationality. Consider the use of an instrumental theory of rationality to explain an individual's behavior in light of his beliefs and desires, or to account for the way an individual's beliefs change with experience.[26] Bobby Shaftoe went to sea because he believed it was the best way to make his fortune, and he wanted above all to make his fortune. Crewmate Reuben Ramsoe came to believe that he wasn't liked by the other deckhands because he saw that they taunted him and greeted his frequent lashings at the hands of the First Mate with unconcealed pleasure. These explanations work because the action or belief in question was quite rational for the agent in the circumstances, and because we correctly suppose both Shaftoe and Ramsoe to have been quite rational.

Facts about degrees of instrumental rationality enter into explanations in other ways as well. First, consider the question why Bobby Shaftoe has had more success than most like-minded individuals in achieving his goals. We may lay his success to the fact that Shaftoe is more instrumentally rational than most—perhaps he has greater-than-average acumen in estimating the probabilities of outcomes, or is more-reliable-than-average at deductive inference, or is more-imaginative-than-average in surveying alternatives.

Second, although we are all imperfect deliberators, our behavior may come to embody habits or strategies that enable us to approximate optimal rationality more closely than our deliberative defects would lead one to expect. The mechanism is simple. Patterns of beliefs and behaviors that do not exhibit much instrumental rationality will tend to be to some degree self-defeating, an incentive to change them, whereas

[25]For a discussion of how informally expressed accounts may nonetheless convey explanatory information, see Section II of my "Probability, Explanation, and Information," *Synthese* 48 (1981), pp. 233–256.

[26]Such explanation uses a naturalized criterion when rationality is defined in terms of relative efficiency given the agent's beliefs and desires. A (more or less) rational agent is thus someone disposed to act in (more or less) efficient ways. There is a deep difficulty about calling such explanation naturalistic, for the constraints placed upon attributions of beliefs and desires by a "principle of charity" may compromise the claim that rational-agent explanations are empirical. Although I believe this difficulty can be overcome, this is hardly the place to start *that* argument.

patterns that exhibit greater instrumental rationality will tend to be to some degree rewarding, an incentive to continue them. These incentives may affect our beliefs and behaviors even though the drawbacks or advantages of the patterns in question do not receive conscious deliberation. In such cases we may be said to acquire these habits or strategies because they *are* more rational, without the intermediation of any *belief* on our part that they are. Thus, cognitive psychologists have mapped some of the unconscious strategies or heuristics we employ to enable our limited intellects to sift more data and make quicker and more consistent judgments than would be possible using more standard forms of explicit reasoning.[27] We unwittingly come to rely upon heuristics in part because they are selectively reinforced as a result of their instrumental advantages over standard, explicit reasoning, that is, in part because of their greater rationality. Similarly, we may, without realizing it or even being able to admit it to ourselves, develop patterns of behavior that encourage or discourage specific behaviors in others, such as the unconscious means by which we cause those whose company we do not enjoy not to enjoy our company. Finally, as children we may have been virtually incapable of making rational assessments when a distant gain required a proximate loss. Yet somehow over time we managed in largely nondeliberative ways to acquire various interesting habits, such as putting certain vivid thoughts about the immediate future at the periphery of our attention, which enable us as adults to march ourselves off to the dentist without a push from behind. Criterial explanation in terms of individual rationality thus extends to behaviors beyond the realm of deliberate action. And, as with the wants/interests mechanism, it is possible to see in the emergence of such behaviors something we can without distortion call learning.

Indeed, our tendency through experience to develop rational habits and strategies may cooperate with the wants/interests mechanism to provide the basis for an *extended* form of criterial explanation, in which an individual's rationality is assessed not relative to his occurrent beliefs and desires, but relative to his objective interests. The examples considered earlier of the wants/interests mechanism in fact involved elements of this sort of explanation, for they showed not only wants being adjusted to interests, but also behavior being adjusted to newly adjusted wants. Without appropriate alteration of behavior to reflect changing wants, the feedback necessary for learning about wants would not occur. With such alteration, the behavior itself may become more rational in the extended sense. An individual who is instrumentally rational is disposed to adjust means to ends; but one result of his undertaking a means—electing a course of study, or accepting a new job—may be a more informed assessment, and perhaps a reconsideration, of his ends.

The theory of individual rationality—in either its simple or its extended form—thus affords an instance of the sort needed to provide an example of normative realism. Evaluations of degrees of instrumental rationality play a prominent role in our explanations of individual behavior, but they simultaneously have normative force for the agent. Whatever other concerns an agent might have, it surely counts for him as a positive feature of an action that it is efficient relative to his beliefs and desires or, in the extended sense, efficient relative to beliefs and desires that would appropriately reflect his condition and circumstances.

The normative force of these theories of individual rationality does not, however, merely derive from their explanatory use. One can employ a theory of instrumental

[27]For a survey of the literature, see Richard Nisbett and Lee Ross, *Human Inference: Strategies and Shortcomings of Social Judgment* (Englewood Cliffs: Prentice-Hall, 1980), where one unsurprisingly finds greater attention paid to drawbacks than advantages.

rationality to explain behavior while rejecting it as a normative theory of reasons, just as one can explain an action as due to irrationality without thereby endorsing unreason.[28] Instead, the connection between the normative and explanatory roles of the instrumental conception of rationality is traceable to their common ground: the human motivational system. It is a fact about us that we have ends and have the capacity for both deliberate action relative to our ends and nondeliberate adjustment of behavior to our ends. As a result, we face options among pathways across a landscape of possibilities variously valenced for us. Both when we explain the reasons for people's choices and the causes of their behavior and when we appeal to their intuitions about what it would be rational to decide or to do, we work this territory, for we make what use we can of facts about what does-in-fact or can-in-principle motivate agents.

Thus emerges the possibility of saying that facts exist about what individuals have reason to do, facts that may be substantially independent of, and more normatively compelling than, an agent's occurrent conception of his reasons. The argument for such realism about individual rationality is no stronger than the arguments for the double claim that the relevant conception of instrumental individual rationality has both explanatory power and the sort of commendatory force a theory of *reasons* must possess, but (although I will not discuss them further here) these arguments seem to me quite strong.

* * *

Passing now beyond the theory of individual rationality, let us ask what criterial explanations involving distinctively moral norms might look like. To ask this, we need to know what distinguishes moral norms from other criteria of assessment. Moral evaluation seems to be concerned most centrally with the assessment of conduct or character where the interests of more than one individual are at stake. Further, moral evaluation assesses actions or outcomes in a peculiar way: the interests of the strongest or most prestigious party do not always prevail, purely prudential reasons may be subordinated, and so on. More generally, moral resolutions are thought to be determined by criteria of choice that are *non-indexical* and in some sense *comprehensive*. This has led a number of philosophers to seek to capture the special character of moral evaluation by identifying a *moral point of view* that is impartial, but equally concerned with all those potentially affected. Other ethical theorists have come to a similar conclusion by investigating the sorts of reasons we characteristically treat as relevant or irrelevant in moral discourse. Let us follow these leads. We thus may say that moral norms reflect a certain kind of rationality, rationality not from the point of view of any particular individual, but from what might be called a social point of view.[29]

By itself, the equation of moral rightness with rationality from a social point of view is not terribly restrictive, for, depending upon what one takes rationality to be, this equation could be made by a utilitarian, a Kantian, or even a non-cognitivist. That is as it should be, for if it is to capture what is distinctive about moral norms, it should be compatible with the broadest possible range of recognized moral theories. However, once one opts for a particular conception of rationality—such as the conception of rationality as efficient pursuit of the non-morally good, or as autonomous and universal

[28]To recall a point from Section II: one may make assessments relative to particular evaluative criteria without thereby valuing that which satisfies them.

[29]I realize that it is misleading to call a point of view that is "impartial, but equally concerned with all those potentially affected" a *social* point of view—some of those potentially affected may lie on the other side of an intersocial boundary. This complication will be set aside until Section V.

self-legislation, or as a noncognitive expression of hypothetical endorsement—this schematic characterization begins to assume particular moral content. Here I have adopted an instrumentalist conception of rationality, and this—along with the account given of non-moral goodness—means that the argument for moral realism given below is an argument that presupposes and purports to defend a particular substantive moral theory.[30]

What is this theory? Let me introduce an idealization of the notion of social rationality by considering what would be rationally approved of were the interests of all potentially affected individuals counted equally under circumstances of full and vivid information.[31] Because of the assumption of full and vivid information, the interests in question will be objective interests. Given the account of goodness proposed in Section III, this idealization is equivalent to what is rational from a social point of view with regard to the realization of intrinsic non-moral goodness. This seems to me to be a recognizable and intuitively plausible—if hardly uncontroversial—criterion of moral rightness. Relative moral rightness is a matter of relative degree of approximation to this criterion.

The question that now arises is whether the notion of degrees of moral rightness could participate in explanations of behavior or in processes of moral learning that parallel explanatory uses of the notion of degrees of individual rationality—especially, in the extended sense. I will try to suggest several ways in which it might.

Just as an individual who significantly discounts some of his interests will be liable to certain sorts of dissatisfaction, so will a social arrangement—for example, a form of production, a social or political hierarchy, etc.—that departs from social rationality by significantly discounting the interests of a particular group have a potential for dissatisfaction and unrest. Whether or not this potential will be realized depends upon a great many circumstances. Owing to socialization, or to other limitations on the experience or knowledge of members of this group, the wants/interests mechanism may not have operated in such a way that the wants of its members reflect their interests. As a result they may experience no direct frustration of their desires despite the discounting of their interests. Or, the group may be too scattered or too weak to mobilize effectively. Or, it may face overawing repression. On the other hand, certain social and historical circumstances favor the realization of this potential for unrest, for example, by providing members of this group with experiences that make them more likely to develop interest-congruent wants, by weakening the existing repressive apparatus, by giving them new access to resources or new opportunities for mobilization, or merely by dispelling the illusion that change is impossible. In such circumstances, one can expect the potential for unrest to manifest itself.

Just as explanations involving assessments of individual rationality were not always replaceable by explanations involving individual *beliefs about* what would be rational, so, too, explanations involving assessments of social rationality cannot be

[30]It also means that the relation of moral criteria to criteria of individual rationality has become problematic, since there can be no guarantee that what would be instrumentally rational from any given individual's point of view will coincide with what would be instrumentally rational from a social point of view.

[31]A rather strong thesis of interpersonal comparison is needed here for purposes of social aggregation. I am not assuming the existence of some single good, such as happiness, underlying such comparisons. Thus the moral theory in question, although consequentialist, aggregative, and maximizing, is not equivalent to classical utilitarianism. I *am* assuming that when a choice is faced between satisfying interest *X* of *A* vs. satisfying interest *Y* of *B*, answers to the question "All else equal, would it matter more to me if I were *A* to have *X* satisfied than if I were *B* to have *Y* satisfied?" will be relatively determinate and stable across individuals under conditions of full and vivid information. A similar, though somewhat weaker, form of comparability-across-difference is presupposed when we make choices from among alternative courses of action that would lead us to have different desires in the future.

replaced by explanations involving *beliefs about* what would be morally right. For example, discontent may arise because a society departs from social rationality, but not as a result of a belief that this is the case. Suppose that a given society is believed by all constituents to be just. This belief may help to stabilize it, but if in fact the interests of certain groups are being discounted, there will be a potential for unrest that may manifest itself in various ways—in alienation, loss of morale, decline in the effectiveness of authority, and so on—well before any changes in belief about the society's justness occur, and that will help explain why members of certain groups come to believe it to be unjust, if in fact they do.

In addition to possessing a certain sort of potential for unrest, societies that fail to approximate social rationality may share other features as well: they may exhibit a tendency toward certain religious or ideological doctrines, or toward certain sorts of repressive apparatus; they may be less productive in some ways (for example, by failing to develop certain human resources) and more productive in others (for example, by extracting greater labor from some groups at less cost), and thus may be differentially economically successful depending upon the conditions of production they face, and so on.

If a notion of social rationality is to be a legitimate part of empirical explanations of such phenomena, an informative characterization of the circumstances under which departures from, or approximations to, social rationality could be expected to lead to particular social outcomes—especially, of the conditions under which groups whose interests are sacrificed could be expected to exhibit or mobilize discontent—must be available. Although it cannot be known *a priori* whether an account of this kind is possible, one can see emerging in some recent work in social history and historical sociology various elements of a theory of when, and how, a persisting potential for social discontent due to persistently sacrificed interests comes to be manifested.[32]

An individual whose wants do not reflect his interests or who fails to be instrumentally rational may, I argued, experience feedback of a kind that promotes learning about his good and development of more rational strategies. Similarly, the discontent produced by departures from social rationality may produce feedback that, at a social level, promotes the development of norms that better approximate social rationality. The potential for unrest that exists when the interests of a group are discounted is potential for pressure from that group—and its allies—to accord fuller recognition to their interests in social decision-making and in the socially-instilled norms that govern individual decision-making. It therefore is pressure to push the resolution of conflicts further in the direction required by social rationality, since it is pressure to give fuller weight to the interests of more of those affected. Such pressure may of course be more or less forceful or coherent; it may find the most diverse ideological expression; and it may produce outcomes more or less advantageous in the end to those exerting it.[33]

[32] See, for example, Barrington Moore, Jr., *The Social Origins of Dictatorship and Democracy: Lord and Peasant in the Making of the Modern World* (Boston: Beacon, 1966) and *Injustice: The Social Bases of Obedience and Revolt* (White Plains, N.Y.: M. E. Sharpe, 1978); E. P. Thompson, *The Making of the English Working Class* (New York: Pantheon, 1963); William B. Taylor, *Drinking, Homicide, and Rebellion in Colonial Mexican Villages* (Stanford: Stanford University Press, 1979); Charles Tilly, *From Mobilization to Revolution* (Reading, Mass.: Addison-Wesley, 1978); and Charles Tilly, et al., *The Rebellious Century, 1830–1930* (Cambridge: Harvard University Press, 1975).

[33] A common theme in the works cited in note 32 is that much social unrest is re-vindicative rather than revolutionary, since the discontent of long-suffering groups often is galvanized into action only when customary entitlements are threatened or denied. The overt ideologies of such groups thus frequently are particularistic and conservative, even as their unrest contributes to the emergence of new social forms that concede

Striking historical examples of the mobilization of excluded groups to promote greater representation of their interests include the rebellions against the system of feudal estates, and more recent social movements against restrictions on religious practices, on suffrage and other civil rights, and on collective bargaining.[34]

Of course, other mechanisms have been at work influencing the evolution of social practices and norms at the same time, some with the reverse effect.[35] Whether mechanisms working on behalf of the inclusion of excluded interests will predominate depends upon a complex array of social and historical factors. It would be silly to think either that the norms of any actual society will at any given stage of history closely approximate social rationality, or that there will be a univocal trend toward greater social rationality. Like the mechanisms of biological evolution or market economics, the mechanisms described here operate in an "open system" alongside other mechanisms, and do not guarantee optimality or even a monotonic approach to equilibrium. Human societies do not appear to have begun at or near equilibrium in the relevant sense, and so the strongest available claim might be that in the long haul, barring certain exogenous effects, one could expect an uneven secular trend toward the inclusion of the interests of (or interests represented by) social groups that are capable of some degree of mobilization. But under other circumstances, even in the long run, one could expect the opposite. New World plantation slavery, surely one of the most brutally exclusionary social arrangements ever to have existed, emerged late in world history and lasted for hundreds of years. Other brutally exclusionary social arrangements of ancient or recent vintage persist yet.

One need not, therefore, embrace a theory of moral progress in order to see that the feedback mechanism just described can give an explanatory role to the notion of social rationality. Among the most puzzling, yet most common, objections to moral realism is that there has not been uniform historical progress toward worldwide consensus on moral norms. But it has not to my knowledge been advanced as an argument against *scientific* realism that, for example, some contemporary cultures and subcultures do not accept, and do not seem to be moving in the direction of accepting, the scientific world view. Surely realists are in both cases entitled to say that only certain practices in certain circumstances will tend to produce theories more congruent with reality, especially when the subject matter is so complex and so far removed from anything like direct inspection. They need not subscribe to the quaint idea that "the truth will out" come what

---

greater weight to previously discounted interests. In a similar way, individuals often fail to notice irrationalities in their customary behavior until they are led by it into uncustomary difficulties, which then arouse a sense that something has gone wrong. For familiar reasons, a typical initial individual response is to attempt to retrieve the *status quo ante,* although genuine change may result from these restorative efforts.

[34]It should be emphasized that these mechanisms do not presuppose a background of democratic institutions. They have extracted concessions even within societies that remained very hierarchical. See, for example, Taylor, *Drinking, Homicide, and Rebellion.*

[35]Indeed, the mechanism just described may push in several directions at once: toward the inclusion of some previously excluded interests, and toward the exclusion of some previously included interests. To be sure, if interests come to be excluded even though their social and material basis remains more or less intact, a new potential for unrest is created. Some groups present a special problem, owing to their inherent inability to mobilize effectively, for example, children and future generations. To account for the pressures that have been exerted on behalf of these groups it is necessary to see how individuals come to include other individuals within their own interests. (Compare the way in which one's future selves, which can exert no pressure on their own behalf, come to be taken into account by one's present self in virtue of one's identification with them.) Unless one takes account of such processes of incorporation and identification, morality (or even prudence) will appear quite mysterious, but I will have little to say about them here. For some preliminary remarks, see Section IX of my "Alienation, Consequentialism, and the Demands of Morality," *Philosophy and Public Affairs* 13 (1984), pp. 134–171.

may. The extended theory of individual rationality, for example, leads us to expect that in societies where there are large conflicts of interest people will develop large normative disagreements, and that, when (as they usually do) these large conflicts of interest parallel large differences in power, the dominant normative views are unlikely to embody social rationality. What is at issue here, and in criterial explanations generally, is the explanation of certain patterns among others, not necessarily the existence of a single overall trend. We may, however, point to the existence of the feedback mechanisms described here as grounds for belief that we can make qualified use of historical experience as something like experimental evidence about what kinds of practices in what ranges of circumstances might better satisfy a criterion of social rationality. That is, we may assign this mechanism a role in a qualified process of moral learning.

The mechanisms of learning about individual rationality, weak or extended, involved similar qualifications. For although we expect that, under favorable circumstances, individuals may become better at acting in an instrumentally rational fashion as their experience grows, we are also painfully aware that there are powerful mechanisms promoting the opposite result. We certainly do not think that an individual must display exceptionless rationality, or even show ever-increasing rationality over his lifetime, in order to apply reason-giving explanations to many of his actions. Nor do we think that the inevitable persistence of areas of irrationality in individuals is grounds for denying that they can, through experience, acquire areas of greater rationality.

The comparison with individual rationality should not, however, be overdrawn. First, while the inclusion-generating mechanisms for social rationality operate through the behavior of individuals, interpersonal dynamics enter ineliminably in such a way that the criteria selected for are not reducible to those of disaggregated individual rationality. Both social and biological evolution involve selection mechanisms that favor behaviors satisfying criteria of relative optimality that are collective (as in prisoner's dilemma cases) or genotypic (which may also be collective, as in kin selection) as well as individual or phenotypic. Were this not so, it is hardly possible that moral norms could ever have emerged or come to have the hold upon us they do.

Second, there are rather extreme differences of degree between the individual and the social cases. Most strikingly, the mechanisms whereby individual wants and behaviors are brought into some congruence with individual interests and reasons operate in more direct and reliable ways than comparable mechanisms nudging social practices or norms in the direction of what is socially rational. Not only are the information demands less formidable in the individual case—that is the least of it, one might say—but the ways in which feedback is achieved are more likely in the individual case to serve as a prod for change and less likely to be distorted by social asymmetries.

Nonetheless, we do have the skeleton of an explanatory theory that uses the notion of what is more or less rational from a social point of view and that parallels in an obvious way uses of assessments of rationality from the agent's point of view in explanations of individual beliefs and behaviors. Like the individual theory, it suggests prediction- and counterfactual-supporting generalizations of the following kind: over time, and in some circumstances more than others, we should expect pressure to be exerted on behalf of practices that more adequately satisfy a criterion of rationality.

Well, if this is a potentially predictive and explanatory theory, how good is it? That is a very large question, one beyond my competence to answer. But let me note briefly three patterns in the evolution of moral norms that seem to me to bear out the predictions of this theory, subject to the sorts of qualifications that the existence of imperfections and competing mechanisms would lead one to expect. I do so with trepidation, however, for although the patterns I will discuss are gross historical trends, it is not essential to the theory that history show such trends, and it certainly is not part of the theory to endorse a set of practices or norms merely because it is a result of them.

Generality. It is a commonplace of anthropology that tribal peoples often have only one word to name both their tribe and "the people" or "humanity." Those beyond the tribe are not deemed full-fledged people, and the sorts of obligations one has toward people do not apply fully with regard to outsiders. Over the span of history, through processes that have involved numerous reversals, people have accumulated into larger social units—from the familial band to the tribe to the "people" to the nation-state—and the scope of moral categories has enlarged to follow these expanding boundaries. Needless to say, this has not been a matter of the contagious spread of enlightenment. Expanding social entities frequently subjugate those incorporated within their new boundaries, and the means by which those thus oppressed have secured greater recognition of their interests have been highly conflictual, and remain—perhaps, will always remain—incomplete. Nonetheless, contemporary moral theory, and to a surprising degree contemporary moral discourse, have come to reject any limitation short of the species.[36]

Humanization. Moral principles have been assigned various origins and natures: as commandments of supernatural origin, grounded in the will or character of a deity, to be interpreted by a priesthood; as formalistic demands of a caste-based code of honor; as cosmic principles of order; as dictates of reason or conscience that make no appeal to human inclinations or well-being; and so on. While vestiges of these views survive in contemporary moral theory, it is typical of almost the entire range of such theory, and of much of contemporary moral discourse, to make some sort of intrinsic connection between normative principles and effects on human interests. Indeed, the very emergence of morality as a distinctive subject matter apart from religion is an instance of this pattern.

Patterns of variation. In addition to seeing patterns that reflect some pressure toward the approximation of social rationality, we should expect to see greater approximation in those areas of normative regulation where the mechanisms postulated here work best, for example, in areas where almost everyone has importantly similar or mutually satisfiable interests, where almost everyone has some substantial potential to infringe upon the interests of others, where the advantages of certain forms of constraint or cooperation are highly salient even in the dynamics of small groups, and where individuals can significantly influence the likelihood of norm-following behavior on the part of others by themselves following norms. The clearest examples have to do with prohibitions of aggression and theft, and of the violation of promises.[37] By contrast, moral questions that concern matters where there are no solutions compatible with protecting the most basic interests of all, where there exist very large asymmetries in the capacity to infringe upon interests, where the gains or losses from particular forms of cooperation or constraint are difficult to perceive, and where individual compliance will little affect general compliance, are less likely to achieve early or stable approximation to social rationality. Clear examples here have to do with such matters as social hierar-

[36]Here and elsewhere, I mean by "contemporary moral theory" to refer to dominant views in the academies, and by "contemporary moral discourse" to refer to widespread practices of public moral argumentation, in those societies that have achieved the highest levels of development of empirical science generally. Again, the moral realist, like the scientific realist, is not committed to worldwide consensus.

[37]However, such prohibitions historically have shown limitations of scope that are no longer recognized as valid. The trend against such limitations is an instance of the first sort of pattern, toward increased generality.

chy—for example, the permissibility of slavery, of authoritarian government, of caste or gender inequalities—and social responsibility—for example, what is the nature of our individual or collective obligation to promote the well-being of unrelated others?

Given a suitable characterization of the conditions that prevailed during the processes of normative evolution described by these patterns, the present theory claims not only that these changes could have been expected, but that an essential part of the explanation of their occurrence is a mechanism whereby individuals whose interests are denied are led to form common values and make common cause along lines of shared interests, thereby placing pressure on social practices to approximate more closely to social rationality.

These descriptions and explanations of certain prominent features of the evolution of moral norms will no doubt strike some as naive at best, plainly—perhaps even dangerously—false at worst. I thoroughly understand this. I have given impossibly sketchy, one-sided, simple-minded accounts of a very complex reality.[38] I can only hope that these accounts will seem as believable as one could expect sketchy, one-sided, simple-minded accounts to be, and that this will make the story I have tried to tell about mechanisms and explanation more plausible.

Needless to say, the upshot is not a complacent functionalism or an overall endorsement of current moral practice or norms. Instead, the account of morality sketched here emphasizes conflict rather than equilibrium, and provides means for criticizing certain contemporary moral practices and intuitions by asking about their historical genesis. For example, if we come to think that the explanation of a common moral intuition assigns no significant role to mechanisms that could be expected to exert pressure toward socially rational outcomes, then this is grounds for questioning the intuition, however firmly we may hold it. In the spirit of a naturalized moral epistemology, we may ask whether the explanation of why we make certain moral judgments is an example of a reliable process for discovering moral facts.

V. LIMITATIONS

Thus far I have spoken of what is morally best as a matter of what is instrumentally rational from a social point of view. But I have also characterized a genuinely moral point of view as one impartial with respect to the interests of all potentially affected, and that is not a socially-bounded notion. In fact, I have claimed that a trend away from social specificity is among the patterns visible in the evolution of moral norms. Part of the explanation of this pattern—and part, therefore, of the explanatory role of degrees of impartial rationality—is that the mechanisms appealed to above are not socially-bounded, either. Societies, and individuals on opposite sides of social boundaries, constrain one another in various ways, much as groups and individuals constrain one another within societies: they can threaten aggression, mobilize resistance to external control, withhold

[38]Moreover, the accounts are highly general in character, operating at a level of description incapable of discriminating between hypotheses based upon the particular account of moral rightness proposed here and others rather close to it. (Roughly, those characterizing moral rightness in terms of instrumental rationality relative to the non-moral good of those affected, but differing on details regarding instrumental rationality—for example, is it straightforwardly maximizing or partly distributive?—or regarding non-moral goodness—for example, is it reducible to pleasure? For a discussion of not-very-close competitors, see Section VI.) If the method I have employed is to be used to make choices from among close competitors, the empirical analysis must be much more fine-grained. Similar remarks apply to the weak and extended theories of individual rationality appealed to above.

cooperation, and obstruct one another's plans; and they are prone to resort to such constraining activities when their interests are denied or at risk. As with intrasocial morality, so in intersocial morality, the best-established and most nearly impartially rational elements are those where the mechanisms we have discussed work most reliably: prohibitions on aggression are stronger and more widely accepted than principles of equity or redistribution. Of course, many factors make intersocietal dynamics unlike intrasocietal ones. . . . But the reader will for once be spared more armchair social science. Still, what results is a form of moral realism that is essentially tied to a limited point of view, an impartial yet human one. Is this too limited for genuine moral realism?

A teacher of mine once remarked that the question of moral realism seemed to him to be the question whether the universe cares what we do. Since we have long since given up believing that the cosmos pays us any mind, he thought we should long since have given up moral realism. I can only agree that if this were what moral realism involved, it should—with relief rather than sorrow—be let go. However, the account offered here gives us a way of understanding how moral values or imperatives might be objective without being cosmic. They need be grounded in nothing more transcendental than facts about man and his environment, facts about what sorts of things matter to us, and how the ways we live affect these things.

Yet the present account is limited in another way, which may be of greater concern from the standpoint of contemporary moral theory: it does not yield moral imperatives that are categorical in the sense of providing a reason for action to all rational agents regardless of their contingent desires. Although troubling, this limitation is not tantamount to relativism, since on the present account rational motivation is not a precondition of moral obligation. For example, it could truthfully be said that I ought to be more generous even though greater generosity would not help me to promote my existing ends, or even to satisfy my objective interests. This could be so because what it would be morally right for me to do depends upon what is rational from a point of view that includes, but is not exhausted by, my own.

In a similar way, it could be said that I logically ought not to believe both a proposition p and a proposition that implies not-p. However, it may not be the case that every rational agent will have an instrumental reason to purge all logical contradictions from his thought. It would require vast amounts of cogitation for anyone to test all of his existing beliefs for consistency, and to insure that every newly acquired belief preserves it. Suppose someone to be so fortunate that the only contradictions among his beliefs lie deep in the much-sedimented swamp of factual trivia. Perhaps his memories of two past acquaintances have become confused in such a way that somewhere in the muck there are separate beliefs which, taken together, attribute to one individual logically incompatible properties. Until such a contradiction rears its head in practice, he may have no more reason to lay down his present concerns and wade in after it than he has to leave his home in suburban New Jersey to hunt alligators in the Okefenokee on the off chance that he might one day find himself stranded and unarmed in the backwaters of southeast Georgia.[39] What an individual rationally ought to do thus may differ from what logic requires of him. Still, we may say that logical evaluation is not subjective or arbitrary,

[39]It is of no importance whether we say that he has *no* reason to do this or simply a vanishingly small one. I suppose we could say that a person has a vanishingly small reason to do anything—even to expend enormous effort to purge minor contradictions from his beliefs or to purge alligators from distant swamps—that might *conceivably* turn out to be to his benefit. But then we would have no trouble guaranteeing the existence of vanishingly small reasons for moral conduct. This would allow naturalized moral rightness to satisfy a Humean thesis of practicality after all, but in a way that would rob the thesis of its interest.

and that good grounds of a perfectly general kind are available for being logical, namely, that logical contradictions are necessarily false and logical inferences are truth-preserving. Since in public discourse and private reflection we are often concerned with whether our thinking is warranted in a sense that is more intimately connected with its truth-conduciveness than with its instrumentality to our peculiar personal goals, it therefore is far from arbitrary that we attach so much importance to logic as a standard of criticism and self-criticism.

By parallel, if we adopt the account of moral rightness proposed above we may say that moral evaluation is not subjective or arbitrary, and that good, general grounds are available for following moral "ought's," namely, that moral conduct is rational from an impartial point of view. Since in public discourse and private reflection we are often concerned with whether our conduct is justifiable from a general rather than merely personal standpoint, it therefore is far from arbitrary that we attach so much importance to morality as a standard of criticism and self-criticism.

The existence of such phenomena as religion and ideology is evidence for the pervasiveness and seriousness of our concern for impartial justification. Throughout history individuals have sacrificed their interests, even their lives, to meet the demands of religions or ideologies that were compelling for them in part because they purported to express a universal—*the* universal—justificatory standpoint. La Rochefoucauld wrote that hypocrisy is the tribute vice pays to virtue,[40] but "hypocrisy" suggests cynicism. We might better say that ideology is the respect partisans show to impartiality. Morality, then, is not ideology made sincere and general—ideology is intrinsically given to heart-felt generalization. Morality is ideology that has faced the facts.

I suspect the idea that moral evaluations must have categorical force for rational agents owes some of its support to a fear that were this to be denied, the authority of morality would be lost. That would be so if one held onto the claim that moral imperatives cannot exist for someone who would not have a reason to obey them, for then an individual could escape moral duties by the simple expedient of having knavish desires. But if we give up this claim about the applicability of moral judgment, then variations in personal desires cannot license exemption from moral obligation.[41]

Thus, while it certainly is a limitation of the argument made here that it does not yield a conception of moral imperatives as categorical, that may be a limitation we can live with and still accord morality the scope and dignity it traditionally has enjoyed. Moreover, it may be a limitation we must live with. For how many among us can convince ourselves that reason is other than hypothetical? Need it also be asked: How many of us would find our sense of the significance of morality or the importance of moral conduct enhanced by a demonstration that even a person with the most thoroughly repugnant ends would find that moral conduct advanced them?

[40]François (duc de) la Rochefoucauld, *Reflexions, ou sentences et maximes morales suivi de reflexions diverses*, ed., Jean Lafond (Paris: Gallimard, 1976), p. 79. La Rochefoucauld apparently borrowed the phrase from the cleric Du Moulin. I am grateful to a remark of Barrington Moore, Jr. for reminding me of it. See his *Injustice*, p. 508.

[41]Contrast Harman's relativism about "ought" in *The Nature of Morality*. Harman adopts the first of the two courses just mentioned, preserving the connection between an individual's moral obligations and what he has (instrumental) reason to do. He defends his approach in part by arguing that, if we suppose that Hitler was engaged in rational pursuit of his ends, an "internal" judgment like "Hitler (morally) ought not to have killed six million Jews" would be "weak" and "odd" compared to an "external" judgment like "Hitler was evil" (see pp. 107 ff). I would have thought the opposite, namely, that it is too "weak" and "odd" to give an account of morality such that Hitler can be judged to be consummately evil (which Harman claims, without explanation, his brand of relativism *can* do) but in which "Hitler (morally) ought not to have acted as he did" is false.

One implication of what has been said is that if we want morality to be taken seriously and to have an important place in people's lives—and not merely as the result of illusion or the threat of repression—we should be vitally concerned with the ways in which social arrangements produce conflicts of interest and asymmetries of power that affect the nature and size of the gap between what is individually and socially rational. Rather than attempt to portray morality as something that it cannot be, as "rationally compelling no matter what one's ends," we should ask how we might change the ways we live so that moral conduct would more regularly be rational given the ends we actually will have.

VI. SUMMARY AND CONCLUSION

I have outlined a form of moral realism, and given some indication of how it might be defended against certain objections. Neither a full characterization of this view, nor full answers to the many objections it faces, can be given within the present essay. Perhaps then I should stop trying to say just a bit more, and close by indicating roughly what I have, and have not, attempted to show.

I have proposed what are in effect reforming naturalistic definitions of non-moral goodness and moral rightness. It is possible to respond: "Yes, I can see that such-and-such an end is an objective interest of the agent in your sense, or that such-and-such a practice is rational from an impartial point of view, but can't I still ask whether the end is good for him or the practice right?" Such "open questions" cannot by their nature be closed, since definitions are not subject to proof or disproof. But open questions may be more or less disturbing, for although definitional proposals cannot be demonstrated, they can fare better or worse at meeting various desiderata.

I have assumed throughout that the drawing up of definitions is part of theory-construction, and so is to be assessed by asking (1) whether the analyses given satisfy appropriate constraints of intelligibility and function, and (2) whether the terms as analyzed contribute to the formulation and testing of worthwhile theories. How do my proposals fit with these criteria?

(1) Beyond constraints of intelligibility, such as clarity and non-circularity, specifically naturalistic definitions of evaluative terms should satisfy two further analytic constraints arising from their intended function. (a) They should insofar as possible capture the normative force of these terms by providing analyses that permit these terms to play their central evaluative roles. In the present setting, this involves showing that although the definitions proposed may not fit with all of our linguistic or moral intuitions, they nonetheless express recognizable notions of goodness and rightness. Further, it involves showing that the definitions permit plausible connections to be drawn between, on the one hand, what is good or right and, on the other, what characteristically would motivate individuals who are prepared to submit themselves to relevant sorts of scrutiny. (b) The naturalistic definitions should permit the evaluative concepts to participate in their own right in genuinely empirical theories. Part of this consists in showing that we have appropriate epistemic access to these concepts. Part, too, (and a related part) consists in showing that generalizations employing these concepts, among others, can figure in potentially explanatory accounts. I have tried to offer reasonably clear definitions and to show in a preliminary way how they might meet constraints (a) and (b).

(2) However, a good deal more must be done, for it remains to show that the empirical theories constructed with the help of these definitions are reasonably good theo-

ries, that is, theories for which we have substantial evidence and which provide plausible explanations. I have tried in the most preliminary way imaginable to suggest this. If I have been wholly unpersuasive on empirical matters, then I can expect that the definitions I have offered will be equally unpersuasive.

It is an attraction for me of naturalism in ethics and epistemology alike that it thus is constrained in several significant dimensions at once. One has such ample opportunities to be shown wrong or found unconvincing if one's account must be responsive to empirical demands as well as normative intuitions. Theorizing in general is more productive when suitably constrained; in ethics especially, constraints are needed if we are to have a clearer idea of how we might make progress toward the resolution of theoretical disputes. Of course, not just any constraints will do. A proposed set of constraints must present itself as both appropriate and useful. Let me say something about (1) the utility of the constraints adopted here, and then a final word about (2) their appropriateness.

(1) Consider three classes of competitors to the substantive moral theory endorsed above, and notice how criticisms of them *naturally* intertwine concerns about normative justification and empirical explanation. *Kantian* conceptions of morality are widely viewed as having captured certain intuitively compelling normative characteristics of such notions as rationality and moral rightness, but it seems they have done so partly at the expense of affording a plausible way of integrating these notions into an empirical account of our reasons and motives in action. Moreover, this descriptive difficulty finds direct expression on the normative side. Not only must any normative "ought" be within the scope of an empirical "can," but a normatively compelling "ought" must—as recent criticisms of Kantianism have stressed—reach to the real springs of human action and concern. *Intuitionist* moral theories also enjoyed some success in capturing normative features of morality, but they have largely been abandoned for want of a credible account of the nature or operation of a faculty of moral intuition. It is too easy for us to give a non-justifying psychological explanation of the existence in certain English gentlemen of something which they identified upon introspection as a faculty of moral insight, an explanation that ties this purported faculty more closely to the rigidity of prevailing social conventions than to anything that looks as if it could be a source of universal truth. *Social choice theories* that take occurrent subjective interests or revealed preferences as given fit more readily than Kantian or intuitionist theories with empirical accounts of behavior, and, unlike them, have found a place in contemporary social science. But they suffer well-known limitations as normative theories, some of which turn out to be bound up with their limitations as explanatory theories: they lack an account of the origin or evolution of preferences, and partly for that reason are unable to capture the ways in which we evaluate purportedly rational or moral conduct by criticizing ends as well as means.

(2) However, the issues at stake when we evaluate competing approaches to morality involve not only this sort of assessment of largish theories, but also questions about which criteria of assessment appropriately apply to definitions and theories in ethics, and about whether definitional systematization and largish theorizing are even appropriate for ethics. I am drawn to the view that the development of theory in ethics is not an artificial contrivance of philosophers but an organic result of the personal and social uses of moral evaluation: time and again individuals and groups have faced difficult questions to which common sense gave conflicting or otherwise unsatisfactory answers, and so they have pressed their questions further and pursued

their inquiry more systematically. The felt need for theory in ethics thus parallels the felt need for theory in natural or social science.[42] It does not follow from this alone that ethical theorizing must run parallel to or be integrable with theorizing in the natural and social sciences. Ethics might be deeply different. Although initially plausible and ultimately irrefutable, the view that ethics stands thus apart is one that in the end I reject. We are natural and social creatures, and I know of nowhere else to look for ethics than in this rich conjunction of facts. I have tried to suggest that we might indeed find it there.[43]

[42]This felt need is also reflected in the codification of laws, and in the development of legal theories. However contrived the law may at times seem, surely the general social conditions and needs that have driven its development are real enough. Indeed, the elaborate artifice of law and its language is in part an indication of how pressing the need to go beyond pretheoretic common sense has been.

[43]I am indebted to a great many people, including Peter Achinstein, Robert Audi, Annette Baier, Michael Bratman, Stephen Darwall, Allan Gibbard, Thomas Nagel, Samuel Scheffler, Rebecca Scott, Nicholas Sturgeon, Nicholas White, and the editors at *The Philosophical Review,* who have kindly provided comments on previous drafts or presentations of this paper.

1991

Why Contractarianism?

David Gauthier

I

> As the will to truth thus gains self-consciousness—there can be no doubt of that—morality will gradually *perish* now: this is the great spectacle in a hundred acts reserved for the next two centuries in Europe—the most terrible, most questionable, and perhaps also the most hopeful of all spectacles.
>
> —NIETZSCHE[1]

Two paragraphs of Section II and most of Section IV are taken from "Morality, Rational Choice, and Semantic Representation—A Reply to My Critics," in E. F. Paul, F. D. Miller, Jr., and J. Paul (eds.), *The New Social Contract: Essays on Gauthier* (Oxford: Blackwell, 1988), pp. 173–4, 179–180, 184–5, 188–9 (this volume appears also as *Social Philosophy and Policy* 5 [1988], same pagination). I am grateful to Annette Baier, Paul Hurley, and Geoffrey Sayre-McCord for comments on an earlier draft. I am also grateful to discussants at Western Washington University, the University of Arkansas, the University of California at Santa Cruz, and the University of East Anglia for comments on a related talk.

[1]*On the Genealogy of Morals,* trans. by Walter Kaufmann and R. J. Hollingdale (New York: Random House, 1967), third essay, sec. 27, p. 161.

Morality faces a foundational crisis. Contractarianism offers the only plausible resolution of this crisis. These two propositions state my theme. What follows is elaboration.

Nietzsche may have been the first, but he has not been alone, in recognizing the crisis to which I refer. Consider these recent statements. "The hypothesis which I wish to advance is that in the actual world which we inhabit the language of morality is in . . . [a] state of grave disorder . . . we have—very largely, if not entirely—lost our comprehension, both theoretical and practical, of morality" (Alasdair MacIntyre).[2] "The resources of most modern moral philosophy are not well adjusted to the modern world" (Bernard Williams).[3] "There are no objective values. . . . [But] the main tradition of European moral philosophy includes the contrary claim" (J. L. Mackie).[4] "Moral hypotheses do not help explain why people observe what they observe. So ethics is problematic and nihilism must be taken seriously. . . . An extreme version of nihilism holds that morality is simply an illusion. . . . In this version, we should abandon morality, just as an atheist abandons religion after he has decided that religious facts cannot help explain observations" (Gilbert Harman).[5]

I choose these statements to point to features of the crisis that morality faces. They suggest that moral language fits a world view that we have abandoned—a view of the world as purposively ordered. Without this view, we no longer truly understand the moral claims we continue to make. They suggest that there is a lack of fit between what morality presupposes—objective values that help explain our behavior, and the psychological states—desires and beliefs—that, given our present world view, actually provide the best explanation. This lack of fit threatens to undermine the very idea of a morality as more than an anthropological curiosity. But how could this be? How could morality *perish?*

II

To proceed, I must offer a minimal characterization of the morality that faces a foundational crisis. And this is the morality of justified constraint. From the standpoint of the agent, moral considerations present themselves as constraining his choices and actions, in ways independent of his desires, aims, and interests. Later, I shall add to this characterization, but for the moment it will suffice. For it reveals clearly what is in question—the ground of constraint. This ground seems absent from our present world view. And so we ask, what reason can a person have for recognizing and accepting a constraint that is independent of his desires and interests? He may agree that such a constraint would be *morally* justified; he would have a reason for accepting it *if* he had a reason for accepting morality. But what justifies paying attention to morality, rather than dismissing it as an appendage of outworn beliefs? We ask, and seem to find no answer. But before proceeding, we should consider three objections.

The first is to query the idea of constraint. Why should morality be seen as constraining our choices and actions? Why should we not rather say that the moral person chooses most freely, because she chooses in the light of a true conception of herself, rather than in the light of the false conceptions that so often predominate? Why should we not link morality with self-understanding? Plato and Hume might be enlisted to support this view, but Hume would be at best a partial ally, for his representation of "virtue

[2]*After Virtue* (Notre Dame, IN: University of Notre Dame Press, 1981), p. 2.

[3]*Ethics and the Limits of Philosophy* (Cambridge, MA: Harvard University Press, 1985), p. 197.

[4]*Ethics: Inventing Right and Wrong* (Harmondsworth: Penguin, 1977), pp. 15, 30.

[5]*The Nature of Morality* (New York: Oxford University Press, 1977), p. 11.

in all her genuine and most engaging charms, . . . talk[ing] not of useless austerities and rigors, suffering and self-denial," but rather making "her votaries . . . , during every instant of their existence, if possible, cheerful and happy," is rather overcast by his admission that "in the case of justice, . . . a man, taking things in a certain light, may often seem to be a loser by his integrity."[6] Plato, to be sure, goes further, insisting that only the just man has a healthy soul, but heroic as Socrates' defense of justice may be, we are all too apt to judge that Glaucon and Adeimantus have been charmed rather than reasoned into agreement, and that the unjust man has not been shown necessarily to be the loser.[7] I do not, in any event, intend to pursue this direction of thought. Morality, as we, heirs to the Christian and Kantian traditions, conceive it, constrains the pursuits to which even our reflective desires would lead us. And this is not simply or entirely a constraint on self-interest; the affections that morality curbs include the social ones of favoritism and partiality, to say nothing of cruelty.

The second objection to the view that moral constraint is insufficiently grounded is to query the claim that it operates independently of, rather than through, our desires, interests, and affections. Morality, some may say, concerns the well-being of all persons, or perhaps of all sentient creatures.[8] And one may then argue, either with Hume, that morality arises in and from our sympathetic identification with our fellows, or that it lies directly in well-being, and that our affections tend to be disposed favorably toward it. But, of course, not all of our affections. And so our sympathetic feelings come into characteristic opposition to other feelings, in relation to which they function as a constraint.

This is a very crude characterization, but it will suffice for the present argument. This view grants that morality, as we understand it, is without purely *rational* foundations, but reminds us that we are not therefore unconcerned about the well-being of our fellows. Morality is founded on the widespread, sympathetic, other-directed concerns that most of us have, and these concerns do curb self-interest, and also the favoritism and partiality with which we often treat others. Nevertheless, if morality depends for its practical relevance and motivational efficacity entirely on our sympathetic feelings, it has no title to the prescriptive grip with which it has been invested in the Christian and Kantian views to which I have referred, and which indeed Glaucon and Adeimantus demanded that Socrates defend to them in the case of justice. For to be reminded that some of the time we do care about our fellows and are willing to curb other desires in order to exhibit that care tells us nothing that can guide us in those cases in which, on the face of it, we do not care, or do not care enough—nothing that will defend the demands that morality makes on us in the hard cases. That not all situations in which concern for others combats self-concern are hard cases is true, but morality, as we ordinarily understand it, speaks to the hard cases, whereas its Humean or naturalistic replacement does not.

These remarks apply to the most sustained recent positive attempt to create a moral theory—that of John Rawls. For the attempt to describe our moral capacity, or more particularly, for Rawls, our sense of justice, in terms of principles, plausible in the light of our more general psychological theory, and coherent with "our considered judgments in reflective equilibrium,"[9] will not yield any answer to why, in those cases in

[6]David Hume, *An Equiry Concerning the Principles of Morals,* 1751, sec. IX, pt. II.

[7]See Plato, *Republic,* esp. books II and IV.

[8]Some would extend morality to the nonsentient, but sympathetic as I am to the rights of trolley cars and steam locomotives, I propose to leave this view quite out of consideration.

[9]John Rawls, *A Theory of Justice* (Cambridge, MA: Harvard University Press, 1971), p. 51.

which we have no, or insufficient, interest in being just, we should nevertheless follow the principles. John Harsanyi, whose moral theory is in some respects a utilitarian variant of Rawls' contractarian construction, recognizes this explicitly: "All we can prove by rational arguments is that anybody who wants to serve our common human interests in a rational manner must obey these commands."[10] But although morality may offer itself in the service of our common human interests, it does not offer itself only to those who want to serve them.

Morality is a constraint that, as Kant recognized, must not be supposed to depend solely on our feelings. And so we may not appeal to feelings to answer the question of its foundation. But the third objection is to dismiss this question directly, rejecting the very idea of a foundational crisis. Nothing justifies morality, for morality needs no justification. We find ourselves, in morality as elsewhere, in mediis rebus. We make, accept and reject, justify and criticize moral judgments. The concern of moral theory is to systematize that practice, and so to give us a deeper understanding of what moral justification is. But there are no extramoral foundations for moral justification, any more than there are extraepistemic foundations for epistemic judgments. In morals as in science, foundationalism is a bankrupt project.

Fortunately, I do not have to defend *normative* foundationalism. One problem with accepting moral justification as part of our ongoing practice is that, as I have suggested, we no longer accept the world view on which it depends. But perhaps a more immediately pressing problem is that we have, ready to hand, an alternative mode for justifying our choices and actions. In its more austere and, in my view, more defensible form, this is to show that choices and actions maximize the agent's expected utility, where utility is a measure of considered preference. In its less austere version, this is to show that choices and actions satisfy, not a subjectively defined requirement such as utility, but meet the agent's objective interests. Since I do not believe that we have objective interests, I shall ignore this latter. But it will not matter. For the idea is clear; we have a mode of justification that does not require the introduction of moral considerations.[11]

Let me call this alternative nonmoral mode of justification, neutrally, deliberative justification. Now moral and deliberative justification are directed at the same objects—our choices and actions. What if they conflict? And what do we say to the person who offers a deliberative justification of his choices and actions and refuses to offer any other? We can say, of course, that his behavior lacks *moral* justification, but this seems to lack any hold, unless he chooses to enter the moral framework. And such entry, he may insist, lacks any deliberative justification, at least for him.

If morality perishes, the justificatory enterprise, in relation to choice and action, does not perish with it. Rather, one mode of justification perishes, a mode that, it may seem, now hangs unsupported. But not only unsupported, for it is difficult to deny that deliberative justification is more clearly basic, that it cannot be avoided insofar as we are rational agents, so that if moral justification conflicts with it, morality seems not only unsupported but opposed by what is rationally more fundamental.

Deliberative justification relates to our deep sense of self. What distinguishes human beings from other animals, and provides the basis for rationality, is the capacity for semantic representation. You can, as your dog on the whole cannot, represent a state of affairs to yourself, and consider in particular whether or not it is the case, and

[10]John C. Harsanyi, "Morality and the Theory of Rational Behavior," in *Utilitarianism and Beyond*, edited by Amartya Sen and Bernard Williams (Cambridge: Cambridge University Press, 1982), p. 62.

[11]To be sure, if we think of morality as expressed in certain of our affections and/or interests, it will incorporate moral considerations to the extent that they actually are present in our preferences. But this would be to embrace the naturalism that I have put to one side as inadequate.

whether or not you would want it to be the case. You can represent to yourself the contents of your beliefs, and your desires or preferences. But in representing them, you bring them into relation with one another. You represent to yourself that the Blue Jays will win the World Series, and that a National League team will win the World Series, and that the Blue Jays are not a National League team. And in recognizing a conflict among those beliefs, you find rationality thrust upon you. Note that the first two beliefs could be replaced by preferences, with the same effect.

Since in representing our preferences we become aware of conflict among them, the step from representation to choice becomes complicated. We must, somehow, bring our conflicting desires and preferences into some sort of coherence. And there is only one plausible candidate for a principle of coherence—a maximizing principle. We order our preferences, in relation to decision and action, so that we may choose in a way that maximizes our expectation of preference fulfillment. And in so doing, we show ourselves to be rational agents, engaged in deliberation and deliberative justification. There is simply nothing else for practical rationality to be.

The foundational crisis of morality thus cannot be avoided by pointing to the existence of a practice of justification within the moral framework, and denying that any extramoral foundation is relevant. For an extramoral mode of justification is already present, existing not side by side with moral justification, but in a manner tied to the way in which we unify our beliefs and preferences and so acquire our deep sense of self. We need not suppose that this deliberative justification is itself to be understood foundationally. All that we need suppose is that moral justification does not plausibly survive conflict with it.

III

In explaining why we may not dismiss the idea of a foundational crisis in morality as resulting from a misplaced appeal to a philosophically discredited or suspect idea of foundationalism, I have begun to expose the character and dimensions of the crisis. I have claimed that morality faces an alternative, conflicting, deeper mode of justification, related to our deep sense of self, that applies to the entire realm of choice and action, and that evaluates each *action* in terms of the reflectively held concerns of its *agent*. The relevance of the agent's concerns to practical justification does not seem to me in doubt. The relevance of anything else, except insofar as it bears on the agent's concerns, does seem to me very much in doubt. If the agent's reflectively endorsed concerns, his preferences, desires, and aims, are, with his considered beliefs, constitutive of his self-conception, then I can see no remotely plausible way of arguing from their relevance to that of anything else that is not similarly related to his sense of self. And, indeed, I can see no way of introducing anything as relevant to practical justification except through the agent's self-conception. My assertion of this practical individualism is not a conclusive argument, but the burden of proof is surely on those who would maintain a contrary position. Let them provide the arguments—if they can.

Deliberative justification does not refute morality. Indeed, it does not offer morality the courtesy of a refutation. It ignores morality, and seemingly replaces it. It preempts the arena of justification, apparently leaving morality no room to gain purchase. Let me offer a controversial comparison. Religion faces—indeed, has faced—a comparable foundational crisis. Religion demands the worship of a divine being who purposively orders the universe. But it has confronted an alternative mode of explanation. Although the emergence of a cosmological theory based on efficient, rather than teleological, causation provided warning of what was to come, the supplanting of teleology in biology by the success of evolutionary theory in providing a mode of explanation that accounted in efficient-causal terms for the *appearance* of a purposive order among living beings, may seem to toll the death knell for religion as an intellectually respectable enterprise. But evolutionary biology and, more generally, modern science do not refute religion. Rather they ignore it, replacing its explanations by ontologically simpler ones. Religion, understood as affirming the justifiable worship of a divine being, may be unable to survive its foundational crisis. Can morality, understood as affirming justifiable constraints on choice independent of the agent's concerns, survive?

There would seem to be three ways for morality to escape religion's apparent fate. One would be to find, for moral facts or moral properties, an explanatory role that would entrench them prior to any consideration of justification.[12] One could then argue that any mode of justification that ignored moral considerations would be ontologically defective. I mention this possibility only to put it to one side. No doubt there are persons who accept moral constraints on their choices and actions, and it would not be possible to explain those choices and actions were we to ignore this. But our explanation of their behavior need not commit us to their view. Here the comparison with religion should be straightforward and uncontroversial. We could not explain many of the practices of the religious without reference to their beliefs. But to characterize what a religious person is doing as, say, an act of worship, does not commit us to supposing that an object of worship actually exists, though it does commit us to supposing that she believes such an object to exist. Similarly, to characterize what a moral agent is doing as, say, fulfilling a duty does not commit us to supposing that there are any duties, though it does commit us to supposing that he believes that there are duties. The skeptic who accepts neither can treat the apparent role of morality in explanation as similar to that of religion. Of course, I do not consider that the parallel can be ultimately sustained, since I agree with the religious skeptic but not with the moral skeptic. But to establish an explanatory role for morality, one must first demonstrate its justificatory credentials. One may not assume that it has a prior explanatory role.

The second way would be to reinterpret the idea of justification, showing that, more fully understood, deliberative justification is incomplete, and must be supplemented in a way that makes room for morality. There is a long tradition in moral philosophy, deriving primarily from Kant, that is committed to this enterprise. This is not the occasion to embark on a critique of what, in the hope again of achieving a neutral characterization, I shall call universalistic justification. But critique may be out of place. The success of deliberative justification may suffice. For theoretical claims about its incompleteness seem to fail before the simple practical recognition that it works. Of course, on the face of it, deliberative justification does not work to provide a place for morality. But to suppose that it must, if it is to be fully adequate or complete as a mode of justification, would be to assume what is in question, whether moral justification is defensible.

If, independent of one's actual desires, and aims, there were objective values, and if, independent of one's actual purposes, one were part of an objectively purposive order, then we might have reason to insist on the inadequacy of the deliberative framework. An objectively purposive order would introduce considerations relevant to practical justification that did not depend on the agent's self-conception. But the supplanting of teleology in our physical and biological explanations closes this possibility, as it closes the possibility of religious explanation.

[12]This would meet the challenge to morality found in my previous quotation from Gilbert Harman.

I turn then to the third way of resolving morality's foundational crisis. The first step is to embrace deliberative justification, and recognize that morality's place must be found within, and not outside, its framework. Now this will immediately raise two problems. First of all, it will seem that the attempt to establish any constraint on choice and action, within the framework of a deliberation that aims at the maximal fulfillment of the agent's considered preferences, must prove impossible. But even if this be doubted, it will seem that the attempt to establish a constraint *independent of the agent's preferences,* within such a framework, verges on lunacy. Nevertheless, this is precisely the task accepted by my third way. And, unlike its predecessors, I believe that it can be successful; indeed, I believe that my recent book, *Morals by Agreement,* shows how it can succeed.[13]

I shall not rehearse at length an argument that is now familiar to at least some readers, and, in any event, can be found in that book. But let me sketch briefly those features of deliberative rationality that enable it to constrain maximizing choice. The key idea is that in many situations, if each person chooses what, given the choices of the others, would maximize her expected utility, then the outcome will be mutually disadvantageous in comparison with some alternative—everyone could do better.[14] Equilibrium, which obtains when each person's action is a best response to the others' actions, is incompatible with (Pareto-)optimality, which obtains when no one could do better without someone else doing worse. Given the ubiquity of such situations, each person can see the benefit, to herself, of participating with her fellows in practices requiring each to refrain from the direct endeavor to maximize her own utility, when such mutual restraint is mutually advantageous. No one, of course, can have reason to accept any unilateral constraint on her maximizing behavior; each benefits from, and only from, the constraint accepted by her fellows. But if one benefits more from a constraint on others than one loses by being constrained oneself, one may have reason to accept a practice requiring everyone, including oneself, to exhibit such a constraint. We may represent such a practice as capable of gaining unanimous agreement among rational persons who were choosing the terms on which they would interact with each other. And this agreement is the basis of morality.

Consider a simple example of a moral practice that would command rational agreement. Suppose each of us were to assist her fellows only when either she could expect to benefit herself from giving assistance, or she took a direct interest in their well-being. Then, in many situations, persons would not give assistance to others, even though the benefit to the recipient would greatly exceed the cost to the giver, because there would be no provision for the giver to share in the benefit. Everyone would then expect to do better were each to give assistance to her fellows, regardless of her own benefit or interest, whenever the cost of assisting was low and the benefit of receiving assistance considerable. Each would thereby accept a constraint on the direct pursuit of her own concerns, not unilaterally, but given a like acceptance by others. Reflection leads us to recognize that those who belong to groups whose members adhere to such a practice of mutual assistance enjoy benefits in interaction that are denied to others. We may then represent such a practice as rationally acceptable to everyone.

[13]See David Gauthier, *Morals by Agreement* (Oxford: Oxford University Press, 1986), especially chaps. V and VI.

[14]The now-classic example of this type of situation is the Prisoner's Dilemma; see *Morals by Agreement,* pp. 79–80. More generally, such situations may be said, in economists' parlance, to exhibit market failure. See, for example, "Market Contractarianism" in Jules Coleman, *Markets, Morals, and the Law* (Cambridge: Cambridge University Press, 1988), chap. 10.

This rationale for agreed constraint makes no reference to the content of anyone's preferences. The argument depends simply on the *structure* of interaction, on the way in which each person's endeavor to fulfill her own preferences affects the fulfillment of everyone else. Thus, each person's reason to accept a mutually constraining practice is independent of her particular desires, aims and interests, although not, of course, of the fact that she has such concerns. The idea of a purely rational agent, moved to act by reason alone, is not, I think, an intelligible one. Morality is not to be understood as a constraint arising from reason alone on the fulfillment of nonrational preferences. Rather, a rational agent is one who acts to achieve the maximal fulfillment of her preferences, and morality is a constraint on the manner in which she acts, arising from the effects of interaction with other agents.

Hobbes's Foole now makes his familiar entry onto the scene, to insist that however rational it may be for a person to agree with her fellows to practices that hold out the promise of mutual advantage, yet it is rational to follow such practices only when so doing directly conduces to her maximal preference fulfillment.[15] But then such practices impose no real constraint. The effect of agreeing to or accepting them can only be to change the expected payoffs of her possible choices, making it rational for her to choose what in the absence of the practice would not be utility maximizing. The practices would offer only true prudence, not true morality.

The Foole is guilty of a twofold error. First, he fails to understand that real acceptance of such moral practices as assisting one's fellows, or keeping one's promises, or telling the truth is possible only among those who are disposed to comply with them. If my disposition to comply extends only so far as my interests or concerns at the time of performance, then you will be the real fool if you interact with me in ways that demand a more rigorous compliance. If, for example, it is rational to keep promises only when so doing is directly utility maximizing, then among persons whose rationality is common knowledge, only promises that require such limited compliance will be made. And opportunities for mutual advantage will be thereby forgone.

Consider this example of the way in which promises facilitate mutual benefit. Jones and Smith have adjacent farms. Although neighbors, and not hostile, they are also not friends, so that neither gets satisfaction from assisting the other. Nevertheless, they recognize that, if they harvest their crops together, each does better than if each harvests alone. Next week, Jones's crop will be ready for harvesting; a fortnight hence, Smith's crop will be ready. The harvest in, Jones is retiring, selling his farm, and moving to Florida, where he is unlikely to encounter Smith or other members of their community. Jones would like to promise Smith that, if Smith helps him harvest next week, he will help Smith harvest in a fortnight. But Jones and Smith both know that in a fortnight, helping Smith would be a pure cost to Jones. Even if Smith helps him, he has nothing to gain by returning the assistance, since neither care for Smith nor, in the circumstances, concern for his own reputation, moves him. Hence, if Jones and Smith know that Jones acts straightforwardly to maximize the fulfillment of his preferences, they know that he will not help Smith. Smith, therefore, will not help Jones even if Jones pretends to promise assistance in return. Nevertheless, Jones would do better could he make and keep such a promise—and so would Smith.

The Foole's second error, following on his first, should be clear; he fails to recognize that in plausible circumstances, persons who are genuinely disposed to a more rigorous compliance with moral practices than would follow from their interests at the time

[15]See Hobbes, *Leviathan*, London, 1651, chap. 15.

of performance can expect to do better than those who are not so disposed. For the former, constrained maximizers as I call them, will be welcome partners in mutually advantageous cooperation, in which each relies on the voluntary adherence of the others, from which the latter, straightforward maximizers, will be excluded. Constrained maximizers may thus expect more favorable opportunities than their fellows. Although in assisting their fellows, keeping their promises, and complying with other moral practices, they forgo preference fulfillment that they might obtain, yet they do better overall than those who always maximize expected utility, because of their superior opportunities.

In identifying morality with those constraints that would obtain agreement among rational persons who were choosing their terms of interaction, I am engaged in rational reconstruction. I do not suppose that we have actually agreed to existent moral practices and principles. Nor do I suppose that all existent moral practices would secure our agreement, were the question to be raised. Not all existent moral practices need be justifiable—need be ones with which we ought willingly to comply. Indeed, I do not even suppose that the practices with which we ought willingly to comply need be those that would secure our present agreement. I suppose that justifiable moral practices are those that would secure our agreement ex ante, in an appropriate premoral situation. They are those to which we should have agreed as constituting the terms of our future interaction, had we been, per impossible, in a position to decide those terms. Hypothetical agreement thus provides a test of the justifiability of our existent moral practices.

IV

Many questions could be raised about this account, but here I want to consider only one. I have claimed that moral practices are rational, even though they constrain each person's attempt to maximize her own utility, insofar as they would be the objects of unanimous ex ante agreement. But to refute the Foole, I must defend not only the rationality of agreement, but also that of compliance, and the defense of compliance threatens to preempt the case for agreement, so that my title should be "Why Constraint?" and not "Why Contractarianism?" It is rational to dispose oneself to accept certain constraints on direct maximization in choosing and acting, if and only if so disposing oneself maximizes one's expected utility. What then is the relevance of agreement, and especially of hypothetical agreement? Why should it be rational to dispose oneself to accept only those constraints that would be the object of mutual agreement in an appropriate premoral situation, rather than those constraints that are found in our existent moral practices? Surely it is acceptance of the latter that makes a person welcome in interaction with his fellows. For compliance with existing morality will be what they expect, and take into account in choosing partners with whom to cooperate.

I began with a challenge to morality—how can it be rational for us to accept its constraints? It may now seem that what I have shown is that it is indeed rational for us to accept constraints, but to accept them whether or not they might be plausibly considered moral. Morality, it may seem, has nothing to do with my argument; what I have shown is that it is rational to be disposed to comply with whatever constraints are generally accepted and expected, regardless of their nature. But this is not my view.

To show the relevance of agreement to the justification of constraints, let us assume an ongoing society in which individuals more or less acknowledge and comply with a given set of practices that constrain their choices in relation to what they would be did they take only their desires, aims, and interests directly into account. Suppose that a disposition to conform to these existing practices is prima facie advantageous, since persons who are not so disposed may expect to be excluded from desirable opportunities by their fellows. However, the practices themselves have, or at least need have, no basis in agreement. And they need satisfy no intuitive standard of fairness or impartiality, characteristics that we may suppose relevant to the identification of the practices with those of a genuine morality. Although we may speak of the practices as constituting the morality of the society in question, we need not consider them morally justified or acceptable. They are simply practices constraining individual behavior in a way that each finds rational to accept.

Suppose now that our persons, as rational maximizers of individual utility, come to reflect on the practices constituting their morality. They will, of course, assess the practices in relation to their own utility, but with the awareness that their fellows will be doing the same. And one question that must arise is: Why these practices? For they will recognize that the set of actual moral practices is not the only possible set of constraining practices that would yield mutually advantageous, optimal outcomes. They will recognize the possibility of alternative moral orders. At this point it will not be enough to say that, as a matter of fact, each person can expect to benefit from a disposition to comply with existing practices. For persons will also ask themselves: Can I benefit more, not from simply abandoning any morality, and recognizing no constraint, but from a partial rejection of existing constraints in favor of an alternative set? Once this question is asked, the situation is transformed; the existing moral order must be assessed, not only against simple noncompliance, but also against what we may call alternative compliance.

To make this assessment, each will compare her prospects under the existing practices with those she would anticipate from a set that, in the existing circumstances, she would expect to result from bargaining with her fellows. If her prospects would be improved by such negotiation, then she will have a real, although not necessarily sufficient, incentive to demand a change in the established moral order. More generally, if there are persons whose prospects would be improved by renegotiation, then the existing order will be recognizably unstable. No doubt those whose prospects would be worsened by renegotiation will have a clear incentive to resist, to appeal to the status quo. But their appeal will be a weak one, especially among persons who are not taken in by spurious ideological considerations, but focus on individual utility maximization. Thus, although in the real world, we begin with an existing set of moral practices as constraints on our maximizing behavior, yet we are led by reflection to the idea of an amended set that would obtain the agreement of everyone, and this amended set has, and will be recognized to have, a stability lacking in existing morality.

The reflective capacity of rational agents leads them from the given to the agreed, from existing practices and principles requiring constraint to those that would receive each person's assent. The same reflective capacity, I claim, leads from those practices that would be agreed to, in existing social circumstances, to those that would receive ex ante agreement, premoral and presocial. As the status quo proves unstable when it comes into conflict with what would be agreed to, so what would be agreed to proves unstable when it comes into conflict with what would have been agreed to in an appropriate presocial context. For as existing practices must seem arbitrary insofar as they do not correspond to what a rational person would agree to, so what such a person would agree to in existing circumstances must seem arbitrary in relation to what she would accept in a presocial condition.

What a rational person would agree to in existing circumstances depends in large part on her negotiating position vis-à-vis her fellows. But her negotiating position is significantly affected by the existing social institutions, and so by the currently accepted moral practices embodied in those institutions. Thus, although agreement may well yield practices differing from those embodied in existing social institutions, yet it will be influenced by those practices, which are not themselves the product of rational agreement. And this must call the rationality of the agreed practices into question. The arbitrariness of existing practices must infect any agreement whose terms are significantly affected by them. Although rational agreement is in itself a source of stability, yet this stability is undermined by the arbitrariness of the circumstances in which it takes place. To escape this arbitrariness, rational persons will revert from actual to hypothetical agreement, considering what practices they would have agreed to from an initial position not structured by existing institutions and the practices they embody.

The content of a hypothetical agreement is determined by an appeal to the equal rationality of persons. Rational persons will voluntarily accept an agreement only insofar as they perceive it to be equally advantageous to each. To be sure, each would be happy to accept an agreement more advantageous to herself than to her fellows, but since no one will accept an agreement perceived to be less advantageous, agents whose rationality is a matter of common knowledge will recognize the futility of aiming at or holding out for more, and minimize their bargaining costs by coordinating at the point of equal advantage. Now the extent of advantage is determined in a twofold way. First, there is advantage internal to an agreement. In this respect, the expectation of equal advantage is assured by procedural fairness. The step from existing moral practices to those resulting from actual agreement takes rational persons to a procedurally fair situation, in which each perceives the agreed practices to be ones that it is equally rational for all to accept, given the circumstances in which agreement is reached. But those circumstances themselves may be called into question insofar as they are perceived to be arbitrary—the result, in part, of compliance with constraining practices that do not themselves ensure the expectation of equal advantage, and so do not reflect the equal rationality of the complying parties. To neutralize this arbitrary element, moral practices to be fully acceptable must be conceived as constituting a possible outcome of a hypothetical agreement under circumstances that are unaffected by social institutions that themselves lack full acceptability. Equal rationality demands consideration of external circumstances as well as internal procedures.

But what is the practical import of this argument? It would be absurd to claim that mere acquaintance with it, or even acceptance of it, will lead to the replacement of existing moral practices by those that would secure presocial agreement. It would be irrational for anyone to give up the benefits of the existing moral order simply because he comes to realize that it affords him more than he could expect from pure rational agreement with his fellows. And it would be irrational for anyone to accept a long-term utility loss by refusing to comply with the existing moral order, simply because she comes to realize that such compliance affords her less than she could expect from pure rational agreement. Nevertheless, these realizations do transform, or perhaps bring to the surface, the character of the relationships between persons that are maintained by the existing constraints, so that some of these relationships come to be recognized as coercive. These realizations constitute the elimination of false consciousness, and they result from a process of rational reflection that brings persons into what, in my theory, is the parallel of Jürgen Habermas's ideal speech situation.[16] Without an argument to

[16]See Raymond Geuss, *The Idea of a Critical Theory: Habermas and the Frankfurt School* (Cambridge: Cambridge University Press, 1981), p. 65ff.

defend themselves in open dialogue with their fellows, those who are more than equally advantaged can hope to maintain their privileged position only if they can coerce their fellows into accepting it. And this, of course, may be possible. But coercion is not agreement, and it lacks any inherent stability.

Stability plays a key role in linking compliance to agreement. Aware of the benefits to be gained from constraining practices, rational persons will seek those that invite stable compliance. Now compliance is stable if it arises from agreement among persons each of whom considers both that the terms of agreement are sufficiently favorable to herself that it is rational for her to accept them, and that they are not so favorable to others that it would be rational for them to accept terms less favorable to them and more favorable to herself. An agreement affording equally favorable terms to all thus invites, as no other can, stable compliance.

V

In defending the claim that moral practices, to obtain the stable voluntary compliance of rational individuals, must be the objects of an appropriate hypothetical agreement, I have added to the initial minimal characterization of morality. Not only does morality constrain our choices and actions, but it does so in an impartial way, reflecting the equal rationality of the persons subject to constraint. Although it is no part of my argument to show that the requirements of contractarian morality will satisfy the Rawlsian test of cohering with our considered judgments in reflective equilibrium, yet it would be misleading to treat rationally agreed constraints on direct utility maximization as constituting a morality at all, rather than as replacing morality, were there no fit between their content and our pretheoretical moral views. The fit lies, I suggest, in the impartiality required for hypothetical agreement.

The foundational crisis of morality is thus resolved by exhibiting the rationality of our compliance with mutual, rationally agreed constraints on the pursuit of our desires, aims, and interests. Although bereft of a basis in objective values or an objectively purposive order, and confronted by a more fundamental mode of justification, morality survives by incorporating itself into that mode. Moral considerations have the same status, and the same role in explaining behavior, as the other reasons acknowledged by a rational deliberator. We are left with a unified account of justification, in which an agent's choices and actions are evaluated in relation to his preferences—to the concerns that are constitutive of his sense of self. But since morality binds the agent independently of the particular content of his preferences, it has the prescriptive grip with which the Christian and Kantian views have invested it.

In incorporating morality into deliberative justification, we recognize a new dimension to the agent's self-conception. For morality requires that a person have the capacity to commit himself, to enter into agreement with his fellows secure in the awareness that he can and will carry out his part of the agreement without regard to many of those considerations that normally and justifiably would enter into his future deliberations. And this is more than the capacity to bring one's desires and interests together with one's beliefs into a single coherent whole. Although this latter unifying capacity must extend its attention to past and future, the unification it achieves may itself be restricted to that extended present within which a person judges and decides. But in committing oneself to future action in accordance with one's agreement, one must fix at least a subset of one's desires and beliefs to hold in that future. The self that agrees and the self that complies must be one. "Man himself must first of all have become *calculable, regular, necessary,* even in his own image of himself, if he is to be able to stand security for *his own future,* which is what one who promises does!"[17]

In developing "*the right to make promises,*"[18] we human beings have found a contractarian bulwark against the perishing of morality.

[17]Nietzsche, *On the Genealogy of Morals,* trans. by Walter Kaufmann and R. J. Hollingdale (New York: Random House, 1967), second essay, sec. 1, p. 58.

[18]Ibid., p. 57.

1993

Goodness and Utilitarianism

Judith Jarvis Thomson

1. Many of us who work in moral philosophy spend a lot of time worrying about utilitarianism.[1] Our problem isn't merely that it continues to have its friends, though it does; our problem is deeper, lying in the fact that we haven't found—and its friends are delighted to draw our attention to the fact that we haven't found—a way of positively killing it off. No amount of mowing and tugging seems to work: it keeps on reappearing, every spring, like a weed with a long root.

One way of bringing out the difficulty is to draw attention to a kind of progress made by utilitarian theorists. I take utilitarianism to be a thesis about the right: it says that the right act is the act that maximizes the good. This constrains the right, but leaves open

[1]Philippa Foot says: "It is remarkable how utilitarianism tends to haunt even those of us who will not believe in it." See her "Utilitarianism and the Virtues," a version of which was her Presidential Address to the American Philosophical Association, Pacific Division; see *Proceedings and Addresses of the American Philosophical Association* 57 (1983). A later version appeared in *Mind* 94 (1985), and is reprinted in *Consequentialism and its Critics*, ed. Samuel Scheffler (Oxford: Oxford University Press, 1988).

Judith Jarvis Thomson, "Goodness and Utilitarianism." Presidential Address for the 89th Annual Eastern Division Meeting of The American Philosophical Association, Washington, DC, 12/29/92. Appeared in *Proceedings and Addresses of the APA* Vol. 67, No. 2 (October 1993): 145–159. Reprinted with the permission of The American Philosophical Association.

what constitutes the good, and some utilitarians have held views about the good which make their thesis about the right seem highly implausible. Suppose, for example, that a utilitarian believes that the good is exhausted by the pleasant. On his view, then, what we ought to do is to maximize the sheer amount of pleasure in the universe. "What," we ask, in our most shocked tone, "kick Alfred in order to amuse Bert? Surely not!" But the sophisticated modern utilitarian does not for a moment believe that the good is exhausted by the pleasant, and this objection flies right past without even causing him to blink.

The sophisticated modern utilitarian may have a theory of the good according to which the good includes the pleasant. If so, he is very likely to think it includes other things too, such as, for example, distributive equality. Or he may think that the good does not include the pleasant. Indeed, he may have no theory of the good at all.

There are three ideas that mark a contemporary moral philosopher as a utilitarian. In the first place, he thinks that some states of affairs are good and some are bad. Second, he thinks that for every instance in which a person can do such and such, there is such a thing as the total outcome—the compound of all of the states of affairs that will obtain if the person does the such and such—the goodness or badness of that total outcome being a function of the goodness or badness of the states of affairs it is a compound of. Third, he thinks that what a person ought to do is to choose that act which, of all the acts open to the person, would issue in the obtaining of the best total outcome.

I want to draw attention to a difficulty for these ideas, which I think has not been adequately appreciated.[2]

2. G. E. Moore took it to be clear that there is such a property as goodness. He said in *Principia Ethica* that

> Ethics is undoubtedly concerned with the question what good conduct is; but, being concerned with this, it obviously does not start at the beginning, unless it is prepared to tell us what is good as well as what is conduct. For "good conduct" is a complex notion: all conduct is not good; for some is certainly bad and some may be indifferent. And on the other hand, other things, besides conduct, may be good; and if they are so, then, "good" denotes some property, that is common to them and conduct; and if we examine good conduct alone of all good things, then we shall be in danger of mistaking for this property, some property which is not shared by those other things. . . .[3]

Thus good conduct is what has the two properties goodness and being conduct, and other things besides good conduct have the property goodness: goodness is the property that all good things have in common. Therefore while ethics is concerned with the question what good conduct is, it begins at the beginning only if it begins by asking what the property goodness itself is.

Now this won't do. (But why has it taken philosophers so *long* to see that it won't do?) Peter Geach drew attention in 1956[4] to the fact that a good car is not something

[2]The difficulty I will be discussing was drawn attention to by Philippa Foot in *op. cit.* [See also John Taurek, "Should the Numbers Count?," *Philosophy and Public Affairs* 6 (1977).] My account of it differs from Mrs. Foot's in ways I cannot go into here.

[3]*Principia Ethica* (Cambridge: Cambridge University Press, 1951), p. 2.

[4]Peter Geach, "Good and Evil," *Analysis* 17 (1956), reprinted in *Theories of Ethics,* ed. Philippa Foot, (Oxford: Oxford University Press, 1967). See also Paul Ziff, *Semantic Analysis* (Ithaca: Cornell University Press, 1960) and Georg Henrik von Wright, *The Varieties of Goodness* (London: Routledge & Kegan Paul, 1963).

W. D. Ross had discussed expressions of the form "good K" but believed that there is also a "predicative use of ['good'], as when it is said that knowledge is good or that pleasure is good." *The Right and the Good* (Oxford: Oxford University Press, 1930), p. 65. He said that "good" has predicative "senses," and that *they* are "the most important for philosophy" p. 73).

that is good and a car just as a big flea is not something that is big and a flea; and he suggested that we should regard "good," like "big," as what many people nowadays call a predicate modifier: what is predicable of a thing is not (just) being good but rather being a good K, for some kind K, just as what is predicable of a thing is not (just) being big, but rather being a big K, for some kind K.

In short, there is no such property as goodness. Geach said: "there is no such thing as being just good or bad, there is only being a good or bad so-and-so."

Alternatively put, the adjective "good" is incomplete in this sense: if a person Alfred says something of the grammatical form "x is good," then either he or the context must supply a kind-term K such that we can take him to be saying about the thing referred to that it is a good K, or else we simply do not know what he is saying about the thing. Here are some examples of what we may discover that Alfred is saying about the thing: it is a

"good" as modifier:
good swimmer
good dancer
good hammer
good sunset

But that is really over-strong—"good" does very often occur as a modifier, but so also does it occur modified, and it would pay us to pay more attention to that fact. We may discover what someone who says something of the form "x is good" is saying about the thing, not by being supplied with a kind-term K for "good" to modify, but by being supplied with an expression that modifies "good." Suppose, for example, that Alfred says "Alice is good." What is he saying about Alice? The context may tell us that what he is saying about her is that she is a good swimmer or a good dancer. But it may tell us instead that what he is saying about her is that she is good *at* doing mental arithmetic. Or that she is good *to* go camping with. Or that she is good *with* small children. Is there a kind K here such that what he is saying about Alice is that she is a good K? I suppose we could force the point: we could say that there is, namely the kind "mental arithmetic doer," or the kind "person to go camping with," or the kind "person to leave your small children with when you go shopping." But there really seems to be no reason to do so. Why shouldn't we allow that Alfred is *not* saying about Alice that she is a good K for some K, and yet that we know what he is saying about her because we know what he is saying she is good at or to or with.

There are expressions of the form "'good' modified" such that predicating them of a person *is* predicating of the person that he or she is a good K for some K. Thus if Alfred tells us that what he is saying about Alice is that she is good at swimming (or dancing), then he is saying about her that she is a good swimmer (or dancer). But that is not true of all of them.

Again, suppose Alfred points to a hammer, and says "That's good." What is he saying about the hammer? The context may tell us that what he is saying about it is that it is a good hammer. But the context may instead tell us that what he is saying about it is that it is good *to use for* holding down a pile of papers which are about to blow all over. Or that it is good *to use in* the collage—to be titled "The Joys of Owning a House"—that we are in process of constructing. If so, Alfred is not saying about the hammer that it is a good hammer. Is there some other K such that he is saying about the hammer that it is a good K? We could (again) force the point: we could say that there is, namely the kind "thing to use for holding down a pile of papers which are about to blow all over," or "thing to use in the collage etc. etc." But why force the point? Why not allow that he is *not* saying about the hammer that it is a good K for some K, and yet that we know what he is saying about the hammer because we know what he is saying it is good to use for or in.

Here are the examples I gave, and some others as well:

"good" modified:
- good *at* doing mental arithmetic, dancing, swimming
- good *to* go camping with, eat, look at
- good *with* small children, the deaf
- good *to use for* holding down a pile of papers, hammering nails
- good *to use in* a collage of tools, making pizza
- good *for* England, Smith, the tree in Jones' backyard
- good *as* an actor, Hamlet

I think it very plausible, moreover, that the role of "good" as modifier on a kind-term is parasitic on the role of "good" modified. It is familiar enough that there are kind terms such that prefixing "good" to them yields something puzzling. If someone says of a thing that it's a good swimmer or a good hammer, we know what is being predicated of the thing; if someone says of a thing that it's a good pebble or a good molecule or a good corpse, we find ourselves at a loss—what *does* the speaker have in mind?[5] Now why this difference? I suggest that we know what is predicated of a thing when it is said to be a good swimmer because we know that a good swimmer is a swimmer who is good at swimming. We know what is predicated of a thing when it is said to be a good hammer because we know that a good hammer is a hammer that is good to use for hammering in nails. (The source of this point does not lie in the fact that "swimmer" and "hammer" are, as they are often said to be, "functional words"; "sunset" is not a functional word, and we nevertheless know what is predicated of a thing when it is said to be a good sunset, that being because we know that a good sunset is a sunset that is good to look at.) In short, we know for *those* kinds K what it is that a good K is good at or to or for and so on. By contrast, we do not know what is predicated of a thing when it is said to be a good pebble or a good molecule or good corpse because we do not know for *these* kinds K what it is that a good K is good at or to or for and so on. Indeed, there doesn't seem to be any such thing. More precisely, while there may well be something that some corpses are good at or to or for, whereas other corpses are not, nothing comes to mind, and it's for *that* reason that "good corpse" puzzles us; and similarly for pebbles and molecules.[6]

That is, of course, entirely compatible with its being the case on a given occasion that the context makes clear what a speaker is saying about a thing when he says it is a good corpse. Consider, for example, an embalmer, who wants to start his apprentice off with one it's particularly easy to work on.

Let's go back to Geach, then. He said: "there is no such thing as being just good or bad, there is only being a good or bad so-and-so." It is very plausible to think we should say that while there certainly is being a good or bad so-and-so, there is also being good at or to or for such and such, and that *where* there is being a good or bad so-and-so that is *because* there is being a so-and-so that is good at or to or for such and such.

[5]"Good pebble" occurs in a lot of places; I take "good molecule" and "good corpse" from Ziff *op. cit.* (Ziff invites us to contrast "good corpse," which is puzzling, with "good cadaver," which is not.)

[6]Perhaps this idea can be connected with the connection Ziff makes between "good" and answering to interests, for perhaps it can be said that the reason why nothing comes to mind is that people do not in general have an interest in the things that some corpses are, and other corpses are not, good at or to or for.

Alternatively put, the adjective "good" is incomplete in this sense: if Alfred says something of the form "x is good," then either he or the context must tell us what he is saying the thing is good at or to or for if we are to know what he is saying about it.[7]

Unfortunately this is still over-strong. For let us now turn to some expressions of the form "good K" for which what I just said won't do. The most striking exceptions are the likes of "good person," "good friend," "good government," and "good act." Suppose I say "Alice is a good person." It can't be said that you don't know what I've said about her unless you know what I am saying she is good at or to or for and so on. Perhaps good people are good at or to or for something; but that she is good at or to or for something wasn't at all what I meant to be saying of her in saying what I did.

We can think of being good at or to or for something as ways in which a thing can be good. What marks a person x as a good person is not that x is good at or to or for something; thus it does not lie in x's being good in one of *those* ways. What marks a person x as a good person is that x is just, reliable, loyal, generous, and so on. And aren't these also ways of being good? A person may be good in some of these ways and not in others; presumably a person is a good person only if he or she is good in enough of them. A government is presumably a good government only if it is good in one of those ways in particular: it has to be just. An act, like a person, may be good in some of these ways and not in others; presumably it is a good act only if it is good in at least one of them.

The expressions "just," "reliable," "loyal" and so on, which I draw attention to here are what Bernard Williams has helpfully called "thick" moral terms. They are, however, only a special case, a sub-class of what might be called

thick evaluative terms:
- moral: just, reliable, loyal
- non-moral: graceful, vigorous, serene, wholesome.

We can think of these too as standing for ways in which a thing can be good.

I suggest, therefore, that we should emend what I said earlier. Where there is being a good or bad so-and-so that is because there is being a so-and-so that is good in this or that way—where the ways include, not merely being good at or to or for such and such, but also being just or reliable or graceful.

Alternatively put, the adjective "good" is incomplete in this sense: if Alfred says something of the form "x is good," then either he or the context must tell us in what way or ways he is saying the thing is good if we are to know what he is saying about it.

Still more compactly put: all goodness is goodness-in-a-way.

[7]I am indebted to Zoltan Szabo for drawing my attention to the possibility of arguing that the expressions on my list headed "'good' modified" must themselves be headed by a kind-term. Suppose Alfred says something of the form "x is good at swimming." It is one thing for a person to be good at swimming, and quite another for a fish to be good at swimming. Shouldn't we conclude that we know what Alfred predicated of the thing only if we know for some K that what he predicated of it was "being a K that is good at swimming"?

There is a larger issue in the offing here, since this kind of consideration can be appealed to in support of saying the same of any number of familiar adjectives and adjective-phrases. For example, it is one thing for a house to be red, and quite another for the paint in a certain bucket to be red. Moreover, the same could also be said of at least some of the expressions on my list headed "'good' as modifier." If it is one thing for a person to be good at swimming, and quite another for a fish to be good at swimming, then so also is it one thing for a person to be a good swimmer, and quite another for a fish to be a good swimmer.

But I prefer to bypass this issue. Anyone who likes may take the appropriate members of both my lists (the list headed "'good' as modifier" as well as a the list headed "'good' modified") to be elliptical: thus "good swimmer" for "K that is a good swimmer," . . . , and "good at swimming" for "K that is good at swimming," . . . And similarly for my third list, shortly to emerge in the text below, headed "thick evaluative terms."

Finally, even if it were agreed that we know what Alfred predicated of the thing only if we know for some K that what he predicated of it was "being a K that is good at swimming," the fact remains that he need not be construed as predicating "being a good K (or L or M)" of it.

I have drawn attention to two kinds of ways of being good: on the one hand, being good at or to or for and so on, on the other hand being just or reliable or graceful and so on. I think these exhaust the kinds. But how do they connect with each other? Well, some ways falling into the second kind are reducible to ways falling into the first. For example, a thing's being wholesome or nourishing just is its being good to eat or drink. But it is clear that the ways falling into the second kind aren't all reducible to ways falling into the first. For example, a reliable person is not one who is good to rely on: a reliable person is one who can be relied on. There seems to be a fundamental difference at work here. In some appropriate sense of the words, being good at or to or for and so on are *external* ways of being good, whereas being just or reliable or graceful and so on are *internal* ways of being good. The external ones are, roughly, aptnesses to purposes, the internal ones are, even more roughly, manners or modes. But what exactly we should take those senses to be seems to me a hard question.

It may have been noticed that I do not offer being desired or liked or admired as itself a way of being good. If we desire a state of affairs we may aim at bringing it about; and then the means we choose may (or may not) be good to use for bringing it about. But I should think that our desiring something is compatible with its not being good in any way at all.

In any case, it pays to stress that my thesis here is not that goodness supervenes on ways of being good: my point is not that a thing is good *because* it is good in this or that way. To say, as I suggest we say, that all goodness is goodness-in-a-way is to say, rather, that a thing's being good just *is* its being good in this or that way. The supervenience is lower down: it is the ways of being good that supervene, and indeed supervene on natural features of the things good in those ways.

One final point. The adjective "good" is certainly not unique in the respect I have been pointing to here. "Interesting" is also incomplete: if we are told that a thing is interesting, we need to know in what way it is being said to be interesting if we are to know what is said about it. Jones is knowledgeable; about what—the Civil War? the class structure of England? Smith is efficient; at what—bookkeeping? beekeeping? Jones and Smith are equal; in what respect—intelligence? tennis-playing ability?[8]

But "big," after all, is different, and in two ways at that, both issuing from the fact that "big" is, and "good" is not, fundamentally comparative. In the first place, a big K just is a K that is bigger than most Ks, and it therefore cannot be the case that most Ks are big Ks. By contrast, a good K is not a K that is better than most Ks. It is not but could have been the case that most, or even all, people are good people, and that most, or even all, hammers are good hammers. More important for our purposes, second, there is such a thing as x's being pure, unadulterated bigger than y; there is no such thing as x's being pure, unadulterated better than y. If, as I am suggesting, all goodness is goodness-in-a-way, then so also is all betterness betterness-in-a-way.

I commend this idea to those who have been saying, in recent years, that goods are, as they put it, 'incommensurable'. Which is better, Russell's Theory of Descriptions or chocolate? Not which do you prefer thinking about when you can't get to sleep at night; rather, which is pure, unadulterated *better*. It's a crazy question. One is good in one way, the other in another, and the incommensurabilists needn't leave the matter to intuition: an argument for their thesis is available, namely that all goodness being goodness-in-a-way, so also is all betterness.

[8]I am indebted to T. Hinton for "equal."

3. These considerations have a bearing on other moral theories, but let us return now to utilitarianism in particular. Can the utilitarian consistently accept the thesis that all goodness is goodness-in-a-way? Yes he can. There are three possibilities open to him—but none is entirely happy.

Why isn't it happy enough for him merely to fix on an appropriate kind? I said that the first of the three ideas that mark a contemporary moral philosopher as a utilitarian is the idea that some states of affairs are good and some are bad. Why shouldn't he merely settle with himself that what he means is that some states of affairs are *good states of affairs* and some are *bad states of affairs?* Well, "good state of affairs" is one respect like "good corpse": help from speaker or context apart, it is puzzling. But in another respect it is unlike "good corpse." The trouble with "good state of affairs" is not that there seems to be no way of being good such that a good state of affairs is a state of affairs that is good in that way; the trouble is that there are too many. "That's a good state of affairs," people often say, and "It's a good thing that such and such." Sometimes they mean that the state of affairs is good for those they are personally interested in, sometimes they mean that it is good for all involved, sometimes they mean that it's just or fair, and I suppose that sometimes they mean more than one of these. We need help from the speaker or context to find out which—or whether some still other way of being good, special to the context, is in question.[9]

So what is the utilitarian to say? One possibility is that he will himself fix on a particular way of being good.

It would be no surprise if he fixed on goodness-for, perhaps goodness for people, perhaps goodness for sentient creatures generally. What is good for a creature is what is on balance in its interest, or constitutes or contributes to its well-being; and what else could matter to morality besides the interest or well-being of humanity? or of sentient creatures generally? The utilitarian who makes this choice, then, says that what we ought to do is to choose that act which, of all the acts open to us, would issue in the obtaining of the total outcome that is on balance best for people, or for sentient creatures generally.[10]

[9]Shelly Kagan says in *The Limits of Morality* (Oxford: Oxford University Press, 1989):

> To say that from the moral standpoint one outcome is objectively better than another, is to say that *everyone* has a reason to choose the better outcome. . . . Thus, on one level, to say that there is a pro tanto reason to promote the good is actually to make a trivial claim. Everyone has a standing reason to promote the objectively best outcome, because the existence of such a reason is in part just what it *is* for something to have objective value. (p. 61)

(Why only "in part"?) The locution "x has a reason to do such and such" is often used in explications of the notion "value," and indeed elsewhere in ethics; but what do the people who use it mean by it? They plainly don't mean something epistemic, as in "x has a reason for believing so and so." They also don't mean something interest-relative, as in "It is in x's interest that x do such and such"; nor do they mean "x actually does have a motive for doing such and such." (Else it would be hard to see how there could be any outcome at all such that everyone has a reason to choose or promote it.) My suspicion is that they mean by it what Ross meant by "x has a prima facie duty to do such and such"—where *this* locution is understood in the second of the two ways I will point to below. It should be clear, however, that anyone who does mean this by it, and then analyses objective value as Kagan does, analyzes the good in terms of the right, and cannot informatively then go on to analyze the right in terms of the good.

[10]Indeed, it is easy to slip into thinking that (non-hedonistic) utilitarianism just *is* this view. Ross says in *The Right and the Good, op. cit.:*

> In fact the theory of "ideal utilitarianism," if I may for brevity refer so to the theory of Professor Moore, seems to simplify unduly our relations to our fellows. It says, in effect, that the only morally significant relation in which my neighbors stand to me is that of being possible *beneficiaries* by my action. (p. 19) (my emphasis)

And when Ross gets down to rebutting that theory, what he begins with is:

It is of great interest that something is lost to the utilitarian who makes this choice. As Philippa Foot said, the chief attraction of utilitarianism for many people is that it sounds like a necessary truth. Suppose it clear that if I do such and such then the world that will come about will be better—just pure, unadulterated better—than the world that will come about if I do so and so. Surely, then, it is clear that I ought to do the such and such. How *could* morality direct me otherwise?[11] (That's the weed's long root.) Well, if all goodness is goodness-in-a-way, then there is no such thing as one world's being pure, unadulterated better than another. Consider, then, the utilitarian I envisage here, who fixes on goodness-for. *He* says that if it is clear that if I do such and such then the world that will come about will be better for people (or sentient creatures) than the world that will come about if I do so and so, then it is clear that I ought to do the such and such. But is that *as* clear? Isn't it in order to think it might matter who wins and who loses in that best world, and to wonder why a world's being better for those winners should be thought to have this moral import? (What if the winners have themselves villainously created the situation in which I have to choose between them and the losers?) Again, isn't it in order to think it might matter how evenly the benefits are distributed in that best world? What emerges is that the theory we are supplied with by the utilitarian I envisage here is not at all plausibly viewable as a necessary truth. People may find it attractive, but if they do, it is a moral judgment which they are finding attractive, a—not at all obvious—moral judgment to the effect that it is goodness-for *alone* that matters to the question what a person ought to do.

I suppose that there are other alternatives as well: goodness for people (or sentient creatures) is presumably not the only possible choice for a utilitarian way of being good which is to be maximized in his theory of the right. Indeed, it is not even essential that the utilitarian fix on one unique way of being good which is to be maximized in his theory of the right. A second possibility for him is to fix on several irreducibly different ways of being good. Then his theory yields no directive for action where the total outcome that will obtain if we do a thing is better in one of those ways but worse in another than the total outcomes that will obtain if he does anything else. I suppose that the utilitarian can live with that consequence of a measure of multiplicity, for he can say that's life, and you shouldn't expect a moral theory to make choice of action easier than it is; but the greater the multiplicity in his theory, the less information his theory yields—and it may be expected to yield no information at all in the most interesting cases, which are precisely those in which ways of being good clash.

A third possibility for the utilitarian is, as I mentioned at the outset, simply to decline to supply any theory of the good at all. "Supply what *you* think the correct account of what makes a state of affairs be good in the way or ways relevant to assessments of what a person ought to do," he may say. "My point is only that what a person ought to

---

> It might seem absurd to suggest that it could be right for any one to do an act which would produce consequences less good than those which would be produced by some other act in his power. (p. 34)

But what he offers by way of demonstration that the suggestion is not absurd is:

> Suppose . . . that the fulfillment of a promise to A would produce 1,000 units of *good for* him, but that by doing some other act I could produce 1,001 units of *good for* B, to whom I have made no promise, the other consequences of the two acts being of equal value; should we really think it self-evident that it was our duty to do the second act and not the first? I think not. (pp. 34–5) (my emphasis)

Plainly "less good than" has turned out to mean "less good for people than." Noticing this helps us to supply a very simple interpretation for Ross' notion 'prima facie duty'—I will return to it in section 5 below.

[11] See Philippa Foot, *op. cit.*, p. 227 in Scheffler reprinting. It is a good question—without an obvious answer—*why* this sounds to people like a necessary truth.

do is what will issue in the total outcome that is best in that way or ways." Utilitarianism so construed yields information about what we ought to do only in so far as we make it do so.

4. I have so far focused primarily on the first of the three ideas that mark a contemporary moral philosopher as a utilitarian, namely the idea that some states of affairs are good and some are bad. Let us turn to the second idea, which is that for every instance in which a person can do such and such, there is such a thing as the total outcome—the compound of all of the states of affairs that will obtain if the person does the such and such—the goodness or badness of that total outcome being a function of the goodness or badness of the states of affairs it is a compound of.

Now one very natural construal of the term "state of affairs" is that states of affairs do not include acts, and thus that the utilitarian's 'total outcome' of an act is the compound of the *effects* of the act—the compound of the states of affairs that are, in Jonathan Bennett's useful metaphor, downstream of the act. This seemed to many people to commit the utilitarian to bizarre conclusions. "Not care by what dreadful act a good outcome would have to be brought about? Surely that won't do!" It is, of course, possible for the utilitarian to stand fast and say "No surely about it." But the sophisticated modern utilitarian does not stand fast. He tells us we are to suppose that what matters is not just what is downstream of an act, but what is everywhere in the stream, including the act itself. We are to take Smith's kicking Jones to be, itself, among the states of affairs whose goodness or badness is relevant to the question whether Smith ought to kick Jones.

It is because the modern utilitarian does wish us to include acts among the states of affairs whose goodness or badness is relevant to the question what a person ought to do that I think "consequentialism"—which is nowadays in wide use as name for this theory—is so unfortunate a name for it. You can of course tell your hearers explicitly that you mean to include the act itself among its own consequences; but why risk misleading those who are not listening as closely as you might like? (G. E. Moore from time to time misled himself on this matter.)

In short, we are, as it were, to step back from the act we are contemplating to the world in which the act occurs. Which act we ought to choose—kicking Alfred or kicking Bert—is to be settled by figuring out whether the world in which we kick Alfred is better than the world in which we kick Bert.

We should ask, however, *why* we should step back from the act to the world. For some ways of being good it can make no difference whether we do. I have in mind in particular goodness-for, and let us fix more particularly still, on goodness for people. Suppose a given act is bad for Smith. Then it is bad for at least one person. Is it bad for people generally? Well, what will happen if the act occurs? Who else, if anyone, will be affected for the better or worse if the act occurs? If on balance, the act contributes to the well-being of those who are affected, then we can if we like say that the world in which the act occurs is on balance good for people; but it is unnecessary to say anything about the world at large—the same information is conveyed by saying, simply, that the act itself is on balance good for people.

What makes this true is, as we might put it, the fact that goodness for people is inheritable. That is, an act which does not itself consist in someone's doing something good for people may nevertheless be good for people, and is so if its consequences downstream are good for people.

Not all ways of being good are inheritable, however, and that a way of being good is not inheritable is an important fact about it. Consider justice, for example. In a kind of case familiar in the literature, I am told that if I do not kill an innocent person, five others will each kill an innocent person. (In one such story, I am a judge, and can see that a mob will lynch five innocents unless I arrange for the quick conviction and execution of one innocent.) My killing the one would be unjust. So also would be the acts of the five others, but my killing the one does not inherit justice from the fact that its consequences downstream include fewer unjust acts.

This means that while for some ways of being good it makes no difference whether we step back from act to world, for others it does. Suppose a utilitarian has fixed on goodness for people as the way of being good to be maximized. Then it makes no difference whether he tells us to choose the act that is best for people or the act such that world in which it occurs is best for people, for an act is on balance best for people if and only if the world in which it occurs is best for people. Suppose a utilitarian has instead fixed on justice as the way of being good to be maximized. (I know of only one utilitarian who has made this decision.[12]) It does make a difference whether *he* tells us to choose the act that is most just or the act such that the world in which it occurs is most just. For in the kind of case I have been pointing to, my act of refusing is more just than my act of killing the one; and if I am to choose the most just act, I must therefore refuse. But the world in which I kill the one is more just than the world in which I refuse, since it contains fewer unjust acts; and if I am to choose the act such that the world in which it occurs is most just, I must therefore kill the one.

Of course a utilitarian might have fixed on both goodness for people and justice as the ways of being good to be maximized. If he does, his theory tells us nothing at all about what I am to do in such a case.

As I said, the third of the three ideas that mark a contemporary moral philosopher as a utilitarian is the idea that what a person ought to do is to choose that act which, of all the acts open to the person, would issue in the obtaining of the best total outcome—or, as I will from now on say, the best world. We should therefore invite the utilitarian, not merely to fix on a way or ways of being good, but also, where he fixes on a way that is not inheritable, to explain why it should be the goodness in that way of the worlds in which acts occur that matters rather than the goodness in that way of the acts themselves. And it is not at all easy to see what his explanation is to consist in. If refusing to kill the one is the best act open to me in *the* way relevant to what a person ought to do, why should we think that the fact that the world will be better in that way if I kill the one makes it right for me to choose the worse act of killing the one?[13]

5. So consider a philosopher who fixes on one or more ways of being good, at least one of which is non-inheritable, and who says we ought to choose the act which is *itself* best in that way or those ways. I call this philosopher merely "a philosopher" and not "a utilitarian," since he rejects the third of the three ideas that mark a contemporary

[12]See Fred Feldman, *Confrontations with the Reaper* (Oxford: Oxford University Press, 1992), pp. 182–190. Feldman, however, makes use also of a notion "intrinsic goodness," whereas if there is no such thing as goodness, then a fortiori, there is no such thing as intrinsic goodness. For more on intrinsic goodness, see my "On Some Ways of Being Good," *Social Philosophy & Policy* 9 (1992).

[13]Samuel Scheffler argues that a certain fundamental and powerful conception of rationality—a maximizing conception—makes opting for "agent-centered restrictions" seem paradoxical. [See his "Agent-Centered Restrictions, Rationality, and the Virtues," *Mind* 94 (1985); this article, which is a commentary on Philippa Foot, *op. cit.*, is reprinted in *Consequentialism and its Critics*, Samuel Scheffler (ed.), *op. cit.*] I think he would say it is equally paradoxical to suppose that I ought to choose the just act even if the world that comes about if I choose it is less just than the world that comes about if I do not. And how is the argument to be thought to go? I model it on Scheffler's own. "You could believe people ought to act justly only if and because you believe 'it is preferable that' (p. 253) no unjust acts occur than that any do. But if *this* is your rationale for believing people ought to act justly, then how can you think it incumbent on you to act justly in a situation in which there will be more unjust acts if you act justly than if you do not?" I fancy that Scheffler's

moral philosopher as a utilitarian. Yet his theory is interestingly similar to utilitarianism, and I will call it quasi-utilitarianism.

This theory has at least one important friend: on one reading of W. D. Ross, *he* is a quasi-utilitarian. For what exactly are we to take Ross' notion "prima facie duty" to consist in? What can he have meant by sentences of the form "A has a prima facie duty to do such and such"? Here is a simple interpretation of what he meant: "A's doing such and such is good in one or more ways."

Let's look at Ross' list of prima facie duties. He lists fidelity, reparation, gratitude, justice, beneficence, self-improvement, and non-maleficence. For brevity, I will shorten the list to the following two: A has a prima facie duty to act justly, and A has a prima facie duty to do good for others. He thought these were conceptual truths, as of course they are if what they mean is "A's acting justly is good in one or more ways," and "A's acting in a way that is good for people is good in one or more ways," since it is a conceptual truth that justice and goodness-for are ways of being good. But some ascriptions of prima facie duty he would not have thought conceptual truths. Thus he would have said that "A has a prima facie duty to give B a banana" is not a conceptual truth. But he would have said it might be true, and on this interpretation of him, he would have said it *is* true if A's giving B a banana is in fact, and in the circumstances, just, or good for people.

Now Ross thought of himself as an anti-utilitarian, and that because he persistently misconstrued utilitarianism as the thesis that we ought to maximize goodness-for,[14] whereas on his own view (however we interpret him), goodness-for is only one among many morally relevant features of an act.

But he was right to think of himself as an anti-utilitarian: it is not worlds, but acts, that he wishes us to focus on. If my refusing to kill one will have as a consequence that five others will each kill one, then the world in which I kill is more just than the world in which I refuse to kill. No matter, from Ross' point of view; what matters on his view is not whether the world that comes about if I kill is just, but rather whether my act of killing is just.

So it suggests itself that his view of our actual (as opposed to merely prima facie) duty is this: we are to choose the act which is *itself* best in the ways he listed. That marks him as a quasi-utilitarian.

There is a problem here, however. If all goodness is goodness-in-a-way, then there is no such thing as x's being pure, unadulterated better than y. So as I said, if a utilitarian fixes on more than one way of being good, then his theory yields no directive for action where the ways of being good clash. Similarly for a quasi-utilitarian. In the kind of case we have been considering, my killing the one is better for people than my refusing, since fewer people die; but my refusing is more just than my killing the one. If Ross is a quasi-utilitarian, then he can supply us with no answer to the question what I ought to do in such a case.[15]

"it is preferable that" means "the world would be pure, unadulterated better if," and that this argument (as well as the argument he gives in his text for the paradoxicality of agent-centered restrictions) will seem plausible to us only if we are prepared to make room for pure, unadulterated betterness. For suppose we fix on a particular way of being good—justice, for example. It is not in the least plausible to suppose that one's rationale for believing people ought to act justly has to (or even can) consist in the (quite trivial) idea that the world would be more just if no unjust acts occur than if any do. Suppose we instead fix on goodness-for. It is not in the least plausible to suppose that one's rationale for believing people ought to act justly has to (or even can) consist in the (very likely false) idea that the world would be better for people if no unjust acts occur than if any do.

[14]See footnote 10 above.

[15]Indeed, he can supply us with no answer to the question what we ought to do in the very case which he thought refuted utilitarianism, namely that in which our doing something for B is better for people than our

Ross himself thought that his theory does supply us with directives for action where prima facie duties clash. He thought that prima facie duties differ in stringency, as he put it; and he thought that actual duty is fixed by assessments of the relative stringency of the relevant prima facie duties. But I do not take this to count against reading him as a quasi-utilitarian, for I think that what explains his having had those thoughts was his thinking that there *is* such a thing as pure, unadulterated betterness or worseness,[16] and thus in particular that an unjust act is pure, unadulterated worse than an act which is good for people—unless the injustice is minor, and the goodness-for great.

There is a second way of reading Ross; or anyway, there are the makings of a second theory lurking in his text. This theory is not quasi-utilitarian, and does yield directives for action where prima facie duties clash.

What I have in mind is a theory according to which we are to interpret "A has a prima facie duty to act justly" and "A has a prima facie duty to do good for others" as conceptual truths, as Ross would have them be, but not because they say that justice, and goodness-for are ways of being good; rather because they say that justice, and goodness-for are among the features of acts that its being the case that A ought to do a thing *supervenes on.*[17]

The idea here is this. As an act's being just, or good for people, supervenes on certain of its natural features, so also, at the next level up, does an act's being the one we ought to choose supervene on its being just, or good for people. So there is a double supervenience here.

And as an act's having one natural feature may count more heavily in support of the conclusion that it is just, or good for people, than its having some other natural feature, so also, at the next level up, may an act's being good in one way count more heavily in support of the conclusion that we ought to choose it than its being good in some other way. Not because being good in the one way is pure, unadulterated better than being good in the other way; rather because of what these ways of being good *are.*

But I can do no more than wave hazily in the direction of the theory I have in mind. What matters about it for present purposes is really only that it says the utilitarian is mistaken in thinking that the right is reducible to the good: it says that independent principles are called for to connect justice, goodness-for, and the other ways of being good with what we ought to do. If, as I have been suggesting, all goodness is goodness-in-a-way, then that at least must be right: such independent principles are needed in a moral theory, if it is to supply directives for action where the ways of being good clash.[18]

---

keeping our promise to A, but our keeping our promise to A is more just than our doing something for B. See footnote 10 above.

[16]See, for example, the passage I quoted in footnote 4 above.

[17]Compare what is very often said to be what Ross had in mind by "x has a prima facie duty to do such and such": other things being equal, x ought to do such and such.

[18]Many people made helpful comments on earlier versions of this material; I am most indebted to the members of my seminar in moral philosophy at MIT in the fall of 1992.